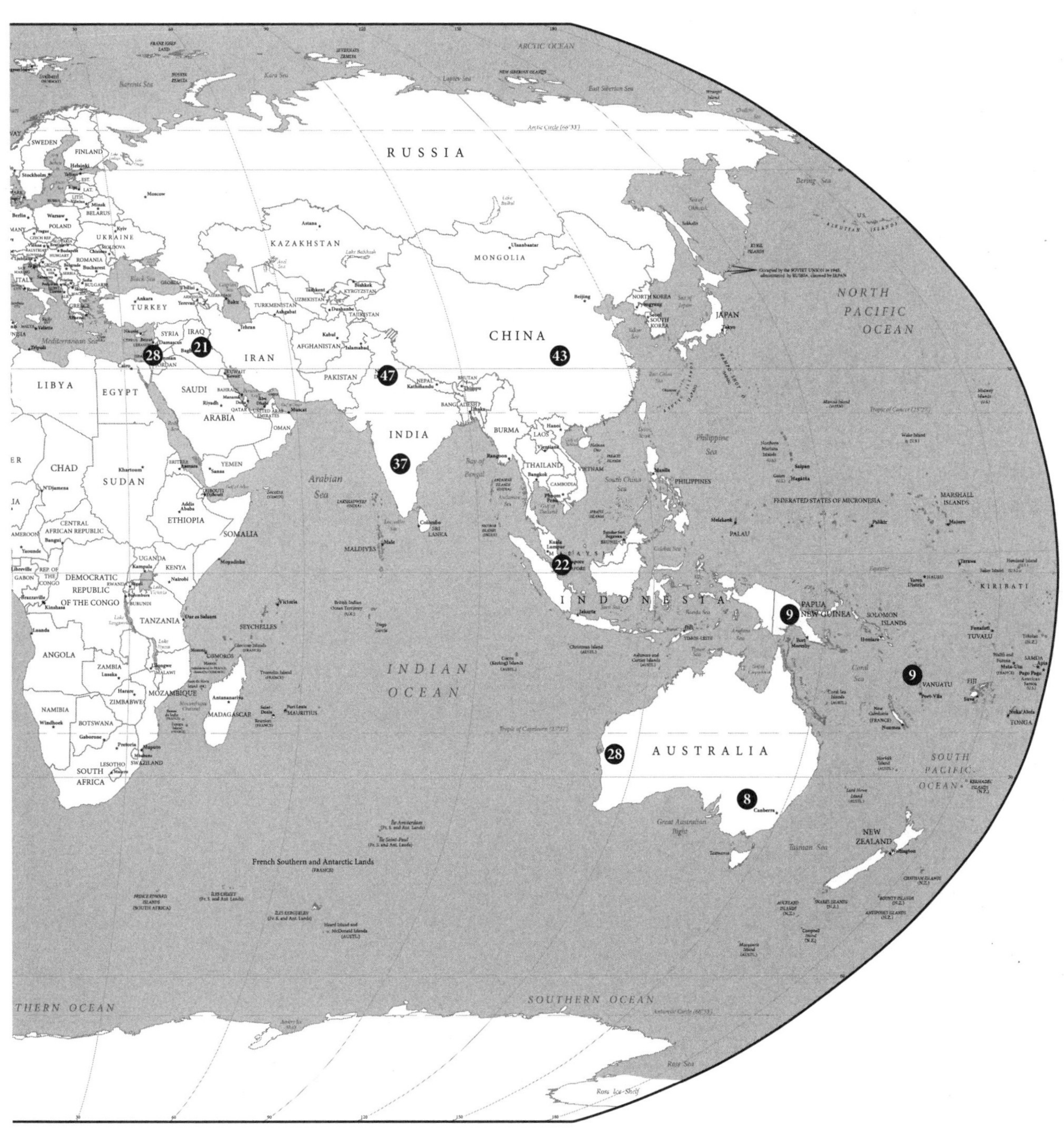


For page numbers, see Table of Contents.

# Making Sense of Language

## Readings in Culture and Communication

*Second Edition*

SUSAN D. BLUM
*The University of Notre Dame*

New York Oxford
OXFORD UNIVERSITY PRESS

To my colleagues, trying to light a match

And to all our students, wishing to catch fire

Oxford University Press, Inc., publishes works that further Oxford University's objective of excellence in research, scholarship, and education.

Oxford New York
Auckland Cape Town Dar es Salaam Hong Kong Karachi
Kuala Lumpur Madrid Melbourne Mexico City Nairobi
New Delhi Shanghai Taipei Toronto

With offices in
Argentina Austria Brazil Chile Czech Republic France Greece
Guatemala Hungary Italy Japan Poland Portugal Singapore
South Korea Switzerland Thailand Turkey Ukraine Vietnam



For titles covered by Section 112 of the US Higher Education Opportunity Act, please visit www.oup.com/us/he for the latest information about pricing and alternate formats.

Published by Oxford University Press, Inc.
198 Madison Avenue, New York, New York 10016
http://www.oup.com



ISBN 978-0-19-984092-2

Printing number: 9 8 7 6 5 4 3 2

Printed in the United States of America
on acid-free paper

# CONTENTS

*** Indicates readings that are new to this edition**

# CONTENTS

*** INDICATES READINGS THAT ARE NEW TO THIS EDITION**

# ANNOTATED CONTENTS

# PREFACE

This reader grows out of my own teaching experience and my quest to find readings on language that are compelling and accessible to undergraduates, even to those who are not planning to specialize in anthropology or the study of language. Some students reading this book may never have taken a course in this field and may never take another one like it. Others may have already taken a more basic course, may be familiar with a four-field approach to anthropology, or may go on to take more advanced courses. Most of the available collections of readings in linguistic anthropology are at a higher level than is accessible to most undergraduates, and many of them focus on particular aspects of linguistic anthropology. I could not find a teaching tool that effectively reached students on various academic paths, so I decided to create one.

My own background is in both cultural and linguistic anthropology; my research focuses on issues of nationalism, identity, ethnicity, multilingualism, stereotypes, naming, truth and deception, and on general pragmatics in China. More recently I have also written about plagiarism, authorship, childhood, education, selfhood, and college culture in the United States. Since 1992 I have been teaching in four-field anthropology departments, where my students often bring me questions from their other classes, and my colleagues often talk about broad issues concerning the nature of humanity. I have become intrigued by the connections among a wide range of topics, and this experience is what I've brought to the choices I've made here.

## The Readings

My intention with this book is to provide a range of topics and viewpoints on the subject of language and its relation to many aspects of being human. Some of the topics are broadly anthropological or even come from fields outside anthropology. (Unit 1 in particular, "What Is Language?," displays a generous curiosity about all things human. This topic is addressed variously by linguistic anthropologists, linguists, biologists, and others, and it is often of great interest to students with backgrounds in biological anthropology, biology, or archaeology.) Some of the readings are classics in the field, and some are contemporary. Some might be obvious choices, and some might be a bit unconventional.

No collection of readings can be all-inclusive. Thus this book does not attempt to cover the entire field of linguistic anthropology, nor does it even begin to address formal linguistics. Some instructors' favorite topics are likely to be omitted, and every academic is likely to argue about whether a particular article is the best example of a specific topic. Fair enough. This field thrives on independence of mind. My hope, though, is that this volume will provide a core set of readings that can be subtracted from or added to as each individual instructor chooses.

The readings run the gamut from many that are short and easily accessible to some that are relatively long, complex, and technical, and will be appropriate only for more advanced students. In some cases, the articles have been edited for space constraints, with a careful eye to retaining the flavor and gist of the author's original work; ellipses mark the omissions.

Many of the readings involve analysis of language in the United States, while the others are distributed (unevenly) across other cultures. This uneven distribution is not meant to imply that the United States is more important than anyplace else, nor does it mean that I assume that my audience consists entirely of students from the United States. Rather, for English-speaking students, many of the most accessible works on language have been written about English-speaking societies. Since the book does not presuppose technical linguistic knowledge, articles relying on grammatical or phonological analysis of languages other than English were overly daunting and had to be omitted.

## Organization

The linear nature of a book requires that topics unfold in a given order, but sections can be taken in any order; sections do not build on one another or assume knowledge from other sections. In my own teaching, I often like to sandwich the topic "What Is Language?" around other topics, so we begin by thinking about what language is, explore it in some detail and variety, and then return to consider it again from a more informed position. Instructors may have different ideas about whether to begin with what is more familiar or more strange, with what is easy to see or with what is more challenging.

Some of the chapters could be placed into several units, because they do more than one thing. Language ideology, for example, is both a unit and a topic addressed by readings in other units. Gender, too, appears in many of the units, as well as in its own.

Chapters are not necessarily set up to provide "for" and "against" positions for most topics. Each reading is meant to open up a window, a way of looking at language. I do not necessarily agree with the arguments presented in some of the articles, but I believe that a multiplicity of perspectives is enriching and that what we gain from them is insight, if not always truth. Rarely do I find any perspective entirely, dismissively wrong.

The topics addressed here are broadly mirrored in the contents of textbooks on language and culture, and a textbook could easily complement this collection of readings. The advantage of using primary sources is that students become familiar with the complexity of actual intellectual work rather than its extract. It's a bit like getting your vitamin C from a juicy orange instead of from a tablet.

### Features

The book includes features intended to be helpful for its various audiences. I've provided introductions to the three parts of the book ("The Nature of Language," "Language and Society," and "Language as Social Action") and to the nine units ("What Is Language?," "Language Origins," "Language and Thought," "Language Socialization," "(New) Media," "Multilingualism," "Language and Identity," "Discourse, Performance, and Ritual," and "Language Ideology"). These introductions provide succinct historical and intellectual contexts for the broad topics, followed by a list of suggested further readings.

Each individual article has an introduction, giving information about the author or the context of the work, along with questions to guide student reading and discussion. There are also post-reading suggestions to help students reflect further; included here are also possible class or individual activities. Following each article is a list of key terms, whose definitions are included in the glossary at the end of the book.

The suggested further reading sections following each part introduction, unit introduction, and article point to foundational readings on each topic, alternative perspectives, or additional examples of the approach provided. Some are more difficult and technical, while others are simply additional.

Even in a reader with as many chapters as this, it is impossible to do more than point to the growing body of knowledge and wisdom regarding the many roles of language in human life. My hope is that this book will serve as an opening, an entrée, an appetizer, to lifelong fascination—whether amateur or professional—with this ubiquitous and mysterious capability that we call language.

## Acknowledgments

This book began when my colleague at Notre Dame, Agustín Fuentes, sent the editor of his book down the hall to see if I had any ideas for a book. I immediately told Jan Beatty, the editor at Oxford University Press, "We need a lower-level collection of readings on language and linguistic anthropology to parallel what's available in the other subfields of anthropology," and even more quickly Jan asked if I'd be interested in doing this project. Several years passed before I had time to do it, but after many more rounds of teaching related courses, many encouraging meetings with Jan at the anthropology meetings, and much helpful input from students, the book is coming to life. I'd like to thank Jan for her steady and knowledgeable guidance.

Also at Oxford were Lauren Mine, Brian Black, and Christine D'Antonio, whose work tracking down final permissions and seeing the manuscript through production were indispensable.

I extend my thanks to the following reviewers commissioned by Oxford University Press: Nobuko Adachi, Illinois State University; Jean-Paul Dumont, George Mason University; Arienne Dwyer, University of Kansas; Douglas Glick, Binghamton University; Rosalyn Howard, University of Central Florida; Janet Dixon Keller, University of Illinois; Emily McEwan-Fujita, University of Pittsburgh; Sue Meswick, Queens College of the City University of New York; John Moore, University of Florida; Susan Rasmussen, University of Houston; Robert Rotenberg, DePaul University; Emily Schultz, St. Cloud State University; H. Stephen Straight, Binghamton University; Cindi Sturtz Streetharan, California State University, Sacramento; Stephen Tyler, Rice University; and Dorothy Wills, California State Polytechnic University, Pomona. Some of their comments pushed me—hard—to define my goals for the book, and I can state without reservation that their critiques were essential in making this book live. Indeed, at least half the entries are different from those in the earlier three versions read by these reviewers. I am grateful that these colleagues read the manuscript for this book so carefully and generously.

This book has had some critical reading from a variety of students at Notre Dame (supported by funding from the College of Arts and Letters, the Department of Anthropology, and the Helen Kellogg Institute for International Studies). David "Day" Zimlich and Kaitlin Ramsey read and commented on several chapters. Kathleen Kennedy Johnson sat with me for several days just before she graduated, giving me her first, informed impression of each chapter. Former student Hillary Brass spent most of an academic year helping me track down permissions for each chapter. Tracy Jennings proofread a version of the manuscript and June Sawyers prepared the index, supported by funding from the Institute for Scholarship in the Liberal Arts, College of Arts and Letters, at the University of Notre Dame.

To these students and their many classmates at both Notre Dame and the University of Colorado Denver (where I also spent almost a decade), I express great appreciation.

My colleagues, present and past, at these two institutions and at the University of Pennsylvania—Jim Bellis, John Brett, Meredith Chesson, Kitty Corbett, Antonio Curet, Linda Curran, Greg Downey, Agustín Fuentes, Roberto Da Matta, Patrick Gaffney, Craig Janes, Satsuki Kawano, Webb

Keane, Steve Koestler, Ian Kuijt, Daniel Lende, John Lucy, Joanne Mack, Cynthia Mahmood, Debra McDougall, Jim McKenna, Lisa Mitchell, Lorna Moore, Carolyn Nordstrom, Duane Quiatt, Karen Richman, Deb Rotman, Mark Schurr, Sue Sheridan, Tammy Stone, David Tracer, Greg Urban, and Cecilia van Hollen—have made me think in broadly anthropological terms about the nature and study of language. In many ways their curiosity and (quite often) self-professed lack of expertise propelled me to locate readings that they might find worthwhile to teach. If a few of them, or their counterparts at other institutions, find this book useful, I'll consider my efforts rewarded.

The Inter-Library Loan (ILL) department of Notre Dame's Hesburgh Libraries, along with Document Delivery, were indispensable in the preparation of this book. Sometimes I requested up to a dozen—or more—articles a day for consideration. Miraculously, sometimes articles would appear on my computer within a few hours of the posting of the request. In this age of criticism of higher education, it is important to point out the bright spots, and ILL is certainly one of them.

Finally, my family great and small provided their usual encouragement and balanced perspective as I plodded through the muddy ground of pedagogy, scholarship, copyright, and economics, my shoes sometimes getting stuck. Lionel, Hannah, and Elena Jensen; Joyce and George Blum; Kathi, David, Leah, and Henry Moss; Bobby, Tracye, Natalie, Madeleine, Cameron, and Weston Blum; Linda, Ken, Veronica, and Sara Long; Barbara Blum and Mitchel Alexander; and Anne Jensen: To all of y'all, I say simply, "Thanks."

I welcome suggestions for improvement. Please let me know what works and what doesn't, and please feel free to suggest concrete ways to make this book a better resource. In addition to understanding the material, students should be able to apply what they learn, to become analysts and observers of life. This, I believe, is one of the most important goals of higher education. How we accomplish it is a work in progress.

## Suggested Further Reading

Here are some popular textbooks, readers, and monographs used in teaching material related to this topic.

### Textbooks


Bonvillain, Nancy. 2011. *Language, Culture, and Communication: The Meaning of Messages.* 6th ed. Upper Saddle River, NJ: Pearson Prentice Hall.

Duranti, Alessandro. 1997. *Linguistic Anthropology.* Cambridge: Cambridge University Press.

Foley, William A. 1997. *Anthropological Linguistics: An Introduction.* Malden, MA: Blackwell.

Greenberg, Joseph H. 1968. *Anthropological Linguistics: An Introduction.* New York: Random House.

Hickerson, Nancy Parrott. 2000. *Linguistic Anthropology.* 2nd ed. Fort Worth, TX: Harcourt.

Ohio State University Department of Linguistics. 2011. *Language Files.* 11th ed. Columbus: Ohio State University Press.

Ottenheimer, Harriet Joseph. 2012. *The Anthropology of Language: An Introduction to Linguistic Anthropology.* 3rd ed. Belmont, CA: Thomson Higher Education. A workbook accompanies this text.

Romaine, Suzanne. 2000. *Language in Society: An Introduction to Sociolinguistics.* 2nd ed. Oxford: Oxford University Press.

Saville-Troike, Muriel. 2003. *The Ethnography of Communication: An Introduction.* 3rd ed. Malden, MA: Blackwell.

Salzmann, Zdenek, James Stanlaw, and Nobuko Adachi. 2011. *Language, Culture and Society: An Introduction to Linguistic Anthropology.* 5th ed. Boulder, CO: Westview Press.


### Readers


Bauman, Richard, and Joel Sherzer, eds. 1989. *Explorations in the Ethnography of Speaking.* 2nd ed. Cambridge: Cambridge University Press.

Blount, Ben G., ed. 1995. *Language, Culture, and Society: A Book of Readings.* 2nd ed. Prospect Heights, IL: Waveland Press.

Brenneis, Donald, and Ronald H. S. Macaulay, eds. 1996. *The Matrix of Language: Contemporary Linguistic Anthropology.* Boulder, CO: Westview Press.

Clark, Virginia P., Paul A. Eschholz, Alfred F. Rosa, and Beth Lee Simon, eds. 2007. *Language: Introductory Readings*, 7th ed. Boston: Bedford/St. Martin's.

Duranti, Alessandro, ed. 2009. *Linguistic Anthropology: A Reader.* Malden, MA: Blackwell.

Duranti, Alessandro, ed. 2004. *A Companion to Linguistic Anthropology.* 2nd ed. Malden, MA: Blackwell.

Giglioli, Pier Paolo, comp. 1972. *Language and Social Context: Selected Readings.* Harmondsworth, UK: Penguin Books.

Gumperz, John J., and Dell Hymes, eds. 1986. *Directions in Sociolinguistics: The Ethnography of Communication.* Oxford: Blackwell.

Jaworski, Adam, and Nikolas Coupland, eds. 2006. *The Discourse Reader.* 2nd ed. London and New York: Routledge.


### Monographs


Basso, Keith H. 1979. *Portraits of "the Whiteman": Linguistic Play and Cultural Symbols Among the Western Apache.* Cambridge: Cambridge University Press.

Everett, Daniel L. 2009. *Don't Sleep, There are Snakes: Life and Language in the Amazonian Jungle.* New York: Vintage.

Graham, Laura R. 2003. *Performing Dreams: Discoveries of Immortality Among the Xavante of Central Brazil.* 2nd ed. Tucson, AZ: Fenestra.

Hymes, Dell. 1974. *Foundations in Sociolinguistics: An Ethnographic Approach.* Philadelphia: University of Pennsylvania Press.

Mendoza-Denton, Norma. 2008. *Homegirls: Language and Cultural Practice Among Latina Youth Gangs.* Malden, MA: Blackwell.

Philips, Susan U. 1983. *The Invisible Culture: Communication in Classroom and Community on the Warm Springs Indian Reservation.* Prospect Heights, IL: Waveland Press.

Urciuoli, Bonnie. 1996. *Exposing Prejudice: Puerto Rican Experiences of Language, Race, and Class.* Boulder, CO: Westview Press.

Wogan, Peter. 2004. *Magical Writing in Salasaca: Literacy and Power in Highland Ecuador.* Boulder, CO: Westview Press.

Zentella, Ana Celia. 1997. *Growing Up Bilingual: Puerto Rican Children in New York.* Malden, MA: Blackwell.

# INTRODUCTION TO THE REVISED EDITION

When Oxford University Press asked me to revise this book, I welcomed the opportunity. I am not only the editor of a book that I hope is useful and appealing to both students and their teachers. I too use the book; I too interact with my students, the world, the Internet, and scholarship. So three years down the road, I was eager for the chance to improve the book. In response to some formal and other informal feedback, I changed a number of the readings, aiming for entries that are perhaps more appropriate for today's students. I was delighted to find so many terrific new resources on language in the last five years or so. Some chapters I deleted with some hesitation; others seemed obvious. I added three entirely new sections: Language Origins, Language Socialization, and (New) Media, in large part because of the explosion of research on all of them and my conviction that students benefit from greater attention paid to these topics. There are also many chapters that concern education. Language ideology is woven throughout.

Financial considerations play a role, but not as you might think; students and faculty at well-endowed universities have easy access to specialized journals, but their counterparts at more modestly resourced schools do not. Libraries everywhere are reducing their subscriptions. Thus, including journal articles is necessary if a broad range of students is to be able to read signal journal articles. In many cases, busy students have no time to track down readings from a range of sources, so it is helpful for them to have readings all in one place.

I have retained a focus on reaching a wide and general student audience, those without specialized expertise in the fields of linguistic anthropology, linguistics, anthropology, or communications. My hope is that these chapters will announce: *This is fascinating, and you can learn more about it!* I see this reader as an array of invitations, a small plates tasting. Not every item will appeal to every person, but there should be something for everyone.

If you are a student, or a professor, and have suggestions for how to improve this book for its next edition, please feel free to contact me or the press. This is not quite crowd-editing or Wiki writing, but to the extent that the audience crafts the work, it is better for us all.

**Acknowledgments**

I am especially grateful to the following individuals who worked on the revised version of the book: Cari Heicklen, Sherith Pankratz, and Marianne Paul at Oxford University Press and Jan Beatty who persuaded me to undertake the revision as well as the initial work; Caitlin Wilson, who will be an excellent contributor to the world of higher education and who pointed out all the infelicities of my introductions and questions and kept track of the permissions for republication; Christina Rogers who helped with word counts, bibliographies, and various miscellaneous tasks; Emily Dawson who appeared in South Bend and helped with the revised Glossary; Christine Finnan who generously explained her thoughts about which components of the first edition were useful and why. I would like to thank the Institute for Scholarship in the Liberal Arts, College of Arts and Letters, University of Notre Dame, for supporting the publication of this resource. And I would particularly like to acknowledge the contributions of three years of students in Anthropology 30104, and the pilot New Media class, at Notre Dame. Even your lack of enthusiasm about some readings was informative—but when you were excited and engaged, it made everything worthwhile.

Thank you to the following reviewers, commissioned by Oxford University Press:

- Robey Callahan, CSU Fullerton
- Claire Cesareo-Silva, Saddleback College
- Janina Fenigsen, University of Wisconsin–Milwaukee
- Sean O'Neill, University of Oklahoma–Norman
- Amy Paugh, James Madison University
- Moore Quinn, College of Charleston
- William Cecil Roberts, St. Mary's College of Maryland
- Richard J. Senghas, Sonoma State University
- William D. Smith, Western Oregon University
- Brian Stross, The University of Texas at Austin

## New in This Edition

THREE UNITS

Language Origins
Language Socialization
(New) Media

A SUBUNIT

Generation

TWENTY-NINE NEW CHAPTERS

MAP

## How to Use This Book

The book is divided broadly into three parts (The Nature of Language, Language and Society, and Language as Social Action), and each part is subdivided into units and sometimes even subunits. The parts can be taken in any order depending on the instructor's particular goals.

The book's components:

- A **map** on the inside cover to locate the readings in space
- **Part introductions**
- **Unit introductions**
- The short **chapter introductions** place the chapter into intellectual or thematic context and, for well-known authors, provide some biographical information.
- **Reading Questions** guide you to pay attention to certain types of information. You may regard this as a set of "what-questions": What did the author say? What did a certain phrase mean?
- The **chapter** itself
- **Critical Thinking and Application** items ask you to look more deeply at the chapter, to connect it to things you know, to wonder about reasons, to evaluate, and to conduct your own research along the lines suggested in the chapter.
- **Vocabulary** items, bolded in the chapter, that are significant in the chapter and that are defined in the **Glossary** at the end of the book.
- **Suggested Further Reading** lists items that are kindred in some sense, sometimes by theoretical extension or context and sometimes by ethnographic or topical connection.

# PART I

# The Nature of Language

Language may not be what you think it is. It is not mostly the perfect, well-formed grammatical sentences that your English teachers have taught you to write, though these are an aspect of language. It does not revolve around spelling and vocabulary tests, though people might analyze those, too. "Language" refers to a range of communicative behavior, and the quintessential form is spoken language, though signed languages, written language, and electronic communication are also language. Many regard the sign as the principal aspect of language. Language is learned principally through interaction, not at school. It always changes, and it interacts with all other aspects of human experience.

In some sense, people have been studying language for hundreds or even thousands of years. The early Sanskrit grammarians such as Panini wrote about Sanskrit grammar in the fifth century B.C.E.; Chinese dictionaries, analyzing the phonetic and semantic (sound and meaning) aspects of words, have been written for 2,000 years; Arabic and Hebrew grammarians wrote about their languages in the early Middle Ages; and the Spanish linguist Antonio de Nebrija wrote a grammar of Castillian in 1492.

The modern study of language is usually traced to the nineteenth-century encounter with the languages of "the Orient" (mostly India and China) and the discovery that the sacred Indian language Sanskrit was related to classical Greek and Latin, the treasure of European education. The stable entities that humans consider "a language," such as French, were understood to have evolved, in this case, from varieties of Latin.

Simultaneously, revolutions in scientific thought, such as the discovery of "geological time"—measuring the earth in billions of years rather than in thousands, because of the understanding of fossils—and the Darwinian revolution in understanding humans' place among biological species, all combined to provide a new way of thinking about language. It could at least be possible that language was not entirely unique in the world. It could be analyzed in its own terms; languages could be compared; human language in general could be compared to nonhuman communication.

With the Age of Exploration leading to anthropological understanding of the nature of peoples other than the European explorers and missionaries, it was recognized that people everywhere "had language" and that their languages were just as complex and even evolved as the European and Semitic languages. Anthropologists such as Franz Boas, himself a polyglot (one who knows many languages), tried to master and analyze the languages of Native Americans, discovering that there were hundreds of such languages, probably more than three hundred, and that they were very sophisticated.

Further advances in the study of language came from a group known as the Prague school, who set modern analytic linguistics on its way with the discovery of the *phoneme* (essentially a psychological image of a sound that had a particular pattern in a language) and other structural aspects of language.

The other major twentieth-century revolution in the study of language is associated with Noam Chomsky, who used an approach called *transformational-generative grammar* to demonstrate the primacy of syntax in the study of language. The study of language as a phenomenon reveals patterns, systems, and order that many find quite elegant and even beautiful.

Other trends in the study of language include a focus not on its structure but on the meanings and functions that emerge from *language in use* and in interaction. This has been facilitated by advances in recording technology. Early in the twentieth century, tape recorders could provide records of sound, permitting detailed transcription of natural speech. More recently, studies of interaction, including nonverbal aspects, have been enabled by video recording.

As the twentieth century unfolded, scholars began to note that since language was always changing, changes in society could be traced through the changes in language. As groups migrated to a particular location, the relations among languages might change entirely, and the language itself might even become extinct, like Hittite and Gothic. Or the languages encountering others could create a kind of blend, a "creole," using elements of the contributing languages. Languages can be born—but they also can die. Scholars estimate that of the 10,000 languages that existed a mere hundred years ago, about half are already extinct.

Efforts are made by many actors to preserve or revitalize endangered languages. Some of such efforts, such as among some groups of Navajos, are considered successful. Others, such as in Wales, are sentimental but have not yielded practical results (see Unit 6).

One of the losses an endangered language risks is the loss of the thought world accompanying it. That's because, as the great linguist and anthropologist Edward Sapir said,

> Human beings do not live in the objective world alone, nor alone in the world of social activity as ordinarily understood, but are very much at the mercy of the particular language which has become the medium of expression for their society.... We see and hear and otherwise experience very largely as we do because the language habits of our community predispose certain choices of interpretation.

How this thing called language affects human thought, which is largely observed in what people say, has perplexed scholars ever since Sapir wrote of language as a "prepared road or groove" for thought.

Yet what exactly language is remains contested. There are not just one or two approaches to it, but dozens, each emphasizing some different aspect, each pointing out what the author regards as the most important thing to know about language: that it is spoken, that it is made of signs, that it enables transmission of culture, that it is similar across all languages, or that it varies greatly across languages.

In this part of the book, we consider the nature of language, from the perspective of a definition (Unit 1, "What Is Language?") and its possible origins (Unit 2, "Language Origins"), as it may or may not affect thought (Unit 3, "Language and Thought") as it is learned through interaction and schooling (Unit 4, "Language Socialization"), and as it is transmitted through an assortment of media (Unit 5, "New Media"). These are broad, foundational issues in understanding this thing so easily contained in the single, simple word, *language*.

## Suggested Further Reading

Aarsleff, Hans. 1982. *From Locke to Saussure: Essays on the Study of Language and Intellectual History*. Minneapolis: University of Minnesota Press.

Harris, Roy, and Talbot J. Taylor. 1989. *The Western Tradition from Socrates to Saussure*. London and New York: Routledge.

Hymes, Dell H. 1974. *Studies in the History of Linguistics: Traditions and Paradigms*. Bloomington: Indiana University Press.

Koerner, E. F. K., and R. E. Asher, eds. 1995. *Concise History of the Language Sciences: From the Sumerians to the Cognitivists*. New York: Pergamon Press.

Lehmann, Winfred P., comp. 1967. *A Reader in Nineteenth Century Historical Indo-European Linguistics*. Bloomington: Indiana University Press.

Robins, R. H. 1990. *A Short History of Linguistics*. 3rd ed. London and New York: Longman.

Seuren, Pieter A. M. 1998. *Western Linguistics: An Historical Introduction*. Oxford and Malden, MA: Blackwell.

# UNIT 1

# What Is Language?

All human societies have had "language" (though only some have had writing), and this is where experts often draw the boundaries between humans and other hominids. But exactly where the line between language and other communicative behavior belongs is a matter for debate. The research and debate on this topic became very lively and multifaceted beginning in the 1990s, with colorful and imaginative suggestions presented from widely differing perspectives. Many focus on the origins of language, relying on differing forms of evidence.

Some scholars regard the essence of language as symbolic behavior. Although obviously this cannot be seen fossilized in human or other primate remains, we can see related examples of symbolic behavior in things like cave paintings, tool manufacture, and deliberate burial. Others see the essence of language as lying in what Charles Hockett calls "duality of patterning," by which small elements, themselves not meaningful, combine in meaningful ways at a higher level. This, too, is invisible in fossils. Some see language as lying on a continuum with other types of communicative behavior, and as stemming from humans' increased brain size (both absolute and relative) compared to our closest primate relatives, chimpanzees and other apes. For this, a deeper understanding of ape communication systems is required. This field alone has given rise to profoundly contested viewpoints.

Some see language as fundamentally spoken, in which case the anatomy of the vocal tract is of interest. Others see it as fundamentally a system of organized signs, with combinations being the most relevant piece. Sign languages may then hearken back to a gestural system of communication, and spoken languages may simply share features with these languages.

Some, such as Noam Chomsky and Steven Pinker, see language as resulting from a genetic mutation, resulting in a language facility as yet undiscovered in the physical brain but permitting all the special characteristics of language: being rule governed, being infinitely productive, employing a finite but quite large set of signifiers, and made up of many smaller "modules" governing negation, semantics, and so forth. Some emphasize the information that can be conveyed through language, and some emphasize the social relations that can be deepened through language. Scholars such as Esther Goody have pointed out that spoken language requires cooperation because it necessarily involves conversational meanings, which emerge only through interaction. Thus, the unit of evolution is not necessarily the individual organism but the social group.

Language occurs in multiple modalities, including speech, signing, and writing. Each of these is regarded as desirable or limited by some people in some circumstances, but those evaluations vary across time and space.

Debates about the nature of language can be intense. This unit presents two attempts to understand the nature of language. This selection is not meant to be exhaustive, merely to provide some outlines of the concepts that must be considered when we try to understand this most unusual faculty of language.

For those intrigued by the question of how humans developed language, it is first necessary to define language, so it can be identified in whatever data are relevant to the question. This evolving discussion involves complex information from genetics, primatology, psychology, neurobiology, paleoanthropology, linguistics, linguistic anthropology, and cultural anthropology. Some is technical and some is more discursive; all is speculative.

## Suggested Further Reading

Aitchison, Jean. 2000. *The Seeds of Speech: Language Origin and Evolution*. Cambridge: Cambridge University Press.

Armstrong, David F., William C. Stokoe, and Sherman E. Wilcox. 1995. *Gesture and the Nature of Language*. Cambridge: Cambridge University Press.

Bickerton, Derek. 1980. *Language and Species*. Chicago: University of Chicago Press.

Burling, Robbins. 2005. *The Talking Ape: How Language Evolved*. Oxford: Oxford University Press.

Byrne, Richard W., and Andrew Whiten, eds. 1988. *Machiavellian Intelligence: Social Expertise and the Evolution of Intellect in Monkeys, Apes and Humans*. Oxford: Clarendon Press.

Calvin, William, and Derek Bickerton. 2000. *Lingua ex Machina: Reconciling Darwin and Chomsky with the Human Brain*. Cambridge, MA: MIT Press.

Cheney, Dorothy L., and Robert M. Seyfarth. 1990. *How Monkeys See the World: Inside the Mind of Another Species*. Chicago: University of Chicago Press.

Chomsky, Noam. 1972. *Language and Mind*. New York: Harcourt Brace Jovanovich.

Christiansen, Morten H., and Simon Kirby, eds. 2003. *Language Evolution*. Oxford: Oxford University Press.

Dessalles, Jean-Louis. 2007 [2000]. *Why We Talk: The Evolutionary Origins of Language*, translated by James Grieve. Oxford and New York: Oxford University Press.

Dunbar, Robin. 1996. *Grooming, Gossip, and the Evolution of Language*. Cambridge, MA: Harvard University Press.

Foley, William. 1997. *Anthropological Linguistics: An Introduction*. Oxford: Blackwell.

Goody, Esther N., ed. 1995. *Social Intelligence and Interaction*. Cambridge: Cambridge University Press.

King, Barbara J., ed. 1999. *The Origins of Language: What Nonhuman Primates Can Tell Us*. Santa Fe, NM: School of American Research Press.

Lieberman, Philip. 1991. *Uniquely Human: The Evolution of Speech, Thought and Selfless Behavior*. Cambridge, MA: Harvard University Press.

Lieberman, Philip. 1998. *Eve Spoke: Human Language and Human Evolution*. New York: Norton.

Oller, D. Kimbrough, and Ulrike Griebel, eds. 2004. *Evolution of Communication Systems: A Comparative Approach*. Cambridge, MA: MIT Press.

Savage-Rumbaugh, E. Sue. 1998. *Apes, Language, and the Human Mind*. New York: Oxford University Press.

Whiten, Andrew. 1991. *Natural Theories of Mind: Evolution, Development and Simulation of Everyday Mindreading*. Oxford: Blackwell.

Whiten, Andrew, and Richard W. Byrne, eds. 1997. *Machiavellian Intelligence II: Extensions and Evaluations*. Cambridge: Cambridge University Press.

# CHAPTER 1

# Smiles, Winks, and Words

## *Robbins Burling*

(2005)

*Robbins Burling has written about languages in Burma and India, about how to learn a field language, and about language origins and many other aspects of language. As much anthropologist as linguist, he looks carefully at how language functions in human interactions to explain how it arose. In this chapter, excerpted from his book* The Talking Ape, *he differentiates among different types of communicative signs, both verbal and gestural, but warns that "gesture" overlooks differences in the ways humans use their bodies communicatively. If we wish to understand the nature of language, it is essential to sort it out from other types of communication.*

### Reading Questions

- In Burling's opening anecdote, how did he figure out that there were two fundamentally different kinds of communicative gestures?
- What does Burling mean by "language"? How is it different from signals of other types?
- How does Burling situate human communication within animal communication?
- What kinds of communication are universal and what kinds are culturally specific?
- What can we do with language that we can't do with other kinds of communication?

Human beings never run out of talk. We relate the events of the day. We gossip about our acquaintances. We speculate about people and power. Children chatter so incessantly that even their talkative parents lose patience. We explain, we cajole, we schmooze, we harangue, and we flirt, all with the help of language. To be sure, we also convey information in many other ways than by talking. We use our voices not only to speak, but to scream, sigh, laugh, hum, and cry. We show our joy with our smiles, and our anger with our scowls. We threaten by standing tall, and show submission by trying to look small. By the way we touch each other, we can show either fury or love. We even learn something from the way others smell. If we are to ask how language emerged in the human species, we need to start by understanding where it fits among the many other ways, audible, visible, olfactory, and tactile, by which humans communicate.

I had a vivid lesson about our different forms of communication when, as a young man, I landed by small boat at the little port of Marmaris on the southern coast of Turkey. Within half an hour of landing, I found myself negotiating for a room with a woman who ran a small guesthouse. She and I had no common language, but the situation made my needs obvious. We stood in a courtyard and she held out her hand, palm downward, with her fingers together and extended toward me. She then bent her hand sharply so that her fingers turned downward, while the back of her hand remained horizontal. This was clearly a stereotyped gesture, intended to convey a specific meaning to me, but I did not understand what that meaning was. I could think of two possibilities. Perhaps she wanted me to follow her or, perhaps, she wanted me to wait. I hesitated for just a moment but then decided to make a test. I deliberately took one step backward, and the woman scowled and looked a bit frustrated. I knew immediately that she wanted me to follow her, and she then led me to a room.

The woman had made two communicative gestures, and even then I was startled at how different they were. Her palm-down beckoning gesture, I would later learn, is used everywhere from Turkey through India and on to Southeast Asia, but as my previous ignorance showed, it is by no means universal. It is conventional, and it has to be learned. Her scowl, on the other hand, needed no learning at all. It was part of the heritage that the woman and I shared with every other human being. I could even use her scowl to help me define the meaning of her hand gesture.

Robbins Burling, Smiles, Winks, and Words. In *The Talking Ape: How Language Evolved*. Oxford: Oxford University Press, 2005, pp. 23–47.

The scowl is an example of a large class of signals that are common to all humanity. These signals need little learning, and they allow us to communicate in quite subtle ways with people of all cultures. They include many of the ways in which we express ourselves with our faces, voices, hands and arms, and even with the posture and movements of our entire bodies: our laughs, screams, smiles, frowns, and shrugs. I will argue that these gestures and vocalizations, which all humans share, should be seen as forming a second kind of human communication, one that is quite different from language. I need a name for this group of signals and I will call them **"gesture-calls."** This is, admittedly, a somewhat contrived term, but it is useful as a way of... [describing] the similarities between these signals and the calls and communicative gestures of other mammals. The word "calls," of course, is not generally used for human signals, but only for the communicative vocalizations of animals. We do not think of human laughs and sobs as "calls" but that is only because we do not usually think of human beings as "animals"; but our laughs, sobs, sighs, and screams can be counted among the distinctive calls of the human species just as pant-hoots and long calls are among the distinctive calls of chimpanzees, and just as barks, growls, and howls are among the distinctive calls of dogs. I cannot fully justify the use of the term "gesture-calls" for human beings [here], but what matters now is to recognize that our human repertory of signals includes many that have meanings that are similar to the signals of other mammals, and that are produced with our voices, our faces, and our postures, just as theirs are.

I will use the word "language" only in its narrow sense, to refer to the system of sounds, words, and sentences to which we give names like "English," "Zulu," or "Chinese." "Body language" is something else. I will begin with an account of some characteristics of language (in this narrow sense) and of the ways in which our other forms of communication are similar to and different from language. These other forms of communication are sometimes referred to simply as our "nonverbal communication," but this expression bundles together too many different kinds of signaling to be very useful. They need to be distinguished not only from language but from one another.

[Eventually I shall conclude] that language could not have evolved from any animal-like form of communication, simply because it is so different from all other animal behavior. The headings used in the following pages identify a series of ways in which language differs from other forms of human communication and from the communication used by other species. It is the evolution of these unique characteristics of language that we must understand if we are ever to know how language originated.

## Digital and Analog Communication

Information can be conveyed in either **analog** or **digital** form, not only inside a computer, but in any medium at all. The steadily sweeping second hand of a clock, the swinging needle of an automobile speedometer, and a slide rule that can be manipulated into an unlimited number of positions are all analog devices. The meanings of a clock hand, speedometer needle, and slide rule vary in proportion to their positions, and in principle, there is no way to count the number of readings these instruments can give. A digital clock that bumps time abruptly from 8:45 to 8:46 but permits no compromise, presents its information with digital rather than analog signals. So does an abacus, where each bead can be positioned either up or down but can never come to rest halfway between. Digital signals have sharp boundaries. They are discrete. Digital devices can assume no more than a finite number of states. The beads of an abacus have a limited number of positions. A pocket calculator has only a finite (though huge) number of possible displays. Human beings communicate with both digital and analog signals.

The sound system of a language, its **phonology**, is prototypically digital. The meaningless units of our phonological systems are the **phonemes** that we represent, imperfectly, by the letters of our wretched spelling system. These phonemes are, as linguists say, in "contrast" with one another. This means that it is no more possible to compromise between the *p* and *b* of *pat* and *bat* than between 11:13 and 11:14 on [the] face of a digital clock. There is always a midpoint between any two positions of a speedometer needle even if the midpoints quickly become microscopic. The contrastive sounds of a language can be joined to form the many thousands of words that language users need, and the words, too, are in contrast. Contrasting words, in turn, allow sentences to be in contrast with one another. It is the digital phonological code that allows us to construct an enormous number of words and an unlimited number of sentences, and to keep them all distinct from one another.

Most of our signals, other than language, are graded rather than discrete. A giggle is not sharply distinct from a laugh, nor is a laugh clearly distinct from a guffaw. A sound that is halfway between a giggle and a laugh means something halfway between them as well. Perhaps giggles even grade into snorts, snorts into cries of objection, cries of objection into cries of anguish, and cries of anguish into sobs. This suggests a continuum that runs all the way from laughs to sobs with no sharp break at any point along the way. This is grading with a vengeance, with no boundaries in sight. The continuum may not reach quite all the way from a laugh to a sob, but human gesture-calls do show extensive grading, and this makes them utterly different from language. A halfway point between two words like *single* and *shingle* simply does not exist. A halfway point between a giggle and a laugh is perfectly real and perfectly understandable.

We can't count the number of our gesture-calls. What happens if we try? We have names for some of our gestures and for some of our calls, and these may tempt us to try to count the signals by counting the words: *laugh, snort, smile, frown, cry, sigh, squint, scream, pout, swagger,* and dozens of others. Listing the names is easy enough, but we soon run into problems. Do we count a giggle and a guffaw as different from a laugh? Or are they simply different forms of a single call? What about something halfway between a giggle and a laugh? What about a cry, a sob, and a whimper? There is an indeterminacy here that is intrinsic to an analog system. We can give names to spots or segments along the continuum, but there is no principled way to decide how many spots or segments to name, or where to draw a line between the end of one and the beginning of the next. There is no way to decide how different two signals must be in order to be counted as different.

The digital system that is provided by linguistic contrast allows human languages to be constructed according to profoundly different principles than what I am calling our "gesture-calls." To say that gesture-calls lack contrast is simply another way of saying that both in their meaning and in the manner by which they are produced, smiles, laughs, frowns, and screams vary along continuous scales. Language is digital, gesture-calls are analog.

Immediately, complications need to be acknowledged. The **intonation** of language, the ups and downs of pitch and emphasis, vary continuously so they form analog signals. On the other hand, the beckoning gesture of the Turkish guesthouse keeper had to be sharply distinct from her other gestures. Clearly, it would be too simple to imagine that language is uniformly digital and that everything else is analog. Examples such as these enormously complicate the description and understanding of human communication, and I will need to return to them later and put them in place. In the meantime, we can still recognize that the phonological and **syntactic** core of language (but not its intonation) is digital, while large parts of the rest of our communication is analog. The difference between digital and analog signals is crucial.

## Reference, Propositions, and Emotions

The digital nature of the phonological code lets us distinguish thousands of words from one another. These words can be used to talk about our ideas, both our ideas about the world and ideas that are pure imagination. With language, we can tell someone where to buy fish. We can extol the virtues of a politician or an applicant for a job. We can whisper a fascinating tidbit about what Velma said to Mervin last night. We can ask questions, make requests, or give orders. We can spin yarns, tell lies, share jokes, and invent imaginary beings. Words give us names, not only for objects but also for actions, qualities, relations, sentiments, and indeed, for anything at all that we can think about. By combining words into sentences we can express propositions, and in this way convey messages about all the things that we name with our words. This kind of propositional information can be easily shared with others, so it conveys information about the state of the world, or at least, about what we imagine the state of the world to be. Our ability to form propositions even allows us to talk about language. We can use language to describe language.

Our analog cries, facial expressions, and postures are of only limited use for describing the world around us. They are much better at conveying delicate shades of emotion and intention. With frowns, smiles, shrugs, sighs, whimpers, and chuckles, we let others know how we feel, and suggest what we are likely to do next. Postures and facial expressions are likely to give a more reliable guide than words about whether to expect a kiss or slap. We use our postures, our gestures, and our facial expressions to ease relationships with others and to show that we know our place in the social world.

We convey many of our feelings more easily, more subtly, and less self-consciously with our calls and facial expressions than we do with language. Many of us dislike discussing serious or sensitive matters over the telephone, in part, at least, because we cannot read the gestures and facial expressions of the person on the other end of the line. We feel crippled by being limited to mere language. We hear one another's words, but we are left uncertain about one another's feelings. Mere language does not make up for the missing gesture-calls.

We can show our anger, our boredom, or our playfulness, with our gesture-calls. We can show others how much we love them. But we cannot tell stories. We cannot describe the difference between a pine tree and an oak, let alone the difference between an odd and even number. We cannot agree on a time and place to meet for lunch. We could easily enough invent gestures with which to plan a lunch date, but the gestures would have to refer to times, places, and events in the world, and in the very act of agreeing on them we would have to devise gestures that have more in common with language than with gesture-calls.

If we find it difficult to form true propositions about the world with our gestures and calls, we find it even more difficult to form false propositions. If we cannot tell true stories, we can hardly tell fairy tales. We cannot lie. We can, to be sure, feign, or at least we can try. The poker player must act as if his cards are different than they really are. The boxer pretends that he is about to hit from the left when he is really planning to hit from the right. We can try to pretend to a happiness we do not really feel or we can try to hide our excitement or pleasure. Feigning emotions, however, is not the same as lying, and most of us are not very good at it. The majority of human beings, who are neither con men nor skilled actors, find it much easier to lie with words than to mislead with gesture-calls.

So the most important thing about language is also the most obvious one. Language allows us, with great ease, to refer to things and events, and to say something about them. Gesture-calls are much better at expressing our emotions and intentions. Nevertheless, the association of digital language with referential messages on the one hand, and analog gestures and calls with emotional messages on the other, while high, is not perfect. Skillful poets can express emotions beautifully with words. Most of us need help from our gesture-calls. When I bite into an apple, my puckered face tells you something about its taste, and my face can also tell you whether something that I have just seen is desirable or frightening. So we can convey some information about the state of the world with our gesture-calls, and we can convey some emotions with language. More often and more easily we use digital language for facts and analog gestures and calls for emotions.

## HEREDITY AND ENVIRONMENT

I need to begin this hoary subject by insisting on one thing: everything that human beings are or do (or that other animals are or do), everything about our bodies, our minds, and our behavior, comes about by the joint action of heredity and environment. Nothing could develop if the genes did not make it possible, and nothing could develop without a suitable environment. It is nonsense to ask whether heredity or environment should be credited for some human trait like stature, language, rock music, spelling, or intelligence. Both heredity and environment have a role in everything.

We find it easier to accept the interaction of inheritance and experience for physical traits like stature or complexion than for behavioral and intellectual traits like aggression, music, or a sense of humor. We feel comfortable with the idea that stature depends on both the genes we inherited from our parents and the food we ate while growing up. Skin color depends not only on how a particular set of genes has instructed a body to produce pigment, but also on how long that body has been exposed to the sun. We have more trouble recognizing that bashfulness, courting behavior, bicycle riding, spoken language, and literacy also emerge from the interaction of hereditary endowment and environmental opportunities, but our behavior is just as much the result of this interaction as is our body. The way we sit depends on both the way our genes have built our bones and the habits of the society in which we have grown up. The food we enjoy depends not only on the inherited nature of human digestion but on our idiosyncratic experiences with food. Our ability to dance, to catch fish, and to do long division, all require both inherited aptitudes and the right experiences. We ask the wrong question when we ask whether heredity or environment is responsible for a piece of our bodies or a bit of our behavior. We can be certain that both have played a role.

What makes us most uncomfortable is to attribute individual differences in behavior to heredity. We accept hereditary variability in the shape of our noses or the amount of hair on our arms, but many of us would like to believe in human perfectibility, to believe that anyone can learn to do anything if only the opportunities are right. Individual differences in inherited aptitude will not go away simply because we wish they did not exist, however, and the world would really be a much duller place if we all started life exactly alike. To make everyone average would call for a lot of dumbing down as well as smarting up, and you and I would be poorer for having no Darwins, Beethovens, and Picassos to show us what is possible.

What, then, do we do about our strong intuitions that nature is more important for some things and nurture for others? Eye color seems pretty well set by the genes. Whether we call the bottom end of our leg our *foot*, *pied*, or *Fuss* seems to have everything to do with experience and nothing at all to do with biology. We can deal with this intuition by asking what proportion of the variation that is found in some physical or behavioral trait is due to differences in heredity and what proportion of that variation is due to differences in experience. A trait whose variability depends on variable genes is said to be **"heritable."** Variability that results from experience is not. Heritability, however, is not an all-or-none matter. Different traits show different degrees of heritability. Stature depends on nutrition as well as inheritance, but it does have a high degree of heritability. The particular name that we use for the end of our leg has a very low heritability. We can legitimately ask how much of the variation that we find in some trait is due to differing kinds of experiences and how much is due to differing innate aptitude, but it is simplistic to ask whether it is one or the other.

My insistence that heredity and environment are every bit as intricately interwoven in our behavior as in our bodies, is needed because it is so terribly tempting, but also so terribly wrong, to suppose that our laughter, our cries, our frowns, and our scowls are determined by inheritance while language has to be learned. Of course we need to learn a particular language, but we could not talk at all if we had not inherited a mind that is designed for language learning. Dogs, even dogs that live in Tanzania, never learn Swahili because they have not been given the right kind of minds. Nor do Japanese very often learn Swahili, but this has nothing to do with Japanese genes or minds. To learn Swahili you need both the right kind of inheritance and the right kind of experience.

What is true for language is also true for our gesture-calls. Once past the first few weeks of life, every reasonably normal human being smiles. The magical ability of babies to smile needs both the right kind of inheritance and the environment of womb and cradle that allows a smile to develop. Short of violence or starvation, it is nearly impossible to stop a baby from smiling, but you and I would not smile under exactly the same circumstances had we grown up in a different culture. We must learn the rules laid down by our own society for the appropriate times, places, and circumstances for smiles, and for all our other gesture-calls.

Both our language and our gesture-calls, then, depend on both genes and experience, but the mixtures differ. The variation from one community to another is much greater for language than for gesture-calls, and this can only mean that language is less narrowly constrained by inheritance than are gesture-calls. Gesture-calls such as laughter are highly heritable. Whatever variability distinguishes the laughs of different individuals depends largely on inherited differences, not on variable experience. The contribution of learning is greater for language. A foreigner understands nothing of Chinese without some learning, and it takes a great deal of learning to understand or to say very much. New arrivals in China can understand much of what is conveyed by Chinese laughs and sobs, giggles and snorts, cries of anguish and all the rest of their gesture-calls, from the moment they step off the plane in Beijing. Because humans everywhere are genetically very much alike, our facial expressions, like our cries and laughs, convey much the same meanings everywhere.

Wherever you travel, a smile will suggest more friendliness than a scowl. Nowhere will you find people who habitually laugh when sad but cry in response to a joke. When anthropologists need to find their way in a new community but have not yet learned much of the language, they can easily judge the reactions of their hosts by reading their facial expressions. They do not need language to know whether people are friendly or hostile.

A half-century ago, the mind of a newborn baby was often imagined to be a "blank slate." It was supposed to contain little when it first entered the world except an ability to absorb whatever the environment offered. Language, like the rest of our behavior, was then attributed almost entirely to learning. If anything called a "mind" was even considered, it was regarded as a sort of general-purpose learning device that could learn one thing about as easily as another. The mind was thought to be pushed in one direction or another by its experiences, and learning seemed to dominate heredity. Nothing was assumed about the inherited nature of the human brain or mind.

Part of the intellectual upheaval brought about by Noam Chomsky was his challenge to this extreme **behaviorism**. He has always insisted that human beings come equipped with a mind and brain that are designed, in highly specific ways, for language. He has insisted that a child could not possibly master the fierce complexities of a language in a few short years if all he had to work with was a blank slate and a generalized ability to learn. Chomsky persuaded a large body of linguists that a successful language learner needs much more built in than generalized learning skills, and he shifted the focus of much of linguistics away from the differences among languages to the universal features that are presumed to arise because of the universal nature of the human mind. The mind came to be thought of as specifically designed for language.

Chomsky succeeded in pushing opinion so far away from the older behaviorism that a few linguists seem almost to have forgotten about learning. Thus, what would otherwise hardly need to be said at all, now needs to be insistently proclaimed: languages do, after all, differ. The differences among them can only result from varying experience, which is to say, from learning. Chomsky is surely right to insist that our genetic inheritance provides us with the capacity to learn a language. It is not simply a metaphor to say that we have a "language instinct." Nevertheless, a vast amount of learning is still needed in order to fulfill the potential of our inheritance. As with all other aspects of our bodies and behavior, we could never speak without both inheritance and learning. Indeed, one of the most interesting questions about human evolution is to ask how our genetic endowment managed to evolve to the point where it lets us learn so much. Our digital and propositional language requires much more learning than our analog and emotional calls and gestures.

## A Massive Vocabulary and Duality of Patterning

Languages have tens of thousands of words. Every one of us has managed to learn a massive vocabulary. This is so utterly unlike anything found in any other communication system that it has to count as one of the most distinctive characteristics of language and, indeed, of humanity.

Our huge stock of words would not be possible without the digital phonological code. Most languages have a thousand or more possible syllables, enough to allow a million distinct two-syllable words. By some counts, to be sure, Hawaiian allows only 160 syllables, but it manages easily because most of its words have at least two syllables and many have three or more. Vocabulary size, obviously, is not limited by the phonological code. Every natural language allows its speakers to name thousands upon thousands of objects, actions, and qualities, and to make whatever subtle distinctions in meaning they need or desire. By our nature, we have the capacity to learn both a phonological code and the thousands of words that are formed with this code. Nothing remotely like this is possible with gesture-calls. These give us no names at all, and they are poorly designed to make the kinds of distinctions in meaning that come so easily with language.

It is not quite accurate to say that we have more words than gesture-calls, however. In principle, gesture-calls have infinite variability. Just as a graded slide rule allows an infinite number of positions, so graded gesture-calls allow an infinite variety of laughs. In practice, of course, we cannot discriminate so many kinds of laughter, and it is words that give us real flexibility. We cannot add new gesture-calls to our repertory in the way we can add new words to our language, and gesture-calls permit nothing like the tens of thousands of words that every adult speaker so easily controls. We ought to regard our huge vocabulary as at least as important as syntax in defining our uniqueness.

The phonological code gives language two distinct levels of organization. This has sometimes been called **"double articulation"** and sometimes **"duality of patterning."** First, we have the contrasting units of the sound system, the phonemes. These are meaningless, but they can be strung together by one set of patterns into larger chunks to which we assign meanings. These larger bits are the **morphemes**. They include the prefixes, suffixes, and word bases that are further organized by a different set of patterns into the words, phrases, and sentences that we toss back and forth to one another. No such dual structure characterizes our gesture-calls. Each call has a characteristic sound and each gesture has a characteristic shape and movement, but they are not constructed from smaller, meaningless parts.

## Arbitrariness

With the phonological code of our language, we can assign a distinct sequence of sounds to every meaning for which we need a name, and we can assign the sounds to the meanings in entirely **arbitrary** ways. As long as everyone else calls it a "shovel," you are well advised to do so too; but if everyone agreed, the same object could just as well be called a "snurk" or a "blongsel." The form of a gesture-call such as a laugh might also be called "arbitrary." A laugh does not, in any objective sense, resemble humor, any more than the word "shovel" resembles a shovel. We can imagine a species where sobbing was a sign of humor and where laughter indicated grief, but human beings are simply not the kind of animals that can switch the meaning of these signs. The meaning and the form of laughter and sobs are narrowly set by our inheritance, with convention making only a very modest contribution. "Shovel" is conventional as well as arbitrary. The same object is called by many other names in other languages. Language is pervasively conventional as well as arbitrary.

## Syntax and Productivity

For many linguists, it is the complexity of **syntax** that gives the most compelling evidence for the unique character of the human mind. Since gesture-calls are not organized by any sort of syntax, they seem, to these linguists, to have little in common with language. You cannot subordinate, embed, or relativize a gesture-call. It is true that two or more gesture-calls can join to convey more precise or more forceful messages than a single one could convey by itself. We can demonstrate anger by combining the right posture with the right facial expression. We can show both anger and fatigue at the same time. But our gesture-calls simply do not meld into the tight syntactic constructions that are so characteristic of all natural spoken or signed languages.

Syntax allows language to escape the limitation of a fixed number of signals. New words can be invented, but not with complete freedom. You may get through the day without hearing a single word that you had never heard before; but unless you neither speak yourself nor listen to anyone else, you will certainly hear many new sentences before you sleep. It is hardly imaginable that the sentences in this paragraph were ever before uttered or written.

Any language with tens of thousands of words that can be joined into long strings allows astronomical numbers of sentences. In fact, thanks to **recursive** rules, there is no limit on the number of possible sentences. Rules are called recursive if they can be used repeatedly. The most trivial recursive rule simply lets a word be repeated. We can say that something is *very very very*... *big* with as many *very*s as we want to toss in. A child who speculates about his *great-great-great-great-*... *grandmother* has discovered the joys of a recursive rule. Only slightly more complex are rules that allow sentences to be joined to one another by means of simple conjunctions: *I saw Bill, so I spoke to him, and we talked for a while, but he got tired, and*.... Such a sentence could, in principle, go on for ever. Languages allow more interesting kinds of recursion than these.... [Here] we need only note that recursive rules, in principle, allow us to produce and use an infinite number of sentences. Recursion is one of the most distinctive characteristics of language.

However subtle our gestures and calls are, they are fixed in form and fixed in meaning. Only over the course of the thousands of generations that are needed for natural selection can a set of gesture-calls be expanded or elaborated. You can never use gesture-calls to say anything that is truly new. Language is open. The system of gesture-calls is closed.

## Voluntary Control

We have a strong sense of having voluntary control over our language. Voluntary control over our gesture-calls is less secure. The ghastly photographs in which people pretend to smile are a tribute to the difficulty so many of us have in producing gesture-calls on demand. We don't naturally smile at inanimate objects, so it isn't easy to smile at a camera. Only something real can make us smile. On other occasions we find it just as hard not to smile, even when keeping a straight face would be more polite. The relatively involuntary nature of our smiles and of our other gesture-calls means that we are in constant danger of revealing ourselves. When people say one thing with language but send a conflicting message with their faces and bodies, they are likely to be branded as liars. It will not be their language that is believed, but their less voluntary gestures and facial expressions. Our calls and gestures sometimes convey our true emotional state considerably more faithfully than we want them to. If you want to lie, you will be well advised to stick to words and be careful to convey as little as possible with your gesture-calls. Photographers may ask us to pretend to smile, but they know better than to ask us to pretend to laugh.

## Immediacy and Displacement

Gesture-calls are limited by what might be called their **"immediacy."** We can use them to express the present state of our emotions and intentions, but not to describe our past or future emotions. They show our reaction to our immediate surroundings but, except when used along with language, we cannot use them to convey our attitude about things that are out of sight or earshot. With language, we can easily describe things that happened long ago or at a great distance, or that never happened at all. This is sometimes described by saying that language allows **"displacement,"** while most other forms of communication do not. Displacement is not totally absent from animal communication. Bees famously tell other bees about where nectar is to be found, but bee dancing is not likely to have much bearing on language. Only with language did human beings overcome the limitation to the immediate situation that is characteristic of all other primate communication.

## Audible and Visible Mediums

Most people, everywhere, use audible languages, and our dependence on visible signals is sufficiently limited that we find it easy to talk in the dark and equally easy to adapt to a telephone. Deaf people who cannot use audible signals can develop rich and flexible visual languages, so spoken languages and **sign languages** each require just one medium, either audible or visible. Gesture-calls often use both. Many facial expressions are exclusively visual, but most of our audible gesture-calls can be seen as well as heard. Across a noisy room we have no trouble seeing that someone is laughing. We do not have to hear the sobs to see that a child is crying. The audible and visible parts of our gesture-call system are so similar and are so often joined closely together that I find it artificial to separate them. This is why I use the term "gesture-call." I find it helpful to be reminded that this part of our own communication includes both audible and... visible signals and that many signals are both. Languages are predominantly expressed by one medium or the other. Gesture-calls exploit both mediums more equally. Nevertheless, spoken language is regularly accompanied by waving hands and it is always accompanied by moving lips, so it cannot be said to be completely lacking a visible component. Spoken language is also accompanied by intonation, which is more like gesture-calls than most of language, both in being analog rather than digital and in being better at expressing emotion than propositional information. Waving hands, moving lips, and intonation all greatly complicate any description of human communication, and a place will eventually have to be found for each of them.

In summary up to this point: As a first approximation, language is digital and allows easy reference. Large parts of language, including its huge vocabulary, have to be learned, and this means that it can vary from one community to another. It is characterized by distinct phonological and syntactic levels of patterning. Its signals are largely arbitrary and conventional, and most languages are predominantly vocal and audible. It can be used productively to describe things distant in time and space. It is subject to a high degree of voluntary control. Our laughs, screams, groans, sobs, scowls, and smiles, like other gesture-calls, form a very different kind of communication. They are analog signals and excellent at conveying emotion. They are less subject to cultural variation than language, and they are less subject to voluntary control.

---

We need to consider some other forms of human communication that share features of both systems. Deaf signing is a visible language. Signs like the beckoning gesture of the Turkish guesthouse keeper are digital rather than analog. The intonation of language is analog, although most of language is digital. We need to find a place for all of these, and for several other kinds of signals by which humans communicate.

## Deaf Signing

For most of us, language is overwhelmingly auditory and vocal. When people with normal hearing learn to read and write, they add a visible form of language to the audible language they started with; but writing is based so closely on spoken language that it needs to be seen as a secondary and specialized skill. Only in very recent times has everyone been expected to become literate, and in some parts of the world literacy is still a minority achievement. Spoken language came first in human history, and it comes first for every hearing child.

People who are deaf, however, need a visible language or they will have no language at all. Deaf people find it exceedingly difficult to learn any sort of spoken language. Without one, written language is a terrible challenge, but communities of deaf people are able to devise visible languages that use manual, instead of spoken, words. These **manual languages** are largely independent of the spoken languages of the wider communities in which they are used; and in the last few decades, we have come to realize that sign languages are as rich in expressive power as spoken languages.

For anyone who can hear well, spoken languages offer several practical advantages. In particular, they interfere less with other activities. We can talk and bathe the baby at the same time. Since a listener does not need to watch the speaker, a spoken language could once have been understood while checking for lions, and a spoken language can still be used while keeping one's eyes on the road. Spoken language can even be used in the dark. It is for practical reasons like these, we presume, that communities of hearing people always choose to use a spoken language rather than a manual language as their primary form of communication. Speech is simply more convenient. When the vocal channel is blocked, however, it is now clear that the human mind is every bit as capable of directing language out through the hands and in through the eyes as it is of sending it out of the mouth and in through the ears.

Sign languages share all the essential characteristics that distinguish spoken languages from our gesture-calls. Signs are as referential as spoken words, and the sentences of a sign language can express the same kinds of propositions as the sentences of spoken language. Just as the words of a spoken language contrast, so do deaf signs. The manual signs of a language such as American Sign Language are as safely distinct from one another as are the words of any spoken language, so sign languages, like spoken languages, are digital systems. Contrasting hand shapes, together with contrasting locations, orientations, and motions of the hands and arms, join to form signed words, much as the phonemes of a spoken language join to form spoken words. Like spoken languages, signed languages need to be learned, so sign languages differ from one part of the world to another, just as spoken languages do.

Sign languages can be used to convey the full range of meanings that spoken languages convey. Signers, like speakers, can agree on where to meet for lunch, discuss the qualifications of politicians, or report the latest scandal. Signers can lie as easily as speakers, and they can as easily use their language to discuss the language itself. Sign languages are as fully productive as spoken languages. New signs can be coined when new things or new ideas need to be discussed,

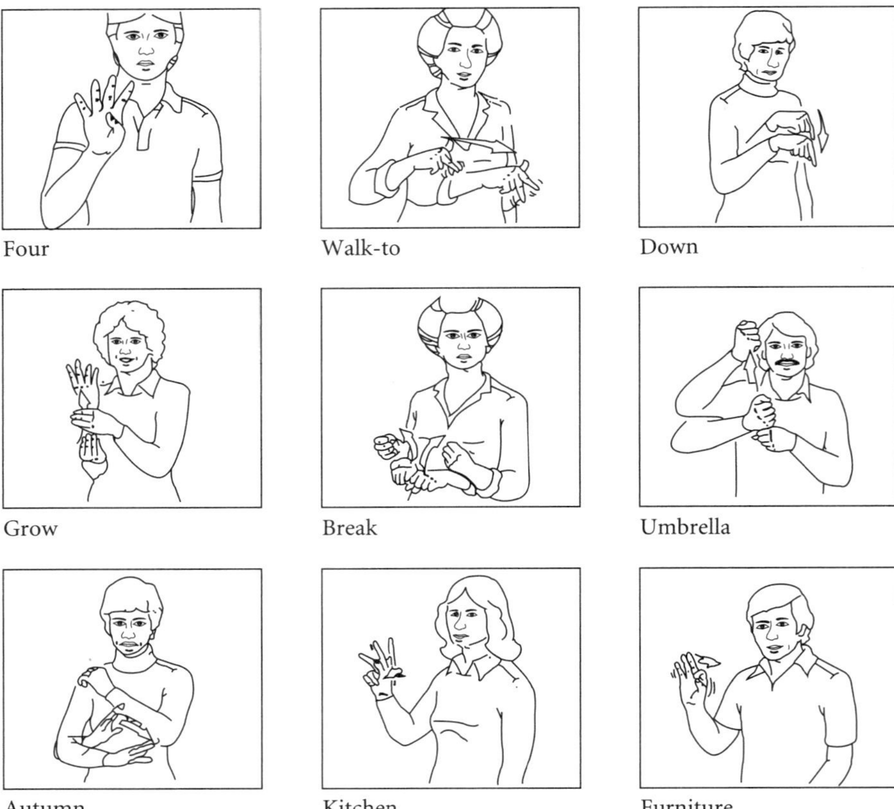


**Figure 1.1** *Signs of American Sign Language. Top row: Highly iconic. Middle row: Semi-iconic. Bottom row: Arbitrary. (Reprinted with permission from T. Humphries, C. Padden, and T. J. O'Rourke,* A Basic Course in American Sign Language, Second Edition *© 1994, T. J. Publishers Inc., Silver Spring, Maryland 20910, USA.)*

and sign languages put no more limits than spoken languages on how many new sentences can be constructed. They are just as subject to voluntary control. In all these respects, signing is utterly different from the nonverbal communication of hearing people. Sign languages are nothing like mime or a game of charades. They are complex and conventional systems that take years to master. Signing has just as much right to be called a "language" as does Chinese or Spanish.

Nevertheless, signing and spoken language are organized in somewhat different ways. Signing takes place in three-dimensional space. Unlike spoken language, it is not confined to the single temporal dimension, and this both imposes limitations and opens opportunities. Visible signs take a bit longer to produce than the average audible word; but the extra dimensions of visible space allow the signer to do several things simultaneously, and this compensates for the time needed to produce each individual sign. When signing about people or objects that are present, signers point to them. When signing about people who are not present, they often assign each person to a different location within their signing space, and then orient their signs toward these assigned spots. A sign meaning "give" can then move from one spot to another, so both the giver and the recipient are shown simultaneously with the sign for "give."

A visual medium invites a degree of iconicity that is impossible in a spoken language, and a considerable proportion of the signs of American Sign Language resemble, in some way, the object that they stand for. Figure 1.1 shows several ASL signs. Those in the top row are almost transparent in meaning. Those in the middle row might not be understood without an explanation, but once their meaning is known, their **iconicity** is clear: a branched plant growing upward, a stick being broken, an umbrella being opened. Those in the bottom row seem to be entirely arbitrary. Spoken words cannot so easily mimic the things they stand for. *Chickadee* and *bob-white* imitate the calls of birds, but the onomatopoeia of spoken languages is marginal when compared with the iconicity of sign languages, although even the languages used by the deaf have many signs that are fully arbitrary.

Because sign languages exploit the special potentials of vision and space while spoken languages exploit the potentials of sound, they are organized differently, but they share their most essential properties. Human beings can devise rich and versatile languages in either a visible or an audible medium. Sign languages show us that it is the brain, rather than the vocal organs, that has made the most important adaptations for language. The human brain can learn to produce a language with either the tongue or the hands, and it can understand with either the eyes or the ears. Which medium each of us prefers is not much more than a matter of convenience.

## Quotable Gestures

We nod and shake our heads, and we use dozens of hand gestures such as the "okay circle" and the "bye-bye wave." These are meaningful signs, but they have to be learned and they are conventional, so they are very different from our laughs and sobs. These learned and stereotypic gestures have sometimes been called "emblems," but I find the term **"quotable gestures"** to be particularly apt. Just as we can quote a word or a sentence, so we can also quote an okay circle or a shake of the head simply by making the same sign. The palm-down beckoning gesture that I learned from the Turkish guesthouse keeper was a quotable gesture. Her scowl was not. Try quoting a scowl. You might imitate a scowl, but it is hard even to know what it would mean to "quote" a scowl.

In both their forms and their meanings, quotable gestures are as conventional as words, and they can convey referential meanings that are as well defined as words. Like words, also, they contrast with one another. It is no more possible to compromise between two quotable gestures than between two words. In spite of the similarity of their form—fingers aimed upward—there can be no compromise, in either meaning or form, between the "finger" and a V-for-Victory sign. The conventional hand signals of a referee need to be unambiguously distinct from one another. Nothing can bridge the gap between a nod and a head shake in the way that transitional laughs bridge the gap between a giggle and a guffaw. It is their contrast that allows these gestures to be quoted, for only a contrastive system lets us know for certain whether two gestures are the same or different. We cannot know whether or not two smiles should count as the same but we do know that two head shakes mean the same thing. Quotable gestures need to be learned. Like language, they form a part of the cultural tradition of a community, and they differ from one community to another. In all these respects quotable gestures are very much like words and very different from gesture-calls. Because they are visible rather than audible, however, they cannot be incorporated into either the phonology or the syntax of spoken language.

Quotable gestures resemble the individual signs of a sign language more closely than they resemble spoken words. Everything that they share with spoken words, they also share with the signs of sign language, but in addition they are, like deaf signs, made with the hands and arms, sometimes with the assistance of facial expressions. Indeed, quotable gestures of the hearing community are sometimes incorporated into the signed languages of the deaf. The usual way to negate a sentence in American Sign Language is with a head shake. Head shakes cannot be incorporated into the audible language of a hearing community, but they can be incorporated into the grammar of sign language, and they can be used systematically within its sentences. In that way, a head shake becomes a word, one among the thousands of other signed words of American Sign Language.

Even for those of us who use spoken languages, the clear meanings and conventionality of quotable gestures make them more like words than like gesture-calls. Although they cannot be used as a part of spoken language, they deserve to be grouped with language in any typology of human communication.

## Quotable Vocalizations

Everyone who uses a spoken language also uses a few expressions such as *oh-oh, tsk-tsk, m-hm*, and *uh-uh* that are meaningful vocal noises, but not really words. These expressions are difficult to spell because they don't conform to ordinary English sound patterns, but these four should be recognizable as meaning "oh dear," "shame on you," "yes," and "no." They have consistent sounds and consistent meanings, but in addition to violating the usual phonological patterns of the language, they cannot be incorporated into its syntax. They don't fit into sentences. We do not have many of these vocalizations, perhaps a dozen or so, but they are unlike any of our other communicative signals. They are discrete rather than graded, for it is no more possible to compromise between the *m-hm* that means "yes" and the *uh-uh* that means "no," than it is to compromise between *yes* and *no* or between a nod and a head shake. Their sounds and meanings are conventional and they have to be learned. All this makes them so much like quotable gestures that they deserve a parallel name, and I will call them **"quotable vocalizations."** Like quotable gestures, these quotable vocalizations are more like words than like gesture-calls, and they belong on the language-like side of our communication.

Since neither quotable vocalizations nor quotable gestures enter the syntactic constructions of spoken language, they cannot contribute to the kind of **productivity** that syntax gives to all languages. We can, however, add new quotable gestures to our repertory. We do not often do so, but the V-for-Victory sign was invented only during the Second World War. It is not difficult to learn the quotable gestures of another culture. It would also be possible to add new quotable vocalizations to our repertory, though this must be even less common than adding quotable gestures. Adding to our existing stock of gesture-calls is impossible.

We can lie with either quotable gestures or quotable vocalizations just as we can lie with language. A nod or a *m-hm* is as surely a lie as is "yes," if the nodder or vocalizer really believes the correct answer should be a head shake or an *uh-uh*. If you try to deceive by shaking your head, you lie; if you laugh at a joke that you do not find funny, you do not. Quotable vocalizations are almost words. They are subject to roughly the same degree of deliberate control as language or quotable gestures, and like words, they have to be learned by participation in the community where they are used. Since quotable vocalizations are produced with the same vocal machinery as spoken language, we usually think of them as closer to language than a shake of the head or a wink of the eye, but the two kinds of quotables are used in almost identical ways, and both exhibit full contrast. In all these respects, both quotable gestures and quotable vocalizations differ from our analog gesture-calls, and both belong with spoken and signed language on the language-like side of our communication.

## Gesticulation, Intonation, and Instrumental Acts

We communicate with several other kinds of gestures and vocalizations, including the intonations of the voice, the **gesticulations** of the hands, and even with instrumental gestures that are not intended to communicate at all. These [are]... introduced briefly....

"Gesticulation" refers to the way we wave our arms and shape our hands as we speak. This hand waving is very different both from the gestural component of our gesture-call system and from quotable gestures, and it is different, also, from the manual gestures of sign language. That gives us four distinct kinds of communicative gestures, and still omits instrumental gestures which are meant for something else than communication. All this makes the word "gesture," if used alone, hopelessly ambiguous. From now on, therefore, I will avoid using "gesture" without qualification, but will, instead, use more specific terms: "gesture-calls," "quotable gestures," "gesticulation," "signing," or "instrumental gesture." Gesticulation differs from the others in its intimate association with speech. It might almost be regarded as a part of language, but its visibility and silence set it apart.

"Intonation" refers to the rhythm, stress, and ups and downs in pitch that accompany ordinary spoken language. Like gesticulation, intonation is used simultaneously with the words and sentences of language, and it is intimately related to them. Generally, we think of intonation as an integral part of language, and it is hardly conventional to set it apart, but it works so differently from the rest of the sound system that it needs special treatment.

Intonation conveys less propositional information than words and sentences generally do, but it reveals more about the attitudes and emotions of the speaker. Intonation also differs from the rest of language in being largely analog rather than digital. Both in its meaning and in its analog form, therefore, intonation is more like our gesture-calls than is the rest of language. Intonation has much in common with gesticulation. Since gesticulation is manual, it seems to be more distinct from spoken language than vocal intonation is, but intonation and gesticulation are closely linked to each other, and they have parallel kinds of involvement with language. It is even difficult to define intonation in a way that makes it a part of language without dragging in gesticulation along with it. Gesticulation and some parts of intonation have sometimes been grouped together as **"paralanguage,"** meaning that they are used "alongside" language. The term recognizes their close connection with language, but still sets them apart....

Finally, we need to leave a place for instrumental acts that are not even meant to be communicative, but that can still be interpreted as meaningful by an observing individual. The business of living requires us to stand up, walk around, search for food, eat, sleep, cooperate, fight, look for mates, and engage in any number of other mundane activities. Our footsteps, our grunts, and even our breathing, can all be heard. Other people can see us and hear us as we perform these activities. These instrumental acts are meant for practical purposes, not for communication, but even if the actors would rather not be seen or heard, others may still be able to glean useful bits of information by watching and listening.

Behavior that starts instrumentally sometimes becomes conventionalized. The arms-up gesture by which babies ask to be picked up starts as an instrumental gesture that allows older hands to slip easily under the baby's arms. Children do not learn this gesture by imitation because older folks never ask a baby to pick them up, and a baby may never see another baby holding out its arms. Instead, each child conventionalizes the gesture by habit, and then exaggerates it to get attention. Adults, in turn, learn to recognize the gesture as a request. The gesture-calls of animals, such as the retracted lip that warns of a bite, also began as instrumental acts....

Figure 1.2 shows our various kinds of communication in a way that is intended to highlight both their similarities and their differences. The figure has two columns, one for visible, and the other for audible, signals, but the dividing line does not extend all the way to the top. This reflects the close association of the visual and audible parts of gesture-calls. Across the middle of the figure is a horizontal line

| | | Visible | Audible |
|---|---|---|---|
| **Emotional-Analog** | Mammalian | Gesture-call System | |
| | Paralinguistic | Gesticulation | Intonation, Tone of voice |
| **Referential-Digital** | Quotable | Quotable Gestures | Quotable Vocalizations |
| | Linguistic | Sign Language | Spoken Language |

**Figure 1.2** *Varieties of Human Communication.*

that divides the analog gesture-call-like forms that are best at conveying emotions and intentions at the top, from the language-like digital communication that is best at conveying referential meaning below. The gesture-call system at the very top is the component of our communication that is most like that of other mammals and least like language. Language, at the bottom, is the most distinctively human. Both the top and bottom halves of the figure are further divided, and the two forms just above the central line and the two just below it all share some features of both language and gesture-calls. Quotable gestures and vocalizations are very much like words, but they are not pulled into either the syntax or phonology of language. Gesticulation and intonation are both used more intimately with language than are either quotable gestures or vocalizations, but they are analog signals and thus quite different from the other parts of language. Instrumental acts are left out of the figure because they are not intended to be communicative at all.

One purpose of Figure 1.2 is to show how very similar to each other audible and visible communication are. Most of what we can do in one **modality** we can do equally well in the other. The distinctiveness of human communication lies not in our specific ability to use vocal language, but rather in our ability to use language, whether audible or visible, to convey referential and propositional meaning, and to do so by means of principles that are very different from our own gesture-calls as well as from any form of animal communication. Linguistic contrast, syntax, and a massive vocabulary are all unique to language, but they are just as characteristic of visible language as of audible language. It is our minds that changed most profoundly as our ability to use language evolved.

## Critical Thinking and Application

- Observe friends talking for a few minutes. How do Burling's distinctions among the various components of the gesture-call system help you analyze the complexity of this (and every) interaction?
- Watch a foreign film without the sound or subtitles. Guess what is occurring. What information do you use to make your inferences? Which gestures are familiar? Are there any gestures that are unfamiliar? Now watch it again with sound or subtitles. How accurate were your guesses?

## Vocabulary

analog
arbitrariness
behaviorism
digital
displacement
double articulation
duality of patterning
gesticulation
gesture-call
heritable, heritability
iconicity
immediacy
intonation
manual language
modality
morpheme
paralanguage
phoneme
phonology
productivity
quotable gestures
quotable vocalizations
recursive
sign language
syntax

## Suggested Further Reading

Aitchison, Jean. 2000. *The Seeds of Speech: Language Origin and Evolution.* Cambridge: Cambridge University Press.

Armstrong, David F., and Sherman E. Wilcox. 2007. *The Gestural Origin of Language.* Oxford and New York: Oxford University Press.

Bickerton, Derek. 1980. *Language and Species.* Chicago: University of Chicago Press.

Burling, Robbins. 2005. *The Talking Ape: How Language Evolved.* Oxford: Oxford University Press.

Calvin, William, and Derek Bickerton. 2000. *Lingua ex Machina: Reconciling Darwin and Chomsky with the Human Brain.* Cambridge, MA: MIT Press.

Christiansen, Morten H., and Simon Kirby, eds. 2003. *Language Evolution.* Oxford: Oxford University Press.

King, Barbara J., ed. 1999. *The Origins of Language: What Nonhuman Primates Can Tell Us.* Santa Fe, NM: School of American Research Press.

Oller, D. Kimbrough, and Ulrike Griebel, eds. 2004. *Evolution of Communication Systems: A Comparative Approach.* Cambridge, MA: MIT Press.

# CHAPTER 2

# Nature of the Linguistic Sign

## *Ferdinand de Saussure*

(1907–1911)

*Ferdinand de Saussure was a linguist working right around the turn of the twentieth century. He is credited with pointing out many important aspects of language, such as that it can be looked at not only historically* **(diachronically)**, *as most linguists including himself were doing at the time, but also at any given moment in time (which he called* **synchronically***). Language forms a* system, *an orderly set of rules and words related to each other.*

*But words are more than just items in a list. One of the important things to note is that they are a kind of* **sign***—a linguistic sign, though there could be other kinds of signs. Linguistic signs have certain properties, most important of which are that they have two aspects and that the two aspects are bonded in an* **arbitrary** *way.*

*The writings we attribute to Saussure were actually compiled from his students' lecture notes after his death. His influence, however, has been unprecedented in the study of language and other cultural phenomena. He proposed a general science of signs, which he termed* **semiology**. *It did not exist at the time, but it does exist now, more commonly as* **semiotics**. *This science can be used to analyze film, literature, clothing, food, and any other aspect of human behavior.*

### Reading Questions

- What is the linguistic sign unit?
- What are the two aspects of a linguistic sign?
- How can looking across languages emphasize that fact?
- What does Saussure mean by "the arbitrary nature of the sign"?

---

### Sign, Signified, Signifier

Some people regard language, when reduced to its elements, as a naming-process only—a list of words, each corresponding to the thing that it names. For example:

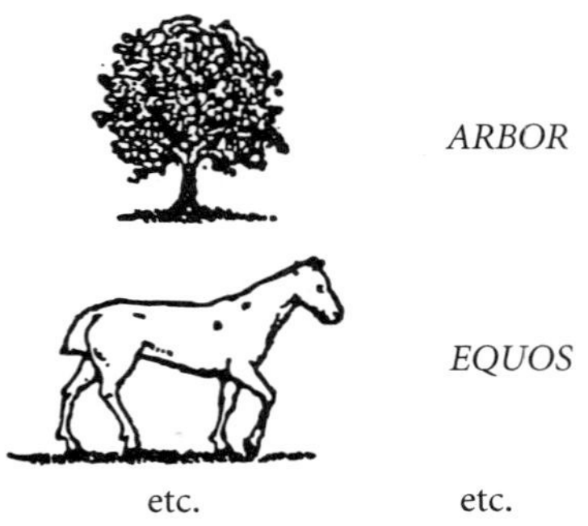


Ferdinand de Saussure, "Nature of the Linguistic Sign," pp. 65–70. Reprinted by permission of McGraw-Hill, New York, from *Course in General Linguistics* by Ferdinand de Saussure, edited by Charles Bally and Albert Sechehaye, translated by Wade Baskin, 

This conception is open to criticism at several points. It assumes that ready-made ideas exist before words...; it does not tell us whether a name is vocal or psychological in nature (*arbor*, for instance, can be considered from either viewpoint); finally, it lets us assume that the linking of a name and a thing is a very simple operation—an assumption that is anything but true. But this rather naive approach can bring us near the truth by showing us that the linguistic unit is a double entity, one formed by the associating of two terms.

We have seen [elsewhere] in considering the speaking-circuit that both terms involved in the linguistic sign are psychological and are united in the brain by an associative bond. This point must be emphasized.

The linguistic sign unites, not a thing and a name, but a concept and a sound-image.[1] The latter is not the material sound, a purely physical thing, but the psychological imprint of the sound, the impression that it makes on our senses. The sound-image is sensory, and if I happen to call it "material," it is only in that sense, and by way of opposing it to the other term of the association, the concept, which is generally more abstract.

The psychological character of our sound-images becomes apparent when we observe our own speech. Without moving our lips or tongue, we can talk to ourselves or recite mentally a selection of verse. Because we regard the words of our language as sound-images, we must avoid speaking of the "phonemes" that make up the words. This term, which suggests vocal activity, is applicable to the spoken word only, to the realization of the inner image in discourse. We can avoid that misunderstanding by speaking of the *sounds* and *syllables* of a word provided we remember that the names refer to the sound-image.

The linguistic sign is then a two-sided psychological entity that can be represented by the drawing:

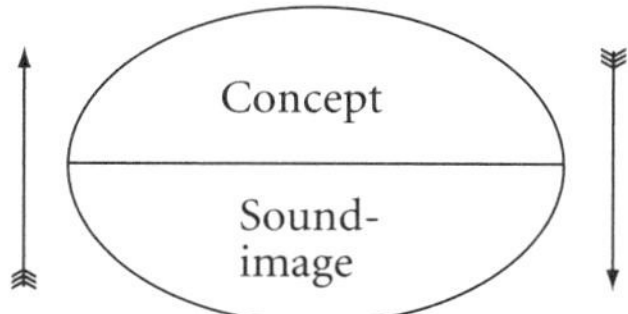


The two elements are intimately united, and each recalls the other. Whether we try to find the meaning of the Latin word *arbor* or the word that Latin uses to designate the concept "tree," it is clear that only the associations sanctioned by that language appear to us to conform to reality, and we disregard whatever others might be imagined.

Our definition of the linguistic sign poses an important question of terminology. I call the combination of a concept and a sound-image a *sign*, but in current usage the term generally designates only a sound-image, a word, for example (*arbor*, etc.). One tends to forget that *arbor* is called a sign only because it carries the concept "tree," with the result that the idea of the sensory part implies the idea of the whole.

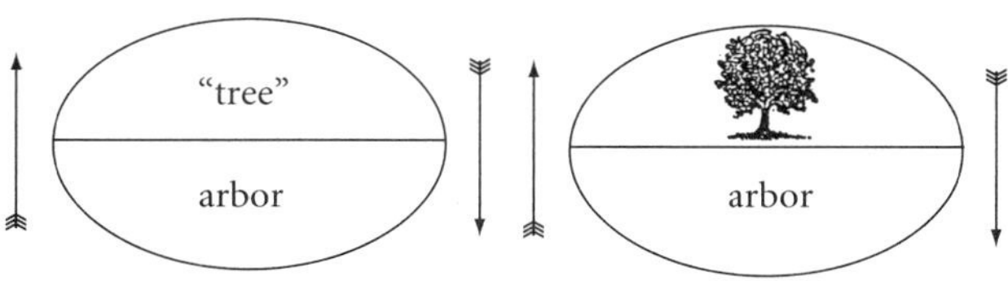


Ambiguity would disappear if the three notions involved here were designated by three names, each suggesting and opposing the others. I propose to retain the word *sign* [*signe*] to designate the whole and to replace *concept* and *sound-image*, respectively, by **signified** [*signifié*] and **signifier** [*signifiant*]; the last two terms have the advantage of indicating the opposition that separates them from each other and from the whole of which they are parts. As regards *sign*, if I am satisfied with it, this is simply because I do not know of any word to replace it, the ordinary language suggesting no other.

The linguistic sign, as defined, has two primordial characteristics. In enunciating them I am also positing the basic principles of any study of this type.

## Principle I: The Arbitrary Nature of the Sign

The bond between the signifier and the signified is arbitrary. Since I mean by sign the whole that results from the associating of the signifier with the signified, I can simply say: *the linguistic sign is arbitrary*.

The idea of "sister" is not linked by any inner relationship to the succession of sounds *s-ö-r*, which serves as its signifier in French; that it could be represented equally by just any other sequence is proved by differences among languages and by the very existence of different languages: the signified "ox" has as its signifier *b-ö-f* on one side of the border and *o-k-s* (*Ochs*) on the other.

No one disputes the principle of the arbitrary nature of the sign, but it is often easier to discover a truth than to assign to it its proper place. Principle I dominates all the linguistics of language; its consequences are numberless. It is true that not all of them are equally obvious at first glance; only after many detours does one discover them, and with them the primordial importance of the principle.

One remark in passing: when semiology becomes organized as a science, the question will arise whether or not it properly includes modes of expression based on completely natural signs, such as pantomime. Supposing that the new science welcomes them, its main concern will still be the whole group of systems grounded on the arbitrariness of the sign. In fact, every means of expression used in society is based, in principle, on collective behavior or—what amounts to the same thing—on convention. Polite formulas, for instance, though often imbued with a certain natural expressiveness (as in the case of a Chinese who greets his emperor by bowing down to the ground nine times), are nonetheless fixed by rule; it is this rule and not the intrinsic value of the gestures that obliges one to use them. Signs that are wholly arbitrary realize better than the others the ideal of the semiological process; that is why language, the most complex and universal of all systems of expression, is also the most characteristic; in this sense linguistics can become the master-pattern for all branches of semiology although language is only one particular semiological system.

The word ***symbol*** has been used to designate the linguistic sign, or more specifically, what is here called the signifier. Principle I in particular weighs against the use of this term. One characteristic of the symbol is that it is never wholly arbitrary; it is not empty, for there is the rudiment of a natural bond between the signifier and the signified. The symbol of justice, a pair of scales, could not be replaced by just any other symbol, such as a chariot.

The word *arbitrary* also calls for comment. The term should not imply that the choice of the signifier is left entirely to the speaker ([since] the individual does not have the power to change a sign in any way once it has become established in the linguistic community); I mean that it is unmotivated, i.e., arbitrary, in that it actually has no natural connection with the signified.

In concluding let us consider two objections that might be raised to the establishment of Principle I:

1. *Onomatopoeia* might be used to prove that the choice of the signifier is not always arbitrary. But onomatopoeic formations are never organic elements of a linguistic system. Besides, their number is much smaller than is generally supposed. Words like French *fouet* "whip" or *glas* "knell" may strike certain ears with suggestive sonority, but to see that they have not always had this property we need only examine their Latin forms (*fouet* is derived from *fāgus* "beech-tree", *glas* from *classicum* "sound of a trumpet"). The quality of their present sounds, or rather the quality that is attributed to them, is a fortuitous result of phonetic evolution.

   As for authentic onomatopoeic words (e.g., *glug-glug, tick-tock*, etc.), not only are they limited in number, but also they are chosen somewhat arbitrarily, for they are only approximate and more or less conventional imitations of certain sounds (cf. English *bow-bow* and French *ouaoua*). In addition, once these words have been introduced into the language, they are to a certain extent subjected to the same evolution—phonetic, morphological, etc.—that other words undergo (cf. *pigeon*, ultimately from Vulgar Latin *pīpiō*, derived in turn from an onomatopoeic formation): obvious proof that they lose something of their original character in order to assume that of the linguistic sign in general, which is unmotivated.
2. *Interjections*, closely related to onomatopoeia, can be attacked on the same grounds and come no closer to refuting our thesis. One is tempted to see in them spontaneous expressions of reality dictated, so to speak, by natural forces. But for most interjections we can show that there is no fixed bond between their signified and their signifier. We need only compare two languages on this point to see how much such expressions differ from one language to the next (e.g., the English equivalent of French *aïe!* is *ouch!*). We know, moreover, that many interjections were once words with specific meanings (cf. French *diable!* "darn"! *mordieu!* "golly"! from *mort Dieu* "God's death", etc.).[2]

Onomatopoeic formations and interjections are of secondary importance, and their symbolic origin is in part open to dispute.

## Principle II: The Linear Nature of the Signifier

The signifier, being auditory, is unfolded solely in time from which it gets the following characteristics: (a) it represents a span, and (b) the span is measurable in a single dimension; it is a line.

While Principle II is obvious, apparently linguists have always neglected to state it, doubtless because they found it too simple; nevertheless, it is fundamental, and its consequences are incalculable. Its importance equals that of Principle I; the whole mechanism of language depends upon it. In contrast to visual signifiers (nautical signals, etc.), which can offer simultaneous groupings in several dimensions, auditory signifiers have at their command only the dimension of time. Their elements are presented in succession; they form a chain. This feature becomes readily apparent when they are represented in writing and the spatial line of graphic marks is substituted for succession in time.

Sometimes the linear nature of the signifier is not obvious. When I accent a syllable, for instance, it seems that I am concentrating more than one significant element on the same point. But this is an illusion; the syllable and its accent constitute only one phonational act. There is no duality within the act but only different oppositions to what precedes and what follows.

### Notes

1. The term sound-image may seem to be too restricted inasmuch as beside the representation of the sounds of a word there is also that of its articulation, the muscular image of the phonational act. But for F. de Saussure language is essentially a depository, a thing received from without. The sound-image is par excellence the natural representation of the word as a fact of potential language, outside any actual use of it in speaking. The motor side is thus implied or, in any event, occupies only a subordinate role with respect to the sound-image. [Ed. (Bally and Sechehaye)]
2. Cf. English *goodness!* and *zounds!* (from *God's wounds*). [Tr.]

---

## Critical Thinking and Application

- Why was it important for Saussure to show that the relationship between sign and signifier is arbitrary? Can you think of an (unmentioned) argument that he is refuting?
- Why does he argue that onomatopoeia and interjections are not central parts of language? What do they have to do with his claims about arbitrariness?
- Pick an aspect of human behavior (clothing, food, art, film, etc.) and see how you might begin to look at it as a set of signs.

## Vocabulary

arbitrary
diachronic
semiology
semiotics
sign
signified
signifier
symbol
synchronic

## Suggested Further Reading

Barthes, Roland. 1982. *The Empire of Signs,* translated by Richard Howard. New York: Hill & Wang.

Bignell, Jonathan. 2002. *Media Semiotics: An Introduction.* 2nd ed. Manchester and New York: Manchester University Press.

Cobley, Paul, ed. 2001. *The Routledge Companion to Semiotics and Linguistics.* London and New York: Routledge.

Saussure, Ferdinand de. 1959. *Course in General Linguistics*, translated by Wade Baskin. New York: Philosophical Society.

# UNIT 2

# Language Origins

Since being banned by the Linguistic Society of Paris in 1866, the topic of the origin of language has drawn periodic attention. It seemed impossible to answer questions about when and how language might have developed; theorists were simply guessing wildly—hence, the century-long ban. Since the 1990s, however, the subject has been picked up by researchers in a wide range of fields. Some of this is made possible by advances in cognitive science, neuroimaging, and deeper comprehension of the human brain. Some is simply a conversation that has taken off. Individual writers must, of course, first define what they mean by *language,* and only then can they begin to identify the evolutionary precursors, the mechanisms and pressures that led to the facility that all humans possess. Researchers in different fields tend to focus on different facets of the entity, and explanations tend to lie squarely at the heart of each researcher's own expertise.

If you were to read the work of linguists, it might resemble not at all that of biologists, which in turn might be entirely different from that of psychologists. Primatologists have still other things to say. Is language biological? cognitive? social? individual? Does it depend on the vocal tract, on the brain, on social organization? Does it have to be spoken, or can it be signed? What is the really critical, essential aspect of language that sets it apart from other species' communication? Should it even be differentiated so sharply? This unit presents a classic treatment in Charles Hockett's work on the design features of language; a consideration by William Stokoe of the relationship between signed and spoken language; and a summary by linguist Derek Bickerton of recent developments in scholarship on the origin of language. These are not conclusive, but will alert you to some of the issues that must be incorporated in any up-to-date discussion of how language originated.

## Suggested Further Reading


Arbib, Michael A. 2005. Interweaving Protosign and Protospeech: Further Developments Beyond the Mirror. *Interaction Studies* 6(2): 145–171.

Cavalli-Sforza, L. L. 2001. *Genes, Peoples, and Languages.* Berkeley: University of California Press.

Cheney, Dorothy L., and Robert M. Seyfarth. 1990. *How Monkeys See the World: Inside the Mind of Another Species.* Chicago: University of Chicago Press.

Chomsky, Noam. 1996. Language and Evolution. *The New York Review of Books* 43 (February 1).

Corballis, Michael C. 2002. *From Hand to Mouth: The Origins of Language.* Princeton, NJ: Princeton University Press.

Deacon, Terrence William. 1997. *The Symbolic Species: The Co-Evolution of Language and the Brain.* New York: Norton.

Dunbar, Robin. 1996. *Grooming, Gossip, and the Evolution of Language.* Cambridge, MA: Harvard University Press.

Hauser, Marc D. 1996. *The Evolution of Communication.* Cambridge, MA: MIT Press.

Hauser, Marc, and W. Tecumseh Fitch. 2003. What Are the Uniquely Human Components of the Language Faculty? In *Language Evolution,* edited by Morten H. Christiansen and Simon Kirby, pp. 158–181. Oxford: Oxford University Press.

Hauser, Marc D., Noam Chomsky, and W. Tecumseh Fitch. 2002. The Faculty of Language: What Is It, Who Has It, and How Did It Evolve? *Science* 298: 1569–1579.

Hawkins, J. A., and M. Gell-Mann, eds. 1992. *The Evolution of Human Languages.* Reading, MA: Addison-Wesley.

Hurford, James R., Michael Studdert-Kennedy, and Chris Knight, eds. 1998. *Approaches to the Evolution of Language: Social and Cognitive Bases.* New York: Cambridge University Press.

Jackendoff, Ray. 2002. *Foundations of Language: Brain, Meaning, Grammar, Evolution.* New York: Oxford University Press.

Ke, Jinyun, and John E. Holland. 2006. Language Origin from an Emergentist Perspective. *Applied Linguistics* 27(4): 691–716.

Kenneally, Christine. 2007. *The First Word: The Search for the Origins of Language.* New York: Penguin.

Knight, Chris, Michael Studdert-Kennedy, and James R. Hurford, eds. 2000. *The Evolutionary Emergence of Language: Social Function and the Origins of Linguistic Form.* Cambridge and New York: Cambridge University Press.

Lieberman, Philip. 1984. *The Biology and Evolution of Language*. Cambridge, MA: Harvard University Press.

Lieberman, Philip. 2006. *Toward an Evolutionary Biology of Language*. Cambridge, MA: Harvard University Press, Belknap.

Mayr, Ernst. 2001. *What Evolution Is*. New York: Basic Books.

Pinker, Steven. 1994. *The Language Instinct*. New York: Morrow.

Pinker, Steven, and Paul Bloom. 1990. Natural Language and Natural Selection. *Behavioral and Brain Sciences* 13: 707–784.

Pinker, Steven, and Ray Jackendoff. 2005. The Faculty of Language: What's Special About It? *Cognition* 95: 201–236.

Savage-Rumbaugh, E. Sue, and Roger Lewin. 1994. *Kanzi: The Ape at the Brink of the Human Mind*. New York: Wiley.

Savage-Rumbaugh, E. Sue, Stuart Shanker, and Talbot J. Taylor. 1998. *Apes, Language, and the Human Mind*. New York: Oxford University Press.

Wray, Alison, ed. 2002. *The Transition to Language*. Oxford: Oxford University Press.

# CHAPTER 3

# The Origin of Speech

## *Charles Hockett*

(1960)

*Before scholars can begin to ask the question of how language arose, we have to know what features of language we actually seek to locate in our evolutionary past. Many such discussions end in pure speculation.*

*Often known as a linguist, Charles Hockett in fact had a PhD in anthropology and considered his work importantly situated within the broadest contours of that field. His classic treatment of the "design features" puts human language on a continuum with—but in some ways distinctive from—the communicative systems of various species. He identifies thirteen aspects of language, all of which apply to human language and only some of which apply to the communication systems of other animals. Most people emphasize, as did Hockett, the features of* discreteness, displacement, productivity, traditional transmission, *and* duality of patterning, *which are unique to humans and hominoids. The goal of this kind of analysis is less to understand human language than to set it apart from other forms of communication. [You'll note, too, that he takes speech, with its features of* broadcast transmission *and* directional reception, rapid fading, *and the* vocal-auditory channel, *as prototypical of human language. Recent work on signed languages suggests orality is not essential for language to exist.]*

### Reading Questions

- What is *displacement*? How do you see it exemplified in ordinary language? Where else might you find it?
- What is *productivity*?
- What is *duality of patterning*? How is it connected to productivity? What are the ramifications of this design feature?
- How does human language differ from other animals' communication systems?
- Why is that important for any discussion of language origins?

---

About 50 years ago the Linguistic Society of Paris established a standing rule barring from its sessions papers on the origin of language. This action was a symptom of the times. Speculation about the origin of language had been common throughout the 19th century, but had reached no conclusive results. The whole enterprise in consequence had come to be frowned upon—as futile or crackpot—in respectable linguistic and **philological** circles. Yet amidst the speculations there were two well-reasoned empirical plans that deserve mention even though their results were negative.

A century ago there were still many corners of the world that had not been visited by European travelers. It was reasonable for the European scholar to suspect that beyond the farthest frontiers there might lurk half-men or man-apes who would be "living fossils" attesting to earlier stages of human evolution. The speech (or quasi-speech) of these men (or quasi-men) might then similarly attest to earlier stages in the evolution of language. The search was vain. Nowhere in the world has there been discovered a language that can validly and meaningfully be called "primitive." Edward Sapir wrote in 1921:

> There is no more striking general fact about language than its universality. One may argue as to whether a particular tribe engages in activities that are worthy of the name of religion or of art, but we know of no people that is not possessed of a fully developed language. The lowliest South African Bushman speaks in the forms of a rich symbolic system that is in essence perfectly comparable to the speech of the cultivated Frenchman.

The other empirical hope in the 19th century rested on the comparative method of historical linguistics, the discovery

Charles Hockett, "The Origin of Speech." *Scientific American* 203(3) (Sept 1, 1960): 88–96.

of which was one of the triumphs of the period. Between two languages the resemblances are sometimes so extensive and orderly that they cannot be attributed to chance or to parallel development. The alternative explanation is that the two are divergent descendants of a single earlier language. English, Dutch, German, and the Scandinavian languages are related in just this way. The **comparative method** makes it possible to examine such a group of related languages and to construct, often in surprising detail, a portrayal of the common ancestor, in this case the **proto**-Germanic language. Direct documentary evidence of proto-Germanic does not exist, yet understanding of its workings exceeds that of many languages spoken today.

There was at first some hope that the comparative method might help determine the origin of language. This hope was rational in a day when it was thought that language might be only a few thousands or tens of thousands of years old, and when it was repeatedly being demonstrated that languages that had been thought to be unrelated were in fact related. By applying the comparative method to all the languages of the world, some earliest reconstructable horizon would be reached. This might not date back so early as the origin of language, but it might bear certain earmarks of primitiveness, and thus it would enable investigators to extrapolate toward the origin. This hope also proved vain. The earliest reconstructable stage for any language family shows all the complexities and flexibilities of the languages of today.

---

These points had become clear a half-century ago, by the time of the Paris ruling. Scholars cannot really approve of such a prohibition. But in this instance it had the useful result of channeling the energies of investigators toward the gathering of more and better information about languages, as they are today. The subsequent progress in understanding the workings of language has been truly remarkable. Various related fields have also made vast strides in the last half-century: zoologists know more about the evolutionary process, anthropologists know more about the nature of culture, and so on. In the light of these developments there need be no apology for reopening the issue of the origins of human speech.

Although the comparative method of linguistics, as has been shown, throws no light on the origin of language, the investigation may be furthered by a comparative method modeled on that of the zoologist. The frame of reference must be such that all languages look alike when viewed through it, but such that within it human language as a whole can be compared with the communicative systems of other animals, especially the other **hominoids,** man's closest living relatives, the gibbons and great apes. The useful items for this sort of comparison cannot be things such as the word for "sky"; languages have such words, but gibbon calls do not involve words at all. Nor can they be even the signal for "danger," which gibbons do have. Rather, they must be the basic features of design that can be present or absent in any communicative system, whether it be a communicative system of humans, of animals, or of machines.

With this sort of comparative method it may be possible to reconstruct the communicative habits of the remote ancestors of the hominoid line, which may be called the protohominoids. The task, then, is to work out the sequence by which that ancestral system became language as the **hominids**—the man-apes and ancient men—became man.

---

A set of 13 **design-features** is presented in [this section]. There is solid empirical justification for the belief that all the languages of the world share every one of them. At first sight some appear so trivial that no one looking just at language would bother to note them. They become worthy of mention only when it is realized that certain animal systems—and certain human systems other than language—lack them.

The first design-feature—the "vocal-auditory channel"—is perhaps the most obvious. There are systems of communication that use other channels: for example, gesture, the dancing of bees, or the courtship ritual of the stickleback. The vocal-auditory channel has the advantage—at least for **primates**—that it leaves much of the body free for other activities that can be carried on at the same time.

The next two design-features—"rapid fading" and "broadcast transmission and directional reception," stemming from the physics of sound—are almost unavoidable consequences of the first. A linguistic signal can be heard by any auditory system within earshot, and the source can normally be localized by binaural direction-finding. The rapid fading of such a signal means that it does not linger for reception at the hearer's convenience. Animal tracks and spoors, on the other hand, persist for a while; so of course do written records, a product of man's extremely recent cultural evolution.

The significance of "interchangeability" and "total feedback" for language becomes clear upon comparison with other systems. In general a speaker of a language can reproduce any linguistic message he can understand, whereas the characteristic courtship motions of the male and female stickleback are different, and neither can act out those appropriate to the other. For that matter in the communication of a human mother and infant neither is apt to transmit the characteristic signals or to manifest the typical responses of the other. Again, the speaker of a language hears, by total feedback, everything of linguistic relevance in what he himself says. In contrast, the male stickleback does not see the colors of his own eye and belly that are crucial in stimulating the female. Feedback is important, since it makes possible the so-called internalization of communicative behavior that constitutes at least a major portion of "thinking."

The sixth design-feature, "specialization," refers to the fact that the bodily effort and spreading sound waves of speech serve no function except as signals. A dog, panting with his tongue hanging out, is performing a biologically essential activity, since this is how dogs cool themselves off and maintain the proper body temperature. The panting dog incidentally produces sound, and thereby may inform other dogs (or humans) as to where he is and how he feels. But this transmission of information is strictly a side effect. Nor does the dog's panting exhibit the design-feature of **"semanticity."** It is not a signal meaning that the dog is hot; it is part of being hot. In language, however, a message triggers the particular result it does because there are relatively fixed associations between elements in messages (e.g., words) and recurrent features or situations of the world around us. For example, the English word "salt" means salt, not sugar or pepper. The calls of gibbons also possess semanticity. The gibbon has a danger call, for example, and it does not in principle matter that the meaning of the call is a great deal broader and more vague than, say, the cry of "Fire!"

In a semantic communicative system the ties between meaningful message-elements and their meanings can be **arbitrary** or nonarbitrary. In language the ties are arbitrary. The word "salt" is not salty nor granular; "dog" is not "canine"; "whale" is a small word for a large object; "microorganism" is the reverse. A picture, on the other hand, looks like what it is a picture of. A bee dances faster if the source of nectar she is reporting is closer, and slower if it is farther away. The design-feature of **"arbitrariness"** has the disadvantage of being arbitrary, but the great advantage that there is no limit to what can be communicated about.

Human vocal organs can produce a huge variety of sound. But in any one language only a relatively small set of ranges of sound is used, and the differences between these ranges are functionally absolute. The English words "pin" and "bin" are different to the ear only at one point. If a speaker produces a syllable that deviates from the normal pronunciation of "pin" in the direction of that of "bin," he is not producing still a third word, but just saying "pin" (or perhaps "bin") in a noisy way. The hearer compensates if he can, on the basis of context, or else fails to understand. This feature of **"discreteness"** in the elementary signaling units of a language contrasts with the use of sound effects by way of vocal gesture. There is an effectively continuous scale of degrees to which one may raise his voice as in anger, or lower it to signal confidentiality. Bee-dancing also is continuous rather than **discrete**.

Man is apparently almost unique in being able to talk about things that are remote in space or time (or both) from where the talking goes on. This feature—**"displacement"**—seems to be definitely lacking in the vocal signaling of man's closest relatives, though it does occur in bee-dancing.

One of the most important design-features of language is **"productivity"**; that is, the capacity to say things that have never been said or heard before and yet to be understood by other speakers of the language. If a gibbon makes any vocal sound at all, it is one or another of a small finite repertory of familiar calls. The gibbon call system can be characterized as closed. Language is open, or "productive," in the sense that one can coin new utterances by putting together pieces familiar from old utterances, assembling them by patterns of arrangement also familiar in old utterances.

Human genes carry the capacity to acquire a language, and probably also a strong drive toward such acquisition, but the detailed conventions of any one language are transmitted **extragenetically** by learning and teaching. To what extent such **"traditional transmission"** plays a part in gibbon calls or for other mammalian systems of vocal signals is not known, though in some instances the uniformity of the sounds made by a species, wherever the species is found over the world, is so great that genetics must be responsible.

The meaningful elements in any language—"words" in everyday parlance, **"morphemes"** to the linguist—constitute an enormous stock. Yet they are represented by small arrangements of a relatively very small stock of distinguishable sounds which are in themselves wholly meaningless. This **"duality of patterning"** is illustrated by the English words "tack," "cat," and "act." They are totally distinct as to meaning, and yet are composed of just three basic meaningless sounds in different permutations. Few animal communicative systems share this design-feature of language—none among the other hominoids, and perhaps none at all.

---

It should be noted that some of these 13 design-features are not independent. In particular, a system cannot be either arbitrary or nonarbitrary unless it is semantic, and it cannot have duality of patterning unless it is semantic. It should also be noted that the listing does not attempt to include all the features that might be discovered in the communicative behavior of this or that species, but only those that are clearly important for language.

It is probably safe to assume that nine of the 13 features were already present in the vocal-auditory communication of the protohominoids—just the nine that are securely attested for the gibbons and humans of today. That is, there were a dozen or so distinct calls, each the appropriate vocal response (or vocal part of the whole response) to a recurrent and biologically important type of situation: the discovery of food, the detection of a predator, sexual interest, need for maternal care, and so on. The problem of the origin of human speech, then, is that of trying to determine how such a system could have developed the four additional properties of displacement, productivity and full-blown traditional transmission. Of course the full story involves a great deal more than communicative behavior alone. The development must be visualized as occurring in the context of the evolution of the primate horde into the primitive society of food-gatherers and hunters, an integral part, but a part, of the total evolution of behavior.

It is possible to imagine a closed system developing some degree of productivity, even in the absence of the other three features. Human speech exhibits a phenomenon that could have this effect, the phenomenon of **"blending."** Sometimes a speaker will hesitate between two words or phrases, both reasonably appropriate for the situation in which he is speaking, and actually say something that is neither wholly one nor wholly the other, but a combination of parts of each. Hesitating between "Don't shout so loud" and "Don't yell so loud," he might come out with "Don't shell so loud." Blending is almost always involved in slips of the tongue, but it may also be the regular mechanism by which a speaker of a language says something that he has not said before. Anything a speaker says must be either an exact repetition of an utterance he has heard before, or else some blended product of two or more such familiar utterances. Thus even such a smooth and normal sentence as "I tried to get there, but the car broke down" might be produced as a blend, say, of "I tried to get there but couldn't" and "While I was driving down Main Street the car broke down."

Children acquiring the language of their community pass through a stage that is closed in just the way gibbon calls are. A child may have a repertory of several dozen sentences, each of which, in adult terms, has an internal structure, and yet for the child each may be an indivisible whole. He may also learn new whole utterances from surrounding adults. The child takes the crucial step, however, when he first says something that he has not learned from others. The only way in which the child can possibly do this is by blending two of the whole utterances that he already knows.

---

In the case of the **closed call-system** of the gibbons or the protohominoids, there is no source for the addition of new unitary calls to the repertory except perhaps by occasional imitation of the calls and cries of other species. Even this would not render the system productive, but would merely enlarge it. But blending might occur. Let AB represent the food call and CD the danger call, each a fairly complex phonetic pattern. Suppose a protohominoid encountered food and caught sight of a predator at the same time. If the two stimuli were balanced just right, he might emit the calls ABCD or CDAB in quick sequence, or might even produce AD or CB. Any of these would be a blend. AD, for example, would mean "both food and danger." By virtue of this, AB and CD would acquire new meanings, respectively "food without danger" and "danger without food." And all three of these calls—AB, CD, and AD—would now be composite rather than unitary, built out of smaller elements with their own individual meanings: A would mean "food"; B, "no danger"; C, "no food"; and D, "danger."

But this is only part of the story. The generation of a blend can have no effect unless it is understood. Human beings are so good at understanding blends that it is hard to tell a blend from a rote repetition, except in the case of slips of the tongue and some of the earliest and most tentative blends used by children. Such powers of understanding cannot be ascribed to man's prehuman ancestors. It must be supposed, therefore, that occasional blends occurred over many tens of thousands of years (perhaps, indeed, they still may occur from time to time among gibbons or the great apes), with rarely any appropriate communicative impact on hearers, before the understanding of blends became speedy enough to reinforce their production. However, once that did happen, the earlier closed system had become open and productive.

It is also possible to see how faint traces of displacement might develop in a call-system even in the absence of productivity, duality, and thoroughgoing traditional transmission. Suppose an early hominid, a man-ape say, caught sight of a predator without himself being seen. Suppose that for whatever reason—perhaps through fear—he sneaked silently back toward others of his band and only a bit later gave forth the danger call. This might give the whole band a better chance to escape the predator, thus bestowing at least slight survival value on whatever factor was responsible for the delay.

Something akin to communicative displacement is involved in lugging a stick or a stone around—it is like talking today about what one should do tomorrow. Of course it is not to be supposed that the first tool-carrying was purposeful, any more than that the first displaced communication was a discussion of plans. Caught in a cul-de-sac by a predator, however, the early hominid might strike out in terror with his stick or stone and by chance disable or drive off his enemy. In other words, the first tool-carrying had a consequence but not a purpose. Because the outcome was fortunate, it tended to reinforce whatever factor, genetic or traditional, prompted the behavior and made the outcome possible. In the end such events do lead to purposive behavior.

Although elements of displacement might arise in this fashion, on the whole it seems likely that some degree of productivity preceded any great proliferation of communicative displacement as well as any significant capacity for traditional transmission. A productive system requires the young to catch on to the ways in which whole signals are built out of smaller meaningful elements, some of which may never occur as whole signals in isolation. The young can do this only in the way that human children learn their language: by learning some utterances as whole units, in due time testing various blends based on that repertory, and finally adjusting their patterns of blending until the bulk of what they say matches what adults would say and is therefore understood. Part of this learning process is bound to take place away from the precise situations for which the responses are basically appropriate, and this means the promotion of displacement. Learning and teaching, moreover, call on any capacity for traditional transmission that the band may have. Insofar as the communicative system itself has survival value, all this bestows survival value also on the capacity for traditional transmission and for displacement. But these in turn increase the survival value of the communicative system. A child can be taught how to avoid certain dangers before he actually encounters them.

---

These developments are also necessarily related to the appearance of large and convoluted brains, which are better storage units for the conventions of a complex communicative system and for other traditionally transmitted skills and practices. Hence the adaptative value of the behavior serves to select genetically for the change in structure. A lengthened period of childhood helplessness is also a longer period of **plasticity** for learning. There is therefore selection for prolonged childhood and, with it, later maturity and longer life. With more for the young to learn, and with male as well as female tasks to be taught, fathers become more domesticated. The increase of displacement promotes retention and foresight; a male can protect his mate and guard her jealously from other males even when he does not at the moment hunger for her.

There is excellent reason to believe that duality of patterning was the last property to be developed, because one can find little if any reason why a communicative system should have this property unless it is highly complicated. If a vocal-auditory system comes to have a larger and larger number of distinct meaningful elements, those elements inevitably come to be more and more similar to one another in sound. There is a practical limit, for any species or any machine, to the number of distinct stimuli that can be discriminated, especially when the discriminations typically have to be made in noisy conditions. Suppose that Samuel F. B. Morse, in devising his telegraph code, had proposed a signal .1 second long for "A," .2 second long for "B," and so on up to 2.6 seconds for "Z." Operators would have enormous difficulty learning and using any such system. What Morse actually did was to incorporate the principle of duality of patterning. The telegraph operator has to learn to discriminate, in the first instance, only two lengths of pulse and about three lengths of pause. Each letter is coded into a different arrangement of these elementary meaningless units. The arrangements are easily kept apart because the few meaningless units are plainly distinguishable.

The analogy explains why it was advantageous for the forerunner of language, as it was becoming increasingly complex, to acquire duality of patterning. However it occurred, this was a major breakthrough; without it language could not possibly have achieved the efficiency and flexibility it has.

One of the basic principles of evolutionary theory holds that the initial survival value of any innovation is conservative in that it makes possible the maintenance of a largely traditional way of life in the face of changed circumstances. There was nothing in the makeup of the protohominoids that destined their descendants to become human. Some of them, indeed, did not. They made their way to ecological niches where food was plentiful and predators sufficiently avoidable, and where the development of primitive varieties of language and culture would have bestowed no advantage. They survive still, with various sorts of specialization, as the gibbons and the great apes.

---

Man's own remote ancestors, then, must have come to live in circumstances where a slightly more flexible system of communication, the incipient carrying and shaping of tools, and a slight increase in the capacity for traditional transmission made just the difference between surviving—largely, be it noted, by the good old protohominoid way of life—and dying out. There are various possibilities. If predators become more numerous and dangerous, any **nonce** use of a tool as a weapon, any co-operative mode of escape or attack might restore the balance. If food became scarcer, any technique for cracking harder nuts, for foraging over a wider territory, for sharing food so gathered or storing it when it was plentiful might promote survival of the band. Only after a very long period of such small adjustments to tiny changes of living conditions could the factors involved—incipient language, incipient tool-carrying and toolmaking, incipient culture—have started leading the way to a new pattern of life, of the kind called human.

---

## Critical Thinking and Application

- How has "traditional transmission" played a role in the development of human society? Where does it come into play in your life?
- After reading this chapter, has your view of the relationship between human language and nonhuman communication changed? How?

## Vocabulary

arbitrary
arbitrariness
blending
closed call-system
comparative method (of historical linguistics)
design feature
discrete, discreteness
displacement
duality of patterning
extragenetic
hominid
hominoid
morpheme
nonce
philology, philological
plasticity
primate
productivity
proto
semanticity
traditional transmission

## Suggested Further Reading

Oller, D. Kimbrough, and Ulrike Griebel, eds. 2004. *Evolution of Communication Systems: A Comparative Approach*. Cambridge, MA: MIT Press.

# CHAPTER 4

# Signing and Speaking
## Competitors, Alternatives, or Incompatibles?

*William C. Stokoe*

(1991)

*William Stokoe, a pioneer in the study of* ***sign languages,*** *points out that in our quest to understand the origins of language, we should not assume that it was spoken and heard. Thus, studies focusing on the vocal tract structures in early hominids and other ancestors of* Homo sapiens, *including* ***Neanderthals*** [Neandertals *in his usage], would miss facets of language that may have been present. He reminds us that sign languages are true languages, that there are different types of signed language, that people in different cultures use a combination of signed and spoken languages, and "that human cultures vary widely and unpredictably." He accepts that language is necessary for humanity, but denies that the crucial feature is vocal. This is a warning that we should not assume that our own ways of regarding language are universal; that holds true as much for our scientific theories as for our daily interactions.*

### Reading Questions

- What kind of language did Neanderthals likely possess?
- What are some examples of signed languages? What are the two types of sign language that Stokoe proposes?
- Why do some societies seem to use spoken language alone and others a combination of spoken and signed language?
- How have supposedly scientific theories been used to support ideas of education for deaf children?

The search for the origins and evolution of language may be frustrated at the outset by shortsightedness of two kinds in the searchers: first, the earliest human languages may not have been spoken and heard and so the earliest evidence of vocal and auditory specialization may be later than the origin of systematic symbolic signalling; second, even when the brain and not the vocal and auditory apparatus is recognized as the language center, we must look beyond biology to culture.

Of course no serious investigation can ignore biology. Human structure differs in significant ways from that of our closest primate relatives. But function as well as structure plays a role: even a single fossil bone may prove whether its owner walked and stood erect or not and had more or less human character. Function alone cannot be trusted: bats fly like birds and cetaceans swim like fish, but when Neandertalers buried the dead and put artifacts into their graves, we have evidence of a culture fully human, not only because such objects are not made by other animals but also because they unmistakably imply a culture that transcends the material, a culture that includes some notions of a life after death.

The question is, how could Neandertal man have lacked the physiology for speech, as Lieberman has suggested he did (1972, 1975), and yet possessed a fully human culture complete with language? Responses to the dilemma Lieberman's experiments pose have either been objections to the methods he used to reconstruct vocal tracts from skulls, or taken the form of denials that a two-tube **superlaryngeal vocal tract** is needed for language. The objectors reason somewhat as follows:

1. Evidence of Neandertal culture implies a human culture;
2. Such a culture requires language;

William C. Stokoe, Signing and Speaking: Competitors, Alternatives, or Incompatibles? *Studies in Language Origins* vol. 2, edited by Jan Wind. Amsterdam: John Benjamins, 1991, pp. 115–121. With kind permission by John Benjamins Publishing Company, Amsterdam/Philadelphia. www.benjamins.com.

3. Therefore Neandertal man could speak and understand; and
4. Lieberman's conclusions must be false.

This train of language origin logic misses two important stations:

> A. Whatever the physiology of the Neandertal superlaryngeal vocal tract, these people had other human attributes, among them true **bipedalism,** human hands with un**pongid** thumb placement, convergent **binocular** vision, human faces....
> B. Despite its one-thousand-to-one distribution in the human population of the earth, spoken language is not the only form of human language.

Taking the logical train over this route, one reaches the conclusion that Neandertalers had a fully human language exactly as the surviving cultural evidence implies. This language may not have been exclusively vocal, but it had to be a complete language, produced by actions of the (human) body and perceived by human vision. This implies that Neandertalers had hands and faces more human than pongid. The binocular vision of the primate order would seem to have evolved with an arboreal way of life—swinging and catching and leaping require a precise perception of distances. But the higher primates use the face for more than a range finder mounting. Close observers can read chimpanzee and gorilla faces accurately and determine, as Darwin made clear (1873), the emotion signified and so communicated. But that is not all that ape faces express. Head turning and lip pointing indicate directions or things worth others' attention, and can be observed not just to signify the pointer's intention but also to communicate it to others.

When the primate range of behavioral patterns is expanded to include some of the behavior and ideation found in human cultures, it is safe to infer that the mobility of the face and the range of what it could express were increased by a quantum leap. Even without anything like a full spoken language, Neandertal man could have possessed a viable language that made use of the potential in the human face and body, and in the information gathering capability of the visual sensory system (Gibson, 1966). How this may have come about is a major question for archaeology and anthropology, but presumably the creatures branching off the primate line lived differently. That is to say they must have expanded the rudimentary toolmaking ability and weapon wielding behavior we can see in chimpanzees. In doing so they would have had to remember past actions, objects other than the one in present attention, to make comparisons and choices, and in short to develop with hand and eye and brain the cognitive base for language.

There are limits, however, to how far one can go with implications, speculation, and bits of physical evidence in reconstructing the past. It does seem certain that Neandertalers had a language, and with or without laryngeal limitations, could have had a language largely if not exclusively read by eye from just those physical changes and actions that characterize the hominid increments to the pongid physiology and capabilities.

On the present scene, sign languages of deaf people have been recognized as true languages since the late nineteen fifties, and for the last three decades the amount and precision of knowledge about them has been on the increase. The impact of knowledge about sign languages on questions of language origins has been various. Some of us see it as strong support for a gestural origin theory; others perceive so much difference between sound and sight that they doubt whether a sign language could have **duality of patterning;** and a few perhaps object that we have not the slightest reason to suppose any of the language-using, language-originating ancestors of the race were deaf.

Quite so. No such implication is intended. The inability to hear at all and to speak unless long and laboriously trained has resulted in deaf people's use of fully articulated sign languages. The study of sign languages used by deaf people, at the very least, provides us with evidence that languages produced gesturally and understood visually are languages. These sign languages also make it quite clear that speech and hearing are not, as many have supposed, essential to language. It is this last point that has been too often overlooked, not only in the search for language origins but in linguistics generally, and in the education and social integration of deaf persons.

A very recent addition to the growing science of signed languages is the work by Adam Kendon, *Sign Language of Aboriginal Australia* (1988). It complements other sign language studies in an important way. Kendon begins by taking note of a very crucial cultural difference: some signed languages are used by groups of persons as their major or sole language; other signed languages are used by persons who also have at their disposal a spoken language, or more than one. The two kinds he calls, respectively, **primary sign languages** and **alternate sign languages.** The importance is that this difference lies more in culture than in language. Primary sign languages are used in most instances by persons whose hearing acuity makes it impossible for them to acquire true spoken language competence—often despite heroic efforts on their part and teachers' to learn to speak and to understand speech by looking at speakers' faces. Although deafness may seem to take away freedom of choice, in fact, many deaf or partially deaf users of primary sign languages have chosen to sign and not to speak in most of their interactions with others.

Alternate sign languages have a more complex relation to culture. Most Americans are aware of the alternate sign language used by the Indian tribes of the plains and learned by mountain men, buffalo hunters, cavalry officers, and their scouts during the era of westward expansion. They may assume, perhaps correctly, that the term "language" may have been misbestowed on a gestural system used only for certain limited purposes when disparate cultures and languages were in constant confrontation. Mallery's work suggests (1880), and some later scholarship agrees, that the practice of gesturally communicating messages commonly spoken may have had a much earlier origin on the North

American continent. Be that as it may, Kendon's work shows conclusively that among the **aboriginal** tribes of Australia the use of signing instead of speech is common practice, that its use is determined by culture not by physical necessity, and that it is not limited to special domains but can be and is used as speech is used, for normal conversation.

Kendon's work shows that signing and speaking are not incompatible. Aboriginal culture not merely permits but strictly requires signing to be substituted for speaking under certain circumstances. Cultural—not physical nor universal psycholinguistic—determinants impose signing; yet no one in that culture feels imposed upon. On the contrary, as Kendon points out, among the older women of the Warlpiri and Warramungu, signing is the preferred medium for prolonged conversational sessions.

We who like to consider the possible origins of language need to give greater heed to cultural differences. In Western cultures sign language is largely confined to deaf persons and those who communicate with them, and until very recently even that evidence of signing was kept away from hearing eyes. Plain signing survives now mainly as a form of intercultural entertainment. Everyone, it is alleged, spoke sign language on Martha's Vineyard (Groce, 1985). Washabaugh (1985) and others have found that deaf signers and their sign language are not despised by hearing people in Caribbean island communities. Hubert Smith has shown on film (in the Smithsonian Film Archives) Yucatec hearing and deaf villagers communicating fluently in sign language. And Du Bois has reported (Lecture Gallaudet College, 1980) that in Yucatan teenagers mix signed words with spoken words in their everyday discourse and so when there are deaf people in a village there they are easily brought into full communication with the hearing because of the alternate sign language (some of whose lexicon Du Bois traces to Mayan carvings).

The indications are plain; human cultures vary widely and unpredictably. The belief that to communicate by speaking is human and communicate by gesturing is subhuman cannot be upheld. It is a belief, in fact, peculiar to recent Western cultures and arose in part from a particular phase of the enlightenment, the oralist-manualist controversy between Heinicke and de l'Épée over the proper way to instruct those born deaf—more generally, over the nature of language itself, whether it is essentially hearing and speech as Heinicke held, or essentially intellectual and indifferent to the particular mode of expression as de l'Épée insisted. (See Garnett in Heinicke, de l'Épée, and Garnett, 1968; Lane, 1984.)

To read onto all cultures the norms and suppositions of one's own is to pervert anthropological science, and yet precisely that is done when the use of a primary sign language is banned from the education of deaf children. Even when signing is permitted, to insist that the signs be **manual** only (without the facial and other components of natural sign language), and must reproduce as exactly as possible the grammatical structure of the teachers' spoken language—this too does more than retard education and deal unfairly with deaf persons who cannot learn to use speech. It also blinds investigators to the truth that language can operate equally well, for those who have competence, in the gestural-visual channel as in the vocal-auditory channel. This is true not only because language is based more deeply in human anatomy than the vocal folds and the cochlea but also because language is as much determined by culture as by physiology.

More research must be directed to the actual communication of those peoples with the least urbanized cultures, but we already have strong evidence that in such cultures there is no tendency to equate talking with language and mental competence and to equate signing with mental incompetence and lack of language. I believe that much of our own culture's readiness to make such equations is simply ethnocentrism. Once this prejudice natural to a literate, print-oriented culture is overcome and real knowledge about signed languages both primary and alternate is more widely diffused, it may be possible to look more closely at gesture and vision as precursors of vocal noise and hearing and the beginnings of human mentality and culture. As James J. Gibson made remarkably clear, vision for primates, especially humans, is the master perceptual system (1966). Current anthropology tells us that the chief physical difference between man and the other apes is that man walks erect. Thus more than other animals, hominids had forearms and hands not only for fighting and foraging but also for signifying and communicating. Still more obvious is the common expression of emotions in man and animals so thoroughly explored by Darwin (1873). But more than emotions will have shown on faces and body postures when members of the new erect walking primate branch began to develop cognitively and culturally by using their vision, forelimb capability, and deep-seated ability to read meaning in each others' actions by watching.

There is nothing to keep us from supposing that, along with this increased use of vision and visible action to signify and communicate the increased complexity of their lives, these folk did not also exploit voice. Quite the reverse; sounds as well as visible signs of what is going on are common to the communication of most mammals and especially important in primate life. However, it is important to note that once there was sufficient hominid ability to adapt to new territory and conditions, a culture could have developed that required the use of a silent language—or the reverse, a vocal language—when one or the other was appropriate to conditions.

I conclude that signing and speaking did not compete in the earliest stages of hominid differentiation; they do not now, unless cultural values and social forces make them (in schools for deaf children). I conclude too that signing and speaking are and always were compatible. Not only do the Aboriginal tribes of Australia use them both, but also there is growing evidence that among un-urbanized societies, signing and speaking (or the use of gestures for more than embellishment) can be and are used in close cooperation. And even among users of primary sign languages there are bilinguals. Some severely deaf persons can and do use speech and lipreading with some success; and many become bilingual, not only reading and writing the language the surrounding community speaks, but also transmitting and receiving it with manual signs representing words or letters. Finally, I conclude that signing and speaking are true alternatives, in the sense of being equally effective input-output devices for the central processor of language. Despite the thousand-to-one disproportion of speaking to signing in primary language use today, the natures of language, physiology, and culture argue that signing is more likely than speaking to have been the means by which language was first transmitted and acquired.

## References

Darwin, C. 1873. *The Expression of Emotion in Man and Animals.* New York: Appleton.

Gibson, J. J. 1966. *The Senses Considered as Perceptual Systems.* New York: Houghton Mifflin.

Groce, N. E. 1985. *Everyone Here Spoke Sign Language.* Cambridge, MA: Harvard University Press.

Heinicke, Samuel, Charles-Michel de L'Epée, and Christopher Browne Garnett. 1968. *The Exchange of Letters Between Samuel Heinicke and Abbe Charles-Michel de L'Epee; A Monograph on the Oralist and Manualist Methods of Instructing the Deaf in the Eighteenth Century, Including the Reproduction in English of Salient Portions of Each Letter.* New York: Vantage Press.

Kendon, A. 1988. *Sign Language of Aboriginal Australia.* Cambridge: Cambridge University Press.

Lane, H. 1984. *When the Mind Hears: A History of the Deaf.* New York: Random House.

Lieberman, P. 1975. *On the Origins of Language.* New York: Macmillan.

Lieberman, P., E. S. Crelin, and D. H. Klatt. 1972. Phonetic ability and related anatomy of the newborn adult human, Neanderthal man, and the chimpanzee. *American Anthropologist* 7, 287–307.

Mallery, G. 1880. *Introduction to the Study of Sign Language Among the North American Indians.* Washington, DC: Government Printing Office.

Washabaugh, W. 1985. *Five Fingers for Survival.* Ann Arbor, MI: Karoma Press.

---

## Critical Thinking and Application

- If language does not have to be spoken to be genuine language, what *is* required for that identification? How would we observe this in the fossil record?
- How does the prejudice against signed languages come into play in the insistence that deaf children learn a "pure" signed language without even facial expressions?
- How does Stokoe's discussion of sign languages challenge conventional theories of language origins?

## Vocabulary

| | | |
|---|---|---|
| aboriginal | duality of patterning | pongid |
| alternate sign languages | hominid | primary sign language |
| binocular | manual | sign languages |
| bipedalism | Neanderthal | superlaryngeal vocal tract |

## Suggested Further Reading

Armstrong, David F., William C. Stokoe, and Sherman E. Wilcox. 1995. *Gesture and the Nature of Language.* Cambridge: Cambridge University Press.

Farnell, Brenda M. 1995. *Do You See What I Mean? Plains Indian Sign Talk and the Embodiment of Action.* Austin: University of Texas Press.

King, Barbara J., ed. 1999. *The Origins of Language: What Nonhuman Primates Can Tell Us.* Santa Fe, NM: School of American Research Press.

Klima, Edward S., and Ursula Bellugi. 1979. *The Signs of Language.* Cambridge, MA: Harvard University Press.

Lieberman, Philip. 1991. *Uniquely Human: The Evolution of Speech, Thought and Selfless Behavior.* Cambridge, MA: Harvard University Press.

Lieberman, Philip. 1998. *Eve Spoke: Human Language and Human Evolution.* New York: Norton.

Meier, Richard P., Kearsy Cormier, and David Quinto-Pozos, eds., with the assistance of Adrianne Cheek, Heather Knapp, and Christian Rathmann. 2002. *Modality and Structure in Signed and Spoken Languages.* Cambridge and New York: Cambridge University Press.

Monaghan, Leila Frances. 2007. *Many Ways to Be Deaf: International Variation in Deaf Communities.* Washington, DC: Gallaudet University Press.

## CHAPTER 5

# Symbol and Structure: A Comprehensive Framework for Language Evolution

*Derek Bickerton*

(2003)

*Derek Bickerton is known for his proposal that language as we know it—as enumerated in Charles Hockett's chapter, "The Origin of Speech" (Chapter 3), but with an emphasis on syntax—was preceded by a phase he called* protolanguage. *This phase came before genuine, full language, and in protolanguage some properties of language such as conveying meaning through symbols may be found. Protolanguage is studied through combining research on ape language, child language acquisition, and pidgins, which all demonstrate some commonalities with protolanguage. This idea, from the 1980s, has been developed over time, and as Bickerton points out in this chapter, developments in the study of the evolution of language have exploded since then. They have come from many directions, including cognitive science, animal behavior, and more, focusing on "social intelligence," mirror neurons, and other new concepts. However, linguists have not necessarily followed these strands of research and may be entirely unaware of them. This chapter is written by Bickerton in his conscious role as a linguist, defining language as consisting of both symbolic units and syntax. Only with a clear understanding of what language is can the issue of biological evolution be addressed.*

*Bickerton's short chapter touches on some strenuous arguments about whether language is a specialized faculty or generalized intelligence; whether language is continuous with other species' communication systems or represents a radical break; what about language made it necessary for increased survival (social interaction? acknowledgment of others' minds? the ability to discuss useful subjects?); when it appeared; what it was like (gesture? sound?). It is unlikely to settle the matter, but it does seem helpful to hear from an expert on language when we wonder about its origins.*

### Reading Questions

- Recall what you know about the classic and contemporary understanding of how biological evolution works. What is "selective pressure"?
- Why is it inadequate to treat language as a "given," or as a "black box"?
- Why have linguists not kept up with the literature about language evolution? Who, instead, has been asking about this? Why do you think this is the case?
- What three things must come together to create language as we know it?
- What are *symbolic units*? What is *syntax*? Why does Bickerton insist that syntax is the most crucial part of human language?

## Speaking as a Linguist[1]

I approach the evolution of language as a linguist. This immediately puts me in a minority, and before proceeding further I think it's worth pausing a moment to consider the sheer oddity of that fact. If a physicist found himself in a minority among those studying the evolution of matter, if a biologist found himself in a minority among those studying the evolution of sex, the world would be amazed, if not shocked and stunned. But a parallel situtation in the evolution of language causes not a hair to turn.

Derek Bickerton, Symbol and Structure: A Comprehensive Framework for Language Evolution. In *Language Evolution*, ed. by Morten H. Christiansen and Simon Kirby. Oxford: Oxford University Press, 2003. pp. 77–93.

Why is this? Several causes have contributed. Linguists long ago passed a self-denying ordinance that kept almost all of them out of the field, until quite recently. Since nature abhors a vacuum, and since the coming into existence of our most salient talent is a scientific question that should concern anyone seriously interested in why humans are as they are, other disciplines rushed to fill that vacuum. Then again, language doesn't look as if it should be all that complex, not like genetics or quantum mechanics. We all speak at least one, that one we acquired without a lick of conscious effort, and most non-linguists, in the unlikely event that they opened a copy of *Linguistic Inquiry* or *Natural Language and Linguistic Theory* only to find stuff every bit as hard going as genetics or quantum mechanics, would in many cases react by saying 'What's all this nonsense about? Why are they making such a fuss about something that's perfectly simple and straightforward?' And they would probably go on to say, 'What do *I* need this stuff for? I'm a systematic biologist/palaeo-anthropologist/evolutionary psychologist/computational mathematician [strike out whichever do not apply]—I do not need this.'

Well, the reason they do need this is simple and straightforward. Language is a means of communication (among many other functions) that differs radically from the means of communication of any other species. At the same time, we are a species that differs radically from other species in our creativity and variability of behaviour (anyone who confuses this statement of plain fact with the claim that we are the pinnacle of evolution or divinely created is herself seriously confused). There is a good chance that these two uniquenesses are not coincidental; in other words, we most likely are the way we are because we have language and no one else does. If that is so, then it must be because there are specific properties of language which, if other species had had them first, would have produced similar results. What we have to do is determine what these properties are, which of them are essential and which accidental. We have to determine how we came to have, not just 'language' in the abstract—whatever that might mean—but the precise set of linguistic properties that happens to correlate with, and most probably causes, our unique nature. We have to do this if we are ever going to explain how humans evolved. But we can't explain why language has the set of properties that it does have, and no other set, if we do not know what those properties are.

## The Interdisciplinary Stance

This is not, yet, a particularly widespread view. A lot of writers believe one can treat language as a given, a black box, in effect, and account for its evolution simply by selecting the selective pressure that gave rise to it. Was it a grooming substitute (Dunbar 1993; 1996)? Or maybe setting up a menstruation ritual for female bonding (Power 1998; 2000)? Or letting men know if their women had cheated on them (Ridley 1993: 229)? Or initiating marriage, so men would know who they weren't supposed to cheat with (Deacon 1997)? The fact that these and similar explanations flourish side by side tells one immediately that not enough constraints are being used to limit possible explanations.

Simply taking into account what we know about language should form an adequate constraint, since all these proposals run up against some language feature quite incompatible with them. Take the grooming proposal. It is far from clear why, if language simply substituted for grooming when group size became too large, language should invariably convey factual information, indeed be incapable of *not* giving factual information, even in flattering someone (*That outfit really suits you—matches your eyes*). Surely a similar result could have been achieved simply by using pleasant but meaningless noises. Lovers often do just that, even now, with all of language at their disposal. Or take the proposal that the driving force behind the emergence of language was gossip and/or some sort of Machiavellian manipulation. Since there undoubtedly was a time when the vocabulary was zero, there must also have been a time when the vocabulary was vanishingly small, no more than three or four units/signs/words, whatever those may have been. The question is simply whether the gossip one could transmit with such a vocabulary would be of any interest whatsoever. It seems unlikely. Similarly, it is highly implausible that, with a small initial stock of symbols, one could do much in the way of social manipulation.

Both gossip and manipulation require a vocabulary of some size, but such a size could hardly have been achieved unless earlier and smaller vocabularies had already served some useful purpose. However, the issue of the minimal vocabulary size required for implementing functions such as these is simply not addressed by those who claim a social-intelligence source for language (see Bickerton 2002 for a fuller treatment of these and related questions).

Ignorance of both language and linguistic theory seemed to me for a long time to be the most serious deficiency among writers on the evolution of language. Then I reviewed two books by linguists (Loritz 1999; Jenkins 2000; see Bickerton 2001) and I'm no longer so sure. Such ignorance now appears as simply a special case (perhaps the most serious, though by no means the only serious one) of a much more widespread tendency. There are at least six fields—linguistics, palaeoanthropology, evolutionary biology, neurology, psychology and primatology—that cannot possibly be ignored in any study of language evolution, and a number of others, such as genetics or palaeo-climatology, that bear on it perhaps somewhat less directly. All too often, a writer whose home is in one or other of these disciplines will make a proposal that is unacceptable in terms of one or more of the other relevant disciplines. This is not inevitable. It certainly does not result from the impossibility of acquiring the necessary knowledge, since anyone of average intelligence should, given goodwill and a little effort, be able to master enough of the literature in all relevant disciplines to avoid making gross errors.[2]

Having mastered linguistics and all the other relevant disciplines, are we now ready to make sense of language evolution? I don't think so. There's something that is implicit in much of my own writing which I fully realized only quite recently. It is that the biggest obstacle to understanding the evolution of language is thinking about it as 'the evolution of language'.

## Divide and Rule

Language as we know it today involves the coming together of three things: **modality, symbolism,** and **structure**. I can see no reason for supposing that all three evolved as a package deal, and good reasons for supposing that they evolved separately. Let's look at each of these three things in turn.

First modality: that includes speech and sign. For many, 'speech' and 'language' are interchangeable; how depressingly often one turns to the index of a book on human evolution to find the damning entry: 'Language: see Speech'. Most recently Mithen (2000: 216) has claimed that Neanderthals had probably acquired 'a degree of vocalization that is most appropriately described as language'. And even some linguists take a similar approach: Lieberman (1984; 1991; 1996), for example, assumes that once speech was there, the rest followed.

However, I take the arguments in Burling (2000) and Sperber and Origgi (2001) to be quite unanswerable. Before any of the three components of language could exist, let alone come together, there had to be comprehension of some kind, however primitive; pre-humans at some stage had to start trying to figure out one another's intentions. This largely solves the problem of what I once called the 'magic moment' (Bickerton 1990): how did the first hearer of a meaningful signal know that it was a meaningful signal (as opposed to a cough, a grunt of pain, or whatever)? Answer: if our ancestors were already trying to interpret the behaviour of their **conspecifics**, even perhaps to the extent of reading meanings where none was intended, they surely wouldn't take long to recognize intentional meanings. It also neatly solves the problem of whether language began as sign or speech. The answer is that it probably began as both—a mixture of anything that might serve to convey meaning. The original mixture of isolated grunts and gestures may have eventually settled on the vocal mode merely through the exigencies of communicating at night, over distance, or in dense vegetation. For a small initial vocabulary, no vocal improvement would have been needed.

Afterwards, as more (and more complex) information gradually came to be exchanged, attempts to convey it would have strongly selected for improved vocal capacities. I think there can be no doubt that the capacity to transmit information was what selected for improved speech capacity, rather than vice versa. Being able to speak more clearly does not, in and of itself, give you more to say. There is thus good reason to believe that the speech modality, far from being the driving force behind language, was entirely contingent on the two other components, the symbolic and the structural, and was developed and refined in response to their development.

Those components, the symbolic and the structural, are also distinct and can also be dissociated from one another. They are actually dissociated in several forms of development that can still be observed in the world around us: in early-stage **pidgins**, in early stage second-language learning, and in the productions of trained apes and other animals.[3] Of course you can't get a double dissociation: **syntactic** structure without symbolic content, the kind of thing you saw in old-fashioned **phrase-structure rules** cannot be used by animate beings to communicate with one another. But symbolic representation does not require any kind of structure—telegrams and headlines are immediately comprehensible with relatively little grammatical structure, and we can perfectly well understand utterances that have no syntactic structure at all, like Pinker's *skid-crash-hospital* (Pinker 1994). Indeed a variety of factors I have discussed at length in earlier work suggest that, in the evolution of our species, symbolism may have preceded syntax by as much as two million years.

Perhaps the clearest evidence for **phylogenetic** dissociation lies in the fact that while symbolic representation (at some level; and under instruction, at a near-human level, see Savage-Rumbaugh 1986) is within the reach of a number of non-human animals, syntax, regardless of the quantity or quality of instruction, remains beyond the reach of any other species ('putting symbols in a regular order' does not, of course, come anywhere close to being syntax). This inevitably suggests that the genetic and neural substrates for the two are quite distinct, and that they therefore must have distinct evolutionary histories. Consequently, explaining how language evolved requires us to answer two separate and quite distinct scientific questions. The first is: how and why one particular primate species, or one primate line of descent, developed a system of communication involving symbolic representation that allowed the transfer of (potentially) unlimited factual information, and the basic principles of which differed from those of all previous systems of communication. The second is how such a system acquired the very specific structural characteristics that the syntax of modern human languages exhibits. If one abbreviates these questions to 'How did meaningful units (words or signs) evolve?' and 'How did syntax evolve?', little is lost. But if only one question is answered, or if the two issues are mixed in together and confused with one another, we will continue to get the conflicting and unsatisfying accounts of language evolution that have predominated to this date. Let us therefore keep them clearly separate and deal with each in turn.

## Symbols

The most crucial thing to grasp about the emergence of symbolic representation is that it must have been primarily a cultural rather than a biological event. This idea, again implicit in some of my earlier work, has not previously been stated in quite these terms. However, it follows inevitably from the fact that a neural substrate adequate for some level of symbolic representation exists not simply in other great apes but among creatures as phylogenetically distant from us as African Grey parrots (Pepperburg 2000). This widespread nature of potential for symbolic representation suggests an **analogous** rather than a **homologous** development, the kind of development that produced fins in sharks, ichthyosaurs, and cetaceans. Probably the potential for symbolism exists in any animal with a brain of sufficient complexity, and this would hardly be surprising, given the still wider spread of **iconic** and **indexical** precursors of symbolism (for Pavlov's dogs, the ringing of a bell was an indexical representation of food, for example).

This view may be disturbing to some who, with Deacon, see the Rubicon between us and other animals as being symbolism rather than syntax. Part of the reason may be that when people think of symbolism, they think of the sophisticated version we enjoy today—a vast branching network of symbols each of which is interpretable in terms of other symbols—and not of the primitive version, compounded mainly of indexical and iconic associations, that may have come into existence two million years ago. Another part may be disbelief that, given the benefits of communication—so visible to us, with the twenty-twenty vision of hindsight—any animal capable of communication would fail to use it under natural conditions. Such a view ignores the essential unreliability of language. Words require little energy to produce; they are 'cheap tokens' and can be used with little or no risk or cost to deceive, just as easily as to inform. Body language is much more reliable for most animal purposes.[4]

I suspect that the only things missing for any relatively large-brained species were the two Ms—modality and motivation. Modality was perhaps the lesser problem, given the low requirement of an initial minimal vocabulary. Any modality capable of differentiating a half-dozen or so symbols would do for a start. Motivation was another matter. To us, able to appreciate the myriad potential uses of language, its possession seems too obvious a boon. But since no species has the gift of foresight, we should ask what benefits this minimal vocabulary would have bestowed on any other species. The answer is simple: none. Solitary species do not need to communicate. Other social species get along fine with non-linguistic methods. Since only one social species has even begun to develop the language mode, the logical place to look for motivation is in circumstances unique to that species. Elsewhere (Bickerton 2002) I have argued in detail that the initial **protolanguage** arose through the exigencies of extractive foraging in mainly dry savannah-type environments. I will not repeat those arguments here; suffice it to say that hunger and a high risk from predation would have engendered social systems in which individuals were more interdependent than they are in most primate societies, and where, accordingly, a degree of trust sufficient to overcome the 'cheap tokens' problem would necessarily be engendered.

Symbolism arose culturally, then, because the minimal necessary biological equipment was already in place and the exploitation of symbolism directly benefited both individuals and groups (groups by optimizing foraging under the fission-fusion constraints that a wide day-range plus vulnerability to predation imposed, individuals by enhancing the status of those who located and led the group to the best food sources). The only question that remains is what the earliest symbols were like.

## Holistic Versus Synthetic

Until quite recently, it was generally assumed that **ontogeny** and **phylogeny**, though far from indissolubly wedded, were at least alike to this extent: the earliest units of pre-human utterances were pretty similar to the earliest units of contemporary infants. That is to say, they were basically single units with ostensively definable referents, perhaps somewhat broader in meaning than the units of an adult vocabulary. Recently, however, this notion has been challenged from a variety of perspectives, all of which converge on the assumption that **holistic** utterances, semantically equivalent to one-clause sentences in modern languages, formed the earliest linguistic utterances.

Wray (2000) sees this proposal as solving the **'continuity paradox'** (Bickerton 1990: 7). Calls can be interpreted holistically, so there could be a seamless transition from a non-linguistic communication system to some form of protolanguage. Carstairs-McCarthy (1999; 2000), assuming syntax to be modelled on the syllable (but see the next section), has to have a holistic protolanguage for the syntactic equivalents of **onset, nucleus,** and **coda** to be factored out of. **Computational linguists** (Batali 1998; Kirby 2000; Briscoe 2002)[5] likewise assume initial holistic utterances, so that, by a process described as 'self-organization', vast quantities of variable and random utterances could gradually converge on fixed forms with fixed meanings. This **holophrastic** approach to initial symbols can even claim some kind of history, since holistic beginnings are implicit in the 'singing ape' conjectures of Darwin, Jespersen, and others.

The approach is, however, beset by a variety of problems. Initially, there is the problem of comprehension: while one can deduce many things about others' intentions from their behaviour, anyone who has visited a country with a strange language knows that such understanding does not extend to linguistic behaviour. Since Quine's discussion (1960; see also Premack 1986) the problem of the speaker who says *Gavagai!* to the researcher when a rabbit runs past has been well known. We may believe, unlike Quine, that the word is rather unlikely to mean 'undissociated rabbit parts.' But that may be largely because we benefit from a history, both ontogenetic and phylogenetic, of learning what words are likely to mean. It is a task of considerable difficulty, although well worth attempting, to try to imagine oneself as not knowing any words at all, not even knowing what words were or could do. Certainly the passage of a rabbit at the moment of utterance is no guarantee that *Gavagai!* has anything to do with the rabbit: events do not occur in a vacuum; something else that might be being referred to is always going on. Even if we could somehow know that *Gavagai!* and the rabbit were connected, they could merely be connected in the way that *God bless you!* is connected with a sneeze.

Now these are problems that would affect understanding even if words or other symbols referred to isolated objects or events and were initially used in the presence of those objects and events (an unlikely proviso—there is little point in talking about what people can see for themselves, and indeed the whole point of language as opposed to animal communication systems in general is that the former, but not the latter, can be used to inform about things that are not physically present). Those problems of understanding are compounded infinitely if the initial utterances of a language do not correspond to anything tangible or easily identifiable, but refer to some set of circumstances that may or may not be apparent from the surrounding context. If the intended meaning is apparent from that context—if, say, initial utterances were things like *Give that to me!* or *Stay away from her!*—you wouldn't need language to express them. Such things are much more unambiguously expressed by behaviour already in an animal's communicative repertoire, such as begging gestures or threat gestures. If the intended meaning is not apparent from that context, the receiver would never be able to select, from a potentially infinite range of possible meanings, the one that the sender meant to express.

It is no accident that in most, if not all, computer simulations of language evolution, the self-organizing 'agents' already *know what their interlocutor means to say.* If the problem space were not limited in this way, the simulations simply wouldn't work—the agents would never converge on a workable system. But such unrealistic initial conditions are unlikely to have applied to our remote ancestors.

Let us suppose, counter to probability, that our ancestors somehow developed a holistic language. They would then have confronted the problem of how to go from such a language to languages that are built up from discrete units with single meanings (as all languages are today). Even today, modern children, equipped with all the bells and whistles of full human language, have a hard time segmenting adult utterances which, though they may sound holistic to the child, consist already of ready-made word units. How much more difficult for creatures with no experience of language to segment strings that were genuinely holistic!

There are two logical possibilities, one of which must be fulfilled by any such holistic utterances. One is that the units that would eventually dissolve into discrete words already contained regularities within the holistic utterance—a phonetic sequence like *-meg-*, for instance, might occur in any holophrase that made reference to 'meat'. This would remove the problem at the same time as it removed any possible justification for supposing that language began in this way. For if such utterances could be straightforwardly decomposed into the equivalent of words, then words as we know them already existed and there would have been no point in starting out with holophrastic units.

The other possibility is that the sequences were truly holistic, in other words that their sound structures bore no relation to one another: 'Give the meat!' might then be *megalup* and 'Take the meat!' might be *kokubar.* From these, or any similar examples, it would simply be impossible to factor out a single symbol for 'meat'.

A holophrastic account has yet more difficulties to face. It may seem easy to translate a **holophrase** (given that we understand it correctly) into an equivalent sentence of discrete words. But suppose some large male **hominid,** in the presence of a female, aggressively utters ***&*&x@**!* We may reasonably take this to mean, 'Stay away from her!' But it could just as easily mean 'Do not go near her!' Or, 'Stay right where you are!' Or even 'You—you, get out of my sight!' How smaller units can be factored out from holophrases when even their global meanings are so potentially ambiguous remains unclear.

But perhaps the biggest problem with the holistic approach is that it doesn't explain anything worth explaining. All the substantive problems in language evolution—how symbolism got started and fixed, how, when, and why structure emerged, where and how and to what extent any of this got instantiated in neural tissue—remain to be solved, whether one accepts a holistic account or not.

Accordingly, it is more parsimonious to assume that language began as it was to go on—that discrete symbols, whether oral or manual, were there from the beginning. I do not know of a single coherent argument why they shouldn't have been. If they were, it is most likely that, once these symbols exceeded the merest handful, they began to be strung together in some ad hoc fashion. One hears frequently of 'proto-syntax', which seems to mean one-clause sentences with fixed word order, and there is a widespread but wholly erroneous belief that this does not merely constitute a step in the direction of real syntax, but that once one has achieved such a level of structure, real syntax follows automatically. In other words, they account for *The cat sat on the mat* and then cross their fingers,[6] confident that 'self-organization' will take care of the rest.

## FEAR OF SYNTAX

Perhaps the most depressing aspect of language evolution studies is fear of syntax, which, the present collection suggests, is as widespread as ever. I know of no other field of study in which the work of a large body of highly intelligent specialists is so systematically misinterpreted, ignored, or even trashed. As a matter of plain fact, we have learned more about syntax in the last forty years than in the preceding 4,000, but you'd never guess that from reading most books on language evolution, including, alas, this one. Syntax forms a crucial part, arguably the most crucial part—since no other species is capable of it—of human language. If we are going to explain how language evolved, we have to explain how syntax evolved. If we are going to explain how syntax evolved, we have to explain how it came to have the peculiar properties it has, and no others. It just will not do to dismiss it as due to self-organization, or the grammaticization of discourse, or analogies with motor systems or syllabic structure, or any of the other one-paragraph explanations that writers on language evolution typically hope to get away with.

The trouble is that most non-syntacticians think syntax is just a matter of regular word order (I wonder what they think syntacticians do all day!) plus perhaps a few prefixes and suffixes. As a corrective to this view, I offer the following brief test on Real Syntax (an asterisk before a word or sentence means that it is ungrammatical):

(1) (a) Bill wants someone to work for.
    (b) Bill wants someone to work for him.

Why does a pronoun at the end of the sentence change the understood subject of *work?*

(2) (a) Who was it you said you didn't wanna/want to see?
    (b) Who was it you said you didn't *wanna/want to see you?

Why does a pronoun at the end of the sentence stop you from contracting *want to* to *wanna?*

(3) (a) Which letter did you throw away without opening?
    (b) That letter you threw away without opening contained anthrax.
    (c) *You were wise to throw away that letter without opening.

Why is it okay to leave out an *it* after *opening* in the first and second sentence but not the third?

(4) (a) We wanted the chance to vote for each other.
    (b) *We wanted the champ to vote for each other.

Why, given that the second sentence is perfectly logical and comprehensible—I wanted the champ to vote for you and you wanted him to vote for me—is it ungrammatical?

Two things need to be emphasized here. First, these sentences do not exhibit weird quirks peculiar to English or other western European languages (it is worth noting that the first full-length **generative grammar** of any language dealt with Hidatsa (a native-American language of North America)—Matthews (1961)—and that there is a vast generative literature on Australian, Austronesian, Native American and countless other non-western European languages that unfortunately doesn't seem to have had a wide readership). To the contrary, the phenomena these sentences illustrate arise from broad general principles familiar to anyone who is up to speed on generative syntax (for those who aren't, I can only refer them to said literature). Second, it should be apparent that phenomena of the type illustrated in these sentences are vanishingly unlikely to have come about through social factors, or self-organization, or the streamlining of discourse, or any of the many alternative explanations currently on offer.

This does not, however, mean that they must remain mysterious. It is a good bet that they are as they are because that is the way the brain works—that when syntax is finally and fully understood, it will become apparent that the **algorithms** the brain actually uses to produce sentences will necessarily produce (as **epiphenomena,** one may suppose) the features of (1)–(4). It should therefore be the task of anyone seriously interested in the evolution of language to work at either one end or both ends of the mystery: finding out the most parsimonious description of syntax that will satisfy the syntactic facts, or trying to determine (through neuroimaging or any other available means) how the brain actually puts sentences together. Once we know exactly what evolved, we may begin to approach a final answer as to how it evolved.

As a linguist, I can only attempt the first course. One promising avenue of inquiry, briefly sketched in the appendix to Calvin and Bickerton (2000), further developed in yet to be published work (Bickerton 2003; in preparation) and now described as 'surface minimalism', would reduce syntax to only three components:

(5) (a) Conditions on the attachment of words to one another.
    (b) Cycles of attachment yielding domains that consist of heads and their modifiers (phrases and clauses).
    (c) Principles derived from the order in which constituents are attached to one another.

If language can run on these resources and these only, nothing like the massive amount of task-specific innate equipment many researchers have very reasonably feared would be required. (5a), or a great deal of it, can be derived directly from semantics. (5b) can be derived via a shift in function of a kind of social score-keeping device such as may have developed in several primate lines: the mapping of every event in episodic memory into a simple schema incorporating who did what to whom (see further Bickerton 2000; Calvin and Bickerton 2000). (5c) can be derived from the way the brain processes any kind of material. The brain is adept at merging series of discrete inputs into coherent wholes (it does this every time you look at anything), and it can keep track of the sequence of its own operations through the gradualness with which neuronal activity decays (Pulvermuller 2002). All that is needed to run such a system is a far higher number of neurons and more of both cortico-cortical and cortico-cerebellar connections than we find in the brains of other primates.

Hurford (2000a: 223) has, very reasonably, expressed doubts as to whether such a stripped-down system could handle 'many of the examples given by Lightfoot [2000].' Consider Lightfoot's *pièce de résistance*, to which he devotes almost half his paper: the asymmetry between subjects and objects that allows much freer **extraction** of the former than the latter (Lightfoot's (11)–(13)):

(6) (a) Who do you think that Ray saw?
    (b) *Who do you think that saw Ray?

(7) (a) Which problem do you wonder how John solved?
    (b) *Who do you wonder how solved which problem?

(8) (a) This is the sweater which I wonder who bought.
    (b) *This is the student who I wonder what bought.

According to Lightfoot, this asymmetry represents a serious dysfunction in language (it 'conflicts with the desire/need to ask questions about the subjects of tensed clauses': Lightfoot 2000: 240), so cannot in itself be adaptive, but must result from some more general condition 'that presumably facilitates parsing' (p. 244). However, he has no explanation for such a condition beyond the suggestion that 'complex, dynamical systems can sometimes go spontaneously from randomness to order' (p. 245).

In surface minimalism, order of attachment (5c) yields two crucial principles, priority and finality (see Bickerton 2002b), which are involved in many different syntactic relations. Only the second of these need concern us here. A constituent X is final in a domain Y if there is no constituent Z such that X could be attached within Y before Z is attached. In other words, final **attachments** (in Lightfoot's examples, final referential attachments, or final **arguments**) mark the boundaries of **domains** (phrases or clauses). Non-final arguments (as in the (a) sentences) can be moved freely, since no information about domain boundaries is lost if they are moved. But if final arguments are moved, as they are in the (b) sentences above, those boundary markers are removed and the sentences consequently become harder to parse, because it is less clear where one clause ends and another begins, and therefore more difficult to assign (unambiguously *and automatically,* as syntax must do) an argument to the domain to which it belongs. Accordingly, restrictions are placed on the mobility of final arguments: the *that* which introduces the **Theme** argument of a verb can't be attached unless a final argument is in place (6b), and question words (*who, which,* etc.) that are final arguments cannot be moved at all if any other question word has been moved (7b, 8b).

## Timing Syntactic Emergence

One question that remains is when syntax emerged. If it emerged gradually, as many (see especially Pinker and Bloom 1990) think it did, there is no problem. A gradually enlarging brain, by providing, not greater intelligence *per se*, but more available neurons and more specialized connections between neurons, could have gradually provided more and more syntax—sentences just got longer and longer, as I once naively supposed (Bickerton 1981:ch. 5).

At least two things are seriously wrong with this. First, the principles involved are across-the-board principles: they apply everywhere, to all structures. At any given time, either they were in place or they weren't. Once they were in place, what was to stop syntax becoming immediately like it is today?

The other involves cognitive development. If we can measure cognitive development by the artefacts our ancestors produced (and what other way do we have?), there was something close to cognitive stagnation over the two million or so years that preceded the appearance of our species....Then, suddenly, creativity blossomed.

Somehow, there is a threshold effect. Somehow, it has to be explained. The advent of fully syntacticized language is the best candidate explanation so far. If anyone can think of a better alternative, or can explain (instead of merely explaining away) the suddenness of the transition, I'll be delighted to hear it. Until then, with all its problems (e.g. why Neanderthals, with bigger brains than ours, didn't win out against us), the best explanation is still that syntax as we know it developed in our species but in no other.

A second timing problem associated with the origins of syntax involves the connection between fully syntacticized language and what has been called the 'Great Leap Forward' (the explosion of human culture that allegedly took place some 30,000–40,000 years ago). If syntax emerged with the human species (say, 120,000 years or more ago), what accounts for the long delay before any tangible consequences appeared?

The answer is, of course, that syntacticized language enables but does not compel. Even today, in the Amazon and Congo jungles, there exist (barely—we are killing them off as quickly as we can) human societies whose toolkits, in an age of spacecraft and supercomputers, show relatively little advance over those of Cro-Magnons. What human language confers is not a technological straitjacket, but freedom—freedom to develop any way you can or think you want to (into societies where you work ever-lengthening hours at some servile and soul-destroyingly repetitive job so that you can afford to buy labour-saving devices, or into societies where you gather all you need for subsistence in fifteen to twenty hours a week and hang out the rest of the time drinking and gossiping). Instead of wondering why culture didn't explode the moment language emerged, maybe we should be wondering why, having acquired language, we chose the path that led to mass poverty, exploitation, perennial warfare, and perennial injustice.

## Conclusion

I have tried in this chapter to present a framework adequate to include all the processes that uniquely produced language in the human species. This framework may be summarized as follows. Driven by climate changes into habitats where predators were fierce and common but food was scarce, at least one primate species began to exchange basic information about the environment in order to survive. But protolanguage is not bee language. Once invented symbols begin to be used, they can be used to describe anything, consequently language can be adapted for social or any other purposes. So symbols multiplied but structure probably did not, prevented from developing by inadequate numbers of neurons and the right kind of connectivity. Once both of these had developed, things the brain could already do enabled protolanguage to develop quite rapidly into language as we know it today. The first group to cross some threshold that allowed unlimited combinations of words *and ideas* happened to be ours. And the rest, as they say, is history.

## Further Reading

The attitude of many non-linguists to linguists who concern themselves with language evolution is expressed by Ingold (1993). The collection that contains his article (Gibson and Ingold 1993) is itself fairly representative of a variety of non-linguistic approaches to the subject. Nowak et al. (2002) illustrates the problems that may arise when a high level of non-linguistic sophistication (in this case, in computer science) mixes with a lower level of linguistic sophistication; linguists (and some biologists too) may boggle at the assertion that 'during primate evolution there was a succession of U(niversal) G(rammar)s that finally led to the UGs of human beings' (p. 615). However, some non-linguists do show a more sophisticated level of understanding, among them Maynard Smith and Szathmáry (1995) and Szathmáry (2001).

The latter source develops the idea that although the language faculty must be biologically determined, it does not rely on hard-wired modules as sensory and motor faculties do. This position is related closely to the position on brain size held by Calvin (1996a; 1996b), who takes as critical the development of 'excess' neurons, which are not committed to any specific function but can be recruited for a number of tasks (including linguistic tasks), depending on what the brain is concerned with at any given moment. This view is consistent with results derived from both brain imaging and lesion studies (Damasio et al. 1996; Crosson 1993; Indefrey et al. 2001). It is also consistent with a view of brain activity held by Dennett (1991; 1997), in which there is no central homunculus or 'executive suite' in the brain. Rather than an individual thinking a thought and expressing it in words (the conventional view), sentences are constantly forming and reforming in the mind, but only the ones that can recruit enough neurons get to be consciously thought or spoken.

Certain developments within the minimalist programme suggest possibilities of reconciling generative syntax with Darwinian evolution. Berwick (1998) is among the few writers who tackle this explicitly, but although they make no reference to evolution, protagonists of the derivational approach to minimalism (Epstein et al. 1998) are producing analyses that are easier to reconcile with biological and neurological constraints than alternative theories.

## Notes

1. Scout's honour, I hadn't read Fritz Newmeyer's contribution to the present volume when I wrote this chapter, nor had he read mine when he wrote his. The impressive similarity of our introductions was quite spontaneous, a highly natural reaction to the circumstances, and should serve as a wake-up call to linguists and non-linguists alike.

2. I speak here with all the zeal of the converted, having myself violated biological probabilities with the 'macro-mutation' scenario of Bickerton (1990) and neurological probabilities with the 'different bits of the brain getting linked' scenario of Bickerton (1995; 1998). Although I know there are neurologists who do not buy them, I know of no evidence, neurological or other, that rules out the proposals of Calvin and Bickerton (2000), which have now replaced those earlier ones, and to which I return later.

3. I have previously claimed early-stage first-language learning as an example (Bickerton 1990). This needs caveatting, if you'll pardon the Haigism. Children learning **inflected** languages can and do acquire **morphological affixes** (they would have a hard time not doing this, in languages where bare **stems** are virtually or completely non-appearing) and at least sometimes use them correctly. They also acquire some basic facts about word order in the target language. But these are not **syntax** (see 'Fear of syntax' for what is).

4. An actual illustration may be relevant here. Karl Muller, a part-Hawaiian who runs a shelter for the homeless in Honolulu, had a confrontation with the shelter's cook. Karl removed his false teeth. The cook ran away. He knew that the removal of the teeth (an expensive set) meant that Karl, an impressive street fighter, was ready to accept serious damage in going the limit with him. No mere verbal threat would have deterred the cook, a skilled amateur boxer ('He could have been a contender', according to Karl).

5. Hurford (2000b: 225–6) claims that his approach to computational evolution is synthetic, rather than analytic. This is somewhat disingenuous, in light of his own statement that 'speakers were prompted to express atomic meanings (e.g. BERTIE, SAY, or GIVE) 50% of the time, and simple or complex whole propositions (e.g. HAPPY (CHESTER), LIKE (JO, PRUDENCE) or SAY (BERTIE (HAPPY (JO))) 50% of the time' (Hurford 2000: 334). The other three authors cited here appear to make their 'speakers' produce holistic propositions 100 per cent of the time.

6. I am not the originator of this sentence, but I have sought in vain for years to find its true begetter. I believed it to be Lila Gleitman, but she (p.c.) has denied authorship; if its real author contacts me, I will be happy to make full acknowledgment.

## References

Batali, J. 1998. Computational simulations of the emergence of grammar. In Hurford et al., 405–26.

Berwick, R. C. 1998. Language evolution and the Minimalist Program: the origins of syntax. In Hurford et al., 320–40.

Bickerton, D. 1981. *Roots of Language*. Ann Arbor, Mich.: Karoma.

Bickerton, D. 1990. *Language and Species*. Chicago: University of Chicago Press.

Bickerton, D. 2000. How protolanguage became language. In Knight et al., 264–84.

Bickerton, D. 2001. Linguists play catch-up with evolution. *Journal of Linguistics* 37: 581–91.

Bickerton, D. 2002. Foraging versus social intelligence in the evolution of language. In Wray, 207–25.

Bickerton, D. 2003. C-command versus surface minimalism. MS. University of Hawaii.

Briscoe, E. 2002. Coevolution of the language faculty and language(s) with decorrelated encodings. Paper presented at Fourth International Conference on the Evolution of Language, Harvard, 2002.

Burling, R. 2000. Comprehension, production and conventionalization in the origins of language. In Knight et al., 27–39.

Calvin, W. H. 1996a. *How Brains Think: Evolving Intelligence, Then and Now.* New York: Basic Books.

Calvin, W. H. 1996b. *The Cerebral Code: Thinking a Thought in the Mosaics of the Mind.* Cambridge, Mass.: MIT Press.

Calvin, W. H., and D. Bickerton 2000. *Lingua Ex Machina: Reconciling Darwin with the Human Brain.* Cambridge, Mass.: MIT Press.

Carstairs-McCarthy, A. 2000. The distinction between sentences and noun phrases: an impediment to language evolution? In Knight et al., 248–63.

Crosson, B. 1992. *Subcortical Functions in Language and Memory.* New York: Guilford Press.

Damasio, H. 1991. Neuroanatomical correlates of the aphasias. In M. T. Sarno (ed.), *Acquired Aphasia,* 2nd edn. New York: Academic Press.

Deacon, T. 1997. *The Symbolic Species: The Coevolution of Language and the Brain.* New York: Norton.

Dennett, D. C. 1991. *Consciousness Explained.* New York: Little, Brown.

Dennett, D. C. 1997. *Darwin's Dangerous Idea: Evolution and the Meanings of Life.* New York: Simon & Schuster.

Dunbar, R. I. M. 1993. The co-evolution of neocortical size, group size and language in humans. *Behavioral and Brain Sciences* 16: 681–735.

Epstein, S. D., E. M. Groat, R. Kawashima, and H. Kitahara 1998. *A Derivational Approach to Syntactic Relations.* New York: Oxford University Press.

Gibson, K. R., and T. Ingold (eds.) 1993. *Tools, Language and Cognition in Human Evolution.* Cambridge: Cambridge University Press.

Hurford, J. R. 2000a. The emergence of syntax. In Knight et al., 219–30.

Hurford, J. R. 2000b. Social transmission favours linguistic generalization. In Knight et al., 324–52.

Hurford, J. R., M. Studdert-Kennedy, and C. Knight (eds). 1998. *Approaches to the Evolution of Language: Social and Cognitive Bases.* New York: Cambridge University Press.

Indefrey, P., C. M. Brown, F. Hellwig, K. Amunts, H. Herzog, R. J. Seitz, and P. Hagoort 2001. A neural correlate of syntactic encoding during speech production. *Proceedings of the National Academy of Sciences* 98: 5933–6.

Ingold, T. 1993. Technology, language, intelligence: a reconsideration of basic concepts. In Gibson and Ingold, 449–72.

Jenkins, L. 2000. *Biolinguistics: Exploring the Biology of Language.* Cambridge: Cambridge University Press.

Kirby, S. 2000. Syntax without natural selection: how compositionality emerges from vocabulary in a population of learners. In Knight et al., 303–23.

Knight, C., M. Studdert-Kennedy, and J. R. Hurford (eds). 2000. *The Evolutionary of Language: Social Function and the Origins of Linguistic Form.* Cambridge: Cambridge University Press.

Liberman, A. M. 1996. *Speech: A Special Code.* Cambridge, Mass.: MIT Press.

Lieberman, P. 1984. *The Biology and Evolution of Language.* Cambridge, Mass.: Harvard University Press.

Lieberman, P. 1991. *Uniquely Human: The Evolution of Speech, Thought, and Selfless Behavior.* Cambridge, Mass.: Harvard University Press.

Lieberman, P., A. Protopapas, E. Reed, and J. W. Youngs 1994. Cognitive defects at altitude. *Nature* 372: 325.

Lieberman, P., and D. H. Klatt 1972. Phonetic ability and related anatomy of the newborn, adult human, Neanderthal man, and the chimpanzee. *American Anthropologist* 74: 287–307.

Lieberman, P., D. H. Klatt, and W. H. Wilson 1969. Vocal tract limitations on the vowel repertoires of rhesus monkeys and other nonhuman primates. *Science* 164: 1185–7.

Lieberman, P., J. T. Laitman, J. S. Reidenberg, and P. J. Gannon 1992. The anatomy, physiology, acoustics and perception of speech. *Journal of Human Evolution* 23: 447–67.

Lightfoot, D. 2000. The spandrels of the linguistic genotype. In Knight et al., 231–47.

Loritz, D. 1999. *How the Brain Evolved Language.* Oxford: Oxford University Press.

Matthews, G. H. 1961. *Hidatsa Syntax.* Cambridge, Mass.: MIT Press.

Maynard Smith, J., and E. Szathmáry 1995. *The Major Transitions in Evolution.* Oxford: Oxford University Press.

Nowak, M. A., N. L. Komarova, and P. Niyogi 2002. Computational and evolutionary aspects of language. *Nature* 417: 611–17.

Pepperberg, I. M. 2000. *The Alex Studies: Cognitive and Communicative Abilities of Grey Parrots.* Cambridge, Mass.: Harvard University Press.

Pinker, S. 1994. *The Language Instinct.* New York: William Morrow.

Pinker, S., and P. Bloom. 1990. Natural language and natural selection. *Behavioral and Brain Sciences* 13: 707–84.

Power, C. 1998. Old wives' tales: the gossip hypothesis and the reliability of cheap signals. In Hurford et al., 111–29.

Premack, D. 1986. 'Gavagai!' or the future history of the animal language controversy. *Cognition* 19: 207–96.

Quine, W. V. O. 1960. *Word and Object.* Cambridge, Mass.: MIT Press.

Ridley, M. 1993. *The Red Queen: Sex and the Evolution of Human Nature.* New York: Macmillan.

Savage-Rumbaugh, S. 1986. *Ape Language: From Conditioned Response to Symbol.* New York: Columbia University Press.

Sperber, D., and G. Origgi 2000. Evolution, communication and the proper function of language. In P. Carruthers and A. Chamberlain (eds.), *Evolution and the Human Mind.* Cambridge: Cambridge University Press.

Szathmáry, E. 2001. Origin of the human language faculty: the language amoeba hypothesis. In J. Trabant and S. Ward (eds.), *New Essays on the Origin of Language.* Berlin: de Gruyter.

Wray, A. 1998. Protolanguage as a holistic system for social interaction. *Language and Communication* 18: 47–67.

Wray, A. (ed.) 2002. *The Transition to Language.* Oxford: Oxford University Press.

## Critical Thinking and Application

- Why does Bickerton argue against *continuism*, or the idea that human language developed from primate calls?
- Why does Bickerton dismiss arguments against "social intelligence" approaches to language origins?
- How did syntax arise? How did it *not* arise?
- When did genuine language likely arise? What is the evidence for this?
- Divide the approaches Bickerton mentions among the students in the class. Have each group read in some depth about the research and theorizing that has been done. Have a class debate and discussion, with each group explaining language origins from its own perspective.

## Vocabulary

affix
algorithm
analogous
argument
attachment
coda
computational linguistics
conspecifics
continuity paradox
domain
epiphenomena, epiphenomenon
extraction
generative grammar
holistic
holophrase
holophrastic
hominid
homologous
iconic
indexical
inflected
modality
morphology
morphological
nucleus
onset
ontogeny
phrase-structure rules
phylogenetic
phylogeny
pidgin
protolanguage
stem
structure
symbolism
syntactic
syntax
theme

## Suggested Further Reading [See also list following Language Origins unit introduction]

Aitchison, Jean. 2000. *The Seeds of Speech: Language Origin and Evolution.* Cambridge: Canto.

Armstrong, David F., William C. Stokoe, and Sherman E. Wilcox. 1995. *Gesture and the Nature of Language.* Cambridge: Cambridge University Press.

Bickerton, Derek. 1981. *Roots of Language.* Ann Arbor, MI: Karoma.

Bickerton, Derek. 1990. *Language and Species.* Chicago: University of Chicago Press.

Calvin, William H., and Derek Bickerton. 2000. *Lingua ex Machina: Reconciling Darwin and Chomsky with the Human Brain.* Cambridge, MA: MIT Press.

Christiansen, Morten H., and Simon Kirby, eds. 2003. *Language Evolution.* Oxford: Oxford University Press.

Lieberman, Philip. 1984. *The Biology and Evolution of Language.* Cambridge, MA: Harvard University Press.

Lieberman, Philip. 1998. *Eve Spoke: Human Language and Human Evolution.* New York: Norton.

# UNIT 3

# Language and Thought

The topic of the relationship between language and thought has captivated writers and readers for centuries. With many precursors, some trace this idea to the nineteenth-century German thinker Humboldt. But the topic is most often associated with the writings of Benjamin Lee Whorf and Edward Sapir. Sometimes the idea that "language determines thought," or its milder form, "language shapes habitual thought," is called the Sapir-Whorf hypothesis, from the two men who wrote sympathetically and foundationally of this view, and sometimes the *linguistic relativity hypothesis*.

Whorf noted, in his paying work as an insurance inspector, that the ways barrels were labeled—"empty" or "full"—affected the ways workers acted around them, despite the fact that barrels "empty" of gasoline were more flammable than full ones. He also studied Mayan and Hopi languages and noted ways of discussing the world quite disparate from those expressed in the European languages with which he was familiar. Edward Sapir had similarly demonstrated that people's habitual thought tends to follow the "grooves" established by their languages.

This suggestion was traced in work by Brent Berlin and Paul Kay, among others, on color terms, which had sometimes been taken to refute Whorf's claims about the power of language to shape thought. However, since the 1980s, new, empirical studies of Whorf's ideas have generated excitement about and refinement of the original concept. John Lucy in particular has attempted to spell out exactly what it would take to confirm or disprove the "hypothesis" that Whorf never quite elucidated and has then carried out such research. Other recent scholarship, such as that of Stephen Levinson at the Max Planck Institute for Psycholinguistics, has been creative in developing empirical methods for testing this hypothesis.

## Suggested Further Reading


Berlin, Brent, and Paul Kay. 1969. *Basic Color Terms: Their Universality and Evolution*. Berkeley: University of California Press.

Bloom, Albert H. 1981. *The Linguistic Shaping of Thought: A Study in the Impact of Language on Thinking in China and the West*. Hillsdale, NJ: Erlbaum.

Boas, Franz. 1966 [1911]. Introduction. In *Handbook of American Indian Languages*, edited by Franz Boas, pp. 1–79. Reprint editor, P. Holder. Lincoln: University of Nebraska Press.

Brown, Penelope, and Stephen C. Levinson. 1993. "Uphill" and "Downhill" in Tzeltal. *Journal of Linguistic Anthropology* 3(1): 46–74.

Friedrich, Paul. 1986. *The Language Parallax: Linguistic Relativism and Poetic Indeterminacy*. Austin: University of Texas Press.

Gentner, Dedre, and Susan Goldin-Meadow, eds. 2003. *Language in Mind: Advances in the Study of Language and Thought*. Cambridge, MA: MIT Press.

Gumperz, John J., and Stephen C. Levinson, eds. 1996. *Rethinking Linguistic Relativity*. Cambridge: Cambridge University Press.

Hill, Jane H. 1985. The Grammar of Consciousness and the Consciousness of Grammar. *American Ethnologist* 12: 725–737.

Hill, Jane H., and Bruce Mannheim. 1992. Language and World View. *Annual Review of Anthropology* 21: 381–406.

Kay, Paul, and W. Kempton. 1984. What Is the Sapir-Whorf Hypothesis? *American Anthropologist* 86: 65–79.

Koerner, E. F. Konrad. 1992. The Sapir-Whorf Hypothesis: A Preliminary History and a Bibliographic Essay. *Journal of Linguistic Anthropology* 2: 173–198.

Lakoff, George. 1987. *Women, Fire, and Dangerous Things: What Categories Reveal About the Mind*. Chicago: University of Chicago Press. See especially the chapter Whorf and Relativism.

Lakoff, George, and Mark Johnson. 1980. *Metaphors We Live By*. Chicago: University of Chicago Press.

Levinson, Stephen C. 1996. Language and Space. *Annual Review of Anthropology* 25: 353–382.

Lucy, John A. 1985. Whorf's View of the Linguistic Mediation of Thought. In *Semiotic Mediation: Sociocultural and Psychological Perspectives*, edited by E. Mertz and R. J. Parmentier, pp. 73–97. Orlando, FL: Academic Press.

Lucy, John A. 1992. *Language Diversity and Thought: A Reformulation of the Linguistic Relativity Hypothesis*. Cambridge: Cambridge University Press.

Lucy, John A. 1992. *Grammatical Categories and Cognition: A Case Study of the Linguistic Relativity Hypothesis*. Cambridge: Cambridge University Press.

Lucy, John A. 1997. Linguistic Relativity. *Annual Review of Anthropology* 26: 291–312.

Lucy, John A., and Richard A. Shweder. 1979. Whorf and His Critics: Linguistic and Nonlinguistic Influences on Color Memory. *American Anthropologist* 81: 581–615.

Martin, Laura. 1986. Eskimo Words for Snow. *American Anthropologist* 88, no. 2 (June): 418–423.

Sapir, Edward. 1964 [1931]. Conceptual Categories in Primitive Languages. In *Language in Culture and Society: A Reader in Linguistics and Anthropology*, edited by Dell H. Hymes. New York: Harper & Row.

Whorf, Benjamin Lee. 1956. *Language, Thought, and Reality: Selected Writings of Benjamin Lee Whorf*, edited by John B. Carroll. Cambridge, MA: MIT Press.

# CHAPTER 6

# The Relation of Habitual Thought and Behavior to Language

*Benjamin Lee Whorf*

(1939)

*For his entire working life, Benjamin Lee Whorf was an insurance inspector attempting to discover the causes of industrial accidents and ways of preventing them. (He worked at the very same company, the Hartford Insurance Company in Hartford, Connecticut, where poet Wallace Stevens worked for his complete paying career.) Whorf was a most unusual character. Not only did he have an active intellectual life completely apart from the work that provided his salary, but he was a theosophist with belief in ESP and other mystical concepts; he also rejected evolution and held deep religious convictions about the literal truth of the Bible. To reconcile the Bible and science, he attempted to learn the original language of the Bible on the hunch that problems of consistency stemmed from poor translations. In the process of learning ancient languages, he became more and more interested in language for its own sake. This led him to study Maya, Aztec, and Hopi on his own, and finally to Yale, where he studied with Edward Sapir. Though he was offered an academic position, he turned it down.*

*This chapter presents the classic piece in which Benjamin Lee Whorf makes his suggestion that different languages give rise to different types of "habitual thought," quoting liberally from his teacher, Edward Sapir. Note that he is not saying that it is not possible to understand things in ways different from what our language predisposes us to; in fact, it would be impossible for him to understand the Hopi if that were the case. Rather, in our ordinary, habitual ways of thinking and acting, we tend to follow the patterns established by our language. He is less interested in single words that label objects or activities than in the powerful, fundamental organizing aspects of language (grammar) such as tense or number. Every time we speak (or sign), we must make use of the grammatical categories of our languages. English speakers, for instance, cannot avoid differentiating singular and plural every time they use a noun or verb, which is to say essentially every time they speak (with trivial exceptions). Chinese speakers, in contrast, because of the way their language works,* may *explicitly label a noun as singular or plural but are not forced by the grammar to do so.*

*Whorf's ideas have been regarded variously as obvious and trivial, as completely wrong, as partially correct, as essentially correct, or as untestable. More recent attempts to sort these positions out by actually* testing *his claims have been proliferating. John Lucy has been especially prominent in teasing out what Whorf meant. You are likely to read more about this in the future.*

## Reading Questions

- How does Whorf explain the risky behavior that people exhibited around "empty" gasoline drums, "spun limestone," kettles of varnish, and other aspects of industrial life? What conclusion does he draw about language and thought from these real-life incidents?

Benjamin Lee Whorf, The Relation of Habitual Thought and Behavior to Language. In *Language, Thought, and Reality*, ed. by John B. Carroll. Cambridge, MA: MIT Press, 1956, pp. 134–159.

- What are some of the ways that concepts of "time" and "matter" vary between Standard Average European (SAE) and Hopi? What cultural accompaniments to the linguistic differences does Whorf point to?

---

Human beings do not live in the objective world alone, nor alone in the world of social activity as ordinarily understood, but are very much at the mercy of the particular language which has become the medium of expression for their society. It is quite an illusion to imagine that one adjusts to reality essentially without the use of language and that language is merely an incidental means of solving specific problems of communication or reflection. The fact of the matter is that the "real world" is to a large extent unconsciously built up on the language habits of the group. . . . We see and hear and otherwise experience very largely as we do because the language habits of our community predispose certain choices of interpretation. —Edward Sapir

There will probably be general assent to the proposition that an accepted pattern of using words is often prior to certain lines of thinking and forms of behavior, but he who assents often sees in such a statement nothing more than a platitudinous recognition of the hypnotic power of philosophical and learned terminology on the one hand or of catchwords, slogans, and rallying cries on the other. To see only thus far is to miss the point of one of the important interconnections which Sapir saw between language, culture, and psychology, and succinctly expressed in the introductory quotation. It is not so much in these special uses of language as in its constant ways of arranging data and its most ordinary everyday analysis of phenomena that we need to recognize the influence it has on other activities, cultural and personal.

## The Name of the Situation as Affecting Behavior

I came in touch with an aspect of this problem before I had studied under Dr. Sapir, and in a field usually considered remote from linguistics. It was in the course of my professional work for a fire insurance company, in which I undertook the task of analyzing many hundreds of reports of circumstances surrounding the start of fires, and in some cases, of explosions. My analysis was directed toward purely physical conditions, such as defective wiring, presence or lack of air spaces between metal flues and woodwork, etc., and the results were presented in these terms. Indeed it was undertaken with no thought that any other significances would or could be revealed. But in due course it became evident that not only a physical situation *qua* physics, but the meaning of that situation to people, was sometimes a factor, through the behavior of the people, in the start of the fire. And this factor of meaning was clearest when it was a linguistic meaning, residing in the name or the linguistic description commonly applied to the situation. Thus, around a storage of what are called "gasoline drums," behavior will tend to a certain type, that is, great care will be exercised; while around a storage of what are called "empty gasoline drums," it will tend to be different—careless, with little repression of smoking or of tossing cigarette stubs about. Yet the "empty" drums are perhaps the more dangerous, since they contain explosive vapor. Physically the situation is hazardous, but the linguistic analysis according to regular analogy must employ the word 'empty,' which inevitably suggests lack of hazard. The word 'empty' is used in two linguistic patterns: (1) as a virtual synonym for 'null and void, negative, inert,' (2) applied in analysis of physical situations without regard to, e.g., vapor, liquid vestiges, or stray rubbish, in the container. The situation is named in one pattern (2) and the name is then "acted out" or "lived up to" in another (1), this being a general formula for the linguistic conditioning of behavior into hazardous forms.

In a wood distillation plant the metal stills were insulated with a composition prepared from limestone and called at the plant "spun limestone." No attempt was made to protect this covering from excessive heat or the contact of flame. After a period of use, the fire below one of the stills spread to the "limestone," which to everyone's great surprise burned vigorously. Exposure to acetic acid fumes from the stills had converted part of the limestone (calcium carbonate) to calcium acetate. This when heated in a fire decomposes, forming inflammable acetone. Behavior that tolerated fire close to the covering was induced by use of the name "limestone," which because it ends in "-stone" implies non-combustibility.

A huge iron kettle of boiling varnish was observed to be overheated, nearing the temperature at which it would ignite. The operator moved it off the fire and ran it on its wheels to a distance, but did not cover it. In a minute or so the varnish ignited. Here the linguistic influence is more complex; it is due to the metaphorical objectifying (of which more later) of "cause" as contact or the spatial juxtaposition of "things"—to analyzing the situation as 'on' versus 'off' the fire. In reality, the stage when the external fire was the main factor had passed; the overheating was now an internal process of convection in the varnish from the intensely heated kettle, and still continued when 'off' the fire.

An electric glow heater on the wall was little used, and for one workman had the meaning of a convenient coathanger. At night a watchman entered and snapped a switch, which action he verbalized as 'turning on the light.' No light appeared, and this result he verbalized as 'light is burned out.' He could not see the glow of the heater because of the old coat hung on it. Soon the heater ignited the coat, which set fire to the building.

A tannery discharged waste water containing animal matter into an outdoor settling basin partly roofed with wood and partly open. This situation is one that ordinarily would be verbalized as 'pool of water'. A workman had occasion to light a blowtorch near by, and threw his match into the water. But the decomposing waste matter was evolving gas under the wood cover, so that the setup was the reverse of 'watery'. An instant flare of flame ignited the woodwork, and the fire quickly spread into the adjoining building.

A drying room for hides was arranged with a blower at one end to make a current of air along the room and thence outdoors through a vent at the other end. Fire started at a hot bearing on the blower, which blew the flames directly into the hides and fanned them along the room, destroying the entire stock. This hazardous setup followed naturally from the term 'blower' with its linguistic equivalence to 'that which blows', implying that its function necessarily is to 'blow'. Also its function is verbalized as 'blowing air for drying', overlooking that it can blow other things, e.g., flames and sparks. In reality, a blower simply makes a current of air and can exhaust as well as blow. It should have been installed at the vent end to DRAW the air over the hides, then through the hazard (its own casing and bearings), and thence outdoors.

Beside a coal-fired melting pot for lead reclaiming was dumped a pile of "scrap lead"—a misleading verbalization, for it consisted of the lead sheets of old radio condensers, which still had paraffin paper between them. Soon the paraffin blazed up and fired the roof, half of which was burned off.

Such examples, which could be greatly multiplied, will suffice to show how the cue to a certain line of behavior is often given by the analogies of the linguistic formula in which the situation is spoken of, and by which to some degree it is analyzed, classified, and allotted its place in that world which is "to a large extent unconsciously built up on the language habits of the group." And we always assume that the linguistic analysis made by our group reflects reality better than it does.

## Grammatical Patterns as Interpretations of Experience

The linguistic material in the above examples is limited to single words, phrases, and patterns of limited range. One cannot study the behavioral compulsiveness of such material without suspecting a much more far-reaching compulsion from large-scale patterning of grammatical categories, such as **plurality**, **gender** and similar classifications (**animate, inanimate**, etc.), **tenses, voices**, and other verb forms, classifications of the type of "parts of speech," and the matter of whether a given experience is denoted by a unit **morpheme,** an **inflected** word, or a syntactical combination. A category such as **number** (singular vs. plural) is an attempted interpretation of a whole large order of experience, virtually of the world or of nature; it attempts to say how experience is to be segmented, what experience is to be called "one" and what "several." But the difficulty of appraising such a far-reaching influence is great because of its background character, because of the difficulty of standing aside from our own language, which is a habit and a cultural *non est disputandum*, and scrutinizing it objectively. And if we take a very dissimilar language, this language becomes a part of nature, and we even do to it what we have already done to nature. We tend to think in our own language in order to examine the exotic language. Or we find the task of unraveling the purely **morphological** intricacies so gigantic that it seems to absorb all else. Yet the problem, though difficult, is feasible; and the best approach is through an exotic language, for in its study we are at long last pushed willy-nilly out of our ruts. Then we find that the exotic language is a mirror held up to our own.

In my study of the Hopi language, what I now see as an opportunity to work on this problem was first thrust upon me before I was clearly aware of the problem. The seemingly endless task of describing the **morphology** did finally end. Yet it was evident, especially in the light of Sapir's lectures on Navaho, that the description of the LANGUAGE was far from complete. I knew for example the morphological formation of plurals, but not how to use plurals. It was evident that the category of plural in Hopi was not the same thing as in English, French, or German. Certain things that were plural in these languages were singular in Hopi. The phase of investigation which now began consumed nearly two more years.

The work began to assume the character of a comparison between Hopi and western European languages. It also became evident that even the grammar of Hopi bore a relation to Hopi culture, and the grammar of European tongues to our own "Western" or "European" culture. And it appeared that the interrelation brought in those large subsummations of experience by language, such as our own terms 'time', 'space', 'substance', and 'matter'. Since, with respect to the traits compared, there is little difference between English, French, German, or other European languages with the POSSIBLE (but doubtful) exception of Balto-Slavic and non-Indo-European, I have lumped these languages into one group called **SAE**, or "Standard Average European."

That portion of the whole investigation here to be reported may be summed up in two questions: (1) Are our own concepts of 'time', 'space', and 'matter' given in substantially the same form by experience to all men, or are they in part conditioned by the structure of particular languages? (2) Are there traceable affinities between (*a*) cultural and behavioral norms and (*b*) large-scale linguistic patterns? (I should be the last to pretend that there is anything so definite as "a correlation" between culture and language, and especially between ethnological rubrics such as 'agricultural, hunting', etc., and linguistic ones like 'inflected', 'synthetic', or 'isolating'.)[1] When I began the study, the problem was by no means so clearly formulated, and I had little notion that the answers would turn out as they did.

## Plurality and Numeration in SAE and Hopi

In our language, that is SAE, plurality and **cardinal numbers** are applied in two ways: to real plurals and imaginary plurals.

Or more exactly if less tersely: perceptible spatial aggregates and metaphorical aggregates. We say 'ten men' and also 'ten days'. Ten men either are or could be objectively perceived as ten, ten in one group perception[2]—ten men on a street corner, for instance. But 'ten days' cannot be objectively experienced. We experience only one day, today; the other nine (or even all ten) are something conjured up from memory or imagination. If 'ten days' be regarded as a group, it must be as an "imaginary," mentally constructed group. Whence comes this mental pattern? Just as in the case of the fire-causing errors, from the fact that our language confuses the two different situations, has but one pattern for both. When we speak of 'ten steps forward, ten strokes on a bell', or any similarly described cyclic sequence, "times" of any sort, we are doing the same thing as with 'days'. CYCLICITY brings the response of imaginary plurals. But a likeness of cyclicity to aggregates is not unmistakably given by experience prior to language, or it would be found in all languages, and it is not.

Our AWARENESS of time and cyclicity does contain something immediate and subjective—the basic sense of "becoming later and later." But, in the habitual thought of us SAE people, this is covered under something quite different, which though mental should not be called subjective. I call it OBJECTIFIED, or imaginary, because it is patterned on the OUTER world. It is this that reflects our linguistic usage. Our tongue makes no distinction between numbers counted on discrete entities and numbers that are simply "counting itself." Habitual thought then assumes that in the latter the numbers are just as much counted on "something" as in the former. This is objectification. Concepts of time lose contact with the subjective experience of "becoming later" and are objectified as counted QUANTITIES, especially as lengths, made up of units as a length can be visibly marked off into inches. A 'length of time' is envisioned as a row of similar units, like a row of bottles.

In Hopi there is a different linguistic situation. Plurals and cardinals are used only for entities that form or can form an objective group. There are no imaginary plurals, but instead **ordinals** used with singulars. Such an expression as 'ten days' is not used. The equivalent statement is an operational one that reaches one day by a suitable count. 'They stayed ten days' becomes 'they stayed until the eleventh day' or 'they left after the tenth day'. 'Ten days is greater than nine days' becomes 'the tenth day is later than the ninth'. Our "length of time" is not regarded as a length but as a relation between two events in lateness. Instead of our linguistically promoted objectification of that datum of consciousness we call 'time', the Hopi language has not laid down any pattern that would cloak the subjective "becoming later" that is the essence of time.

## Nouns of Physical Quantity in SAE and Hopi

We have two kinds of nouns denoting physical things: individual nouns, and mass nouns (e.g., 'water, milk, wood, granite, sand, flour, meat'). Individual nouns denote bodies with definite outlines: 'a tree, a stick, a man, a hill'. Mass nouns denote homogeneous continua without implied boundaries. The distinction is marked by linguistic form; e.g., mass nouns lack plurals,[3] in English drop articles, and in French take the partitive article *du, de la, des*. The distinction is more widespread in language than in the observable appearance of things. Rather few natural occurrences present themselves as unbounded extents; 'air' of course, and often 'water, rain, snow, sand, rock, dirt, grass'. We do not encounter 'butter, meat, cloth, iron, glass', or most "materials" in such kind of manifestation, but in bodies small or large with definite outlines. The distinction is somewhat forced upon our description of events by an unavoidable pattern in language. It is so inconvenient in a great many cases that we need some way of individualizing the mass noun by further linguistic devices. This is partly done by names of body-types: 'stick of wood, piece of cloth, pane of glass, cake of soap'; also, and even more, by introducing names of containers though their contents be the real issue: 'glass of water, cup of coffee, dish of food, bag of flour, bottle of beer'. These very common container formulas, in which 'of' has an obvious, visually perceptible meaning ("contents"), influence our feeling about the less obvious type-body formulas: 'stick of wood, lump of dough,' etc. The formulas are very similar: individual noun plus a similar relator (English 'of'). In the obvious case this relator denotes contents. In the inobvious one it "suggests" contents. Hence the 'lumps, chunks, blocks, pieces', etc., seem to contain something, a "stuff," "substance," or "matter" that answers to the 'water', 'coffee', or 'flour' in the container formulas. So with SAE people the philosophic "substance" and "matter" are also the naïve idea; they are instantly acceptable, "common sense." It is so through linguistic habit. Our language patterns often require us to name a physical thing by a binomial that splits the reference into a formless item plus a form.

Hopi is again different. It has a formally distinguished class of nouns. But this class contains no formal subclass of mass nouns. All nouns have an individual sense and both singular and plural forms. Nouns translating most nearly our mass nouns still refer to vague bodies or vaguely bounded extents. They imply indefiniteness, but not lack, of outline and size. In specific statements, 'water' means one certain mass or quantity of water, not what we call "the substance water." Generality of statement is conveyed through the verb or predicator, not the noun. Since nouns are individual already, they are not individualized by either type-bodies or names of containers, if there is no special need to emphasize shape or container. The noun itself implies a suitable type-body or container. One says, not 'a glass of water' but *kə·yi* 'a water', not 'a pool of water' but *pa·hə*,[4] not 'a dish of cornflour' but *ŋəmni* 'a (quantity of) cornflour', not 'a piece of meat' but *sikʷi* 'a meat'. The language has neither need for nor analogies on which to build the concept of existence as a duality of formless item and form. It deals with formlessness through other symbols than nouns.

## Phases of Cycles in SAE and Hopi

Such terms as 'summer, winter, September, morning, noon, sunset' are with us nouns, and have little formal linguistic difference from other nouns. They can be subjects or objects, and we say 'at sunset' or 'in winter' just as we say 'at a corner' or 'in an orchard'.[5] They are pluralized and numerated like nouns of physical objects, as we have seen. Our thought about the referents of such words hence becomes objectified. Without objectification, it would be a subjective experience of real time, i.e., of the consciousness of "becoming later and later"—simply a cyclic phase similar to an earlier phase in that ever-later-becoming duration. Only by imagination can such a cyclic phase be set beside another and another in the manner of a spatial (i.e., visually perceived) configuration. But such is the power of linguistic analogy that we do so objectify cyclic phasing. We do it even by saying 'a phase' and 'phases' instead of, e.g., 'phasing'. And the pattern of individual and mass nouns, with the resulting binomial formula of formless item plus form, is so general that it is implicit for all nouns, and hence our very generalized formless items like 'substance, matter', by which we can fill out the binomial for an enormously wide range of nouns. But even these are not quite generalized enough to take in our phase nouns. So for the phase nouns we have made a formless item, 'time'. We have made it by using 'a time', i.e., an occasion or a phase, in the pattern of a mass noun, just as from 'a summer' we make 'summer' in the pattern of a mass noun. Thus with our binomial formula we can say and think 'a moment of time, a second of time, a year of time'. Let me again point out that the pattern is simply that of 'a bottle of milk' or 'a piece of cheese'. Thus we are assisted to imagine that 'a summer' actually contains or consists of such-and-such a quantity of 'time'.

In Hopi however all phase terms, like 'summer, morning', etc., are not nouns but a kind of adverb, to use the nearest SAE analogy. They are a formal part of speech by themselves, distinct from nouns, verbs, and even other Hopi "adverbs." Such a word is not a case form or a locative pattern, like 'des Abends' or 'in the morning'. It contains no morpheme like one of 'in the house' or 'at the tree'.[6] It means 'when it is morning' or 'while morning-phase is occurring'. These "temporals" are not used as subjects or objects, or at all like nouns. One does not say 'it's a hot summer' or 'summer is hot'; summer is not hot, summer is only WHEN conditions are hot, WHEN heat occurs. One does not say 'THIS summer,' but 'summer now' or 'summer recently'. There is no objectification, as a region, an extent, a quantity, of the subjective duration-feeling. Nothing is suggested about time except the perpetual "getting later" of it. And so there is no basis here for a formless item answering to our 'time'.

## TEMPORAL FORMS OF VERBS IN SAE AND HOPI

The three-tense system of SAE verbs colors all our thinking about time. This system is amalgamated with that larger scheme of objectification of the subjective experience of duration already noted in other patterns—in the binomial formula applicable to nouns in general, in temporal nouns, in plurality and numeration. This objectification enables us in imagination to "stand time units in a row." Imagination of time as like a row harmonizes with a system of THREE tenses; whereas a system of TWO, an earlier and a later, would seem to correspond better to the feeling of duration as it is experienced. For if we inspect consciousness we find no past, present, future, but a unity embracing complexity. EVERYTHING IS in consciousness, and everything in consciousness IS, and is together. There is in it a sensuous and a nonsensuous. We may call the sensuous—what we are seeing, hearing, touching—the 'present' while in the nonsensuous the vast image-world of memory is being labeled 'the past' and another realm of belief, intuition, and uncertainty 'the future'; yet sensation, memory, foresight, all are in consciousness together—one is not "yet to be" nor another "once but no more." Where real time comes in is that all this in consciousness is "getting later," changing certain relations in an irreversible manner. In this "latering" or "durating" there seems to me to be a paramount contrast between the newest, latest instant at the focus of attention and the rest—the earlier. Languages by the score get along well with two tenselike forms answering to this paramount relation of "later" to "earlier." We can of course CONSTRUCT AND CONTEMPLATE IN THOUGHT a system of past, present, future, in the objectified configuration of points on a line. This is what our general objectification tendency leads us to do and our tense system confirms.

In English the present tense seems the one least in harmony with the paramount temporal relation. It is as if pressed into various and not wholly congruous duties. One duty is to stand as objectified middle term between objectified past and objectified future, in narration, discussion, argument, logic, philosophy. Another is to denote inclusion in the sensuous field: 'I SEE him.' Another is for **nomic,** i.e., customarily or generally valid, statements: 'We SEE with our eyes.' These varied uses introduce confusions of thought, of which for the most part we are unaware.

Hopi, as we might expect, is different here too. Verbs have no "tenses" like ours, but have **validity-forms** ("assertions"), **aspects,** and clause-linkage forms (modes), that yield even greater precision of speech. The validity-forms denote that the speaker (not the subject) reports the situation (answering to our past and present) or that he expects it (answering to our future)[7] or that he makes a nomic statement (answering to our nomic present). The aspects denote different degrees of duration and different kinds of tendency "during duration." As yet we have noted nothing to indicate whether an event is sooner or later than another when both are REPORTED. But need for this does not arise until we have two verbs: i.e., two clauses. In that case the "modes" denote relations between the clauses, including relations of later to earlier and of simultaneity. Then there are many detached words that express similar relations, supplementing the modes and aspects. The duties of our three-tense system and its tripartite linear objectified "time" are distributed among various verb categories, all different from our tenses; and there is no more basis for an objectified time in Hopi verbs than in other Hopi patterns; although this does not in the least hinder the verb forms and other patterns from being closely adjusted to the pertinent realities of actual situations.

## Duration, Intensity, and Tendency in SAE and Hopi

To fit discourse to manifold actual situations, all languages need to express durations, intensities, and tendencies. It is characteristic of SAE and perhaps of many other language types to express them metaphorically. The **metaphors** are those of spatial extension, i.e., of size, number (plurality), position, shape, and motion. We express duration by 'long, short, great, much, quick, slow', etc.; intensity by 'large, great, much, heavy, light, high, low, sharp, faint', etc.; tendency by 'more, increase, grow, turn, get, approach, go, come, rise, fall, stop, smooth, even, rapid, slow'; and so on through an almost inexhaustible list of metaphors that we hardly recognize as such, since they are virtually the only linguistic media available. The nonmetaphorical terms in this field, like 'early, late, soon, lasting, intense, very, tending,' are a mere handful, quite inadequate to the needs.

It is clear how this condition "fits in." It is part of our whole scheme of OBJECTIFYING—imaginatively spatializing qualities and potentials that are quite nonspatial (so far as any spatially perceptive senses can tell us). Noun-meaning (with us) proceeds from physical bodies to referents of far other sort. Since physical bodies and their outlines in PERCEIVED SPACE are denoted by size and shape terms and reckoned by cardinal numbers and plurals, these patterns of denotation and reckoning extend to the symbols of nonspatial meanings, and so suggest an IMAGINARY SPACE. Physical shapes 'move, stop, rise, sink, approach,' etc., in perceived space; why not these other referents in their imaginary space? This has gone so far that we can hardly refer to the simplest nonspatial situation without constant resort to physical metaphors. I "grasp" the "thread" of another's arguments, but if its "level" is "over my head" my attention may "wander" and "lose touch" with the "drift" of it, so that when he "comes" to his "point" we differ "widely," our "views" being indeed so "far apart" that the "things" he says "appear" "much" too arbitrary, or even "a lot" of nonsense!

The absence of such metaphor from Hopi speech is striking. Use of space terms when there is no space involved is NOT THERE—as if on it had been laid the taboo teetotal! The reason is clear when we know that Hopi has abundant conjugational and lexical means of expressing duration, intensity, and tendency directly as such, and that major grammatical patterns do not, as with us, provide analogies for an imaginary space. The many verb "aspects" express duration and tendency of manifestations, while some of the "voices" express intensity, tendency, and duration of causes or forces producing manifestations. Then a special part of speech, the "tensors," a huge class of words, denotes only intensity, tendency, duration, and sequence. The function of the tensors is to express intensities, "strengths," and how they continue or vary, their rate of change; so that the broad concept of intensity, when considered as necessarily always varying and/or continuing, includes also tendency and duration. Tensors convey distinctions of degree, rate, constancy, repetition, increase and decrease of intensity, immediate sequence, interruption or sequence after an interval, etc., also QUALITIES of strengths, such as we should express metaphorically as smooth, even, hard, rough. A striking feature is their lack of resemblance to the terms of real space and movement that to us "mean the same." There is not even more than a trace of apparent derivation from space terms.[8] So, while Hopi in its nouns seems highly concrete, here in the tensors it becomes abstract almost beyond our power to follow.

## Habitual Thought in SAE and Hopi

The comparison now to be made between the habitual thought worlds of SAE and Hopi speakers is of course incomplete. It is possible only to touch upon certain dominant contrasts that appear to stem from the linguistic differences already noted. By "habitual thought" and "thought world" I mean more than simply language, i.e., than the linguistic patterns themselves. I include all the analogical and suggestive value of the patterns (e.g., our "imaginary space" and its distant implications), and all the give-and-take between language and the culture as a whole, wherein is a vast amount that is not linguistic but yet shows the shaping influence of language. In brief, this "thought world" is the microcosm that each man carries about within himself, by which he measures and understands what he can of the macrocosm.

The SAE microcosm has analyzed reality largely in terms of what it calls "things" (bodies and quasibodies) plus modes of extensional but formless existence that it calls "substances" or "matter." It tends to see existence through a binomial formula that expresses any existent as a spatial form plus a spatial formless continuum related to the form, as contents is related to the outlines of its container. Nonspatial existents are imaginatively spatialized and charged with similar implications of form and continuum.

The Hopi microcosm seems to have analyzed reality largely in terms of EVENTS (or better "eventing"), referred to in two ways, objective and subjective. Objectively, and only if perceptible physical experience, events are expressed mainly as outlines, colors, movements, and other perceptive reports. Subjectively, for both the physical and nonphysical, events are considered the expression of invisible intensity factors, on which depend their stability and persistence, or their fugitiveness and proclivities. It implies that existents do not "become later and later" all in the same way; but some do so by growing like plants, some by diffusing and vanishing, some by a procession of metamorphoses, some by enduring in one shape till affected by violent forces. In the nature of each existent able to manifest as a definite whole is the power of its own mode of duration: its growth, decline, stability, cyclicity, or creativeness. Everything is thus already "prepared" for the way it now manifests by earlier phases, and what it will be later, partly has been, and partly is in act of being so "prepared." An emphasis and importance rests on this preparing or being prepared aspect of the world that may to the Hopi correspond to that "quality of reality" that 'matter' or 'stuff' has for us.

## Habitual Behavior Features of Hopi Culture

Our behavior, and that of Hopi, can be seen to be coordinated in many ways to the linguistically conditioned microcosm. As in my fire casebook, people act about situations in ways which are like the ways they talk about them. A characteristic of Hopi behavior is the emphasis on preparation. This includes announcing and getting ready for events well beforehand, elaborate precautions to insure persistence of desired conditions, and stress on good will as the preparer of right results. Consider the analogies of the day-counting pattern alone. Time is mainly reckoned "by day" (*taLk*, *-tala*) or "by night" (*tok*), which words are not nouns but tensors, the first formed on a root "light, day," the second on a root "sleep." The count is by ORDINALS. This is not the pattern of counting a number of different men or things, even though they appear successively, for, even then, they COULD gather into an assemblage. It is the pattern of counting successive reappearances of the SAME man or thing, incapable of forming an assemblage. The analogy is not to behave about day-cyclicity as to several men ("several days"), which is what WE tend to do, but to behave as to the successive visits of the SAME MAN. One does not alter several men by working upon just one, but one can prepare and so alter the later visits of the same man by working to affect the visit he is making now. This is the way the Hopi deal with the future—by working within a present situation which is expected to carry impresses, both obvious and occult, forward into the future event of interest. One might say that Hopi society understands our proverb 'Well begun is half done,' but not our 'Tomorrow is another day.' This may explain much in Hopi character.

This Hopi preparing behavior may be roughly divided into announcing, outer preparing, inner preparing, covert participation, and persistence. Announcing, or preparative publicity, is an important function in the hands of a special official, the Crier Chief. Outer preparing is preparation involving much visible activity, not all necessarily directly useful within our understanding. It includes ordinary practicing, rehearsing, getting ready, introductory formalities, preparing of special food, etc. (all of these to a degree that may seem overelaborate to us), intensive sustained muscular activity like running, racing, dancing, which is thought to increase the intensity of development of events (such as growth of crops), mimetic and other magic, preparations based on esoteric theory involving perhaps occult instruments like prayer sticks, prayer feathers, and prayer meal, and finally the great cyclic ceremonies and dances, which have the significance of preparing rain and crops. From one of the verbs meaning "prepare" is derived the noun for "harvest" or "crop": *na'twani* 'the prepared' or the 'in preparation.'[9]

Inner preparing is use of prayer and meditation, and at lesser intensity good wishes and good will, to further desired results. Hopi attitudes stress the power of desire and thought. With their "microcosm" it is utterly natural that they should. Desire and thought are the earliest, and therefore the most important, most critical and crucial, stage of preparing. Moreover, to the Hopi, one's desires and thoughts influence not only his own actions, but all nature as well. This too is wholly natural. Consciousness itself is aware of work, of the feel of effort and energy, in desire and thinking. Experience more basic than language tells us that, if energy is expended, effects are produced. WE tend to believe that our bodies can stop up this energy, prevent it from affecting other things until we will our BODIES to overt action. But this may be so only because we have our own linguistic basis for a theory that formless items like "matter" are things in themselves, malleable only by similar things, by more matter, and hence insulated from the powers of life and thought. It is no more unnatural to think that thought contacts everything and pervades the universe than to think, as we all do, that light kindled outdoors does this. And it is not unnatural to suppose that thought, like any other force, leaves everywhere traces of effect. Now, when WE think of a certain actual rosebush, we do not suppose that our thought goes to that actual bush, and engages with it, like a searchlight turned upon it. What then do we suppose our consciousness is dealing with when we are thinking of that rosebush? Probably we think it is dealing with a "mental image" which is not the rosebush but a mental surrogate of it. But why should it be NATURAL to think that our thought deals with a surrogate and not with the real rosebush? Quite possibly because we are dimly aware that we carry about with us a whole imaginary space, full of mental surrogates. To us, mental surrogates are old familiar fare. Along with the images of imaginary space, which we perhaps secretly know to be only imaginary, we tuck the thought-of actually existing rosebush, which may be quite another story, perhaps just because we have that very convenient "place" for it. The Hopi thought-world has no imaginary space. The corollary to this is that it may not locate thought dealing with real space anywhere but in real space, nor insulate real space from the effects of thought. A Hopi would naturally suppose that his thought (or he himself) traffics with the actual rosebush—or more likely, corn plant—that he is thinking about. The thought then should leave some trace of itself with the plant in the field. If it is a good thought, one about health and growth, it is good for the plant; if a bad thought, the reverse.

The Hopi emphasize the intensity-factor of thought. Thought to be most effective should be vivid in consciousness, definite, steady, sustained, charged with strongly felt good intentions. They render the idea in English as 'concentrating, holding it in your heart, putting your mind on it, earnestly hoping.' Thought power is the force behind ceremonies, prayer sticks, ritual smoking, etc. The prayer pipe is regarded as an aid to "concentrating" (so said my informant). Its name, *na'twanpi*, means 'instrument of preparing.'

Covert participation is mental collaboration from people who do not take part in the actual affair, be it a job of work, hunt, race, or ceremony, but direct their thought and good will toward the affair's success. Announcements often seek to enlist the support of such mental helpers as well as of overt participants, and contain exhortations to the people to aid with their active good will.[10] A similarity to our concepts of a sympathetic audience or the cheering section at a football game should not obscure the fact that it is primarily the power of directed thought, and not merely sympathy or encouragement, that is expected of covert participants. In fact these latter get in their deadliest work before, not during, the game! A corollary to the power of thought is the power of wrong thought for evil; hence one purpose of covert participation is to obtain the mass force of many good wishers to offset the harmful thought of ill wishers. Such attitudes greatly favor cooperation and community spirit. Not that the Hopi community is not full of rivalries and colliding interests. Against the tendency to social disintegration in such a small, isolated group, the theory of "preparing" by the power of thought, logically leading to the great power of the combined, intensified, and harmonized thought of the whole community, must help vastly toward the rather remarkable degree of cooperation that, in spite of much private bickering, the Hopi village displays in all the important cultural activities.

Hopi "preparing" activities again show a result of their linguistic thought background in an emphasis on persistence and constant insistent repetition. A sense of the cumulative value of innumerable small momenta is dulled by an objectified, spatialized view of time like ours, enhanced by a way of thinking close to the subjective awareness of duration, of the ceaseless "latering" of events. To us, for whom time is a motion on a space, unvarying repetition seems to scatter its force along a row of units of that space, and be wasted. To the Hopi, for whom time is not a motion but a "getting later" of everything that has ever been done, unvarying repetition is not wasted but accumulated. It is storing up an invisible change that holds over into later events.[11] As we have seen, it is as if the return of the day were felt as the return of the same person, a little older but with all the impresses of yesterday, not as "another day," i.e., like an entirely different person. This principle joined with that of thought-power and with traits of general Pueblo culture is expressed in the theory of the Hopi ceremonial dance for furthering rain and crops, as well as in its short, piston-like tread, repeated thousands of times, hour after hour.

## Some Impresses of Linguistic Habit in Western Civilization

It is harder to do justice in few words to the linguistically conditioned features of our own culture than in the case of the Hopi, because of both vast scope and difficulty of objectivity—because of our deeply ingrained familiarity with the attitudes to be analyzed. I wish merely to sketch certain characteristics adjusted to our linguistic binomialism of form plus formless item or "substance," to our metaphoricalness, our imaginary space, and our objectified time. These, as we have seen, are linguistic.

From the form-plus-substance dichotomy the philosophical views most traditionally characteristic of the "Western world" have derived huge support. Here belong materialism, psychophysical parallelism, physics—at least in its traditional Newtonian form—and dualistic views of the universe in general. Indeed here belongs almost everything that is "hard, practical common sense." Monistic, holistic, and relativistic views of reality appeal to philosophers and some scientists, but they are badly handicapped in appealing to the "common sense" of the Western average man—not because Nature herself refutes them (if she did, philosophers could have discovered this much), but because they must be talked about in what amounts to a new language. "Common sense," as its name shows, and "practicality" as its name does not show, are largely matters of talking so that one is readily understood. It is sometimes stated that Newtonian space, time, and matter are sensed by everyone intuitively, whereupon relativity is cited as showing how mathematical analysis can prove intuition wrong. This, besides being unfair to intuition, is an attempt to answer offhand question (1) put at the outset of this [discussion], to answer which this research was undertaken. Presentation of the findings now nears its end, and I think the answer is clear. The offhand answer, laying the blame upon intuition for our slowness in discovering mysteries of the Cosmos, such as relativity, is the wrong one. The right answer is: Newtonian space, time, and matter are no intuitions. They are recepts from culture and language. That is where Newton got them.

Our objectified view of time is, however, favorable to historicity and to everything connected with the keeping of records, while the Hopi view is unfavorable thereto. The latter is too subtle, complex, and ever-developing, supplying no ready-made answer to the question of when "one" event ends and "another" begins. When it is implicit that everything that ever happened still is, but is in a necessarily different form from what memory or record reports, there is less incentive to study the past. As for the present, the incentive would be not to record it but to treat it as "preparing." But OUR objectified time puts before imagination something like a ribbon or scroll marked off into equal blank spaces, suggesting that each be filled with an entry. Writing has no doubt helped toward our linguistic treatment of time, even as the linguistic treatment has guided the uses of writing. Through this give-and-take between language and the whole culture we get, for instance:

1. Records, diaries, bookkeeping, accounting, mathematics stimulated by accounting.
2. Interest in exact sequence, dating, calendars, chronology, clocks, time wages, time graphs, time as used in physics.
3. Annals, histories, the historical attitude, interest in the past, archaeology, attitudes of introjection toward past periods, e.g., classicism, romanticism.

Just as we conceive our objectified time as extending in the future in the same way that it extends in the past, so we set down our estimates of the future in the same shape as our records of the past, producing programs, schedules, budgets. The formal equality of the spacelike units by which we measure and conceive time leads us to consider the "formless item" or "substance" of time to be homogeneous and in ratio to the number of units. Hence our prorata allocation of value to time, lending itself to the building up of a commercial structure based on time-prorata values: time wages (time work constantly supersedes piece work), rent, credit, interest, depreciation charges, and insurance premiums. No doubt this vast system, once built, would continue to run under any sort of linguistic treatment of time; but that it should have been built at all, reaching the magnitude and particular form it has in the Western world, is a fact decidedly in consonance with the patterns of the SAE languages. Whether such a civilization as ours would be possible with widely different linguistic handling of time is a large question—in our civilization, our linguistic patterns and the fitting of our behavior to the temporal order are what they are, and they are in accord. We are of course stimulated to use calendars, clocks, and watches, and to try to measure time ever more precisely; this aids science, and science in turn, following these well-worn cultural grooves, gives back to culture an ever-growing store of applications, habits, and values, with which culture again directs science. But what lies outside this spiral? Science is beginning to find that there is something in the Cosmos that is not in accord with the concepts we have formed in mounting the spiral. It is trying to frame a NEW LANGUAGE by which to adjust itself to a wider universe.

It is clear how the emphasis on "saving time" which goes with all the above and [its] very obvious objectification of time, leads to a high valuation of "speed," which shows itself a great deal in our behavior.

Still another behavioral effect is that the character of monotony and regularity possessed by our image of time as an evenly scaled limitless tape measure persuades us to behave as if that monotony were more true of events than it really is. That is, it helps to routinize us. We tend to select and favor whatever bears out this view, to "play up to" the routine aspects of existence. One phase of this is behavior evincing a false sense of security or an assumption that all will always go smoothly, and a lack in foreseeing and protecting ourselves against hazards. Our technique of harnessing energy does well in routine performance, and it is along routine lines that we chiefly strive to improve it—we are, for example, relatively uninterested in stopping the energy from causing accidents, fires, and explosions, which it is doing constantly and on a wide scale. Such indifference to the unexpectedness of life would be disastrous to a society as small, isolated, and precariously poised as the Hopi society is, or rather once was.

Thus our linguistically determined thought world not only collaborates with our cultural idols and ideals, but engages even our unconscious personal reactions in its patterns and gives them certain typical characters. One such character, as we have seen, is CARELESSNESS, as in reckless driving or throwing cigarette stubs into waste paper. Another of a different sort is GESTURING when we talk. Very many of the gestures made by English-speaking people at least, and probably by all SAE speakers, serve to illustrate, by a movement in space, not a real spatial reference but one of the nonspatial references that our language handles by metaphors of imaginary space. That is, we are more apt to make a grasping gesture when we speak of grasping an elusive idea than when we speak of grasping a doorknob. The gesture seeks to make a metaphorical and hence somewhat unclear reference more clear. But, if a language refers to nonspatials without implying a spatial analogy, the reference is not made any clearer by gesture. The Hopi gesture very little, perhaps not at all in the sense we understand as gesture.

It would seem as if kinesthesia, or the sensing of muscular movement, though arising before language, should be made more highly conscious by linguistic use of imaginary space and metaphorical images of motion. Kinesthesia is marked in two facets of European culture: art and sport. European sculpture, an art in which Europe excels, is strongly kinesthetic, conveying great sense of the body's motions; European painting likewise. The dance in our culture expresses delight in motion rather than symbolism or ceremonial, and our music is greatly influenced by our dance forms. Our sports are strongly imbued with this element of the "poetry of motion." Hopi races and games seem to emphasize rather the virtues of endurance and sustained intensity. Hopi dancing is highly symbolic and is performed with great intensity and earnestness, but has not much movement or swing.

Synesthesia, or suggestion by certain sense receptions of characters belonging to another sense, as of light and color by sounds and vice versa, should be made more conscious by a linguistic metaphorical system that refers to nonspatial experiences by terms for spatial ones, though undoubtedly it arises from a deeper source. Probably in the first instance metaphor arises from synesthesia and not the reverse; yet metaphor need not become firmly rooted in linguistic pattern, as Hopi shows. Nonspatial experience has one well-organized sense, HEARING—for smell and taste are but little organized. Nonspatial consciousness is a realm chiefly of thought, feeling, and SOUND. Spatial consciousness is a realm of light, color, sight, and touch, and presents shapes and dimensions. Our metaphorical system, by naming nonspatial experiences after spatial ones, imputes to sounds, smells, tastes, emotions, and thoughts qualities like the colors, luminosities, shapes, angles, textures, and motions of spatial experience. And to some extent the reverse transference occurs; for, after much talking about tones as high, low, sharp, dull, heavy, brilliant, slow, the talker finds it easy to think of some factors in spatial experience as like factors of tone. Thus we speak of "tones" of color, a gray "monotone," a "loud" necktie, a "taste" in dress: all spatial metaphor in reverse. Now European art is distinctive in the way it seeks deliberately to play with synesthesia. Music tries to suggest scenes, color, movement, geometric design; painting and sculpture are often consciously guided by the analogies of music's rhythm; colors are conjoined with feeling for the analogy to concords and discords. The European theater and opera seek a synthesis of many arts. It may be that in this way our metaphorical language that is in some sense a confusion of thought is producing, through art, a result of far-reaching value—a deeper esthetic sense leading toward a more direct apprehension of underlying unity behind the phenomena so variously reported by our sense channels.

## Historical Implications

How does such a network of language, culture, and behavior come about historically? Which was first: the language patterns or the cultural norms? In main they have grown up together, constantly influencing each other. But in this partnership the nature of the language is the factor that limits free plasticity and rigidifies channels of development in the more autocratic way. This is so because a language is a system, not just an assemblage of norms. Large systematic outlines can change to something really new only very slowly, while many other cultural innovations are made with comparative quickness. Language thus represents the mass mind; it is affected by inventions and innovations, but affected little and slowly, whereas TO inventors and innovators it legislates with the decree immediate.

The growth of the SAE language-culture complex dates from ancient times. Much of its metaphorical reference to the nonspatial by the spatial was already fixed in the ancient tongues, and more especially in Latin. It is indeed a marked trait of Latin. If we compare, say Hebrew, we find that, while Hebrew has some allusion to not-space as space, Latin has more. Latin terms for nonspatials, like *educo, religio, principia, comprehendo*, are usually metaphorized physical references: lead out, tying back, etc. This is not true of all languages—it is quite untrue of Hopi. The fact that in Latin the direction of development happened to be from spatial to nonspatial (partly because of secondary stimulation to abstract thinking when the intellectually crude Romans encountered Greek culture) and that later tongues were strongly stimulated to mimic Latin, seems a likely reason for a belief, which still lingers on among linguists, that this is the natural direction of semantic change in all languages, and for the persistent notion in Western learned circles (in strong contrast to Eastern ones) that objective experience is prior to subjective. Philosophies make out a weighty case for the reverse, and certainly the direction of development is sometimes the reverse. Thus the Hopi word for "heart" can be shown to be a late formation within Hopi from a root meaning think or remember. Or consider what has happened to the word "radio" in such a sentence as "he bought a new radio," as compared to its prior meaning "science of wireless telephony."

In the Middle Ages the patterns already formed in Latin began to interweave with the increased mechanical invention, industry, trade, and scholastic and scientific thought. The need for measurement in industry and trade, the stores and bulks of "stuffs" in various containers, the type-bodies in which various goods were handled, standardizing of measure and weight units, invention of clocks and measurement of "time," keeping of records, accounts, chronicles, histories, growth of mathematics and the partnership of mathematics and science, all cooperated to bring our thought and language world into its present form.

In Hopi history, could we read it, we should find a different type of language and a different set of cultural and environmental influences working together. A peaceful agricultural society isolated by geographic features and nomad enemies in a land of scanty rainfall, arid agriculture that could be made successful only by the utmost perseverance (hence the value of persistence and repetition), necessity for collaboration (hence emphasis on the psychology of teamwork and on mental factors in general), corn and rain as primary criteria of value, need of extensive PREPARATIONS and precautions to assure crops in the poor soil and precarious climate, keen realization of dependence upon nature favoring prayer and a religious attitude toward the forces of nature, especially prayer and religion directed toward the ever-needed blessing, rain—these things interacted with Hopi linguistic patterns to mold them, to be molded again by them, and so little by little to shape the Hopi world-outlook.

To sum up the matter, our first question asked in the beginning (p. 45) is answered thus: Concepts of "time" and "matter" are not given in substantially the same form by experience to all men but depend upon the nature of the language or languages through the use of which they have been developed. They do not depend so much upon ANY ONE SYSTEM (e.g., tense, or nouns) within the grammar as upon the ways of analyzing and reporting experience which have become fixed in the language as integrated "fashions of speaking" and which cut across the typical grammatical classifications, so that such a "fashion" may include lexical, morphological, syntactic, and otherwise systemically diverse means coordinated in a certain frame of consistency. Our own "time" differs markedly from Hopi "duration." It is conceived as like a space of strictly limited dimensions, or sometimes as like a motion upon such a space, and employed as an intellectual tool accordingly. Hopi "duration" seems to be inconceivable in terms of space or motion, being the mode in which life differs from form, and consciousness *in toto* from the spatial elements of consciousness. Certain ideas born of our own time-concept, such as that of absolute simultaneity, would be either very difficult to express or impossible and devoid of meaning under the Hopi conception, and would be replaced by operational concepts. Our "matter" is the physical subtype of "substance" or "stuff," which is conceived as the formless extensional item that must be joined with form before there can be real existence. In Hopi there seems to be nothing corresponding to it; there are no formless extensional items; existence may or may not have form, but what it also has, with or without form, is intensity and duration, these being nonextensional and at bottom the same.

But what about our concept of "space," which was also included in our first question? There is no such striking difference between Hopi and SAE about space as about time, and probably the apprehension of space is given in substantially the same form by experience irrespective of language. The experiments of the Gestalt psychologists with visual perception appear to establish this as a fact. But the CONCEPT OF SPACE will vary somewhat with language, because, as an intellectual tool,[12] it is so closely linked with the concomitant employment of other intellectual tools, of the order of "time" and "matter," which are linguistically conditioned. We see things with our eyes in the same space forms as the Hopi, but our idea of space has also the property of acting as a surrogate of nonspatial relationships like time, intensity, tendency, and as a void to be filled with imagined formless items, one of which may even be called 'space.' Space as sensed by the Hopi would not be connected mentally with such surrogates, but would be comparatively "pure," unmixed with extraneous notions.

As for our second question (p. 45): There are connections but not correlations or diagnostic correspondences between cultural norms and linguistic patterns. Although it would be impossible to infer the existence of Crier Chiefs from the lack of tenses in Hopi, or vice versa, there is a relation between a language and the rest of the culture of the society which uses it. There are cases where the "fashions of speaking" are closely integrated with the whole general culture, whether or not this be universally true, and there are connections within this integration, between the kind of linguistic analyses employed and various behavioral reactions and also the shapes taken by various cultural developments. Thus the importance of Crier Chiefs does have a connection, not with tenselessness itself, but with a system of thought in which categories different from our tenses are natural. These connections are to be found not so much by focusing attention on the typical rubrics of linguistic, ethnographic, or sociological description as by examining the culture and the language (always and only when the two have been together historically for a considerable time) as a whole in which concatenations that run across these departmental lines may be expected to exist, and, if they do exist, eventually to be discoverable by study.

## Notes

1. We have plenty of evidence that this is not the case. Consider only the Hopi and the Ute, with languages that on the overt morphological and lexical level are as similar as, say, English and German. The idea of "correlation" between language and culture, in the generally accepted sense of correlation, is certainly a mistaken one.

2. As we say, 'ten at the SAME TIME', showing that in our language and thought we restate the fact of group perception in terms of a concept 'time', the large linguistic component of which will appear in the course of this [discussion].

3. It is no exception to this rule of lacking a plural that a mass noun may sometimes coincide in lexeme with an individual noun that of course has a plural; e.g., 'stone' (no pl.) with 'a stone' (pl. 'stones'). The plural form denoting varieties, e.g., 'wines' is of course a different sort of thing from the true plural; it is a curious outgrowth from the SAE mass nouns, leading to still another sort of imaginary aggregates, which will have to be omitted from this [discussion].

4. Hopi has two words for water quantities; *kə· yi* and *pa ·hə*. The difference is something like that between 'stone' and 'rock' in English, *pa·hə* implying greater size and "wildness"; flowing water, whether or not outdoors or in nature, is *pa·hə*; so is 'moisture'. But, unlike 'stone' and 'rock', the difference is essential, not pertaining to a connotative margin, and the two can hardly ever be interchanged.

5. To be sure, there are a few minor differences from other nouns, in English for instance in the use of the articles.

6. 'Year' and certain combinations of 'year' with name of season, rarely season names alone, can occur with a locative morpheme 'at', but this is exceptional. It appears like historical detritus of an earlier different patterning, or the effect of English analogy, or both.

7. The expective and reportive assertions contrast according to the "paramount relation." The expective expresses anticipation existing EARLIER than objective fact, and coinciding with objective fact LATER than the status quo of the speaker, this status quo, including all the subsummation of the past therein, being expressed by the reportive. Our notion "future" seems to represent at once the earlier (anticipation) and the later (afterwards, what will be), as Hopi shows. This paradox may hint of how elusive the mystery of real time is, and how artificially it is expressed by a linear relation of past–present–future.

8. One such trace is that the tensor 'long in duration', while quite different from the adjective 'long' of space, seems to contain the same root as the adjective 'large' of space. Another is that 'somewhere' of space used with certain tensors means 'at some indefinite time.' Possibly however this is not the case and it is only the tensor that gives the time element, so that 'somewhere' still refers to space and that under these conditions indefinite space means simply general applicability, regardless of either time or space. Another trace is that in the temporal (cycle word) 'afternoon' the element meaning 'after' is derived from the verb 'to separate'. There are other such traces, but they are few and exceptional, and obviously not like our own spatial metaphorizing.

9. The Hopi verbs of preparing naturally do not correspond neatly to our "prepare"; so that *na'twani* could also be rendered 'the practiced-upon, the tried-for,' and otherwise.

10. See, e.g., Ernest Beaglehole, *Notes on Hopi economic life* (Yale University Publications in Anthropology, no. 15, 1937), especially the reference to the announcement of a rabbit hunt, and on p. 30, description of the activities in connection with the cleaning of Toreva Spring—announcing, various preparing activities, and finally, preparing the continuity of the good results already obtained and the continued flow of the spring.

11. This notion of storing up power, which seems implied by much Hopi behavior, has an analog in physics: acceleration. It might be said that the linguistic background of Hopi thought equips it to recognize naturally that force manifests not as motion or velocity, but as cumulation or acceleration. Our linguistic background tends to hinder in us this same recognition, for having legitimately conceived force to be that which produces change, we then think of change by our linguistic metaphorical analog, motion, instead of by a pure motionless changingness concept, i.e., accumulation or acceleration. Hence it comes to our naïve feeling as a shock to find from physical experiments that it is not possible to define force by motion, that motion and speed, as also "being at rest," are wholly relative, and that force can be measured only by acceleration.

12. Here belong "Newtonian" and "Euclidean" space, etc.

## Critical Thinking and Application

- Try to understand the Hopi examples that Whorf gives of, for instance, differentiating real and imaginary plurals. Is this easy or hard? Why do you think this is the case?
- Think about time. What images come to mind? Do these line up with what Whorf says about SAE time? Can you think of time without the words to do so?
- Why does Whorf emphasize that "language is a system, not just an assemblage of norms"? How well does an observer have to know a language and culture to be able to see its systematicity?
- Identify someone who is a native speaker of a non-Indo-European language. Ask her or him about learning English and where the difficulties lie. Does the answer support or refute Whorf's thesis?

## Vocabulary

animate
aspect
cardinal numbers
gender
inanimate
inflected
inflection
isolating
metaphor
morpheme
morphological
morphology
nomic
number
ordinals
plurality
SAE
synthetic
tense
validity-forms
voice

## Suggested Further Reading [See also list following Language and Thought unit introduction]

Lavery, David. N.d. *The Benjamin Lee Whorf WWW.* Website. http://mtsu32.mtsu.edu:11072/Whorf/

Ridington, Robin. 1987. Models of the Universe: The Poetic Paradigm of Benjamin Lee Whorf. *Anthropology and Humanism Quarterly* 12(1): 16–24.

Witherspoon, Gary. 1977. *Language and Art in the Navaho Universe.* Ann Arbor: University of Michigan Press.

# CHAPTER 7

# Metaphors We Live By

## *George Lakoff and Mark Johnson*

(1980)

*George Lakoff and Mark Johnson's book,* Metaphors We Live By, *sparked a lively conversation when it was published in 1980. The authors pointed out that all language is metaphoric; that there is no such thing as pure, transparent language; and that the metaphors work together in systematic ways. In this short excerpt from their book, you are introduced to the basic idea of conceptual metaphors.*

### Reading Questions

- Where do Lakoff and Johnson see evidence of metaphor in everyday life? What claims do they make about "our ordinary conceptual system"?
- Why is it important that they claim that human thought processes are largely metaphorical?
- Consider their claims about TIME IS MONEY. Do you experience time this way? Can you think of it any other way? Have you ever read about a culture in which time is conceived of differently? What do you think would happen if people from cultures with two different concepts of time encountered each other?

---

**Metaphor** is for most people a device of the poetic imagination and the rhetorical flourish—a matter of extraordinary rather than ordinary language. Moreover, metaphor is typically viewed as characteristic of language alone, a matter of words rather than thought or action. For this reason, most people think they can get along perfectly well without metaphor. We have found, on the contrary, that metaphor is pervasive in everyday life, not just in language but in thought and action. Our ordinary conceptual system, in terms of which we both think and act, is fundamentally metaphorical in nature.

The concepts that govern our thought are not just matters of the intellect. They also govern our everyday functioning, down to the most mundane details. Our concepts structure what we perceive, how we get around in the world, and how we relate to other people. Our conceptual system thus plays a central role in defining our everyday realities. If we are right in suggesting that our conceptual system is largely metaphorical, then the way we think, what we experience, and what we do every day is very much a matter of metaphor.

But our conceptual system is not something we are normally aware of. In most of the little things we do every day, we simply think and act more or less automatically along certain lines. Just what these lines are is by no means obvious. One way to find out is by looking at language. Since communication is based on the same conceptual system that we use in thinking and acting, language is an important source of evidence for what that system is like.

Primarily on the basis of linguistic evidence, we have found that most of our ordinary conceptual system is metaphorical in nature. And we have found a way to begin to identify in detail just what the metaphors are that structure how we perceive, how we think, and what we do.

To give some idea of what it could mean for a concept to be metaphorical and for such a concept to structure an everyday activity, let us start with the concept ARGUMENT and the conceptual metaphor ARGUMENT IS WAR. This metaphor is reflected in our everyday language by a wide variety of expressions:

ARGUMENT IS WAR

> Your claims are *indefensible*.
> He *attacked every weak point* in my argument.
> His criticisms were *right on target*.
> I *demolished* his argument.
> I've never *won* an argument with him.
> You disagree? Okay, *shoot!*
> If you use that *strategy*, he'll *wipe you out*.
> He *shot down* all of my arguments.

It is important to see that we don't just *talk* about arguments in terms of war. We can actually win or lose arguments.

---

George Lakoff and Mark Johnson, Metaphors We Live By and The Systematicity of Metaphorical Concepts. In *Metaphors We Live By*. Chicago and London: University of Chicago Press, 1980, pp. 3–9.

We see the person we are arguing with as an opponent. We attack his positions and we defend our own. We gain and lose ground. We plan and use strategies. If we find a position indefensible, we can abandon it and take a new line of attack. Many of the things we *do* in arguing are partially structured by the concept of war. Though there is no physical battle, there is a verbal battle, and the structure of an argument—attack, defense, counterattack, etc.—reflects this. It is in this sense that the ARGUMENT IS WAR metaphor is one that we live by in this culture; it structures the actions we perform in arguing.

Try to imagine a culture where arguments are not viewed in terms of war, where no one wins or loses, where there is no sense of attacking or defending, gaining or losing ground. Imagine a culture where an argument is viewed as a dance, the participants are seen as performers, and the goal is to perform in a balanced and aesthetically pleasing way. In such a culture, people would view arguments differently, experience them differently, carry them out differently, and talk about them differently. But *we* would probably not view them as arguing at all: they would simply be doing something different. It would seem strange even to call what they were doing "arguing." Perhaps the most neutral way of describing this difference between their culture and ours would be to say that we have a discourse form structured in terms of battle and they have one structured in terms of dance.

This is an example of what it means for a **metaphorical concept,** namely, ARGUMENT IS WAR, to structure (at least in part) what we do and how we understand what we are doing when we argue. *The essence of metaphor is understanding and experiencing one kind of thing in terms of another.* It is not that arguments are a subspecies of war. Arguments and wars are different kinds of things—verbal discourse and armed conflict—and the actions performed are different kinds of actions. But ARGUMENT is partially structured, understood, performed, and talked about in terms of WAR. The concept is metaphorically structured, the activity is metaphorically structured, and, consequently, the language is metaphorically structured.

Moreover, this is the *ordinary* way of having an argument and talking about one. The normal way for us to talk about attacking a position is to use the words "attack a position." Our conventional ways of talking about arguments presuppose a metaphor we are hardly ever conscious of. The metaphor is not merely in the words we use—it is in our very concept of an argument. The language of argument is not poetic, fanciful, or rhetorical; it is literal. We talk about arguments that way because we conceive of them that way—and we act according to the way we conceive of things.

The most important claim we have made so far is that metaphor is not just a matter of language, that is, of mere words. We shall argue that, on the contrary, human *thought processes* are largely metaphorical. This is what we mean when we say that the human conceptual system is metaphorically structured and defined. Metaphors as linguistic expressions are possible precisely because there are metaphors in a person's conceptual system. Therefore, whenever . . . we speak of metaphors, such as ARGUMENT IS WAR, it should be understood that *metaphor* means *metaphorical concept.*

---

Arguments usually follow patterns; that is, there are certain things we typically do and do not do in arguing. The fact that we in part conceptualize arguments in terms of battle systematically influences the shape arguments take and the way we talk about what we do in arguing. Because the metaphorical concept is systematic, the language we use to talk about that aspect of the concept is systematic.

We saw in the ARGUMENT IS WAR metaphor that expressions from the vocabulary of war, e.g., *attack a position, indefensible, strategy, new line of attack, win, gain ground,* etc., form a systematic way of talking about the battling aspects of arguing. It is no accident that these expressions mean what they mean when we use them to talk about arguments. A portion of the conceptual network of battle partially characterizes the concept of an argument, and the language follows suit. Since metaphorical expressions in our language are tied to metaphorical concepts in a systematic way, we can use metaphorical linguistic expressions to study the nature of metaphorical concepts and to gain an understanding of the metaphorical nature of our activities.

To get an idea of how metaphorical expressions in everyday language can give us insight into the metaphorical nature of the concepts that structure our everyday activities, let us consider the metaphorical concept TIME IS MONEY as it is reflected in contemporary English.

TIME IS MONEY

You're *wasting* my time.
This gadget will *save* you hours.
I don't *have* the time to *give* you.
How do you *spend* your time these days?
That flat tire *cost* me an hour.
I've *invested* a lot of time in her.
I don't *have enough* time to *spare* for that.
You're *running out* of time.
You need to *budget* your time.
*Put aside* some time for ping pong.
Is that *worth your while?*
Do you *have* much time *left?*
He's living on *borrowed* time.
You don't *use* your time *profitably.*
I *lost* a lot of time when I got sick.
*Thank you for* your time.

Time in our culture is a valuable commodity. It is a limited resource that we use to accomplish our goals. Because of the way that the concept of work has developed in modern Western culture, where work is typically associated with the time it takes and time is precisely quantified, it has become customary to pay people by the hour, week, or year. In our culture TIME IS MONEY in many ways: telephone message units, hourly wages, hotel room rates, yearly budgets, interest on loans, and paying your debt to society by "serving time." These practices are relatively new in the history of the human race, and by no means do they exist in all cultures. They have arisen in modern industrialized societies and structure our basic everyday activities in a very profound way. Corresponding to the fact that we *act* as if time is a valuable commodity—a limited resource, even money—we *conceive of* time that way. Thus we understand and experience time as the kind of thing that can be spent, wasted, budgeted, invested wisely or poorly, saved, or squandered.

TIME IS MONEY, TIME IS A LIMITED RESOURCE, and TIME IS A VALUABLE COMMODITY are all metaphorical concepts. They are metaphorical since we are using our everyday experiences with money, limited resources, and valuable commodities to conceptualize time. This isn't a necessary way for human beings to conceptualize time; it is tied to our culture. There are cultures where time is none of these things.

The metaphorical concepts TIME IS MONEY, TIME IS A RESOURCE, and TIME IS A VALUABLE COMMODITY form a single system based on subcategorization, since in our society money is a limited resource and limited resources are valuable commodities. These subcategorization relationships characterize entailment relationships between the metaphors. TIME IS MONEY entails that TIME IS A LIMITED RESOURCE, which entails that TIME IS A VALUABLE COMMODITY.

We are adopting the practice of using the most specific metaphorical concept, in this case TIME IS MONEY, to characterize the entire system. Of the expressions listed under the TIME IS MONEY metaphor, some refer specifically to money (*spend, invest, budget, profitably, cost*), others to limited resources (*use, use up, have enough of, run out of*), and still others to valuable commodities (*have, give, lose, thank you for*). This is an example of the way in which metaphorical entailments can characterize a coherent system of metaphorical concepts and a corresponding coherent system of metaphorical expressions for those concepts.

---

## Critical Thinking and Application

- Why do you think we tend to be unaware of the systematic metaphors that Lakoff and Johnson point out? How aware are we, in general, of the way our language works?
- Analyze a text, looking for conceptual metaphors. What metaphors do you find? Could the concepts be expressed without the metaphors?
- For native speakers of languages other than English: do you have equivalents in your language to the English metaphors mentioned by Lakoff and Johnson? Are there other metaphors that English does not have?
- What is the relationship between reality, our concepts, and our metaphorical linguistic expressions? Do humans who speak different languages live in the same reality?

## Vocabulary

metaphor metaphorical concept

## Suggested Further Reading

Black, Max. 1962. *Models and Metaphors: Studies in Language and Philosophy*. Ithaca, NY: Cornell University Press.

Fernandez, James W. 1991. *Beyond Metaphor: The Theory of Tropes in Anthropology*. Stanford, CA: Stanford University Press.

Holland, Dorothy C., and Naomi Quinn, eds. 1987. *Cultural Models in Language and Thought*. Cambridge and New York: Cambridge University Press.

Kittay, Eva Feder. 1987. *Metaphor: Its Cognitive Force and Linguistic Structure*. Oxford: Clarendon Press.

Kuhn, Thomas S. 1970. *The Structure of Scientific Revolutions*. Chicago: University of Chicago Press.

Lakoff, George. 1987. *Women, Fire, and Dangerous Things: What Categories Reveal About the Mind*. Chicago: University of Chicago Press.

Lakoff, George. 2004. *Don't Think of an Elephant! Know Your Values and Frame the Debate: The Essential Guide for Progressives*. White River Junction, VT: Chelsea Green.

Lakoff, George, and Mark Johnson. 1980. *Metaphors We Live By*. Chicago and London: University of Chicago Press.

Ortony, Andrew, ed. 1979. *Metaphor and Thought*. Cambridge and New York: Cambridge University Press.

Pepper, Stephen C. 1942. *World Hypotheses: A Study in Evidence*. Berkeley and Los Angeles: University of California Press.

Sacks, Sheldon, ed. 1979 [1978]. *On Metaphor*. Chicago: University of Chicago Press.

## CHAPTER 8

# Language and Mind
## Let's Get the Issues Straight!

*Stephen C. Levinson*
(2003)

*Stephen Levinson has been very much involved in the revival and empirical assessment of the linguistic relativity hypothesis that began in the 1990s. He has worked at the Max Planck Institute for Psycholinguistics in the Netherlands since 1991, serving as director for many years. Psycholinguistics is the study of the relationship between language and thought, including the neurobiological dimensions of cognition. Much of this research is technologically sophisticated and laboratory based, but some of it relies on in-depth ethnographic studies of people, their language, and their behavior, especially in its cross-cultural dimension.*

*Levinson's work on this topic has been especially focused on the relationship between language and space, comparing the ways different languages discuss space, whether in locating something relative to something else (*to the left of the house*) or in absolute terms (*north of the house*) or in discussing the proximity and relationship of various objects (*in the box, on the shelf*). These systems vary quite prominently across languages, and Levinson has shown that there are cognitive consequences of these linguistic differences. In other words, we think the way our language prepares us to think. One of the most striking findings is that people with absolute spatial systems are many times better at finding their location than people with relative spatial systems. (English has both, but the relative system is more widespread and powerful.)*

*Levinson argues for the principle of "coevolution" (biology and culture [and language]) and against the doctrine of "Simple Nativism," which holds that the essence of human language is syntax, that language is innate, and that the world's thousands of languages simply apply different labels to the same shared concepts. Levinson sees the great diversity among languages as more than simple "noise" but rather as providing evidence about something profound. Further, he emphasizes that humans have evolved to have culture but a specific, not a general human, culture.*

### Reading Questions

- Levinson summarizes a body of research that has shown that children's first task is to figure out the sounds of the particular language into which they are born. By eighteen months, they have sorted this out quite thoroughly. How does this support Levinson's broader point?
- What evidence does Levinson provide to dispute Li and Gleitman's claim that "the grammars and lexicons of all languages are broadly similar"?
- What sorts of things vary across languages? Why does Levinson regard this as "*the fundamentally interesting thing* about language"?

---

Stephen C. Levinson, "Language and Mind: Let's Get the Issues Straight!" In *Language in Mind: Advances in the Study of Language and Thought*. Edited by Dedre Gentner and Susan Goldin-Meadow. Cambridge, MA, and London: MIT Press, 2003, pp. 25–46.

- What are linguistic universals? Are there any specific ones? What conclusion does Levinson draw from this? How does he interpret the implications of Berlin and Kay's studies of color?

---

Current discourse on the topic of language and mind is at about the intellectual level of a chat show on the merits of democracy. Ideological nonsense, issued by famous scholars, fills the air, even the scientific journals. Serious scholars tend to leave well enough alone, since such exchanges reveal a banal underlying lack of analysis. It is as if the topic of **"Whorfianism"** is a domain where anybody can let off steam, go on mental holiday, or pounce upon an ideological enemy. This is a pity, because the issues are deeply relevant to understanding our place in nature, and how we should understand our unique language capacity. Further, the issues are entirely open to careful analysis and empirical investigation, using the normal methods of the linguistic and psychological sciences.

In this chapter, I try to spell out in the simplest terms what the underlying issues are (but see Levinson 1996, 1997a, 2000, 2001, 2003, for deeper discussion). We have to establish some kind of sensible mode of discourse before empirical results can be appreciated for what they are. As I outline at the end of the chapter, there is an accumulated body of such results, but first we had better try to establish the foundations for rational discourse.

## The Doctrine of Simple Nativism and Its Coevolutionary Alternative

There is a widespread presumption in the **cognitive sciences** that language is essentially **innate**. All the other species have innate communication systems, so why not humans too? Of course, languages don't all sound alike, but that's a matter of superficial clothing. Underneath, it's the very same flesh and blood. There are two basic tenets to the doctrine. The first holds that the **syntax** of language is fundamentally universal and innate, a view of course associated with Chomsky. The second (of central interest to this chapter) holds that the semantics is given by an innate "language of thought," a view ably defended by Fodor (1975). Put them together and one has the widespread presumption, which I will dub ***Simple Nativism,*** which curiously enough is not generally associated with any adaptational or evolutionary argument for language (see Levinson 2000). The central property of Simple Nativism is the claim that all the major properties of language, the object of study, are dictated by inbuilt mental apparatus. The observable variation is simply "noise," and nothing much can be learned from it. Protagonists of this view can be found across the cognitive sciences, including linguists like Jackendoff (see Landau and Jackendoff 1993), cognitive psychologists like Pinker (1994) or Gleitman (see, e.g., Li and Gleitman 2002), and the so-called evolutionary psychologists like Tooby and Cosmides (1992).

Despite its prominence, this doctrine is peculiar. First, it is impossible to reconcile with the facts of variation across languages. Second, it is a theory of innate (thus biological) endowment outside biology. There is no biological mechanism that could be responsible for providing us with all the meanings of all possible words in all possible languages—there are only 30,000 genes after all (about the number of the most basic words in just one language), and brain tissue is not functionally specific at remotely that kind of level. Third, it misses the most fundamental biological specialization of our species: the species has coevolved with culture—we cannot survive without it, but with it we have evolved a method of adapting to new ecological niches with much greater rapidity than our genome.

This last point is worth developing a little further. Human evolution has been shaped by the development of two distinct types of information transfer across generations, genetic and cultural, with systematic interactions between them (Durham 1991). Just look at the evolution of our hands and the progression of the tools to be found in the archaeological record. Language is an obvious central part of this gene-culture coevolution—it is culture, responding to its particular ecological niche, that provides the bulk of the conceptual packages that are coded in any particular language. The contents of language, and much of its form, are thus largely the products of cultural tradition—but at the same time those cultural elements are constrained in many different ways by the biological nature of the organism, particularly its learning capacity. Rather precise information about this kind of interaction has now been provided by the study of infant speech perception. Infants are highly sensitive to the initial speech sounds around them, and they seem to have an innate fine-grained categorical system of perception shared with monkeys and other mammals. But by six months after birth infants have done something no monkey can do: they have warped this system of categories into line with the local language they are hearing around them. In that short time, they have acquired a cultural acoustic landscape. It is hard to escape the conclusion that human infants are "built" to expect linguistic diversity and have special mechanisms for "tuning in" to the local variety (Kuhl and Meltzoff 1996, 1997). We can expect to find exactly the same sort of interaction between prelinguistic perceptual distinctions and linguistically variable semantic distinctions. Thus, Choi et al. (2000; see also McDonough, Choi, and Mandler, 2003; Bowerman and Choi, 2003) have shown that 9-month-old infants have equal facility to make, for example, English versus Korean spatial distinctions, while by 18 months they are tuned into the local language-specific distinctions. By the time we reach adulthood, just as we find alien language distinctions hard to hear, so English-speaking adults have lost the ability to make Korean distinctions even in nonlinguistic implicit categorization. Infants, unlike monkeys, are preadapted for cultural variation, for discovering the local system and specializing in it.

This alternative coevolutionary account, with psychology and cultural variation locked in mutual adaptation, is much better suited than Simple Nativism to understanding linguistic and cultural variation. It makes us think differently about what the biological endowment for language must be like. Instead of expecting that endowment to predict all the interesting properties of observable languages, we need rather to think about it as a learning mechanism wonderfully adapted to discerning the variability of culturally distinctive systems—a mechanism that simultaneously puts limits on the variation that those systems can throw at it. On this account, the essential properties of language are divided between two inheritance systems, biological and cultural, and the long-term interactions between them.

Simple Nativism has blocked sensible and informed discussion of the relation between language and thought for decades. Once the facts about linguistic diversity are properly appreciated, it will be clear that Simple Nativism ceases to be of any real interest.

## Linguistic Variation

Simple Nativists hold that linguistic categories are a direct projection of universal concepts that are native to the species:

> Knowing a language, then, is knowing how to translate mentalese into strings of words and vice versa. People without a language would still have mentalese, and babies and many nonhuman animals presumably have simpler dialects. (Pinker 1994, 82)

Learning a language is on this view simply a matter of learning the local projection, that is, finding the local phonetic clothing for the preexisting concepts. Or as Li and Gleitman (2002, 266) put it:

> Language has means for making reference to the objects, relations, properties, and events that populate our everyday world. It is possible to suppose that these linguistic categories and structures are more or less straightforward mappings from a preexisting conceptual space, programmed into our biological nature: Humans invent words that label their concepts.

Hence, they hold, "the grammars and lexicons of all languages are broadly similar."

The view just sketched is simply ill informed. There is no sense of "broad" under which "the grammars and lexicons of all languages are broadly similar." If there were, linguists could produce a huge range of absolute linguistic universals—but they cannot do so. As Greenberg (1986, 14) has put it, either language universals are trivial ("All spoken languages have vowels"), or they are conditional generalizations with statistical generality. It is fundamentally important to cognitive science that the true range of human language variation is not lost sight of.

It may be useful to review some of the fundamental parameters of variation. Natural languages may or may not be in the **vocal-auditory** channel—they can be shifted to the **visual-manual** one, as in sign languages. When they are broadcast in an acoustic medium, they may have as few as 11 or as many as 141 distinctive sounds or **phonemes** (Maddieson 1984). Languages may or may not have **morphology,** that is, inflection or derivation. Languages may or may not use **constituent structure** (as in the familiar tree-diagrams) to encode fundamental grammatical relations (Austin and Bresnan 1996; Levinson 1987). Thus, they may or may not have syntactic constraints on word or phrase order. Languages may or may not make use of such basic word class distinctions as adjective, adverb, or even, arguably, noun and verb (Mithun 1999, 60–67). If they do, the kind of denotation assigned to each may be alien from an English point of view. Languages force quite different sets of conceptual distinctions in almost every sentence: some languages express **aspect,** others don't; some have seven tenses, some have none; some force marking of visibility or honorific status of each noun phrase in a sentence, others don't; and so on and so forth. Linguists talk so often about universals that nonlinguists may be forgiven for thinking that they have a huge list of absolute universals in the bag; but in fact they have hardly any that have even been tested against all of the 5%–10% of languages for which we have good descriptions. Almost every new language that is studied falsifies some existing generalization—the serious comparative study of languages, and especially their semantic structures, is unfortunately still in its infancy.

I emphasize the range of linguistic variation because *that's the fundamentally interesting thing* about language from a comparative point of view. We are the only known species whose communication system is profoundly variable in both form and content (thus setting aside, e.g., minor dialects in bird song form; Hauser 1997, 275–276). So we can't have the same kind of theory for human communication that we have for bee or even monkey communication; fixed innate schemas are not going to give us a full explanation of language. Of course, the human innate system must be superbly equipped to expect and deal with the variation—and so it is. This is what Kuhl (1991) has so nicely shown in the realm of speech sounds, as noted above: infants, unlike monkeys, are built to specialize early in the local sound-system.

Let us now pursue the subject of special interest to this chapter: semantic variation across languages. Take the spatial domain. On first principles, this is a conceptual domain where we would least expect major semantic variation; after all, every higher animal has to be able to find its way home, and mammals share a great many specialized anatomical and neurophysiological systems dedicated to telling them where they are and where things are with respect to them. So if the Fodor, Pinker, or Gleitman story is correct anywhere, it should be so here: spatial categories in language should be direct projections of shared innate conceptual categories. But it turns out that there is not the slightest bit of evidence for this.

We may take a few simple examples of spatial concepts where universal agreement on spatial categories has been expected. Let us start with **deixis,** often presumed universal in all essentials. It has been supposed that all languages have demonstratives that make at least a contrast between 'this' and 'that', but even spoken German seems to falsify that (some German dialects arguably have no demonstratives at all, but only articles). And for languages that do have two demonstratives, it turns out that there are at least four semantic types; more generally, research shows almost as many semantic distinctions in demonstratives as languages investigated (Dunn and Meira, in preparation). Likewise, it has been supposed that all languages make a basic distinction between 'come' and 'go' verbs. But in fact not all languages handle this distinction in lexical verbs (instead, e.g., using 'hither', 'thither' particles), and, when they do, there is tremendous variation in exactly what is coded. Typically, but not always, 'go' has no deictic coding, merely pragmatically contrasting with 'come', and the 'come' verb may or may not entail arrival at the deictic center, and may or may not allow motion continued beyond this center (Wilkins and Hill 1995).

Next, let us turn to the subdomain of so-called topological spatial relations. These are relations of contact or propinquity (like English *on, at, in, near*), which, following Piaget and Inhelder (1956), have been taken to be the simplest kind of spatial relation. Landau and Jackendoff (1993) have suggested that closed-class spatial expressions in languages are highly restricted in conceptual type, referring only to "the very gross geometry of the coarsest level of representation of an object—whether it is a container or a surface" (p. 227). On the basis of English prepositions, they confidently make universal claims of the following sort: no language will have spatial relators expressing specific volumetric shapes of ground objects—for example, there will be no preposition or closed-class spatial relator *sprough* meaning 'through a cigar-shaped object' (p. 226). But the Californian language Karuk has precisely such a spatial [suffix] *-vara* 'in through a tubular space' (Mithun 1999, 142)! The whole set of claims is based on woeful ignorance of the crosslinguistic facts.

Still, however rich the rest of the semantic distinctions, it could be that every language encodes a notion precisely like English *on* and *in*. Not so: many languages fractionate these notions and indeed have much more specific notions, like 'in a hemispherical container' versus 'in a cylindrical container.' Tzeltal makes many such distinctions in spatial predicates (Brown 1994). But perhaps we simply need to qualify the claim: if a language encodes spatial relations in prepositions (or postpositions), then every such language encodes a notion precisely like English *on* or *in*. This is not remotely true either. In current work, Sergio Meira and I have mapped the adpositions (prepositions or postpositions) of a dozen languages of different stocks onto exactly the same set of 70 spatial scenes, each scene depicting a subtype of a topological relation.[1] What emerges quite clearly is that there is no basic agreement on what constitutes an 'in' scene, a spatial relation of containment, or any other basic topological relation. It is simply an empirical matter that spatial categories are almost never the same across languages, even when they are as closely related as English and Dutch.

Finally, we have also surveyed a wide sample of languages for the kinds of coordinate systems or frames of reference they use for describing the location of objects widely separated from a reference object (Levinson, 2003). In these situations, some kind of angular specification on the horizontal plane is called for—as in 'The ball is behind the tree'. It turns out that although languages vary greatly in the detailed geometry employed, there are three main families of solutions: an egocentric (or more accurately viewpoint-dependent) **relative system** (as in 'The ball is left of the tree'), a geocentric **absolute system** (as in 'The ball is north of the tree'), and an object-centered **intrinsic system** (as in 'The ball is at the front of the truck'). These three are all polar coordinate systems and constitute the best claim for universals in the spatial domain. But there are some important caveats. First, not all languages use all three systems. Rather, they form an inventory from which languages must choose at least one—all combinations are possible, except that a relative system entails an intrinsic system. That means there are languages without words for 'left' or 'right' directions, but where all spatial directions must be specified in terms of cardinal directions like 'east' (so one has to say things like 'Pass the northern cup', 'There's a fly on your northern leg', etc.). Second, as mentioned, the local instantiation of any one system may be of a unique kind. Consider for example relative systems, which if fully developed involve a 'left', 'right', 'front', 'back' set of distinctions. Now, these distinctions are very variously mapped. They involve a projection of viewer-centered coordinates onto a landmark object, so that, for example, the ball can be said to be behind the tree. In English, this projection involves a reflection of the viewer's own left-right-front-back coordinates onto (in this case) the tree, so the tree's *front* is the side facing us, and its *back* is the side away from us, but its *left* and *right* are on the same side as the viewer's. In Hausa and many other languages, this projection involves translation, so 'left' and 'right' remain as in English, but 'front' and 'back' are reversed ('The ball is behind the tree' means it is between the viewer and the tree). In some dialects of Tamil, the projection involves rotation, so 'front' and 'back' are like in English, but 'left' and 'right' are reversed. And so on and so forth—there is plenty of semantic variation. Although the choices between different frames of reference are limited, they are quite sufficient to induce the very strongest "Whorfian" effects, as described below (and see Levinson 1996; Pederson et al. 1998).

To sum up: the Simple Nativist idea (as voiced by Pinker and Gleitman) that universal concepts are directly mapped onto natural language words and morphemes, so that all a child-learner has to do is find the local name as it were, is simply false. There are vanishingly few universal notions, if any, that every language denotes with a simple expression. Even the renowned case of the color words only substantiates this fact: languages vary substantially in the number of color words they have, and what they actually denote (Kay and McDaniel 1978; Kay, Berlin, and Merrifield 1991). A term glossed as 'red' may—according to the standard theory—actually include brown, yellow, and related hues, and 'black' may include blue and green. But some languages have at best only incipient color words (Levinson 2000), and this has required substantial weakening of the standard theory (Kay and Maffi 1999). There is really no excuse for continued existence of the myth of a rich set of lexically packaged semantic universals. Removing that myth opens the way for entertaining seriously a heretical idea.

## The Very Thought: Could the Language We Speak Influence the Way We Think?

There is an ideological overtone to Simple Nativism: the independence of thought from language opens up to us the freedom of will and action ("[S]ince mental life goes on independently of particular languages, concepts of freedom and equality will be thinkable even if they are nameless" Pinker 1994, 82). So Whorfianism and **linguistic determinism** *have* to be impossible! This moral imperative is beside the point, not only because we are not in the preaching business, but also because, despite some incautious language, no one, not even Whorf, ever held that our thought was in the infernal grip of our language. Whorf's own idea was that certain grammatical patterns, through making obligatory semantic distinctions, might induce corresponding categories in habitual or nonreflective thought in just the relevant domains (see Lucy 1992b for careful exposition). Now that idea, generalized also to lexical patterns, seems neither anti-American nor necessarily false. More generally still, it seems fairly self-evident that the language one happens to speak affords, or conversely makes less accessible, certain complex concepts. There are languages with no or very few number words, and without a generative system of numerals—it seems unlikely that the speakers of such a language would ever entertain the notion 'seventy-three', let alone that of a logarithm, and certainly their fellows would never know if they did. As mentioned, there are languages that only use cardinal direction terms for spatial directions, where one must constantly be able to unerringly locate the center of a quadrant at, say, 15 degrees east of north—speakers of such languages can be shown to have a developed sense of direction of a different order of magnitude from speakers of languages that lack such constant reference to geocentric coordinates (Levinson, 2003). If they didn't have such competence, they couldn't communicate; the language affords, even requires, certain underlying computations (see "The Issues in the Light of Empirical Evidence," below). In this sort of way, languages can differentially impede, facilitate, or require underlying mental operations.

In this section, I want to show that the web of theoretical commitments we already have in the linguistic and psychological sciences seem to converge on the presumption that speaking specific languages does indeed have cognitive consequences for the speakers of those languages.

First, take the simple question "Do we think the same way that we speak?" Making various classical assumptions (e.g., accepting the notion of a *representation*), this question can reasonably be rendered as the more specific "Are the representations we use in serious nonlinguistic thinking and reasoning the very same representations that underlie linguistic meanings?" The answer, I have shown (Levinson 1997a), has to be no. The reasons are various, but conclusive: semantic representations have to be decoupled from conceptual representations to allow for various properties of linguistic meaning like deixis, anaphora, very limited lexica, linearization, and so on, which are clearly not properties of conceptual representations. Besides, there are many different kinds of conceptual representation, from the imagistic to the propositional. But there are also quite persuasive arguments to the effect that though linguistic and nonlinguistic representations are distinct, there must be at least one level of conceptual representation that is closely aligned to a semantic level; otherwise, we couldn't transform the one into the other with the facility we have, as shown by the speed of language encoding and comprehension. Further, any semantic distinctions must be supported by the underlying conceptual distinctions and processes that are necessary to compute them (if you have a lexical concept 'seven'—and not all languages do—you had better be able to count to 7 if you are going to use it correctly). So, overall, that level of conceptual representation is close to, but not identical to, a level of semantic representation.

Our next simple question is, "Do all humans think alike?" Given that there are multiple representation systems (for vision, touch, smell, etc.), many of them specialized to the sensory modalities, and given that many human sensory experiences are basically similar (given the world we all inhabit), there is no doubt that there is a broad base of "psychic unity" in the species. But we are interested in the more abstract representations in which we think and reason, which are closest to language. We can transform the basic question then into the more specific "Is the conceptual representation system closest to semantic representation universal in character?" The answer to that question is—perhaps surprisingly—almost certainly no. The answer can be derived from both first principles and empirical investigation. Here I concentrate on the reasoning from first principles, postponing the empirical arguments to the following section.

Why must the conceptual representations closest to semantic representations be nonuniversal? Because languages vary in their semantic structure, as we saw [earlier: "Linguistic Variation"]. Simply put, the fact is that there are few if any lexical concepts that universally occur in all the languages of the world; not all languages have a word (or other expression) for 'red' or 'father' or 'in' or 'come' or even 'if'. Now the consequences of that basic fact are easily enough appreciated. Let us pursue a *reductio*. We have established that semantic representations map fairly directly, but not exactly, onto the closest level of conceptual representation (CR). Assume now that CR is universal. Then, allowing for some slippage, semantic representations (SR) must be roughly universal too. But they are not. Therefore, we must abandon the assumption that CR is universal.

Approaching the problem from the other direction, we know that languages code different concepts at the lexical level. Now assume—as Fodor and many psychologists do—that corresponding to a lexical item is a single holistic concept (Fodor, Fodor, and Garrett 1975). Further assume, as they do, that SR and CR are coextensive. Then, since we think in CR, users of different languages think differently. So, it follows that "nondecompositionalists" (i.e., those who do not think that lexical concepts decompose into subconcepts) are implicit Whorfians—a fact that they do not seem to have appreciated.[2]

Linguists tend to be decompositionalists—they tend to think that lexical concepts are complex, composed out of atomic concepts. Naturally, they are not always so naive about semantic variation as the psychologists. But they think they can escape the immediate Whorfian consequence: languages encode different concepts at the lexical level, but they "compose" those semantical concepts from a universal inventory of atomic concepts. Even assuming that SR and CR are closely related, as seems to be the case, it no longer seems to follow that different languages require different conceptual relations, or that speaking a language would induce different ways of thinking: both SR and CR could be universal at the level of conceptual primes or primitives. So we can cook our varied semantic cakes out of the same old universal flour and sugar.

Though I am sympathetic with the decompositional move, it is hardly the intellectual triumph that it may seem. Suppose I hypothesize a universal inventory of 20 or 100 primes, and now I come across a language that has words that won't decompose into those primes. What will I do? Add to the universal inventory the features we need for that language, of course. So what makes them universal? At least one language uses them! How would you falsify such a theory? There isn't any way to falsify a theory of universals that consists in an augmentable list of features that any one language may freely select from. It's the weakest possible kind of theory—it would need to be supplemented with a theory that tells us why *just those features* and no others are in the inventory, and we are in no position to do that because we have as yet no idea of the real extent of semantic variation.

But there's another problem with decomposition. Psycholinguistic evidence shows that when words are activated, the concept as a whole is activated, not little bits of it. And the psychologists have compelling evidence that we don't think at that atomic level—we think at the macrolevel of conceptual wholes, the level reflected in lexical concepts. The reasons for this lie partly in properties of short-term memory, the major bottleneck in our computing system. For short-term memory is limited to, say, five chunks at a time, while not caring a jot about how complex the underlying chunks are—or, put another way, what they can be decomposed into (Miller 1956; Cowan 2001). We don't have to think about a *hundred* as 'ten tens' when doing mental arithmetic, or *aunt* as 'mother's sister, or father's sister, or father's brother's wife, or mother's brother's wife' when greeting Aunt Mathilda. Composing complex concepts gives enormous power to our mental computations, and most of those complex concepts are inherited from the language we happen to speak. So the linguists are wrong to think that lexical decomposition will let them off the Whorfian hook. Sure, it allows them to hold a remoter level of universal concepts, and it might help to explain how we can learn complex cultural concepts, but the conceptual level closest to the semantic representations, and the level in which we compute, seems likely to be heavily culture specific.

So, given the facts of semantic variation, and what we know about mental computation, it is hard to escape the conclusion that, yes, the ways we speak—the kinds of concepts lexically or grammatically encoded in a specific language—are bound to have an effect on the ways we think. And this conclusion is going to be general over all the different kinds of theory scholars are likely to espouse: noncompositional or compositional representational theories, and equally of course connectionist theories, where activation patterns are a direct reflection of input patterns.

## The Issues in the Light of Empirical Evidence

So now at last we might be prepared to accept the idea that it is worth empirically investigating the kinds of influence a specific language might have on our mental coding of scenes and events, our nonlinguistic memory and inference. In fact, there is already a quite impressive body of evidence that demonstrates significant effects here. I will review a few examples, concentrating on our own work.

Curiously enough, the color work in the tradition of Berlin and Kay (1969), which has been taken to indicate simple universals of lexical coding, has also yielded evidence for the impact of linguistic categories on memory and perceptual discriminations. As noted above, the lexical universals are of a conditional sort; for example, if a language has just three color words, one will cover the "cool" range (black, green, blue), another the "warm" range (red, yellow, orange), and another the "bright" range (white, pink, pale blue, etc.) (see Kay and McDaniel 1978). So it is easy to find languages that differ in their color coding. Lenneberg and Roberts (1956) had earlier shown that having specific terms for, say, 'yellow' versus 'orange', helped English speakers memorize colors, compared to Zuni speakers who have no such lexical discrimination. Lucy (1981) showed similar effects for Yucatec versus Spanish versus English speakers, and Davidoff, Davies, and Roberson (1999) did the same for English versus Berinmo. Kay and Kempton (1984) explored the effects of linguistic coding on perceptual discriminability and found that if a language like English discriminates 'blue' and 'green', while another like Tarahumara does not, English speakers but not Tarahumara speakers will exaggerate the perceptual differences on the boundary. This suggests that our visual perception may be biased by linguistic categorization just as our auditory perception clearly is by the specific phonemes in a language (which is why of course late second language learners have difficulty perceiving and producing the alien speech sounds).

Turning to our own work, in a large-scale, long-term collaborative enterprise involving two score researchers, we have researched linguistic differences in the spatial domain. Our goals have been first, to understand the linguistic differences here, and second, to then explore the relation of those linguistic differences to nonlinguistic cognition. I have already outlined above some of the quite surprising linguistic differences to be found across languages; in general, it is hard to find any pair of spatial descriptors with the same denotation across languages (see, e.g., Levinson and Wilkins 2006). In the subdomain of frames of reference, we have pursued the nonlinguistic correlates in detail. The following is a synopsis of much detailed work (see Levinson 1996, 1997b, 2003; Pederson et al. 1998; and references therein).

As mentioned above, languages make different use of the three basic frames of reference. Some languages, like English or other European languages, employ the relative frame of reference (involving left/right/front/back terms projected from a viewpoint) along with the intrinsic (involving properties of the landmark or reference object, e.g., its intrinsic top, back, sides, etc.). Other languages, like Tzeltal or Arrernte, use no relative frame of reference, but instead supplement an intrinsic system with an absolute one—that is, a cardinal-direction type system. In languages like these, speakers can't say 'Pass me the cup to your left', or 'Take the first right', or 'He's hiding behind the tree'—the relevant spatial expressions simply don't exist. Instead, they have to say 'Pass me the cup to the west', or 'Take the first turn to the south', or 'He's hiding east of the tree', as appropriate. Such cardinal-direction systems are actually quite diverse (e.g., they may have arbitrary directions unrelated to the earth's poles) and are always different from the English speaker's use of map coordinates (e.g., in the English system there is no linguistic convention about how many degrees on either side of grid-north still constitutes 'north', and English speakers only use this system on a geographic scale).

We made the following predictions. First, speakers of languages with absolute coordinates should have a better sense of direction than speakers of relative languages: they not only have to know where, say, 'south' is at any one moment (otherwise they couldn't speak the language), but they also need to know, for example, that place B is south of A, because they may have a verb 'go-south' properly used for any motion from A to B. We transported people from three absolute communities to novel locations and got them to point to a range of other locations at varying distances. They can do this with remarkable accuracy, but speakers of relative languages cannot (Levinson 2003). We have also examined unreflective gesture while speaking: for absolute speakers, gestures to places are geographically accurate; for relative speakers, are not. Second, we supposed that speakers of absolute languages would have to maintain internal representations of space in terms of fixed bearings, rather than egocentric coordinates. That is because if memories were coded in egocentric coordinates, there would be no way to describe them in the relevant language: there is no translation algorithm from egocentric coordinates to geocentric ones, or vice versa (you can't get from the description 'The knife was north of the fork' to the description 'The knife was left of the fork', or vice versa). Since one might want to talk about any observed situation, it had better be memorized in coordinates appropriate to the language. To test this, we invented a rotation paradigm, with which it is possible to distinguish nonlinguistic mental coding in any of the frames of reference. For example, subjects see an arrow on a table pointing to their left, or south. They are now rotated 180 degrees and are asked to place the arrow on another table so it is just as before. If they point it to their left, they thought about it in terms of egocentric coordinates; if to their right (i.e., south), in geocentric coordinates. This paradigm allows examination of different psychological capacities, and we designed a battery of tests exploring recognition memory, recall, and inference of different kinds, all conducted under rotation. The tasks were carried out in four relative and six absolute language communities. The results are quite startling: overwhelmingly, subjects follow the coding pattern in their language when performing these entirely nonlinguistic tasks (Levinson 1996, 2003).

We find these results to be convincing evidence that linguistic coding is both a facilitator of a specific cognitive style and a bottleneck, constraining mental representations in line with the output modality. It seems that preferred frames of reference in language deeply affect our mental life. They affect the kind of mental coding of spatial relations in memory, and the way in which we reason about space, since the different frames of reference have different logical properties (see Levinson 1996). They affect the kinds of mental maps we maintain (as shown by the navigation experiments mentioned above), even the kind of mental imagery we use when we gesture. These are anything but superficial correlates of a mode of linguistic coding.

In a recent paper, Li and Gleitman (2002) try to resist these conclusions and reassert a Simple Nativist perspective. They carried out one simplified version of one of our tasks with an American student population and claimed that they could induce absolute or relative coding by manipulating the conditions of the task. First, the task yielded a relative result indoors, but a mixed relative/absolute result outdoors. Second, by placing salient landmarks or spatial cues at alternate ends of the stimulus and response tables, subjects could be made to construct the response in line with the landmark cue. Li and Gleitman conclude that we all think equally in relative or absolute frames of reference; it just depends on the conditions under which one coding system or another becomes more appropriate. Unfortunately, their results are either not replicable (the outdoors condition) or betray a misunderstanding of the nature of the three frames of reference (the landmark cues condition). When they used salient spatial cues on the stimulus and response tables, what they were actually doing was invoking a response in the intrinsic frame of reference, not the absolute one. We showed this by reproducing their experiment and introducing a new condition: subjects were now rotated 90 degrees instead of 180 degrees (Levinson et al. 2002). If you see a row of animals headed leftward, or south, on table 1 toward a jug, and are then rotated to face table 2 at 90 degrees, and are asked to place the animals just as they were (with an emphasis on remembering which animals were in which order), a response that preserves them heading left or heading south or heading toward the jug can easily be distinguished. English- or Dutch-speaking subjects will place the animals so they are heading either left (relative) or toward the jug (intrinsic), not south (absolute). That's because English and Dutch offer both the relative and intrinsic frames of reference—although the relative is dominant, as can be shown by increasing the memory load (e.g., by adding to the number of animals), whereupon the relative is selected over the intrinsic. In short, pace Li and Gleitman, the evidence remains that the frames of reference used in people's language match those used in their nonlinguistic cognition.

There are many other results that support the idea that linguistic coding has an effect on nonlinguistic cognition. Special mention should be made of the work of John Lucy (1992a; see also Lucy and Gaskins, 2003), which demonstrates that the original ideas of Whorf can be verified—namely, the idea that grammatical patterning with semantic correlates may have an especially powerful effect on implicit categorization. English has obligatory number marking (singular vs. plural) on countable nominals, while Yucatec has only optional number marking, mostly only on animates. Following the hypothesis that this insistent number marking in English might have nonlinguistic effects, Lucy showed that English speakers are better at remembering number in nonlinguistic stimuli. In work with Suzanne Gaskins, he has gone on to show that this lack of number marking in Yucatec is associated with nominals whose semantics are unspecified for quantificational unit (Lucy and Gaskins 2001). They tend to denote not bounded units, but essence or "stuff"; thus, the term used for 'banana' actually denotes any entity made of banana-essence (e.g., the tree or the leaf or the fruit). On sorting tasks, Yucatec speakers behave differently than English speakers: English speakers tend to sort by shape or function, Yucatec speakers by the material out of which things are made. The suggestion is that the pattern in the grammar has far-reaching correlations with implicit mental categories.

## Conclusion

Where are we? I have tried to establish that (1) languages vary in their semantics just as they do in their form, (2) semantic differences are bound to engender cognitive differences, (3) these cognitive correlates of semantic differences can be empirically found on a widespread basis. As a consequence, the semantic version of Simple Nativism ought to be as dead as a dodo. But it isn't.

Why not? One reason is that its proponents think they have an argument that it *just has to be right,* so no negative evidence will be seriously entertained! The argument of course is a learnability argument. Consider what the poor child has to do: find the meaning corresponding to some acoustic signal—the child must segment the signal, find the word forms, and then hypothesize the meanings. Suppose, as Fodor, Pinker, and Gleitman hold, that the child is already provided with the relevant conceptual bundles; then all she has to do is map strings of phonemes to ready-made conceptual bundles. This is already difficult, since there are lots of those bundles. Now, suppose the picture was radically different, and the child had to construct the bundles—not a chance! Even worse, suppose that the child has not only to construct the possible meanings for words, but even to figure out how the adults *think*, since they think differently in different cultures. Now the child first has to learn the local cognitive style, and then construct the relevant meanings in line with the cognitive style, before finally being in a position to map the acoustics onto the meanings. The picture is hopeless—Simple Nativism just has to be right!

We can disarm this argument (but see Levinson 2001 for the full counterargument). First, the Fodorean picture doesn't really help. If languages only label antecedently existing concepts, the set of those concepts must include every possible concept lexicalizable in every possible language—a billion or more to be sure. So how will knowing that the needle is already in the haystack help the child find the one correct concept to match to a particular acoustic wave? Second, the picture of the child thumbing through her innate lexicon to find the right antecedently existing concept is surely absurd in the first place; once the lexicon gets to any size at all, it will be much easier to construct the concept than to find it. What the child is going to do is try and figure out what those peculiar adults or elder siblings are really preoccupied with. She will use every clue provided to her, and there are plenty. And some of the most valuable clues will be provided in many different ways by the fact that the adults *think* in a way tightly consistent with the semantics of the language they speak. For example, suppose the adults speak a language where the relative frame of reference predominates. Every aspect of the environment will reflect that fact—the way doors or books open, the arrangement of things (knife always to the right of the fork, socks in the left drawer), the nature of gesture (pointing to the side the referent was on when they were looking at it, not where it actually is from here now), the preferred side of the sidewalk they choose to walk on. In contrast, suppose the adults speak a language where the absolute frame of reference predominates. Now they won't care about preserving egocentric constancies; they will only care that one sleeps with one's head always to the north, builds windbreaks to the east, and, when pointing, points in the veridical direction. A thousand little details of the built environment and, more importantly, the conduct of interaction (see Tomasello 2003) will inform the discerning toddler again and again till she gets the message. It is just *because* we think in line with how we speak, that the clues are not all in the language but are distributed throughout the context of language learning. This new picture doesn't banish the puzzles of how children perform the incredible feat of learning a language, but one thing is certain: it doesn't make it any *more* of an impossible feat than it was on the old picture given to us by the Simple Nativists.

So the overall message is that Simple Nativism has outlived its utility; it blocks a proper understanding of the biological roots of language, it introduces incoherence into our theory, it blinds us to the reality of linguistic variation and discourages interesting research on the language-cognition interface. As far as its semantic tenets go, it is simply false—semantic variation across languages is rich in every detail. We don't map words onto antecedently existing concepts, we build them according to need. That's why cognitive development in children exists, and why the history of science shows progress. The reason we have a developed vocabulary (instead of the limited repertoire of other animals) is that we have found it helps us to *think*. How it does that is explained by that foundational cornerstone of cognitive psychology, Miller's (1956) theory of recoding as a method of increasing computational power by getting around the bottleneck of short-term memory (see Cowan 2001 for an update). Linguistically motivated concepts are food for thought.

## Notes

1. The scenes were devised by Melissa Bowerman, with additions by Eric Pederson, and are available as the stimulus set Topological Relations Picture Series of the Max Planck Institute for Psycholinguistics, Nijmegen. For a preliminary report, see the Annual Report 2001, Max Planck Institute for Psycholinguistics (<http://www.mpi.nl>).

2. Fodor himself adopts the only way out of this dilemma, which is to say that every lexical concept in every language that ever has been and ever will be is already sitting there in our heads. So Cro-Magnon man already had the notions 'neutrino' and 'piano', but probably hadn't gotten around to giving them phonetic form!

## References


Austin, P., and Bresnan, J. 1996. Non-configurationality in Australian Aboriginal languages. *Natural Language and Linguistic Theory* 14: 215–68.

Berlin, B., and Kay, P. 1969. *Basic color terms: Their universality and evolution.* Berkeley and Los Angeles: University of California Press.

Bowerman, M., and Choi, S. 2003. Space under construction: Language-specific spatial categorization in first language acquisition. In D. Gentner and S. Goldin-Meadow (Eds.), *Language in mind: Advances in the study of language and thought* (pp. 387–427). Cambridge, MA, and London: MIT Press.

Bowerman, M., and Levinson, S. C. (Eds.). 2001. *Language acquisition and conceptual development.* Cambridge: Cambridge University Press.

Brown, P. 1994. The INs and ONs of Tzeltal locative expressions: The semantics of static descriptions of location. *Linguistics* 32: 743–90.

Choi, S., McDonough, L., Mandler, J., and Bowerman, M. (2000, May). *Development of language-specific semantic categories of spatial relations: From prelinguistic to linguistic stage.* Paper presented at the workshop "Finding the Words." Stanford University.

Cowan, N. 2001. The magical number 4 in short-term memory: A reconsideration of mental storage capacity. *Behavioral and Brain Sciences* 24: 87–114.

Davidoff, J., Davies, I., and Roberson, D. 1999. Colour in a Stone-Age tribe. *Nature* 398: 203–04.

Dunn, M., and Meira, S. In preparation. *Demonstratives in use.*

Durham, W. 1991. *Coevolution.* Stanford, CA: Stanford University Press.

Fodor, A. J. 1975. *The language of thought.* New York: Crowell.

Fodor, J. D., Fodor, J. A., and Garrett, M. F. 1975. The unreality of semantic representations. *Linguistic Inquiry* 6: 515–31.

Greenberg, J. 1986. On being a linguistic anthropologist. *Annual Review of Anthropology* 15: 1–24.

Hauser, M. 1997. *The evolution of communication.* Cambridge, MA: MIT Press.

Kay, P., Berlin, B., and Merrifield, W. 1991. Biocultural implications of systems of color naming. *Journal of Linguistic Anthropology* 1: 12–25.

Kay, P., and Kempton, W. 1984. What is the Sapir-Whorf hypothesis? *American Anthropologist* 86: 65–79.

Kay, P., and Maffi, L. 1999. Color appearance and the emergence and evolution of basic color lexicons. *American Anthropologist* 101: 743–60.

Kay, P., and McDaniel, C. K. 1978. The linguistic significance of the meanings of basic color terms. *Language,* 54: 610–46.

Kuhl, P. 1991. Perception, cognition and the ontogenetic and phylogenetic emergence of human speech. In S. E. Brauth, W. S. Hall, and R. J. Dooling (Eds.), *Plasticity of development* (pp. 73–106). Cambridge, MA: MIT Press.

Kuhl, P., and Meltzoff, A. N. 1996. Infant vocalizations in response to speech: Vocal imitation and developmental change. *Journal of the Acoustical Society of America,* 100: 2425–438.

Kuhl, P. K., and Meltzoff, A. N. 1997. Evolution, nativism and learning in the development of language and speech. In M. Gopnik (Ed.), *The inheritance and innateness of grammars* (pp. 7–44). New York: Oxford University Press.

Landau, B., and Jackendoff, R. 1993. "What" and "where" in spatial language and spatial cognition. *Behavioral and Brain Sciences* 16: 217–38.

Lenneberg, E., and Roberts, J. 1956. *The language of experience: A study in methodology.* Memoir 13. Indiana University Publications in Anthropology and Linguistics. Baltimore, MD: Waverly Press.

Levinson, S. C. 1987. Pragmatics and the grammar of anaphora. *Journal of Linguistics* 23: 379–434.

Levinson, S. C. 1996. Frames of reference and Molyneux's question: Cross-linguistic evidence. In P. Bloom, M. Peterson, L. Nadel, and M. Garrett (Eds.), *Language and space* (pp. 109–69). Cambridge, MA: MIT Press.

Levinson, S. C. 1997a. From outer to inner space: Linguistic categories and non-linguistic thinking. In J. Nuyts and E. Pederson (Eds.), *Language and conceptualization* (pp. 13–45). Cambridge: Cambridge University Press.

Levinson, S. C. 1997b. Language and cognition: The cognitive consequences of spatial description in Guugu Yimithirr. *Journal of Linguistic Anthropology* 7: 98–131.

Levinson, S. C. (2000). Language as nature and language as art. In R. Hide, J. Mittelstrass, and W. Singer (Eds.), *Changing concepts of nature and the turn of the millennium* (pp. 257–87). Vatican City: Pontifical Academy of Science.

Levinson, S. C. 2001. Covariation between spatial language and cognition, and its implications for language learning. In M. Bowerman and S. C. Levinson (Eds.), *Language acquisition and conceptual development* (pp. 566–88). Cambridge: Cambridge University Press.

Levinson, S. C. 2003. *Space in language and cognition: Explorations in cognitive diversity*. Cambridge: Cambridge University Press.

Levinson, S. C., Kita, S., Haun, D., and Rasch, B. 2002. Returning the tables: Language affects spatial reasoning. *Cognition* 84: 155–88.

Levinson, S. C., and Wilkins, D. (Eds.). 2006. *Grammars of space*. Cambridge: Cambridge University Press.

Li, P., and Gleitman, L. 2002. Turning the tables: Language and spatial reasoning. *Cognition* 83: 265–94.

Lucy, J. 1981. *Cultural factors in memory for color: The problem of language usage*. Paper presented at AAA.

Lucy, J. 1992a. *Grammatical categories and cognition: A case study of the linguistic relativity hypothesis*. Cambridge: Cambridge University Press.

Lucy, J. 1992b. *Language diversity and thought: A reformulation of the linguistic relativity hypothesis*. Cambridge: Cambridge University Press.

Lucy, J., and Gaskins, S. 2001. Grammatical categories and the development of classification preferences: A comparative approach. In M. Bowerman and S. C. Levinson (Eds.), *Language acquisition and conceptual development* (pp. 257–83). Cambridge: Cambridge University Press.

Lucy, J., and Gaskins, S. 2003. Interaction of language type and referent type in the development of nonverbal classification preferences. In D. Gentner and S. Goldin-Meadow (Eds.), *Language in mind: Advances in the study of language and thought* (pp. 465–92). Cambridge, MA, and London: MIT Press.

Maddieson, I. 1984. *Patterns of sounds*. Cambridge: Cambridge University Press.

McDonough, L., Choi, S., and Mandler, J. 2003. Understanding spatial relations: Flexible infants, lexical adults. *Cognitive Psychology* 46(3): 229–59.

Miller, G. A. 1956. The magical number seven, plus or minus two: Some limits on our capacity for processing information. *Psychological Review* 63: 81–97.

Mithun, M. 1999. *The languages of Native North America*. Cambridge: Cambridge University Press.

Pederson, E., Danziger, E., Wilkins, D., Levinson, S., Kita, S., and Senft, G. 1998. Semantic typology and spatial conceptualization. *Language*, 74: 557–89.

Piaget, J., and Inhelder, B. 1956. [1948] *The child's conception of space*. London: Routledge and Kegan Paul.

Pinker, S. 1994. *The language instinct*. New York: Morrow.

Tomasello, M. 2003. The key is social cognition. In D. Gentner and S. Goldin-Meadow (Eds.), *Language in mind: Advances in the study of language and thought* (pp. 47–57). Cambridge, MA, and London: MIT Press.

Tooby, J., and Cosmides, L. 1992. The psychological foundations of culture. In J. H. Barkow, L. Cosmides, and J. Tooby (Eds.), *The adapted mind* (pp. 19–136). Oxford: Oxford University Press.

Wilkins, D., and Hill, D. 1995. When 'GO' means 'COME': Questioning the basicness of basic motion verbs. *Cognitive Linguistics* 6: 209–59.

## Critical Thinking and Application

- Consider the two primary approaches to the study of language origins that Levinson outlines: Simple Nativism and the coevolutionary account. Be sure you understand how they differ, especially with regard to language universals and diversity. How does each approach explain linguistic and cultural diversity? Is biological evolution an appropriate analogy for language? Compare the two approaches to the views of the nature of language in Unit 1.
- What did Levinson's own work with frames of reference show?
- Try to carry out one of Levinson's experiments. Compare your results to his claims.

## Vocabulary

absolute coordinate system
aspect
cognitive sciences
constituent structure
deixis
innate
intrinsic coordinate system
linguistic determinism
morphology
nativism
phoneme
relative coordinate system
Simple Nativism
syntax
visual-manual
vocal-auditory
Whorfianism

## Suggested Further Reading [See also list following Language and Thought unit introduction]

Levinson, Stephen C. 2003. *Space in Language and Cognition: Explorations in Cognitive Diversity*. Cambridge: Cambridge University Press.

Levinson, Stephen C., and David Wilkins, eds. 2006. *Grammars of Space: Explorations in Cognitive Diversity*. Cambridge: Cambridge University Press.

# UNIT 4

# Language Socialization

How children learn language has long been a research focus in linguistics, anthropology, and psychology under the rubric of *language acquisition*, often part of *psycholinguistics*. In this guise, it is regarded as an individual's natural endowment, needing to be "triggered" by exposure to data. Noam Chomsky convincingly demonstrated, through an argument known as "the poverty of the stimulus," that it was not possible for children to learn language through standard classical conditioning, such as reinforcement, or behaviorist approaches, as people like B. F. Skinner had proposed. Rather, there had to be something already present in the brain. Children were not presented with well-formed sentences, he argued. Further, they produced sentences such as *Me goed* that they had never heard before. This showed that the children were creating theories about what they heard, such as: *past tense equals verb plus {-ed}* (in English). Chomsky wrote of the Language Acquisition Device, a part of the brain somehow devoted to the learning of language, which came naturally to all humans (of normal intelligence and hearing etc.). The actual physical workings of mind were left to others to discover.

Using this paradigm, from the 1960s until the 1980s, much subtle, careful, powerful research on language acquisition was conducted. This was part of Chomskyan linguistics, generative linguistics, and defined the field. *Universal Grammar* (UG) was assumed to be part of the human mental endowment, part of mind; it simply had to be activated so that the appropriate specific language could be selected, but the details of specific and different languages were deemed uninteresting.

At the same time, another approach to children learning language was developing, most notably under the pen of Elinor Ochs and Bambi Schieffelin. They named this approach *language socialization*, which they explained as examining how children were socialized *into* and *through* language. In this sense, language was no longer an individual capability but rather something that involved social groups. Language socialization studies tended to uncover not the uniformities and universals that work on language acquisition had demonstrated but rather cultural variation. It turned out that many assumptions, such as that mothers focused on their babies' talk (equating *baby talk* and *motherese* and *caregiver registers*), were not observed everywhere. There was an enormous range of people involved in even young babies' care, from young siblings to grandparents to "allomothers." Sometimes children were attended to, and other times they were ignored. Sometimes children were addressed with simplified language, and other times they were not addressed at all. In every society, however, children learned the language expected of them and the ways to use it appropriately.

This research program was also hugely productive. Scholars went all around the globe studying the ways children were incorporated into social lives. Since the 1980s, a rich body of scholarship has been published examining language socialization beyond the first few years and extending into adolescence and beyond, as well as looking at language socialization among bilingual and multilingual populations. An especially exciting line of inquiry is in literacy and schooling. In many of these research projects, the unit of study is not the isolated individual but activity engaged in by a "community of practice."

Much of the research, thus, intersects with that on other rich topics, such as the nature of community, identity, power, relationships, and more. As with any study of language, it is strongest when seen in its fullest human, dynamic context. And the work on language socialization demonstrates the full range of human meaning, thus illuminating clearly several perspectives on the nature of language.

## Suggested Further Reading

Besnier, Niko. 1995. *Literacy, Emotion, and Authority: Reading and Writing on a Polynesian Atoll.* Cambridge: Cambridge University Press.

Bloom, Paul. 2000. *How Children Learn the Meanings of Words.* Cambridge, MA: MIT Press.

Blum-Kulka, Shoshana. 1997. *Dinner Talk: Cultural Patterns of Sociability and Socialization in Family Discourse.* Mahwah, NJ: Erlbaum.

Bowerman, Melissa, and Stephen C. Levinson. 2001. *Language Acquisition and Conceptual Development.* Cambridge and New York: Cambridge University Press.

Brown, Roger. 1973. *A First Language: The Early Years.* Cambridge, MA: Harvard University Press.

Chomsky, Noam. 1959. A Review of B. F. Skinner's *Verbal Behavior. Language* 35(1): 26–58.

Clark, Herbert H., and Eve V. Clark. 1977. *Psychology and Language.* New York: Harcourt Brace Jovanovich.

Collins, James. 1995. Literacy and Literacies. *Annual Review of Anthropology* 24: 75–93.

De Villiers, Jill G., and Peter A. De Villiers. 1978. *Language Acquisition.* Cambridge, MA: Harvard University Press.

Duff, Patricia, and Nancy H. Hornberger. 2008. *Language Socialization.* 2nd ed. New York: Springer.

Dunn, Cynthia D. 1999. Coming of Age in Japan: Language Ideology and the Acquisition of Formal Speech Registers. In *Language and Ideology: Selected Papers from the Sixth International Pragmatics Conference*, edited by Jef Verschueren, 1: 89–97. Antwerp: International Pragmatics Association.

Ferguson, Charles A., and Dan Slobin. 1973. *Studies of Child Language Development.* New York: Holt, Rinehart & Winston.

Garrett, Paul B., and Patricia Baquedano-López. 2002. Language Socialization: Reproduction and Continuity, Transformation and Change. *Annual Review of Anthropology* 31: 339–361.

Goodwin, Marjorie H. 1990. *He-Said-She-Said: Talk as Social Organization Among Black Children.* Bloomington: Indiana University Press.

Heath, Shirley Brice. 1983. *Ways with Words: Language, Life, and Work in Communities and in Classrooms.* Cambridge: Cambridge University Press.

Kramsch, Claire J. 2002. *Language Acquisition and Language Socialization: Ecological Perspectives.* London and New York: Continuum.

Larson, Karen A. 1985. *Learning Without Lessons: Socialization and Language Change in Norway.* Lanham, MD: University Press of America.

Lee, Namhee. 2009. *The Interactional Instinct: The Evolution and Acquisition of Language.* New York: Oxford University Press.

McCune, Lorraine. 2008. *How Children Learn to Learn Language.* New York: Oxford University Press.

Mendoza-Denton, Norma. 2008. *Homegirls: Language and Cultural Practice Among Latina Youth Gangs.* Malden, MA: Blackwell.

Ochs, Elinor. 1988. *Culture and Language Development: Language Acquisition and Socialization in a Samoan Village.* New York: Cambridge University Press.

Rampton, Ben. 1995. *Crossing: Language and Ethnicity Among Adolescents.* London: Longman.

Piaget, Jean, and Noam Chomsky. 1980. *Language and Learning: The Debate Between Jean Piaget and Noam Chomsky.* Cambridge, MA: Harvard University Press.

Rymes, Betsy. 2001. *Conversational Borderlands: Language and Identity in an Urban Alternative High School.* New York: Teachers College Press.

Schieffelin, Bambi I. 1990. *The Give and Take of Everyday Life: Language Socialization of Kaluli Children.* Cambridge and New York: Cambridge University Press.

Schieffelin, Bambi B., and Elinor Ochs, eds. 1986. Language Socialization. *Annual Review of Anthropology* 15: 163–191.

Schieffelin, Bambi B., and Elinor Ochs. 1986. *Language Socialization Across Cultures.* Cambridge and New York: Cambridge University Press.

Tomasello, Michael. 2003. *Constructing a Language: A Usage-Based Theory of Language Acquisition.* Cambridge, MA: Harvard University Press.

Tomlinson, Brian. 2007. *Language Acquisition and Development: Studies of Learners of First and Other Languages.* London and New York: Continuum.

Wenger, Etienne. 1998. *Communities of Practice: Learning, Meaning, and Identity.* Cambridge: Cambridge University Press.

Zentella, Ana Celia. 1997. *Growing Up Bilingual: Puerto Rican Children in New York.* Malden, MA: Blackwell.

# CHAPTER 9

# Language Acquisition and Socialization: Three Developmental Stories and Their Implications

*Elinor Ochs and Bambi B. Schieffelin*

(1984)

*Elinor Ochs and Bambi Schieffelin essentially invented the field of* language socialization, *consolidating lines of inquiry that had been conducted by many researchers over time but without any sense that they were embarking on a common research platform. Ochs and Schieffelin brought together questions about cultural variation, households and families, language acquisition, human development, and power, demonstrating that all these components had to be studied if we were to genuinely understand how the young were socialized into their own particular social world. Granting some degree of universal biological and psychological commonality, they nonetheless showed that without a serious commitment to the empirical study of how children are socialized across the world, it is premature to make claims about how language is socialized.*

*The chapter presented here derives from their own combined experience in studying children in Papua New Guinea (Kaluli) and Western Samoa, as well as studies of white, middle-class American children, showing strong contrasts in many aspects of their lives with and beyond language. This is anthropology at its best: showing that assumptions must be challenged because, if we look outside our own world, we find people doing things differently. Children have to learn to speak—and all children, essentially, do—but their relations with their caregivers, their daily activities, their interactions with and without language—all this is breathtakingly variable. Simply taking these three societies as an indication of potential human variation, we see that we must continue to ask how little people are treated and what the expectations are for language and other symbolic interactions.*

## Reading Questions

- Before you read the chapter, think about what you consider normal or ideal in terms of interacting with very young children. Where did your model come from?
- Be sure you understand the contrasts in these three societies in terms of:
  - baby-talk register
  - babies as conversational partners
  - interpretation, if any, of preverbal expressions
  - verbal environment
  - questions asked of preschoolers
  - caregivers' guesses, if any, of infants' intentions
  - explicit and direct linguistic instruction
  - talk used primarily for...
  - gender differences in language socialization
  - housing
  - sleeping

Elinor Ochs and Bambi B. Schieffelin. Language Acquisition and Socialization: Three Developmental Stories and Their Implications. In *Culture Theory: Essays on Mind, Self, and Emotion*, edited by Richard A. Shweder and Robert A. LeVine. New York: Cambridge University Press, 1984. pp. 276–320.

- baby-carrying position
- number of participants in typical conversations
- direction of accommodation
- How do the authors draw on social interactions beyond language in their explanation of what occurs with language? Could they convincingly make the case if they studied linguistic interactions, say, from a transcript of the words spoken? Why or why not?

---

This chapter addresses the relationship between communication and culture from the perspective of the *acquisition of* language and socialization *through language*. Heretofore the processes of language acquisition and socialization have been considered as two separate domains. Processes of language acquisition are usually seen as relatively unaffected by cultural factors such as social organization and local belief systems. These factors have been largely treated as "context," something that is *separable* from language and its acquisition. A similar attitude has prevailed in anthropological studies of socialization. The language used both *by* children and *to* children in social interactions has rarely been a source of information on socialization. As a consequence, we know little about the role that language plays in the acquisition and transmission of sociocultural knowledge. Neither the forms, the functions, nor the message content of language have been documented and examined for the ways in which they *organize* and *are organized by* culture.

Our own backgrounds in cultural anthropology and language development have led us to a more integrated perspective. Having carried out research on language in several societies (Malagasy, Bolivian, white-middle-class American, Kaluli [Papua New Guinea], and Western Samoan), focusing on the language of children and their **caregivers** in three of them (white middle-class American, Kaluli, Western Samoan), we have seen that the primary concern of caregivers is to ensure that their children are able to display and understand behaviors appropriate to social situations. A major means by which this is accomplished is through language. Therefore, we must examine the language of caregivers primarily for its socializing functions, rather than for only its strict grammatical input function. Further, we must examine the prelinguistic and linguistic behaviors of children to determine the ways they are continually and selectively affected by values and beliefs held by those members of society who interact with them. What a child says, and how he or she says it, will be influenced by local cultural processes in addition to biological and social processes that have universal scope. The perspective we adopt is expressed in the following two claims:

1. The process of acquiring language is deeply affected by the process of becoming a competent member of a society.
2. The process of becoming a competent member of society is realized to a large extent through language, by acquiring knowledge of its functions, social distribution, and interpretations in and across socially defined situations, i.e., through exchanges of language in particular social situations.

In this chapter, we will support these claims through a comparison of social development as it relates to the communicative development of children in three societies: Anglo-American white middle class, Kaluli, and Samoan. We will present specific theoretical arguments and methodological procedures for an ethnographic approach to the development of language. Our focus at this point cannot be comprehensive, and therefore we will address developmental research that has its interests and roots in language development rather than anthropological studies of socialization. For current socialization literature, the reader is recommended to see Briggs 1970; Gallimore, Boggs, & Jordon 1974; Geertz 1959; Hamilton 1981; Harkness & Super 1980; Korbin 1978; Leiderman, Tulkin, & Rosenfeld 1977; LeVine 1980; Levy 1973; Mead & MacGregor 1951; Mead & Wolfenstein 1955; Montagu 1978; Munroe & Munroe 1975; Richards 1974; Wagner & Stevenson 1982; Weisner & Gallimore 1977; Whiting 1963; Whiting & Whiting 1975; Williams 1969; and Wills 1977.

## Approaches to Communicative Development

Whereas interest in language structure and use has been a timeless concern, the child as a language user is a relatively recent focus of scholarly interest. This interest has been located primarily in the fields of linguistics and psychology, with the wedding of the two in the establishment of developmental psycholinguistics as a legitimate academic specialization. The concern here has been the relation of language to thought, both in terms of conceptual categories and in terms of cognitive processes (such as perception, memory, recall). The child has become one source for establishing just what that relation is. More specifically, the language of the child has been examined in terms of the following issues:

1. The relation between the relative complexity of conceptual categories and the linguistic structures produced and understood by young language-learning children at different developmental stages (Bloom 1970, 1973; Bowerman 1977, 1981; Brown 1973; Clark 1974; Clark & Clark 1977; Greenfield & Smith 1976; Karmiloff-Smith 1979; MacNamara 1972; Nelson 1974; Schlessinger 1974; Sinclair 1971; Slobin 1979).

2. Processes and strategies underlying the child's construction of grammar (Bates 1976; Berko 1958; Bloom, Hood, & Lightbown 1974; Bloom, Lightbown, & Hood 1975; Bowerman 1977; Brown & Bellugi 1964; Brown, Cazden, & Bellugi 1969; Dore 1975; Ervin-Tripp 1964; Lieven 1980; MacWhinney 1975; Miller 1982; Scollon 1976; Shatz 1978; Slobin 1973).
3. The extent to which these processes and strategies are language universal or particular (Berman in press; Bowerman 1973; Brown 1973; Clancy in press; Clark in press; Johnston & Slobin 1979; MacWhinney & Bates 1978; Ochs 1982b, in press; Slobin 1981, in press; Asku & Slobin in press).
4. The extent to which these processes and strategies support the existence of a language faculty (Chomsky 1959, 1968, 1977; Fodor, Bever, & Garrett 1974; Goldin-Meadow 1977; McNeill 1970; Newport 1981; Newport, Gleitman, & Gleitman 1977; Piattelli-Palmarini 1980; Shatz 1981; Wanner & Gleitman 1982).
5. The nature of the prerequisites for language development (Bates et al. in press; Bloom 1973; Bruner 1975, 1977; Bullowa 1979; Carter 1978; de Lemos 1981; Gleason & Weintraub 1978; Golinkoff 1983; Greenfield & Smith 1976; Harding & Golinkoff 1979; Lock 1978, 1981; Sachs 1977; Shatz in press; Slobin 1973; Snow 1979; Snow & Ferguson 1977; Vygotsky 1962; Werner & Kaplan 1963).
6. Perceptual and conceptual factors that inhibit or facilitate language development (Andersen, Dunlea, & Kekelis 1982; Bever 1970; Greenfield & Smith 1976; Huttenlocher 1974; Menyuk & Menn 1979; Piaget 1955/1926; Slobin 1981; Sugarman 1984; Wanner & Gleitman 1982).

Underlying all these issues is the question of the *source* of language, in terms of not only what capacities reside within the child but the relative contributions of biology (nature) and the *social* world (nurture) to the development of language. The relation between nature and nurture has been a central theme around which theoretical positions have been oriented. B. F. Skinner's (1957) contention that the child brings relatively little to the task of learning language and that it is through responses to specific adult stimuli that language competence is attained provided a formulation that was subsequently challenged and countered by Chomsky's (1959) alternative position. This position, which has been termed **nativist**, **innatist**, rationalist (see Piattelli-Palmarini 1980), postulates that the adult verbal environment is an inadequate source for the child to inductively learn language. Rather, the rules and principles for constructing grammar have as their major source a genetically determined language faculty:

> Linguistics, then, may be regarded as that part of human psychology that is concerned with the nature, function, and origin of a particular "mental organ." We may take UG (**Universal Grammar**) to be a theory of the language faculty, a common human attribute, genetically determined, one component of the human mind. Through interaction with the environment, this faculty of mind becomes articulated and refined, emerging in the mature person as a system of knowledge of language. (Chomsky 1977:164)

It needs to be emphasized that an innatist approach does not eliminate the adult world as a source of linguistic knowledge; rather, it assigns a different role (vis-à-vis the behaviorist approach) to that world in the child's attainment of linguistic competence: The adult language presents the relevant information that allows the child to select from the Universal Grammar those grammatical principles specific to the particular language that the child will acquire.

One of the principal objections that could be raised is that although "the linguist's grammar is a theory of this [the child's] attained competence" (Chomsky 1977:163), there is no account of *how* this linguistic competence is attained. The theory does not relate the linguist's grammar(s) to processes of acquiring grammatical knowledge. Several psycholinguists, who have examined children's developing grammars in terms of their underlying organizing principles, have argued for similarities between these principles and those exhibited by other cognitive achievements (Bates et al. 1979; Bever 1970).

A second objection to the innatist approach has concerned its characterization of adult speech as "degenerate," fragmented, and often ill formed (McNeill 1966; Miller & Chomsky 1963). This characterization, for which there was no empirical basis, provoked a series of observational studies (including tape-recorded documentation) of the ways in which caregivers speak to their young language-acquiring children (Drach 1969; Phillips 1973; Sachs, Brown, & Salerno 1976; Snow 1972). Briefly, these studies indicated not only that adults use well-formed speech with high frequency but that they modify their speech to children in systematic ways as well. These systematic modifications, categorized as a particular speech **register** called **baby-talk register** (Ferguson 1977), include the increased (relative to other registers) use of high pitch, exaggerated and slowed intonation, a baby-talk lexicon (Garnica 1977; Sachs 1977; Snow 1972, 1977b) diminutives, reduplicated words, simple sentences (Newport 1976), shorter sentences, interrogatives (Corsaro 1979), vocatives, talk about the "here-and-now," play and politeness routines – peek-a-boo, hi–good-bye, say "thank you" (Andersen 1977; Gleason & Weintraub 1978), cooperative expression of propositions, repetition, and expansion of one's own and the child's utterances. Many of these features are associated with the expression of positive affect, such as high pitch and diminutives. However, the greatest emphasis in the literature has been placed on these features as evidence that caregivers *simplify* their speech in addressing young children (e.g., slowing down, exaggerating intonation, simplifying sentence structure and length of utterance). The scope of the effects on grammatical development has been debated in a number of studies. Several studies have supported Chomsky's position by demonstrating that caregiver speech facilitates the acquisition of only language-specific features but not those features widely (universally) shared across languages (Feldman, Goldin-Meadow, & Gleitman 1978; Newport, Gleitman, & Gleitman 1977). Other studies, which do not restrict the role of caregiver speech to facilitating only language-specific grammatical features (Snow 1977b, 1979), report that caregivers appear to adjust their speech to a child's cognitive and linguistic capacity (Cross 1977). And as children become more competent, caregivers use fewer features of the baby-talk register. Whereas certain researchers have emphasized the direct facilitating role of caregiver speech in the acquisition of language (van der Geest 1977), others have linked the speech behavior of caregivers to the caregiver's desire to communicate with the child (Brown 1977; Snow 1977a, 1977b, 1979). In this perspective, caregivers simplify their own speech in order to make themselves understood when speaking to young children. Similarly, caregivers employ several verbal strategies to understand what the child is trying to communicate. For example, the caregiver attends to what the child is doing, where the child is looking, and the child's behavior to determine the child's communicative intentions (Foster 1981; Golinkoff 1983; Keenan, Ochs, & Schieffelin 1976). Further, caregivers often request clarification by repeating or paraphrasing the child's utterance with a questioning intonation, as in Example 1 (Bloom 1973:170):

EXAMPLE 1*

| *Mother* | *Allison* (16 mos 3 wks) |
|---|---|
| (*A* picks up a jar, trying to open it)<br>(*A* holding jar out to *M*) | more wídə̀/ə wídə̀/<br>ə wídə̀/ə wídə̀/<br>up/ Mama/ Mama/<br>Mama ma ə wídə̀/<br>Mama Mama ə wídə̀/ |
| What, darling? | |
| | Mama wídə̀/ Mama/<br>Mama wídə̀/ Mama<br>Mama wídə̀/ |
| What do you want<br>Mommy to do? | |
| | —/ ə wídə̀ ə wídə̀/ |
| (*A* gives jar to *M*) | |
| | —/here/ |
| (*A* tries to turn top on<br>jar in *M*'s hand) | |
| | Mama/Mama/ə wídə̀t/ |
| Open it up? | |
| | up/ |
| Open it? OK.<br>(*M* opens it) | |

In other cases, the caregiver facilitates communication by jointly expressing with the child a proposition. Typically, a caregiver asks a question to which the child supplies the missing information (often already known to the caregiver), as in Example 2 (Bloom 1973:153):

EXAMPLE 2

| *Mother* | *Allison* |
|---|---|
| What's Mommy have<br>(*M* holding cookies)<br>(*A* reaching for cookie) | |
| | cookie/ |
| Cookie! OK. Here's a cookie for you<br>(*A* takes cookie; reaching with other<br>hand toward others in bag) | |
| | more/ |
| There's more in here. We'll have<br>it in a little while.<br>(*A* picking up bag of cookies) | |
| | bag/ |

These studies indicate that caregivers make extensive **accommodations** to the child, assuming the perspective of the child in the course of engaging him or her in conversational dialogue. Concurrent research on interaction between caregivers and prelinguistic infants supports this conclusion (Bruner 1977; Bullowa 1979; Lock 1978; Newson 1977, 1978; Schaffer 1977; Shotter 1978). Detailed observation of white middle-class mother-infant **dyads** (English, Scottish, American, Australian, Dutch) indicates that these mothers attempt to engage their very young infants (starting at birth) in "conversational exchanges." These so-called protoconversations (Bullowa 1979) are constructed in several ways. A protoconversation may take place when one party responds to some facial expression, action, and/or vocalization of the other. This response may be nonverbal, as when a gesture of the infant is "echoed" by his or her mother.

> As a rule, prespeech with gesture is watched and replied to by exclamations of pleasure or surprise like "Oh, my my!", "Good heavens!", "Oh, what a big smile!", "Ha! That's a big one!" (meaning a story), questioning replies like, "Are you telling me a story?", "Oh really?", or even agreement by nodding "Yes" or saying "I'm sure you're right"....A mother evidently perceives her baby to be a person like herself. Mothers interpret baby behavior as not only intended to be communicative, but as verbal and meaningful. (Trevarthen 1979a:339)

On the other hand, mother and infant may respond to one another through verbal means, as, for example, when a mother expresses agreement, disagreement, or surprise following an infant behavior. Social interactions may be sustained over several exchanges by the mother assuming both speaker roles. She may construct an exchange by responding on behalf of the infant to her own utterance, or she may verbally interpret the infant's interpretation. A combination of several strategies is illustrated in Example 3 (Snow 1977a:12).

* Examples 1–5 follow transcription conventions in Bloom and Lahey 1978.

EXAMPLE 3

| *Mother* | *Ann* (3 mos) |
|---|---|
| | (smiles) |
| Oh what a nice little smile! | |
| Yes, isn't that nice? | |
| There. | |
| There's a nice little smile. | (burps) |
| What a nice wind as well! | |
| Yes, that's better, isn't it? | |
| Yes. | |
| Yes. | (vocalizes) |
| Yes! | |
| There's a nice noise. | |

These descriptions capture the behavior of white middle-class caregivers and, in turn, can be read for what caregivers believe to be the capabilities and predispositions of the infant. Caregivers evidently see their infants as sociable and as capable of intentionality, particularly with respect to the intentional expression of emotional and physical states. Some researchers have concluded that the mother, in interpreting an infant's behaviors, provides meanings for those behaviors that the infant will ultimately adopt (Lock 1981; Ryan 1974; Shotter 1978) and thus emphasize the active role of the mother in socializing the infant to her set of interpretations. Other approaches emphasize the effect of the infant on the caregiver (Lewis & Rosenblum 1974), particularly with respect to the innate mechanisms for organized, purposeful action that the infant brings to interaction (Trevarthen 1979b).

These studies of caregivers' speech to young children have all attended to what the child is learning from these interactions with the mother (or caregiver). There has been a general movement away from the search for *direct* causal links between the ways in which caregivers speak to their children and the emergence of grammar. Instead, caregivers' speech has been examined for its more general communicative functions, that is, how meanings are negotiated, how activities are organized and accomplished, and how routines and games become established. Placed within this broader communicative perspective, language development is viewed as one of several achievements accomplished through verbal exchanges between the caregiver and the child.

## THE ETHNOGRAPHIC APPROACH

### Ethnographic Orientation

To most middle-class Western readers, the descriptions of verbal and nonverbal behaviors of middle-class caregivers with their children seem very familiar, desirable, and even natural. These descriptions capture in rich detail what goes on, to a greater or lesser extent, in many middle-class households. The characteristics of caregiver speech (baby-talk register) and comportment that have been specified are highly valued by members of white middle-class society, including researchers, readers, and subjects of study. They are associated with good mothering and can be spontaneously produced with little effort or reflections. As demonstrated by Shatz and Gelman (1973), Sachs and Devin (1976), and Andersen and Johnson (1973), children as young as 4 years of age often speak and act in these ways when addressing small children.

From our research experience in other societies as well as our acquaintance with some of the cross-cultural studies of language socialization (Blount 1972; Bowerman 1981; Clancy in press; Eisenberg 1982; Fischer 1970; Hamilton 1981; Harkness 1975; Harkness & Super 1977; Heath 1983; Miller 1982; Philips 1983; Schieffelin & Eisenberg in press; Scollon & Scollon 1981; Stross 1972; Ward 1971; Watson-Gegeo & Gegeo 1982; Wills 1977) the general patterns of white middle-class caregiving that have been described in the psychological literature are characteristic neither of all societies nor of all social groups (e.g., all social classes within one society). We would like the reader, therefore, to reconsider the descriptions of caregiving in the psychological literature as **ethnographic** descriptions.

By ethnographic, we mean descriptions that take into account the perspective of members of a social group, including beliefs and values that underlie and organize their activities and utterances. Ethnographers rely heavily on observations and on formal and informal elicitation of members' reflections and interpretations as a basis for analysis (Geertz 1973). Typically, the ethnographer is not a member of the group under study. Further, in presenting an ethnographic account, the researcher faces the problem of communicating world views or sets of values that may be unfamiliar and strange to the reader. Ideally, such statements provide for the reader a set of organizing principles that give coherence and an analytic focus to the behaviors described.

Psychologists who have carried out research on the verbal and nonverbal behavior of caregivers and their children draw on both methods. However, unlike most ethnographers, the psychological researcher *is* a member of the social group under observation. (In some cases, the researcher's own children are the subjects of study.) Further, unlike the ethnographer, the psychologist addresses a readership familiar with the social scenes portrayed.

That the researcher, reader, and subjects of study tend to have in common a white middle-class literate background has had several consequences. For example, by and large, the psychologist has not been faced with the problem of cultural translation, as has the anthropologist. There has been a tacit assumption that readers can provide the larger cultural framework for making sense out of the behaviors documented, and, consequently, the cultural nature of the behaviors and principles presented have not been explicit. From our perspective, language and culture as bodies of knowledge, structures of understanding, conceptions of the world, and collective representations are extrinsic to any individual and contain more information than any individual could know or learn. Culture encompasses variations in knowledge between individuals, but such variation, although crucial to what an individual may know and to the social dynamic between individuals, does not have its locus within the individual. Our position is that culture is not something that can be considered separately from the accounts of caregiver–child interaction; rather, it is what organizes and gives meaning to that interaction. This is an important point, as it affects the definition and interpretation of the behaviors of caregivers and children. How caregivers and children speak and act toward one another is linked to cultural patterns that extend and have consequences beyond the specific interactions observed. For example, how caregivers speak to their children may be linked to other institutional adaptations to young children. These adaptations, in turn, may be linked to how members of a given society view children more generally (their "nature," their social status and expected comportment) and to how members think children develop.

We are suggesting here that the sharing of assumptions between researcher, reader, and subjects of study is a mixed blessing. In fact, this sharing represents a paradox of familiarity. We are able to apply without effort the cultural framework for interpreting the behavior of caregivers and young children in our own social group; indeed, as members of a white middle-class society, we are socialized to do this very work, that is, interpret behaviors, attribute motives, and so on. Paradoxically, however, in spite of this ease of effort, we can not easily isolate and make explicit these cultural principles. As Goffman's work on American society has illustrated, the articulation of norms, beliefs, and values is often possible only when faced with violations, that is, with gaffes, breaches, misfirings, and the like (Goffman 1963, 1967; Much & Shweder 1978).

Another way to see the cultural principles at work in our own society is to examine the ways in which *other* societies are organized in terms of social interaction and of the society at large. In carrying out such research, the ethnographer offers a point of contrast and comparison with our own everyday activities. Such comparative material can lead us to reinterpret behaviors as cultural that we have assumed to be natural. From the anthropological perspective, every society will have its own cultural constructs of what is natural and what is not. For example, every society has its own theory of procreation. Certain Australian Aboriginal societies believe that a number of different factors contribute to conception. Von Sturmer (1980) writes that among the Kugu-Nganychara (West Cape York Peninsula, Australia) the spirit of the child may first enter the man through an animal that he has killed and consumed. The spirit passes from the man to the woman through sexual intercourse, but several sexual acts are necessary to build the child (see also Hamilton 1981; Montagu 1937). Even within a single society there may be different beliefs concerning when life begins and ends, as the recent debates in the United States and Europe concerning abortion and mercy killing indicate. The issue of what is nature and what is nurtured (cultural) extends to patterns of caregiving and child development. Every society has (implicitly or explicitly) given notions concerning the capacities and temperament of children at different points in their development (see, e.g., Dentan 1978; Ninio 1979; Snow, de Blauw, & van Roosmalen 1979), and the expectations and responses of caregivers are directly related to these notions.

## Three Developmental Stories

At this point, using an ethnographic perspective, we will recast selected behaviors of white middle-class caregivers and young children as pieces of one "developmental story." The white middle-class developmental story that we are constructing is based on various descriptions available and focuses on those patterns of interaction (both verbal and nonverbal) that have been emphasized in the literature. This story will be compared with two other developmental stories from societies that are strikingly different: Kaluli (Papua New Guinea) and Western Samoan.

A major goal in presenting and comparing these developmental stories is to demonstrate that communicative interactions between caregivers and young children are **culturally constructed**. In our comparisons, we will focus on three facets of communicative interaction: (1) the social organization of the verbal environment of very young children, (2) the extent to which children are expected to adapt to situations or that situations are adapted to the child, (3) the negotiation of meaning by caregiver and child. We first present a general sketch of each social group and then discuss in more detail the consequences of the differences and similarities in communicative patterns in these social groups.

These developmental stories are not timeless but rather are linked in complex ways to particular historical contexts. Both the ways in which caregivers behave toward young children and the popular and scientific accounts of these ways may differ at different moments in time. The stories that we present represent ideas currently held in the three social groups.

The three stories show that there is more than one way of becoming social and using language in early childhood. All normal children will become members of their own social group, but the process of becoming social, including becoming a language user, is culturally constructed. In relation to this process of construction, every society has its own developmental stories that are rooted in social organization, beliefs, and values. These stories may be explicitly codified and/or tacitly assumed by members.

**An Anglo-American White Middle-Class Developmental Story** The middle class in Britain and the United States includes a broad range of lower middle-, middle middle-, and upper middle-class white-collar and professional workers and their families.[1] The literature on communicative development has been largely based on middle middle- and upper middle-class households. These households tend to consist of a single nuclear family with one, two, or three children. The primary caregiver almost without exception is the child's natural or adopted mother. Researchers have focused on communicative situations in which one child interacts with his or her mother. The generalizations proposed by these researchers concerning mother–child communication could be an artifact of this methodological focus. However, it could be argued that the attention to two-party encounters between a mother and her child reflects the most frequent type of communicative interaction to which most young middle-class children are exposed. Participation in two-party as opposed to multiparty interactions is a product of many considerations, including the physical setting of households, where interior and exterior walls bound and limit access to social interaction.

Soon after an infant is born, many mothers hold their infants in such a way that they are face-to-face and gaze at them. Mothers have been observed to address their infants, vocalize to them, ask questions, and greet them. In other words, from birth on, the infant is treated as a *social being* and as an ***addressee*** in social interaction. The infant's vocalizations and physical movements and states are often interpreted as meaningful and are responded to verbally by the mother or other caregiver. In this way, protoconversations are established and sustained along a **dyadic**, turn-taking model. Throughout this period and the subsequent language-acquiring years, caregivers treat very young children as communicative partners. One very important procedure in facilitating these social exchanges is the mother's (or other caregiver's) taking the perspective of the child. This perspective is evidenced in her own speech through the many simplifying and affective features of the baby-talk register that have been described and through the various strategies employed to identify what the young child may be expressing.

Such perspective taking is part of a much wider set of accommodations by adults to young children. These accommodations are manifested in several domains. For example, there are widespread material accommodations to infancy and childhood in the form of cultural artifacts designed for this stage of life, for example, baby clothes, baby food, miniaturization of furniture, and toys. Special behavioral accommodations are coordinated with the infant's perceived needs and capacities, for example, putting the baby in a quiet place to facilitate and ensure proper sleep; "baby-proofing" a house as a child becomes increasingly mobile, yet not aware of, or able to control, the consequences of his or her own behavior. In general, the pattern appears to be one of prevention and intervention, in which situations are adapted or modified to the child rather than the reverse. Further, the child is a focus of attention, in that the child's actions and verbalizations are often the starting point of social interaction with more mature persons.

Although such developmental achievements as crawling, walking, and first words are awaited by caregivers, the accommodations have the effect of keeping the child dependent on, and separate from, the adult community for a considerable period of time. The child, protected from those experiences considered harmful (e.g., playing with knives, climbing stairs), is thus denied knowledge, and his or her competence in such contexts is delayed.

The accommodations of white middle-class caregivers to young children can be examined for other values and tendencies. Particularly among the American middle class, these accommodations reflect a discomfort with the competence differential between adult and child. The competence gap is reduced by two strategies. One is for the adult to simplify her/his speech to match more closely what the adult considers to be the verbal competence of the young child. Let us call this strategy the self-lowering strategy, following Irvine's (1974) analysis of intercaste demeanor. A second strategy is for the caregiver to richly interpret (Brown 1973) what the young child is expressing. Here the adult acts *as if* the child were more competent than his behavior more strictly would indicate. Let us call this strategy the child-raising (no pun intended!) strategy. Other behaviors conform to this strategy, such as when an adult cooperates in a task with a child but treats that task as an accomplishment of the child.

For example, in eliciting a story from a child, a caregiver often cooperates with the child in the telling of the story. This cooperation typically takes the form of posing questions to the child, such as "Where did you go?" "What did you see?" and so on, to which the adult knows the answer. The child is seen as telling the story even though she or he is simply supplying the information the adult has preselected and organized (Greenfield & Smith 1976; Ochs, Schieffelin & Platt 1979; Schieffelin & Eisenberg 1984). Bruner's (1978) description of **scaffolding**, in which a caregiver constructs a tower or other play object, allowing the young child to place the last block, is also a good example of this tendency. Here the tower may be seen by the caregiver and others as the child's own work. Similarly, in later life, caregivers playing games with their children let them win, acting as if the child can match or more than match the competence of the adult.

The masking of incompetence applies not only in white middle-class relations with young children but also in relations with mentally, and to some extent to physically, handicapped persons as well. As the work of Edgerton (1967) and the recent film *Best Boy* indicate, mentally retarded persons are often restricted to protected environments (family households, sheltered workshops or special homes) in which trained staff or family members make vast accommodations to their special needs and capacities.

A final aspect of this white middle-class developmental story concerns the willingness of many caregivers to interpret unintelligible or partially intelligible utterances of young children (cf. Ochs 1982c), for example, the caregiver offers a paraphrase (or **"expansion"**; Brown & Bellugi 1964; Cazden 1965), using a question intonation. This behavior of caregivers has continuity with their earlier attributions of intentionality to the ambiguous utterances of the infant. For both the prelinguistic and language-using child, the caregiver provides an explicitly verbal interpretation. This interpretation or paraphrase is potentially available to the young child to affirm, disconfirm, or modify.

Through exposure to, and participation in, these clarification exchanges, the young child is socialized into several cultural patterns. The first of these recognizes and defines an utterance or vocalization that may not be immediately understood. Second, the child is presented with the procedures for dealing with ambiguity. Through the successive offerings of possible interpretations, the child learns that more than one understanding of a given utterance or vocalization may be possible. The child is also learning who can make these interpretations and the extent to which they may be open to modification. Finally, the child is learning how to settle upon a possible interpretation and how to show disagreement or agreement. This entire process socializes the child into culturally specific modes of organizing knowledge, thought, and language.[2]

**A Kaluli Developmental Story** A small (population approximately 1,200), nonliterate egalitarian society (Schieffelin 1976), the Kaluli people live in the tropical rain forest on the Great Papuan Plateau in the southern highlands of Papua New Guinea.[3] Most Kaluli are monolingual, speaking a non-Austronesian verb-final ergative language. They maintain large gardens and hunt and fish. Traditionally, the sixty to ninety individuals that comprise a village lived in one large longhouse without internal walls. Currently, although the longhouse is maintained, many families live in smaller dwellings that provide accommodations for two or more extended families. It is not unusual for at least a dozen individuals of different ages to be living together in one house consisting essentially of one semipartitioned room.

Men and women use extensive networks of obligation and reciprocity in the organization of work and sociable interaction. Everyday life is overtly focused around verbal interaction. Kaluli think of, and use, talk as a means of control, manipulation, expression, assertion, and appeal. Talk gets you what you want, need, or feel you are owed. Talk is a primary indicator of social competence and a primary means of socializing. Learning how to talk and become independent is a major goal of socialization.

For the purpose of comparison and for understanding something of the cultural basis for the ways in which Kaluli act and speak to their children, it is important first to describe selected aspects of a Kaluli developmental story that I have constructed from various ethnographic data. Kaluli describe their babies as helpless, "soft" (*taiyo*), and "having no understanding" (*asugo andoma*). They take care of them, they say, because they "feel sorry for them." Mothers, the primary caregivers, are attentive to their infants and physically responsive to them. Whenever an infant cries, it is offered the breast. However, while nursing her infant, a mother may also be involved in other activities, such as food preparation, or she may be engaged in conversation with individuals in the household. Mothers never leave their infants alone and only rarely with other caregivers. When not holding their infants, mothers carry them in netted bags suspended from their heads. When the mother is gardening, gathering wood, or just sitting with others, the baby sleeps in the netted bag next to the mother's body.

Kaluli mothers, given their belief that infants "have no understanding," never treat their infants as partners (speaker/addressee) in dyadic communicative interactions. Although they greet their infants by name and use expressive vocalizations, they rarely address other utterances to them. Furthermore, a mother and infant do not gaze into each other's eyes, an interactional pattern that is consistent with adult patterns of not gazing when vocalizing in interaction with one another. Rather than facing their babies and speaking to them, Kaluli mothers tend to face their babies outward so that they can see, and be seen by, other members of the social group. Older children greet and address the infant, and the mother responds in a high-pitched nasalized voice "for" the baby while moving the baby up and down. **Triadic** exchanges such as that in Example 4 are typical (Golinkoff 1983).

EXAMPLE 4

Mother is holding her infant son Bage (3 mo). Abi (35 mo) is holding a stick on his shoulder in a manner similar to that in which one would carry a heavy patrol box (the box would be hung on a pole placed across the shoulders of the two men).

| *Mother* | *Abi* |
|---|---|
| (*A* to baby) | Bage/ do you see my box here?/<br>Bage/ ni bokisi we badaya?/<br>Do you see it?/<br>olibadaya?/ |
| (high nasal voice talking as if she is the baby, moving the baby who is facing Abi):<br>My brother, I'll take half, my brother.<br>nao, hεbɔ ni diεni, nao.<br>(holding stick out) | mother give him half/<br>nɔ hεbɔ emɔ dimina/<br>mother,<br>my brother here/here take half/<br>nao we/we hεbɔ dima/ |
| (in a high nasal voice as baby):<br>My brother, what half do I take?<br>nao, hεbɔ diεni hεh?<br>What about it? my brother, put it on the shoulder!<br>Wangaya? nao, kεlεnɔ wεla diεfoma!<br>(to Abi in her usual voice):<br>Put it on the shoulder.<br>kεlεnɔ wεla diεfɔndo.<br>(Abi rests stick on baby's shoulder)<br>There, carefully put it on. | |

ko dinafa diɛfoma. (stick
accidently pokes baby)
Feel sorry, stop.
Heyɔ, kadɛfoma.

When a mother takes the speaking role of an infant she uses language that is well formed and appropriate for an older child. Only the nasalization and high-pitch mark it as "the infant's." When speaking as the infant to older children, mothers speak assertively, that is, they never whine or beg on behalf of the infant. Thus, in taking this role the mother does for the infant what the infant cannot do for itself, that is, appear to act in a controlled and competent manner, using language. These kinds of interactions continue until a baby is between 4 and 6 months of age.

Several points are important here. First, these triadic exchanges are carried out primarily for the benefit of the older child and help create a relationship between the two children. Second, the mother's utterances in these exchanges are not based on, nor do they originate with, anything that the infant has initiated—either vocally or gesturally. Recall the Kaluli claim that infants have no understanding. How could someone with "no understanding" initiate appropriate interactional sequences?

However, there is an even more important and enduring cultural construct that helps make sense out of the mother's behaviors in this situation and in many others as well. Kaluli say that "one cannot know what another thinks or feels." Although Kaluli obviously interpret and assess one another's available behaviors and internal states, these interpretations are not culturally acceptable as topics of talk. Individuals often talk about their own feelings (I'm afraid, I'm happy, etc.). However, there is a cultural dispreference for talking about or making claims about what another might think, what another might feel, or what another is about to do, especially if there is no external evidence. As we shall see, these culturally constructed behaviors have several important consequences for the ways in which Kaluli caregivers verbally interact with their children and are related to other pervasive patterns of language use, which will be discussed later.

As infants become older (6–12 months), they are usually held in the arms or carried on the shoulders of the mother or an older sibling. They are present in all ongoing household activities, as well as subsistence activities that take place outside the village in the bush. During this time period, babies are addressed by adults to a limited extent. They are greeted by a variety of names (proper names, kin terms, affective and relationship terms) and receive a limited set of both negative and positive imperatives. In addition, when they do something they are told not to do, such as reach for something that is not theirs to take, they will often receive such rhetorical questions . . . as "who are you?!" (meaning "not someone to do that") or "is it yours?!" (meaning "it is not yours") to control their actions by shaming them (*sasidiab*). It should be stressed that the language addressed to the preverbal child consists largely of "one-liners" that call for no verbal response but for either an action or termination of an action. Other than these utterances, very little talk is directed to the young child by the adult caregiver.

This pattern of adults treating infants as noncommunicative partners continues even when babies begin babbling. Although Kaluli recognize babbling (*dabedan*), they call it noncommunicative and do not relate it to the speech that eventually emerges. Adults and older children occasionally repeat vocalizations back to the young child (age 12–16 months), reshaping them into the names of persons in the household or into kin terms, but they do not say that the baby is saying the name nor do they wait for, or expect, the child to repeat those vocalizations in an altered form. In addition, vocalizations are not generally treated as communicative and given verbal expression except in the following situation. When a toddler shrieks in protest of the assaults of an older child, mothers say "I'm unwilling" (using a quotative particle), referring to the toddler's shriek. These are the only circumstances in which mothers treat vocalizations as communicative and provide verbal expression for them. In no other circumstances did the adults in the four families in the study provide a verbally expressed interpretation of a vocalization of a preverbal child. Thus, throughout the preverbal period very little language is directed to the child, except for imperatives, rhetorical questions, and greetings. A child who by Kaluli terms has not yet begun to speak is not expected to respond either verbally or vocally. As a result, during the first 18 months or so very little sustained dyadic verbal exchange takes place between adult and infant. The infant is only minimally treated as an addressee and is not treated as a communicative partner in dyadic exchanges. Thus, the conversational model that has been described for many white middle-class caregivers and their preverbal children has no application in this case. Furthermore, if one defines language input as language directed to the child then it is reasonable to say that for Kaluli children who have not yet begun to speak there is very little. However, this does not mean that Kaluli children grow up in an impoverished verbal environment and do not learn how to speak. Quite the opposite is true. The verbal environment of the infant is rich and varied, and from the very beginning the infant is surrounded by adults and older children who spend a great deal of time talking to one another. Furthermore, as the infant develops and begins to crawl and engage in play activities and other independent actions, these actions are frequently referred to, described, and commented upon by members of the household, especially older children, to each other. Thus the ongoing activities of the preverbal child are an important topic of talk among members of the household, and this talk about the here-and-now of the infant is available to the infant, though it is not talk addressed to the infant. For example, in referring to the infant's actions, siblings and adults use the infant's name or kin term. They say, "Look at Seligiwo! He's walking." Thus the child may learn from these contexts to attend [to] the verbal environment in which he or she lives.

Every society has its own ideology about language, including when it begins and how children acquire it. The

Kaluli are no exception. Kaluli claim that language begins at the time when the child uses two critical words, "mother" (*nɔ*) and "breast" (*bo*). The child may be using other single words, but until these two words are used, the beginning of language is not recognized. Once a child has used these words, a whole set of interrelated behaviors is set into motion. Once a child has begun to use language, he or she then must be "shown how to speak" (Schieffelin 1979). Kaluli show their children language in the form of a teaching strategy, which involves providing a model for what the child is to say followed by the word *ɛlɛma*, an imperative meaning "say like that." Mothers use this method of direct instruction to teach the social uses of assertive language (teasing, shaming, requesting, challenging, reporting). However, object labeling is never part of an *ɛlɛma* sequence, nor does the mother ever use *ɛlɛma* to instruct the child to beg or appeal for food or objects. Begging, the Kaluli say, is natural for children. They know how to do it. In contrast, a child must be taught to be assertive through the use of particular linguistic expressions and verbal sequences.

A typical sequence using *ɛlɛma* is triadic, involving the mother, child (20–36 months), and other participants, as in Example 5 (Schieffelin 1979).

EXAMPLE 5

Mother, daughter Binalia (5 yrs), cousin Mama (3 1/2 yrs), and son Wanu (27 mos) are at home, dividing up some cooked vegetables. Binalia has been begging for some, but her mother thinks that she has had her share.

M → W →> B:*
Whose is it?! say like that.
Abɛnowo?! ɛlɛma.

whose is it?!/
abɛnowo?!/

Is it yours?! say like that.
Gɛnowo?! ɛlɛma.

is it yours?!/
gɛnowo?!/

Who are you?! say like that.
ge oba?! ɛlɛma.

who are you?!/
ge oba?!/

Mama → W →> B:
Did you pick?! say like that.
gi suwo?! ɛlɛma.

did you pick?!/
gi suwo?!/

M → W →> B:
My grandmother picked! say like that.
ni nuwɛ suke! ɛlɛma.

My grandmother picked!/
ni nuwɛ suke!/

Mama → W →> B:
This my g'mother picked! say like that
we ni nuwɛ suke! ɛlɛma.

This my g'mother picked!/
we ni nuwɛ suke!/

*→ = speaker → addressee
→> = addressee → intended addressee

In this situation, as in many others, the mother does not modify her language to fit the linguistic ability of the young child. Instead, her language is shaped so as to be appropriate (in terms of form and content) for the child's intended addressee. Consistent with the way she interacts with her infant, what a mother instructs her young child to say usually does not have its origins in any verbal or nonverbal behaviors of the child but in what the mother thinks should be said. The mother pushes the child into ongoing interactions that the child may or may not be interested in and will at times spend a good deal of energy in trying to get the child verbally involved. This is part of the Kaluli pattern of fitting (or pushing) the child into the situation rather than changing the situation to meet the interests or abilities of the child. Thus mothers take a directive role with their young children, teaching them what to say so that they may become participants in the social group.

In addition to instructing their children by telling them what to say in often extensive interactional sequences, Kaluli mothers pay attention to the form of their children's utterances. Kaluli correct the phonological, morphological, or lexical form of an utterance or its pragmatic or semantic meaning. Because the goals of language acquisition include the development of a competent and independent child who uses mature language, Kaluli use no baby-talk lexicon, for they said (when I asked about it) that to do so would result in a child sounding babyish, which was clearly undesirable and counterproductive. The entire process of a child's development, of which language acquisition plays a very important role, is thought of as a hardening process and culminates in the child's use of "hard words" (Feld & Schieffelin 1982).

The cultural dispreference for saying what another might be thinking or feeling has important consequences for the organization of dyadic exchanges between caregiver and child. For one, it affects the ways in which meaning is negotiated during an exchange. For the Kaluli, the responsibility for clear expression is with the speaker, and child speakers are not exempt from this. Rather than offering possible interpretations or guessing at the meaning of what a child is saying, caregivers make extensive use of clarification requests such as "huh?" and "what?" in an attempt to elicit clearer expression from the child. Children are held to what they say and mothers will remind them that they in fact have asked for food or an object if they don't act appropriately on receiving it. Because the responsibility of expression lies with the speaker, children are also instructed with *ɛ̀lɛma* to request clarification (using similar forms) from others when they do not understand what someone is saying to them.

Another important consequence of not saying what another thinks is the absence of adult expansions of child utterances. Kaluli caregivers put words into the mouths of their children, but these words originate from the caregiver. However, caregivers do not elaborate or expand utterances initiated by the child. Nor do they jointly build propositions across utterances and speakers except in the context of sequences with *ɛlɛma* in which they are constructing the talk for the child.

All these patterns of early language use, such as the lack of expansions and the verbal attribution of an internal state to an individual are consistent with important cultural conventions of adult language usage. The Kaluli avoid gossip and often indicate the source of information they report. They make extensive use of direct quoted speech in a language that does not allow indirect quotation. They use a range of **evidential markers** in their speech to indicate the source of speakers' information, for example, whether something was said, seen, heard, or gathered from other kinds of evidence. These patterns are also found in a child's early speech and, as such, affect the organization and acquisition of conversational exchanges in this face-to-face egalitarian society.

**A Samoan Developmental Story** In American and Western Samoa, an archipelago in the southwest Pacific, Samoan, a verb-initial Polynesian language, is spoken.[4] The following developmental story draws primarily on direct observations of life in a large, traditional village on the island of Upolu in Western Samoa; however, it incorporates as well analyses by Mead (1927), Kernan (1969), and Shore (1982) of social life, language use, and childhood on other islands (the Manu'a islands and Savai'i).

As has been described by numerous scholars, Samoan society is highly **stratified**. Individuals are ranked in terms of whether or not they have a title, and if so, whether it is an orator or a chiefly title – bestowed on persons by an extended family unit (*aiga potopoto*) – and within each **status**, particular titles are reckoned with respect to one another.

Social **stratification** characterizes relationships between untitled persons as well, with the assessment of relative **rank** in terms of generation and age. Most relevant to the Samoan developmental story to be told here is that caregiving is also socially stratified. The young child is cared for by a range of untitled persons, typically the child's older siblings, the mother, and unmarried siblings of the child's mother. Where more than one of these are present, the older is considered to be the higher ranking caregiver and the younger the lower ranking caregiver (Ochs 1982c). As will be discussed in the course of this story, ranking affects how caregiving tasks are carried out and how verbal interactions are organized.

From birth until the age of 5 or 6 months, an infant is referred to as *pepemeamea* (baby thing thing). During this period, the infant stays close to his or her mother, who is assisted by other women and children in child-care tasks. During this period, the infant spends the periods of rest and sleep near, but somewhat separated from, others, on a large pillow enclosed by a mosquito net suspended from a beam or rope. Waking moments are spent in the arms of the mother, occasionally the father, but most often on the hips or laps of other children, who deliver the infant to his or her mother for feeding and in general are responsible for satisfying and comforting the child.

In these early months, the infant is talked *about* by others, particularly in regard to his or her physiological states and needs. Language addressed *to* the young infant tends to be in the form of songs or rhythmic vocalizations in a soft, high pitch. Infants at this stage are not treated as conversational partners. Their gestures and vocalizations are interpreted for what they indicate about the physiological state of the child. If verbally expressed, however, these interpretations are directed in general not to the infant but to some other more mature member of the household (older child), typically in the form of a directive.

As an infant becomes more mature and mobile, he or she is referred to as simply *pepe* (baby). When the infant begins to crawl, his or her immediate social and verbal environment changes. Although the infant continues to be carried by an older sibling, he or she is also expected to come to the mother or other mature family members on his or her own. Spontaneous language is directed to the infant to a much greater extent. The child, for example, is told to "come" to the caregiver.

To understand the verbal environment of the infant at this stage, it is necessary to consider Samoan concepts of childhood and children. Once a child is able to locomote himself or herself and even somewhat before, he or she is frequently described as cheeky, mischievous, and willful. Very frequently, the infant is negatively sanctioned for his actions. An infant who sucks eagerly, vigorously, or frequently at the breast may be teasingly shamed by other family members. Approaching a guest or touching objects of value provokes negative directives first and mock threats second. The tone of voice shifts dramatically from that used with younger infants. The pitch drops to the level used in casual interactions with adult addressees and voice quality becomes loud and sharp. It is to be noted here that caregiver speech is largely talk directed *at* the infant and typically caregivers do not engage in "conversations" *with* infants over several exchanges. Further, the language used by caregivers is not lexically or syntactically simplified.

The image of the small child as highly assertive continues for several years and is reflected in what is reported to be the first word of Samoan children: *tae* (shit), a curse word used to reject, retaliate, or show displeasure at the action of another. The child's earliest use of language, then, is seen as explicitly defiant and angry. Although caregivers admonish the verbal and nonverbal expression of these qualities, the qualities are in fact deeply valued and considered necessary and desirable in particular social circumstances.

As noted earlier, Samoan children are exposed to, and participate in, a highly stratified society. Children usually grow up in a family compound composed of several households and headed by one or more titled persons. Titled persons conduct themselves in a particular manner in public, namely, to move slowly or be stationary, and they tend to disassociate themselves from the activities of lower status persons in their immediate environment. In a less dramatic fashion, this demeanor characterizes high ranking caregivers in a household as well, who tend to leave the more active tasks, such as bathing, changing, and carrying an infant to younger persons (Ochs 1982c).

The social stratification of caregiving has its reflexes in the verbal environment of the young child. Throughout the day, higher ranking caregivers (e.g., the mother) direct lower ranking persons to carry, put to sleep, soothe, feed, bathe, and clothe a child. Typically, a lower ranking caregiver waits for such a directive rather than initiate such activities spontaneously. When a small child begins to speak, he or she learns to make his or her needs known to the higher ranking caregiver. The child learns not to necessarily expect a direct response. Rather, the child's appeal usually generates a conversational sequence such as the following:

> Child appeals to high ranking caregiver (A → B)
> High ranking caregiver directs lower ranking caregiver (B → C)
> Lower ranking caregiver responds to child (C → A)

These verbal interactions differ from the ABAB dyadic interactions described for white middle-class caregivers and children. Whereas a white middle-class child is often alone with a caregiver, a Samoan child is not. Traditional Samoan houses have no internal or external walls, and typically conversations involve several persons inside and outside the house. For the Samoan child, then, multiparty conversations are the norm, and participation is organized along hierarchical lines.

The importance of status and rank is expressed in other uses of language as well. Very small children are encouraged to produce certain speech acts that they will be expected to produce later as younger (i.e., low ranking) members of the household. One of these speech acts is reporting of news to older family members. The reporting of news by lower status persons complements the detachment associated with relatively high status. High status persons ideally (or officially) receive information through reports rather than through their own direct involvement in the affairs of others. Of course, this ideal is not always realized. Nonetheless, children from the one-word stage on will be explicitly instructed to notice others and to provide information to others as Example 6 illustrates.

EXAMPLE 6

> Pesio, her peer group including Maselino 3 yrs 4 mos, and Maselino's mother, Iuliana, are in the house. They see Alesana (member of research project) in front of the trade store across the street. Iuliana directs the children to notice Alesana.

| *Pesio* (2 yrs 3 mos) | *Others* |
|---|---|
| | Iuliana: Va'ai Alesana.<br>Look (at) Alesana! |
| ā?/<br>Huh? | |
| | Iuliana: Alesana<br>Maselino: Alesaga/ |
| ai Alesaga/<br>Look (at) Alesana | |
| | Iuliana: Vala'au Alesana<br>Call (to) Alesana. |
| ((very high, loud))<br>SAGA?/<br>Alesana! | |
| | ((high, soft))<br>Iuliana: Mālō.<br>(Greeting) |
| ((loud))<br>ALŌ<br>(Greeting) | |
| | Iuliana: (Fai) o Elegoa lea.<br>(Say) prt. Elenoa here.<br>(say "Elenoa [is] here.") |
| Sego lea/<br>Elenoa here<br>(Elenoa [is] here.) | |

The character of these instructions is similar to that of the triadic exchanges described in the Kaluli developmental story. A young child is to repeat an utterance offered by a caregiver to a third party. As in the Kaluli triadic exchanges, the utterance is designed primarily for the third party. For example, the high, soft voice quality used by Iuliana expresses deference in greeting Alesana, the third party. Caregivers use such exchanges to teach children a wide range of skills and knowledge. In fact, the task of repeating what the caregiver has said is *itself* an object of knowledge, preparing the child for his or her eventual role as messenger. Children at the age of 3 are expected to deliver *verbatim* messages on behalf of more mature members of the family.

The cumulative orientation is one in which even very young children are oriented toward others. In contrast to the white middle-class tendencies to accommodate situations to the child, the Samoans encourage the child to meet the needs of the situation, that is, to notice others, listen to them, and adapt one's own speech to their particular status and needs.

The pervasiveness of social stratification is felt in another, quite fundamental aspect of language, that of ascertaining the meaning of an utterance. Procedures for clarification are sensitive to the relative rank of conversational participants in the following manner. If a high status person produces a partially or wholly unintelligible utterance, the burden of clarification tends to rest with the hearer. It is not inappropriate for high status persons to produce such utterances from time to time. In the case of orators in particular, there is an expectation that certain terms and expressions will be obscure to certain members of their audiences. On the other hand, if a low status person's speech is unclear, the burden of clarification tends to be placed more on the speaker.

The latter situation applies to most situations in which young children produce ambiguous or unclear utterances. Both adult and child caregivers tend not to try to determine the message content of such utterances by, for example, repeating or expanding such an utterance with a query intonation. In fact, unintelligible utterances of young children will sometimes be considered as not Samoan but another language, usually Chinese, or not language at all but the sounds of an animal. A caregiver may choose to initiate clarification by asking "What?" or "Huh?" but it is up to the child to make his or her speech intelligible to the addressee.

Whereas the Samoans place the burden of clarification on the child, white middle-class caregivers assist the child in clarifying and expressing ideas. As noted in the white middle-class developmental story, such assistance is associated with good mothering. The good mother is one who responds to her child's incompetence by making greater efforts than normal to clarify his or her intentions. To this end, a mother tries to put herself in the child's place (take the perspective of the child). In Samoa good mothering or good caregiving is almost the reverse: A young child is encouraged to develop an ability to take the perspective of higher ranking persons in order to assist them and facilitate their well-being. The ability to do so is part of showing *fa'aaloalo* (respect), a most necessary demeanor in social life.

We can not leave our Samoan story without touching on another dimension of intelligibility and understanding in caregiver–child interactions. In particular, we need to turn our attention to Samoan attitudes toward motivation and intentionality (cf. Ochs 1982c). In philosophy, social science, and literary criticism, a great deal of ink has been spilled over the relation between act and intention behind an act. The pursuit and ascertaining of intentions is highly valued in many societies, where acts are objects of interpretation and motives are treated as explanations. In traditional Samoan society, with exceptions such as teasing and bluffing, actions are not treated as open to interpretation. They are treated for the most part as having one assignable meaning. An individual may not always know what that meaning is, as in the case of an oratorical passage; in these cases, one accepts that there is one meaning that he may or may not eventually come to know. For the most part as well, there is not a concern with levels of intentions and motives underlying the performance of some particular act.

Responses of Samoan caregivers to unintelligible utterances and acts of young children need to be understood in this light. Caregivers tend not to guess, hypothesize, or otherwise interpret such utterances and acts, in part because these procedures are not generally engaged in, at least explicitly, in daily social interactions within a village. As in encounters with others, a caregiver generally treats a small child's utterances as either clear or not clear, and in the latter case prefers to wait until the meaning becomes known to the caregiver rather than initiate an interpretation.

When young Samoan children participate in such interactions, they come to know how "meaning" is treated in their society. They learn what to consider as meaningful (e.g., clear utterances and actions) procedures for assigning meaning to utterances and actions, and procedures for handling unintelligible and partially intelligible utterances and actions. In this way, through language use, Samoan children are socialized into culturally preferred ways of processing information. Such contexts of experience reveal the interface of language, culture, and thought.

## Implications of Developmental Stories: Three Proposals

**Interactional Design Reexamined** We propose that infants and caregivers do not interact with one another according to one particular "biologically designed choreography" (Stern 1977). There are many choreographies within and across societies, and cultural as well as biological systems contribute to their design, frequency, and significance. The biological predispositions constraining and shaping the social behavior of infants and caregivers must be broader than thus far conceived in that the use of eye gaze, vocalization, and body alignment are orchestrated differently in the social groups we have observed. As noted earlier, for example, Kaluli mothers do not engage in sustained gazing at, or elicit and maintain direct eye contact with, their infants as such behavior is dispreferred and associated with witchcraft.

Another argument in support of a broader notion of a biological predisposition to be social concerns the variation observed in the participant structure of social interactions. The literature on white middle-class child development has been oriented, quite legitimately, toward the two-party relationship between infant and caregiver, typically infant and mother. The legitimacy of this focus rests on the fact that this relationship is primary for infants within this social group. Further, most communicative interactions are dyadic in the adult community. Although the mother is an important figure in both Kaluli and Samoan developmental stories, the interactions in which infants are participants are typically triadic or multiparty. As noted, Kaluli mothers organize triadic interactions in which infants and young children are oriented away from their mothers and toward a third party. For Samoans, the absence of internal and external walls, coupled with the expectation that others will attend to, and eventually participate in, conversation, makes multiparty interaction far more common. Infants are socialized to participate in such interactions in ways appropriate to the status and rank of the participants.

This is not to say that Kaluli and Samoan caregivers and children do not engage in dyadic exchanges. Rather, the point is that such exchanges are not accorded the same significance as in white middle-class society. In white middle-class households that have been studied, the process of becoming social takes place predominantly through dyadic interactions, and social competence itself is measured in terms of the young child's capacity to participate in such interactions. In Kaluli and Samoan households, the process of becoming social takes place through participation in dyadic, triadic, and multiparty social interactions, with the latter two more common than the dyad.

From an early age, Samoan and Kaluli children must learn how to participate in interactions involving a number of individuals. To do this minimally requires attending to more than one individual's words and actions and knowing the norms for when and how to enter interactions, taking into account the social identities of at least three participants. Further, the sequencing of turns in triadic and multiparty interactions has a far wider range of possibilities vis-à-vis dyadic exchanges and thus requires considerable knowledge and skill. Whereas dyadic exchanges can only be ABABA..., triadic or multiparty exchanges can be sequenced in a variety of ways, subject to such social constraints as speech content and the status of speaker (as discussed in the Samoan developmental story). For both the Kaluli and the Samoan child, triadic and multiparty interactions constitute their earliest social experiences and reflect the ways in which members of these societies routinely communicate with one another.

**Caregiver Register Reexamined** A second major proposal based on these three developmental stories is that the simplifying features of white middle-class speech are not necessary input for the acquisition of language by young children. The word "input" itself implies a directionality toward the child as information processor. The data base for the child's construction of language is assumed to be language directed *to* the child. It is tied to a model of communication that is dyadic, with participation limited to the roles of speaker and addressee. If we were to apply this strict notion of input (language addressed to the child) to the Kaluli and Samoan experiences, we would be left with a highly restricted corpus from which the child is expected to construct language. As we have emphasized in these developmental stories, the very young child is less often spoken to than spoken about. Nonetheless, both Kaluli and Samoan children become fluent speakers within the range of normal developmental variation.

Given that the features of caregivers' speech cannot be accounted for primarily in terms of their language-facilitating function, that is, as input, we might ask what can account for the special ways in which caregivers speak to their children. We suggest that the particular features of the caregiver register are best understood as an expression of a basic sociological phenomenon. Every social relationship is associated with a set of behaviors, verbal and nonverbal, that set off that relationship from other relationships. Additionally, these behaviors indicate to others that a particular social relationship is being actualized. From this point of view, the "special" features of caregiver speech are not special at all, in the sense that verbal modifications do occur wherever social relationships are called into play. This phenomenon has been overlooked in part because in describing the language of caregivers to children it is usually contrasted with a generalized notion of the ways in which adults talk to everyone else. The most extreme example of this is found in interviews with adults in which they are asked to describe special ways of talking to babies (Ferguson 1977). A less extreme example is found in the procedure of comparing caregiver speech to children with caregiver speech to the researcher/outsider (Newport, Gleitman, & Gleitman 1977). In the latter case, only one adult-adult relationship is used as a basis of comparison, and this relationship is typically formal and socially distant.

The social nature of caregiver speech has been discussed with respect to its status as a type of speech register. Nonetheless, the language-simplifying features have been emphasized more than any other aspect of the register. The dimension of simplification is significant with respect to the white middle-class caregiver registers documented; however, the notion of simplification has been taken as synonymous with the caregiver register itself. More to the point of this discussion is the apparent tendency to see simplification as a universal, if not natural, process. Ferguson's insightful parallel between caregiver speech and foreigner talk (1977) has been taken to mean that more competent speakers everywhere spontaneously accommodate their speech to less competent interactional partners, directly influencing language change in contact situations (pidgins in particular) as well as in acquisition of a foreign language. Ferguson's own discussion of "simplified registers" does not carry with it this conclusion, however. Further, the stories told here of Kaluli and Samoan caregiver speech and comportment indicate that simplification is culturally organized in terms of when, how, and extent. In both stories, caregivers do not speak in a dramatically more simplified manner to very young children. They do not do so for different cultural reasons: The Kaluli do not simplify because such speech is felt to inhibit the development of competent speech, the Samoans because such accommodations are dispreferred when the addressee is of lower rank than the speaker.

The cultural nature of simplification is evidenced very clearly when we compare Samoan speech to young children with Samoan speech to foreigners (*palagi*). As discussed by Duranti (1981), "foreigner talk" *is* simplified in many ways, in contrast to "baby talk." To understand this, we need only return to the social principle of relative rank. Foreigners typically (and historically) are persons to whom respect is appropriate – strangers or guests of relatively high status. The appropriate comportment toward such persons is one of accommodation to their needs, communicative needs being basic. The Samoan example is an important one, because we can use it to understand social groups for whom speaking to foreigners is like speaking to children. That is, we can at least know where to *start* the process of understanding this speech phenomenon: to see the phenomenon as expressive of cultural beliefs and values. Just as there are cultural explanations for why and how Samoans speak differently to young children and foreigners, so there are cultural explanations for why and how white middle-class adults modify their speech in similar ways to these two types of addressees. These explanations go far beyond the attitudes discussed in the white middle-class story. Our task here is not to provide an adequate cultural account but rather to encourage more detailed research along these lines. An understanding of caregiver or baby-talk register in a particular society will never be achieved without a more serious consideration of the sociological nature of register.

**What Caregivers Do with Words** In this section we build on the prior two proposals and suggest that:

1. A functional account of the speech of both caregiver and child must incorporate information concerning cultural knowledge and expectations;
2. Generalizations concerning the relations between the behavior and the goals of caregivers and young children should not presuppose the presence or equivalent significance of particular goals across social groups.

In each of these developmental stories we saw that caregivers and children interacted with one another in culturally patterned ways. Our overriding theme has been that caregiver speech behavior must be seen as part of caregiving and socialization more generally. What caregivers say and how they interact with young children are motivated in part by concerns and beliefs held by many members of the local community. As noted earlier, these concerns and beliefs may not be conscious in all cases. Certain beliefs, such as the Kaluli notions of the child as "soft" and socialization as "hardening" the child, are explicit. Others, such as the white middle-class notions of the infant and small child as social and capable of acting intentionally (expressing intentions), are not explicitly formulated.

To understand what any particular verbal behavior is accomplishing, we need to adopt ethnographic procedures, namely, to relate particular behaviors to those performed in other situations. What a caregiver is doing in speaking to a child is obviously related to what she or he does and/or others do in other recurrent situations. We have suggested, for example, that the accommodations that middle-class (particularly American) caregivers make in speaking to young children are linked patterned ways of responding to incompetence in general (e.g., handicapped persons, retardates). Members of this social group appear to adapt situations to meet the special demands of less competent persons to a far greater extent than in other societies, for example, Samoan society. We have also suggested that the heavy use of expansions by middle-class caregivers to query or confirm what a child is expressing is linked to culturally preferred procedures for achieving understanding, for example, the recognition of ambiguity, the formulation and verification of hypotheses (interpretations, guesses). In participating in interactions in which expansions are used in this way, the child learns the concepts of ambiguity, interpretation, and verification, and the procedures associated with them.

A common method in child language research has been to infer function or goal from behavior. The pitfalls of this procedure are numerous, and social scientists are acutely aware of how difficult it is to establish structure–function relations. One aspect of this dilemma is that one cannot infer function on the basis of a structure in isolation. Structures get their functional meaning through their relation to contexts in which they appear. The "same" structure may have different functions in different circumstances. This is true within a society, but our reason for mentioning it here is that it is true also across societies and languages. Although caregivers in two different societies may expand their children's utterances, it would not necessarily follow that the caregivers shared the same beliefs and values. It is possible that their behavior is motivated by quite different cultural processes. Similarly, the absence of a particular behavior, such as the absence of expansions among caregivers, may be motivated quite differently across societies. Both the Kaluli and the Samoan caregivers do not appear to rely on expansions, but the reasons expansions are dispreferred differ. The Samoans do not do so in part because of their dispreference for guessing and in part because of their expectation that the burden of intelligibility rests with the child (as lower status party) rather than with more mature members of the society. Kaluli do not use expansions to resay or guess what a child may be expressing because they say that "one cannot know what someone else thinks," regardless of age or social status.

Our final point concerning the structure–function relation is that the syntax of our claims about language acquisition must be altered to recognize variation across societies. The bulk of research on communicative development has presupposed or asserted the universality of one or another function, for example, the input function, the communicative function, and the illustrated verbal and nonverbal behaviors that follow from, or reflect, that function. Our three stories suggest that generalizations must be context-restricted. Thus, for example, rather than assuming or asserting that caregivers desire to communicate with an infant, the generalization should be expressed: "Where caregivers desire communication with an infant, then..." or "If it is the case that caregivers desire communication with an infant then..."

## A Typology of Socialization and Caregiver Speech Patterns

At this point, with the discussion nearing its conclusion, we have decided to stick our necks out a bit further and suggest that the two orientations to children discussed in the developmental stories – adapting situations to the child and adapting the child to situations – distinguish more than the three societies discussed in this chapter. We believe that these two orientations of mature members toward children can be used to create a **typology** of socialization patterns. For example, societies in which children are expected to adapt to situations may include not only Kaluli and Samoan but also white and black working-class Anglo-Americans (Heath 1983; Miller 1982; Ward 1971).

The typology of course requires a more refined application of these orienting features. We would expect these orientations to shift as children develop; for example, a society may adapt situations to meet the needs of a very small infant, but as the infant matures, the expectation may shift to one in which the child should adapt to situations. Indeed, we could predict such a pattern for most, if not all, societies. The distinction between societies would be in terms of *when* this shift takes place and in terms of the *intensity* of the orientation at any point in developmental time.

Having stuck our necks out this far, we will go a little further and propose that these two orientations will have systematic reflexes in the organization of communication between caregivers and young children across societies: We predict, for example, that a society that adapts or fits situations to the needs (perceived needs) of young children will use a register to children that includes a number of simplifying features, for example, shorter utterances, with a restricted lexicon, that refer to here-and-now. Such an orientation is also compatible with a tendency for caregivers to assist the child's expression of intentions through expansions, clarification requests, cooperative proposition building and the like. These often involve the caregiver's taking the perspective of a small child and correlate highly with allowing a small child to initiate new topics (evidencing child-centered orientation).

On the other hand, societies in which children are expected to meet the needs of the situation at hand will communicate differently with infants and small children. In these societies, children usually participate in multiparty situations. Caregivers will socialize children through language to notice others and perform appropriate (not necessarily polite) speech acts toward others. This socialization will often take the form of modeling, where the caregiver says what the child should say and directs the child to repeat. Typically, the child is directed to say something to someone other than the caregiver who has modeled the original utterance. From the Kaluli and Samoan cases, we would predict that the utterances to be repeated would cover a wide range of speech acts (teasing, insulting, greeting, information requesting, begging, reporting of news, shaming, accusations, and the like). In these interactions, as in other communicative contexts with children, the caregivers do not simplify their speech but rather shape their speech to meet situational contingencies (Table 9.1).

**Table 9.1** Two Orientations Toward Children and Their Corresponding Caregiver Speech Patterns

| Adapt Situation to Child | Adapt Child to Situation |
|---|---|
| Simplified register features baby-talk lexicon | Modeling of (unsimplified) utterances for child to repeat to third party (wide range of speech act, not simplified) |
| Negotiation of meaning via expansion and paraphrase | |
| Cooperative proposition building between caregiver and child | Child directed to notice others |
| Utterances that respond to child-initiated verbal or nonverbal act | Topics arise from range of situational circumstances to which caregiver wishes child to respond |
| Typical communicative situation: two-party | Typical communicative situation: multiparty |

## A Model of Language Acquisition Through Socialization (The Ethnographic Approach)

### Cultural Organization of Intentionality

Like many scholars of child language, we believe that the acquisition of language is keyed to accomplishing particular goals (Bates et al. 1979; Greenfield & Smith 1976; Halliday 1975; Lock 1978; Shotter 1978; Vygotsky 1962). As Bates and her colleagues (1979) as well as Carter (1978) and Lock (1981) have pointed out, small children perform communicative acts such as drawing attention to an object and requesting and offering before conventional morphemes are produced. They have acquired knowledge of particular social acts before they have acquired language in even the most rudimentary form. When language emerges, it is put to use in these and other social contexts. As Bates and her colleagues suggest, the use of language here is analogous to other behaviors of the child at this point of development; the child is using a new means to achieve old goals.

Although not taking a stand as to whether or not language is like other behaviors, we support the notion that language is acquired in a social world and that many aspects of the social world have been absorbed by the child by the time language emerges. This is not to say that functional considerations determine grammatical structure but rather that ends motivate means and provide an orienting principle for producing and understanding language over developmental time. Norman (1975), as well as Hood, McDermott, and Cole (1978), suggests that purpose/function is a mnemonic device for learning generally.

Much of the literature on early development has carefully documented the child's capacity to react and act intentionally (Harding & Golinkoff 1979). The nature and organization of communicative interaction is seen as integrally bound to this capacity. Our contribution to this literature is to spell out the social and cultural systems in which intentions participate. The capacity to express intentions is human but which intentions can be expressed by whom, when, and how is subject to local expectations concerning the social behavior of members. With respect to the acquisition of competence in language use, this means that societies may very well differ in their expectations of what children can and should communicate (Hymes 1967). They may also differ in their expectations concerning the capacity of young children to understand intentions (or particular intentions). With respect to the particular relationship between a child and his or her caregivers, these generalizations can be represented as follows:

SOCIAL EXPECTATIONS AND LANGUAGE ACQUISITION

| Expectations | *Influence* | Participation in social situations | How & which intentions are expressed by child *Influences* How & which intentions are expressed by caregiver | Structure of child language *Influence* Structure of caregiver language |
|---|---|---|---|---|

Let us consider examples that illustrate these statements. As noted in the Samoan development story, Samoans have a commonly shared expectation that a child's first word will be *tae* (shit) and that its communicative intention will be to curse and confront (corresponding to the adult [word] for *'ai tae* (eat shit). Whereas a range of early consonant-vowel combinations of the child are treated as expressing *tae* and communicative, other phonetic strings are not treated as language. The Kaluli consider that the child has begun to use language when he or she says "mother" and "breast." Like the Samoans, the Kaluli do not treat other words produced before these two words appear as part of "language," that is, as having a purpose.

Another example of how social expectations influence language acquisition comes from the recent work by Platt (1980) on Samoan children's acquisition of the deictic verbs "come," "go," "give," "take." The use of these verbs over developmental time is constrained by social norms concerning the movement of persons and objects. As noted in the Samoan story, higher ranking persons are expected to be relatively inactive in the company of lower ranking (e.g., younger) persons. As a consequence, younger children who are directed to "come" and who evidence comprehension of this act, tend not to perform the same act themselves. Children are socially constrained not to direct the more mature persons around them to move in their direction. On the other hand, small children are encouraged to demand and give out goods (particularly food). At the same developmental point at which the children are *not* using "come," they *are* using "give" quite frequently. This case is interesting because it indicates that a semantically more complex form ("give" – movement of object and person toward deictic center) may appear in the speech of a child earlier than a less complex form ("come" – movement of person toward deictic center) because of the social norms surrounding its use (Platt 1980).

Although these examples have focused on children's speech, we also consider caregiver speech to be constrained by local expectations and the values and beliefs that underlie them. The reader is invited to draw on the body of this chapter for examples of these relationships, for example, the relation between caregivers who adapt to young children and use of a simplified register. Indeed, the major focus of our developmental stories has been to indicate precisely the role of sociocultural processes in constructing communication between caregiver and child.

## Sociocultural Knowledge and Code Knowledge

In this section we will build on our argument that children's language is constructed in socially appropriate and culturally meaningful ways. Our point will be that the process of acquiring language must be understood as the process of integrating code knowledge with sociocultural knowledge.

Sociocultural knowledge is generative in much the same way that knowledge about grammar is generative. Just as children are able to produce and understand utterances that they have never heard before, so they are able to participate in social situations that don't exactly match their previous experiences. In the case of social situations in which language is used, children are able to apply both grammatical and sociocultural principles in producing and comprehending novel behavior. Both sets of principles can be acquired out of conscious awareness.

Developmental time ↑

Sociocultural → code
knowledge ← knowledge

In the case of infants and young children acquiring their first language(s), sociocultural knowledge is acquired hand-in-hand with the knowledge of code properties of a language. Acquisition of a foreign or second language by older children and adults may not necessarily follow this model. In classroom foreign-language learning, for example, a knowledge of code properties typically precedes knowledge of the cultural norms of code use. Even where the second language is acquired in the context of living in a foreign culture, the cultural knowledge necessary for appropriate social interaction may lag behind or never develop, as illustrated by Gumperz (1977) for Indian speakers in Great Britain.

Another point to be mentioned at this time is that the sociocultural principles being acquired are not necessarily shared by all native speakers of a language. As noted in the introduction, there are variations in knowledge between individuals and between groups of individuals. In certain cases, for example, children who are members of a nondominant group, growing up may necessitate acquiring different cultural frameworks for participating in situations. American Indian and Australian Aboriginal children find themselves participating in interactions in which the language is familiar but the interactional procedures and participant structures differ from earlier experiences (Philips 1983). These cases of growing up monolingually but biculturally are similar to the circumstances of second-language learners who enter a cultural milieu that differs from that of first socialization experiences.

## On the Unevenness of Language Development

The picture we have built up suggests that there is quite a complex system of norms and expectations that the young language acquirer must attend to, and does attend to, in the process of growing up to be a competent speaker-hearer. We have talked about this system as affecting structure and content of children's utterances at different points in developmental time. One product of all this is that children come to use and hear particular structures in certain contexts but not in others. In other words, children acquire forms in a subset of contexts that has been given "priority" by members.

Priority contexts are those in which children are encouraged to participate. For example, Kaluli and Samoan children use affect pronouns, for example, "poor-me," initially in begging, an activity they are encouraged to engage in. The use of affect pronouns in other speech acts is a later development. Similarly, many white middle-class children use their first nominal forms in the act of labeling, an activity much encouraged by caregivers in this social group. Labeling is not an activity in which Kaluli and Samoan caregivers and children engage in. Each social group will have its preferences, and these, in turn, will guide the child's acquisition of language.

## On Lack of Match Between Child and Caregiver Speech

Those who pursue the argument concerning how children acquire language often turn to correlational comparisons between children's and caregivers' speech strategies. Lack of match is taken as support for some input-independent strategy of the child and as evidence that some natural process is at work. We suggest that this line of reasoning has flaws.

If the reader has accepted the argument that societies have ideas about how children can and should participate in social situations and that these ideas differ in many respects from those concerning how more mature persons can and should behave, then the reader might further accept the conclusion that children may speak and act differently from others because they have learned to do so. Why should we equate input exclusively with imitation, that is, with a match in behavior? Of course there are commonalities between child and adult behavior, but that does not imply that difference is not learned. In examining the speech of young children, we should not necessarily expect their speech and the functions to which it is put to match exactly those of caregivers. Children are neither expected nor encouraged to do many of the things that older persons do, and, conversely, older persons are neither expected nor encouraged to do many of the things that small children do. Indeed, unless they are framed as "play," attempts to cross these social boundaries meet with laughter, ridicule, or other forms of negative sanctioning.

## A Note on the Role of Biology

Lest the reader think we advocate a model in which language and cognition are the exclusive product of culture, we note here that sociocultural systems are to be considered as *one* force influencing language acquisition. Biological predispositions, of course, have a hand in this process as well. The model we have presented should be considered as a subset of a more general acquisition model that includes both influences.

| | | |
|---|---|---|
| Social expectations | | Language over developmental time |
| | Influence | |
| Biological predispositions | | |

## CONCLUSIONS

This is a chapter with a number of points but one message: That the process of acquiring language and the process of acquiring sociocultural knowledge are intimately tied. In pursuing this generalization, we have formulated the following proposals:

1. The specific features of caregiver speech behavior that have been described as simplified register are neither universal nor necessary for language to be acquired. White middle-class children, Kaluli children, and Samoan children all become speakers of their languages within the normal range of development and yet their caregivers use language quite differently in their presence.
2. Caregivers' speech behavior expresses and reflects values and beliefs held by members of a social group. In this sense, caregivers' speech is part of a larger set of behaviors that are culturally organized.
3. The use of simplified registers by caregivers in certain societies may be part of a more general orientation in which situations are adapted to young children's perceived needs. In other societies, the orientation may be the reverse, that is, children at a very early age are expected to adapt to requirements of situations. In such societies, caregivers direct children to notice and respond to [others'] actions. They tend not to simplify their speech and frequently model appropriate utterances for the child to repeat to a third party in a situation.
4. Not only caregivers' but children's language as well is influenced by social expectations. Children's strategies for encoding and decoding information, for negotiating meaning, and for handling errors are socially organized in terms of who does the work, when, and how. Further, every society orchestrates the ways in which

> children participate in particular situations, and this, in turn, affects the form, the function, and the content of children's utterances. Certain features of the grammar may be acquired quite early, in part because their use is encouraged and given high priority. In this sense, the process of language acquisition is part of the larger process of socialization, that is, acquiring social competence.

Although biological factors play a role in language acquisition, sociocultural factors have a hand in this process as well. It is not a trivial fact that small children develop in the context of organized societies. Cultural conditions for communication organize even the earliest interactions between infants and others. Through participation as audience, addressee, and/or "speaker," the infant develops a range of skills, intuitions, and knowledge enabling him or her to communicate in culturally preferred ways. The development of these faculties is an integral part of becoming a competent speaker.

## Coda

This chapter should be in no way interpreted as proposing a view in which socialization determines a fixed pattern of behavior. We advocate a view that considers human beings to be flexible and able to adapt to change, both social and linguistic, for example, through contact and social mobility. The ways in which individuals change is a product of complex interactions between established cultural procedures and intuitions and those the individual is currently acquiring. From our perspective, socialization is a continuous and open-ended process that spans the entire life of an individual.

## Notes

This chapter was written while the authors were research fellows at the Research School of Pacific Studies, the Australian National University. We would like to thank Roger Keesing and the Working Group in Language and Its Cultural Context. Ochs's research was supported by the National Science Foundation and the Australian National University. Schieffelin's research was supported by the National Science Foundation and the Wenner-Gren Foundation for Anthropological Research. We thank these institutions for their support.

1. This story is based on the numerous accounts of caregiver-child communication and interaction that have appeared in both popular and scientific journals. Our generalizations regarding language use are based on detailed reports in the developmental psycholinguistic literature, which are cited throughout. In addition, we have drawn on our own experiences and intuitions as mothers and members of this social group. We invite those with differing perceptions to comment on our interpretations.

2. We would like to thank Courtney Cazden for bringing the following quotation to our attention: "It seems to us that a mother in expanding speech may be teaching more than grammar; she may be teaching something like a world-view" (Brown & Bellugi 1964).

3. This analysis is based on the data collected in the course of ethnographic and linguistic fieldwork among the Kaluli in the Southern Highlands Province between 1975 and 1977. During this time, E. L. Schieffelin, a cultural anthropologist, and S. Feld, an ethnomusicologist, were also conducting ethnographic research. This study of the development of communicative competence among the Kaluli focused on four children who were approximately 24 months old at the start of the study. However, an additional twelve children were included in the study (siblings and cousins in residence), ranging in age from birth to 10 years. The spontaneous conversations of these children and their families were tape-recorded for one year at monthly intervals with each monthly sample lasting from 3 to 4 hours. Detailed contextual notes accompanied the taping, and these annotated transcripts, along with interviews and observations, form the data base. A total of 83 hours of audio-tape were collected and transcribed in the village. Analyses of Kaluli child acquisition data are reported in Schieffelin 1981, in press-a, and in press-b.

4. The data on which this analysis is based were collected from July 1978 to July 1979 in a traditional village in Western Samoa. The village, Falefa, is located on the island of Upolu, approximately 18 miles from the capital, Apia. The fieldwork was conducted by Alessandro Duranti, Martha Platt, and Elinor Ochs. Our data collection consisted of two major projects. The first, carried out by Ochs and Platt, was a longitudinal documentation, through audio- and videotape, of young children's acquisition of Samoan. This was accomplished by focusing on six children from six different house holds, from 19 to 35 months of age at the onset of the study. These children were observed and taped every five weeks, approximately three hours each period. Samoan children live in compounds composed of several households. Typically, numerous siblings and peers are present and interact with a young child. We were able to record the speech of seventeen other children under the age of 6, who were part of the children's early social environment. A total of 128 hours of audio and 20 hours of video recording were collected. The audio material is supplemented by handwritten notes detailing contextual features of the interactions recorded. All the audio material has been transcribed in the village by a family member or family acquaintance and checked by a researcher. Approximately 18,000 pages of transcript form the child language data base. Analyses of Samoan child language are reported in Ochs 1982a, 1982b, and in press.

## References

Aksu, A., & Slobin, D. I. In press. Acquisition of Turkish. In D. I. Slobin, ed., *The Crosslinguistic Study of Language Acquisition*. Hillsdale, N.J.: Erlbaum.

Andersen, E. 1977. *Learning to speak with style*. Unpublished doctoral dissertation, Stanford University.

Andersen, E. S., Dunlea, A., & Kekelis, L. 1982. *Blind children's language: resolving some differences*. Paper presented at the Stanford Child Language Research Forum, Stanford, Calif.

Andersen, E. S., & Johnson, C. E. 1973. Modifications in the speech of an eight-year-old to younger children. *Stanford Occasional Papers in Linguistics*, No. 3: 149–60.

Bates, E. 1976. *Language and Context: the Acquisition of Pragmatics*. New York: Academic Press.

Bates, E., Beeghly-Smith, M., Bretherton, I., & McNew, S. In press. Social bases of language development: a reassessment. In H. W. Reese & L. P. Lipsitt, eds., *Advances in Child Development and Behavior*, vol. 16. New York: Academic Press.

Bates, E., Benigni, L., Bretherton, I., Camaioni, L., & Volterra, V. 1979. *The Emergence of Symbols*. New York: Academic Press.

Berko, J. 1958. The child's learning of English morphology. *Word* 14: 150–77.

Berman, R. In press. Acquisition of Hebrew. In D. I. Slobin, ed., *The Crosslinguistic Study of Language Acquisition*. Hillsdale, N.J.: Erlbaum.

Bever, T. 1970. The cognitive basis for linguistic structure. In J. R. Hayes, ed., *Cognition and the Development of Language*. New York: Wiley.

Bloom, L. 1970. *Language Development: Form and Function in Emerging Grammars*. Cambridge, Mass.: MIT Press.

Bloom, L. 1973. *One Word at a Time*. The Hague: Mouton.

Bloom, L., Hood, L., & Lightbown, P. 1974. Imitation in language development: if, when, and why? *Cognitive Psychology* 6: 380–420.

Bloom, L., & Lahey, M. 1978. *Language Development and Language Disorders*. New York: Wiley.

Bloom, L., Lightbown, P., & Hood, L. 1975. Structure and variation in child language. *Monographs of the Society for Research in Child Development* 40 (2, serial no. 160).

Blount, B. 1972. Aspects of socialization among the Luo of Kenya. *Language in Society* 1: 235–48.

Bowerman, M. 1973. *Early Syntactic Development: A Crosslinguistic Study with Special Reference to Finnish*. Cambridge: Cambridge University Press.

Bowerman, M. 1977. Semantic and syntactic development: a review of what, when, and how in language acquisition. In R. Schiefelbusch, ed., *Bases of Language Intervention*. Baltimore: University Park Press.

Bowerman, M. 1981. Language development. In H. Triandis & A. Heron, eds., *Handbook of Cross-cultural Psychology*, vol. 4. Boston: Allyn & Bacon.

Briggs, J. L. 1970. *Never in Anger: Portrait of an Eskimo Family*. Cambridge, Mass.: Harvard University Press.

Brown, R. 1973. *A First Language: The Early Stages*. Cambridge, Mass.: Harvard University Press.

Brown, R. 1977. Introduction. In C. Snow & C. Ferguson, eds., *Talking to Children: Language Input and Acquisition*. Cambridge: Cambridge University Press.

Brown, R., & Bellugi, U. 1964. Three processes in the child's acquisition of syntax. *Harvard Educational Review* 34: 133–51.

Brown, R., Cazden C., & Bellugi, U. 1969. The child's grammar from I to III. In J. P. Hill, ed., *Minnesota Symposium on Child Psychology*, vol. 2. Minneapolis: University of Minnesota Press.

Bruner, J. S. 1975. The ontogenesis of speech acts. *Journal of Child Language* 2: 1–19.

Bruner, J. S. 1977. Early social interaction and language acquisition. In H. R. Schaffer, ed., *Studies in Mother-Infant Interaction*. London: Academic Press.

Bruner, J. S. 1978. The role of dialogue in language acquisition. In A. Sinclair, R. J. Jarvella, & W. J. M. Levelt, eds., *The Child's Conception of Language*. New York: Springer-Verlag.

Bullowa, M. 1979. Introduction: prelinguistic communication: a field for scientific research. In M. Bullowa, ed., *Before Speech: The Beginnings of Interpersonal Communication*. Cambridge: Cambridge University Press.

Carter, A. L. 1978. From sensori-motor vocalizations to words. In A. Lock, ed., *Action, Gesture and Symbol: The Emergence of Language*. London: Academic Press.

Cazden, C. 1965. *Environmental assistance to the child's acquisition of grammar*. Unpublished doctoral dissertation, Harvard University.

Chomsky, N. 1959. Review of *Verbal Behavior* by B. F. Skinner. *Language* 35: 26–58.

Chomsky, N. 1965. *Aspects of the Theory of Syntax*. Cambridge, Mass.: MIT Press.

Chomsky, N. 1968. *Language and Mind*. New York: Harcourt Brace Jovanovich.

Chomsky, N. 1975. *Reflections on Language*. Glasgow: Fontana/Collins.

Chomsky, N. 1977. *Essays on Form and Interpretation*. New York: North Holland.

Clancy, P. In press. Acquisition of Japanese. In D. I. Slobin, ed., *The Cross-linguistic Study of Language Acquisition*. Hillsdale, N.J.: Erlbaum.

Clark, E. V. 1974. Some aspects of the conceptual basis for first language acquisition. In R. L. Schiefelbusch & L. Lloyd, eds., *Language Perspectives: Acquisition, Retardation and Intervention*. Baltimore: University Park Press.

Clark, E. V. In press. Acquisition of Romance, with special reference to French. In D. I. Slobin, ed., *The Crosslinguistic Study of Language Acquisition*. Hillsdale, N.J.: Erlbaum.

Clark, H. H., & Clark, E. V. 1977. *Psychology and Language*. New York: Harcourt Brace Jovanovich.

Corsaro, W. 1979. Sociolinguistic patterns in adult-child interaction. In E. Ochs & B. B. Schieffelin, eds., *Developmental Pragmatics*. New York: Academic Press.

Cross, T. 1977. Mothers' speech adjustments: the contributions of selected child listener variables. In C. Snow & C. Ferguson, eds., *Talking to Children: Language Input and Acquisition*. Cambridge: Cambridge University Press.

de Lemos, C. 1981. Interactional processes in the child's construction of language. In W. Deutsch, ed., *The Child's Construction of Language*. London: Academic Press.

Dentan, R. K. 1978. Notes on childhood in a nonviolent context: the Semai case. In A. Montagu, ed., *Learning Non-aggression: The Experience of Nonliterate Societies*. Oxford: Oxford University Press.

Dore, J. 1975. Holophrases, speech acts and language universals. *Journal of Child Language* 2: 21–40.

Drach, K. 1969. *The language of the parent.* Working paper 14, Language Behavior Research Laboratory, University of California, Berkeley.

Duranti, A. 1981. *The Samoan Fono: A Sociolinguistic Study.* Pacific Linguistic Series B, vol. 80. Canberra: Australian National University.

Edgerton, R. 1967. *The Cloak of Competence: Stigma in the Lives of the Mentally Retarded.* Berkeley: University of California Press.

Eisenberg, A. 1982. *Language acquisition in cultural perspective: talk in three Mexicano homes.* Unpublished doctoral dissertation, University of California, Berkeley.

Ervin-Tripp, S. 1964. Imitation and structural change in children's language. In E. Lenneberg, ed., *New Directions in the Study of Language.* Cambridge, Mass.: MIT Press.

Feld, S., & Schieffelin, B. B. 1982. Hard words: A functional basis for Kaluli discourse. In D. Tannen, ed., *Analyzing Discourse: Talk and Text.* Washington, D.C.: Georgetown University Press.

Feldman, H., Goldin-Meadow, S., & Gleitman, L. 1978. Beyond Herodotus: the creation of language by linguistically deprived deaf children. In A. Lock, ed., *Action, Gesture and Symbol.* London: Academic Press.

Ferguson, C. 1977. Baby talk as a simplified register. In C. Snow & C. Ferguson, eds., *Talking to Children: Language Input and Acquisition.* Cambridge: Cambridge University Press.

Fischer, J. 1970. Linguistic socialization: Japan and the United States. In R. Hill & R. Konig, eds., *Families in East and West.* The Hague: Mouton.

Fodor, J., Bever, T., & Garrett, M. 1974. *The Psychology of Language.* New York: McGraw-Hill.

Foster, S. 1981. The emergence of topic type in children under 2: 6: a chicken and egg problem. *Papers and Reports in Child Language Development*, No. 20. Stanford, Calif.: Stanford University Press.

Gallimore, R., Boggs, J., & Jordan, C. 1974. *Culture, Behavior and Education: a Study of Hawaiian Americans.* Beverly Hills, Calif.: Sage.

Garnica, O. 1977. Some prosodic and para-linguistic features of speech to young children. In C. Snow & C. Ferguson, eds., *Talking to Children: Language Input and Acquisition.* Cambridge: Cambridge University Press.

Geertz, C. 1973. *The Interpretation of Cultures.* New York: Basic Books.

Geertz, H. 1959. The vocabulary of emotion: a study of Javanese socialization processes. *Psychiatry* 22: 225–37.

Gleason, J. B., & Weintraub, S. 1978. Input language and the acquisition of communicative competence. In K. Nelson, ed., *Children's Language*, vol. 1. New York: Gardner Press.

Goffman, E. 1963. *Behavior in Public Places.* New York: Free Press.

Goffman, E. 1967. *Interaction Ritual: Essays on Face to Face Behavior.* Garden City, N.Y.: Doubleday (Anchor Books).

Goldin-Meadow, S. 1977. Structure in a manual language system developed without a language model: language without a helping hand. In H. Whitaker & H. A. Whitaker, eds., *Studies in Neurolinguistics*, vol. 4. New York: Academic Press.

Golinkoff, R., ed. 1983. *The Transition from Prelinguistic to Linguistic Communication.* Hillsdale, N.J.: Erlbaum.

Goody, E. 1978. Towards a theory of questions. In E. Goody, ed., *Questions and Politeness.* Cambridge: Cambridge University Press.

Greenfield, P. 1979. Informativeness, presupposition and semantic choice in single-word utterances. In E. Ochs & B. B. Schieffelin, eds., *Developmental Pragmatics.* New York: Academic Press.

Greenfield, P. M., & Smith, J. H. 1976. *The Structure of Communication in Early Language Development.* New York: Academic Press.

Gumperz, J. 1977. The conversational analysis of interethnic communication. In E. L. Ross, ed., *Interethnic Communication. Proceedings of the Southern Anthropological Society.* Athens: University of Georgia Press.

Halliday, M. A. K. 1975. *Learning How to Mean: Explorations in the Development of Language.* London: Arnold.

Hamilton, A. 1981. *Nature and Nurture: Aboriginal Childrearing in North-Central Arnhem Land.* Canberra, Australia: Institute of Aboriginal Studies.

Harding, C., & Golinkoff, R. M. 1979. The origins of intentional vocalizations in prelinguistic infants. *Child Development* 50: 33–40.

Harkness, S. 1975. Cultural variation in mother's language. In W. von Raffler-Engel, ed., *Child Language – 1975, Word* 27: 495–8.

Harkness, S., & Super, C. 1977. Why African children are so hard to test. In L. L. Adler, ed., *Issues in Cross Cultural Research: Annals of the New York Academy of Sciences* 285: 326–31.

Harkness, S., & Super, C. eds. 1980. *Anthropological Perspectives on Child Development.* New Directions for Child Development, no. 8. San Francisco: Jossey-Bass.

Heath, S. B. 1983. *Ways with Words: Language, Life and Work in Communities and Classrooms.* Cambridge: Cambridge University Press.

Hood, L., McDermott, R., & Cole, M. 1978. *Ecological niche-picking* (Working Paper 14). Unpublished manuscript, Rockefeller University, Laboratory of Comparative Human Cognition, New York.

Huttenlocher, J. 1974. The origins of language comprehension. In R. L. Solso, ed., *Theories of Cognitive Psychology.* Hillsdale, N.J.: Erlbaum.

Hymes, D. 1967. Models of the interaction of language and social setting. *Journal of Social Issues* 23(2): 8–28.

Hymes, D. 1974. *Foundations in Sociolinguistics: An Ethnographic Approach.* Philadelphia: University of Pennsylvania Press.

Irvine, J. 1974. Strategies of status manipulation in the Wolof greeting. In R. Bauman & J. Sherzer, eds., *Explorations in the Ethnography of Speaking.* Cambridge: Cambridge University Press.

Johnston, J. R., & Slobin, D. I. 1979. The development of locative expressions in English, Italian, Serbo-Croatian and Turkish. *Journal of Child Language* 6: 529–45.

Karmiloff-Smith, A. 1979. *A Functional Approach to Child Language*. Cambridge: Cambridge University Press.

Keenan, E., Ochs E., & Schieffelin, B. B. 1976. Topic as a discourse notion: a study of topic in the conversations of children and adults. In C. Li, ed., *Subject and Topic*. New York: Academic Press.

Kernan, K. T. 1969. *The acquisition of language by Samoan children*. Unpublished doctoral dissertation, University of California, Berkeley.

Korbin, J. 1978. *Caretaking patterns in a rural Hawaiian community*. Unpublished doctoral dissertation, University of California, Los Angeles.

Leiderman, P. H., Tulkin, S. R., & Rosenfeld, A., eds. 1977. *Culture and Infancy*. New York: Academic Press.

LeVine, R. 1980. Anthropology and child development. *Anthropological Perspectives on Child Development*. New Directions for Child Development, no. 8. San Francisco: Jossey-Bass.

Levy, R. 1973. *The Tahitians*. Chicago: University of Chicago Press.

Lewis, M., & Rosenblum, L. A., eds. 1974. *The Effect of the Infant on Its Caregiver*. New York: Wiley.

Lieven, E. 1980. Different routes to multiple-word combinations? *Papers and Reports in Child Language Development*, no. 19, Stanford University, Stanford, Calif.

Lock, A. 1978. *Action, Gesture and Symbol*. London: Academic Press.

Lock, A. 1981. *The Guided Reinvention of Language*. London: Academic Press.

MacNamara, J. 1972. The cognitive basis of language learning in infants. *Psychological Review* 79: 1–13.

MacWhinney, B. 1975. Rules, rote and analogy in morphological formation by Hungarian children. *Journal of Child Language* 2: 65–77.

MacWhinney, B., & Bates, E. 1978. Sentential devices for conveying givenness and newness: a cross-cultural developmental study. *Journal of Verbal Learning and Verbal Behavior* 17: 539–58.

McNeill, D. 1966. The creation of language by children. In J. Lyons & R. J. Wales, eds., *Psycholinguistic Papers*. Edinburgh: Edinburgh University Press.

McNeill, D. 1970. *The Acquisition of Language*. New York: Harper & Row.

Mead, M. 1927. *Coming of Age in Samoa*. New York: Blue Ribbon Books.

Mead, M. 1975. *Growing Up in New Guinea*. New York: Morrow. Originally published, 1935.

Mead, M., & MacGregor, F. 1951. *Growth and Culture*. New York: Putnam.

Mead, M., & Wolfenstein, M. 1955. *Childhood in Contemporary Cultures*. Chicago: University of Chicago Press.

Menyuk, P., & Menn, L. 1979. Early strategies for the perception and production of words and sounds. In P. Fletcher & M. Garman, eds., *Language Acquisition*. Cambridge: Cambridge University Press.

Miller, G., & Chomsky, N. 1963. Finitary models of language users. In R. Bush, E. Galanter, & R. Luce, eds., *Handbook of Mathematical Psychology*, vol. 2. New York: Wiley.

Miller, P. 1982. *Amy, Wendy and Beth: Learning Language in South Baltimore*. Austin: University of Texas Press.

Montagu, A. 1937. *Coming into Being Among the Australian Aborigines: A Study of the Procreation Beliefs of the Native Tribes of Australia*. London: Routledge.

Montagu, A., ed. 1978. *Learning Non-aggression: The Experience of Nonliterate Societies*. Oxford: Oxford University Press.

Much, N., & Shweder R. 1978. Speaking of rules: the analysis of culture in breach. In W. Damon, ed., *Moral Development*. New Directions for Child Development, no. 2. San Francisco: Jossey-Bass.

Munroe, R. L., & Munroe, R. N. 1975. *Cross Cultural Human Development*. Monterey, Calif.: Brooks/Cole.

Nelson, K. 1974. Concept, word and sentence: interrelations in acquisition and development. *Psychological Review* 81: 267–85.

Newport, E. L. 1976. Motherese: The speech of mothers to young children. In N. J. Castellan, D. B. Pisoni, & G. R. Potts, eds., *Cognitive Theory*, vol. 2. Hillsdale, N.J.: Erlbaum.

Newport, E. L. 1981. Constraints on structure: evidence from American sign language and language learning. In W. A. Collins, ed., *Minnesota Symposium on Child Psychology*, vol. 14. Hillsdale, N.J.: Erlbaum.

Newport, E. L., Gleitman, H., & Gleitman, L. R. 1977. Mother, I'd rather do it myself: some effects and non-effects of maternal speech style. In C. Snow & C. Ferguson, eds., *Talking to Children: Language Input and Acquisition*. Cambridge: Cambridge University Press.

Newson, J. 1977. An intersubjective approach to the systematic description of mother-infant interaction. In H. R. Schaffer, ed., *Studies in Mother-Infant Interaction*. London: Academic Press.

Newson, J. 1978. Dialogue and development. In A. Lock, ed., *Action, Gesture and Symbol*. London: Academic Press.

Ninio, A. 1979. The naive theory of the infant and other maternal attitudes in two subgroups in Israel. *Child Development* 50: 976–80.

Norman, D. A. 1975. Cognitive organization and learning. In P. M. A. Rabbitt & S. Dornic, eds., *Attention and Performance V*. New York: Academic Press.

Ochs, E. 1982a. *Affect in Samoan child language*. Paper presented to the Stanford Child Language Research Forum, Stanford, Calif.

Ochs, E. 1982b. Ergativity and word order in Samoan child language: a sociolinguistic study. *Language* 58: 646–71.

Ochs, E. 1982c. Talking to children in Western Samoa. *Language in Society* 11: 77–104.

Ochs, E. In press. Variation and error: a sociolinguistic study of language acquisition in Samoa. In D. I. Slobin, ed., *The Crosslinguistic Study of Language Acquisition*. Hillsdale, N.J.: Erlbaum.

Ochs, E., Schieffelin, B. B., & Platt, M. 1979. Propositions across utterances and speakers. In E. Ochs & B. B. Schieffelin, eds., *Developmental Pragmatics*. New York: Academic Press.

Philips, S. 1983. *The Invisible Culture*. New York: Longman.

Phillips, J. 1973. Syntax and vocabulary of mothers' speech to young children: age and sex comparisons. *Child Development* 44: 182–5.

Piaget, J. 1955. *The Language and Thought of the Child*. London: Routledge & Kegan Paul. Originally published, 1926.

Piattelli-Palmarini, M., ed. 1980. *Language and Learning: The Debate Between Jean Piaget and Noam Chomsky*. Cambridge, Mass.: Harvard University Press.

Platt, M. 1980. The acquisition of "come," "give," and "bring" by Samoan children. *Papers and Reports in Child Language Development*, no. 19. Stanford, Calif.: Stanford University.

Richards, M. P. M., ed. 1974. *The Integration of a Child into a Social World*. Cambridge: Cambridge University Press.

Ryan, J. 1974. Early language development: towards a communicational analysis. In M. P. M. Richards, ed., *The Integration of a Child into a Social World*. Cambridge: Cambridge University Press.

Sachs, J. 1977. Adaptive significance of input to infants. In C. Snow & C. Ferguson, eds., *Talking to Children: Language Input and Acquisition*. Cambridge: Cambridge University Press.

Sachs, J., Brown, R., & Salerno, R. 1976. Adults' speech to children. In W. von Raffler Engel & Y. Lebrun, eds., *Baby Talk and Infant Speech*. Lisse: Riddler Press.

Sachs, J., & Devin, J. 1976. Young children's use of age-appropriate speech styles. *Journal of Child Language* 3: 81–98.

Schaffer, H. R., ed. 1977. *Studies in Mother-Infant Interaction*. London: Academic Press.

Schieffelin, B. B. 1979. Getting it together: an ethnographic approach to the study of the development of communicative competence. In E. Ochs & B. B. Schieffelin, eds., *Developmental Pragmatics*. New York: Academic Press.

Schieffelin, B. B. 1981. A developmental study of pragmatic appropriateness of word order and case marking in Kaluli. In W. Deutsch, ed., *The Child's Construction of Language*. London: Academic Press.

Schieffelin, B. B. In press-a. Acquisition of Kaluli. In D. I. Slobin, ed., *The Crosslinguistic Study of Language Acquisition*. Hillsdale, N.J.: Erlbaum.

Schieffelin, B. B. In press-b. *How Kaluli Children Learn What to Say, What to Do and How to Feel*. Cambridge: Cambridge University Press.

Schieffelin, B. B., & Eisenberg, A. 1984. Cultural variation in children's conversations. In R. L. Schiefelbusch & J. Pickar, eds., *Communicative Competence: Acquisition and Intervention*. Baltimore: University Park Press.

Schieffelin, E. L. 1976. *The Sorrow of the Lonely and the Burning of the Dancers*. New York: St. Martin's Press.

Schlesinger, I. M. 1974. Relational concepts underlying language. In R. Schiefelbusch & L. Lloyd, eds., *Language Perspectives – Acquisition, Retardation and Intervention*, Baltimore: University Park Press.

Scollon, R. 1976. *Conversations with a One Year Old*. Honolulu: University Press of Hawaii.

Scollon, R., & Scollon, S. 1981. The literate two-year old: the fictionalization of self. Abstracting themes: a Chipewyan two-year-old. *Narrative, Literacy and Face in Interethnic Communication*. Vol. 7 of R. O. Freedle, ed., *Advances in Discourse Processes*. Norwood, N.J.: Ablex.

Shatz, M. 1978. The relationship between cognitive processes and the development of communication skills. In C. B. Keasey, ed., *Nebraska Symposium on Motivation*, vol. 25. Lincoln: University of Nebraska Press.

Shatz, M. 1981. Learning the rules of the game: four views of the relation between social interaction and syntax acquisition. In W. Deutch, ed., *The Child's Construction of Language*. London: Academic Press.

Shatz, M. In press. Communication. In J. Flavell & E. Markman, eds., *Cognitive Development*, P. Mussen, gen. ed., *Carmichael's Manual of Child Psychology*, 4th ed. New York: Wiley.

Shatz, M., & Gelman, R. 1973. The development of communication skills: modifications in the speech of young children as a function of listener. *Monographs of the Society for Research in Child Development*, 152 (38, serial no. 5).

Shore, B. 1982. *Sala' Ilua: A Samoan Mystery*. New York: Columbia University Press.

Shotter, J. 1978. The cultural context of communication studies: theoretical and methodological issues. In A. Lock, ed., *Action, Gesture and Symbol*. London: Academic Press.

Sinclair, H. 1971. Sensorimotor action patterns as a condition for the acquisition of syntax. In R. Huxley & E. Ingram, eds., *Language Acquisition: Models and Methods*. New York: Academic Press.

Skinner, B. F. 1957. *Verbal Behavior*. New York: Appleton-Century-Crofts.

Slobin, D. I., ed. 1967. *A Field Manual for Cross-cultural Study of the Acquisition of Communicative Competence*. Language Behavior Research Laboratory, University of California, Berkeley.

Slobin, D. I. 1973. Cognitive prerequisites for grammar. In C. Ferguson & D. I. Slobin, eds., *Studies in Child Language Development*. New York: Holt, Rinehart and Winston.

Slobin, D. I. 1979. *Psycholinguistics*, 2nd ed. Glenview, Ill.: Scott Foresman.

Slobin, D. I. 1981. The origin of grammatical encoding of events. In W. Deutsch, ed., *The Child's Construction of Language*. London: Academic Press.

Slobin, D. I. 1982. Universal and particular in the acquisition of language. In E. Wanner & L. R. Gleitman, eds., *Language Acquisition: The State of the Art*. Cambridge: Cambridge University Press.

Slobin, D. I., ed. In press. *The Crosslinguistic Study of Language Acquisition.* Hillsdale, N.J.: Erlbaum.

Snow, C. 1972. Mothers' speech to children learning language. *Child Development* 43: 549–65.

Snow, C. 1977a. The development of conversation between mothers and babies. *Journal of Child Language* 4: 1–22.

Snow, C. 1977b. Mothers' speech research: from input to inter-action. In C. Snow & C. Ferguson, eds., *Talking to Children: Language Input and Acquisition.* Cambridge: Cambridge University Press.

Snow, C. 1979. Conversations with children. In P. Fletcher & M. Garman, eds., *Language Acquisition.* Cambridge: Cambridge University Press.

Snow, C., de Blauw, A., & van Roosmalen, G. 1979. Talking and playing with babies: the role of ideologies of child-rearing. In M. Bullowa, ed., *Before Speech: The Beginnings of Interpersonal Communication.* Cambridge: Cambridge University Press.

Snow, C., & Ferguson, C., eds. 1977. *Talking to Children: Language Input and Acquisition.* Cambridge: Cambridge University Press.

Stern, D. 1977. *The First Relationship: Infant and Mother.* Cambridge, Mass.: Harvard University Press.

Stross, B. 1972. Verbal processes in Tzeltal speech socialization. *Anthropological Linguistics* 14: 1.

Sugarman, S. 1984. The development of preverbal communication: its contribution and limits in promoting the development of language. In R. L. Schiefelbusch & J. Pickar, eds., *Communicative Competence: Acquisition and Intervention.* Baltimore: University Park Press.

Trevarthen, C. 1979a. Communication and cooperation in early infancy: a description of primary intersubjectivity. In M. Bullowa, ed., *Before Speech: The Beginnings of Interpersonal Communication.* Cambridge: Cambridge University Press.

Trevarthen, C. 1979b. Instincts for human understanding and for cultural cooperation: their development in infancy. In M. von Cranach, K. Foppa, W. Lepenies, & D. Ploog, eds., *Human Ethology: Claims and Limits of a New Discipline.* Cambridge: Cambridge University Press.

van der Geest, T. 1977. Some interactional aspects of language acquisition. In C. Snow & C. Ferguson, eds., *Talking to Children: Language Input and Acquisition.* Cambridge: Cambridge University Press.

von Sturmer, D. E. 1980. *Rights in nurturing.* Unpublished master's thesis, Australian National University, Canberra.

Vygotsky, L. S. 1962. *Thought and Language.* Cambridge, Mass.: MIT Press.

Wagner, D., & Stevenson, H. W., eds. 1982. *Cultural Perspectives on Child Development.* San Francisco: Freeman.

Wanner E., & Gleitman, L. R., eds. 1982. *Language Acquisition: The State of the Art.* Cambridge: Cambridge University Press.

Ward, M. 1971. *Them Children: A Study in Language Learning.* New York: Holt, Rinehart and Winston.

Watson-Gegeo, K., & Gegeo, D. 1982. *Calling out and repeating: two key routines in Kwara'ae children's language acquisition.* Paper presented at the American Anthropological Association meetings, Washington, D.C.

Weisner, T. S., & Gallimore, R. 1977. My brother's keeper: child and sibling caretaking. *Current Anthropology* 18(2): 169–90.

Werner, H., & Kaplan, B. 1963. *Symbol Formation.* New York: Wiley.

Whiting, B., ed. 1963. *Six Cultures: Studies of Child Rearing.* New York: Wiley.

Whiting, B., & Whiting, J. 1975. *Children of Six Cultures.* Cambridge, Mass.: Harvard University Press.

Williams, T. R. 1969. *A Borneo Childhood: Enculturation in Dusun Society.* New York: Holt, Rinehart and Winston.

Wills, D. 1977. *Culture's cradle: social structural and interactional aspects of Senegalese socialization.* Unpublished doctoral dissertation, University of Texas, Austin.

## Critical Thinking and Application

- What do Ochs and Schieffelin mean about "the sharing of assumptions between researcher, reader, and subjects of study [being] a mixed blessing" and representing a "paradox of familiarity"? What is gained and what is lost by researchers studying their own society?
- How can a careful comparative study challenge assumptions about what is "natural"?
- Why is there a correspondence between adapting to young children and the existence of simplified registers? Would you expect other consistencies between cultural patterns and forms of interaction with young children? Give examples.
- Given the range of observed variation in language socialization, do you think there is any common, universal aspect to development? What, if any, is the role of biology?
- Observe children interacting with their caregivers. (If you wish, you can watch movies that include child/caregiver interactions.) Describe the situation carefully, modeling your account on one of those given by Ochs and Schieffelin.

## Vocabulary

accommodation
addressee
baby-talk register
caregiver
culturally constructed
dyad, dyadic
ethnographic, ethnography
evidential marker
expansion
innatist
nativist
rank
register
scaffolding
status
stratified, stratification
triadic
typology
Universal Grammar

## Suggested Further Reading [See also list following Language Socialization unit introduction]

Bloom, Lois. 1970. *Language Development: Form and Function in Emerging Grammars*. Cambridge, MA: MIT Press.

Bloom, Lois, Erin Tinker, and Ellin Kofsky Scholnick. 2001. *The Intentionality Model and Language Acquisition: Engagement, Effort, and the Essential Tension in Development*. Boston: Blackwell.

Bowerman, Melissa. 1973. *Early Syntactic Development: A Cross-Linguistic Study with Special Reference to Finnish*. Cambridge: Cambridge University Press.

Ferguson, Charles A. 1977. Baby Talk as a Simplified Register. In *Talking to Children: Language Input and Acquisition*, edited by Catherine E. Snow and Charles A. Ferguson, pp. 209–234. Cambridge: Cambridge University Press.

Golinkoff, Roberta M., and Kathy Hirsh-Pasek. 1999. *How Babies Talk: The Magic and Mystery of Language in the First Three Years of Life*. New York: Dutton.

Greenfield, Patricia Marks, and Joshua H. Smith. 1976. *The Structure of Communication in Early Language Development*. New York: Academic Press.

Halliday, M. A. K. 1975. *Learning How to Mean: Explorations in the Development of Language*. London: Arnold.

Harkness, Sara, and Charles M. Super. 1980. *Anthropological Perspectives on Child Development*. San Francisco: Jossey-Bass.

Harkness, Sara, and Charles M. Super. 1996. *Parents' Cultural Belief Systems: Their Origins, Expressions, and Consequences*. New York: Guilford Press.

Scollon, Ronald. 1976. *Conversations with a One Year Old: A Case Study of the Developmental Foundation of Syntax*. Honolulu: Hawaii University Press.

Slobin, Dan Isaac, ed. 1985. *The Cross-Linguistic Study of Language Acquisition*. Hillsdale, NJ: Erlbaum.

Snow, Catherine E., and Charles A. Ferguson, eds. 1977. *Talking to Children: Language Input and Acquisition*. Cambridge: Cambridge University Press.

Ward, Martha. 1971. *Them Children: A Study in Language Learning*. New York: Holt, Rinehart & Winston.

Whiting, Beatrice Blyth, ed. 1963. *Six Cultures: Studies of Child Rearing*. New York: Wiley.

Whiting, Beatrice Blyth, and John Wesley Mayhew Whiting. 1975. *Children of Six Cultures: A Psycho-Cultural Analysis*. Cambridge, MA: Harvard University Press.

# CHAPTER 10

# What No Bedtime Story Means: Narrative Skills at Home and at School

*Shirley Brice Heath*

(1982)

*Shirley Brice Heath's detailed work on the nature of language and literacy in three nearby but differing Appalachian societies opened up the study of what is now considered, in the plural,* literacies. *It is evident from her work that different social and ethnic groups even within the same country might have different attitudes toward children and their speech, toward writing and reading, toward authority, toward the nature of asking questions, toward learning, and virtually everything else. Each subsociety imbues behavior with morality, but sometimes the morality is the reverse valance of someone else's. Of course, cultural relativism—the idea that differences are merely neutral—is not entirely possible when the values and practices of one of the groups are institutionalized into schools and present a standard against which all groups are measured. Thus, "understanding" the differences may be a starting point, but it is necessary to suggest a practical way of navigating a world where some groups are doomed to "fail" simply because their ways of interacting are not those of the dominant group. Heath has done that as well. (She describes it in detail in the book-length treatment of this subject.) In the affluent and optimistic days of the 1970s, she suggested an approach that could both respect the practices of the nondominant group and assist them in succeeding within a school system that is largely unconscious of difference. Those days, sadly, seem to be long over.*

*Heath's work, like that of Ochs and Schieffelin, has served as the inspiration for a rich body of research modeled on it (see, e.g., Mahiri, Chapter 17 in this book). The results have been nuanced and probing, pointing to differences in children's language and literacy practices that may not usually be attributed to culture but are often seen as individual failure to conform to absolute norms. These analytic tools provide another way of looking at people we may interact with daily.*

## Reading Questions

- Compare the three societies analyzed in this chapter on the basis of their practices regarding:
  - baby-talk register
  - babies as conversational partners
  - questions asked of preschoolers
  - caregivers' guesses with regard to infants' intentions
  - talk used primarily for...
  - gender differences in language socialization
  - housing, room decorations, and arrangements
  - sleeping arrangements
  - baby-carrying position
  - number of participants in typical conversations
  - direction of accommodation
  - types of stories
  - when reading is done

Shirley Brice Heath. What No Bedtime Story Means: Narrative Skills at Home and at School. *Language in Society* 11 (1), 1982: 49–76.

- what reading is used for
- relationship between content of books and the world
- use of written sources in everyday life (by adults and children)
- attentiveness to books
- questions about books
- ideas of truth and lies, reality and fiction, and their places in books
- books as entertainment
- preschoolers' factual and fictional narrative openings
- age at which child becomes an audience for reading a book
- attitudes toward the use of and care of books
- types of toys
- children's incorporation into or separation from adults' activities
- how children are taught to accomplish tasks
- What is the relationship between Maintown's "bedtime story" and school success? Which specific aspects of book-related behavior in Roadville and Trackton are antagonistic to school practices, at least in certain grades? Which are supportive of school practices in other grades?
- How do religious and moral ideas intersect with ideas about literacy?

---

In the preface to *S/Z*, Roland Barthes' work on ways in which readers read, Richard Howard writes: "We require an education in literature... in order to discover that *what we have assumed* - with the complicity of our teachers - *was nature is in fact culture, that what was given is no more than a way of taking*" (emphasis not in the original; Howard 1974:ix).[1] This statement reminds us that the *culture* children learn as they grow up is, in fact, **"ways of taking"** meaning from the environment around them. The means of making sense from books and relating their contents to knowledge about the real world is but one "way of taking" that is often interpreted as "natural" rather than learned. The quote also reminds us that teachers (and researchers alike) have not recognized that ways of taking from books are as much a part of learned behavior as are ways of eating, sitting, playing games, and building houses.

As school-oriented parents and their children interact in the pre-school years, adults give their children, through modeling and specific instruction, ways of taking from books which seem natural in school and in numerous institutional settings such as banks, post offices, businesses, or government offices. These *mainstream* ways exist in societies around the world that rely on formal educational systems to prepare children for participation in settings involving literacy. In some communities these ways of schools and institutions are very similar to the ways learned at home; in other communities the ways of school are merely an overlay on the home-taught ways and may be in conflict with them.[2]

Yet little is actually known about what goes on in story-reading and other literacy-related interactions between adults and preschoolers in communities around the world. Specifically, though there are numerous diary accounts and experimental studies of the preschool reading experiences of mainstream middle-class children, we know little about the specific literacy features of the environment upon which the school expects to draw. Just how does what is frequently termed "the literate tradition" envelope the child in knowledge about interrelationships between oral and written language, between knowing something and knowing ways of labelling and displaying it? We have even less information about the variety of ways children from *non-mainstream* homes learn about reading, writing, and using oral language to display knowledge in their preschool environment. The general view has been that whatever it is that mainstream school-oriented homes have, these other homes do not have it; thus these children are not from the literate tradition and are not likely to succeed in school.

A key concept for the empirical study of ways of taking meaning from written sources across communities is that of ***literacy events:*** occasions in which written language is integral to the nature of participants' interactions and their interpretive processes and strategies. Familiar literacy events for mainstream preschoolers are bedtime stories, reading cereal boxes, stop signs, and television ads, and interpreting instructions for commercial games and toys. In such literacy events, participants follow socially established rules for verbalizing what they know from and about the written material. Each community has rules for socially interacting and sharing knowledge in literacy events.

This paper briefly summarizes the ways of taking from printed stories families teach their preschoolers in a cluster of mainstream school-oriented neighborhoods of a city in the Southeastern region of the United States. We then describe two quite different ways of taking used in the homes of two English-speaking communities in the same region that do not follow the school-expected patterns of bookreading and reinforcement of these patterns in oral storytelling. Two assumptions underlie this paper and are treated in detail in the ethnography of these communities (Heath forthcoming b): (1) Each community's ways of taking from the printed word and using this knowledge are interdependent with the ways children learn to talk in their social interactions with caregivers. (2) There is little or no validity to the time-honored dichotomy of "the literate tradition" and "the oral tradition." This paper suggests a frame of reference for both the community patterns and the paths of development children in different communities follow in their literacy orientations.

## Mainstream School-Oriented Bookreading

Children growing up in mainstream communities are expected to develop habits and values which attest to their membership in a "literate society." Children learn certain customs, beliefs, and skills in early enculturation experiences with written materials: the bedtime story is a major literacy event which helps set patterns of behavior that recur repeatedly through the life of mainstream children and adults.

In both popular and scholarly literature, the "bedtime story" is widely accepted as a given—a natural way for parents to interact with their child at bedtime. Commercial publishing houses, television advertising, and children's magazines make much of this familiar ritual, and many of their sales pitches are based on the assumption that in spite of the intrusion of television into many patterns of interaction between parents and children, this ritual remains. Few parents are fully conscious of what bedtime storyreading means as preparation for the kinds of learning and displays of knowledge expected in school. Ninio and Bruner (1978), in their longitudinal study of one mainstream middle-class mother-infant **dyad** in joint picture-book reading, strongly suggest a universal role of bookreading in the achievement of labelling by children.

In a series of "reading cycles," mother and child alternate turns in a dialogue: the mother directs the child's attention to the book and/or asks **what-questions** and/or labels items on the page. The items to which the what-questions are directed and labels given are two-dimensional representations of three-dimensional objects, so that the child has to resolve the conflict between perceiving these as two-dimensional objects and as representations of a three-dimensional visual setting. The child does so "by assigning a privileged, autonomous status to pictures as visual objects" (1978: 5). The arbitrariness of the picture, its decontextualization, and its existence as something which cannot be grasped and manipulated like its "real" counterparts is learned through the routines of structured interactional dialogue in which mother and child take turns playing a **labelling game.** In a **"scaffolding"** dialogue (cf. Cazden 1979), the mother points and asks "What is x?" and the child vocalizes and/or gives a nonverbal signal of attention. The mother then provides verbal feedback and a label. Before the age of two, the child is socialized into the **"initiation-reply-evaluation sequences"** repeatedly described as the central structural feature of classroom lessons (e.g., Sinclair and Coulthard 1975; Griffin and Humphry 1978; Mehan 1979). Teachers ask their students questions which have answers prespecified in the mind of the teacher. Students respond, and teachers provide feedback, usually in the form of an evaluation. Training in ways of responding to this pattern begins very early in the labelling activities of mainstream parents and children.

### Maintown Ways

This patterning of "incipient literacy" (Scollon and Scollon 1979) is similar in many ways to that of the families of fifteen primary-level school teachers in Maintown, a cluster of middle-class neighborhoods in a city of the Piedmont Carolinas. These families (all of whom identify themselves as "typical," "middle-class," or "mainstream") had preschool children, and the mother in each family was either teaching in local public schools at the time of the study (early 1970s), or had taught in the academic year preceding participation in the study. Through a research dyad approach, using teacher-mothers as researchers with the ethnographer, the teacher-mothers audio-recorded their children's interactions in their primary network – mothers, fathers, grandparents, maids, siblings, and frequent visitors to the home. Children were expected to learn the following rules in literacy events in these nuclear households:

(1) As early as six months of age, children *give attention to books and information derived from books.* Their rooms contain bookcases and are decorated with murals, bedspreads, mobiles, and stuffed animals which represent characters found in books. Even when these characters have their origin in television programs, adults also provide books which either repeat or extend the characters' activities on television.

(2) Children, from the age of six months, *acknowledge questions about books.* Adults expand nonverbal responses and vocalizations from infants into fully formed grammatical sentences. When children begin to verbalize about the contents of books, adults extend their questions from simple requests for labels (What's that? Who's that?) to ask about the attributes of these items (What does the doggie say? What color is the ball?)

(3) From the time they start to talk, children *respond to conversational allusions to the content of books; they act as question-answerers who have a knowledge of books.* For example, a fuzzy black dog on the street is likened by an adult to Blackie in a child's book: "Look, there's a Blackie. Do you think *he's* looking for a boy?" Adults strive to maintain with children a running commentary on any event or object which can be book-related, thus modelling for them the extension of familiar items and events from books to new situational contexts.

(4) Beyond two years of age, children *use their knowledge of what books do to legitimate their departures from "truth."* Adults encourage and reward "book talk," even when it is not directly relevant to an ongoing conversation. Children are allowed to suspend reality, to tell stories which are not true, to ascribe fiction-like features to everyday objects.

(5) Preschool children *accept book and book-related activities as entertainment.* When preschoolers are "captive audiences" (e.g., waiting in a doctor's office, putting a toy together, or preparing for bed), adults reach for books. If there are no books present, they talk about other objects as though they were pictures in books. For example, adults point to items, and ask children to name, describe, and compare them to familiar objects in their environment. Adults often ask children to state their likes or dislikes, their view of events, and so forth, at the end of the captive audience period. These affective questions often take place while the next activity is already underway (e.g., moving toward the doctor's office, putting the new toy away, or being tucked into bed), and adults do not insist on answers.

(6) Preschoolers *announce their own factual and fictive narratives* unless they are given in response to direct adult elicitation. Adults judge as most acceptable those narratives which open by orienting the listener to setting and main character. Narratives which are fictional are usually marked by formulaic openings, a particular prosody, or the borrowing of episodes in story books.

(7) When children are about three years old, adults discourage the highly interactive participative role in bookreading children have hitherto played and children *listen and wait as an audience.* No longer does either adult or child repeatedly break into the story with questions and comments. Instead, children must listen, store what they hear, and on cue from the adult, answer a question. Thus, children begin to formulate "practice" questions as they wait for the break and the expected formulaic-type questions from the adult. It is at this stage that children often choose to "read" to adults rather than to be read to.

A pervasive pattern of all these features is the authority which books and book-related activities have in the lives of both the preschoolers and members of their primary network. Any initiation of a literacy event by a preschooler makes an interruption, an untruth, a diverting of attention from the matter at hand (whether it be an uneaten plate of food, a messy room, or an avoidance of going to bed) acceptable. Adults jump at openings their children give them for pursuing talk about books and reading.

In this study, writing was found to be somewhat less acceptable as an "anytime activity," since adults have rigid rules about times, places, and materials for writing. The only restrictions on bookreading concern taking good care of books: they should not be wet, torn, drawn on, or lost. In their talk to children about books, and in their explanations of why they buy children's books, adults link school success to "learning to love books," "learning what books can do for you," and "learning to entertain yourself and to work independently." Many of the adults also openly expressed a fascination with children's books "nowadays." They generally judged them as more diverse, wide-ranging, challenging, and exciting than books they had as children.

**The Mainstream Pattern** A close look at the way bedtime story **routines** in Maintown taught children how to take meaning from books raises a heavy sense of the familiar in all of us who have acquired mainstream habits and values. Throughout a lifetime, any school-successful individual moves through the same processes described above thousands of times. Reading for comprehension involves an internal replaying of the same types of questions adults ask children of bedtime stories. We seek ***what-explanations***, asking what the topic is, establishing it as predictable and recognizing it in new situational contexts by classifying and categorizing it in our mind with other phenomena. The what-explanation is replayed in learning to pick out topic sentences, write outlines, and answer standardized tests which ask for the correct titles to stories, and so on. In learning to read in school, children move through a sequence of skills designed to teach what-explanations. There is a tight linear order of instruction which recapitulates the bedtime story pattern of breaking down the story into small bits of information and teaching children to handle sets of related skills in isolated sequential hierarchies.

In each individual reading episode in the primary years of schooling, children must move through what-explanations before they can provide ***reason-explanations*** or ***affective commentaries***. Questions about why a particular event occurred or why a specific action was right or wrong come at the end of primary-level reading lessons, just as they come at the end of bedtime stories. Throughout the primary grade levels, what-explanations predominate, reason-explanations come with increasing frequency in the upper grades, and affective comments most often come in the extra-credit portions of the reading workbook or at the end of the list of suggested activities in text books across grade levels. This sequence characterizes the total school career. High school freshmen who are judged poor in compositional and reading skills spend most of their time on what-explanations and practice in advanced versions of bedtime story questions and answers. They are given little or no chance to use reason-giving explanations or assessments of the actions of stories. Reason-explanations result in configurational rather than hierarchical skills, are not predictable, and thus do not present content with a high degree of redundancy. Reason-giving explanations tend to rely on detailed knowledge of a specific domain. This detail is often unpredictable to teachers, and is not as highly valued as is knowledge which covers a particular area of knowledge with less detail but offers opportunity for extending the knowledge to larger and related concerns. For example, a primary-level student whose father owns a turkey farm may respond with reason-explanations to a story about a turkey. His knowledge is intensive and covers details perhaps not known to the teacher and not judged as relevant to the story. The knowledge is unpredictable and questions about it do not continue to repeat the common core of content knowledge of the story. Thus such configured knowledge is encouraged only for the "extras" of reading—an extra-credit oral report or a creative picture and story about turkeys. This kind of knowledge is allowed to be used once the hierarchical what-explanations have been mastered and displayed in a particular situation and, in the course of one's academic career, only when one has shown full mastery of the hierarchical skills and subsets of related skills which underlie what-explanations. Thus, reliable and successful participation in the ways of taking from books that teachers view as natural must, in the usual school way of doing things, precede other ways of taking from books.

These various ways of taking are sometimes referred to as "cognitive styles" or "learning styles." It is generally accepted in the research literature that they are influenced by early socialization experiences and correlated with such features of the society in which the child is reared as social organization, reliance on authority, male-female roles, and so on. These styles are often seen as two contrasting types, most frequently termed **"field independent-field dependent"** (Witkin et al. 1966) or "analytic-relational" (Kagan, Sigel, and Moss 1963; Cohen 1968, 1969, 1971). The analytic field-independent style is generally presented as that which correlates positively with high achievement and general academic and social success in school. Several studies discuss ways in which this style is played out in school—in preferred ways of responding to pictures and written text and selecting from among a choice of answers to test items.

Yet, we know little about how behaviors associated with either of the dichotomized cognitive styles (field-dependent/relational and field-independent/analytic) were learned in early patterns of socialization. To be sure, there are vast individual differences which may cause an individual to behave so as to be categorized as having one or the other of these learning styles. But much of the literature on learning styles suggests a preference for one or the other is learned in the social group in which the child is reared and in connection with other ways of behaving found in that culture. But how is a child socialized into an analytic/field-independent style? What kinds of interactions does he enter into with his parents and the stimuli of his environment which contribute to the development of such a style of learning? How do these interactions mold selective attention practices such as "sensitivity to parts of objects," "awareness of obscure, abstract, nonobvious features," and identification of "abstractions based on the features of items" (Cohen 1969: 844–45)? Since the predominant stimuli used in school to judge the presence and extent of these selective attention practices are written materials, it is clear that the literacy orientation of preschool children is central to these questions.

The foregoing descriptions of how Maintown parents socialize their children into a literacy orientation fit closely those provided by Scollon and Scollon for their own child Rachel. Through similar practices, Rachel was "literate before she learned to read" (1979:6). She knew, before the age of two, how to focus on a book and not on herself. Even when she told a story about herself, she moved herself out of the text and saw herself as author, as someone different from the central character of her story. She learned to pay close attention to the parts of objects, to name them, and to provide a running commentary on features of her environment. She learned to manipulate the contexts of items, her own activities, and language to achieve book-like, decontextualized, repeatable effects (such as puns). Many references in her talk were from written sources; others were modelled on stories and questions about these stories. The substance of her knowledge, as well as her ways of framing knowledge orally, derived from her familiarity with books and bookreading. No doubt, this development began by labelling in the dialogue cycles of reading (Ninio and Bruner 1978), and it will continue for Rachel in her preschool years along many of the same patterns described by Cochran-Smith (1981) for a mainstream nursery school. There teacher and students negotiated story-reading through the scaffolding of teachers' questions and running commentaries which replayed the structure and sequence of story-reading learned in their mainstream homes.

Close analyses of how mainstream school-oriented children come to learn to take from books at home suggest that such children learn not only how to take meaning from books, but also how to talk about it. In doing the latter, they repeatedly practice routines which parallel those of classroom interaction. By the time they enter school, they have had continuous experience as information-givers; they have learned how to perform in those interactions which surround literate sources throughout school. They have had years of practice in interaction situations that are the heart of reading – both learning to read and reading to learn in school. They have developed habits of performing which enable them to run through the hierarchy of preferred knowledge about a literate source and the appropriate sequence of skills to be displayed in showing knowledge of a subject. They have developed ways of decontextualizing and surrounding with explanatory prose the knowledge gained from selective attention to objects.

They have learned to listen, waiting for the appropriate cue which signals it is their turn to show off this knowledge. They have learned the rules for getting certain services from parents (or teachers) in the reading interaction (Merritt 1979). In nursery school, they continue to practice these interaction patterns in a group rather than in a dyadic situation. There they learn additional signals and behaviors necessary for getting a turn in a group, and responding to a central reader and to a set of centrally defined reading tasks. In short, most of their waking hours during the preschool years have enculturated them into: (1) all those habits associated with what-explanations, (2) selective attention to items of the written text, *and* (3) appropriate interactional styles for orally displaying all the know-how of their literate orientation to the environment. This learning has been finely tuned and its habits are highly interdependent. Patterns of behaviors learned in one setting or at one stage reappear again and again as these children learn to use oral and written language in literacy events and to bring their knowledge to bear in school-acceptable ways.

## Alternative Patterns of Literacy Events

But what corresponds to the mainstream pattern of learning in communities that do not have this finely tuned, consistent, repetitive, and continuous pattern of training? Are there ways of behaving which achieve other social and cognitive aims in other sociocultural groups?

The data below are summarized from an ethnography of two communities—Roadville and Trackton—located only a few miles from Maintown's neighborhoods in the Piedmont Carolinas. Roadville is a white working-class community of families steeped for four generations in the life of the textile mill. Trackton is a working-class black community whose older generations have been brought up on the land, either farming their own land or working for other landowners. However, in the past decade, they have found work in the textile mills. Children of both communities are unsuccessful in school; yet both communities place a high value on success in school, believing earnestly in the personal and vocational rewards school can bring and urging their children "to get ahead" by doing well in school. Both Roadville and Trackton are literate communities in the sense that the residents of each are able to read printed and written materials in their daily lives, and on occasion they produce written messages as part of the total pattern of communication in the community. In both communities, children go to school with certain expectancies of print and, in Trackton especially, children have a keen sense that reading is something one does to learn something one needs to know (Heath 1980). In both groups, residents turn from spoken to written uses of language and vice versa as the occasion demands, and the two modes of expression seem to supplement and reinforce each other. Nonetheless there are radical differences between the two communities in the ways in which children and adults interact in the preschool years; each of the two communities also differs from Maintown. Roadville and Trackton view children's learning of language from two radically different perspectives: in Trackton, children "learn to talk," in Roadville, adults "teach them how to talk."

### Roadville

In Roadville, babies are brought home from the hospital to rooms decorated with colorful, mechanical, musical, and literacy-based stimuli. The walls are decorated with pictures based on nursery rhymes, and from an early age, children are held and prompted to "see" the wall decorations. Adults recite nursery rhymes as they twirl the mobile made of nursery-rhyme characters. The items of the child's environment promote exploration of colors, shapes, and textures: a stuffed ball with sections of fabrics of different colors and textures is in the crib; stuffed animals vary in texture, size, and shape. Neighbors, friends from church, and relatives come to visit and talk to the baby, and about him to those who will listen. The baby is fictionalized in the talk to him: "But this baby wants to go to sleep, doesn't he? Yes, see those little eyes gettin' heavy." As the child grows older, adults pounce on word-like sounds and turn them into "words," repeating the "words," and expanding them into well-formed sentences. Before they can talk, children are introduced to visitors and prompted to provide all the expected politeness formulas, such as "Bye-bye," "Thank you," and so forth. As soon as they can talk, children are reminded about these formulas, and book or television characters known to be "polite" are involved as reinforcement.

In each Roadville home, preschoolers first have cloth books, featuring a single object on each page. They later acquire books which provide sounds, smells, and different textures or opportunities for practicing small motor skills (closing zippers, buttoning buttons, etc.). A typical collection for a two-year-old consisted of a dozen or so books—eight featured either the alphabet or numbers, others were books of nursery rhymes, simplified Bible stories, or "real-life" stories about boys and girls (usually taking care of their pets or exploring a particular feature of their environment). Books based on Sesame Street characters were favorite gifts for three- and four-year-olds.

Reading and reading-related activities occur most frequently before naps or at bedtime in the evening. Occasionally an adult or older child will read to a fussy child while the mother prepares dinner or changes a bed. On weekends, fathers sometimes read with their children for brief periods of time, but they generally prefer to play games or play with the children's toys in their interactions. The following episode illustrates the language and social interactional aspects of these bedtime events; the episode takes place between Wendy (2;3 at the time of this episode) and Aunt Sue who is putting her to bed.

[Aunt Sue (AS) picks up book, while Wendy (W) crawls about the floor, ostensibly looking for something]

W: uh uh

AS: Wendy, we're gonna read, uh, read this story, come on, hop up here on this bed.
[Wendy climbs up on the bed, sits on top of the pillow, and picks up her teddy bear]
[Aunt Sue opens book, points to puppy]

AS: Do you remember what this book is about? See the puppy? What does the puppy do?
[Wendy plays with the bear, glancing occasionally at pages of the book, as Aunt Sue turns. Wendy seems to be waiting for something in the book]

AS: See the puppy?
[Aunt Sue points to the puppy in the book and looks at Wendy to see if she is watching]

W: uh huh, yea, yes ma'am

AS: Puppy sees the ant, he's a li'l
[Wendy drops the bear and turns to book.]
fellow. Can you see that ant? Puppy has a little ball.

W: ant bite puppy
[Wendy points to ant, pushing hard on the book]

AS: No, the ant won't bite the puppy, the [turns page] puppy wants to play with the ant, see?
[Wendy tries to turn the page back; AS won't let her, and Wendy starts to squirm and fuss]

AS: Look here, here's someone else, the puppy
[Wendy climbs down off the bed and gets another book]

W: read this one

AS: Okay, you get back up here now. [Wendy gets back on bed]

AS: This book is your ABC book. See the A, look, here, on your spread there's an A. You find the A. [The second book is a cloth book, old and tattered, and long a favorite of Wendy's. It features an apple on the cover, and its front page has an ABC block and ball. Through the book, there is a single item on each page, with a large representation of the first letter of the word commonly used to name the item. As AS turns the page, Wendy begins to crawl about on her quilt, which shows ABC blocks interspersed with balls and apples. Wendy points to each of the A's on the blanket and begins talking to herself. AS reads the book, looks up, and sees Wendy pointing to the A's in her quilt.]

AS: That's an A, can you find the A on your blanket?

W: there it is, this one, there's the hole too. [pokes her finger through a place where the threads have broken in the quilting]

AS: [AS points to ball in book] Stop that, find the ball, see, here's another ball.

This episode characterizes the early orientation of Roadville children to the written word. Bookreading time focuses on letters of the alphabet, numbers, names of basic items pictured in books, and simplified retellings of stories in the words of the adult. If the content or story plot seems too complicated for the child, the adult tells the story in short, simple sentences, frequently laced with requests that the child give what-explanations.

Wendy's favorite books are those with which she can participate: that is, those to which she can answer, provide labels, point to items, give animal sounds, and "read" the material back to anyone who will listen to her. She memorizes the passages and often knows when to turn the pages to show that she is "reading." She holds the book in her lap, starts at the beginning, and often reads the title "Puppy."

Adults and children use either the title of the book or phrases such as "the book about a puppy" to refer to reading material. When Wendy acquires a new book, adults introduce the book with phrases such as "This is a book about a duck, a little yellow duck. See the duck. Duck goes quack quack." On introducing a book, adults sometimes ask the child to recall when they have seen a "real" specimen such as that one treated in the book: "Remember the duck on the College lake?" The child often shows no sign of linking the yellow fluffy duck in the book with the large brown and grey mallards on the lake, and the adult makes no efforts to explain that two such disparate looking objects go by the same name.

As Wendy grows older, she wants to "talk" during the long stories, Bible stories, and carry out the participation she so enjoyed with the alphabet books. However, by the time she reaches three and a half, Wendy is restrained from such wide-ranging participation. When she interrupts, she is told:

> Wendy, stop that, you be quiet when someone is reading to you. You listen; now sit still and be quiet.

Often Wendy immediately gets down and runs away into the next room saying "no, no." When this happens, her father goes to get her, pats her bottom, and puts her down hard on the sofa beside him. "Now you're gonna learn to listen." During the third and fourth years, this pattern occurs more and more frequently; only when Wendy can capture an aunt who does not visit often does she bring out the old books and participate with them. Otherwise, parents, Aunt Sue, and other adults insist that she be read a story and that she "listen" quietly.

When Wendy and her parents watch television, eat cereal, visit the grocery store, or go to church, adults point out and talk about many types of written material. On the way to the grocery, Wendy (3;8) sits in the backseat, and when her mother stops at a corner, Wendy says "Stop." Her mother says "Yes, that's a stop sign." Wendy has, however, misread a yield sign as *stop*. Her mother offers no explanation of what the actual message on the sign is, yet when she comes to the sign, she stops to yield to an oncoming car. Her mother, when asked why she had not given Wendy the word "yield," said it was too hard, Wendy would not understand, and "it's not a word we use like *stop*."

Wendy recognized animal cracker boxes as early as 10 months, and later, as her mother began buying other varieties, Wendy would see the box in the grocery store and yell "Cook cook." Her mother would say, "Yes, those are cookies. Does Wendy want a cookie?" One day Wendy saw a new type of cracker box, and screeched "Cook cook." Her father opened the box and gave Wendy a cracker and waited for her reaction. She started the "cookie," then took it to her mother, saying "You eat." The mother joined in the game and said "Don't you want your *cookie*?" Wendy said "No cookie. You eat." "But Wendy, it's a cookie box, see?", and her mother pointed to the C of *crackers* on the box. Wendy paid no attention and ran off into another room.

In Roadville's literacy events, the rules for cooperative discourse around print are repeatedly practiced, coached, and rewarded in the preschool years. Adults in Roadville believe that instilling in children the proper use of words and understanding of the meaning of the written word are important for both their educational and religious success. Adults repeat aspects of the learning of literacy events they have known as children. In the words of one Roadville parent: "It was then that I began to learn... when my daddy kept insisting I *read* it, *say* it right. It was then that I *did* right, in his view."

The path of development for such performance can be described in three overlapping stages. In the first, children are introduced to discrete bits and pieces of books—separate items, letters of the alphabet, shapes, colors, and commonly represented items in books for children (apple, baby, ball, etc.). The latter are usually decontextualized, not pictured in their ordinary contexts, and they are represented in two-dimensional flat line drawings. During this stage, children must participate as predictable information-givers and respond to questions that ask for specific and discrete bits of information about the written matter. In these literacy events, specific features of the two-dimensional items in books which are different from their "real" counterparts are not pointed out. A ball in a book is flat; a duck in a book is yellow and fluffy; trucks, cars, dogs, and trees talk in books. No mention is made of the fact that such features do not fit these objects in reality. Children are not encouraged to move their understanding of books into other situational contexts or to apply it in their general knowledge of the world about them.

In the second stage, adults demand an acceptance of the power of print to entertain, inform, and instruct. When Wendy could no longer participate by contributing her knowledge at any point in the literacy event, she learned to recognize bookreading as a performance. The adult exhibited the book to Wendy: she was to be entertained, to learn from the information conveyed in the material, and to remember the book's content for the sequential followup questioning, as opposed to ongoing cooperative participatory questions.

In the third stage, Wendy was introduced to preschool workbooks which provided story information and was asked questions or provided exercises and games based on the content of the stories or pictures. Follow-the-number coloring books and preschool "push-out and paste" workbooks on shapes, colors, and letters of the alphabet reinforced repeatedly that the written word could be taken apart into small pieces and one item linked to another by following rules. She had practice in the linear, sequential nature of books: begin at the beginning, stay in the lines for coloring, draw straight lines to link one item to another, write your answers on lines, keep your letters straight, match the cutout letter to diagrams of letter shapes.

The differences between Roadville and Maintown are substantial. Roadville adults do not extend either the content or the habits of literacy events beyond bookreading. They do not, upon seeing an item or event in the real world, remind children of a similar event in a book and launch a running commentary on similarities and differences. When a game is played or a chore done, adults do not use literate sources. Mothers cook without written recipes most of the time; if they use a recipe from a written source, they do so usually only after confirmation and alteration by friends who have tried the recipe. Directions to games are read, but not carefully followed, and they are not talked about in a series of questions and answers which try to establish their meaning. Instead, in the putting together of toys or the playing of games, the abilities or preferences of one party prevail. For example, if an adult knows how to put a toy together, he does so; he does not talk about the process, refer to the written material and "translate" for the child, or try to sequence steps so the child can do it.[3] Adults do not talk about the steps and procedures of *how* to do things; if a father wants his preschooler to learn to hold a miniature bat or throw a ball, he says "Do it this way." He does not break up "this way" into such steps as "Put your fingers around here," "Keep your thumb in this position," "Never hold it above this line." Over and over again, adults do a task and children observe and try it, being reinforced only by commands such as "Do it like this," "Watch that thumb."

Adults at tasks do not provide a running verbal commentary on what they are doing. They do not draw the attention of the child to specific features of the sequences of skills or the attributes of items. They do not ask questions of the child, except questions which are directive or scolding in nature ("Did you bring the ball?" "Didn't you hear what I said?"). Many of their commands contain idioms which are not explained: "Put it up," or "Put that away now" (meaning to put it in the place where it usually belongs), or "Loosen up," said to a four-year-old boy trying to learn to bat a ball. Explanations which move beyond the listing of names of items and their features are rarely offered by adults. Children do not ask questions of the type "But I don't understand. What is that?" They appear willing to keep trying, and if there is ambiguity in a set of commands, they ask a question such as "You want me to do this?" (demonstrating their current efforts), or they try to find a way of diverting attention from the task at hand.

Both boys and girls during their preschool years are included in many adult activities, ranging from going to church to fishing and camping. They spend a lot of time observing and asking for turns to try specific tasks, such as putting a worm on the hook or cutting cookies. Sometimes adults say "No, you're not old enough." But if they agree to the child's attempt at the task, they watch and give directives and evaluations: "That's right, don't twist the cutter." "Turn like this." "Don't try to scrape it up now, let me do that." Talk about the task does not segment its skills and identify them, nor does it link the particular task or item at hand to other tasks. Reason-explanations such as "If you twist the cutter, the cookies will be rough on the edge" are rarely given, or asked for.

Neither Roadville adults nor children shift the context of items in their talk. They do not tell stories which fictionalize themselves or familiar events. They reject Sunday School materials which attempt to translate Biblical events into a modern-day setting. In Roadville, a story must be invited or announced by someone other than the storyteller, and only certain community members are designated good storytellers. A story is recognized by the group as a story about one and all. It is a true story, an actual event which occurred to either the storyteller or to someone else present. The marked behavior of the storyteller and audience alike is seen as exemplifying the weaknesses of all and the need for persistence in overcoming such weaknesses. The sources of stories are personal experience. They are tales of transgressions which make the point of reiterating the expected norms of behavior of man, woman, fisherman, worker, and Christian. They are true to the facts of the event.

Roadville parents provide their children with books; they read to them and ask questions about the books' contents. They choose books which emphasize nursery rhymes, alphabet learning, animals, and simplified Bible stories, and they require their children to repeat from these books and to answer formulaic questions about their contents. Roadville adults also ask questions about oral stories which have a point relevant to some marked behavior of a child. They use proverbs and summary statements to remind their children of stories and to call on them for simple comparisons of the stories' contents to their own situations. Roadville parents coach children in their telling of a story, forcing them to tell about an incident as it has been pre-composed or pre-scripted in the head of the adult. Thus, in Roadville, children come to know a story as either an accounting from a book, or a factual account of a real event in which some type of marked behavior occurred and there is a lesson to be learned. Any fictionalized account of a real event is viewed as a *lie;* reality is better than fiction. Roadville's church and community life admit no story other than that which meets the definition internal to the group. Thus children cannot decontextualize their knowledge or fictionalize events known to them and shift them about into other frames.

When these children go to school they perform well in the initial stages of each of the three early grades. They often know portions of the alphabet, some colors and numbers, can recognize their names, and tell someone their address and their parents' names. They will sit still and listen to a story, and they know how to answer questions asking for what-explanations. They do well in reading workbook exercises which ask for identification of specific portions of words, items from the story, or the linking of two items, letters, or parts of words on the same page. When the teacher reaches the end of story-reading or the reading circle and asks questions such as "What did you like about the story?", relatively few Roadville children answer. If asked questions such as "What would you have done if you had been Billy [a story's main character]?", Roadville children most frequently say "I don't know" or shrug their shoulders.

Near the end of each year, and increasingly as they move through the early primary grades, Roadville children can handle successfully the initial stages of lessons. But when they move ahead to extra-credit items or to activities considered more advanced and requiring more independence, they are stumped. They turn frequently to teachers asking "Do you want me to do this? What do I do here?" If asked to write a creative story or tell it into a tape recorder, they retell stories from books; they do not create their own. They rarely provide emotional or personal commentary on their accounting of real events or book stories. They are rarely able to take knowledge learned in one context and shift it to another; they do not compare two items or events and point out similarities and differences. They find it difficult either to hold one feature of an event constant and shift all others or to hold all features constant but one. For example, they are puzzled by questions such as "What would have happened if Billy had not told the policemen what happened?" They do not know how to move events or items out of a given frame. To a question such as "What habits of the Hopi Indians might they be able to take with them when they move to a city?", they provide lists of features of life of the Hopi on the reservation. They do not take these items, consider their appropriateness in an urban setting, and evaluate the hypothetical outcome. In general, they find this type of question impossible to answer, and they do not know how to ask teachers to help them take apart the questions to figure out the answers. Thus their initial successes in reading, being good students, following orders, and adhering to school norms of participating in lessons begin to fall away rapidly about the time they enter the fourth grade. As the importance and frequency of questions and reading habits with which they are familiar decline in the higher grades, they have no way of keeping up or of seeking help in learning what it is they do not even know they don't know.

## Trackton

Babies in Trackton come home from the hospital to an environment which is almost entirely human. There are no cribs, car beds, or car seats, and only an occasional high chair or infant seat. Infants are held during their waking hours, occasionally while they sleep, and they usually sleep in the bed with parents until they are about two years of age. They are held, their faces fondled, their cheeks pinched, and they eat and sleep in the midst of human talk and noise from the television, stereo, and radio. Encapsuled in an almost totally human world, they are in the midst of constant human communication, verbal and nonverbal. They literally feel the body signals of shifts in emotion of those who hold them almost continuously; they are talked about and kept in the midst of talk about topics that range over any subject. As children make cooing or babbling sounds, adults refer to this as "noise," and no attempt is made to interpret these sounds as words or communicative attempts on the part of the baby. Adults believe they should not have to depend on their babies to tell them what they need or when they are uncomfortable; adults know, children only "come to know."

When a child can crawl and move about on his own, he plays with the household objects deemed safe for him—pot lids, spoons, plastic food containers. Only at Christmastime are there special toys for very young children; these are usually trucks, balls, doll babies, or plastic cars, but rarely blocks, puzzles, or books. As children become completely mobile, they demand ride toys or electronic and mechanical toys they see on television. They never request nor do they receive manipulative toys, such as puzzles, blocks, take-apart toys or literacy-based items, such as books or letter games.

Adults read newspapers, mail, calendars, circulars (political and civic-events related), school materials sent home to parents, brochures advertising new cars, television sets, or other products, and the Bible and other church-related materials. There are no reading materials especially for children (with the exception of children's Sunday School materials), and adults do not sit and read to children. Since children are usually left to sleep whenever and wherever they fall asleep, there is no bedtime or naptime as such. At night, they are put to bed when adults go to bed or whenever the person holding them gets tired. Thus, going to bed is not framed in any special routine. Sometimes in a play activity during the day, an older sibling will read to a younger child, but the latter soon loses interest and squirms away to play. Older children often try to "play school" with younger children, reading to them from books and trying to ask questions about what they have read. Adults look on these efforts with amusement and do not try to convince the small child to sit still and listen.

Signs from very young children of attention to the nonverbal behaviors of others are rewarded by extra fondling, laughter, and cuddling from adults. For example, when an infant shows signs of recognizing a family member's voice on the phone by bouncing up and down in the arms of the adult who is talking on the phone, adults comment on this to others present and kiss and nudge the child. Yet when children utter sounds or combinations of sounds which could be interpreted as words, adults pay no attention. Often by the time they are twelve months old, children approximate words or phrases of adults' speech; adults respond by laughing or giving special attention to the child and crediting him with "sounding like" the person being imitated. When children learn to walk and imitate the walk of members of the community, they are rewarded by comments on their activities: "He walks just like Toby when he's tuckered out."

Children between the ages of twelve and twenty-four months often imitate the tune or "general Gestalt" (Peters 1977) of complete utterances they hear around them. They pick up and repeat chunks (usually the ends) of phrasal and clausal utterances of speakers around them. They seem to remember fragments of speech and repeat these without active production. In this first stage of language learning, the repetition stage, they imitate the intonation contours and general shaping of the utterances they repeat. Lem 1;2 in the following example illustrates this pattern.

| | |
|---|---|
| Mother: | [talking to neighbor on porch while Lem plays with a truck on the porch nearby] But they won't call back, won't happen = |
| Lem: | = call back |
| Neighbor: | Sam's going over there Saturday, he'll pick up a form = |
| Lem: | = pick up on, pick up on [Lem here appears to have heard *form* as *on*] |

The adults pay no attention to Lem's "talk," and their talk, in fact, often overlaps his repetitions.

In the second stage, repetition with variation, Trackton children manipulate pieces of conversation they pick up. They incorporate chunks of language from others into their own ongoing dialogue, applying productive rules, inserting new nouns and verbs for those used in the adults' chunks. They also play with rhyming patterns and varying intonation contours.

| | |
|---|---|
| Mother: | She went to the doctor again. |
| Lem (2;2): | [in a sing-song fashion] went to de doctor, doctor, tractor, dis my tractor, doctor on a tractor, went to de doctor. |

Lem creates a monologue, incorporating the conversation about him into his own talk as he plays. Adults pay no attention to his chatter unless it gets so noisy as to interfere with their talk.

In the third stage, participation, children begin to enter the ongoing conversations about them. They do so by attracting the adult's attention with a tug on the arm or pant leg, and they help make themselves understood by providing nonverbal reinforcements to help recreate a scene they want the listener to remember. For example, if adults are talking, and a child interrupts with seemingly unintelligible utterances, the child will make gestures, extra sounds, or act out some outstanding features of the scene he is trying to get the adult to remember. Children try to create a context, a scene, for the understanding of their utterance.

This third stage illustrates a pattern in the children's response to their environment and their ways of letting others know their knowledge of the environment. Once they are in the third stage, their communicative efforts are accepted by community members, and adults respond directly to the child, instead of talking to others about the child's activities as they have done in the past. Children continue to practice for conversational participation by playing, when alone, both parts of dialogues, imitating gestures as well as intonation patterns of adults. By 2;6 all children in the community can imitate the walk and talk of others in the community, or frequent visitors such as the man who comes around to read the gas meters. They can feign anger, sadness, fussing, remorse, silliness, or any of a wide range of expressive behaviors. They often use the same chunks of language for varying effects, depending on nonverbal support to give the language different meanings or cast it in a different key (Hymes 1974). Girls between three and four years of age take part in extraordinarily complex stepping and clapping patterns and simple repetitions of hand clap games played by older girls. From the time they are old enough to stand alone, they are encouraged in their participation by siblings and older children in the community. These games require anticipation and recognition of cues for upcoming behaviors, and the young girls learn to watch for these cues and to come in with the appropriate words and movements at the right time.

Preschool children are not asked for what-explanations of their environment. Instead, they are asked a preponderance of **analogical questions** which call for non-specific comparisons of one item, event, or person with another: "What's that like?" Other types of questions ask for specific information known to the child but not the adults: "Where'd you get that from?" "What do you want?" "How come you did that?" (Heath 1982). Adults explain their use of these types of questions by expressing their sense of children: they are "comers," coming into their learning by experiencing what knowing about things means. As one parent of a two-year-old boy put it: "Ain't no use me tellin' 'im: learn this, learn that, what's this, what's that? He just gotta learn, gotta know; he see one thing one place one time, he know how it go, see sump'n like it again, maybe it be the same, maybe it won't." Children are expected to learn how to know when the form belies the meaning, and to know contexts of items and to use their understanding of these contexts to draw parallels between items and events. Parents do not believe they have a tutoring role in this learning; they provide the experiences on which the child draws and reward signs of their successfully coming to know.

Trackton children's early stories illustrate how they respond to adult views of them as "comers." The children learn to tell stories by drawing heavily on their abilities to render a context, to set a stage, and to call on the audience's power to join in the imaginative creation of story. Between the ages of two and four years, the children, in a monologue-like fashion, tell stories about things in their lives, events they see and hear, and situations in which they have been involved. They produce these spontaneously during play with other children or in the presence of adults. Sometimes they make an effort to attract the attention of listeners before they begin the story, but often they do not. Lem, playing off the edge of the porch, when he was about two and a half years of age, heard a bell in the distance. He stopped, looked at Nellie and Benjy, his older siblings, who were nearby and said:

Way
Far
Now
It a church bell
Ringin'
Dey singin'
Ringin'
You hear it?
I hear it
Far
Now.

Lem had been taken to church the previous Sunday and had been much impressed by the church bell. He had sat on his mother's lap and joined in the singing, rocking to and fro on her [lap], and clapping his hands. His story, which is like a poem in its imagery and line-like prosody, is in response to the current stimulus of a distant bell. As he tells the story, he sways back and forth.

This story, somewhat longer than those usually reported from other social groups for children as young as Lem,[4] has some features which have come to characterize fully-developed narratives or stories. It recapitulates in its verbal outline the sequence of events being recalled by the storyteller. At church, the bell rang while the people sang. In the line "It a church bell," Lem provides his story's topic, and a brief summary of what is to come. This line serves a function similar to the formulae often used by older children to open a story: "This is a story about (a church bell)." Lem gives only the slightest hint of story setting or orientation to the listener; where and when the story took place are capsuled in "Way, Far." Preschoolers in Trackton almost never hear "Once upon a time there was a ______" stories, and they rarely provide definitive orientations for their stories. They seem to assume listeners "know" the situation in which the narrative takes place. Similarly, preschoolers in Trackton do not close off their stories with formulaic endings. Lem poetically balances his opening and closing in an inclusio, beginning "Way, Far, Now." and ending "Far, Now." The effect is one of closure, but there is no clearcut announcement of closure. Throughout the presentation of action and result of action in their stories, Trackton preschoolers invite the audience to respond or evaluate the story's actions. Lem asks "You hear it?" which may refer either to the current simulus or to yesterday's bell, since Lem does not productively use past tense endings for any verbs at this stage in his language development.

Preschool storytellers have several ways of inviting audience evaluation and interest. They may themselves express an emotional response to the story's actions; they may have another character or narrator in the story do so often using alliterative language play; or they may detail actions and results through direct discourse or sound effects and gestures. All these methods of calling attention to the story and its telling distinguish the speech event as a story, an occasion for audience and storyteller to interact pleasantly, and not simply to hear an ordinary recounting of events or actions.

Trackton children must be aggressive in inserting their stories into an ongoing stream of discourse. Storytelling is highly competitive. Everyone in a conversation may want to tell a story, so only the most aggressive wins out. The content ranges widely, and there is "truth" only in the universals of human experience. Fact is often hard to find, though it is usually the seed of the story. Trackton stories often have no point —no obvious beginning or ending; they go on as long as the audience enjoys and tolerates the storyteller's entertainment.

Trackton adults do not separate out the elements of the environment around their children to tune their attentions selectively. They do not simplify their language, focus on single-word utterances by young children, label items or features of objects in either books or the environment at large. Instead, children are continuously contextualized, presented with almost continuous communication. From this ongoing, multiple-channeled stream of stimuli, they must themselves select, practice, and determine rules of production and structuring. For language, they do so by first repeating, catching chunks of sounds, intonation contours, and practicing these without specific reinforcement or evaluation. But practice material and models are continuously available. Next the children seem to begin to sort out the productive rules for speech and practice what they hear about them with variation. Finally, they work their way into conversations, hooking their meanings for listeners into a familiar context by recreating scenes through gestures, special sound effects, etc. These characteristics continue in their story-poems and their participation in jump-rope rhymes. Because adults do not select out, name, and describe features of the environment for the young, children must perceive situations, determine how units of the situations are related to each other, recognize these relations in other situations, and reason through what it will take to show their correlation of one situation with another. The children can answer questions such as "What's that like?" ["It's like Doug's car"] but they can rarely name the specific feature or features which make two items or events alike. For example, in the case of saying a car seen on the street is "like Doug's car," a child may be basing the analogy on the fact that this car has a flat tire and Doug's also had one last week. But the child does not name (and is not asked to name) what is alike between the two cars.

Children seem to develop connections between situations or items not by specification of labels and features in the situations, but by configuration links. Recognition of similar general shapes or patterns of links seen in one situation and connected to another, seem to be the means by which children set scenes in their nonverbal representations of individuals, and later in their verbal chunking, then segmentation and production of rules for putting together isolated units. They do not decontextualize; instead they heavily contextualize nonverbal and verbal language. They fictionalize their "true stories," but they do so by asking the audience to identify with the story through making parallels from their own experiences. When adults read, they often do so in a group. One person, reading aloud, for example, from a brochure on a new car decodes the text, displays illustrations and photographs, and listeners relate the text's meaning to their experiences asking questions and expressing opinions. Finally, the group as a whole synthesizes the written text and the negotiated oral discourse to construct a meaning for the brochure (Heath forthcoming a).

When Trackton children go to school, they face unfamiliar types of questions which ask for what-explanations. They are asked as individuals to identify items by name, and to label features such as shape, color, size, number. The stimuli to which they are to give these responses are two-dimensional flat representations which are often highly stylized and bear little resemblance to the "real" items. Trackton children generally score in the lowest percentile range on the Metropolitan Reading Readiness tests. They do not sit at their desks and complete reading workbook pages; neither do they tolerate questions about reading materials which are structured along the usual lesson format. Their contributions are in the form of "I had a duck at my house one time." "Why'd he do that?" or they imitate the sound effects teachers may produce in stories they read to the children. By the end of the first three primary grades, their general language arts scores have been consistently low, except for those few who have begun to adapt to and adopt some of the behaviors they have had to learn in school. But the majority not only fail to learn the content of lessons, they also do not adopt the social interactional rules for school literacy events. Print in isolation bears little authority in their world. The kinds of questions asked of reading books are unfamiliar. The children's abilities to metaphorically link two events or situations and to recreate scenes are not tapped in the school; in fact, *these abilities often cause difficulties,* because they enable children to see parallels teachers did not intend, and indeed, may not recognize until the children point them out (Heath 1978).

By the end of the lessons or by the time in their total school career when reason-explanations and affective statements call for the creative comparison of two or more situations, it is too late for many Trackton children. They have not picked up along the way the composition and comprehension skills they need to translate their analogical skills into a channel teachers can accept. They seem not to know how to take meaning from reading; they do not observe the rules of linearity in writing, and their expression of themselves on paper is very limited. Orally taped stories are often much better, but these rarely count as much as written compositions. Thus, Trackton children continue to collect very low or failing grades, and many decide by the end of the sixth grade to stop trying and turn their attention to the heavy peer socialization which usually begins in these years.

## From Community to Classroom

A recent review of trends in research on learning pointed out that "learning to read through using and learning from language has been less systematically studied than the decoding process" (Glaser 1979: 7). Put another way, how children learn to use language to read to learn has been less systematically studied than decoding skills. Learning how to take meaning from writing before one learns to read involves repeated practice in using and learning from language through appropriate participation in literacy events such as exhibitor/questioner and spectator/respondent dyads (Scollon and Scollon 1979) or group negotiation of the meaning of a written text. Children have to learn to select, hold, and retrieve content from books and other written or printed texts in accordance with their community's rules or "ways of taking," and the children's learning follows community paths of language socialization. In each society, certain kinds of childhood participation in literacy events may precede others, as the developmental sequence builds toward the whole complex of home and community behaviors characteristic of the society. The ways of taking employed in the school may in turn build directly on the preschool development, may require substantial adaptation on the part of the children, or may even run directly counter to aspects of the community's pattern.

**At Home** In *Maintown* homes, the construction of knowledge in the earliest preschool years depends in large part on labelling procedures and what-explanations. Maintown families, like other mainstream families, continue this kind of classification and knowledge construction throughout the child's environment and into the school years, calling it into play in response to new items in the environment and in running commentaries on old items as they compare to new ones. This pattern of linking old and new knowledge is reinforced in narrative tales which fictionalize the teller's events or recapitulate a story from a book. Thus for these children the bedtime story is simply an early link in a long chain of interrelated patterns of taking meaning from the environment. Moreover, along this chain, the focus is on the individual as respondent and cooperative negotiator of meaning from books. In particular, children learn that written language may represent not only descriptions of real events, but decontextualized logical propositions, and the occurrence of this kind of information in print or in writing legitimates a response in which one brings to the interpretation of written text selected knowledge from the real world. Moreover, readers must recognize how certain types of questions assert the priority of meanings in the written word over reality. The "real" comes into play only after prescribed decontextualized meanings; affective responses and reason-explanations follow conventional presuppositions which stand behind what-explanations.

*Roadville* also provides labels, features, and what-explanations, and prescribes listening and performing behaviors for preschoolers. However, Roadville adults do not carry on or sustain in continually overlapping and interdependent fashion the linking of ways of taking meaning from books to ways of relating that knowledge to other aspects of the environment. They do not encourage decontextualization; in fact, they proscribe it in their own stories about themselves and their requirements of stories from children. They do not themselves make analytic statements or assert universal truths, except those related to their religious faith. They lace their stories with synthetic (nonanalytic) statements which express, describe, and synthesize actual real-life materials. Things do not have to follow logically so long as they fit the past experience of individuals in the community. Thus children learn to look for a specific moral in stories and to expect that story to fit their facts of reality explicitly. When they themselves recount an event, they do the same, constructing the story of a real event according to coaching by adults who want to construct the story as they saw it.

*Trackton* is like neither Maintown nor Roadville. There are no bedtime stories; in fact, there are few occasions for reading to or with children specifically. Instead, during the time these activities would take place in mainstream and Roadville homes, Trackton children are enveloped in different kinds of social interactions. They are held, fed, talked about, and rewarded for nonverbal, and later verbal, renderings of events they witness. Trackton adults value and respond favorably when children show they have come to know how to use language to show correspondence in function, style, configuration, and positioning between two different things or situations. Analogical questions are asked of Trackton children, although the implicit questions of structure and function these embody are never made explicit. Children do not have labels or names of attributes of items and events pointed out for them, and they are asked for reason-explanations not what-explanations. Individuals express their personal responses and recreate corresponding situations with often only a minimal adherence to the germ of truth of a story. Children come to recognize similarities of patterning, though they do not name lines, points, or items which are similar between two items or situations. They are familiar with group literacy events in which several community members orally negotiate the meaning of a written text.

**At School** In the early reading stages, and in later requirements for reading to learn at more advanced stages, children from the three communities respond differently, because they have learned different methods and degrees of taking from books. In comparison to Maintown children, the habits Roadville children learned in bookreading and toy-related episodes have not continued for them through other activities and types of reinforcement in their environment. They have had less exposure to both the content of books and ways of learning from books than have mainstream children. Thus their need in schools is not necessarily for an intensification of presentation of labels, a slowing down of the sequence of introducing what-explanations in connection with bookreading. Instead they need *extension of these habits to other domains* and to opportunities for practicing habits such as producing running commentaries, creating exhibitor/questioner and spectator/respondent roles. Perhaps most important, Roadville children need to have articulated for them *distinctions in discourse strategies and structures.* Narratives of real events have certain strategies and structures; imaginary tales, flights of fantasy, and affective expressions have others. Their community's view of narrative discourse style is very narrow and demands a passive role in both creation of and response to the account of events. Moreover, these children have *to be reintroduced to a participant frame of reference to a book.* Though initially they were participants in bookreading, they have been trained into passive roles since the age of three years, and they must learn once again to be active information-givers, taking from books and linking that knowledge to other aspects of their environment.

Trackton students present an additional set of alternatives for procedures in the early primary grades. Since they usually have few of the expected "natural" skills of taking meaning from books, they must not only learn these, but also *retain their analogical reasoning practices* for use in some of the later stages of learning to read. They must *learn to adapt the creativity in language, metaphor, fictionalization, recreation of scenes and exploration of functions and settings of items they bring to school.* These children already use narrative skills highly rewarded in the upper primary grades. They distinguish a fictionalized story from a real-life narrative. They know that telling a story can be in many ways related to play; it suspends reality, and frames an old event in a new context; it calls on audience participation to recognize the setting and participants. They must now *learn as individuals to recount factual events in a straightforward way* and *recognize appropriate occasions for reason-explanations and affective expressions.* Trackton children seem to have skipped learning to label, list features, and give what-explanations. Thus they need to *have the mainstream or school habits presented in familiar activities with explanations related to their own habits of taking meaning* from the environment. Such "simple," "natural" things as distinctions between two-dimensional and three-dimensional objects may need to be explained to help Trackton children learn the stylization and decontextualization which characterizes books.

To lay out in more specific detail how Roadville and Trackton's ways of knowing can be used along with those of mainstreamers goes beyond the scope of this paper. However, it must be admitted that a range of alternatives to ways of learning and displaying knowledge characterizes all highly school-successful adults in the advanced stages of their careers. Knowing more about how these alternatives are learned at early ages in different sociocultural conditions can help the school to provide opportunities for *all* students to avail themselves of these alternatives early in their school careers. For example, mainstream children can benefit from early exposure to Trackton's creative, highly analogical styles of telling stories and giving explanations, and they can add the Roadville true story with strict chronicity and explicit moral to their repertoire of narrative types.

In conclusion, if we want to understand the place of literacy in human societies and ways children acquire the literacy orientations of their communities, we must recognize two postulates of literacy and language development.

(1) Strict dichotomization between oral and literate traditions is a construct of researchers, not an accurate portrayal of reality across cultures.
(2) A unilinear model of development in the acquisition of language structures and uses cannot adequately account for culturally diverse ways of acquiring knowledge or developing cognitive styles.

Roadville and Trackton tell us that the mainstream type of literacy orientation is not the only type even among Western societies. They also tell us that the mainstream ways of acquiring communicative competence do not offer a universally applicable model of development. They offer proof of Hymes' assertion a decade ago that "it is impossible to generalize validly about 'oral' vs. 'literate' cultures as uniform types" (Hymes 1973: 54).

Yet in spite of such warnings and analyses of the uses and functions of writing in the specific proposals for comparative development and organization of cultural systems (cf. Basso 1974: 432). the majority of research on literacy has focused on differences in class, amount of education, and level of civilization among groups having different literacy characteristics.

"We need, in short, a great deal of ethnography" (Hymes 1973: 57) to provide descriptions of the ways different social groups "take" knowledge from the environment. For written sources, these ways of taking may be analyzed in terms of *types of literacy events,* such as group negotiation of meaning from written texts, individual "looking things up" in reference books, writing family records in Bibles, and the dozens of other types of occasions when books or other written materials are integral to interpretation in an interaction. These must in turn be analyzed in terms of the specific *features of literacy events,* such as labelling, what-explanation, affective comments, reason-explanations, and many other possibilities. Literacy events must also be interpreted in relation to the *larger sociocultural patterns* which they may exemplify or reflect. For example, ethnography must describe literacy events in their sociocultural contexts, so we may come to understand how such patterns as time and space usage, caregiving roles, and age and sex segregation are interdependent with the types and features of literacy events a community develops. It is only on the basis of such thoroughgoing ethnography that further progress is possible toward understanding cross-cultural patterns of oral and written language uses and paths of development of communicative competence.

## Notes

1. First presented at the Terman Conference on Teaching at Stanford University, 1980, this paper has benefitted from cooperation with M. Cochran-Smith of the University of Pennsylvania. She shares an appreciation of the relevance of Roland Barthes' work for studies of the socialization of young children into literacy; her research (1981) on the story-reading practices of a mainstream school-oriented nursery school provides a much needed detailed account of early school orientation to literacy.

2. Terms such as *mainstream* or *middle-class* cultures or social groups are frequently used in both popular and scholarly writings without careful definition. Moreover, numerous studies of behavioral phenomena (for example, mother-child interactions in language learning) either do not specify that the subjects being described are drawn from mainstream groups or do not recognize the importance of this limitation. As a result, findings from this group are often regarded as universal. For a discussion of this problem, see Chanan and Gilchrist 1974, Payne and Bennett 1977. In general, the literature characterizes this group as school-oriented, aspiring toward upward mobility through formal institutions, and providing enculturation which positively values routines of promptness, linearity (in habits ranging from furniture arrangement to

entrance into a movie theatre), and evaluative and judgmental responses to behaviors which deviate from their norms.

In the United States, mainstream families tend to locate in neighborhoods and suburbs around cities. Their social interactions center not in their immediate neighborhoods, but around voluntary associations across the city. Thus a cluster of mainstream families (and not a community—which usually implies a specific geographic territory as the locus of a majority of social interactions) is the unit of comparison used here with the Trackton and Roadville communities.

3. Behind this discussion are findings from cross-cultural psychologists who have studied the links between verbalization of task and demonstration of skills in a hierarchical sequence, e.g., Childs and Greenfield 1980; see Goody 1979 on the use of questions in learning tasks unrelated to a familiarity with books.

4. Cf. Umiker-Sebeok's (1979) descriptions of stories of mainstream middle-class children, ages 3–5 and Sutton-Smith 1981.

## References


Basso, K. 1974. The ethonography of writing. In R. Bauman & J. Sherzer (eds.), *Explorations in the ethnography of speaking.* Cambridge: Cambridge University Press.

Cazden, C. B. 1979. Peekaboo as an instructional model: Discourse development at home and at school. *Papers and Reports in Child Language Development* 17: 1–29.

Chanan, G., & Gilchrist, L. 1974. *What school is for.* New York: Praeger.

Childs, C. P., & Greenfield, P. M. 1980. Informal modes of learning and teaching. In N. Warren (ed.), *Advances in cross-cultural psychology*, vol. 2 London: Academic Press.

Cochran-Smith, M. 1981. The making of a reader. Ph.D. dissertation. University of Pennsylvania.

Cohen, R. 1968. The relation between socio-conceptual styles and orientation to school requirements. *Sociology of Education* 41: 201–20.

Cohen, R. 1969. Conceptual styles, culture conflict, and nonverbal tests of intelligence. *American Anthropologist* 71(5): 828–56.

Cohen, R. 1971. The influence of conceptual rule-sets on measures of learning ability. In C. L. Brace, G. Gamble, & J. Bond (eds.), *Race and intelligence.* (Anthropological Studies, No. 8, American Anthropological Association). 41–57.

Glaser, R. 1979. Trends and research questions in psychological research on learning and schooling. *Educational Researcher* 8(10): 6–13.

Goody, E. 1979. Towards a theory of questions. In E. N. Goody (ed.), *Questions and politeness: Strategies in social interaction.* Cambridge: Cambridge University Press.

Griffin, P., & Humphrey, F. 1978. Task and talk. In *The study of children's functional language and education in the early years.* Final report to the Carnegie Corporation of New York. Arlington, Va.: Center for Applied Linguistics.

Heath, S. 1978. *Teacher talk: Language in the classroom.* (Language in Education 9.) Arlington, Va.: Center for Applied Linguistics.

Heath, S. 1980. The functions and uses of literacy. *Journal of Communication* 30(1): 123–33.

Heath, S. 1982. Questioning at home and at school: A comparative study. In G. Spindler (ed.), *Doing ethnography: Educational anthropology in action.* New York: Holt, Rinehart & Winston.

Heath, S. (forthcoming a). Protean shapes: Ever-shifting oral and literate traditions. To appear in D. Tannen (ed.), *Spoken and written language: Exploring orality and literacy.* Norwood, N.J.: Ablex.

Heath, S. (forthcoming b). *Ways with words: Ethnography of communication in communities and classrooms.*

Howard, R. 1974. A note on S/Z. In R. Barthes, *Introduction to S/Z.* Trans. Richard Miller. New York: Hill and Wang.

Hymes, D. H. 1973. On the origins and foundations of inequality among speakers. In E. Haugen & M. Bloomfield (eds.), *Language as a human problem.* New York: W. W. Norton & Co.

Hymes, D. H. 1974. Models of the interaction of language and social life. In J. J. Gumperz & D. Hymes (eds.), *Directions in sociolinguistics.* New York: Holt, Rinehart and Winston.

Kagan, J., Sigel, I., & Moss, H. 1963. Psychological significance of styles of conceptualization. In J. Wright & J. Kagan (eds.), *Basic cognitive processes in children.* (Monographs of the society for research in child development.) 28(2): 73–112.

Mehan, H. 1979. *Learning lessons.* Cambridge, Mass.: Harvard University Press.

Merritt, M. 1979. Service-like events during individual work time and their contribution to the nature of the rules for communication. NIE Report EP 78-0436.

Nino, A., & Bruner, J. 1978. The achievement and antecedents of labelling. *Journal of Child Language* 5: 1–15.

Payne, C., & Bennett, C. 1977. "Middle class aura" in public schools. *The Teacher Educator* 13(1): 16–26.

Peters, A. 1977. Language learning strategies. *Language* 53: 560–73.

Scollon, R., & Scollon, S. 1979. The literate two-year old: The fictionalization of self. *Working Papers in Sociolinguistics.* Austin, TX: Southwest Regional Laboratory.

Sinclair, J. M., & Coulthard, R. M. 1975. *Toward an analysis of discourse.* New York: Oxford University Press.

Sutton-Smith, B. 1981. *The folkstories of children.* Philadelphia: University of Pennsylvania Press.

Umiker-Sebeok, J. D. 1979. Preschool children's intraconversational narratives. *Journal of Child Language* 6(1): 91–110.

Witkin, H., Faterson, F., Goodenough, R., & Birnbaum, J. 1966. Cognitive patterning in mildly retarded boys. *Child Development* 37(2): 301–16.

## Critical Thinking and Application

- Compare media accounts of the "achievement gap" between majority and minority students in school with Heath's chapter. How did Heath apply the understanding of the "ways of taking" meaning used by different groups to explain their differing success within a monolithic school system?
- Observe interactions of families from groups different from your own using the types of topics listed above. What is surprising? What do you think you would not have noticed had you not read this work? How might the home practices of the group you observed conflict with the dominant schooling ethos? How might children from this background be taught to function within such an alien system while retaining self-respect?

## Vocabulary

affective commentaries
analogical questions
dyad
field dependent
field independent
initiation-reply-evaluation sequence
labeling game
literacy event
reason-explanations
routine
scaffolding
"ways of taking"
what-explanations
what-question

## Suggested Further Reading [See also list following Language Socialization unit introduction]*


Barton, David. 1988. Problems with an Evolutionary Account of Literacy. *Lancaster Papers in Linguistics* 49.

Barton, David, and Mary Hamilton. 1990. *Researching Literacy in Industrialized Countries: Trends and Prospects*. Hamburg: UNESCO Institute for Education.

Barton, David, Mary Hamilton, and Roz Ivanic, eds. 2000. *Situated Literacies: Reading and Writing in Context*. London and New York: Routledge.

Barton, David, and Roz Ivanič, eds. 1991. *Writing in the Community*. Newbury Park, CA: Sage.

Basso, Keith H. 1974. The Ethnography of Writing. In *Explorations in the Ethnography of Speaking*, edited by Richard Bauman and Joel Sherzer, pp. 425–432. Cambridge: Cambridge University Press.

Berggren, Carol, and Lars Berggren. 1975. *The Literacy Process: A Practice in Domestication or Liberation*. London: Writers and Readers Publishers' Cooperative.

Besnier, Niko. 1989. Literacy and Feelings: The Encoding of Affect in Nukulaelae Letters. In *Cross-Cultural Approaches to Literacy*, edited by Brian V. Street, pp. 62–86. Cambridge: Cambridge University Press.

Besnier, Niko. 1991. Literacy and the Notion of Person on Nukulaelae Atoll. *American Anthropologist* 93: 570–587.

Biber, Douglas. 1988. *Variation Across Speech and Writing*. Cambridge: Cambridge University Press.

Bledsoe, Caroline, and Kenneth M. Robey. 1986. Arabic Literacy and Secrecy Among the Mende of Sierra Leone. *Man* 21: 202–226.

Bloch, Maurice. 1993. The Uses of Schooling and Literacy in a Zafimaniry Village. In *Cross-Cultural Approaches to Literacy*, edited by Brian V. Street, pp. 87–109. Cambridge: Cambridge University Press.

Bloome, David, ed. 1989. *Classrooms and Literacy*. Norwood, NJ: Ablex.

Cazden, Courtney B. 1978. Learning to Read in Classroom Interaction. In *Theory and Practice in Early Reading* (vol. 3), edited by L. B. Resnick and P. A. Weaver, pp. 295–306. Hillsdale, NJ: Erlbaum.

Chafe, Wallace L., and Deborah Tannen. 1987. The Relation Between Written and Spoken Language. *Annual Review of Anthropology* 16: 383–407.

Cole, Michael, and Angeliki Nicolopoulou. 1992. Literacy: Intellectual Consequences. In *International Encyclopaedia of Linguistics* (vol. 2), edited by William Bright, pp. 343–346. New York and Oxford: Oxford University Press.

Collins, James. 1986. Differential Treatment and Reading Instruction. In *The Social Construction of Literacy*, edited by Jenny Cook-Gumperz, pp. 138–164. Cambridge: Cambridge University Press.

Collins, James. 1988. Language and Class in Minority Education. *Anthropology and Education Quarterly* 19(4): 299–326.

Cook-Gumperz, Jenny, ed. 1986. *The Social Construction of Literacy.* Cambridge: Cambridge University Press.

Crump, Thomas. 1988. Alternative Meanings of Literacy in Japan and the West. *Human Organization* 47: 138–145.

Eisomon, Thomas O. 1988. *Benefitting from Basic Education, School Quality and Functional Literacy in Kenya.* Oxford: Pergamon.

Erikson, Frederick. 1984. School Literacy, Reasoning and Civility: An Anthropologist's Perspective. *Review of Educational Research* 54(4): 525–546.

Everhardt, Robert B. 1983. *Reading, Writing and Resistance: Adolescence and Labour in a Junior High School.* London: Routledge & Kegan Paul.

Ferguson, Charles A. 1987. Literacy in a Hunting-Gathering Society: The Case of the Diyari. *Journal of Anthropological Research* 43: 223–237.

Finnegan, Ruth H. 1988. *Literacy and Orality: Studies in the Technology of Communication.* Oxford: Blackwell.

Fishman, Andrea R. 1991. "Because This Is Who We Are": Writing in the Amish Community. In *Writing in the Community*, edited by David Barton and Roz Ivanič, pp. 14–37. London: Sage.

Goody, Jack, ed. 1968. *Literacy in Traditional Societies.* Cambridge: Cambridge University Press.

Goody, Jack. 1977. *The Domestication of the Savage Mind.* Cambridge: Cambridge University Press.

Goody, Jack. 1986. *The Logic of Writing and the Organization of Society.* Cambridge: Cambridge University Press.

Goody, Jack. 1987. *The Interface Between the Written and the Oral.* Cambridge: Cambridge University Press.

Goody, Jack, and Ian Watt. 1963. The Consequences of Literacy. *Comparative Studies in Society and History* 5: 304–345.

Graff, Harvey J. 1979. *The Literacy Myth: Literacy and Social Structure in the Nineteenth Century.* New York: Academic Press.

Graff, Harvey J. 1987. *The Legacies of Literacy: Continuities and Contradictions in Western Culture and Society.* Bloomington: Indiana University Press.

Hansen, Judith Friedman. 1979. *Sociocultural Perspectives on Human Learning: An Introduction to Educational Anthropology.* Englewood Cliffs, NJ: Prentice Hall.

Havelock, Eric. 1976. *Origins of Western Literacy.* Toronto: Ontario Institute of Education.

Heath, Shirley Brice. 1983. *Ways with Words: Language, Life, and Work in Communities and Classrooms.* Cambridge: Cambridge University Press.

Heath, Shirley Brice, and Brian V. Street. 2007. *On Ethnography: Approaches to Language and Literacy Research.* New York: Teachers College Press.

Hornberger, Nancy. 2003. *Continua of Biliteracy: An Ecological Framework for Educational Policy, Research, and Practice in Multilingual Settings.* Bristol: Multilingual Matters.

Houston, Robert A. 1988. *Literacy in Early Modern Europe: Culture and Education 1500–1800.* London: Longman.

Hunter, Carmen St. John, and David Harman. 1979. *Adult Illiteracy in the United States.* New York: McGraw-Hill.

Jackson, Michael D. 1975. Literacy, Communications, and Social Change: A Study of the Meaning and Effect of Literacy in Early Nineteenth Century Maori Society. In *Conflict and Compromise: Essays on the Maori Since Colonization*, edited by Ian Hugh Kawheru, pp. 27–54. Wellington: Reed.

Kimberley, Keith, Margaret Meek, and Jane Miller. 1992. *New Readings: Contributions to an Understanding of Literacy.* London: Black.

Kintgen, Eugene R., Barry M. Kroll, and Mike Rose, eds. 1988. *Perspectives on Literacy.* Carbondale: Southern Illinois University Press.

Kulick, Don, and Christopher Stroud. 1990. Christianity, Cargo and Ideas of Self: Patterns of Literacy in a Papua New Guinea Village. *Man* (NS) 25: 286–304.

Lankshear, Colin, and Moira Lawler. 1987. *Literacy, Schooling and Revolution*. Brighton: Falmer Press.

Larson, Joanne, ed. 2007. *Literacy as Snake Oil: Beyond the Quick Fix*. New York: Lang.

Leap, William L. 1991. Pathways and Barriers to Indian Language Literacy-building on the Northern Ute Reservation. *Anthropology and Education Quarterly* 22: 21–41.

Levine, Kenneth. 1986. *The Social Context of Literacy*. London: Routledge & Kegan Paul.

Lewis, I. M. 1986. Literacy and Cultural Identity in the Horn of Africa: The Somali Case. In *The Written Word: Literacy in Transition*, edited by Gerd Baumann, pp. 133–150. Oxford: Clarendon Press.

Mace, Jane. 1979. *Working with Words*. London: Chameleon.

Mace, Jane. 1992. *Talking About Literacy*. London: Routledge.

McDermott, R. P., Hervé Varenne, and Vera Hamid-Buglione. 1982. *"I Teach Him Everything He Learns in School": The Acquisition of Literacy for Learning in Working Class Families*. New York: Teachers College Press.

McLaren, Peter L. 1988. Culture or Canon? Critical Pedagogy and the Politics of Literacy. *Harvard Educational Review* 58(2): 213–234.

McLaren, Peter L. 1999 [1986]. *Schooling as a Ritual Performance: Toward a Political Economy of Educational Symbols and Gestures*. 3rd ed. Lanham, MD: Rowman & Littlefield.

McLaughlin, Daniel. 1989. The Sociolinguistics of Navajo Literacy. *Anthropology and Education Quarterly* 20: 275–290.

Meek, Margaret. 1991. *On Being Literate*. London: Bodley Head.

Mercer, Neil, ed. 1988. *Language and Literacy from an Educational Perspective: A Reader*. Milton Keynes: Open University Press.

Michaels, Sarah, and Courtney Cazden. 1986. Teacher/Child Collaboration as Oral Preparation for Literacy. In *The Acquisition of Literacy: Ethnographic Perspectives*, edited by Bambi B. Schieffelin and Perry Gilmore, pp. 132–153. Norwood, NJ: Ablex.

Ong, Walter J. 1982. *Orality and Literacy: The Technologizing of the Word*. London and New York: Methuen.

Oxenham, John. 1980. *Literacy: Writing, Reading and Social Organization*. London: Routledge & Kegan Paul.

Pahl, Kate, and Jennifer Rowsell, eds. 2006. *Travel Notes from the New Literacy Studies: Instances of Practice*. Clevedon: Multilingual Matters.

Parsonson, G. S. 1967. The Literate Revolution in Polynesia. *Journal of Pacific History* 2: 169–190.

Pattison, Robert. 1982. *On Literacy: The Politics of the Word from Homer to the Age of Rock*. New York and Oxford: Oxford University Press.

Philips, Susan U. 1975. Literacy as a Mode of Communication on the Warm Springs Indian Reservation. In *Foundations of Language Development: A Multidisciplinary Approach* (vol. 2), edited by Eric Heinz Lenneberg and Elizabeth Lenneberg, pp. 367–381. New York: Academic Press.

Reder, Stephen, and Karen Reed. 1983. Contrasting Patterns of Literacy in an Alaskan Fishing Village. *International Journal of the Sociology of Language* 42: 9–39.

Roberts, Joan, and Sherrie K. Akinsaya, eds. 1976. *Schooling in the Cultural Context: Anthropological Studies of Education*. New York: McKay.

Rogers, Alan, ed. 2005. *Urban Literacy: Communication, Identity, and Learning in Development Contexts*. Hamburg, Germany: UNESCO Institute for Education.

Säljö, Roger, ed. 1988. *The Written World: Studies in Literate Thought and Action*. Berlin and New York: Springer.

Schieffelin, Bambi B., and Marilyn Cochran-Smith. 1984. Learning to Read Culturally: Literacy Before Schooling. In *Awakening to Literacy*, edited by Hillel Goelman, Antoinette Oberg, and Frank Smith, pp. 3–23. Exeter, NH: Heinemann.

Schieffelin, Bambi B., and Perry Gilmore, eds. 1986. *The Acquisition of Literacy: Ethnographic Perspectives*. Norwood, NJ: Ablex.

Scollon, Ron, and Suzanne B. K. Scollon. 1981. *Narrative, Literacy, and Face in Interethnic Communication.* Norwood, NJ: Ablex.

Scribner, Sylvia, and Michael Cole. 1981. *The Psychology of Literacy*. Cambridge, MA: Harvard University Press.

Shuman, Amy. 1986. *Storytelling Rights: The Uses of Oral and Written Texts by Urban Adolescents.* Cambridge: Cambridge University Press.

Smith, Frank. 1983. *Essays into Literacy.* Exeter, NH: Heinemann.

Street, Brian V. 1984. *Literacy in Theory and Practice.* Cambridge: Cambridge University Press.

Street, Brian V. 1987. Literacy and Social Change: The Significance of Social Context in the Development of Literacy Programmes. In *The Future of Literacy in a Changing World*, edited by Daniel A. Wagner, pp. 55–72. Oxford: Pergamon Press.

Street, Brian V., ed. 1993. *Cross-Cultural Approaches to Literacy.* Cambridge: Cambridge University Press.

Street, Brian V., ed. 2001. *Literacy and Development: Ethnographic Perspectives.* London and New York: Routledge.

Street, Brian V. 2003. What's "New" in New Literacy Studies? Critical Approaches to Literacy in Theory and Practice. *Current Issues in Comparative Education* 5(2): 77–91.

Street, Brian V., ed. 2005. *Literacies Across Educational Contexts: Mediating Learning and Teaching.* Philadelphia: Caslon.

Street, Brian V., and Niko Besnier. 1994. Aspects of Literacy. In *Companion Encyclopedia of Anthropology*, edited by Tim Ingold, pp. 527–562. London and New York: Routledge.

Street, Brian V., and Adam Lefstein. 2007. *Literacy: An Advanced Resource Book.* London and New York: Routledge.

Stubbs, Michael. 1980. *Language and Literacy: The Sociolinguistics of Reading and Writing.* London and Boston: Routledge & Kegan Paul.

Szwed, John F. 1981. The Ethnography of Literacy. In *Writing: The Nature, Development, and Teaching of Written Communication* (vol. 1), edited by Marcia Farr Whiteman, pp. 13–23. Hillsdale, NJ: Erlbaum.

Tannen, Deborah. 1985. Relative Focus on Involvement in Oral and Written Discourse. In *Literacy, Language, and Learning: The Nature and Consequences of Reading and Writing*, edited by David R. Olson, Nancy Torrance, and Angela Hildyard, pp. 124–147. Cambridge: Cambridge University Press.

Taylor, Denny. 1985. *Family Literacy*. London: Heinemann.

Teale, William H., and Elizabeth Sulzby, eds. 1986. *Emergent Literacy: Writing and Reading.* Norwood, NJ: Ablex.

Varenne, Hervé, and H. P. McDermott. 1986. "Why" Sheila Can Read: Structure and Indeterminacy in the Reproduction of Familial Literacy. In *The Acquisition of Literacy: Ethnographic Perspectives*, edited by Bambi B. Schieffelin and Perry Gilmore, pp. 188–210. Norwood, NJ: Ablex.

Wagner, Daniel A., ed. 1987. *The Future of Literacy in a Changing World.* Oxford: Pergamon Press.

Wagner, Daniel A. 1989. Literacy Campaigns: Past, Present, and Future. *Comparative Educational Review* 33(2): 256–260.

Weinstein-Shr, Gail. 1993. Literacy and Social Process: A Community in Transition. In *Cross-Cultural Approaches to Literacy*, edited by Brian V. Street, pp. 272–293. Cambridge: Cambridge University Press.

Willinsky, John. 1990. *The New Literacy: Redefining Reading and Writing in the Schools.* New York: Routledge.

Willis, Paul. 1977. *Learning to Labour.* Farnborough: Saxon House.

Wortham, Stanton, and Betsy Rymes, eds. 2003. *Linguistic Anthropology of Education.* Westport, CT: Praeger.

* With contributions from Brian Street and Niko Besnier.

# CHAPTER 11

# The Pragmatics of Reading Prayers

## Learning the Act of Contrition in Spanish-based Religious Education Classes (*Doctrina*)

*Patricia Baquedano-López*

(2008)

*Research on language socialization (LS) has blossomed since Ochs and Schieffelin named the field in the 1980s. While they focused especially on early childhood and sometimes on nonliterate societies, their students and others have extended the inquiry to examine the ways children are socialized into culture and language both in schools and out. A lively and powerful branch of this involves the linguistic anthropology of education and the question of literacies, often associated with Stanton Wortham, Brian Street, Niko Besnier, and Nancy Hornberger.*

*Patricia Baquedano-López has been conducting fieldwork for many years on Spanish-based Catholic religious training for Mexican immigrant children. Her work looks at a range of questions involved in examining how children are socialized and intersects with many central anthropological questions such as the nature of ritual and identity, the meaning of religion, and what is being taught in schools besides the curricular content.*

### Reading Questions

- What are the goals of *doctrina* education?
- How does the author support her claim that the Act of Contrition (AOC), the text being studied, is constructed as sacred even though it is not considered the "Word of God"?
- What are the meanings of both ethnic and national and of religious identities?
- What are the actions undertaken by children (novices) and their teachers (experts)?
- How does reading play a part in the children's religious and social training?
- How are the children supposed to interact with the text? How *do* they interact with it?

### Introduction

In this [chapter] I examine the practice of reading prayers in Spanish-based Catholic children's religious education (*doctrina*) classes. These Saturday classes have been the focus of my language and literacy socialization studies of Latino immigrant children in Catholic parishes in California. For the span of seven years I investigated the literacy and language socialization practices of *doctrina* instruction in Southern California, at St. Paul's Catholic Church (1994–1998),[1] and in the East Bay of the greater San Francisco Metropolitan Area, at Faith Catholic Church (2001–2004) (Baquedano-López 1997, 2000, 2004). In this [chapter], I examine the convergence of linguistic, interactional, and textual resources, in short, the pragmatics involved in the reading of the Act of Contrition (AOC),[2] a prayer that *doctrina* students must memorize and say during the religious ritual that involves the confession and absolution of sins. Through an analysis of a sample reading activity of the AOC I discuss how a teacher and her students engage [in] a *ritualization* process that focuses and constructs text as sacred. Their reading activity illustrates this process through (i) parallel reframing and interpretation on the words being read and (ii) verbalizations of **cognitive** activity related to ways of reading text. The analysis of this activity also exemplifies the importance placed on grammatical correctness and the appropriate delivery of religious text, where attention to text and to other participants is promoted.

Building on the widely accepted notion in contemporary social theory that institutions play a significant role in socializing individuals to the norms of comportment and

Patricia Baquedano-López, The Pragmatics of Reading Prayers: Learning the Act of Contrition in Spanish-based Religious Education Classes *(Doctrina)*. *Text & Talk* 28–5 (2008): 581–602.

knowledge that are historically valued by society, I analyze how the local negotiation and organization of the activity of reading the AOC in *doctrina* constitute examples of variability in this process. That is, institutions vary in the way that they organize behavior and knowledge, and in the way they instill dispositions toward that knowledge. In his discussion of collective ritualized activity, Pierre Bourdieu (1990: 69) noted the ways both body and language 'function as depositories of deferred thoughts that can be triggered off at a distance in space and time by the simple effect of re-placing the body in an overall posture which *recalls* the associated thoughts and feelings'. Collective rituals thus provide ways to remember, *re*-cognize, and act according to already internalized patterns of conduct. These acts, in turn, keep the boundaries of the group stable and provide the mechanisms for **reproduction.** Similarly, in his analysis of the social and **discursive** mechanisms that institutions develop to organize and control behaviors, Michel Foucault (1997: 200) discussed how 'discursive practices are not purely and simply ways of producing discourse', rather, 'they are embodied in technical processes, in institutions, in patterns of general behavior, in forms of transmission and diffusion, and in pedagogical forms which, at once, impose and maintain them'. These processes account for the continued supply of discourses that maintain the status quo. From this perspective, the power of the institution rests on the historically organized and embodied actions that uphold it.

While we need to account for the role of institutions in organizing social practices that are reproductive in nature, we need to be mindful that social reproduction is never entirely predictable or homogeneous in its outcome. In the context of the Catholic Church, for example, there are varied ways that its branches (the archdioceses, the parishes, the classrooms) create versions of practices that are relevant to their local contexts of interaction constituting cultural improvisations, to use Renato Rosaldo's terms (1999 [1989]). These actions are not always necessarily forms of 'resistance' to the institution, to invoke Foucault's (1990 [1976]: 95) dictum 'where there is power, there is resistance'.[3] Attention to everyday activity, its discourses and practices, can help illuminate the ways participants in interaction manage the local contingencies of their joint activities as they socialize each other to the **emergent** norms of their interaction. The outcomes of such socialization interactions may very well serve to support the institution that produced them, but they may also challenge or disrupt it.

## Religious Socialization: A Perspective from Language Socialization Research

I begin this discussion of religious socialization by recognizing the fact that the expansionist program of the Church has played a determinant role in upholding and reproducing religious **epistemologies** and expectations across societies and sociopolitical orders and epochs. Accounts of the discursive detail of this reproductive force as it has impacted and influenced cultural practices and texts are on the increase.[4] There is a strong tradition in the field of linguistic anthropology investigating the study of a variety of religious genres (and their blends) for the cultural insights they offer (Hanks 2006; Keane 1997; Poveda et al. 2005; Robbins 2001; Shoaps 2002; Silverstein 2004; Tambiah 1985; Wilce 2001; among others). Within the discipline, a growing group of language socialization scholars has been examining the ways locally managed discursive practices around religious texts and activities serve the broader goals of religious literacy and socialization (see Aminy 2004; Baquedano-López 2000; Capps and Ochs 2002; Duranti et al. 1995; Fader 2001, 2007; Heath 1983; Jacobs-Huey 2006; Moore 2006a, 2006b; Ochs 1988; Schieffelin 2002). This is the theoretical starting point of this analysis of ritualization. The linguistic practices of *doctrina* instruction around the AOC socialize skill and comportment in children's participation in the cultural practices of their religious community.

Language socialization research is concerned with the ways in which people learn cultural competencies through language, while simultaneously they are socialized into ways of using language (Schieffelin and Ochs 1986). This perspective also presupposes that there is an **intersubjective** component in this process that includes negotiations between novices or newcomers and expert-others (Lave and Wenger 1991; Rogoff 1990).[5] The outcomes of this socialization process are varied, that is, some practices fully realize the goals of social institutions and thus serve as a vehicle for continuity of practice, but they may very well promote innovation, transformation, or they may also produce outcomes that disrupt that which is normative within the institution (see Garrett and Baquedano-López 2002). The study of practices in religious settings such as *doctrina* can help illuminate how these aspects of competency and participation are realized, how engagement in momentary learning activity, such as reading a text, is always an instantiation and realignment of relations of expertness and affiliation.

The following sections are organized in two parts. The first includes a brief ethnographic description of *doctrina* instruction and an overview of the AOC's origins. The second consists of an analysis of the text, that is, of the **pragmatics** of reading the AOC, which draws from examples of transcribed video-recorded interactions during reading and memorization of the AOC by four female students under the supervision of a teacher aide. This approach is consistent with the main perspective taken here, that there is a reciprocal relationship between the details of moment-to-moment interaction and the larger social context in which it occurs.

## Children's Catholic Education: *Doctrina* Practices

Religious education classes for children are offered in response to the Catholic Church mandate to teach the tenets of Catholicism and prepare young children (ages 6–8) to participate in two important sacraments or Catholic rites of passage: Reconciliation (also known as First Confession) and First Communion (also First Eucharist). On weekends, Catholic parishes across the United States provide religious instruction to young school-age children who attend secular schools during the week. Children enrolled in the private parochial schools normally receive religious training as part of the regular school curriculum and thus do not need to attend the weekend classes. Students attending *doctrina* are in their majority Spanish-speaking children living within the parish's jurisdiction. Teachers of religious instruction include clergy and laity affiliated with the national office of the Confraternity of the Christian Doctrine or CCD.[6] CCD in effect serves as an outreach initiative for children and adults new to Catholicism. At both St. Paul's and Faith Catholic Church, CCD classes were offered in English and in Spanish given their large Spanish-speaking congregations. This is not to say that the enactment of these practices in the context of US Catholicism or immigration debates is conflict-free. Elsewhere I have discussed how ideologies of language use and their speakers influenced pedagogical practice to the point of near elimination of the *doctrina* program in the Southern California parish (Baquedano-López 1997, 2004). The persistence of these classes in US parishes illustrates a form of continuity of practices that are at once religious, but also linguistic and cultural.

*Doctrina* is also the term employed in Mexico and Latin America for young children's Catholic religious education that follows the same Catholic Church mandate. It is also the term used to refer to the program in US parishes by Spanish-speaking parishioners, although sometimes *catecismo* (catechism) is used. *Doctrina* instruction in Mexico, however, is inextricably tied to the colonization processes of the Spanish Crown during the sixteenth century which underlie the development of modern Mexico (Frye 1996; Hanks 1996). The diasporic nature of Mexican Catholicism in the United States is a topic of growing interest in the study of collective political and religious Mexican identity (Dolan and Figueroa Deck 1994; Matovina and Riebe-Estrella 2002). In the broader context of the education of immigrant Mexican children in the United States, *doctrina* instruction offers a number of opportunities for children to develop Spanish skills. In the classes I observed, the learning of religious tenets and beliefs was carried out through a number of **literacy practices** almost entirely in Spanish, the **home** or **heritage language** of students, and which is not always the language of the public schools they attend during the week.

## Prayers and Reading Activity in *Doctrina*

Religious language, and within the genre, prayer in particular, holds a myriad of meanings for those who engage it. From a language-based perspective, prayer can be said to provide a link between the human and the spiritual (the divine). As Keane (1997: 49) has noted, 'Language is one medium by which the presence and activity of beings that are otherwise unavailable to the senses can be made presupposable, even compelling'. Prayers vary greatly in structure. They can be situational or spontaneous (scripted or prescribed), written or oral, individual or collective, said for those present or for absent others. In this way they are also **dialogic** (Bahktin 1981), evoking a multiplicity of voices and perspectives. Prayers can embody the 'word of God' (as in the Lord's Prayer or the Qur'an) or they can be products of a religious institution as in the case of the AOC. Rather than being a bounded genre, prayer has a **liminal** structure that blends into other genres such as divination, dance, lament, narrative, or poetry (see also Baquedano-López 2001; Capps and Ochs 2002; Shoaps 2002) and in some educational contexts, prayers become **laminated** onto other literacy activities and events (Poveda et al. 2005).

Across the two-year curriculum of *doctrina* instruction, teachers and students engage a variety of prayer forms ranging from situational to scripted that invoke different 'speaking' perspectives. Drawing on Goffman's (1974) analytic framework for speaker and hearer positions in interaction, the roles constructed during prayer in *doctrina* included as the primary **addressees** God/Jesus and Mary (Jesus's mother). The **author** or **principal** included teachers and students or in some cases, these roles were attributed to authors of sacred texts (i.e., Jesus as the author of the Lord's Prayer). Prayers were **animated** by those present while the **beneficiaries** varied from those present to absent others.[7] Prayers received various forms of instructional attention, sometimes they were read or memorized. They were recited if scripted or said spontaneously if situational, that is, when they arose from the current moment (e.g., praying for a good class or for a sick classmate). Reading activity, memorization, and interpretation of scripted text engaged a **recursive** instructional process until the target text was recited from memory.

Prayers often constituted the content of reading activity. Reading ability was developmentally (maturationally) expected of all students. Children who failed to read at the same rate as their peers were never considered to have cognitive delay. These children did not experience exclusion from the group and were expected to join their peers in all activities, including reading and recitation of prayers. The social interactive and linguistic complexity of reading in educational contexts has been amply recognized (Bloome 1987; Barton and Hamilton 1998; Cushman 1998; Heath 1983; Sterponi 2007; Street 2003). From this perspective, reading refers to actions that are beyond having **decoding** and **inference-making skills** to arrive at the appropriate interpretation of texts (Alverman et al. 2007). This process is not always conflict-free. Indeed, it is the case that literacy practices of the school do not always account for conflicting expectations of what should count as literacy in the home and vice versa, especially in religious communities in contact with secular practices (see, for example, Fader 2008 and Sarroub 2002, 2007). While reading and literacy research highlights the act of reading in interaction, my investigation of the reading practices of the AOC suggests that reading activities privilege the text being read. That is, the text itself is central and the act of reading has primarily a **sacralizing** function.

Like other religious practices around text, *doctrina* reading practices illustrate how the language of the text and the language used to talk about text are inextricably related, as Jonathan Boyarin (1992: 229) has noted, '[t]he voices around the text are the voices in the text'.[8] In the discussion of the Yeshiva of his anthropological studies, Boyarin explains how in that setting equal importance was placed on 'text and speech' so that texts were both literal and oral. *Doctrina* instruction engaged a ritualization process that created 'a ritual of the text'. That is, reading activity of the AOC included a notable separation between knowledge and creation of a sacred text and the cognitive and performative mastery needed to engage 'reading' the text.

## The Act of Contrition: History of a Sacrament

While not a text 'of divine revelation', that is, the AOC is not considered the 'Word of God', it is nonetheless a sacralized text that is read, studied, memorized, and recited as part of the preparation to receive the Sacrament of Reconciliation. Sanctioned by the Council of Trent, the AOC became part of a religious rite where priests mediate the absolution of sins upon its recitation and commitment to moral rectification. During the Counter-Reformation period, a response to the growing Protestant movement of Europe, the Church of Rome redefined its system of beliefs and practices. The Council of Trent, a series of meetings held over a period of almost twenty years (1545–1563) produced the panoply of documents and rulings that became the foundation of what we know today as Catholicism. The Council of Trent defined the seven sacraments—Baptism, Confirmation, Penance (today generally known as Reconciliation or Confession), Eucharist (Holy Communion), Marriage, Extreme Unction (the Last Rites), and Holy Orders—as well as the practices around their investment (Bowker 1997; *The New American Bible* 1993 [1987]). As rites, the sacraments mark the life cycle and provide explicit opportunities to reaffirm one's faith in the Catholic Church. As instructed in the Council of Trent documents, attention to the education of young children was to be the responsibility of all dioceses or the administrative units under the leadership of a bishop.[9] Of significance, the decrees and canons explicitly indicated the use of the local **vernacular** in the teaching of young children to ensure understanding of the content being taught.

Reconciliation and its attendant rites and practices represent an act of purification of the soul prior to taking the Holy host. Through a tripartite model that involves introspection, confession, and penance, a penitent or confessant is absolved of sins by the confessor (an ordained priest). This discursive aspect of the confession is a unique example of how institutions shape individual action and vice versa. There is already important work that provides a social analysis of the institution of the Church (Foucault 1990 [1976], 1995 [1977]) and I briefly reference this work as it discusses

**Table 11.1** Act of Contrition (Spanish and English)

| Acto de Contrición | Act of Contrition |
|---|---|
| Dios mío, con todo mi corazón me arrepiento de todo el mal que he hecho y de todo lo bueno que he dejado de hacer. Al pecar, te he ofendido a ti, que eres el supremo bien y digno de ser amado sobre todas las cosas. Propongo firmen ente, con la ayuda de tu gracia, hacer penitencia, no volver a pecar y huir de las ocasiones de pecado. Señor, por los méritos de la pasión de nuestro Salvador Jesucristo, apiádate de mí. Amén. | My God, I am sorry for my sins with all my heart. In choosing to do wrong and failing to do good, I have sinned against you whom I should love above all things. I firmly intend, with your help, to do penance, to sin no more, and to avoid whatever leads me to sin. Our Savior Jesus Christ suffered and died for us. In his name, my God, have mercy. Amen. |

how through the verbalization of sins and transgressions, the rules and ideals of the institution are made visible and are upheld. Table 11.1 contains the Spanish and English versions of the AOC as listed in the students' textbooks. (Note: The versions are not an exact word-for-word translation.)

## Ritualization: The Process of Creating Sacred Text and Ritual Practice

At the outset of this [chapter] I suggested that the activity of learning the AOC in *doctrina* instruction is part of a process of ritualization. That is, the various activities involved in the learning [of] the AOC (reading, memorization, and recitation) constitute features of collective ritual action. Repetition, individual turns at reading, and choral readings of the AOC accomplish a larger goal of preparing and socializing children, and preparing children's bodies in particular, to religious ritual practice. As it has been argued in the anthropology of ritual, ritual practice organizes behavior (Rappaport 1999) and supports social structure (Turner 1995 [1969]), but perhaps more instrumentally, ritual practice controls the body—it controls attention and encourages focused concentration. A focus on ritualization as a process invites a departure from seeing ritual as the end goal or as (an automatic) routine and to consider it as an activity involving sustained concentration and cognitive engagement (Liénard and Boyer 2006; Boyer and Liénard 2006).[10] There is also a small but significant body of research on ritual in schooling contexts, notably the work of McLaren (1999 [1986]) and Rampton (2002). The basis of the arguments presented in both of these authors' work is that schools and their **metaphors** and **signifiers** create ritual systems that **reify** students' institutional identities.[11]

While there is variation in the ways teachers organize reading activities across *doctrina* instruction, there are clear patterns in practice. Teachers would normally start the activity leading a choral, whole-class reading of the prayer and then they would ask individual students to read aloud or recite the memorized prayer to the whole class. Figure 11.1 is a reproduction of the page of the students' textbook in the

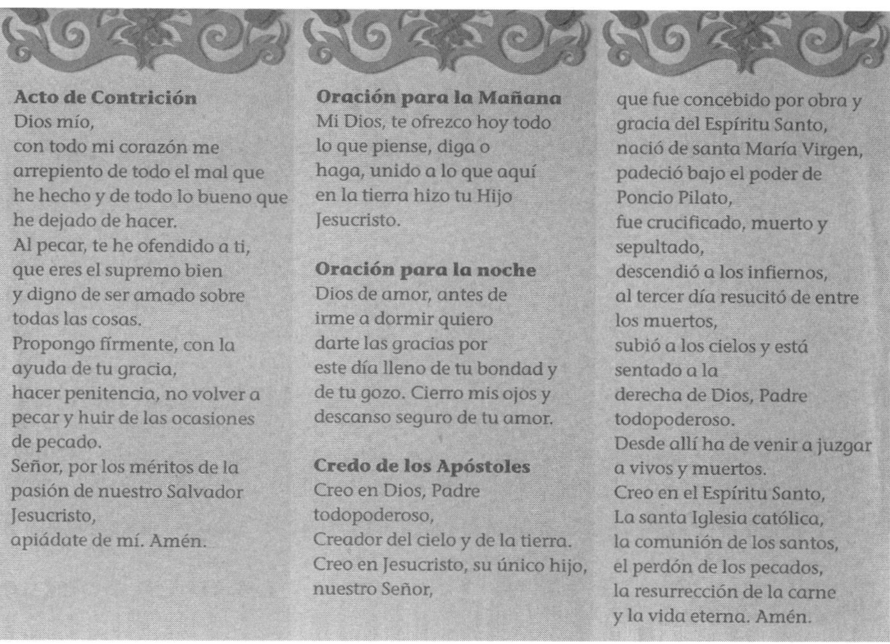

**Acto de Contrición**
Dios mío,
con todo mi corazón me
arrepiento de todo el mal que
he hecho y de todo lo bueno que
he dejado de hacer.
Al pecar, te he ofendido a ti,
que eres el supremo bien
y digno de ser amado sobre
todas las cosas.
Propongo firmente, con la
ayuda de tu gracia,
hacer penitencia, no volver a
pecar y huir de las ocasiones
de pecado.
Señor, por los méritos de la
pasión de nuestro Salvador
Jesucristo,
apiádate de mí. Amén.

**Oración para la Mañana**
Mi Dios, te ofrezco hoy todo
lo que piense, diga o
haga, unido a lo que aquí
en la tierra hizo tu Hijo
Jesucristo.

**Oración para la noche**
Dios de amor, antes de
irme a dormir quiero
darte las gracias por
este día lleno de tu bondad y
de tu gozo. Cierro mis ojos y
descanso seguro de tu amor.

**Credo de los Apóstoles**
Creo en Dios, Padre
todopoderoso,
Creador del cielo y de la tierra.
Creo en Jesucristo, su único hijo,
nuestro Señor,
que fue concebido por obra y
gracia del Espíritu Santo,
nació de santa María Virgen,
padeció bajo el poder de
Poncio Pilato,
fue crucificado, muerto y
sepultado,
descendió a los infiernos,
al tercer día resucitó de entre
los muertos,
subió a los cielos y está
sentado a la
derecha de Dios, Padre
todopoderoso.
Desde allí ha de venir a juzgar
a vivos y muertos.
Creo en el Espíritu Santo,
La santa Iglesia católica,
la comunión de los santos,
el perdón de los pecados,
la resurrección de la carne
y la vida eterna. Amén.

**Figure 11.1** *Act of Contrition on students' textbook*

class analyzed here at Faith Catholic Church that depicts the AOC. The page also includes a morning prayer, an evening prayer, and the Nicene Creed—originally authorized in the year 325 as a statement of Christian faith.

In addition to organizing tasks for students to work individually or in **dyads,** teachers also engaged students in collaborative small-group reading activities. Normally an adult expert (teacher, teacher aide, or parent volunteer) would join a group of students sitting at a table or in a small circle and would lead them through reading, memorization, and recitation of the AOC. In these small group activities, adult and children read chorally or would take turns reading the prayer's stanzas. In the examples of transcribed video-recorded exchanges below,[12] I examine the interactions of a teacher aide, Señora Paz, with a group of four female students engaged in this last activity. I focus my analysis on how the participants in this event negotiated language, their ongoing interaction, and the meanings that were derived from the text they were reading and the activity they were engaging.

## Text-generated Interpretations and Elaborations

After circulating around the classroom to supervise individual students, the teacher aide, Señora Paz, joined a small group at a table and began to lead the group in a choral reading of the prayer. The group was composed of Jane, Irma, Laura, and Celia and they had all been, textbooks in hand, reading and reciting lines by memory to each other. . . .

In what follows I focus on the collaborative reading of the AOC. In the transcribed excerpt of this choral reading of the AOC, Señora Paz and Jane's interpretations and elaborations are placed inside the 'more than/less than' degree signs to indicate the fast-paced nature of their production:

(1)

1 All: *'Al pecar te he ofendido'*
Whenever I have sinned I have offended you.
2 Paz: *>Hemos ofendido a Dios<*
We have offended God.
((punctuates words with hand))
3 All: *'que eres el supremo bien'*
You are the supreme good
4 Paz: *>él es el supremo bien de nosotros, ¿verdad?<*
He is the supreme good for us, right?
5 *>El nos da todo ¿eh?<*
he gives us everything, you know?
6 All: *'y digno de ser amado sobre todos las cosas.'*
And worthy of being loved above all things.
7 Jane: *>Como el primer mandamiento.<*
Like the First Commandment.
8 *Eso dice el mandamiento<*
That's what the commandment says.
9 All: *'Propongo firmemente con la ayuda de tu gracia'*
I firmly intend with your grace

The interpretations offered by Señora Paz while the students are reading reframe grammatically, **prosodically,** and conceptually the lines of the text being read. Earlier I alluded to

Goffman's (1974) production format to indicate the different roles that interactants take in communicative exchanges. The parallel and grammatical contrast were created by changing the first-person-singular pronoun 'I' of the supplicant and beneficiary in the written text to a plural 'we' and 'us' to now include those engaged in the ongoing reading activity. It is important to note here that Spanish is a pro-drop language, that is, personal pronouns are not always overt; see line 1, *Al pecar* [yo] *te he ofendido* ('whenever I have sinned I have offended you') and line 9, [yo] *Propongo firmemente con la ayuda de tu gracia* ('I firmly intend with your grace'). The shift in pronoun makes explicit the third-person pronoun referring to God (*él* 'him'). Of significance, while normally scripted prayers animate the voice of a different author, the AOC challenges this assumption. In its **metapragmatic function,** the AOC is a form of ritualized apology that is embodied when the confessant tells a priest her or his personal transgressions. In its ritual manifestation, then, the AOC also involves a second co-present human party, a mediator, a priest who listens and absolves sins. Rather than the 'empty I' slot common in scripted prayers (see DuBois 1992 and Shoaps 2002), the 'I' in the AOC appears to articulate what could be described as a second-order *indexical ground* (Hanks 1990), which in essence aligns author and animator (or emitter) participant frameworks, an ordering which is made corporeal through the act of confessing sins with its required bodily manifestations (kneeling down, crossing oneself with hands, a quiet voice). The relational property of this style of reading of the AOC also reveals a relation of simultaneity and **dialogism** (see Holquist 2002 [1990]) in the alignment of first-person singular into a collective voice *Al pecar te he ofendido / Hemos ofendido a Dios* ('whenever I have sinned / we have offended God', lines 1 and 2). Similarly, the 'You' addressed to God in the written text is changed to a third person 'He' to match the collective voice animated now.

The prosodic features and rhythmic parsing of the AOC are all recognized features of religious language (DuBois 1986; Keane 1997; Robbins 2001; Shoaps 2002). The process of **prosodic** reorganization of text is consistent with description of ritualized behavior where activity is ordered, scripted, and, thus, eventually repeatable (Rappaport 1971, 1979). The prosodic contour also overlapped with a conceptual parsing out of the text, facilitating **'apprehension'.** As Baker (1992: 108) has posited, apprehension is an activity of the reading process where a reader 'confronts and takes hold of what there is to know and remember'. A next level of reading activity in his model is that of comprehension, exemplified in Jane's contribution to the exchange we have been considering. Jane's interpretations in line 7, *Como el primer mandamiento* ('like the First Commandment') and in line 8, *Eso dice el mandamiento* ('that's what the commandment says') provide a link to another religious text that the students have already studied—the Ten Commandments. Jane's comments illustrate a 'creative competence to use words with conventional meanings to talk about things in one's terms' (Baker 1992: 108), and in this case, an intertextual relationship between the AOC and the Ten Commandments.

Finally, the interpretations provided by Señora Paz provide a way to also read the text in the context of everyday experience: *El nos da todo, ¿eh?* ('He gives us everything, no?', line 5). This **socio-semiotic** dimension of their reading activity was central across the collaborative reading activities that teachers carried out with students. Every idea, every line of a written text provided an opportunity to discuss the social meanings of the words being read (Halliday 1994), in this case, also against the rhythmic cadence of their choral reading. Taken together, the prosodic juxtapositions in the text read out loud and the elaborations and impromptu commentaries that accompany the reading of the text, constructed ritualized activity. In this excerpt, a written text and the language to engage it are reordered to facilitate the *re*-cognition, as it were, of what students must 'take' from the AOC in order to memorize it.

## Text and Cognitive Activity

The collaborative reading of the AOC also provided teacher and students with opportunities to comment on the learning processes taking place. Excerpt (2) depicts the continuation of the interaction just analyzed and illustrates the ways Jane verbalizes the cognitive task of memorizing the AOC. After the group had read chorally a few of the stanzas, Señora Paz assigned individual stanzas to be read by each student in the group, round-robin sequence. Of interest, note that Señora Paz's directive 'to pray' is a synonym of 'to read'. As Señora Paz is about to nominate the first reader of the group, Jane tells the group what she has learned up to that point:

(2)

1 Paz: *A ver ustedes ahora van a rezar=*
Let's see, now you are going to pray
2 Jane: *=Yo nomás me aprendí este-esta poquito*
I only learned this little bit
3 Paz: *Eh? una parte.*
Uh a part of it. ((offered as an alternative for '*esta poquito*'))
4 Jane: *Hasta aquí*
Up to here
((pointing at book))
5 *Desde el principio. Yo desde el principio*
From the beginning. From the beginning
6 *hasta el punto y ya me lo aprendí.*
to the period and I have learned it already.
7 Paz: *Ya ves. Para que veas. Si estudian (más xxx–)*
There. You see. If you study more- ((inaudible))
8 Jane: *Lo tengo que aprender todo.*
I have to learn it all.

Jane's statement in line 8, *'lo tengo que aprender todo'* (I have to learn it all) outlines a learning curve for the group. In other words, she provides a yardstick against which the other members of the group can measure their own competency. Reminiscent of Gee's (1999: 124) paradigm of I-statements,[13] which are associated with expressions of knowledge, including such positioning as 'I can/can't do x', 'I have/don't have to do x', or 'I challenge myself', Jane's disclosure of her memorization progress reveals a cognitive state. It indicates a disposition toward the text, as well as a trajectory of the unfolding and ultimate goals of the activity (memorizing the AOC).

When Jane points to an exact referent on the page of her textbook, she also visually displays what she knows (or has memorized or learned). She thus 'transposes' the already verbalized expression in line 4, *hasta aquí* ('up to here') to two visible and identifiable end points on the printed text. The use of transpositions has been documented across a myriad of discursive acts (Hanks 1990; Haviland 1996) to illustrate how speakers utilize different **communicative modalities,** which may include narratives, reported speech, or gestures, to reorient an ongoing perspective toward past or expected goals and actions. These discursive strategies have been also documented in classroom discourse as a way to match present actions to curricular or cognitive expectation (Solís et al. forthcoming). Transpositions have also been examined in religious language to illustrate more particularly the processes of **entextualization** or the process of reorganizing discourse in another context and thus producing 'text-in-context' (Silverstein and Urban 1996; Shoaps 2002).[14] Thus Jane's expression 'up to here', while simultaneously pointing to the lines in the text, locate her accomplishments, her readings and recitations of the text, as now part of the text before her. Under the constant supervision of the adult in the group, the students heard each other's accomplishments, which turned the less tangible process of memorization into an objectified segment of the text before them.

Señora Paz's corrections exemplify an ideological orientation to Spanish language proficiency in this class (and of the *doctrina* program in general). For example, she does not hesitate to correct Jane's utterance *esta-este poquito* (line 2), similar to the English phrase 'this little bit', and she provides the more contextually appropriate expression *una parte* ('a section') (line 3). In these and other ways, the focus on grammatical correctness punctuates reading activity and supports learning the code. As the group continues their round-robin reading, it is Celia's turn to read. Celia, however, cannot yet read with fluency in either English or Spanish. In Excerpt (3) below, Celia is assigned a stanza from the AOC:

(3)

1 Paz: *Ahora tú*
Now you
((touches Celia's arm))
2 Celia: *(xx- )*
((inaudible))
3 Paz: *Te quiero oir eh, reciecito. Reciecito*
I want to hear you, uh, a bit louder, louder
4 Celia: *(xx- )*
((inaudible)
5 Paz: *Mira, en tu casa? Come bien hija.*
Look, at home? Eat well my child
6 *Para que-que cuando vengas=*
So that when you come [to school]
7 Jane: *=Yo no la escucho*
I can't hear her
8 Paz: *vienes bien desayunada.*
You come having had breakfast
9 *Para que puedas hablar no? mi'ja?*
So that you can talk, okay? my child?

Here the teacher attributes Celia's inability to read not to cognitive skill but to a physical, somatic cause. Celia often displayed what has been termed 'procedural display' or the actions that indicate that students are 'getting the lesson done' and which may be evidenced in vocalizations or hands being raised in response to questions, but whether learning actually occurs is not always immediately apparent (Bloome 1987, 1990). What the exchange more poignantly illustrates is the construction of the body as the vessel of prayer, and perhaps more fundamentally, as a vessel of ritual action. In my year-long observation of Celia in this class, she was never questioned about her reading skills even when she could not read aloud. And when I asked the main teacher, Señora Luz, about Celia's reading abilities, she responded confidently that Celia would be reading by the time of the class's First Confession (a mere month away). Celia eventually memorized the AOC and was able to participate in First Confession and Communion, but it was not until the end of the academic year that she began decoding and doing independent **chunking** of words. The insistence that students recite the AOC even before they can decode it illustrates the primacy of the verbal over the text and the value placed on memorization. Baker's (1992) processes of 'apprehension' also seem to be exemplified here as Celia is not able 'to take from text' or to creatively read text to make other interpretive links based on it. The excerpt of interaction just analyzed reveals an orientation in early *doctrina* instruction and in other religious education settings where rote memorization is a valued skill (see Fader 2008 and also Moore 2008). Reading ability is not as important as the ability to first recite sacred text. And as this excerpt also illustrates, the cultivation of certain body orientations and dispositions (speaking clearly, eating well) expresses a proper way of relating to sacred text.

The intensity of the reading act being accomplished by students and teacher, in particular the timing and segmentation of the text, and their sustained attention to text and to each other, socialized ritualized behavior (Liénard and Boyer 2006). The socialization to total engagement of cognitive activity is reminiscent of notions of entering or achieving 'flow' during the course of ritual performance (Csikszentmihalyi 1975; Beeman 1993). Thus simultaneously, as students apprehended and comprehended text, they also learned the performance that satisfied the conditions of the ritual of the confession of sins.

## CONCLUSION

Students in *doctrina* participate in an educational setting where they learn to engage a range of cognitive and social skills as part of a ritualization process. These learning activities include reading, writing, interpreting text, memorizing and reciting facts, and comparing texts. They learn to link this knowledge (or 'comprehend') to everyday experiences and activities outside the classroom (understanding the bountifulness of God or the importance of eating well). The socialization to ritualized activity evidenced in the reading tasks examined here will no doubt be reinforced in other aspects of their religious experience, such as during confession or the weekly mass. That is, the early familiarity with texts, religious language, and other cultural artifacts, will give novices the necessary legitimacy and authority for later participation in collective and routine religious rituals (Keane 1997; Robbins 2001). Teachers in *doctrina* play an important role guiding, promoting, and interpreting religious knowledge and activities. Señora Paz, as many other teachers in classes I observed, was attentive to student actions, constantly supervising, and at times intervening, to ensure the appropriate ways of engaging religious activity.

I would like to return to an earlier point made on the importance of studying the routine as the locus of socialization. Given the examples of interaction analyzed here, I argue that ritual action is different from routine or routinized behavior. Language socialization research places a premium on the study of routine as a site where the structuring of learning tasks and skills occurs and where social roles are learned (Peters and Boggs 1986). Certainly, the activities that Señora Paz organized for her students, such as work in pairs or choral readings, were recurrent and in many ways structured, predictable, and routine. Yet it would be limiting to say that children were being socialized to and through routines or perhaps more problematic, that routine was ritual. I believe this stance can lose sight of the most important aspect that the exchanges I analyzed illustrated—a way to acquire competencies in and of ritual. As Boyarin (1992) and Silverstein and Urban (1996) discuss in their treatment of text, there is an inextricable relationship between text and context. Relevant to this discussion is Halliday's (1994) notion of texts existing not as utterances or sentences, but as embedded in utterances and sentences. The interactions of *doctrina* reading activity illustrate this view. While attending to text, students and teachers *construct* text; they create a unique version of how that text matters to them in the present moment and as a blueprint for future action.

In this [chapter] I have examined how a group of students and their teacher engaged reading of a text (created more than five hundred years ago) that is historicized, repeated, and rendered accessible through its varied intertextual features (Bakhtin 1981). I examined how participants attended to text and to each other and in the process produced a vernacular of the social order that made religious experience tangible and relevant. In *doctrina* classes, learning the AOC engages a pragmatics of reading that includes 'readings' of the immediate context of interaction, as well as of the sociohistorical embeddings of text. Indeed, the work students and teachers do as they work on religious text illustrate how they reach the divine and in so doing they create a version of ritual practice.

**Appendix: Transcription Conventions**

Transcription conventions follow those outlined by Gail Jefferson in Atkinson and Heritage (1984).

| | |
|---|---|
| >talk< | More than and less than degree marks indicate speech faster than normal cadence. |
| 'talk' | Utterances placed inside quotation marks indicate text being read aloud. |
| ? | Question mark indicates rising intonation, not necessarily a question. |
| . | A period indicates falling intonation. |
| , | A comma indicates slight rising intonation, as if listing items. |
| - | A dash at the end of a word indicates a cut-off or a stop in the flow of talk. |
| = | An equal sign at the end and beginning of a turn indicates latched speech or immediately contiguous utterance within or between turns. |
| (talk) | Material in parentheses indicates inaudible speech. |
| ((words)) | Material in double parentheses captures a description of gestures or of the quality of the talk being produced. |

## Notes

The research reported here received the generous support of the Wenner Gren Foundation for Anthropological Research, the Spencer Foundation, the University of California Berkeley Committee on Research, and the University of California All Campus Consortium on Research for Diversity (UC ACCORD). I am grateful to Laura Sterponi and Shlomy Kattan for their thoughtful reading of earlier drafts. I thank three anonymous reviewers of *Text & Talk* for their time and comments. Any errors and misrepresentations remaining are solely my own.

1. All names used in this [chapter] are pseudonyms.
2. I draw on a general understanding of pragmatics that refers to the way people use language to produce and interpret meaning and draw inferences from their context of interaction (Brown and Yule 1983; Levinson 1983).
3. I have certainly seen this aspect of resistance to the institution in *doctrina* practices. In an earlier publication I described an example of these 'tactics' (de Certeau 1984) during the failed merger of the Spanish and English tracks at the parish in Southern California. In that instance, the director of *doctrina* became the director of a new parish program (which in effect eliminated *doctrina* instruction) yet utilized her position and the temporary disinterest of the parish council to continue to offer instruction in Spanish (Baquedano-López 2004).
4. There are important debates on the division between secularity and religion that I cannot take up here. The reader is directed

to Asad (2003), Taylor (2007), and Mahmood (2005). A much earlier debate on religious and secular rituals is discussed in Rappaport (1971).

5. These perspectives have influenced recent language socialization research. The notion of 'becoming competent members of community' draws on aspects from these models (see Garrett and Baquedano-López 2002).

6. *Report 14: Catechesis, Religious Education, and the Parish*, by Susan Raftery and David C. Leege, in the University of Notre Dame series of studies published from 1981 to 1989 (www.nd.edu/~icl/study_reports/report14.pdf).

7. See also DuBois (1992), Keane (1997), Shoaps (2002), Poveda et al. (2005) for additional perspectives on participant frameworks across prayer and other forms of religious discourse.

8. Here J. Boyarin makes reference to D. Boyarin's explanations of the multivocality of rabbinic texts (D. Boyarin, 'Voices in the text', *Revue Biblique* 93, pp. 581–597, 1986).

9. Larger units or historically important units are archdioceses and they are supervised by an archbishop.

10. These authors have spurred much debate on ritualized behavior and go as far as to posit that it is an adaptive response toward self- and group preservation.

11. For McLaren, ritualization involved . . . 'the incarnation of symbols' through body gesture that is tied to a political economy of symbols that socially orders students inside schools. Rampton discusses the discursive features of the ritual language of foreign-language lessons and the improvised responses of students to those lessons, which ranged from pleasure to parody.

12. See the appendix for transcription conventions.

13. This is not to be confused with the earlier discussion of the 'I slot' of the participation framework. Gee's framework evolved from an analysis of interviews with working-class and middle-class teenagers and the development of socially situated identities about work and life (see Gee 1999).

14. See also Michael Silverstein's response to Robbins' (2001) review of ritual communication in *Current Anthropology*, vol. 43 (5), pp. 606–607. Here Silverstein reiterates rituals as indexical and 'actional texts-in-context'.

## References

Alverman, D., Phelps, S., and Ridgeway, V. 2007. *Content Area Reading and Literacy: Succeeding in Today's Diverse Classrooms*, 5th ed. Boston, MA: Allyn and Bacon.

Aminy, M. 2004. Constructing the moral identity: Literacy practices and language socialization in a Muslim community. Unpublished Ph.D. dissertation, University of California, Berkeley, California.

Asad, T. 2003. *Formations of the Secular: Christianity, Islam, Modernity*. Stanford, CA: Stanford University Press.

Atkinson, J. and Heritage, J. 1984. *Structures of Social Action: Studies in Conversation Analysis*. New York: Cambridge University Press.

Baker, J. 1992. The presence of the name: Reading scripture in an Indonesian village. In J. Boyarin (ed.), *The Ethnography of Reading*, 98–138. Berkeley: University of California Press.

Bakhtin, M. 1981. *The Dialogic Imagination: Four Essays*, M. Holquist (ed.). Austin: University of Texas Press.

Baquedano-López, P. 1997. Creating social identities through *doctrina* narratives. *Issues in Applied Linguistics* 8(1): 27–45.

Baquedano-López, P. 2000. Narrating community in *doctrina* classes. *Narrative Inquiry* 10(2): 429–452.

Baquedano-López, P. 2001. Prayer. In *Key Terms in Language and Culture*, A. Duranti (ed.), 193–196. Malden, MA: Blackwell.

Baquedano-López, P. 2004. Traversing the center: The politics of language use in a Catholic religious education program for immigrant Mexican children. *Anthropology and Education Quarterly* 35(2): 212–232.

Barton, D. and Hamilton, M. 1998. *Local Literacies: Reading and Writing in One Community*. New York: Routledge.

Beeman, W. O. 1993. The anthropology of theater and spectacle. *Annual Review of Anthropology* 22: 369–393.

Bloome, D. 1987. Reading as a social process in a middle school classroom. In *Literacy and Schooling*, D. Bloome (ed.), 123–149. Norwood, NJ: Ablex.

Bloome, D. 1990. Toward a more delicate elaboration of procedural display: A rejoinder to Atkinson and Delamon. *Curriculum Inquiry* 20(1): 71–73.

Bourdieu, P. 1990. *The Logic of Practice*. Stanford, CA: Stanford University Press.

Bowker, J. 1997. Roman Catholic Church. In *The Oxford Dictionary of World Religions*, J. Bowker (ed.), 821. New York: Oxford University Press.

Boyarin, J. 1992. Voices around the text: The ethnography of reading at Mesivta Tifereth Jerusalem. In *The Ethnography of Reading*, J. Boyarin (ed.), 212–237. Berkeley: University of California Press.

Boyer, P. and Liénard, P. 2006. Why ritualized behavior? Precaution systems and action parsing in developmental, pathological and cultural rituals. *Behavioral and Brain Sciences* 29: 1–56.

Brown, P. and Yule, G. 1983. *Discourse Analysis*. New York: Cambridge University Press.

Capps, L. and Ochs, E. 2002. Cultivating prayer. In *The Language of Turn and Sequence*, C. Ford, B. Fox, and S. Thompson (eds.), 39–55. Cambridge: Oxford University Press.

Csikszentmihalyi, M. 1975. *Beyond Boredom and Anxiety*. San Francisco: Jossey-Bass.

Cushman, E. 1998. *The Struggle and the Tools: Oral and Literate Strategies in an Inner City Community*. Albany, NY: SUNY Press.

de Certeau, M. 1984. *The Practice of Everyday Life*. Berkeley: University of California Press.

Dolan, J. and Figueroa Deck, A. (eds.) 1994. *Hispanic Catholic Culture in the U.S.: Issues and Concerns*. Notre Dame, IN: Notre Dame University.

DuBois, J. 1986. Self-evidence in ritual speech. In *Evidentiality: The Linguistic Coding of Epistemology*, W. Chafe and J. Nichols (eds.), 313–336. Norwood, NJ: Ablex.

DuBois, J. 1992. Meaning without intentions: Lessons from divination. In *Responsibility and Evidence in Oral Discourse*, J. Hill and J. Irvine (eds.), 45–90. Hillsdale, NJ: Lawrence Erlbaum.

Duranti, A., Ochs, E., and Ta'ase, E. 1995. Change and tradition in literacy instruction in a Samoan American Community. *Educational Foundations* 9: 57–74.

Fader, A. 2001. Literacy, bilingualism, and gender in a Hasidic community. *Linguistics and Education* 12: 261–283.

Fader, A. 2007. Reclaiming sacred sparks: Linguistic syncretism and gendered language shift among Hasidic Jews in New York. *Journal of Linguistic Anthropology* 17(1): 1–22.

Fader, A. 2008. Reading Jewish signs: The socialization of multilingual literacies among Hasidic women and girls in Brooklyn, New York. *Text & Talk* 28(5): 621–641.

Foucault, M. 1990 [1976]. *The History of Sexuality: An Introduction*. New York: Vintage/Random House.

Foucault, M. 1995 [1977]. *Discipline and Punish: The Birth of the Prison*. New York: Vintage/Random House.

Foucault, M. 1997. *Language, Counter-Memory, Practice: Selected Essays and Interviews*, D. Bouchard (ed.). Ithaca, NY: Cornell University Press.

Frye, D. 1996. *Indians into Mexicans: History and Identity in a Mexican Town*. Austin: Texas University Press.

Garrett, P. and Baquedano-López, P. 2002. Language socialization: Reproduction and continuity, transformation and change. *Annual Review of Anthropology* 31: 339–361.

Gee, J. P. 1999. *An Introduction to Discourse Analysis: Theory and Method*. London/New York: Routledge.

Goffman, E. 1974. *Frame Analysis: An Essay on the Organization of Experience*. Boston: Northeastern University Press.

Halliday, M. A. K. 1994. Language as social semiotic. In *Language and Literacy in Social Practice*, J. Maybin (ed.), 23–43. Clevedon: Multilingual Matters/The Open University.

Hanks, W. 1990. *Referential Practice: Language and Lived Space among the Maya*. Chicago: University of Chicago Press.

Hanks, W. 1996. *Language and Communicative Practices*. Boulder, CO: Westview.

Hanks, W. 2006. Joint commitment and common ground in a ritual event. In *Roots of Human Sociality: Culture, Cognition, and Interaction*, N. Enfield and S. Levinson (eds.), 299–328. Oxford/New York: Berg.

Haviland, J. 1996. Projections, transpositions, and relativity. In *Rethinking Linguistic Relativity*, J. Gumperz and S. Levinson (eds.), 271–323. Cambridge: Cambridge University Press.

Heath, S. 1983. *Ways with Words: Language, Life, and Work in Communities and Classrooms*. Cambridge: Cambridge University Press.

Holquist, M. 2002 [1990]. *Dialogism*. London/New York: Routledge.

Jacobs-Huey, L. 2006. *From the Kitchen to the Parlor: Language and Becoming in African American Women's Hair Care*. New York: Oxford University Press.

Keane, W. 1997. Religious language. *Annual Review of Anthropology* 26: 47–71.

Lave, J. and Wenger, E. 1991. *Situated Learning: Legitimate Peripheral Participation*. New York: Cambridge University Press.

Levinson, S. C. 1983. *Pragmatics*. Cambridge: Cambridge University Press.

Liénard, P. and Boyer, P. 2006. Whence collective rituals? A cultural selection model of ritualized behavior. *American Anthropologist* 108(4): 814–827.

Mahmood, S. 2005. *Politics of Piety: The Islamic Revival and the Feminist Subject*. Princeton, NJ: Princeton University Press.

Matovina, T. and Riebe-Estrella, G. (eds.) 2002. *Horizons of the Sacred: Mexican Traditions in U.S. Catholicism*. Ithaca, NY: Cornell University Press.

McLaren, P. 1999 [1986]. *Schooling as Ritual Performance: Toward a Political Economy of Educational Symbols and Gestures*. Lanham, MD: Rowman & Littlefield.

Moore, L. C. 2006a. Learning by heart in Koranic & public schools in northern Cameroon. *Social Analysis: The International Journal of Cultural & Social Practice* 50(3): 109–126.

Moore, L. C. 2006b. Changes in folktale socialization in a Fulbe community. In *West African Linguistics: Descriptive, Comparative, & Historical Studies in Honor of Russell G. Schuh*. (Supplement to *Studies in African Linguistics*.) P. Newman and L. Hyman (eds.), 176–187.

Moore, L. C. 2008. Body, text, and talk in Maroua Fulbe Qur'anic schooling. *Text & Talk* 28(5): 643–665.

Ochs, E. 1988. *Culture and Language Development: Language Acquisition and Language Socialization in a Samoan Village*. New York: Cambridge University Press.

Peters, A. and Boggs, S. 1986. International routines as cultural influences upon language socialization. In *Language Socialization across Cultures*, B. Schieffelin and E. Ochs (eds.), 80–96. New York: Cambridge University Press.

Poveda, D., Cano, A., and Palomares-Valera, M. 2005. Religious genres, entextualization, and literacy in Gitano children. *Language in Society* 34: 87–115.

Rampton, B. 2002. Ritual and foreign language practices at school. *Language in Society* 31: 491–525.

Rappaport, R. 1971. The sacred in human evolution. *Annual Review of Ecology and Systematics* 2: 23–44.

Rappaport, R. 1979. *Ecology, Meaning, and Religion*. Richmond, CA: North Atlantic Books.

Rappaport, R. 1999. *Ritual and Religion in the Making of Humanity*. Cambridge: Cambridge University Press.

Robbins, J. 2001. Ritual communication and linguistic ideology: A reading and partial reformulation of Rappaport's theory of ritual. *Current Anthropology* 42(5): 591–599.

Rogoff, B. 1990. *Apprenticeship in Thinking: Cognitive Development in Social Context.* New York: Cambridge University Press.

Rosaldo, R. 1999 [1989]. *Culture and Truth: The Remaking of Social Analysis.* Boston: Beacon Press.

Sarroub, L. K. 2002. In-betweenness: Religion and conflicting visions of literacy. *Reading Research Quarterly* 37(2): 130–148.

Sarroub, L. 2007. *All American Yemeni Girls: Being Muslim in an American School.* Philadelphia: University of Pennsylvania Press.

Schieffelin, B. 2002. Marking time. *Current Anthropology* 43: 5–17.

Schieffelin, B. and Ochs, E. (eds.) 1986. *Language Socialization across Cultures.* New York: Cambridge University Press.

Shoaps, R. 2002. 'Pray earnestly': The textual construction of personal involvement in Pentecostal prayer and song. *Journal of Linguistic Anthropology* 12(1): 34–71.

Silverstein, M. 2004. 'Cultural' concepts and the language-culture nexus. *Current Anthropology* 45(5): 621–645.

Silverstein, M. and Urban, G. 1996. The natural history of discourse. In *Natural Histories of Discourse*, M. Silverstein and G. Urban (eds.), 1–20. Chicago: University of Chicago Press.

Solis, J., Kattan, S., and Baquedano-López, P. (forthcoming). Locating time in science classroom activity: Adaptation as a theory of learning and change. In *Talking Science, Writing Science: The Work of Language in Multicultural Classrooms*, K. Richardson Bruna and K. Gomez (eds.). Mahwah, NJ: Erlbaum.

Sterponi, L. 2007. Clandestine interactional reading: Intertextuality and double-voicing under the desk. *Linguistics and Education* 18: 1–2.

Street, B. 2003. What's 'new' in New Literacy Studies? Critical approaches to literacy in theory and practice. *Current Issues in Comparative Education* 5(2): 77–91.

Tambiah, S. 1985. *Culture, Thought and Social Action.* Cambridge, MA: Harvard University Press.

Taylor, C. 2007. *A Secular Age.* Cambridge, MA: Harvard University Press.

*The Council of Trent: The Canons and Decrees of the Sacred and Ecumenical Council of Trent.* 1848. Waterworth, J. (ed. and trans.). London: Dolman. Scanned documents available online at URL: <http://history.hanover.edu/texts/trent.html>.

*The New American Bible.* 1993 [1987]. Wichita, KS: Catholic Bible Publishers.

Turner, V. 1995 [1969]. *The Ritual Process: Structure and Anti-structure.* New York: Aldine de Gruyter.

Wilce, J. 2001. Divining troubles or divining troubles? Gender, conflict, and polysemy in Bangladeshi divinations. *Anthropological Quarterly* 74(4): 190–199.


## Critical Thinking and Application

- How is the reading activity in this *doctrina* class similar to and different from reading in secular classes?
- Besides teaching the Act of Contrition (AOC), what other aspects of socialization are being conveyed by this class?
- Look carefully at the interaction between Señora Paz and Celia (Excerpt 3). Why do you think Señora Paz explains Celia's inability to recite the text as a consequence of not having had breakfast?
- Observe a classroom. Note the attention of the students, their interactions with the teacher, and their interactions with other students. Consider the role of texts, if relevant. Can you conclude anything about how children or older students are being socialized?

## Vocabulary

addressee
animated
apprehension (in reading)
author
beneficiary
chunking
cognitive
decoding
dialogic
dialogism
discursive
dyad
emergent
entextualization
epistemology
heritage language
home language
inference-making skills
intersubjective
laminated
liminal
literacy practices
metaphor
metapragmatic function
modality, communicative modality
pragmatics
principal
prosodic, prosodically
recursive
reify
reproduction
sacralize
signifiers
socio-semiotic
vernacular

## Suggested Further Reading [See also list following Language Socialization unit introduction]

Bloome, David, ed. 1987. *Literacy and Schooling*. Norwood, NJ: Ablex.

Bourdieu, Pierre, and Jean-Claude Passeron. 1977. *Reproduction in Education, Society, and Culture*, translated by Richard Nice. London and Beverly Hills, CA: Sage.

Goody, Jack, and Ian Watt. 1963. The Consequences of Literacy. *Comparative Studies in Society and History* 5(3): 304–345.

Lancy, David F., John Bock, and Suzanne Gaskins, eds. 2010. *The Anthropology of Learning in Childhood*. Lanham, MD: AltaMira (Rowman & Littlefield).

Lave, Jean, and Etienne Wenger. 1991. *Situated Learning: Legitimate Peripheral Participation*. New York: Cambridge University Press.

McLaren, Peter. 1999 [1986]. *Schooling as Ritual Performance: Toward a Political Economy of Educational Symbols and Gestures*. Lanham, MD: Rowman & Littlefield.

Rogoff, Barbara. 1990. *Apprenticeship in Thinking: Cognitive Development in Social Context*. New York: Cambridge University Press.

Street, Brian. 2003. What's "New" in New Literacy Studies? Critical Approaches to Literacy in Theory and Practice. *Current Issues in Comparative Education* 5(2): 77–91.

Wortham, Stanton, Enrique G. Murillo, and Edmund T. Hamann, eds. 2002. *Education in the New Latino Diaspora: Policy and the Politics of Identity.* Westport, CT: Ablex.

Wortham, Stanton, and Betsy Rymes, eds. 2003. *Linguistic Anthropology of Education*. Westport, CT: Praeger.

# UNIT 5

# (New) Media

Why the parentheses around *new*?

A *medium* is something that lies between two entities. In the study of communication, a medium may be something as widespread as language in general (lying between two or more speakers) or as specific as a cell phone. The plural of *medium* is *media*, though many people often speak of *the media* in the singular, especially when speaking of newspapers, radio, and television. This reflects the unease English speakers feel with words of Latin origin and their plurals, as well as a common impression that especially mainstream media operate as if with a single voice. In the twenty-first century, we often hear about *new media* such as the Internet. But I believe it is helpful to place this innovation within a broader context, with other media also having been introduced and with several effects. Thus, to genuinely understand what are regarded as *new* media, it is essential to grasp the functions of media in a broader sense.

In the study of media, scholars identify several revolutionary moments that have had transformative power in society:

Language itself
Writing
Printing
Telegraph
Telephone
Radio, Television, Cinema
Computers, the Internet
Mobile telephony

We could certainly delve into each of these media and the many devices connected with each one. Writing itself has provoked much curiosity, and you may be surprised to learn that no less a luminary than Socrates expected writing itself to lead to negative effects such as the decline of memory.

Each new medium tends to be celebrated by some (*cyberoptimists*, today) and deplored by others (*cyberpessimists* today, Luddites in the past).

There are also different scholarly theories about the ways media operate. Some people, known as *technological determinists*, tend to see the media as having necessary and inherent—and often negative—consequences. Some of the predictions might now strike us as overly alarmist: writing leads to lack of reliance on memory; printing leads to democratization as individuals no longer rely on others' interpretations (as in the Protestant Reformation); the telephone will lead to the erosion of family life as others can freely interrupt; television will lead to mind-numbing passivity; the Internet makes our attention spans short and reduces reading; mobile telephony means we are constantly connected to people remote from us and not attending to what is in front of us. There is no shortage of contemporary lamentations and celebrations: the Internet caused the Arab Spring revolutions in 2011. We will be liberated; we will be enslaved.

Others see technology as shaped by its users. People like Clay Shirky write of the many ways the Internet can be harnessed by ordinary people to do extraordinary things.

Still others see multiple versions of technologies, with cultural differences in how they are used, just as *literacy* is not a single, uniform, universal capacity but better conceptualized as multiple literacies, different in different contexts (as Shirley Brice Heath demonstrated so persuasively in Chapter 10), or different versions of mobile phones, computer use, and ideas of freedom and constraint. It is time for students to develop critical and analytical skills regarding this sea that is increasingly the nature of our surroundings. If we fail to understand, we may tread water, but we probably won't swim.

## Suggested Further Reading


Adorno, Theodor, and Max Horkheimer. 1944. The Culture Industry: Enlightenment as Mass Deception. From their book *The Dialectic of Enlightenment*. http://www.marxists.org/reference/archive/adorno/1944/culture-industry.htm

Agre, Philip E. 2003 [1994]. Surveillance and Capture: Two Models of Privacy. In *The New Media Reader*, edited by Noah Wardrip-Fruin and Nick Montfort, pp. 737–760. Cambridge, MA, and London: Routledge.

Baron, Dennis. 2009. *A Better Pencil: Readers, Writers, and the Digital Revolution*. Oxford and New York: Oxford University Press.

Baron, Naomi S. 2008. *Always On: Language in an Online and Mobile World*. Oxford and New York: Oxford University Press.

Bauerlein, Mark. 2008. *The Dumbest Generation: How the Digital Age Stupefies Young Americans and Jeopardizes Our Future [Or, Don't Trust Anyone Under 30].* New York: Tarcher/Penguin.

Benjamin, Walter. 1968 [1955]. The Work of Art in the Age of Mechanical Reproduction. In *Illuminations*, edited by Hannah Arendt, translated by Harry Zohn, pp. 217–251. New York: Schocken Books.

Berger, Arthur Asa. 2005. *Making Sense of Media: Key Texts in Media and Cultural Studies.* Malden, MA: Blackwell.

Berger, Arthur Asa. 2007. *Media and Society: A Critical Perspective.* 2nd ed. Lanham, MD: Rowman & Littlefield.

Berkman Center for Internet and Society's OpenNet Initiative. http://cyber.law.harvard.edu/; http://opennet.net/; http://opennet.net/research/profiles

Berry, Wendell. 1987. Why I Am Not Going to Buy a Computer. *New England Review and Bread Loaf Quarterly* 10(1) (Autumn): 112–113.

Bolter, J. David. 2003 [1991]. Seeing and Writing. In *The New Media Reader*, edited by Noah Wardrip-Fruin and Nick Montfort, pp. 679–690. Cambridge, MA, and London: Routledge.

Bolter, Jay David, and Richard Grusin. 2000. *Remediation: Understanding New Media.* Cambridge, MA, and London: MIT Press.

Briggs, Asa, and Peter Burke. 2009. *A Social History of the Media: From Gutenberg to the Internet.* 3rd ed. Cambridge and Malden, MA: Polity.

Carr, Nicholas. 2008. *The Big Switch: Rewiring the World, From Edison to Google.* New York and London: Norton.

Carr, Nicholas. 2008. Is Google Making Us Stupid? *The Atlantic Monthly* (July/August). http://www.theatlantic.com/doc/200807/google

Clark, Andy. 2009. Technologies to Bond With. In *Rethinking Theories and Practices of Imaging*, edited by Timothy H. Engström and Evan Selinger, pp. 164–183. Basingstoke: Palgrave Macmillan.

Coover, Robert. 2003 [1992]. The End of Books. In *The New Media Reader*, edited by Noah Wardrip-Fruin and Nick Montfort, pp. 705–709. Cambridge, MA, and London: Routledge.

Croteau, David, and William Hoynes. 2003. *Media Society: Industries, Images, and Audiences.* 3rd ed. Thousand Oaks, CA: Pine Forge Press.

Crowley, David, and Paul Heyer, eds. 2007. *Communication in History: Technology, Culture, Society.* 5th ed. Boston: Pearson.

Crystal, David. 2008 *Txtng: The Gr8 Db8.* New York: Oxford University Press.

Dalsgaard, Steffen. 2008. Facework on Facebook: The Presentation of Self in Virtual Life and Its Role in the US Elections. *Anthropology Today* 24(6): 8–12.

Deresiewicz, William. 2009. Faux Friendship. *The Chronicle of Higher Education* (December 6). http://chronicle.com/article/Faux-Friendship/49308/#top

Erickson, Tamara. 2008. *Plugged In: The Generation Y Guide to Thriving at Work.* Boston: Harvard Business Press.

Fallows, James. 2008. The Connection Has Been Reset. *The Atlantic Monthly* (March). http://www.theatlantic.com/doc/200803/chinese-firewall

Fischer, Claude S. 1992. *America Calling: A Social History of the Telephone to 1940.* Berkeley and Los Angeles: University of California Press.

Fuller-Seeley, Kathryn H. 2007. Learning to Live with Television: Technology, Gender, and America's Early TV Audiences. In *The Columbia History of American Television*, edited by Gary R. Edgerton, pp. 91–110. New York: Columbia University Press.

Grant, August E., and Jennifer H. Meadows, eds. 2008. *Communication Technology Update and Fundamentals.* 11th ed. Amsterdam and Boston: Elsevier.

Horst, Heather A., and Daniel Miller. 2006. *The Cell Phone: An Anthropology of Communication.* Oxford and New York: Berg.

Ito, Mizuko, Heather Horst, Matteo Bittanti, danah boyd, Becky Herr-Stephenson, Patricia G. Lange, C. J. Pascoe, and Laura Robinson. 2008. *Living and Learning with New Media: Summary of Findings from the Digital Youth Project.* Cambridge, MA: MIT Press.

Ito, Mizuko, Daisuke Okabe, and Misa Matsuda. 2005. *Personal, Portable, Pedestrian: Mobile Phones in Japanese Life.* Cambridge, MA: MIT Press.

Ito, Mizuko, et al. 2010. *Hanging Out, Messing Around, and Geeking Out: Kids Living and Learning with New Media.* Cambridge, MA: MIT Press.

Jackson, Maggie. 2009. *Distracted: The Erosion of Attention and the Coming Dark Age.* New York: Prometheus Books.

Jenkins, Henry. 2006. *Convergence Culture: Where Old and New Media Collide.* New York and London: New York University Press.

Katz, James E. 2006. *Magic in the Air: Mobile Communication and the Transformation of Social Life.* New Brunswick, NJ: Transaction.

Katz, James E., and Mark Aakhus, eds. 2002. *Perpetual Contact: Mobile Communication, Private Talk, Public Performance.* Cambridge: Cambridge University Press.

Lessig, Lawrence. *Free Culture.* http://www.free-culture.cc/

Lethem, Jonathan. 2007. The Ecstasy of Influence: A Plagiarism. *Harper's Magazine* (February). http://harpers.org/archive/2007/02/0081387

Lethem, Jonathan. *Promiscuous Materials Project.* http://www.jonathanlethem.com/promiscuous.html

Levinson, Paul. 2009. *New New Media.* Boston: Allyn & Bacon.

Ling, Rich. 2008. *New Tech, New Ties: How Mobile Communication Is Reshaping Social Cohesion.* Cambridge, MA: MIT Press.

Lister, Martin, Jon Dovey, Seth Giddings, Iain Grant, and Kieran Kelly. 2009. *New Media: A Critical Introduction.* 2nd ed. London and New York: Routledge.

Manovich, Lev. 2001. *The Language of New Media*. Cambridge, MA: MIT Press.

McLagan, Meg. 2002. Spectacles of Difference: Cultural Activism and the Mass Mediation of Tibet. In *Media Worlds: Anthropology on New Terrain*, edited by Faye D. Ginsburg, Lila Abu-Lughod, and Brian Larkin, pp. 90–111. Berkeley and Los Angeles: University of California Press.

McLuhan, Marshall. 1964. *Understanding Media: The Extensions of Man*. New York: McGraw-Hill.

McLuhan, Marshall. 2003. *Understanding Media: The Extensions of Man*. Critical edition, edited by W. Terrence Gordon. Corte Madera, CA: Gingko Press.

McLuhan, Marshall, and Quentin Fiore. 1967. *The Medium Is the Message: An Inventory of Effects*, produced by Jerome Agel. Berkeley, CA: Gingko Press.

Miller, Daniel, and Don Slater. 2000. *The Internet: An Ethnographic Approach*. Oxford and New York: Berg.

Montgomery, Kathryn C. 2007. *Generation Digital: Politics, Commerce, and Childhood in the Age of the Internet*. Cambridge, MA, and London: MIT Press.

Palfrey, John, and Urs Gasser. 2008. *Born Digital: Understanding the First Generation of Digital Natives*. New York: Basic Books.

Postman, Neil. 2006 [1986]. *Amusing Ourselves to Death: Public Discourse in the Age of Show Business*. 20th anniversary edition. New York: Penguin.

Rafael, Vicente L. 2006. The Cell Phone and the Crowd: Messianic Politics in the Contemporary Philippines. In *New Media, Old Media: A History and Theory Reader*, edited by Wendy Hui Kyong Chun and Thomas Keenan, pp. 297–313. New York and London: Routledge

Shirky, Clay. 2008. *Here Comes Everybody: The Power of Organizing Without Organizations*. New York: Penguin.

Spitulnik, Debra. 2002. Mobile Machines and Fluid Audiences: Rethinking Reception Through Zambian Radio Culture. In *Media Worlds: Anthropology on New Terrain*, edited by Faye D. Ginsburg, Lila Abu-Lughod, and Brian Larkin, pp. 337–354. Berkeley and Los Angeles: University of California Press.

Tait, Robert, and Matthew Weaver. 2009. How Neda Soltani Became the Face of Iran's Struggle. *The Guardian* (June 22). http://www.guardian.co.uk/world/2009/jun/22/neda-soltani-death-iran

Tapscott, Don. 2009. *Grown Up Digital: How the Net Generation Is Changing Your World*. New York: McGraw-Hill.

Theall, Donald F. 2001. Introduction: Why/What Is Marshall McLuhan? In *The Virtual Marshall McLuhan*, pp. 21–37. Montreal and Kingston: McGill-Queen's University Press.

Turkle, Sherry. 2011. *Alone Together: Why We Expect More from Technology and Less from Each Other*. New York: Basic Books.

van Dijk, Jan. 2006. *The Network Society: Social Aspects of New Media*. 2nd ed. London and Thousand Oaks, CA: Sage.

Watkins, S. Craig. 2009. *The Young and the Digital: What the Migration to Social-Network Sites, Games, and Anytime, Anywhere Media Means for Our Future*. Boston: Beacon Press.

Williams, Raymond. 2003 [1972]. The Technology and the Society. In *The New Media Reader*, edited by Noah Wardrip-Fruin and Nick Montfort, pp. 289–300. Cambridge, MA, and London: Routledge.

Wu, Tim. 2010. *The Master Switch: The Rise and Fall of Information Empires*. New York: Knopf.

# CHAPTER 12

# What Is Writing?

## *John DeFrancis*

(1989)

*Those of us who have always been surrounded by writing may never have wondered how it was invented. But try. Imagine being surrounded by a stream of sound and having to figure out a way to record it. What would you attend to? What would be important to freeze? What would be included, and what would be excluded? What medium would you use? How would others retrieve the original utterance?*

*John DeFrancis, a formidable linguist and scholar of Chinese, provides a general discussion of the context within which writing occurs, placing it alongside multiple modalities of human communication. He challenges many erroneous assumptions about some writing systems, which may be regarded as "pictorial" despite the fact that all full writing systems necessarily convey the* sounds *of the language. The surface differences of writing systems are evident and striking, but they all share fundamental principles.*

### Reading Questions

- What are some of the modalities of communication that DeFrancis mentions? Which does he regard as the grounding of all full systems of communication? Why?
- What is the difference between "full" and "partial" writing systems? Give examples of each. What are the two means by which writing systems convey meaning? What is the *Duality Principle*?
- How do languages manage if there is an imperfect correspondence between sound and symbol?

## Definitions and Dichotomies

One useful way to look at writing is to view it within the total framework of human communication. In this context speech must be placed first among the various **modalities,** followed by writing and, much farther behind, other means which, taken together, use all of our five senses. Some of the last are of only marginal utility, as in the case of smell. . . .

In approaching writing and related modalities it should be carefully noted that there are two main schools of thought whose adherents might be labeled **inclusivists** and **exclusivists** on the basis of their support for one or the other of two definitions of writing:

> Inclusivists: Writing includes *any* system of graphic symbols that is used to convey *some amount of thought.*

> Exclusivists: Writing includes *only* those systems of graphic symbols that can be used to convey *any and all thought.*

The inclusivist definition of writing includes such limited systems as mathematical notation and chemical formulas. It also includes petroglyphs, Amerindian pictographs, and international symbols such as those for "No Parking" and "No Smoking." The exclusivist definition of writing excludes these symbols on the grounds that while they permit partial expression of thought, they are far too limited and cannot be expanded into complete systems that would enable us to write a poem or a philosophical treatise or a manual on how to operate a word processor. Exclusivists point out that not all the sounds we produce are music, and not all the motions we make are dance. So why then must all the marks we make be considered writing? Just as all that glitters is not gold, so all that's written is not writing.

It appears that we can distinguish between ***partial writing*** and ***full writing*** by how much of human thought they can represent. These terms can be defined in this way:

John DeFrancis, What Is Writing? From *Visible Speech: The Diverse Oneness of Writing Systems*. Honolulu: University of Hawaii Press, 1989, pp. 3–9, 49–56.

> Partial writing is a system of graphic symbols that can be used to convey only some thought.
> Full writing is a system of graphic symbols that can be used to convey any and all thought.

Inclusivists believe that both partial and full writing should be called writing. Exclusivists believe that only full writing deserves this label. The failure to agree, or even to note that there is a fundamental difference of opinion, is one of the main sources of confusion in discussions of writing.

In a way it doesn't much matter which definition we adopt, *so long as we do not confuse the two*. This means in particular that we should not unthinkingly assume that there is a relationship between partial writing and full writing, or that the former represents an early stage of the latter. In some cases elements of partial writing are part of a broader full system of writing. Thus an ordinary text in English can contain numerical and other special symbols (e.g., "The book costs $19.95"). In other cases partial writing represents a dead-end system that stands completely apart and has nothing to do with full writing. Only superficially do the two have any resemblances. At a more basic level they are essentially unrelated, since they are based on fundamentally different and opposing principles. This is the case with Amerindian pictographs . . ., as opposed to Chinese characters and other full systems of writing. Confusion and error often arise from overlooking these facts.

The attempt of the exclusivists to restrict the definition of writing to full writing parallels the attempt of scientific linguists to restrict the definition of language to speech. Neither appears to have much chance of success. People insist on calling all sorts of things writing, and even many linguists refer to "spoken language" and "written language." Bowing to these realities, I shall extend the use of *language* to include "written language," "sign language," and even "touch language," and shall apply the dichotomy of partial and full to all.

The same dichotomy applies to all forms of human communication. Figure 12.1 provides a graphic overview of all communication from this perspective. It shows the two main branches, partial and full, of the communication tree. Full communication starts with spoken language. This leads into three other modes of full communication. Partial communication possibly involves all our senses, but the branches depicted are limited to those of real importance. Even so, our communication tree is limited since there are many more forms of communication than those dealt with here. A more comprehensive and detailed classification would also have to take care of such exotic forms as drum and whistle surrogates for speech (Umiker 1974).

The various modes of communication are not mutually exclusive. Scholars sometimes read papers containing diagrams and charts to academic audiences who follow the oral presentation from written handouts and slides. One can point and shout at the same time. And it is possible for full communication to make use of the partial modes, especially those of the same modality. Thus materials written in standard **orthography** frequently contain charts, mathematical notation, and other graphic symbols. Despite these mixtures

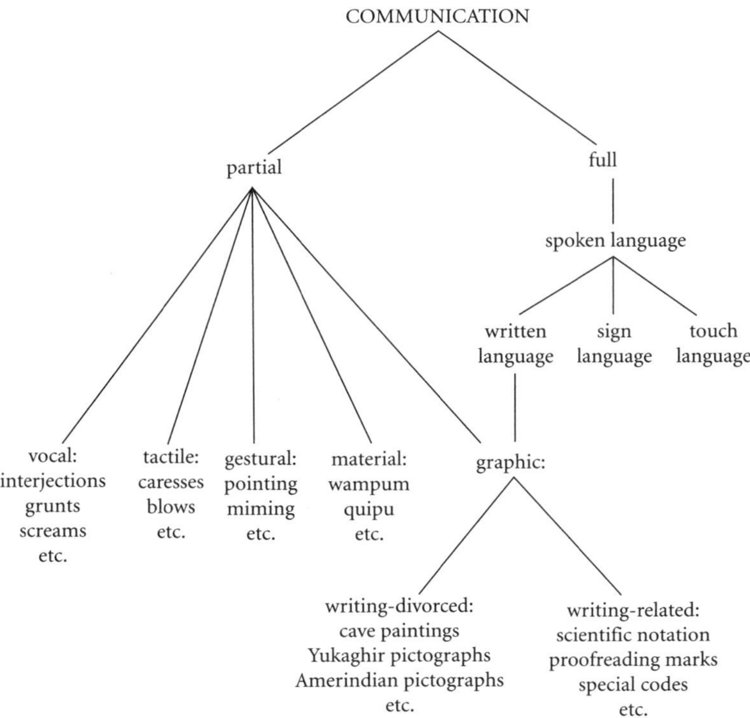


**Figure 12.1** *Communication Classification Scheme*

and overlaps, the various mediums retain their distinctive identities.

Figure 12.1 supports my central thesis that all full systems of communication are based on speech. Further, no full system is possible unless so grounded. . . .

## Spoken Language

As human beings we are unique in the way we think and express our thoughts in speech. Our ability to think is superior to and qualitatively different from the instinctual behavior of animals in general. The same is true of spoken language as compared to human and nonhuman vocalizations that fall far short of full speech. Dogs answer when their masters whistle and growl menacingly if strangers intrude. We instinctively express pain with groans, grief with sobs, joy with other sounds. But only full spoken language enables us as human beings to express any and all thought.

Full spoken language is the defining characteristic of the human species. Other species can be defined by other, more limited, communicative abilities—bats by their ability to produce and detect sonar, bees to perform dances that communicate elaborate messages, and so on through the gamut of our coinhabitants on planet earth. In all of these cases the medium is unalterably part of the genetic make-up of the species. The same is true of language in human beings.[1]

It can hardly be accidental that speech was the most fully developed means of communication of *Homo sapiens.* It was, to be sure, not the sole means of communication, nor was it the first to emerge. The prevailing view among students of the subject is that in the first few million years of their existence our ancestors communicated chiefly by gestures. These were supplemented by such vocalizations as grunts and screams, gross acoustic signals that were all that could be produced—given the still undeveloped state of the vocal tract, the higher neural programs which control the anatomy, and the social organization that would require a more advanced means of exchanging information. The spiral of evolutionary progress in all these related and mutually reinforcing areas eventually led, some 50,000 years ago, to the emergence of speech as the dominant medium among the multimodal channels of communication (Hockett 1978; Wang 1979).

The switch in channels that resulted in the ascendancy of speech, and the significance of all this in human evolution, are vividly summarized in the following statement that concludes a review of literature dealing with the origins of language:

> Consider, now, that hand-carrying, hunting, and tools and technology... gave the hands many things to do. As time passed there was more and more to communicate about, and an ever larger number of occasions when the hands were much too busy to be used even for vitally important semaphor. As a ridiculously trivial example, imagine two or three folks gathered around a heavy object to lift it; when all are ready, how can the leader's hand signal *"Now!"*? So, more and more it was necessary for our ancestors to eke out their lives with grunts, and more and more it was crucial for the grunts to be specific and unambiguous.
>
> That could easily have led nowhere (and for many homonid groups doubtless did), for in organic evolution there is never any advance guarantee that selection will successfully adapt a species to the environmental and social demands it faces. In fact, however, it led to the birth of true language, because here we are [Hockett 1978:300–301].

Yes, here we are, at the top of the heap, thanks in large measure to the fact that full speech enabled our ancestors to out-communicate rivals who had only gestures and rudimentary grunts at their command. Speech was a major factor leading to the ascendancy of the human animal in the process of natural selection, and today speech, supplemented by other modalities, continues to be the primary means of communication. All human communication is based on one of the several thousands of spoken languages now in existence.

All these languages possess two essential design features that distinguish speech from other vocalizations. The specific details of these design features differ from language to language.

One design feature is an inventory of basic distinctive sounds that linguists refer to as ***phonemes.*** For example, four such basic sounds are contained in the English word conventionally spelled "Fred." The unconventional spelling "Phred" of the *Doonesbury* comic strip illustrates the point that the same basic sound can be represented by different individual symbols or combinations of symbols. Phonemes, and the symbols used to represent them, are the basic building blocks used to form words, sentences, and extended discourse.

Languages vary widely in the number of these basic sounds, from around 20 for Hawaiian and Japanese, to about 40 for English, and over 60 for several languages spoken in the Caucasus. One of the largest numbers of phonemes is found in the language spoken by a branch of the Southeast Asian people variously known as Hmong or Miao or Meo. The White Meo language has no fewer than 80 phonemes—57 consonants, 15 vowels, and 8 tones (Heimbach 1966, 1:8–17).

The second essential design feature of spoken language is the stringing together of the phonemes, and the words and other extensions, in various sequences that are peculiar to each individual language. Thus English and Korean permit the sequence *pap*, with a *p* in both initial and final position in a word, whereas Mandarin Chinese and Japanese limit the use of *p* to initial position, as in *pa*. The principal word order of English is subject-verb-object (SVO), whereas in Japanese it is subject-object-verb (SOV), and in Pharaonic Egyptian it was verb-subject-object (VSO). Within individual languages, variations in sequencing of linguistic items are related to variations in meaning. In English, *pat* has one meaning, *tap* another, and *apt* still another. The same is true of *John loves Mary* and *Mary loves John*.

Speaking a particular language involves emitting from the mouth a series of sounds whose sequence follows the rules peculiar to the individual language. When our ears hear speech they receive the sounds in the same order in which they came from the speaker's mouth. The ability to process speech by ear and by mouth is normally acquired in early childhood and is an accomplishment that surely ranks among the marvels of human achievement. . . .

If all full systems of writing are based on speech, and none is possible unless so grounded, then we must examine how writing represents speech. And because writing cannot represent speech with complete fidelity, we also need to examine how and to what extent it departs from the straight and narrow path of phonetic representation. The details, since they vary from system to system, are taken up [elsewhere]. Here I pave the way with some general comments.

By and large one can say that all writing systems convey meaning by two means. The first is by the use of symbols which represent sounds and function as surrogates of speech. The second is by the use of symbols that add nonphonetic information. These two together are combined in different proportions in different scripts. Together they comprise what I call the "Duality Principle" that forms the basis for all true systems of writing.

The pervasive tendency to exaggerate the nonphonetic aspect of writing leads to several related errors that can culminate in a belief in the existence of full systems of writing based on pictographs. One error is to think that pictographic symbols necessarily have a pictographic function, that is that pictographic symbols are always used to convey whatever ideas the pictographs as pictographs may evoke. This error can be described in other words as the failure to distinguish between form and function. Because of this failure many people are blind to the significance of the epoch-making invention that marked the birth of true writing. That invention was the ***rebus principle,*** whereby a pictographic symbol was used not for its original meaning value but specifically to represent the sound evoked by the name of the symbol. The change in function that results from using a picture as a rebus can be illustrated by the use of a picture for a bee followed by that for a leaf to express the sounds of the word *belief*.

The two pictures involved in this simple illustration are just as much phonetic symbols, syllabic ones in this case, as are the letters in our conventional way of writing the word. One who continues to refer to them simply as pictographs misses the central point about the nature of writing and overlooks one of the greatest inventions in human history.

Pictographs used as pictographs lead nowhere. Pictographs used as phonetic symbols lead to full writing. All inventions of full writing originated from pictographs. Not all pictographs lead to writing. The history of writing is as full of dead ends as is the history of human evolution.

The rebus principle formed the basis of three systems of writing, generally thought to have been independently developed, which were created at intervals of about fifteen hundred years: first by the Sumerians about 3000 B.C., then by the Chinese about 1500 B.C., and last by the Mayas about the beginning of our era. The systems developed by these peoples were based on exactly the same basic principle despite the differences in how their symbols look.

The particular form that phonetic symbols take, whether they look like pictures or have no resemblance to anything, is a matter of quite secondary importance. Certainly, other considerations, such as aesthetics and efficiency, are also involved. But efficiency is mostly a modern concept, and it was certainly not a major concern of the specialized scribes and elitist groups that have been primarily concerned with writing. Much more basic than these matters is the ability of all phonetic symbols of whatever shape to function as the basis of full systems of writing.

In the matter of phonetic representation, *all* systems are incomplete, since they all fail to take account of some things that are present in speech. There are significant features such as intonation, stress, and tempo which are virtually never represented in standard orthographies and are dealt with, if at all, only in specialized studies by scholars. With regard to the phonetic representation that does occur, there is a very wide range of completeness and efficiency.

In general we can say that what might be called the "phoneticity" of a system of writing, that is, the detailed fit of symbols to sounds, falls within a range that theoretically extends from 1 to 99 percent. One hundred percent efficiency in representing speech can be achieved only by nongraphic means, such as tape recorders and other acoustic recording devices. Zero percent representation likewise means we are dealing with something other than writing, or, if you will, full writing, since it encompasses such pseudowriting as that of the Yukaghir and the North American Indians.

As far as real writing is concerned, the efficiency rating starts at near the top for scientific systems created by highly skilled phoneticians, such as the system called "Visible Speech" that was developed by Alexander Melville Bell. Among actually existing orthographies, Finnish ranks very high because of its close correspondence between sounds and symbols. It decreases somewhat for systems such as German, Spanish, and Russian. It drops further for French, still further for English, and even further for Chinese. An eminent Chinese linguist has suggested that English is 75 percent phonetic, Chinese only 25 percent (Chao 1976: 92). Many people mistakenly think that the figure is actually zero for Chinese. This ranking, impressionistic though it doubtless is, nevertheless comprises a suggestive ranking of writing systems on the basis of their phoneticity.

Amplifying on the "Duality Principle" enunciated earlier, we can say that the poorer a writing system is in phonetic representation, the more it compensates, either by design or by historical accident, by greater use of nonphonetic devices. Some of these essentially mnemonic devices have been noted: visual puns and numerical expressions. Other devices include capitalization, grammatical hints such as punctuation, and semantic clues such as those of Chinese notoriety. Still others are the outright pictographic symbols used in Egyptian writing.

Students of writing are at odds in trying to explain these non-phonetic phenomena. At the heart of their disagreement is the question of how to relate levels of writing to levels of speech.

With respect to levels of speech, there is general agreement that utterances consist of a hierarchy of phonological units. The smallest of these is the phoneme. Various numbers of phonemes (1–2 in Hawaiian, 1–4 in Chinese, 1–7 in English) make up syllables. Various numbers of syllables make up words, phrases, sentences, and so on.

The symbols used in writing can be considered in relation to the levels of speech just mentioned. If a system of writing represents phonemes, it is said to be a phonemic system, and its symbols are collectively referred to as an alphabet. Finnish, German, Russian, English, Korean, and many other languages have phonemic or alphabetic scripts. If a system of writing represents syllables, it is said to be a syllabic system, and its symbols, which can individually be called syllabograms, are collectively referred to as a syllabary. The simple Japanese script called kana is the best-known representative of syllabic systems; it comprises a syllabary of fewer than fifty symbols. . . .

[Many scholars] have seriously undervalued the phonetic element in Chinese writing. As noted earlier, estimates of the phoneticity of the Chinese script range from a high of 25 percent to a low of zero. The 25 percent figure is, to my mind, much too low, and the zero estimate is based on ignorance.

. . . I present below, as an appetizer, a character which is used independently to represent the word *mǎ* 'horse' but is also used as a component in a compound character, where it is used solely for its sound. Joined with this *mǎ* character is another character that functions as a semantic "determinative" meaning 'female' and gives a clue to the meaning of the whole complex character.

馬 *mǎ* 'horse'
媽 *mā* 'mother'

The meaning of the complex character is not determined by the sum of the meanings of the two elements of which it is composed. That is to say, it does not mean 'female horse,' though it would be possible to invent, as is often done, a ***false etymology*** for *mā* 'mother' based on the idea of a female who works like a horse. However appealing such an etymology might be, especially to hard-working mothers, the reality is that the *mǎ* 'horse' component in *mā* 'mother' is merely a phonetic symbol, just as we might use the picture of a horse to represent the word *hoarse*. We distinguish homophonous *horse* and *hoarse* by differences in spelling. Chinese distinguishes more or less homophonous *mǎ* 'horse' and *mā* 'mother' by the device of semantic determinatives.[2]

The problem of how extensive, and how significant, these phonetic elements are in Chinese is crucially important, but here we need only note that the precise figure of phoneticity of Chinese characters is really beside the point, because even if the figure of 25 percent were to turn out to be only an educated guess needing drastic reduction, it would still be necessary to classify Chinese as a phonetic system of writing of the syllabic type. For what determines the level of a writing system is the indispensable operational unit that enables the script to function. In Chinese that unit is a graphic symbol that represents a syllable.

The concept "operational unit that enables a script to function" is essential to counter the imprecise phraseology used by most students of writing, who say that such-and-such element in writing "represents" this or that element in speech. Thus it is often said of the Korean writing system, which has letter-symbols and combines these into groups corresponding to syllables and words, that it "represents" phonemes, syllables, and words (Taylor 1980). This is true, but it is only true in the same sense that English orthography "represents" both phonemes and words.

The confusion and ambiguity inherent in the multiple use of the word "represents" can be avoided if we establish a dichotomy between two units: (1) The meaningless graphic unit that corresponds to the smallest segment of speech represented in the writing. This is the basic operational unit without which a script simply could not function. I call this unit a ***grapheme.*** (2) The basic unit of writing that is surrounded by white space on the printed page. I call this unit a ***frame,*** following the terminology suggested by William S.-Y. Wang (1981:226–228).

English graphemes are letters that either singly or in combination represent phonemes (e.g., *s, sh*). They may themselves constitute frames (e.g., *I* and *a* in *"I have a dream."*) or combine to form frames representing words. It has become the convention, especially since the advent of printing, to separate words by white space, a practice which, while not carried out with scientific accuracy or consistency, contrasts with theearlierpracticeofrunningallthewordstogether.

Chinese graphemes are characters that singly represent whole syllables. They may themselves constitute frames (e.g., the character for *mǎ* 'horse'), or combine with other nonphonetic elements to form more complex characters representing frames (e.g., the character for *mā* 'mother').

It is important to note that in English, apart from a few one-letter frames such as the pronoun *I* and the article *a*, frames always consist of more than one grapheme—as many as twenty-three in a long word like *disestablishmentarianism*. In addition to differing in number of phonetic components, the graphemes and frames also differ in the amount of space that they occupy. These self-evident disparities bring out in strong relief and constantly reinforce the difference between the two units in English.

In contrast, Chinese frames invariably contain only one grapheme and are so written as to occupy exactly the same amount of space as an independent grapheme (e.g., the characters for 'horse' and 'mother' cited above). These obvious but secondary similarities between the two units contribute to the general failure to make a clear distinction between grapheme and frame in Chinese, which in turn leads to the common mistake of concentrating attention on the frame as the more conspicuous and ubiquitous unit.

In all writing systems the grapheme is by far the most important of the two units. What happens beyond the grapheme is of quite secondary importance, as demonstrated by the fact that English would be able to function, though with different degrees of efficiency, whether it separated words or ran them together. The same is true of Chinese and of all other writing systems.

The ability of writing systems to function without the use of frames is well illustrated by the case of Japanese. In most Japanese publications, apart from division of text by means of punctuation marks, all the graphic symbols are strung together like a continuous string of beads without any regard to dividing them into groups on the basis of semantic considerations. Delimitation of frames is largely restricted to primers and dictionaries, where the graphic elements are grouped together, surrounded by white space, to form lexical items.

Indeed, it is probably true for all writing systems that frames are most clearly evidenced in the entries found in their dictionaries. This being so, perhaps frames might better be defined as the items occurring in lexical lists such as dictionaries, and hence might better be renamed ***lexemes***—words in English (e.g., *horse, hoarse,* and *disestablishmentarianism*), and characters in Chinese (e.g., the characters for *horse* and *mother*). Dictionaries are late additions to writing systems, however, so that their lexemes play a secondary role to the more basic graphemes.[3]

English functions fairly well with its imperfect system of graphemes of the phonemic or alphabetic type. It could function also with a system of graphemes of the syllabic type, but with much greater difficulty, because its inventory of spoken syllables, over 8,000 in number, is too large to be represented simply in this way. Chinese functions, though not easily, with graphemes of the syllabic type. Its inventory of spoken syllables—only 1,277 counting tones and 398 not counting them—is small enough to be represented in this way and still allow for the cumbersome addition of semantic elements to compensate for the imperfections of the phonetic base. It could, of course, be written very simply with an alphabetic system, such as **Pinyin,** the auxiliary romanization scheme adopted in 1958.

Neither English nor Chinese writing, nor the writing of any other language, can function with graphemes based on any of the semantic levels—discourse, words, or even morphemes. For the number of the equivalent spoken items at the command of the average speaker of any language is so enormous that the human mind has shown no evidence of being able to represent them with graphemes of this sort, despite its ability to manipulate them by mouth and by ear.

In the light of all this it should be clear that the key question to ask about writing systems is not the ambiguous one of what they "represent" but the more precise query as to what are the basic units—the graphemes—that make the systems work. In Finnish and English, it is alphabetic symbols that represent the phonemes of these languages. In Japanese and Chinese, it is graphic symbols that represent their respective syllables. Finnish does its job with almost one-to-one correspondence between sound and symbol. English writing has poor sound–symbol correspondence but makes up for this in various ways. The Japanese kana system does its job in a fairly simple and efficient manner by its good correspondence between syllabic sounds and syllabic symbols. Chinese has even poorer sound–symbol correspondence than does English but makes up for this by various nonphonetic clues.

The parallelism between the foregoing pairs of languages leads me to set up dichotomies of "pure" phonetic writing and "meaning-plus-sound" scripts. So we have "pure" phonemic scripts (Finnish) versus "meaning-plus-sound" phonemic scripts (English) on the one hand, and "pure" syllabic scripts (Japanese kana) and "meaning-plus-sound" syllabic scripts (Chinese) on the other. In between these pairs I sandwich "pure" consonantal scripts (Arabic) versus "meaning-plus-sound" consonantal scripts (Egyptian at the time of the pharaohs).

No script with a zero phonetic component can function as a full system of writing. One with only a small percentage can. The phonetic operational unit, that is the grapheme, is the heart of the system. In the total weight of the human body, the heart counts for little. In the functions that sustain life, it counts for everything. No heart, no life. No phonetics, no writing. Weak hearts can be doctored in various ways. And so . . . can weak phonetic systems.

## Notes

1. I owe the ideas, and much of the phrasing, in this paragraph to S. Robert Ramsey (personal communication, 5/24/1988).

2. *Horse* and *hoarse* are homophonous in my dialect. But Ramsey (personal communication, 5/24/1988) says they are not homophonous in his speech, and he also notes that the two words are given separate pronunciations in Webster. He further notes that the differences in spelling reflect earlier differences in pronunciation. Hence the disambiguating techniques involved in the spellings for *horse-hoarse* and in the characters for *mǎ-mā* may not be completely analogous.

3. The relationship between graphemes and frames or lexemes, and the way they are handled in dictionaries, are complicated matters that merit special attention. Detailed study of these matters would throw much light on the workings of individual systems of writing. It is important to note, for example, that the lexemes in English dictionaries, as in those of most other languages, are arranged by their graphemes (that is, by the letters that comprise their graphemes), whereas the lexemes in Chinese dictionaries are arranged not by their graphemes but by their secondary semantic keys or radicals. The dictionary handling of lexemes in Chinese is a major factor leading to the common error of minimizing the phonetic aspect and exaggerating the semantic aspect in the Chinese system of writing (DeFrancis 1984: 93–97).

## References

Chao, Yuen Ren. 1976. *Aspects of Chinese Sociolinguistics.* Ed. Anwar S. Dil. Stanford: Stanford University Press.

DeFrancis, John. 1984. *The Chinese Language: Fact and Fantasy.* Honolulu: University of Hawaii Press.

Heimbach, Ernest E. 1966. *White Meo-English Dictionary.* 2 vols. Chiengmai: Overseas Missionary Fellowship.

Hockett, Charles F. 1978. In Search of Jove's Brow. *American Speech* 53(4): 243–313.

Taylor, Insup. 1980. The Korean Writing System: An Alphabet? A Syllabary? A Logography? In Paul A. Kolers, Merald E. Wrolstad, and Herman Bouma, eds., *Processing of Visible Language 2.* Pp. 67–82. New York: Plenum Press.

Umiker, Donna Jean. 1974. Speech Surrogates: Drum and Whistle Systems. In Thomas A. Sebeok, ed., *Current Trends in Linguistics* 12(1): 497–536. The Hague: Mouton.

Wang, William S.-Y. 1979. Review of J. F. Kavanagh and J. E. Cutting, eds., *The Role of Speech in Language.* (Cambridge: MIT Press, 1975). *Language* 55(4): 941–945.

Wang, William S.-Y. 1981. Language Structure and Optimal Orthography. In Ovid J. L. Tzeng and Harry Singer, eds., *Perception of Print. Reading Research in Experimental Psychology.* Pp. 223–236. Hillsdale, N.J.: Lawrence Erlbaum Associates.

---

## Critical Thinking and Application

- DeFrancis discusses the rebus principle. Give examples of this from electronic media. Are words and phrases formed using the rebus principle harder or easier to process than those formed using phonetic means? Why do you think this is the case?
- DeFrancis explains that English has about forty phonemes (basic units of sound). How many symbols does the English alphabet use? What is the result of this mismatch? If some languages have as many as eighty phonemes, what kind of writing system might suit them best?
- Why is there so much confusion and misunderstanding about the nature of writing? What is the important thing to understand about writing?

## Vocabulary

exclusivist
false etymology
frame (of writing)
full writing
grapheme
inclusivist
lexeme
modality
orthography
partial writing
phoneme
pinyin
rebus principle

## Suggested Further Reading [See also list following (New) Media unit introduction]

Coe, Michael D. 1992. *Breaking the Maya Code.* New York: Thames & Hudson.

Coulmas, Florian. 1989. *The Writing Systems of the World.* Oxford: Blackwell.

DeFrancis, John. 1984. *The Chinese Language: Fact and Fantasy.* Honolulu: University of Hawaii Press.

DeFrancis, John. 1989. *Visible Speech: The Diverse Oneness of Writing Systems.* Honolulu: University of Hawaii Press.

Diringer, David. 1968. *The Alphabet: A Key to the History of Mankind.* 3rd ed. London: Hutchinson.

Gaur, Albertine. 1984. *A History of Writing.* London: British Library.

Gelb, Ignace J. 1963. *A Study of Writing.* 2nd ed. Chicago: University of Chicago Press.

Goody, Jack. 1987. *The Interface Between the Written and the Oral.* Cambridge: Cambridge University Press.

Harbsmeier, Michael. 1988. Inventions of Writing. In *State and Society: The Emergence and Development of Social Hierarchy and Political Centralization,* edited by John Gledhill, Barbara Bender, and Mogens Trolle Larsen. One World Archaeology 4. London: Unwin Hyman.

Harris, Roy. 1986. *The Origin of Writing.* London: Duckworth.

Harris, William V. 1989. *Ancient Literacy.* Cambridge, MA: Harvard University Press.

Havelock, Eric Alfred. 1986. *The Muse Learns to Write: Reflections on Orality and Literacy from Antiquity to the Present*. New Haven, CT: Yale University Press.

Hornberger, Nancy, ed. 1996. *Indigenous Literacies in the Americas: Language Planning from the Bottom Up*. Berlin and New York: Mouton de Gruyter.

Idema, W. L. 2009. *Heroines of Jiangyong: Chinese Narrative Ballads in Women's Script*. Seattle: University of Washington Press.

Illich, Ivan, and Barry Sanders. 1988. *ABC: The Alphabetization of the Popular Mind*. San Francisco: North Point Press.

Innis, Harold Adams. 1972. *Empire and Communications*, 2nd ed. Toronto: University of Toronto Press.

Kalman, Judy. 1999. *Writing on the Plaza: Mediated Literacy Practice Among Scribes and Clients in Mexico City*. Cresskill, NJ: Hampton Press.

Keightley, David N. 1978. *Sources of Shang History: The Oracle-Bone Inscriptions of Bronze Age China*. Berkeley: University of California Press.

Lounsbury, F. G. 1989. The Ancient Writing of Middle America. In *The Origins of Writing*, edited by Wayne M. Senner. Lincoln: University of Nebraska Press.

Olsen, David R. 1994. *The World on Paper: The Conceptual and Cognitive Implications of Writing and Reading*. Cambridge and New York: Cambridge University Press.

Omniglot.com. *Writing Systems and Languages of the World*.

Ong, Walter J. 1982. *Orality and Literacy: The Technologizing of the Word*. London and New York: Methuen.

Sampson, Geoffrey. 1985. *Writing Systems: A Linguistic Approach*. London: Hutchinson.

Schmandt-Besserat, Denise. 1992. *Before Writing*. Austin: University of Texas Press.

Schmandt-Besserat, Denise. 1996. *How Writing Came About*. Austin: University of Texas Press.

Senner, Wayne M., ed. 1989. *The Origins of Writing*. Lincoln: University of Nebraska Press.

CHAPTER 13

# How the Brain Adapted Itself to Read

## The First Writing Systems

*Maryanne Wolf*

(2007)

*Writing was one of the most profound technologies that humans have ever invented, even though most of us raised in literate societies take it completely for granted. But at one time, humans had to figure out how to represent the fleeting sounds of spoken language in an enduring, physical form. This required subtle analysis of the nature of speech and language. Only some elements of speech, typically, are recorded, even in phonetic alphabets. The rest is filled in by the readers, who then appeal to their fuller knowledge of the spoken language.*

*The ability to write and the ability to read represent profound accomplishments. But it is only with the capacity to analyze the human brain as it actually works that we are beginning to note all the components of the brain and mind that are involved in this—with things that can go wrong at any point. The integration of a number of skills and an appeal to stored knowledge of various sorts must occur if reading is to be effortless.*

*It is not the case that all people celebrated literacy. As long ago as Greek times, Socrates warned against all kinds of dire consequences if people began to rely on written records rather than on their own cultivated memories. We rarely hear arguments* against *literacy in our world, yet Socrates' objections strike a familiar tone as another new form of media arises.*

*In* Proust and the Squid, *the book from which this chapter is selected, Maryanne Wolf explains how reading works cognitively and neurobiologically to understand what goes right—or wrong—when we read.*

### Reading Questions

- How did writing first develop? What was its function? Who invented it?
- What are the cognitive, linguistic, and cultural changes that have accompanied the invention of reading and writing?
- What three breakthroughs have occurred each time writing was invented?
- How was writing transformed over time? What are the major components of writing systems?
- What parts of the brain are involved in reading? How does this differ depending on what kind of writing system is being read?

---

And so I ambitiously proceed from my history as a reader to the history of the act of reading. Or rather, to a history of reading, since any such history—made up of particular institutions and private circumstances—must be only one of many. —Alberto Manguel

The invention of writing, which occurred independently in distant parts of the world at many times, even occasionally in the modern era, must rank among mankind's highest intellectual achievements. Without writing, human culture as we know it today is inconceivable.—O. Tzeng and W. Wang

Maryanne Wolf, How the Brain Adapted Itself to Read. From *Proust and the Squid: The Story and Science of the Reading Brain*. New York: HarperCollins, 2007, pp. 24–48.

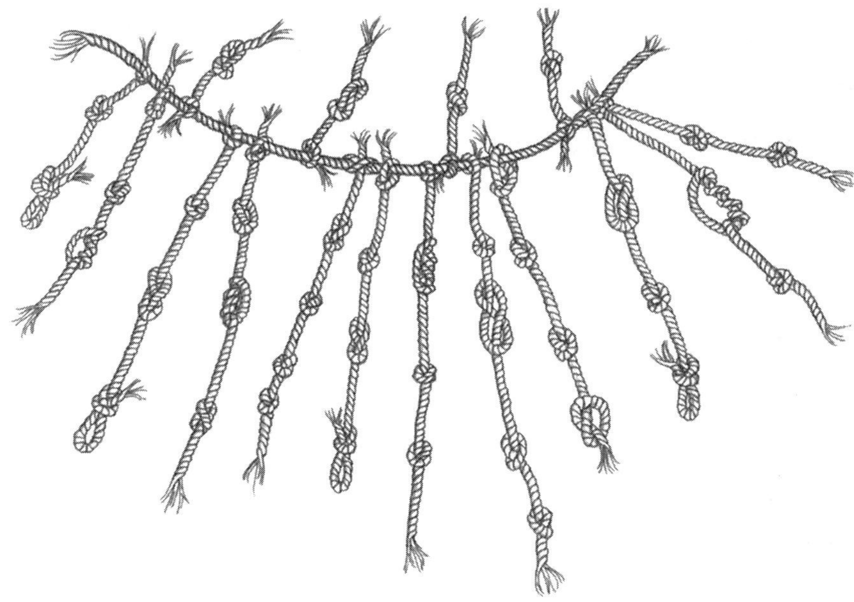

**Figure 13.1** *Example of Incan Quipus*

Little tokens in hardened clay envelopes, intricate dyed knots of twine in Incan *quipus* (see Figure 13.1), graceful designs scratched on the surface of turtle shells: the origins of writing took wondrously various shapes and forms over the last 10,000 years, all over the earth. Crosshatched lines on stones thought to be 77,000 years old were found recently under layers of earth in the Blomos Cave in South Africa and may prove to be still earlier signs of the first human efforts to "read."

Wherever and however it occurred, reading never "just happened." The story of reading reflects the sum of a series of cognitive and linguistic breakthroughs occurring alongside powerful cultural changes. Its colorful, spasmodic history helps reveal what our brain had to learn, one new process and insight at a time. It is a history not only of how we learned to read, but also of how different forms of writing required different adaptations of the brain's original structures and in the process helped to change the way we think. From the contemporary perspective of our own unfolding changes in communication, the story of reading offers a unique documentation of how each new writing system contributed something special to our species' intellectual development.

Across every known system, writing began with a set of two or more epiphanies. First came a new form of *symbolic representation*, one level of abstraction more than earlier drawings: the amazing discovery that simple marked lines on clay tokens, stones, or turtle shells can represent either something concrete in the natural world, such as a sheep; or something abstract, such as a number or an answer from an oracle. With the second breakthrough came the insight that a system of **symbols** can be used to communicate across time and space, preserving the words and thoughts of an individual or an entire culture. The third epiphany, the most linguistically abstract, did not happen everywhere: *sound-symbol correspondence* represents the stunning realization that all words are actually composed of tiny individual sounds and that symbols can physically signify each of these sounds for every word. Examining how several of our ancestors made these leaps into early writing provides us with a special lens on ourselves. Understanding the origins of a new process helps us see, as the neuroscientist Terry Deacon put it, "how it works." Understanding how it works, in turn, helps us know what we possess and what we need to preserve. . . .

## THE FIRST WRITTEN EUREKA: SYMBOLIC REPRESENTATION

> By the mere fact of looking at these tablets, we have prolonged a memory from the beginning of our time, preserved a thought long after the thinker has stopped thinking, and made ourselves participants in an act of creation that remains open for as long as the incised images are seen, deciphered, read. —ALBERTO MANGUEL

The chance discovery of little clay pieces, no larger than a quarter, marks the birth of modern efforts to learn about the history of writing. Called tokens, some of these pieces came enclosed in clay envelopes (see Figure 13.2) that bore markings representing their contents. We now know that these pieces date back to the period between 8000 and 4000 B.C.E., and formed a kind of accounting system used across many parts of the ancient world. The tokens primarily recorded the number of goods bought or sold, such as sheep, goats, and bottles of wine. A lovely irony of our species' cognitive growth is that the world of letters may have begun as an envelope for the world of numbers.

Simultaneously, the development of numbers and letters promoted both ancient economies and our ancestors'

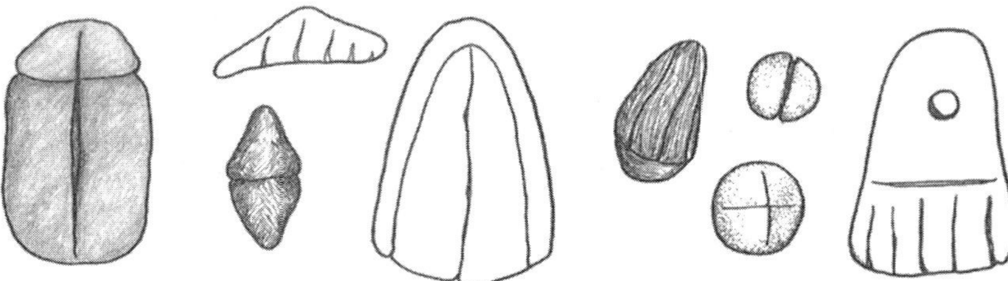

**Figure 13.2** *Tokens*

intellectual skills. For the first time "stock" could be counted with no necessity for the sheep, goats, or wine to be present. The precursor of stored data, a permanent record came into existence, accompanied by new cognitive capacities. For example, along with cave drawings like those in France and Spain, tokens reflected the emergence of a new human ability: the use of a form of symbolic representation, in which objects could be symbolized by marks for the eye. To "read" a symbol demanded two sets of novel connections: one cognitive-linguistic and the other cerebral. Among the long-established brain circuits for vision, language, and conceptualization, new connections developed and new retinotopic pathways—between the eye and specialized visual areas—became assigned to the tiny token marks.

We will never have a brain scan of our ancestors reading a token, but by using present knowledge of brain function, we can extrapolate to make a decent guess about what went on in their brains. The neuroscientists Michael Posner and Marcus Raichle, and Raichle's research group at Washington University, conducted a pioneering series of brain imaging studies to observe what the brain does when we look at a continuum of symbol-like characters with and without meaning. Their range of tasks included meaningless symbols, meaningful symbols that make up real letters, meaningless words, and meaningful words. Although clearly designed for other purposes, these studies provide a remarkable glimpse of what happens when the brain encounters ever more abstract and demanding writing systems—millennia ago and today.

Raichle's group found that when humans look at lines which convey no meaning, we activate only limited visual areas located in the occipital lobes at the back of the brain. This finding exemplifies some aspects of retinotopic organization... The cells in the retina activate a group of specific cells in the occipital regions that correspond to discrete visual features such as lines and circles.

When we see these same circles and lines and interpret them as meaningful symbols, however, we need new pathways. As Raichle's work showed, the presence of real-word status and meaning doubles or triples the brain's neuronal activity. Becoming familiar with the basic pathways used in a token-reading brain is an excellent foundation for understanding what happens in more complex reading brains. Our ancestors could read tokens because their brains were able to connect their basic visual regions to adjacent regions dedicated to more sophisticated visual and conceptual processing. These adjacent regions are found in other **occipital** and nearby **temporal** and **parietal** areas of the brain. The temporal lobes are involved in an impressive range of auditory and language-based processes, which contribute to our ability to comprehend the meanings of words. Similarly, the parietal lobes participate in a wide range of language-related processes, as well as spatial and computational functions. When a visual symbol like a token is imbued with meaning, our brain connects the basic visual areas to both the language system and the conceptual system in the temporal and parietal lobes and also to visual and auditory specialization regions called "association areas."

Symbolization, therefore, even for the tiny token, exploits and expands two of the most important features of the human brain—our capacity for specialization and our capacity for making new connections among association areas. One major difference between the human brain and the brain of any other primate is the proportion of our brain devoted to these association areas. Essential to reading symbols, these areas are responsible both for more demanding sensory processing and for making mental representations of information for future use (think of "representations"). Such a representational capacity is profoundly important for the use of symbols and for much of our intellectual life. It helps humans remember and retrieve stored representations of all sorts, from visual images like predators' footprints and tokens to auditory sounds like words and a tiger's growl. Further, this representational ability prepares the foundation for our evolutionary capacity to become virtually automatic at recognizing patterns in information all about us. All this enables us to become specialists in identifying various sensory information—whether tracks of woolly mammoths or tokens for goats. It is all of a piece.

Reading symbols required more than the visual specialization of our ancestors. Linking visual representations to linguistic and conceptual information was critical. Located at the juncture of the three posterior lobes of the brain, the ***angular gyrus*** area, described as the "association area of the association areas" by the great behavioral neurologist Norman Geschwind, is ideally located for linking different kinds of sensory information. The nineteenth-century French neurologist Joseph-Jules Déjerine observed that an injury to the angular gyrus region produced a loss in reading and writing. And

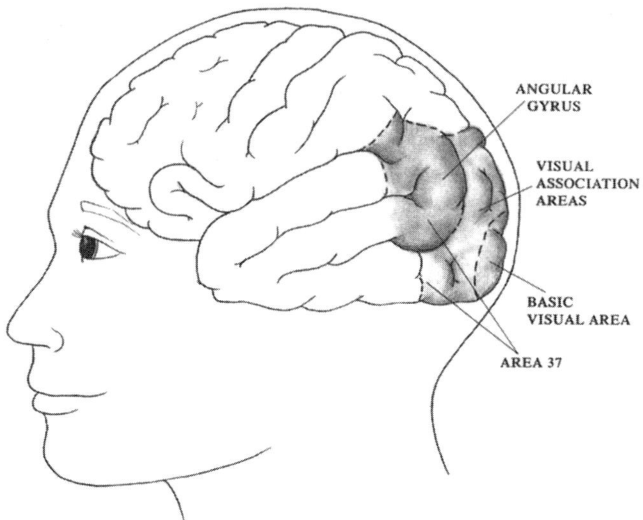


**Figure 13.3** *First "Token-Reading Brain"*

today, the neuroscientists John Gabrieli and Russ Poldrack and their groups at MIT and UCLA find, through their imaging research, that pathways to and from the angular gyrus region become intensely activated during reading development.

From Raichle's, Poldrack's, and Gabrieli's work, we can infer that the likely physiological basis of our ancestors' first reading of tokens was a tiny new circuitry connecting the angular gyrus region with a few nearby visual areas and if Dehaene is correct, a few parietal areas involved in **numeracy** and occipital-temporal areas involved in object recognition (i.e., area 37) (Figure 13.3). However rudimentary, a novel form of connectivity began with the use of tokens, and with it came our species' earliest cognitive breakthrough in reading. By teaching new generations to use an increasing repertoire of symbols, our ancestors essentially passed on knowledge about the brain's capability for adaptation and change. Our brain was preparing to read.

## From the Mouths of Kings and Queens: The Second Breakthrough into Cuneiform and Hieroglyphic Writing Systems

> Have you noticed how picturesque the letter Y is and how innumerable its meanings are? The tree is a Y, the junction of two roads forms a Y, two converging rivers, a donkey's head and that of an ox, the glass with its stem, the lily on its stalk and the beggar lifting his arms are a Y. This observation can be extended to everything that constitutes the elements of the various letters devised by man.
>
> —VICTOR HUGO

Toward the end of the fourth millennium B.C.E. (3300–3200), a second breakthrough occurred: individual Sumerian inscriptions developed into a **cuneiform** system and Egyptian symbols became a **hieroglyphic** system. Whether or not the Sumerians or the Egyptians are the inventors of writing is increasingly debated. But there is no debate that the Sumerians invented one of the first and most revered systems for writing, whose influence continued through the great Akkadian system throughout all of Mesopotamia. The word "cuneiform" derives from the Latin word *cuneus*, "nail," which refers to the script's wedge-like appearance. Using a pointed reed stylus on soft clay, our ancestors created a script that looks, to the untutored eye, a lot like bird tracks (Figure 13.4).

The discovery of these strange-looking symbols is comparatively recent and a testimony to the lengths to which some intrepid linguists go to understand the origins of language. Contemporary language scholars like to recount how the nineteenth-century scholar and soldier Henry Raulinson risked life and limb to examine ancient writing in what is now Iran. Raulinson dangled on a rope 300 feet in the air to copy some of the first Sumerian writings carved into the side of a cliff.

Mercifully, the 5,000 extant Sumerian tablets are much more accessible. Found in Sumerian palaces, temples, and warehouses, this writing was originally invented and used largely for administration and accounting. The ancient inhabitants of the Tigris-Euphrates delta themselves had a far more romantic notion of how their writing came to be. In one epic tale a messenger from the lord of Kulab arrived at a distant kingdom, too exhausted to deliver an important oral message. So as not to be frustrated by mortal failings, the lord of Kulab had also "patted some clay and set down the words as on a tablet... it verily was so." And so the first written words came into being, although the Sumerians sidestepped the awkward matter of who was able to read the lord of Kulab's words.

Less uncertain is the place of the Sumerian writing system as a milestone in the evolution of writing. It was a true system, with all that this implies for emerging cognitive

**Figure 13.4** *Examples of Cuneiform*

skills in writer, reader, and teacher. Although far more comprehensive than tokens, the earliest signs in Sumerian cuneiform demanded only slightly more abstraction because they were generally pictographic (images that visually resembled the object represented). The pictographic characters were easily recognized by the visual system, which would require only a further match with an object name in the spoken language. Stanislas Dehaene observes that many of the symbols and letters used in writing and numerical systems around the world incorporate highly common visual shapes and features that correspond to objects in nature and our world. The French novelist Victor Hugo, quoted above, observed as much at the turn of the twentieth century. Hugo proposed that all letters originated from Egyptian hieroglyphs, which, in turn, stemmed from images in our world such as rivers, snakes, and lily stalks. These similar ideas between novelist and neuroscientists remain conjectural but they highlight the question of how the brain learned to recognize letters and words in the first place with such alacrity. In Dehaene's evolutionary terms, early pictographic symbols, which utilized known shapes in the external world, "recycled" the circuits used for object recognition and naming.

This simple state of affairs didn't last long, however. Soon after it originated, Sumerian cuneiform, mysteriously and rather astonishingly, became sophisticated. Symbols rapidly became less pictographic and more **logographic** and abstract. A logographic writing system directly conveys the concepts in the oral language, rather than the sounds in the words. Over time many of the Sumerian characters also began to represent some of the syllables in oral Sumerian. This double function in a writing system is classified by linguists as a ***logosyllabary***, and it makes a great many more demands on the brain.

In fact, to fulfill these double functions, the circuits of the Sumerian reading brain must have crisscrossed it. First, considerably more pathways in the visual and visual association regions would be necessary in order to decode what would eventually become hundreds of cuneiform characters. Making such accommodations in the visual areas is basically the equivalent of adding memory to our hard drive. Second, the conceptual demands of a logosyllabary would inevitably involve more cognitive systems, which, in turn, would require more connections to visual areas in the occipital lobes, to language areas in the temporal lobes, and to the **frontal lobes.** The frontal lobes become involved because of their role in "executive skills" such as analysis, planning, and focused attention, all of which are necessary to process the tiny syllables and sounds within words and the many semantic categories like human, plant, and temple.

Attending to individual sound patterns inside words must have been very new for our ancestors, and it came about because of something extremely clever. As they began to add new words, the Sumerians incorporated what is called a ***rebus principle*** in their writing. This occurs when a symbol (for example, "bird") represents not its meaning but rather its sound, which in Sumerian was a word's first syllable. In this way, the symbol for "bird" could do double duty—as its meaning or its speech sound. Disambiguating the two, of course, required still more new functions, including specific markers both for sounds and for common categories of meaning. These phonetic and semantic markers, in turn, required more elaborate cerebral circuitry.

To imagine what the Sumerian brain eventually looked like, we can do two tricky things. First, we can return to the findings of Raichle's group, who looked at what happens when meaning is added to words. For example, they studied how the brain reads pseudo words like "mbli" and real words like "limb," in which the letters were the same but only one combination of them was meaningful. In each case, the same visual areas initially activated, but the pseudo words stimulated little activity beyond their identification in the visual association regions. For real words, however, the brain became a beehive of activity. A network of processes went to work: the visual and visual association areas responded to visual patterns (or representations); frontal, temporal, and parietal areas provided information about the smallest sounds in words, called **phonemes;** and finally areas in the temporal and parietal lobes processed meanings, functions, and connections to other real words. The difference between the two arrangements of the same letters—only one of which was a word—was almost half a cortex. When encountering words written in cuneiform and hieroglyphs, the first readers—both the Sumerians and the Egyptians—undoubtedly used parts of these same regions, as they set about creating the first two writing systems.

As further evidence of this scenario, I have a second trick up my sleeve. To get another glimpse of the ancient Sumerian reading brain, we can extrapolate from a living, flourishing, similarly constructed writing system (i.e., logosyllabary). One language today has a similar history of shifts from pictographic symbols to logographic symbols, uses phonetic and semantic markers to help disambiguate its symbols, and has ample brain images: Chinese. John DeFrancis, a scholar of ancient languages and Chinese, classifies both Chinese and Sumerian as logosyllabic writing systems, with many similar elements, though of course also some dissimilar ones. (See also Chapter 12.)

Thus a Chinese reading brain (Figure 13.5) offers a contemporary, fairly reasonable approximation of the brains of the first Sumerian readers. A vastly expanded circuit replaces the little circuit system of the token reader. This new adaptation by the brain requires far more surface area in visual and visual association regions, and in both hemispheres. Unlike other writing systems (such as **alphabets),** Sumerian and Chinese show considerable involvement of the right hemisphere areas, known to contribute to the many spatial analysis requirements in logographic symbols and also to more global types of processing. The numerous, visually demanding logographic characters require much of both visual areas, as well as an important occipital-temporal region called area 37, which is involved in object recognition and which Dehaene hypothesizes is the major seat of "neuronal recycling" in literacy.

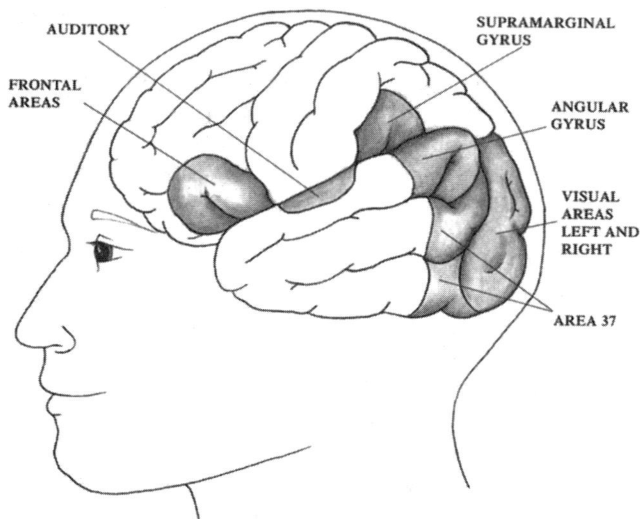


**Figure 13.5** *Logosyllabary—Reading Brain*

Although all reading makes use of some portions of the frontal and temporal lobes for planning and for analyzing sounds and meanings in words, logographic systems appear to activate very distinctive parts of the frontal and temporal areas, particularly regions involved in motoric memory skills. The cognitive neuroscientists Li-Hai Tan and Charles Perfetti and their research group at the University of Pittsburgh make the important point that these motoric memory areas are far more activated in reading Chinese than in reading other languages, because that is how Chinese symbols are learned by young readers—by writing, over and over. This is also how Sumerian characters were learned—on little clay practice tablets, over and over again: "it verily was so."

## The Story Within a Story: How Sumerians Taught Their Children to Read

The Sumerians taught all new pupils to read with lists of words on little clay tablets. This small fact does not sound like a momentous event in the intellectual history of *Homo sapiens*, but it was. The act of teaching not only requires a firm knowledge of the subject, but also forces the teacher to analyze what goes into the learning of a particular content. Moreover, good teaching renders the multiple dimensions of the subject to be taught more visible—in this case, the complex nature of language in its written form. The gradual process of learning how to teach the earliest writing systems forced our world's first reading instructors to also become the world's earliest linguists.

Ancient records recently analyzed by the Assyriologist Yori Cohen of Tel Aviv University indicate how long it took Sumerian pupils before they could read and write—virtually years of study in their *e-dubba* or "tablet house" schools. This name refers to an essential part of the Sumerian instructional methods: teachers would write the cuneiform symbols on one side of a clay tablet, and students would copy the symbols on the reverse side. New readers learned to read text that included both logographic and phonetic information—sometimes in the same word. To do so, young readers had to have rich contextual background knowledge, well-honed automatic skills, and no small amount of cognitive flexibility to decide what value to give a particular written sign—logographic, phonetic-syllabic, or semantic—if they were to understand the texts at all fluently. This took years of practice. It is little wonder that newly discovered practice tablets depict miserable students in each year with their teacher, followed by the oft-repeated line "And then he caned me."

But frequent canings are not the real surprise. These first teachers of reading utilized highly analytical, linguistic principles for teaching that would be useful in any era. From early on, Cohen observed that novice readers learned lists of words based on one of several particular linguistic principles. Some lists taught *semantic*, or meaning-based, categories, with each category identified by specific markers. As the Sumerian writing system began to incorporate symbols for syllables, a second set of word lists was grouped on the basis of shared pronunciations. This meant that Sumerians were analyzing the sound-based or ***phonological*** system—the emphasis of most phonics-based reading programs today. In other words, long before twentieth-century educators would debate whether reading is best taught by phonics or by meaning-based methods, the Sumerians were incorporating elements of both in their early instruction.

A major contribution of early Sumerian writing is the way that teaching methods promoted conceptual development. Requiring Sumerian pupils or any children to learn semantically and phonetically related words helped them recall the words more efficiently, increase their vocabulary, and increase their conceptual knowledge. In current terms, the Sumerians used the first known **metacognitive** strategy to teach reading. That is, Sumerian teachers gave their pupils tools that made *explicit* how to learn something, and how to remember it.

Over time, the novice Sumerian readers also learned words that illustrated the common ***morphological*** properties of language (e.g., how two symbolic units can come together to make a new related word). **Morphology** is a system of rules for forming words from the smallest meaningful parts of a language, called **morphemes.** For example, in English the word "bears" is composed of two morphemes: the root word, "bear"; and the "s," which indicates either a plural noun or the present tense of the verb "to bear." Without this profoundly important capacity for combination in language, our vocabulary and conceptual possibilities would be severely narrowed, with dramatic implications for our intellectual evolution and for the cognitive differences between our primate cousins and ourselves.

The call system of one of our primate relatives, Nigerian putty-nosed monkeys, illustrates the importance of this type of combinatorial capacity in language. The putty-nosed monkey, like the vervet monkey, has two separate warning calls for its major predators. "Pyow" means that a leopard is nearby, and a "hacking sound" indicates the approach of the eagle. Recently, two Scottish zoologists observed that the monkeys have combined the two calls to make a new call, indicating to the young monkeys that it's time "to leave a site." Such an innovation among the putty-nosed monkeys is analogous to our use of morphemes to create new words, as the Sumerians frequently did in their writing system.

What is historically humbling about Sumerian writing and pedagogy is not their understanding of morphological principles, but their realization that the teaching of reading must begin with explicit attention to the principal characteristics of oral language. This is exactly what takes place today in the supposedly "cutting-edge" curricula in our own lab where we incorporate all major aspects of language in our reading instruction. It makes perfect sense. If you believe you are the first reading people on earth, and have no prior methods to influence how you teach, you try to figure out all the characteristics of your oral language in order to create a written version. For the first Sumerian teachers this resulted in a long-lasting set of linguistic principles that facilitated teaching and learning and also accelerated the development of cognitive and linguistic skills in literate Sumerians. Thus, with the Sumerians' contributions to teaching our species to read and write, the story began of how the reading brain changed the way we all think.

*All* of us. One of the less known but felicitous aspects of the Sumerian legacy has to do with the discovery that the women of the royal houses learned to read. Women possessed their own dialect, called Emesal, or the "fine tongue," as distinguished from the standard dialect Emegir, the "princely tongue." The feminine dialect differed in the pronunciation of many of its own separate words. We can only imagine the cognitive complexity required by pupils who had to switch dialects between passages where the goddesses spoke the "fine tongue" and the gods used their "princely" one. It is beautiful testimony to this ancient culture that some of the world's first recorded love songs and lullabies were composed by their women:

> Come sleep, come sleep
> Come to my son
> Hurry sleep to my son
> Put to sleep his restless eyes,
> Put your hand on his sparkling eyes,
> And as for his babbling tongue
> Let not the babbling hold back his sleep.

## From Sumerian to Akkadian

It is also a testimony to the Sumerian writing system that at least fifteen peoples, including the early Persians and Hittites, adopted the Sumerian cuneiform script and the related teaching methods long after Sumerian ceased to be used. Just as cultures die out, so, too, do languages. By the beginning of the second millennium B.C.E., Sumerian was dying as a spoken language, and new readers began to learn "bilingual lists" for words in the increasingly dominant Akkadian language. By 1600 B.C.E., no speakers of Sumerian remained. All the more impressive, therefore, is the fact that the Akkadian writing system and its teaching methods continued to preserve many Sumerian written symbols and methods. Sumerian learning methods contributed to the educational process throughout Mesopotamian history. Indeed, there are memorable scenes as late as 700 B.C.E. showing two scribes working intently side by side, one on clay tablets and one on papyrus—one with the ancients' writing, and one with the new.

Only around 600 B.C.E. did Sumerian writing disappear. And even then, its impact remained, inside some of the characters and within the methods of Akkadian, the lingua franca from the third to the first millennium B.C.E. Akkadian became the language used and adapted by most of the peoples of Mesopotamia for some of the most important ancient documents in recorded history, beginning with the timeless descriptions of the human condition in the Akkadian *Epic of Gilgamesh*:

> For whom have I labored? For whom have I journeyed?
> For whom have I suffered? I have gained absolutely
> Nothing for myself.

Discovered in twelve stone tablets in the Nineveh library of Ashurbanipal, king of Assyria between 668 and 627 B.C.E., the *Epic of Gilgamesh* bears the name of Shin-eq-unninni, one of the first known authors in history. In this epic, which undoubtedly has motifs from far earlier oral legends, the hero Gilgamesh battles terrible foes, overcomes horrific obstacles, loses his beloved friend, and learns that no one, including himself, can escape the ultimate enemy of all humans—mortality.

*Gilgamesh* and the flurry of Akkadian writing that followed exemplify several important changes in the history of writing. The sheer volume of writing and the flowering of literary genres contributed hugely to the knowledge base of the second millennium B.C.E. The titles of these works tell their own story—from touching didactic texts like *Advice of a Father to His Son* and spiritual works like *Dialogue of a Man with His God* to mythic legends like *Enlil and Nilil*. The impulse to codify led to what is probably the first encyclopedia, modestly titled *All Things Known About the Universe*. Similarly, the *Code of Hammurabi* in 1800 B.C.E. gave the world a brilliant codification of the laws of society under this great ruler, and the *Treatise of Medical Diagnostics and Prognostics* classified all known medical writings. The level of conceptual development, organization, abstraction, and creativity in Akkadian writing inevitably shifts any previous focus on what is cognitively required by an individual writing system to what aspects of cognitive development are being advanced.

Some features of Akkadian made it somewhat easier to use, with a caveat. Ancient languages like Akkadian, and other languages like Japanese and Cherokee, have a rather simple, tidy syllabic structure. Such oral languages lend themselves well to the type of writing system called a **syllabary,** in which each syllable, rather than each sound, is denoted by a symbol. (For example, when the Native American leader Sequoya decided to invent a writing system, he used a syllabary, a system well suited for the eighty-six syllables of Cherokee.) A perfectly rendered, "pure" syllabary for Akkadian, however, would have meant giving up the old Sumerian logograms and their ties with the past—something unacceptable to the Akkadians. Over time a linguistic compromise emerged, often used in other languages. The Akkadian writing system retained some of the old Sumerian logograms for common, important words like "king," but rendered its other words in the syllabary. In this way the ancient Sumerian language and culture survived—a matter of great pride to the Akkadian culture—even though the resulting writing system became more complex. Underlying most convoluted writing systems around the world can be found the wish of one culture to preserve a previous culture or language that shaped it.

The English language is a similar historical mishmash of homage and pragmatism. We include Greek, Latin, French, Old English, and many other roots, at a cost known to every first- and second-grader. Linguists classify English as a ***morphophonemic*** writing system because it represents both morphemes (units of meaning) and phonemes (units of sound) in its spelling, a major source of bewilderment to many new readers if they don't understand the historical reasons. To illustrate the morphophonemic principle in English, the linguists Noam Chomsky and Carol Chomsky use words like "muscle" to teach the way our words carry an entire history within them—not unlike the Sumerian roots inside Akkadian words. For example, the silent "c" in "muscle" may seem unnecessary, but in fact it visibly connects the word to its origin, the Latin root *musculus*, from which we have such kindred words as "muscular" and "musculature." In the latter words the "c" is pronounced and represents the *phonemic* aspect of our alphabet. The silent "c" of "muscle," therefore, visually conveys the *morphemic* aspect of English. In essence, English represents a "trade-off" between depicting the individual sounds of the oral language and showing the roots of its words.

An intellectually and physiologically demanding writing system confronted young readers of ancient Akkadian, because of similar trade-offs. It is hardly a surprise that the Akkadian writing system, like the earlier Sumerian system, took between six and seven years to master. This length of time and powerful political factors restricted literacy to a small, exclusive group of people in the temple and court—those who could afford the luxury of learning something for several years. Nowhere are such political forces lived out more vividly or more disastrously than in the parallel story of the other "first" writing system—the Egyptian hieroglyphs, which some recent scholarship suggests predated the Sumerian system by perhaps a century or more.

## Another "First"? The Invention of Hieroglyphic Writing

For many years most scholars have assumed that the Sumerians invented the first system for recording language, and that the Egyptian script was partially derived from the Sumerian writing system. New linguistic evidence, however, suggests that an entirely independent invention of writing in Egypt took place either around 3100 B.C.E.; or, on the basis of still controversial evidence from German Egyptologists in Abydos, as early as 3400 B.C.E.—earlier than the Sumerian script. If this finding proves correct, hieroglyphs would be the first major adaptation in the evolution of the reading brain.

Because the evidence is not yet certain, I want to present the Egyptian hieroglyphic system (Figure 13.6) as a separate adaptation. Largely logographic and aesthetically beautiful, the earliest hieroglyphs were visually very unlike the Sumerian bird-feet style. Anyone who has tried to decipher some of this early writing soon becomes enamored of its sheer artistry. Both scripts employed the unusual rebus principle, and both were considered gifts from the gods.

Over time the hieroglyphic script evolved into a mixed system with both logographic signs for a core of word meanings and also special signs for consonantal sounds (called phonograms). For example, the hieroglyphic sign for "house" looks a lot like a house seen from above—as the gods were thought to see it. This sign can be used as a simple, imagistic logogram meaning "house," or it can be read as the consonantal blend "pr." Or it can be placed after other logograms to ensure that those signs are pronounced with "pr." This is the *phonetic marker* or *complement*, seen also in Sumerian. Or the sign can be placed with semantically similar, related words like "temple" and "palace" to ensure that the reader knows the classification of the word (see Figure 13.6).

With regard to cognitive requirements, the Egyptian system, like Sumerian, must have presented a formidable challenge to the novice reader. The early readers had to figure out exactly how a given sign was being used. Once again, the variety of strategies required by these different uses, combined with the cognitive judgment and flexibility involved in deciding when to use what, makes for a very active brain. To recognize a logogram required visual-conceptual connections; to recognize consonantal signs required connections between the visual, auditory, and phonological systems; and to recognize phonetic and semantic markers required additional abstraction and classification capacities, along with phonological and semantic analysis.

Furthermore, early Egyptian writing appeared neither punctuated nor consistently arranged from left to right or right to left. Egyptian and some other early systems were written in the *boustrophedon* style (Greek for "the turning around of the ox") in which one line moves from left to right and then right to left, the way oxen plow a field. Instead of

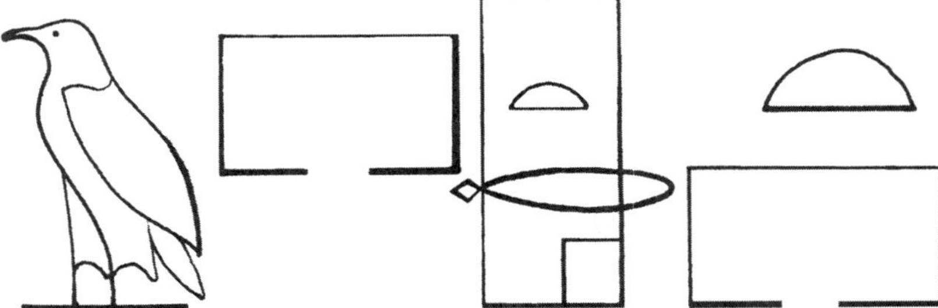

**Figure 13.6** *Egyptian Hieroglyphs of Bird, House, and Temple*

scanning in one linear direction as we do today, the eye just moves down a notch at the end of a line and continues to read in the other direction. Egyptians also wrote from top to bottom or vice versa, depending on the architecture of the structure they were inscribing. The upshot is that the reader of hieroglyphs had to possess a spectrum of skills, including a highly developed visual memory, auditory and phoneme analysis, and considerable cognitive and spatial flexibility.

Over the centuries, like the Sumerian system and most other major early **orthographies,** the Egyptian system added many new signs and some new features. Unlike other systems, however, the Egyptian underwent two major transformations. First, for those charged with writing and copying, the hieroglyphic system evolved to include two cursive forms of writing. This first transformation added efficiency to the act of writing and copying texts, something which must have delighted all scribes. These ancient scribes, however, must have been even more pleased with the second transformation.

Basically, the Egyptians discovered the equivalent of the phoneme. There may have been no dancing in the streets, but for scribes this invention was very important indeed, for it helped them more easily denote new names of cities and members of the royal family, and also to spell foreign words and names. The clever rebus principle could take this task only so far. A similar phenomenon can be seen much later in Japanese's two writing systems—its older Chinese-based, logographic system, **kanji;** and the later syllabary, **kana.** (Like the Egyptian partial alphabet, the kana syllabary was designed as a supplement to kanji, to enable the written language to record new words, foreign words, and names.)

We know that this linguistic discovery was made in early Egyptian writing because it began to incorporate a tiny subset of characters that could depict the consonants of the Egyptians' oral language. As the linguist Peter Daniels described it, this was a marvel in the history of writing—the birth of a "partial *alphabet* for consonants." This new group of characters by the Egyptians marked the earliest glimmerings of what would later become the third cognitive breakthrough in writing history: a system of writing based on the internal, sound-based structure of words. But just as Moses would be unable to live in the promised land, the Egyptians themselves would never fully exploit this alphabetic precursor. For reasons cultural, political, and religious, the hieroglyphic system never evolved in more efficient directions, despite the possibilities given to it by the partial alphabet. From some 700 standard signs in the Middle Egyptian period, the number of Egyptian hieroglyphs grew over the next millennium to several thousand, some of which became weighed down with layer after layer of religiously encrypted meanings, learnable by fewer and fewer people. These changes meant that hieroglyphic reading grew more, rather than less, conceptually demanding, and became restricted to fewer and fewer people.

We know from millions of Chinese readers, who daily acquire fluent reading also using thousands of characters, that the decline and fall of the Egyptian writing system cannot be explained simply by the quantitative demands on visual memory. By the first millennium B.C.E., the brain of an Egyptian scribe may well have needed far more cortical activation and cognitive resources to handle the encrypted meanings than was required for most other writing systems in all of history. Paradoxically, the Egyptian partial consonantal system—which may have first come into being because of the complexities of hieroglyphs—might prove to be the single most important contribution to the evolution of the alphabet in the early history of writing systems.

## Dragon Bones, Turtle Shells, and Knots: The Curious Signs of Other Early Writing Systems

The very different histories of the Egyptian and the Sumerian systems do not resolve whether writing was invented separately by each culture, or whether one system traveled to the other. Cumulative evidence around the world suggests that writing was invented at least three times in the last part of the fourth millennium B.C.E., and at least three more times in different parts of the world in later periods. In addition to the Egyptian and Sumerian systems, the Indus people's system of writing evolved from potters' marks around 3300 B.C.E. to a full script around 2500 B.C.E. This script remains undeciphered, and continues to defy valiant efforts to crack its code.

The first of the later writing systems appeared in Crete, in the second millennium B.C.E. Presumably influenced by the Egyptians, it included a pictographic, Cretan hieroglyphic script called Linear A, and the famous script Linear B.... A very different, rich logosyllabary system created originally by the Zapotecs was used by them, the Mayans, and the

Olmecs throughout Mesoamerica. For decades, the stunning Mayan writing system, like the Greek Linear B, defied every attempt to decipher it. Then, quite remarkably, a relatively isolated scholar in Stalinist Russia with little access to most of the relevant materials broke the seemingly uncrackable code. Told in superb detail by Michael Coe in his book *Breaking the Maya Code*, the little-known story of Yuri Valentinovich Knorosov's breakthrough is one of the riveting intellectual whodunits of the twentieth century. Knorosov figured out that the brilliant ancient Mayans applied linguistic principles such as phonetic and semantic markers that were similar to those of the Sumerians and Egyptians, but that were even more similar to the way Japanese combined its two types of logographic and syllabary systems.

Another great Mesoamerican mystery, however, is still on the horizon. Recently, Gary Urton, an anthropologist at Harvard University, and his colleague Jeffrey Quilter suggested a new way of understanding the beautiful, mysterious quipus (or khipus), the ancient dyed fibers and twine shaped into patterns with extremely intricate systems of knots and attachments (refer back to Figure 13.1). Urton surprised linguists and Inca scholars with his hypothesis that the 600 or so quipus that still exist represent an undeciphered Incan written language system. Each type of knot, each direction of the knot, and each color may denote linguistic information, just as each knot in the Jewish tallith, or shawl, does. Until now, quipus were thought to have functioned like an abacus, although some records from Spanish historians in the sixteenth century described how the Incas told missionaries that entire cultures were recorded on them. (The missionaries promptly burned all the quipus they could find, to rid the Incas of their ties to past gods!) Today, Urton and his colleagues are trying to use the remaining quipus to decipher what may well be the equivalent of another complex ancient written language.

Yet another mystery can be found in the ancient Chinese writing system. Although its beginnings are usually dated from the Shang period (1500–1200 B.C.E.), some scholars believe that a Chinese writing system existed much earlier. Another example of serendipity is the discovery of early Chinese writing in, of all places, nineteenth-century pharmacies. At the time people clamored to buy **"dragon bones,"** which were believed to have magical healing properties, and someone noticed a system of marks on the old bones and the turtle shells. It is now thought that questions for the deities were written in an early Chinese script on turtle shells and the shoulder bones of cows; then the shells were split with a hot poker to reveal the gods' answers, given through the patterns of cracks that appeared inside the shells. A complete oracle bone inscription would ask the question, give the date, describe the gods' answers, and then tell what happened. For example, a 3,000-year-old inscription from the Shang dynasty recounts that King Wu Ding wanted to know whether his wife's pregnancy would be a "happy event." The gods answered that it would be happy only if the wife, Hao, gave birth on certain dates. She did not. The last inscription confirmed the prognostication of the deities: "The birthing was not a happy event. It was a girl."

## Critical Thinking and Application

- How did writing transform the societies in which it was invented?
- Sumerians appear to have taught reading through explicit attention to the nature of spoken language. How did you learn to read? What aspects of spoken language did you learn about?
- Which aspects of English writing are phonemic and which are morphemic? Would this be useful for young spellers to know? Why or why not?
- Research debates on "whole language" versus "phonics" as ways to teach writing and reading. Have a class debate about these philosophies and their efficacy.

## Vocabulary

| | | |
|---|---|---|
| alphabet | logographic | orthography |
| *angular gyrus* | logosyllabary | parietal lobe |
| cuneiform | metacognition | phoneme |
| dragon bones | morpheme | phonology, phonological |
| frontal lobes | morphological, morphology | rebus principle |
| hieroglyphic writing | morphophonemic | syllabary |
| *kana* | numeracy | symbol |
| *kanji* | occipital area | temporal lobe |

## Suggested Further Reading [See also list following (New) Media unit introduction]

Coe, Michael D. 1992. *Breaking the Maya Code*. New York: Thames & Hudson.

Coulmas, Florian. 1989. *The Writing Systems of the World*. Oxford: Blackwell.

DeFrancis, John. 1989. *Visible Speech: The Diverse Oneness of Writing Systems.* Honolulu: University of Hawaii Press.

Diringer, David. 1968. *The Alphabet: A Key to the History of Mankind.* 3rd ed. London: Hutchinson.

Finnegan, Ruth H. 1988. *Literacy and Orality: Studies in the Technology of Communication.* Oxford: Blackwell.

Gaur, Albertine. 1984. *A History of Writing.* London: British Library.

Gelb, Ignace J. 1963. *A Study of Writing.* 2nd ed. Chicago: University of Chicago Press.

Goody, Jack. 1987. *The Interface Between the Written and the Oral.* Cambridge: Cambridge University Press.

Harbsmeier, Michael. 1988. Inventions of Writing. In *State and Society: The Emergence and Development of Social Hierarchy and Political Centralization*, edited by John Gledhill, Barbara Bender, and Mogens Trolle Larsen. One World Archaeology 4. London: Unwin Hyman.

Harris, Roy. 1986. *The Origin of Writing.* London: Duckworth.

Harris, William V. 1989. *Ancient Literacy.* Cambridge, MA: Harvard University Press.

Havelock, Eric Alfred. 1986. *The Muse Learns to Write: Reflections on Orality and Literacy from Antiquity to the Present.* New Haven, CT: Yale University Press.

Hornberger, Nancy, ed. 1996. *Indigenous Literacies in the Americas: Language Planning from the Bottom Up.* Berlin and New York: Mouton de Gruyter.

Idema, W. L. 2009. *Heroines of Jiangyong: Chinese Narrative Ballads in Women's Script.* Seattle: University of Washington Press.

Illich, Ivan, and Barry Sanders. 1988. *ABC: The Alphabetization of the Popular Mind.* San Francisco: North Point Press.

Innis, Harold Adams. 1972. *Empire and Communications.* 2nd ed. Toronto: University of Toronto Press.

Kalman, Judy. 1999. *Writing on the Plaza: Mediated Literacy Practice Among Scribes and Clients in Mexico City.* Cresskill, NJ: Hampton Press.

Keightley, David N. 1978. *Sources of Shang History: The Oracle-Bone Inscriptions of Bronze Age China.* Berkeley: University of California Press.

Lord, Albert B. 1960. *The Singer of Tales.* Cambridge, MA: Harvard University Press.

Lounsbury, F. G. 1989. The Ancient Writing of Middle America. In *The Origins of Writing*, edited by Wayne M. Senner. Lincoln: University of Nebraska Press.

Olsen, David R. 1994. *The World on Paper: The Conceptual and Cognitive Implications of Writing and Reading.* Cambridge and New York: Cambridge University Press.

Omniglot.com. *Writing Systems and Languages of the World.*

Ong, Walter J. 1982. *Orality and Literacy: The Technologizing of the Word.* London and New York: Methuen.

Parry, Milman. 1971. *The Making of Homeric Verse: The Collected Papers of Milman Parry*, edited by Adam Parry. Oxford: Clarendon Press.

Sampson, Geoffrey. 1985. *Writing Systems: A Linguistic Approach.* London: Hutchinson.

Schmandt-Besserat, Denise. 1992. *Before Writing.* Austin: University of Texas Press.

Schmandt-Besserat, Denise. 1996. *How Writing Came About.* Austin: University of Texas Press.

Scribner, Sylvia, and Michael Cole. 1981. *The Psychology of Literacy.* Cambridge, MA: Harvard University Press.

Senner, Wayne M., ed. 1989. *The Origins of Writing.* Lincoln: University of Nebraska Press.

Tannen, Deborah. 1982. *Spoken and Written Language: Exploring Orality and Literacy.* Norwood, NJ: Ablex.

Vygotskii, Lev. 1986. *Thought and Language.* Cambridge, MA: MIT Press.

Wolf, Maryanne. 2007. *Proust and the Squid: The Story and Science of the Reading Brain.* New York: HarperCollins.

# CHAPTER 14

# The Peek-a-Boo World

*Neil Postman*

(1985)

*Neil Postman's* Amusing Ourselves to Death *was a succinct and learned tirade against the modern world, with the apogee in television. He traced historical changes from Guttenberg's Bible and the popularization of print, through the widespread literacy and orality of the early United States, and finally discussed the profound transformation in human experience wrought first by the telegraph, then by photography, and later by television. (The computer had not yet made its way into the heart and soul of our world.) Though telegraph lines have not been entirely removed, and some countries continue to use telegrams as another form of communication, the last Western Union telegram in the United States was sent in 2006, and most experts consider e-mail and other forms of electronic communication to have displaced the telegram.*

*But to understand the world in which television and other media are taken for granted, it is first necessary to point out the revolution that occurred when messages could travel, unaccompanied by humans, to any place connected by the network of wires that had been constructed with so much effort. Prior to the existence of the telegraph, some humans had to physically transport the message, sometimes quickly by horse-and-rider relays (one example is the Pony Express) or by railroad. The conceptual breakthrough of the telegraph should not be underestimated; we are still relying on it conceptually now. Postman does not think this is all beneficial, however. Your first instinct may be to scoff at him as hopelessly romantic, but consider what he is saying. Is something lost by our instant connection to the entire world? What could it be?*

### Reading Questions

- What does Postman mean about telegraphy introducing "context-free information"? Has this increased or decreased, do you think, since he wrote this in the middle 1980s?
- What is the relationship between telegraphy, newspapers, and the elevation of irrelevant information?
- How does Postman compare the way books contain and manage information or ideas to the more rapid dissemination in telegraph-aided newspapers?

Toward the middle years of the nineteenth century, two ideas came together whose convergence provided twentieth-century America with a new metaphor of public discourse. Their partnership overwhelmed the Age of Exposition, and laid the foundation for the Age of Show Business. One of the ideas was quite new, the other as old as the cave paintings of Altamira. We shall come to the old idea presently. The new idea was that transportation and communication could be disengaged from each other, that space was not an inevitable constraint on the movement of information.

Neil Postman, The Peek-a-Boo World. From *Amusing Ourselves to Death: Public Discourse in the Age of Show Business*. New York: Penguin, 1985, pp. 64–80.

Americans of the 1800's were very much concerned with the problem of "conquering" space. By the mid-nineteenth century, the frontier extended to the Pacific Ocean, and a rudimentary railroad system, begun in the 1830's, had started to move people and merchandise across the continent. But until the 1840's, information could move only as fast as a human being could carry it; to be precise, only as fast as a train could travel, which, to be even more precise, meant about thirty-five miles per hour. In the face of such a limitation, the development of America as a national community was retarded. In the 1840's, America was still a composite of regions, each conversing in its own ways, addressing its own interests. A continentwide conversation was not yet possible.

The solution to these problems, as every school child used to know, was electricity. To no one's surprise, it was an American who found a practical way to put electricity in the service of communication and, in doing so, eliminated the problem of space once and for all. I refer, of course, to Samuel Finley Breese Morse, America's first true "spaceman." His telegraph erased state lines, collapsed regions, and, by wrapping the continent in an information grid, created the possibility of a unified American discourse.

But at a considerable cost. For telegraphy did something that Morse did not foresee when he prophesied that telegraphy would make "one neighborhood of the whole country." It destroyed the prevailing definition of information, and in doing so gave a new meaning to public discourse. Among the few who understood this consequence was Henry David Thoreau, who remarked in *Walden* that "We are in great haste to construct a magnetic telegraph from Maine to Texas; but Maine and Texas, it may be, have nothing important to communicate.... We are eager to tunnel under the Atlantic and bring the old world some weeks nearer to the new; but perchance the first news that will leak through into the broad flapping American ear will be that Princess Adelaide has the whooping cough."[1]

Thoreau, as it turned out, was precisely correct. He grasped that the telegraph would create its own definition of discourse; that it would not only permit but insist upon a conversation between Maine and Texas; and that it would require the content of that conversation to be different from what Typographic Man was accustomed to.

The telegraph made a three-pronged attack on typography's definition of discourse, introducing on a large scale irrelevance, impotence, and incoherence. These demons of discourse were aroused by the fact that telegraphy gave a form of legitimacy to the idea of context-free information; that is, to the idea that the value of information need not be tied to any function it might serve in social and political decision-making and action, but may attach merely to its novelty, interest, and curiosity. The telegraph made information into a commodity, a "thing" that could be bought and sold irrespective of its uses or meaning.

But it did not do so alone. The potential of the telegraph to transform information into a commodity might never have been realized, except for the partnership between the telegraph and the press. The penny newspaper, emerging slightly before telegraphy, in the 1830's, had already begun the process of elevating irrelevance to the status of news. Such papers as Benjamin Day's *New York Sun* and James Bennett's *New York Herald* turned away from the tradition of news as reasoned (if biased) political opinion and urgent commercial information and filled their pages with accounts of sensational events, mostly concerning crime and sex. While such "human interest news" played little role in shaping the decisions and actions of readers, it was at least local—about places and people within their experience—and it was not always tied to the moment. The human-interest stories of the penny newspapers had a timeless quality; their power to engage lay not so much in their currency as in their transcendence. Nor did all newspapers occupy themselves with such content. For the most part, the information they provided was not only local but largely functional—tied to the problems and decisions readers had to address in order to manage their personal and community affairs.

The telegraph changed all that, and with astonishing speed. Within months of Morse's first public demonstration, the local and the timeless had lost their central position in newspapers, eclipsed by the dazzle of distance and speed. In fact, the first known use of the telegraph by a newspaper occurred *one day* after Morse gave his historic demonstration of telegraphy's workability. Using the same Washington-to-Baltimore line Morse had constructed, the *Baltimore Patriot* gave its readers information about action taken by the House of Representatives on the Oregon issue. The paper concluded its report by noting: "...we are thus enabled to give our readers information from Washington up to two o'clock. This is indeed the annihilation of space."[2]

For a brief time, practical problems (mostly involving the scarcity of telegraph lines) preserved something of the old definition of news as functional information. But the foresighted among the nation's publishers were quick to see where the future lay, and committed their full resources to the wiring of the continent. William Swain, the owner of the *Philadelphia Public Ledger*, not only invested heavily in the Magnetic Telegraph Company, the first commercial telegraph corporation, but became its president in 1850.

It was not long until the fortunes of newspapers came to depend not on the quality or utility of the news they provided, but on how much, from what distances, and at what speed. James Bennett of the *New York Herald* boasted that in the first week of 1848, his paper contained 79,000 words of telegraphic content[3]—of what relevance to his readers, he didn't say. Only four years after Morse opened the nation's first telegraph line on May 24, 1844, the Associated Press was founded, and news from nowhere, addressed to no one in particular, began to crisscross the nation. Wars, crimes, crashes, fires, floods—much of it the social and political equivalent of Adelaide's whooping cough—became the content of what people called "the news of the day."

As Thoreau implied, telegraphy made relevance irrelevant. The abundant flow of information had very little or nothing to do with those to whom it was addressed; that is, with any social or intellectual context in which their lives were embedded. Coleridge's famous line about water everywhere without a drop to drink may serve as a metaphor of a decontextualized information environment: In a sea of information, there was very little of it to use. A man in Maine and a man in Texas could converse, but not about anything either of them knew or cared very much about. The telegraph may have made the country into "one neighborhood," but it was a peculiar one, populated by strangers who knew nothing but the most superficial facts about each other.

Since we live today in just such a neighborhood (now sometimes called a "global village"), you may get a sense of what is meant by context-free information by asking yourself the following question: How often does it occur that information provided you on morning radio or television, or in the morning newspaper, causes you to alter your plans for the day, or to take some action you would not otherwise have taken, or provides insight into some problem you are required to solve? For most of us, news of the weather will sometimes have such consequences; for investors, news of the stock market; perhaps an occasional story about a crime will do it, if by chance the crime occurred near where you live or involved someone you know. But most of our daily news is inert, consisting of information that gives us something to talk about but cannot lead to any meaningful action. This fact is the principal legacy of the telegraph: By generating an abundance of irrelevant information, it dramatically altered what may be called the "information-action ratio."

In both oral and typographic cultures, information derives its importance from the possibilities of action. Of course, in any communication environment, input (what one is informed about) always exceeds output (the possibilities of action based on information). But the situation created by telegraphy, and then exacerbated by later technologies, made the relationship between information and action both abstract and remote. For the first time in human history, people were faced with the problem of information glut, which means that simultaneously they were faced with the problem of a diminished social and political potency.

You may get a sense of what this means by asking yourself another series of questions: What steps do you plan to take to reduce the conflict in the Middle East? Or the rates of inflation, crime and unemployment? What are your plans for preserving the environment or reducing the risk of nuclear war? What do you plan to do about NATO, OPEC, the CIA, affirmative action, and the monstrous treatment of the Baha'is in Iran? I shall take the liberty of answering for you: You plan to do nothing about them. You may, of course, cast a ballot for someone who claims to have some plans, as well as the power to act. But this you can do only once every two or four years by giving one hour of your time, hardly a satisfying means of expressing the broad range of opinions you hold. Voting, we might even say, is the next to last refuge of the politically impotent. The last refuge is, of course, giving your opinion to a pollster, who will get a version of it through a desiccated question, and then will submerge it in a Niagara of similar opinions, and convert them into—what else?—another piece of news. Thus, we have here a great loop of impotence: The news elicits from you a variety of opinions about which you can do nothing except to offer them as more news, about which you can do nothing.

Prior to the age of telegraphy, the information-action ratio was sufficiently close so that most people had a sense of being able to control some of the contingencies in their lives. What people knew about had action-value. In the information world created by telegraphy, this sense of potency was lost, precisely because the whole world became the context for news. Everything became everyone's business. For the first time, we were sent information which answered no question we had asked, and which, in any case, did not permit the right of reply.

We may say then that the contribution of the telegraph to public discourse was to dignify irrelevance and amplify impotence. But this was not all: Telegraphy also made public discourse essentially incoherent. It brought into being a world of broken time and broken attention, to use Lewis Mumford's phrase. The principal strength of the telegraph was its capacity to move information, not collect it, explain it or analyze it. In this respect, telegraphy was the exact opposite of typography. Books, for example, are an excellent container for the accumulation, quiet scrutiny and organized analysis of information and ideas. It takes time to write a book, and to read one; time to discuss its contents and to make judgments about their merit, including the form of their presentation. A book is an attempt to make thought permanent and to contribute to the great conversation conducted by authors of the past. Therefore, civilized people everywhere consider the burning of a book a vile form of anti-intellectualism. *But the telegraph demands that we burn its contents.* The value of telegraphy is undermined by applying the tests of permanence, continuity or coherence. The telegraph is suited only to the flashing of messages, each to be quickly replaced by a more up-to-date message. Facts push other facts into and then out of consciousness at speeds that neither permit nor require evaluation.

The telegraph introduced a kind of public conversation whose form had startling characteristics: Its language was the language of headlines—sensational, fragmented, impersonal. News took the form of slogans, to be noted with excitement, to be forgotten with dispatch. Its language was also entirely discontinuous. One message had no connection to that which preceded or followed it. Each "headline" stood alone as its own context. The receiver of the news had to provide a meaning if he could. The sender was under no obligation to do so. And because of all this, the world as depicted by the telegraph began to appear unmanageable, even undecipherable. The line-by-line, sequential, continuous form of the printed page slowly began to lose its resonance as a metaphor of how knowledge was to be acquired and how the world was to be understood. "Knowing" the facts took on a new meaning, for it did not imply that one understood implications, background, or connections. Telegraphic discourse permitted no time for historical perspectives and gave no priority to the qualitative. To the telegraph, intelligence meant knowing *of* lots of things, not knowing *about* them.

Thus, to the reverent question posed by Morse—What hath God wrought?—a disturbing answer came back: a neighborhood of strangers and pointless quantity; a world of fragments and discontinuities. God, of course, had nothing to do with it. And yet, for all of the power of the telegraph, had it stood alone as a new metaphor for discourse, it is likely that print culture would have withstood its assault; would, at least, have held its ground. As it happened, at almost exactly the same time Morse was reconceiving the meaning of information, Louis Daguerre was reconceiving the meaning of nature; one might even say, of reality itself. As Daguerre remarked in 1838 in a notice designed to attract investors, "The daguerreotype is not merely an instrument which serves to draw nature... [it] gives her the power to reproduce herself."[4]

Of course both the need and the power to draw nature have always implied reproducing nature, refashioning it to make it comprehensible and manageable. The earliest cave paintings were quite possibly visual projections of a hunt that had not yet taken place, wish fulfillments of an anticipated subjection of nature. Reproducing nature, in other words, is a very old idea. But Daguerre did not have this meaning of "reproduce" in mind. He meant to announce that the photograph would invest everyone with the power to duplicate nature as often and wherever one liked. He meant to say he had invented the world's first "cloning" device, that the photograph was to visual experience what the printing press was to the written word.

In point of fact, the daguerreotype was not quite capable of achieving such an equation. It was not until William Henry Fox Talbot, an English mathematician and linguist, invented the process of preparing a negative from which any number of positives could be made that the mass printing and publication of photographs became possible.[5] The name "photography" was given to this process by the famous astronomer Sir John F. W. Herschel. It is an odd name since it literally means "writing with light." Perhaps Herschel meant the name to be taken ironically, since it must have been clear from the beginning that photography and writing (in fact, language in any form) do not inhabit the same universe of discourse.

Nonetheless, ever since the process was named it has been the custom to speak of photography as a "language." The metaphor is risky because it tends to obscure the fundamental differences between the two modes of conversation. To begin with, photography is a language that speaks only in particularities. Its vocabulary of images is limited to concrete representation. Unlike words and sentences, the photograph does not present to us an idea or concept about the world, except as we use language itself to convert the image to idea. By itself, a photograph cannot deal with the unseen, the remote, the internal, the abstract. It does not speak of "man," only of *a* man; not of "tree," only of *a* tree. You cannot produce a photograph of "nature," any more than a photograph of "the sea." You can only photograph a particular fragment of the here-and-now—a cliff of a certain terrain, in a certain condition of light; a wave at a moment in time, from a particular point of view. And just as "nature" and "the sea" cannot be photographed, such larger abstractions as truth, honor, love, falsehood cannot be talked about in the lexicon of pictures. For "showing of" and "talking about" are two very different kinds of processes. "Pictures," Gavriel Salomon has written, "need to be recognized, words need to be understood."[6] By this he means that the photograph presents the world as object; language, the world as idea. For even the simplest act of naming a thing is an act of thinking—of comparing one thing with others, selecting certain features in common, ignoring what is different, and making an imaginary category. There is no such thing in nature as "man" or "tree." The universe offers no such categories or simplifications; only flux and infinite variety. The photograph documents and celebrates the particularities of this infinite variety. Language makes them comprehensible.

The photograph also lacks a syntax, which deprives it of a capacity to argue with the world. As an "objective" slice of space-time, the photograph testifies that someone was there or something happened. Its testimony is powerful but it offers no opinions—no "should-have-beens" or "might-have-beens." Photography is preeminently a world of fact, not of dispute about facts or of conclusions to be drawn from them. But this is not to say photography lacks an epistemological bias. As Susan Sontag has observed, a photograph implies "that we know about the world if we accept it as the camera records it."[7] But, as she further observes, all understanding begins with our *not* accepting the world as it appears. Language, of course, is the medium we use to challenge, dispute, and cross-examine what comes into view, what is on the surface. The words "true" and "false" come from the universe of language, and no other. When applied to a photograph, the question, Is it true? means only, Is this a reproduction of a real slice of space-time? If the answer is "Yes," there are no grounds for argument, for it makes no sense to disagree with an unfaked photograph. The photograph itself makes no arguable propositions, makes no extended and unambiguous commentary. It offers no assertions to refute, so it is not refutable.

The way in which the photograph records experience is also different from the way of language. Language makes sense only when it is presented as a sequence of propositions. Meaning is distorted when a word or sentence is, as we say, taken out of context; when a reader or listener is deprived of what was said before, and after. But there is no such thing as a photograph taken out of context, for a photograph does not require one. In fact, the point of photography is to isolate images from context, so as to make them visible in a different way. In a world of photographic images, Ms. Sontag writes, "all borders... seem arbitrary. Anything can be separated, can be made discontinuous, from anything else: All that is necessary is to frame the subject differently."[8] She is remarking on the capacity of photographs to perform a peculiar kind of dismembering of reality, a wrenching of moments out of their contexts, and a juxtaposing of events and things that have no logical or historical connection with each other. Like telegraphy, photography recreates the world as a series of idiosyncratic events. There is no beginning, middle, or end in a world of photographs, as there is none implied by telegraphy. The world is atomized. There is only a present and it need not be part of any story that can be told.

That the image and the word have different functions, work at different levels of abstraction, and require different modes of response will not come as a new idea to anyone. Painting is at least three times as old as writing, and the place of imagery in the repertoire of communication instruments was quite well understood in the nineteenth century. What was new in the mid-nineteenth century was the sudden and massive intrusion of the photograph and other iconographs into the symbolic environment. This event is what Daniel Boorstin in his pioneering book *The Image* calls "the graphic revolution." By this phrase, Boorstin means to call attention to the fierce assault on language made by forms of mechanically reproduced imagery that spread unchecked throughout American culture—photographs, prints, posters, drawings, advertisements. I choose the word "assault" deliberately here, to amplify the point implied in Boorstin's "graphic *revolution*." The new imagery, with photography at its forefront, did not merely function as a supplement to language, but bid to replace it as our dominant means for construing, understanding, and testing reality. What Boorstin implies about the graphic revolution, I wish to make explicit here: The new focus on the image undermined traditional definitions of information, of news, and, to a large extent, of reality itself. First in billboards, posters, and advertisements, and later in such "news" magazines and papers as *Life, Look*, the New York *Daily Mirror* and *Daily News*, the picture forced exposition into the background, and in some instances obliterated it altogether. By the end of the nineteenth century, advertisers and newspapermen had discovered that a picture was not only worth a thousand words, but, where sales were concerned, was better. For countless Americans, seeing, not reading, became the basis for believing.

In a peculiar way, the photograph was the perfect complement to the flood of telegraphic news-from-nowhere that threatened to submerge readers in a sea of facts from unknown places about strangers with unknown faces. For the photograph gave a concrete reality to the strange-sounding datelines, and attached faces to the unknown names. Thus it provided the illusion, at least, that "the news" had a connection to something within one's sensory experience. It created an apparent context for the "news of the day." And the "news of the day" created a context for the photograph.

But the sense of context created by the partnership of photograph and headline was, of course, entirely illusory. You may get a better sense of what I mean here if you imagine a stranger's informing you that the illyx is a subspecies of vermiform plant with articulated leaves that flowers biannually on the island of Aldononjes. And if you wonder aloud, "Yes, but what has that to do with anything?" imagine that your informant replies, "But here is a photograph I want you to see," and hands you a picture labeled *Illyx on Aldononjes*. "Ah, yes," you might murmur, "now I see." It is true enough that the photograph provides a context for the sentence you have been given, and that the sentence provides a context of sorts for the photograph, and you may even believe for a day or so that you have learned something. But if the event is entirely self-contained, devoid of any relationship to your past knowledge or future plans, if that is the beginning and end of your encounter with the stranger, then the appearance of context provided by the conjunction of sentence and image is illusory, and so is the impression of meaning attached to it. You will, in fact, have "learned" nothing (except perhaps to avoid strangers with photographs), and the illyx will fade from your mental landscape as though it had never been. At best you are left with an amusing bit of trivia, good for trading in cocktail party chatter or solving a crossword puzzle, but nothing more.

It may be of some interest to note, in this connection, that the crossword puzzle became a popular form of diversion in America at just that point when the telegraph and the photograph had achieved the transformation of news from functional information to decontextualized fact. This coincidence suggests that the new technologies had turned the age-old problem of information on its head: Where people once sought information to manage the real contexts of their lives, now they had to invent contexts in which otherwise useless information might be put to some apparent use. The crossword puzzle is one such pseudo-context; the cocktail party is another; the radio quiz shows of the 1930's and 1940's and the modern television game show are still others; and the ultimate, perhaps, is the wildly successful "Trivial Pursuit." In one form or another, each of these supplies an answer to the question, "What am I to do with all these disconnected facts?" And in one form or another, the answer is the same: Why not use them for diversion? for entertainment? to amuse yourself, in a game? In *The Image*, Boorstin calls the major creation of the graphic revolution the "pseudo-event," by which he means an event specifically staged to be reported—like the press conference, say. I mean to suggest here that a more significant legacy of the telegraph and the photograph may be the pseudo-*context*. A pseudo-context is a structure invented to give fragmented and irrelevant information a seeming use. But the use the pseudo-context provides is not action, or problem-solving, or change. It is the only use left for information with no genuine connection to our lives. And that, of course, is to amuse. The pseudo-context is the last refuge, so to say, of a culture overwhelmed by irrelevance, incoherence, and impotence.

Of course, photography and telegraphy did not strike down at one blow the vast edifice that was typographic culture. The habits of exposition, as I have tried to show, had a long history, and they held powerful sway over the minds of turn-of-the-century Americans. In fact, the early decades of the twentieth century were marked by a great outpouring of brilliant language and literature. In the pages of magazines like the *American Mercury* and *The New Yorker*, in the novels and stories of Faulkner, Fitzgerald, Steinbeck, and Hemingway, and even in the columns of the newspaper giants—the *Herald Tribune*, the *Times*—prose thrilled with a vibrancy and intensity that delighted ear and eye. But this was exposition's nightingale song, most brilliant and sweet as the singer nears the moment of death. It told, for the Age of Exposition, not of new beginnings, but of an end. Beneath its dying melody, a new note had been sounded, and photography and telegraphy set the key. Theirs was a "language" that denied interconnectedness, proceeded without context, argued the irrelevance of history, explained nothing, and offered fascination in place of complexity and coherence. Theirs was a duet of image and instancy, and together they played the tune of a new kind of public discourse in America.

Each of the media that entered the electronic conversation in the late nineteenth and early twentieth centuries followed the lead of the telegraph and the photograph, and amplified their biases. Some, such as film, were by their nature inclined to do so. Others, whose bias was rather toward the amplification of rational speech—like radio—were overwhelmed by the thrust of the new epistemology and came in the end to support it. Together, this ensemble of electronic techniques called into being a new world—a peek-a-boo world, where now this event, now that, pops into view for a moment, then vanishes again. It is a world without much coherence or sense; a world that does not ask us, indeed, does not permit us to do anything; a world that is, like the child's game of peek-a-boo, entirely self-contained. But like peek-a-boo, it is also endlessly entertaining.

Of course, there is nothing wrong with playing peek-a-boo. And there is nothing wrong with entertainment. As some psychiatrist once put it, we all build castles in the air. The problems come when we try to *live* in them. The communications media of the late nineteenth and early twentieth centuries, with telegraphy and photography at their center, called the peek-a-boo world into existence, but we did not come to live there until television. Television gave the epistemological biases of the telegraph and the photograph their most potent expression, raising the interplay of image and instancy to an exquisite and dangerous perfection. And it brought them into the home. We are by now well into a second generation of children for whom television has been their first and most accessible teacher and, for many, their most reliable companion and friend. To put it plainly, television is the command center of the new epistemology. There is no audience so young that it is barred from television. There is no poverty so abject that it must forgo television. There is no education so exalted that it is not modified by television. And most important of all, there is no subject of public interest—politics, news, education, religion, science, sports—that does not find its way to television. Which means that all public understanding of these subjects is shaped by the biases of television.

Television is the command center in subtler ways as well. Our use of other media, for example, is largely orchestrated by television. Through it we learn what telephone system to use, what movies to see, what books, records and magazines to buy, what radio programs to listen to. Television arranges our communications environment for us in ways that no other medium has the power to do.

As a small, ironic example of this point, consider this: In the past few years, we have been learning that the computer is the technology of the future. We are told that our children will fail in school and be left behind in life if they are not "computer literate." We are told that we cannot run our businesses, or compile our shopping lists, or keep our checkbooks tidy unless we own a computer. Perhaps some of this is true. But the most important fact about computers and what they mean to our lives is that we learn about all of this from television. Television has achieved the status of "meta-medium"—an instrument that directs not only our knowledge of the world, but our knowledge of *ways of knowing* as well.

At the same time, television has achieved the status of "myth," as Roland Barthes uses the word. He means by myth a way of understanding the world that is not problematic, that we are not fully conscious of, that seems, in a word, natural. A myth is a way of thinking so deeply embedded in our consciousness that it is invisible. This is now the way of television. We are no longer fascinated or perplexed by its machinery. We do not tell stories of its wonders. We do not confine our television sets to special rooms. We do not doubt the reality of what we see on television, are largely unaware of the special angle of vision it affords. Even the question of how television affects us has receded into the background. The question itself may strike some of us as strange, as if one were to ask how having ears and eyes affects us. Twenty years ago, the question, Does television shape culture or merely reflect it? held considerable interest for many scholars and social critics. The question has largely disappeared as television has gradually *become* our culture. This means, among other things, that we rarely talk about television, only about what is *on* television—that is, about its content. Its ecology, which includes not only its physical characteristics and symbolic code but the conditions in which we normally attend to it, is taken for granted, accepted as natural.

Television has become, so to speak, the background radiation of the social and intellectual universe, the all-but-imperceptible residue of the electronic big bang of a century past, so familiar and so thoroughly integrated with American culture that we no longer hear its faint hissing in the background or see the flickering gray light. This, in turn, means that its epistemology goes largely unnoticed. And the peek-a-boo world it has constructed around us no longer seems even strange.

There is no more disturbing consequence of the electronic and graphic revolution than this: that the world as given to us through television seems natural, not bizarre. For the loss of the sense of the strange is a sign of adjustment, and the extent to which we have adjusted is a measure of the extent to which we have been changed. Our culture's adjustment to the epistemology of television is by now all but complete; we have so thoroughly accepted its definitions of truth, knowledge, and reality that irrelevance seems to us to be filled with import, and incoherence seems eminently sane. And if some of our institutions seem not to fit the template of the times, why it is they, and not the template, that seem to us disordered and strange.

It is my object in [*Amusing Ourselves to Death*] to make the epistemology of television visible again. [There] I...try to demonstrate by concrete example that television's way of knowing is uncompromisingly hostile to typography's way of knowing; that television's conversations promote incoherence and triviality; that the phrase "serious television" is a contradiction in terms; and that television speaks in only one persistent voice—the voice of entertainment. Beyond that, I...try to demonstrate that to enter the great television conversation, one American cultural institution after another is learning to speak its terms. Television, in other words, is transforming our culture into one vast arena for show business. It is entirely possible, of course, that in the end we shall find that delightful, and decide we like it just fine. That is exactly what Aldous Huxley feared was coming, fifty years ago.

## Notes

1. Thoreau, p. 36.
2. Harlow, p. 100.
3. Czitrom, pp. 15–16.
4. Sontag, p. 165.
5. Newhall, p. 33.
6. Salomon, p. 36.
7. Sontag, p. 20.
8. Sontag, p. 20.

## References

Czitrom, Daniel. *Media and the American Mind: From Morse to McLuhan*. Chapel Hill: University of North Carolina Press, 1982.

Harlow, Alvin Fay. *Old Wires and New Waves: The History of the Telegraph, Telephone and Wireless*. New York: Appleton-Century, 1936.

Newhall, Beaumont. *The History of Photography from 1839 to the Present Day*. New York: Museum of Modern Art, 1964.

Salomon, Gavriel. *Interaction of Media, Cognition and Learning*. San Francisco: Jossey-Bass, 1979.

Sontag, Susan. *On Photography*. New York: Farrar, Straus and Giroux, 1977.

Thoreau, Henry David. *Walden*. Riverside Editions. Boston: Houghton Mifflin, 1957.

## Critical Thinking and Application

- Postman charges photography and the proliferation of images with an array of wrongs. Discuss their negative consequences in Postman's view and weigh this argument. What media are positive in their effects and why?
- What is the basis of Postman's critique of the "peek-a-boo world"? Does it apply more or less to the world in the twenty-first century? What does he wish for?
- Collect an assortment of critiques of modern technologies. On what basis do they claim negative consequences? What would the benefits be of each medium?

## Suggested Further Reading

Berger, Arthur Asa. 2005. *Making Sense of Media: Key Texts in Media and Cultural Studies*. Malden, MA: Blackwell.

Berger, Arthur Asa. 2007. *Media and Society: A Critical Perspective*. 2nd ed. Lanham, MD: Rowman & Littlefield.

Briggs, Asa, and Peter Burke. 2009. *A Social History of the Media: From Gutenberg to the Internet*. 3rd ed. Cambridge and Malden, MA: Polity.

Burns, Eric. 2010. *Invasion of the Mind Snatchers: Television's Conquest of America in the Fifties*. Philadelphia: Temple University Press.

Crowley, David, and Paul Heyer, eds. 2007. *Communication in History: Technology, Culture, Society*. 5th ed. Boston: Pearson.

Edgerton, Gary R. 2007. *The Columbia History of American Television*. New York: Columbia University Press.

Gabler, Neal. 1998. *Life the Movie: How Entertainment Conquered Reality*. New York: Knopf.

Grant, August E., and Jennifer H. Meadows, eds. 2008. *Communication Technology Update and Fundamentals*. 11th ed. Amsterdam and Boston: Elsevier.

Mander, Jerry. 1978. *Four Arguments for the Elimination of Television*. New York: Morrow.

Mankiewicz, Frank, and Joel L. Swerdlow. 1978. *Remote Control: Television and the Manipulation of American Life*. New York: Times.

McLuhan, Marshall. 1964. *Understanding Media: The Extensions of Man*. New York: McGraw-Hill.

Postman, Neil. 1985. *Amusing Ourselves to Death: Public Discourse in the Age of Show Business*. New York: Penguin.

Sontag, Susan. 1977. *On Photography*. New York: Farrar, Straus & Giroux.

Spigel, Lynn. 2001. *Welcome to the Dreamhouse: Popular Media and Postwar Suburbs*. Durham, NC: Duke University Press.

# CHAPTER 15

# The Quest for Authentic Connection

*John Durham Peters*

(1999)

*Communication always involves connecting one or more people with one or more others. Yet as Peters points out, the fact that other selves differ from us is both tragic and wonderful.*

*As each of the new media that are so familiar to us was introduced, critics and partisans alike expected enormous social transformation. As the telegraph had been revolutionary in permitting communication without physical contact (see Chapter 14), so the telephone was revolutionary; people could be summoned in their own houses and obliged to interact. The radio broadcast its words to all, whether they wished to receive them or not. Here we learn about the origins of the Federal Communications Commission (FCC) and the early discussions about what constituted a "common carrier" and many more facts. But beyond the historical details is a profound question of what all this means for us as human beings.*

*This chapter comes from a remarkable book called* Speaking into the Air, *in which John Durham Peters, a professor of communication studies at the University of Iowa, ruminates through history, literature, psychology, and communications about the effects and meanings of various forms of communication. His insight regarding the erotic dimension of communication—a yearning for contact—may help explain why people sleep with their cell phones: we crave contact, yet often remain ever unsatisfied, thus constantly seeking contact. Can "'communication' without bodies or presence" be genuine? How do we achieve authentic communion with others? How do we know when the others are sincere if we can't see or touch them? How, ultimately, do we navigate the risks in our disembodied world? Peters writes*

> *Communication is ultimately unthinkable apart from the task of establishing a peaceable kingdom in which each may dwell with the other. Given our condition as mortals, communication will always remain a problem of power, ethics, and art. Short of some redeemed state of angels or porpoises, there is no release from the discipline of the object in our mutual dealings. This fact is not something to lament: it is the beginning of wisdom. To treat others as we would want to be treated means performing for them in such a way not that the self is authentically represented but that the other is caringly served. This kind of connection beats anything the angels may offer. Joy is found not in the surpassing of touch but in its fullness.*

*As humans—not angels, not other animals—we must work hard to contact others, knowing it will remain imperfect, no matter what the device or medium used. But this is our great possibility.*

## Reading Questions

- What is the meaning of "broadcast"? What is new about broadcast media?
- How do radio and telephone intrude into people's domestic and private lives?
- Compare one-to-many, many-to-one, and point-to-point communication. Who initiates each interaction? Who has the option to accept or refuse interaction? What are the goals of each interaction? How does commerce intersect with the meaning and effect of such communicative interactions?

---

John Durham Peters, The Quest for Authentic Connection. From *Speaking into the Air: A History of the Idea of Communication*. Chicago: University of Chicago Press, 1999, pp. 195–225.

The telephone, after fits and starts, has solidified its use as a means of staying in personal touch with individuals who are not immediately at hand, while wireless technologies (radio and television) have largely gone in the opposite direction of having a diffuse and general addressee. In principle, both telephone and wireless technologies can be either a central exchange for many voices (party lines or radio broadcasting) or a means of point-to-point contact (cellular phones or ham radio). The issue is not so much the inherent properties of the medium as the social constellation of speakers and hearers that became enforced as normative. Radio became the carrier of messages aimed for low-resolution address, and the telephone, of those for high-resolution.

In the dawn of telephone systems, the personal touch was omnipresent. Every call was placed with the aid of a human operator, and up to the 1880s there were no telephone *numbers:* operators simply used the names of subscribers to track the slots on the switchboard. It took the Bell system several years, in fact, to persuade all its customers to switch to numbers. Even then many local exchanges had prefixes based on a sense of local geography—Pennsylvania 6–5000, for example. Even so, the idea of confidential conversation heard only by two people was slow in coming, just as it was in the mails. One technical problem resolved early was how to get only one specific telephone in a networked system to ring, for all would ring when one was called. The telephone, like all media of multiplication (transmission and recording), was essentially a public medium. Just as Warren and Brandeis in the 1890s sought to establish a right to privacy and the anonymously posted letter arose in the 1850s, telephone managers in the 1890s and early 1900s sought to secure private channels of contact between unique addresses.[1] The task again was to domesticate the plurality of media by the singularity of "communication."

Before automated switching, the routine medium of routing telephone calls was the switchboard operator. We have met this figure before—passive, neutral or feminine gender identity, servicing an apparatus of message delivery—in the spiritualist medium and in Bartleby the scrivener. An Ontario newspaper in the 1890s reported on operators: "The girls then, are automata. . . . They looked as cold and passionless as icebergs," and an early training manual prescribed that each "operator must now be made as nearly as possible a paragon of perfection, a kind of human machine, the exponent of speed and courtesy; a creature spirited enough to move like chain lightning, and with perfect accuracy; docile enough to deny herself the privilege of the last word."[2] These descriptions have the virtue, at least, of explicitness: the operator's body—her voice, gestures and fatigue—was, like that of typists as well, a key site of psychotechnical discipline.[3] The telephone operator antedates the **cyborg**, a plastically gendered creature formed of electrical wiring and the organic body.[4] Like spiritualist mediums, operators inhabit a profoundly liminal space. The female body hidden at the heart of a national communications network, appearing only in impersonal voice, is an archetypal figure. In popular culture the operator was often treated as a heroine who, knowing everyone's habits, could bring people together in emergencies: the operator as matchmaker, lifeguard, or angel of mercy. She was always betwixt and between.[5]

Like Diotima's **Eros**, operators had the job of managing the gaps and ferrying messages back and forth across the chasm. Indeed, there was something sexy about operators, with their voices traveling across the expanses. As an American manager wrote in 1905, "There is something about the sound of the voice of a girl on the wire that sets a young man into a wooing mood."[6] The telephone itself has been sung and lamented as an agent of romantic coupling and haunting, being a classic go-between for lovers. Marriages were performed over the telephone, as over the radio, an obligatory coming-of-age event for each new medium of distance communication.[7] The arrows of Eros and of electrical circuit diagrams here converge. Note too that the couplet—public radio, private telephone—has made the notion of a radio-sex industry sound laughable, but with 900 numbers there is, alas, a thriving phone-sex business.

Once the switchboard connection was made, there were still address gaps. Without access to the bodily presence of the other, initial interaction on the telephone dramatized the likelihood that one did not know whom one was addressing. In face-to-face interaction we usually know whom we are speaking to, save in cases of imposture or more difficult philosophical questions of identity. Negotiations of identity became routine in telephone etiquette. When my second son was younger, he would call a friend's house and speak to whoever answered as if that person were his friend and knew who was calling. He hadn't yet learned to identify himself or the interlocutor, failing to recognize the need for connection management in a medium that cloaks presence. Different styles of decorum arose to manage the missing persons over the telephone. In the Netherlands, telephone speakers are expected to identify themselves at once: those answering must answer with their names, and the callers must do so as well. In the United States norms of self-identification are far more relaxed, and some callers never bother to identify themselves at all, assuming their voice is recognized. In habitual face-to-face interaction, such work at initial coupling is always implicit; thanks to the media-stimulated dream of wondrous contact, we have grown accustomed in the twentieth century to finding such problems everywhere in communication.

In early telephone culture modes of interaction were sought that dispensed with the need for cues of presence.[8] The telephone could be both a handicap (in its blindness) and a sensory extension (a hearing aid and voice amplification device). A 1915 piece states the telephone's deficiencies with remarkable economy: "Conversation by telephone is talk shorn of all the adventitious aids that spring from the fact of physical and visual proximity." The undifferentiated totality of the face-to-face setting is redescribed according to the new audiovisual order of silent cinema and pictureless telephones. "There is no flashing glance to 'register,' as the movie actors have it, wrath; no curling lip to betoken scorn; no twinkling eye to suggest whimsicality; none of the charm of personal presence that might give substance to an attenuated argument or power to a feeble retort. The voice must do it all."[9]

The telephone could be strange indeed. In it, the face-to-face setting could be redefined as a communication problem, with its "adventitious aids" of "physical and visual proximity" that had never before been distinct channels. The historian Catherine Covert argued that the telephone served cultural critics as an ordinary baseline against which to measure the weirdness of radio in the years after the Great War. In contrast to the supernatural world of radio was "the quite worldly experience of Americans with the telephone—as a direct connection between human beings."[10] In fact, the telephone evoked many of the same anxieties as radio: strange voices entering the home, forced encounters, the disappearance of one's words into an empty black hole, and absent faces of the listeners. An *Atlantic Monthly* piece from 1920, written in the voice of a neurasthenic woman, notes: "It is bad to hear myself talk on any occasion. It is worse to talk into an empty black hole, without the comfort and guide of a responsive face before me." The telephone's lack of manners also irks her. "It makes no preambles and respects no privacies," rings without regard to how occupied one may be in other tasks, and pulls one into "unexplained encounters" with strangers.[11] Our writer notes the classic features of dissemination; Socrates too was worried about odd encounters and indifference to the personal situation.

The looseness of personal identification lies at the core of the telephone's eeriness. Even today, there is nothing quite so unnerving as a caller who repeatedly calls and hangs up or who never identifies himself (it is usually a he) and simply breathes into the phone. Such violations of etiquette call forth the primal uncanniness of the medium. Taking "obscene" in the original sense of something appearing that is supposed to be concealed (off-scene), the notion of an obscene phone call is a redundancy. In ways that foreshadow recent concerns about how loosened markers of personal identity allow abusive discourse in cyberspace, such as the tirades known as "flames," commentators attributed telephone rudeness to the loss of instantaneous recognition in the face-to-face setting.[12] In the words of one 1918 writer, "There are men who, as someone has put it, take advantage of their 'low visibility' over the telephone to act as they never would if face to face with you."[13] The relative anonymity of the Internet, it is similarly argued, allows people to get away with vituperative modes of discourse they would never dare in person.

The telephone also contributed to the modern derangement of dialogue by splitting conversation into two halves that meet only in the cyberspace of the wires. Dialogue, despite its reputation for closeness and immediacy, occurs over the telephone in a no-man's-land as elusive as writing itself. The effect of such flayed discourse has been compared to schizophrenia and to crosscutting in film editing.[14] Mark Twain caught both schizoid and comic dimensions in his satire "A Telephonic Conversation":

> Then followed that queerest of all the queer things in this world—a conversation with only one end to it. You hear questions asked; you don't hear the answer. You hear invitations given; you hear no thanks in return. You have listening pauses of dead silence, followed by irrelevant or unjustifiable exclamations of glad surprise or sorrow or dismay. You can't make head or tail of the talk, because you never hear anything that the person at the other end of the wire says.

The piece then offers an account of one such "conversation," a premise for Twain to indulge in a series of droll nonsequiturs, such as:

> Pause.
>
> It's forty-ninth Deuteronomy, sixty-fourth to ninety-seventh inclusive. I think we ought all to read it often.
>
> Pause.
>
> Perhaps so; I generally use a hair-pin.[15]

The subtext of the story, corroborating other comments of the period, is the contrast between masculine gruffness and abruptness on the phone and feminine talkativeness; it is the male narrator, for instance, who is asked to ring the central office for a female member of his household.

Two one-sided conversations that couple only in virtual space: this is the nature of speech on the telephone. Naturally, the question arises whether such coupling ever occurs. In Dorothy Parker's early 1930s monologue, "A Telephone Call," a woman pleads frenziedly with God to have a man friend call, but in the course of the monologue he does not; the title of the story names what never takes place. Waiting for a call that never comes exemplifies not only the loneliness of the neglected lover but the whole problem of how to know that one has made contact at all; it is not by accident that the monologue is addressed to God. Parker gives us a neat communication circuit: she places a call that seeks as its answer another call. The voice of desire seeks another voice of desire. Aldous Huxley's "Over the Telephone" from the same era reverses the gender of the supplicant: a young poet mentally rehearses his grandiloquent invitation to a woman friend to attend the opera, imaginatively taking the entire evening to its happy conclusion as the lovers kiss in his flat. When after many mishaps the operator finally makes the connection with the woman, however, he stumbles hopelessly and she declines owing to a previous engagement: "Despairingly, Walter took the receiver from his ear. The voice squeaked away impotently into the air like the ghost of a Punch and Judy show." The breach in telephonic communication, like that of the planned date, is marked as an erotic failure, squeaking impotently into the air.[16] Such an attempt at "communication" is at best a situation of hermeneutic rupture, two sides barred from each other by some deep distance.

**Kafka and the Telephone** The spookiest of all explorers of the telephone, and of "communication" as two monologues that may never connect, even in imagined space, was Franz

Kafka. All **hermeneutics** is the art of reading texts by an unintended audience; it is a mode of eavesdropping. Facing the dead, or a partner who cannot, will not, or does not respond, can leave one in a tizzy of guesswork. Mediated communication, as by the telephone, teaches us that we are always eavesdropping. How is the voice of Parker's monologue to know what the lack of a call signifies—rejection, a lost number, or nothing at all? All that separates desolation from elation is a phone call. The exploding of dialogue into two remotely linked halves makes the validity of interpretation obscure. The inability to distinguish inner projections from outer messages flourishes in conditions where interpreters have to bear the weight of the entire communication circuit. This inability, psychologically conceived, is called paranoia; socially conceived, we should call it mass communication. Those who have ears to hear will hear. Kafka is our guide to these conditions.

In a short parable called "The Neighbor," Kafka extends the idealist architecture by making the walls too thin rather than too thick.[17] The narrator, a young businessman, tells how an identical office adjacent his own is rented by another young businessman named Harras, whose business is mysterious but seems the same as his own. The two never meet, only brush past each other on the stairs. Their only relations are mediated and imagined; they never actually converse with each other. The walls are so miserably thin, however, that everything can be heard in the neighboring office. Even worse, on the common wall of the two offices, the narrator has a telephone; even if it were placed on the opposite wall, Harras could still hear everything. Ever unsure whether the neighbor is listening, the narrator adopts a roundabout style of speech in his dealings over the phone and studiously never mentions the names of customers. Yet he is sure he is still betraying secrets. "If I really wanted to exaggerate—as people often do, to make things clearer to themselves—I could say: Harras needs no telephone, he uses mine."

Harras is no wiretapper. This is a story of a doppelgänger and a telephone, both of which involve enigmatic splittings of identity and conversation. Harras (as the narrator surmises) eavesdrops on the ghosts that proliferate in the space between the two termini of the telephone conversation. Thus he is able to outsmart the narrator: by figuring out who and where the person on the other end of the line is. Harras speeds through the city and meets the customer before the narrator is even off the phone, working against him (or so fantasizes the narrator). In a new twist on telephone harras-ment, Harras uses the telephone not simply to breathe or threaten, but to transport his person as fleetly as electrical speech. The parable is not only a meditation on surveillance and the futility of coded speech to conceal secrets, but a fantasy on the comparative advantage of presence. Kafka catches the horror of speaking on the phone when one's double—the proxy of the voice—goes streaking through the wires to appear in the presence of the telephone partner. Anyone who has ever used a phone to discuss a sensitive matter knows how your double can arrive on the other end and work against you. The narrator's paranoia—literally, the sense of other minds—is appropriate to a system of mechanically multiplied personal tokens.

Another telephone scene occurs in the beginning of Kafka's posthumous *The Castle* (1926). "K" enters a village inn and finds himself accosted by a representative of the Castle, a vaporous entity whose identity remains permanently veiled throughout the book and thus functions as an allegory of infinity and bureaucracy. Haughtily K claims to be "the surveyor," summoned by the Castle, and the representative checks twice with the Castle by telephone. On being recognized by the Castle the second time, K reflects that this is propitious (since it gets him off the hook from the representative, who had wanted to banish him from the country) but also unpropitious (because it means the Castle is on to him and is giving him the chance to make his next move). K does not know, cannot know, whether he has been recognized or is only party to a fabrication.

This interpretive wavering before an enigmatic answer is a fundamental experience in the modern world: carrying on a fencing match either with a partner who seems to be responding but whose motives are inscrutable or with one whose responses can never be verified as responses. Modern men and women stand before bureaucracies and their representations or wait by telephones in the same way that sinners stood before the God who hides his face: anxiously sifting the chaos of events for signs and messages. The *deus absconditus* (hidden god) of theology no longer hides in the farthest corners of the universe; his successor has moved into the infernal machines of administration. Dante's vision of the place beyond the heavens was a kaleidoscopic reflection of spheres against spheres, a multifoliate rose of infinitely refracted light. K, like the rest of us, peers into a place where the reverberations are not optical but informational. (Game theory, uniquely appropriate for twentieth-century organizational culture, is the scientized form of this experience.) K does not know whether the permission to stay in the village is a mandate from the Castle itself, from some sleepy bureaucrat on the other end of the line trying to cover a possible failure to note K's arrival, or from the representative himself, fascinated by K's haughty certitudes. K must interpret the gestures from the Castle (if they indeed come from the Castle at all) with the same attentiveness with which augurs once monitored the sky above the *templum* for the flight of birds or the fall of stars. He must follow them with the falsificationist rationality of the modern scientist, carefully peeling away alternative hypotheses, checking the data for clerical errors, strenuously trying to avoid fudging the data with his own unconscious visions, wondering if the instrument was flawed or tapped the right information. To survive in the modern world, men and women must become diviners of inscrutable others, interpret the moods of secretaries, the words of department heads, the decisions of deans and CEOs, and shake-ups in the organization of the Kremlin, White House, or Vatican as if they were the language of some hidden, murky, remote god, content to speak only in darkness and in dreams.

Walter Benjamin once said that there are two wrong ways to read Kafka: naturally and supernaturally.[18] The point is Kafka's astounding ability to hover between the two, infinitely postponing a decision. He is the greatest theorist of organizational communication of this century. As Benjamin says, "The world of offices and registries, of musty, shabby, dark rooms, is Kafka's world."[19] Kafka is the premier existential student of bureaucracy, better than Max Weber at interpreting the dark weight of official maneuvers. Kafka's world is not quite a world of conspiratorial deceptions and evil lies that might in principle be uncovered; it is a world in which the ultimate source of all messages is hidden. He knows what is at stake in deciding what is a message, what is a projection, and what is some strange undecidable charade of people in mutual collusion who do not know it or never admit it. In bureaucratic mazes, how is one to know if the memo is a disclosure or a ruse, signal or noise? K, a surveyor, one who must read the marks of ownership, never knows if such marks express a coherent design or if whatever design exists is only a paranoid projection of an overactive interpreter.

The signs are all around us; they simply refuse to tell us how to read them. We hesitate, caught between the fear of being paranoid ("everything's a message") and the fear of missing a revelation if we act as if nothing is a message. The inability to make certain whether a sign is a projection of the self or an utterance of the other, an interpretive artifact or an objective pattern in the world, confronts a variety of social types: wizards who read tea leaves or entrails, believers who receive answers to prayers, takers of the Turing test who wager on whether the conversant is a human or a smart machine, and anyone who talks with another person on any passionate, painful, or delicate topic. . . .

Kafka ponders the strange communication circuit of the telephone to reveal potentials for trouble in face-to-face interaction that often are skillfully kept out of sight. He explores the twilight zones in which the signal-to-noise ratio approaches zero or infinity. In both "The Neighbor" and *The Castle*, the telephone foregrounds potentials for schizophrenia, paranoia, dissimulation, and eavesdropping that lurk in everyday speech. The common world may be habitual and sound, but breakdown allows all the primal uncanniness to return. In a blackout, or the telephone's suddenly going dead, or the static caught between the stations, we discover the gaps, not the bridges. To quote a thinker whose sensibility is often akin to Kafka's, "Pathology, with its magnification and exaggeration, can make us aware of normal phenomena which we should otherwise have missed."[20]

The historicity of Kafka's insights is beyond doubt. He dwelled in a zone where the level of message scatter was unbearable, though he died (1924) before the full splendor of radio's bazaar could be appreciated. Today most communications are voices crying in the wilderness. Turn on the radio or television and you will instantly discover a limbo of missed connections: pitch artists waxing earnest about "rock-hard abs" or engagement rings, newscasters describing the latest trauma to life and limb, songsters lamenting lost love in the musical dialects of opera and country. The paraphernalia of dead letters is no longer on display only at auctions: it is the daily stuff of public communication in our time. There are so many kinds of voices in the world, said Saint Paul. Or as Sherlock Holmes sniffed concerning the "agony columns" (personals) in turn of the century London newspapers: "'Dear me!' said he, turning over the page, 'what a chorus of groans, cries, and bleatings! What a ragbag of singular happenings! . . . Bleat, Watson—unmitigated bleat!'"[21] Unmitigated bleat mixed with the rare voice of truth crying in the wilderness: this is the formula for so much of modern communications, in spiritualism, the broadcast **ether**, and much of what we say to each other.

## Radio: Broadcasting as Dissemination (and Dialogue)

For ye shall speak into the air.

—1 COR. 14:9 KJV

In the 1920s and 1930s the radio was undoubtedly a leading source of unmitigated bleat. Radio's early history stages, with some starkness, all the issues facing communication in our time: the longing for an assured delivery and the desire to touch over long distances.

The radio signal is surely one of the strangest things we know; little wonder its ability to spirit intelligence through space elicited immediate comparisons to telepathy, séances, and angelic visitations. At any point on the earth's surface in the twentieth century, silent streams of radio voices, music, sound effects, and distress signals fill every corner of space. In any place you are reading this, messages surround and fly past you, infinitely inconspicuous, like the cicadas in the *Phaedrus*, who sing of things we cannot hear with our unaided ears. The remarkable property of the radio signal (discovered in the 1890s, the same decade when Warren and Brandeis wrote of privacy) is its inherent publicity. Electromagnetic signals radiate "to whom it may concern"; they are no respecters of persons, and they rain on the just and the unjust.

Early developers found the omnipresent quality of the radio signal a defect, seeing only dialogue as a legitimate form of communication. Like the phonograph, radio technology was first conceived as a means of point-to-point communication. Marconi was characteristic of his generation in thinking of the new technology as a wireless telegraph. But the telegraph had single termini; the airwaves did not. The looming obstacle, as with the mails before envelopes and anonymous sending and with the party line years of the telephone, was the lack of confidentiality. Anyone with a receiver set potentially had, as the parable of the sower put it, "ears to hear." Reception of the signal was inherently open-ended. As the adman Bruce Barton wrote in 1922, "Radio telephone messages can never be secret. They go out in all directions; and anyone with a machine tuned to the proper wave length can hear what you are saying to your partner in New Orleans or your sweetheart in Kenosha."[22] The inability to bar unintended recipients was a major hindrance to the profitability of wireless telegraphy and, after the audion tube in 1907, wireless telephony as well. The quest for a confidential channel, sometimes called "syntony" or "selectivity," was a preoccupation of early radio engineers.[23] Wanted was person-to-person connection, not a **party line**.[24] The quest for "private service on a party line" was an aim for both telephone and radio in this period.[25] Sought was the electromagnetic equivalent of the postal envelope. The term "listening in," the eventual verb for describing audience behavior in commercial radio, even borrowed the notion of eavesdropping on party lines, as if radio audiences were overhearing messages not originally intended for their ears.[26]

An exhibit of the principle that cultural preconception shapes the uses of technology as much as its internal properties do, radio "broadcasting" was not embraced until wireless technology had been in use for a quarter of a century.[27] The origins of the term are obscure, but all fingers point to an agricultural use not far from the *Phaedrus*, the parable of the sower, and the nervous metaphors of Comstock and Warren and Brandeis: the scattering of seeds. In nineteenth-century American literature, "broadcast" was most often used as an adjective meaning scattered. In *Tom Sawyer*, "A sweep of chilly air passed by, rustling all the leaves and snowing the flaky ashes broadcast about the fire." Thoreau wrote that "Nature strews her nuts and flowers broadcast, and never collects them into heaps" (*A Week on the Concord and Merrimack Rivers*). Whitman's *Leaves of Grass* praises the United States for being "essentially the greatest poem. In the history of the earth hitherto the largest and most stirring appear tame and orderly to their ampler largeness and stir. Here at last is something in the doings of man that corresponds with the broadcast doings of the day and night." The term *broadcasting* did not at first refer to any organized social practice. The free character of things broadcast naturally fit the radio signal's tendency to stray.

The discovery of radio as an agency of broadcasting is often attributed to David Sarnoff, future head of the National Broadcasting Company. In a now famous 1915–16 memo Sarnoff described the wireless as a household music box.[28] The "ether" would be filled not with the cacophony of amateur operators making point-to-point transmissions, but with music "broadcast" to a nation of listeners—who would then want to purchase Westinghouse radio sets. One obstacle, of course, to the development of radio as pure broadcasting was the question of how to make money from a communication circuit that seemed to be a continuous potlatch or gift to the public.[29] Sarnoff lit on the idea that desirable programming would fuel acquisition of radio hardware; he had not yet discovered the eventually victorious, lamentable practice of advertiser support for programs. Sarnoff saw the ether's lack of privacy as an opportunity rather than an obstacle. The lack of a specific addressee, he thought, would be the specialty rather than a defect of radio, speaking to the great audience invisible.[30] Sarnoff's memo was a dead letter in its impact on his Westinghouse superiors, though in retrospect it seems prophetic. Maybe, like Socrates, they were suspicious of forms of communication whose reception was open-ended and whose addressees were anonymous.

World War I saw power wrested from radio amateurs by the military, the state, and large corporations. The amateur vision of the ether as a cacophonous public forum in which anyone could take part was losing ground by the 1920s and was preserved largely in the efforts of noncommercial broadcasters, themselves pushed decisively aside by the early 1930s.[31] Herbert Hoover, who as secretary of commerce was probably the chief agent in making American radio a corporate, federally regulated entity, spoke in 1922 against the wireless as a means of person-to-person contact: "The use of the radio telephone for communication between single individuals, as in the case of the ordinary telephone, is a perfectly hopeless notion. Obviously, if ten million subscribers are crying through the air for their mates they will never make a junction."[32] Like Socrates' concerns about writing, Hoover was worried about the inability of "broadcasting" to achieve "junction." The Iowa-born, Stanford-trained engineer is not usually thought of as a particularly erotic thinker, but here **eros** looms, trying as ever to "bridge the chasm." Imagine the myriad crisscrossing of radio telephone voices crying for their loves, lost in transit, incomplete passes, the very air full of undelivered longings. Ah, Bartleby! Ah, humanity! Saint Paul's warning to the Corinthians who practiced **glossolalia** without interpreters could be motto of every broadcaster: You will be speaking into the air (1 Cor. 14:9). Like Paul, Hoover wanted to control the confusion of tongues.

Eventually radio became officially defined as an agent of public communication. The key question in the 1920s and early 1930s was its regulatory status: Was radio a common carrier or something else? This question involved the old couplet of dialogue and dissemination. "Common carriage" was a nineteenth-century category that included shipping lines, elevators, and above all railroads. The Interstate Commerce Act (1887) gave the Interstate Commerce Commission (ICC) jurisdiction over "common carriers," which were ceded a "natural monopoly" in return for which they had to offer all comers equal service and submit their rates to the ICC for approval. The Mann-Elkins Act (1910) and the Transportation Act (1920) expanded the definition of "common carrier" to include "transmission of intelligence by wire or wireless," thus placing the telegraph and telephone under ICC jurisdiction.[33]

But radio had difficulty fitting the point-to-point model. Heather Wessely captures the contrast well: "Rail transport is not a service designed with a potential terminus in every household."[34] Radio spoke into the blue yonder. A key case before the ICC, *Sta-Shine Products Co. v. Station WGBB* (1932), raised the question whether radio broadcasts entailed a "transmission of intelligence." Should the ICC treat radio stations as common carriers, thus regulating advertising rates? The decision declared radio outside the ICC's jurisdiction, since "no service is performed at the receiving end by the broadcasting company, similar to the service performed by common carriers." Broadcasting lacked "the boy in the blue uniform who rings the door bell and who brings the message itself." Common carriers saw to it that people receive their cargoes or messages, but broadcasting made no effort to ensure delivery. "Unless one has a radio receiving set properly attuned, he will never get and is not expected to get the intelligence, whether it be instruction, entertainment, or advertising, sent out from the broadcasting station."[35] By the standards of common carriage, broadcasting was a deformed communication circuit, since the "transmission of intelligence" was left to chance.

The conclusive definition of broadcasting was left to the jurisdiction of a New Deal agency, the Federal Communications Commission (FCC). The contrast between broadcasting and common carriage became a cornerstone of United States broadcasting policy in the Communications Act of 1934. According to section 3(h) of the act, "A person engaged in radio broadcasting shall not, insofar as such person is so engaged, be deemed a common carrier."[36] Common carriers operate point-to-point, deliver their goods to a definite address, and must be accessible to anyone and accountable for the tariffs they charge. A common carrier is characterized by "the separation of the content from the conduit" and lacks editorial discretion over the messages private people send.[37] Thus, if you shout obscenities into a phone, the phone company is exempt from prosecution; if you do so into a radio microphone, the station may have to answer to the FCC. Common carriers must be message blind and sender blind, but never receiver blind. Broadcasters, if not quite audience blind, see their audiences through a glass darkly.[38] Broadcasting, as legally defined, involves privately controlled transmission but public reception, whereas common carriage involves publicly controlled transmission but private reception. The two models possess striking symmetry. A common carrier offers universal access to transmission and restricted access to reception, whereas broadcasting offers restricted access to transmission and universal access to reception. Like Socrates in the *Phaedrus*, common carriage seeks to guarantee the delivery of the seed; like Jesus in the parable of the sower, broadcasting focuses on scattering the message to all (even if the actual reception is spotty).

The Communications Act of 1934 thus installed the ancient notion of dissemination in the heart of a modern technology in the guise of "broadcasting." As it developed, however, the term acquired a double sense. In its generic use, it refers to transmission over the air, but "broadcasting" as a legal term refers not to the diverse practices of the airwaves but to an idealized configuration among speakers and audiences. It conjures visions of the agora, the town meeting, or the "public sphere"; broadcasting is supposed to be more a town crier summoning citizens to assembly than a midway barker inviting the curious to spend their nickels on the freak show. By defining broadcasting in terms of the public interest, the 1934 Communications Act articulated a vision of the audience—a civic one, the audience as disinterested public—that fit the technology's lack of confidentiality and gave a lofty lineage to a set of practices that owed as much to the circus as to the polis. In fact, by the 1930s, commercial broadcasters had developed a number of techniques for routing audiences and managing the junction. The brief shining moment of dissemination was washed over by a flood of **dialogism**.[39]

**"They Will Never Make a Junction"** William James had compared the brains of sitters at séances to Marconi stations that pick up and amplify impossibly faint and distant signals of departed minds, just as Rudyard Kipling had compared very early radio communications to a séance. The question in both realms was similar: authentication in psychical research, identification and intimacy in early radio. The issue was how to make sure you reach the one you really want to reach. Throughout the interwar years, theorists and practitioners of radio recognized its strange ability, like the telephone, to put speaker and hearer in "contact" without physical presence or personal acquaintance. Radio carried what Rudolf Arnheim in 1936 called "voices without bodies" and breached limits of space, time, and audibility that had once seemed natural. Organizing radio's connection to the bodies of the communicants was a chief prerequisite of its naturalization into daily life. Without attempting anything close to a cultural history of broadcasting here, I will argue that securing mainstream acceptance for radio required means to close the obvious gaps of distance, disembodiment, and dissemination. Hence the history of commercial radio in the interwar years is of central interest for understanding the twentieth-century obsession with communication breakdown and its remedies. This history is a kind of moving meditation on how to reduce radio's uncanniness quotient.[40]

The distance between speaker and audience in radio replayed idealism's separate rooms and telephony's severing of a conversation into two disconnected halves. DX-ing in particular, the quest for a signal from remote stations and still a common sport among ham radio operators, reveals something about the curious ontology of the radio signal and the longings associated with communication at a distance. Communication afar is always erotic in the broad sense—a yearning for contact. The key call in DX-ing is "CQ," from the phrase "seek you." One fictional account of a 1924 family's DX listening describes it as "a sacrificial rite." A son adjusts the dials with excruciating precision to a spot where he hopes to catch the signal of a distant station; instead he hears emanations from the great beyond: "Out of the air comes the sizzle of static. The carrying wave of station after station whistles shrilly, cheerful mischievous devils signaling to presumptuous mortal man from somewhere in the empyrean." It is an evident challenge to find the one true signal, in spite of interference from other stations, the weather, and celestial beings. "Now he catches the murmur of a voice so faint and far that it might be in sober earnest a message from another world."[41] Such "DX-fishing," with its goal to hear the call letters of far-off stations, was a kind of quest for extraterrestrial intelligence *avant la lettre*: the search for the distant transmission amid the shrieks and pops of space. "Behind the music one still hears a wailing of winds lost somewhere in the universe and very unhappy about it."[42] In the early years of radio static was often heard as a sign of distant worlds; "celestial caterwauling," Bruce Bliven called it.[43] Another commentator noted, "The delicate mechanism of the radio has caught and brought to the ears of us earth dwellers the noises that roar in the space between the worlds."[44] Like Dorothy Parker's telephone call to God, or William James's quest to discern the will to communicate, DX-ing is an allegory of faith in our times.

Radio's gaps between transmission and reception could mean comic mockery as well as rites of supplication. As with the telephone, radio invited a new decorum for behavior in conditions of mutual absence.[45] The invisibility and domestic setting of the radio listening experience made for loosened norms of attentiveness compared with those that had developed in bourgeois theater. Bruce Bliven noted in 1924 that most political orators, if aware of "the ribald comments addressed to the stoical loud-speaker" of the home receiver, would seek other jobs. "The comments of the family range from Bill's, 'Is *that* so!' down to Howard's irreverent, 'Aw, shut your face, you poor hunk of cheese!' "[46] Home listening allowed oratory to be received in a mood of chronic flippancy. Likewise, one could exit live performances midstream without embarrassing anyone. "If the whole audience 'signed off' (disconnected the instruments) Miss Altenbrite would be none the wiser, and would send her trills just as sweetly through ninety thousand square miles of night."[47] More serious questions were raised in England about whether radio audiences should wear hats or sit when hearing an address from the queen.[48] In each case the question was, How binding is a relationship that lacks any contract of mutuality? What kind of moral or political obligation can ethereal contact compel? What is "communication" without bodies or presence?

Anxieties about contact were not confined to the receiving end; senders also faced the prospect of barriers to communication. Having to speak into a soulless microphone was a common complaint in the 1920s and 1930s from entertainers used to performing before live audiences. The microphone replaced the faces and souls of the listeners. In a 1924 radio address, Herbert Hoover worried again about the lack of junction, complaining about having to speak into "the deadly inexpressive microphone.... We need a method by which a speaker over the radio may sense the feelings of his radio audience. A speaker before a public audience knows what hisses and applause mean; he cuts his speech short or adjusts himself to it."[49] Critic Gilbert Seldes in 1927 noted the queasy feeling of the radio performer before an invisible audience in even more graphic terms: "The microphone, which seems so alive with strange vital fluids when you begin, goes suddenly dead; you think that somewhere in the next room the operator has cut off the current; that everywhere everyone has tuned out. You wonder who these people are who may be listening, in what obscurity, with what hostility. And when you listen to the radio yourself, you know no more."[50] Seldes was concerned, like other critics of dissemination, about the loss of "strange vital fluids," the current's being turned off, the enigma of the missing audience. He found himself in the position of speaker to the dead. His concerns—the unknown listeners, the lack of interaction, the speaking into the air—replicate the larger fears of solipsism and communication breakdown raging through the art, literature, and philosophy of the interwar years.[51] Indeed, the philosophical concerns of a Bradley or Hocking, that the other may be utterly inaccessible, recur in the mundane setting of the radio studio. Broadcasting restages the scenario of idealist philosophy: communicating deaf and blind through impermeable walls. Both broadcasters and audiences ran the risk of sending dead letters to each other. The twentieth century is full of discourses produced in what Paul Ricoeur would call situations of exploded dialogue.

**Compensatory Dialogism** How to compensate for the fact that people could be in touch without appearing "in person" was an acute question in the early history of radio and its development into a huge commercial entertainment empire. New forms of authenticity, intimacy, and touch not based on immediate physical presence had to be found. The hunt for communicative prostheses—compensations for lost presences—was vigorous in the culture of commercial radio in the 1920s and 1930s. Broadcasters quickly recognized the risk of alienating the affections of listeners and invented diverse strategies to replace what had apparently been taken away: the presence of fellow listeners, a conversational dynamic, and a personal tone. Commercial broadcasting was quite self-conscious about overcoming the listener's sense of being stuck in a mass audience without mutual interaction or awareness, with one-way flow of communication and anonymous styles of talk. New discursive strategies were designed to compensate for the medium's structural lacks. The aim was to restore lost presence.

"The pivotal fact," writes Paddy Scannell, "is that the broadcasters, while they control the discourse, do not control the communicative context." That the site of reception lies beyond the institutional authority of the broadcaster "powerfully drives the communicative style and manner of broadcasting to approximate to the norms not of public forms of talk, but to those of ordinary, informal conversation." He stunningly argues that radio broadcasting marked not the beginning but the end of mass communication as the address of large undifferentiated audiences.[52] Intimate sound spaces, domestic genres, cozy speech styles, and radio personalities all helped bridge the address gap in radio. In clear contrast to the regulatory language of the FCC, which stipulated that all broadcasting be done in the public interest, one observer noted that on the radio you "are not speaking to the Public. You are speaking to a family much like the families that live on the next block."[53] A 1931 article in the *Journal of Home Economics* put it bluntly: "Radio is an extension of the home."[54] Little wonder the light domestic drama and the soap opera have been the staples of broadcasting: like their audiences, the genres are set in living rooms. If official policy defined radio as a public space, those who actually used the new medium knew better. The styles of address in radio talk that evolved in the United States were a far cry from the stump orator or the Enlightenment public sphere. The heroes of radio in the 1930s were crooners, comics, and avuncular politicians, people who knew how to "reach out and touch" their audiences. The system's lifeblood was advertising, and audiences were its product. Some kind of interaction with them was crucial. Audience ratings and radio research aimed to play Eros by bridging the chasm.[55] The fostering of "we-ness," dialogical inclusion, and intimate address have remained at the core of broadcast discourse to this day.

The glad-handing joviality of much of American commercial radio culture in the 1930s and beyond was not, of course, a natural outgrowth of the technology but a cultural adaptation to specific political economic conditions. Broadcast culture could have remained starkly impersonal; up to the mid-1920s, for instance, most announcers were literally anonymous, known largely by code names, in what was a conscious policy of station owners to suppress radio "personalities" (lest their fame lead to greater salary demands, as of course occurred).[56] Announcers could have remained in the paradigm of telephone operators, passive channels for connecting other people, which was in fact more the model for the BBC. Instead, a policy of "unmitigated bleat" ensued.

One prong of the policy was a new chatty tone. Intimate forms of talk were to replace the harsh open-air soapbox voice. "The normal tone of transmission," wrote Rudolf Arnheim, "has to be that of a light, intimate conversation between broadcaster and listener." Many speakers "bellow through the microphone to an audience of millions," but Arnheim seriously doubted that radio appealed to the millions as masses: radio "talks to everyone individually, not to everyone together.... the radio-speaker should proceed softly and as if 'à deux.'" Arnheim prescribed bonhomie rather than bombast.[57] One writer said of educational radio, "I don't want a lecture, I just want a chat in my everyday language."[58]

Dialogic forms were another technique of simulating presence. In such techniques as crooning, direct address of listeners, dramatic dialogue, "feuds" between stars, fan letters, fan clubs, contests and promotional giveaways, or radio comedy, the remote audience was invited to become an imaginary participant in the world of the characters and of its fellow auditors. Radio comedy discovered the live studio audience and the stooge as solutions to the lack of live rapport. The in-house audience was a sounding board for the comic, and the stooge served as "straight man" for gags, both incorporating an internal circuit of sending and receiving in the broadcast. Since a mutual loop of talk could not be achieved with the dispersed listeners, it was simulated within the radio program. Radio programs not only transmitted voices but pretended to receive them back from the great audience invisible. Entertainers learned how to work one end of the telephone line when the other was piped into the millions. The ventriloquistic technique of keeping up both sides of the conversation persists in broadcast discourse. Perhaps the best emblem of such dialogism is the immensely popular comedy duo of the late 1930s and 1940s, Edgar Bergen and Charlie McCarthy. Two voices in dialogue, both produced by the same body. Two characters, one of them a dummy. It would be hard to find a more perfect symbol of radio's communication circuit.

Finally, techniques were explored to provide listeners with a sense of membership in a live audience. As Hadley Cantril and Gordon W. Allport noted in their very astute *Psychology of Radio* (1935), "No crowd can exist, especially no radio crowd, unless the members have a 'lively impression of universality.' Each individual must believe that others are thinking as he thinks and are sharing his emotions." A "consciousness of kind" had to be raised, via "social facilitation," such as the sound of laughter, applause, interaction, coughing, ahems, heckling, or other audible signs of a live assembly. Tapping into the older contrast between crowds and publics, and anticipating the more recent notion of imagined communities, they argued that radio audiences were distinctly "consociate" rather than "congregate" assemblies: united in imagination, not in location. But they also noted that a very different "social contract" prevailed in each type of collectivity; they did not forget the insuperability of touch.[59]

Ironically, the concept of "mass communication," as minted in the 1950s, suggests only the ways that mass media seem to fall short of face-to-face talk: vast audiences, one-way messages, and impersonal address.[60] What it misses is the very lifeblood of commercial media culture as we have come to know it. The early history of broadcast talk consisted largely in the attempt to create a world in which audiences would feel like participants. Today both the programming and reception of most commercial media, in the United States at least, actively cultivate a sense of intimate relations between persona and audience. Media culture is a lush jungle of fictional worlds where "everyone knows your name," celebrities and politicians address audiences by first names, and conversational formats proliferate. The conventional concept of "mass communication" captures only the abstract potential for alienation in large-scale message systems, not the multiple tactics of interpersonal appeal that have evolved to counter it.[61] Early broadcasters saw "mass society" looming and tried to stop it.

***Hoc Est Corpus,* Hocus-Pocus** But it could not be stopped entirely. Despite the many compensations to make up for the loss of face-to-face communication, including a tonal shift toward snugger modes of address and the simulation of personal interaction, the relationship of body to body could not be restored fully over the ether any more than a telephone marriage could be consummated by wire. A creepy surplus remained. The unease about the new spectral bodies of broadcasting could not always be suppressed. A few genres—horror drama, for instance—played radio's uncanny potential to the hilt. The Shadow knew that under commercial broadcasting's carefully wrought artifice of intimate familiarity lurked the loneliness of the long gaps, the eerie calls of distant voices, and the touch of oozing ectoplasm, strange flesh from afar. American radio in the 1920s and 1930s was explicitly a "live" medium, and the effort to breathe life into the spirits emerging from the loudspeaker after a long journey often involved the strangest of resurrectionist techniques.

Liveness in radio was the effort to break the connection between death and distance. The term "live" arose as life's uncontested dominion, its naturalness, ended. The *Oxford English Dictionary* gives such phrases as "two live plants in flower pots" (1856), a locution presumably motivated by plants such as immortelles, flowers that retain their color after death, and "live cattle" (1897), presumably in contrast to the slaughtered. In both cases, "live" explicitly contrasts with something dead. "Live" could also mean "containing unexpended energy," as in a live shell, cartridge, or match. A "live wire" carried electrical current and could provide power or shocks. An 1875 dictionary of mechanics defined a "live-axle," one year before the telephone and two years before the phonograph, as "one communicating power; in contradistinction to a dead or blind axle." Finally, the more recent term "live action" means the filming of actors and events as opposed to animation, titling, or other kinds of image manipulation. "Live" is the prosthetic form of life, something that announces its authenticity against potentially deceptive substitutes. Its fundamental sense is contrastive: "live" means "not dead."

"Live" also means "communicating power," and such is crucial to modern communications. Because life could be simulated by recording and transmitting media, liveness became something eagerly sought. Notions of life were important in the terminology of early moving image technologies: zoetrope, bioscope, vitagraph, cinema (from Greek *kineo*, to move, as in "kinetic"), motion pictures, and movies. By the 1920s, "live" came to mean simultaneous broadcasting. A sociologist in 1928, predicting a greater future for the radio than the phonograph, made the explicit equation of simultaneity with life and recording with death: "The radio does not transmit 'dead' material as does the phonograph, but present and 'living' events."[62] In a "live" performance, the body is present in the flesh. "Live" means that contingency is still possible, that the energy is actual, and that a new and singular event can take place. Here again, in the bowels of the new machines of simulation, the old marker of authenticity—the mortal body itself—reappeared.

Freud wrote *Civilization and Its Discontents* in 1929, amid such transformations in the shape of the solo body and the body politic. For Freud, eros and civilization were forever at odds. Eros was the force of coupling and was essentially dyadic, but civilization demanded a larger scope and lowered intensity of affective bonds. "Sexual love is a relationship between two individuals in which a third can only be superfluous or disturbing, whereas civilization depends on relationships between a considerable number of individuals." He could have been talking about the mass address of radio, but he was not. He thought the work of civilization was inevitably to bind individuals, families, nations, and races into larger and larger libidinal units. But the stinger in his story was that an authentically democratic eros was impossible: its price was repression. Nature had loaded the deck against human happiness; the scale of our affections was mismatched with the demands of social order. Civilization sought to rechannel our finite libidinal energy onto its approved objects.

We ought to count Freud as one of the most prescient thinkers of mass communication, of what happens when dyadic form (communication) is technologically stretched to a gigantic degree (mass). His comments on modern media featured the stubborn fact of human embodiment, our twin entanglements in biology and culture. He made a point more commonly associated with McLuhan thirty-five years later, but with a more tragic twist: that media are extensions of the human body. Each medium for Freud was an attempt to cover a human lack, to fill the gap between ourselves and the gods. Telephony has extended our ears, allowing us to hear our distant loved ones, as photography and phonography have substituted for memory. And yet we are none the happier. Finitude recurs with a vengeance. "Man has, as it were, become a kind of prosthetic god. When he puts on all his auxiliary organs he is truly magnificent; but those organs have not grown onto him and they still give him much trouble at times." Freud knew what struggles it took to fit our bodies into the new auxiliary organs of the media.[63]

In addition to the deep reasons for nervousness about radio—its distance, deathliness, disembodiment, and dissemination—there were sound substantive reasons as well. Radio was the latest chapter in American hucksterism. Resistance to advertising on radio was widespread in the 1920s and 1930s and waning but still strong in the 1940s.[64] Radio called forth not only entertainers and journalists but confidence men whose goat-gland operations and mind cures promised health and rejuvenation to the millions. What Cooley thought had disappeared was back with a vengeance: the need to differentiate between the ghosts and the frauds.

Many of the most successful performers exploited liveness, in the sense of either simultaneity or nondeath, to cut through public anxieties about fakery and duplication in the radio world. A token of the live body was extended across the waves to assure truthfulness. During one of his first fireside chats, for instance, the consummate radio performer President Franklin Delano Roosevelt "suddenly burst forth with 'Where's that glass of water?'" After a pause to drink, he explained to his listeners: "My friends, it's very hot here in Washington tonight."[65] Erik Barnouw's embellished account of the episode calls this "a simple human action that may have been sophisticated showmanship."[66] The gesture was powerful because a "simple human" need was enough to interrupt a presidential address. In the Elizabethan language of the king's two bodies, the body mortal briefly trumped the body politic.[67] By letting his audience in on his thirst and thus revealing the finitude he shared with them, FDR proved his sincerity. He was "one of us." FDR not only wove policies, he interrupted their enunciation to affirm something more profound. Polished words would be too slick. Imperfection was the guarantee of truth in a medium in which the polio-stricken body of the president could be converted into a Voice that reassured Americans everywhere. The intrusion of thirst is a classic reality effect, an undercutting of the medium that actually plays to its strengths. Take, he said, *hoc est corpus meum*.

FDR, like other radio performers who secured the trust or adoration of their audiences, learned—to use James's distinction—to assert the "will to communicate" over the "will to personate." A synecdoche of one's unique human individuality could lift the veil of the commodity.[68] The body and its pain became the last frontier of authenticity, the bedrock immune to fakery, a source of private fact. The flesh provided the ultimate ethos. The religious notion (much older than the mass media per se) that a larger social body could be formed by distributing tokens of an individual body recurs in radio. We ought not to forget that "mass" in "mass communication" can be taken as a noun as well as an adjective.[69]

Like Freud, Theodor W. Adorno thought all such compensations ill-fitting annoyances. There was no more formidable critic of the commercialized culture of sincerity. Simulated community among colisteners or staged interaction between audiences and radio stars were, he thought, so much hocus-pocus (a term that derives from a cynical misunderstanding of the phrase from the Latin Mass, *hoc est corpus*). Adorno's view of media audiences was more subtle than the frequent caricature as brainwashed zombies or infantilized masses. The danger of radio was not its rabble-rousing, but its individualizing ability, its skill at tucking the listener into a cocoon of unreflective security or sadistic laughter. Mass culture did not instill passivity; rather, it shunted enormous energies into shock absorption. Solidarity within the audience was at best a **fetish**, as was audience participation in the radio world. His rogues' gallery of "regressive listeners" jitterbugging their way into false ecstasy is the epitome of idolatrous interaction with distant objects. The radio ham, for instance, "is only interested in the fact that he hears and succeeds in inserting himself, with his private equipment, into the public mechanism, without exerting even the slightest influence on it."[70] This extraordinary description (an accurate rendering of Adorno's German) complains of the perversion of an authentic and fertile erotic **dyad**. As in Seldes's description and the *Phaedrus*, the specter of wasted seed recurs. Like Freud, with whom he found much to dispute, Adorno took the dyad as the insuperable site of genuine eros. The libidinal structure of radio, however, could only be either solitary or plural. Ever the Hegelian Marxist, he thought authentic interaction could occur only when one subject encountered another in its objectivity. Radio address had to be structurally insincere owing to the generality of its solicitations. Like Marx on money, Adorno saw in radio a form of pimpery. As Adorno's colleague Leo Lowenthal complained, attempts at personal address involved a slippage between general and individual address: "Especially for you means all of you."[71] Like Socrates, Adorno is concerned about mass eros as one prominent communication disorder.

If Adorno's radio studies exposed the failure to craft symbolic participation at a distance, Robert K. Merton's (1946) study of the all-American singer Kate Smith examined a successful ritual performance. Smith's smashing success at mass persuasion in a one-day war bond drive on 21 September 1943 stemmed, Merton argued, from what audiences perceived as her sincerity. Many Hollywood stars had gone on the air to raise funds for the war effort, but few had achieved Smith's success. Merton borrowed George Herbert Mead's definition of sincerity as a speaker's use of "verbal symbols which evidently affect himself as he intends them to affect his audience. Sincerity provides for a mutual experience."[72] For Merton, Smith was not just staging an interaction; her audience really was getting something from her.

The key to her link with the audience was her "propaganda of the deed." Smith did not exempt herself from the sacrifice she asked of her audience. Her own live radio performance, eighteen hours in a single day, put her body on the line, just as she asked her audiences to put their money on the line. Doing a physically exhausting radio campaign without complaint allayed suspicions of fakery well enough to bind a national audience in a moment of crisis. A recorded performance would have lost the crucially persuasive presence of the live body. If, somehow, it was revealed that it had all been transcribed and her responses to listener calls had been fabricated, Smith's sincerity would have vanished, even if the two performances were identical. The audience may have believed in the metaphysics of presence, but bad metaphysics may still be the basis of persuasive rhetoric. Smith was a sacrificial surrogate who modeled behavior for the listening audience in the best style of ancient expiation. Her lack of sex appeal, Merton found, was also part of her credibility. Kate Smith was not Rita Hayworth; no glamour corrupted her sincerity. The irreality of Hollywood faded, as Merton argued, in the drama of a voice in a race against exhaustion. From the Greeks onward, suffering has been taken as a guarantee of truth; the words of the dying are still given special testimonial value. Pain is often still taken to limit the motive to fabricate.[73] Kate Smith had found the mother lode of communicative authenticity: the body speaking from its pain. . . .

The politics of mass communication theory turn on one's vision of the possibility of media-made community. The question is, Can you take part without being there in the flesh? Can an audience be said to participate in a remote event? The bodily context of all communication is inescapable. Merton's argument that symbols working at a distance can afford authentic sociability has an elective affinity with the interests of the media industries, whose economic well-being depends on convincing audiences to trust the sincerity of distant testimonials. Yet Adorno's thesis that all distant relationships are false can give us no antidote to the mutual distrust that eats at us all, for which relationships are untouched by distance (as he well knew)? The analysis of the falsity can be interminable. Adorno's negative dialectics constantly undermines the dream of reconciliation between people—in the name of that dream.

Removing false hope is a fine service so long as it does not damage our animal faith, since all action rests on strategic illusion. The decision as to which thinker is right may turn on whether we are more afraid of being suckered by power or deprived of hope.

In the apparently innocuous questions whether Kate Smith can be sincere over the air and whether such a performance can afford a "mutual" experience, then, is found the intellectual and political heart of mass communication theory, the question of mediation—in other words, the possibility of interaction without personal or physical contact. Adorno finds the idea of audience participation in the radio world the worst kind of projection; Merton finds it to be a ritual act of solidarity with real consequences. Merton believed in the possibility, at least on extraordinary occasions, of an expanded social body, joined at a distance. Adorno was suspicious of any attempt to expand the human symbolically or technically. For him no "auxiliary organs," as Freud called media, could heal the body's displacement in mass communication; they were at best clumsy prostheses to restore a bodily wholeness that may never even have existed. Merton's erotics—his vision of how bodies can be coupled—allowed for real communication across distance; Adorno's insisted on the face-to-face, seeing only illusion or perversion in distended ties. In Maxwell's terms, Merton believed in action at a distance; Adorno believed that all immediacy was laced with infinitesimal gaps.

These questions are rich in implication for our public and private lives today. Democracy and eros remain the twin frames for popular reception of each new medium. Talk about the Internet today, for instance, is rife with dreams of new bodies politic (participatory democracy) and horrors of new bodies pornographic (children preyed on). The meaning of communicative connections, large scale and small, is an ongoing conundrum. We continue to play out Maxwell's options: bodies joined at a distance and bodies that, even when pressed tightly together, are not in absolute contact. If success in communication was once the art of reaching across the intervening bodies to touch another's spirit, in the age of electronic media it has become the art of reaching across the intervening spirits to touch another's body. Not the ghost in the machine, but the body in the medium is the central dilemma of modern communications.

## Notes

1. See Michèle Martin, *"Hello, Central?" Gender, Technology, and Culture in the Formation of Telephone Systems* (Montreal: McGill-Queen's University Press, 1991).

2. Martin, *"Hello, Central?"* 70, 73.

3. See Helmut Gold and Annette Koch, eds., *Fräulein vom Amt* (Munich: Prestel, 1993), and Friedrich A. Kittler, *Grammophon, Film, Typewriter* (Berlin: Brinkmann und Bose, 1986), 273–89.

4. Donna J. Haraway, *Simians, Cyborgs, and Women: The Reinvention of Nature* (New York: Routledge, 1991), and Claudia Springer, *Electronic Eros: Bodies and Desire in the Post-industrial Age* (Austin: University of Texas Press, 1996).

5. See Herbert N. Casson, "The Social Value of the Telephone," *Independent*, 26 October 1911, 899–906; "How the Hotel Telephone Girl Sizes You Up," *American Magazine*, August 1923, 23, 70, 72; "When the 'Hello Girl' Tries Hand at Detective Work," *Literary Digest*, 5 November 1927, 52–54.

6. Martin, *"Hello, Central?"* 95. Besides the general point that distance breeds eros, Rick Altman suggests the sexiness of the female voice may owe to the suppression of high frequencies in telephone sound (designed on the model of the male voice), thus tending to make female telephone voices into sultry contraltos.

7. One example of telephone marriage is given in Mary B. Mullett, "How We Behave When We Telephone," *American Magazine*, November 1918, 44–45, 94, at 45. A 1995 *National Geographic* article pictures "first virtual reality wedding" as a physically separated couple "embracing" in virtual reality. And yet the meeting in the flesh cannot be postponed forever: "There was no question about the ending though: a real kiss after the virtual one." Joel L. Swerdlow, Louis Psihoyos, and Allen Carroll, "Information Revolution," *National Geographic Magazine* 188, 4 (1995): 35.

8. Lana Rakow, *Gender on the Line: Women, the Telephone, and Community Life* (Urbana: University of Illinois Press, 1992), 43, treats the relative ineptitude of men in the town of "Prospect" at managing telephone talk.

9. "On Conversation by Telephone," *Independent*, 10 May 1915, 229–30.

10. Catherine L. Covert, "'We May Hear Too Much': American Sensibility and the Response to Radio, 1919–1924," in *Mass Media between the Wars*, 1918–1941, ed. Catherine L. Covert and John D. Stevens (Syracuse: Syracuse University Press, 1984), 202.

11. "Telephone Terror," *Atlantic Monthly*, February 1920, 279–81.

12. Mark Dery, ed., *Flame Wars: The Discourse of Cyberculture* (Durham: Duke University Press, 1994).

13. Mullett, "How We Behave When We Telephone," 45.

14. Ronell, *Telephone Book;* Frank Kessler, "Bei Anruf Rettung!" in *Telefon und Kultur: Das Telefon im Spielfilm*, ed. B. Debatin and H. J. Wulff (Berlin: Volker Spiess, 1991), 167–73.

15. Mark Twain, "A Telephonic Conversation," in *"The $30,000 Bequest" and Other Stories* (1880; New York: Harpers, 1917), 204–8.

16. Parker, "Telephone Call," 333–39; Aldous Huxley, "Over the Telephone," in *The Smart Set Anthology*, ed. Burton Rascoe (New York: Reynal and Hitchcock, 1934), 122–28.

17. Franz Kafka, "Der Nachbar," in *Beschreibung eines Kampfes: Novellen, Skizzen, Aphorismen aus dem Nachlaß* (Frankfurt am Main: Fischer, 1989), 100–101.

18. Walter Benjamin, "Franz Kafka," in *Illuminations*, ed. Hannah Arendt (New York: Schocken, 1968), 127.

19. Benjamin, "Franz Kafka," 112.

20. Sigmund Freud, *New Introductory Lectures on Psycho-analysis*, Great Books of the Western World, ed. Robert Maynard

Hutchins, vol. 54 (1932; Chicago: Encyclopaedia Britannica, 1952), 830.

21. Arthur Conan Doyle, "The Adventure of the Red Circle," in *The Complete Sherlock Holmes* (Garden City, N.Y.: Doubleday, 1930), 2:904.

22. Bruce Barton, "This Magic Called Radio: What Will It Mean in Your Home in the Next Ten Years?" *American Magazine*, June 1922, 11–13, 70–71, at 70.

23. Hugh G. J. Aitken, *Syntony and Spark: The Origins of Radio* (New York: Wiley, 1976), and "Radio Wave Band for Every Country," *New York Times*, 23 August 1921, 4.

24. The development of cryptography before and during World War II made it technically possible to destine messages for a specific address via the airwaves. Alan Turing played a key role in this in Great Britain, as did Claude Shannon in the United States.

25. Phrase taken from "To Stop Telephone-Eavesdropping," *Literary Digest*, 17 October 1914, 733.

26. Covert, "'We May Hear Too Much,'" 203.

27. See Susan J. Douglas, *Inventing American Broadcasting* (Baltimore: Johns Hopkins University Press, 1987), and Susan Smulyan, *Selling Radio: The Commercialization of American Broadcasting, 1920–1934* (Washington, D. C.: Smithsonian Institution Press, 1994).

28. David Sarnoff, "Memorandum to E. J. Nally," in *Documents of American Broadcasting*, ed. Frank J. Kahn (Englewood Cliffs, N.J.: Prentice-Hall, 1984), 23–25.

29. Smulyan, *Selling Radio*.

30. Daniel J. Boorstin, *The Americans: The Democratic Experience* (New York: Vintage, 1973), 391.

31. Robert W. McChesney, *Telecommunications, Mass Media, and Democracy: The Battle for the Control of U. S. Broadcasting, 1928–1935* (New York: Oxford University Press, 1993).

32. Quoted in Richard A. Schwarzlose, "Technology and the Individual: The Impact of Innovation on Communication," in *Mass Media Between the Wars, 1918–1941*, ed. Catherine L. Covert and John D. Stevens (Syracuse: Syracuse University Press, 1984), 100.

33. The relevant documents can be found in Bernard Schwartz, *The Economic Regulation of Business and Industry: A Legislative History of U. S. Regulatory Agencies*, 5 vols. (New York: Chelsea House, 1973). Congressman James R. Mann also wrote the Mann Act of 1910, prohibiting "the transportation of women across state lines for immoral purposes." His legislation dealt with all sorts of common carriers.

34. Heather A. Wessely, "Culture, History and the Public Interest: Developing a Broadcasting Service for the United States" (manuscript, Department of Communication Studies, University of Iowa, 1993), 54.

35. *Sta-Shine Products Company, Inc. v. Station WGBB of Freeport NY* 188 ICC 271 (1932); quotations from 276, 277–78.

36. As Justice White put it in 1979: "The language of § 3 (h) is unequivocal; it stipulates that broadcasters shall not be treated as common carriers." *FCC v. Midwest Video Corporation*, in *Documents of American Broadcasting*, ed. Frank J. Kahn (Englewood Cliffs, N.J.: Prentice-Hall, 1984), 364.

37. T. Barton Carter, Marc A. Franklin, and Jay B. Wright, *The First Amendment and the Fifth Estate: Regulation of Electronic Mass Media* (Mineola, N.Y.: Foundation, 1986), 395.

38. This legal distinction may in part be a post hoc version of the division of labor agreed upon in 1926 between RCA and AT&T, leaving the former with the air/broadcasting and the latter with wires/telephony. See Noobar R. Danielian, *AT&T: The Story of Industrial Conquest* (New York: Vanguard, 1939).

39. Thus far I have used "dialogism" to mean the ideology that dialogue is the morally supreme form of communication. Here I use it in a different sense, closer to Mikhail Bakhtin, to refer to the multiple voices that layer discourse.

40. My account will regrettably be limited largely to United States sources.

41. Bruce Bliven, "The Legion Family and the Radio: What We Hear When We Tune In," *Century Magazine*, October 1924, 811–18, at 814. On the numinous overtones of early radio static, see Douglas, *Inventing American Broadcasting*, 304–5.

42. Bruce Bliven, "The Ether Will Now Oblige," *New Republic*, 15 February 1922, 328.

43. Bliven, "Ether Will Now Oblige," 328. A wonderful account of the literary and metaphysical aspects of radio static is James A. Connor, "Radio Free Joyce: *Wake* Language and the Experience of Radio," *James Joyce Quarterly* 30–31 (summer-fall 1993): 825–43.

44. A. Leonard Smith, "Broadcasting to the Millions," *New York Times*, 19 February 1922, sec. 7, 6, quoted in Douglas, *Inventing American Broadcasting*, 304.

45. The most sensitive students of the social contract between audiences and broadcast events are Daniel Dayan and Elihu Katz, *Media Events: The Live Broadcasting of History* (Cambridge: Harvard University Press, 1992), esp. chap. 5, and Paddy Scannell, "Public Service Broadcasting and Modern Public Life," *Media, Culture, and Society* 11, 2 (1989): 135–66.

46. Bliven, "Legion Family," 817.

47. Bliven, "Ether Will Now Oblige," 329.

48. Scannell, "Public Service Broadcasting."

49. Radio Talk by Secretary Hoover, 26 March 1924, box 48, Herbert Hoover Presidential Library; quoted in Wessely, *Culture, History and the Public Interest*, 44–45.

50. Gilbert Seldes, "Listening In," *New Republic*, 23 March 1927, 140–41.

51. See Douglas Kahn and Gregory Whitehead, eds., *The Wireless Imagination: Sound, Radio, and the Avant-Garde* (Cambridge: MIT Press, 1992).

52. Paddy Scannell, "Introduction: The Relevance of Talk," in *Broadcast Talk*, ed. Paddy Scannell (Newbury Park, Calif.: Sage, 1991), 1–9, at 3.

53. Morse Salisbury, "Writing the Home Economics Radio Program," *Journal of Home Economics* 24 (1932): 954–60, at 957.

54. Morse Salisbury, "Signs of the Times," *Journal of Home Economics* 23 (1931): 847.

55. Paul F. Lazarsfeld and Frank N. Stanton, "Introduction," in *Radio Research, 1941* (New York: Sloan, Duell, and Pearce, 1942), vii, make this point explicitly. On the historical centrality of the ratings to the broadcasting industry, see Eileen R. Meehan, "Heads of Households and Ladies of the House: Gender, Genre, and Broadcast Ratings, 1929–1990," in *Ruthless Criticism: New Perspectives in U. S. Communications History*, ed. William S. Solomon and Robert W. McChesney (Minneapolis: University of Minnesota Press, 1993), 204–21.

56. Erik Barnouw, *A Tower in Babel: A History of Broadcasting in the United States to 1933* (New York: Oxford University Press, 1966), 163–67.

57. Rudolf Arnheim, *Radio* (1936; New York: Arno Press, 1986), 71, 72.

58. Salisbury, "Signs of the Times," 851.

59. Hadley Cantril and Gordon W. Allport, *The Psychology of Radio* (New York: Harper, 1935).

60. Charles R. Wright, *Mass Communication: A Sociological Perspective* (New York: Random House, 1959), 11–14, offers a classic definition of "mass communication" in this way.

61. Donald Horton and Richard R. Wohl, "Mass Communication and Para-social Interaction: Observations on Intimacy at a Distance" (1956), in *Inter/Media: Interpersonal Communication in a Media World*, ed. Gary Gumpert and Robert Cathcart (New York: Oxford University Press, 1982), 188–211.

62. E. W. Burgess, "Communication," *American Journal of Sociology* 33 (1928): 125.

63. Sigmund Freud, *Civilization and Its Discontents*, trans. Joan Riviere (1930; New York: Norton, 1961), 39–45. During the writing of the book, Freud wore an irritating prosthesis in the roof of his mouth as a consequence of his throat cancer.

64. Smulyan, *Selling Radio*, and Paul F. Lazarsfeld and Patricia L. Kendall, *Radio Listening in America* (New York: Prentice-Hall, 1948), 59–80.

65. "The President Broadcasts: Confronted with Mikes, Cameras, and Radio Engineers, Roosevelt Pauses for a Glass of Water," *Broadcasting* 5, 3 (1933): 8. This outburst is not recorded in the official record of the fireside chats. Thanks to Joy Elizabeth Hayes for advice on FDR and radio.

66. Erik Barnouw, *The Golden Web: A History of Broadcasting in the United States, 1933–1953* (New York: Oxford University Press, 1968), 8.

67. Ernst H. Kantorowicz, *The King's Two Bodies: A Study in Mediaeval Political Theology* (Princeton: Princeton University Press, 1957).

68. Allison McCracken, "White Men Can't Sing Ballads: Crooning and Cultural Anxiety, 1927–1933" (manuscript, American Studies Program, University of Iowa, 1998).

69. John Durham Peters, "Beyond Reciprocity: Public Communication as a Moral Ideal," in *Communication, Culture, and Community: Liber Amicorum James Stappers*, ed. Ed Hollander, Coen van der Linden, and Paul Rutten (Houten, Netherlands: Bohn, Stafleu, van Loghum, 1995), 41–50.

70. Theodor W. Adorno, "On the Fetish-Character in Music and the Regression of Listening," in *The Essential Frankfurt School Reader*, ed. Andrew Arato and Eike Gebhardt (1938; New York: Continuum, 1982), 270–99, 286–99, 293. See also Adorno, "Analytical Study of the NBC *Music Appreciation Hour*," *Musical Quarterly* 78, 2 (1994): 325–77 (written 1938–41).

71. Leo Lowenthal, "Biographies in Popular Magazines," in *Radio Research, 1942–1943*, ed. Paul F. Lazarsfeld and Frank N. Stanton (New York: Sloan, Duell, and Pearce, 1944), 507–48, 581–85.

72. Robert K. Merton, with Marjorie Fiske and Alberta Curtis, *Mass Persuasion: The Social Psychology of a War Bond Drive* (New York: Harper, 1946), 105.

73. Page DuBois, *Torture and Truth* (London: Routledge, 1991); Elaine Scarry, *The Body in Pain: The Making and Unmaking of the World* (New York: Oxford University Press, 1985).

## Critical Thinking and Application

- Peters writes of the need for radio to appear intimate. How does current talk radio fit with this mandate?
- Peters summarizes a debate between two important social theorists, Theodor Adorno and Robert Merton. Adorno sees nothing but falsity in distant, mediated relations, whereas Merton sees the possibility of genuine relationship. Where do you stand on this question?
- Why does Peters claim that "the body in the medium is the central dilemma of modern communications"? How do we resolve this dilemma?
- Peters write here of telephony and radio, but many of his points can be extended beyond these two media. Make a similar analysis of other media.
- Observe your own interactions for a portion of a day. Note which are with physically present others and which are with physically absent others. Which did you initiate? Which "summoned" you? Which were one-to-many, which many-to-one, and which point-to-point? Does it make a difference? Did any feel more "authentic" than others? Why?

## Vocabulary

| | | |
|---|---|---|
| cyborg | eros | glossolalia |
| dialogism | ether | hermeneutics |
| dyad | fetish | party line |

## Suggested Further Reading [See also list following (New) Media unit introduction]

Adorno, Theodor W. 1974 [1944–1951]. *Minima Moralia: Reflections from Damaged Life*, translated by E. F. N. Jephcott. London: Verso.

Blanchard, Margaret A. 1998. *History of the Mass Media in the United States: An Encyclopedia*. Chicago: Fitzroy Dearborn.

Douglas, Susan J. 1999. *Listening In: Radio and the American Imagination: From Amos 'n' Andy and Edward R. Murrow to Wolfman Jack and Howard Stern*. New York: Times Books.

Fisher, Marc. 2007. *Something in the Air: Radio, Rock, and the Revolution That Shaped a Generation*. New York: Random House.

Gergen, Kenneth J. 1991. *The Saturated Self: Dilemmas of Identity in Contemporary Life*. New York: Basic Books.

Gladstone, Brooke, and Josh Neufeld. 2011. *The Influencing Machine: Brooke Gladstone on the Media*. New York: Norton.

Goffman, Erving. 1983. Radio Talk: A Study of the Ways of Our Errors. In *Forms of Talk*, pp. 197–330. Philadelphia: University of Pennsylvania Press.

Lewis, Tom. 1991. *Empire of the Air: The Men Who Made Radio*. New York: Burlingame Books.

Merton, Robert K. 1946. *Mass Persuasion: The Social Psychology of a War Bond Drive*. New York: Harper.

Peters, John Durham. 1999. *Speaking into the Air: A History of the Idea of Communication*. Chicago: University of Chicago Press.

# CHAPTER 16

# Why All the Fuss?

## *David Crystal*

(2008)

*When texting first became widespread—first in Asia and Europe and in North America early in the twenty-first century—there was consternation that it was destroying... civilization? brains? writing? thinking? I remember getting a phone call around 2006 from a journalist who asked if I agreed that texting was ruining schooling. I dismissed her alarm, but there had been little research published on the subject at the time. By the time Crystal writes, and of course even more when you are reading this, there are more complicated and sophisticated ways of viewing the writing that occurs through text. There is more of it—in 2010, data surpassed voice use on cellular phones in the United States (Wortham 2010)—and given smart phones and other devices, the abbreviations, initialisms, and other linguistic phenomena that Crystal identifies have changed. (iPhones, for instance, autocorrect spelling, sometimes to hilarious and sometimes to mortifying effect.) Crystal is right, though, that media and technology affect the language—and that people have significant social, aesthetic, and moral reactions to other people's changing language. This usually applies to youth, who tend to be at the forefront of language change. Deborah Cameron has written of* verbal hygiene, *in which people evaluate others' linguistic usage, aiming for some kind of purity or ideal that usually corresponds with that of the observer and her or his own generation, social group, occupational niche, or social class. Sociologists write of* moral panics, *in which some problem grips the public's imagination, usually fed by "the media," often out of proportion to the actual harm being inflicted, because it reflects some other, deeper fear of change that is more difficult to identify or observe.*

*So the prolific and learned linguist David Crystal wonders here, why all the fuss about texting?*

### Reading Questions

- What are some of the particular features of texting that Crystal identifies? Are they still relevant?
- How is the language of texting different from the language of other written forms? Be specific.
- Though a common complaint is that texting decreases writing ability, Crystal claims that literacy awareness helps people become adept texters. Why do you think this is the case? What skills are required to text well?
- What are some of the benefits of text messaging? What are some of the drawbacks?

---

A remarkable number of doom-laden prophecies arose during the opening years of the new millennium, all relating to the linguistic evils which would be unleashed by texting. The prophecies went something like this:

- Texting uses new and nonstandard **orthography**.
- This will inevitably erode children's ability to spell, punctuate, and capitalize correctly – an ability already thought to be poor.
- They will inevitably transfer these new habits into the rest of their schoolwork.
- This will inevitably give them poorer marks in examinations.

David Crystal, Why All the Fuss? From *Txtng: The Gr8 Db8*. Oxford: Oxford University Press, 2008, pp. 151–175.

- A new generation of adults will inevitably grow up unable to write proper English.
- Eventually the language as a whole will inevitably decline.

There was never any clear evidence supporting these assertions, but that did not stop them being made. And when someone found a piece of writing which did seem to support the argument – the child who supposedly wrote her essay entirely in a texting style... it was immediately publicized as being typical of a generation. The one extract from that essay was reproduced in hundreds of newspapers and websites all over the world. The full essay, if it existed, was never presented. And no other examples of this kind have since been found. Every time I talk to groups of teachers and examiners, I ask them whether they have encountered anything remotely similar. None of them ever has.

In 2007 I had the opportunity to work with some groups of teenagers studying for **A-levels** at various schools in the UK. They all texted. I asked them whether they would use text abbreviations in their schoolwork. They looked at me with blank incomprehension. One said, 'Why would you ever want to do that?' They were perfectly clear in their minds that texting was for mobile phones and not for other purposes. 'You'd have to be pretty stupid not to see the difference', said another. The point was affirmed many times in a BBC forum which followed the report on the child's essay in 2003, such as this comment from 11-year-old Charlotte:[1]

> I write all my notes in txt, like from a video, if I were going 2 do an essay on it (which I do in normal language), but I wouldn't do it for proper work, ESPECIALLY IN EXAMS.

Or this one from 15-year-old Terri:

> I have never heard of anyone using 'text language' for an essay or anything, and if I did, I'd probably hurt them horribly. But, it's not my problem if you get horrendous grades for something ridiculously stupid you did if you happen to use it. I don't understand how people can't tell the difference between what CAN be used in English (which is correct English, duh) and what can't, like text language or whatever.

Doubtless there are some children who can't 'tell the difference', and who therefore introduce the occasional text spelling or abbreviation into their written work. Teachers and examiners have told me of cases, and I have seen some examples of work in which a few abbreviations appear. But the instances were few and sporadic, evidence of carelessness or lack of thought rather than a systematic inability to spell and punctuate. I also got the impression, from the general appearance of the handwriting, that some of the writers were simply in a hurry, and in their rush to get ideas down and complete a paper in time used some abbreviations in much the same way as anyone might replace *for example* by *e.g.* or use an *etc.* to replace some items in a list.

The formal examination reports are not much help, for they present an unclear picture, and their conclusions are distorted by media hype. For example, in 2006, the chief examiner's report of the Irish State Examination Commission drew attention to a concern over one section of the Junior Certificate:[2]

> Expertise in text messaging and email in particular would appear to have affected spelling and punctuation. Text messaging, with its use of phonetic spelling and little or no punctuation, seems to pose a threat to traditional conventions in writing.

The comment was made in relation to the 'Personal Writing' section of the examination; no similar comments were made in relation to the other six sections of the exam. The conclusion in the second sentence – even allowing for its cautious phrasing – hardly seems warranted, therefore. But it takes very little to rouse the prophets of doom.[3] And not surprisingly it was the 'threat' which motivated all the headlines, in which the language of possibility was transformed into the language of definite fact:

> Shock: text messages blamed for declining standards in written language (*Mobile Digest*)
> Text messages destroying our language (*The Daily Opinion*: see p. 7 above)

Also in 2006, the Scottish Qualifications Authority commented that text abbreviations were appearing, but only in a 'very small' percentage of exam papers.[4] In relation to the task of 'Folio Writing', they comment on things that some candidates found 'demanding':

> observance of the conventions of written expression and, in a few cases, the avoidance of the inappropriate use of the informalities of talk and, occasionally, 'text language'

It was a comment made for the Standard Grade only, not for the Intermediate 1 and 2, Higher, or Advanced Higher. Note the qualifications: 'few cases', 'occasionally'. This was not enough to stop adverse political reaction and media comment about the language being 'murdered' (to take a headline from *The Sunday Times*).[5]

Tim Shortis, a former chief examiner for English language A-level at the exam board AQAB, said he had rarely seen **textisms** used in A-level papers, though they were more common at **GCSE** level. He commented:[6]

> There's a **moral panic** about young people and language, a populist alarm. But the examples you see in the media are rarely used. You get **initialisms** such as *LOL* for 'laugh out loud' and letter and number homophones such as *r* and *2*, but they are not as widespread as you think. There are also remarkably few casual misspellings.

It would be strange if it were otherwise. As [I have shown elsewhere], very few words in a language are abbreviated by texters – we are talking about a few dozen common words and phrases, and certainly not hundreds. Not all young texters use the abbreviated forms. And those who do use them do not use them very much – in as few as 6 per cent of messages, in [a] Norwegian study[7]... People who talk of texting as a 'new language', implying that the whole of the writing system is altered, are inculcating a myth.

None of this is to doubt the frequently reported observation that there are many instances of poor written work in schools. But it is crucial to recognize the various causes of inadequate literacy. There are indeed children who are weak at writing, poor spellers, and bad punctuators. There always have been. Possibly up to 10 per cent of the child population have learning difficulties (such as dyslexia) in which reading and writing are specifically affected. The problems facing these children are increasingly being recognized. But there is nothing new about them. They were there long before texting was invented.

Another group of children are said to be poor writers and spellers, compared with previous generations, for a whole host of other reasons – too much television, too many video games, too much internet, not enough reading... It is not my purpose [here] to explore these issues. All I want to point out is that these reasons pre-date texting. The claim that there has been a decline in writing skills, whatever its merits, goes back decades. It is the theme of the opening pages of the Bullock Report on English.[8] That was in 1975. This report quoted several firms complaining about the poor levels of spoken and written English in their employees. One firm said that they were having 'great difficulty in obtaining junior clerks who can speak and write English clearly and correctly, especially those aged from 15 to 16 years'. That was in 1921.

I do not see how texting could be a significant factor when discussing children who have real problems with literacy. If you have difficulty with reading and writing, you are hardly going to be predisposed to use a technology which demands sophisticated abilities in reading and writing. And if you do start to text, I would expect the additional experience of writing to be a help, rather than a hindrance.

There is a curious ambivalence around. Complaints are made about children's poor literacy, and then, when a technology arrives that provides fresh and motivating opportunities to read and write, such as email, chat, blogging, and texting, complaints are made about that. The problems associated with the new medium – such as new abbreviation styles – are highlighted and the potential benefits ignored. I heard someone recently complaining that 'children don't keep diaries any more'. The speaker was evidently unaware of the fact that the online diary – the blog – is one of the most popular areas of internet activity among young people.

A couple of axioms might be usefully affirmed at this point. I believe that any form of writing exercise is good for you. I also believe that any form of **tuition** which helps develop your awareness of the different properties, styles, and effects of writing is good for you. It helps you become a better reader, more sensitive to nuance, and a better writer, more sensitive to audience. Texting language is no different from other innovative forms of written expression that have emerged in the past. It is a type of language whose communicative strengths and weaknesses need to be appreciated. If it were to take its place alongside other kinds of writing in school curricula, students would soon develop a strong sense of when it is appropriate to use it and when it is not. It is not as if the school would be teaching them something totally new.... [M]any websites are already making texters aware that there are some situations in which it is inappropriate to use texting abbreviations, because they might not be understood.

This might seem to be self-evident, yet when a text-messaging unit was included as an option in the English curriculum in schools in Victoria, Australia, for students in years 8 to 10, it was condemned by no less a person than the federal minister of education.[9] The students were being taught to translate **SMS** texts, write glossaries of abbreviations, and compare the language of texting with that of formal written English. Stylistic comparisons of this kind have long proved their worth in English classes; their value is repeatedly asserted in the documents which led to the UK English National Curriculum, for example, and the comparative study of standard and nonstandard varieties of language is now a regular event in the English classroom – and not only in the UK.[10] The minister was reported as urging a return to 'basics'. But what could be more basic, in terms of language acquisition, than to focus on students' developing sense of linguistic appropriateness?

The knee-jerk antagonism to texting as a variety of language is fostered by the misinformation about it in the media. For example, on 9 November 2006 Wikipedia accepted an entry which was headed 'New Zealand students able to use txt language in exams'.[11] It began:

> The New Zealand Qualifications Authority (NZQA) has announced that a shorter version of English known as txt language will be acceptable in the external end of year exams.

This seems absolutely clear-cut, and if it were true – given the widespread suspicion of texting – likely to provoke an outcry. But the NZQA site the next day told a very different story:[12]

> The Qualifications Authority is actively discouraging candidates in NCEA exams from using abbreviations, including text-style abbreviations. Deputy Chief Executive, Qualifications, Bali Haque said there had been no change in the Authority's policy in regard to use of abbreviations in examinations. Where an examination requires candidates to demonstrate language use – i.e. sentence structure, grammar, spelling – they would be penalised for using abbreviations, Mr Haque said... [because] use of abbreviations creates a risk of answers not being understood.

Far more people find the Wikipedia site than the NZQA one, of course, so the error lives on.

Misinformation of this kind can be crushed only by solid research findings. And research is slowly beginning to show that texting actually benefits literacy skills. The studies are few, with small numbers of children, so we must be cautious; but a picture is emerging that texting does not harm writing ability and may even help it. Here are the findings of some recent studies:

- Veenal Raval, a speech and language therapist working at the City University in London, compared a group of 11- to 12-year-old texters with a similar group of non-texters.[13] She found that neither group had noticeably worse spelling or grammar than the other, but that both groups made some errors. She also noted that text abbreviations did not appear in their written work.
- A team of Finnish researchers found that the informal style of texting was an important motivating factor, especially among teenage boys, and provided fresh opportunities for linguistic creativity.[14]
- In a series of studies carried out in 2006–7, Beverly Plester, Clare Wood, and others from Coventry University found strong positive links between the use of text language and the skills underlying success in standard English in a group of pre-teenage children.[15] The children were asked to compose text messages that they might write in a particular situation – such as texting a friend to say that they had missed their bus and they were going to be late. The more text abbreviations they used in their messages, the higher they scored on tests of reading and vocabulary. The children who were better at spelling and writing used the most texting abbreviations. Also interesting was the finding that the younger the children received their first phone, the higher their scores.

These results surprise some people. But why should one be surprised? Children could not be good at texting if they had not already developed considerable literacy awareness. Before you can write abbreviated forms effectively and play with them, you need to have a sense of how the sounds of your language relate to the letters. You need to know that there are such things as alternative spellings. You need to have a good visual memory and good motor skills. If you are aware that your texting behaviour is different, you must have already intuited that there is such a thing as a standard. If you are using such abbreviations as *lol* ('laughing out loud') and *brb* ('be right back'), you must have developed a sensitivity to the communicative needs of your textees, because these forms show you are responding to them. If you are using *imho* ('in my humble opinion') or *afaik* ('as far as I know'), you must be aware of the possible effect your choice of language might have on them, because these forms show you are self-critical. Teenage texters are not stupid nor are they socially inept within their peer group. They know exactly what they are doing.

What teenagers are not good at is fully understanding the consequences of what they are doing, in the eyes of society as a whole. And this is where teaching (in the broadest sense of the word) comes in. They need to know when it would be appropriate to text and when it would not be. They need to know when textisms are effective and when they are not. They need to appreciate the range of social reactions which texting, in its various forms, can elicit. This knowledge is slowly acquired from parents, peers, text etiquette websites, and (in the narrow sense) teachers. Teenagers have to learn to manage this new behaviour, as indeed do we all. For one thing is certain: texting is not going to go away, in the foreseeable future.

These arguments are not unique to texting. They apply equally to the other 'literacies' which children need to acquire if they are to achieve a fluent command of their language as readers and writers. Here are three sentences from the previous paragraph, but with the texting terminology replaced by terms relating to a different variety of language:

> They need to know when it would be appropriate to use scientific language and when it would not be. They need to know when scientific jargon is effective and when it is not. They need to appreciate the range of social reactions which scientific jargon, in its various forms, can elicit.

You could replace 'scientific language' by many other terms: 'literary language', 'poetic language', 'journalistic language', 'advertising language', 'nonstandard language', 'regional dialect'... The aim of language education is to put all these literacies under the confident control of the student, so that when they leave school they are able to cope with the linguistic demands made upon them.

Texting is just another variety of language, which has arisen as a result of a particular technology. It takes its place alongside the other mediums of electronic communication which have resulted from the internet revolution. Texting is not alone, and many of its linguistic properties are shared by other kinds of computer-mediated communication. For example, text messages are short; but so are several other forms of electronic expression. In fact they are not the most succinct form: that record is held by instant messaging. A comparative study by Richard Ling and Naomi Baron showed that almost 60 per cent of text messages contained more than one sentence while only 34 per cent of instant messages did.[16] Sentences were longer in texting and there were more characters per message. Texts are more autonomous. This is unsurprising: it would be awkward and uneconomical to continue a lengthy chat dialogue by mobile phone. Because each text message has an individual cost, messages tend to be fuller and more self-contained. Instant messaging, by contrast, readily spreads the content of a message serially over several transmissions, with no cost implications, so that individual transmissions tend to be short and incomplete in character.

In the end, whatever the strengths and weaknesses of texting as a variety of language, it is in the classroom that matters need to be managed. If there are children who are unaware of the difference between texting and standard English, then it is up to teachers to make them aware. If there are children whose discourse skills are being hampered by texting, then it is up to teachers to show them how to improve. Some methods will work well and some will not. As the old song might have said, it's not what you teach but the way that you teach it. The point is made succinctly by Jill Attewell in a paper for *Literacy Today* in 2003:[17]

> there are reports of examiners finding SMS abbreviations and slang in GCSE English papers. This is worrying, although enquiries should perhaps focus on how teachers have prepared their pupils for the examinations rather than on the students' use of mobile phones.

It would indeed be worrying if students entered an examination hall unaware of the difference between formal and informal English, or between standard and nonstandard English. Fortunately, all the evidence from examiners and others suggests that the vast majority of students are well aware of the difference, and do not use textisms in their writing.

The research findings are promising, but we do not yet know if the positive results will be replicated across all ability levels of children and all aspects of linguistic structure. And the emergence of these findings does not mean that we can be blasé about maintaining a balance between texting and other aspects of linguistic behaviour. For example, the use of the phone keypad, along with the ready availability of predictive texting, reinforces the point made in the 1990s that the internet is reducing the opportunities, and thus the ability, of children to use handwriting. Teaching – and examining – needs to take this into account. The need to maintain a clear and fluent handwriting style is of great importance – and not only to guard against the day when there is a power-cut.

Research reports also repeatedly draw attention to the reduced grammatical complexity of text messages – as indeed of some other kinds of electronic communication, such as chat and instant messaging. Text messages are quite short, compared with emails, blogging, and other kinds of forum activity, and certainly much shorter than most traditional forms of written expression, such as the letter, diary entry, or essay. The sentences are also shorter, making use of elliptical constructions in the manner of conversational speech (e.g. *Getting the 4 pm bus* rather than *I'm getting the 4 pm bus*). Grammatical words are often omitted, in the manner of a telegram (*bus arriving 7.10*). The danger here, it is suggested, is that the constraint to write in short sentences might make children think in correspondingly short bursts, so that they become less able to handle notions which require more complex elucidation. One of Veenal Raval's findings was that texters wrote less than non-texters when asked to describe a picture. If this turns out to be a genuine effect – that text messaging is fostering a reduction in discourse skills – then this is certainly something which needs to be compensated for in classroom activity. But findings are mixed. One research team found considerable collaborative discourse activity in using mobile phones, with young people often sitting together and exchanging text content in what they refer to as 'gift-giving rituals'.[18] And another study concluded that texting actually helps the development of communication skills such as the ability to summarize and express oneself concisely.[19] The same study also suggested that texting motivates people to sharpen their diplomatic skills, for, as with all written activity, it allows more time to formulate thoughts and express them carefully.

As with any new technology, people have to learn to manage it. There are undoubtedly problems in relation to the use of texting, but they seem to be social or physiological, not linguistic, in character. For example, one report, by Jan Van den Bulck from the Catholic University of Leuven in Belgium, found that text messages interrupted the sleep of most adolescents.[20] Among 13-year-olds, 13.4 per cent reported being woken up one to three times a month, 5.8 per cent were woken up once a week, 5.3 per cent were woken up several times a week, and 2.2 per cent were woken up every night. Among 16-year-olds, the interference was greater: 20.8 per cent were woken up between one and three times a month, 10.8 per cent were woken up at least once a week, 8.9 per cent were woken up several times a week, and 2.9 per cent were woken up every night. This is an issue that goes well beyond the linguistic.

The issues raised by texting also go well beyond children in schools. Another report, by Glenn Wilson from the University of London, commissioned by technology firm Hewlett Packard, identified problems of reduced concentration, productivity, and even IQ among employees who spent too much time texting while at work.[21] The practice was evidently also causing some harm to personal relations: half the employees said they always responded immediately to a message – notwithstanding the fact that most people think it highly discourteous to read or answer a text message or email during a face-to-face meeting. The problems carried over into the outside world, with most employees reporting that they checked work-related text messages and emails even when at home or on holiday.

The press have made much use of the term 'addiction', when reporting such findings; and indeed, there have been reports of people booking themselves into clinics for help. In 2003 the Priory clinics were reporting a sharp rise in 'technology addiction', with some people evidently texting up to seven hours a day.[22] There have also been reports of undesirable physical effects. Physiotherapists have begun to notice cases of text message injury (TMI), a form of repetitive stress injury caused by excessive use of the thumb to type text messages.[23] There is also a risk of damage to the hand, wrist, and arm. They advise texters to use both hands when texting, to hold the phone higher up and as close to the body as possible to avoid neck and shoulder strain, to keep the phone as close to the body as possible to avoid extra strain on the arms, and to take regular breaks.

Anything which reduces the number of keystrokes is seen as a good thing, such as predictive texting – or, of course, abbreviating.

At the same time, other reports are more positive. Texting has proved valuable in giving children a discreet way of reporting when they are being bullied.[24] Several teachers have stories of reserved, introverted, or nervous pupils who have had their expressive confidence boosted by their use of texting. The point has long been appreciated with reference to the use of the internet to provide chat forums in distance learning;[25] and it seems to be just as relevant here.

A national survey carried out by Kate Fox in 2001 for the Social Issues Research Centre in the UK drew attention to the important role played by texting as part of the 'gossip' of a speech community.[26] Most of her focus-group participants saw texting as an important means of maintaining contact in a large social network:

> they found texting an ideal way to keep in touch with friends and family when they did not have the time, energy, inclination or budget for a 'proper' phone conversation or visit.

Her main conclusion in relation to the teenagers she interviewed supported the point made above:

> texting can help them to overcome their awkwardness and develop their social and communication skills: they communicate with more people, and communicate more frequently, than they did before having access to mobile texting.

Fox's conclusions about texting formed part of a larger study of the important role of gossip in maintaining social networks. Texting dialogue reminded her of village-green conversations where little content may be exchanged but personal connections are made. And the supporting technology for mobile phones has a similar social effect in other parts of the world. In Africa, for example, limited electricity supply has brought people together in an unexpected way:[27]

> In the town centre there is one phone shop that sells airtime and phones. This is where many people also charge their phones. Many have to wait for their phones because there have been incidents of phones disappearing, and there are no guarantees or insurances... It is common to find mostly professionals, like teachers, chatting near the shop as they wait because their schools do not have electricity; new social networks develop from this; discussions range from sharing expertise, development issues to politics...
>
> [in another village] I have observed a few people who come specifically to charge their phones, mostly retirees who do not want to walk to the village shop, maybe to save their money and airtime. They are not charged for this but I have seen them discuss issues from their experience with those in the vicinity and others working in the compound like veterinarians and children. From a cultural aspect, it reminds me of how the old used to sit around the fire with the young and impart knowledge. This culture has gradually died in many communities but maybe this charging of mobile phones may partially replace it.

Texting is one of the most innovative linguistic phenomena of modern times, and perhaps that is why it has generated such strong emotions – 'a kind of laziness', 'an affectation', 'ridiculous'[28] – and why we have seen [a] 'moral panic.'... Yet all the evidence suggests that belief in an impending linguistic disaster is a consequence of a mythology largely created by the media. Children's use of text abbreviations has been hugely exaggerated, and the mobile phone companies have played a part in this by emphasizing their 'cool' character, compiling dictionaries, and publishing usage guides – doubtless, thereby, motivating sales.

Texting has been blamed for all kinds of evils that it could not possibly have been responsible for. Virtually any piece of nonstandard English in schoolwork is now likely to be considered the result of texting, even if the evidence is incontrovertible that the nonstandardism has been around for generations. The other day I read about someone condemning *would of* (for *would have*) as a consequence of texting. That mis-spelling has been around for at least 200 years. You will find it in Keats. I have encountered similar misapprehensions in Japan, Finland, Sweden, and France, and it is probably present in every country where texting has become a feature of daily communication.

In a logical world, text messaging should not have survived. Imagine a pitch to a potential investor. 'I have this great idea. A new way of person-to-person communication, using your phone. The users won't have a familiar keyboard. Their fingers will have trouble finding the keys. They will be able to send messages, but with no more than 160 characters at a time. The writing on the screens will be very small and difficult to read, especially if you have a visual handicap. The messages will arrive at any time, interrupting your daily routine or your sleep. Oh, and every now and again you won't be able to send or receive anything because your battery will run out. Please invest in it.' What would you have done?

But, it was direct, avoiding the problem of tracking down someone over the phone. It was quick, avoiding the waiting time associated with letters and emails. It was focused, avoiding time-wasting small-talk. It was portable, allowing messages to be sent from virtually anywhere. It could even be done with one hand, making it usable while holding on to a roof-strap in a crowded bus. It was personal, allowing intimacy and secrecy, reminiscent of classroom notes under the desk. It was unnoticed in public settings, if the user turned off the ringtone. It allowed young people to overcome the spatial boundary of the home, allowing communication with the outside world without the knowledge of parents and siblings. It hugely empowered the deaf, the shared writing system reducing the gap between them and hearing people. And it was relatively cheap (though, given the quantity of messaging, some parents still had an unpleasant shock when their phone bill arrived). It wasn't surprising, therefore, that it soon became the preferred method of communication among teenagers. Youngsters valued its role both as a badge of identity, like accents and dialects, and as a **ludic** linguistic pastime. And in due course adults too came to value its discreetness and convenience. The interruption caused by the arrival of a text message is disregarded. To those who text, the beep heralding a new message invariably thrills, not pains.

How long will it last? It is always difficult to predict the future, when it comes to technology. Perhaps it will remain as part of an increasingly sophisticated battery of communicative methods, to be used as circumstances require. Or perhaps in a generation's time texting will seem as archaic a method of communication as the typewriter or the telegram does today, and new styles will have emerged to replace it. For the moment, texting seems here to stay, though its linguistic character will undoubtedly alter as its use spreads among the older population.

Some people dislike texting. Some are bemused by it. Some love it. I am fascinated by it, for it is the latest manifestation of the human ability to be linguistically creative and to adapt language to suit the demands of diverse settings. In texting we are seeing, in a small way, language in evolution.

## Notes

1. <http://news.bbc.co.uk/cbbcnews/hi/chat/your_comments/newsid_2814000/2814357.stm>

2. <http://www.examinations.ie/archive/examiners_reports/cer_2006/JC_English_2006. pdf>

3. For an excellent collection of media quotations along these lines, see Crispin Thurlow, 'From statistical panic to moral panic: the metadiscursive construction and popular exaggeration of new media language in the print media', *Journal of Computer-Mediated Communication* 11 (3). <http://jcmc.indiana.edu/vol11/issue3/thurlow.html>

   The term 'moral panic' is the watchword of Stan Cohen, *Folk Devils and Moral Panics* (Routledge, 1972, 3rd edn 2002).

4. <http://www.sqa.org.uk/files_ccc/CourseReportEnglish2006.pdf> <http://www.sqa.org.uk/files_ccc/PAReportEnglish-StandardGrade2006.pdf>

5. Katie Grant, 'Our language is being murdered', *The Sunday Times*, 5 November 2006. <http://www.timesonline.co.uk/tol/newspapers/sunday_times/scotland/article624235.ece>

6. <http://www.tes.co.uk/search/story/?story_id=2341958>

7. 'The socio-linguistics of SMS: An analysis of SMS use by a random sample of Norwegians', in R. Ling and P. Pedersen (eds.), *Mobile Communications: Renegotiation of the Social Sphere* (London: Springer, 2005), 335–49.

8. *A Language for Life* (London: HMSO, 1975).

9. <http://www.abc.net.au/worldtoday/content/2006/s1760068.htm>

10. For example, in the Kingman Report (London: HMSO, 1988), section 4.29, and many other places.

11. <http://en.wikinews.org/wiki/New_Zealand_students_able_to_use_txt_language_in_exams>

12. <http://www.nzqa.govt.nz/news/releases/2006/101106.html>

13. <http://www.city.ac.uk/marketing/dps/Citynews/email_bulletin/0060%20Citynews%20email%20bulletin%20-%2010%20January%202005.pdf>

14. E.-L. Kasesniemi and P. Rautiainen (2002), 'Mobile culture of children and teenagers in Finland', in J. E. Katz and M. Aakhus (eds.), *Perpetual Contact: Mobile Communication, Private Talk and Public Performance* (Cambridge: Cambridge University Press), 170–92.

15. Beverly Plester, Clare Wood, and Victoria Bell (2008), 'Txt msg n school literacy: does mobile phone use adversely affect children's attainment?' *Literacy* 42, 137–44 and Beverly Plester, Clare Wood, and Puja Joshi (2009), 'Exploring the relationship between children's knowledge of text message abbreviations and school literacy outcomes', *British Journal of Developmental Psychology* 27, 145–61.

16. Naomi Baron and Richard Ling, 'IM and SMS: a linguistic comparison', paper given at the International Conference of the Association of Internet Researchers, Toronto, October 2003.

17. <http://www.literacytrust.org.uk/Pubs/attewell.html>

18. A. S. Taylor and R. Harper, 'Age-old practices in the "new world": a study of gift giving between teenage mobile phone users', paper given at the Conference on Human Factors and Computing Systems, Minneapolis, April 2002.

19. Kate Fox, 'Evolution, alienation and gossip: the role of mobile telecommunications in the 21st century', *Social Issues Research Centre, 2001*. <www.sirc.org/publik/gossip.shtml>

20. Jan Van den Bulck, 'Text messaging as a cause of sleep interruption in adolescents, evidence from a cross-sectional study', *Journal of Sleep Research* 12 (2003), 263.

21. <http://www.timesonline.co.uk/tol/life_and_style/education/student/news/article384086.ece>

22. Report in <http://news.bbc.co.uk/1/hi/uk/3165546.stm>.

23. <http://www.csp.org.uk/director/newsandevents/news.cfm?item_id=117F52FABA0EFD81E11F1670148A480C>

24. <http://www.bteducation.org/news/newsitem.ikml?-id=376&PHPSESSID=13a3584ee0>

25. For example, by Boyd H. Davis and Jeutonne P. Brewer, *Electronic Discourse: Linguistic Individuals in Virtual Space* (Albany: State University of New York Press, 1997).

26. See Fox (note 19).

27. C. N. Adeya, 'Wireless technologies and development in Africa', in *Wireless Communication and Development: a Global Perspective*, 2005. <http://arnic.info/workshop05.php>

28. <http://www.student.nada.kth.se/~ulslxvti/SPRAKT/sms.pdf>

## Critical Thinking and Application

- What are the forms of "moral panic" regarding texting that Crystal summarizes? Why do you think people are so uneasy about new forms of communication?
- Do you agree with the claim that "texting is just another variety of language, which has arisen as a result of a particular technology"? Why or why not?
- Think about different forms of communication (e-mail, texting, Twitter, Skype, IM, phone, etc.). How do the norms of interaction differ? What kinds of politeness, correctness, humor or irony, seriousness, spelling, grammar, and so forth are appropriate for each one? What happens if you violate the norms and use the wrong level of politeness?
- What are the rules of etiquette that apply to texting? For example, ask your classmates or conduct a survey about such topics as: where is it appropriate and where inappropriate? Does someone have to respond immediately to a text? (Think of your own questions, too.)
- Collect a dozen conversations that occur through texting from yourself or—with the permission of both parties—from your classmates or friends. Analyze the language: Is it similar to other written forms? Are there any linguistic features unique to texting? Why do you think they occur?

## Vocabulary

| | | |
|---|---|---|
| A-Level | ludic | SMS |
| GCSE | moral panic | textism |
| initialism | orthography | tuition |

## Suggested Further Reading

Baron, Dennis. 2009. *A Better Pencil: Readers, Writers, and the Digital Revolution*. Oxford and New York: Oxford University Press.

Baron, Naomi S. 2008. *Always On: Language in an Online and Mobile World*. Oxford and New York: Oxford University Press.

Bauerlein, Mark. 2008. *The Dumbest Generation: How the Digital Age Stupefies Young Americans and Jeopardizes Our Future [or, Don't Trust Anyone Under 30]*. New York: Tarcher/Penguin.

Cameron, Deborah. 1995. *Verbal Hygiene*. London and New York: Routledge.

Cohen, Stanley. 1980. *Folk Devils and Moral Panics: The Creation of the Mods and Rockers*. New York: St. Martin's Press.

Crystal, David. 2008. *Txtng: The Gr8 Db8*. New York: Oxford University Press.

Horst, Heather A., and Daniel Miller. 2006. *The Cell Phone: An Anthropology of Communication*. Oxford and New York: Berg.

Ito, Mizuko, Heather Horst, Matteo Bittanti, danah boyd, Becky Herr-Stephenson, Patricia G. Lange, C. J. Pascoe, and Laura Robinson. 2008. *Living and Learning with New Media: Summary of Findings from the Digital Youth Project*. Cambridge, MA: MIT Press.

Ito, Mizuko, Daisuke Okabe, and Misa Matsuda. 2005. *Personal, Portable, Pedestrian: Mobile Phones in Japanese Life*. Cambridge, MA: MIT Press.

Ito, Mizuko, et al. 2010. *Hanging Out, Messing Around, and Geeking Out: Kids Living and Learning with New Media*. Cambridge, MA: MIT Press.

Katz, James E. 2006. *Magic in the Air: Mobile Communication and the Transformation of Social Life*. New Brunswick, NJ: Transaction.

Katz, James E., and Mark Aakhus, eds. 2002. *Perpetual Contact: Mobile Communication, Private Talk, Public Performance*. Cambridge: Cambridge University Press.

Ling, Rich. 2008. *New Tech, New Ties: How Mobile Communication Is Reshaping Social Cohesion*. Cambridge, MA: MIT Press.

Tapscott, Don. 2009. *Grown Up Digital: How the Net Generation Is Changing Your World*. New York: McGraw-Hill.

Turkle, Sherry. 2011. *Alone Together: Why We Expect More from Technology and Less from Each Other*. New York: Basic Books.

Wortham, Jenna. 2010. Cellphones Now Used More for Data Than for Calls. *The New York Times* (May 14), p. B1.

# CHAPTER 17

# Literacies in the Lives of Urban Youth

## *Jabari Mahiri*

(2008)

*Statistics are often given of literacy rates. But building on the work of Shirley Brice Heath and others (see Chapter 10), Jabari Mahiri demonstrates that literacy varies. We can study its specific forms in a variety of settings, looking at the ways writing and reading are incorporated into daily life and how they intersect with various forms of digital media. The old absolute dichotomy between "literacy" and "orality," or "literacy" and "illiteracy," was shown by Heath and Brian Street, among others, as irrelevant to the ways people interact with words. Here we find more complex questions again as we broaden our gaze to include the entire range of semiotic domains—written texts, digital texts, images, games, music, and more.*

### Reading Questions

- What is usually meant by "literacy"? How is it usually measured?
- What are "multimodal texts"? How is music relevant to the discussion of literacies?
- How does Mahiri challenge the idea that conventional accounts of "print-based literacy" fail to do justice to "the richness and complexity of actual literacy practices in young people's lives enabled by new technologies that magnify and simplify access to and creation of multimodal texts"? Do you agree?

## Introduction

A period of approximately 30 years from the late 1970s through 2006 frames the discussion in this chapter of out-of-school literacy practices. Young people born during this period can be seen as "natives" of the digital age. A key feature of this age is that "new media" enabled by digital computer technologies greatly increased the mobility, interchangeability, and accessibility of texts and signs while magnifying and simplifying processes for their production and dissemination. Video games, instant or text messages, blogs, zines, email, ipods, ichat, and Internet sites like myspace are digitized places that many young people inhabit. Importantly, these new media have enabled "new literacies" (see also Leander and Lewis, 2008; Street, 2008; Schultz and Hull, 2008). Another consideration for this period is its overlap and reciprocal influences with the hip-hop generation—youth around the world who utilize particular styles of music, language, dress, and other practices linked to hip-hop culture for core representations of meaning and identity. During the early part of this period, ways that youth were framed in public discourse contrasted with ways young people have begun to use new media to enact alternative frames. Finally, this period reflected fundamental changes in how literacy itself was conceptualized, moving from traditional literacy models that focused on writing and speech as the central forms of representation to new literacy and new media models that explore **multimodal** and multi-textual representational practices and forms "situated" in specific social contexts.

Jabari Mahiri, Literacies in the Lives of Urban Youth. *Encyclopedia of Language and Education*, volume 2, *Literacy*, 2nd ed., edited by Brian V. Street and Nancy H. Hornberger. New York: Springer Science+Business Media, 2008, pp. 299–307.

## Early Developments

Earlier theories of literacy as static skills that had pervasive cognitive consequences by scholars like Jack Goody and Ian Watt, David Olsen, and Walter Ong began to encounter challenges in the late 1970s and early 1980s from a number of scholars like Ruth Finnegan, Sylvia Scribner, Michael Cole, Denny Taylor, and Marcia Farr who reported ethnographic research on actual literacy practices in various social contexts. Heath (1983) was a classic example of these studies that described the range of **literacy events** and **practices** of different participants acting together in social situations. She explored the language socialization of children in two communities she called Trackton and Roadville and compared these processes in conjunction with a third community of townspeople. Among other things, she found very different literacy events occurring.

Storytelling, for example, varied considerably from community to community. The black residents of Trackton saw the facts of a story very differently from the white residents of Roadville. Although Trackton storytellers may have based their stories on actual events, they liberally fictionalized the details such that the outcome of the story might bear no resemblance to what really happened. These highly elaborated tales were greatly valued. However, parents in this community almost never read stories to their children. In Roadville, on the other hand, stories were read to children and stories would also stick to the facts. There residents usually waited to be invited to tell their stories where in Trackton stories were self-initiated in order to reveal personal status and power. These literacy events had different functions and different social meanings in the different communities. This work by Heath and others during the late 70s and early 80s made early contributions to re-conceptualizing non-school literacy practices by delineating distinct and culturally specific ways of making and receiving meaning in a variety of textual mediums.

Extending the re-conceptions of literacy that were emerging from various ethnographic studies, Street (1984) argued that earlier theories claiming that literacy was a universal and decontextualized set of skills that did not change significantly from one social setting to another reflected an **"autonomous model"** that was severely limited for understanding actual literacy practices. He put forth an **"ideological model"** as an alternative framework for understanding literacy in terms of concrete social practices embedded in and given meaning through different ideologies. He chose the term "ideological" to denote that these practices were aspects of power structures as well as of cultures. In further developing this framework, Street (1993) began to outline a "new literacy studies" approach to focus more comprehensively on how literacy is linked to social and cultural contexts. In this edited volume, Street brought together research from a variety of world cultures to investigate and demonstrate the different meanings and uses of literacy in different cultures and societies. This work globalized what Heath (1983) had done with local communities and families in one geographical region.

One early revision of the autonomous model of literacy was a "continuum model" that challenged the notion of a great divide between orality and written texts. Yet, this model also tended to reify "literacy in itself at the expense of recognition of its location in structures of power and ideology" (Street, 1993, p. 4). Street co-founded a group of international scholars (see Gee, 1990; Barton and Hamilton, 1998; Barton, Hamilton and Ivanic, 1999; Pahl and Rowsell, 2006; etc.) called the New Literacy Studies Group who took the view that literacies were multiple rather than a monolithic concept, and that they should be studied as variably and historically "situated" practices within social, cultural, economic, and political contexts. The contributions reviewed in the following section reflect this new literacy perspective.

## MAJOR CONTRIBUTIONS

A wave of qualitative research and critique influenced by the early developments in studying and theorizing non-school literacy practices began to explore sociocultural contexts like transnational communities (Guerra, 1998, 2004; Gutierrez, 1997; Lam, 2004), families (Cushman, 1998), churches (Moss, 1994), sports (Mahiri, 1994), youth social and peer groups (Finders, 1996; Smith and Wilhelm, 2002; Willis, 1990) youth organizations (Heath and McLaughlin, 1993; Maira and Soep, 2005), gangs (Cowan, 2004), rap music and spoken word venues (Miller, 2004; Rose, 1994), and digital mediated spaces like the Internet (Alvermann, 2002), video games (Gee, 2004), and other electronic media (Johnson, 2005). This work documented and analyzed literacy practices and built additional, grounded theories about learning and literacy in non-school settings.

For example, Guerra's (1998) transnational fieldwork with a Mexicano social network of several hundred people residing both in Chicago and in a rural *rancho* in Mexico further problematized notions of dichotomies between orality and literacy. His research indicated that both were highly overlapping linguistic (rhetorical) practices that resisted any clear characterization of fixed boundaries between them. Furthering this analysis, he used the literacy practices of one young woman in this social network to demonstrate her use of overlapping, situated literacies and a "nomadic consciousness" (shaped by continual physical and linguistic border crossings) to enact what he termed "transcultural repositioning"—a rhetorical ability to productively move back and forth between different languages, literacies, dialects, social settings, and ways of seeing and thinking (Guerra, 2004). Transcultural repositioning elides the simplicity of dichotomous models of literacy and can be connected to Gutierrez (1997) and her collaborators' notion of a "third space" for language and literacy learning. Moving beyond discourses that position literacies as oppositional and hierarchical, these researchers posited a third space in which less distinction is placed on formal versus informal learning and more emphasis is placed on normalizing multiple pathways and literacies as learning resources. Lam (2004) utilized a slightly different third space metaphor in her research on the transnational discourse of Chinese youth to illuminate the nature of their reading and discussion of international comic books as a fundamental social practice linked to literacy learning and the transformation of their cultural identity. Here the third space was the site of new or emerging frames of reference and processes of signification afforded between cultures of transnational youth.

A number of significant contributions followed leads from Heath (1983) to look further at community literacy practices revealed in families, churches, youth social groups, and neighborhood based organizations serving youth. Cushman (1998) showed the rich repertoire of literacy practices that poor black women exhibit as they interact with societal institutions from which they need to get resources. Moss's

(1994) work on black sermons delivered from full, partial, or no texts continued the complication of intersections between oral and written language. Mahiri (1994) described and assessed an array of spontaneous and adaptive literacy practices of preadolescent African American males linked to their involvement in a community sports program. Smith and Wilhelm (2002) looked at boys and young men from a variety of backgrounds to investigate why males disproportionately underperform in literacy and found wide-ranging practices of literacy that usually do not get valued in schools. Cowan (2004) researched the low-rider car culture of some Latino males (who are often assumed to be gang members) and found unique literacy practices associated with constructing reading cars as symbolic texts and powerful identity markers. By contrast, Willis (1990) noted that traditional conceptions of symbolic creativity "have no real connection with most young people or their lives" (p. 1). Focusing on adolescent girls, Finders (1996) captured both visible and "hidden" literacies that girls use to construct personal identity and to maintain friendship groups. All of these studies or critiques acknowledged the contrast of their copious findings of complex and expansive practices of literacy to how little is known or utilized from these practices in schools and other societal institutions.

Other more recent contributions have explored the workings and implications of novel literacy practices connected to and often enabled by digital technologies. Manovich (2001) described how earlier visual media eventually converged with (or was consumed by) digital computer technologies through the expanding capability of computers to translate all existing media into numerical data. The result was a "new media" that incorporated graphics, moving images, sounds, shapes, and other forms of texts into data that was computable and thereby interchangeable. These qualities allowed for new forms of authorial assemblage through re-mixing, sampling, and cutting-and-pasting of highly mutable and (through the Internet) highly accessible texts. It created what Miller (2004) termed a "gift economy" that supplies abundant textual raw materials that allow consumers of all kinds of literacy texts to easily become producers of them. Johnson (2005) argued that as these kinds of transformations in **meaning making** are taking place, "the culture is getting more intellectually demanding, not less" (p. 9). Gee (2003), in his analysis of how these transformations play out specifically in the domain of video games noted that the theory of learning reflected in these digital environments actually "fits better with the modern, high-tech, global world today's children and teenagers live in than do the theories (and practices) of learning that they see in school" (p. 7).

A number of studies have attempted to understand how and what intellectual demands and literacy practices are engaged by youth in digital environments. For the studies in her edited volume Alvermann (2002) broadened "the term *literacies* to include the performative, visual, aural, and **semiotic** understandings necessary for constructing and reconstructing print-and-nonprint-based texts" (p. viii). Chapters in [Street and Hornberger 2008] describe the new "attention" economy that is becoming increasingly pervasive; they portray literacies in the lives of people defined as "millennial" adolescents or "Shape-Shifting Portfolio People"; and, they argue that youth participation in digital technologies offers dramatically new ways of constructing meanings and identities.

An illuminating example of some of these considerations was provided in a study by Fleetwood (2005). Her description and analysis of the production process for a narrative video about youth life in San Francisco's Mission District that was to be shot from the youth's perspective revealed provocative issues connected to practices of literacy and the creation and representation of identity through digital visual media. The question this study raised was could this visual media be utilized by youth for "authentic" projections, or did the larger community and organizational context surrounding the use of this media inherently work to mainly racialize and contrive youth identity? It was a question of could practices of literacy associated with visual media production work to transform rather than merely conform perceptions of youth. Fleetwood concludes that youth media production does provide possibilities for alternative representations of youth, but it does not resolve the complicated problems of youth being represented authentically.

## Work in Progress

In attempting to apprehend more authentic youth practices and representations, recent research has worked to counter characterizations of youth in mainstream media and political discourse as a "transitional" category and often marked as violent, or dangerous, or weird: "the devious computer hacker, the fast-talking rapper, the ultra-fashionable Japanese teenager teetering on platform heels. Youth in these incarnations personify a given society's deepest anxieties" (Maira and Soep, 2005, p. xv). The on-going work of these researchers attempts to capture and critique "the transnational imaginaries of youth culture" facilitated by the global reach of technology, but "always in dialectical tension with both national ideologies and local affiliations" (p. xxvi).

Other on-going research on learning and literacy of youth outside of schools attempts to capture their authentic textual productions and symbolic representations at the intersection of new or alternative digital media and the local and global manifestations of hip-hop culture. Miller (2004) continues to demonstrate the cross-fertilizing connections between hip-hop and technology noting, for example, that rap artists were quickest to exploit digital samplers and sequencers when these and other technologies suited their cultural purposes. A decade earlier Rose (1994) had argued that "hip hop transforms stray technological parts intended for cultural and industrial trash heaps into sources of pleasure and power. These transformations have become a basis of digital imagination all over the world" (p. 22). Now, contemporary youth in the U.S and globally are utilizing technological resources to sample, cut and paste, and re-mix multimedia and multimodal texts for replay in new configurations, just as hip hop DJs reconfigure images, words, and sounds to play anew (see Richardson, 2008).

Work by Mahiri and a group of collaborators (2007) is one example of research at the intersection of digital media and hip-hop culture. One of the originators of hip-hop, DJ Here, claimed that it "has given young people a way to understand their world" (Quoted in Chang, 2005, p. xi). It is widely considered to be a salient voice of contemporary youth—a voice that is electrified, digitized, and spoken through rappers' mikes, DJ music mixes, dance styles, and graffiti. The mic of the music DJ or the rap and spoken word MC is a potent symbol at the intersection of power and pleasure on hand inside this dynamic and comprehensive aspect of youth culture. The mic also marks the intersection and interaction of production and consumption of hip-hop texts and styles. Mahiri and his collaborators are documenting and analyzing the wide-ranging practices of literacy inside hip-hop culture focused on how these practices are manifested on both sides of the mic by producers and consumers who are writing and reading the world though vibrant, provocative, music-centric lenses.

Other work in progress by a group of distinguished literacy researchers under the direction of Banks (2007) is focused on understanding and theorizing the nature of learning that is "life-long, life-wide, and life-deep." This research is comprehensively addressing the nature of learning in the multiple contexts and valued practices of everyday life across the life span and attempting to connect the different and continuously changing "whats" of learning to the different and continually changing "whos" of learners. One strand of this research contends that for youth particularly, the complexity of rapidly changing repertoires of practice might be best understood as "semiotic domains" that Gee (2003) noted as "any set of practices that recruit one or more modalities (e.g., oral or written language, images, equations, symbols, sounds, gestures, graphs, artifacts, etc.) [to create] and communicate distinctive types of meaning" (p. 18). This research on learning for youth that is life-long, life-wide, and life-deep is attempting to understand semiotic domains that are increasingly linked to interactive, web compatible, digital technologies like cell phones, ipods, video games, audio and video recording and playback devices, as well as computers.

## Problems and Difficulties

Traditional conceptions of print-based literacy do not account for the richness and complexity of actual literacy practices in young people's lives enabled by new technologies that magnify and simplify access to and creation of multimodal texts. Similarly, traditional research processes (that intimately link to traditional conceptions of print-based literacy) are not well suited to capture these widely variable, highly changeable, temporal, and local acts of meaning making and identity construction. The novel, diverse, and transient text production and utilization we attempt to document, analyze, and publish are only realized long "after the fact" and thereby increase the possibility that the fact has significantly changed.

How do we bridge the generational divide between researchers and researched? If our informants are digital natives, we are more like digital tourists who are recognized immediately as if we were wearing fanny packs and white running shoes. I have tried to circumvent this problem by working with young graduate student researchers, but even they are quickly reminded that they are "old school." More importantly, how do we bridge conceptual divides that distort our views of youth practices as they are filtered through our more static cultural models? Particularly the primacy of modes of meaning making and representation for youth seem to have shifted from written texts to more dynamic and interactive visual, tactile, and sonic texts, yet the primacy of modes for attempting to report these shifts seems not to be affected at all by these changes.

## Future Directions

A key challenge for the future seems to be to imagine and implement new ways to more fully and more accurately capture and reflect the significance of everyday practices of youth in part through their textual productions. Willis (1990) noted, "that there is a vibrant symbolic life and symbolic creativity in everyday life, everyday activity and expression—even if it is sometimes invisible, looked down on or spurned. We don't want to invent it or propose it. We want to recognize it—literally re-cognize it" (p. 1).

One thing that needs to be "re-cognized" in research on the literacy and learning of youth is the centrality of practices of meaning making and representation through musical texts the selection of which enact narratives—sonic significations—that are increasingly enabled by digital technologies. "Sound," Miller (2004) claimed, "has become a digital **signifier** whose form adjusts its shape in front of us like an amorphous cloud made of zeros and ones" (p. 5). His point and intent (that more literacy researchers may also need to engage) is to create a "rhythm science"—"a forensic investigation of sound as a vector of coded language that goes from the physical to the informational and back again" (pp. 4–5).

### References

Alvermann, D. E. (ed.). 2002. *Adolescents and literacies in a digital world*, Peter Lang Publishing, New York.

Banks, J. 2007. Learning: Life-long, life-wide, life-deep. Center for Multicultural Education, University of Washington.

Barton, D. and Hamilton, M. 1998. *Local literacies: reading and writing in one community*, Routledge, London.

Barton, D., Hamilton, M., and Ivanic, R. (eds.). 1999. *Situated literacies: Reading and writing in context*, Routledge, London.

Chang, J. 2005. *Can't stop won't stop: A history of the hip-hop generation*, St Martin's Press, New York.

Cowan, P. 1994. 'Devils or angels: Literacy and discourse in lowrider culture', in J. Mahiri (ed.), *What they don't learn in school: Literacy in the lives of urban youth*, Peter Lang Publishing, New York, 47–74.

Cushman, E. 1998. *The struggle and the tools: Oral and literate strategies in an inner city community*, State University of New York Press, Albany, New York.

Finders, M. 1996. *Just girls: Hidden literacies and life in junior high*, Teachers College Press, New York.

Fleetwood, N. R. 2005. 'Authenticating practices: Producing realness, performing youth,' in S. Maira and E. Soep (eds.), *Youthscapes: The popular, the national, the global*, University of Pennsylvania Press, Philadelphia, 155–72.

Gee, J. P. 1990. *Social linguistics and literacy: Ideology in discourses*, Falmer Press, London.

Gee, J. P. 2004. *What video games have to teach us about learning and literacy*, Palgrave Macmillan, New York.

Guerra, J. 1998. *Close to home: Oral and literate strategies in a transnational Mexicano community*, Teachers College Press, New York.

Guerra, J. 2004, 'Putting literacy in its place: Nomadic consciousness and the practice of transnational repositioning', in C. Gutierrez-Jones (ed.), *Rebellious reading: The dynamics of Chicana/o cultural literacy*. Center for Chicana/o Studies, Santa Barbara, CA.

Gutierrez, K. D., Baquedano-Lopez, P., and Turner, M. G. 1997. 'Putting language back into language arts: When the radical middle meets the third space', *Language Arts* 74(5), 368–78.

Heath, S. B. 1983. *Ways with words: Language, life, and work in communities and classrooms*, Cambridge University Press, Cambridge.

Johnson, S. 2005. *Everything bad is good for you: How today popular culture is actually making us smarter*, Riverhead Books, New York.

Lam, E. 2004. 'Border discourses and identities in transnational youth culture', in J. Mahiri (ed.), *What they don't learn in school: Literacy in the lives of urban youth*, Peter Lang Publishing, New York, 79–98.

Leander, K. M., and Lewis, C. 2008. 'Literacy and Internet technologies', in B. V. Street and Hornberger, N. H. (eds.), *Encyclopedia of language and education*, 2nd ed., vol. 2, *Literacy*, Springer Science+Business, New York, 53–70.

Mahiri, J. 1994. 'Reading rites and sports: Motivation for adaptive literacy of young African American males', in B. Moss (ed.), *Literacy across communities*, Hampton Press, Cresskill, NJ.

Mahiri, J., Ali, M., Scott, A., Asmerom, B., and Ayers, R. 2007. 'Both sides of the mic: Digital natives in the age of hip-hop', in J. Flood, D. Lapp, and S. B. Heath (Vol. II Eds.), *Handbook of research on teaching literacy through the communicative, visual, and performing arts*, Lawrence Erlbaum, Mahwah, NJ.

Maira, S. and Soep, E. (eds.). 2005. *Youthscapes: The popular, the national, the global*, University of Pennsylvania Press, Philadelphia.

Manovich, L. 2001. *The language of new media*, MIT Press, Cambridge, MA.

Miller, P. 2004. *Rhythm science*, MIT Press, Cambridge, MA.

Moss, B. 1994. Creating a community: Literacy events in African American Churches, in B. Moss (ed.), *Literacy across communities*, Hampton Press, Cresskill, NJ.

Pahl, K. and Rowsell, J. (eds.). 2006. *Travel notes from the New Literacy Studies: Case studies in practice*, Multilingual Matters Ltd, Clevedon.

Richardson, E. 2008. 'African American literacies', in B. V. Street and Hornberger, N. H. (eds.), *Encyclopedia of language and education*, 2nd ed., vol. 2, *Literacy*, Springer Science+Business, New York, 335–46.

Rose, T. 1994. *Black noise: Rap music and black culture in contemporary America*, Wesleyan University Press, Middletown, CT.

Schultz, K., and Hull, G. 2008. 'Literacies in and out of school in the United States', in B.V. Street and Hornberger, N. H. (eds.), *Encyclopedia of language and education*, 2nd ed., vol. 2, *Literacy*, Springer Science+Business, New York, 239–50.

Smith, M. W. and Wilhelm, J. D. 2002. *"Reading don't fix no Chevys": Literacy in the lives of young men*, Heinemann, Portsmouth, NH.

Street, B. 1984. *Literacy in theory and practice*, Cambridge University Press, Cambridge.

Street, B. (ed.). 1993. *Cross-cultural approaches to literacy*, Cambridge University Press, Cambridge.

Street, B. V. 2008. 'New literacies, new times: Developments in literacy studies', in B. V. Street and Hornberger, N. H. (eds.), *Encyclopedia of language and education*, 2nd ed., vol. 2, *Literacy*, Springer Science+Business, New York, 3–14.

Street, B. V., and Hornberger, N. H. (eds.). 2008. *Encyclopedia of language and education*, 2nd ed., vol. 2, *Literacy*, Springer Science+Business, New York.

Willis, P. 1990. 'Symbolic creativity', in *Common culture: Symbolic work at play in the everyday cultures of the young*, Westview Press, Boulder, CO, 1–83.

## Critical Thinking and Application

- Mahiri suggests that some forms of modern music, such as hip-hop, blur the distinction between producer and consumer. What does this mean? How has this changed the ways youth interact with music?
- Do you think "digital natives" differ from their elders in their use of texts? Is this a fundamental difference or something that can be regarded just as a change of form?

- Given the realities of the ways urban youth employ texts, how does school fit into this? Might there be some way that school could play a role in preparing youth for their real lives?

## Vocabulary

| | | |
|---|---|---|
| autonomous model | literacy practice | semiotic |
| ideological model | meaning making | signifier |
| literacy event | multimodal | |

## Suggested Further Reading [See also list following (New) Media unit introduction]


Barton, David. 1988. *Problems with an Evolutionary Account of Literacy*. Lancaster Papers in Linguistics no. 49. Department of Linguistics, University of Lancaster.

Barton, David, Mary Hamilton, and Roz Ivanič, eds. 2000. *Situated Literacies: Reading and Writing in Context*. London and New York: Routledge.

Basso, Keith H. 1974. The Ethnography of Writing. In *Explorations in the Ethnography of Speaking*, edited by Richard Bauman and Joel Sherzer, pp. 425–432. Cambridge: Cambridge University Press.

Baynham, Mike. 1993. Code Switching and Mode Switching: Community Interpreters and Mediators of Literacy. In *Cross-Cultural Approaches to Literacy*, edited by Brian V. Street, pp. 294–314. Cambridge: Cambridge University Press.

Chang, Jeff. 2005. *Can't Stop, Won't Stop: A History of the Hip-Hop Generation*. New York: St. Martin's Press.

Collins, James. 1995. Literacy and Literacies. *Annual Review of Anthropology* 24: 75–93.

Cook-Gumperz, Jenny, ed. 1986. *The Social Construction of Literacy*. Cambridge: Cambridge University Press.

Everhart, Robert B. 1983. *Reading, Writing and Resistance: Adolescence and Labour in a Junior High School*. London: Routledge & Kegan Paul.

Finnegan, Ruth. 1988. *Literacy and Orality: Studies in the Technology of Communication*. Oxford: Blackwell.

Goody, Jack. 1977. *The Domestication of the Savage Mind*. Cambridge: Cambridge University Press.

Goody, Jack, and Ian Watt. 1963. The Consequences of Literacy. *Comparative Studies in Society and History* 5: 304–345.

Graff, Harvey J. 1979. *The Literacy Myth: Literacy and Social Structure in the Nineteenth Century City*. New York: Academic Press.

Heath, Shirley Brice. 1983. *Ways with Words: Language, Life, and Work in Communities and Classroom*. Cambridge: Cambridge University Press.

Heath, Shirley Brice, and Brian V. Street. 2007. *On Ethnography: Approaches to Language and Literacy Research*. National Conference on Research in Language and Literacy. New York: Teachers College Columbia.

Jenkins, Henry. 2006. *Convergence Culture: Where Old and New Media Collide*. New York and London: New York University Press.

Kimberly, Keith, Margaret Meek, and Jane Miller. 1992. *New Readings: Contributions to an Understanding of Literacy*. London: Black.

Kintgen, Eugene R., Barry M. Kroll, and Mike Rose, eds. 1988. *Perspectives on Literacy*. Carbondale: Southern Illinois University Press.

Lankshear, Colin, and Moira Lawler. 1987. *Literacy, Schooling and Revolution*. Brighton: Falmer Press.

Levine, Kenneth. 1986. *The Social Context of Literacy*. London: Routledge & Kegan Paul.

Mace, Jane. 1979. *Working with Words*. London: Chameleon.

Mace, Jane. 1992. *Talking About Literacy*. London: Routledge.

McDermott, R. P., Hervé Varenne, and Vera Hamid-Buglione. 1982. *"I Teach Him Everything He Learns in School": The Acquisition of Literacy for Learning in Working Class Families*. New York: Teachers College Press.

McLaren, Peter L. 1986. *Schooling as a Ritual Performance*. London: Routledge & Kegan Paul.

Meek, Margaret. 1991. *On Being Literate*. London: Bodley Head.

Mercer, Neil, ed. 1988. *Language and Literacy from an Educational Perspective: A Reader*. Milton Keynes: Open University Press.

Morgan, Marcyliena. 2001. "Nothin' but a G Thang": Grammar and Language Ideology in Hip Hop Identity. In *Sociocultural and Historical Contexts of African American English*, edited by Sonja L. Lanehart, pp. 187–209. Amsterdam and Philadelphia: Benjamins.

Morgan, Marcyeliena. 2002. *Language, Discourse, and Power in African American Culture*. Cambridge: Cambridge University Press.

Ong, Walter. 1982. *Orality and Literacy: The Technologizing of the Word*. London: Methuen.

Pahl, Kate, and Jennifer Rowsell, eds. 2006. *Travel Notes from the New Literacy Studies: Instances of Practice*. Clevedon: Multilingual Matters.

Rampton, Ben. 1995. *Crossing: Language and Ethnicity Among Adolescents*. London and New York: Longman.

Rogers, Alan, ed. 2005. *Urban Literacy: Communication, Identity, and Learning in Development Contexts*. Hamburg, Germany: UNESCO Institute for Education.

Schieffelin, B., and Perry Gilmore, eds. 1986. *The Acquisition of Literacy: Ethnographic Perspectives*. Norwood, NJ: Ablex.

Shuman, Amy. 1986. *Storytelling Rights: The Uses of Oral and Written Texts by Urban Adolescents*. Cambridge: Cambridge University Press.

Smith, Frank. 1983. *Essays into Literacy*. Exeter, NH: Heinemann.

Smith, Marc Kelly, and Mark Eleveld. 2003. *The Spoken Word Revolution: Slam, Hip-Hop, and the Poetry of a New Generation*. Naperville, IL: Sourcebooks MediaFusion.

Street, Brian V. 1984. *Literacy in Theory and Practice*. Cambridge Studies in Oral and Literate Cultures no. 9. Cambridge: Cambridge University Press.

Street, Brian V., ed. 1993. *Cross-Cultural Approaches to Literacy*. Cambridge Studies in Oral and Literate Cultures. Cambridge: Cambridge University Press.

Street, Brian. 2003. What's "New" in New Literacy Studies? Critical Approaches to Literacy in Theory and Practice. *Current Issues in Comparative Education* 5(2): 77–91.

Street, Brian V., and Niko Besnier. 1994. Aspects of Literacy. In *Companion Encyclopedia of Anthropology*, edited by Tim Ingold, pp. 527–562. London and New York: Routledge.

Street, Brian V., and Adam Lefstein. 2007. *Literacy: An Advanced Resource Book*. London and New York: Routledge.

Szwed, J. F. 1981. The Ethnography of Literacy. In *Writing: The Nature, Development, and Teaching of Written Communication*, Vol. 1, edited by Marcia Farr Whiteman, pp. 13–23. Hillsdale, NJ: Erlbaum.

Watkins, S. Craig. 2005. *Hip Hop Matters: Politics, Pop Culture, and the Struggle for the Soul of a Movement*. Boston: Beacon Press.

Willinsky, John. 1990. *The New Literacy: Redefining Reading and Writing in the Schools*. New York: Routledge.

Willis, Paul. 1977. *Learning to Labour: How Working Class Kids Get Working Class Jobs*. Farnborough: Saxon House.

# CHAPTER 18

# *Homo Somnians*: Humanity in the Age of the Internet

*Marshall T. Poe*

(2011)

*Everybody wants to know: Is the Internet good or bad? Is the world becoming a blissful paradise because of the possibilities now freely available online, or is it becoming hellish and miserable because humans live their lives through screens? Is human life completely transformed, or is it just a speeded-up, connected version of what preceded?*

*This chapter stems from a longer work,* A History of Communications, *devoted to a complete comparative analysis of a range of forms of communication. Its author, historian Marshall Poe, develops a comprehensive theory about the kinds of connections made in a range of media, and their place within the sweep of human history, beginning with speech itself, moving through the invention of writing, and then of printing and audiovisual media. Each type of communication is analyzed carefully. The Internet, too, shares much with other forms of media, while offering some notable innovations. Poe asks genuinely fundamental questions, such as: what is the purpose of communicating? His answer may surprise you.*

### Reading Questions

- What are the technological precursors to the Internet? What needs and desires did the Internet meet?
- What are the factors that Poe suggests "pulled" people toward the Internet, and what are those that "pushed" them toward it?
- How do "Old Media" and "New Media" coexist?
- What are the benefits of the Internet? What are the dangers?

---

Next then, I said... Picture people as dwelling in a cavernous underground chamber, with the entrance opening upward to the light, and a long passageway running down the whole length of the cave. They have been there since childhood, legs and necks fettered so they cannot move: they see only what is in front of them, unable to turn their heads because of the bonds.

A strange image, he said, and strange prisoners.

Like ourselves, I replied.[1]

—PLATO, THE REPUBLIC, 514A

## The Internet Before the Internet

The story of the Web properly begins in sixteenth-century Europe during the Scientific Revolution, for it was then and there that the project that would end in the Internet was conceived in its modern form. That project was the systematic collection, classification, and dissemination of knowledge for the purpose of scientific progress.[2] The initial spurs that urged European thinkers to pay close attention to data gathering, classification, and dissemination were two. The first spur was the revival of ancient Greek scientific interests and practices. Aristotle and his peers stimulated Europeans to think anew about the world of the senses, the more so now that their many works were widely available thanks to print. No better example of the new attention to data collection, classification, and dissemination can be given than that of Tycho Brahe, whose exact observations of celestial bodies helped his assistant, Johannes Kepler, formulate his eponymous laws of planetary motion and revolutionize our understanding of cosmology.[3] The second spur was imperialism. The people of the Renaissance had the good fortune of "discovering" (to put it very mildly) new worlds,

Marshall T. Poe, *Homo Somnians*: Humanity in the Age of the Internet. From *A History of Communications: Media and Society from the Evolution of Speech to the Internet*. Cambridge: Cambridge University Press, 2011, pp. 202–250.

and when they did, they imported new things from them by the ton. These novelties were often categorized and displayed in early museums of natural history – cabinets of curiosities (*Kunstkammern* or *Wunderkammern*). Scientifically minded elites created the first such institutions in the mid-sixteenth century.[4] By all reports they were big hits. The impulse to collect and catalogue was a characteristic of the age, as we can see in the pathbreaking methodological writings of Francis Bacon, proto-information scientist *par excellence*. Bacon is most famous for the saying "knowledge is power."[5] He seems to have believed it. In a number of still-read books, Bacon outlined a program to banish ignorance and superstition by collecting, measuring, analyzing, and comparing everything. Like so many ambitious programs, it proved largely unworkable.

Happily, some of Bacon's fellows and followers were rather more practical than he. The founders of the early scientific societies not only theorized about collecting and exchanging data, they created organizations to do it. The result of their handiwork can be seen in the Italian *Accademia dei Lincei* (founded 1603), the English Royal Society (founded 1660), the French *Académie des sciences* (founded 1666), the Prussian *Akademie der Wissenschaften* (founded 1724), and the Russian *Akademiia nauk* (founded 1724).[6] Before these societies, natural philosophers had only very limited means to discuss their work with like-minded colleagues. The early scientific societies and state-sponsored institutions – especially research universities – improved this situation dramatically. Together they created the basic structure for handling scholarly information that persisted until the birth of the Internet. This system comprised three institutions. The first was the *library*, which allowed scientific information to accumulate in one place for easy access. The second was the *index*, which permitted information in the library to be retrieved. And the third was the *article* (in a book or journal), which allowed scientists to share information at a distance. The entire system worked in a loop: scientists produced journals that fed the libraries that were indexed by bibliographers who then supplied them to scientists who produced more journals, and so on.

The new system of scholarly communications constituted a real step forward, but it was by no means perfect. Far from it. Libraries concentrated information, which was good. But they also isolated it, which was bad. You had to go to the library, it could not come to you. So if you weren't near the library you needed or if you were near and couldn't get in, you were out of luck. Indexes helped you find information, which was good. But they also hid it from you, which was bad. Alphabetical or subject indexes generally do not penetrate – or do not penetrate very far – the items they index. In an ordinary card catalogue, you get the author, title, a few subject headings, and the book's location in the stacks. Almost everything between the covers is obscured. This is to say that you really had to know exactly what you were looking for before you started to look, and this is inconvenient if you don't know quite what you want. Articles provided a convenient means to share scientific information on a specific topic, which was good. But they shared the deficiencies of the library and the index, which was bad. That is, if you didn't have access to the article for whatever reason – a subscription cost too much, the library lost it, your dog ate it – it might as well not exist. And even if you did have access to it, there was no really efficient method to find out exactly what was in it other than to read it carefully – not a very efficient way to track down specific facts. In short, the entire thing didn't work well for people who: (a) didn't have access to a big library; (b) didn't know exactly what they were looking for; and (c) didn't have the time or patience to read everything that might have what they wanted. That pretty much describes everyone who wasn't a student or professor at a university.

The problem was recognized. As early as the eighteenth century, enlightened souls were trying to figure out ways to improve scholarly communications and bring trustworthy knowledge to the people who needed it. The French *encyclopédistes* felt that the existing mechanism of separating truth from superstition, disseminating the former and discarding the latter, was wanting. To rectify this sorry situation, Denis Diderot, Jean le Rond d'Alembert, and their *philosophe* allies revived an old (Greek, as it happens) idea – the encyclopedia.[7] They set themselves the task of compiling all that was true and useful in one place for all time. The result was the epoch-making thirty-five-volume *Encyclopédie, ou dictionnaire raisonné des sciences, des arts et des métiers* (1751–). Yet the *Encyclopédie* and its imitators (especially the *Encyclopedia Britannica* [1768–] and the *Brockhaus Enzyklopädie* [1796–]) were limited by the **medium** in which they were produced, namely print. Books are fine for many purposes, but if your object is to provide a universal store of knowledge in which anything can be found instantly and anything can be amended as needed, they are not ideal. Anyone who has ever used a print encyclopedia knows that they are big but not complete; well-indexed, though not well enough; and often updated, though never really current.

Print not only limited the degree to which scholarly communications could be perfected, it also limited the imaginations of the men and women who were trying to perfect it. Diderot, d'Alembert, and the Enlightenment gang just couldn't conceive of a way to store, find, and transmit information outside the ink-and-paper paradigm. A bit later, however, some began to see past the printed book. One such visionary was the French bibliographer and information scientist Paul Otlet.[8] Otlet didn't much like books. He felt – correctly – that they concealed as much as they revealed. They were full of data that was basically hidden from researchers and, more importantly to the progressive, Internationalist Otlet, hidden from humankind in general. To Otlet, the existing means of storing, categorizing, and conveying information hindered human progress. But Otlet had a solution – the humble 3 × 5 index card. Otlet and his colleagues wanted to use the index card to crack the book, that is, to extract from the standard scientific print medium every bit of discrete information it held. According to Otlet's plan, these unique bits would be recorded on 3 × 5 cards and classified according to an exhaustive universal index so that information could be found and easily retrieved. He called his index the "Universal Decimal Classification." It was a kind of Dewey Decimal System on steroids. Otlet even dreamed of creating a Rube Goldberg-esque workstation in which scholars would use levers to find and extract cards from his massive universal card catalogue. It was all quite mad. The engineering problems presented by print made Otlet's vision utterly impractical. For all that he was ahead of his time, Otlet was still thinking in terms of print.

New technologies such as microfilm inspired his followers to think past print, sort of. One of the most obvious problems with print as a mode of communications is its bulk and weight. A piece of paper is small, but thousands of pieces of paper are big. A piece of paper is light, but thousands of pieces of paper are heavy. Big, heavy things are expensive to transport. This makes them unattractive as **media** (cf. stone tablets). One way to surmount this problem, however, is to shrink the big heavy thing into a small light thing. Publishers have known this trick for centuries, and they have endeavored to test the limits of human vision by publishing ever smaller books with ever smaller type. Interestingly, if you are really devoted (not to say crazy), you can pack a lot of text into a very small place by hand. According to legend, followers of Mao inscribed the entire contents of his *Little Red Book* on a six-sided die. Such feats are impressive, but not very practical. The real breakthrough in tiny text came with the invention of practical photography by Louis Daguerre in 1839.[9] It took less than a year for one of Daguerre's admirers, the lens grinder John Benjamin Dancer of Manchester, to begin miniaturizing photographs for viewing under microscopes. In its early days, microphotography was nothing but a novelty. Rene Dagron of Paris was given the first microphotography patent in 1859. His chief product was a tiny image embedded in a tiny viewer embedded in a tiny trinket. Yet a few forward-thinking people at the time recognized that microphotography might be made to serve more practical purposes. In 1859, the same year Dagron patented his bauble, the *Photographic News* wrote that microphotography might allow "the whole archives of a nation [to be] packed away in a small snuff box."[10] Given the state of miniaturization at the time, it would have had to have been a very big snuff box. But no one needed to build such a box, because no one was really thinking of putting government archives on tiny bits of photographic paper – governments had more important things to think about.

Businesses didn't. In the early twentieth century, banks – theretofore used largely by rich folks and merchants – became truly retail businesses. Everyone began to use them, and thus they found themselves having to track millions of transactions, not only deposits and withdrawals (done at the bank, so easily recorded), but also checking activity (done off site with third parties, so more difficult to record). In the mid-1920s, New York banker George McCarthy saw in microphotography a potential solution to the bank's paperwork problem.[11] With this in mind, the plucky money man invented the "Checkograph," a device that produced microfilm copies of checks flowing through financial institutions. For obvious reasons, Eastman Kodak loved the Checkograph, bought it from McCarthy in 1928, and began to sell microfilming services under its Recordak brand. By the 1940s, governments, university libraries, and corporations began to microfilm their holdings. They did so with some urgency. Even as Recordak filmed, entire cities were being wiped off the map in World War II, taking entire government archives, academic libraries, and corporate vaults with them. The ordinarily upbeat President Franklin Roosevelt stressed that the United States needed to microfilm everything "so that if any part of the country's original archives are destroyed a record of them will exist in some other place."[12] He uttered these words a bit over a month after the Pearl Harbor attack in which, as a matter of fact, "original archives" had been destroyed by Japanese bombers. It seems he expected more of this to come. If he did, he was right.

The notion that microfilm might be used to preserve and disseminate *some* knowledge – banking records, government archives, and such – rather naturally led the futurist H. G. Wells to the idea that it might be used to preserve and disseminate *all* knowledge. Wells proposed the creation of a "Permanent World Encyclopedia" that would capture and convey all of the world's wisdom by means of very tiny text.[13] "At the core of such an institution," he writes, "would be a world synthesis of bibliography and documentation with the indexed archives of the world. A great number of workers would be engaged perpetually in perfecting this index of human knowledge and keeping it up to date. Concurrently, the resources of micro-photography, as yet only in their infancy, will be creating a concentrated visual record." Such a record is, he says, already being created by "American microfilm experts" who are making "facsimiles of the rarest books, manuscripts, pictures and specimens, which can then be made easily accessible upon the library screen." By means of this remarkable technology, he gushes, "there is no practical obstacle whatever now to the creation of an efficient index to all human knowledge, ideas and achievements, to the creation, that is, of a complete planetary memory for all mankind." One suspects that Wells did not have much hands-on experience of the "practical obstacles" presented by microfilm. Indeed, as anyone who has ever used it can attest, such enthusiasm for microfilm can only have been born of never having used it. Wells, it seems, never touched the stuff.

The next wave of information scientists had probably used microfilm, so they knew to look elsewhere for inspiration. The elsewhere in question was in the rapidly developing field of information-handling machines. The notion that one could use mechanical means – wedges, gears, levers, etc. – to store information and even solve mathematical problems was hardly new. The people who built Stonehenge over 4,000 years ago knew it; the Greeks who built devices to predict the position of celestial bodies in the second century BC knew it; the inventors of the slide rule in the seventeenth century knew it. So did one Vannevar Bush, engineer, science tsar, and technological visionary.[14] In the first of these capacities, Bush built the "Differential Analyzer" in 1927, a device that could solve complicated differential equations very quickly and accurately. In the second capacity, Bush ran the Office for Scientific Research and Development, the bureau that oversaw the Manhattan Project and all military research in the United States during World War II. In the final capacity, Bush wrote "As We May Think," an essay published in the *Atlantic Monthly* in 1945.[15]

Today Bush is remembered primarily for "As We May Think." It's little wonder, for it is a remarkably prescient essay. In it, he plainly says that gummed-up scientific communications are a huge problem. "Professionally," he writes, "our methods of transmitting and reviewing the results of research are generations old and by now are totally inadequate for their purpose." Researchers produce more useful information than ever, but more than ever is simply lost due to an antiquated system of storage, search, and retrieval. "The summation of human experience," Bush complains, "is being expanded at a prodigious rate, and the means we use for threading through the consequent maze to the momentarily important item is the same as was used in the days of square-rigged ships." In a word, the print paradigm – libraries, indexes, and articles – just wasn't doing the job anymore, if it ever did.

Bush proposed that the basic problem was the linear way that information was stored, indexed, and retrieved in print. Finding a "record" in a library catalogue was like walking a narrow, confined path: you could go forward or backward, but you couldn't leave the trail. "The human mind," Bush pointed out, "does not work that way. It operates by association. With one item in its grasp, it snaps instantly to the next that is suggested by the association of thoughts, in accordance with some intricate web of trails carried by the cells of the brain." Bush dreamed of a workstation that could store and retrieve huge volumes of information, but which mimicked the way the brain related bits of data by subtle "associations." In the former aspect, Bush's "Memex" looks a lot like Otlet's data contraption, replete with levers, gears, buttons, and plenty of microfilm. It is the latter aspect – sorting by fuzzy, expandable, and user-directed association – that makes Bush's Memex noteworthy. Like Otlet, Bush dreamed of cracking the book, that is, finding a way to extract and isolate every bit of useful information in it. But his "associations" went beyond Otlet, for they allowed researchers to freely create new sources that could then be cracked by other researchers. "It is exactly," Bush wrote, "as though the physical items had been gathered together from widely separated sources and bound together to form a new book."

Bush was ahead of his time, not only in terms of his ideas but also in terms of the technology available to realize them. Yet help was on the way. It came from the U. S. Defense Department.[16] After World War II – which, as you will recall, had gone pretty badly for all sides involved, though worse for some than others – the American military became concerned about preventing "another Pearl Harbor." The U. S. generals had good reason to be worried, as the potential consequences of a sneak attack had grown much more terrible in the terrible nuclear age. So, they wisely set up a system of radar installations designed to detect airborne incursions from sea to shining sea. The radar bases worked fine, as radar itself had been thoroughly battle-tested during the aforementioned world war. In fact, the bases worked a little too well, that is, they provided too much information too fast for even the smartest generals to handle in a reasonable amount of time. And said generals did not, in fact, have a reasonable amount of time to sort through the reams of data and decide what to do, for the attacking planes – flying very fast – would arrive at their targets only minutes after the radars detected their presence. Something needed to be done to improve what the military calls "command and control" or, they said, we'd all be blown to hell. So the defense establishment decided to build a computer-aided information network, the world's first. Made operational in 1959, SAGE (Semi-Automatic Ground Environment) brought everything the decision makers needed to know – including radar images, an innovation – to central locations so the deciding could be done. SAGE also assisted the decision makers – via automation, another innovation – in scrambling fighters and guiding them to their airborne targets.[17] Once again, science and technology had made America safe.

But then another problem arose, a hypothetical one posed by one of the many professionally paranoid people governments employ to dream up nightmarish hypothetical scenarios. What would happen, this thinker of the unthinkable asked, if one of the enemy's bombers got through the radar-based, electronically linked, computer-assisted early-warning system and managed to drop a bomb on the system itself?[18] The answer was plain: the system would crash and take America's ability to make good decisions about what to do next with it. This just wouldn't do. So, in the early 1960s, the government decided to invest some effort in creating a more robust **network**, one that wouldn't collapse like a house of cards if one of its cards were pulled away (or blown to bits, as the case may be). Happily, there were some very smart young scientists working on just this problem at various well-thought-of universities around the globe. They proposed an ingenious solution: break the system's messages up into chunks, send the chunks through multiple paths in the network, and reassemble them at the end. That way, if any path were destroyed, the several parts of the message would still get through by traveling along other paths and could be reassembled as if nothing had happened. Humpty Dumpty *could* be put back together again. This disassembly-reassembly system was called "packet switching" over a "distributed network."[19] It seemed to be a good solution to the problem of network fragility, and the American government was pleased to fund and implement it.

But scientists working on the new communications system pointed out yet another problem, as scientists will. It's fine to switch packets and distribute networks, but the computers doing the switching and distributing have to be able to talk to one another. Computers, you may recall, were sort of new at the time, and a lot of people were building them. Computer companies generally built computers that could talk to the ones they built, but not to the ones that other people built. So there were a lot of computers that couldn't talk to one another, many of them in the American defense establishment itself, as it was the primary market for expensive computers. This was bad. But it wasn't the only difficulty, the scientists warned. Rather more selfishly, they noted that not only were mute computers bad for the nation's defense, they were also bad for science itself. You see, mathematicians, engineers, and physicists – all the folks who are so vital to America's security – love to talk to one another. They must do so, and often, in order to accomplish their work efficiently and effectively. If their computers couldn't talk to one another, neither could they, and science would suffer. So the scientists proposed a solution that would solve both the generals' problem and theirs: a set of computers and computer protocols (a sort of *lingua franca* for machines) that would link not only the defense establishment's computers in a distributed network, but theirs (or rather, those owned by their research institutes and universities) as well. The American government, being wealthy, worried, and respectful of scientists, decided to fund and implement this program too. So was the Advanced Research Projects Agency Network (ARPANET) born in 1969.[20]

Alas, neat though it was, ARPANET wasn't very useful if you weren't a general or a computer scientist. This was true for a variety of reasons, but the chief one was that you couldn't get to ARPANET from your network, wherever your network was. And there were several good ones in different places around the country and world. Just as a lot of computer companies were producing computers that couldn't talk to one another, there were serious establishments (especially scientific institutes and universities) creating networks that couldn't talk to one another. The military didn't care much, because it had its own network and, prizing secrecy as military folk will, didn't really want anyone else on it. But communications-hungry scientists did care, because they wanted to trade information in the service of scientific progress. What was needed, they said, was a network of networks, a massive grid that would enable every scientist to talk to every other scientist no matter what network he or she was on. As many parties and interests were involved, it took well over a decade, a lot of negotiation, and a boatload of money to create this "inter-network." But by the mid-1980s, the network of networks – the "Internet" – was alive and well, linking most big institutes and universities in the nation, and some overseas.[21]

Although the Internet was much bigger and more accessible than ARPANET, it was still pretty hard to use. You could exchange messages, files, and even run some programs remotely, but beyond that you couldn't really do much unless you were an expert. This bothered an English fellow named Tim Berners Lee. He worked at a big Swiss physics laboratory, and it was his job to make it simple for scientists to collaborate. Since it plainly wasn't simple, he set about designing a way to make the Internet useful as a collaborative tool. He figured that what people really wanted out of a network was access to things on computers, not computers themselves. After all, when you use the phone, you want to talk to someone, not simply connect to another phone. It's the same with the Internet. You want to use it to get information in documents, not to connect to computers. So in the early 1990s, he and a French colleague designed a system that used the Internet to store, receive, and send documents, and he called his invention the "World Wide Web."[22] On the World Wide Web, you seem to move from document to document, reading what you want and moving on. The computers are just where they should be, in the background. Technical people almost immediately recognized that the Web was extremely useful, and they made it a kind of a standard.

At this point, the Internet and the Web that ran on top of it were still obscure. People in the computer industry knew about it, because they make their living building gadgetry. Scientists knew about it, because they enjoy collaborating with colleagues in distant places. And, finally, geeks – especially young geeks – knew about it, because young geeky people make it their business to know about the latest technical advances. While the computer-builders were busy building networked computers for the collaborating scientists, a team of young geeks in Illinois had a monumental insight.[23] First, they noted that a lot of people were buying desktop PCs running the Windows or Macintosh operating systems, not UNIX, which was standard in "serious" computing. Second, they noted that these PCs could be hooked up to the Internet by phone lines. Third, they noted that our frustrated English fellow in Switzerland had already created a kind of software that made it easy to send, receive, and store multimedia documents on the Internet, although his program was kind of clunky and not very pretty. So these college students put one, two, and three together and set about creating a really intuitive, clean, multimedia "Web browser" for users of PCs. The browser was something like a combination of a glossy magazine – full of pictures and text – and a TV beamed right into your home. It made the Internet easy to understand. In 1993, these college students *cum* entrepreneurs began to give their graphical Web browser away under the name "Mosaic." Suddenly it was not only easy to get on the Internet, but once you were there, it was easy to get around. By the mid-1990s, "surfing the net" was an activity like reading the newspaper, listening to radio, or watching TV, although there wasn't much in the way of newspapers, radio, or TV on it.

## "Pulling" the Internet into Existence

And so the Internet was born. Its deepest roots, as we've pointed out, were scientific. In this sense, the Internet is the fulfillment of the 400-year-old dream that information might be collected, stored, and sifted easily, efficiently, and endlessly. Yet science itself did not **"pull"** the Internet into existence in the last quarter of the twentieth century. No, there were larger systemic forces at work, all of which are hinted at in the story we have just told. Generalizing, they were three: information capitalism, the surveillance state, and cultural privatism.

First, there was information capitalism.[24] Industrial capitalism, a product of the eighteenth century and one of the motive forces behind the spread of audiovisual media, is about producing goods. It still exists, as we still need things produced industrially, for there is no more efficient way to make them. But, beginning in the twentieth century, industrial capitalists noted two things. First, they saw that the data-handling requirements of modern business were becoming a drag on productivity and, more important, on profitability. Second, they understood that the return on investment in research and development could be significant, particularly in a legal framework that protected intellectual property and an economic framework – the public company – that allowed rapid financing and development. These two insights put a new and higher premium on information production, manipulation, and storage. Knowledge might be power, but information was money. Companies became interested in what were aptly called "business machines." Calculating engines had been around since the seventeenth century. Both Pascal and Leibniz built them.[25] By the 1880s, they were being produced commercially, and by the 1890s, they were becoming common in offices throughout the developed world. The companies that made calculators and other early data-processing machines (punchers, tabulators, sorters) are still with us today: IBM, NCR, Burroughs (now Unisys).[26] They invested resources in researching and developing new products and supplied a steady stream of them to businesses seeking to make their operations more efficient. Somewhat surprisingly, computers were a relatively late addition to the game. First built in the 1940s, they – "mainframes" – long remained much too expensive for most businesses. With the advent of time-sharing by dial-up connection in the 1960s, more businesses began to use computers in their operations. But it was really only after the introduction of the PC in the late 1970s that computers become a staple of office work.

It was the spread of the PC that was to be businesses' primary contribution to the rise of the Internet, for, by giving computer manufacturers an incentive to produce low-cost, portable, easy-to-use machines, they put computers within reach of large numbers of consumers. This provided a kind of mass "base" for the rapid take-off of the Web in the 1990s. Some thought was given to how networked computers might aid collaborative work, in business and out. Examples include Ted Nelson's "Project Xanadu" (1960s), Murray Turoff's "Electronic Information Exchange System" (1976), Irene Greif and Paul Cashman's "Computer Supported Cooperative Work" (1984), and Charles Findley's "Collaborative Networked Learning" (1986).[27] But, by and large, businesses were caught off guard by the rapid expansion of the Internet. However, once they saw it for what it was – both a new place and a new way to conduct business – they very quickly exploited the opportunity it provided, thereby hastening its expansion.

The "pull" of information capitalism, however, paled before that of the surveillance state.[28] The welfare state was all about providing goods and services at a minimum level to its citizenry. In order to fulfill this mission, however, it needed to collect and crunch a huge amount of data. If you are going to send pension payments to everyone over 65 years of age, you need to know (a) where the money is going to come from; (b) who is going to process it and how; and (c) where the money is going to go. That might not seem like a lot of information until you consider that it requires you to know a host of other things: who works where, what they do, how much they earn, where they live, what they own, what they owe, what sorts of families they live in, to whom they are related, how old they are, and sundry other difficult-to-anticipate items. Then multiply the task by many tens of millions. As the scope of the "safety net" expanded to include educational entitlements, health insurance, unemployment insurance, survivor's benefits, and all the other "rights" afforded to citizens, so too did the information-handling requirements of the state grow. It's not surprising that the enterprise that became IBM got its start building machines to tabulate the results of the U.S. censuses of 1890 and 1900.[29] Neither should it be unexpected that government bureaucracies remained the best customers of the makers of business machines throughout the twentieth century.

The pursuit of national welfare, however, was not the only reason modern states needed to ramp up their information-collecting and data-handling capacities. There were less savory grounds as well. One we have already touched on was the need to find more efficient ways to kill people and prevent them from being killed. The U.S. Defense Department funded virtually all of the research that led to the production of the first American computers, the first American computer networks, and the immediate forerunner of the Internet, ARPANET.[30] This investment was by far the most powerful factor "pulling" the Web into being in the second half of the twentieth century. Another factor was "state security," or rather insecurity. Governments have been spying on their subjects for eons, but the scope and intensity of clandestine state surveillance expanded radically during the twentieth century. This was especially true in the socialist world, where enemies were suspected under every rock, and party dictatorship ensured that every rock would be picked up without objection from the public. But it was also the case in democracies and semi-democracies, particularly during the periodic "Red Scares" that marked the century. Time and again, free governments set civil liberties aside in order to surreptitiously surveil the free citizens in whose interest they supposedly governed. Sometimes they had reason. Sometimes they didn't. But in either case the task of surveillance put an additional load on the state's information-handling capacity, and thereby helped "pull" the Internet into existence.

Finally, there was cultural **hedonism**.[31] In the first half of the twentieth century, cultural liberalism helped bring the modern audiovisual media into being by putting a fig leaf on impropriety. You could show most anything in public, so long as bodies remained clothed, speech clean, and messages "wholesome." The Hay's Code and its fellows made most everyone a hypocrite, which was fine with most everyone. Appearances had to be maintained. Until the 1950s. For reasons that go far beyond the scope of this book, polite hypocrisy began to fall out of favor in that decade in much of the Western world. Like Holden Caulfield, a lot of people suddenly found themselves surrounded by "phonies."[32] Some of these people are cultural icons today: Hugh Heffner, who founded *Playboy* in 1953; Aldous Huxley, who issued *The Doors of Perception* in 1954; Jack Kerouac, who published *On the Road* in 1957.[33] In a sense, all three of these men were hinting at the same thing: appearances don't need to be maintained because they aren't being maintained as it is. We should, therefore, do away with appearances and openly embrace what is "real." And that, for the proto-pornographer, the advocate of drug use, and the poet of loafing about, was raw experience. The rising generation, it turned out, was very receptive to this notion.[34] It became central to the shift in mores that took place during the 1960s, the wake of which we still live in today. Heffner's, Huxley's, and Kerouac's philosophy (if it can be called such) rested on a utilitarian logic that was as compelling as it was simple: all you know and are is what you feel, and therefore the "good life" should be spent in the pursuit of feelings, especially the good ones. Combined with a convenient cynicism toward "the man" – that is, the real world – this doctrine exploded into full-blown hedonism under the thin guise of "mental expansion," "consciousness-raising," and "getting back to nature." Whether any minds were expanded, consciousnesses raised, or natures gotten back to in the 1960s and 1970s is not at all clear. It is certain, though, that a lot of sex was had, drugs were taken, and loafing about done. Not surprisingly, the people who, moving far past anything Heffner, Huxley, and Kerouac ever imagined, trumpeted the virtues of radical hedonism became heroes to the merrymakers and were made celebrities by the press. The names of Timothy Leary, Ken Kesey, and Hunter Thompson still ring today.[35] They were, after a fashion, serious people, or at least famous people, which increasingly amounted to the same thing. The intellectuals of hedonism added a veneer of high-mindedness to the pursuit of raw experience.

The problem, however, was that once right-thinking people had agreed to condone high-minded hedonism, they were defenseless against the low-minded variety. Any such differentiation would make them hypocrites, and recall that it was the fight against hypocrisy that started the slide into hedonism in the first place. If you approved of Hugh Heffner, Aldous Huxley, and Jack Kerouac, it was hard to consistently disapprove of Larry Flint, Snoop Dogg, and Charles Bukowski. These "free spirits" were all just "doing their own thing," which is what everyone was supposed to do. The courts more or less agreed. By the mid-1970s, only two classes of expressions could be constitutionally censored in the United States: (1) those that were likely to promote "imminent lawless action" (*Brandenburg v. Ohio*, 1969); and (2) those that a community deems obscene *and* a reasonable observer would find lacking in any serious "literary, artistic, political or scientific value" (the Miller Test, 1973).[36] In practice, this meant that nothing beyond credible death threats and kiddy porn was banned. The FCC could censor more, but really only on the public airwaves. The 1960s and the birth of cultural hedonism set the stage for the Internet. By the moment of its birth, people were ready for a channel in which they could hear, see, and say anything. Print and audiovisual media could not supply this. The Internet could and did.

## Human Nature and the Internet

. . . Whereas writing and printing spread slowly, audiovisual media took off in a few decades. The reason . . . was in part because we have a natural disinclination to read and write and an inborn inclination to watch and listen. Interestingly, the Internet took off even more quickly than the audiovisual media. In the span of a few years, it covered the globe and penetrated every nation on earth. The preexistence of an audiovisual infrastructure explains much of this rapid spread and remarkable reach: the Internet "piggybacked" on other networks, and so did not have to wait for new networks to be built, as was the case with audiovisual media. But that doesn't explain the entire phenomenon. It seems sensible to say that there is something about the Internet that appeals to our natures, a drive that makes us want it. Is there?

The answer would seem to be "yes." While it would not be fair to say that the Internet **pushes** all our evolutionary buttons, it certainly pushes more of them than any other single device in history. . . . Humans were designed to look for anomalies and solve puzzles. The Internet is full of anomalies and puzzles. The world is a very big place and people are doing all kinds of things. You don't know about most of them. But now they are putting them on the Internet for you to find. Just about any search you perform, no matter how specific, is likely to return results that surprise you and present you with things to figure out. It's all there: the odd, the weird, the strange, the peculiar, the curious, the bizarre, the uncanny, the mysterious – everything. What is more, because you are on the Internet, you can quickly and easily do some research to clear things up. That's the idea, at least. So you surf from link to link to link, uncovering more and more and more information. Yet, as you do, you uncover new anomalies and puzzles that lead you in new directions. A book is a machine for focusing attention; the Internet is a machine for diffusing it. A book takes you on a trip from here to there; the Internet takes you on a trip from here to God-knows-where. Getting lost is half the fun of it. Most of us have had the experience of casually going to look something up on Wikipedia and ending up, an hour or more later, in a place we never imagined, learning about something we never knew existed. In truth, you don't so much look things up on the Internet as just look at things. This is something we clearly like to do, an end in itself. So compelling is our desire for anomalies and puzzles that some of the most popular sites on the Web are devoted to their collection. Some of them are low-brow, like Fark.com, and some are high-brow, like Metafilter.com, but they all exist precisely because we naturally find the unusual, curious, and just plain weird entertaining.

These link-presentation sites exist for another reason, also evolutionary in origin. Not only do we need to find what we called "relevance," but we are driven beyond reason to share what we find with others. We usually do this by talking, but the Internet has provided us with a much larger forum in which to present our trophies. Some commentators make the mistake of calling what happens on the Internet "exchange" and wax lyrical about how the Internet has unleashed a long-repressed human desire to "collaborate."[37] But the truth is that both exchange and collaboration on the Internet are *results* of the native drive to present relevance to others, not the cause. Ultimately speaking, we do not talk because we want to trade information or work together; rather, we talk because we naturally enjoy it, and we naturally enjoy it because talking – the presentation of relevance – increased our fitness eons ago. Similarly, we do not put things on the Internet because we desire to swap information or cooperate with each other; rather, we do it because we naturally enjoy putting things on the Internet, and we naturally enjoy it because this sort of behavior – the presentation of relevance – increased our fitness eons ago. Posting is the continuation of talking by other means.

This is easy to demonstrate. People often wonder why anyone contributes to Wikipedia. Indeed, it's something of a puzzle if you look at it in terms of cost-benefit analysis, at least as cost and benefit are usually understood. What are the costs? Well, there is the time and effort you spend editing. But you spend a lot of time on the Internet anyway, so that's a minor expense. More significantly, there is the very real possibility that your edits will be erased *and*, to add insult to injury, that you will be abused by angry strangers whose hardheadedness is matched only by their ignorance. Wikipedia can be a rough place. What are the benefits? Well, you certainly don't get paid, which is the way most people who work expect to be rewarded. Neither do you attain glory, for most contributors edit Wikipedia anonymously or at least pseudonymously. Contributing just doesn't add up. Yet thousands of people do it. There are probably many reasons – the desire to participate in something "bigger than yourself," the fellowship of the "collaborative community," or the simple alleviation of boredom. But the basic reason people contribute is that they find it enjoyable, and they find it enjoyable for easy-to-understand evolutionary reasons. The Internet is like a great game of show-and-tell, and we like show-and-tell a lot.

Another button that the Internet pushes is our desire to experience what [are] called "intrusive stimuli." These . . . are a class of sounds and sights that we are preprogrammed to pay close attention to, whether we like it or not. They include depictions of sex, food, drink, power, wealth, conflict, and violence. From an evolutionary point of view, these stimuli are always relevant and therefore instinctively draw our ears and eyes. It goes without saying that the Internet is brimming over with material of this sort. Obviously, there is more pornography in more flavors than one can easily comprehend. But not only that. Even "mainstream" sites often have a quasi-pornographic visual style. They show you things that you want to see but don't have the opportunity or stomach to see in "real life." In the former category – opportunity – one would put all the commodity porn that populates so many commercial sites: gadgets, cars, houses, clothes, and "bling" of every kind. In the latter category – stomach – one would put the frequently disturbing pictures and videos of misfortune that litter the Web: pratfalls, car accidents, airplane crashes, and even people being beheaded. Looking at the one and the other you often get a kind of rush. The feeling may be superficially pleasurable or unpleasurable. But in either case it is a feeling, a kind of stimulation, that you desire on some very deep psychological level. If you didn't, you wouldn't look. And you always do.

Information capitalism, the surveillance state, and cultural hedonism "pulled" the modern Internet into existence. They succeeded in doing so rapidly and thoroughly in large measure because we are inclined by nature to like – even to the point of personal harm – what the Internet allows us to do. Once the door to the audiovisual media was opened, we ran through it. Once the door to the Internet was opened, we ran through it and, sometimes, stumbled.

## What the Internet Did (and Is Doing)

Not even two decades ago, then, the world of the "Old Media" – talking, manuscript-writing, printing, broadcasting – became the world of the "New Media" – those carried by the Internet. In truth, that's a bit of an exaggeration in two senses. First, despite what you might have heard, the "Old Media" have not and probably will not disappear, *ever*. All the historical evidence suggests that major media are remarkably persistent: new media don't displace the old, they join them. Second, and again despite what you may have heard, the Internet is not the dominant mode of human communications today. Far from it. About 80 percent of Americans currently use the Internet regularly. On average, they spend 17 hours a week online.[38] Almost all Americans chat, read, and watch TV. Every week they spend on average 13 hours chatting, 2.5 hours reading "for pleasure," and 23 hours playing couch potato.[39] Assuming they aren't doing these things simultaneously, Americans live in the world of the "Old Media" a lot more than they live in the world of the "New Media" (21.5 hours a week more, to be exact). . . .

### Accessibility

There was a time, now dimly remembered, when computers were very expensive and Internet access was rare. The IBM PC, released in 1981, cost around $2,000;[40] the original Apple Macintosh, released in 1984, ran $2,500.[41] Neither had modems. These cost around $225 in 1980.[42] The Internet was in its infancy and there were no Internet service providers (ISPs), but you could access bulletin board systems (BBSs) for a few dollars a month. Today, you can buy any number of new, fully functional PCs – computer, screen, keyboard, mouse, modem – for less than $400.[43] The philanthropic organization "One Laptop per Child" is building a machine that will cost around $200.[44] If you don't mind used computers, you can get one for the price of shipment. Internet access will cost you about $10 a month at home, but you won't have any trouble finding someplace where it's free if you live in the developed world. Every school, public library, café, and many cities offer *gratis* wired or wireless access. And of course you get it at work for nothing, if you don't count the working part.

There was also a time, perhaps not so dimly remembered, in which learning to use a PC and navigate the Internet was hard. Many of us remember the wonders of config.sys, autoexec.bat, and the "blue screen of death." More of us, alas, know what TCP/IP and DHCP stand for. In the main, however, the tendency has been for both "usability" and "connectivity" to increase – that is, become easier – over time. Many computers are now truly "plug and play," though occasionally they have to be re-plugged and re-played. The era in which the tech guy was a god-king is not gone entirely, but it's fading fast. Proof that PCs and Internet access have become less costly in financial and training terms is borne out by the number of people who use them. It's estimated that there are more than one billion PCs in use worldwide today, and that number will double by 2015.[45] Something on the order of 1.4 billion people have Internet access.[46] Both numbers are rising. There are 6.7 billion people on the planet.[47] The digital divide, it would seem, is closing rapidly.[48] We should add that would-be monopolists will have a hard time making Internet access any more expensive than it naturally is, for the Internet's logistical chain has no readily exploitable bottleneck. Computers are made in too many places for production to be controlled. They are small enough that they can be transported relatively easily and secretly. Once in operation, they can be hidden. Some Internet traffic moves over telephone and cable lines, which can be cut, but only at the loss of other important services. Internet signals that are transmitted over satellites and picked up wirelessly are difficult to interrupt. Some tyrannical states have attempted to limit Internet access.[49] Not surprisingly, only North Korea has been really successful, largely because it has no telecommunication infrastructure to speak of.[50] The country code for North Korea is +850, but don't try to call because almost no one has a phone.[51] Satellite dishes and even cell phones are periodically banned. The frightened leaders of China, Iran, Cuba, and other shackled countries censor the Internet, but their ability to do so in the long haul as satellite-delivered service expands seems doubtful.

The Internet is a marvel of accessibility. If you want to get on it and use it, you probably can. If you can't now, you'll be able to soon. Accessible media foster diffused networks, that is, ones in which the ability to send and receive messages is shared by a large proportion of the population. In the developed world – Canada, the United States, Western Europe, Japan, South Korea, Australia – 40 to 80 percent of the population have Internet access.[52] In the less developed though developing world – Mexico, South America, the Middle East, Russia, China – 20 to 40 percent of the population have it. In the undeveloped world – Africa, Central Asia, Southern Asia, Southeast Asia – between 0 percent and 20 percent do. Overall, about 20 percent of the earth's population can get on the Internet. According to our theory, diffused networks *equalize* social practices and values evolved in and around them. Diffused networks give everyone roughly equal power to send and receive messages. Thus, it is difficult for any particular sender or receiver to monopolize communications and use unequal control to create unequal power.

There are ways in which the Internet is not democratic at all. Governments regulate it, telecom companies own it, search engines dominate it, and big corporations manipulate it. But having said all that, it's probably the most democratic "place" in the world, at least in the sense of having equalized social practices. In the real world, you are a person with lots of traits – gender, race, class, and all of their subspecies – that differentiate you from others; on the Web, however, you are most often just a "user" like any other. Offline, Bill Gates is very rich and you aren't. But online, Bill Gates is a "user" and so are you. Citizenship is to offline democracy as "userhood" is to online democracy. Since both you and Bill are "users," everything you do together online – play games, talk software, write encyclopedia articles – is going to be on a "peer-to-peer" basis. Actually, *all* virtual social practices are equalized in the sense of "more equal than in the real world." They are not, however, equal for at least two reasons. First, the real world bleeds into the online world. So Bill's offline cred – if the "user" is *really* offline Bill Gates – is going to win him points in the software discussion site that you can't score. Second, reputation matters in the online world. Bill might really know what he's talking about and develop a good reputation, while you might be a "troll" and develop a bad one. Bill's online "peers" are going to listen to him and they aren't going to listen to you (in fact, they may ask the "mods" – moderators – to ban you). If you behave, however, you and everyone else will get a voice, just like your "peer," Bill Gates. . . .

## Privacy

It's the most famous cartoon ever produced about the Internet. It's been reprinted thousands of times. Everyone has seen it. "On the Internet, no one knows you're a dog."[53] In the real world, everyone knows who you are. Here's why. First, you don't get to decide who you are. Others do that for you. You can't elect to be blue if you're born green. You can try to pass as someone you aren't, and some have. But the difficulty and psychological toll are great. Witness Michael Jackson. Second, you only get one identity at a time. You can try to lead a double (or triple, or quadruple) life. This feat, however, is notoriously difficult to pull off, and usually ends in divorce, incarceration, or an extended stay in a mental hospital. Third, you don't get to change identities. You can attempt to remake yourself. But if you really want a new identity, you have to enter the FBI's witness protection program. That, alas, involves saying bad things about some very mean people, a risky endeavor in itself. Finally, you often have to present your identity to others in person. You can avoid the *tête-à-tête* with intermediaries, letters, and the telephone. But when the deal is finally done, you are often going to have to look the other fellow in the eye.

None of these rules applies on the Internet. You get to decide who you are. Just pick a user name, "Bob," and make up a false profile. You get to have multiple identities simultaneously. Just make up another user name, "Betty," and another false profile. You can switch from one identity to another easily. Toggle back and forth: Bob-Betty-Bob-Betty. You never have to meet anyone face to face, for everything you want to do can be done at a distance. Even having sex (of an electronic sort). This doesn't mean that you can't be tracked down. Unless you're an expert, you can be found. But it's going to take a lot of effort to get from Bob and Betty to you if you are at all careful. As for your correspondence, it's relatively easy to conceal. Imagine some unauthorized someone wanted to see a file you've placed on the Internet. They would have to know where the file is. Happily, there is software available that will make a file functionally invisible. If they knew where the file was, they would need to get to it. Firewalls can stop them. If they manage to get to it, they would have to be able to open it. Passwords can prevent them from doing that. If they managed to open it, they'd have to be able to read it. Encryption will prevent that. Someone really dedicated and smart will probably be able to hack the file, but, again, they are going to have to go to a lot of trouble.

The Internet, then, is very private indeed. With just a little effort, you can hide who you are and what you've communicated behind multiple layers of deception and security. People do it routinely. Private media engender segmented networks, that is, ones in which information can flow in confined, restricted spaces but not between them. According to our theory, segmented networks will *close* social practices evolved in and around them. For a whole variety of reasons – some noble and some base – people like to hide what they do, and the Internet enables them to do this like no medium before it.

The Internet has allowed people to accomplish something unprecedented: the creation of private though public social space. This may seem like a contradiction in terms, but that's only because most of us have never had the experience of being unidentifiable in public. If you've been to a masked ball, then you've come close. But even there, you can probably be identified because masks don't mask very well. On the Internet, however, you can achieve true anonymity: your offline self will remain private, while your online self – your "avatar" as it is sometimes called – remains open for all to see. When you are anonymous, *all* of the social practices in which you engage are closed in the sense that they cannot be identified with your offline self. If you want a partial "second life," all you need do is pick a pseudonym. If you want a complete "second life," you can find it in any number of online virtual worlds.[54] In either case, you needn't worry at all about what others think of you, because "you" are separated from your actions. You – that is, the real you – are not accountable.[55] It's well understood that when people are not accountable, they do things they ordinarily wouldn't and probably shouldn't. "When the cat's away, the mice will play," as the proverb has it. It's no surprise, then, that the Internet is full of such bad behavior, or at least behavior that is deemed bad by offline standards.[56] Yet, even if you decide to enter the online world using your true offline identity, you can still easily create a closed space and a closed social practice within it. You simply build what is commonly referred to as a "walled garden," that is, a network that cannot be penetrated from the "outside." Within the garden, you and the other "users" will be able to do as they please without regard for "public" censure. Clearly, the possibilities for such closed "collaboration" are endless and somewhat disturbing. . . .

## Fidelity

Many people speak of the Internet as if it were a radically new mode of communication. In some ways it is... But in other ways, it's not new at all. Take the kinds of data it delivers. There's speech: you can talk to people over the Web using Skype. There's writing: you can correspond with them using email. There's print: you can read all manner of printed material on the Web. And there are audiovisual media: you can listen to music, look at pictures, and watch videos on the Web. The Internet, then, is a telephone, a post office, a library, a radio, a photo album, and a TV all rolled into one. Which of these is new? None of them. "New" would be a medium that carries tastes, smells, and feeling. Sense-o-Rama may be coming, but the Internet isn't it. Despite what the boosters say, what we have in the case of the Internet is old wine in new bottles, at least in terms of data-type. On the Internet, speech, writing, and print are still five-to-one codes: they reduce every kind of experience to linguistic symbols born by sound (speech) or vision (writing and print). Internet "word pictures" still aren't pictures. On the Internet, audiovisual media are still one-to-one codes. Internet sounds are sounds; Internet pictures are pictures. Enthusiasts will object that the Web enables people to do all kinds of artsy new things with these media, things that were impossible in the old world. At best, that's an exaggeration. At worst, it's just untrue. Decades before the Internet, artists were mixing, mashing, and otherwise manipulating speech, writing, print, and audiovisual media for fun and profit. Go to MOMA or any collection of modern art and see. What is definitely true is that *computers* – not the Internet – have made messing about with the traditional media a lot easier than it was when Andy Warhol made art out of soup labels. If Andy had had Illustrator and Photoshop, he could have saved himself a lot of trouble. But the Internet wouldn't have made much difference.

In terms of the kinds of information it delivers, the Internet is nothing but the sum of its parts. These are two: a low-fidelity channel carrying speech, writing, and print, and a high-fidelity channel carrying audiovisual messages. Hence, we have a dual network. When used to send and receive messages through the low-fidelity channel, the Internet will generate symbolic networks. Users on these networks have to "know the code" – that is, how to read – in order to use them effectively. Some of them will, some of them won't, and some of them will fall in between. When used to send and receive messages through the high-fidelity channel, the Internet will generate iconic networks. Users on these networks have to know a code, but it is so natural – listening and watching things "as they are" – that no conscious decoding will be required. They will just "get it," and they will all do so to roughly the same degree. According to [my] theory, **symbolic** networks *conceptualize* social practices developed in and around them, while **iconic** networks *sensualize* them. The Internet is a dual network, so it should do both.

It does, but even this is not entirely new. The Internet is not the first medium to deliver two channels, one low- and the other high-fidelity. In principle, writing can deliver two: a writer, for example, can draft text *and* draw pictures in a sketchbook. In principle, audiovisual media can deliver two: a TV producer can create a broadcast with both text and images, for example, a film with subtitles. These, however, are really marginal cases, for in the instance of writing, words dominate, while in the instance of TV, pictures do. We read writing and watch TV; we almost never watch writing and read TV. The first medium to approach a balance between the two channels was print, especially in recent times. The modern glossy magazine – *Time, Sports Illustrated, Playboy* – definitely has two channels. You get words and you get pictures. You never get one without the other, even in really wordy magazines like *The Atlantic Monthly, The New Yorker*, or *The Economist*. These considerations suggest a surprising conclusion: the Internet looks a lot like a "slick," as they say in the magazine trade. It's pretty hard to find web pages that are *only* words or *only* sounds and images. You almost always get both. Yet there is a difference between the way channels are employed in print and on the Internet. It's one of weighting. By and large, in print the low-fidelity channel (text) dominates, thus print networks are primarily symbolic, and therefore the most pronounced effect is the conceptualization of social practices and values. In contrast, on the Internet the high-fidelity channel (sounds and images) dominates, thus Internet networks are primarily iconic, and therefore the most pronounced effect is the sensualization of social practices and values.

And sensualization is just what we find. [Elsewhere I showed] that audiovisual media engendered social practices centered on the consumption of "cheap thrills," that is, stimulating, low-cost entertainments. The Web continues and amplifies this trend by further reducing the costs of the production and consumption of "cheap thrills." Some of these are genuinely new – the multiplayer online games, for example – but most are traditional, which is to say they are images, music, or video. On the production side, the Internet (and attendant computer technologies) enables almost anyone to create or at least copy a picture, a song, or a movie. These items, in turn, can be distributed to millions upon millions of "users" via "file-sharing" sites. Thus, we find millions of amateur "cheap thrills" on the Internet, as well as many that would seem to be made by professionals and nominally protected by the laws of copyright. On the consumption side, everything on offer, whether copyrighted or not, is free because all the "users" were doing was sharing. Add the fact that all of these free "cheap thrills" could be consumed in private, outside the censorious gaze of the public, and you have the recipe for an explosion of entertainment unprecedented in the history of the media. If you find it stimulating, you can find it on the Internet – all the time, for free, and probably in quantities and varieties you never imagined. . . .

## Volume

. . . Surfing the Internet is like watching captioned TV, with one crucial difference: there are millions of channels on the Web. Just how many millions, no one knows. More than 100 million registered domain names are currently active.[57] According to one recent estimate, there are in excess of 170 million websites (although only about 700,000 are active).[58] Since any of these sites can have many pages, and many do, the number of total web pages runs well into the billions. One rough estimate is that there are over 27 billion pages on the indexed Web.[59] And that's only the part of the Web search engines can see. The "Deep Web," that part which has been hidden (see "Privacy"), is probably much larger.[60]

The Internet, then, has extraordinarily high volume. It currently has too many channels to comprehend, and more are being added at a fantastic rate. This is hardly surprising. Anyone with a wired computer, a little know-how, and something to say can add their own drop to this electronic ocean. Since just about everybody has all three, the electronic ocean is expanding rapidly. High-volume media engender unconstrained networks, that is, ones that have plenty of spare capacity above and beyond what is deemed necessary for essential communications. According to our theory, unconstrained networks will *hedonize* social practices and values developed in and around them. The reason is this: people are pleasure-seeking. Thus, if a medium has extra bandwidth, people will use it for the purposes of pleasure. The Internet has ample spare capacity and has, as a result, hedonized social practices and values. . . .

The Internet has even more excess capacity [than audiovisual media], so we shouldn't be surprised to learn that it engendered even more "leisure." It did this in two ways: by changing the way entertainment is made and changing the way it's delivered.

First, consider entertainment production. In the Talking, Manuscript, and Print Eras, we generally made our own fun and little of it involved the media. In the Audiovisual

Era, we paid people to make our fun for us and it was the media. In terms of entertainment, the Internet Era is like the one and the other: we make our own fun, but we use the media – or rather the Web – to do it. This isn't to say we don't hire people to entertain us on the Web. We certainly do. All the traditional entertainment companies – publishers, record companies, film studios, radio stations, TV channels – make their products available on the Web, usually for a fee. The difference is that they do not dominate the Internet in the way they ruled print and audiovisual media. The reason is simple: bandwidth. Print and audiovisual media don't have much of it, comparatively speaking, so only big companies can afford it. The Internet has an infinite amount of it, so anyone can get into the entertainment game. You've written the great American novel but can't get a contract? Post it online. You've penned the greatest song since "Puff the Magic Dragon" but can't find a distributor? Post it online. Your one-minute remake of *Star Wars* isn't getting any attention from the studios? Post it online. We tell our children to think they are geniuses-in-the-making, teach them to emulate geniuses-in-fact, and then tell them to sit down and shut up. It's hardly a surprise that there have long been millions of frustrated Hemingways, Dylans, and Scorseses out there who just needed a break. Now the Internet has given it to them and to all of us.

Second, there's delivery. In the Audiovisual Era, entertainment was what we might call "then-and-there." *I Love Lucy* was on at 6:00 PM on Mondays in your "TV room." You had to be "then-and-there" to enjoy it. This being so, audiovisual companies made sure that their best programming was broadcast when and where people had free time at home. Thus TV, for example, colonized evenings, that is, "prime-time." On the Internet, however, entertainment is "always-and-everywhere." You don't have to enjoy it at a particular time and place; you can enjoy it any time and any place, or some approximation thereof. You, not some programmer at a big media company, decide when and where to look, listen, or watch. The liberation of entertainment from time and space, however, had a peculiar effect: it allowed "leisure" to colonize all the times that were not otherwise occupied by work and traditional media. These periods tended to be short: a few minutes waiting for the doctor, riding the bus, or between tasks at the office. But "short" is just what the Internet offers. Articles, picture essays, songs, games, videos – they can all be enjoyed in a few minutes. The result is that the Internet has increased the total time people spend at "leisure." Since a lot of this increased "down-time" is spent at work, employers and economists are worried about the cost of "workplace Internet leisure browsing," or "cyberslacking," as it's sometimes called. . . .[61]

## Velocity

Email and chat have always been fast. It doesn't take long to compose messages and, once sent, they arrive almost instantly if everything is running according to spec. Thus, you can easily "talk" to someone over them. Web pages are a different story, or at least were. For most of the 1990s, making and editing web pages was a slow process because every alteration had to be hand-coded, that is, you had to write the HTML. If you didn't know HTML, and most people didn't, then updates were especially slow. "Slow" here means hours, which may be fast to you and me, but is an eternity in Internet time. In any case, hours between updates meant that you couldn't really have a conversation on or between web pages. Rather, you could have a series of monologues, and that really isn't very satisfying. So, in the late 1990s, some impatient programmers with a lot to say invented tools that allowed them to edit web pages quickly and easily.[62] Thus was the Blog born, and with it the flood of read/write web pages that are now ubiquitous on the Web. You've probably heard the term "Web 2.0."[63] You may not have heard the phrase "read/write Web." They mean the same thing – it's just that the former is an opaque buzzword promoted to sell electronic soap, while the latter is a pretty good description of what many people do on the Web today, and have since the early 2000s. You read something on a web page and then you write something about what you read on the same web page. Then other people read what you just wrote and they write back. The back-and-forth can happen instantly, just like talking to someone; or it can be drawn out, like an email exchange. But in either case it is what it is: a conversation. These days you are not limited to reading web pages and writing to them. You can listen, look, or watch, and then respond in kind. So a more accurate description of the Web today would be the read-listen-look-watch/write-record-photograph-video Web. One doubts that clumsy tag will catch on, but the point is the same: the Internet allows you to create and transmit messages in several formats very quickly, and thereby facilitates discussion.

The Internet, then, is a high-velocity medium: you can compose and send messages very quickly, and others can respond to them. This you cannot really do with writing, print, and audiovisual media. High-velocity media generate **dialogic** networks, ones in which messages can be quickly and easily exchanged between nodes. The "turn-around time" on such networks is short, or at least can be short. You compose a message and send it. It arrives quickly and is understood. And the recipient composes and sends a response. Thus, messages flow back and forth over the network rapidly and easily. According to our theory, dialogic networks *democratize* social practices developed in and around them. By "democratize" we mean to encourage deliberative and consensual decision making. People like to talk, and they like to be heard. Dialogic networks give them the opportunity to do both at a low cost.

The Internet is a huge dialogic network made up of millions of smaller dialogic networks – an Inter-network, a network of networks. Wikipedia, for example, is one of them. Most people would say Wikipedia is an online encyclopedia. It sure looks like one. It's comprised of short descriptive entries, just like an encyclopedia. They are written in a "stick-to-the-facts" style, just like an encyclopedia. They cover a remarkably broad range of topics, just like an encyclopedia. Wikipedia, however, clearly isn't an encyclopedia in the traditional sense, and some critics say it's not an encyclopedia at all. The reason most commonly cited for Wikipedia's "un-encyclopedia-ness" is that it is written by amateurs rather than experts. But that can't really be right, for in point of fact many amateurs contribute to *Britannica* and many experts to Wikipedia, though the proportion of each is surely different in the one case and the other. The real difference between traditional encyclopedias and Wikipedia is the medium in which they are realized and the way in which those media shape their form.

As we've said, writing and print are inherently monologic because they do not permit the rapid production and exchange of messages. The traditional encyclopedia is a perfect example. An artifact like *Britannica* takes many years to organize, write, edit, typeset, print, and distribute. And once it's done, it's done: the articles themselves cannot be edited. It is true that the production of the next edition will involve an exchange of information. The new authors will enter into a "conversation" of sorts with the old authors – and the "literature" in general – as they go about updating entries. But is a "conversation" that takes place over decades or even centuries really worthy of the name? No matter what we call it, one thing is clear: the lag between "call" and "response" – a function of the logistical characteristics of the medium – seems unnaturally long. In contrast, the Internet as it exists today is inherently dialogic in that it not only permits rapid exchange of information but encourages it. Imagine you've been asked to write a *Britannica* entry. It might take you a short time – you just slap something together. Or it might take you a long time – you write a carefully crafted, informed article. When you're done, as we said, you are done. Now imagine you want to write a Wikipedia entry. The goal is the same, and it's your choice how you want to pursue it. You can settle for "good enough" or strive for excellence. The difference is that when you're done, you aren't done. In fact, you – or rather the article you've started – is never done. Ever. This is because anyone can edit "your" article at any time or leave comments about it. It is this ceaseless back-and-forth about articles that really makes one wonder whether Wikipedia is an "encyclopedia" and its articles are really "articles." Might it not be more accurate to say that Wikipedia is a never-ending discussion about everything, neatly topically arranged for everyone's convenience? And might not one say the same of the Internet in general? What is it but a boundless forum for dialogue, discourse, and conversation, for negotiation, cooperation, and collaboration, for deliberation, disputation, and debate? Imagine a space so large as to comfortably accommodate everyone in the world. A space in which everyone is near everyone else, but no one can touch anyone. What do you think people would do there? They'd talk, of course. . . .

## Range

When we talk about the Internet, we usually mean the World Wide Web. The former is a system of pipes; the latter is one of the kinds of data – HTML documents – that runs through the pipes. The distinction, however, is now largely lost. Most people use the terms "Internet" and "Web" synonymously. In a way, that's good, because as a descriptor "Internet" is obscure. It's short for "Internetwork," a non-word that isn't really much clearer. "Web" is much more telegraphic, as it is metaphorically connected to things with which we are all familiar – weaving, fabric, and even spiders. It's easy to imagine the Internet as a gigantic spider's web blanketing the earth, connecting everything to everything else through multiple, interconnected strands. Of course, the "web" – in the generic sense of a communications network – is not new. It was brought into being hundreds of thousands of years ago the moment one human talked to another. Over time, humans invented new media and used them to create new webs, each larger than the last. They superimposed the new webs on the old: writing on talking, print on writing, audiovisual media on print, and finally the Internet – *the* Web – on audiovisual media. Although the Internet web is probably larger geographically than the audiovisual web, the two are very roughly the same size. You can retrieve HTML files from servers all over the world; but you can also place calls all over the world, listen to radio stations from all over the world, and watch TV from all over the world. What really makes the Internet web different from the audiovisual web is not its extent, but rather its density. The Internet web is thicker, bushier, woollier than the audiovisual web. More people are connected to more places at fewer removes more of the time on the Internet than on, say, a telephone, radio, or TV web. This relates to our previous discussion of channels. The Internet's billions of channels are "served" from computers all over the world. You can go to any of them, any time. The audiovisual networks have thousands of "broadcasts" from stations over most of the world. You can go to some of them, some of the time. Audiovisual channels typically have much larger audiences than Internet channels, but the coverage of the Internet web as a whole is greater than that of the audiovisual web. As the audiovisual channels themselves migrate to the Internet (so-called convergence), the superiority of the Web will become all the greater.

The Internet, then, has global range and unexcelled coverage. It goes everywhere and soon will reach everyone. Media with these characteristics engender extensive networks, which is to say networks that bring diverse places and peoples together. According to our theory, extensive networks *diversify* social practices and values evolved in and around them. On extensive networks, strangers confront one another, learn from one another, and assimilate one another to their worldviews. What was smooth becomes rough, what was plain becomes mixed, what was monochrome becomes multicolored. It's not always pretty. Sometimes this confrontation leads to conflict. But over extended periods of time it often leads to the softening of edges and the acceptance of diversity.

There is no doubt that the Internet mixes things up in a new way. Everything is there: every nationality, culture, language, dialect, creole; every political viewpoint, economic theory, scientific school; every religious creed, spiritual belief, and ritual practice; every taste, aesthetic, and sensibility; every ethic, moral code, and law. All and more are found together on the Web. Some are real; some are imaginary. Some are serious; some are silly. Some are sensible; some are so wacky as to confound belief. But they are all there, each exactly one click away from the other. The Web scotched the notion that people and things are the same, or even similar, everywhere for good. But it also engendered a new kind of voyeurism. In the Print and Audiovisual Eras, the presentation of documentary exotica – that is, depictions of the strange that were uncontrived or "natural" – was enough to satisfy the curiosity of most readers, listeners, and viewers. There seemed to always be more of it, so what was on offer simply created anticipation for what came next. The Internet, however, demonstrated that the well of "natural" variation was not bottomless. In fact, it was quite finite, and that which is finite and known is not as interesting as that which is infinite and unknown. The finitude of "natural" variation, then, created a desire for what we might call "artificial" variation, that is, exotica that is purposely contrived simply to surprise, astonish, or shock. Some of this is benign, or at least relatively so, for example the "virtual worlds" created by online gamers. But some of it is very disturbing, particularly that which involves real people doing dangerous, degrading, or disgusting things simply for the sake of attention. You can see such material in abundance on YouTube and any number of fetish porn sites. . . .

### Persistence

In spring 2007, Bear Stearns hedge-fund managers Ralph Cioffi and Matthew Tannin were pretty bullish about the prospects of the securities they were hawking. At least that's what they told the investors who bought them. Secretly, however, they knew the funds were dogs. Tannin told Cioffi so in an email:

> [T]he subprime market looks pretty damn ugly. . . . If we believe [our internal modeling] is ANYWHERE CLOSE to accurate I think we should close the funds now. The reason for this is that if [our internal modeling] is correct then the entire subprime market is toast. . . . If AAA bonds are systematically downgraded then there is simply no way for us to make money – ever.[64]

They didn't close the funds – they kept on pitching. And they didn't make any money – ever. But they did get indicted on charges of conspiracy, securities fraud, and wire fraud. Thus, Cioffi and Tannin joined the ranks of Henry Blodget (Merrill Lynch), Jack Grubman (Citigroup), Frank Quattrone (Credit Suisse First Boston), and other Wall Street crooks who, while quite smart, forgot one of the basic rules of life on the Internet: email is forever. So is most everything else on the Internet. It's not really the case that the Internet never forgets. It does. But it remembers a heck of a lot.

The reason is twofold. First, it can. Unlike spoken words, writing, printing on paper, and audiovisual signals on tape, digital files – the kind that are stored on the Internet – can be copied and archived very quickly, very accurately, and very cheaply. Practically speaking, there is no limit to the amount of information that can be stored on the vast array of devices that make up the Web. Second, we live in a world where archiving information is the safe bet, at least most of the time. You never know when you are going to need that document for some purpose. So you archive it. Many people, however, are lazy about backing up their files. Horror stories abound. Don't worry, though, there are powerful organizations making sure that everything gets saved. Your company, for example, has probably hired people to make sure that its digital files are routinely archived. That includes the emails you send from your work address. Then there are the folks at the Internet Archive. They've been taking periodic "snapshots" of the Web since 1996 and making them available to the public. Although the Internet Archive is not complete, it's still awfully large. As of 2008, it contained 2,000 terabytes of data and over 85 billion web pages.[65] According to one estimate, an academic research library – the kind with millions of books – holds about two terabytes.[66] The print collection of the Library of Congress, arguably the largest library in the world, contains about 10 terabytes.[67] And then there are all the private corporations that record and archive what you do on the Internet in order to sell you more soap. They do this using "tracking cookies" – little pieces of software that are downloaded to your computer – that essentially spy on you. Google's cookies, for example, tell the main office what you searched for, when you searched, which of the results you selected, and so on. They save it all, mix it up with other user data, crunch it, and then use the results to try to figure out what sort of soap you and people like you want. Then they sell advertising space on your browser to your soap company. That's a good trick. Just how long all of this data will last we don't exactly know, but it will probably be a long time. The medium in which it is recorded doesn't decay very rapidly. The means used to read it – hardware, software – changes from time to time, but engineers are for the most part pretty aware of the need for "backward compatibility." And the languages recorded are very big and stable: English, Chinese, Japanese, etc. Besides, any file in danger of becoming illegible due to decay, format obsolescence, or language change can be recopied, re-formatted, and translated. It wouldn't be surprising if the "snapshots" of the Internet taken by the Internet Archive today were legible in 1,000 years. If we're still here to read them.

The Internet, then, is a persistent medium. It's like a trillion elephants all linked together in a sort of Vulcan mind-meld. Don't forget that next time you decide to bilk your investors out of their hard-earned cash. Persistent media engender additive networks. These are networks with a significant capacity to accumulate information. Like your crazy grandmother, they don't throw anything away – they just put it in the basement. According to our theory, additive networks will *historicize* social practices and values developed in and around them. This means that both awareness and the importance of the past will be heightened. The past – represented in artifacts or imagined – will be in a constant dialogue with the present.

. . . Since at least 1996, the Internet has been recording a good percentage of the *new* spoken, written, printed, recorded, photographed, or filmed messages that passed over it. Thus, it comprises a remarkable record of what we have done online for the past decade or so. But just as significantly, the Web is assimilating the pre-Internet past as well. For well over a decade now, institutions of every shape, size, and purpose have busied themselves with the digitization and posting of artifacts that were not "born digital." The scope of this project is mind boggling: every government record, every corporate record, every clerical record – pretty much everything ever written, printed, or photographed by an agency of one sort or another. Google and a consortium of academic libraries alone plan to scan and make available somewhere around 32 million books.[68] This may seem like a lot of information, but it may be exceeded as individuals and their families get into the act. People are already scanning and uploading their family photo albums to the Web. It won't be long before they begin to scan old letters, personal paper, and even the family Bible. Like some enormous gravitational force, the Internet is sucking the past into its vast memory banks. That digitized past will be affixed to the ever-expanding present of born-digital information, at which point the "what came before" will be one seamless digital archive.

The Internet will enable us to preserve more of the past than ever before. It will also expand the capacity for mass surveillance by creating a vast permanent record for every "user."[69] Every email you send, every post you make, every site you visit, every search you conduct, every profile you view, every article you read, every file you download, every file you upload – all of it can be recorded and stored for "later reference." And it's not only your online behavior that will find its way online. All of the "real world" records you generate will be there as well: your commute times, your arrival and departure from work, your credit card purchases, all of your other bills, your phone records, and all those video surveillance tapes that you appear on. Interestingly, none of this – or almost none of it – is Big Brother's doing. We are active participants in the creation and maintenance of the permanent record machine. We don't mind the cookies, we like the nifty transaction records, and we feel safer because of the security cameras. Of course, the collectors of this information assure us that it is secure and will never be used for nefarious purposes. Not everyone is convinced.[70] The creation of the electronic dossier has led, predictably enough, to an expansion of the practice of "reputation management." In the Audiovisual Era, corporations used reputation management in order to protect their brands.[71] They needed to do this because they were public entities and were, therefore, closely watched. Any misstep could cost them dearly. In the Internet Era, everybody needs to practice reputation management because everyone is a public entity and is closely watched. You, so the business gurus say, are a brand.[72] If you let someone sully your image, you may not be able to clean it up. That, of course, could cost you dearly. So you need to monitor and perhaps even edit, say, your Wikipedia entry to make sure that it tells your version of the truth. But don't get caught managing your reputation in this way, for that in itself could damage your reputation.[73] . . .

## Searchability

The ability to store a lot of information is useless if you can't find anything in it. As we've said, written, print, and audiovisual archives can be quite capacious, but it's hard to find anything in them. The reason is that we don't have a special tool we can use to look through the data – all we have are our eyes and ears, and they were designed to do other things. In contrast, computers, which can store even more information, do have a specialized tool to search for data in their archives – the find command or something similar. As everyone knows, computers store all their data as zeros and ones – the two digits in "digital." The find command tells the computer to go through data looking for a specific series of these zeros and ones. Functionally speaking, this is no different than you looking for a string of characters on a page, in a book, or in a library. The difference is that the computer can do the operation really, really fast. We can't. Since we can't, we construct indexes: tables of one sort or another that tell us where the information we want is. Computers do the same thing – they just do it much faster and arguably better. Librarians laboriously construct indexes – catalogues – that tell us where every book in the library is. By analogy, the computer automatically constructs an index that tells it where every word in every book in the library is, as well as where many possible combinations of words are. In a sense, a search engine works like a computer. It "crawls" across the Internet gathering information and then uses that information to construct a massive index. When you tell the engine to find something – such as a string of characters like "William" – it mechanically looks through the indexes and return addresses – URLs – to web pages that you might want.

The crucial term here is "might," for given that your search term is probably short and the index is very large, you are probably going to get a lot of URLs that have nothing to do with what you are actually searching for. If your intention in searching the string "William" was to get web pages about William Shakespeare, you might be disappointed. The engine could return a lot about "William" and only a little, if any, about William Shakespeare. Here, however, the search engine has an advantage over the personal computer, because it can anticipate what you were looking for even when you were vague, as in the previous example. It does this by comparing your behavior to everyone else's. We noted that a search engine records all the strings everyone searches and what they select after the results are returned. This enables it to compile a ranking based on click-through rate. If it turns out that many people who search the string "William" click a link having to do with William Shakespeare, then the search engine will respond to your "William" query by presenting you with William Shakespeare pages on the sensible presumption that you are more or less like everyone else. Since you are, you will get what you want despite the fact that you were vague. Click-through rate is only one of the factors that the search engine can consider when deciding how to rank URLs returned. It might also consider the amount of traffic a site gets, the number of inbound links a site has, the amount of time people spend on a site, the number of pages they look at on a site, or the rate at which they return to the site. All of these factors are packed together in a search algorithm, a kind of formula the engine uses to guess what you are really looking for when you type "William" into the search box. The results can be sort of spooky, because the search engine seems to know something about you that you didn't tell it. That's because it does.

The Internet is a supremely searchable medium. Unlike, say, the British Library, its doors are always open. Unlike the British Library, it has a remarkably detailed index. Unlike the British Library, its index can be searched with blinding speed. And, unlike the British Library, the search results are highly relevant and the materials themselves are immediately accessible. It's no wonder that the British Library and every other library on earth is rushing to put its holdings online. Searchable media generate mapped networks, that is, ones that have a fine-grained address system that allows users to locate archived items easily. These sorts of networks *amateurize* social practices developed in and around them. By allowing anyone the ability to find and retrieve what they need to know, they blunt the attempts of "experts" to monopolize special knowledge and use it as a basis for professionalization. The line between amateurs and experts thus becomes blurred.

The Internet is blurring this line remarkably quickly. Only a quarter century ago, if you wanted to learn something specific and specialized on your own, you were going to have a hard time doing it. Most people didn't have access to those great repositories of knowledge, academic research libraries. Even if they managed to get in, they probably didn't have the background knowledge to find what they wanted and, more important, needed. And even if they located it in a book or article, they wouldn't likely be able to retrieve it without special permission. None of that is true today. If the Internet has not already supplanted the academic research library as the primary archive of knowledge, it soon will. In some cases, the institutions that control these repositories are themselves abetting this process of democratization, as in the case of the consortium of libraries that have joined the Google Books project.[74] In other cases, they are resistant, as in the case of many academic publishers. In the end, it won't matter because the information will "leak" out of these sources through multiple channels. The same forces that are pushing copyright-protected audiovisual materials onto the Internet will force copyright-protected intellectual materials there as well. They may not be in a form that can easily be traced or recognized, for example in Wikipedia entries or on blog posts, but the substance will be the same. You can be pretty sure that what you need to know is somewhere on the Internet. To find it, all you will need is some "Googlefu" – the ability to use a search engine efficiently – and a search engine.[75] You may not know exactly what you need to know – that is, be faced with what former U.S. Secretary of Defense Donald Rumsfeld called an "unknown unknown."[76] The search engines, however, know what people *like you* typically need to know and will lead you in that direction. If this "wisdom of crowds" technique fails, you can rely on the wisdom of individuals to tell you what you need. There are, as we've already noted, thousands of communities of interest on the Internet in which real people are trading knowledge of every kind, from how to deal with cancer to how to get a date. On these sites you can ask very general or very specific questions and receive tailored advice. If you don't learn what you need here, then you can take a final step and ask an expert directly. There are countless thousands of credentialed experts on the Web who are giving away advice. They do it for various reasons: because they want attention, because it makes them feel good, because they are bored. The remarkable thing is that they are there and will provide you a professional service for free. . . .

---

People have been waiting for virtual reality for years. They needn't wait any longer, because it's here. It's not an immersive environment, but rather a set of web pages through which we can "live." On these web pages we can chat up strangers, go on dates, have sex. We can read books, watch movies, and play games. We can go to museums, visit foreign countries, or land on the moon. We can go to school, do our work, and get paid. We can buy stuff, sell stuff, and trade stuff. We can be professors, lawyers, and doctors, or at least "know" what they know. We can do all this and never leave our seat in front of the computer. Of course, as Plato would point out, it's all a sort of illusion, for none of it gets to the essence of things, none of it is True. Nonetheless, it has many real-world implications, some of which we have tried to flesh out in this chapter. The Internet is a new medium, but it is a medium all the same. As such, it has physical attributes that permit people to use it in certain ways and prevent them from using it in others. These logistical characteristics, we argued, predictably led to the formation of certain sorts of media networks, and these media networks in turn engendered specific social practices and values. . . .

Most of the world's nations seem to have learned the lesson taught by print and audiovisual media: media will do what media do, and attempting to go against their grain will probably lead to nothing but trouble and failure. This acceptance is one of the reasons the Internet is now virtually everywhere, and virtually everywhere the same. There are nations that have not learned this lesson. They are uniformly the last remaining illiberal, undemocratic, tyrannies left on the planet. And – with the exception of those that almost completely block access to the Internet – none of them is succeeding in bending the Internet to its will, at least to any great degree. Moreover, where they have succeeded, we can be reasonably sure they will eventually fail, and suffer for their failure. For the Internet will do there what the Internet has naturally done everywhere else. It will spread until almost everyone has it and everyone believes everyone should have it. It will foster the formation of many private groups and a belief that individuals have the natural-born right to opt in or out of these groups. It will be used primarily for pleasure and without penalty or shame. It will engender dialogues both within and between groups at a level heretofore unimaginable, and it will lead to a general (though not necessarily laudable) democratization of everything. It will grow to include everyone, everywhere, and thereby break down barriers. It will save everything, make everything saved findable, and thereby make us at once vulnerable and knowledgeable.

This, then, is Internet Culture, brought into being by the Web and the organized interests that "pulled" it into existence. Whether its run will be long and whether it will be good for humanity, we do not know. . . .

## Notes

1. *The Republic*, translated by R. E. Allen (New Haven and London: Yale UP, 2006), 227.

2. For a recent survey, see John Henry, *The Scientific Revolution and the Origins of Modern Science*, third edition (New York: Palgrave Macmillan, 2008).

3. There are many accounts of Brahe and Kepler. A standard version is Alexandre Koyré, *The Astronomical Revolution: Copernicus, Kepler, Borelli*, translated by R. E. W. Maddison (Ithaca: Cornell UP, 1973), 159ff. For a more recent view, see James R. Voelkel, *The Composition of Kepler's Astronomia nova* (Princeton: Princeton UP, 2001), 93ff.

4. See Paula Findlin, *Possessing Nature: Museums, Collecting, and Scientific Culture in Early Modern Italy* (Berkeley: University of California Press, 1994). For a broader view, see Arthur MacGregor, *Curiosity and Enlightenment: Collectors and Collections from the Sixteenth to Nineteenth Century* (New Haven: Yale UP, 2008).

5. Francis Bacon, *Religious Meditations. Places of perswasion and disswasion, seene and allowed* (London: Printed [by John Windet] for Humfrey Hooper, and are to be sold at the blacke Beare in Chauncery Lane, 1597).

6. On early modern European scientific societies, see Martha Ornstein, *The Role of Scientific Societies in the Seventeenth Century* (New York: Columbia UP, 1913); James E. McClellan, *Science Reorganized: Scientific Societies in the Eighteenth Century* (New York: Columbia UP, 1985); and Mordechai Feingold, "Tradition Versus Novelty. Universities and Scientific Societies in the Early Modern Period," in *Revolution and Continuity: Essays in the History and Philosophy of Early Modern Science*, edited by P. Barker and R. Ariew (Washington, DC: Catholic University of America Press, 1991), 45–59.

7. On the *Encyclopédie*, see Robert Darnton, *The Business of Enlightenment: A Publishing History of the Encyclopédie, 1775–1800* (Cambridge: Harvard UP, 1979). The idea may have been Greek in origin, but there were plenty of contemporary examples at hand. See Lawrence E. Sullivan, "Circumscribing Knowledge: Encyclopedias in Historical Perspective," *Journal of Religion* 70:3 (1990), 315–339; and Richard Yeo, *Encyclopedic Visions: Scientific Dictionaries and Enlightenment Culture* (New York: Cambridge UP, 2001).

8. On Otlet, see Trudi Bellardo Hahn and Michael Keeble Buckland, eds., *Historical Studies in Information Science* (Medford: Information Today, 1998), 22–50; Ronald E. Day, *The Modern Invention of Information Science: Discourse, History, and Power* (Carbondale: Southern Illinois UP, 2001), 7–37; and Françoise Levie, *L'homme qui voulait classer le monde: Paul Otlet et le Mundaneum* (Brussels: Impressions nouvelles, 2006).

9. On the history of microfilm, see Fredric Luther, *Microfilm: A History, 1839–1900* (Annapolis: National Microfilm Association, 1959); Susan A. Cady, "Machine Tool of Management: A History of Microfilm Technology" (Ph.D. dissertation, Lehigh University, 1994); and Alistair Black, Dave Muddiman, and Helen Plant, *The Early Information Society: Information Management in Britain Before the Computer* (Aldershot: Ashgate Publishers, 2007), 14–23.

10. "Micro-Photography," *Photographic News* 1:22 (February 4, 1859), 262.

11. Willard Detering Morgan, *The Encyclopedia of Photography*, 20 vols. (New York: Graystone Press, 1970), vol. 12: 2286.

12. "Letter from Franklin D. Roosevelt to R. D. W. Conner" (February 13, 1942), *American Archivist* 5 (April, 1942), 119–120.

13. H. G. Wells, "The Idea of a Permanent World Encyclopedia," in H. G. Wells, *World Brain* (Garden City: Doubleday-Doran, 1938).

14. On Bush, see G. Pascal Zachary, *Endless Frontier: Vannevar Bush, Engineering the American Century* (New York: Free Press, 1997); and James N. Nyce and Paul Kahn, eds., *From Memex to Hypertext: Vannevar Bush and the Mind's Machine* (Boston: Academic Press, 1991).

15. Vannevar Bush, "As We May Think," *Atlantic Monthly* (July, 1945), 101–108.

16. The following is based on Janet Abbate, *Inventing the Internet* (Cambridge: MIT Press, 1999); and Katie Hafner and Andrew Lyon, *Where the Wizards Stay Up Late: The Origins of the Internet* (New York: Simon & Schuster, 1998). For a good (if now a bit dated) review of the literature, see Roy Rosenzw[illegible], "Wizards, Bureaucrats, Warriors, and Hackers: Writing the History of the Internet," *American Historical Review* 103:5 (1998), 1530–1552. For a more recent, broader treatment of the history of the Internet and related telecommunications technologies, see Gerald W. Brooks, *The Second Information Revolution* (Cambridge: Harvard UP, 2003).

17. On SAGE, see Kent C. Redmond and Thomas M. Smith, *From Whirlwind to MITRE: The R&D Story of the SAGE Air Defense Computer* (Cambridge: MIT Press, 2000). For a short, readable account, see Robert Buderi, *The Invention That Changed the World: How a Small Group of Radar Pioneers Won the Second World War and Launched a Technological Revolution* (New York: Simon & Schuster, 1996), 380–406.

18. Herman Kahn, *On Thermonuclear War* [1960] (New Brunswick: Transaction Publishers, 2007), 278.

19. On the origins of "packet switching," see Abbate, *Inventing the Internet*, 7–42.

20. On the origins of ARPANET, see Abbate, *Inventing the Internet*, 43–82. Abbate makes clear that ARPANET was first and foremost a research network, not a "military command and control system." See her "Government, Business and the Making of the Internet," *Business History Review* 75:1 (2001), 150. For an interesting collection of documents related to the founding of ARPANET, see Peter H. Salus, ed., *The ARPANET Sourcebook: The Unpublished Foundations of the Internet* (Charlottesville: Peer-to-Peer Communications, 2008).

21. On the formation of the "network of networks," see Abbate, *Inventing the Internet*, 113–146.

22. On the origins of the World Wide Web, see Abbate, *Inventing the Internet*, 214ff. The story has been told by the very people who invented the Web. See Tim Berners-Lee, *Weaving the Web: The Original Design and Ultimate Destiny of the World Wide Web by Its Inventor* (San Francisco: HarperSanFrancisco, 1999); and James Gillies and Robert Caliliau, *How the Web Was Born: The Story of the World Wide Web* (Oxford: Oxford UP, 2000).

23. On the origins of the browser, see Abbate, *Inventing the Internet*, 217ff. Also see Jim Clark and Owen Edwards, *Netscape Time: The Making of the Billion-Dollar Start-Up That Took on Microsoft* (New York: St. Martin's Press, 1999).

24. On information capitalism, see Muddiman and Plant, *The Early Information Society: Information Management in Britain Before the Computer*; James W. Cortada, *Before the Computer: IBM, NCR, Burroughs, and Remington Rand and the Industry They Created, 1865–1956* (Princeton: Princeton UP, 1993); Thomas Haigh, "Inventing Information Systems: The Systems Men and the Computer, 1950–1968," *Business History Review* 75:1 (2001), 15–61; James W. Cortada, *The Digital Hand: How Computers Changed the Work of American Manufacturing, Transportation, and Retail Industries* (New York: Oxford UP, 2003); and James W. Cortada, *The Digital Hand*: Volume II: *How Computers Changed the Work of American Financial, Telecommunications, Media, and Entertainment Industries* (New York: Oxford UP, 2005). For critical perspectives, see David Lyon and Elia Zuriek, eds., *Computers, Surveillance, and Privacy* (Minneapolis: University of Minnesota Press, 1996); and Jim Davis, Thomas Hirschl, and Michael Stack, *Cutting Edge: Technology, Information, Capitalism and Social Revolution* (London: Verso, 1997).

25. See Arno Borst, *The Ordering of Time: From Ancient Computus to the Modern Computer* (Chicago: University of Chicago Press, 1994), especially 106ff.

26. See especially Cortada, *Before the Computer*.

27. On "Project Xanadu," see Gary Wolf, "The Curse of Xanadu," *Wired*, 3.06 (June 1995). On the "Electronic Information Exchange System," see Howard Rheingold, *The Virtual Community: Homesteading on the Electronic Frontier*, revised edition (Cambridge: MIT Press, 2000), 113ff. On "Computer Supported Cooperative Work," see Paul Wilson, *Computer Supported Cooperative Work: An Introduction* (Oxford: Kluwer Academic Publishers, 1991). On "Collaborative Networked Learning," see Peter Goodyear et al., eds., *Advances in Research on Networked Learning* (Oxford: Kluwer Academic Publishers, 2004).

28. On the surveillance state, see Christopher Dandeker, *Surveillance, Power and Modernity: Bureaucracy and Discipline from 1700 to the Present Day* (Cambridge: Polity Press, 1990); Andrew Polsky, *The Rise of the Therapeutic State* (Princeton: Princeton UP, 1991); David Lyon, *The Electronic Eye: The Rise of Surveillance Society* (Minneapolis: University of Minnesota Press, 1994); Jon Agar, *The Government Machine: A Revolutionary History of the Computer* (Cambridge: MIT Press, 2003); Helen Margetts, *Information Technology in Government: Britain and America* (New York: Routledge, 1998); John Gilliom, *Overseers of the Poor: Surveillance, Resistance, and the Limits of Privacy* (Chicago: University of Chicago Press, 2001); and Sandra Brama, *Change of State: Information, Policy and Power* (Cambridge: MIT Press, 2006). Unfortunately, much of the literature on government-sponsored efforts to gather information on citizens is reliant on Foucault and his exaggerated image of modern society as "panopticon."

29. Cortada, *Before the Computer*, 53.

30. On Defense Department subsidies of the computer industry during the Cold War, see Paul N. Edwards, *The Closed World: Computers and the Politics of Discourse in Cold War America* (Cambridge: MIT Press, 1996); and Arthur L. Norberg and Judy E. O'Neill, *Transforming Computer Technology: Information Processing for the Pentagon, 1962–1986* (Baltimore: Johns Hopkins UP, 1996).

31. On the notion that "hedonism" or "self-fulfillment" has come to dominate postwar Western culture, see Daniel Bell, *The Cultural Contradictions of Capitalism* (New York: Basic Books, 1976); Christopher Lasch, *The Culture of Narcissism* (New York: Norton, 1979); and Robert Bellah et al., *Habits of the Heart: Privatism and Commitment in American Life* (Berkeley: University of California Press, 1984). For a revision, see Paul Lichterman, "Beyond the Seesaw Model: Public Commitment in a Culture of Self-Fulfillment," *Sociological Theory* 13:3 (1995), 275–300. On postwar permissiveness, see Arthur Marwick, *The Sixties: Cultural Transformation in Britain, France, Italy and the United States, c. 1958–c. 1974* (New York: Oxford UP, 2000). Also of interest is Ronald K. L. Collins and David M. Skover, "The Pornographic State," *Harvard Law Review* 107:6 (1994), 1374–1399.

32. J. D. Salinger, *The Catcher in the Rye* (Boston: Little, Brown, 1951).

33. Aldous Huxley, *The Doors of Perception* (New York: Harper, 1954); Jack Kerouac, *On the Road* (New York: Viking Press, 1957).

34. See Bill Osgerby, *Playboys in Paradise: Masculinity, Youth and Leisure-style in Modern America* (Oxford: Berg Publishers, 2001); Martin Torgoff, *Can't Find My Way Home: America in the Great Stoned Age, 1945–2000* (New York: Simon & Schuster, 2004); and Tom Lutz, *Doing Nothing: A History of Loafers, Loungers, Slackers and Bums in America* (New York: Macmillan, 2007), 215ff.

35. See Peter O. Whitmer with Bruce VanWyngarden, *Aquarius Revisited: Seven Who Created the Sixties Counterculture That Changed America* (New York: Macmillan, 1987). The "seven" in question are: William S. Burroughs, Allen Ginsberg, Ken Kesey, Timothy Leary, Norman Mailer, Tom Robbins, and Hunter S. Thompson.

36. On these cases, see Terry Eastland, ed., *Freedom of Expression in the Supreme Court: The Defining Cases* (Lanham: Rowman & Littlefield, 2000), 192–194 and 218–234.

37. See Howard Rheingold, *Smart Mobs: The Next Social Revolution* (New York: Basic Books, 2003); Yochai Benkler, *The Wealth of Networks: How Social Production Transforms Markets and Freedom* (New Haven: Yale UP, 2006); Cass Sunstein, *Infotopia: How Many Minds Produce Knowledge* (New York: Oxford UP, 2006); Dan Tapscott and Anthony D. Williams, *Wikinomics: How Mass Collaboration Changes Everything* (New York: Portfolio, 2008); Clay Shirky, *Here Comes Everyone: The Power of Organizing Without Organization* (New York: Penguin Press, 2008). One should probably also include the many books of Lawrence Lessig.

38. "2009 Digital Future Report," Center for the Digital Future, USC Annenberg School of Communications (2009).

39. For chatting ("socializing and communicating") and TV watching, see *The American Time Use Survey, 2007* (Washington, DC: Bureau of Labor Statistics, 2008), table A-1. On reading "for pleasure," see *The American Time Use Survey, 2007*, table 11.

40. Website: "IBM Personal Computer. Model 5150," Obsolete Technology Website. Retrieved on August 10, 2009.

41. Website: "Apple Macintosh. Model M0001," Obsolete Technology Website. Retrieved on August 10, 2009.

42. For example, the 300 Baud Texas Instruments TI-99/4 modem, introduced in 1980. See Website: "Texas Instruments CC-40." Retrieved August 10, 2009.

43. Jen Aronoff, "Retailers Say Computers Hot-to-Go This Weekend," *Charlotte Observer* (August 8, 2009).

44. Stuart Kennedy, "Cheap PCs for Kids Starts a Chain Reaction," *The Australian* (July 28, 2009).

45. Simon Yates et al., "Worldwide PC Adoption Forecast, 2007 to 2015," Forrester Research (June 11, 2007).

46. Website: "Internet World Stats." Retrieved July 23, 2008.

47. Website: U.S. Census Bureau, "WorldPOPClock Projection." Retrieved July 23, 2008.

48. David Buckinham and Rebekah Willett, *Digital Generations: Children, Young People, and New Media* (London: Routledge, 2006), 255.

49. Christine Ogan, "Communications Technology and Global Change," in *Communication Technology and Social Change*, edited by Carolyn A. Lin and David J. Atkin (London: Routledge, 2007), 29. Also see Ronald Deibert et al., eds., *Access Denied. The Practice and Policy of Global Internet Filtering* (Cambridge: MIT Press, 2008).

50. See "North Korea," in *Access Denied*, 347ff. Also see Stacey Banks, "North Korean Telecommunications: On Hold," *North Korean Review* 1 (2005), 88–94; and Marcus Noland, "Telecommunications in North Korea: Has Orascom Made the Connection?" *North Korean Review* 5 (2009), 62–74.

51. According to Nolan, North Korea has about five telephone lines for each 100 inhabitants, and "most of these are installed in government offices, collective farms, and state-owned enterprises." See Noland, "Telecommunications in North Korea."

52. For the statistics that follow, see Website: "Internet World Stats." Retrieved July 23, 2008.

53. Cartoon by Peter Steiner, *New Yorker* 69:20 (July 5, 1993), 61.

54. See Edward Castronova, *Synthetic Worlds: The Business and Culture of Online Games* (Chicago: University of Chicago Press, 2005); Tim Guest, *Second Lives: A Journey Through Virtual Worlds* (New York: Random House, 2008); Tom Boellstorff, *Coming of Age in Second Life: An Anthropologist Explores the Virtually Human* (Princeton: Princeton UP, 2008); Wagner James Wu, *The Making of Second Life: Notes from the New World* (New York: HarperBusiness, 2008); and Edward Castronova, *Exodus to the Virtual World: How Online Fun Is Changing Reality* (New York: Palgrave, 2008).

55. On the implications of online anonymity, see Daniel J. Solove, *The Future of Reputation: Gossip, Rumor, and Privacy on the Internet* (New Haven: Yale UP, 2007), 125–160.

56. The relationship between online anonymity and "disinhibitive" behavior is well documented. See Michael Tresca, "The Impact of Anonymity on Disinhibitive Behavior Through Computer-Mediated Communication" (Master's Thesis, Department of Communications, Michigan State University, 1998); Adam N. Joinson, "Causes and Implications of Disinhibited Behavior on the Internet," in *Psychology and the Internet: Intrapersonal, Interpersonal, and Transpersonal Implications*, edited by Jayne Gackenbach (Amsterdam: Academic Press, 1998), 43–60; John Suler, "The Online Disinhibition Effect," *CyberPsychology & Behavior* 7:3 (2004), 321–326.

57. Website: DomainTools, "Domain Counts & Internet Statistics." Retrieved July 23, 2008.

58. Website: Netcraft, "June 2008 Web Server Survey." Retrieved July 23, 2008.

59. Website: WorldWideWebSize, "The Size of the World Wide Web." Retrieved July 23, 2008.

60. Bin He et al., "Accessing the Deep Web," *Communications of the ACM* 50:5 (2007), 94–1001; and Alex Wright, "Exploring a 'Deep Web' That Google Can't Grasp," *New York Times* (February 22, 2009).

61. Kathryn Leger, "Stealing Time at Work on the Net; Companies Cracking Down on Cyberslacking," *The Gazette* (Montreal) (April 4, 2008); "Personal Web Use at Work Is 'Costing UK GB10.6bn a Year'," *Financial Advisor* (June 26, 2008). More generally see Patricia M. Wallace, *The Internet in the Workplace: How New Technology Is Transforming Work* (Cambridge: Cambridge UP, 2004), 226–229.

62. A brief history of the origins of blogging software can be found in Biz Stone's *Who Let the Blogs Out: A Hyperconnected Peek at the World of Weblogs* (New York: Macmillan, 2004), 13ff.

63. There are many books on "Web 2.0." See Bradley L. Jones, *Web 2.0 Heroes: Interviews with Web 2.0 Influencers* (New York: John Wiley & Sons, 2008).

64. "Two Senior Managers of Failed Bear Stearns Hedge Funds Indicted on Conspiracy and Fraud Charges," U.S. Department of Justice press release, June 19, 2008.

65. J. Scott Orr, "Trying to Preserve Today's Web for Future Generations," *Seattle Times* (April 7, 2008).

66. Website: Peter Lyman and Hal R. Varian, "How Much Information? 2003." Retrieved July 24, 2008.

67. Website: Peter Lyman and Hal R. Varian, "How Much Information? 2003." Retrieved July 24, 2008.

68. On Google Books, see Jeffrey Toobin, "Google's Moon Shot: The Quest for the Universal Library," *New Yorker* (February 5, 2007), 30–35; and Matthew Rimmer, *Digital Copyright and the Consumer Revolution: Hands Off My iPod* (Northampton: Edward Elgar Publishing, 2007), 225–260.

69. For a brief introduction, see Daniel J. Solove, *The Digital Person: Technology and Privacy in the Information Age* (New York: NYU Press, 2004). Also see Daniel J. Solove, Marc Rothenberg, and Paul M. Schwartz, *Privacy, Information, and Technology* (New York: Aspen Publishers, 2006).

70. See James B. Rule, *Privacy in Peril: How We Are Sacrificing a Fundamental Right in Exchange for Security and Convenience* (New York: Oxford UP, 2007); David Holtzman, *Privacy Lost: How Technology Is Endangering Your Privacy* (San Francisco: Jossey-Bass, 2006); Christopher Slobogin, *Privacy at Risk: The New Government Surveillance and the Fourth Amendment* (Chicago: University of Chicago Press, 2007); and Jon J. Mills, *Privacy: The Lost Right* (New York: Oxford UP, 2008).

71. See John M. T. Balmer and Stephen A. Greyser, eds., *Revealing the Corporation: Perspectives on Identity, Image and Reputation, Corporate Branding, and Corporate-Level Marketing. An Anthology* (London: Routledge, 2003).

72. See Tom Peters, among many others, *The Brand You 50, Or Fifty Ways to Transform Yourself from an 'Employee' into a Brand That Shouts Distinction, Commitment, and Passion!* (New York: Knopf, 1999).

73. Plenty of people – especially politicians and corporate flacks – have been caught "managing" their Wikipedia pages. For an overview, see Solove, *The Future of Reputation*, 142–146.

74. See Toobin, "Google's Moon Shot," 30–35; and Rimmer, *Digital Copyright and the Consumer Revolution*, 225–260.

75. "Google-fu," in Andrew Peckham, *Urban Dictionary: Fularius Street Slang Defined* (Kansas City: Andrews McMeel Publishing, 2005), 59.

76. Website: "News Transcript: DoD New Briefing–Secretary Rumsfeld and Gen. Myers" (February 12, 2002), U. S. Department of Defense. Retrieved August 13, 2009.

## Critical Thinking and Application

- In the section titled "Fidelity," Poe concludes that the Internet is not really new. It is made of bits and pieces of other forms of communication. Why does he make this claim? Do you accept it?
- Poe claims that "we do not talk because we want to trade information or work together; rather, we talk because we naturally enjoy it because talking... increased our fitness eons ago.... Posting [on the Internet] is the continuation of talking by other means." This view of the reasons for communicating is quite fundamental, as well as at odds with common views of the goals humans have for communicating. Discuss this theory of human nature and communication.
- Do you think the Internet is changing human society and interactions? How? What are the mechanisms for this change? What is your evidence?

## Vocabulary

dialogic
hedonism
iconic
media, medium
network
pull theory of media evolution
push theory of media evolution
symbolic

## Suggested Further Reading [See also list following (New) Media unit introduction]

Peters, John Durham. 1999. *Speaking into the Air: A History of the Idea of Communication*. Chicago: University of Chicago Press.

Poe, Marshall T. 2011. *A History of Communications: Media and Society from the Evolution of Speech to the Internet*. Cambridge: Cambridge University Press.

# PART II

# Language and Society

If you are reading this, you are a user of English. You may be a native speaker of English, or you may have learned English well after you learned another language. You may have learned English as a young child along with another language or two. You may know English from residing in the United States, but you could just as easily have learned it by growing up and becoming educated in Singapore, the Philippines, India, South Africa, Australia, Canada, England, the Netherlands, or Thailand. (If I haven't included your home, that just reinforces my point about English being available in multiple locations.) English dominates communicative interactions in today's world, much as French, Dutch, or Latin did in the past. We don't really know how long its hegemony will last; some predict that Chinese will overtake English as a world language.

But we do know that it is possible for a world language to be used for some purposes while another or several other language varieties are used for other purposes. That is the basic insight that governs this part of the book, "Language and Society."

It is tempting to ask "How many languages are there in the world?" That seems like a basic enough starting point if we wish to explore relations of language and society. But it turns out the question is very complicated, and forces us to ask more questions, such as "How do we define *a language*?" and "How do people in any speech community use the multiple linguistic resources around them?"

Language is not just a tool to be had. It is a tool used by somebody, and by somebodies as members of groups, not simply as individuals. Humans are social by nature, and we signal our social identities largely through the ways we speak. Language is intimately involved in all social interactions, from the largest entities such as nation-states to the smallest and most intimate interactions such as those among friends or family. The study of language and society is rich and multifaceted, and moves outward to a range of topics from education to stereotypes. When we look at the social meanings of language, we learn about the nature of identity and society as they affect all humans.

There are, by most estimates, approximately 6,000 languages extant in the world. Languages have always been born and have died through the movement and change of their speakers.

But to speak of "a language" is far too simple. If we count "English" with its billion speakers as a single language, and also count the Hezhe language with its 4,000 speakers as a single language, and conclude that there are "two languages," we have overlooked a great deal of the complexity in the world. Further, English has uncountable varieties, from the upper-class variety spoken by the educated in England to the Rastafarian English spoken in Jamaica, from African American Vernacular English spoken in the urban United States, to the Appalachian English spoken in rural Kentucky. There are also *Englishes* spoken in Malaysia, India, Africa, and so on.

Many people are speakers of more than one language variety. They acquire multiple languages in complex ways and use them for subtle communicative purposes. Sometimes languages used by decreasing numbers of speakers become endangered, and efforts must be made to maintain or revive them if they are to survive.

So, trying to account for the question "How many languages are there in the world?" requires attention to the realities of how language is used and how it varies within and across societies. It is too simple to state that "The French speak French"; there are multiple varieties of French spoken by people within France and in Francophone Africa and the Caribbean, and there are multiple languages spoken within the boundaries of each country besides just the *official language*.

Beyond even the nameable language varieties such as Malaysian Chinese, there are variations in how exactly language is used, variations that index speakers' identities. These may be social identities, such as social class or gender, or they could be regional or religious identities. Speakers have multiple facets to their identities and can draw on varying resources as they interact in different spheres.

If we think ecologically, that is, within a system (though a system without clear boundaries), we can look at language varieties and variants as resources that are called upon for particular purposes in particular circumstances.

This sounds like something people might do in a very calculating way: "use resources for a purpose" almost as if one were manufacturing a machine. But of course, one of the mysteries of language is that we can do all this without ever having to think about it consciously.

Some people do think about it, though, especially when they are charged with *language planning* or *language revitalization*.

This section takes as its basic premises that (1) multilingualism is the norm, (2) societies and individuals use and value their diverse languages in a variety of ways, (3) languages change and their relative power and value change, (4) identities are enacted at least in large part through language, and (5) status and solidarity are two poles of a continuum.

## Vocabulary

language planning
language revitalization
official language

# UNIT 6

# Multilingualism

Is it a blessing or a curse that most societies everywhere are multilingual? It is the case that for most of human history, all groups interacted with other groups. Attitudes about this differ; sometimes this diversity and divergence are celebrated, sometimes they are ignored, and sometimes they are repressed. Many societies, such as Judeo-Christian societies, have creation myths explaining such linguistic diversity (as in the Tower of Babel story, in which it was deplored).

The term *multilingualism* encompasses a range of behavior from *bilingualism* and *diglossia* (a special kind of bilingualism in which often-related languages such as Arabic and the vernaculars are divided by function) to tri- and quadrilingualism and more. Further, we might distinguish between *societal multilingualism*, in which the society as a whole permits the use of two or more official languages, and *individualism multilingualism*, in which a particular person commands two or more languages.

Some nation-states specify in their constitutions an official or national language and sometimes also what linguistic rights minority groups retain. India's constitution, for instance, specifies Hindi as the official language, stating that English was to be the medium for official purposes for a limited time, and naming a variety of other national languages, for a total of twenty-two officially recognized languages. In China, minority groups are allowed by law to have an education and to publish in their own languages and scripts. (These rights are not always granted in fact.) Canada is officially bilingual, but the province of Quebec is monolingual (French only). The United States has no official statement on language, but several states have since the 1980s passed legislation making English the official language.

Language planning and standardization involve the determination of which language can be recognized for official purposes, such as government communication and education.

Some nations, most famously France and Spain, have academies (the *Académie Française* was founded in 1635, and the French language has been identified with the French nation in the classical case) that determine not only which language is official but specifics about how that language should change or be prevented from changing. The Real Academia Española, founded in 1713, has a modern website that permits users to ascertain which forms are proper in Spanish.

However societies and individuals resolve the issue of multilingualism, it is a fact of human life everywhere.

Individuals can also be multilingual. They can switch from one language to another in appropriate settings, as when they move to a new country or speak to a different person. Or they can switch mid-utterance, for emphasis or to convey a different feeling or because different languages are used for different functions. Hearers also make inferences about speakers' use of their various languages.

Increasingly, languages with fewer speakers and those with less power are being abandoned in favor of more powerful languages and those associated with greater educational or economic opportunities. Estimates of language endangerment and even language death are alarming. Some efforts are being made, however, to resist this trend.

## Suggested Further Reading


Edwards, John R. 1994. *Multilingualism*. London and New York: Routledge.

Ferguson, Charles. 1972 [1959] Diglossia. In *Language and Social Context*, edited by Pier Paolo Giglioli, pp. 232–251. Middlesex: Penguin.

Fishman, Joshua A. 1991. *Reversing Language Shift: Theoretical and Empirical Foundations of Assistance to Threatened Languages*. Clevedon and Philadelphia: Multilingual Matters.

Gal, Susan. 1979. *Language Shift: Social Determinants of Linguistic Change in Bilingual Austria*. New York: Academic Press.

Grosjean, François. 1982. *Life with Two Languages: An Introduction to Bilingualism*. Cambridge, MA: Harvard University Press.

Gumperz, John J. 1982. *Discourse Strategies*. Cambridge: Cambridge University Press.

Heller, Monica, ed. 1988. *Codeswitching: Anthropological and Sociolinguistic Perspectives*. Berlin and New York: Mouton de Gruyter.

Myers-Scotton, Carol. 1988. Codeswitching as Indexical of Social Negotiations. In *Codeswitching: Anthropological and Sociolinguistic Perspectives*, edited by Monica Heller, pp. 151–186. Berlin and New York: Mouton de Gruyter.

Ramaswamy, Sumathi. 1997. *Passions of the Tongue: Language Devotion in Tamil India, 1891–1970*. Berkeley: University of California Press.

Romaine, Suzanne. 1989. *Bilingualism*. New York: Blackwell.

Schiffman, Harold F. 1996. *Linguistic Culture and Language Policy*. London and New York: Routledge.

Terralingua. http://www.terralingua.org/. This website is devoted to maintenance and restoration of biological, cultural, and linguistic diversity.

Terralingua. http://www.terralingua.org/TLUNLetterLHR.htm. This provides Terralingua's presentation to the United Nations about linguistic rights.

UNESCO. http://www.unesco.org/most/ln2pol.htm. MOST Clearing House on Linguistic Rights.

Woolard, Kathryn. 1985. *Double Talk: Bilingualism and the Politics of Ethnicity in Catalonia*. Stanford, CA: Stanford University Press.

Zentella, Ana Celia. 1997. *Growing Up Bilingual: Children in El Barrio*. Malden, MA: Blackwell.

# Societal Multilingualism

## CHAPTER 19

# Chinese, English, Spanish—and the Rest

*Tom McArthur*

(2005)

*When empires were ruled by European nations, the question of language was often pressing: How could the colonial rulers communicate with the local people? How could the various local peoples, speaking a wide range of languages, communicate efficiently and trade effectively? One solution was to develop a* lingua franca, *a language like Latin, that would serve as a shared medium of expression, even if it was a second (or third) language for most of its speakers. The choice of which variety to select as a lingua franca involved understanding local power relations and history and a good dose of chance.*

*At various times in the past, certain languages rose to dominance because of the widespread economic and political power of their speakers. Though many have tried to explain this dominance in terms of some intrinsic virtue of the language itself (French as nuanced and appropriate for diplomacy, English as having a wide vocabulary), it is clear that empires took their languages with them and imposed them on the populations they ruled.*

*Since the end of colonialism, we can see a different dynamic at work. For example, Melayu (a variety of Malay) was deliberately developed as a lingua franca in what was later to become the new nation of Indonesia (and Melayu became the national language, Indonesian). The Dutch who ruled the Dutch East Indies selected it for a variety of reasons.*

*Tom McArthur, editor of the journal* English Today, *categorizes the languages of the world in the twenty-first century, singling out English as a unique language (actually as a set of languages collected as "Englishes"). Though it is not the first language of the majority of the world's speakers, it is the language used for many affairs of the world, constituting a "world language." People who speak English, perhaps quite well, nonetheless frequently speak a number of other languages in addition. Native speakers of English are the least likely to feel obliged to learn other languages.*

*McArthur's seven levels of languages help make sense of the varying breadth and power of the languages in the world, with the largest number of speakers focused in the top three levels and the largest number of languages focused in the bottom four levels. As many of the authors in Unit 6 do implicitly, McArthur writes explicitly of an "ecology" of languages.*

### Reading Questions

- What are the characteristics of a "world language"? Which languages have had that designation in the past? What are the reasons for English having become one recently?
- Why does McArthur write of the "English language complex" rather than simply the "English language"?
- What is the difficulty in determining the difference between *language* and *dialect*?
- Look carefully at the evidence by which McArthur singles out English from, say, Spanish and Chinese. Does this make sense to you? What other evidence might you amass?

---

The second edition of the *Oxford Dictionary of English* (2003) defines *ecology* as "the branch of biology that deals with the relations of organisms to one another and to their physical surroundings." I would, however, like to extend this definition here to include an "ecology of communication," covering the nature and evolution of language, the media, and such technologies as radio, telephony, television, and

Tom McArthur, Chinese, English, Spanish – and the Rest. *English Today* 83 (vol. 21, no. 3), July 2005: 55–61.

the net/web. This discussion will not, however, deal with an ecology of communication at large, but five particular, related matters: English and the rest of the world's languages; the idea of a "world language"; the interaction of the world's languages and communicative technologies; the millions of people who use English and at least one other language; and the size, security, and health of our global linguistic inheritance.

## The English Language Complex

English is a paradox. In traditional terms it is a single language, but in recent centuries it has become so large and varied that it has taken on the features of a family of languages: like the *Semitic languages* (origin, West Asia) or the *Romance languages* (which might more properly be called the *Latin languages*: cf. Wright 2004). Anyone concerned after the 1980s with *world* or *international* or *global* English also knows (and may use) the form *Englishes*, promoted with marked success by the Indian American linguist Braj B. Kachru. However, although phrases like *the Englishes* and *world Englishes* imply a family, Kachru has not (to my best recollection) explicitly proposed that any of the Englishes are, or might become, distinct languages. One wonders, therefore, whether his "Englishes" constitute a single complex entity or a family of entities.

Since bringing out *The English Languages* in 1998 I have continued to hold the plural view expressed there. However, I have also felt the need for a further phrase: *the English language complex*, which retains the tradition of *English* as a single entity, while allowing for both *the Englishes* and *the English languages* as terms for handling a multiplicity that includes *African English, African-American English, American English, British English, China English, Indian English,* and *Nigerian English*. Yet wherever one looks there are semantic complications. For example:

- The label *British English* can be ambiguous if not overtly clarified: it may mean upper- and middle-class British usage with an **RP** accent (as conventionally on offer in **ELT** textbooks and dictionaries) *or* all English as used in England alone *or* all English as used in England, Scotland, Wales, and Northern Ireland.
- The label *Indian English* has a range of sub-divisions that includes *Anglo-Indian English, Bengali English,* and is at the same time (uncontentiously) part of *Asian English,* yet we do not usually say that *British English* is part of *European English,* although oddly enough (since there are now many such entities as *Dutch English* and *Swedish English*) this is the case. To complicate matters further, people now talk (often disparagingly) of a European Union kind of English, used especially in Brussels, that is often called *Euro-English,* but explicitly *not* what either the British or the Irish use.

Containing by definition these and other (often confusing) ***varieties,*** the English language complex is, as it were, a system of systems whose membership is unclear, because commentators can always find another English to add to the list: for example, *Afghan English* or *United Nations English.* One cannot predict or apparently exhaust the number of such terms, whether they are geographic, educational, professional, social, or a mix of these, as with *British English* (as above), *Business English, British Business English, American Business English, Anglo-American Business English* (note: much more likely than *British-American Business English), Californian English, Californian Media English, China English,* and *Chinese English* (delicately contrasted in recent issues of *ET*), *Jamaican English Creole,* and indeed that really difficult pair, *X* ***Standard*** *English* and *Standard X English* (where we can replace the *X* with whatever nation, region, ethnicity, business, or other activity we wish) ad infinitum et nauseam.

We *can* say, however, that for some time there have been two universally agreed nation-based standards of English, one cent*red* on the UK, the other center*ed* on the US. It has become increasingly clear, however, over the last half-century, that these are no longer alone. Most Australians, Canadians, and New Zealanders now assume that they too have standard varieties, and there are dictionaries to demonstrate the fact. And indeed, the Irish Republic, South Africa, India, and Singapore can arguably be added to this list (with or without national dictionaries).

In a major everyday sense, however, English remains a language among languages. Yet, even so, many would agree that, since at least the mid-twentieth century, it has not been a language in the way that Danish, Hungarian, Korean, Maori, or Nahuatl are languages, for at least *six* reasons: its scale, its distribution, the number and range of its varieties, its technical and professional applications, and the number of its users and would-be users, whether as a mother tongue or an other tongue. One reason for calling it a *complex* is that many of its varieties are *not*, and never have been, **dialects**. No one talks of an *Indian dialect of English,* or sub-dialects within Indian English. They do, however, talk about *Punjabi English, Bengali English,* and such like, as (sub)varieties of *Indian English,* each of them influenced by at least one major regional language and/or the vagaries of regional life, and *not* by isolation from the mother source, as was the case for example with the usage of Newfoundland and the Falkland Islands.

In traditional terms, dialects are seldom sharply separated, but are areas within continua: that is, Dialects A and B do not usually "meet" at a boundary line: rather, an area of A shades into an area of B, until A-ness becomes B-ness. In certain politico-cultural instances, however, one area in such a continuum acquires prestige and a script in which records can be kept, orders issued, and books written, becoming because of this the primary and perhaps sole official tool for national record-keeping, news, policy, and officially-received culture, as with *le bon français* or the *King's English.* When a speech form becomes like that, linguists call it an ***acrolect*** (Greek: "high dialect") and the rest become ***basilects*** ("low dialects"), maybe with an intermediate layer or two, the ***mesolects*** ("middle dialects"). Such names make commentary more clinical, but *acro* and *basi* are just Greek elements in English that mean "high" and "low"—verging (dare I say it?) on a cosmetic exercise. The distance between Standard English and the **vernacular** Englishes, between Mandarin Chinese [Putonghua] and the Han dialects, or Classical Arabic and the vernacular Arabics remains great however the scale is calibrated.

## Standard, Dialect, Variety, Accent, Pidgin, Creole

By and large, the standard and near-standard forms of British and American English are **mutually intelligible** (especially in print): in effect "the same language" while differing in ways which do not invoke questions about which is a dialect of the other. Many British people have of course insisted that US usage is derivative and therefore secondary, but an overwhelming reversal of global roles in the course of the twentieth century has gravely damaged that particular argument. Linguists, however, agree that neither is a lect of the other and each has lects of its own—and that, in any case, the US is vastly larger and more populous, and carries a bigger stick.

After 1945, there was no reason for Americans to feel secondary to anyone in any aspect of their lives, even if some might defer to British niceties. The rest of the twentieth century simply affirmed a state of affairs that seems likely to last well into the twenty-first. But by and large none of this affected other kinds of English elsewhere, including entities far more exotic than traditional dialects and mildly different standard varieties. English-based **pidgins** and **creoles** have sometimes been called "dialects", but usually they have been described not just as "barbarous" or "uncouth" (as dialects have often been described) but as "broken" and "debased": not real English but bastard offshoots to be regretted, and kept at arm's length.

In such a world climate the term *variety* has been immensely reassuring (but at times a copout) for linguists and language teachers. Although I find the term invaluable, I worry about its catch-all blandness: any distinctive spoken, written, printed, electronic or other aspect of a language, and especially English, can be a "variety." And the term has not helped much in avoiding the original problem: In everyday life, *variety* is not much used for talking about language, and the term *dialect* is far more likely to be applied to mesolects and basilects than to acrolects (which are or become the "standard" language that is blessed with **orthography** and print). Meanwhile, the term *pidgin* remains low, often negative, and at best neutral (despite having been adopted by linguists as a technical term), and *creole* is hardly known outside the Caribbean, Louisiana, and linguistics libraries.

There is more, however. In addition to dialects, pidgins, and creoles, English in all its varieties has long been mixing with other languages, producing a range of, as it were, *Anglo-hybrids*. Such entities may seem chaotic to an outsider meeting them for the first time, but blends of this kind are inevitable in locales where two or more avowed languages are in wide daily contact. Such outcomes as *franglais* and *Spanglish* are not, however, chaotic to their users but are pragmatic blends in which the most immediately recalled and relevant material takes pride of place. Many social commentators deplore such hybridization, but deploring it has never put an end to it, any more than it has put an end to dialect.

When people of different backgrounds within "the same" language come together, the amount of adjustment needed for adequate communication may range from minimal to massive, but by and large exposure to such media as TV and films/movies and news services such as BBC World and CNN appears to have made encounters with variation easier than in the past. Even so, however, remoteness from the world's main travel routes and lack of exposure to the media may make some varieties of a language like English as exotic as the flora and fauna of their locale, as, say, with *Caribbean Creole* and *Tok Pisin* in Papua New Guinea.

## Seven Levels

English is a vast language, whereas Scottish Gaelic now has about 70,000 speakers left. A thousand years ago Gaelic was the primary language of Scotland, accumulating a strong tradition of orature and literature that only a few can now access. I was born into a family whose last Gaelic speaker died in the 1930s. My children know only a few words (such as *slainte* "health," and also a toast which few know, and *glen*, which many know because it became an English word). Both my father and I wanted to acquire it, but life got in the way. However, all three of my children know English, and also French, from living in Quebec; my older daughter is fluent in Japanese, and my son is competent in Italian. Alas, however, none speaks Persian, their mother's language, because she chose not to use it with them. Crucially, however, neither set of grandparents when young could have predicted the languages their grandchildren would know, and this seems increasingly to be the way of the world.

The following is a seven-level model that seeks to represent the world's languages in terms of size and "clout" (if any). The first five levels "contain" the largest and safest languages, and here I spend more time on them (alas), while the lowest two levels contain the many languages worldwide suffering diminution and facing extinction (cf. Crystal 2000).

### Level 1: English

A vast, unevenly but widely distributed language complex with two globalized national varieties (American and British), each with a standard form, three further major national varieties (Australian, Canadian, New Zealand), and many varieties worldwide. Around a billion people use it, as a first, second, or other language, and its standard varieties are taught to further millions. It can be heard or read almost everywhere, and is the world's primary vehicle for the media, commerce, technology, science, medicine, education, popular and youth culture, travel, trade in armaments, and United Nations peace-keeping. In terms of its widest reach it is often called *World, International,* or *Global English,* and there is a multitude of regional and other *Englishes,* known more or less formally as, say, *South African English* and *Japanese English,* or informally and often facetiously as, say, *Japlish* and *Taglish* (English mixed with Tagalog, in the Philippines).

### Level 2: Chinese, Spanish, Hindi-Urdu

Three language complexes covering hundreds of millions of people. *Chinese,* the largest, has over a billion users, the vast majority in the People's Republic of China, Hong Kong, and Taiwan. *Spanish* is widely disseminated in the Americas, with a limited role in Europe (its continent of origin, as with English). Despite the prestige of Castilian usage in Spain, the language has no single strong centre, like Chinese, or centres, like English. Its geopolitical focus, like English, is the western hemisphere, from Argentina to the US. It is also spoken in Morocco and Equatorial Guinea in Africa and the Philippines in Asia. The vast majority of users of *Hindi-Urdu* are in northern India and Pakistan, with **diaspora** populations elsewhere. Hindi-Urdu is more or less one entity in speech but not in sociocultural terms. Its Hindi component is the official language of India, uses the Devanagari script, and is largely a medium for northern (not southern) Hindus. Its Urdu component uses the Perso-Arabic script and is primarily a medium for Muslims in India and Pakistan. All three complexes are world-regional, with little (though increasing) wider diffusion.

### Level 3: Arabic, French, German, Japanese, Malay

The *Arabic* complex is used across North Africa and in much of the Middle East, throughout which it is the primary medium of ethnic Arabs. In addition, from Europe and North Africa to the Philippines it is the historic vehicle of Islam. It has both a Classical form and a range of colloquial, and not necessarily mutually intelligible, forms in Bahrain, Dubai, Egypt, the Emirates, Iraq, Jordan, Kuwait, Lebanon, Morocco, Qatar, Saudi Arabia, Sudan, Syria, and Yemen. *French* has traditionally been in cultural competition with English, German, and Italian, and until the mid-twentieth century was the elite language of diplomacy. After the Second World War, it lost ground to *les anglo-saxons* (the Americans and British viewed as a unity in which the British formerly dominated and the Americans now dominate). The community of *le français mondial* ("World French") is known as *La Francophonie* ("the French-speaking world"). *German,* formerly strong in Europe and some African colonies, and in academic-cum-scientific writing, lost influence as a consequence of the defeat of Germany and Austria in two world wars, but retains strength in business and technology. *Japanese* has never had a world role, despite Japan's global commercial success. *Malay,* however, has begun to develop a higher profile in Asia because of its role in Malaysia, Indonesia, Brunei, Singapore, and southern Thailand.

### Level 4: Significant Nationally and/or Regionally

This level includes such flourishing strong regional languages as Ashanti, Hausa, Ibo, and Yoruba in West Africa; Amharic, Swahili, Somali, and Kikuyu in East Africa; Dutch, Hungarian, Polish, Romanian, and Swedish in Europe; Portuguese in Brazil, Portugal, Angola, Mozambique, East Timor, and Macao; Turkish and Persian in Western and Central Asia; Bengali, Gujarati, Kannada, Konkani, Marathi, Oriya, Punjabi, Tamil, Telugu, and Malayalam in India: all used in communities with large populations, complex social histories, and thriving cultures. Most of the languages at this level are robustly healthy, and many have diaspora communities.

### Level 5: Locally and Socially Strong

Languages within one or more nations or territories, such as Berber in Morocco, Catalan in Spain and France, Danish in Denmark, Finnish in Finland, Maya in Mexico and Central America, Guarani in Paraguay, Tagalog and Ilocano in the Philippines, Nahuatl in Mexico, Quechua in Peru, and, as an exceptional case, the vibrant small language Icelandic. Some languages at this level are secure in national terms (as with Danish and Finnish, although English is in use for professional, higher-educational, and international purposes), while others occupy a mid-position in their local hierarchy (as with Catalan and Ilocano), and others have large numbers of users but little or no international prominence (as with Berber, Maya, and Quechua).

### Level 6: Small and (Perhaps) Managing

Hundreds of languages used mainly in politically or geographically non-metropolitan areas, or among migrant workers, whose speakers number in the low millions, hundreds of thousands, or less. They may or may not be well-situated nationally, regionally, continentally, socioculturally, or in educational terms, and in many cases have been depleted by social change, including emigration of speakers and immigration of non-speakers. They may, however, be sustaining themselves, sometimes in secure situations, such as Faroese in Denmark's Faroe Islands, sometimes in situations less negative than formerly, as with Maori in New Zealand, sometimes under politically neutral conditions, such as Welsh in Wales (within the UK), Gallego in Spain, and more secure Amerindian languages such as Navajo.

### Level 7: Extremely Small and Endangered

Some thousands of languages in the Americas, Asia, Africa, Australasia, Europe, and the Pacific whose speakers number in the thousands, hundreds, or tens and less, often in communities that are shrinking for various reasons (including migration and intermarriage) or disrupted and sometimes demoralized, within and ranging across the boundaries of nation-states, and therefore semi-assimilated into more socially and economically powerful societies. Some manage to sustain themselves, as with Lapp in northern Scandinavia, while others have for many years been in dire straits, particularly the remaining Aboriginal languages of Australia, the "heritage languages" of Canada's "Native Peoples," such as Ojibwa and Inuit; and comparable "American Indian" languages in the US, such as Cherokee and Mohawk. Some may be dichotomous, where for example Irish Gaelic (or Irish) is somewhat sustained by government effort and a national education policy in the Irish Republic, but Scottish Gaelic has no official role or protection, and dwindles despite efforts to promote it (including through internet lessons). Some groups are stable and fairly secure but many are socially disrupted, the numbers of active speakers dwindling, and many probably will not survive the next half-century.

Discussion of the languages in Categories 1 and 2 of this list is difficult without bringing in the languages of 3 to 7, because in many instances multilingual individuals and communities use both large languages alongside their own local-cum-ethnic languages, or have given up a local tongue, or are using it less, or see the next generation giving it up in favour of one or more languages offering better prospects. Significantly, for our purposes here, if users of a language at the sixth or seventh level are not only learning and using a language of wider local distribution but also learning English at school or using it in their work, then *two* kinds of pressure are being exerted on small languages that may not yet be endangered, but could become so in, say, fifty years' time.

Millions of busy people worldwide *can* and *do* become successful trilinguals. In India this is often the norm: mother tongue, other Indian tongue, and English ("the window on the world"). Many native-speakers of English, however, do not use any other language beyond, say, school-days French. It is often therefore difficult for them to imagine or take seriously competition among languages *inside* a nation-state. I don't have Gaelic because local work and migration patterns meant that Highlanders and Islanders moved to the Lowland cities, where they acquired Lowland Scots as the language of work and their children learned Scottish English in school while using versions of Scots vernacular in the street and playground. Nothing simple there, nor anything simple elsewhere. **Language ecologies** are like bio-ecologies: they normally function well enough, but can be thrown off balance. I don't speak Gaelic, but I *do* know Scots and English natively, plus French and Persian non-natively. Maybe two out of three isn't too bad. And probably Lowland Scots will survive, partly because many people don't accept that it's a language. It may therefore manage to sneak around for quite some time, heavily disguised as bad English.

## Meanwhile, at the Big End of the Scale

The spread since 1945 of "world" or "international" or "global English" has been remarkable, which is why it has Category 1 to itself. Yet even if I'd put Levels 1 and 2 of 7 levels together as 1 of 6 levels, it would have made no difference to language reality. I didn't do this because the distributions are so different: Spanish, Chinese, and Hindi-Urdu massively concentrated in particular regions, with limited impact elsewhere, and Hindi-Urdu not well known as a single entity, even in India. As a result, this vast complex removes itself from the world discussion, despite its scale and significance. The following three factors apply to it, but in global terms relate more to Chinese, Spanish, and English:

1. Far more users of Chinese and Spanish are learning English than there are users of English learning Spanish and Chinese.
2. Far more users of Chinese and Spanish are learning English than are learning one another's language.
3. Far more users of other languages are learning English than are learning Chinese and Spanish.

However, we can note that Spanish occupies a unique role as the only language currently making inroads into the English-speaking world, and in its most powerful locale, the United States. The demographic and linguistic advance of Latino migrants into the US (from Mexico and further south) has been so marked in recent times that alarmed US linguistic conservatives campaign for English to be made the official federal language (as if this would make much difference). Ironically, in the most powerful fortress of English, enough people have been nervous enough to band together to protect the one language on the planet that is least in need of protection.

The Chinese complex is vast, but the majority of its speakers are Han (ethnic Chinese) living in the People's Republic of China. The vast majority of the world's non-native learners of Chinese are non-Han citizens of the PRC, with however a small but growing number of learners in neighbouring East Asia, their eyes on trade. Like Hindi-Urdu and Spanish, therefore, Chinese is (despite its size) a world-regional language, whereas English (with all its built-in spelling and other hurdles) is the closest we have come to universality in the use of a language, and so, even if English has nearly destroyed Gaelic and long ago upstaged Scots (which was my mother's tongue), I have learned to live with it, and, like my revered English teacher Miss Frances Anderson, at Woodside Senior Secondary School in Glasgow, love it as much as I love Scots. Not to forget French, Latin, Greek, and Persian.

In *The Future of English?* (1997), David Graddol suggests three options for English as a lingua franca in Asia: that it might keep this role indefinitely; that it might be supplanted by Mandarin; or that there might not in future be any Asian lingua franca. A few years further on, in 2005, it would seem that English will sustain its transnational role in Asia, as illustrated by recent developments in the Association of South East Asian Nations (ASEAN), which since its formation in 1967 has used English as its common medium. One must suppose that, when ASEAN members meet such prospective regional trading partners as China and India, English will continue in its current role. In that role, however, it will not be operating as an Atlantic language, but as an Asian lingua franca. And when in the nearish future ASEAN will be dealing with both India and China, English will be the broker language, working together with Hindi-Urdu, Chinese, and Malay as key languages in South and East Asia.

One might call this *English Plus*. In the Americas it will be English plus Spanish (plus Portuguese for Brazil, and French for Quebec). In North and West Africa, it will be English plus Arabic (plus French). In West Asia, it will be Arabic plus English. In South Asia, it will be English plus Hindi-Urdu (South Indians preferring English to Hindi; Pakistanis comfortable with Urdu and English; Sri Lankans opting for English). In parts of Eastern Europe and Central Asia, it will be English plus Russian (with French in the wings in Romania, and German in the Balkans). In western Europe, however, it looks as though English will be the lingua franca (even for the French). That is, English will be everywhere, but often in partnership with other large languages. Not much help (alas) for the languages in Level 7, but less monolithic than some may fear. And maybe an ecology in which people from traditionally multilingual backgrounds can work towards reducing the downward drift.

## References and Related Reading


Crystal, David. 1997 (2nd ed., 2003). *English as a Global Language*. Cambridge: Cambridge University Press.

Crystal, David. 2000. *Language Death*. Cambridge: Cambridge University Press.

Graddol, David. 1997. *The Future of English?* London: The British Council.

Kachru, Braj B. 1982. *The Other Tongue: English Across Cultures*. Urbana: University of Illinois Press.

Kachru, Braj B. 1992. *The Other Tongue: English Across Cultures*. [new collection]. Urbana & Chicago: University of Illinois Press.

Kachru, Braj B. 2005. *Asian Englishes: Beyond the Canon*. Hong Kong: Hong Kong University Press.

McArthur, Tom. 1998. *The English Languages*. Cambridge: Cambridge University Press.

McArthur, Tom. 2002. *Oxford Guide to World English*. Oxford: Oxford University Press.

Wright, Roger. 2004. "Latin and English as world languages." In *English Today* 80 (20:4).


## Critical Thinking and Application

- Have you studied a foreign language? Which level does that language occupy? Have you learned about the force and power of the nations associated with that language? Could *every* language be portrayed as important and significant? In what sense?
- How can you account for the languages taught in schools in your country? On what basis are they selected? Have those languages changed since your parents were students? Would you expect the next generation to be learning the same or different languages? What languages do you think *should* be taught? Why?
- What is the role of the media in determining which languages have world dominance?

## Vocabulary

| | | | |
|---|---|---|---|
| accent | dialect | mesolect | RP |
| acrolect | diaspora | mutually intelligible | standard |
| basilect | ELT | orthography | variety |
| creole | language ecology | pidgin | vernacular |

## Suggested Further Reading


Edwards, John R. 1994. *Multilingualism*. London and New York: Routledge.

McCrum, Robert. 2010. *Globish: How the English Language Became the World's Language*. New York: Norton.

Romaine, Suzanne. 1989. *Bilingualism*. New York: Blackwell.

Schiffman, Harold F. 1996. *Linguistic Culture and Language Policy*. London and New York: Routledge.

# CHAPTER 20

# Bad Language—Bad Citizens

*Edwin L. Battistella*

(2005)

*Is some language better than other language? Most people in most places feel that the answer is obviously "yes," while anthropologists and linguists see the answer as "no." Edwin Battistella looks at different kinds of language that tend to be evaluated negatively in his book* Bad Language: Are Some Words Better Than Others? *He considers bad writing, bad grammar, bad words, bad citizens, and bad accents. Judgments of all five of these could be regarded as arbitrary; they are socially determined, and they vary across time and space. But people within any given society see their judgments as natural, inevitable, and* right.

*Linguists often distinguish between* **prescriptive** *and* **descriptive grammar**. Prescriptive *grammar is what we learn in school, telling us what we* should *say or write: "Don't say* Him and me *went; the proper form is* He and I." *"Make sure the items in a list are parallel."* Descriptive *grammar, by contrast, analyzes what people actually say.*

*In many places in the world, multilingualism gives rise to formulas and policies that have value judgments attached to them, giving preferential treatment to one language or another. Some nations have officially designated languages while others—including the United States—do not. The Académie Française in France and the Real Academia Española in Spain offer pronouncements about how to protect, preserve, and improve their languages. In some countries, such as China, minority language rights are recognized in the constitution. In some countries, such as India, the officially recognized national languages are enumerated in the constitution. Some countries, such as Israel, recognize several official languages (Hebrew, Standard Arabic, English).*

*There are clear decisions that must be made when institutions such as government or education are involved: Which language(s) should be used? What are the positions of other languages? Should efforts be made to protect minority languages? Are national efforts primarily directed toward assimilation or toward diversity and pluralism?*

*How linguistic diversity is regarded depends on a number of underlying principles, and in many countries, these principles change over time, along with other historical factors. In this chapter, Battistella chronicles some of the ways multilingualism has been regarded in the United States.*

## Reading Questions

- What were the dominant concerns of the founders of the United States with regard to language?
- What attitudes did pre-twentieth-century Americans display toward linguistic diversity? What attitudes did they hold toward assimilation or cultural pluralism?

Edwin L. Battistella, Bad Language: Bad Citizens. From *Bad Language: Are Some Words Better Than Others?* Oxford and New York: Oxford University Press, 2005, pp. 101–123.

- What seems to account for waves of concern about an official language?
- What are the similarities and differences among attitudes toward foreign language learning, deaf manualism, Native American language, bilingual education, and English-only legislation?

In a 1917 speech, Theodore Roosevelt famously made the link between speaking the English language and good American citizenship, saying that

> We must have one flag. We must also have one language.... The greatness of this nation depends on the swift assimilation of the aliens she welcomes to her shores. Any force which attempts to retard that assimilative process is a force hostile to the highest interests of our country.[1]

For Roosevelt, language was both a symbol of national unity, like the flag, and a means of creating that unity, by swift assimilation of immigrants to American language, customs, and values. For many, the foreign languages of immigrants, to the extent that they were maintained rather than given up, were a form of bad language that got in the way of their adoption of American speech and values.

[Elsewhere] I have examined how differences of grammar and vocabulary lead to judgments about speakers. The same is true of retention of foreign languages, which has often been seen as unpatriotic, uneducated, or separatist. [Here] I focus on American attitudes toward languages other than English, beginning with some history and case studies and moving forward to contemporary issues of English-only and **bilingual education**. In looking at the urge to assimilate other languages, my aim is to explore why some see foreign languages as making bad citizens.

## Birth of a Nation

The United States began as a developing nation. Much early American discussion of language issues focused on the relative merits of American versus British usage and whether British English should continue to be the standard in the United States. Writers like Benjamin Franklin, who helped to set standards for American prose style—and who were successful writers in part because their prose style satisfied English critics—argued for British standards. As historian Daniel Boorstin notes, Franklin wrote to his friend David Hume in 1760 that he hoped that "we in America make the best English of this Island our standard."[2] John Pickering likewise argued that attention to English standards was necessary for literary appreciation, scientific communication, and international respect. Pickering cited English criticisms of American usage and remarked that, while the American language had changed less than might have been expected, "it has in so many instances departed from the English standard, that our scholars should lose no time in endeavoring to restore it to its purity, and to prevent further corruption."[3]

On the other hand, writers like Thomas Jefferson and Noah Webster were proponents of an American language. Jefferson argued that language planning should look to the future by expanding the vocabulary so that English would be an appropriate vehicle for new knowledge. In a letter of 1813 stressing usage and innovation over grammar and tradition, Jefferson suggested that the new United States would require a certain amount of new vocabulary and that language, like government, ought to follow the will of the people.[4] Jefferson's own writing was criticized for using novel words and, in an 1820 letter to John Adams, Jefferson wrote, "I am a friend to neology. It is the only way to give a language copiousness and euphony," adding that "Dictionaries are but the depositories of words legitimated by usage."[5]

Noah Webster had a businessman's interest in creating an independent American economy. He also had a revolutionary's interest in creating a unified and independent American culture and language.[6] He wrote that "Custom, habits, and *language*, as well as government, should be national. America should have her *own* language distinct from all the world."[7] In addition, Webster saw American usage as reflecting a conservatism that had been given up by British grammarians. In his view, the best speech was that of the American gentleman farmers, whom he saw as different from the English peasants—as better educated, landowning, and independent.

Webster also feared that copying British manners would mean carrying over British linguistic vices to the new American nation. As literary scholar David Simpson emphasizes, Webster saw the establishment of an American language as a way to recapture the former purity of the English language before its corruption by the London court and the English theater.[8] This view arose in part from Webster's Puritan suspicion of ornamentation, though disdain for the language of the court was also characteristic of reformers like Bishop Lowth. Webster's distaste was particularly aimed at the language of writers like Samuel Johnson, which he viewed as pompous and antiquated. He believed that freed of British vices, educated usage in America would reflect principles of rational analogy and would preserve a uniformity of American speech against both literary affectation and dialect variation. And he hoped that adopting such a version of English, together with access to land and an egalitarian commercial environment, would preserve the social and moral health of America. As Simpson explains, Webster worried that Americans who adopted contemporary British speech habits would create disharmony in their own communities by introducing the class distinctions of England. Historian Kenneth Cmiel notes that such attitudes were common—many expressed a "fear of aristocratic overrefinement, of using civil forms solely to maintain social distinctions."[9] But fears of refinement were balanced by a sense that eloquence was necessary for participation in political affairs. Cmiel notes that "even radicals understood that entrance to public life demanded verbal felicity."[10]

The dispersion of the population in America and the distance from British cultural standards also raised concerns that linguistic corruption would follow from the lack of a cultural center. **Standardization** of usage was a concern to some of the political founders of the United States. One solution entertained was the establishment of a legal authority to govern language, with John Adams advocating that Congress establish a national academy to **standardize** usage and pronunciation. Adams feared a natural degeneration of English and saw a national academy promoting the study of English (and other languages) as key to diplomatic goals.[11] Adams, who was often characterized as a monarchist, was careful to stress the democratic effect of a common standard. In 1780 he wrote that, with a public standard in place, "eloquence will become the instrument for recommending men to their fellow citizens, and the principal means of advancement through the various ranks and offices of society."[12] Adams also stressed that he was not advocating a new American language. He wrote that "[w]e have not made war against the English Language, any more than against the old English character," and he suggested that an academy would be an American accomplishment of something that England had not succeeded in doing.[13] The Continental Congress, however, did not place a high priority on a national academy, and the proposal never emerged from the committee studying it. While an official English Academy was never established, there does not seem to have been much doubt that English was intended as the de facto **standard language**. As John Jay noted in the *Federalist Papers:* "Providence has been pleased to give this one connected country to one united people—a people descended from the same ancestors, speaking the same language, professing the same religion, attached to the same principles of government."[14]

In colonial and post-Revolution discussions of language, we find the familiar theme of choosing a standard. Here the choice was between British and American styles and involved considerations of simplicity, commonness, and refinement. The discussion of an American language was embedded in larger discussions of American and British culture, and language played an important role in defining an American identity that could be linked to the best of English values and culture yet remain separate from perceived English vices. A separate American language was seen as a means of representing and maintaining international status and of accommodating new knowledge and situations.

## Native American Languages

The founders of America understood the need to accommodate various European linguistic groups, as a means of fostering support for the revolution and as a means of encouraging settlement. While many of the founders were sympathetic toward the learning of other languages, broader public attitudes toward foreign and minority languages have often been indifferent or hostile. In this section and the next, I look at two case studies of attempts at assimilation—Native American languages and the sign language of the deaf. While these cases are very different, what stands out is the way that language differences are seen as a social problem.

From colonial times, European settlers' attitudes toward Native Americans often focused on civilizing and Christianizing, in part by forcing Native Americans to speak English. From the early 1800s, Congress provided funds for missionary Indian schools that promulgated official government views about land holding and resettlement. By the late 1800s, as the military was more capable of policy enforcement in the West, the government became much more directive toward Native Americans. As John Reyhner notes, when Congress ended treaty making in 1871, policy shifted from relocation to assimilation, and the government became involved in the operation of Indian schools.[15] A report of the Commissioner for Indian Affairs in 1878 advocated removal of children from the influence of reservation life (and from parents) and proposed the creation of boarding schools. Prototype schools were developed in 1878 at the Hampton Institute in Virginia and in 1879 at the Carlisle Indian School in Pennsylvania, a converted army barracks. By 1902 almost 10,000 children had been relocated to twenty-five Indian boarding schools where English-only rules were enforced by corporal punishment. Also during this period, mission schools that had been instructing students in Bible studies using their native languages were forced to conduct instruction only in English in order to retain federal funds.

Federal policy of the late 1800s was exemplified by the views of J. D. C. Atkins, Commissioner of Indian Affairs. In his 1887 annual report, Atkins cited the report of a commission on Indian conditions the previous year, which advocated that "barbarous dialects should be blotted out, and the English language substituted." The report also linked assimilation of language to assimilation of thought and behavior, in language that foreshadows Orwell's theme of language as a mechanism of conformity and social control:

> Through sameness of language is produced sameness of sentiment, and thought; customs, and habits are moulded and assimilated in the same way, and thus in process of time the differences producing trouble would have been gradually eliminated.[16]

Adopting the majority language, in his view, would assimilate Indians to the majority perspective. Atkins went on to say that Indians "must be taught the language which they must use in transacting business with the people of this country. No unity or community of feeling can be established among different peoples unless they are brought to speak the same language."[17]

Assimilationism remained the main policy direction in Indian affairs well into the twentieth century, though a shift away from the assimilationist perspective did occur in the 1930s. The Meriam Report of 1928, an extensive survey of social and economic conditions sponsored by the Institute of Government Research, criticized the practice of breaking up Native American families and the practices of the boarding schools. The report led to such federal legislation as the Indian Reorganization Act of 1934, which promoted self-determination and cultural pluralism. Federally sponsored day schools were also established to provide English training with less disruption of the family and community. During World War II, however, funding was reallocated to the war effort. After the war, assimilationism reemerged as a way of encouraging Native American urbanization, and a policy of terminating reservations emerged in the 1950s.

During the New Frontier and Great Society era, termination efforts were challenged and policy again shifted to ways of combining federal assistance with self-determination. President Lyndon Johnson called for the end to termination efforts in his March 1968 Special Message to Congress, "The Forgotten American," and won passage of the Indian Civil Rights Act of 1968. The Nixon administration continued efforts to support self-determination, with the Indian Education Act of 1972 strengthening Indian control of education in their communities. In addition, the tribal college movement begun in the 1960s expanded Native American higher education. Most recently, the 1990 Native American Languages Act made it policy to "preserve, protect, and promote the rights and freedom of Native Americans to use, practice, and develop Native American languages."[18] Among other things, the act encouraged Native American language survival and recognized the rights of tribes to use Native American languages as a medium of instruction in federally funded schools.

The support for Native American languages is a case in which the policy of assimilation and termination was recognized as counterproductive in a variety of ways—socially, educationally, and culturally. Earlier policies of relocation to boarding schools, restraint of language traditions, and termination of reservations have been supplanted by perspectives that give communities more voice in how schools educate youth and that encourage the use of native languages and cultures to strengthen educational opportunities for Native American students.

## Manualism Versus Oralism

Education of the deaf in the United States provides an interesting parallel to the assimilationist theme apparent in attitudes toward Native American languages. As historian Douglas Baynton points out in *Forbidden Signs: American Culture and the Campaign Against Sign Language*, attitudes toward sign language changed dramatically at the end of the nineteenth century. Deafness had been viewed as an affliction that isolated the deaf from religion and prayer. But after the Civil War period, it came to be seen as a social condition, isolating groups from the nation as a whole.[19] Baynton remarks that "the ardent nationalism that followed the Civil War—the sense that the divisions or particularisms within the nation were dangerous and ought to be suppressed—provided most of the initial impetus for a new concern about what came to be called the 'clannishness' of deaf people."[20] The deaf were treated essentially as immigrant communities and sign was referred to as a foreign language by Alexander Graham Bell and others. Bell in fact warned of the dangers of intermarriage of deaf adults creating a separatist race of deaf people.

The sentiment that deafness was a social problem as well as an individual affliction was reflected in a shift in the methods of teaching the deaf from **manualism** to **oralism.** Manualism, the use of sign language as a means of communication, had arisen from the work of reformers like Thomas Gallaudet, an evangelical minister who founded the American Asylum for the Deaf and Dumb in Hartford, Connecticut, in 1817. Gallaudet and others believed that the deaf could not acquire moral understanding without taking part in group religious exercises, which sign made possible. Gallaudet's manualism reflected a somewhat romantic view of the deaf as in need of salvation, but at the same time it acknowledged that the deaf were a cohesive community. By contrast, oralists tended to see community among the deaf as a danger and viewed sign as encouraging the deaf to communicate primarily among themselves. As Baynton notes, the focus of oralism was not on the individual but, as with the assimilation of Native Americans, on "national unity and social order through homogeneity in language and culture."[21]

Oralism focused instruction on the goal of speaking. It drew support from popular ideas from the emerging theory of evolution: sign language was seen as reflecting lower orders of communication and oral language as one of evolution's higher achievements. In fact, the view that oral language had arisen from gesture was taken as evidence that sign represented an evolutionary step back.[22] With its apparent progressive flavor and with advocates like Alexander Graham Bell, the oralist position took hold in the education system. According to Baynton, by 1899 sign was prohibited in about 40 percent of schools for the deaf and by 1920, in about 80 percent, establishing a pattern that held for the first half of the twentieth century.[23]

During the twentieth century, advocates of oralism also stressed pedagogical and psychological factors. Alexander and Ethel Ewing's 1964 *Teaching Deaf Children to Talk*, for example, argued that "the highest priority for deaf children is learning to talk, this not only in terms of speech as a means of communication, but because the spoken language is a prime factor in social development (from its very beginning with the mother-child relationship) in thought-patterning and the development of intelligence."[24] And as Marc Marschark notes, until the late 1960s many hearing people still saw sign as "a relatively primitive communication system that lacked extensive vocabulary and the means to express subtle or abstract concepts."[25]

Like Native American languages, sign has enjoyed a resurgence in the last forty years. One factor in this was a critical mass of studies in the 1960s and 1970s confirming that oralism had failed. Education researcher Herbert Kohl, for example, in his 1966 study *Language and Education of the Deaf*, described deaf education as dismal. Kohl drew on government statistics showing that of the 1,104 sixteen-year-old students leaving deaf schools in 1961–1962, 501 graduated (with a mean grade level of 7.9) and 603 left without graduating (at a mean grade level of 4.7). He characterized the deaf child as isolated from the start of life, likely to show "outbursts of anger, rage, and frustration" in school, and to be "further frustrated by their failure in language" due to oral instruction.[26]

There may be other factors as well in the renewed viability of sign. Marschark notes that the number of deaf children experienced a tremendous growth in the 1960s due to the rubella epidemic of 1962–1965, which left close to 40,000 infants born deaf. This undoubtedly focused attention on improving deaf education. In addition, linguistic researchers from the 1970s on have emphasized the affinities of sign with spoken language. And members of the deaf community themselves have become very effective at making the case for sign language and deaf culture and at pointing out the failures of oralism.[27] Federal legislation has also benefited sign users: the Rehabilitation Act of 1973 required programs receiving federal aid to provide access to individuals with disabilities, with sign interpretation as a possible way of doing this for the deaf. And the 1990 Americans with Disabilities Act required comparable access in all state and local government schools, regardless of whether or not the schools get federal assistance.[28] For a variety of reasons, sign language has survived the assimilationist efforts of the oralist movement. Sign is accepted by many universities as meeting a second language requirement and major sign research centers exist at the Rochester Institute of Technology, the Salk Institute, and of course Gallaudet University. As with Native American languages, issues of access, education, and culture have reversed an earlier trend toward assimilating language communities.

## Restrictions on Foreign Languages

So far we have seen how late-nineteenth-century thinking reflected the assimilationist ideology of "one nation–one language." The national language impetus of colonial times evolved so that minority languages such as sign language and Native American languages came to be treated as diversity problems—as barriers to efficiency, national unity, and civic participation. The tension between assimilation and pluralism also provides a context from which to consider language issues that arise from immigration and settlement. In the early twentieth century, concerns about assimilation reached a fever pitch after the influx of immigration that lasted from 1880 to 1919. Some reactions, such as literacy tests and proposals for the deportation of immigrants who failed to learn English, were clearly exclusionary.[29] Other initiatives, such as those that focused on Americanization, were motivated by concern for the newcomers' welfare, as well as for promoting American ideas.

During this period public schools increasingly focused on Americanization and civics, and civics instruction included fostering certain attitudes toward language. There was an increased pressure to ensure that English was the language of the classroom by restricting foreign language instruction. The most famous incident of this sort is the case of *Meyer v. Nebraska*.[30] The *Meyer* case arose in the context of anti-German sentiment following World War I. Several states adopted laws that restricted the use of foreign languages in public, that prohibited foreign language parochial schools, and that proscribed the teaching of modern foreign languages to young children. Nervous about its state's German-speaking population, the Nebraska legislature passed two laws restricting foreign languages. In 1919 legislators passed an open meeting law which required that meetings concerning "political or non-political subjects of general interest... be conducted in the English language exclusively." The other law, known as the Siman Law after its legislative sponsor, prohibited the teaching of any foreign language before the completion of the eighth grade and provided for a fine of up to $100 and a jail sentence of up to 30 days.[31]

The Siman Law was challenged when parochial school teacher Robert Meyer was fined for teaching German during the school's lunch hour. Meyer, who had been reading a Bible story in German to a student, claimed that he was merely providing religious instruction outside of normal school hours. While extracurricular religious instruction was allowable under the law, state prosecutors noted that the school had extended its lunch recess specifically to permit the lunchtime study of German. The Nebraska Supreme Court, voting 4–2, ruled that the school curriculum was within the state's jurisdiction and took the view that the teaching of foreign languages was harmful to the country and to young children. The Nebraska Court wrote:

> To allow the children of foreigners, who had emigrated here, to be taught from early childhood the language of the country of their parents was to rear them with that language as their mother tongue. It was to educate them so that they must always think in that language, and, as a consequence, naturally inculcate in them the ideas and sentiments foreign to the best interests of this country.[32]

The case was appealed to the United States Supreme Court, which ruled in 1923 that the restrictions on foreign language instruction were unconstitutional abridgements of liberty. Justice James McReynolds wrote the majority opinion voiding the Siman Law on the basis of the Fourteenth Amendment. McReynolds wrote that "the protection of the Constitution extends to all—to those who speak other languages as well as to those born with English on the tongue."[33] He agreed that all citizens needed to be literate in English, writing that the Court appreciated "the desire of the legislature to foster a homogeneous people with American ideals, prepared readily to understand current discussions of civic matters." But he maintained that English literacy could not be promoted through an unconstitutional ban on foreign language instruction. McReynolds argued in addition that the state could not interfere with parents' natural duty to provide for the education of their children. The decision was not unanimous, however. Justice Oliver Wendell Holmes, Jr., dissented in the concurrent case of *Nebraska District of Evangelical Lutheran Synod v. McKelvie*, drawing on the idea that childhood is a critical time in establishing language skills:

> Youth is the time when familiarity with a language is established and if there are sections in the State where a child would only hear Polish or French or German spoken at home I am not prepared to say that it is unreasonable to provide that in his early years he shall hear and speak only English at school. But if it is reasonable it is not an undue restriction of the liberty of either of teacher or scholar.

*Meyer v. Nebraska* provides a good illustration of the way in which foreign language issues were seen by policy makers in the first quarter of the twentieth century. Foreign languages were seen as promoting a heterogeneity at odds with good citizenship. Even as it accepted the rights of parents to have foreign languages taught to children, the Court asserted the desire of the majority for English literacy and for, in McReynolds's words, "a homogeneous people."

## Bilingual Education

Just as earlier controversies about the teaching of foreign languages prefigure some of today's English-only debates, the issue of bilingualism and bilingual education has an interesting history as well. Though some of us may associate debates over bilingualism with issues arising in the last forty years, it has actually been a policy concern since the founding of the nation. In fact, the eighteenth-century and early nineteenth-century discussions of the role of German in Pennsylvania are similar to discussions heard today regarding Spanish. Benjamin Franklin worried about the third of the state's population who were German-speaking, fearing that Pennsylvania would become a German-dominated colony. Fears of political and cultural domination—and of possible sedition—led to proposals for Americanization of German areas and for English requirements for public discourse. But some early policy makers also advocated bilingual education as a means to assimilate the German population to English political and religious ideas, while at the same time providing them with an education in a language they could understand. Bilingualism came to be an important issue in the Pennsylvania Constitutional Convention of 1837–1838, at which Charles Ingersoll proposed that schools provide education in both English and German. According to linguist Dennis Baron, objections to Ingersoll's proposal included the fear that other languages would need similar provisions. Concerns were also expressed that bilingual teachers were generally less qualified and that bilingual education would corrupt schoolroom English. Some delegates also argued that there was little need for bilingual education because most Germans had been already assimilated to English and that educated Germans themselves favored assimilation. The Pennsylvania Constitutional Convention rejected Ingersoll's bilingualism proposal by fewer than ten votes.[34] As we will see, similar objections recur today in debates about bilingual education and English-only legislation.

The impetus for modern bilingual education efforts came from studies in the 1960s showing that schools were ignoring the language barrier between Spanish-speaking children and English-speaking teachers, and in some cases even punishing children for speaking Spanish. The 1968 Bilingual Education Act, sponsored by Senator Ralph Yarborough of Texas, was originally proposed as part of President Lyndon Johnson's Great Society programs aimed at improving school success and economic opportunity. In his January 1967 speech introducing the act, Senator Yarborough spoke of the disparities in the education of Mexican-American children in the Southwest in language echoing that of the Supreme Court's 1954 *Brown v. Board of Education* decision outlawing school segregation:

> Little children, many of whom enter school knowing no English and speaking only Spanish, are denied the use of their language. Spanish is forbidden to them, and they are required to struggle along as best they can in English, a language understood dimly by most and not at all by many.
>
> Thus the Mexican American child is wrongly led to believe from the first day of school that there is something wrong with him, because of his language. This misbelief soon spreads to the image he has of his culture, of the history of his people, and of his people themselves. This is a subtle and cruel form of discrimination because it imprints upon the consciousness of young children an attitude which they will carry with them all the days of their lives.[35]

The 1968 Bilingual Education Act established federal jurisdiction over bilingual education and provided financial assistance for new programs, though without specifically defining what bilingual education was. Later amendments to the act, in 1974 and 1978, emphasized assimilation but also promoted **language maintenance** as well. Equally important in determining educational policy was Title VI of the 1964 Civil Rights Act, which prohibited discrimination on the basis of race or national origin in federally funded programs.

The view that equal treatment alone did not address the needs of students with limited English proficiency led to lawsuits such as *Lau v. Nichols* in 1974. In the Lau case, parents of about 3,000 students in San Francisco filed a class-action suit that argued that the city of San Francisco had not provided sufficient supplementary instruction in English to students whose primary language was Chinese. The U.S. Supreme Court ultimately reversed a Federal District Court ruling that having access to the same curriculum entailed lack of discrimination.[36] However, the Supreme Court's opinion did not provide a specific remedy; it only required that the Board of Education solve the problem. The Lau decision was extended to all public schools as part of the 1974 Equal Educational Opportunity Act but again without identifying solutions. In 1975, the Department of Health, Education, and Welfare began outlining so-called Lau remedies, which included a requirement that students' native languages be used in instruction and that native cultures be taken into account as well. Compliance to the Lau ruling was monitored by the U.S. Office of Civil Rights. But as many states adopted bilingual education measures, school systems often were compelled to develop bilingual programs whether or not they had any expertise in doing so. As linguist Lily Wong Fillmore has noted, many programs that arose this way were perfunctory and understaffed, leading to poor results.[37]

As English language education became more central to the work of schools, various types of programs developed. English as a second language instruction is typically geared to classes that are made up of students from many different languages and often focuses specifically on English skills. By contrast, **transitional bilingual education** programs involve classes of students who share the same second language. In such cases, instruction in school subjects takes place in the native language but time is also spent on English. **English immersion** approaches are ones in which instruction is entirely in English (often simplified) and which focus both on English skills and on other academic subjects. Still another approach is **dual-immersion** (or two-way bilingual education), where instruction is given in two languages. Here classes include native speakers of two languages, for example, English and Spanish, with the goal being dual proficiency.

Transitional bilingual education came under increasing attack in the 1980s as Hispanic and Asian immigration increased and as social programs lost federal funding. Such critics as Education Secretary William Bennett argued that there was no evidence that bilingual education programs helped students learn English. In 1980, an English-only Lau remedy had been approved in Virginia because the number of language groups made bilingual education less feasible than intensive English instruction. Soon Congressional amendments began to focus on the possibility of adding English-only immersion methods to Lau remedies, and a 1988 reauthorization designated up to 25 percent of the federal funding for immersion methods. Amendments to the Bilingual Education Act in 1994 increased emphasis on bilingual education, bilingual proficiency, and language maintenance, but funding was then cut by over 30 percent in 1996.

The broad policy goal of bilingual education programs remains educational opportunity and assimilation of minorities to English. Opponents of bilingual education often see it as unnecessarily delaying the learning of English and as unrealistically assuming that minority children can be comfortable in both cultures. Arguments are often focused on the effectiveness of bilingual programs and the claim that they are costly diversions from English instruction that reduce incentives to learn English. Opponents also argue that bilingual education serves more as a means of preserving ethnic cultures than of assimilating speakers to English and American culture. Bilingual education has been characterized by some as a cultural program for minorities rather than an educational program aimed at fluency in English. In a 1985 opinion piece in the *New York Times*, writer Richard Rodriguez argued that bilingual education efforts, despite the outward focus on learning English, reflect ethnic identity movements that romanticize dual culture. In Rodriguez's view, the cost of bilingual efforts is the embarrassment and silence of working-class immigrant children who do not succeed in mastering English.[38]

In June of 1998, 61 percent of California voters approved Proposition 227 (*English Language in the Public Schools*), which required that students from non-English backgrounds be taught in intensive immersion classes rather than bilingual programs. The initiative was part of a broader "English for the Children" campaign initiated by California activist Ron Unz. As a result, California law now requires that schools place children with limited English skills in an English immersion program for at least a year. As the name of Unz's campaign suggests, the rationale is that early literacy in English is fostered by rapid exposure to native speakers of English in mainstream classrooms. In 2002 Massachusetts voters followed, overwhelmingly rejecting bilingual education in favor of English immersion classes. Massachusetts had been the first state to enact bilingual education in 1971, but 70 percent of voters approved ballot Question 2, funded by Unz.[39] Like the California measure, Question 2 called for placing most non-English-speaking students in English immersion classes for a year. Under the Massachusetts bilingual education plan that had existed, about 30,000 non-English-speaking students took subjects like math or science in their native languages, easing into English over time. In California, bilingual programs served about 30 percent of that state's 1.3 million limited-English-proficiency students. Critics of these measures have expressed concern about inflexible, state-mandated curricula and about the potential difficulty of obtaining waivers for parents who choose not to have their children participate in immersion. Educators have concerns as well. One is the effect that mainstreaming limited English speakers after just one year of English instruction might have on the broader learning environment. Another is the consequence of grouping students by English proficiency rather than age.

Proponents of transitional bilingual education often view sink-or-swim approaches as ineffective and unfair, arguing that non-English-speaking children fall behind in early learning and cognitive development when they are unable to comprehend classroom language. Supporters of bilingual education may also argue that rejection of the home language in English-only immersion affects children's self-perception, as Senator Ralph Yarborough did in introducing the act. In addition, proponents often stress bilingual education as a positive factor in developing a workforce competent in languages other than English, and see support for bilingualism in childhood as a way to foster adult second-language proficiency.

Does bilingual education work? Is it better or worse than immersion programs? A review commissioned by the

National Research Council and the Institute of Medicine assessed the success of various types of bilingual and second-language learning efforts. Chaired by Stanford University psychologist Kenji Hakuta and directed by Diane August of the National Research Council, the study was unable to answer the question of what type of program was best. Hakuta and August found beneficial effects to both bilingual programs and structured immersion programs, and noted that successful bilingual and immersion programs had elements in common. They concluded that questions of effectiveness needed to be community based. Equally significant, the study condemned the "extreme politicization" of the research process by advocates, noting that "most consumers of the research are not researchers who want to know the truth, but advocates who are convinced of the absolute correctness of their positions."[40]

## English-Only

In the background of the debate over bilingual education and immersion is the recent campaign to make English the official language of many states. The origins of this English-only effort began with California Senator S. I. Hayakawa's unsuccessful English Language Amendment to the U.S. Constitution. In the early 1980s, Hayakawa and others believed such an amendment was necessary to prevent language differences from becoming divisive. Following the defeat of that amendment, Hayakawa and John Tanton of the Federation for American Immigration Reform founded the group U.S. English in 1983.[41] This group saw a number of political successes including initiatives that made English the official language of various states (in Virginia, Indiana, Kentucky, Missouri, Alaska, Tennessee, California, Georgia, Arkansas, Mississippi, North Dakota, North Carolina, South Carolina, Arizona, Colorado, Florida, Alabama, New Hampshire, Montana, Utah, South Dakota, Iowa, and Wyoming). Some of these initiatives were characterized by proponents as merely symbolic. Others, however, were intended to curtail demands for bilingual services. As linguist Geoffrey Nunberg reports, English-only advocates have petitioned for limits on the number of licenses for foreign-language radio stations and have attempted to halt the publication of such resources as the *Hispanic Yellow Pages*.[42]

While the U.S. English group has been successful in promoting English-only legislation at the state level, restrictive legislation has been challenged in courts. Arizona's 1988 English-only amendment, for example, was struck down in 1990 because it required the use of English by state employees on the job. Judge Paul Rosenblatt ruled that by prohibiting state legislators from speaking to their constituents in languages other than English, the state amendment abridged First Amendment rights. Judge Rosenblatt noted that while the government may regulate the speech of public employees in the interests of efficiency, "a state may not apply stricter standards to its legislators than it may to private citizens, ... nor may a state require that its officers and employees relinquish rights guaranteed them by the First Amendment as a condition of public employment."[43] Rosenblatt stopped short, however, of ruling that the plaintiff had a First Amendment right to speak Spanish at work.

The arguments of English-only proponents draw on the idea of English as having an economic and civic value, but also on fears about linguistic diversity.[44] English-only rhetoric casts English as the bond that unites us as a nation and sees that unity as threatened by bilingual services, foreign-language mass media, and the preservation of heritage languages. Such services and efforts are seen as a disincentive to the transition to English and as serving the interests of separatist ethnic leaders. For example, a U.S. English fund-raising brochure from the mid-1980s describes English as being "under attack" and raises fears of "institutionalized language segregation and a gradual loss of national unity."[45] The brochure also refers disapprovingly to "new civil rights assertions" such as bilingual ballots and voting instructions, to "record immigration ... reinforcing language segregation and retarding language assimilation," and to the availability of foreign-language electronic media as providing "a new disincentive to the learning of English." In addition to the English-only constitutional amendment, the brochure called for elimination of bilingual ballots, curtailment of bilingual education, enforcement of English language requirements for naturalization, and the expansion of opportunities for learning English.[46]

English-only rhetoric also draws on the fears of the kind of violence and fragmentation that have affected Canada. In the 1960s the Canadian province of Quebec became the focus of militant efforts to establish a separate French-speaking nation. Beginning in 1969, a series of riots and terrorist acts, including the kidnapping and murder of Quebec's minister of labor and immigration, led the Canadian government to temporarily suspend civil liberties in 1970. After a political accommodation was reached, French became the official language of Quebec in 1974. In 1976 Quebec separatists won the provincial election and soon passed a charter that restricted education in English-language schools, changed English place-names, and established French as the language of government and public institutions. While Quebec voters rejected referenda to make the province an independent country in 1980 and again in 1995, the earlier pattern of violence, legislation, and separatism has made many Americans nervous about heritage language retention, especially in the Southwest where there are large numbers of Hispanic speakers.

English-only rhetoric incorrectly assumes that today's immigrants refuse to learn English and that official status is an effective means of fostering identification with the majority culture. Sociologist Carol Schmid has summarized a number of surveys of immigrant attitudes which suggest that there is little danger of English losing its desirability for nonnative speakers, and which dispel the fallacy that Spanish speakers don't want to learn English.[47] She notes that surveys of Hispanics find that they overwhelmingly support the idea that speaking and understanding English is necessary for citizenship and economic success, a fact that is also supported by the robustness of advertisements for English training on Spanish-language television. And there is also evidence that speakers of other languages shift to English over time. Schmid cites the well-known study by Calvin Veltman which found that about three-quarters of Spanish-speaking immigrants were speaking English regularly after about fifteen years of residence.[48] She also emphasizes that language loyalty rates of Spanish speakers in the Southwest actually declined between 1970 and 1990. The idea that English is in danger from Spanish is not supported by such data.

The English-only movement of the 1980s and 1990s has been counterbalanced to some extent by the work of groups such as the English Plus Clearinghouse and the English Plus Coalition, both of which were established in 1986. These groups see the learning of languages as a resource and argue that English-only restrictions are counterproductive both economically and politically. They have also argued that English-only laws are unnecessary as a means of fostering assimilation. As linguist Robert King has emphasized, linguistic diversity does not necessarily entail political violence.[49] The English-only rhetoric ignores the many linguistically heterogeneous nations that lack the separatist violence that has existed in Belgium, Sri Lanka, and Canada. Switzerland, for example, has a long tradition of language rights, decentralization, and power sharing among groups, and the Swiss very successfully accommodate multilingualism. Schmid sees the Swiss adaptation to multilingualism as an instructive model for both the United States and Canada.[50] Switzerland arose from a military confederacy of German states dating from 1291, which gradually added French, Italian, and Romansch allies. Though German remained the alliance's official language until 1798, there was little linguistic conflict among the various cantons, and a tradition of local autonomy and diversity was an important factor in attracting new groups to the confederation. An 1848 constitution established the equality of French, German, and Italian in the Swiss confederation by making them all national languages. And while today's French-speaking minority in Switzerland has a strong linguistic identity, the intensity of that identity is attenuated by Swiss national pride and the allegiance of French and German speakers to a common civic culture. There are also important differences between the language situations in the United States and in Canada which suggest that the Canadian experience is not likely to be repeated in the United States. Schmid emphasizes that the dominance of English has historically been much stronger in the United States than in Canada, and she notes the strong interest that nonnative speakers in the United States have had in learning English. She attributes the interest in separatism in Canada to French-Canadians' worries over assimilation, to optimism about the sustainability of a separate existence, and to the failure of Canadian political institutions to accommodate the collective identity of a French-speaking region. These different conditions suggest that the United States is in no danger of being overcome by linguistic separatism.

## One Flag, One Language

The ideology of language assimilation arises from several factors. It is motivated by the belief that a common language is necessary for national unity and for economic productivity. It is also motivated by the assumption that a common language resolves social differences and builds understanding among those of different backgrounds. And it is motivated by the fear that language diversity will lead to political disunity and potential violence. In the United States there have also been sustained periods in which foreign and minority languages have been stigmatized, suppressed, and seen as problems to be overcome rather than resources to be fostered. As a result, foreign languages and minority languages have been the focus of social engineering that often attempts to legislate a process of assimilation already underway and to dictate its nature as monolingual rather than bilingual. The acceptance of sign language and the preservation and revitalization of Native American language are areas where progress has been seen. But the perception of foreign languages seems to have changed little since Theodore Roosevelt's 1917 statement extolling language as the symbol of national unity.

### Notes

1. Theodore Roosevelt's "Children of the Crucible" speech is reprinted in *Language Loyalties: A Source Book on the Official English Controversy*, ed. James Crawford (Chicago: University of Chicago Press, 1992), 84–85.

2. Daniel J. Boorstin's *The Americans: The Colonial Experience* (New York: Vintage, 1958), chs. 41 and 42, is the source for background on colonial attitudes and for the citation to Franklin's 1760 letter to Hume (278); for Boorstin's views on descriptive linguistics, see *The Americans: The Democratic Experience* (New York: Vintage, 1973), pp. 452–62.

3. The quote from John Pickering's "Essay on the Present State of the English Language in the United States" is excerpted in C. Merton Babcock's *The Ordeal of American English* (Boston: Houghton Mifflin, 1961), 30.

4. David Simpson's *The Politics of American English, 1776–1850* (New York: Oxford University Press, 1988), p. 32, is the source for the citation to Jefferson's 1813 letter. Writers such as John Witherspoon also advocated an American style. Witherspoon saw the issue as a contest between the more cultured nature of British speech and the potential for uniformity that an American language might foster, particularly in light of the mobility of Americans. He saw the common speech in America as less parochial than the common speech of England, but nevertheless cautioned against too common a style, arguing for a language that expressed neither "bombast and empty swelling" nor "low sentiments and vulgar terms." See the excerpts of *The Druid*, no. 5, collected in Babcock's *The Ordeal of American English*, 74.

5. See Adrienne Koch, *The Philosophy of Thomas Jefferson* (Gloucester, MA: Peter Smith, 1957), 109, for the citation to Jefferson's 1820 letter to Adams. As Julie Tetel Andresen notes in her *Linguistics in America, 1769–1924: A Critical History* (London: Routledge, 1990), pp. 57–62, Jefferson also advocated spelling reform and the resurrection of provincial archaisms.

6. Webster is most famous for his spelling reforms, and as a publisher he was sometimes accused of self-interest for these since he would profit from Americanized editions of books. Webster saw spelling reform as a means to reduce the gap between speaking and writing and to foster communication and opportunities for unified political action. Webster's own reforms were largely unsuccessful in his lifetime, and his greatest influence may have been the association of correct language with American values, which ensured the success of his competitors Murray, Brown, and Kirkham.

7. Webster, quoted in Simpson, 65.

8. Simpson, *The Politics of American English, 1776–1850*, 52–72, is the source for the summary of Noah Webster's views. Both Webster and Jefferson were influenced by the revival of interest in Anglo-Saxon as a source of English political and linguistic traditions. Webster, in particular, was influenced by the Saxonist speculations of John Horne Tooke. See Simpson, 81–90.

9. Kenneth Cmiel, *Democratic Eloquence* (New York: William Morrow, 1990), 45.

10. Cmiel, 47.

11. As Shirley Brice Heath notes, antimonarchists in the United States were skeptical of a centralized authority setting cultural norms, so proponents focused the debate on the role of language in education and law. See Shirley Brice Heath, "A National Language Academy? Debate in the New Nation," *Linguistics* 10.189 (1977), 9–43.

12. Simpson (30) is the source for this quote from John Adams.

13. Heath (21) is the source for this quote from Adams and for information generally on the language academy issue.

14. The quote from John Jay is cited in Carol Schmid's *The Politics of Language: Conflict, Identity, and Cultural Pluralism in Comparative Perspective* (New York: Oxford University Press, 2001), 18.

15. The sketch of Native American language policy draws on John Reyhner's "Policies Toward American Indian Languages: A Historical Sketch," in *Language Loyalties: A Source Book on the Official English Controversy*, ed. James Crawford (Chicago: University of Chicago Press, 1992), 41–47, and William Leap's "American Indian Languages," in *Language in the USA*, ed. Charles Ferguson and Shirley Brice Heath (Cambridge: Cambridge University Press, 1981), 116–44.

16. The report of the 1868 commission on Indian conditions is cited by Atkins (48).

17. J. D. C. Atkins, Annual Report [of the Federal Commissioner of Indian Affairs] (excerpted as "Barbarous Dialects Should Be Blotted Out" in Crawford, *Language Loyalties*, 50).

18. The Native American Languages Act is Public Law 101–477 (Oct. 30, 1990). For a report on the Native American educational experience, see *Indian Nations at Risk: An Educational Strategy for Action* (Washington, DC: U.S. Department of Education, 1991, ERIC Document Reproduction Service No. ED339587).

19. See Douglas Baynton, *Forbidden Signs: American Culture and the Campaign Against Sign Language* (Chicago: University of Chicago Press, 1996), pp. 15–26. Baynton's book was a key source for many of the facts in this section: Alexander Graham Bell's views (30–31), Thomas Gallaudet's beliefs (17–20, 113–14), John Tyler's comments (36–38), the influence of evolution (38–44), and teacher statistics (25).

20. Baynton, 29.

21. Baynton, 16. The impetus for assimilation in the post–Civil War period reform mentality was also connected to "widespread fears of unchecked immigration and expanding, multiethnic cities."

22. Baynton cites an 1899 keynote address by John Tyler to the American Association to Promote the Teaching of Speech to the Deaf, which characterized sign language as brutish and advocated education based on the characteristics that evolution had promoted, namely speech. Baynton notes also that religious advocates of sign interpreted the origin of language differently, some seeing sign as closer to creation and thus representing a morally superior state.

23. In his 1943 book *Deafness and the Deaf in the United States* (New York: Macmillan, 524), Harry Best notes that opponents of sign continued to stress the social dangers of separatism.

24. Alexander Ewing and Ethel Ewing, *Teaching Deaf Children to Talk* (Manchester: Manchester University Press, 1964), viii.

25. Marc Marschark, *Raising and Educating a Deaf Child* (New York: Oxford University Press, 1997), 54.

26. Herbert Kohl's observations are from his *Language and Education of the Deaf* (New York: Center for Urban Education, 1966), 4–5; for citations to other summaries of the research on sign language and oralism, see Baynton 166, n.11.

27. Baynton (155) suggests that another factor in changing attitudes toward sign was a cultural shift in the 1960s in the way people viewed physicality. He notes that this included "such things as new and more sensuous forms of dance, a greater openness concerning sexuality, and an expanded tolerance for nudity and the celebration of the body, . . . [a] renewed fascination with "body language" generally, . . . more open expressions of passion and personal feelings, . . . [and] the popularity of new psychotherapies."

28. Earlier, the Bilingual Education Act of 1988 had included sign language for the first time.

29. The 1917 Immigration Act, passed over Woodrow Wilson's veto, excluded immigrants over the age of sixteen who were physically capable of reading but could not. Earlier literacy restrictions had been vetoed by Grover Cleveland and William Howard Taft.

30. Jack Rodgers's review of the "The Foreign Language Issue in Nebraska" (*Nebraska History*, 39.1 [1958], 1–22) was a source for the facts of *Meyer v. Nebraska*.

31. The relevant statues can be found in *Nebraska Laws* 1919, chapter 234 (Nebraska's open meeting law) and chapter 249 (the Siman Law).

32. The 1922 Nebraska Supreme Court ruling can be found at 187 *Northwestern Reporter* 100, 1922.

33. The Supreme Court's *Meyer v. Nebraska* ruling may be found at 262 U.S. 390 (1923) and its *Nebraska District of Evangelical Lutheran Synod v. McKelvie* ruling may be found at 262 U.S. 404 (1923).

34. Dennis Baron's *The English-Only Question: An Official Language for Americans* (64–83) was a valuable source for background on

the colonial German questions and on the origins of bilingual education policy, including the objections to Ingersoll's proposal (74–77) and Franklin's comments (66).

35. The quote from Ralph Yarborough's 1967 speech is from Crawford, *Language Loyalties*, 324.

36. The Supreme Court's *Lau v. Nichols* decision may be found at 414 U.S. 56 (1974).

37. Lily Wong Fillmore, "Against Our Best Interest: The Attempt to Sabotage Bilingual Education," in Crawford, *Language Loyalties*, 369.

38. Richard Rodriguez, "Bilingualism Con: Outdated and Unrealistic," *New York Times*, Nov. 10, 1985, sec. 12, 83. See also his *The Hunger of Memory* (Boston: David R. Godine, 1981).

39. Similar efforts passed in Arizona in 2000 and failed in Colorado in 2002.

40. Diane August and Kenji Hakuta, *Educating Language-Minority Children* (Washington, DC: National Academic Press, 1998), 61. The National Academy of Sciences is a private, nonprofit group operating under a congressional charter.

41. Tanton was also associated with the Federation for American Immigration Reform. He resigned from U.S. English in 1988 after the release of a controversial anti-immigration memo. See James Crawford's "What's Behind the Official English Movement," in *Language Loyalties*, 171–77.

42. Geoffrey Nunberg, "Linguistics and the Official Language Movement," *Language* 65.3 (1989), 580–81, was the source of the observations on the range of official English laws and some of their intended consequences. For discussion of English-only workplace rules and legal challenges to these, see Carol Schmid, *The Politics of Language* (New York: Oxford University Press, 2001), 65–68.

43. Judge Paul Rosenblatt's opinion appears as *Yniguez v. Mofford*, 730 F. Supp. 309 (D. Ariz. 1990). Rosenblatt rejected Arizona's position that the amendment was merely intended to be used by the state in its official capacity and that it was not intended as a blanket prohibition on state officials and employees.

44. Geoffrey Nunberg, for example, notes that English-only assumes that "acquisition of English and assimilation to the majority culture are incompatible with retention of the native language and cultural values; that people will not learn a second language as long as the native language is kept available as a 'crutch' and so on" ("Linguistics and the Official Language Movement," 583–84).

45. Reprinted as "In Defense of Our Common Language..." in Crawford, *Language Loyalties*, 143–48.

46. Journalist James Crawford also points out that English-only proponents assume that English is best learned by immersion and assume that ethnic leaders who argue for bilingual programs do so out of self-interest (for example, to provide jobs for bilingual educators). See his "What's Behind the Official English Movement," in *Language Loyalties*, 171–77.

47. Schmid, *Politics of Language*, 88–89. Surveys conducted in 1984, 1988, and 1990 found 61 percent, 66 percent, and 90 percent of Hispanics agreeing that it was important for citizens to speak and understand English. A 1985 Miami survey found 98 percent of Hispanic parents agreeing that English was essential for children's success.

48. Schmid, *Politics of Language*, 47–48. She also reports on surveys about the relation between education and assimilation. See also Calvin Veltman's *The Future of the Spanish Language in the United States* (Washington, DC: Spanish Policy Development Project, 1988). For a study of African-American attitudes toward English-only, see Geneva Smitherman, *Talkin That Talk* (London: Routledge, 2000), 297–302. Smitherman reports on a survey of 216 African-Americans in five cities in which over half (64.6 percent) said that they would not support English-only laws.

49. Robert King, "Should English Be the Law?" *Atlantic Monthly*, April 1997, 55–64.

50. Schmid, *Politics of Language*, 195–97.

## Critical Thinking and Application

- Is maintenance of a language—as for Native Americans—necessary for cultural survival?
- Contrast the outcomes, motives, and contexts of the French Canadian and English-only movements.
- What is the difference between bilingual education and English-immersion education? What are the arguments in favor of each? How could their effectiveness be measured? Why do you think advocates and opponents are so passionate?
- Research English-only, English-plus, bilingual education, and the Unz amendment. What kinds of arguments is each group using (moral, psychological, pedagogical, etc.)? Are they addressing the same issues? How could someone decide between their positions? What are the participants' assumptions about the relationship between linguistic diversity and national unity? Do they use evidence from other societies to support their position? How do they evaluate individual and collective needs and rights?

## Vocabulary

bilingual education
descriptive grammar
dual immersion
English immersion
language maintenance
manualism
oralism
prescriptive grammar
standard language
standardization, standardize
transitional bilingual education

## Suggested Further Reading

Center for Applied Linguistics. http://www.cal.org/

Crawford, James, ed. 1992. *Language Loyalties: A Source Book on the Official English Controversy*. Chicago: University of Chicago Press.

Edwards, John R. 1994. *Multilingualism*. London and New York: Routledge.

Ethnologue: Languages of the World. http://www.ethnologue.com/web.asp

Schmid, Carol. 2001. *The Politics of Language*. New York: Oxford University Press.

# CHAPTER 21

# Language Education Policy—Arabic Speaking Countries

*Y. Suleiman*
(1999)

*Arabic is the dominant language in Arab League countries, but it always coexists with local vernacular forms of Arabic and often shares a linguistic ecosystem with other entirely unrelated languages. As Charles Ferguson pointed out in his 1959 article, "Diglossia," Classical Arabic has a level of prestige as the "H" (high) language that makes it more visible and evident than other more widely used "L" (low) languages, to the point that people sometimes deny using L because they believe they are supposed to be using H. Multilingualism always poses a problem for school policy, as multiple, sometimes conflicting goals must be accommodated: the goal of national unity and respect for local practices, the goal of encouraging use of a language of wider communication, and the maintenance of a language with local identity.*

*In many countries, language is explicitly mentioned in the constitution, which spells out the roles played by each language. Sometimes the language has symbolic power. Sometimes a former colonial language is retained as an* official *language, even if it is not regarded as a* national *language. In all cases, considerations of utility and modernity need to be weighed against the desire for national, religious, and traditional ideals. Education, then, is a key component in all countries that take up language questions.*

### Reading Questions

- What is the difference between a *national* and an *official* language? Why does Suleiman claim that "the national language is always an official language, but not vice versa"?
- How do the linguistic situations differ, broadly speaking, among the countries of North Africa and those of the Middle East? How have they been influenced by their colonial histories?
- What are the two meanings of *ta'rīb*? What is the difference between *Arabicization* and *Arabization*? What are the implications of this difference?
- How are policies with regard to teaching foreign languages determined? What factors (prestige, usefulness, history, etc.) seem most influential?

Language education policies in the Arabic speaking countries are embedded in their overall educational policies. These policies have as their aim aiding the development of students intellectually, socially, emotionally, and physically. They also strive to instill in the learners the values of their society and culture to enable them to grow up into good citizens who can live in harmony in their environment.

Y. Suleiman, Language Education Policy—Arabic Speaking Countries. In *Concise Encyclopedia of Educational Linguistics*, edited by Bernard Spolsky. Amsterdam: Elsevier, 1999, pp. 106–116.

## Preliminaries

The position of Arabic as the dominant language in the Arabic speaking world is enshrined in the existing constitutions of the countries which make up the Arab League (Jabbūr 1976). The existence of coterritorial languages with sizeable numbers of speakers—particularly Berber in Algeria and Morocco, Kurdish in Iraq, and the plethora of African languages in Southern Sudan—does not challenge the overall validity of this characterization (Abu Bakr 1995; Abuhamdia 1995; Blau and Suleiman 1996; Bell 1989; Faiq 1999; Miller and Abu-Manga 1992; Qindīl 1989; Rouchdy 1991; Tilmatine and Suleiman 1996;

Zaborski 1997). Attention in this [chapter] will therefore be directed mainly towards describing **language policy** as it pertains to Arabic in its written form, utilizing for this purpose the two organizing categories of **status planning** and **corpus planning**. Foreign language policy will be dealt with under **acquisition planning** (Cooper 1989).

In dealing with status planning, this article will be restricted to language policy in Arabic speaking countries in the second half of the twentieth century. This restriction coincides with events in modern Arab history which have had an impact on the functional allocation of languages, including (a) the formation of the Arab League (1945); (b) the independence from French colonial rule of the **francophone** countries of North Africa (Morocco 1956; Tunisia 1956; and Algeria 1962); (c) the independence of Sudan from Britain in 1956; and (d) the establishment of Israel in 1948, which led to a radical change in the status of Arabic in that part of mandatory Palestine on which the state was established. The discussion of corpus planning will have a wider time frame, covering much of the twentieth century. The position of Arabic outside the Arabic speaking world will not be considered here (Akinnaso and Ogunbiyi 1990; Ghalādant 1982; Kenny 1992; Sātī 1995; Sawaie 1992; Shohamy 1994; Spolsky and Shohamy 1997; Versteegh 1997; Walbridge 1992). Adult literacy policies will also be excluded, albeit Arabic is invariably the target language in status planning terms in this enterprise (Al-Sāfī 1989).

Although a distinction is drawn in the literature between **language planning** and language policy, the two terms will be used interchangeably here to cover the 'deliberate efforts' (Cooper 1989: 45) of governmental organizations and 'nongovernmental innovators' (ibid: 148)—sometimes called 'language strategists'—to bring about changes in language use. The intention here being to influence the acquisition of foreign languages in a speech community (acquisition planning), the orthographic representation and grammatical structure of the **national language** (corpus planning), and the functional allocation of languages to communicative domains (status planning). The following discussion of these issues in the Arabic speaking countries will be of a general nature owing to (a) the differences which exist between these countries in each of the areas of language education policy mentioned above; (b) the absence of coherent and fully worked out official language policies in these countries; (c) the difficulty of obtaining up-to-date information which can enable the researcher to draw firm conclusions from these policies, especially of the governmental type; and (d) the difficulty of separating the three types of planning from each other, since status planning decisions may have a direct impact on acquisition planning ones or corpus planning initiatives may be motivated by considerations stemming from status planning orientations.

## Status Planning: General Considerations

Discussions of status planning in the Arabic speaking countries are informed by a few considerations. First, planning of this type is motivated by extralinguistic or ideological concerns pertaining to national liberation and nation-building, the formation of new elites or the preservation of old ones, social and economic modernization and development, the maintenance of extraterritorial ties of religious solidarity, and the incorporation of non-Arab ethnic groups into the nascent nation-state project. Broadly speaking, status planning in the Arabic speaking countries is as much about inclusion as it is about exclusion in sociopolitical terms. Rarely, if ever, does status planning aim at solving purely linguistic problems. Second, discussions of status planning in the Arabic context are invariably embedded in the much wider debate about the roles of authenticity/tradition (*al-aṣāla*) and modernity (*al-mu'āṣara/al-ḥadātha*) in modern Arabic sociopolitical thought and practice (Al-Ḫamzāwī 1986). The former, authenticity, revolves around the role of the past and its set of symbolic values in setting a point of reference for national self-definition. Modernity, on the other hand, involves the injection of an external element of a Western origin into the project of generating or fine-tuning a new definition of the national self. Third, the colonial legacy and its projections of postindependence dependence sometimes play a decisive role in setting the parameters within which decisions about status planning are made. Fourth, the **diglossic** nature of the Arabic language situation (Ferguson 1959) invariably favors the written standard over the spoken **colloquial** or any approximation between the two, because of the functional role and symbolic significance of the former as the language of religion, high culture, and pannational unity conceptualizations. It is this attitude towards the written standard language, rather than linguistic behavior per se, that justifies the description of the speakers of the various Arabic colloquials as members of the same **speech community** and which, in turn, justifies treating the Arabic speaking countries as one area for language education policy purposes.

As a starting point in pursuing the discussion of status planning in the Arabic speaking countries, we must distinguish between four concepts: national language (*lugha waṭaniyya* or *qawmiyya*), **official language** (*lugha rasmiyya*), **semiofficial language,** which may or may not be an indigenous language, and **working language**. This classification overlaps with Cooper's classification of language functions into statutory, working, and symbolic (1989: 100), but differs from it in four ways. First, both the national and official language categories coincide with the statutory function in Cooper's classification. Although the distinction between national and official language may not be relevant in all cases of status planning in the Arabic context, the fact that this distinction is explicitly articulated in some cases underlies the decision to separate the two functions methodologically. Second, a semiofficial language in this framework is a working language in Cooper's classification, the only difference being that in the present framework the language concerned enjoys some constitutional backing. Third, a working language in the scheme proposed above is one which is widely used in the community, although it does not enjoy any constitutional backing. Fourth, Cooper's symbolic function is not methodologically recognized in the present framework because it may accrue to any of the above language types, albeit in differing ways and with different sociolinguistic connotations, rather than just to the national language (statutory language in Cooper's tripartite classification).

To demonstrate the role of the above language categories in setting out the parameters for status planning in the Arabic speaking countries this [chapter] will consider those articles which impinge on this issue in the constitutions of Arab states (Jabbūr 1976: 31–36). Arabic is declared as an official language in the constitutions of all member states of the Arab League, including, by implication, Saudi Arabia in which the Qur'an functions as the ultimate source of legality in organizing the statutes of the state. Although the Palestinian National Charter is silent on the issue of the national and official language for any future Palestinian state, Arabic already functions in this capacity in the West Bank (including Arab East Jerusalem) and Gaza. The status of being official is attributed to other languages in some constitutions. In Iraq, Kurdish is given this status in the Kurdish speaking areas only. In Mauritania, French is established as an official language with Arabic, and is, in fact, listed before Arabic when referred to in this capacity only. The constitution of Mauritania additionally describes Arabic as the national language, to distinguish it from the other official language, French. The postindependence Algerian constitution described Arabic as the national language, but allowed the use of French temporarily as a semiofficial language. The 1943 Lebanese constitution establishes Arabic as the national and official language. The same constitution describes French as an official language, but stipulates that a special law will be promulgated to define the domains in which it may be used. When the constitution was later amended, French ceased to be an official language of the state, and turned into a named semiofficial language whose use is to be regulated by a special law. In Sudan, Arabic is established as the sole official language, but the constitution leaves the possibility open for the use of other semiofficial languages—presumably southern Sudanese languages and/or English—provided that special permission is obtained for this purpose from the parliament. In Somalia, Arabic is a second official language after the Somali language. As a matter of fact the role played by Arabic in Somalia is largely symbolic, reflecting its membership in the Arab League, in which the official status of Arabic functions as the lowest common denominator between the member states. Although French is not specified in the constitutions of Tunisia and Morocco as an official or semiofficial language, nevertheless it is widely used in education, the media, the private and public sectors, and many walks of life to warrant being referred to as a working language in Cooper's sense (Gallagher 1968). In language planning terms, French has the status of official, semiofficial, and working language in the Arabic speaking countries.

The following observations may be launched, based on the information in the preceding paragraph. First, the national language is always an official language, but not vice versa. Second, the distinction between national and official language is not sanctioned when Arabic serves exclusively in both capacities. Third, the concept of national language is posited to make possible the constitutional incorporation of another language as an official language alongside the national language. Fourth, the concept of national language is not used to refer to the dominant official language when the other official language is an indigenous language, as in the case of Kurdish in Iraq. Fifth, a semiofficial language is a constitutionally named language, or one whose establishment as such is constitutionally permissible, whether indigenous (as in Sudan) or not (as in Algeria and Lebanon). Although these observations may need some fine-tuning, because of the deliberate ambiguities which the articles of the various constitutions embody, they are sound in their broad outline.

## Arabicization or Arabization?

Broadly speaking, the promotion of Arabic as the primary language of communication in all spheres of life in the Arabic speaking countries is referred to as *taʿrīb* in Arabic. This term is often rendered as Arabicization and Arabization in English, which, more often than not, are used interchangeably with little regard for the subtle difference in meaning between them in language education policy or the ethnolinguistic sphere. In Arabic the term *taʿrīb* refers to two phenomena. One is more applicable to the Arabic speaking countries in Asia, Egypt, and Libya; the other is more, if not exclusively, applicable to the francophone countries of North Africa. The Sudan represents a special case which, while combining features of both situations, has its own specific character as will be explained below.

In its first sense, *taʿrīb* refers to two major phenomena: the incorporation of foreign terms or, preferably, their newly coined native equivalents, into the Arabic lexicon, which is a corpus planning issue (Khalīfa 1987); and the use of Arabic in the delivery of higher education in the sciences, especially medical science (Dūs 1997; Nuʿayamī 1997; Al-Zayn 1997). In this sense, *taʿrīb* has a linguistic and educational dimension which, directly or indirectly, is informed by the need to achieve non-linguistic ends. This sense of *taʿrīb* is referred to as *Arabicization* to highlight the importance of promoting the language as the immediate target of status planning (Khasāra 1994). Arabicization is underpinned by the work of the **language academies** (Abuhamdia 1984; Altoma 1974; Holes 1995; Al-Jamīʿī 1983) in Damascus (1919), Cairo (1932), Baghdad (1947), and Amman (1976), as well as the Arab League sponsored Bureau of Arabicization in Rabat (1961) which, through its journal *Al-Lisān al-ʿArabī*, has done quite a lot to coin new terms in the sciences and technology using English and French as source languages.

In its second sense *taʿrīb* is more inclusive. Using the definition of this phenomenon which the Moroccan government proposed at the first education conference held in Rabat in 1961 (Aḥmad 1986: 43; Wannās 1995: 164–65), it is possible to isolate the following features of *ta'rīb*: (a) using Arabic in place of foreign languages in education; (b) expanding the **lexical** resources of the Arabic language—which is a corpus-planning issue; (c) using Arabic exclusively in government administration; (d) promoting Arabic as the language of everyday communication and opposing all those who refuse to use it in this capacity; (e) the net result of these steps is to make Arabic suitable for articulating the emotional and intellectual life of its speakers in an age of technological advancement (*'aṣr al-dharra wa-l-ṣawārīkh*: the age of the atom and the rocket). This sense of *ta'rīb* is referred to as *Arabization* to highlight its nonlinguistic ends. In this context, Arabization goes beyond the lexical revitalization of the language and its use in the educational process to its deployment as an instrument that can help create a new elite who, in turn, can fashion a new North African identity in which Arabism (*al-'urūba*) acts as a major formative impulse. This linkage of *ta'rīb* with an Arab-bound sense of national identity was opposed by members of the old elite and the indigenous Berber community in Algeria and, to a lesser extent, Morocco (Faiq 1999; Tilmatine and Suleiman 1996).

As explained earlier the situation in Sudan combines aspects of both senses of *ta'rīb* set out above, but it has its own special features. In addition to Arabicization in its two dimensions above, Sudan exhibits a modulated sense of Arabization whose operational contours ebb and flow in a way which reflects the ever-changing political environment, and in a manner that is sometimes reminiscent of the language situation during the British colonial period (1889–1956) in its broad outline. A similar situation applies to Arabization in North Africa, especially in Tunisia, but the main difference between the two cases is that while the avowed objective of Arabization in North Africa is to replace a *foreign* language, French, by a national language, Arabic, the main challenge in the Sudan is twofold. On the one hand, Arabization is aimed at stemming the influence of English and replacing it by Arabic as a medium of education throughout the whole country—but especially in the South—although proficiency in English in the Sudan is most probably not at the same level, quantitatively and qualitatively, as proficiency in French in the countries of North Africa. On the other hand, Arabization in the Sudan is aimed at promoting Arabic as a medium of education and in government administration over the 100 or more *indigenous* languages, especially in the South, as the basis of a truly unified Sudan. This mode of bringing about national unity has been advocated by no less than the idealogue of the present Sudanese government, Ḥassan al-Turābī who, in an interview with the Jordanian newspaper *al-Dustūr* on 7 April 1996, declared that 'The Arabic language is the [only] basis for building a united Sudan.' However, because of high illiteracy rates, religious and ethnic differences, physical isolation, political conflicts, and even war, the number of people who are competent in Arabic as a spoken or written language in Southern Sudan (Jernudd 1968; Miller and Abu-Manga 1992) is very small in comparison with the almost universal knowledge of Arabic, especially as a spoken language, in North Africa. This makes the implementation of Arabization in the Sudan a task of gargantuan proportions in comparison with the same project in North Africa. In addition, while Arabic is regarded as the major national language in North Africa and the language of the religion of the vast proportion of the population in that region, it is at best viewed with apathy by some Southern Sudanese elite and as a language of a different religion by others. Arabization is therefore resisted because it is taken to mean what its root meaning actually implies: transforming the population into Arabs culturally.

The seeds of this situation were sown during the British colonial period, in which a policy of linguistically divide and rule was deliberately and openly espoused (Abū Bakr 1995; Bashīr 1970; Al-Sayyid 1975). The aims of this policy were to weaken Arabic in the South, and ultimately exclude it from schools and government administration; promote English as the language of education beyond the initial stages of primary schooling; and introduce selected local languages in the first 2 years of primary schooling. For the latter purpose, the British administration developed Roman alphabets for the languages concerned to distance them graphically from Arabic and to bring them closer to English.

## Arabization in North Africa

The French policy in North Africa had a strong linguistic dimension whose aim was to support the colonial administration in its endeavors to tighten its grip over the territories it controlled (Aḥmad 1986; Bin Nu'mān 1981; al-Jābirī 1990; Wannās 1991, 1996, n.d.). This linguistic dimension revolved around the twin objectives of weakening Arabic in the schools and government administration, and supplanting it by French, within an overall policy of ethnically divide and rule. As a result, Arabization became a rallying cry in the struggle for independence, although its fortunes ebbed and flowed in Morocco, Algeria, and Tunisia in the postindependence period. The intensity of this cry was particularly pronounced in Algeria, because of the length of colonial rule, the bloody nature of the war of independence, the fact that some prominent members of the counter elite were Arabophones who had no competence in French, and, finally, the fact that Arabic did not enjoy the protection of a traditional and prestigious seat of learning similar to al-Qarawiyyīn in Morocco or al-Zaytūna in Tunisia. This latter factor led to the intense politicization of the language issue, as manifest in the most recently promulgated Algerian constitution (1997), in which Arabic is set out as the only official and national language, in spite of some Berber opposition.

Arabization in North Africa was embedded in government policies which, additionally, aimed at the following: (a) unifying the educational system by bringing the different types of ethnic, traditional and modern schools into a single system; (b) promoting universal education; and (c) employing the nationals of each country only as teachers in schools. However, the lack of financial and human resources to implement these policies, the huge number of school age children whose educational needs had to be met more or less immediately after independence, resistance by the old elite, and the lack of will to pursue Arabization vigorously by the new elite meant that the progress of Arabization in postindependence North African countries fell short of the high expectations which the framers of those policies had in mind in the preindependence period.

But these are not the only reasons for the variable success of Arabization in North Africa in the field of education and in government administration. The generally peaceful progress to independence in Morocco and Tunisia, compared with Algeria's bloody war of independence, meant that opposition to French in the former two countries in the preindependence and postindependence period was not imbued with the same connotations of domination and resistance it had in the latter country. In addition, the linking of French with economic development, labor migration to France, and modernity (Gill 1999) gave a new impetus to the calls by the new elite to preserve and, even, promote the language in the educational system. In Tunisia, the promotion of French, even when it was counter to the Arabization policy, was imbued with politicolinguistic meanings of resisting the encroachment of Arab nationalism during the period of bad relations between Bourguiba's Tunisia and Nasser's Egypt in the mid-1960s. One may even speak of de-Arabization in the education context of this period.

In Algeria, Arabization faced enormous obstacles because of the resistance of the francophone elements of the new elite, who stressed the economic advantages of French and the need for the gradual implementation of Arabization to avoid the reduction in standards in schools and universities, and who, in pursuing their aims, were even able to thwart the implementation of presidential decrees on the implementation of Arabization. The lack of coordinated policies meant that Arabization did not work through the entire educational system up to university level. It was therefore not possible to ensure educational continuity for those schooled in Arabic across the range of subjects offered by institutes of higher education. This led to impoverished job opportunities for these graduates in comparison with French language educated ones. And, to cap it all, the ethnic connotations of Arabization did lead to some resistance from members of the Berber speaking community. The combined effect of these factors meant that Arabization in Algeria, although in some ways more advanced than Arabization in Tunisia and Morocco, did not achieve its stated objectives. The same is true of the Arabization of government administration in all three countries of North Africa (Aḥmad 1986).

Three models were used to implement Arabization in schools. The first, called the horizontal model, aimed at Arabizing the teaching year by year, starting from primary one upwards. When this proved difficult to implement throughout the whole school system, an alternative model was employed. This second model, called the vertical model, consisted of the staged Arabization of one or more areas of the curriculum, particularly in the humanities, leaving French as the language of instruction in the sciences. The third model aimed at the wholesale Arabization of the teaching in a particular school or set of schools whenever possible. While the first two models were implemented in all three countries of North Africa, the last model was implemented in Algeria only, which, as was pointed [out] earlier, reflects the sociopolitical potency of Arabization in this country.

## Corpus Planning

The discussion in this section will be organized around three topics: writing system, grammar, and lexicon. Unlike status planning, most of the initiatives in corpus planning are the work of individual innovators, or what has been referred to as 'strategic planners' earlier. These initiatives are part of what is generally referred to in Arabic discourse as the language reform movement (*ḥarakat al-iṣlāḥ al-lughawī*) or, in the area of word derivation (Ḥamādī 1980), the language correction movement (*ḥarakat al-taṣḥīḥ al-lughawī*). In this they answer to Cooper's concept of 'renovation' (1989: 154). A characteristic feature of these initiatives is that they rarely get implemented. Their value therefore is mainly in highlighting the kind of issues which corpus planning policy may choose to focus on if it were to be officially launched in the Arabic speaking countries.

Corpus planning initiatives in the Arabic speaking countries share two major properties with similar plans elsewhere. On the one hand, they tend to be based on no more than an impressionistic assessment of the problems they are designed to solve. On the other hand, they cannot be divorced from the ideologically motivated nonlinguistic ends which constitute their ultimate, albeit often undeclared, goals. A bold statement of these ends is provided by the well-known Egyptian writer Salama Moussa who declared that the Romanization of Arabic would 'mark a change in [the] psychological attitude [of the Arabs, who would, as a result] welcome modern industrial civilization, with its moral, cultural and spiritual values.' (1955: 44)

### Writing System

The reform of the Arabic writing system has been the subject of intense debate in the twentieth century (Altoma 1961, 1974; Makdesi 1955; Moussa 1955). The avowed aim of the large number of proposals to reform this system is to deal with the educational and economic problems caused by two perceived defects in the script. The first defect concerns the positionally determined multiplicity of letter shapes in the writing system which, according to one estimate, number over 400. The second defect concerns the reliance of this system on **diacritical** marks, which are usually not included in hand-written or printed materials.

Two major types of reform were put forward in the literature. The first type calls for the use of a modified form of the Latin script in writing Arabic. A proposal to this effect was submitted to the Arab Language Academy in the 1940s by the once minister of education in Egypt, ʿAbd al-ʿAzīz Fahmī. The Lebanese linguist Frayḥa (1955) also supported Romanization. The second type consisted of developing a modified form of the Arabic script, either to address the problem of the high costs of producing printed materials, or to deal with perceived learning difficulties, or both. However, predictions that the Arabs will eventually opt for Romanization (Moussa 1955) have so far proved unwarranted, as have the hopes for the adoption of a modified form of the Arabic script which the Moroccan educationalist Aḥmad Lakhḍar devised, and for which he seems to have received semiofficial pan-Arab backing in the late 1950s and early 1960s (Altoma 1961).

## Grammar

The reform of Arabic grammar, called *taysīr al-naḥw* in Arabic (Ḍayf 1986a; Al-Jawārī 1984; Khalīfa 1986; Stetkevych 1970), is principally related to the role of **diglossia** in depressing the speakers' grammatical competence in the standard language; this is typically reflected in the problem of the incorrect manipulation (*laḥn*) of the **desinential inflections** (*iʿrāb*). The complex and unwieldy nature of pedagogic grammars, which tend to be organized around the twin principles of form and grammatical governance rather than semantic or communicative function, is said to exacerbate this problem, as does the fact that these grammars tend to be filled with attested materials (*shawāhid*) that are difficult to interpret and understand. The lack of qualified teachers who can use the language correctly in their teaching across the full range of the curriculum is said to make the above problem even more intractable.

Broadly speaking, grammatical reforms fall into two types. One type has as its objective bridging the gap between the standard language and the colloquials in a two-directional movement of leveling down (standard to colloquial) and leveling up (colloquial to standard). This type of reform was supported by Al-Ḥuṣrī (1985), the most prominent thinker of pan-Arab nationalism (Suleiman 1994, 1997), although his ideas remained at the level of theoretical articulation only. A similar position was advocated by Frayḥa. In a series of publications (1951, 1952, 1955, 1980), he called for simplifying the Arabic language by adopting a set of measures which, in addition to developing a middle language between the standard and the colloquial, also included as an interim step implementing radical changes in pedagogic grammars and the way the standard language is taught in schools (Al-Batal 1994). Most of Frayḥa's ideas, however, remained at the level of broad theoretical articulation.

The second type of reform aims at recasting Arabic grammar, in the post-descriptive sense (Suleiman 1996), in a new way which eliminates most of the problems it is thought to generate at the pedagogic level. By far the best known proposal of this type was put forward in 1937 by the Egyptian linguist Ibrāhīm Muṣṭafā in his book *Iḥyāʾ al-naḥw* (1959). In this book, the author advocates a new scheme for dealing with the desinential inflections to give them grammatical coherence, based not on the concept of governance but on semantic considerations of a very general nature (Omran 1991). Although the book contains no direct reference to the fact, it is clearly inspired by the work of the twelfth century Andalusian linguist Al-Qurṭubī (1982), which goes to show the historical depth of the notion of grammatical reform in the Arabic grammatical tradition. In recent times, this same work has served as the inspiration for a series of publications on the topic by Ḍayf (1986a, 1986b, 1990, 1994). However, none of these efforts succeeded in bringing about a radical change, if any at all, in pedagogic grammar by adopting grammatical categories and classificatory schemata in language teaching that are different from the ones they set out to replace. The same fate befell the proposal which the Arabic Language Academy in Cairo developed, in response to an invitation by the Ministry of Education in 1938. Conservatism, inertia and, later in 1956, opposition from the Syrian part of the United Arab Republic (whose other part was Egypt) put paid to any hope of implementing this proposal.

## Lexicon

Sustained contact with Europe, brought about by the Napoleonic invasion of Egypt (1798–1801), had a major impact on Arabic in a variety of fields, but the intensity of this impact was no more apparent than in the lexical arena. The need to find new terms to designate new inventions and concepts was a driving force behind the efforts to modernize the language, at both the individual and official level through, in the latter case, the work of the academies and the Bureau of Arabicization which were set up only in the twentieth century. A major factor in this drive was the ideologically anchored commitment to preserve the purity of the language. In practical terms this meant a preference for native terms over borrowed ones wherever possible.

The following overall strategy seems to underlie the work of individual innovators and the academies in coining new terms. Utilizing the lexical resources of the language is the preferred option. This usually involves applying one of the following measures: (a) creating a new term out of the existing root configurations of the language; (b) using an existing term which is not in common use to designate the new concept or invention; (c) extending the semantic scope of an existing word to designate the new concept or invention; (d) loan translation or paraphrase; (e) blending (*naḥt*), which involves forming composite words by coalescing parts of existing words; and (f) using the colloquials as a quarry from which words can be extracted and circulated after carrying out the necessary **phonological** and **morphological** modifications to make them conform to the standard. The second option is foreign language borrowing, mainly from English and French, which is more prevalent in scientific texts than in the humanities. Borrowed terminologies undergo a process of naturalization to bring them in line with the phonological and morphological patterns of the language.

Approved new terminologies are published in the journals of the language academies, but there is no information as to the take-up rate of new terms whenever these are not already in circulation. Other methods of dissemination employed by the academies, which may involve utilizing the media or communicating their decisions directly to government departments and private businesses, are not known. The academies sometimes take the line of least resistance and approve borrowed terms whenever these have become established in the speech community. Here, they play a legitimizing role rather than a leading one in which they set the trend.

Dictionary making is a major aspect of language planning in the lexical field. Most of the initiatives in this area originate with individuals, although the Arab League sponsored Bureau of Arabization in Morocco has been at the forefront of the attempts to provide Arabic language equivalents for scientific and technical terms in a number of fields. The fast expanding number of bilingual dictionaries in the Arabic speaking countries, especially in the sciences, is symptomatic of an acute awareness of the need to try to rejuvenate the lexicon of the language. The intensity of this activity mirrors that of compiling monolingual dictionaries in the second half of the nineteenth century and the first half of the twentieth century (Yaʿqūb 1981), when the issue seems to have been one of codification in the face of what was sometimes projected as serious deviations from the strict norms of the language (Ḥamādī 1980). Dictionary makers, in compiling these dictionaries, debated whether to arrange entries alphabetically or by following the traditional root arrangement system. Although dictionaries were compiled in both modes, nevertheless the latter system predominated, as in *Al-Muʿjam al-Wasīṭ* (1972), which the Arabic Language Academy in Cairo sponsored and promoted for use in schools.

## Acquisition Planning: Foreign Language Education Policy

The aims of foreign language education policy are generally subsumed under the aims of educational policy as a whole in Arabic speaking countries (Ismāʿīl 1989; Al-Jābirī 1990; Qindīl 1989; Riḥā 1998). Special laws normally spell out the specific aims of foreign language education policy in terms of aiding intercultural communication, professional development, enhanced job opportunities in an increasingly competitive and globalized market place, scientific and technical progress, and economic development at the national level. To implement these aims foreign language education policy in Arabic speaking countries is operationalized by defining a set of stated objectives which relate to attainment levels in the four language skills. On the whole, these levels are of a general nature. As a result, it is often difficult to monitor and evaluate the policy in terms of institutional implementation and whether or not it has achieved its stated objectives.

Six considerations of a general nature relate to foreign language education policy in Arabic speaking countries. The first concerns the absence of a fully worked out policy in this field in individual Arab countries, of the kind developed in Holland (van Els 1994) or Australia (Ingram 1994). Second, the choice of foreign languages in individual Arab countries is to a great extent determined by historical accident, defined in terms of the colonial legacy, although this cannot be divorced from the need factor. This explains the predominance of English as the primary foreign language in Egypt, Jordan, Libya, Palestine, Oman, Qatar, Sudan, and the United Arab Emirates. It also explains the predominance of French in Algeria, Lebanon, Mauritania, Morocco, and Tunisia. The same applies to the presence of Spanish in Morocco, although this is additionally aided by the imperatives of geographical proximity which makes Spain Morocco's gateway to Europe. Need is the second defining factor in the choice of foreign language. This explains the predominance of English in Saudi Arabia and Yemen which escaped Western colonial rule, as it explains the position of the same language in Lebanon as a result of missionary work in the nineteenth century and contact with migrant Lebanese communities in North America. The shift from French to English in Syria and the serious encroachments made by English in Morocco in recent years constitute a further expression of the role of need in shaping foreign language education policy, owing to the unrivaled position of this language as the foremost international language. The continued presence of French in Egypt springs from the cultural prestige of this language among Egyptians, which goes back to Napoleon's invasion of the country (1798–1801) and the longstanding cultural and scientific contact with France this short-lived event initiated. Third, the Eurocentric bias of foreign language education policy, which favors English and French as the main foreign languages in the Arabic speaking countries, reflects the positive image of these languages in sociocultural terms and the fact that they are spoken by high-prestige groups at the national level, be they the old colonial elite or the new elite (cf. Trim 1994). Fourth, foreign language education policy in the Arabic speaking countries of the Middle East is almost completely divorced from its regional context. This explains the little interest there is in Hebrew, Persian, and Turkish in this part of the Arab world, although the exact reasons for this situation in each case are complex and varied. Fifth, in extreme and isolated cases foreign language education policy may be suddenly altered to suit the political imperatives of the moment, as happened in Libya when English was banned from schools in the late 1980s following the American air attacks on the country. Finally, foreign language proficiency is to a great extent dependent not so much on whether the foreign language is the target of instruction, but whether it is the language *through* which the instruction of parts of the curriculum is carried out. This is typically the case in the leading private schools, faculties of science and technology, and foreign universities in the Middle East. In North Africa the situation is different because of the almost universal use of French in teaching science subjects in state schools and the universities.

## Language Education Policy: The Ethnic Dimension

Lambert (1995) distinguishes three types of country from the perspective of the development of national language policy: (a) homogeneous countries (containing a small number of ethnolinguistic groups that are marginal in geographical and social terms); (b) dyadic countries (possessing a small number of two or more ethnolinguistic groups that are geographically and socially cohesive); and (c) mosaic countries (containing a substantial number of ethnolinguistic groups). As explained above ("Arabicization or Arabization"), Sudan is the only Arabic speaking country which belongs to the mosaic type. Most Arabic speaking countries belong to the homogeneous type, not withstanding the presence of such languages as Nubian in Egypt, Mahrī and Baluchi in Oman, or Armenian in Lebanon, Palestine, and Syria, to give just a few examples. It is, however, mainly in the context of Iraq and both Algeria and Morocco that we can legitimately speak of dyadic countries.

In Iraq, Kurdish is declared as an official language, alongside Arabic, but only in the Kurdish speaking areas. This fact distinguishes Iraq from Iran and Turkey in which sizable Kurdish communities do exist, but in which the language is not recognized as official. In Iraq, Kurdish is, therefore, taught in schools and at the university level at the University of Sulay-māniyya in Northern Iraq. Kurdish is also present in the media, both press (using the Arabic script) and electronic.

In Algeria and Morocco, the situation is different with respect to Berber, which is spoken by a sizable proportion of the population. Owing to the fact that Berber is not recognized as an official language in these two countries, only minimal concessions are made to its propagation, in spite of internal and external pressures (from Berberophones in France) to do so (Tilmatine and Suleiman 1986). This means that in these two countries there does not exist a Berber language education policy to speak of.

## Future Work

Much work is needed to establish the exact nature of the language situation in the Sudan, Mauritania, Somalia, and Djibouti as well as in other Arab countries where ethnolinguistic groups exist. Information yielded from such research is necessary before any comprehensive picture of language education policy in the Arabic speaking countries can emerge. Empirical studies are also needed to determine the validity or otherwise of some of the claims made in connection with corpus planning initiatives in the Arabic speaking countries, especially in light of the success in introducing standard Arabic as a spoken language in children's TV programs, most notably *Iftaḥ yā Simsim*, the Arabic adaption of Sesame Street (Abu-Absi 1990, 1991; Palmer 1979).

On the prescriptive side, better coordination in areas of common concern, particularly in the field of corpus planning, is needed between the Arabic speaking countries. A language education policy that is in tune with its regional context is a developmental priority in the Arab world, as is the need to introduce major foreign languages into the curriculum which 'buck the trend' of the North–South bias, in favor of a more balanced policy in which a South–South dimension is given due recognition, at least at university level.

### References

*References in Arabic have been deleted to save space.*


Abu-Absi, S. 1990. A characterization of the language of *Iftaḥ yā Simsim*: Sociolinguistic and educational implications for Arabic. *Language Problems and Language Planning* 14: 33–46.

Abu-Absi, S. 1991. The 'simplified Arabic' of *Iftaḥ yā Simsim*: Pedagogical and sociolinguistic implications. *Al-'Arabiyya* 24: 111–21.

Abuhamadia, Z. 1984. The dilemma of academies of Arabic: The case of the Jordan academy of Arabic. *Muslim Education Quarterly* 1: 57–84.

Abuhamadia, Z. 1995. Orthography policy-making by fiat: The policy to Romanize Somali. *Journal of King Saud University* 7: 49–69.

Akinnaso, N., Ogunbiyi, I. A. 1990. The place of Arabic in education and language planning in Nigeria. *Language Problems and Language Planning* 14: 1–19.

Altoma, S. J. 1961. The Arabic writing system and proposals for its reform. *The Middle East Journal* 15: 403–15.

Altoma, S. J. 1974. Language education in Arab countries and the role of the academies. In: Fishman, J. (ed.) *Advances in Language Planning*. Mouton, The Hague, pp. 279–313.

Al-Batal, M. 1994. The Lebanese linguist Anīs Frayḥa (1902–1993) and his contribution to Arabic language reform. In: Rammuny, R. M., Parkinson, D. B. (eds.). *Investigating Arabic: Linguistic, Pedagogical and Literary Studies in Honor of Ernest N. McCarus*. Greyden Press, Columbus, OH, pp. 155–72.

Bell, H. 1989. Language and ethnic identity in the Sudan and the Soviet Union: A comparative study. In: Hurreiz, S. H., Abdel Fatih, S. E. A. (eds.). *Ethnicity Conflict and National Integration in the Sudan*. Institute of African and Asian Studies, Khartoum, pp. 186–95.

Blau, J., Suleiman, Y. 1996. Language and ethnic identity in Kurdistan: An historical overview. In: Suleiman, Y. (ed.) *Language and Identity in the Middle East and North Africa*. Curzon Press, Richmond, UK, pp. 153–64.

Cooper, R. L. 1989. *Language Planning and Social Change.* Cambridge University Press, Cambridge.

Faiq, S. 1999. The status of Berber: A permanent challenge to language policy in Morocco. In: Suleiman, Y. (ed.) *Language and Society in the Middle East and North Africa: Studies in Variation and Identity.* Curzon Press, Richmond, UK, pp. 137–53.

Ferguson, C. 1959. Diglossia. *Word* 15: 325–40.

Gallagher, C. F. 1968. North African problems and prospects: Language and identity. In: Fishman, J., Ferguson, C., Das Gupta, J. (eds.) *Language Problems of Developing Nations.* Wiley, New York, pp. 129–50.

Gill, H. 1999. Language choice, language policy and the tradition-modernity debate in culturally mixed postcolonial communities: France and the 'Francophone' Maghreb as a case study. In: Suleiman, Y. (ed.) *Language and Society in the Middle East and North Africa: Studies in Variation and Identity.* Curzon Press, Richmond, UK, pp. 122–36.

Harrison, W., Prator, C., Tucker, G. R. 1975. *English-Language Policy Survey of Jordan: A Case Study in Language Planning.* Center for Applied Linguistics, Arlington, VA.

Holes, C. 1995. *Modern Arabic: Structures, Functions and Varieties.* Longman, London.

Ingram, D. E. 1994. Language policy in Australia in the 1990s. In: Lambert, R. (ed.) *Language Planning Around the World: Contexts and Systemic Change.* National Foreign Language Center, Washington, DC, pp. 69–109.

Jernudd, B. 1968. Linguistic integration and national development: A case study of the Jebel Marra area, Sudan. In: Fishman, J., Ferguson, C., Das Gupta, J. (eds.) *Language Problems of Developing Nations.* Wiley, New York, pp. 167–81.

Kenny, D. 1992. Arab-Americans learning Arabic: Motivation and attitudes. In: Rouchdy, A. (ed.) *The Arabic Language in America.* Wayne State University Press, Detroit, MI, pp. 119–61.

Lambert, R. D. 1995. Language policy: An overview. Paper presented at the International Symposium on Language Policy. Language Policy Research Center, Bar-Ilan University.

Makdesi, N. 1955. Facts and figures: Arabic type simplified. *Middle Eastern Affairs* 6: 51–53.

Miller, C., Al-Amin, A. M. 1992. *Language Change and National Integration: Rural Migrants in Khartoum.* Ithaca Press, Reading, UK.

Moussa, S. 1955. Arabic language problems. *Middle Eastern Affairs* 6: 41–44.

Omran, E. M. H. 1991. Arabic grammar: Problems and reform efforts. In: Kinga, D. K., Iványi, T. (eds.) *Proceedings of the Colloquium on Arabic Grammar: The Arabist, Budapest Studies in Arabic* 3–4: 297–311.

Palmer, E. 1979. Linguistic innovation in the Arabic adaptation of 'Sesame Street.' In: Altais, J., Tucker, G. (eds.) *Language in Public Life.* Washington, DC, pp. 287–94.

Rouchdy, A. 1991. *Nubians and the Nubian Language in Contemporary Egypt: A Case of Cultural and Linguistic Contact.* E. J. Brill, Leiden.

Sawaie, M. 1992. Arabic in the melting pot: Will it survive? In: Rouchdy, A. (ed.) *The Arabic Language in America.* Wayne State University Press, Detroit, MI, pp. 83–99.

Shohamy, E. 1994. Issues of language planning in Israel. In: Lambert, R. (ed.) *Language Planning Around the World: Contexts and Systemic Change.* National Foreign Language Center, Washington, DC, pp. 131–42.

Spolsky, B., Shohamy, E. 1997. Planning foreign-language education: An Israeli perspective. In: Bongaerts, T., de Bot, K. (eds.) *Perspectives on Foreign-Language Policy: Studies in Honour of Theo van Els.* John Benjamins, Amsterdam and Philadelphia, pp. 99–111.

Stetkeyvch, J. 1970. *The Modern Arabic Literary Language: Lexical and Stylistic Developments.* University of Chicago Press, Chicago.

Suleiman, Y. 1994. Nationalism and the Arabic language: An historical overview. In: Suleiman, Y. (ed.) *Arabic Sociolinguistics: Issues and Perspectives.* Curzon Press, Richmond, UK, pp. 3–24.

Suleiman, Y. 1996. The simplification of Arabic grammar and the problematic nature of the sources. *Journal of Semitic Studies* XLI: 99–119.

Suleiman, Y. 1997. The Arabic language in the fray: A sphere of contested identities. In: Jones, A. (ed.) *University Lectures in Islamic Studies* (Vol. I). Al-Tajir World of Islam Trust, London, pp. 127–48.

Tilmatine, M., Suleiman, Y. 1996. Language and identity: The case of the Berber. In: Suleiman, Y. (ed.) *Language and Identity in the Middle East and North Africa.* Curzon Press, Richmond, UK, pp. 165–80.

Trim, J. L. M. 1994. Some factors influencing national language policymaking in Europe. In: Lambert, R. (ed.) *Language Planning Around the World: Contexts and Systemic Change.* National Foreign Language Center, Washington, DC, pp. 1–15.

van, Els, T. J. M. 1994. Foreign language planning in the Netherlands. In: Lambert, R. (ed.) *Language Planning around the World: Contexts and Systemic Change.* National Foreign Language Center. Washington, DC, pp. 47–68.

Versteegh, K. 1997. *The Arabic Language.* Edinburgh University Press, Edinburgh.

Walbridge, L. 1992. Arabic in the Dearborn mosques. In: Rouchdy, A. (ed.) *The Arabic Language in America.* Wayne State University Press, Detroit, MI, pp. 184–204.

Zaborski, A. 1997. Minority languages in Arab countries. In: Synak, S., Wicherkiewicz, T. (eds.) *Language Minorities and Minority Languages in the Changing Europe.* Wydawnictwo Uniwersytetu Gdanskiego, Gdansk, pp. 385–94.

## Critical Thinking and Application

- Why do you think languages such as French are not included in the constitutions of Tunisia or Morocco despite its widespread use? What does this suggest about the factors influencing whether a language receives official or semiofficial status?
- How does the choice of a language affect national identity?
- Compare the policies that Suleiman describes with what you know of your own country's policies with regard to language and education.
- Select one of the countries mentioned in this chapter, and look carefully at its policies with regard to multilingualism, language status, and education.

## Vocabulary

acquisition planning
colloquial
corpus planning
desinential inflections
diacritical
diglossia, diglossic
francophone
language academy
language planning
language policy
lexicon, lexical
morphology
morphological
national language
official language
phonology, phonological
semiofficial language
speech community
status planning
working language

## Suggested Further Reading

Anderson, Benedict. 1983. *Imagined Communities: Reflections on the Origin and Spread of Nationalism*. London: Verso.

Cooper, Robert Leon. 1989. *Language Planning and Social Change*. Cambridge: Cambridge University Press.

Creese, Angela, Peter Martin, and Nancy H. Hornberger, eds. 2008. Ecology of Language. *Encyclopedia of Language and Education* (Vol. 9). New York: Springer.

Edwards, John R. 1994. *Multilingualism*. London and New York: Routledge.

Ferguson, Charles A. 1959. Diglossia. *Word* 15: 325–340.

Schiffman, Harold F. 2002. *Linguistic Culture and Language Policy*. London and New York: Routledge.

# CHAPTER 22

# The Language Ecology of Singapore

*Anthea Fraser Gupta*

(2008)

*Singapore isn't* the *most complicated place in the world, but for an island nation, a city-state that achieved independence from the Malaysian Federation only in 1965, with a population of only 4.7 million, it is plenty complicated. With three official languages—and one of them, Chinese, with multiple versions—this ultramodern, prosperous, and sophisticated country has grappled with its policies and the places of its three powerful languages. This has stemmed especially from education policy. We might also look at the English spoken in Singapore (sometimes called* Singlish*) in the context of the New Englishes that Tom McArthur discusses in Chapter 19.*

*Chinese is a family of languages, with Mandarin the official language of Mainland China and southern varieties in wide usage, especially throughout Southeast Asia. Most Chinese in Singapore initially spoke southern varieties, particularly Hokkien—also spoken in Taiwan—but with the growing influence and opportunities of China, Mandarin has become increasingly favored.*

*In this chapter, Gupta uses the concept* language ecology*—an intertwining set of languages within an environment—to discuss the complex linguistic reality of Singapore. We might take this as a laboratory for linguistic planning and complexity throughout the contemporary world.*

## Reading Questions

- How have the dominant languages of Singapore changed since its independence? What factors are responsible for these changes?
- What are the regulations with regard to the language within which children are educated? What reasons are behind these regulations?
- Why is it difficult to distinguish "free choice" and "coercion" with regard to language use in Singapore?

## Introduction

The **language ecology** of Singapore has been shaped by educational policy, which in turn has been a response to a particularly complex language ecology. Concepts of **indigeneity** are meaningless in this city state, which has been a multicultural trading port since at least the fourteenth century (Gupta, 1994; Miksic, 2004), and whose present language make-up is the result of British **colonialism** and associated immigration in the nineteenth century (Gupta, 1994; Platt and Weber, 1980). The colonial government manipulated the delivery of education as a tool of ethnic management and **social engineering**, and this policy has been continued by the government of independent Singapore (Benjamin, 1976; Bloom, 1986; Chua, 1995; Gopinathan, Pakir, Ho and Saravanan (eds), 1998; Gupta, 1994; Murray, 1971; Pennycook, 1994; PuruShotam, 1998; Tan, Gopinathan and Ho (eds), 1997; Tremewan, 1994).

The extreme societal and individual multilingualism of the early twentieth century (Kuo, 1976; Murray, 1971; Platt

Anthea Fraser Gupta, The Language Ecology of Singapore. In *Encyclopedia of Language and Education*, vol. 9, *Ecology of Language*, 2nd ed., edited by Angela Creese, Peter Martin, and Nancy H. Hornberger. New York: Springer Science+Business Media, 2008, pp. 99–111.

and Weber, 1980) has given way to a linguistically more homogeneous society, in which the norm is for everyone to be able to use English and the official language associated with their officially defined race (either Malay, Mandarin Chinese or Tamil). Considerable **language shift** to English and Mandarin, mostly from non-official languages, has taken place. The entire population is now much more linguistically united than it was, through English, and the Chinese population is also more united than in the past, through English and Mandarin. Those born after independence are likely to know fewer languages, and are less likely to have some knowledge of a language associated with another ethnic group than are those born in the 50 years before independence.

Some aspects of the linguistic ecology of Singapore are shared with the whole Malay world (potentially extending as far as modern Thailand and modern Australia), and even more is shared with (modern) Malaysia and Brunei Darussalam, to which Singapore has close historical and geographical links. But Singapore has always been, to varying degrees, politically distinct from the wider region, and in this [chapter] I will link it to the wider region only when that is unavoidable.

## Developments

Modern Singapore is a city state, about 640 sq km in area, built across over 30 islands, many of them very small. It is located in calm waters at the southern tip of mainland Asia, where the monsoons of the South China Sea and the Indian Ocean meet, at a crucial point on the trade routes that link China, India, and Arabia. In this small corner of the Malay region, there are cities and the ruins of cities that are or were international trading posts, such as Sri Vijaya, Malacca, Banten, Banda Aceh, and Singapore (the classic history is Wheatley, 1961). Some of these cities (especially Sri Vijaya and Malacca) at their height controlled a wide region. Groups of foreign traders settled in the cities in districts that were set aside for them, and the cities were open to influence by the cultures and languages of India, Arabia, China and Europe. Miksic (2004) argues that although Singapore fits into this 'port of trade' category, it is possible that the foreigners in Singapore may have had more freedom to mix with the local population than was usually the case. In Singapore, we see what seems like rapid change in the twentieth century, but this should be placed in the context of two millennia (at least) of cosmopolitan trading ports in the immediate region, and 600 years in Singapore itself.

There are a number of early Chinese (quoted by Miksic, 2004; Wheatley, 1961) and European accounts of pre-colonial Singapore in the context of the wider region of the Malay peninsula and archipelago. The language which gave rise to most attention was Malay. De Houtman van Gouda (1603) supplied the first European treatment, and Marsden's became the classic account (1812a, b). Malay was the **lingua franca** of the entire region, and its adaptations as a lingua franca were a considerable source of fascination (especially Bowrey, 1701). The negotiation of multilingualism in the region was to be a central topic of much of the writing on the area.

In 1819, Stamford Raffles and William Farquhar made an agreement with Singapore's Malay rulers and began a formal connection with Britain that was responsible both for its later ethnolinguistic composition and for the prominence that English came to have. Because of the trade established under British control, many immigrants were attracted to Singapore, most of them from groups that had been associated with the region for centuries, and many coming to Singapore from other cosmopolitan cities in the region, especially Malacca. As a result, the population is still dominated by three groups, all of them internally diverse, which in Singapore are officially labelled[1] as follows:

- Chinese: people of Chinese ancestry, mostly from Southern regions of China now part of the People's Republic of China. Brought with them a range of varieties of Chinese, the largest of which are the closely related Hokkien (Amoy) and Teochew. Also large numbers of Cantonese speakers.
- Malay: people whose ancestors formed the majority population in the Malay Region. Most spoke dialects of Malay, which was also the lingua franca of the whole region, but there were substantial groups who spoke other related languages, especially Javanese and Boyanese.
- Indian: people of South Asian ancestry (modern Bangladesh, India, Pakistan and Sri Lanka). Most were from Southern India, a small majority being Tamil speakers. Other groups included Malayalees and Punjabis.

There are also a number of groups that are identified as resulting from a genetic and cultural mixture before the nineteenth century, some of which (especially those descended from Arab or Indian Muslim men) were partly absorbed into the Malay population, adopting Malay, and some of which developed **contact varieties** of Malay (Malacca Chitty, Straits Chinese) or Portuguese (Malacca Portuguese). Some nineteenth century migrants came from smaller groups, often via India, and some of these people (Arabs, Armenians, Europeans, Eurasians and Jews) were important in the development of English in Singapore (Gupta, 1994).

Singapore was briefly (1963–1965) a part of Malaysia, and became a fully independent country in 1965, since when the *People's Action Party* has been returned as the governing party at every election. The government of Singapore is active in social engineering, and has used language, especially as expressed in educational policy, as a major tool in shaping Singapore society (Bloom, 1986; Chua, 1995; Gopinathan, Pakir, Ho and Saravanan (eds), 1998; Gupta, 1994; PuruShotam, 1998; Tan, Gopinathan and Ho (eds), 1997; Tremewan, 1994).

The British colonial power was concerned to classify and manage the population of Singapore, which it did through its decennial censuses (from 1871) and annual reports on education (from 1856). Gazetteers of the region (such as Crawfurd, 1856; Hamilton, 1815) outlined the salient features of people and languages. Many of those working on the sociolinguistic situation of Singapore (such as Bloom, 1986; Chua, 1995; Gupta, 1994; PuruShotam, 1998) are indebted to Benjamin (1976) for an insight on how multiculturalism is a powerful cultural and social institution in Singapore. Singapore's multiracialism is one in which the state is seen as being composed of the three main constituent 'races' (Malays, Chinese, Indians), with a 'stereotypical list of defining characteristics ascribed to it' (Benjamin 1976, p. 124): an individual's full Singaporean identity depends on membership of a 'race'. A citizen's official racial classification is allocated at birth, based on paternal ancestry: it is expressed as membership of a 'race' (such as 'Chinese') and a 'dialect group' (such as 'Hokkien'). Official race has consequences in allocation of housing, school, and, probably most crucially, in allocating languages studied at school (see below). The sharp official classifications mask the amount of blurring of boundaries that has happened, though most Singaporeans do have a sense of belonging to (at least) one of these subgroups, and will attribute cultural traits to this ancestry (such as appearance, how festivals are celebrated, the style of domestic cuisine, taste in clothes). The younger a person is the less likely they are to speak the language associated with their official dialect group, especially if it is one of the smaller varieties.

The categories used by the British have been persistent into the censuses and the thinking of modern Singapore (Gupta, 1994; Kuo, 1976; Lau, 1993; Leow, 2001; Saw, 1981; Tay, 1983). There are accurate records of officially classifiable race and ethnicity, but the data on language use and knowledge is patchy. It is important to remember that as a result of language shift and intermarriage, it cannot be assumed that a person can speak their official 'dialect group', let alone that it is their native or best language. Censuses do have information on literacy in the official languages, and, since 1980, they have had limited information on language of the home. The way these questions are asked ('what is the main language you speak to....?') underestimates the amount of domestic bilingualism. The Ministry of Education collects some information on home languages of children coming into Primary School, which are released annually. The censal and Ministry figures taken together represent the most accurate data on current language ecology that there is, but they are based on self-report, and limited in scope. There has never been reliable information on native language patterns in Singapore: rather researchers use intelligent guesses triangulated with what is available.

In a place as complex as Singapore, the choice of code is highly rule-governed. The home is a place of freedom and knowledge. Members of a family know the repertoires of the individuals and choose a code that is appropriate to either include or exclude other family members. Mixing of codes is routine and expected in the family setting, as is the use of colloquial varieties of the languages. In interactions with strangers, codes are selected on the basis of an assessment of the ethnic and social characteristics of the speaker, the **interlocutor** and the setting. The rules are complex and subtle. Many Singaporeans habitually use two or three or even four or more languages on a daily basis. This is an area of Singapore behaviour that has been little studied.

## Major Contributions and Work in Progress: Education and Language Shift

The story of languages in Singapore is one of language shift motivated by pragmatism and linked to educational policy, which in turn is linked to the politics of race. Until the middle of the twentieth century, most people spoke the language their ancestors had brought to Singapore, and often several other languages as well. Bazaar Malay had been established for centuries as a lingua franca over a wide region, and most of those who lived in Singapore had to learn it. The largest single Chinese dialect, Hokkien, was known by most of the Chinese population, and even by many non-Chinese, and also functioned as a lingua franca, especially within the Chinese population.

The colonial education policy provided education in the medium of Malay for Malays, and gave some support to education in English for the rest of the population. Most education in the mediums of English and Chinese was fee-paying, with a great deal of charitable and church involvement. Much of the Chinese-**medium education** was provided by community associations of various types and was in the medium of the dialect associated with the association. By 1900, about half of all boys had some education, but the literacy rate in females was less than 20% (there are details of this history in Bloom, 1986; Gupta, 1994). Between 1900 and 1920, participation in education rose dramatically and was extended to more social and ethnic groups, and both genders. Recruitment in English-medium schools increased faster than in any other medium. The effects of the change can still be seen in census reports: the younger you are, the more likely you are to be literate, and the more likely it is that one of the languages in which you are literate is English.

Education is a major tool of social engineering and is also the principal route of social and economic advancement: the bulk of the population is enthusiastic about education and keen for their children to achieve. **Tertiary education** in the medium of English became available in Singapore from 1929 and was available in Chinese from 1958. By the 1950s, girls were as likely to go to school as boys, more children were enrolled in English-medium schools than in any other medium, and someone who was literate in Chinese was likely to know Mandarin. There are two cornerstones of the racially based policy that has shaped modern Singapore:

- There are four official languages, but English is the language of government;
- There are three main 'racial' groups, each of which is recognised as distinct and whose culture is validated. Each group is associated with one of the official languages other than English (Malay, Mandarin Chinese, Tamil).

Education is highly controlled in Singapore, and it is usually not possible for Singaporean children to be privately educated in Singapore. In March 2004, the Ministry of Education announced that it would allow privately funded schools to be established that Singaporeans could attend, but these schools have not yet been developed: it is still best to think of private schools as being principally schools for foreigners. In 2003, education became compulsory for children over 6 years and below 15 years, but it was nearly half a century before it became compulsory.

Until the 1950s, education in the medium of English competed with education in the mediums of (Mandarin) Chinese, Tamil, and Malay. However, over the twentieth century, English-medium education became the most popular, and, from the 1950s onwards, all children were required to learn English, even if they were educated in some other medium. By the 1980s almost no children were educated in any other medium, and from 1987, all education under government control (which means all education for Singaporeans) was required to be principally or solely in the medium of English. Tertiary education in Chinese-medium had ended by 1978.

Since the 1950s it has been required that all children study a language in addition to English. Until 1981, children could choose any of the official languages, the main consequence of which was that, while most children studied the language congruent with their ancestry, some children of Chinese and Indian ancestry studied Malay. Malay, Mandarin, and Tamil are articulated by policy as being associated with the maintenance of culture and cohesiveness in the three racial groups, as providing 'cultural ballast'. Confusingly, the ethnically representative language is often referred to as the 'mother tongue': this does not imply anything about the child having grown up speaking the language, and Mandarin was rarely a native language until the 1970s. In 1979, the government began to strenuously promote Mandarin, encouraging its use by Chinese people in domains where formerly southern dialects were used. In line with this philosophy, the educational policy has been tightened up, so that (with rare exceptions) children are required to study the language associated with their official race. Virtually all Chinese children now study Chinese, and Malay is studied by few non-Malays.

The prescription of the language to be studied presents problems mainly to people of mixed ancestry, and to members of minority groups that have no affiliation to any of the three languages: the situation is especially fraught for the Indian community (PuruShotam, 1998; Schiffman, 2002). It also presents practical problems for Malays and Indians, because Malay and Tamil cannot be offered in as many schools as Chinese is. A further negative consequence is the emergence of many schools that are attended only by Chinese children. Regulations cap the proportion of minority children allowed in a school: there are no schools that are dominated by minority ethnic groups. Like minorities everywhere, the ethnic minorities of Singapore are more familiar with the majority than the majority are with them (Gupta, 1994).

The lack of opportunity for non-Chinese children in the school system to learn Mandarin, the language linked to the largest ethnic group, has often been commented on in the press, many members of minority groups feeling that they are linguistically excluded from some commercial and social activities dominated by Chinese-speakers. The policy has also resulted, in the 20 years of its operation, in a decrease in the knowledge of Malay by non-Malays, something that was commented on in the Singapore press (Straits Times, 18 February 2005) when Singapore sent help to victims of the Pacific tsunami of 26 December, 2004. Senior members of the government came to the realisation that non-Malays could not communicate with Indonesian authorities in Aceh (Sumatra is visible from Singapore), as the only younger Singaporeans to know Malay now are Malays. The decline in knowledge of cross-ethnic languages arises partly from the education policy having halted a move to Malay that had happened at the expense of Chinese and Indian languages, and partly because English is now available as a universal lingua franca in Singapore.

There has in recent years been some move to redress the ethnic separation that resulted from the prescription of the language to be studied. Within the state education system it has for some years been possible for only the most able students to study a third language formally, from the age of 12 years. Initially the languages offered were Malay, French, German and (for those who already knew Chinese) Japanese. Following a suggestion from the then Prime Minister, Goh Chok Tong in 2002, Chinese became available to academically able non-Chinese in this way from 2004. In response to continuing concerns expressed about the lack of cross-ethnic language knowledge, and in recognition of the fact that '[t]he ability to speak a third language is useful, and will help young Singaporeans of all races operate effectively in the region and beyond', there has been an extension of this third language scheme, so that '[f]rom 2007, Sec[ondary] One students will be allowed to offer another M[other] T[ongue] L[anguage] in addition to their native M[other] T[ongue] L[anguage], as long as they have the interest and inclination' (Ministry of Education, 2004). This means that students of all levels of ability may study Chinese or Malay, or, if there is demand, Tamil, as a third language, even if they do not have high marks in their primary school subjects. The extension of this scheme does make it possible in a limited way for children to learn cross-ethnic languages in school: it is not clear how many will take up the opportunity. Some schools also now have limited 'programmes for students to pick up conversational skills in either Malay language or Chinese language' (Ministry of Education, 2006).

The selection of English as the medium of education for all Singaporean children had an inevitability about it once Singapore broke away from Malaysia in 1965. English was already the dominant medium of education and it unified the racial groups. The negotiation of a potentially difficult racial situation is central to Singapore's politics. The People's Action Party has faced the difficult balancing act of being a small country with a clear Chinese majority enclosed by two large Malay nations (Gupta, 1994). The Chinese population of Singapore is the successor of a division between

'Chinese-educated' and 'English-educated' that is still to some extent linked to a class division, the 'English-educated' having been on average of higher social class, as are the English-focused of today (Kuo, 1976). The better educated you are, the better English you are likely to know, the richer you are likely to be, and the more likely you are to speak English to your parents. The move to universal English-medium education has broken this down to some extent, but there is still a perception that the Chinese of the 'HDB heartlands' or 'neighbourhoods' are Chinese-focused and perhaps chauvinistic. English is the bulwark against this, and Mandarin is the gesture towards this majority group.

The language policy has supplied a universal lingua franca, English, but has unfortunately produced some mono-ethnic (Chinese-only) schools and has reduced the opportunity to learn languages associated with racial groups other than one's own. The situation is a difficult one, and is under constant political discussion. The academic studies referenced here are a mixture of critiques of policy, and studies of how policies are being implemented.

Whenever a language is used as a medium of education, it is likely to become someone's best language. As education was extended to the whole population, the languages of education attracted speakers at the expense of other languages. It is not surprising that English should recruit people who prefer to speak it to any other language, and who speak it to their spouses and friends. And as a result of Mandarin being the variety of Chinese used in education, and because of the government's attacks on other Chinese dialects from 1979 onwards, the ancestral dialects of Chinese came to be seen as low prestige. Parents who can speak both school languages are likely to use them to their children because they think it is an advantage for their children to be able to speak the languages of education before they go to school. Moreover, most parents of school-age children now can speak both school languages, so that most children now come to kindergarten already able to speak both school languages.

Patterns of intermarriage have long promoted language shift in the cosmopolitan cities of the Malay region. There is widespread intermarriage of different 'dialect groups' within the Chinese community, facilitated by the post-1960 breaking up of the ethnic residential enclaves and by the spread of education. Intermarriage across ethnic boundaries within the Muslim population (84% of whom were officially Malay in 2000) has been commonplace for centuries and through processes of assimilation Malay has also largely displaced related languages like Javanese and Boyanese. English-focused Chinese and Indian Singaporeans of high social class are also likely to intermarry, especially if they are Christian. The fact that only paternal ancestry is recorded makes it hard to estimate just what proportion of the population is mixed in some sense. The languages that benefit from intermarriage are English, Mandarin and Malay.

The use of Mandarin in education from the 1920s created a Chinese population that had a latent knowledge of Mandarin, but used it little. As a result of the drive to switch to Mandarin, over the 1980s oral use of Mandarin in social interaction rocketed, and it is now probably the single largest native language of children under 10 (Gupta, 1994).

Over the generations, the languages passed down to children have changed – Mandarin and English have gained many native and non-native speakers; Malay has gained native speakers but is less commonly learnt as a non-native language; and all other languages (especially Indian languages, languages closely related to Malay, and dialects of Chinese other than Mandarin) have lost native and (especially in the case of Hokkien) non-native speakers. New lingua francas have emerged. In the nineteenth century, the main lingua franca across racial lines was (Bazaar) Malay, while among the Chinese it was Hokkien. Now, English is the main lingua franca, with Mandarin an important lingua franca in the Chinese community. English, and even more so Mandarin, are relatively new in the linguistic ecology of Singapore.

English spread to the whole population over the course of the twentieth century. It is hard to find a Singaporean under 60 who cannot speak English, but in a snapshot of the present we see the past—the younger you are, and the higher your social status, the more likely you are to have English as a native language and to speak it in more domains. However, by the late twentieth century, English was not *restricted* to the social elite, as it had been in earlier generations. The link of English with particular ethnic groups is relatively weak, though the minority groups (Malays and, especially, Indians) are more likely to use English in more domains. The rise of Mandarin has promoted unity among the Chinese population, but Mandarin has spread in some domains at the expense of English, giving rise to some dissatisfaction in other ethnic groups.

Those born roughly 1930–1960 were the most multilingual generation, especially the Chinese, who were typically able to speak English, two or three varieties of Chinese, and Bazaar Malay (Murray, 1971; Platt and Weber, 1980). Their parents and grandparents may have spoken just the ancestral language, plus one or two lingua francas (English, Hokkien, Malay), and their children probably speak just English and the official language of their race, possibly making them unable to converse with their own grandparents, which is the tragic consequence of rapid language shift.

## FUTURE DIRECTIONS

Singapore continues to change. One of the most apparent recent changes is that a remarkably high proportion of those who live in modern Singapore are now non-citizens. There has been a considerable rise in the number of foreigners living in Singapore, from 10% of the population in 1970 and 14% in 1990 to 26% of the population in 2000, and the revelation of this in the 2000 census returns was the subject of extensive comment in the press.

In the reports on the 2000 census, information on most questions is recorded only for Singapore 'residents', who are defined as Singapore citizens plus foreigners with a permanent right to reside in Singapore. Apart from visitors, and children at boarding schools in Singapore, there are two groups of 'non-resident' foreigners living in Singapore—low-paid 'work permit holders' and high-paid 'employment pass holders'. The overwhelming majority of 'non-resident' foreigners living in Singapore are work permit holders in low-paid manual and domestic jobs, most of them from Indonesia, South Asia, and the Philippines. There is legal and societal discrimination against them, although, according to the ILO the conditions under which they work compare favourably to conditions for similar workers elsewhere (Ofori, 1998). The status of the (diverse) higher prestige group of foreigners is closer to that of the Singaporean population, and as they are allowed to be accompanied by family members, some groups have established private schools following, for example, the British, American, Canadian, French, German, Japanese and Swiss curricula.

Foreigners who become Singapore residents still come predominantly from the three traditional sources: the Malay region, India and China. Some of the 'resident' population born outside Singapore are the children of citizens temporarily overseas, but the majority are likely to have, or to have been born with, another nationality. The world's population has become highly mobile, and especially the Chinese. 82% of Singapore 'residents' born outside Singapore are described as 'Chinese:' Singapore is attracting diasporic Chinese from all over the world. The effect on language ecology is likely to further strengthen the two strongest languages, English and Mandarin.

There are moral, hegemonic and ideological issues around the choice of medium of education and associated language shift, which will continue to be explored in relation to Singapore (Pennycook, 1994; Phillipson, 1992; Skutnabb-Kangas, 2000). Language shift in Singapore appears to have taken place rapidly in relatively happy circumstances, associated with the rise in participation in education, and in a context of increasing prosperity and social equity. It has also taken place in a region with a long tradition of openness to multiple cultures and languages: Singapore is the latest in a long line of cosmopolitan trading ports in the Malay Region, and pragmatism is what it is about. At the moment the dominant languages in Singapore are English and Mandarin, but, should the need arise, Singapore could just as rapidly adjust to a Chinese, Malay, or even Arabic, focus.

The identification of Mandarin Chinese, Malay and Tamil as 'Mother Tongues' reflects past and current patterns of migration, and shapes what is seen as 'Singaporean'. There is still an ambivalence towards English, which is a vital language in Singapore, but which is still seen within Singapore as in some senses 'foreign'. At official and unofficial levels, for example, it is not accepted that a large proportion of Singaporeans are native speakers of English: when the government discusses the use of 'native speakers of English' in education, they mean people from countries such as the UK, USA and Australia.

The central role of education in a directed policy of language shift is unusually clearly articulated in Singapore. It is hard to know what constitutes free choice of language and what constitutes coercion, and this is something that scholars need to continue to explore. Perhaps the distinction is meaningless. De Swaan (2001) shows how individuals make choices, defend their rights to choice, and shows how individuals will only respond to governmental decisions on language if they correspond with the actual communication value of a language. He celebrates 'complex language constellations' and bilingualism, and the fact that lingua francas have increased 'the coherence of the human species in its entirety' (p. 186). I personally endorse these views. I do not think our present is determined by our ancestral endowment: nearly all of us must have ancestors who at one point or another were engaged in language shift, and each generation changes the culture of its parents. Language shift need not damage the individual or the society that engages in it. We are actors in a real world of functional language, and of change, and that is the context in which the language ecology of Singapore has taken place, and will continue to take place.

## Notes

1. The terms used for ethnic groups, languages and dialects are always problematic. I have used the terms currently used in official Singapore documents and glossed them by alternatives. The variety called 'Mandarin Chinese' can also be called 'Modern Standard Chinese' and is also known as *guoyu* ('national language'), though this implies a political evaluation that would be regarded as inappropriate in modern Singapore. I use 'Malay' in its widest sense, to refer to all dialects, including the standard varieties of Malaysia, Brunei, Singapore and Indonesia. Singapore designates English, Malay, Mandarin and Tamil as its official languages. Malay is the 'national language', which is a ceremonial designation.

## References


Benjamin, G. 1976. 'The cultural logic of Singapore's 'multiracialism',' in R. Hassan (ed.), *Singapore: A Society in Transition*, Oxford University Press, Kuala Lumpur, 115–33.

Bloom, D. 1986. 'The English language and Singapore: A critical survey', in B. K. Kapur (ed.) *Singapore Studies*, Singapore University Press, Singapore, 337–458.

Bowrey, T. 1701. *A Dictionary of English and Malayo, Malayo and English*, for the author, London.

Chua, B-H. 1995. *Communitarian Ideology and Democracy in Singapore*, Routledge, London/New York.

Crawfurd, J. 1856. *A Descriptive Dictionary of the Indian Isles and Adjacent Countries*, Bradbury and Evans, London.

de Houtman van Gouda, F. 1603. *Spraekende woord-boeck Inde Maleysche ende Madgaskarische Talen*, Jan Ebertsz, Amsterdam.

de Swaan, A. 2001. *Words of the World*, Polity, Cambridge.

Gopinathan, S., Pakir, A., Ho W. K., and Saravanan, V. (eds.) 1998. *Language, Society and Education in Singapore: Issues and Trends* (second edition), Times Academic Press, Singapore.

Gupta, A. F. 1994. *The Step-Tongue: Children's English in Singapore*, Multilingual Matters, Clevedon.

Hamilton, W. 1815. *The East Indian Gazeteer*, John Murray, London.

Kuo, E. C. Y. 1976. 'A sociolinguistic profile', in R. Hassan (ed.), *Singapore: A Society in Transition*, Oxford University Press, Kuala Lumpur, 135–48.

Lau Kak En. 1993. Singapore Census of Population 1990, Department of Statistics, Singapore (especially Statistical Release 1: Demographic characteristics and Statistical Release 3: Literacy, Languages Spoken and Education).

Leow Bee Geok. 2001. Census of Population 2000, Singapore Department of Statistics, Singapore (especially Statistical Release 2: Education, language and religion).

Marsden, W. 1812a. A Dictionary of the Malayan Language, for the author, London.

Marsden, W. 1812b. A Grammer of the Malayan Language, Longman, London.

Miksic, J. N. 2004. '14th-century Singapore: A port of trade', in J. N. Miksic and C-A. Low Mei Gek (eds.), *Early Singapore: 1300s–1819*, Singapore History Museum, Singapore, 41–54.

Ministry of Education. 2004. Non-Native Mother Tongue Language as a Third Language, Press release, 29 September. www.moe.gov.sg/press/2004/pr20040929c.htm

Ministry of Education. 2006. FY 2006 Committee of Supply Debate, 4th Reply by MOS Chan on Gifted Education, Pre-School Education, Mother Tongue Languages etc., 8 March. www.moe.gov.sg/speeches/2006/sp20060308a.htm [Accessed August 2006]

Murray, D. 1971. *Multilanguage Education and Bilingualism: The Formation of Social Brokers in Singapore*, PhD, Stanford University.

Ofori, G. 1998. *Foreign Construction Workers in Singapore*, International Labour Organization. www.ilo.org/public/english/dialogue/sector/papers/forconst/forcon5.htm. [Accessed March 2005]

Pennycook, A. 1994. *The Cultural Politics of English as an International Language*, Longman, London/New York.

Phillipson, R. 1992. *Linguistic Imperialism*, Oxford University Press, Oxford.

Platt, J. and Weber, H. 1980. *English in Singapore and Malaysia*, Oxford University Press, Kuala Lumpur.

PuruShotam, N. S. 1998. *Negotiating Language, Contructing Race: Disciplining Differences in Singapore*, Mouton de Gruyter, Berlin/New York.

Saw Swee-Hock. 1981. *Demographic Trends in Singapore, Census Monograph No. 1*, Department of Statistics, Singapore.

Schiffman, H. 2002. 'Tamil linguistic culture and Malaysian national culture', *Language and Communication* 22(2), 159–69.

Skutnabb-Kangas, T. 2000. *Linguistic Genocide in Education—or Worldwide Diversity and Human Rights?*, Lawrence Erlbaum, Mahwah, NJ.

Tan, J., Gopinathan, S., and Ho Wah Kam (eds.). 1997. *Education in Singapore: A Book of Readings*, Prentice Hall, Singapore.

Tay, M. W. J. 1983. *Trends in Language, Literacy and Education in Singapore, Census Monography No. 2*, Department of Statistics, Singapore.

Tremewan, C. 1994. *The Political Economy of Social Control in Singapore*, St Martin's Press, Basingstoke/London.

Wheatley, P. 1961. *The Golden Khersonese*, University of Malaya Press, Kuala Lumpur.

## Critical Thinking and Application

- Why do you think English was selected as the medium within which all Singaporean children are educated, no matter what their national, "racial," or ethnic background?
- How have changing world politics affected language policy and education policy within Singapore? How might you expect them to change in the near future?
- What social values are negotiated through education policy?
- Research the language ecology of other complex settings in the world, looking especially for information about the census, education policy, language shift, and the relative power of each language.

## Vocabulary

colonialism
contact variety
indigeneity
interlocutor
language ecology
language shift
lingua franca
-medium school
social engineering
tertiary education

## Suggested Further Reading

Anderson, Benedict. 1983. *Imagined Communities: Reflections on the Origin and Spread of Nationalism*. London: Verso.

Creese, Angela, Peter Martin, and Nancy H. Hornberger, eds. 2008. Ecology of Language. *Encyclopedia of Language and Education* (Vol. 9). New York: Springer.

Foley, Joseph. 1988. *New Englishes: The Case of Singapore*. Singapore: Singapore University Press.

Haugen, Einar Ingvald. 1972. *The Ecology of Language*. Stanford, CA: Stanford University Press.

Lian, Kwen Fee. 2006. *Race, Ethnicity, and the State in Malaysia and Singapore*. Leiden: Brill.

Lim, Lisa. 2004. *Singapore English: A Grammatical Description*. Philadelphia: Benjamins.

McCrum, Robert. 2010. *Globish: How English Became the World's Language*. New York: Norton.

Schiffman, Harold F. 2002. *Linguistic Culture and Language Policy*. London and New York: Routledge.

Seargeant, Philip. 2009. *The Idea of English in Japan: Ideology and the Evolution of a Global Language*. Bristol: Multilingual Matters.

## Individual Multilingualism

# CHAPTER 23

# Bilingualism *en casa*

*Ana Celia Zentella*

(1997)

*Bilingualism is a special case of multilingualism, which is the norm around the world. Like multilingual people, bilingual individuals employ two languages in very subtle ways. They know in which situations to use one language or the other, or when they converse with fellow bilinguals which topics, or which aspects of which topics, call for a specific language. This knowledge is gained very young, as they move from setting to setting and interact with others.*

*Ana Celia Zentella conducted a careful study of a Puerto Rican community in New York City, looking at patterns of language use among not just "English" and "Spanish" in a neighborhood in Spanish Harlem (East Harlem). In her book,* Growing Up Bilingual: Puerto Rican Children in New York, *from which this chapter is derived, she identified three different varieties of Spanish (Popular Puerto Rican Spanish, Standard Puerto Rican Spanish, and English-dominant Spanish) and four different varieties of English (Puerto Rican English, African American Vernacular English, Hispanized English, and Standard New York City English), as well as "Spanglish." For a period of about eighteen months, she interacted with and observed numerous families and their children, using participant observation and interviews to get to know intimately how people used language.*

*What is clear from the complexity of Zentella's account in this chapter is that bilinguals do not simply throw in random phrases or words from one language or another, but they must master a subtle set of patterns and rules for gauging the linguistic capacities and identities of the people with whom they converse. As in many settings where bilingualism is the result of migration, children are more learned in the language of the new society (English, in this case) than their elders are. While their caregivers might address them in Spanish (as is common), children might respond in either Spanish or English, and they frequently speak English among themselves. Gender, level of involvement in the outside English-speaking world, type of employment, age, and many other factors are involved in people's mastery and use of various codes.*

*An old view of bilinguals is that they often suffered cognitive deficiency as a result of their bilingualism, but it is evident from more recent data that navigating this complex world calls for very detailed social and linguistic knowledge.*

*It is not only impersonal rules that govern which language should be employed at any given moment but also speakers' individual preferences. Some people are directed inwardly, toward* el bloque, *while others spend more time and attention at activities in the English-dominant world.*

*The term* code-switching *(also written as* codeswitching *or* code switching*) refers to the movement from one language ("code") to another, whether in different situations or even within the same sentence ("intrasentential code switches"). Scholars accounting for the switches have observed many important things about this phenomenon, including the fact that it follows precise grammatical rules and gives evidence of the speaker's attitude toward what is said.*

### Reading Questions

- Why do some siblings differ in their linguistic preferences?
- How does gender play a role in determining which language is most likely to be used?

Ana Celia Zentella, Bilingualism *en casa*. From *Growing Up Bilingual: Puerto Rican Children in New York*. Malden, MA: Blackwell, 1997, pp. 56–79.

- What rules of politeness come into play when people are deciding which language to use with a new conversational partner?
- What educational experiences do you see described in this chapter?
- Zentella writes of Lolita's "meta-linguistic awareness." What is this? Why does she have it? How might this be channeled into academic success more broadly for other bilingual children?

---

A knock on the door of any of the apartments that housed the families of *el bloque* was greeted by "WHO?" or "*¿Quién es*?" ("Who is it?"), or both. The lone English interrogative was most popular, even with Spanish-dominant occupants. Children greeted me in English because they knew that I was a teacher, but they ran to call an adult in Spanish. Inside the door, residents addressed visitors predominantly in English or Spanish, in a consistent pattern. The bilingual-multidialectal repertoire of the home approximated that of the block, with some limitations: standard and non-standard Puerto Rican Spanish **(SPRS/NSPRS)**, Hispanized English **(HE)**, and Puerto Rican English **(PRE)** predominated. The vernacular of African Americans **(AAVE)** was heard less frequently than on the street, and no one spoke standard English consistently at home. PRS, PRE, and alternating between them, constituted the basic verbal repertoire for the four communication **dyads** at home:

1. the language(s) that caretakers spoke to each other
2. the language(s) that caretakers spoke to children
3. the language(s) that children spoke to caretakers
4. the language(s) that children spoke to each other

Theoretically, a large number of patterns was possible, since each dyad could be realized by one of nine combinations:

| | | |
|---|---|---|
| Span-Eng | Span-Span | Span-Both |
| Eng-Eng | Eng-Span | Eng-Both |
| Both-Eng | Both-Span | Both-Both |

In practice, the 20 homes of *el bloque's* families fell under six major language configurations (see Table 23.1).

The major patterns at home can be described as follows:

1. Caregivers spoke Spanish among themselves and addressed children in Spanish. Children answered adults in Spanish but spoke English and Spanish to each other.
2. Caregivers were fluent in both English and Spanish. They spoke both languages among themselves (except single mothers, #s 2 and 8) and to children. Children responded predominantly in English, and favored English among themselves.
3. Caregivers spoke Spanish to each other. One spoke to the children in Spanish and the other spoke Spanish and English. The children talked Spanish and English to their caregivers and among themselves.
4. All communication among caregivers and children was carried out in Spanish, but the children were too young to speak more than a few words.
5. Caregivers communicated in English with each other and the males spoke English to the children, but mothers talked to them in Spanish and English. The children in 5a in Table 23.1 spoke English to their parents and to each other, but

**Table 23.1** Language Dyads Within *el bloque's* Families

| Caregiver(s) to Each Other | Caregiver(s) to Child(ren) | Child(ren) to Caregiver(s) | Children to Each Other |
|---|---|---|---|
| 1 Families #4, 5, 7, 9, 10, 11<br>Spanish | Spanish | Spanish | English and Spanish |
| 2 Families #2, 8, 17, 18, 19<br>English and Spanish | English and Spanish | English | English |
| 3 Families #12, 13, 15<br>Spanish | One = Spanish,<br>One = Spanish and English | Spanish and English | English and Spanish |
| 4 Families #3, 14<br>Spanish | Spanish | Spanish | Spanish |
| 5a Family #16<br>English | One = English<br>One = Spanish and English | English | English |
| 5b Family #20<br>English<br>(Anglo male) | Anglo = English only<br>Mother, Spanish and English | English to Anglo<br>Spanish and English to mother | Spanish and English |
| 6a Family #6<br>(mother alone) | Spanish | Spanish and English | English |
| 6b Family #1<br>(mother alone) | Spanish and English | Spanish and English | (only child) |

those in 5b distinguished between their caregivers by interacting with the Anglo male in English and with the mother in Spanish and English. They talked both languages to each other.

6. The mothers were single and Spanish dominant. One mother (#6) spoke Spanish to her children but the other (#1) spoke Spanish and English to her child. Children in both families talked to their mothers in Spanish and English, but they preferred English with their siblings and/or friends.

This overview necessarily obscures many differences among and within families; ultimately there were almost as many language patterns as families because of the unique configurations of several variables, including the number of caregivers and children, and differences in language proficiency, education, bilingual literacy skills, years in the US, gender and age of each speaker. Even if every caregiver-caregiver, caregiver-child, and child-child communication dyad were specified, other crucial input in the linguistic development of the children would be missing. The following profiles of three families, representative of categories 1, 3, and 5 in Table 23.1, respectively, bring to life the multiple, contrasting, and ever changing linguistic demands that were made on the children of *el bloque* at home.

## PROFILE I PACA AND HERMAN AT HOME WITH MAGDA

The ideal Puerto Rican family includes at least one *parejita* ("couple"), a boy and a girl, born in that order approximately two or more years apart. Very few women wanted more than two or three children, but some who bore only males or females continued to have children until a girl or a boy was born. Magda was fortunate; two years after she had Herman at age 20, her daughter Paca was born. In 1979, Magda was living apart from her husband, Paca was six years old and had just completed one year of half-day kindergarten in the local public school, and eight-year-old Herman had completed third grade in the same school's bilingual program. During the following year, a number of changes in their home and school lives produced contrasting language experiences which alternately strengthened their English and weakened their Spanish, and vice versa.

Paca and Herman were the only children on the first floor of the building sandwiched between one of the *bodegas* and the pinball storefront.... Their two-bedroom apartment was at the end of the hall—a dangerous location because their windows faced the back alley—but advantageous in other respects. They did not have to climb stairs, and all who went up or down the five flights were forced to pass their door, so they knew everyone's whereabouts. Also, children played in the hall all year long; its narrow passageway was ideal for a junior version of baseball, learning how to maneuver a bicycle, and racing battery-operated toys. No traditional Puerto Rican games were known to the children, and all play was carried on without adult participation, in English with some Spanish code switches.

The next door neighbors were elderly Spanish speakers, whom Paca and Herman greeted with short Spanish phrases. When the children were drafted to help carry groceries or strollers, those interactions occurred in Spanish and English. On errands to the *bodega*, they repeated the adult's Spanish request. The different language backgrounds of the people Paca and Herman encountered in the hall, the *bodega*, and on the street required constant code switching in accordance with the addressee's dominant language.

Because Paca and Herman had excellent access to the main areas for congregating, they spent a good deal of time with other children. In fair weather they were often outside until 9 P.M. after Magda returned from work and on weekends. Herman was allowed to go around the corner to the pizza shop, because he was older and because he was a boy, although he was supposed to ask permission to do so. As the year progressed, Herman roller skated and rode his bicycle further distances on forays away from *el bloque*. On one occasion Paca petulantly pointed out that her brother was not restricted as she was, but her older cousin Dylcia said, "*Déjalo, él es macho*" ("Let him, he's a male"). Paca usually was with a female adult; Herman often was nowhere in sight.

Paca and Herman underwent dramatic changes in their daily routine in the course of one year. They changed apartments three times, they changed baby sitters twice, and Paca changed schools. One person remained constant—their mother Magda. Due to her efforts, their schooling proceeded with few interruptions. Their daily routine began at 7 A.M.: Magda woke, fed, and dressed them as the Spanish radio warned her of the fleeting time at five-minute intervals. Magda dropped Paca off at school on her way to her job as housekeeper for a shut-in who lived ten blocks away. Paca was picked up from school at 3 o'clock by her baby sitter, with whom she stayed until about 6 or 7 P.M. when her mother called for her. Herman walked the three blocks to another school in the morning with children from the block. He was in a bilingual class and attended an after-school program conducted in English. Magda picked him up on her way home from work at 5.30 P.M. Paca's baby sitter also looked after Herman during the summer and on all school holidays.

When the study began, the household also included Magda's 23-year-old niece Dylcia, who had migrated from Puerto Rico with her 12-month-old daughter Jennie seven months earlier. Dylcia, a high school graduate, was three months pregnant, spoke no English, and had no job or income. She helped her aunt with the chores and the children, and in turn Paca and Herman helped with Jennie. Dylcia could not be counted on as a permanent baby sitter because her future plans were up in the air. Four months later she moved into an empty apartment on the fifth floor with Luís, the college student who had introduced me to *el bloque*.

For five years, Paca and Herman were looked after by one of the block's most beloved residents, Dolores, a good-natured woman in her forties who had raised six children of her own and 13 others over a period of 20 years on the block. Dolores was credited with having nursed Paca to health after doctors had given her slim chances for survival shortly after birth. Magda trusted and loved Dolores as if she were an older sister, and she lavished the best gifts on her that her limited salary allowed. To Paca and many other children Dolores was *Mamá*. The children she helped raise dropped by regularly and three of her former charges came from Puerto Rico to spend their summer vacation with her. During the years when she was taking care of Paca and Herman, Dolores' apartment—really two apartments with a wall broken through to connect them—was constantly full with some of the 22 members of her family who were part of *el bloque*. Participation in this setting demanded rapid alternation of Spanish and English. Paca and Herman learned the **intra-sentential code switching** that was common among the second generation, but they also got practice in speaking Spanish to Dolores.

When the city began a limited housekeeping service for indigent shut-ins, Dolores began to clean and cook for some of *El Barrio*'s senior citizens, a paying job which could be performed in Spanish. Dolores had worked at home raising others' children along with her own, but she did not always charge for her services. Magda, for example, had not been able to pay her a regular salary because she could not find a steady job. She had completed three years of high school in Puerto Rico and had lived in NYC for eight years, but like Dolores, Magda had never carried on a conversation in English. Stable employment was out of her reach until the housekeeping program hired her upon Dolores' recommendation. When Dolores and Magda found jobs, Paca and Herman had to be left with a new baby sitter, one who was trustworthy, available, and nearby. One of Dolores' daughters-in-law, 20-year-old Vicky, fulfilled the prerequisites. She lived in the same building with Dolores' son, Güiso, and was known to take good care of their three-year-old boy, Eddie. Vicky was unable to work outside of the home because she was expecting another baby.

Several aspects of the new baby sitting arrangement were different. Paca and Herman were no longer immersed in an extended Spanish-English family; Vicky and Güiso, both US born, spoke English to each other and to their toddler (see Profile III). Afternoons and school vacations were spent playing with Eddie in English, watching English television programs, and singing along with the radio's English lyrics. The importance of Spanish in their lives diminished further when Dolores' long-standing application for public housing was granted, and she moved seven blocks away. Paca and Herman no longer saw her every day, although they spent some weekends with her. Eight months later, a fire set by a disturbed alcoholic left many apartments uninhabitable. Magda and her children were relocated in a hotel across town, and then they moved three more times: to another hotel, to the father's basement apartment, and to Dolores' project apartment. Traveling was expensive, time-consuming, and painful in the cold, but they made daily trips to the block to watch over their belongings in their burned-out home. After three months, the city began to repair the building, and Magda, Paca, and Herman returned to the block. During this period of upheaval, the children missed several days of school despite Magda's strenuous efforts to get them to class every day and to get to her own job. Vicky took care of them after school. Paca became Vicky's little helper, carefully dressing and feeding the boys. She was gentle and patient with demanding Eddie, who at three years of age weighed more than Paca and tended to grab and punch a lot. Herman and Paca always spoke to the boys in English, and their English vocabulary and syntax increased notably over the year. As the school year progressed, Paca and Herman spoke more English than Spanish to each other.

After six years of predominantly Spanish-filled days, Paca participated in a full school day in English in the local Catholic school's first grade. She stayed with Vicky until Magda completed her errands after work, and did her homework under Vicky's supervision in English. When winter darkness and cold set in, Paca and Herman spent more time indoors, playing with separate groups of friends or alone, but rarely with each other. Paca went to bed by 9 p.m. but Herman stayed up late watching television in English. When his mother had visitors, he played with toys or watched television, never participating in the conversations. Dylcia dubbed him "*el rey de la casa*" ("the king of the house") because he had few responsibilities and generally determined his own schedule.

Magda's day began at 6 a.m. and often ended after midnight. After work, she shopped, cooked, swept, washed and ironed clothes. Paca and Herman always were smartly and neatly dressed in the latest fashions, which—along with baby sitting fees—ate up a good part of her salary. Her cramped two-bedroom apartment had no closets, little furniture or decorations, many leaks, cracks, and roaches, and her chores took most of her free time. She rarely sat, except to see a *novela*. She was interested in many topics, but was a quiet woman who listened more than she spoke, perhaps because of a speech impediment. Neighbors who dropped by stood in the kitchen doorway while she went on with tasks similar to the ones she did all day for an invalid.

The tiny kitchen had no table, so each child was given a plate of food and ate in the living room, often at different times. Paca was a poor eater, and received weekly injections for anemia; the refrigerator door was full of her medicines. Magda usually fed her frail daughter to make sure she ate, and those feedings included mother-daughter chats in Spanish. When visitors came, Paca often sat and listened to the women talk. Magda spent blocks of time with her children only on weekends. She never played with them, but she took them to visit Dolores or their father, and on shopping trips downtown. She also sought out organized excursions and was the only parent who ever joined my outings to zoos, beaches, puppet shows, and parks. On those trips she was constantly concerned for their welfare and safety getting on and off subways or crossing the street. She did not take on a "teacher" role, that is, expounding, explaining, comparing, or asking questions meant to instruct, and she depended on Herman to interpret for her. A good reader, he read signs, asked questions and directions, made purchases and explained procedures to his mother. Magda was left out of the conversation when the children competed for my hand and attention with constant questions in English. Whenever Paca and Herman played with other children, they spoke in English, and she did not understand what they were talking about. They spoke Spanish only when addressing her, usually for short comments or requests. Magda was a concerned, responsible, and hardworking mother whose Spanish monolingualism left her at the periphery of most of her children's activities; she was more a provider and a watchdog than a participant.

Magda chose Catholic school for her daughter because Herman had been in several fights in the public school, and after looking into [the incidents] she characterized the school as lacking in discipline. Fearing that the diminutive Paca would not be well protected there, she sacrificed to pay for Catholic school. Paca cried often during the first three weeks in her English-only classroom, and said she had no friends there. By October she seemed to have adjusted, although Catholic school did not turn out to be a totally safe environment. There were schoolyard incidents in which others took advantage of her slight build, but she defended herself and claimed victory in at least one instance. Those narratives were vividly reported in Spanish to her mother and in English to her playmates. She was getting so accustomed to English that she even called to her mother in English one day, asking her to corroborate her age; "I'm six [said five times], Mami, right I'm six?" No one commented on the fact that Paca had addressed her mother in English, and I never heard her do it again.

The nuns sent Paca home with a preliminary progress report which indicated she was about average in most areas, although she had not kept up with all homework assignments. The report became the only wall adornment in the apartment; it was taped near the entrance and visitors commented on it. Paca's given name was written at the top—Ivón. A few months later Paca said she preferred Yvonne /ivan/, i.e., the English spelling and pronunciation. On the block, everyone continued to call her by her nickname, Paca, with its Spanish pronunciation. Once a friend jokingly used exaggerated English phonology (/pha:kha:/); Paca looked amazed and repeated it in a disbelieving tone. Still, she continued to prefer the English /ivan/ over the Spanish /ibon/, just like her friends Lolita, Isabel, Blanca, and Elli preferred the English pronunciations of their names. Toward the end of the year Paca also commented on Puerto Rican nicknames: "*¿Por qué la gente en español tiene* funny names?" ("Why do people in Spanish have funny names?"). Her code switching was increasing along with her awareness of dominant cultural norms, and her distancing from those of the home culture. During the first months of taping, Paca rated herself a better Spanish than English speaker, "or both a little." She used to greet me and other bilingual adults in Spanish, and adhered to the community norm by responding in Spanish if she was addressed in it. By the summer of the following year, she greeted us in English and she did not always switch to Spanish if it was directed at her, unless the addressee was a monolingual Spanish speaker.

A house guest from Puerto Rico, Magda's sister, offset the English avalanche. The older woman often played with her young niece, and she was an articulate speaker with captivating narratives about family incidents and superstitions in their home town. Paca was an eager listener, and she asked about topics or words unknown to her, for example, "*¿Qué son 'leyendas'?*" ("What are 'legends'?"), "*¿Qué es 'cariño'?*" ("What is 'affection'?"), and "*¿Qué es 'relación'?*" ("What is 'relationship'?"). Paca made developmental errors, for example, "*juegaba*" and "*sueñé*" instead of *jugaba* ("I used to play") and *soñé* ("I dreamt"), which went uncorrected. A few of her errors caused laughter, for example when Magda told the group: "*A Herman le gusta més Puerto Rico porque quiere que le compre un caballo.*" ("Herman likes Puerto Rico better because he wants me to buy him a horse"), Paca piped up with: "*Uy mami! ¿Tú me puedes comprar una caballa?*" ("Oh mommy! Can you buy me a horse-feminine?") Her aunt laughingly commented "*porque es femenina*" ("because it's/she's? feminine"), but no one explained the joke to Paca, and she did not ask why everyone had laughed.

When Paca sat in on the conversations of her Spanish-speaking elders, she behaved according to appropriate Puerto Rican norms for children. She did not break into the conversation precipitously, often waiting up to six turns, tentatively attempting to speak at turn exchange points with "*y-y-y*" ("and-and-and"), softly calling the names of the speakers, and asking permission, e.g., "*con permiso*" ("excuse me"). Despite her increasing preference for English with me, Paca honored the language of adult Spanish conversations by addressing me in Spanish when she intended to participate in such a discussion. Switching languages for parts of sentences was rare in either her Spanish or English contributions in that setting. Her short exchanges in English either were not related to the adult topic or were asides meant specifically for someone who was English-dominant.

Paca's turn-taking behavior and the pitch of her voice during the Spanish discussions contrasted sharply with her English contributions in group settings. The latter were often high-pitched or shrill, and competitive; she interrupted others in a loud demanding tone. Since most of the English conversations in which she participated were with children (because she was not exposed to similar gatherings of monolingual English-speaking adults), we can assume that her more aggressive linguistic behavior in English was a function of what Philips (1972) called the "participant structures," that is, Paca learned that interacting with female adults required not only Spanish but certain respectful behaviors regarding the way Spanish was spoken, but she talked with peers in English and in a more contentious manner.

Herman always referred to himself with the English version of his name and spoke more fluent English than Paca, but he too had the opportunity to strengthen his command of Spanish during 1979–80. He was in a bilingual class, and he had Spanish monolingual friends for a while when three boys emigrated from Puerto Rico, with whom he communicated easily. After four months, however, two of the families returned to Puerto Rico, and the father of the remaining boy severely curtailed his son's activities. Herman resumed hanging out with long-time block residents who spoke more English than Spanish. By the end of the year, Herman, like Paca but even more so, initiated Spanish and responded in it only when he had to talk with a diminishing number of Spanish monolinguals. Nevertheless, Herman's mother was proud of the fact that he could read and write Spanish and English, skills learned in the bilingual program. He read the Spanish newspapers and cards and letters that arrived from Puerto Rico. His English reading ability was at grade level in school, and he read comic books, game instructions, subway signs, and Monopoly Community Chest cards with ease. Herman himself claimed he spoke both languages equally well, and this appeared to be the case; he was a more balanced bilingual than Paca. After observing them for two years, I thought that both Herman and Paca would grow up to be English-dominant bilinguals, but that Paca's skills in Spanish would be better than Herman's as he became more disconnected from the family and *el bloque* and Paca became more immersed in the Spanish-dominant female networks....

No Spanish-speaking adult ever stopped Herman and Paca from speaking English to each other, and only rarely did they ask for translations of what was said in that language. The implicit rule seemed to be that if the children had anything to say that concerned the adults, they would say it in Spanish. English was another "channel" for children and their activities. This acceptance of English at home contradicted Magda's response to a question concerning the appropriate domains for Spanish and English. When she was asked whether there were any times or places when the children should speak only Spanish or only English, she answered that they should speak Spanish at home and English outside whenever there was anyone around who did not understand Spanish. In fact, Magda never insisted that the children speak only Spanish at home, but they were expected to speak it to her and to their relatives from Puerto Rico. Most of the parents expressed a greater concern for accommodating English speakers who could not understand Spanish than for accommodating Spanish monolinguals. This imbalance may be interpreted as an indication that the need to speak Spanish was a given, especially *en casa*, but the repeated concern for the predicament of English monolinguals pointed to the symbolic dominance exerted by English. It paralleled the frequent refrain that "It is important to know English" or "Everybody should know English"; similar expressions about the importance of knowing Spanish were rarer. Paca's family spoke positively about being bilingual, but they referred to it in terms of adding English to one's linguistic repertoire, not in terms of adding Spanish.

## Profile II Lolita and Marta at Home with Armando and Lourdes

Lolita, eight years old, was born and raised on the block and lived with her 16-year-old sister Marta, her mother Lourdes (36), and her father Armando (40). Armando had lived there for several years before his 17-year marriage and was one of the best-known members of the community. He was a high school graduate, had some college credits, had been an army officer, and was a skilled electrician, but because of the massive layoffs that occurred when the city almost declared bankruptcy in the mid-seventies, he had been unemployed for four years when we met. His problems with alcohol worsened as the years went by. Armando spent most of his time with Spanish-speaking men in the *bodega* network, but he was fluent in English and was the only block resident who spoke of extensive contacts with Black residents of the projects across the street.[1]

Lolita's father was recognized as a good speaker of standard Spanish and he held strong opinions about language; for example, he was very vocal about the value of being bilingual: "*Son dos personas en una.*" ("They are two people in one.") His pride in his own fluency in both languages, and that of his children, was stated often. Armando reproached Puerto Ricans for a lack of linguistic ability and language consciousness, claiming that Puerto Ricans did not speak real Spanish ("*el español verdadero*"), and that they did not prepare for tomorrow's world. He laid special blame at the feet of Puerto Rican parents; if their children did not speak Spanish, parents should stress it: "*Los padres no hacen énfasis.*" ("The parents don't emphasize it.") Armando reported that he required Spanish at home, and that he corrected his daughters often. As for the disparity in the girls' abilities ("*Marta mata el español, ésta no. Esta lo lee, lo escribe, todo bien.*" ... "Marta kills Spanish, but not this one [Lolita]. She reads it, writes it, all well."), he credited the difference to school programs. Lolita had learned her skills in three years of bilingual classes, but Marta had never been in a bilingual program and was now in a public high school outside of *El Barrio*. She spent her free time off the block, and her language abilities and preferences reflected her position outward, toward the external, English-dominant, world. Lolita's activities and networks were confined to *el bloque*.

Armando exerted a tight rein on his daughters' movements and behavior. Lolita requested his permission to go anywhere, visit anyone, do anything—even to put on the television in the morning if he was listening to a Spanish radio station. She was on constant alert for his distinctive whistle; it meant that she had to leave whatever she was doing and run to his side. When she spoke in his presence, her father corrected her for how she carried herself more than for what she said. He was concerned about her posture ("*Párate bien.*" ... "Stand up right."), her mouth ("*Cierra la boca.*" ... "Close your mouth."), her attentiveness ("*Te están hablando.*" ... "They're talking to you."), and her grimaces ("*Los monos están en el circo.*" ... "Monkeys are in the zoo.").

In contrast, he did not correct her when she alternated Spanish and English ten times in one half-hour tape, although Marta reported that her father disapproved of code switching and insisted that she speak one language or the other.

In his own speech, Armando usually kept both codes strictly apart despite frequent switching for **interlocutors** who spoke Spanish or English. Only three intra-sentential code switches by him were recorded throughout the study—all directed at his daughters:

1. *Tú* share *con los demás.* ("You share with the rest.")
2. *Tráeme un* flashlight. ("Bring me a flashlight.")
3. *No me gusta ese* neighborhood. ("I don't like that neighborhood.")

In these sentences the switches to English were for single words, not the larger constituents or whole phrases that characterized the switching of the second generation [see Zentella (1997), Chapter 5, Honoring the Syntactic Hierarchy]. Armando usually spoke to his children in standard Spanish, but he addressed them in English too. The girls heard their father speak English most often when he talked with the Anglo male who lived on the block.

The girls spent less time with their virtually monolingual mother because of her long day, first at a factory in New Jersey and then at beauty school in the Bronx. A baby sitter picked Lolita up after school and took her to the block where she played within earshot of her father until her mother returned. In cold weather, Lolita went home with the baby sitter and played with her daughter in English, but she spoke Spanish with the child's mother, as she normally did with her own mother.

Lourdes had remained Spanish-dominant despite having lived for 17 years in NYC because her daily activities did not provide opportunities to participate in English conversations. She knew enough English to buy what she needed, as recordings of two exchanges with monolingual English-speaking merchants revealed, but otherwise she never initiated speaking it on her own. Unlike her husband, she had never been in a job or a classroom that developed her proficiency and her self-confidence in English. For the previous 14 years, her factory job in New Jersey, where her co-workers were Spanish speakers, required her to leave the block before 7 A.M. and return at 5.30 P.M. Three nights a week and on Saturdays she travelled to a Beautician's Academy in the Bronx where classes were conducted in Spanish. Her time on the block was spent cooking, washing clothes, and shopping for food, clothes, and school supplies for the girls. She was a quiet person and rarely had time for standing around with the other women, but they all expressed admiration for her as a hard worker, a loyal wife, and a devoted mother. Everyone could see that Lourdes' relationship with her children was close and warm, despite the fact that her obligations restricted her time with them.

Lourdes, like her husband, produced a few examples of the community-wide practice of code switching:

1. *¿Costó* dollar seventy two? ("It cost dollar seventy two?")
2. *Allí,* across the street. ("Over there, across the street.")

Switches by Spanish-dominant but long-term residents of *el bloque* like Lourdes and Armando reflected the influence that constant interaction with code-switching children had on their parents' language behavior.

Lolita and Marta spoke to their mother in Spanish, often followed up with English. [However], Lolita and her mother communicated in Spanish on occasion, but they were more likely to engage in non-reciprocal language dyads. Lolita understood everything her mother said in Spanish and Lourdes understood what her daughters said in English, but each preferred to respond in her stronger language. Lourdes did not insist that the girls speak to her in Spanish; she concentrated on the content instead of the form of their messages. In contrast to her husband, she never held forth on the importance of Spanish, but she was a more consistent source of uninterrupted Spanish in their lives than he was. Also, because of her close ties to her siblings and mother in Puerto Rico and the fact that she was the one who accompanied the girls on visits to the island, Lourdes embodied her children's most intense link between Spanish and Puerto Rico. That connection did not necessarily translate into an overt expression of Puerto Rican identity for Lolita and Marta when they were young.

Lolita's very first words to me reflected the identity conflict faced by second and third generation Puerto Ricans that has been the subject of some research and much debate (Seda Bonilla 1975; Fitzpatrick 1971). When I told Armando (with Lolita at his side) that I was interested in observing his daughters and other children in order "to understand how Puerto Rican children learn to speak two languages," Lolita's reaction was, "But I'm not Puerto Rican, I'm American." Her statement reflected the popular notion that Puerto Ricans are those born on the island of Puerto Rico, but those born in the United States are "Americans." Lolita identified herself as a US American, but her environment and behavior, linguistic and otherwise, would not have been deemed characteristic of the "typical American child" by anyone who subscribed to the "Leave It to Beaver" or "Family Ties" television models. The extent to which Lolita was representative of eight-year-old, island-born-and-raised Puerto Rican girls cannot be ascertained because of the lack of contemporary ethnographies of children's socialization in Puerto Rico. I once visited with Lolita and her cousins in Puerto Rico and did not note any dramatic differences, but prolonged observation undoubtedly would have revealed behaviors in addition to language that distinguished her from her island cousins. Lolita was, after all, a product of both worlds—her parents' Puerto Rico and her *bloque* in NYC—and both were reflected in her ways of speaking and everyday activities.

Lolita was attractive, outgoing, bright, talented, and respectful, and she was selected for activities which marked her as special both in and out of school and which expanded her bilingual/multidialectal repertoire. Her third grade bilingual class at the local public school was labeled IGC—for Intellectually Gifted Children. A prestigious African American dance company had selected her for its weekly classes, and Lolita's petite frame was also in the front line of her school's baton twirling troupe. Her tiny stature and her dependence on her parents made her seem younger than her years. Still, she was not anemic like Paca, and she danced, sang, and partook in many physical games. Her linguistic abilities were among her principal accomplishments; she was proud of and confident in her ability to speak, read, and write both English and Spanish. My observations and taping corroborated that she was adept at the following:

1. switching rapidly from one language to another;
2. describing the language dyads in all the block families, that is, she knew who spoke what to whom;
3. determining whether a stranger was bilingual or not;
4. correcting the English and Spanish of peers;
5. knowing the linguistic limitations of others and translating to meet them;
6. meeting a variety of reading and writing demands for herself and her friends;
7. combining the **morphological** and **phonological** systems of both languages for comic effect.

Lolita, a quick and accurate judge of the linguistic abilities of those who addressed her, generally accommodated others by speaking to them in their dominant language, especially if their English was noticeably weak. She spoke Spanish to her father's friends, the older women, and the infant children of Spanish-dominant parents. Conversations with her sister, peers, the block teenagers, and the infant children of English-oriented parents, were in English. The ability to shift from one language to the other developed as a natural consequence of constant interaction with members of different networks, which demanded rapid alternation between English and Spanish, as in the following episode:

> [Context: Lolita (L) was in the *bodega* with another eight-year-old, Corinne (C), who barely spoke and understood Spanish. The two-year-old daughter of a recent migrant, Jennie (J), followed them into the store. The *bodeguero* (B) belonged to her father's network of Spanish-dominant men.]

| | |
|---|---|
| *C to L:* | Buy those. |
| *L to C:* | No, I buy those better. |
| *L* to *bodeguero:* | *Toma la quora.* ("Take the quarter.") |
| *L to C:* | What's she doing here? [referring to Jennie] |
| *L to J:* | *Vete pa(-ra) dentro.* ("Go inside.") |

The three switches in rapid succession in this excerpt accommodated the linguistic abilities of three different addressees. Lolita spoke to her nearly monolingual English friend in English, to the Spanish-dominant male in Spanish, and to the child of a recent immigrant in Spanish. Her control of the pronunciation, grammar, and vocabulary of each segment was native, that is, she sounded like a native PRS speaker in Spanish and like a native PRE speaker in English. Switching without hesitation from one language to another when they interacted with members of different networks became a mark of in-group community membership. Ultimately, the switches were not limited to accommodating addressees who had distinct levels of linguistic proficiency; bilinguals switched with other bilinguals in the same conversation or sentence to accomplish a variety of discourse strategies [see Zentella (1997), Chapter 5, Conversational Strategies]. Toddlers like Jennie who were exposed to this bilingual style from infancy could be expected to acquire the same ability.

Lolita knew what every member of *el bloque* spoke because she had been a part of it all her life, but she also deduced which language newcomers were most comfortable with. Like a "junior ethnographer" (Fantini 1985), she determined how to address them guided by three observables:

1. Physical features: Spanish for Latinos and English for others.
2. Gender: Spanish for women and English for men.
3. Age: Spanish for infants and the elderly, English for others.

Because these factors determined who spoke what to whom on the block, all older Latinas were expected to speak Spanish, and young African American or Anglo-looking men were expected to know English.

Lolita seemed incredulous of those for whom this process of deduction was not second nature. Doris, a nine-year-old who, like Lolita, was born and raised in *el bloque*, listened to my description, in English, of my interest in bilingual children and asked:

| | |
|---|---|
| *D to ACZ:* | You talk two languages? |
| *L to D:* | Of course she does! |
| *D to L* | Some people don't. [said defensively] |
| *L to D:* | I know, like this girl in my class.... |

Whereas Doris hesitated to assume that I was bilingual, Lolita was surprised that Doris could not tell that I spoke Spanish—given my gender, looks, and age—just as she was surprised that a Puerto Rican classmate of hers, in a bilingual class, was not bilingual. Lolita was very sure of herself, albeit not very clear, when she told me another way she could tell if someone was not bilingual:

| | |
|---|---|
| *ACZ:* | How do you know if somebody doesn't talk two languages? |
| *L:* | By the looks sometimes. |
| *ACZ:* | How come? |
| *L:* | Because sometimes English people don't look like they were um—like if they were too glad to talk—if they wasn't glad—if they ain't glad because they won't talk Spanish. That's one way. And every time we go to Spanish in class, they say that Spanish is cancelled. And everybody says "Yeaa, that's good!" because they don't like Spanish. |

| | |
|---|---|
| *ACZ*: | Who? |
| *L*: | The children in my class. And my teacher says that you should be proud because like that if you go to Puerto Rico and you don't know Spanish you won't be able to talk their language, and to other places. |
| *ACZ*: | How come the children don't like it? |
| *L*: | Because they got mean teachers. I got Ms.—, she's meean! She pulls hair, and pulls ears too. |

Despite Lolita's difficulty with the verb ("if they were too glad," "if they wasn't glad," "if they ain't glad"), her first point is that "English people" do not like to be addressed in Spanish. Her second point is that the other third graders in her bilingual class did not enjoy Spanish, presumably because of the teacher's harsh methods. She went on, however, to disassociate herself from their negative attitudes: "But I like Spanish because sometimes she tells us stories, about what she used to do in Cuba."

Lolita not only reported on the attitudes of schoolmates toward English and Spanish, she also described the abilities and attitudes of most of the members of *el bloque*. While Paca was mulling over what language she spoke to whom, Lolita anticipated her answers and, in one instance, corrected her:

| | |
|---|---|
| *ACZ to Paca*: | *¿Qué me hablas a mi?* ("What do you speak to me?") |
| *P to ACZ*: | To you? In Spanish. |
| *L to P*: | And in English. |
| *P to L*: | No, in Spanish. |
| *L to P*: | You just spoke to her in English! |

Lolita's **meta-linguistic awareness**, which exceeded that of her friends, was heightened by her father's preoccupation with language standards and her participation in a bilingual class; both made explicit references to language and bilingualism that she adopted.

Lolita had a special mentor-like relationship with her two closest friends, and language caregiving was part of it. She spent most of her time with Isabel, who was her age but who had been left back and spoke both languages with non-standard and unique forms [see Zentella (1997), Chapter 6, Standards, Constraints, and Transfers]. Lolita often translated for Isabel; she tended to interpret anybody's "What?" or questioning look in response to a statement by Isabel as a request for a translation. She helped Isabel with her homework, and took over most of her reading and writing tasks. When I gave each child some pictures of our trip to the zoo and suggested they write the date and comments on the back, Lolita realized that Isabel was not up to the task. Immediately, she offered to write whatever Isabel wanted to say on another paper, from which Isabel could copy onto her pictures. Isabel spoke, Lolita wrote down, and Isabel copied: "It was fun. We saw lots of animals. Ana was the one who took me." For Valentine's Day, Isabel's valentine to a friend was written with Lolita's help. In March, Isabel's birthday party invitations were filled in by Lolita and another girl; Isabel signed them. When we play-acted a visit to the doctor, Lolita wrote out the diagnosis ("ulcers"), the prescription ("mylanta"), and the appointment slips for "Dr. Isabel." She added a note from "Walfar" [Welfare] for me, the patient: "Ana is too poor to pay. So don't acks for money." It was unclear whether Isabel's literacy was aided by her friend's efforts as much as Lolita's own literacy was.

Lolita's translations for Isabel were most often from English into Spanish, while Corinne required translations from Spanish into English. For example, Lolita translated the quoted price of a mango for Corinne because "sometimes she doesn't understand numbers." In deference to Corinne's limitations, Lolita's code switching was curtailed whenever Corinne joined the otherwise bilingual group of children. In contrast, Lolita was more likely to initiate Spanish with Isabel; for example, in one tape, the only Spanish utterance she initiated (total $n = 169$) was directed at Isabel. It took the form of a solicitous "*¿No quieres?*" ("Don't you want any?") after Isabel turned down her offer of candy, made in English. Switching to Spanish for the purpose of mothering exemplified one of the role-changing strategies that the children accomplished by alternating languages with the same speaker [see Zentella (1997), Chapter 5, Footing].

Lolita met school and community literacy demands in both languages confidently. She beamed when she reported a fifth grade reading score in Spanish at the end of the third grade, and 3.9 in English. On the block, she read everything that came her way, including record album covers, greeting cards, advertisements, and prayer cards in Spanish, and joke books, birthday invitations, game instructions, report cards, product labels in English. On one occasion she switched **phonology** with ease when she read a bilingual announcement aloud despite words such as "hospital," which often trip up bilingual readers because they are spelled alike in English and Spanish but pronounced differently.

Never hesitant about writing in either language, Lolita frequently asked for paper and pencil when she wanted to entertain herself, and she took on little writing projects such as labeling my tapes with the date, time, and names of speakers. On Christmas and Valentine's Day she made her own impromptu cards, and she wrote out my *bloque* Christmas card list including name, address, and apartment number of each family. Occasions to write Spanish arose less frequently, but they presented no problems when they did. When I described—in Spanish—the pattern for a blouse with the aid of folded pieces of paper, Lolita wrote *manga* ("sleeve"), *frente* ("front"), and *espalda* ("back") on the papers with no help.

Lolita was the only child in the study who played with Spanish and English for special effects. She comically exaggerated a request that her friends not grab a package of candy she was about to open by imitating a US American speaking Spanish: "No touch-ey, Es-pear-uh-tay" (*No toque. Espérate.* "Don't touch. Wait."). On another occasion, she demonstrated that she was attuned to the role of Spanish phonology in expressing politeness. The *bodeguero* made an elaborate gesture to take Lolita's money for a purchase, and carefully enunciated "*GraciaS*" ("Thank you"). In keeping with his exaggerated formality—obvious because of his emphasis on the syllable-final -s—Lolita's response was "*De nadaS,*" that is, she added and stressed a final -s in a phrase that does not have one (*De nada.* "You're welcome."). Puerto Rican jokes often derive their humor from the same **hypercorrection** that Lolita captured with "*de nadaS*"; the juxtaposition of formal and informal styles for comic effect is part of every native speaker's knowledge of the sociolinguistic rules of his/her language.

It appeared that Lolita would continue to develop her proficiency in English and Spanish for several reasons. She was promoted to the fourth grade bilingual class for gifted children and looked forward to three more years in a school with many bilingual teachers and pupils, she spent two weeks in Puerto Rico after six years of not visiting and her family planned to return on a yearly basis, and life on the block continued to require both languages. By the end of 1980, however, her future bilingual development was in question. Lolita's mother astonished *el bloque* by leaving her husband unexpectedly. Lolita left *El Barrio,* its bilingual school, and her lifelong friends, and she was not allowed to reveal her new address or have visitors. Her new neighborhood, school, friends, and baby sitter were predominantly English-speaking. Asked whether her ability in Spanish was Excellent, Good, Fair, or Poor, she chose Fair; 15 months earlier she had rated it as Good. . . .

## Profile III Eddie and Davey at Home with Vicky and Güiso

Vicky and Güiso, both 20 years old, were the youngest couple with children. They had lived together for four years and had two boys: three-year-old Eddie, and Davey, born three months into the study. Güiso said he wanted to have two more children but Vicky was reluctant, although both of them longed for a girl. Each came from a large family: Vicky was one of five children and Güiso had one older brother and four younger sisters, all of whom had been born in *el bloque* and had never been to Puerto Rico. Until his mother Dolores moved to the projects and a fire forced out two married sisters, most of Güiso's family lived in his building. Even after the fire, he could count on various kin among his neighbors, and whenever his mother or his sisters visited, the clan gathered in his apartment. These gatherings were characterized by conversations that alternated rapidly between English and Spanish, especially among the younger women. One sister accurately observed that the girls often spoke Spanish to each other and to their mother, but that the boys "stuck to English."

Güiso spoke English to all his siblings; when he spoke to his mother, he struggled with his limited Spanish. Dolores gave this version of her son's attempt to explain what he would do if he were to have a third child and it did not turn out to be a girl:

> *Me estaba hablando en español. El habla mucho español pero algunas palabras se le—que él cogía una nena y que la adoptaba. Ve, entonces cuando me dijo así, que si iba a tener otro nene, otro, y si le salía nene cogía* "girls *y lo* adopt," *tú sabe(-s), eso me lo metió en inglés.*
>
> ("He was talking to me in Spanish. He talks a lot of Spanish but some words [escape] him—that he would take a little girl and adopt her. See, when he told me that, that if he was going to have another baby, another, and if it came out a little boy he was going to get 'girls and adopt it [masculine singular]', you know, that part he stuck in in English.")

Güiso was insecure about his Spanish, and reported that as a child he stuttered and "wouldn't talk at all." It is unclear to what extent his problems were normal, or whether they contributed to the acting-out behavior that led to his removal from the fourth grade. After a few years in one of the notorious 600 schools for discipline problems, he dropped out when he was 15.

In addition to extended family, Güiso had lifelong friends on the block, especially among the young dudes who whiled away most summer evenings and winter weekends discussing and playing sports, drinking, and listening to *salsa* music until the wee hours. Güiso's newfound sense of responsibility as a father did not allow him to "break night" anymore, but he still socialized with his *panas* ("buddies") for long hours. Their conversations were always in English—either PRE or AAVE.

Ironically, Güiso rated himself a poor speaker of Spanish but it was his ability to speak Spanish that landed him his job, guarding the wares at a local Korean-owned market and serving as interpreter. The job helped reinforce positive attitudes nurtured as an adolescent when he had longed to "rap to the beautiful Spanish-speaking girls," mainly recent immigrants. As an adult, he defended the benefits of bilingualism to his African American friends: "This is a Spanish-speaking community, you need both." Güiso and Vicky, both dark-skinned Puerto Ricans, identified with the racial concerns of their African American friends, but they identified with Puerto Ricans culturally. Consequently, Güiso was trying to learn to speak better Spanish, and he practiced reading bilingual advertisements and palm cards. Despite proclaiming that his children would be bilingual and that "it's up to the parents," all of his conversations with his wife and children were in English.

Vicky shared Güiso's confidence in their children's bilingual future, but she too helped maintain the English-speaking atmosphere of their household. Her television was always on English channels, as was her radio. She spoke English to Güiso, the old girl friends who visited, her two sons, and her baby sitting charges. Vicky reported that she spoke Spanish to the children most often when she was angry, and observations bore her out. Most of her Spanish comments to the children were commands or threats that followed the English version and served to underscore them, as in the following example:

> *V to Eddie*: See that chair over there, go squash your seat in it. Go sit down, go.
> *¡Deja eso y sién-ta-te!*
> ("Leave that and sit down!")

Most often she addressed her sons in English only.

Outside her home, Vicky had many occasions to speak Spanish, for example, when she picked up or dropped off

Paca, when she visited Güiso's mother, aunt, or cousin, when she stopped to chat on the stoop with the first-generation women, or when she made a new friend of a recent arrival from Puerto Rico. Vicky's first language as a child had been Spanish, but she had learned English quickly from her brothers and sisters because she was the youngest of the brood. She still spoke Spanish to her parents, but English to her brothers and sisters. Unlike her husband, she had close relationships with several Spanish monolinguals, including two of her seven *comadres*. As a result, although Vicky's Spanish included non-standard forms and she asked help for unknown words, she was a much more confident Spanish speaker than Güiso. But she could not read or write Spanish because she had dropped out of school at 16 and had never had a job that required literacy skills in any language. A year after we met, she replaced her husband at the vegetable stand while he recuperated from a lingering foot ailment; that job increased her oral proficiency in Spanish, but made few demands on literacy in Spanish or English.

With their father in charge, Eddie and Davey heard almost no Spanish at home, and very little was directed to them outside of their home; everyone on the block knew them to be English speakers. Nonetheless, their parents overrated the children's language abilities and were optimistic about their future as bilinguals. Vicky was counting on the school's bilingual program, unaware that its classes were off limits to English monolinguals. Her claim that Eddie understood Spanish and that he spoke to Güiso's aunts and mother in Spanish conflicted with my observations: I never heard him speak it and he looked blank whenever someone addressed him in Spanish. In fact, much of what Eddie spoke was garbled until he was four years old. Paca translated for Eddie when she understood him. Vicky did not express alarm over her son's speech, perhaps because of her own pronounced lisp and her husband's similar language history, but her concern surfaced in her unwillingness to interfere in his choice of language. She was the only parent who felt that there were no situations which should require that her child speak only English or only Spanish:

> "It's really up to him. I can't tell him just speak to this person in Spanish, this person in English. That's really up to him. The language that he understands best, that's the one he should speak."

Vicky and Güiso were the first of *el bloque's* parents to favor English at home with each other and their children, although they voiced a strong belief in the importance of being bilingual and were convinced that their children would be able to speak, read, and write both Spanish and English. Because the principal settings, social networks, and activities in which the children participated were dominated by English, their parents' aspirations seemed unrealistic. Still, it was possible that the boys' lives might change in ways that would bring them into closer contact with Spanish monolinguals, or otherwise expand their limited knowledge of Spanish. That, after all, had been the case with their parents, whose ability to speak Spanish strengthened as they took on parental roles and jobs in *El Barrio*....

## CONCLUSION

The larger socio-political context in which bilingualism *en casa* was enmeshed pitted the children's strong, intimate links with Puerto Rico, Puerto Ricans, and Spanish-speaking elders against the ever expanding and authority-laden role of English. Given the "symbolic domination" (Bourdieu and Passeron 1977) of English, English became the language not only of the children's channel, it also seeped into their parents' formerly monolingual Spanish channel. Together, old and new generations forged a joint way of speaking that "spoke to" the experiences of both. Like the push-pull forces that propel the NYC-Puerto Rico circulatory migration pattern, the increasing power of English in the homes of *el bloque* is a statement about the economic, social, and political forces propelling children towards English.

At the beginning of the 1980s, *el bloque* was between stages five and six on Fishman's (1991) eight-level measure of community **language shift,** the Graded Intergenerational Disruption Scale (GIDS), and there were signs that it was moving in the direction of greater **language loss** (at GIDS eight, only a few old speakers are left). Principal among these were the reluctance of parents to insist that they be addressed in Spanish, and the widespread use of English in all children's activities. Even when second-generation parents resurrected their childhood Spanish via participation in adult networks, they used it more for communicating with their elders than with their siblings or children. If Fishman (1991: 91) is right that, for **language maintenance,** nothing "can substitute for the re-establishment of young families of child-bearing age in which Xish [Spanish in this case] is the normal medium or co-medium of communication and/or of other culturally appropriate home, family, neighborhood, and community intergenerational vernacular activity," then the likelihood of maintaining Spanish beyond the second generation in the NYPR community looks bleak. Ethnography provided a complex portrait of the factors that made parents and children favor English or Spanish.

In *el bloque*, six principal communication patterns existed among the 20 families with children; they differed in terms of the language(s) that parents spoke to each other, the language(s) parents spoke to children and vice versa, and the language(s) children spoke among themselves. The presence of Spanish was related to the migration history of the caretakers, as follows:

1. In the majority of families (12/20 in Table 23.1), children heard their parents speak Spanish at home to each other and were always spoken to in Spanish by at least one parent. Those parents had migrated to the United States after spending their youth, including early adolescence, in Puerto Rico.
2. When one or more parents was Puerto Rican born but had migrated before late adolescence, Spanish and English were alternated in the home. This occurred in six families which included 14 children.

3. English was the predominant language among parents and children in two families, with two children each: in one there was an Anglo male who could not speak Spanish and in the other both parents, Vicky and Güiso, had been born and raised in *El Barrio* and had never been to Puerto Rico.

Children's English increased in proportion to the amount of English understood and spoken by their parents. Parents who had migrated to the US as adolescents or young adults continued to speak to their siblings in Spanish. This held true even for sisters and brothers who had lived more years in NYC than in Puerto Rico, so that many of those who had arrived at 14 and 16 years old still spoke Spanish to each other at 42 and 44, at 62 and 64. When they spoke to their children, however, some used English and those who did not allowed their children to respond in English as they came to understand it more. As a result, children's comprehension skills in Spanish and parents' comprehension skills in English outdistanced their ability to speak, read, or write their second language. Every adult knew some survival English, but there was already one child who did not understand enough Spanish to participate fully in the life of the community.

Schooling was the most important promoter of English dominance, whether children were in an all–English class or in a bilingual program. After one year in school, young children spoke to each other increasingly in English, even when their primary caretakers had not made any visible improvement in their knowledge of English. The children in bilingual programs had one major advantage: they were the only ones who learned to read and write in Spanish as well as English, skills that were valued and useful in the community.

Despite the impact of family migration histories and schooling, children from the same type of background could differ markedly in their ability to speak, read, and/or write Spanish or English. Some visited Puerto Rico more frequently or for longer stays than others, some were enrolled in a bilingual program or in an English-only class, some were allowed to spend many hours out on the block whereas others were confined to their apartment and female networks, some identified more with African Americans than with Puerto Ricans, some participated in religious activities that required literacy in English or Spanish, etc. As the profiles of three families proved, specifying the language dyads, or who speaks what to whom in each family, as listed in Table 23.1, provides a limited view of children's linguistic input. *El bloque's* children were not raised behind closed doors in nuclear families isolated from their neighbors. It is incorrect to assume that children with monolingual Spanish parents did not speak English with adults, or that those whose parents spoke only English heard no Spanish conversations. The presence of overlapping networks guaranteed constant visiting, sharing, and exposure to both languages. Children could emerge from any number of apartment doors, behind which they might have been taking part in English, Spanish, or Spanish and English conversations.

More than anything else in their lives, the frequent interspersal of sentences and words from both languages was the primary symbol of membership in *el bloque* and reflected the children's dual cultural identification....

## Note

1. Only "Black" was heard in the community; I use "African American" when I am not quoting community members.

## References

Bourdieu, P. and Passeron, J. C. 1977. *Reproduction in Education, Society, and Culture.* Beverly Hills, CA: Sage.

Fantini, A. 1985. *Language Acquisition of a Bilingual Child: A sociolinguistic perspective.* San Diego: College Hill Press.

Fishman, J. A. 1991. *Reversing Language Shift.* Clevedon: Multilingual Matters.

Fitzpatrick, J. 1971. *Puerto Rican Americans: The meaning of migration to the mainland.* Englewood Cliffs, NJ: Prentice Hall.

Philips, S. U. 1972. Participant structures and communicative competence: Warm Springs children in community and classroom. In C. B. Cazden, D. H. Hymes, and V. John (eds.), *Functions of Language in the Classroom,* New York: Teachers College Press 370–94.

Seda Bonilla, E. 1975. Qué somos: puertorriqueños, neorriqueños, o niuyorriqueños? *The Rican: Journal of contemporary Puerto Rican thought* 2(2–3): 81–107.

Zentella, A. C. 1997. *Growing Up Bilingual: Puerto Rican Children in New York.* Malden, MA: Blackwell.

---

## Critical Thinking and Application

- Why does Zentella focus on families rather than individuals? How are linguistic practices learned by a researcher?
- Zentella herself is bilingual, having grown up in a New York Puerto Rican community. Do you think that a person without this membership could have learned what she did? Why or why not? She writes that being a member of the group under investigation brings with it both assets and liabilities. What kinds of liabilities do you think this would have?

- Zentella identifies six principal communication patterns among the 20 families with children that she knew best. List the factors that make people more likely to use Spanish, and those that make people more likely to use English.
- Interview someone who is bilingual and try to figure out what the uses of each language are (as reported by the speaker). How does your subject feel about his or her languages?

## Vocabulary

| | | |
|---|---|---|
| AAVE | intra-sentential code switching | morphological |
| dyad | language loss | NSPRS |
| HE | language maintenance | phonological, phonology |
| hypercorrection | language shift | PRE |
| interlocutor | meta-linguistic awareness | SPRS |

## Suggested Further Reading

Dewaele, Jean-Marc, Alex Housen, Li Wei, and Hugo Baetens Beardsmore, eds. 2003. *Bilingualism: Beyond Basic Principles*. Clevedon and Buffalo: Multilingual Matters.

Edwards, John R. 1994. *Multilingualism*. London and New York: Routledge.

Grosjean, François. 1982. *Life with Two Languages: An Introduction to Bilingualism*. Cambridge, MA: Harvard University Press.

Gumperz, John J. 1982. *Discourse Strategies*. Cambridge: Cambridge University Press.

Heller, Monica, ed. 1988. *Codeswitching: Anthropological and Sociolinguistic Perspectives*. Berlin and New York: Mouton de Gruyter.

Myers-Scotton, Carol. 1988. Codeswitching as Indexical of Social Negotiations. In *Codeswitching: Anthropological and Sociolinguistic Perspectives*, edited by Monica Heller, pp. 151–186. Berlin and New York: Mouton de Gruyter.

Romaine, Suzanne. 1989. *Bilingualism*. New York: Blackwell.

Stavans, Ilan. 2003. *Spanglish: The Making of a New American Language*. New York: Rayo.

Urciuoli, Bonnie. 1996. *Exposing Prejudice: Puerto Rican Experiences of Language, Race, and Class*. Boulder, CO: Westview Press.

Woolard, Kathryn. 1985. *Double Talk: Bilingualism and the Politics of Ethnicity in Catalonia*. Stanford, CA: Stanford University Press.

Zentella, Ana Celia. 1997. *Growing Up Bilingual: Children in El Barrio*. Malden, MA: Blackwell.

CHAPTER 24

# Serious Games:[1] Code-Switching and Gendered Identities in Moroccan Immigrant Girls' Pretend Play

*Inmaculada M. García-Sánchez*
(2010)

*Code-switching (codeswitching, or code switching) is the use of more than one linguistic variety by a single individual. This phenomenon has been studied thoroughly throughout the world, with a variety of effects but a single conclusion: code-switching demonstrates great mastery over linguistic and social features of language in its social context. John Gumperz showed in his 1982 article, "Conversational Code Switching," that code-switching in every case was rule governed, not the haphazard tossing of a few words of one variety or another into sentences. In the intervening years, significant theories of code-switching have been developed by specialists such as Monica Heller and Carol Myers-Scotton, and by others such as Alexandra Jaffe, to ask the questions: Why this specific switch? Why here? Why now? Why with these particular people? Why about this particular subject?*

*Migration has always characterized the human condition, ever since humans wandered out of Africa and settled in every corner of the globe. We have always encountered others and have had varieties of responses to that otherness: fascination, repulsion, convergence, war, and more. In the twentieth and twenty-first centuries, migration has become especially salient to social theorists. In the study of social power and inevitable inequalities, many types of researchers, including those who study language, provide insights. Traditionally phrased as "power" and "solidarity" by sociolinguists, we can observe tension between the forces that pull people outward toward social prestige and those that draw them toward their home practices. The study of code-switching often reveals precisely this tension.*

*This chapter examines the ways Moroccan immigrant girls in Spain use play among friends to figure out their identities. Play, in this sense, is serious because the stakes are quite high: who are they and who will they become?*

## Reading Questions

- García-Sánchez attributes functions to the two languages used by the children she studied. What are these functions? How does she determine the interactional roles played by the codes?
- In some cases, the children voice ideas and concepts that would be forbidden in their own families. From where does their knowledge of such practices derive?
- What knowledge of Spanish and Moroccan Arabic is evident in the examples provided in this chapter? Do you see evidence of a lack of linguistic competence?
- What is *heteroglossia*? Where do you see this concept applied here? Is this unique to bilingual populations?

Inmaculada M. García-Sánchez. 2010. Serious Games: Code-Switching and Gendered Identities in Moroccan Immigrant Girls' Pretend Play. *Pragmatics* 20 (4): 523–555.

## Introduction

In recent years, the complex relationship between children and their multiple languages as intertwined with the multifaceted identities they have to negotiate in different arenas of their social life has been emphasized in language socialization research in multilingual, **diasporic** communities undergoing rapid change (e.g. Baquedano-López 2000; Garrett 2007b; He 2001; Paugh 2005). Understanding how immigrant children develop a sense of self is particularly important in hybrid, multilingual communities where these children juggle not only multiple linguistic codes and their social valences but also conflicting sociocultural expectations, moral frameworks and notions of personhood (Fader 2001, 2009). Sociocultural research in immigrant communities emphasizes the daily complex acts of cultural negotiation involved when immigrant youth attempt to traverse contradictory influences on their sense of self (Hall 1995, 2002, 2004). Yet, few studies have paid close attention to the everyday communicative practices involved in these daily acts of negotiation, or *acts of cultural translation* (Bhabha 1990). Many sociologists of immigration point to the need to understand how immigrant youth navigate the countervailing influences and scrutiny of elder generations in their heritage communities and a host society attempting to re-enculturate them (Samad 2007). Yet, little is understood about the on-the-ground ways in which immigrant children create autonomous arenas for action that may give rise to hybrid *processes of identification* (Brubaker and Cooper 2000).

Drawing on Bakhtin's (1981, 1986) notions of **heteroglossia** and **hybridity**, this [chapter] examines ways in which Moroccan immigrant children in Spain create imagined, alternative life worlds and explore possible forms of identification, through an investigation of these children's hybrid language practices in the midst of play. In particular, the analysis focuses on **codeswitching** practices and clandestine *tactics* (De Certeau 1988) that Moroccan immigrant girls deploy in pretend-play to construct desirable female identities in the context of Spanish idealizations of femininity, but which are transgressional in Moroccan diaspora communities.

## Communicative Practices and Play in Children's Peer Groups

Previous research on children's communicative practices in peer networks has shown these contexts to be crucial for processes of language socialization, in that these contexts allow children to construct autonomous arenas for action where they can develop competencies as language users and social actors relatively free from adult censure, disapproval, and scrutiny (e.g. Aronsson and Thorell 1999; Blum-Kulka and Snow 2004; Corsaro 1988a, 1988b, 1994, 2000; Goodwin 2000, 1998, 1997, 1990a, 1990b; Goodwin and Kyratzis 2007; Kyratzis 2004). Children use the multiple languages available in their linguistic repertoires to structure games and other activities, as well as to challenge, transform and reproduce societal ideologies about languages and ethnic relations (Evaldsson and Cekaite 2010; Howard 2007; Minks 2010). Hybrid linguistic practices, in particular, have been shown to socialize peers into alternative notions of morality, and facilitate the negotiation of hierarchies and multiple, fluid identities (e.g. Cekaite and Aronsson 2005; Evaldsson 2005; García-Sánchez 2005; Jørgenssen 1998; Kyratzis 2010; Rampton 1995, 1998; Reynolds 2002, 2010; Zentella 1997, 1998).

More specifically, children's codeswitching has been described to differentiate between '*negotiation of the play*' and '*in-character play*', as well as the negotiation of ongoing social interaction – teasing, by-play, displays of power or anger, participants roles and topic changes (e.g. Cromdal and Aronsson 2000; Cromdal 2004; Ervin-Tripp and Reyes 2005; Gudal 1997). Codeswitching is used to signal different *sub-registers* during play, i.e. '*in-character play*' and '*negotiation of the play*', and to enact different *voices*, i.e. the voice of the child, the voice of the role-character, and the voice of the director. In this regard, a number of studies has consistently found that in multi- or bilingual situations, play characters speak and are spoken to in one language, while running **metacommentary** on the game is usually carried out in a different code (Kwan-Terry 1992; Halmari and Smith 1994). Codeswitching during play has also been shown to be an important resource for children's constructions of their emerging understandings of how contrasting languages **index** social identities, activities, and **language ideologies** (Garrett 2007b; Minks 2010). In Dominica, for instance, where children's use of Patwa is closely monitored and forbidden by adults, Paugh (2005) found that, in peer group contexts where children are free from this linguistic surveillance, they use Patwa to enact specific adult roles and activities, such as bus driver, and English to enact other roles, such as the role of teacher.

A second important line of inquiry for the present analysis is sociolinguistic research on youth peer groups of North African immigrant descent and other ethnic minorities in Europe, since these youth groups also come to be under heavy adult surveillance and are frequently racialized as '*young delinquents*' and '*trouble-makers*'. Drawing on Corsaro's notion of *interpretive reproduction*,[2] Poveda and Marcos (2005), for instance, have argued that Spanish Romani minority children use playful transformations of popular songs and rhymes in the safe contexts of their peer groups as a way to assert themselves socially against the larger backdrop of social exclusion and discrimination. These playful interactions provide them with resources to confront racially marked facets of their daily experiences.

Tetreault (2007, 2008, 2009) investigated the hybrid language practices of adolescent peer groups of Algerian descent in France and the importance of these practices for articulating ties to immigrant origins and emergent adolescent subcultures. From her analysis of parental name calling in ritual insults (2007) to her recent study of these youths' use of mock style French TV host **register** (2009), Tetreault illustrates how communicative practices in the peer group constitute an intricate web of personal and cultural relations in the self-presentations of these adolescents. More importantly, these interactional practices also reveal how French adolescents of

North African descent subvert, transgress, and reinforce different forms of identification and gendered expectations in both French dominant discourses and their immigrant communities. For female adolescents of North African descent, in particular, gendered identifications are fraught with anxieties and moral ambivalence, involving complex processes of simultaneous identification and dis-identification with their choices of self-representation (Tetreault 2008). Similarly, Hall's (1995, 2002) descriptions of how British Sikh youth negotiate—and often subvert—gendered expectations across the cultural worlds of their families, peer groups, and other ethnic communal arrangements, have shown how the process is profoundly conflictual and ambivalent for these youth.

## The Ethnographic Context of the Girls' Lives

This analysis is part of a two year ethnographic, **language socialization** study, investigating the **linguistic ecology** of the lives of Moroccan immigrant children (8 to 11 years old) in South-Central Western Spain. This study examines these children's communicative practices in relation to the extent to which they are able to juggle languages and social practices against the backdrop of rising levels of tension against immigrants from North Africa. During 2005–2007, I conducted fieldwork in a rural Spanish town, located approximately 125 miles southwest of Madrid urban area, with a total population of 10,815. This rural Spanish community has been a major settlement area for Moroccan immigrants since the early 1990's, when, initially single males, and subsequently entire families, came looking for jobs in the booming agricultural sector. The total immigrant population makes up 37% of the total population of the town, with the bulk of this percentage being overwhelmingly of Moroccan origin. The current geopolitical, as well as local, climate of suspicion surrounding immigrants from North Africa and the Muslim world, in addition to historical, economic, sociocultural, and linguistic factors, make the intergroup dynamics between immigrants and locals in this community difficult and fraught with tension.

These delicate and precarious interethnic relations impinge upon the life of Moroccan immigrant children in complex and consequential ways. For instance, at the public school, Moroccan immigrant children are ethnicized as the 'Other' and constituted as 'outsiders' through routine participation in exclusionary interactional practices with teachers and peers and through linguistically mediated regimes of surveillance. One characteristic of these practices of social exclusion is the active monitoring of Moroccan immigrant children's behavior that, in many ways, echo the intense surveillance to which the Moroccan immigrant community as a whole is subjected at the national and local levels (García Sánchez 2007, 2009). Another important form of social exclusion to which these children are subjected is that Spanish girls avoid contact with Moroccan immigrant girls in social settings at school and also outside school. A telling example of the distinct boundaries of separation that Spanish girls attempt to build around Moroccan girls is an episode that occurred as the whole fourth grade class was preparing their costumes to celebrate the annual Carnival Festival at the school. Children were supposed to design and craft their own costumes during Plastic Arts class. Although the whole fourth grade class was dressing up as birds, children had the prerogative to choose the dominant color of their feather design. A group of the most socially popular Spanish girls requested pink as their dominant color. Immediately, Wafiya and Sarah, two of the Moroccan girls followed in this study, asked the teacher whether they could also have pink. When the teacher also granted Wafiya and Sarah's request to have pink, the group of Spanish girls approached the teacher and informed her that they had changed their minds and now wanted blue as the dominant color of their outfit design.

Moroccan immigrant girls may sometimes experience additional layers of social constraints and surveillance by members of their own diaspora communities. Gender inequality has been documented in other immigrant communities around the world, for example, among Hmong immigrant families in the United States (Lee 2005). In Europe, more specifically, higher levels of social restrictions for girls, such as avoiding spending too much time outdoors and adopting appropriate styles of dress, have also been reported for adolescent girls of Algerian descent in North African diaspora communities in France (Tetreault 2008). In this community, adults and older male siblings in the Moroccan community often monitor girls' actions and behaviors, sometimes curtailing the girls' participation in certain extracurricular activities, such as school field trips, or in recreational activities, such as going to the swimming pool, to the weekly outdoor market, or to the town's annual fair. In this community, in particular, male siblings often behave towards their sisters in a more authoritarian way than the girls' own parents, i.e. controlling their ways of dressing and speaking, as well as their peer group activities, sometimes even disciplining the girls on their own accounts, without necessarily having parental authorization (or parental knowledge) to do so.[3] In fact, during the course of my fieldwork, I observed a number of instances of older siblings getting in trouble with their parents for disciplining their sisters on their own. Many of the **focal** girls, in particular, Worda, Sarah, and Wafiya, repeatedly complained about what they considered their brothers' *nagging* behavior in videotaped interviews and in more private conversations.

Moroccan girls' and boys' participation in certain extracurricular activities was often further limited by the tight financial circumstances that many of the immigrant families in this community faced. As children of economic migrants, they and their families tend to occupy **subaltern** positions in the socio-political structure of the town's social hierarchy.

The powerful convergence of all the influences described above (discrimination and social exclusion; economic exclusion; and gendered exclusion) is crucial to understand the constraints and affordances of Moroccan immigrant girls' lives, as crystallized in communicative practices and peer group pretend-play.

## DATA AND METHODOLOGY

### Data Collection and Analysis

In documenting the linguistic ecology of the lives of Moroccan immigrants, I focused on the everyday, face-to-face communicative and social practices that the children participated in with extended family, peers, teachers, and other community members in the diverse settings that make up their daily lives and activities.[4] The six focal children in the study were relatively recent immigrants to the country, ranging from one to five years of residence. The naturally occurring interactional routines of this group of children were systematically observed and video/audio-recorded over a period of 12 consecutive months. The audio and videotaped corpus yielded by this body of data collection was transcribed according to the system developed by Sacks, Schegloff, and Jefferson (1974), as adapted by Goodwin (1990).[5] The transcripts were further ethnographically annotated with the help of two Moroccan Arabic native speaker assistants, who provided nuanced **metalinguistic** commentary of children's language use and insights into cultural ideologies and attitudes toward that use (Garrett 2007a; Schieffelin 1990). In addition, questions concerning the actions and speech of the children, as well as the situations in which these occurred, were addressed to the children's caregivers during several interviews and consultation periods over the course of the study. The transcripts were also annotated with the information gained in these consultations.

During the course of the recordings I adopted the role of observer and minimized my participation in any of the activities that the children themselves organized in the context of their interactions with peers; for instance, I never elicited any speech or form of language use, and I never directed or made decisions regarding peer group activities. In a few occasions, some children participating in these activities, particularly those friends of the focal children who were not as accustomed to my presence and systematic observation, tried to recruit my intervention in games and on-going interactions, especially when conflict and disagreement erupted among themselves, but also for **ludic** purposes. However, even in this handful of occasions, I reminded the children that I was interested in knowing how they played and learned together, and I did not intervene in any subsequent course of action the children took.

### The Peer Group as a Unit of Analysis

Moroccan immigrant children in this rural Spanish community spend a significant amount of their out-of-school time with other Moroccan immigrant children in the local park, on the street pavement near their homes, or in several building-free plots of land scattered in various places around the town. From an early age they spend at least an average of three hours daily playing and interacting with school friends, neighborhood children, siblings and other children in their extended families, an amount that increases during holidays and school breaks. Most Moroccan parents do not consider the household an appropriate domain for children to engage in ludic interactions and usually do not allow peer groups into the homes. Home and street/park are clearly delineated spaces not only by physical boundaries, but also by the activities that routinely take place in them. The home is restricted for household and other adult-dominated activities, while children's games are seen as an interference[6] to those activities. This distinct delineation of spaces allows Moroccan children to carry out their peer group activities with little interference and surveillance from adults.

With very few exceptions, peer groups are distinctly divided along ethnic and gender lines in this community. Moroccan girls play with other Moroccan girls and Moroccan boys play with other Moroccan boys; Spanish girls play with other Spanish girls and Spanish boys with other Spanish boys. Small boys are sometimes present in Moroccan female peer groups because, starting in middle childhood, Moroccan girls are often assigned the responsibility of caring for younger siblings. If the girls go out to play with friends they bring with them their younger brothers. In these cases, the young boy is rarely a participant of the focal activities of the female peer group, remaining on the sidelines either as an observer or engaging in his own forms of play.

Although similar gender-segregated arrangements have been described in children's cultures and peer groups across a wide range of settings and speech communities (Goodwin 1990; Thorne 1993), what is striking about the organization of peer groups in this town is the pervasive lack of multi-ethnic children's groups in informal settings,[7] which can be seen as a reverberation of the complex and tense interethnic dynamics of this community, as well as an extension of the pervasive practices of social exclusion and surveillance that Moroccan immigrant children are subjected to by their own Spanish peers at school.

Moroccan immigrant peer groups are composed of children of different ages who often possess varying degrees of expertise and experience with Spanish and Moroccan cultures and languages. A peer group may include a child who has been born in Spain, a child who has spent most of his/her childhood in Morocco and has just recently arrived in Spain, and a child who came to Spain when s/he was just a toddler. The intergenerational, mixed-expertise character of Moroccan immigrant children's peer groups allows for an original range of possible types of participation as experts and/or novices that blur the age distinctions usually associated with these roles. This characteristic, along with the minimal adult supervision of peer group activities, also underscore the importance of the peer group as an autonomous arena for action in which immigrant children are agents of language socialization into communicative practices and sociocultural norms.

Moroccan immigrant children peer groups are usually fluid in their composition. While a handful of children in the study remained in peer groups, there was also an ebb and flow of participants present at any given recording of peer group interactions. Often different neighborhood children, cousins, or siblings would join in the play activities. The size of a peer group could range from three to eight children, and even sometimes more, although this was not very common.

Two focal children, Worda and Wafiya, both 9 years old, are the main participants in the pretend-play games analyzed below. They both arrived in Spain as toddlers: Worda had been living in the country for five years and Wafiya for four years. They were friends at school, where they both attended fourth grade, and teammates in the local Track-and-Field team. They spent most of their out-of-school time together, either training, playing, doing homework, or hanging out. The core of Worda and Wafiya's[8] peer group—the group that I was able to follow more consistently—was composed of Salma, age 10, who is Worda's oldest sister; Dunia, age 4, Worda's youngest sister, who had been born in Spain; and Manal, age 11, a neighbor of Worda's who had arrived in Spain after kindergarten. Also, apart from being neighbors, Worda and Manal's mothers were close friends. In addition, a number of other girls were *part-time* members of this peer group, participating on and off in different games and activities. Among the most important is Sarah, age 9, who was in the same fourth class as Wafiya and also one of the focal children. She had spent most of her childhood in Morocco and was a recent arrival into the country, having been in Spain for less than one year. Other part-time participants were: Houriya, aged 11, who was a member of the local Track-and-Field team and trained with Worda and Wafiya; Lamia, aged 8, Worda's next door neighbor; and Leila, aged 8, a distant relative of Wafiya's family who also attended the track-and-field training sessions from time to time.

In the context of their peer groups, these and other children engaged in a wide variety of activities, such as pretend-play, marbles, soccer, hopscotch, jump rope games, singing nursery rhymes and traditional and popular songs, clapping rhymes, tag and other chasing games. Children's discursive practices were also varied and include: Word play, arguing, negotiating, reciting, gossiping, and explaining game rules. The prevailing feature of these activities is their hybrid nature. These activities are characterized by a high incidence of codeswitching between Spanish and Moroccan Arabic.

## Interactional Frames and Identity Construction in Pretend-Play

Pretend-play is frequent in Moroccan immigrant girls' peer groups. Girls enact pretend-play sequences related to the ordinary contexts of their lives, including school and mass media and popular culture, e.g. role-playing T.V. soap operas and sitcoms and popular movies. Whether enacting everyday or extraordinary situations, what Moroccan immigrant girls bring to pretend-play activities is the double orientation of the cultural and linguistic dispositions of their heritage community and of the larger Spanish community. Linguistic practices in pretend-play, in particular, the high rate of codeswitching between Spanish and Moroccan Arabic, are primordial means by which this double orientation is accomplished. Codeswitching also evidences the **double-voicedness** of this hybrid linguistic practice (Bahktin 1981), in that instances of codeswitching point to girls' ambivalent, transgressional, and clandestine orientation towards the activities they enact in play. The **reflexivity** inherent in how this group of girls enacts the tensions between activities and linguistic varieties can be clearly seen in their keen awareness that they could be '*discovered*'.

Role-play interaction involving dolls figures prominently in Moroccan immigrant girls' games of pretend. This type of pretend-play activity is particularly interesting because, as they construct imaginary life worlds for their dolls, the girls interweave ordinary routines and settings with the extraordinary, idealized life styles that female characters are likely to lead in T.V. sitcoms. The following analysis focuses on two extended doll-play sequences involving five participants: Worda and Wafiya, Salma, Dunia, and Lamia.[9] In both occasions, the girls are playing a few houses down the street from Worda's family's home, where they often meet on weekend afternoons while their mothers are at home either tending to house chores or having tea and visiting with other female neighbors and relatives, and their fathers are in the town square or locally-run Moroccan coffee shops meeting other male friends.

### Patterns of Code Choice and Use: Managing Play and Interactional Frames

This group of girls uses Spanish and Moroccan Arabic in most social situations of their daily lives. At school they use only Spanish in their encounters with teachers and Spanish peers, but they often use Moroccan Arabic to interact among themselves.[10] Similarly, at home while Moroccan Arabic tends to predominate in most interactions between the children and their parents, the children among themselves, particularly those who have spent a long period of time in Spain, frequently use Spanish. In the context of their pretend-play, they overwhelmingly use Spanish—and more specifically a stylized register of Spanish—when ventriloquizing their dolls and for stage-setting and narrative emplotment (Kyratzis and Ervin-Tripp 1999). Conversely, Moroccan Arabic is used (1) to negotiate the specifics of the game; (2) for metacommentary on the play frame; (3) to resolve conflict among the girls (usually conflict springing from the game); (4) to monitor and control the behavior of younger siblings who are present in the interaction, even if they are not fully **ratified participants** of the game sequence; and (5) to interact with passers-by (usually other Moroccan neighbors, family members or acquaintances). Thus, codeswitching between Spanish and Moroccan Arabic is essential to create and sustain interactional and play frames during doll games. **Figure 24.1** summarizes the distribution of code use and codeswitching patterns during pretend-play activities. As mentioned above, a similar distribution of code labor has also been observed in children's games in bi/multilingual play in other speech communities (e.g. Cromdal 2004; Gudal 1997; Halmari and Smith 1994; Kwan-Terry 1992; Paugh 2005).

**Figure 24.1** Distribution of Code Choice and Use

| Spanish | Moroccan Arabic |
|---|---|
| In-character Dialogue<br>Stage-setting<br>Narrative Emplotment | Negotiating parameters of the game<br>Metacommentary on the play frame<br>Resolving conflict among participants<br>Monitoring the behavior of younger siblings<br>Interacting with passers-by |

In the present study, there are also important differences with regards to language choice and use between enacting the voices of the dolls and creating a fantasy play space on the one hand, and interactions among the children to negotiate parameters of the play frame and solve intra-group conflicts on the other (See **Figure** below). Interestingly, the issue of which code to use when speaking *in character* is in itself a matter of metalinguistic awareness among the girls. Indeed, the choice of Spanish to ventriloquize the dolls is one of the parameters of the game that the girls themselves settle early on in their play interaction. The following example takes place towards the beginning of the play sequence. Immediately before the beginning of this excerpt, the girls had been speaking in Moroccan Arabic about the different hairstyles of their dolls and about the array of props and doll accessories that they have brought to play with. This excerpt inaugurates the play frame, in that this is the first time that the girls ventriloquize the voices of the dolls [Example 1]:

Worda and Wafiya stage a scenario in which their dolls have run into each other on the street. The sequence opens with an exchange of greetings that is realized both verbally (lines 1–3) and kinetically with a mutual exchange of kisses on the cheek (see frame grab above).[13] It is important to note that, although the girls perform this initial greeting in Moroccan Arabic, Worda explicitly instructs Wafiya to speak in Spanish

EXAMPLE # 1: Key: Spanish (Regular Font) — Moroccan Arabic (***Bold Italics***)[11]

**Participants:**
**Worda**
**Wafiya**
**Salma**

**((Worda and Wafiya pretend their dolls have met on the street and greet each other))**

| | |
|---|---|
| **1. WAFIYA:** | ***Sala:::m***<br>**Hello** |
| **2. WORDA:** | ***Kiraki dayra?***<br>**How are you?** |
| **3. WAFIYA:** | ***labas***<br>**Fine** |

→

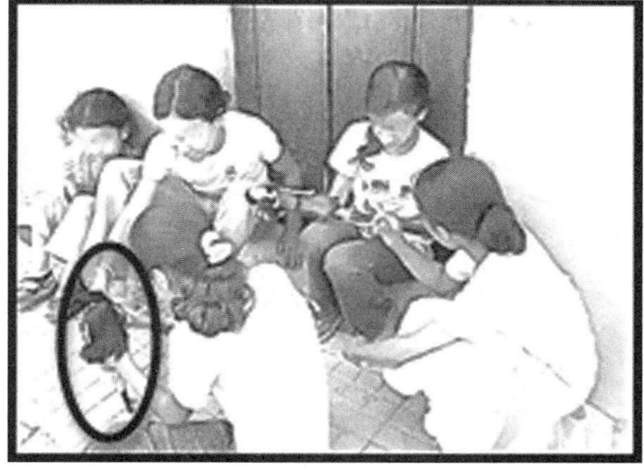

**4. WORDA:** ***Hadri aSbanyouliya Hadri***
**Speak Spanish Speak**

**5. WAFIYA:** Hola
**Hello**

**6. WORDA:** qué tal?
**how are you?**

**7. SALMA:** **Nn::: ((Vocalizes to signal to Wafiya that she has dropped her doll's purse))**[12]

**8. WORDA:** Se te ha caído el bolso?
**Did you drop the purse?**

**9. WAFIYA:** y yo también
**and me too**

**10. WORDA:** Te vas a la playa?
**Are you going to the beach?**

**11. WAFIYA:** Sí vamos
**Yes, let's go**

**12. WORDA:** vale
**ok**

in line 4 with a bold, repeated imperative in Moroccan Arabic "Haḍri aSbanyouliya Haḍri" (Speak Spanish Speak). Wafiya orients positively to this command by initiating a second greeting exchange in Spanish in line 5—"Hola" (Hello)—that closely mirrors her initial greeting in Moroccan Arabic in line 1—"Sala:::m" (Hello:::). Similarly, Worda responds to this new

EXAMPLE # 2: Key: Spanish (Regular Font) — Moroccan Arabic (***Bold Italics***)

**Participants:**
**Worda**
**Wafiya**
**Salma**
**Lamia**

**1. WORDA:** ***šuf druk raha žayya Hsan man gbila, yaki?***
**Look now, she's better than before, right? ((Referring to Salma's Doll))**

**((Wafiya communicates with Salma with gestures expressing that the doll looks very pretty.))**

**2. SALMA:** **Nn::::**
**((Salma vocalizes, still unhappy))**

**3. WORDA:** ***iwa haki, go 'di***
**Listen take it, sit down**

**4. SALMA:** **Nn:::: Nn:::**
**((Salma vocalizes, still unhappy))**

**5. WORDA:** ***mabġitiš? iwa ruHi barra***
**you don't want?, ok Go away**

**6. WORDA:** Estamos tardando mucho, eh?
**We're taking a long time, ah?**

**7. WAFIYA:** Y el collar te lo has traído?
**And the necklace did you bring it?**

(...)

**8. WORDA:** Vamos, vamos que hemos tardao mucho
**Come on, come on. It's already taken us a long time**

**9. WORDA:** Uy ya hemos llegao. Me voy a dormir así la siesta
**We have already arrived. I'm going to take a nap.**

**10. WORDA:** Vamos a qued- ***matšaddihaš man š'ar tfu (xxx)***
**Let's stay- don't grab her by the hair (xxx)**

greeting in Spanish with a sequentially appropriate "Qué tal?" (How are you?) in line 6 that is equivalent to her greeting in line 2—"Kiraki dayra?" (How are you?). After this second greeting exchange in Spanish, code alternation between Spanish and Moroccan Arabic is fairly consistent throughout the game, and the girls speak in Spanish only when speaking *for the dolls*. In addition, it is important to mention that some of the activities the girls begin to enact in this opening excerpt—in Line 10, "Te vas a la playa?" (Are you going to the beach?) and Line 11, "Sí vamos" (Yes, let's go)—could be assessed negatively by adults. Unlike their male siblings, some of the girls participating in this doll-play, in particular Worda and her sisters and Wafiya, were not allowed to go to the municipal swimming pool during the summer.[14]

The pattern of code choice, as established by the girls themselves in the opening sequence of their pretend game, is crucial not only to sustain and signal shifts between *in-play* and *off-play* **interactional frames** but also to mark children's changes in **footing** (Goffman 1981) and **affective stances** towards the game itself and towards each other. For instance, although in their daily lives interactions with siblings often take place in Spanish, *off-play* interactions among siblings throughout the game are carried out in Moroccan Arabic. In particular, negotiating disagreement and controlling the rogue behavior of siblings as well as the mischievous behavior of other girls are two activities that very often trigger switches into Moroccan Arabic. In this sense, codeswitching can also be considered as playing an important interactional role in the construction and enforcement of in-group norms of behavior that regulate interactions among peers. In addition, older siblings' linguistic behavior also has important implications for intergenerational sociocultural and language maintenance.

Example 2 illuminates ways in which codeswitching is a crucial linguistic resource not only for signaling shifts between on-play and off-play interactional frames but also for this group of girls' interactional management of sibling conflict and appropriate conduct during the game. The excerpt opens with an exchange in Moroccan Arabic between Worda and her sister Salma. Salma has repeatedly refused to participate with her doll in the pretend-play that her sister and the other girls are enacting, and, furthermore, is upset because of the way her doll looks. Worda has been trying to calm her down and to convince her to participate in the game. In Line 1, Worda attempts to convince her sister one more time to participate in the game. Immediately before this excerpt, Worda has been dressing and styling Salma's doll.

Worda responds to Salma's refusals to participate in the game with a series of bold directives in line 3 "iwa haki, go'di" (Listen, take it, sit down) and line 5—"ruHi barra" (Go away). This last directive is particularly aggravated, as it can also be seen in Worda's gesture in the frame grab above, and results in Salma being asked to leave the group. Immediately following this last directive, Worda code-switches into Spanish in line 6, closing the *off-play* sequence and resuming *in-character dialogue*. Moreover, in ventriloquizing the voice of the doll as saying "Estamos tardando mucho, eh?" (We are taking a long time, ah?—Line 6), Worda is not only effectively shifting frames but also constructing the *on-play* interactional frame as the main activity. She treats the preceding exchange with her sister as a parenthetical insertion, clearly separate and distinct from the *on-play* interactional frame. A second interesting instance of codeswitching takes place a few turns later in line 10. Worda and Wafiya are engaged in *in-character dialogue* and are enacting a play scene between their dolls involving a trip to the beach. In the midst of their dialogue, Wafiya grabs Worda's doll by her hair with a forceful movement. Worda then interrupts her turn in mid-sentence and code-switches into Moroccan Arabic with the bold directive "matšaddihaš man š'ar tfu" (Don't grab her by the hair), rebuking Wafiya for her careless handling of the doll.

The previous examples demonstrate the interactional importance of codeswitching between Spanish and Moroccan Arabic for the on-going organization of distinct interactional and play frames, for social control of siblings and other girls, and for management of pretend-play peer norms, preferences, and expectations. The following sections examine how codeswitching also plays a crucial role in girls' construction of gendered identities for their play characters.

## Linguistic Resources for the Construction of Social Identities and Life Worlds

The **indexical** meanings (or **metaphorical meanings**, Gumperz 1982) of children's codeswitching practices to create social identities for play characters, as well as of children's own metacommentary on these enactments, is particularly relevant in multilingual immigrant contexts. Because these contexts are not only linguistically complex, but socially, culturally, and politically complicated as well, Bakhtin's (1981) notion of heteroglossia is particularly useful to get at all the socio-ideological layers of children's hybrid voicing. To examine how all the layers in these immigrant girls' codeswitching practices co-occur to indexicalize class-, ethnicity-, and gender-inflected social identities, it is important to pay attention to three aspects of language-use in codeswitching: Naming practices, in-character dialogue, and stage-setting narration.

### Naming Practices

The power inherent in naming, as both a language and an identity act, has been highlighted cross-culturally in studies on names and naming practices (Alford 1988; Blum 1997; Eid 1995; Markstrom and Iborra 2003; Rymes 1996). Far from being arbitrary or a one-time fixed label, a name can be constitutive of personal and social identity, in that naming is thoroughly embedded in the way people constitute relationships with themselves, with one another and with the world that surrounds them (Blum 1997).[15] Choosing 'appropriate' names for their dolls and for other imaginary play characters is an important activity in Moroccan immigrant girls' pretend-play. The social and indexical meanings of this group of girls' naming practices become even more relevant against the backdrop of transgressional socio-cultural and linguistic subversion that characterize their peer-group codeswitching practices and interactions. Example 3 is excerpted from one of the negotiation sequences involving the assignation of names for play characters. As part of this negotiation, different names of Spanish and Arabic origins are proposed; the first are accepted and ratified, while the latter are invariably rejected. In this sense, the excerpt illustrates both the indexical values of codes for the construction of the social identities of the play characters. The segment starts in Spanish, since the girls have been ventriloquizing their dolls in the previous turns. In line 3, Worda codeswitches into Moroccan Arabic, shifting frames as the girls begin a negotiation sequence to decide the names of their dolls. This negotiation ends in line 14 when all the girls have chosen *appropriate* names for their dolls, and Worda codeswitches again into Spanish, resuming *in-character play*. In addition to codeswitching, this shift in frame is also achieved by the Spanish **discourse marker**[16] "vale," which is often used as a closing sequence device to signal that agreement has been reached by all parties in an interaction about a particular topic.

EXAMPLE # 3: Key: Spanish (Regular Font) — Moroccan Arabic (***Bold Italics***)

| **Participants:** |
|---|
| **Worda** |
| **Wafiya** |
| **Dunia** |
| **Lamia** |

**1. WORDA:** Cómo te llamas? Yo Carolina
**Wafiya, what's your name? I am Carolina**

**2. LAMIA:** Yo (Lidia/Lilia) ((Laughing))
**I am (Lidia/Lilia)**

**3. WORDA:** Lidia ***goli*** Lidia ***ba'da***
**Lidia call her Lidia at least**

**4. WAFIYA:** ***ana*** Lidia, ***ana*** Lidia
**I am Lidia, I am Lidia**

**5. LAMIA:** ***ana*** Lidia, ***anti?***
**I am Lidia, you are?**

**6. LAMIA:** [Lidia ((pointing at herself))

**7. WAFIYA:** [***wana ana Zora-Suriya=***
**And I am Zora-Suriya=**

**8. LAMIA:** =***Zoraida=***
=***Zoraida=***

**9. WORDA:** =***la, la, la***
**=no, no, no**

**10. LAMIA:** =*Soraya*
=**Soraya**

**11. WAFIYA:** Tsk, Tsk, Tsk ((Shaking her head)) E:::h
**Tsk, Tsk, Tsk ((Shaking her head)) E:::h**

**12. WORDA:** ***ana*** Rosi
**I am Rosi**

**13. WAFIYA:** ***ana*** Carolina
**I am Carolina**

**14. WORDA:** [Vale? Carolina yo me voy
**Ok? Carolina I am leaving**

**15. LAMIA:** [el pelo como está- es rubia o-
**My hair how it is- It's blond or**

**16. WAFIYA:** Pos adiós
**Then, good-bye**

**17. WORDA:** Te vas a quedar?
**Are you staying?**

**18. WAFIYA:** No yo también [me voy
**No, I am also [leaving**

**19. WORDA:** [Qué- qué tonta eres!
**[How- how silly you are**

The act of naming that these girls perform during role-play is crucial for imparting an identity for their play characters. In negotiating what names are acceptable for their dolls, the girls construct specific ethnic and gendered social identities, while simultaneously rejecting other identities associated with first generation Moroccan immigrants. Only Spanish names are ratified and accepted, while names of Arabic origin, such as Suriya or Zoraida, are repeatedly rejected (in lines 9 and 11, respectively), paralleling the girls' choice of Spanish to ventriloquize the dolls. Through Spanish naming practices, girls attempt to access *technologies of power* (Foucault 1982/1988). Thus, in the play frame, they become full-fledged host society '*insiders*' able to exert power and agency.

Their local versions of Spanish femininity (or what being a Spanish female means to them), become more subtle and complex as the interaction unfolds. In addition to their choices of name and code, it is important to pay attention to girls' shift to a highly stylized feminine register of Spanish during *in-character dialogue* and to the dreamy life worlds that the girls construct for the dolls through the combination of *in-character dialogue* and *stage-setting narration*. The language practices described which the girls bring to bear in *the voices* they enact *for the dolls*, are crucial in unpacking how social identities encapsulated in these names are related to the girls' perceptions of the links between language, social roles, status, and expectations.

### Register shifts in 'In-Character Dialogue'

Many times when voicing the play characters, the girls shift to a stylized register of Spanish that is highly distinct from the Spanish variety that the girls use in most contexts of their daily lives. Girls' **enregisterment** when voicing their play characters is consequential for their construction of idealized versions of Spanish femininity, in that the indexical value of this register is rooted in its recognizable association with upper class, *fashionable* women (Agha 2005). This *in-character dialogue* register is characterized by exaggerated affectation of manners and stance. This heightened affective orientation and artificial posturing operates concurrently at several levels of linguistic structure: **Phonological, morphological** and **discursive**

(Ochs and Schieffelin 1989). At the phonological level, the register is characterized by use of exaggerated intonation contours, amplified pitch, and vowel elongation, such as in:

(a) **WORDA:** ↑Eduardo::: (.) ya ha venido mi marido Eduardo
**↑Eduardo::: (.) my husband Eduardo has already arrived**

And, also, by the hyper-pronunciation of final sounds (i.e. /s/), as in

(b) **WAFIYA:** yo- lo que pidaS, pidelo
**I- what you order, order it**
**(=meaning whatever you order, order it for me as well)**

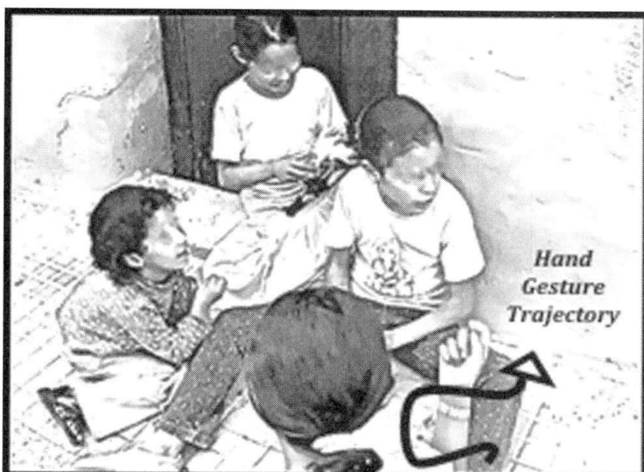


This hyper-pronunciation of final /s/ is particularly salient in the sociolinguistic environment of Southwestern Spain, where one of the most widespread **dialectal** features is the systematic **aspiration** or dropping of all final sounds. In addition, the affectation indexed by this kind of hyper-pronunciation is rendered more powerful by its co-occurrence with equally affected gestures and other non-verbal behavior. Although it is difficult to convey the full range of a hand gesture in a single image, the frame grab above captures the endpoint of a continuous hand gesture, whose upward and outward trajectory is rendered by the curvy arrow. This gesture is frequently used to affect women of higher class. Girls' linguistic and corporeal behavior, in this regard, is reminiscent of **hypercorrection** phenomena documented as common among socially insecure groups of low socio-economic status (Labov 1964, 1966), who appropriate linguistic features of socio-economic dominant groups in an attempt to *gain* **social** and **cultural capital** (Bourdieu 1991).

At the morphological level, there is a conspicuous use of affect-loaded suffixes, such as '-ito,' as in:

(c) **WORDA:** = ↑UY que cafeci:to me voy a tomar!
**= ↑UY what a good little coffee I am going to have!**

Finally, at the discourse level, the affected quality of this register is accomplished by the deployment of stereotypical speech genres of girl talk, such as the *demure* or *fake-embarrassment* genre. In Example 4, one of the girls enacts this appearance-conscious genre when voicing her doll's repeated requests for attention to the way in which she is wearing her imaginary bikini.

EXAMPLE # 4: Key: Spanish (Regular Font)

**Participants:**
**Worda**
**Wafiya**
**Dunia**
**Lamia**

1. **WORDA:** ↑O:::H, Me lo he puesto al revés. Me lo he puesto al revés o no? (1.5) Di:::!
**↑O:::H, I have put it inside out. Have I put it inside out or not? (1.5) Te:::ll me!**
2. **WAFIYA:** Qué?
**What?**
3. **WORDA:** Que si me lo he puesto al revés?
**Whether I have put it inside out?**
4. **WAFIYA:** Qué es?
**What is it?**
5. **LAMIA:** Qué?
**What?**
6. **WORDA:** El bikini
**My bikini**
**((Girls laugh))**
7. **WAFIYA:** °No:
**No**
8. **WORDA:** Vaya
**Oh, well.**

As noted above, many of these girls, including Worda, are not allowed to wear swimwear in public. In this respect, what is also striking about this excerpt is that the doll is actually not wearing a bikini. Yet, Worda performs this genre in an affected and emphatic manner as evidenced by the initial, phonologically salient "O:::H" in Line 1 and by her repeated requests for other girls' attention in Line 1 "Di:::!" (Te:::ll me!) and in Line 3 "Que si me lo he puesto al revés?" (Whether I have put it inside out?). Once she has secured other participants' undivided attention, Worda delivers the *punch line* with maximal effect in Line 6 "El bikini" (My bikini). The subsequent eruption of laughter indexes [the] girls' embarrassment and their awareness of the transgressional possibilities of their game.

### Emplotment Through Stage-Setting Narration and In-Character Dialogue

Although some facets of emplotment of play dramas are accomplished in Moroccan Arabic, much stage setting of the activities the dolls are to perform is carried out in Spanish. Narratives enacted through the voices of the play characters create an idealized Spanish high society life style, with independence, access to financial resources, professional success, and a lively social agenda of activities that take place outside of home domains.

The doll characters, as performed by the girls, spend much of their time socializing with their *friends* (i.e. the other dolls): They go to the beach and the swimming pool; they go out to have coffee, dinners, and to nighttime parties. The dolls are portrayed as financially well off and go on several shopping trips for cell phones and clothes. In addition, they make plans to go to a nearby town to look for an apartment to rent, since they have just gotten jobs as '*directora*' (manager) and '*profesora*' (professor). In a later iteration of this game the dolls turn out to be married to Spanish men; the choice of names for the dolls' *husbands* (Eduardo, Miguel, and Alfredo, respectively) is also crucial in establishing identifications for these other imaginary characters. Example 5 is part of a larger sequence in which the girls enact a social outing to have coffee and dinner with friends.

EXAMPLE # 5: Key: Spanish (Regular Font) — Moroccan Arabic (***Bold Italics***)

**Participants:**
**Worda**
**Wafiya**
**Lamia**
**Dunia**

**1. WORDA:** Estamos en la cafetería=
**We're in the cafeteria**

**2. WAFIYA:** =VaMOS ((inaudible))
**=Let's go ((inaudible))**
**((Worda and Wafiya sit their dolls in a circle they have created with their legs))**

**3. WORDA:** ***alla alkašni dyal hadi a Wafiya***
**((She returns the shawl to Lamia))**
**No, no that's the shawl of this one**

**4. WAFIYA:** He he he ((laughing))

**5. WORDA:** ***A Wafiya*** ((inaudible))
**Wafiya ((inaudible))**

**6. WAFIYA:** Qué tal?
**How are you?**

**7. WORDA:** Bien
**Fine**

**8. WAFIYA:** °Estamos aquí
**°We are here**

**9. WAFIYA:** Te lo pongo?
**Do I put it on for you?=**
**((Referring to Lamia's doll's shawl))**

**10. WORDA:** = ↑UY qué cafeci:to me voy a tomar!
**= ↑UY what a good little coffee I am going to have!**

**11. WAFIYA:** Y yo también
**And me too**

**12. DUNIA:** Toma, toma **((Giving a toy purse to Lamia))**
**Take it, take it**

**13. DUNIA:** Se te [cayó **((Still speaking to Lamia))**
**It [fell**

**14. WORDA:** [Qué guay
**How cool**

(...)

**15. WORDA:** No. Yo he pedido na mas ketchup con pollo y::: pescado
**No. I have ordered anything else. Ketchup with chicken and fish**

**16. WAFIYA:** Pollo, pescado [patatas fritas
**Chicken, fish, [French fries**

**17. WORDA:** [y, y
**[and, and**

**18. WORDA:** y whisky
**And whisky**

**19. WAFIYA:** Yo whisky y patatas fritas con ketchup y pollo y pescado
**I whisky and French fries with ketchup and chicken and fish**

This excerpt illustrates how these idealized life worlds are created in both *in-character dialogue* (Lines 6–11, and line 14. See also, lines 15–19) and *stage-setting narration* (Line 1 and Line 8).[17] As they dramatize this cafeteria outing and, through the voices of the dolls, engage in transgressional behaviors, such as drinking alcohol, the girls are also exploring imagined possibilities that are part of their repertoires of selves, identities, and moral worlds. The imagined possibilities that the pretend-play and the dolls, as part of the girls' material culture, afford are constrained in the real world by family expectations, monitoring and control over girls' behavior, by unequal structures of the Spanish society which considers them outsiders, and by the socio-economic positions of their families within these structures. Yet, as the girls construct through the voices of the dolls alternative social realities and life worlds in which they hold decision-making authority, they momentarily challenge, subvert, and transform restrictions and conflicts they experience in other everyday environments. In this sense, *in-character dialogue* and *stage setting* function as powerful counter-narratives to subject and economic subaltern positions assigned to them by the host society and to other cultural narratives about female behavior in their diasporic communities.

The role of the peer group as a relatively autonomous arena for action with limited, if any, adult supervision is critical for these immigrant girls' explorations of ways of being in the world that their families could consider transgressional, such as drinking alcohol, attending night time parties, or exposing themselves in swimwear. Furthermore, the extraordinarily dreamy life worlds that the girls construct for their play characters, along with the highly stylized register of Spanish with which they enact the social voices (Agha 2005; Bahktin 1981, 1986) of the dolls, also suggests an idealization of Spanish femininity as desirable. Desire often reverberates interactionally when the girls, *through the voices of the dolls*, make evaluations of the activities they enact, as in example 7.5: "Qué guay!" (How cool! Line 14).

## Ambivalent Stances and the Moral Inflection of Codes

Although a positive stance of playfulness and desire dominates pretend-play, a closer analysis of girls' codeswitching practices reveals a more ambivalent stance towards the actions and gendered identifications that they are performing in their games. The ambivalent stances that permeate Moroccan immigrant girls' doll play are reminiscent of other ethnographically situated accounts of identity formation among immigrant youth in other communities across Europe (Hall 1995, 2002; Treteault, 2008).

Codeswitching into Moroccan Arabic to make metacommentaries about girls' own behavior, the behavior of the other girls, and the actions they are enacting in their imaginary play serve as an important function for the interactional management of the girls' conflicting affective stances towards their *Spanish* gendered identifications. Instances of metacommentaries interspersed throughout the game indicate a high level of *reflexivity* (Bakhtin 1981) in that girls are aware that they are acting transgressionally. Example 6 opens with the girls ventriloquizing the voices of the dolls as they are getting ready to leave for the beach. When Salma refuses to join in the pretend-play, an explosion of laughter follows. Lamia happens to laugh particularly boisterously. Worda then codeswitches into Moroccan Arabic to reprimand Lamia's noisy behavior, because it has the potential *to give them away*.

This metacommentary marks the pretend-play they are engaged in as a *clandestine interaction* (De Certeau 1988; Sterponi 2004: 96–97) meant to take place surreptitiously away from the gaze and the ears of adult authority figures. Central to the construction of the doll-play as *clandestine* is the semantics of the verb 'fḍeH' (to give away), used when one has a secret to protect or is doing something stealthily. Making too much noise is in this context dangerous, because it may attract the attention of parents and others to the activities of the girls in the peer group. Girls' own construction of their pretend-play as a clandestine activity and the ambivalence this reveals towards the actions they perform as part of the game infuses the social meanings of codes in this peer group. Use of Moroccan Arabic and Spanish in this pretend-play results in a heteroglossic polyphony of voices imbued with moral tensions (Bahktin 1981, 1986). The struggle (in Bakhtin's sense) between the Moroccan voices of the girls in their metacommentaries and the Spanish voices they enact for their play characters inflects the codes with ethical valences. Moroccan Arabic is the code in which the girls voice their moral ambiguity, and Spanish is the furtive language that they bring to bear in their clandestine explorations of imagined transgressional possibilities, repertoires of selves, and ways of being in the world. The hybrid linguistic practices allow the voice of the *characters*, the voice of the *narrator*, and the voice of the *director* to represent distinct points of view on the world.

EXAMPLE # 6: Key: Spanish (Regular Font) — Moroccan Arabic (***Bold Italics***)

**Participants:**
**Worda**
**Wafiya**
**Salma**
**Lamia**
**Dunia**

**1. WORDA:** Yo me voy, eh? Vamo:s
**I'm leaving, ah? Let's go**

**2. WAFIYA:** Vamo:::s
**Let's go!**

**3. WORDA:** ((inaudible)) ***yalla*** **((To Salma))**
**((inaudible)) let's go**

**4. SALMA:** **Nn::: Nn:::: ((Shaking her head))**

**((Wafiya starts laughing and Lamia laughs extremely loud))**

**5. WORDA:** ***a Lamia ġadi tfaḍHina***
**Lamia is going to give us away**

***((To Lamia))ruHi galsi alhiha falbab adyalna***
**go sit down by our door**

## The Peer Group as a Context for Language Socialization into Communicative Practices and Gendered Identities

The examples discussed in this paper illustrate immigrant children's acute sensitivity to the power of contrasting languages and registers to index and construct stances, acts, activities, and social identities (Ochs 1992, 1993, 2002). How do children learn the complex linguistic and socio-cultural knowledge that they deploy in ludic interactions among peers? As noted above, in pretend-play girls interweave ordinary aspects of their lives with '*high society*' and glamorous behaviors, actions, and even ways of speaking. Some of the behaviors that the girls make relevant in their pretend-play can be traced to girls' everyday activities, such as training for and running in public arena races, watching T.V., going to the store and so on. Codeswitching as a practice is itself part of the girls' repertoire of everyday ways of speaking. At the same time, the girls' role enactments include a range of behaviors (including ways of speaking, such as the highly stylized register of Spanish that they use when ventriloquizing the dolls) that are far removed from their daily lives. They are, after all, enacting *being adult women* whose conducts are barred for them, because of socio-economic constraints or moral expectations. I would like to consider further these more extraordinary enactments.

Some enactments in pretend-play were remote for the girls due to the difficult socio-economic situation of many of these immigrant families (e.g. expensive shopping trips for clothes and technology), or to family prohibitions for female behavior (e.g. going to the local swimming pool or participating in some of the festivities that take place annually in the town). Parental sanctions are particularly relevant because, as Kulick and Schieffelin (2004: 335) have discussed in their account of language socialization in relation to culturally-discouraged subject positions or 'bad subjects', prohibitions may act as an instigator of desire: "verbal admonitions which are intended to discourage particular desires, in fact often sustain them" (2004: 357). This dynamic may partially account for the idealization and stance of desire that permeates the Spanish-dominant doll pretend-play interactions analyzed in this paper. Alternatively, although their mothers or older sister would very rarely go out to coffee shops or engage in the kind of social outings that the girls perform in the course of the doll-play, the girls would observe many other groups of women going to bars, restaurants and coffee shops on weekend afternoons and early evenings. They were also exposed to their female teachers' conversations in informal school settings, where plans and weekend activities were often discussed. In addition, they would also frequently overhear exchanges among the most socially popular female peers in their classes about shopping trips to near, larger cities, where many of them often went to purchase clothes and school materials.

Another crucial aspect to consider in the girls' constructions and idealizations of the dolls' femininity is the role that TV sitcoms and soap operas may play in these girls' imaginative play. Many of the girls that I studied were avid consumers of these types of programs. As mentioned, characters and plots from these television programs were some of the most common themes of pretend-play in these girls' peer groups. Discussion about the 'previous day's episode' was common in school during class breaks and other social venues not only among Moroccan immigrant girls but also among their Spanish female peers. The girls' exposure to varied ways of speaking and possible ways of being in the world as females, through mass media, observation and vicarious participation in adult and classmate-organized activities affords their socialization into host society (1) gendered identities, (2) socio-economic hierarchies, and (3) indexical associations for different codes and language practices.

An important dimension that I would like to highlight is how the peer group itself is a crucial context for children's socialization into communicative practices and processes of identification (Goodwin and Kyratzis 2007; Goodwin 2000; García-Sánchez 2005; Paugh 2005). As noted, Moroccan immigrant peer groups are composed of children of different ages and with different levels of expertise in and experience with Moroccan and Spanish linguistic and socio-cultural practices (See "The Peer Group as a Unit of Analysis"). In pretend-play, older girls, or girls with longer migratory histories, also expose and socialize younger children and children with shorter lengths of stay in the country into hybrid uses of language varieties available to them and into ways of (re)fashioning alternative social identities.

The significance of play for children's socio-cultural learning has been highlighted in a number of fields. Goodwin (1985: 316–317) has argued that a continuity exists between hierarchical forms of interaction within games and non-game domains of experience. Moroccan girls' play allows them to experiment with the meaning of socio-cultural processes in game domains and with the meaning of those processes in other domains of their daily lives. In addition, Rogoff (1998) has pointed out that in play children contribute to each other's learning as well as to their own development. *Intent participation*, in particular (Rogoff, Paradise, Mejía Arauz, Correa-Chávez, and Angelillo 2003), entails keen observation of an on-going activity in which the novice is already participating or is expected to participate and is a pervasive and effective way of learning in children's lives. Intent participation involves collaboration between experts and novices in a shared endeavor.

In the pretend-play sequences under analysis, intent participation organizes the learning process of child novices in powerful ways. Throughout the games, children novices, such as Dunia, Worda's youngest sister, can be seen keenly observing the actions of her older peers, often in anticipation of participation (See image on opposite page.). Many times in these pretend-play sequences, Dunia picks up her sister's and other girls' dolls, while the rest argued and negotiated different parameters of the game, to practice and rehearse the actions that she had seen the other girls previously enact, often carrying out quasi-whispering self-dialogues with the dolls. Dunia always ran after her peers whenever they went to their houses or to the near-by construction site to pick up further props for their games. In addition, Dunia's emerging participation and understanding of the practices enacted in this doll-play interaction can be observed in her self-appointed role as a 'look-out', collecting dolls'

*Dunia's Observation and Intent Participation*

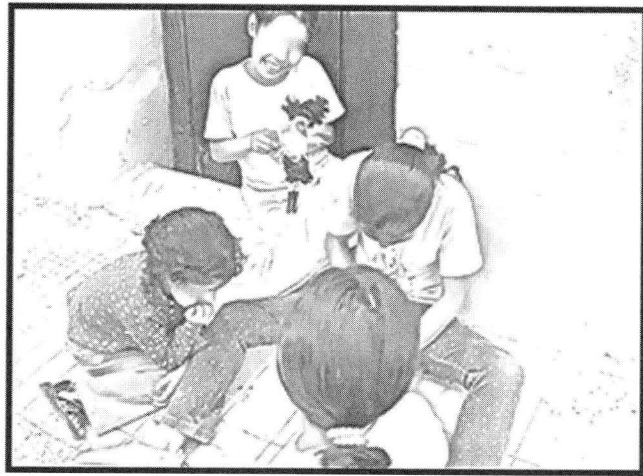

props, such as toy purses or glasses that fell off the dolls in the midst of play, and most importantly, warning her sister and the other girls whenever any adult or adolescent boys approached the peer group.

The peer group is a primordial locus for immigrant children's language socialization as well when they share stories with each other about some of the social outings in which they were allowed to participate. They would often incorporate events of these outings in their games. Not all Moroccan girls in this study experience the same levels of restriction and monitoring. While some parents would not permit the daughters' participation in extra-curricular school field trips, other parents did not object to such occasions. One of the field trips that took place during my fieldwork was an outing to a movie theater in a nearby, larger city to see the popular movie *The Chronicles of Narnia.* A day after this field trip took place, a large number of Moroccan girls gathered in the park after school. Among them were three of the participants in this doll pretend-play (Worda, Wafiya, and Dunia). Those girls who had been allowed to go to the movies started telling the other girls their experiences in the theater and described the plot of the movie. Eventually, all the girls decided that they were going to pretend-play *The Chronicles of Narnia*, which I had the opportunity to record. In these ways, pretend-play with peers offers a prime context for immigrant children's socio-cultural and linguistic learning, and socialization into dominant cultural dispositions and practices otherwise out of reach for many of the girls in this study.

## Conclusion

The minimal adult supervision of peer group activities makes pretend-play a crucial context for immigrant children to become active agents in their own and other children's socialization into communicative practices and socio-cultural norms. The rich verbal and socio-cultural environments of peer groups provide an excellent window to investigate how immigrant children negotiate and subvert through play the different, and often incongruous, socio-cultural and linguistic expectations and constraints that they encounter on a daily basis. Codeswitching between Spanish and Moroccan Arabic plays a critical role in these processes. This analysis has highlighted the importance of these hybrid linguistic practices in immigrant girls' explorations of alternative processes of gendered identification and future life paths in multilingual, culturally-syncretic environments where, not only languages, but also ways of being in the world enter into conflict. This research underscores the implications of children's language use and choice in pretend-play for larger processes of cultural continuity and transformation in transnational, diasporic communities undergoing rapid change (See also Paugh 2005).

In addition, the indexically-complex linguistic practices in this immigrant girls' peer group illuminate important aspects of the relation between codeswitching and social identity. Many instances of codeswitching, particularly those involving shifts to a register highly distinct from the Spanish that the girls use in the communicative contexts that make up their daily lives are more related to the dynamic aspects of translingual phenomena, such as Rampton's (1995, 1998) description of **crossing,**[18] than to the one-to-one mapping between codeswitching and social identity, such as solidarity-distance and in-group/out-group dichotomies, that characterized some of the earlier research on codeswitching (See Woolard 2004 and Auer 1998 for a review and critique of this literature).

Narrative emplotment, in-character dialogue, and running metacommentary inflect the codes with sociopolitical and moral values. The girls' own ideological interpretations of and stances towards these values mobilized in their codeswitching practices offer a vantage point into their developing gendered and ethnic subjectivities and socio-cultural consciousness (Hill 1985; Gal 1987), as well as into their incipient political consciousness. The investigation of children's development of gender, socio-cultural, and political consciousness, particularly the role that everyday linguistic and social practices play in them, may be particularly important for immigrant girls' complex and ambiguous processes of identification. As Hall (1995: 244) noted in her discussion of how young British Sikh imagine their futures in relation to numerous possible identities, as they contend with the contrasting ideologies of their families and host country: "Identity formation is not simply a matter of preserving a cultural tradition handed down by one's parents. For ethnic minorities marginalized by the forces of racism and nationalism as well as forms of class and gender inequality, cultural-identity formation, I will argue, is an inherently political process."

Finally, although outside of the scope of the present paper, peer play involving toys, and dolls in particular, also have important implications for the affordances that material culture has in the life of children and how children exploit these affordances as they learn to navigate their own ways through societal structures and hierarchies (Thorne *Forthcoming*).

## Notes

1. The first part of the title of this [chapter] makes reference to Ortner's formulation of *serious games* (Ortner 1996, 1999, 2006) as a way of understanding how in social life and relations, "social actors through their living, on the ground, variable practices, reproduce, transform—and usually some of each—the culture that made them" (2006: 129). Although the social activity that this group of immigrant girls is engaged in is indeed a *game*, the metaphorical notion of *serious games* is particularly useful for the purposes of this [chapter] because it takes into account both the complex dimensions of the subjectivity of social actors and the complex forms of social relations of power, inequality, and solidarity. In this sense, the notion captures the constraints and affordances of individuals as agents in relation to the larger forces of formation, reproduction, and transformation of social and cultural life. Much like the doll-pretend play that this group of immigrant girls enacts, a *serious games* perspective considers the possibility of how the engagement of social actors with others in the play of *serious games* (or the micropolitics of social life, involving both routine and intentionalized action), "contain the potential to disrupt particular plays of the game in the case of individuals, and the very continuity of the game as a social and cultural formation over the long run" (2006: 151).

2. Corsaro's (1994, 1997) notion of *interpretive reproduction* suggests that in the peer cultures in which children participate and create, children do not just merely reproduce aspects of the adult social world. Rather, by creatively appropriating information and knowledge about the larger social world, they are able to extend it and transform it, as well as reproduce it.

3. In documenting patterns of sociological change observed in Moroccan youth in the last few decades, El Harras (2004: 41–42) has discussed a similar phenomenon in Morocco. He has claimed that, although the control of parents over female children seems to have weakened in the last few decades, the control of male siblings over their sisters has tightened and increased. Many male youth adopt the self-appointed role of guardians of the moral conduct of their sisters and, in general, of the family honor.

4. In addition to children's interactions with peers, I videotaped the children's participation in routine activities with members of their extended households once a month. Because a central goal of this study was to investigate how children juggled languages and social practices to meet different situational expectations, once a week I also videotaped focal children's linguistic practices in different institutional learning contexts (the town public school and Koranic classes at the local mosque) and formal after-school activities (training sessions with the local track and field team). Finally, I also had the opportunity to videotape children at the local health center where they would often translate for their parents during visits to the pediatrician. This last set of data is the least systematically recorded due to the unpredictability of medical needs and/or children's availability to act as language brokers in these encounters. Accompanying the video record, there are comprehensive ethnographic notes, along with photographs, maps and charts, children's textbooks and other printed material collected during fieldwork, about family and social interactions in the community, including celebrations, professional meetings, and special events, as well as more quotidian aspects of the community life. In-depth ethnographic interviews were also conducted over a period of several months with focal children, parents, teachers, and school officials.

5. Transcription conventions adapted from Goodwin (1990), pp. 25–26:

| | |
|---|---|
| : | Lengthening |
| ° | Low Volume |
| . | Falling contour |
| ? | Rising contour |
| ↑ | Higher Pitch |
| [ | Overlap |
| = | Latching (no interval between turns) |
| ~ | Rapid speech |
| - | Sudden cut-off |
| (.) | Brief Pause |
| () | Material in parenthesis indicate a hearing the transcriber was unsure about |
| (()) | Comment by the transcriber. Not part of the talk being transcribed |
| **BOLD UNDERLINED CAPITALS** | Increased volume |

6. Paugh (2005) has also discussed the significance of place and spatial restrictions on children's language use in her study of children's multilingual play in Dominica. See also Schieffelin's (2003) discussion of language and play in children's worlds.

7. The only out-of-school context in which both Moroccan immigrant children and Spanish children of mixed genders came together in a socially shared space of action was the track-and-field team. In this arena, boys and girls of multiple ethnicities participated jointly in weekly training and weekend competitions. However, these endeavors cannot be considered peer group activities *per se* since they are supervised by adults, namely two male coaches and several parents, who would sometimes accompany the children in some of the most geographically removed competitions. In addition, even in these contexts, I was able to document a tendency for Spanish children and Moroccan children (again, segregated by gender) to cluster separately during training breaks or down-times before and after the competition. Certainly, during the often long bus rides that would take the children to different competition sites, Moroccan and Spanish children rarely sat together.

8. These are not the children's real names. In order to safeguard the anonymity and privacy of the children who participated in the study, all the names in this [chapter] are pseudonyms that the girls themselves chose.

9. For more ethnographic information about these girls and the composition of this peer group, see "The Peer Group as a Unit of Analysis" above.

10. It is also important to mention that Moroccan immigrant children also attend Arabic Heritage Language classes at school once a week as part of a first-language maintenance program that is jointly funded by the Moroccan and Spanish Ministries of Education.

11. See Appendix I for Arabic transliteration symbols.

12. Salma suffered a serious ear infection as a baby. As a consequence, she lost most of her auditory ability and cannot speak.

13. Kissing on both cheeks is a pervasive, ritualistic feature of greetings among friends and acquaintances in both Moroccan and Spanish communities.

14. In conversations with the girls and their mothers, I learned that this prohibition was related to parents' concern about their daughters exposing themselves publicly in swimwear. Interestingly, the issue of swimwear is also made relevant by the girls later in the game (See Example 4 below).

15. The importance of names has been particularly emphasized in research on naming in relation to gender and identity (Alford 1988; Eid 1995). For example, in their study of Navajo female rites of passage, Markstrom and Iborra (2003) have discussed how the new names adopted in these ceremonies defined adolescent girls' changing identities, as well as new social roles and expectations.

16. Discourse markers have also been described as an important interactional resource by which children in monolingual contexts manage different interactional and play frames in peer interaction (See Kyratzis and Ervin-Tripp 1999).

17. Lines 3–5 involve negotiation of conflict over a piece of clothing for the doll. As mentioned earlier when discussing play and interactional frames, negotiations interspersed in the emplotment of the pretend-play are carried out in Moroccan Arabic. Lines 12–13 are part of a concurrent interaction between Dunia and Lamia. Lamia is dressing up her doll to meet the other dolls in the cafeteria, and Dunia gives her a toy purse that Lamia had dropped.

18. Rampton's (1995) notion of crossing refers to the act of codeswitching into a code or linguistic variety (usually a minority language) that is not 'owned' by the speaker, but rather belongs to a group which they cannot legitimately claim to be part of.

## References

Agha, A. 2005. Voice, footing, enregisterment. *Journal of Linguistic Anthropology* 15(1): 38–59.

Alford, R. 1988. *Naming and Identity. A cross-cultural study of personal naming practices.* New Haven: HRAF Press.

Aronsson, K., and M. Thorell 1999. Family politics in children's play directives. *Journal of Pragmatics* 31: 25–47.

Auer, P. (ed.). 1998. *Code-switching in Conversation: Language, interaction, and identity.* London: Routledge.

Bhabha, H. 1990. The third space: Interview with Homi Bhabha. In Jonathan Rutherford (ed.). *Identity, Community, Culture, Difference.* London: Lawrence and Wishart, pp. 207–21.

Bakhtin, M. M. 1981. *The Dialogic Imagination: Four essays.* Ed. by M. Holquist, translated by C. Emerson & M. Holquist. Austin: University of Texas Press.

Bakhtin, M. M. 1986. *Speech Genres & Other Late Essays.* Austin: University of Texas Press.

Baquedano-Lopez, P. 2000. Narrating community in Doctrina classes. *Narrative Inquiry* 10(2): 429–52.

Blum, S. 1997. Naming practices and the power of words in China. *Language in Society* 26(3): 357–79.

Blum-Kulka, S., and C. Snow 2004. Introduction: The potential for peer talk. *Discourse Studies* 6(3): 291–306.

Bourdieu, P. 1991. *Language and Symbolic Power.* Cambridge, MA: Harvard University Press.

Brubaker, R., and F. Cooper 2000. Beyond "identity." *Theory and Society* 29: 1–47.

Cekaite, A., and K. Aronsson 2005. Language play, a collaborative resource in children's L2 learning. *Applied Linguistics* 26(2): 169–91.

Corsaro, W. 1988a. Routines in the peer cultures of American and Italian nursery school children. *Sociology of Education* 61(1): 1–14.

Corsaro, W. 1988b. Peer culture in the preschool. *Theory into Practice* 27(1): 19–24.

Corsaro, W. 1994. Discussion, debate, and friendship processes: Peer discourse in U.S. and Italian nursery schools. *Sociology of Education* 67(1): 1–26.

Corsaro, W. 1997. *The Sociology of Childhood.* Thousand Oaks, CA: Pine Forge Press.

Corsaro, W. 2000. Early childhood education, children's peer cultures, and the future of childhood. *European Early Childhood Education Research Journal* 8(2): 89–102.

Cromdal, J. 2004. Building bilingual oppositions: Notes on code-switching in children's disputes. *Language in Society* 33: 33–58.

Cromdal, J., and K. Aronsson 2000. Footing in bilingual play. *Journal of Sociolinguistics* 4: 435–57.

De Certeau, M. 1988. *The Practice of Everyday Life.* Berkeley and Los Angeles, CA: University of California Press.

Eid, M. 1995. What's in a name?: Women in Egyptian obituaries. In Y. Suleiman (ed.), *Arabic Sociolinguistics: Issues and perspectives.* New York: Routledge, pp. 81–100.

El Harras, M. 2004. La juventud marroquí ante el siglo XXI: Cambios y desafios. In B. López García and M. Berriane (eds.), *Atlas de la Inmigración Magrebí en España.* Taller de Estudios Internacionales Mediterráneos. Madrid: UA Eduçiones, pp. 41–3.

Ervin-Tripp, S., and I. Reyes 2005. Child codeswitching and adult content contrasts. *International Journal of Bilingualism* 9(1): 85–102.

Evaldsson, A. C. 2005. Staging insults and mobilizing categorizations in a multiethnic peer group. *Discourse & Society* 16(6): 763–86.

Evaldsson, A. C., and A. Cekaite 2010. "Schwedis' He can't even say Swedish" – Subverting and reproducing institutionalized norms for language use in multilingual peer groups. *Pragmatics* 20(4): 587–604.

Fader, A. 2001. Literacy, bilingualism, and gender in a Hasidic community. *Linguistics and Education* 12(3): 261–83.

Fader, A. 2009. *Mitzvah girls: Bringing up the next generation of Hasidic Jews in Brooklyn.* Princeton: Princeton University Press.

Foucault, M. 1982. Technologies of the self. In Luther H. Martin, Huck Gutman and Patrick H. Hutton (eds.), *Technologies of the Self: A seminar with Michel Foucault.* Amherst: The University of Massachusetts Press, pp. 16–49.

Gal, S. 1987. Codeswitching and consciousness in the European periphery. *American Ethnologist* 14(4): 637–53.

García-Sánchez, I. M. 2005. More than just games: Language socialization in an immigrant children's peer group. *Texas Linguistic Forum: Proceedings of the Thirteenth Annual Symposium About Language and Society* 49: 61–71.

García-Sánchez, I. M. 2007. Practices of social exclusion of Moroccan immigrant children in Spain. *Thirteenth Annual Conference on Language, Interaction, and Social Organization (LISO)*. University of California, Santa Barbara.

García-Sánchez, I. M. 2009. Moroccan immigrant children in a time of surveillance: Navigating sameness and difference in contemporary Spain. Unpublished Ph.D. dissertation. Department of Applied Linguistics. University of California, Los Angeles.

Garrett, P. 2007a. Language socialization. In P. Duff and N. H. Hornberger (eds.), *Elsevier Encyclopedia of Language and Education*, Second Edition: Volume 10. Heidelberg: Springer, pp. 189–201.

Garrett, P. 2007b. Language socialization and the reproduction of bilingual subjectivities. In Monica Heller (ed.), *Bilingualism: A social approach*. New York: Palgrave McMillan, pp. 233–56.

Goffman, E. 1981. Footing. In *Forms of Talk*. Philadelphia: University of Pennsylvania Press, pp. 124–59.

Goodwin, M. H. 1985. The serious side of jump rope: Conversational practices and social organization in the frame of play. *Journal of American Folklore* 98 (389), July-September, 315–30.

Goodwin, M. H. 1990a. *He-said-she-said: Talk as social organization among Black children*. Bloomington and Indianapolis: Indiana University Press.

Goodwin, M. H. 1990b. Tactical uses of stories: Participation frameworks within girls' and boys' disputes. *Discourse Processes* 13: 33–71.

Goodwin, M. H. 1997. Children's linguistic and social worlds. *Anthropology Newsletter* 38: 4.

Goodwin, M. H. 1998. Games of stance: Conflict and footing in hopscotch. In S. Hoyle and C. Temple Adger (eds.), *Kids' Talk: Strategic language use in later childhood*. New York: Oxford University Press, pp. 23–46.

Goodwin, M. H. 2000. Morality and accountability in girls' play. *Texas Linguistic Forum: Proceedings of the seventh annual Symposium About Language and Society – Austin* 43: 77–86.

Goodwin, M. H., and A. Kyratzis 2007. Introduction. Children socializing children: Practices for negotiating the social order among peers. *Research on Language and Social Interaction* 40(4): 279–89.

Gudal, T. 1997. Three children, two languages: The role of code-selection in organizing conversation. Unpublished Ph.D. dissertation. Norwegian University of Science and Technology at Trondheim.

Gumperz, J. J. 1982. *Language and Social Identity*. Cambridge: Cambridge University Press.

Hall, K. 1995. There's a time to act English and there's a time to act Indian: The politics of identity among British Sikh teenagers. In S. Stephen (ed.), *Children and the Politics of Culture*. Princeton: Princeton University Press, pp. 243–64.

Hall, K. 2002. *Lives in Translation: Sikh youth as British citizens*. Philadelphia: University of Pennsylvania Press.

Hall, K. 2004. The ethnography of imagined communities: The cultural production of Sikh and British ethnicity. *Annals of the American Academy AAPSS* 595: 108–21.

Halmari, H., and W. Smith 1994. Code-switching and register shift: Evidence from Finnish-English child bilingual conversation. *Journal of Pragmatics* 21: 427–45.

He, A. W. 2001. The Language of ambiguity: Practices in Chinese heritage language classes. *Discourse Studies* 3(1): 75–96.

Hill, J. H. 1985. The grammar of consciousness and the consciousness of grammar. *American Ethnologist* 12(4): 725–37.

Hirschfeld, L. 1996. *Race in the Making: Cognition, culture, and the child construction of human kinds*. London: Bradford/MIT Press.

Howard, K. 2007. Kinship usage and hierarchy in Thai children's peer groups. *Journal of Linguistic Anthropology* 17(2): 204–30.

Jørgenssen, J. N. 1998. Children's acquisition of code-switching for power wielding. In P. Auer (ed.), *Code-switching in Conversation: Language, interaction and identity*. New York: Routledge, pp. 237–58.

Kulick, D., and B. B. Schieffelin 2004. Language socialization. In A. Duranti (ed.), *A Companion to Linguistic Anthropology*. Malden, MA: Blackwell Publishing, pp. 349–68.

Kwan-Terry, A. 1992. Code-switching and code-mixing: The case of a child learning English and Chinese simultaneously. *Journal of Multilingual and Multicultural Development* 13: 243–59.

Kyratzis, A. 2004. Talk and interaction among children and the co-construction of peer groups and peer cultures. *The Annual Review of Anthropology* 33: 625–49.

Kyratzis, A. 2010. Latina girls' peer play interactions in a bilingual Spanish-English U.S. preschool: Heteroglossia, frame-shifting, and language ideology. *Pragmatics* 20(4): 557–86.

Kyratzis, A., and S. M. Ervin-Tripp 1999. The development of discourse markers in peer interaction. *Journal of Pragmatics* 31: 1321–338.

Labov, W. 1964. Hypercorrection by the lower middle class as a factor in linguistic change. In W. Bright (ed.), *Sociolinguistics, Proceedings of the UCLA Sociolinguistics Conference, 1964*. Los Angeles: UCLA.

Labov, W. 1966. The effect of social mobility on linguistic behavior. *Sociological Inquiry* 36(2): 186–203.

Lee, S. 2005. *Up Against Whiteness: Race, School, and Immigrant Youth*. New York: Teachers College Press.

Markstrom, C. A., and A. Iborra 2003. Adolescent identity formation and rites of passage: The Navajo Kinaaldá ceremony for girls. *Journal of Research on Adolescence* 13(4): 399–425.

Minks, A. 2010. Socializing heteroglossia among Miskitu children on the Caribbean coast of Nicaragua. *Pragmatics* 20(4): 495–522.

Ochs, E., and B. B. Schieffelin 1989. Language has a heart. *Text* 9(1): 7–25.

Ochs, E. 1992. Indexing gender. In A. Duranti and C. Goodwin (eds.), *Rethinking Context*. New York: Cambridge University Press, pp. 335–58.

Ochs, E. 1993. Constructing social identity: A language socialization perspective. *Research on Language and Social Interaction* 26(3): 287–306.

Ochs, E. 2002. Becoming a speaker of culture. In C. Kramsch (ed.), *Language Socialization and Language Acquisition: Ecological perspectives*. New York: Continuum Press, pp. 99–120.

Ortner, S. 1996. Making gender: Toward a feminist, minority, postcolonial, subaltern... etc. theory of practice. In S. Ortner, *Making Gender: The politics and erotics of culture*. Boston: Beacon Press, pp. 1–20.

Ortner, S. 1999. *Life and Death on Mt Everest: Sherpas and Himalayan mountaineering*. Princeton: Princeton University Press.

Ortner, S. 2006. Power and projects: Reflections on agency. In S. Ortner (ed.), *Anthropology and Social Theory: Culture, power, and the acting subject*. Durham: Duke University Press, pp. 129–53.

Paugh, A. L. 2005. Multilingual play: Children's code-switching, role play, and agency in Dominica, West Indies. *Language in Society* 34: 63–86.

Poveda, D., and T. Marcos 2005. The social organization of a 'stone fight': Gitano children's interpretive reproduction of ethnic conflict. *Childhood* 12(3): 327–49.

Rampton, B. 1995. *Crossing: Language and ethnicity among adolescents*. London: Longman.

Rampton, B. 1998. Crossing: Language and ethnicity among adolescents. In P. Auer (ed.), *Language, Interaction and Identity*. New York: Routledge, pp. 290–317.

Reynolds, J. 2002. Maya children's practices of the imagination. Unpublished Ph.D. dissertation. Department of Anthropology, University of California, Los Angeles.

Reynolds, J. 2010. Enregistering the voices of discursive figures of authority in Antonero children's soci-dramatic play. *Pragmatics* 20(4): 467–93.

Rogoff, B. 1998. Cognition as a collaborative process. In W. Damon, D. Kuhn & R. S. Siegler (eds.), *Handbook of child psychology. Vol. 2: Cognition, perception, and language*. New York: Wiley, pp. 679–744.

Rogoff, B., R. Paradise, R. Mejía Arauz, M. Correa-Chávez, and C. Angelillo 2003. First hand learning through intent participation. *Annual Review of Psychology* 54: 175–203.

Rymes, B. 1996. Naming as a social practice: The case of Little Creeper from Diamond Street. *Language in Society* 25(2): 237–60.

Sacks, H., E. A. Schegloff, and G. Jefferson. 1974. A simplest systematics for the organization of turn-taking for conversation. *Language* 50: 696–735.

Samad, Y. 2007. Ethnicization of religion. In Y. Samad and S. Kasturi (eds.), *Islam in the European Union: Transnationalism, youth and the War on Terror*. Oxford: Oxford University Press, pp. 159–70.

Schieffelin, B. B. 1990. *The Give and Take of Everyday Life: Language socialization of Kaluli children*. Cambridge: Cambridge University Press.

Schieffelin, B. 2003. Language and place in children's worlds. *Proceedings of the Tenth Annual Symposium About Language and Society. Texas Linguistic Forum* 45: 152–66.

Sterponi, L. 2004. Reading as involvement with text. Unpublished Ph.D. dissertation. Department of Applied Linguistics. University of California, Los Angeles.

Tetreault, C. 2007. Collaborative conflicts: Teens performing aggression and intimacy in a French Cité. Paper presented at the *American Anthropological Association Annual Meetings*. Washington, D.C.

Tetreault, C. 2008. La racaille: Figuring gender, generation, and stigmatized space in a French cité. *Gender and Language* 2(2): 141–70.

Tetreault, C. 2009. Cité teens entextualizing French TV host register: Crossing, voicing, and participation frameworks. *Language in Society* 38: 201–31.

Thorne, B. (1993/1995) *Gender Play: Girls and boys in school*. New Brunswick, NJ: Rutgers University Press.

Thorne, B. 2008. 'The Chinese girls' and 'the Pokemon kids': Children constructing difference in urban California. In Jennifer Cole and Deborah Durham (eds.), *Figuring the Future: Globalization and the temporalities of children and youth*. Santa Fe, NM: SAR Press, pp. 73–97.

Woolard, K. A. 2004. Codeswitching. In A. Duranti (ed.), *A Companion to Linguistic Anthropology*. Malden, MA: Blackwell Publishing Ltd, pp. 73–94.

Zentella, A. C. 1997. *Growing Up Bilingual: Puerto Rican children in New York*. Oxford: Blackwell.

Zentella, A. C. 1998. Multiple codes, multiple identities: Puerto Rican children in New York City. In S. M. Hoyle and C. T. Adger (eds.), *Kids Talk: Strategic language use in later childhood*. New York: Oxford University Press, pp. 95–112.

## Appendix I

### Arabic Transliteration Symbols**

| | |
|---|---|
| ا = ā | ظ = ṭ |
| ب = b | ع = ‘ |
| ت = t | غ = ġ |
| ث = z | ف = f |
| ج = ž | ق = g/q |
| ح = H | ك = k |
| خ = kh | ل = l |
| د = d | م = m |
| ذ = D | ن = n |
| r/rr = ر | ه = h |
| ز = ẓ | ي = ī/y |
| س = s | ء = ’ |
| ش = š | َ = a/e |
| ص = S | ُ = u/o |
| ض = ḍ | ِ = i |
| ط = T | |

## Critical Thinking and Application

- How did the children García-Sánchez studied deploy their two languages? How might this be similar to other settings or unique to this setting?
- What is *serious* about the *pretend-play* of these young Moroccan girls?
- Record conversation among bilingual or multilingual people. Where do switches occur? Can you account for them either in terms of relations between speakers or their stance toward the topic of their conversation?

## Vocabulary

affective stance
aspiration
code-switching
crossing
cultural capital
dialectal
diasporic
discourse marker
discursive
double-voiced
enregisterment
focal
footing
heteroglossia
hybridity
hypercorrection
index, indexical
interactional frame
language ideology
language socialization
linguistic ecology
ludic
metacommentary
metalinguistic
metaphorical meaning
morphological
phonological
ratified participant
reflexive, reflexivity
register
social capital
subaltern

## Suggested Further Reading

Atkinson, David, and Helen Kelly-Holmes. 2011. Codeswitching, Identity, and Ownership in Irish Radio Comedy. *Journal of Pragmatics* 43: 251–260.

Auer, Peter, ed. 1988. *Code-Switching in Conversation: Language, Interaction and Identity*. London: Routledge.

Backus, Ad, J. Normann Jørgensen, and Carol Pfaff. 2010. Linguistic Effects of Immigration: Language Choice, Codeswitching, and Change in Western European Turkish. *Language and Linguistics Compass* 4(7): 481–495.

Callahan, Laura. 2007. Spanish/English Codeswitching in Service Encounters: Accommodation to the Customer's Language Choice and Perceived Linguistic Affiliation. *Southwest Journal of Linguistics* 26(1): 15–38.

Gumperz, John J. 1982. Conversational Code Switching. From *Discourse Strategies*, pp. 59–99. Cambridge: Cambridge University Press.

Heller, Monica, ed. 1988. *Codeswitching: Anthropological and Sociolinguistic Perspectives*. New York: Mouton de Gruyter.

Higgins, Christina. 2007. Constructing Membership in the In-Group: Affiliation and Resistance Among Urban Tanzanians. *Pragmatics* 17(1): 49–70.

Jaffe, Alexandra. 2007. Codeswitching and Stance: Issues in Interpretation. *Journal of Language, Identity, and Education* 6(1): 53–77.

Myers-Scotton, Carol. 1993. *Social Motivations for Code Switching: Evidence from Africa*. Oxford: Oxford University Press.

Myers-Scotton, Carol. 1998. *Codes and Consequences: Choosing Linguistic Varieties*. New York: Oxford University Press.

Omoniyi, Tope. 2006. Hip-Hop Through the World Englishes Lens: A Response to Globalization. *World Englishes* 25(2): 195–208.

Poplack, Shana. 1980. Sometimes I'll Start a Sentence in English y Termino en Español. *Linguistics* 18: 581–618.

Rampton, Ben. 1995. *Crossing: Language and Ethnicity Among Adolescents*. London: Longman.

Woolard, Kathryn A. 2004. Codeswitching. In *A Companion to Linguistic Anthropology*, edited by Alesssandro Duranti, pp. 73–94. Malden, MA: Blackwell.

## CHAPTER 25

# Most of the World's Languages Went Extinct

*John H. McWhorter*

(2001)

*Since human language began, perhaps 100,000 to 150,000 years ago, new languages have formed and old languages have "died." Humans have migrated as part of our species' heritage, until we began to settle down following the Neolithic revolution—the invention/discovery of agriculture (at different times in different parts of the world). Some experts believe that sedentism has been accompanied by increasing language loss. Migrants may learn the language of groups they encounter, or the two languages may form a hybrid (a creole). People may add more languages to those they already know, or they may delete old ones as they learn new ones. When small groups speak an isolated language, its fate is intertwined with their biological and cultural fate; if they die off, the language dies with them.*

*Experts speculate that prior to the advent of agriculture, humans spoke a vastly greater number of different languages, perhaps as many as 100,000! Now that number is down to about 6,000, but many of them are spoken only by very small numbers of people.*

*Of course, "language death" is a metaphor, but it is the one commonly used to discuss this phenomenon. Language death begins with multilingualism, followed by "language shift," when people begin to move to another language for many of their communicative needs.*

*Using the analogy of biological evolution, in this chapter John McWhorter discusses the tragedy of linguistic extinction. He adds that linguistic extinction is even more complete than biological extinction because languages have left no trace at all, while organisms have had the chance to remain as fossils or as genetic constructs from offspring DNA.*

*McWhorter begins with a discussion of the reasons one language may give way to another over a brief period of time. He details many cases of languages known to have died both in the remote past and in very recent time. Moreover, even cases when languages have not completely disappeared cannot compensate for the fact that the vast majority of the people in the world—96 percent—speak just twenty powerful languages (maybe along with an indigenous language). McWhorter further argues that with the growth of cities and of national cultures, it is unrealistic to expect anything like the 6,000 currently spoken languages to endure, sad though that prospect is.*

*McWhorter pleads the case that what is lost when a language dies is not so much the cultural knowledge associated with that language but rather the specifics of the* language, *the details of its structure, the delicate, elaborate rules. So he urges linguists and others who love language at the very least to record dying languages so that in the future we can know what they were.*

### Reading Questions

- What is the general pattern of language death?
- What evidence do we have of earlier languages that have died?

---

John H. McWhorter, Most of the World's Languages Went Extinct. From *The Power of Babel: A Natural History of Language*. New York: Times Books, 2001, pp. 253–86.

- What causes languages to die? How can this be resisted, if it can? What cases have been successful?
- How have the specifics of industrialization and urbanization contributed to language death? What is the future likely to hold in terms of linguistic diversity?

---

[This discussion is part of a larger work] dedicated to an analogy between biological evolution and human language. Like animals and plants, languages change, split into subvarieties, hybridize, revivify, evolve functionless features, and can even be genetically altered. The analogy continues in that languages, like animals and plants, can go extinct.

As animals and plants drive one another to extinction by nosing one another out of ecological niches in competition for sustenance, in the past languages have usually gone extinct when one group conquers another or when a group opts for a language that it perceives as affording it greater access to resources it perceives as necessary to survival. Typically, a generation of speakers of a language becomes bilingual in one spoken by a group that is politically dominant or endowed with valuable goods or access to same. This bilingual situation can persist across several generations, but as often as not, the inevitable tendency for languages to be **indexed** to social evaluations takes its toll. Usually, through time new generations come to associate the outside language with status and upward mobility and the indigenous one with "backwardness." This is especially the case when the dominant language is a First World "tall building" language associated with money, technology, and enshrinement in the media while the indigenous one is an obscure tongue spoken only in villages.

A point arrives when one generation speaks the outside language better than the indigenous language, largely using the latter to speak with older relatives and in ritual functions. As such, these people do not speak the indigenous language much better than many Americans might speak French or Spanish after a few years of lessons in high school. One is unlikely to speak to one's child in a language one is not fully comfortable in and does not consider an expression of oneself. It is here that a language dies, because a language can only be passed on intact as a mother tongue to children. Once it is spoken only by adults and is no longer being passed on to children, even though it will be "spoken" in the strict sense for another several decades, it will die with its last fluent speakers.

Our natural sense is to suppose that, as long as the language has been written down or codified in a grammar, then it need not be dead forever. However, grammar writing is a relatively recent practice, and in the absence of a grammar, a dead language's full apparatus is only evident when there is a considerable volume of writings. This is in turn only the case for a small number of "big actors" such as Latin. Because writing itself is a relatively recent invention—as it has been put, if humans had existed for just one day, then writing would have been invented about 11:00 P.M.—obviously even these potential paths of rescue have been unavailable to human language for most of its existence. Until 11:00 P.M., once a language went extinct, it was gone forever.

An extinct language before the advent of writing is even more unrecoverable than an extinct life form. Life forms may leave their impressions as fossils, and technology gets ever closer to allowing us to someday at least partially resurrect ancient life forms through remains of their DNA. However, a language could not leave an "imprint" before writing existed, because an individual language is not encoded in a person's genes. If the ability to speak is genetically encoded, we can be quite sure that this inheritance is a generalized one allowing someone to speak any language on earth. The particular word shapes, grammatical configurations, and various irregularities that characterize any one language are the result of largely random accretions through the millennia, no more reproducible from basic human materials than the form of an individual snowflake is from the water droplets that it began as.

And even when a language is preserved in writing, there is a long trip indeed between the tales, recipes, battle accounts, and poetry preserved on the page and the language being used daily by living, breathing human beings as an expression of their souls. Many of us can attest to this from our exposure to Latin—no matter how good you may have gotten at those declensions, conjugations, and ablative absolutes, even this was a long way from speaking the language fluently, and what life conditions can we even imagine, outside of the clergy, where fluent Latin would be natural or necessary? Languages die when others take their place—we don't *need* Latin or any dead language, because we've got languages of our own. As often as not, a revived language hovers in the realm of the "undead"—part of the revivification effort entails gamely making space for the language in lives already quite full without it and sometimes even vaguely discomfited by its return.

## World History: A Treadmill to Linguistic Oblivion?

### It Was Ever Thus—To an Extent

Like biological extinctions, **language death** has been a regular and unsung occurrence throughout human history. We have records of Indo-European languages now no longer spoken, such as Hittite from present-day Turkey and Syria, and Tocharian, spoken by Europeans who penetrated as far east as present-day China. There was once a Romance language spoken on the Adriatic shores called Dalmatian, a kind of transition between Italian and Romanian, whose last speaker died in 1898.[1] The Romance languages in general spread in a continuous patch from Portugal eastward until a break after Italy, turning up again only in Romania, with the exception of some dots of odd Romanian dialects spoken in the interim. As was Dalmatian, these dots are remnants of what once were many other Romance languages filling in today's gap—languages that died in the face of encroaching Slavic varieties now spoken in the former Yugoslavia. A Slavic language called Sorbian (or Wendish) is spoken within German borders and, predictably, has lost in the competition with German and is now only spoken by a few elderly people. King Arthur represented the Celtic peoples who once inhabited all of the British Isles and significant swaths of Iberia and present-day France. The onslaught of the Romans and then the Vikings pushed the languages they spoke to the margins. Gaelic hangs on tenuously in Ireland, as does an offshoot variety in Scotland; Welsh does so in Wales; and Breton is fighting for life in northwestern France. But the Gaulish that the *Asterix* characters are supposed to be speaking has not been heard from since about A.D. 500, the last full speaker of Cornish of Cornwall died in 1777, and Manx of the Isle of Man died in 1974.

In other cases, language deaths in the past are only reconstructable by inference. In Africa, where languages often change from one small region to another, the Maa language is relatively unusual in being spoken across a belt of territory incorporating two countries, stretching from the top of Kenya to the middle of Tanzania. Peculiarities among various groups of its speakers attest to Maa having "killed" local languages in its spread, the Maa being a traditionally successful pastoral people who migrated widely in the past in search of grazing lands.

In northern Kenya, there are Maa speakers who stand out in being hunter-gatherers instead of pastoralists. These Dorobo peoples assist the Maa of the area in their herding, and the Maa's oral tradition mentions having met hunter-gatherers in the past. Presumably before the meeting, the Dorobo spoke their own language, this made even more likely by the cultural distinctiveness they retain today. Southward there are other Maa speakers whose cultural distinctiveness tips us off to language death in days of yore. The Camus people on Lake Baringo of Kenya farm and fish, traits alien to and even looked down on by traditional Maa peoples; the Arusa of Tanzania also remain farmers, though speaking Maa. In other cases, the death of languages in the face of Maa is concretely visible as speakers remain who speak a shredded version of the original language: the Elmolo, Yaaku, and Omotik languages are now only spoken by the very old, their communities having opted for Maa in connection with the benefits of the pastoral life style.

It was ever thus, then. No more ammonites, *Pteranodon*, or eighteen-foot-tall rhinoceroses;[2] no more Hittite, Dalmatian, or Elmolo. There is a sense in which we cannot help but regret the demise of any of the endlessly marvelous permutations of life or language, and surely the demise of each creature or language is in the strict sense a tale of marginalization and erasure. Animals and plants have vanished as often in catastrophic grand extinctions as through gradual outnumbering by more successful competitors, and languages have often died as the result of violent conquest, enslavement, and oppression. However, under ordinary conditions, we could perhaps congratulate ourselves that naked conquest of this sort is no longer officially sanctioned by the world community (even if, sadly, conditions too often leave such events to be allowed passively to proceed, especially when the people in question are not perceived as commercially important) and that our enlightened awareness of the value of diversity combined with the availability of writing will further help ensure that languages will no longer disappear at nearly the rate that they used to.

This, however, is an understandable but mistaken view. Our parallel with animals and plants unfortunately extends to the fact that, today, languages are in fact disappearing at a rate as alarmingly rapid as that of flora and fauna. The same geopolitical forces that are raping the global environment are also vaporizing not just the occasional obscure tongue spoken in remote regions, but most of the world's six thousand languages. Today, a subset of the "top twenty" languages (Chinese, English, Spanish, Hindi, Arabic, Bengali, Russian, Portuguese, Japanese, German, French, Punjabi, Javanese, Bihari, Italian, Korean, Telugu, Tamil, Marathi, and Vietnamese)[3] are imposed as languages of education and wider commerce throughout the world. The result is that ninety-six percent of the world's population speaks one or more of these top twenty; that is, these people speak one of these languages in addition to an indigenous one, and there is a threat that succeeding generations will learn only the dominant one and let the indigenous one die. This means that only *four percent* of the world's population is living and dying speaking *only* an indigenous language.

This imbalance of power leads to some rather gruesome predictions. By one reasonable estimate, ninety percent of the world's languages will be dead by 2100—that is, about fifty-five hundred full, living languages will no longer be spoken about 1,125 months from when you are reading this. As David Crystal puts it, this means that a language is dying roughly every two weeks.

Many of the languages we are most exposed to are among the top twenty or will be among the five-hundred-odd "medium" languages that will likely survive the impending mass extinction (Catalan, Finnish, Wolof, Thai, Tagalog, etc.), and all of these languages have been so richly documented in writing and in recordings that, even if they lost all of their native speakers, their revival, or at least maintenance on life support, would be at least technically feasible. Thus it can be difficult to appreciate the massive loss that more widespread language death will entail.

The Native American situation is illustrative. Before the arrival of Europeans, there were about three hundred separate languages spoken by Native Americans in what is today the continental United States. Today, a third of those languages are no longer spoken, whereas all but a handful of the rest are spoken only by the very old and will surely be extinct within a decade or so. The current situation is as if, in Europe, Albanian, Frisian, Romanian, Basque, Catalan, Occitan, Welsh, Lithuanian, Latvian, and Irish and Scottish

Gaelic were no longer spoken, and meanwhile only English, German, and Russian were still being passed on to children, with Swedish, Norwegian, Danish, Icelandic, Dutch, French, Spanish, Italian, Portuguese, Serbo-Croatian, Macedonian, Polish, Bulgarian, Finnish, Estonian, and Hungarian only spoken by very old people, viewed as "quaint" and backward by young people jetting around in sports cars.

Each of these Native American languages was an astoundingly complex and remarkably beautiful conglomeration, presenting the glorious kinds of baroquenesses we [might see] in Cree. Europe is covered mostly by languages of one family such that all are based on a common general "game plan," but the Native American languages spoken north of Mexico constituted at the very least two dozen families, with a range of variation across the continent as broad as that on the entire Eurasian landmass, taking in Indo-European, Chinese, Japanese, Arabic, and others.

## The First Crack in the Dam: The Neolithic Revolution

The trend toward a decrease in the number of the world's languages is, in large view, not an isolated phenomenon but one symptom of general trends in human development in the past several millennia. Until just about eleven thousand years ago, humanity worldwide consisted of relatively small groups of hunter-gatherers. This life style was not one inherently geared toward population increase and spread, and thus the world was feasibly shareable by large numbers of such groups, with minimum occasion for one group to exterminate another one along with its language. We can be sure such things happened but generally on a very local scale, counterbalanced by the birth of new languages as groups that reached a certain size spawned offshoot groups who moved away from the original group, their speech eventually developing into a new language. It has been estimated that this world could have harbored as many as one hundred thousand languages, and the scenario has been termed ***linguistic equilibrium.***

Large-scale language death began with the development of agriculture in many societies, starting in about 9000 B.C. Agriculture required large expanses of land, and its greater yield of food led to hitherto unknown population growth. Cultivation allows the amassing of food surpluses, which, freeing certain classes of people from hand-to-mouth subsistence, is the basis of the development of hierarchies of specialization that breed technological advances. Armed with these, and in constant need of extra space as their populations burgeoned, agricultural societies quickly began overrunning hunter-gatherer groups worldwide.

Even the way in which the world's language families are distributed today makes it clear that language death has been a regular part of human existence for several millennia. In India, roughly speaking, the languages spoken in the top half are Indo-European languages such as Hindi, Bengali, and Marathi, whereas in the bottom half, languages of another family called Dravidian are spoken, including Tamil, Kannada, Telugu, and Malayalam. However, the subdivision of space is not perfect: there is the occasional Dravidian language spoken way up in northern India or even as far northwest as present-day Pakistan. What are those people doing way up there? From our present-day perspective, it looks as if certain Dravidian speakers decided at some point to pack up and move thousands of miles away from their homelands. Much more likely, and supported archaeologically, is that Indo-European speakers slowly moved southward, with formerly spoken Dravidian languages dying along the way as their speakers were incorporated into the invaders' societies for generations and gave up their original languages. Life is never tidy, and naturally some pockets remain that the invaders never happened to get to. Thus the Dravidian "outliers" are remnants of a once greater variety of Dravidian languages spoken in southern Asia.

A similar case is the Dahalo language of Kenya, unusual in having the **clicks** otherwise found only way down in the south of Africa, among a small group of languages called Khoi-San and a few Bantu languages spoken near them such as Xhosa and Zulu. It is easy to see why the Bantu languages have the clicks—language contact long ago with Khoi-San speakers. However, what are clicks doing way up in Kenya? Clicks are so extremely rare cross-linguistically—otherwise found only in one Australian language, and even there, only in a special "secret" variety of that language—that it is unlikely that the clicks developed in Kenya merely by chance. Most likely, Khoi-San "click" languages were once spoken more widely in Africa, and Dahalo is one of the only remnants of that situation. What this means is that untold numbers of click languages must have died as Bantu and other peoples spread into what began as click-language territory. Again, archaeological evidence supports this scenario: skulls of people of the ethnicity who today speak Khoi-San languages have been found as far north as Zambia, and the Bantu takeover apparently occurred within a mere few centuries' time after 1000 B.C.

In the New World and Australia, Europeans similarly overwhelmed Native American and Aboriginal languages, assisted by the germs that living among livestock had immunized them to but that quite often decimated indigenous hunter-gatherer populations on impact.

## Situation Critical: The Downsides of the Global Economy

Thus even today's six thousand languages constitute a vast decrease in the number of languages that existed before the Neolithic revolution. Today, however, a second revolution, which some leftist political commentators term the imperialist one, is having an even starker effect on how many languages are spoken in the world.

During the Neolithic revolution, when a language spread across an area, it generally did so relatively slowly such that, by the time the spread was complete, the language had already developed into several new ones, which continued to spawn new ones in turn. For example, by the time

Latin was disseminated throughout the Roman Empire, its progenitor Proto-Indo-European had elsewhere in Europe already split into several branches such as Germanic, Slavic, Celtic, Hellenic (Greek). Then Latin itself developed into more than a dozen new languages, the Romance languages, while at the same time Proto-Slavic was developing into several new tongues. Thus, though Europe was once covered by languages now lost forever, this original diversity was replaced at least partly by new diversity. Furthermore, until recently, Europeans were unable to physically take over tropical and subtropical regions, where farming methods developed for temperate climates were ineffective and diseases Europeans had no immunity to tended to kill them, just as their own diseases tended to kill Native Americans and Australian Aborigines.

However, in the past few hundred years, the development of capitalism and the Industrial Revolution, and its resultant technological advances and encouragement of strongly centralized nationalist governments, have led a certain handful of languages to begin gradually elbowing not just many but *most* of the world's remaining languages out of existence. The urgencies of capitalism require governments to exact as much work and allegiance from their populations as possible, and the imposition of a single language has traditionally been seen as critical to this goal, especially within the nationalist models that have ruled since the 1700s. [Relevent is] the active hostility of the French government to the Occitan dialects and other "patois" of France, in favor of a scenario under which everyone in France spoke French.

In our era, climatological boundaries present few barriers to the onslaught. Today, language death is often caused less by physical conquest than by gradually yoking indigenous peoples into a centralized cash economy. This is often done by transforming their traditional life styles on site according to what their local topography can bear, with the aid of advances in agricultural technology. In other cases, the dominant power renders much of the population migrant laborers, spending half of their lives working in cities, this facilitated by modern transportation technology (assembling part-time work forces drawn from afar was more difficult before the invention of trains, for example). In the past few centuries, a great many human societies have been drawn from independent subsistence on the land into dependent relationships with capitalist superstructures, with traditional ways of life often actively discouraged in favor of new practices geared toward supplying the central government with salable resources.

## A Skeleton of Its Former Self: A Language Withers Away

What happens to a language as it dies? Generally, the last generation of fluent speakers has learned it only partly, never truly living in the language, using it only in the corners of their lives. As a result, the language is slightly **pidginized.** However, whereas in many cases a **pidgin** has been a temporary "setback" on the way to its expansion into a new language, the moribund variety of a dying language is a step along the way to permanent demise.

### "I Wish I Had the Words": Atrophied Vocabulary

Just as pidgins such as early Tok Pisin had restricted vocabularies, dying languages' vocabularies are constricted, with many single words pinch-hitting for concepts that were expressed by several more specific ones in the living language. Cayuga is a Native American language originally spoken in New York State. Under the Jackson Administration in the 1830s, as *you was* popped up in letters written by white clerks in New York City, many Native Americans were relocated to Oklahoma, intended as a delineated Indian Territory, and Cayugas were among them. By 1980, only a few elderly people spoke any Cayuga but had been thoroughly English-dominant all of their lives, and their Cayuga was seriously frayed around the edges as a result. The Oklahoma Cayuga had a word for *leg* but none for *thigh*, a word for *foot* but none for *ankle* or *toe*, words for *face* and *eye* but none for *cheek* or *eyebrow*. Where full Cayuga had a word specifically meaning *enter*, these old people substituted the more general word *go*, such that *Come into the house* was rendered as *Go into the house*. The nuance of where the speaker was in relation to the house—determining whether one would say from the porch ***Come** in* or say from a hill up yonder ***Go** in*—was left to context.

### The Genericization of a Language: The Demise of the "Hard Stuff"

Just as pidgins strip away aspects of language not necessary to basic communication, dying languages are marked by a tendency to let drop many of the accreted "frills" languages drift into developing through time. In a language that one uses little, the first thing to start wearing away in the grammar is, predictably, the "hard stuff" that takes lifelong daily practice to learn and retain.

**The Death of Inflections** One "frill" in a language is the inflectional **prefix** or **suffix**, which quite a few languages do without. **Inflections** arise accidentally through time from what begin usually as separate words, which as inflections become one of the challenging aspects of language to learn, entailing lists of arbitrarily shaped bits of stuff signaling concepts such as gender, person, and number that are in any case either clear from context or unnecessary to communication. People who use an inflected language day in and day out learn the inflections with ease and have no trouble retaining them throughout their lives; they become as ingrained as walking. But in dying languages speakers have often never mastered the inflections fully or have lost control of them in time, and thus to them the inflections become "hard," just as they would be to a foreigner learner.

Thus speakers of a dying inflected language often avoid using inflections in favor of more immediately transparent constructions, just as an English speaker feels as if he has gotten a kind of break when finding out that, in Spanish, instead of *hablaré* "I will speak" he can also say *Voy a hablar*, which allows him to get around calling up the ending in favor of using a form of the verb *go* that he has already learned. In traditional forms of Pipil, spoken in Guatemala and El Salvador, there were future inflections, such that *I will pass* was:

Ni-panu-**s**
I- pass- will

But today we mostly see this in old texts; elderly living speakers might cough it up for money, but in the Pipil they speak, stripped down in comparison with the living language of yore, the future is expressed with a "going to" construction. *I'm going to do it* is:

**Ni-yu** ni-k-chiwa
I- go I- it-do

Thus Pipil has moved in the direction of pidginhood, paralleling the tendency in pidgins to express the future with "going" expressions (although many old languages happen to express the future this way as well).

**The Soul of Celtic Melts Away** In Welsh, ... the first consonant of a noun often changes, depending on which possessive word comes before. The word for *cat* is *cath*, but the word takes on a different form as used with the word for *my*:

| | |
|---|---|
| *eu cath* | "their cat" |
| *fy* ***ngh****ath* | "my cat" |

The *his* and *her* case is particularly interesting because the same word is used for both: only the change in the consonant shows whether *his* or *her* is intended in the meaning:

| | |
|---|---|
| *ei* ***g****ath* | "his cat" |
| *ei* ***ch****ath* | "her cat" |

In Welsh's relative Gaelic—namely, the Scottish variety spoken in Sutherland County—speakers in their forties were the last generation of fluent speakers left in the early 1970s. Gaelic has the same kinds of consonant changes as Welsh does, and one sign of the decay of the Sutherland speakers' Gaelic was the gradual breakdown of these rules. To say *She was kept in* in living Scottish Gaelic, laid as all Celtic languages are on a basic foundation quite different from English's, one says literally "Was she on her keeping in":

Bha i air a cùmail.
was she on her keeping-in

This is a little challenging to wrap our heads around, but for our purposes concentrate on the last two words:

Bha i air **a** **cùmail**.
was she on **her** **keeping-in**

To say ***He*** *was kept in*—that is, "Was he on his keeping in"—one uses the same word as for *her*, but the consonant in the following verb changes:

Bha e air a **ch**ùmail.
was he on his keeping-in

And to say ***They*** *were kept in*, there is a different consonant change:

Bha iad air an **g**ùmail.
was they on their keeping-in

In the moribund Scottish Gaelic of Sutherland County, however, as often as not, in all three cases the form ***ch****ùmail*, properly used with *his*, was used for all three:

| | |
|---|---|
| Bha i air a **ch**ùmail. | "She was kept in." |
| Bha e air a **ch**ùmail. | "He was kept in." |
| Bha iad air an **ch**ùmail. | "They were kept in." |

These speakers have a general sense that there is some consonant change after possessive words but have not mastered the particular changes that each possessive pronoun requires or does not require. Thus just as we might do in trying to learn to speak Scottish Gaelic, these speakers simply generalized one kind of change to all persons.

**There's Speaking and There's Speaking** The last generation to speak a language is often incapable of being *articulate* in it as well, a crucial indication that the language is no longer capable of expressing full humanity.

There are scattered examples in English of concepts that are expressed as a single word incorporating both the object and the verb together: *He sat the baby for her* is more often rendered as *He babysat for her*. In many Native American languages, however, this process is central to basic expression, usable for just about any commonly occurring verb–object combination. In Cayuga, to say *She has a big house*, one might say "It house-bigs her," in the sense of "Things have it that she has a big house." Moreover, all of this is one word: *Konǫhsowá:neh*. When to use expressions like this and when not to are central to manipulating language artfully in these cultures, in the same vein as word choice and relative clauses are for us.

Of course, as we in particular know, a language can do just fine without this sort of thing, which evolves accidentally in certain languages through time—[elsewhere I show] it having done so just in the past century with "camp-sat" in Ngan'gityemerri in Australia. It's an extra and, as such, one of the first things to start wearing away as a language containing it dies. In living Cayuga, to render *She has a big onion* within a narrative, one would likely say "It onion-bigs her." In dying Cayuga, however, speakers are more likely to just say something like *The onion is big* or *Her onion is big*.

When a language is dying, then, its last speakers typically render it in the very way that we or another foreigner might, taking the easy ways out, avoiding the kinky stuff, reducing complexities to one-size-fits-all. The moribund version of a language is like one of those 1920s 78 rpm records of a symphony orchestra playing, recorded acoustically rather than electrically. You get the basics, but no matter how carefully we enhance the recording with modern techniques, it's nothing like having been at the performance.

All of this is to say that, when a language dies, one of the thousands of offshoots of the first language simply grinds to a halt, after having thrived and morphed and mixed with abandon for 150,000 years.

## How Do You Solve a Problem Like Revival?

### Language Revival Meets the Realities of Language in Time and Space

In response to all of this, there are attempts proceeding worldwide to halt the death of minority languages, with a particularly concerted effort by many linguists in the past ten years to call worldwide attention to the problem. The effort serving as a primary inspiration is the example of Hebrew, which by the late 1800s had essentially been used only in writing and for liturgical purposes for more than two thousand years—Hebrew was an archaic-looking language encountered in weighty books, not something you had dinner in. The movement to make it the official language of Israel was so successful that today it is spoken natively by a nation of six million people. There are movements to similarly resuscitate threatened languages such as Irish Gaelic, which in many areas is taught, and taught in, in schools, with radio and television time set aside for broadcasts in the language and various activities in the language encouraged for young people. There are similar movements for Breton, Occitan, Maori, Hawaiian, and other languages. Yet these efforts, laudable as they are, face many imposing obstacles, posed in large part by the realities of how languages live in the world as we know it.

For one, . . . most "languages" are actually clusters of dialects. The form of a dying language taught in school is often a single, standardized variety, which can be quite different from the various dialects that constitute the "language" as it actually exists. If there is still a healthy population of people speaking the language natively and well, this "school" variety that children learn may sound rather sanitized and even imposed from without. This is a special problem in communities where the impending death of the language is a symptom of historical oppression by a surrounding power, as has been the case in Brittany with Breton. France's former policy was to discourage the use of Breton in favor of French, treating Breton as a primitive "patois" only suitable for talking to livestock. The Breton nationalist movement in response has occasionally been a violent one, and to its partisans, the alien air of "school" Breton often suffers by association with the martinet French educational tradition that has been so hostile to the language rights of Breton peoples.

[It is also important to see] how languages mix, often when speakers are shifting from one language to another one through time. Typically, speakers leave footprints from their old language in their version of the new one (the peculiarities of Irish English come largely from Gaelic) while at the same time, during the twilight of their old language, they speak it with heavy influence from the new one. This means that, in many cases, the dying language we encounter is no longer its true self, having been tinted by the one its speakers are now dominant in.

Gros Ventre was a Native American language of Montana. When its last speakers were interviewed in the 1960s, their Gros Ventre showed evidence of remodeling on an English template. In the living language, there was no way to express the word for a body part in isolation. One could not simply say *eye*; one had to say *my eye, your eye, his eye*. The closest you could come to just *eye* was "someone's eye." Thus, to express the root *síitheh* "eye" alone would be pidgin Gros Ventre; one would have to at least say ***bi**-síitheh* "someone's eye." In true Gros Ventre, *my eye* was ***ne**síitheh*. In dying Gros Ventre, however, it was ***ne-bi**-síitheh*, where the speaker tacked the prefix for *my* onto the word meaning "someone's eye." To this speaker, more comfortable with English, in which we can say just *eye*, ***bi**-síitheh* had come to mean simply *eye* rather than "someone's eye," such that it felt natural to him to render *my eye* as ***ne**-bi-síitheh*, although to a tribal elder this would have meant the nonsensical "my someone's eye."[4]

Because it is harder for adults to learn new languages well than it is for children, when adults are forced to learn a new language quickly, the result is often various degrees of pidginization, utilizing just the bare bones of a language. This becomes a problem in revival efforts because, even when adults of a given nationality desire strongly to have their ethnic language restored to them, the mundane realities of a busy life can make it difficult to get beyond a pidgin-level competence in the language.

This is especially crucial in the **language-revival** case, because the languages in most immediate danger of death tend to be those spoken by previously isolated groups—for example, the peoples who were isolated enough by geography that Europeans could not transform their lands into plantation colonies in the middle of the past millennium. As we have seen, languages spoken by such groups, having had millennia to complexify without intermediation by large numbers of second-language speakers to keep the overgrowth in check, tend to be more imposingly complex than the "big dude" languages.

To the English speaker, Spanish presents its challenges with its gender marking, conjugations, and occasional quirks like *Me gusta el libro* instead of the "Yo gusto el libro" that would feel "normal" to us. But in general, one senses oneself as "still in Kansas"—there are plenty of similar word shapes, and how thoughts are put together is generally akin to how we do so in English. Go to languages beyond familiar ones like this and things get rockier. Someone I know who emigrated from Romania at fourteen speaks English perfectly (with a lovely hint of accent), and learning French was no problem for her. But during a stay in the Czech Republic, she ultimately decided that it was hopeless trying to pick up any Czech because, as she put it, there was simply nothing familiar: word shapes are usually unlike anything we are used to in Germanic or Romance (remember Romanian is a Romance, not Slavic, language); there is a sound or two that one essentially has to be born hearing to render properly; the nouns are declined as fiercely as the verbs are conjugated; and then there are the notorious Slavic verb pairs, where each verb takes arbitrarily different prefixes or suffixes or even changes its root according to whether actions are continuous or abrupt.

And my Romanian friend was still within Indo-European. With Native American languages, for example, one is confronted not simply with learning extremely unfamilar word shapes, but with ways of putting words together to render even the most basic of thoughts that an English speaker might barely believe humans could spontaneously resort to in running speech. *She has a big house* in Spanish translates almost word for word: *Ella tiene una casa grande*. In Czech, it is similar; typically of Slavic languages, no word for *a*, but that's not hard to get used to: *Ona má velký dům*. In general Czech "puts" things in ways that make intuitive sense to an English speaker. But then recall Cayuga's "It house-bigs her"—that's just off the scale, and remember that this is not just one wrinkle but a general way of phrasing things throughout the grammar. "Someone's eye" instead of just "eye"; having to specify just how you broke something—these are the sorts of things that confront the now English-dominant Native Americans seeking to reacquire the language of their ancestors. Here is Mohawk for *Suddenly, she heard someone give a yell from across the street:*

> *Tha'kié:ro'k iá:ken' ísi' na'oháhati iakothón:te' ónhka'k khe tontahohén:rehte'.*

Literally translated, with an attempt to make this sound the *least* needlessly "exotified," what this comes out as is "Suddenly, by what you could hear, there, it's beyond the street, the ear went to who just then made-shouted back toward her."

It's not impossible to learn a Native American language after childhood, and one can gradually wrap one's head around such ways of putting things. The language makes its own sense once one masters various general principles distinguishing such languages from ours. There are success stories of young Native Americans acquiring competence in their tribe's language from tutelage by elders, as in a long-term project directed by Leanne Hinton at the linguistics department of the University of California, Berkeley, pairing Native Americans with elders in an attempt to save as many Californian indigenous languages as possible. But learning one of these languages or an Australian Aboriginal language is hard work for someone raised in English or a related language, much harder work than picking up Spanish, and quite a job to expect of whole communities of people.

This difficulty relates to the fact that living languages are developed far beyond the strict necessities of communication and that incomplete learning guarantees that some of these baubles will be stripped away. Children learning an indigenous language in school but more comfortable in a dominant one such as English typically speak a rather simplified variety, just as do American students who learn French or Spanish in school. There is a perhaps universal tendency for elders to view youngsters as insufficiently mindful of tradition, which is heightened when the youngsters in question are assimilating to a dominant culture. This area of tension extends into children's version of a threatened language, when older fluent speakers often disparage the new version as "not real X," sometimes putting a damper on enthusiasm for the revival itself.

One of the notorious "Dammits" in Polynesian languages such as Maori and Hawaiian, for example, is the often arbitrary classification of nouns as taking either an *o* or an *a* possessive marker, and young speakers are often unsure which class a given noun belongs to. To a fluent Maori or Hawaiian speaker, this sounds like "bad" speech, just as saying *speaked* or *squoze* sounds to an English speaker. One can only imagine what schoolchildren's version of an immensely elaborated language such as Fula would sound like. The truth is that a revived language, if it "takes" and is passed on to children, will almost certainly be a considerably simplified version of the language as it was once spoken.

Finally, just as writing tends to give a language an air of "legitimacy," the converse also is true—a language that has not been traditionally written is often considered "less of a language" even by its speakers if they have been reared in a written, standardized "top twenty" language. Whereas to the scholar or social services worker, the indigenous language appears, quite properly, an exotic treasure to be cherished, to a person for whom the language is a mundane aspect of daily life, sociological realities intrude and often stamp the language as a lowly vehicle, associated with the elderly, parochialism, and a world many consider—for better or worse—a lesser option than the world of tall buildings.

Scholars have not always been immune to shades of this view. Before cultural pluralism was as overtly valued in mainstream educated discourse in America, even a linguist might describe Occitan in this fashion, this passage being from a generally masterful 1944 book on the world's languages (or the pipe-smoking Western professor of the period's conception thereof, with a Eurocentric bias focusing on standardized languages): "This *Provençal* has a flourishing culture of romantic poetry greatly influenced by Moorish culture. Its modern relatives are hayseed dialects."

If this was the best even some scholars could do until recently, then certainly lay speakers traditionally tend toward the same equation of "written" with "real." The very sound of the indigenous language immediately conveys a social context considered orthogonal to prestige, just as, no matter how Politically Correct we are and no matter what race we happen to be, we would be hard pressed to see the Declaration of Independence written in inner-city Black English as a document equal in gravity to the one Thomas Jefferson wrote. Such judgments are thoroughly arbitrary but noisomely deeply ingrained, and many communities resist efforts to revive their dying languages out of a sense that the languages are incompatible with the upward mobility they seek.

## Language Versus Prosperity

And this brings us to a very important matter regarding language death: why people give up their languages.

To be sure, indigenous languages have often been actively discouraged, by school policies calling for corporal punishment on any Native American student heard conversing in his home language, a practice especially common in the United States until the middle of the twentieth century, and by governmental positions declaring minority languages antithetical to national unity (witness France in the 1700s). My first office at Berkeley looked out on a courtyard called Ishi Court, named after a man who found himself the last living speaker of his native language, Yahi, after all of the other Yahis had been massacred. Many Native Americans died after similar massacres carried out by presidential administrations in the nineteenth century and depicted so placidly in the history books. Dozens of these languages expired under the watch of the Millard Fillmores and Chester Alan Arthurs by extermination or when groups were forced to live among others or to scatter, thus making it impossible to pass their languages on to enough children to keep them alive.

It is not difficult to make a case that people must not have their languages forcibly taken from them or beaten out of them. But in reality, just as often the reason groups abandon their traditional languages is ultimately a desire for resources that their native communities do not offer. Sometimes this occurs "naturally," as with the groups who now speak Maa in Kenya and Tanzania, a by no means unusual case that Western linguists would be unlikely to decry as an injustice. But more often today, it happens as a result of the pervasive effects of First World imperialism: the language of the dominant power—written, spoken by the wealthy, and broadcast constantly on radio and television—quite often comes to be associated with legitimacy, the cosmopolitan, and success. Almost inevitably, the home language is recast as, basically, *not* that—and thus antithetical to survival under the best possible conditions. This judgment is ultimately as unrelated to the stuff of the language itself as our evaluation of nonstandard dialects as "backward" is. But that's something only linguists know, for the most part, and in the meantime, many languages of Papua New Guinea, for instance, are gradually being replaced by Tok Pisin within their own largely self-subsisting villages, not through active outside imposition but because the villagers themselves have come to see this language and the access to the outside world that it offers as "cool."

**Urbanization: Linguistic Slurry** The trend toward urban migration that this cultural co-optation encourages is particularly lethal for language diversity. There is a short step from spending half of one's life working in a city to relocating there permanently in search of larger opportunities, especially when the degradation by large-scale logging, mining, monoculture, and other resource extractions destroys the environment a group formerly inhabited. For better or for worse, the modern geopolitical trend is toward general population intermixture in multiethnic polities. This could be termed "diversity," and indeed one potential aim might be that peoples speaking different languages will coexist within large cities, maintaining their native languages at home while using the dominant top twenty languages as utilitarian **lingua francas** in the realms of education, politics, and the workplace. This is the goal stated by many language revivalists, who certainly do not wish to bar indigenous peoples from the world economy.

This vision seems unobjectionable enough on its face but in reality simply could not support six thousand distinct languages. Certainly there are cities and countries where two or more languages coexist, such as English and French in Canada, Spanish and Catalan in the Catalonian region of Spain, or even more than a dozen in India. However, it is impossible, by the dictates of sheer logic, that *six thousand* languages, or anything even close, could thrive and be passed on generation after generation within the world's cities.

This is because if a city is to contain ethnic groups in a state of harmony—and presumably this is the ideal—then a phenomenon inherent to harmony is intermarriage. Love knows no boundaries, and world history eloquently demonstrates that intermarriage can only be prevented under conditions of virulent enmity between groups or, at the very least, stringent caste relations such as those in India, designating certain groups as unsuitable for intimate contact with others. The problem is that, if a couple speaking different native languages but both fluent in the dominant lingua franca marry and have children, then the children almost inevitably become more competent and comfortable in the lingua franca than in the language spoken by either parent. This is partly because the parents are more likely to speak the lingua franca to each other. Furthermore, even if the parents dutifully make sure to speak to the children only in their respective native languages, once the children are exposed to the lingua franca in school and in the world outside of the home, social evaluations kick in. Young children are exquisitely sensitive to such metrics, and quite commonly, as the child gets older, he or she begins to reject the parents' home languages in favor of the "cool" language, the one spoken by playmates, heard incessantly on television, and in general the marker of success and acceptance in the only society they have ever known. Many are the people we know who say that they spoke their parents' native language or languages when they were young but have since forgotten most of it—even when they still live with the parents and hear the language constantly. Social evaluations play a crucial role in a child's receptivity to linguistic input and orientation toward it.

Finally, even in rare cases when parents are diligent enough to maintain their child's fluency in the home language or languages, when that child himself marries, the chances of his marrying someone who speaks the same language (or certainly languages) are slim, and hence the chances that *their* children will speak a language they hear only occasionally from one parent and otherwise only when grandparents visit is nil.

**The Grass Is Always Greener: The Mundane Realities of the "Exotic"** What this means is that a world where all six thousand of today's languages thrived would be, properly speaking, one where a great many peoples remained rooted to isolated hunter-gatherer, pastoral, or small-scale cultivational existences, untouched by the First World. There is perhaps a certain romance in that idea: we are trained to emphasize the downsides of our First World existences, which are certainly many, such that a picture of a globe peopled by smallish groups living on the land may seem "the way things should be." Yet for all of the pernicious injustices and psychological dislocation inherent to Western life, there is perhaps a danger in romanticizing Third World cultures as well. The rain forest–dwelling Amazonians whose cultures and languages are dying at an alarming rate are, after all, also societies where life expectancy is often brief, diseases easily cured in the West are often rampant and lethal, there is a high infant mortality rate, and the treatment of women would be unthinkable to anyone reared in a "modern" society, especially since the 1970s. It is not accidental that it is often women in rural and indigenous societies who are in the vanguard of opting out of the native language in favor of the linguistic key to success in the surrounding culture, where women have more freedom of choice about child rearing and more control over their relationships with men.

In the conclusion of a much-discussed article in academic linguistics' signature journal *Language*, the eminent linguist Peter Ladefoged described a Dahalo-speaking father who was proud that his son now spoke only Swahili, because this was an index of his having moved beyond the confines of village life into material success beyond. "Who am I to say that he was wrong?" writes Ladefoged. Certainly we cannot prefer that the son opt for poverty; he was most likely moving away from a context in which few Westerners, language revivalists or not, could even conceive of living if other options were available. This last point is crucial: even if the Dahalo speaker was seduced by attractions of city life and the cash economy that in our eyes are of superficial value, we put ourselves in a tenuous position when we argue that the son should resist the very life style that none of us, downsides fully acknowledged, would even consider giving up.

The possible objection that it would be preferable for his son to move to a city but be bilingual in Dahalo and Swahili would most likely be a stopgap solution: dozens of languages are spoken in Tanzania, and the chances that the son will marry a fellow Dahalo speaker in the city are slim. In response, Nancy Dorian, who spearheaded the study of language death with seminal work on the demise of Scottish Gaelic, answered Ladefoged by noting that the generations sired by the one that let its language go often come to resent their parents for not passing on such a precious inheritance. But the sad question is whether their having tried to pass the language on would have been effective in a context where those very children would have been lapping up the dominant language as eagerly as all children do—and if they had, would the children have been able to pass the language on to *their* children?

## Practical Solutions

Cognizant of these problems and paradoxes, Daniel Nettle and Suzanne Romaine argue in *Vanishing Voices*, the most deeply thought of the various book-length treatments of the language-death matter, that any realistic worldwide language-revival effort must take place within a general initiative allowing indigenous groups to continue living on their lands within their own cultures. Nettle and Romaine view language death as a symptom of the larger process of the rape of the world's landscapes and the destruction of the cultures that once thrived within them, driven by the insatiable capitalist thirst for natural resources and the often brutally centralized control necessary to ensure its continual slaking. By no means so utopian as to require that native groups not acquire top twenty languages in order to participate to some extent in the world economy, Nettle and Romaine propose that such groups be ushered into a **diglossic** use of dominant languages and their native ones. Their point is that only if such groups are encouraged and allowed to stay in their traditional settings will such **diglossia** not be a mere stopgap along the way to the abandonment of the "low" language forever in favor of the "high."

Nettle and Romaine's message is as depressing as it is sensible, because at its heart is the belief that the preservation of any significant number of the world's languages will require a significant transformation in the global economy, which is driven largely by governments for whom such notions as cultural diversity have been anathema at worst and of low priority at best. The sad fact is that Western scholars' earnest musings on the value of linguistic diversity are ultimately a luxury of the prosperity created by the very destructive policies at the heart of the extinctions in question. It is not accidental, for example, that to date almost all of the seminal books and anthologies on language death have been published by Cambridge University Press, an entity representing and founded on an institution made possible only through the wealth generated by what was once one of the world's most nakedly imperialist, exploitative powers.

Developing countries, constrained by limited budgets, pressing poverty, and poor educational systems, and too frequently run by despotic dictatorships as little concerned with minority rights as the monarchies that created today's First World countries, generally only pay lip service to European calls that they preserve their lands and indigenous cultures. After all, the very European countries urging "multiculturalism" on, say, an Indonesia only developed their own broad-horizoned intelligentsia on the basis of resources derived from deforesting and polluting their own countries, as well as others, and often exterminating other cultures in the process.

This is not to say that we coddled Western intellectuals are wrong in our exhortations. It is clear to many that cultural relativism has its limits, and I believe that we can assert that the preservation of environments and indigenous cultures is a desirable pathway for humankind without censuring ourselves for imposing "ethnocentric" conceptions. I for one can quite confidently reject the notion that the erasure of the entire Amazonian rain forest be treated as a legitimate expression of a "different culture." I would love to see Nettle and Romaine's articulate exhortation and its general frame of reference serve as the foundation of increased efforts to prevent most of the world's peoples from being subsumed into a slurry of multiethnic urban misery and exploitation voiced in just a couple of dozen big fat languages.

## What Will Happen to the First Language's Children?

Yet it is clear in view of modern realities that a great many languages now technically alive will not be saved. A sober yet progressive assessment of the situation might be that today's endangered languages constitute three main sets having potential viability.

### Many Will Either Survive or Become Thriving "Taught" Languages

In the relatively successful language revivals of Irish, Breton, Maori, Welsh, and Hawaiian, large numbers of children are learning the languages in school, the media have joined the effort, and there are increasing amounts of printed materials available in the languages. However, it is also true that these languages remain very much the second languages of most of the learners, not much spoken at home or in casual situations. Whether these languages will survive as natively spoken ones is at this writing essentially a question mark.

Hebrew was indeed revived from the page at the founding of Israel—but the fact that today this case remains the only one commonly referred to as a success story signifies that it was unusual. The revival of Hebrew was favored by its occurrence within a new country where the language was explicitly designated as the intended official one, with the government expressly committed to the effort rather than setting aside occasional funds for the use of Hebrew "alongside" another language. Furthermore, the original immigrants to Israel spoke various languages and thus there was a motivation for a new language to express the new national identity, in contrast with Welsh, Irish, Hawaiian, or Maori people who, for better or for worse, can only adopt the indigenous language as an "add-on," English having long been their primary language. Finally, the adoption of Hebrew was assisted by its link to a religious tradition, virtually a covenant: even though Hebrew was declared the official language of Israel from on high, the success of the movement was determined by a powerful sentiment within the families themselves that the use of this language was critical to the establishment of a Jewish state. It has been said that the revival would not have succeeded without this crucial element—a sense of learning Hebrew as an imperative of, again, one's very soul, not just as a kind of party trick or "local custom."

Conditions in Ireland, Wales, New Zealand, or Hawaii only approximate the spiritual ones that reanimated Hebrew. The indigenous languages are not connected to religions still alive and deeply felt by most, nor are the revival efforts taking place among a people committed so starkly and universally to cultural sovereignty as to relocate to a brand-new nation or be allowed by sociohistorical serendipity to found one. Yet many of the people learning these languages feel that they are not fully expressing their souls without speaking the indigenous language. This is a hopeful sign. In all of these places, increasing numbers of homes are passing the language on to their children as a first one.

Yet even if these success stories remain too scattered to revive the languages generally, their situation is not quite as hopeless as is claimed by various commentators who have declared the Irish revival movement a failure because of the unlikelihood that significant numbers of families will pass the language on to children as a mother tongue. It is a central tenet of the language-revival movement that a language is only truly alive when it is regularly passed on to children, but this is not necessarily true. More properly, throughout human history thus far, this has been the case. Yet it is conceivable that languages such as Irish, Welsh, Maori, and Hawaiian could be passed on as second languages, taught in school and spoken nonnatively but proficiently, *in perpetuo*. Under such conditions, the languages could persist as cultural indicators, the very learning of the language in school itself constituting a hallmark of cultural identity. As such, the population would surely speak the language with varying degrees of proficiency, some excellently, others only controlling the basics (as do many Americans in California who "speak Spanish" as the result of a few years of classes in school followed by constant exposure to the language from the large Latino population), and many people falling somewhere between these poles.

This is, after all, the case with many lingua francas in Third World countries, with more speakers having learned the languages as teenagers or later than having learned them natively; Swahili has long been an example. Many languages born as pidgins have been spoken as nonnative languages for centuries, learned mostly by men in work contexts and quickly expanding through constant use of this kind into **creoles,** suitable for precise and modulated expression. It is perhaps something of a Western conceit to suppose that a language is not "a language" unless it is spoken from the cradle. This requirement, after all, would imply that clergy speaking Latin or Sanskrit are not really "speaking the language," because they did not learn the language as infants, a claim that would ultimately seem to be rather arbitrary.

Similarly, Africans typically "speak" many languages that were not spoken to them until adolescence or later; even if a speaker's version of a language constitutes only, say, seventy-five percent of what a natively transmitted version consists of, it is unclear that this African "does not speak" the language.

For better or for worse, the cultural conditions are present to preserve, for example, Irish within what could be considered a domain for minority languages commensurate with new world conditions: a living *taught* language. The invention of writing, which has threatened minority languages in tending to anoint the dominant languages chosen to write in as "legitimate," can ironically be of assistance here, in allowing the transcription and dissemination of language-teaching materials.

## Many Will Likely Survive Only as Living "Taught" Languages

Then there are the languages concentrated in tropical regions that are threatened by the encroachments of global capitalism—the Dahalos of the world, such as the Ugong language that Thai is edging away, and the more than eight hundred fabulously complex and variegated languages of Papua New Guinea. In these cases, the glass-half-full perspective suggests hope that national governments can be persuaded to assist in preserving the cultures speaking these languages, because only this will allow them to continue to be spoken natively. On the other hand, a constructive response to the glass-half-empty perspective, conceding that brutal realities make it likely that such attempts will not be able to save anything approaching all of these languages, would be to adopt the "taught language" perspective, providing for a time when descendants of today's native speakers will at least be able to acquire some proficiency in their languages through schooling, to the extent that the descendants remain a coherent enough entity to ensure a suitable demand.

## A Historically Unprecedented Number Will Die

On the other hand, almost all of the indigenous languages of North America and Australia would appear to be lost forever as living languages. All but a handful are spoken only by the very elderly, as foreign and imposing to many of their English-dominant children and grandchildren as they are to us. In most cases, surviving descendants of a given group are too few and too geographically scattered for there to be significant demand for revival of any kind in the future.

## A Really Good Chinese Restaurant in San Francisco

In general it would appear that the linguistic landscape of the future will be a less diverse and somewhat blander one than has existed until now. Many of the languages that survive as natively spoken will be mostly geopolitically dominant ones, and such languages, by the very nature of having through the ages been learned by large numbers of adults and as often as not used as secondary rather than primary languages, are often somewhat "streamlined" in regard to grammatical elaborations. This means that a certain "vanilla" quotient will be overrepresented among the surviving languages— . . . Swahili is somewhat watered down in complexity as Bantu languages go; it has even been argued that the Romance languages, representing Latin learned as a second language by subjugated populations, are slightly "pidginized" in comparison with other Indo-European languages. Note also that Wolof, in becoming the lingua franca of Senegal, is probably on the way to seeing its array of noun class markers severely reduced as a "price" to pay for its new broadened sway—power corrupts! Meanwhile, a substantial number of minority languages will persist in use as "taught" languages—but then in this guise these languages will be somewhat less elaborated than they were when spoken natively.

One might analogize the linguistic landscape of the future to a world where the dazzling variety and subtlety of native Chinese cuisines, the product of thousands of years of accumulated skills, evolutions, branchings, and mixture, are represented only by Chinese food as available in the United States. Certainly, a great deal of excellent Chinese food is available here, but not in the protean richness available in China, and a great deal of what Americans are accustomed to eating as "Chinese" food is actually better described as Chinese ingredients adapted to a beef-stew palate. Yet just as this is surely better than nothing (there was no won ton soup, sushi, coconut milk soup, or even spaghetti and meatballs served on the *Titanic* in 1912), the admittedly blanched language palate that even our most dedicated language-revival efforts will most likely leave behind is certainly better than what would remain if we did nothing.

## The Task Ahead and Why It Must Be Done

It is therefore urgent that we record as many languages as possible before they no longer exist so that, even if they are not actively spoken anymore, we have their essences preserved for posterity for the benefit of descendants of speakers who want to make contact with their heritage by learning some of the language; for research; and for sheer wonder.

It is here that linguists, the people most qualified to carry out this task, will be crucial, but only if there is a fundamental recasting of current attitudes in the discipline. People often suppose that linguists are either professional **polyglots** or arbiters of "proper grammar." Neither is the case; in fact, precisely what most linguists are engaged in would surprise many people by virtue of the extremely specific nature of the enterprise, focused on a particular issue barely perceptible at all to the layperson.

The linguistics discipline as it is today configured is centered on identifying through elegant induction the precise structure of our innate neurological endowment for language, sparked by a paradigm founded by Noam Chomsky in the late 1950s. There are many other branches of linguistics and a great many linguists with no serious interest in the Chomskyan approach. However, the paradigm looms over the field with a sociological "capital" analogous to the domination of the music composition field decades ago by atonalists despite their never having been a numerical majority.

One's basic training focuses on the Chomskyan framework, and there is a tacit but powerful sense in the field that this subarea is not only the "sexiest," but also the most intellectually substantial. For example, there are some departments where students are trained in nothing but the Chomskyan paradigm, but none where students are grounded entirely in any other subfield—the other subfields are ultimately regarded as "other," the icing rather than the cake. Regardless of the caliber of his work in another subfield, the linguist who does not display at least token interest in the Chomskyan endeavor is not considered "a *linguist* linguist" in the back of the minds of a great many in the field, and the most general respect is accorded the linguist in an "icing" subfield who is invested in showing the implications of his work for the latest developments in the Chomsky bailiwick. For example, it is safe to say that to most modern linguists in America the phenomena I [cover in many of my books] are perhaps "interesting" in a passing way, but generally not considered "real linguistics."

To be sure, Chomskyan linguistics is a thoroughly fascinating investigation. Steven Pinker's book *The Language Instinct* should in my opinion, along with Jared Diamond's *Guns, Germs, and Steel* (a rare example of a book that tells us what we want to hear and is empirically correct in the bargain), be required reading for all thinking people. It is not for nothing that the Chomskyan paradigm took our field by storm to such an extent in the 1960s and has obsessed so many fine minds since. Properly, however, illuminating the possibility that we possess a neural mechanism calibrated to produce basic sentences is but one of dozens of ways that one might study the multifarious thing known as human language. In our moment, as linguist R. M. W. Dixon eloquently calls for in his book *The Rise and Fall of Languages*, linguists should be trained to go out and document at least one dying language before it disappears forever from the earth—I myself will be embarking on such work as soon as I finish this book. This is particularly appropriate given that the study of such a language inestimably enriches the study of the possibility of an innate language competence, often furnishing a career's worth of relevant data. (Notice my sense of obligation to say that, so powerful is the sense of "Chomsky—smart/other—also-ran" in modern academic linguistics in the United States.)

It is often said that we must preserve the world's languages because each one reflects a particular culture. Although this is true in itself, I have always felt that to elevate this as a guiding motivation for preserving languages is based on an oversimplified conception of the relationship between language and culture. It is true that when a group loses its language millennia of accumulated knowledge regarding the medicinal properties of plants, the subtleties of managing crops, the life cycles of fishes, and other phenomena are lost. However, in the strict sense, the linkage of language revival with cultures seems to imply that once researchers recorded the cultural aspects of language for posterity, then it would no longer be important whether or not the language as a whole continued to be spoken.

And in any case, as I have noted previously, most of a given language has evolved less on the basis of culture than through the structured randomness of an evolution bounded only by human physiognomy and cognitive requirements. All but a few pages of any written grammar of a language is taken up with elaborate rules, lists, and exceptions that no more reveal anything specific to the culture that uses them than a pattern of spilled milk reveals anything specific about the bottle it came from.

Linguists are quite aware of this, and in fact most linguists' scholarship on languages has little to do with charting links between grammars and cultures. It is safe to say that most, although not all, linguists largely cherish languages because of the sheer marvel of their various architectures, elegantly combining structure and chaos in six thousand different ways. I surmise that the emphasis on culture among linguists active in the language-revival movement stems from a sense that the purely linguistic wonder of human speech is less accessible to the general public than arguments founded on more easily perceived concepts such as culture.

Yet... I have hoped to usher the reader into the very awareness animating linguists that human speech is a truly wondrous thing in itself. In this vein, it pays to note that the Dahalo language that Peter Ladefoged referred to is the one with clicks spoken far from the territory where the other click languages are spoken—the language the farmer thinks of as a sign of backwardness is, with all due respect to his justifiable relationship to his immediate circumstances, a language with a wondrous sound system. A great many of the Native American languages dying before our eyes were so complex that children were not fully competent in them until they were ten years old. It is truly sad that world history cannot allow all of these languages to continue to be spoken, transform themselves into new ones, overgrow, and mix with one another. But at the very least we can make sure that as many of them as possible are written down as thoroughly as possible before their demise as living systems and that at least a healthy number of lucky ones can be passed along as secondary but essential languages across generations.

Let's take a look at one last descendant of the world's first language. Because prefixes and suffixes generally evolve in a language from what begin as full, separate words, the first language can be assumed to have had no prefixes or suffixes at all (or tones or a great many other complications of a grammar that only arise through gradual reinterpretations of material). Yet 150,000 years later, gradual evolution produced a remarkable array of prefixes in the Central Pomo language of California. English speakers associate prefixes with relatively basic meanings such as repetition (*re-*) and opposition (*un-*, *in-*, *mis-*). But in Central Pomo, prefixes carry much more robust and specific meanings:

*ba-* orally
*s-* by sucking
*š-* with a handle
*ča-* by slicing
*č*$^{h}$*-* pertaining to vegetative growth
*da-* by pushing with the palm
*h-* by poking
*m-* with heat
*qa-* by biting
*ša-* by shaking
*'-* by fine hand action, such as using the fingers

The root *yól* means "to mix." Each of its combinations with these eleven prefixes yields a particularly useful word:

***ba**yól* to insert words suddenly while humming; that is, mix orally
***s**yól* to wash down cookies or doughnuts with coffee; that is, to mix by sucking
***š**yól* to stir with a spoon; that is, to mix with a "handle"
***ča**yól* to chop up several things together, such as celery and onions for stew
***č***$^{h}$*yól* to plant things close together
***da**yól* to fold in dry ingredients while baking
***h**yól* to add salt or pepper (I guess they "poke" it in)
***m**yól* to throw various ingredients into a pot; that is, to mix by heating
***qa**yól* to eat several things together, such as meat and potatoes; that is, to mix by biting
***ša**yól* to sift dry ingredients
*'yól* to throw ingredients into a bowl with the fingers

Of course, the prefixes create new words with each verb; *'ól*, with a glottal stop as its first consonant, means "to summon," and here are some of its prefixed versions:

***ba**'ól* to call; that is, to summon orally
***š**'ól* to set a fishing line; that is, to summon by manipulating a handle
***č***$^{h}$*'ól* to comb hair; that is, to summon vegetative growth (by analogy with the flowing motion of some vegetation)
***da**'ól* to dig for; that is, to summon by pushing with the palm
***h**'ól* to probe for a creature with a stick; that is, to summon by poking

It is this kind of thing, then, that we are losing when languages die—the last known fluent speakers of Central Pomo have died since these data were collected. Just as we would be inestimably poorer to be denied the opportunity to see giraffes, roses, bombardier beetles, tulips, and little black house cats with white spots on their chests that sit on our laps as we write, we lose one of the true wonders of the world every time one of these glorious variations on a theme set by the first language slips away unrecorded for posterity. We will never encounter a stegosaur, but we can be thankful that fossils allow us to know what it was like. In the same way, if we cannot enjoy all six thousand of the world's languages alive for much longer, let us at least make sure to afford them high-quality preservation.

In the Central Pomo case, certainly the loss of the language entailed the loss of a vehicle of cultural expression. But surely all of us value sucking, poking, and shaking as much as the Central Pomo speakers did: it's just that our languages chose not to index such things with prefixes. Most likely the reader's native language chose instead to genuflect to marking each noun as definite or indefinite. Both the Central Pomo prefixes and the European languages' articles are fascinating in their own right as alternate methods of packaging information in order to talk about this thing called living, and both are only the tip of the iceberg in regard to the endless ways in which humans can express themselves in speech.

Each variant of the first language is festooned with gloriously random remnants of things caught in the cracks in the course of transformations long forgotten, and most of them exist in an array of subvariants on the theme related to one another rather like Barbara Cartland's hundreds of romance novelettes. All carry mementoes of past liaisons with other dialects of other languages; some of them once rose from the ashes; most of them developed as far beyond the call of duty as the Cathedral of Notre Dame. A select few even sit swathed in a Dorian Gray complex as a by-product of the invention of the printing press. The world's riffs on basic materials that emerged in East Africa around 148,000 B.C. represent six thousand ways of being human.

## Notes

1. Unfortunately he died toothless, rendering the data elicited from him somewhat fuzzy around the edges—particularly awkward because he was the only source of the language ever recorded.

2. Yes, there *were!* Just imagine that.

3. Notice that India is so populous that languages many of us have never heard of are spoken by more people than almost any others in the world (Bihari, Telugu, Marathi).

4. Which in itself sounds like a song cut from *The Music Man* on the road to New York.

## Critical Thinking and Application

- Do you agree that it is tragic to lose a language? Why? What is lost with it?
- Analogies help us think about unfamiliar things in more familiar terms, which provides advantages. At the same time, they may urge us to overlook differences. Discuss the advantages and disadvantages of using biological evolution as an analogy for human language.
- Poll the students in your class. How many generations back did their forebears speak languages other than English? How many languages were spoken? How many languages can your classmates speak and how well? Are any of their ancestors' languages endangered?
- What does it mean for a language to be genuinely spoken?
- Research an endangered language and the activities being done to combat its loss.

## Vocabulary

click
creole
diglossia, diglossic
index
inflection
language death
language revival
linguistic equilibrium
lingua franca
pidgin, pidginized
polyglot
prefix
suffix

## Suggested Further Reading

Abley, Mark. 2003. *Spoken Here: Travels Among Threatened Languages.* Boston and New York: Houghton Mifflin.

Dorian, Nancy C. 1981. *Language Death: The Life Cycle of a Scottish Gaelic Dialect.* Philadelphia: University of Pennsylvania Press.

Dorian, Nancy C., ed. 1989. *Investigating Obsolescence: Studies in Language Contraction and Death.* Cambridge: Cambridge University Press.

McWhorter, John H. 2001. *The Power of Babel: A Natural History of Language.* New York: Times Books.

Nettle, Daniel, and Suzanne Romaine. 2000. *Vanishing Voices: The Extinction of the World's Languages.* Oxford: Oxford University Press.

Walsh, Michael. 2005. Will Indigenous Languages Survive? *Annual Review of Anthropology* 34: 293–315.

CHAPTER 26

# Indigenous Language Endangerment and the Unfinished Business of Nation States

*Donna Patrick*

(2007)

*Canada has faced its colonial legacy full-on and has worked hard with First Nations and other aboriginal groups to demonstrate respect and to bolster their cultural and economic survival. Language is more difficult than some other topics because it requires a critical mass of speakers to maintain the vibrancy of a particular variety. If a language isn't useful because it no longer has many functions, multilingual speakers will shift to a more widely used language. And then the "smaller" language will become endangered.*

*As in the United States, Canadian indigenous groups (called Aboriginal peoples, including First Nations, Inuit, and Métis groups) are regarded as autonomous nations on a par with Canada. Treaties between nations must be worked out with mutual respect and compromise. Canada has recognized that restitution is owed its aboriginal peoples because of past disregard of their rights, with residential schools a prime cause of the loss of traditional knowledge, language, and culture. To restore what had been lost through assimilationist policies that lasted a century, though, is no simple task.*

## Reading Questions

- What is the current situation with regard to aboriginal languages in Canada? How has this come about?
- What are some of the arguments for protecting or supporting indigenous languages?
- How is indigenous language discourse in Canada similar to and different from national minority language mobilization?
- What is *strategic essentialism*, and how has it been used to make the case for language rights? What links are made between aboriginal groups' spirituality, culture, land, traditional knowledge, and language?

---

We believe that protecting First Nation, Inuit and Métis languages is another step in the continual process of Canada's nation building. As the Supreme Court of Canada and others, including the Royal Commission on Aboriginal Peoples, have noted, Canada has unfinished business with the First Nations, Inuit and Métis peoples of this country.

—Report of the Task Force on Aboriginal Languages and Cultures (2005: 74)

Donna Patrick, Indigenous Language Endangerment and the Unfinished Business of Nation States. In *Discourses of Endangerment: Ideology and Interest in the Defence of Languages*, edited by Alexandre Duchêne and Monica Heller. London and New York: Continuum, 2007, pp. 35–56.

**Indigenous** mobilization in the late twentieth and early twenty-first centuries has been conceived largely as part of a continuous struggle against colonization, land appropriation, broken treaty promises, assimilation, marginalization and genocide. At the international level, concerns over language in particular have given rise to a supranational discourse, which has made **language endangerment** and **language rights** issues part of international agendas in both governmental and non-governmental arenas, and brought the plight of Indigenous languages to the attention of a growing public. The international prominence of these issues can be traced to the 1953 UNESCO document *The Use of Vernacular Languages in Education*, and can be seen today not only in the work of such non-governmental organizations (NGOs) as Terralingua, Linguapax and the Foundation for Endangered Languages, but also in the considerable amount of academic research devoted to them (see e.g. Grenoble and Whaley 1998; Henze and Davis 1999; Crystal 2000; Nettle and Romaine 2000; Fishman 2001; Hinton and Hale 2001; Maffi 2001; Stuknabb-Kangas *et al.* 2003; Freeland and Patrick 2004; May 2005; Muehlmann and Duchene, in press).

Yet, despite this supranational turn, endangered language issues remain largely a matter for nation states. This is because these issues remain, to a large degree, shaped by national concerns and constructed through national spaces, which provide openings for mobilization and for the legitimization of Indigenous claims. Accordingly, many of these concerns have been taken up at national and local levels. As Smith notes, 'some communities [have] focused primarily on cultural revitalization', while 'others, either as separate organizations or as small groups of individuals, [have become] much more intent on engaging in reorganizing political relations with the state' (1999: 111). While a description of activist work in terms of this division of labour might well reflect how such work has been conceived, it overlooks the extent to which Indigenous political and cultural activism, and the discourses associated with them, have overlapped in practice. Moreover, it overlooks the importance of language and language rights as a mobilizing force that is both political and cultural, uniting Indigenous activists and their communities in the twin goals of achieving 'nationhood' and cultural 'survival', and allowing them to tap into international discourses, including a number of **conventions** and covenants on language endangerment and protection, which provide further support for their goals.

In what follows, I shall be trying to spell out how language rights, and the discourses surrounding them, have acted as just such a 'mobilizing force' in the struggle of Indigenous groups for greater autonomy. My focus will be language endangerment discourse in Canada, a country in which the politics of language, land claims, and **Aboriginal**[1] mobilization is well established, and where language endangerment discourse echoes that found elsewhere.

While the Indigenous language discourse to be examined here is, to some extent, unique to the political, economic and historical conditions of Canada, there are nevertheless a number of points that pertain to language endangerment discourse in general. In other words, the Canadian Indigenous language discourse has similarities with both Indigenous language and minority language movements found elsewhere, including language movements of national minorities, such as French in Canada, Welsh in the United Kingdom or Corsican in France. In both Indigenous and national minority language mobilization, smaller political collectivities are vying for a social, cultural and economic space and some form of territorial integrity within the nation state. While each collectivity might aim for a particular kind of minority or Indigenous relationship with the state—from outright separation, to retaining some kind of nation-like status (i.e. remaining within the jurisdiction of the larger nation state), or holding some form of regional or local control over institutions and municipalities—the common underlying drive to gain 'territory' or a land base is at the root of the language mobilization.

In addition to this underlying link to land, language endangerment discourse also tends to highlight particular facts about language in order to build a case for language promotion (and thereby promotion for the group itself). Some of these facts include the high rates of language attrition and the concomitant loss of (1) local knowledge and culture associated with the language; (2) cultural diversity that enriches the nation; and (3) crucial tangible and intangible cultural heritage that defines the nation. Also key to this discourse are the appeals at times to **linguistic essentialism**, which ties particular language varieties to 'authentic' cultural practices and socio-cultural groups, inhabiting particular social places and localities.

Despite these similarities found in language endangerment discourses, there are some important differences between Indigenous groups and national minorities. For one thing, Indigenous groups tend to form a more fragmented social category, often more marginalized and with smaller numbers than national minorities. In large part, this marginalization is rooted in the oppositional nature of Indigenous economies and notions (or lack of notions) of land 'ownership'—economies which have largely been at odds with the economic and material beliefs and practices of the colonizers. In other words, non-Western, non-capitalist Indigenous economies have often been subjugated by the aggressive, expanding, market-oriented colonial settlers. Harvesting practices have not only been grounded in different forms of land tenure, but also in different cosmologies governing social and cultural meanings and human relationships to the natural world. For many Indigenous groups, the idea of unifying around a cohesive, unifying nationalistic discourse and using state apparatuses to gain control, 'ownership' or 'rights' to land is in direct opposition and conflict with the Indigenous values and beliefs that the groups want to protect. This paradox and complexity can lead to greater fragmentation in the group, but it also means that the way that language and land become discursively linked in language endangerment discourse can vary among groups as well.

Despite the variation, however, there are also common links in Indigenous language discourse. In order to gain clout and support for Indigenous languages and Indigenous movements within and beyond the nation state, the discourses have relied on moral appeals to human and Indigenous rights, social justice and protecting biodiversity. As we shall see, certain discursive strategies emphasizing such appeals also draw on the importance of protecting 'traditional knowledge' (as opposed to other forms of 'cultural knowledge') and linking linguistic diversity to biodiversity.

That being said, what is arguably distinctive about language endangerment discourse in Canada, particularly as constructed by Aboriginal groups themselves, is the specific highlighting of the 'unfinished business' of land negotiations and the reconciliation between Aboriginal groups and the Canadian state. This need for reconciliation stems from decades of **assimilationist** paternalistic policies and the need for the federal government to recognize (1) past mistakes in the colonization process; (2) rights to land and territories that include rights to resources and economic development on these lands; and (3) the need to renegotiate new relationships between **First Nations**, Inuit and Métis and the Canadian state—relationships that are rooted in the nation-to-nation relationships established in the treaty-making of the past.

Language becomes important in this discourse, since language was lost through colonial practices, which included residential schooling, the banning of particular rituals and cultural practices, land appropriation and economic degradation. Language has thus gained importance in cultural and spiritual revitalization movements, and these in turn are linked to the need for greater autonomy and control over lands within the Canadian state.

In the discussion to follow, we shall examine a recent instance of such language endangerment discourse, exemplified in the June 2005 *Report to the Minister of Canadian Heritage*, prepared by the *Task Force on Aboriginal Languages and Cultures*, a group of ten First Nation, Inuit and Métis representatives that was formed in 2003. As we shall see, this report has provided a space for the Aboriginal language survival movement in Canada to promote itself at the national level in the context of official bilingualism and heritage language promotion. However, while the Aboriginal language movement broadly echoes that of the French language movement in Canada for increased rights and recognition, there are differences. For one thing, the way that language and land are linked in the Aboriginal discourse is somewhat different from the French language debates that have characterized the country, including the Quebec movement for increased linguistic and territorial autonomy within Canada. The Aboriginal discourse is different not only because of the hundreds of outstanding land claims cases waiting to be legally settled between Aboriginal groups and the Crown, but also because of the diversity among Aboriginal populations and groups. This fragmentation among Aboriginal groups is based on different social and geographical realities and means that there is a more complex language movement at play with particular consequences for different groups of speakers.

Significantly, the **essentializing** of a link between Aboriginal language and Aboriginal land, though of great strategic value in the struggle for language preservation, risks excluding certain Aboriginal groups from the language endangerment discourse. Among these are members of urbanized Aboriginal communities, created as the result of significant levels of migration of Aboriginal peoples to cities. While such migration has tended not to involve a complete de-territorialization of people from their Aboriginal homeland 'territories', given considerable movement back and forth between these territories and cities, it has nevertheless sparked the construction of new identities and new cultural and linguistic practices that are shaping new forms of community. Thus, new forms of place-making—not necessarily linked to dominant interests in traditional, territorialized 'nationhood'—are creating new forms of 'locality' and 'community' in which First Nations, Inuit and Métis in Canada can thrive. This makes the question of what Aboriginal language is being saved for whom a pressing one, which indicates the need to create a more inclusive and radicalized discourse of language endangerment, consistent not only with the need for political reconciliation and **restitution**, but with increasing diversity within Aboriginal groups.

The rest of this chapter is organized as follows. The next section will review some of the historical forces that led to the current state of Aboriginal languages and of Aboriginal communities more generally. The third section will offer an analysis of language endangerment discourse, as it is exemplified in the *Task Force Report on Aboriginal Languages and Cultures* (hereafter the *Task Force Report*). The fourth section will provide a discussion of this discourse, drawing particular attention both to its social effects and to its limits, and briefly address the question 'What languages are being saved, and for whom?' The final section will offer some concluding remarks, including the need for sociolinguistics to widen the scope of what is seen as 'language revitalization'.

## The Historical Roots of Indigenous Language Endangerment in Canada

A useful place to start an investigation of the discourse of language endangerment in Canada is to consider the current situation of Aboriginal languages. Of the 50 or so Aboriginal languages still spoken in Canada, all but a handful have been classified as 'endangered', indicating that their chances of survival beyond this century are limited (Kincade 1991; Kirkness 1998; Cook 1998; *Task Force Report* 2005). One response to this situation, which has come from Aboriginal groups in particular, has been to make appeals for institutional support for **language revitalization** and protection. These appeals and the discourse constructed around them can thus be seen as integral parts of the revitalization movement. Before considering them in more detail, however, it is important to recognize the historical context that has led to **language shift** and language endangerment in the first place.

Prior to the arrival of Europeans, North America was populated by hundreds of distinct Indigenous groups, differing greatly not only in the languages that they spoke, but in their political, economic and social organization, which ranged from autonomous, rather isolated groups to vast confederacies. The cultural, political and economic knowledge of these groups was conveyed by means of oral traditions; this knowledge permitted these groups, 'as distinct as they were' with respect to language and culture, to develop 'shared diplomatic protocols which allowed for a free flow of trade on a continental scale' (Office of the Treaty Commissioner 1998: 14). In fact, when Europeans arrived in North America, they were able to adopt the east–west trade routes already established by the people living there.

During this period of initial European contact, alliances were forged between Europeans and Indigenous groups, primarily to ensure trade routes for the competing colonial trade companies. French and English interests in the fur trade resulted in particular trade patterns which sustained a more-or-less equal trade partnership between Europeans and Indigenous groups. This balanced relation, however, 'soon gave way to imbalance' when the lessening of hostilities between French and English resulted in a decline in the 'politically motivated flow of goods from European authorities to native American allies' (Wolf 1982: 194). Indigenous trappers became more dependent on the trading post, not only for guns and ammunition, but also for foodstuffs such as tea, flour and sugar, and other common trade items, such as cloth and tobacco. In the nineteenth century, as wildlife became depleted and contagious diseases decimated Aboriginal populations, economic conditions worsened for Aboriginal peoples. This was exacerbated by increased settlement, expansionist threats by the United States and the declining importance of the fur trade. In addition, pressure to settle Western Canada, which increased after the signing of the *British North America Act* (*BNA Act*) and the establishment of Canadian confederation in 1867, led in turn to an increase in treaty negotiations between First Nations and the Crown (see Morris 1991; Office of the Treaty Commissioner 1998; Ray *et al.* 2000).

Since the signing of the *BNA Act*, the federal government has held responsibility for 'Indians and lands reserved for Indians', as prescribed in section 91(24) of the Act. This section was the legislative basis for the *Indian Act* of 1876 and the repressive Aboriginal policies that followed, which restricted movement, property rights, political rights, cultural practices, and the items that Aboriginal peoples were permitted to possess (McCarthy and Patrick 2005).[2] The *Indian Act* has had a profound effect on Aboriginal political, cultural and economic life, not least because it was the basis for the federal government's grouping of all Aboriginal peoples in Canada into a single legal–racial category—a grouping that ignores the tremendous heterogeneity of Aboriginal groups, with their distinct histories, languages and cultures.

The *Indian Act* and its revisions throughout the late nineteenth and early twentieth centuries set up the framework that governed Indians on the reserves created through the treaty process.[3] The provisions of the Act had the effect of: (1) formalizing the residential school system;[4] (2) stifling cultural and economic activity on reserves; (3) inhibiting the movement of Aboriginal peoples; and (4) depriving them both of recourse to legal action and of the ability to organize politically (McCarthy and Patrick 2005). These consequences of the Act are now widely recognized to have been dire, and political and legal action in recent years has sought to expose and redress the abuses and injustices for which it was directly or indirectly responsible. The brutality of the residential school system has been a particular target of legal action,[5] not only because this system required children to be separated from their families, and permitted them to be subjected to physical and psychological abuse, including punishment for speaking Aboriginal languages, but also because such abuses meant that the federal government had failed to provide adequate education to Aboriginal peoples, one of their fiduciary duties under the *BNA Act*.

After the Second World War, the international mobilization of Indigenous peoples (Smith 1999; Feldman 2001) and the rise of other social movements set in motion efforts to restore to Aboriginal peoples in Canada the material and symbolic resources, including land, languages and cultural heritage, that they had lost through assimilationist government policy. Efforts also were taken to foster respect for and to promote forms of Aboriginal 'nationhood' and to heal the relations between Aboriginal groups and the state. A milestone here was the entrenchment of Aboriginal rights in the 1982 *Constitution Act*,[6] the nature and extent of the land, hunting, fishing and other rights granted there being clarified through a series of court cases, such as *R v. Van der Peet* (1996), with significant implications for the conceptualization of Aboriginal culture and language in Canadian law (see Vallance 2003; Patrick 2005). Another milestone was the establishment of the Royal Commission on Aboriginal Peoples (RCAP) (1991–1996),[7] set up to examine Aboriginal state relations and Aboriginal relations with Canadian society as a whole, during a period of intense politicization of Aboriginal groups in Canada (see Dickason 2002: 393–431 for an overview). This commission produced a five volume report, which included recommendations concerning language. Specifically, it called for community-driven, community-managed initiatives, leading ideally to a Canadian Aboriginal Languages Foundation (RCAP vol. 3, ch. 6 sec. 2.5, recommendation 3.6.10). Although this foundation has still not been established, the concept seems to have re-emerged in the form of the Aboriginal Languages and Cultures Centre proposed in the *Task Force Report* (2005: 13, to be described in more detail below).

The growing prominence of Aboriginal rights as a national issue can also be traced to efforts begun in 1987 to establish a Canadian Heritage Languages Institute, to promote languages other than French and English.[8] This heritage language initiative coincided with the *Canadian Multiculturalism Act* (1988), intended to reflect and promote Canadian cultural and racial diversity.[9] One key failing of the Canadian Heritage Languages Institute initiative was its high degree of 'centralization' (as voiced by grassroots community representatives in consultations), as well as its exclusion of Aboriginal organizations (Paron 2005). Bill C-37 (1989), the heritage language legislation that finally resulted from this initiative, did include Aboriginal groups, but this inclusion was achieved without consultation with these groups, which was unacceptable to them.

This problem was rectified, to some extent, by the recent establishment by the Ministry of Canadian Heritage of an Aboriginal Language Task Force, consisting of ten Aboriginal representatives from First Nations, Inuit and Métis communities, which was set up in 2003 with a mandate to 'propose a national strategy to preserve, revitalize and promote First Nation, Inuit and Métis languages and cultures' (*Task Force Report* 2005: i). Despite this greater accommodation of Aboriginal concerns within the Department of Canadian Heritage, Aboriginal language issues nevertheless remain distinct from those of French and heritage languages in at least one important respect: namely, in how efforts to preserve and promote them can be justified. More specifically, the justification for promoting French and heritage languages has rested primarily on the link between language and culture and the unquestioned assumption that 'if the language is lost, then the culture is lost'—such a loss being highly undesirable in an officially pluralistic and multicultural society. However, such justifications are inadequate in the context of Aboriginal claims to language and cultural rights. This is, in particular, because these claims are rooted in the historical, political and economic relations of the First Peoples with Europeans and the way in which Canada has developed as a nation, which has meant that cultural and linguistic revitalization remains bound up with the continuing political and social struggles reflected in the hundreds of still unsettled land claims and other kinds of 'unfinished Constitutional business' in the country. However, problems also arise because of the unique difficulties associated with defining and securing Aboriginal rights. As far as the Supreme Court of Canada is concerned, Aboriginal 'culture' is preserved only through the continuation of specific traditional practices such as hunting or fishing, and is not tied in any direct way to language use (see Patrick 2005). Since Aboriginal languages are facing 'extinction' even though many cultural practices have persisted, one needs to find arguments in addition to those that invoke links between language and culture in order to justify Aboriginal language promotion and revitalization. As it happens, such arguments have been advanced in the *Task Force Report*, which we shall be turning to in the next section.

## The Construction of Language Endangerment Discourse in Canada

As just noted, the goal of promoting Aboriginal languages in Canada requires a language endangerment discourse that goes beyond the assumption that cultures die when languages die. This does not mean, however, that this discourse has eschewed a link between language and culture, which still figures prominently in the construction of Aboriginal identity and in the discourse on Aboriginal language endangerment in Canada. This can be seen in examples of this discourse that appear in the media as well as in 'official' discourse produced by political organizations, language activists and political leaders. In what follows, we shall be examining two examples of this discourse, both of which offer an Aboriginal perspective on how language revitalization and protection can be achieved in a linguistically politicized Canada; one text focuses more narrowly on the link between language and culture, while the other offers a broader and more complex treatment of language endangerment.

### Language Endangerment and the Media

We can gather some sense of the role that the link between Aboriginal languages and cultures continues to play in language endangerment discourse in Canada from recent media coverage of language issues, which have arisen in the context of legislated French and English language use. For example, a 2004 article in Montreal's *Le Devoir*[10] describes how at the Second Conference on Aboriginal Languages, held in St. Sauveur, north of Montreal, in October of that year, the regional chief of the Assembly of First Nations of Quebec and Labrador asserted that Indigenous groups in Quebec need a law similar to Bill 101, the Quebec provincial legislation aimed at protecting the French language. What we see here is a parallel, made by an Aboriginal leader and affirmed in the newspaper article, between Aboriginal languages and French, which has benefited from provincial 'official language' laws, including those that aim to support its use in education, the workplace, and other institutional spheres. What we also find in this article is (the reporting of) an attempt to derive support for local efforts to protect linguistic diversity by invoking commonly held assumptions about the desirability of cultural diversity, by making a 'natural' link of language to culture. At the same time, there are appeals to existing language rights initiatives, already in place in Quebec, Canada and internationally. The former point is echoed in the assertion of a spokesperson for the Canadian Commission for UNESCO that 'la source de la diversité culturelle se trouve dans les langues. C'est à travers elles qu'on peut explorer d'autres façons de voir le monde. En les perdant, on perd des connaissances et des compétences'. ['the source of cultural diversity is in languages. It is through languages that we are able to explore other ways of seeing the world. When we lose languages, we lose knowledge and abilities'.] (Doyon 2004). The latter point is echoed in the assertion of the director of the conference that it is now necessary to see 'les initiatives nationales et internationales existantes' ['existing national and international initiatives'] and to put forward 'un plan d'action pour que le gouvernement reconnaisse la nécessité de preserver les langues autochtones' ['a plan of action so that the government recognizes the need to preserve Aboriginal languages']. The 'plan of action' suggested here, encompassing both federal and international levels, alludes to the existence of international covenants and conventions pertaining to language rights, promotion and revitalization.

Even this brief consideration of Aboriginal language endangerment discourse as reported in the popular media reveals how this discourse serves to naturalize the links between language, culture, ethnicity and nationhood, through references to the specific historical, social and political context of Canada and to the international sphere. Yet, those aspects of language endangerment discourse just reviewed hardly do justice to the complexity of this discourse, with its layering of elements related to national and international issues, including constitutional issues, the federal government's fiduciary duties and land rights, in the former case, and the covenants and conventions concerning traditional knowledge, biodiversity and indigenous rights in the latter.[11]

## The 2005 Task Force Report and Strategic Uses of Essentialism

The 2005 *Task Force Report*, already mentioned in the previous section, offers a clearer picture of the complexity of language endangerment discourse in Canada. The report provides a comprehensive treatment of Aboriginal language issues and exemplifies a systematic use of strategic **essentialism**, linking spiritual and healing aspects of language revitalization to cultural revitalization, legal and political reconciliation to Aboriginal and constitutional rights and language to 'the land'. The following sections will examine these linkages more closely, in order to see how language endangerment is broadly conceived as political and cannot be factored out of the larger concerns of restitution of land, resources and autonomy of First Nations, Inuit and Métis within Canada.

### Language, Land and Spirituality

Arguably, the key link made in the *Task Force Report*, as in Aboriginal language endangerment discourse in Canada more generally, is between 'the people, their languages and the land' (2005: 20). While this, in itself, is not unique from other language struggles, such as the nationalistic movement in Quebec, which discursively connects people, language and a territory, the Aboriginal discourse is different in some key respects.

In the report, this particular linkage is made by emphasizing how Aboriginal groups' spirituality, cultural relationships and connection to the land (and thus, in turn, their legal and political struggles over land rights) are all tied to 'sacred and traditional knowledge', and particularly oral traditions, transmitted through Aboriginal languages. As such, these languages are constructed as a crucial part of Aboriginal existence—and also crucial for understanding the 'historic continuity' of Aboriginal peoples with the land and for interpreting treaties and other historical events related to the land (2005: 20).

The *Task Force Report* begins with an assertion of the central role of spirituality in Aboriginal cultural practices and the importance of language to spirituality. Language revitalization in this context is seen as part of a process of individual and community healing, both of which involve spiritual reconnection with the past and the land. Thus land, spirituality, healing and language are all interconnected: the land serves as a spiritual link between languages and those who speak them; and languages, as 'gifts from the Creator' and carriers of 'unique, irreplaceable values and spiritual beliefs', 'allow speakers to relate with their ancestors and to take part in sacred ceremonies'.[12] In short, language is constructed as the key to fostering certain 'principles and values' and 'spiritual beliefs', and as a dynamic element in healing rituals and other practices that have become part of community-based First Nations, Inuit and Métis rehabilitation and other social service programmes.

The importance of language in this spiritual conception of the world is further emphasized by the claim that language encodes relationships and maintains the 'web of identities' that connect people—for example, through the use of particular words for introducing speakers (*Task Force Report* 2005: 22)—and by the claim that the meanings of particular words in a language are easily lost in translation. Thus, the word for 'land' in Aboriginal languages, which may have a holistic sense that includes its flora and fauna and 'the people's spiritual and historical relationship with it' (*ibid.*: 23), does not find a close parallel in its English translation equivalent.

The importance of Aboriginal languages in cultural practices also emerges from a consideration of the importance of oral traditions and oral history for Aboriginal groups. This importance is related not only to the recognition by the courts 'that oral history must have a role in Aboriginal rights and treaty cases' (*ibid.*: 24), but also to the fact that oral tradition has survived as a separate way of describing the human experience of this world' (*ibid.*: 25) and 'to its role in establish[ing] and maintain[ing] important relationships and pass[ing] them on intact to future generations' (*ibid.*: 24–25). The report notes, in particular, that oral history is used to 'educate the listener for a moral purpose, pass on aspects of culture through stories or sacred songs, or perhaps establish the claim of a family or clan to a territory or to social authority or prestige' (*ibid.*: 24). It thus describes unique experiences and stories of the world, which further justifies the preservation of the Aboriginal languages that have served these functions.

In a similar vein, the report asserts that languages harbour 'different philosophies' that 'are key to forming Aboriginal identities and [...] tied to distinctive languages and cultures' (*ibid.*: 24). Not only is language thus seen as the 'primary vehicle for culture' (*ibid.*: 7), but language and culture are viewed as 'inseparable concepts for First Nations, Inuit and Métis peoples' (*ibid.*: 25). This is because for 'many First Nation, Inuit and Métis languages are largely languages of relationship' (*ibid.*: 7)—reinforcing their tight connection to the land and their identities as the First Peoples of Canada, and enabling them to participate in sacred ceremonies. Moreover, since these languages are integral to 'the history of First Nation, Inuit and Métis peoples', they are also an integral part of Canadian identity and heritage, and thus should be revitalized and protected 'for all Canadians' (*ibid.*: 71).

Stepping back from the particular assertions about language and culture contained in the *Task Force Report*, we can see them not merely as articulating a particular cultural perspective but—given their appearance in a government task force report—also serving to justify and promote, first, the salience of 'land' in the preservation of language and culture and, second, the use of Aboriginal languages in practices that are part of individual and community decolonization and healing processes, through revitalized spiritualism. Strategic uses of linguistic essentialism, binding language to culture, and culture to land, are thus prevalent in the discourse in order to promote the idea that only certain worldviews connect human beings so closely to the land. Not only land, but also these worldviews need to be protected—something that is possible only if the languages encoding these worldviews are themselves protected.

That these assertions about language and culture have considerable strategic importance can also be seen in the *Task Force Report's* seeking of further support for them in national and international discourses, including those that promote the preservation of traditional ecological knowledge, biodiversity, cultural and linguistic diversity and Indigenous rights. For example, the report cites the finding of the *Red Book on Endangered Languages*, produced by the United Nations Educational, Scientific and Cultural Organization (UNESCO), 'that at least half of the world's languages are in danger of extinction by the end of this century', the 'vast majority [of which] are Indigenous' (*Task Force Report* 2005: 71). In addition, the report builds its case that Aboriginal languages should be revitalized because of their intimate connection to traditional Aboriginal knowledge, 'each people and their language represent[ing] a unique way of organizing information and knowledge about the ecosystem', by appealing to national and international discourses on biodiversity and to the need for Canada to fulfil its 'international obligations to protect cultural heritage' (*ibid.*: 82). These appeals to protecting 'intangible heritage' resonate with the previously mentioned links between language and culture and of culture to the land.

Also of strategic importance in the *Task Force Report* are national and international appeals to environmental protection and biological diversity. These appeals are tied to the protection of Aboriginal languages by emphasizing how these languages serve as repositories of traditional ecological knowledge. For example, the report cites Environment Canada and UNESCO statements about the importance of 'Aboriginal traditional knowledge', which 'encompasses all aspects of the environment—biophysical, economic, social, cultural and spiritual—and sees humans as an intimate part of it' (2005: 72). It also invokes Canada's status 'as a signatory to the international Convention on Biological Diversity', which requires the Canadian government to '[p]rotect and encourage customary use of biological resources in accordance with traditional cultural practices that are compatible with conservation or sustainable use requirements' (*ibid.*: 73). The report further emphasizes the need for Canada to also 'preserve and maintain knowledge, innovations and practices of indigenous and local communities embodying traditional lifestyles relevant for the conservation and sustainable use of biological diversity...with the approval and involvement of the holders of such knowledge (Article 8(j) of the *Convention on Biodiversity* cited in the *Task Force Report* 2005: 73).

International conventions provide necessary clout to national pleas to provide resources to 'protect' languages; as the *Task Force Report* notes, Canada is falling behind 'international standards, such as UNESCO's yardstick on explicit and implicit government and institutional policy and attitudes to language' (2005: 75). To remedy this, action must be taken, such as fulfilling Canada's commitment to 'The Action Plan for the Implementation of the Declaration on Cultural Diversity...[which] calls on member states to support and promote linguistic diversity and protect traditional knowledge' (*ibid.*: 82). This is in line with UNESCO's 'action plan for endangered languages'. What is arguably at the heart of this discourse is the idea that linguistic diversity is a desirable human 'good', with the richness of forms both within and across languages suggesting the richness of the natural world, just as biological diversity does.

The point in making these international appeals is that Canadian national identity has in part been constructed around its international commitments to human rights and to its national, liberal cultural policies that promote cultural diversity. That said, the *Task Force Report* makes it clear that if these international commitments are not upheld, as a nation 'Canada could well be characterized as continuing to promote, either actively or passively, assimilation of First Nation, Inuit, and Métis peoples' (2005: 75). Crucially tied to these appeals is the argument that the national discourse of Canada, through the entrenchment of First Nations, Inuit and Métis rights in the 1982 *Constitution Act*, affirms that 'government support of language revitalization is to be grounded in the principle that all First Nation, Inuit and Métis languages must be protected and promoted' (2005: 71). This issue will be explored in the next section.

### Language and Legal–Political Restitution

In addition to the link that the *Task Force Report* makes between language, land and spiritual values is the link that it makes between the revitalization of Aboriginal languages and the achievement of legal and political goals, such as the restitution of Aboriginal rights and Aboriginal 'nationhood'. The idea here, seen in strategic terms, is that Aboriginal language revitalization is a natural part of broader political goals of Aboriginal groups, which are achievable within the established Canadian political–legal framework. This means that 'enduring institutional support for First Nation, Inuit and Métis languages' and for the 'principles and values' embedded in these goes hand in hand with support for other Aboriginal rights and aspirations and with languages (consistent with the Canadian *Charter of Rights and Freedoms*), and with the Canadian federation.

Two intertwined ideas have a prominent place in this discussion. One is that treaties and the Canadian constitutional structure have provided the political space for Aboriginal nationhood, and for undertaking the task of resolving the 'unfinished business' between Aboriginal peoples and the Canadian government over land and other resources as well as over wrongs done to the language, culture and well-being of Aboriginal communities through assimilationist policies. The other, closely related, is that the First Nations, Inuit and Métis were founding peoples alongside the French and the English and that the Canadian government, with the settlement of the country, has a fiduciary duty to Aboriginal peoples to look after their interests, including support for their languages. Together, these ideas lead the report to conclude that the government should recognize Aboriginal linguistic rights and place Aboriginal languages on an equal footing with English and French, particularly as regards funding for language programmes.

The *Task Force Report* emphasizes that First Nations, Inuit and Métis each legitimize their status as distinct 'nations' through 'common bonds of language, culture, ethnicity and a collective will to maintain their distinctiveness' (2005: 26). This idea of Aboriginal nationhood, the report points out, is hardly a new one, but instead 'has been a key element of the relationship between First Nation, Inuit and Métis people and the Crown since the beginning', which has been 'expressed in the form of political autonomy and [...] reflected in the treaty process' (*ibid.*: 25). That is, the idea of Aboriginal nationhood is one with real legal force, and is consistent with the need for nation-to-nation agreements between Canadian Aboriginal groups and the federal government (and for government-to-government agreements between Aboriginal governments and the federal, provincial and territorial governments of Canada) to resolve ongoing disputes. However, Canada has in the past 'failed to honour the nation-nation relationship reflected in the Royal Proclamation[13] and the treaties' and adopted assimilationist policies (*ibid.*: 26), which had the result of 'suppressing [Aboriginal] languages and cultures' (*ibid.*: v).[14] Accordingly, it is now Canada's duty to resolve the 'unfinished business' related to its commitments to the Aboriginal nations.

Indeed, the Canadian government's 'duty of loyalty and protection to the First Peoples of Canada' (*ibid.*: 27) looms large in the report, where this duty is understood to include not only the recognition of Aboriginal rights, as expressed in the *Constitution Act* (1982), s. 35(1), but also the recognition and protection of 'the equality of languages' (*Task Force Report* 2005: 71). Canada has yet to grant 'federal legislative recognition to promote and protect' Aboriginal languages (*ibid.*: v), spoken well before the arrival of the French and the English. What is required, then, is the treatment of these languages on an equal footing with French and English, to 'reverse the perception that First Nation, Inuit and Métis languages have less value than French or English'. This means rectifying the disparity 'between the national funding provided for French and English and that provided for First Nation, Inuit and Métis languages' (p. v), with funding for the latter languages to be brought, 'at a minimum, [to] the same level as that provided for the French and English languages' (*ibid.*: 75), as required to implement Aboriginal language immersion programmes (*ibid.*: 88).

Canada's 'duty of loyalty and protection' impinges on another key concern of Aboriginal nations, also closely tied to Aboriginal language and culture. This is the need for restitution for assimilative state policies and practices, such as those of the residential school system, which bear a large responsibility for ruptures in the transmission of knowledge about Aboriginal language, culture and traditional harvesting practices. As the *Task Force Report* points out, Indian Residential School and Indian Day School policies were 'meant to assimilate Indian children into Canadian society' by having 'them "un-learn" their indigenous language, culture, heritage and beliefs and to re-learn a foreign language, religion and way of life' (2005: 44). Such policies and practices instilled low self-esteem in Aboriginal children, severed their 'connection to their people', thus having an intergenerational impact, and led them to accept an inferior status for the Aboriginal languages (*ibid.*: v). Accordingly, compensation claims serving to redress these past injustices, the report asserts, must include claims for resources to restore the Aboriginal linguistic and cultural knowledge of which residential school students and their communities were deprived.

## Implications of Aboriginal Language Endangerment Discourse

As the discussion above has made clear, language endangerment issues in Canada are embedded in a highly political discourse centred on land and the role that land plays in Aboriginal cultures, including their spiritual values and languages. What also emerges from an examination of this discourse is the large number of outstanding court cases related to land claims and treaty rights in Canada and to compensation sought for abuse in the residential school system and for 100 years of assimilative policy. While the report makes clear that any legal compensation should be separate from funding for language protection and revitalization, the reasons why compensation has been sought in the first place figure prominently in language endangerment discourse. With the decline in trade and the weakening of political alliances, the Aboriginal–state relationship became, throughout the nineteenth and twentieth centuries, one that was dominated by assimilationist state policies and practices. Current efforts to heal the wounds created by this relationship involve efforts to make the government acknowledge the harm done and compensate for it. In this political context, Aboriginal language revitalization is clearly distinct from French, English and heritage language issues in Canada; that is, it is clearly not limited to retaining, revitalizing and promoting culture. Even with regards to the mobilization for the protection of French language, which also arose in response to economic English-language colonization and assimilation, the substance of the language discourse is different. For Aboriginal groups, language revitalization is linked to individual and community healing practices, the reclaiming of ties to land and place and constitutionally entrenched Aboriginal rights.

Although the above discussion of Indigenous language endangerment discourse in Canada has attempted to lay out the key elements, the complexities surrounding this discourse have still left us with at least one very basic question: namely, what kinds of language will be revitalized, and for whom? Given the highly 'territorialized' nature of the discourse, and the fact that language revitalization is largely justified through its connections to land, history and place, it is reasonable to ask where such a discourse leaves 'de-territorialized' Aboriginal individuals and communities, who risk being left out of the language survival/endangerment equation. The individuals and communities in question include, in particular, urban dwellers who have no close connection to those Aboriginal groups with claims to 'land', and who might speak highly urbanized versions of Aboriginal languages or engage in cultural practices that reflect strong urban Aboriginal identities, but at the same time might lead to exclusion from more 'authentic' cultural and linguistic practices, associated more closely with land-based spiritual and community relationships. In other words, would one be seen as less 'Aboriginal' if one engaged in non-traditional, urban cultural and linguistic practices? If language is so connected to spirituality, can one be as 'authentically' spiritual without speaking the traditional language? To a large extent, these questions can find answers only through an investigation of lived local experiences and of the nature of this locality with respect to larger state and global processes, such investigation of a 'living' language making crucial use of fluid notions of language, including less 'standard', newer and culturally inventive ways of speaking. Such investigation would, therefore, be the next step in understanding the nature and broader implications of current Aboriginal language endangerment discourse in Canada.

## Conclusion

The aim of this chapter has been to explore the discourse of language endangerment in Canada, the specific historical, political and economic conditions that have given rise to it, and the ideologies, practices and language issues associated with it. What we have found is that this discourse is part of a political strategy of Aboriginal groups in Canada to redress the wrongs created, in particular, from years of assimilationist federal government policy and practice and the government's failure to honour its treaty and other legal obligations to Aboriginal peoples; and that its basic goal is the resolution of 'unfinished business' related to these failures, which includes the revitalization of endangered Aboriginal languages. Finally, we have found that the discourse designed to promote these goals makes strategic use of certain assertions about the relation between Aboriginal languages and Aboriginal spirituality, culture and land.

What, I believe, we can hope to gain from such an investigation is some insight not only into this specific discourse and language revitalization movement, but also into similar language movements in other locales. However, ... there are many other questions which must be answered before we can achieve a serious understanding of this discourse. Among these are how the legitimacy of particular Indigenous languages is tied to other forms of legitimacy; who is engaged, and how, in the discourses and actions to 'save' these languages and who is not, and what is at stake for each group; and finally, what the consequences of these discourses are for the distribution of material and symbolic resources, including the maintenance of an Indigenous language in a community. Satisfying answers to these questions will depend on a fluid concept of language and a broadening of our conception of what counts as 'authentic' language revitalization in the twenty-first century.

## Notes

1. In Canadian usage, the term *Aboriginal* refers to First Nations, Inuit and Métis people, who are recognized in the Canadian *Constitution Act* (1982), s. 35.

2. Since its establishment, the *Indian Act* has been continually revised through a series of amendments. However, the most comprehensive and significant revisions occurred in 1951, 1961 and 1985. These revisions included the removal of most discriminatory provisions, permitting the free movement off reserves, the right to organize politically, and the right to vote (which was legislated in 1962).

3. One issue in treaty negotiations was the use and occupancy of certain parcels of land and access to the resources that they contained. Although it remains an open question whether this included a ceding of territory, what is clear is that negotiations determined that specific portions of lands would be 'reserved' for the exclusive use of Aboriginal peoples.

4. According to the Ministry of Indian and Northern Affairs, '[t]he term "residential schools" generally refers to a variety of institutions which have existed over time, including: industrial schools, boarding schools, student residences, hostels, billets and residential schools' (www. inac.gc.ca, specifically, *Backgrounder: The Residential School System*, www.ainc-inac.gc.ca/gs/schl_e.html accessed September 2005). The residential school system predates Confederation, having grown out of Canada's experience with various missionary organizations. The Federal Government became significantly involved in developing and administering this school system as early as 1874, mainly to meet its obligation, under the *Indian Act*, to provide an education to Aboriginal people. A second goal was integration and assimilation into the dominant English-speaking, capitalist society.

5. Documentation of legal compensation and reconciliation claims can be found on the Assembly of First Nations website (www.afn.ca).

6. The three groups that constitute Aboriginal peoples in Canada (see n. 1)—namely, the First Nations, Inuit and Métis—have, as a result of their categorization as distinct groups in Canadian political-legal discourse, officially become distinct political entities, represented by the Assembly of First Nations (AFN), Inuit Tapiriit Kanatami (ITK) and the Métis National Council (MNC), respectively. Three other national organizations, the Native Women's Association of Canada (NWAC), Pauktutiit (the Inuit Women's organization) and the Congress of Aboriginal People (CAP), are also prominent in Aboriginal national politics. CAP is mandated to represent Aboriginal people regardless of their status or residency, one of its goals being the inclusion of non-status and urban Aboriginal people in the political process.

7. The five-volume report issued in November 1996 is commonly referred to as RCAP and is regarded as one of the most extensive Aboriginal perspectives on 'Canadian history and the role that aboriginal peoples should play in modern society' (Doerr 2000: 3).

8. The role of French and English was dealt with in the Royal Commission on Bilingualism and Biculturalism (B&B Commission), initiated in 1963 (which led to the *Official Languages Act* of 1969). Book 4 of the Royal Commission, published in 1969 under the title *The Cultural Contribution of other Ethnic Groups*, led to the establishment of official multiculturalism

policy in 1971, which later became entrenched in the *Multiculturalism Act* (1988).

9. Since then, there have been critiques concerning the contradictory nature of Canadian multiculturalism, which can be seen primarily as a homogenizing policy with the effect of transforming cultural diversity into a manageable entity (Mackey 2002).

10. The article, written by Frédérique Doyon and entitled 'S.O.S. langues autochtones—vers une loi 101 des Premières Nations?' ['SOS Aboriginal languages: Towards a Bill 101 for First Nations?'], appeared in the 18 October 2004 edition of *Le Devoir*, a French-language daily.

11. There are numerous international conventions relating to indigenous rights, culture and language. These include the *Universal Declaration of Human Rights* (1948), the *International Covenant on Civil and Political Rights* (1976), the International Labour Organization (ILO) *Convention 169 concerning Indigenous and Tribal Peoples in Independent Countries*, the *Convention of the Rights of the Child* (1989), the *Convention on Biological Diversity* (1992), the *Draft Declaration on the Rights of Indigenous Peoples* (1994), the *Universal Declaration of Cultural Diversity* (2001) and the UNESCO *Convention for the Safeguarding of the Intangible Cultural Heritage* (2003) (See *Task Force Report* 2005: 131).

12. All of these excerpts are taken from the Executive Summary of the Report, pp. i–xiv.

13. The Royal Proclamation of 1763 essentially ensured that lands held by 'several nations or tribes of Indians' were 'protected' as the 'hunting grounds' of these said groups by King George III of England. The Indian groups could sell their land to the British Crown but not to any private person. This established the constitutional basis for future treaty negotiations (Hall 2000: 2047).

14. The importance of treaties for Aboriginal peoples in Canada is a recurrent theme in the report, which figures both in various claims that it makes and even in its language. Most notable here is the use of phrases that echo those uttered at the conclusion of treaty negotiations, where they 'support[ed] the notion that the treaty relationship forged between parties was forever' (Morris 1991: 202; Office of the Treaty Commissioner 1998). We find such language in the assertion that restoring languages and cultures would ensure that Aboriginal nations remain strong for 'as long as the sun shines, the grass grows and the river flows' (Morris 1991: viii).

## References


Cook, E.-D. 1998. 'Aboriginal languages: History', in J. Edwards (ed.), *Language in Canada*. Cambridge: Cambridge University Press.

Crystal, D. 2000. *Language Death*. Cambridge: Cambridge University Press.

Dickason, O. P. 2002. *Canada's First Nations: A History of Founding Peoples from Earliest Times* (3rd edn). Oxford: Oxford University Press.

Doerr, A. 2000. 'Aboriginal Peoples, Royal Commission on', in *The Canadian Encyclopedia: Year 2000 Edition*. Toronto: McClelland & Stewart, pp. 3–4.

Doyon, F. 2004. 'S.O.S. langues autochtones – vers une loi 101 des Premières Nations?', *Le Devoir*, 18 October.

Feldman, A. 2001. 'Transforming peoples and subverting states', *Ethnicities* 1: 147–78.

Fishman, J. (ed.). 2001. *Can Threatened Languages Be Saved? Reversing Language Shift, Revisited: A 21st Century Perspective*. Clevedon, UK: Multilingual Matters.

Freeland, J. and Patrick, D. (eds) 2004. *Language Rights and Language Survival*. Manchester, UK: St. Jerome Publishing.

Grenoble, L. and Whaley, L. (eds). 1998. *Endangered Languages: Language Loss and Community Response*. Cambridge: Cambridge University Press.

Hall, A. J. 2000. 'Royal Proclamation of 1763', in *The Canadian Encyclopedia: Year 2000 Edition*. Toronto: McClelland & Stewart, pp. 2047–48.

Henze, R. M. and Davis, K. A. 1999. 'Authenticity and identity: lessons from Indigenous language education'. *Anthropology and Education Quarterly*, 30: 3–21.

Hinton, L. and Hale, K. (eds). 2001. *The Green Book of Language Revitalization in Practice*. San Diego: Academic Press.

Kincade, D. M. 1991. 'The decline of native languages in Canada', in R. H. Robins and E. M. Uhlenbeck (eds), *Endangered Languages*. Oxford: Berg, pp. 157–76.

Kirkness, V. J. 1998. 'The critical state of Aboriginal languages in Canada'. *Canadian Journal of Native Education*, 22(1): 93–105.

Mackey, E. 2002. *The House of Difference: Cultural Politics and National Identity in Canada*. Toronto: University of Toronto Press.

Maffi, L. (ed.). 2001. *On Biocultural Diversity: Linking Language, Knowledge, and the Environment*. Washington, DC: Smithsonian Institution Press.

May, S. (ed.). 2005. 'Debating Language Rights'. Theme issue of *Journal of Sociolinguistics*, 9(3).

McCarthy, A. and Patrick, D. 2005. 'Urban aboriginality and the changing political landscape in Canada'. Paper presented to the British Association of Canadian Studies, Canterbury, UK, April 2005.

Morris, A. 1991. *The Treaties of Canada with the Indians of Manitoba and the North-West Territories Including the Negotiations on Which They Were Based*. Saskatoon: Fifth House Publishers.

Muehlmann, S. and Duchêne, A. in press. 'Beyond the Nation-States: International agencies as new sites of discourses on bilingualism', in M. Heller (ed.), *Bilingualism: A Social Approach*. London: Palgrave.

Nettle, D. and Romaine, S. 2000. *Vanishing Voices: The Extinction of the World's Languages*. Oxford: Oxford University Press.

Office of the Treaty Commissioner. 1998. *Statement of Treaty Issues: Treaties as a Bridge to the Future*. Saskatoon, Saskatchewan.

Paron, M. 2005. 'Managing Language, maintaining authenticity: Mapping approaches to language conservation initiatives in Canada, from the Canadian Heritage Language Institute to the Language and Cultures Council'. (MA Research Essay, School of Canadian Studies, Carleton University).

Patrick, D. 2005. 'Language rights in Indigenous communities: The case of the Inuit of Arctic Quebec'. *Journal of Sociolinguistics*, 9(3): 369–89.

*R. v. Van der Peet* 1996. Supreme Court of Canada ruling, volume 2, 507. Available at www.lexum.umontreal.ca.

Ray, A. J., Miller, J. and Tough, F. J. 2000. *Bounty and Benevolence: A History of Saskatchewan Treaties*. Montreal: McGill-Queen's University Press.

*Royal Commission on Aboriginal Peoples* 1996. 5 volumes. Ottawa: Minister of Supply and Services.

Skutnabb-Kanga, T., Maffi, L. and Harmon, D. 2003. 'Sharing a World of Difference: The Earth's Linguistic and Cultural and Biological Diversity'. UNESCO. Terralingua, and World Wide Fund for Nature. Available (19 September 2005) at (www.terralingua.org).

Smith, L. T. 1999. *Decolonizing Methodologies: Research and Indigenous Peoples*. London, New York: Zed Books.

Task Force on Aboriginal Languages and Cultures. 2005. *Towards a New Beginning: A Foundational Report for a Strategy to Revitalize First Nation, Inuit and Métis Languages and Cultures*. Report to the Minister of Canadian Heritage, June 2005.

UNESCO 1953. document on *The Use of Vernacular Languages in Education*. Paris: UNESCO.

Vallance, N. 2003. 'A comparison of the use of 'culture' by the Supreme Court of Canada in the recognition of Aboriginal rights and the protection of minority language education rights'. Paper presented to the Symposium on *Diversity and Equality: Understanding and Resolving the Conflicts Between Minorities and the Protection of Fundamental Freedoms in Canada*, University of Victoria, British Columbia.

Wolf, E. 1982. *Europe and the People Without History*. Berkeley: University of California Press.

## Critical Thinking and Application

- Patrick frames the article in the context of past wrongs done to indigenous peoples and the agreed-upon need for restitution to be made in the name of justice. Can restitution be made?
- Research other cases of governments' attempts to restore language rights after a period of assimilationist policies. Which have been successful? What has "success" meant?
- Debate the need for retaining language to retain culture.

## Vocabulary

aboriginal
assimilationist
convention
essentialism; linguistic essentialism; essentialize
First Nation
indigenous
language endangerment
language revitalization
language rights
language shift
restitution

## Suggested Further Reading

Bradley, David, and Maya Bradley, eds. 2002. *Language Endangerment and Language Maintenance*. London and New York: RoutledgeCurzon.

Crystal, David. 2000. *Language Death*. Cambridge: Cambridge University Press.

Cultural Survival. http://www.culturalsurvival.org/

Dalby, A. 2003. *Language in Danger: The Loss of Linguistic Diversity and the Threat to Our Future*. New York: Columbia University Press.

Fishman, Joshua. 1991. *Reversing Language Shift: Theoretical and Empirical Foundations of Assistance to Threatened Languages*. Clevedon: Multilingual Matters.

Hinton, Leanne. 1994. *Flutes of Fire: Essays on California Indian Languages*. Berkeley, CA: Heyday Books.

Hinton, Leanne. 1998. Language Loss and Revitalization in California: Overview. *International Journal of the Sociology of Language* 132: 83–93.

Hinton, Leanne, and Kenneth L. Hale, eds. 2001. *The Green Book of Language Revitalization in Practice*. San Diego: Academic Press.

Nettle, Daniel, and Suzanne Romaine. 2000. *Vanishing Voices: The Extinction of the World's Languages*. Oxford: Oxford University Press.

Terralingua.org. *Index of Linguistic Diversity*. http://www.terralingua.org/linguisticdiversity

Terralingua.org. *Langscape.* http://www.terralingua.org/publications/Langscape/langscape.html

UNESCO: *MOST Clearing House: Linguistic Rights.* http://www.unesco.org/most/ln2int.htm

UNESCO: *Universal Declaration on Cultural Diversity.* http://portal.unesco.org/culture/en/ev.php=URL_ID=35232&URL_DO=DO_TOPIC&URL_SECTION=201.htm

Walsh, Michael. 2005. Will Indigenous Languages Survive? *Annual Review of Anthropology* 34: 293–315.

Wolf, Eric. 1982. *Europe and the People Without History*. Berkeley: University of California Press.

## CHAPTER 27

# *Français, Acadien, Acadjonne*: Competing Discourses on Language Preservation Along the Shores of the Baie Sainte-Marie

*Annette Boudreau and Lise Dubois*

(2007)

*Languages are used to communicate, but beyond that, they often, as has been spelled out effectively by Pierre Bourdieu, have* symbolic power. *That is to say, a language gets you understood by some people but also gets you identified as a particular kind of person. In multilingual communities, such as parts of francophone (French-speaking) Canada, since the late twentieth century there have been struggles not only between French and English but between different varieties of French, each claiming to be superior on some ground. A local variety spoken in part of Nova Scotia* (acadjonne) *claims to be the original eighteenth-century variety of French, while other forms of French (Acadian) have evolved away from the original variety. Ironically, even the "standard" forms of Canadian French, such as those spoken in Quebec, are often regarded as nonstandard by those who take the French spoken in France as the ideal form—something made official by entities such as L'Académie française. In this chapter, we follow some debates about which language is "best" in a complex and self-conscious community, where language minorities battle among themselves.*

### Reading Questions

- What are the languages spoken in Baie Sainte-Marie? What is the status of each variety?
- What is the difference between bilingualism and a French- or English-only policy, whether political or educational? Why would individuals defend one or the other?
- Trace the different kinds of "purity" in the debates described by Boudreau and Dubois. What is the role of English in debates about varieties of French?

## Introduction

Behind every discourse on an **endangered language** there are not only a definition of what that endangered language is, but also various social and cultural issues attached to that definition. This supports the ideas that language and the criteria defining boundaries between languages are ideological constructions, and that discourses on **language endangerment** are fertile ground for understanding the issues at stake. Furthermore, discourses on language endangerment and **preservation** almost invariably recreate the same type of power struggles between speakers that the preservation is supposed to eliminate.

In the following chapter, our main goal is to shed some light on how linguistic debates in general and the question of language survival in particular become ideologized and politicized in conjunction with the symbolic values attributed to languages and linguistic varieties, and to show that the major stakes in these debates carried out on the terrain of language are indeed social. We will attempt to describe the different **language ideologies** that prevail in the region where we conducted our research, i.e. the municipality of Clare in southwestern Nova Scotia (otherwise known as the Baie Sainte-Marie; see below for a brief description). To do so, we will of course have to refer to language ideologies in Canada as a whole and in **Francophone** minority communities in particular. We will

Annette Boudreau and Lise Dubois, *Français, Acadien, Acadjonne*: Competing Discourses on Language Preservation Along the Shores of the Baie Sainte-Marie. In *Discourses of Endangerment: Ideology and Interest in the Defence of Languages*, edited by Alexandre Duchêne and Monica Heller. London and New York: Continuum, 2007, pp. 99–120.

then examine the broad social conditions that have led to the destabilization of a traditional **hegemonic** discourse on language by a discourse of contestation in the Baie Sainte-Marie area, and the consequences that this shift has had so far on the construction of Acadian identity in the region. Our data comes from **ethnographic** observation of community events, analysis of documents regarding community events, institutions and debates and interviews with key producers of discourse on language and identity, notably, in this case, those involved in education, the arts, community organization, community associations, community radio and key sectors of economic activity. We will then focus on how various actors from both sides of the debate appeal to discourses concerning threats to the survival of their language, how they define the variety that they defend as being the legitimate one and how they define themselves as legitimate stakeholders in the power struggle. Special attention will be paid to the strong influence that standard French has on speakers' representations of French, of their variety and of their own linguistic competence.

Since 1996, both authors are part of a research group examining how minority Francophones in Canada,[1] and in particular Franco-Albertans, Franco-Ontarians and Acadians, build discursive spaces in which they can articulate their **'francité'**, why they do it, what is at stake when they do it, what are the consequences for those included in these processes and for those who are excluded from them, and, finally, how social categories based on language are constructed. A three-pronged approach based on ethnographic field work was developed: we collect documentation on the community under study (books, music, media reports, etc.), do ethnographic observation and interview key social actors.

All the participants interviewed spontaneously broached the subject of the public use of the French local **vernacular**, a **marked** variety called *acadjonne* which creates controversy and debate within the community. Some of them defend it, others categorically reject it. The debates concerning this language variety inevitably touch upon language survival and resonate in many sectors of the community. We became interested in language ideologies as a means to understand how language acts as a catalyst for social and political debates. Indeed, language ideologies shed light on power struggles taking place on broader levels, and the ones described in this chapter illustrate that the minority experience and reaction to what appears to be domination by the English-speaking population is ambivalent and certainly not uniform (Blommaert 1999).

## CONTEXT

### Canada and Its Two Official Languages

Canada has two **official languages**, French and English. The number of Canadians who in 2001 stated having French as their first language is a little over 6.7 million (23 per cent of the general population), of which almost 5.8 million (85 per cent of all Canadian Francophones) live in the province of Québec (Census of Canada 2001). The other 950,000 are unequally distributed among the nine remaining provinces, in what is generally called in Canada 'official language minority communities'. Francophones therefore constitute an important majority in Québec while maintaining a minority status elsewhere, except in New Brunswick, the only officially bilingual province, where Francophones make up almost 33 per cent of the population. The Canadian Charter of Rights and Freedoms (adopted with the *Constitution Act* of 1982) guarantees various rights for official linguistic communities, such as the right to be educated in the minority language in schools managed by the minority community.

Minority French-speaking communities outside Québec define their 'francité' (Heller 2002; Heller and Labrie 2003) in the context of categories of similarity and difference, that is, through defining relationships with a range of relevant others: the dominant **Anglophone** society, Québec and its State-territorial model of 'francité', other Canadian Francophone minority communities and the larger world of **'la francophonie'**. These relationships also shape their representations of French and its varieties, and of bi- or multilingualism. As we will see, these relationships are key to understanding how people in the Baie Sainte-Marie position themselves.

The minority status of the French language in Canadian communities outside Québec has generated over the last 50 years, both inside and outside these communities, an intense debate on the efforts needed to 'save' them from language attrition and assimilation **(language transfer)** to English, the dominant language, and, therefore, to guarantee their reproduction and durability. In this debate, the survival of the community is intimately linked to the maintenance of French as the language of use among its members. Questions raised in this debate invariably touch upon issues of legitimacy, exclusion and representations of language: which variety of French spoken in these communities should legitimately be saved; who is legitimately empowered to determine this and who is excluded from the debate; how and by whom are the discourses on legitimacy constructed; what discursive strategies do protagonists develop around the power struggles taking place in these communities as they pertain to the circulation of discourses on endangerment?

#### The Acadian Community of the Baie Sainte-Marie

The Acadian community where we conducted our ethnographic work is made up of a dozen villages strung along the eastern shore of the Baie Sainte-Marie in southwestern Nova Scotia, where Acadia was originally founded by French settlers in 1604. These villages, the first Acadian villages in the Maritimes to be resettled by returning Acadians after the British deported them between 1755 and 1763, have recently been amalgamated into one larger municipality, called Clare, which has a population of approximately 9,000 people, 67 per cent of whom have declared French as their first language (Census of Canada 2001). The French-speaking population of Nova Scotia today makes up about 4 per cent of its total population. The main economic activities of the Baie Sainte-Marie region are the fishing and forestry industries. The narrative of the Deportation (called 'le Grand Dérangement' by Acadians) and of the return of the exiled Acadians to this area is constructed, reproduced and claimed as collective memory through various storytelling, cultural and community events and annual celebrations, e.g. the 'Joseph and Marie Dugas Festival' named after the first couple who resettled from Grand Pré, where they had been deported, to Belliveau Cove in 1768.

In recent years, language issues have generated debate within the community. For instance, in the 1980s, after the Charter of Rights and Freedoms was adopted, the right to manage education was effectively handed over to the minority community, which until then had had to operate in the form of **bilingual education** within the constraints of English-dominated school boards. This triggered a debate between those who lobbied (eventually successfully) for a change to French-only (so-called 'linguistically homogeneous') schools, and those who had felt comfortable with the status quo, or who at least wished to preserve bilingual schools, fearing that all-French schools would jeopardize their children's competency level in English (Ross 2001). Canada's linguistic duality is characterized by dual education systems, a system for Francophones where subjects are taught mostly in French and another for Anglophones where subjects are taught in English except for second language classes. Because of their minority status outside Québec, Francophones have a very high rate of bilingualism throughout the Anglo-dominant provinces, whereas Anglophones are not generally bilingual (Heller 2003: 70–74, 106–12).

In the 1990s, the Baie Sainte-Marie's francophone community radio station, which had been struggling to survive, started to broadcast programmes and to advertise in the local French vernacular, which increased its popularity and its ratings, making it one of the most successful community radio stations in the country (Boudreau and Dubois 2003; Dubois 2003). Up until then, only standard French and English had been heard on the airwaves, either through public radio stations (which are operated by a federal agency) or through various public radio stations. To this day, the public use of this variety is a bone of contention within the community, as well as outside it, as we shall explain in the following pages.

It is generally accepted among descriptive linguists who have studied the Baie Sainte-Marie variety that the French spoken in the region represents the oldest variety of French spoken in North America (Flikeid 1994). Among its salient features are the widespread use of archaic forms, which have survived since the colonization period, as well as English forms which were introduced into this variety because of the community's close contact with the surrounding dominant English community and its isolation from other Acadian communities over long periods of time. Because contact with other Francophone communities has increased since the middle of the twentieth century, speakers of this variety are acutely aware of the differences in their speech when confronted with speakers of other varieties of French, be they Canadian, Québécois, French or from other parts of the francophone world. Paradoxically, these same features which are stigmatized by defenders of the **standard** and by some speakers themselves become symbolic of the quest to construct a new Acadian language, acadjonne. In reaction to the values attributed to the standard, which is seen by some members of the community as the only variety appropriate for teaching and for broadcasting, defenders of acadjonne have developed a discourse of survival around these features.

Proponents on both sides of the debate want the same thing: the survival of the community as a French-speaking community. At the heart of the debate is the issue of which variety of French is best suited to guarantee the community's survival: the standard variety traditionally used by the educated and moneyed elite, or the local variety which has just recently been introduced during the 1990s into the public **linguistic market** through the community radio station. Like all public debates in small communities, this one goes beyond the community radio where it originated, and has since been taken into other areas such as education, economic development and associative organizations.

## Language Ideologies

Before describing the main economic, social and cultural changes which occurred in the Baie Sainte-Marie region and which made a heated language debate possible, we will briefly present the language ideologies which prevail.

Language ideologies are usually defined as a set of beliefs on language or a particular language shared by members of a community (Watts 1999; Milroy 2001). These beliefs come to be so well established that their origin is often forgotten by speakers, and are therefore socially reproduced and end up being 'naturalized', or perceived as natural or as common sense, thereby masking the social construction processes at work. Ideologies become political when they are embedded in the social principles on which a community organizes itself institutionally (Watts 1999).

In this region of Nova Scotia Acadia (as elsewhere for that matter), the ideologies of language that circulate may sometimes compete with each other, while at other times or in certain linguistic markets, one of them may become dominant, but all of them exert pressure on linguistic and non-linguistic issues. In this section, we will present briefly the ideologies that are generally shared by other Canadian francophones; then we will discuss an emerging competing ideology of language which seems to us to be entirely endemic to the Baie Sainte-Marie community.

The ideology of bilingualism posits the social, cultural and economic advantages of being bilingual as an individual and as a country. Canada has developed a positive image of itself as a bilingual, therefore tolerant and progressive country, and its most ardent defenders are various government departments, the media and the Francophone communities themselves. For example, the official site of Nova Scotia's Tourism Department bids tourists to visit the Baie Sainte-Marie region (which is part of the 'Evangeline Trail' tourist area) this way:

> The Municipality of Clare, often referred to as the Acadian Shore, hugs Baie Ste-Marie (...). Route 1 passes through twelve picturesque French-speaking villages (...). The bilingual inhabitants along this shore are descendants of the first European settlers, who came from France in the early 1600's (http://novascotia.com/en/ home/planatrip/travel_guides/downloads.aspx.)

Another website attracts the attention of would-be tourists by pointing out the particularities of the local vernacular: 'The spoken language still rings of 17th century French with a new world twist including Mi'kmaq Indian and English words' (www.evangelinetrail.com/churchpoint.html). But in reality, bilingualism as it is practiced in Nova Scotia is more ideological than it is real; at the very least, it is an **asymmetrical bilingualism**. Indeed, the only truly bilingual populations are the Acadian ones, who speak English fluently with very little linguistic markers. A visitor to the province of Nova Scotia attracted by the promotional material on Nova Scotia Acadia would be hard-pressed to 'see' and 'hear' bilingualism, as well as to get service in French anywhere other than in the Acadian communities. In fact, in ordinary daily activities, one is led to believe that the ideology of **monolingualism** is at work here, since the Anglophone majority expects that Acadian French-speakers use English in all public activities, an expectation which does not allow Francophones to exercise their right to use French if they wish to do so.

Another ideology which acts upon language behaviour is the ideology of the standard, which is linked to the perception of language as an essentialized object, that is as a rigid and unchanging system. Despite the fact that it is difficult to define what the standard language is, the idea of its existence is well established in the minds of French speakers and influences how they judge languages, speakers and their own performances.

Lodge (1997) reminds us that French is one of the most **standardized** languages in the world, and that its speakers have developed strong representations of a unified language with little room for diversity and variation. Furthermore, various studies on French speakers in peripheral regions (peripheral here meaning not in France) have also shown that the idea of a standard is part of the linguistic imagination of Francophones all over the world (see Francard 1993; Francard *et al.* 2001). Because standard French is regarded as prestigious, those who speak vernacular varieties most often accept the symbolic dominance of 'legitimate speakers' since they too aspire to acquire 'an imagined standard language' in order to have access to the economic and social capital associated with standard languages and to a wider range of linguistic markets (Bourdieu 1982).

The ideology of the standard exerts pressure on linguistic practices and on the construction of identity. First, Francophones from minority communities in Canada who have lived in an anglophone dominant environment inevitably show in their linguistic practices the traces of this close linguistic contact through English **borrowings** and **calques**. In addition, they have often maintained archaic or older French **lexical** and **syntactic** forms.

They are acutely aware of the distance between their variety and the standard. **Linguistic insecurity** is commonplace in Acadia (Boudreau and Dubois 1991, 2001), and we have found in other studies that some Acadians go as far as to invent various personas to escape negative reactions from other Francophones. For example, in a call centre in Moncton (New Brunswick), where we conducted research on how linguistic skills were used in the new economy, we interviewed a Francophone voice operator who, when dealing with Francophone callers from outside the Maritime Provinces, claimed she was an Anglophone learning French to avoid being criticized by those who preferred dealing with someone speaking a more standard French rather than someone speaking with an obvious southeast New Brunswick accent.

The last ideology presented here, and the one that we posit is unique to the Baie Sainte-Marie within the Canadian context, is the ideology of the **dialect**. Indeed, we discovered in this community ardent defenders of the dialect who aspire to make it the legitimate language of the community and who have managed to open up the linguistic markets to the local variety by taking control of the community radio. The justifications for their stance regarding this variety are partly historical in nature, claiming that the vernacular was the language spoken by their ancestors when they reclaimed residency in the province at the end of the eighteenth century. According to Watts (1999), when this ideology is acted upon, dialects are then used in the education system (at least in their spoken form) and in certain media, such as radio and television, which is the case in the Baie Sainte-Marie. Language ideologies are therefore linked to the myths that circulate within a community about language (Watts 1999: 72–4). Myths are transmitted and disseminated through shared stories that contribute to the (re)construction of a given cultural group (i.e. the storytelling about the return of the deported mentioned above), and are usually endowed with an explanatory force that can historically frame various group behaviours, including language behaviour and practices. We will see further how the myth of the origins of the Baie Sainte-Marie community is construed today by some of its members as an answer to the various discourses on languages that circulate in the region, and especially how it is being used in the discourses on the survival of French in southwestern Nova Scotia.

## Changing Social Conditions in the Baie Sainte-Marie

There have been many changes over the past 30 years in the Baie Sainte-Marie that can explain the current linguistic debate. The conflict over the increased use of French in the region's schools which emerged in the early 1980s lasted for almost 20 years, divided the community and set the scene for what was to come. The school conflict had indeed polarized the community into two major camps: those in favour of linguistically homogeneous schools where all subjects are taught in standard French and those in favour of maintaining bilingual schools, where only some of the subjects were taught in French in mixed classes (see above). The move towards homogeneous schools was based on the widespread belief that the vitality and the preservation of Francophone minority communities depends largely on the community's access to French-only institutions, schools being the most important. This belief is largely circulated by the communities' traditional educated elites, whereas other groups within the community support bilingual education as a means to upward social mobility. The lines between groups were therefore drawn before the current conflict around the radio station emerged in the late 1990s, in an entirely new context in terms of the community's position within the Canadian 'Francophonie' and within a more globalized economic environment.

In 1994, Acadians organized the first 'Congrès mondial acadien' (CMA – World Acadian Congress), a large popular gathering which unfolded over a period of several weeks, included many types of activities such as large family reunions, concerts, conferences, etc. and has been held every five years since. The 1994 CMA, held in Moncton (New Brunswick, about a six-hour drive from the Baie Sainte-Marie) has come to be regarded as a watershed moment in Acadia's history and in Acadians' awareness of their specificity in the Maritime Provinces and in Canada in general. The CMA's objective was to gather the Acadians from the **diaspora** (which refers to those of Acadian descent who live outside of the Maritime Provinces) and from all of Acadia in one place: approximately 500,000 people attended and the event generated much enthusiasm. Most importantly, the CMA resulted in the creation of all types of transprovincial and transnational networks – cultural, academic, political and economic – which have not only persisted but have flourished. The second Congress was held in 1999 in Louisiana, and the third, in 2004, in the Baie Sainte-Marie itself. Thus, at the time of our fieldwork, many members of the community were increasingly understanding themselves in the context of discourses, institutions and networks connected to this particular discursive space. The discourses, institutions and networks in question are largely constituted around ideas of language, identity and culture.

If Acadian culture has enabled Acadians to take part in successful cultural exchanges among Canadian Francophones, and between Francophone Canada and connected areas in the United States (notably Louisiana and parts of New England), it has also enabled them to participate in international exchanges, especially within the 'francophonie internationale'. Acadian artists perform regularly in Europe, and a variety of institutions and networks have developed to facilitate this. For example, since 1996, Moncton has been hosting a regional 'Franco-fête', an annual event in various parts of French Canada, spread over several days, whose purpose is to showcase Francophone artists in the fostering of a market for Francophone artistic and cultural products. Several artists and musicians from the Baie Sainte-Marie are now known throughout Acadia, North America and parts of Europe.

Globalization has also enabled traditional businesses from the region to branch out into international markets: one family fish processing business has become in recent years a multinational business exporting its products all over the world, while another small shipyard has specialized in the building of luxury yachts, which again are sold internationally.

Globalization has enabled Francophones from peripheral areas such as the Baie Sainte-Marie to establish links and networks with other communities and interests. These outlying communities have thus been able to redefine their identity and their place in the world without going through traditional channels, such as the State or other agencies dominated by their Anglo-Canadian compatriots. Increased contacts through networking and through increased mobility have deeply modified not only their relationship with the State and with the Anglo-dominant society but also their perception of themselves and of their language.

## Discourses on the Survival of French in the Baie Sainte-Marie[2]

In the following section, we will attempt to answer the questions raised in the introduction, that is who constructs the discourses on legitimacy, what discursive strategies do protagonists develop around the power struggles taking place, who benefits from the debate and why, and what the repercussions are for Acadians and for other French speakers around them. While our corpus includes a wide variety of forms of data on the debates surrounding linguistic variation and identity in the Baie Sainte-Marie, we will focus here on interviews with key actors in a specific debate surrounding the community radio, which concerns the public use of the local dialect on the airwaves. When we arrived in the region for our fieldwork, we were unaware of the deep divisions within this community caused by the radio station. The use of English words in predominantly French utterances is what offends the majority of participants in the study who oppose the public use of acadjonne, while the use of older archaic forms is more easily accepted. We have heard radio ads using the words 'shirt' for *chemise*, 'pants' for *pantalon*, 'chicken' for *poulet*, etc., which is a source of concern for many participants.

The participants we quote here are those who expressed very strong stances on language as a way of gaining access to important social and economic resources, although they have very different views on how to get there; as such, they represent the extreme positions in the debate. At the outset of our research in the region, we were surprised and intrigued by the strong feelings expressed over the use of a local dialect, which seemed to us to be no more than another variety of language. We were soon to find out that language was at the heart of larger debates connected, on the one hand, to the creation of social categories (who is a real and 'pure' Acadian), and on the other hand, to the redefinition of social structures at the heart of economic developments in the region (what French gets to be legitimized when it comes to attracting tourists in the region, how is acadjonne supposed to be seen as the *real* and authentic language).

The defenders and promoters of acadjonne come from different backgrounds; some are intellectuals like Marcel, who studied abroad and uses his knowledge to reinvent a language aimed at legitimizing what he sees as the 'real Acadian French', while others, who are slightly more educated than the average and who have spent a large part of their lives elsewhere, defend it as they feel that acadjonne is the language through which they construct their sense of belonging in a tight-knit community. The defenders of the standard, such as Paul and Louise, who are members of the intellectual elite, truly believe that the only way for Acadians to have access to social status, good jobs and to be able to be a part of a bigger 'francophonie' is to speak a standard language, even one with some regional features. They feel that not knowing the standard will contribute to further building borders with francophones from elsewhere. Paul was educated by clerics who used standard French as criteria for deciding who belonged to the elite, thus creating social categories based on language, which Paul himself reproduces. Louise is a Quebecker who settled in the area over ten years ago and who believes that people who speak acadjonne are at risk of being trapped in a linguistic ghetto.

As mentioned above, the regional variety of French spoken in the Baie Sainte-Marie was for a long time and is to a large extent today a stigmatized variety. Louise relates that very few people in the Baie Sainte-Marie area were educated enough to teach in the local college. Therefore, a large number of teachers were imported from elsewhere, mostly clerics from Québec, who adopted a superior attitude. Louise, who mostly endorses the pro-standard stance, explains:

EXTRACT 1

| | |
|---|---|
| Louise | ils sont allés chercher énomément de profs au Québec qui disaient 'il faut montrer à ces gens-là à parler français' ou encore 'il faut parler un français standard' (...) les Québécois qui sont venus se sont posés comme des maîtres de la discipline et des policiers de la langue (...) ils (les Acadiens) n'avaient pas le droit d'utiliser les expressions acadiennes |
| *Louise* | *they brought in a lot of teachers from Québec who said 'we have to teach these people how to talk' or 'we have to speak Standard French' (...) the people from Québec who came claimed to be masters of the discipline and the language police (...) Acadians did not have the right to use Acadian expressions when speaking* |

When the community radio station was launched, the language used on the air was standard French. After a short period, it almost went bankrupt. Marcel, a very active voice in the promotion of acadjonne explains that:

EXTRACT 2

| | |
|---|---|
| Marcel | toute l'élite du coin était là-dedans et puis ils ont décidé d'être normatifs et pis à la place de parler *akadjonne* / ils avont décidé de parler le bon français et puis la population l'a boudée |
| *Marcel* | all of the area's elite was involved in the station and they decided to use the standard instead of acadjonne / they decided to speak good French and the population turned away |

What is interesting in this statement is the fact that Marcel, who moves fluently from one **register** to the next throughout the entire interview, makes ostentatious use of certain salient features of acadjonne, such as 'ils avont décidé' when speaking of the former management of the station. Marcel explained that acadjonne was always criticized in schools and Acadians developed a negative attitude towards their own language. When acadjonne became the dominant language on the community airwaves, the ratings rose and the station became the most listened-to station in the region.

As pointed out above, Francophones in the province of Nova Scotia are a small minority, but in this sub-region (Clare), they are the majority. Fortified by their unique historic legitimacy as the direct descendants of the first Europeans to settle in North America, a certain number of Acadians from this region have reclaimed these facts and made them the basis of their distinct identity. To legitimize their way of speaking, they promote the most archaic features of their variety.[3] Marcel explains: 'notre mission c'est de conserver la langue de l'ancienne capitale et de continuer le rêve et la mission de nos ancêtres.' ['*our mission is to conserve the language of the old capital and to continue our ancestors' dream and mission*'.]

According to Marcel, not only does the language need to be conserved, but the ancestors' dream also needs to be pursued. Watts has explained that ideologies are born from the right historical circumstances (Watts 1999). The idea of deliberately bringing back to life this 'old language', as Marcel calls it, by increasing the awareness of what makes it distinct, progressively took hold after the CMA in 1994 and the 'Sommet de la francophonie', held in Moncton in 1999, two events which provided Acadians from all three Maritime provinces with a new legitimacy. Furthermore, the idea of constructing acadjonne as a distinct language is meant to lift it from anonymity, to give it a new beginning, but at the same time this idea gives much importance to the historical origins of the community, which are particularly valued by Acadians of the diaspora.

Conserving the archaic forms is one aspect of the intentional construction of acadjonne; another aspect is the acceptance and sometimes deliberate use of English words in French utterances, which, as we mentioned, is what offends the majority of participants in the study who oppose the public use of acadjonne, while the use of older archaic forms is more easily accepted. The arguments used to re-invent a distinct and unique language are based on the idea of a need to distinguish the community from other Francophone communities; to distinguish its speech from other varieties; and, most of all, to distinguish it from standard French. As Marcel puts it, acadjonne is: 'un outil du tonnerre / un outil ultra-moderne qui s'appelerait l'acadjonne et qui se distancierait du français standard' ['*a terrific tool / an ultramodern tool which would be called acadjonne and which would distance itself from standard French*'.]

Very active in this fight, Marcel states that Nova Scotia Acadians will never become French from France, Québécois from Québec nor Acadians from New Brunswick; they might just as well stress their differences by asserting their specificity, therefore their origins. This ideology has given rise to debates, and continues to do so, within the community, especially since ads on the community radio are written in acadjonne (mostly by Marcel). Up until then, because acadjonne was confined to private spaces, there had not been much strife. From the moment that acadjonne was used outside of the family and informal markets, it was condemned by the defenders of the standard. These debates have since been taken into the schools, where once again there are stormy controversies taking place. Parents opposed to 'homogeneous' schools (see above), are now opposing teachers who attempt to eliminate **mixed codes** from their students' speech, acting out the ideology of the dialect. One of the participants in the study tells the story of his wife, who is a teacher in these schools and whose attempts at correcting her pupils' speech are often met with **resistance:** students say, 'c'est acadjonne Madame' [*it's acadjonne ma'am*]. Moreover, one of the disc jockeys working at the community radio station who was interviewed claims that more listeners phone in to complain that they do not understand some everyday standard French words than there are listeners who phone in to complain about the use of mixed codes. He alleges that not comprehending standard French is not the problem because in public meetings, these same speakers will speak up to express their opinions to those who have said what they had to say in standard French.

EXTRACT 3

Leo ils vont dire 'moi je comprends pas le français (standard)' / c'est pas vrai / ils vont aller dans une réunion pis quelqu'un va s'exprimer dans un français standard et si il dit quelque chose qu'ils n'aiment pas / ils ont compris (...) ils vont à l'église le dimanche et puis si le prêtre dit quelque chose que ils sont pas d'accord euh je t'assure qu'ils vont pas dire qu'ils ont pas compris le français

*Leo they will say 'me, I don't understand (standard) French' / it's not true / they'll go to a meeting and if someone says something in standard French and if it's something they don't like / they understood (...) they go to church on Sunday and if the priest says something they do not agree with euh I can assure you that they will not say that they have not understood*

The problem is therefore not one of comprehension, but one of resistance. We see here that the comprehension argument is a discursive strategy used to (re)position oneself within the 'francophonie' and to (re)define what is meant by being Acadian. This is comparable to the situation of German Swiss illustrated by Watts, who tells of a mother who says to her child who wishes to buy a book written in German: 'No, don't be silly dear. That's written in Standard German. You won't be able to understand' (Watts 1999: 85). Contrary to the situation in Switzerland, l'acadjonne is rarely written, though it is currently used in songs and has been portrayed in a film (*Les gossipeuses*, 1978), to denounce the parochial mentality of some of the characters in the film. But, in both cases, the comprehension argument is put forward as a discursive strategy to resist the hegemonic influences of those who support the use of the standard.

These discourses on language are linked to strategies to save the language. Some proponents of the dialect think that if the people in the Baie Sainte-Marie were to become confident in their language, they would be better positioned to resist Anglicization and assimilation. However, the public defence of acadjonne has erected yet other language barriers between speakers. Some participants have claimed that speakers who use standard forms are now **stigmatized** and rejected. Even Marcel, a militant of acadjonne, who attended university outside his community and is capable of using various linguistic registers, says that the typical Acadian:

EXTRACT 4

Marcel adore entendre un Québécois parler québécois, un Français de France parler son français, le Néo-Brunswickois parler avec son accent, le Chéticamptain le Louisianais, il adore ça // mais si il y a quelque chose qui fait tenir les cheveux à pique sur la tête c'est quand ce qu'il y a un des leurs qui s'en va en dehors pis qui s'en revient et puis tout d'un coup qu'il peut plus parler dans l'Anse ou Meteghan [two villages along the Baie Sainte-Marie] ou une affaire de même / la langue acadjonne pour un Acadjen de la Baie c'est de quoi de sacré

*Marcel loves to hear a Quebecker speak québécois, a Frenchman speak his French, a New Brunswicker speak with his accent, a person from Chéticamp or from Louisiana, he loves that // but if there is something that makes his hair stand on its ends it's when one of theirs goes outside then comes back and all of a sudden can no longer speak in the Cove or in Meteghan or something like that / the acadjonne language for an Acadian from the Baie is sacred*

In this case, maintaining regional structures that were stigmatized in the past instead of using standard forms displays loyalty to the community. Marcel himself reports that he has been excluded, but endorses nonetheless the restrictions of this stance and has even become one of its most ardent defenders:

EXTRACT 5

Marcel beaucoup de fois je me ferais radorsé[4] / t'as dit la poubelle / c'est la garbage can // j'ons tout le temps dit la garbage can (...) es-tu en train de te comporter comme un traître

*Marcel I have been told to straighten up many times // you said poubelle / it's a garbage can / we have always said garbage can (...) are you being a traitor*

The opponents of the ideology of the dialect say they are worried by the social and cultural restrictions put on the members of the community by the widespread use of acadjonne. They feel that using a variety that is too far from standard French may lead to the creation of a linguistic ghetto. Paul, a proponent of the standard, believes that the Baie Sainte-Marie lost its bid to host the *Jeux de l'Acadie*, an annual sporting event in which all Acadian schools of the three Maritimes Provinces have participated since 1978, because of the language issue (which of course we can't confirm).

EXTRACT 6

Paul l'acadjonne c'est une langue de communication **pour ici** / ça disparaîtra jamais dans les foyers / mais pour les jeunes qui veulent se lancer sur le marché du travail // de faiT nous étions la région française de la Nouvelle-Écosse // pendant des siècles // pis aujourd'hui c'est Halifax qui est la région française de la Nouvelle-Écosse avec le Carrefour du Grand Havre // c'est Halifax qui est la région / on ne l'est plus on ne l'est plus ici (...) parce que: il y a trop d'anglais // il y a /// ben on dit: // les finales des Jeux de l'Acadie ont eu lieu à presque toutes les régions / de l'Acadie // deux ou trois ans passés // Clare ici la municipalité / a fait un gros effort pour avoir la finale ici // ils ont dépensé même dix mille dollars là juste pour préparer un document / pour aller le présenter pour attirer les Jeux de l'Acadie ici / Edmundston les avait déjà eu: // ils sont allés là et la décision c'est que les Jeux iraient à Edmundston /// pis ils se demandaient pourquoi /// à quelques-uns uns j'ai dit: 'regardez les deux personnes qui sont allées là pis écoutez-les s'exprimer' / pis les Jeux de l'Acadie c'est pour promouvoir la langue chez les jeunes / et / simplement en les écoutant parler ils ont dit 'on peut pas aller là' /// ils l'ont pas dit (rire) le comité au Nouveau-Brunswick l'a pas dit // mais c'est facile à voir on avait toutes les facilités ici avec l'université pis l'école / tout ce qu'il fallait / et puis la municipalité avait dépensé de l'argent les Jeux étaient jamais venus ici // mais les Jeux sont pas venus ici // alors c'est ce que je vous dis que: // on ne s'attire pas en voulant promouvoir euh / l'acadjonne comme on l'appelle

*Paul acadjonne is a language of communication for here / it will never disappear from the homes / but for the young people who want to go into the job market // in fact we were the first French region of Nova Scotia // for centuries // but today it is Halifax that is the first French region of Nova Scotia with the Carrefour du Grand Havre (name of the French school in Halifax) // it is Halifax that is the region / we are no longer it here (...) because there is too much English // there is /// well it is said // the Jeux de l'Acadie finals have taken place in almost all the regions of Acadia // two or three years ago // the municipality of Clare made a huge effort to have the finals here // they even spent ten thousand dollars just to prepare a document / to go present to bid for the Jeux de l'Acadie here / Edmundston had already gotten them // they went there and the decision was to give them to Edmundston /// and then they wanted to know why /// I told a couple of them 'look at the two people who went there and listen to them speak' / well les Jeux de l'Acadie exist to promote the language with the young people / and / simply to listen to them talk they said to themselves we can't go there /// they didn't say (laugh) the New Brunswick committee didn't say // but it is easy to see that we had all the facilities here with the university and the school / all that was needed / and the municipality had spent all that money because the Games had never come here // but the Games did not come here // that's why I tell you this // we do not attract by wanting to promote acadjonne, like we call it here*

Extract 6 summarizes the position of those who oppose the use and promotion of acadjonne. They fear that speakers of this variety will be barred access to activities taking place in the 'Francophonie' and to the job market. In opposition to the regional variety, Paul speaks of his conception of what is Acadian French:

EXTRACT 7

Lise qu'est-ce qui vous choque dans le dans les la publicité / de la radio communautaire

Paul c'est pas français / c'est que c'est / on prend des mots anglais ou même on // on invente des mots // tu sais

Lise avez-vous des exemples

Paul je devrais en avoir à conter tu sais là pis je peux pas y penser

Lise vous avez dit quelque chose d'intéressant vous avez dit qu'ils pensent que c'est de l'acadien mais ça ne l'est pas vraiment / qu'est-ce que c'est pour vous l'acadien

Paul **l'acadien: / c'est le français classique // du dix-septième siècle** // alors si dire: / si pour du pain je vas dire du 'ponne' (pain) ou à matin je vas dire 'à matonne' (matin) / nous sommes les seuls Acadiens au monde maintenant Nouveau-Brunswick vous êtes pas des Acadiens ni l'Île-du-Prince-Édouard ni Chéticamp // tu sais parce qu'on est on est les seuls qui parlent comme ça alors si on dit si on dit que ça c'est de l'acadien /// ça veut dire qu'on /// on est on est les seuls Acadiens au monde

Lise *what is it that offends you about the advertisement on the community radio*

Paul *it's not French / it's that it's / English words are used or even new words are invented you know*

Lise *do you have any examples*

Paul *I should have some to tell but now I can't think of any*

Lise *you said something interesting you said that they thought that it was Acadian but it isn't really / what is Acadian for you*

Paul *Acadian / it's classic French // from the 17th century // so to say / if for bread I say ponne or for morning I say à matonne / we are the only Acadians in the world today now NewBrunswick you are not Acadian neither is Prince-Edward Island nor Cheticamp // you know because we are the only ones who speak that way therefore if we say that that is Acadian /// then that means that /// we are the only Acadians in the world*

To establish a link between Acadian French and French spoken in France during North America's colonization indicates a fixed and rigid conception of language and a certain nostalgia for the origins of the French language considered to be 'pure, clear and elegant' (Joseph 1987: 158; Walter 1988: 100–14). Language here is seen as detached from real language practices, which explains Paul's difficulty in accepting the particular status given to a regional variety by the community radio station.

This debate on language shows that, in the context under study, the simple choice of using one word over another is filled with significance which cannot be grasped by linguistic analysis alone. The choice to say *ponne* instead of *pain* (bread) is not only an act of identity: it is also taking a stance in relation to a social and political project constructed around the **reappropriation** of a language, which is seen as the core of the construction of community identity. In this case, the choice to use acadjonne is politically charged and a source of conflict among members of the community.

What is interesting to note here is the fact that positive values attributed to the 'language of the ancestors' are common to both camps and are at the heart of the arguments used for justifying completely different views on language. For the defenders of acadjonne (participants who feel excluded from social structures revolving around the standard), the Acadian language goes back to the beginnings of the colony, and its speakers are the 'purest' of representatives of that state of language which should be conserved even if it means adding English words in order to adapt the language to modern times. For those who oppose acadjonne (the intellectual elite, who exert symbolic power through their use of the legitimate language and who are most aware of the cultural capital gained through the standard, and artists who are now travelling to other parts of the Francophonie and want to diversify their linguistic resources), the Acadian language is also connected to eighteenth-century French as it is imagined, and it cannot be modified without losing its characteristic 'purity'.

Needless to say that the positions presented here are not clear-cut and any single individual's position on the matter is often quite ambivalent; in other words, the different discourses concerning the preservation of language sometimes overlap. In fact, on the question of the 'purity' of the language inherited from the ancestors, the two discourses converge, though they diverge considerably on the intended outcome: on the one hand, the aim is to promote the use of a regional language; on the other hand, it is to reassert the value of the standard. This convergence/divergence illustrates the power struggle between two groups who wish to gain social advantages on the terrain of language. Therefore, the value attributed to archaisms differs. The proponents of acadjonne seek to assert their identity and their distinctiveness through the concrete use of archaisms derived from a language imagined as being authentic, whereas those who defend the standard pay lip service to the value of maintaining archaisms, distancing themselves from the actual use of these 'old words' and conforming their practices to a fictional standard.

The most obvious aspects of this struggle centre around the language issue, but the real stakes reside in the unequal access to material and symbolic resources in the community. In other words, which group will obtain the funding to operate the community radio and thus to define the community image that is broadcast? Which variety of French will be valued in the various linguistic markets and in individual and collective identity building processes? The most legitimate discourse in the eyes of both groups is the one linked to the historical dimension that is often referred to by politicians and intellectuals alike who value the authenticity of the Baie Sainte-Marie community for various reasons: for example, as a way to promote tourism, as a way to obtain special cultural funding (i.e. the 400th anniversary of the establishment of Acadia), or as a way to participate in the debate surrounding the first French presence on North American soil.

## CONCLUSION

The debate surrounding the 'coming out' of a particular variety of language, a variety which is doomed to be seen by outsiders as impure and contrary to the traditional 'bon usage', is as much about social issues as it is about language. The discourse on the preservation of French via acadjonne can be labelled as a discourse of resistance against the **hegemony** of standard French whose defenders once monopolized resources in media and educational realms. It challenges long-standing power structures which had been accessed until now only through standard French. However, well-intentioned promoters of the standard language are (aiming as they do at greater access to jobs, social mobility, prestige), many speakers of Acadian French feel left out because of their way of speaking, characterized by **hybridity** and archaic features. In both cases, language and values attributed to language varieties serve as the bases for social stratification and processes of identity.

In this chapter, we have attempted to show that different groups of social actors from an 'imagined community' have multiple stakes and interests in preserving what they perceive as 'their' variety of French and how they develop different discourses in order to save the language from attrition. In other words, as we stated in the introduction, discourses on language endangerment recreate the power struggles between members of the community that exist already. Discourses aimed at defending a language vary in this case precisely because of the different representations that speakers have of what a language should be ideally, and also because these same speakers develop different language ideologies that shape their political and social actions aimed at preserving the kind of language they want to preserve, imagined as a 'pure' language or as a 'hybrid' one regardless of whether it is rooted in the seventeenth century or not. This case study illustrates that language issues are central to the shaping of a society, especially in minority settings.

TRANSCRIPTION GUIDELINES

1. The apostrophe is used to mark an elision, as it is usually used in French.
2. Capital letters at the end of certain words indicates pronunciation.
3. The slash is used to indicate pauses: one slash indicates a brief pause, two slashes a longer one, three slashes indicate a 4-second pause. The slash also indicates hesitation, such as *la mai/la maison*.
4. Brackets have three functions: (xxx) indicate incomprehensible parts; (laughter) or (ringing), etc. give additional information which cannot be transcribed; (...) truncated parts of the interview.

## Notes

1. The research projects were *Prise de parole 1* (1996–1999) which was funded by the Social Sciences and Humanities Research Council of Canada (SSHRC) (main researcher: Normand Labrie; co-researchers: Jürgen Erfurt and Monica Heller) and *Prise de parole 2: la francophonie canadienne et la nouvelle économie mondialisée* (2000–2003), which also received funding from SSHRC (main researcher: Monica Heller; co-researchers: Annette Boudreau, Lise Dubois, Normand Labrie, Patricia Lamarre and Deirdre Meintel).
2. The translation of each interview extract presented in this section follows each extract.
3. We are not saying that these features were not used before. The fact that they recognize these features as archaic makes their use emblematic.
4. Note: the word 'radorser' is an old French word for 'to straighten up'. The 'j'ons' form in the extract, the first person singular conjugated as the first person plural, is a typical Baie Sainte-Marie structure used as a first person plural 'we'.

## References


Blommaert, J. 1999. 'The debate is open', in J. Blommaert (ed.), *Language Ideological Debates*. Berlin: Mouton de Gruyter, pp. 1–38.

Boudreau, A. and Dubois, L. 1991. 'L'insécurité linguistique comme entrave à l'apprentissage du français'. *Bulletin de l'Association canadienne de linguistique appliquée*, 13(2): 37–50.

Boudreau, A. and Dubois, L. 2001. 'Langues minoritaires et espaces publics: le cas de l'Acadie'. *Estudios de Sociolingüistica*, 2(1): 37–60.

Boudreau, A. and Dubois, L. 2003. 'Le cas de trois radios communautaires en Acadie', in M. Heller and N. Labrie (eds.), *Discours et identités. La francité canadienne entre modernité et mondialisation*. Cortil-Wodon: Éditions Modulaires Européennes [coll. Proximités], pp. 269–97.

Bourdieu, P. 1982. *Ce que parler veut dire. L'économie des échanges linguistiques*. Paris: Fayard.

Canada. *2001 Census of Canada*. (www12.statcan.ca/english/census01/home/ index.cfm).

Dubois, L. 2003. 'Radios communautaires acadiennes: idéologies linguistiques et pratiques langagières', in A. Magord (ed.), *L'Acadie plurielle. Dynamiques identitaires collectives et développement au sein des réalités acadiennes*. Moncton: Centre d'études acadiennes, Université de Moncton; Poitiers: Institut d'études acadiennes et québécoises, Université de Poitiers, pp. 307–23.

Flikeid, K. 1994. 'Origines et évolution du français acadien à la lumière de la diversité contemporaine', in R. Mougeon and E. Béniak (eds.), *Les origines du français québécois*. Sainte-Foy: Les Presses de l'Université Laval, pp. 275–326.

Francard, M. 1993. 'L'insécurité linguistique dans les communautés francophones périphériques'. Actes du Colloque Louvain-la-Neuve, 10–12 November 1993. *Cahiers de l'Institut de linguistique de Louvain-la-Neuve*, 19(3–4).

Francard, M., Geron, G. and Wilmet R. 2001. 'Le français de référence. Construction et appropriation d'un concept'. Actes du Colloque Louvain-la-Neuve, 3–5 November 1999. *Cahiers de l'Institut de linguistique de Louvain-la-Neuve*, 27(1–2).

Heller, M. 2002. *Éléments d'une sociolinguistique critique*. Paris: Didier.

Heller, M. 2003. *Crosswords. Language, Education and Ethnicity in French Ontario*. Berlin: Mouton de Gruyter (1st edition: 1994).

Heller, M. and Labrie, N. 2003. 'Langue, pouvoir et identité: une étude de cas, une approche théorique, une méthodologie', in M. Heller and N. Labrie (eds.), *Discours et identités. La francité canadienne entre modernité et mondialisation*. Cortil-Wodon: Éditions Modulaires Européennes [coll. Proximités], pp. 9–39.

Joseph, J. E. 1987. *Eloquence and Power. The Rise of Language Standards and Standard Languages*. New York: Basil Blackwell.

Lodge, A. 1997. *Le français. Histoire d'un dialecte devenu langue*. Paris: Fayard.

Milroy, L. 2001. 'The social categories of race and class', in N. Coupland, S. Sarangi and C. Candlin (eds.), *Sociolinguistics and Social Theory*. London: Longman, pp. 235–60.

Ross, S. 2001. *Les écoles acadiennes en Nouvelle-Écosse, 1758–2000*. Moncton: Centre d'études acadiennes, Université de Moncton.

Walter, H. 1988. *Le français dans tous les sens*. Paris: Éditions Robert Laffont.

Watts, R. 1999. 'The Ideology of Dialect in Switzerland', in J. Blommaert (ed.), *Language Ideological Debates*. Berlin: Mouton de Gruyter, pp. 67–103.

## Critical Thinking and Application

- Boudreau and Dubois point out a debate about whether people in Baie Sainte-Marie support standard (Canadian) French or the local variety of Acadian French. What is the basis of the arguments on each side?
- Why do some people claim not to understand standard French, while others claim that the first group in fact does understand it? What is at stake? Why would people claim not to understand a language that they do understand? Can you imagine other cases where this might occur?
- Some people argue that the study of language should be "descriptive," that is, stating the facts about how things are. In debates about which linguistic variety should be promoted and which left to its own devices, scholars often present sympathies for one or another variety. Try to establish a principle for when it is best simply to describe and when it is appropriate to "prescribe."

## Vocabulary

anglophone
asymmetrical bilingualism
bilingual education
borrowing
calque
dialect
diaspora
endangered language
ethnographic, ethnography
francité
francophone
hegemonic, hegemony
hybridity
la francophonie
language endangerment
language ideology
language preservation
language transfer
lexical
linguistic insecurity
linguistic market
marked
mixed codes
monolingualism
official language
reappropriation
register
resistance
standard
standardized
stigmatized
syntactic
vernacular

## Suggested Further Reading

Blommaert, Jan, ed. 1999. *Language Ideological Debates*. Berlin: Mouton de Gruyter.

Blommaert, Jan, and Jef Verschueren. 1998. *Debating Diversity: Analysing the Discourse of Tolerance*. London and New York: Routledge.

Bourdieu, Pierre. 1991 [1982]. *Language and Symbolic Power*, translated by John B. Thompson. Cambridge, MA: Harvard University Press.

Edwards, John. 1994. *Multilingualism*. London and New York: Routledge.

Heller, Monica, ed. 2007. *Bilingualism: A Social Approach*. Basingstoke: Palgrave Macmillan.

Lambert, Wallace E. 1972. *Language, Psychology, and Culture*. Stanford, CA: Stanford University Press.

Moogk, Peter N. 2000. *La Nouvelle France: The Making of French Canada. A Cultural History*. East Lansing: Michigan State University Press.

## CHAPTER 28

# Stop, Revive, Survive: Lessons from the Hebrew Revival Applicable to the Reclamation, Maintenance and Empowerment of Aboriginal Languages and Cultures

*Ghil'ad Zuckermann and Michael Walsh*

(2011)

*Can "dead" languages be brought back to life? This is a pressing issue in the world, as scholars estimate that* most *of the world's languages are currently endangered and will be squeezed out by languages of wider communication (see also Chapters 19, 25, 26).*

*Hebrew is usually considered the only genuinely successful case of language revival. From its use solely as a sacred language by Jews in Diaspora whose everyday language (often Yiddish) was related to that of their neighbors, it became the living language in the state of Israel which was founded as a place that would gather Jews and others from widely scattered homes. This case has been much studied, as those working to revive Irish, Hawaiian, Native American languages, Maori, and other languages seek the critical factors that will permit their own case to become another success. As in many other postcolonial settings, aboriginal languages in Australia—aboriginal,* ab origine, *from the beginning—have been abandoned in large numbers, leaving their speakers feeling guilty and bereft.*

*Here, Zuckermann and Walsh inquire into the specific reasons that led to the success of Hebrew. Zuckermann elsewhere sets up a distinction between* Hebrew, *the ancient language, and* Israeli, *the modern version, which is notably different from its historic and sacred ancestor. The authors hope to release contemporary people—and in particular, those who wish to see aboriginal revival efforts succeed—from the unrealistic burden of believing that they must not transform languages to make them suit their current needs. Emphasizing that* linguistic *features of languages are quite different from* cultural *and* political *dimensions, they show that in the Hebrew-Israeli case, only some aspects of languages, such as words, have been retained even if others, such as sounds, are replaced. If grammar is not regarded as untouchable, the revived language—in reality, a deliberately invented hybrid—may be effective. Aiming for realism rather than purism may be a route to greater success in revitalizing languages.*

*The title of this chapter comes from an Australian safety campaign against driving fatigued. Is this advice applicable to anyone about to run out of energy after a long road? Imagine the long journey of trying to revive a language; what would the necessary tools be to keep going?*

### Reading Questions

- What are some of the specific factors that led to the reclamation of Hebrew in the twentieth century?
- What is the situation now with regard to indigenous Australian (aboriginal) languages? What are the benefits, according to the authors, of language revitalization?

Ghil'ad Zuckermann and Michael Walsh, Stop, Revive, Survive: Lessons from the Hebrew Revival Applicable to the Reclamation, Maintenance and Empowerment of Aboriginal Languages and Cultures. *Australian Journal of Linguistics* 31 (1), January 2011: 111–127.

- What do Zuckermann and Walsh mean by "purism" in language revival efforts? Why do they argue that this can be an obstacle in language revitalization?
- What are the challenges in classifying Israeli? What three approaches have been suggested?
- Which *linguistic* features of Hebrew were, in reality, incorporated into modern Israeli? Where did the other features come from?

---

> I must study politics and war that my sons may have liberty to study mathematics and philosophy. My sons ought to study mathematics and philosophy, geography, natural history, naval architecture, navigation, commerce, and agriculture, in order to give their children a right to study painting, poetry, music, architecture, statuary, tapestry, and porcelain. (John Adams, 1735–1826, second president of the United States)

The main aim of this article is to suggest that there are perspicacious lessons applicable from the relatively successful Hebrew revival to the reclamation, maintenance and empowerment of Aboriginal languages and cultures. 'Language is power; let us have ours', wrote Aboriginal politician Aden Ridgeway on 26 November 2009 in the *Sydney Morning Herald*. Previous revival efforts have largely failed (for obvious reasons, we are not going to single out specific failures here). While there have been some good results from several projects since 1992 (e.g. Kaurna, see below), **Aboriginal** people overall do not see as many positive outcomes from revival programmes as they would like. In large part this is the result of shortage of sufficient (continuity of) funding, lack of technical expertise, and lack of integration of school-based programmes with community language programmes. However, there are purely linguistic reasons too: many revival efforts were not supported by a sound theoretical understanding of how successful language revival works. As pointed out by Thieberger (2002), decisions about the appropriate target for language maintenance programmes are too often driven by **structural linguistics**, where the supposed ideal is intergenerational transmission of the language with all its original structural complexity retained, thus creating unrealistic expectations among the Aboriginal community.

This article is the first of its kind as it will innovatively draw crucial insights from 'Modern Hebrew' (henceforth, Israeli—see Zuckermann 1999), so far the most successful known **reclamation** attempt of a sleeping tongue. Zuckermann's (2005, 2008a, 2009, 2010, 2011) research on Israeli demonstrates which language components are more revivable than others. Words and conjugations, for example, are easier to revitalize than intonation, discourse, associations and connotations. We should encourage revivalists and Aboriginal leaders to be realistic rather than puristic, and not to chastise English **loanwords** and pronunciation, for example, within the emergent language. Applying such precious conclusions from Hebrew will closely assist Australian revivalists in being more efficient, urging them not to waste time and resources on Sisyphean efforts to resuscitate linguistic components that are unlikely to be revivable.

While the results of the endeavours we are proposing here have considerable value as a research enterprise, one can also consider them in terms of a cost–benefit analysis (Mühlhäusler & Damania 2004; Walsh 2008): **language revitalization** contributes to social reconciliation, cultural tourism (Clark & Kostanski 2005), capacity building, and improved community health for **Indigenous** peoples (Walsh forthcoming). In the process of language revival, some Aboriginal people will go from being dysfunctional (cf. Sutton 2009) to well-balanced, positive people. The benefits to the wider community and to Australian society are immense.

**Reversing language shift (RLS)** (Fishman 1991, 2001; Hagège 2009; Evans 2010; Walsh 2005; Zuckermann 2011) is thus of great social benefit. Language revival does not only do historical justice and address inequality but can also result in the empowerment of people who have lost their heritage and purpose in life.

Some Aboriginal people distinguish between usership and ownership. There are even those who claim that they own a language although they only know one single word of it: its name. Consequently, some Indigenous Australians do not find it important to revive their comatose tongue. We, on the other hand, have always believed in Australia's very own roadside dictum: *'Stop, revive, survive!'*

## Background: The Hebrew Revival

> I suppose the process of acceptance will pass through the usual four stages: 1. This is worthless nonsense. 2. This is an interesting, but perverse, point of view. 3. This is true, but quite unimportant. 4. I always said so (Haldane 1963: 464).

'Hebrew' is the most quoted example of a successful language revival. On the other hand, if we are to be brutally truthful with ourselves, the modern-day vernacular spoken in downtown Tel Aviv is a very different language—both typologically and genetically—to that of the Hebrew Bible (Old Testament) or of the Mishnah, the first major redaction of Jewish oral traditions.

Hebrew was spoken since approximately the fourteenth century B.C.E. It belonged to the Canaanite division of the northwestern branch of the Semitic languages, which constitute a branch of the Afro-Asiatic language family. Following a gradual decline, it ceased to be spoken by the second century C.E. The failed Bar-Kokhba Revolt against the Romans in Judea in 132–135 C.E. marks the *symbolic* end of the period of spoken Hebrew. We believe that the Mishnah was codified around 200 C.E. because Hebrew was then dying as a mother tongue. Rabbi Judah haNasi and his collaborators might have realized that if they did not act then to redact the oral tradition, it would soon have been too late because Jews were already speaking languages other than Hebrew. (In fact, the Gemara, the other component of the Babylonian Talmud, which was codified around 500 C.E., was written in Aramaic rather than in Hebrew.)

For approximately 1,750 years thereafter, Hebrew was 'clinically dead'. A most important liturgical and literary language, it occasionally served as a ***lingua franca***—a means of communication between people who do not share a mother tongue—for Jews of the **Diaspora**, but not as a native language.

Fascinating and multi-faceted Israeli, which emerged in Palestine (*Eretz Israel*) at the end of the nineteenth century, possesses distinctive socio-historical characteristics such as the lack of a continuous chain of native speakers from spoken Hebrew to Israeli, the non-Semitic mother tongues spoken by the Hebrew revivalists, and the European impact on literary Hebrew. Consequently, it presents the linguist with a unique laboratory in which to examine a wider set of theoretical problems concerning language genesis, social issues like language, identity and politics, and important practical matters, such as whether it is possible to revive a no-longer-spoken language.

The genetic classification of Israeli has preoccupied scholars since its genesis. The still regnant traditional *thesis* suggests that Israeli is *Semitic*: Hebrew *revived*. The revisionist *antithesis* defines Israeli as *Indo-European*: Yiddish *relexified*; that is, Yiddish, the revivalists' mother tongue, is the **'substratum'**, whilst Hebrew is the **'superstratum'** providing the vocabulary (cf. Horvath & Wexler 1997). According to Zuckermann's m*osaic* (rather than M*osaic*) *synthesis*, Israeli is not only multi-layered but also multi-parental. A Semito-European, or Eurasian, hybrid, Israeli is both Semitic (Afro-Asiatic) and (Indo-) European. It is based simultaneously on 'sleeping beauty'/'walking dead' Hebrew and '*máme lóshn*' (mother tongue) Yiddish, which are both *primary contributors* to Israeli, and a plethora of other tongues spoken by Jewish pioneers in Palestine in the 1880s–1930s, e.g. Russian, Polish, Arabic, Ladino (Judeo-Spanish), Turkish, German, French and English.

### The Success Rate of the Hebrew Revival

The vernacularization of Hebrew was partially a success and partially a failure. It is hard to provide an exact quantification for such a multi-variable enterprise, but we would roughly estimate that on a 1–10 scale, 10 being a complete success and one being a complete failure, the Hebrew revival is at seven. More specifically, we propose the following continuum approximations for the extent to which Israeli can be considered Hebrew: mindset/spirit: 1 (i.e. European); discourse (communicative tools, speech acts): 1; sounds (phonetics and phonology): 2; semantics (meaning, associations, connotations, semantic networkings): 3; constituent/word order (syntax): 4; general vocabulary: 5; word formation: 7; verbal conjugations: 9; and basic vocabulary: 10 (i.e. Hebrew).

The factors leading to the partial failure of the Hebrew revival have little to do with a lack of motivation or zealousness, or with economic or political variables—not even with the fact that the revivalists, such as the symbolic father of Israeli, Eliezer Ben-Yehuda (born Perelman, 1858–1922), were not as linguistically sophisticated as contemporary linguists. It is simply the case that one cannot negate one's most recent roots, be they cultural or linguistic, even if one is keen to deny one's parents' and grandparents' heritage (diasporic Yiddish) in search of cultural antiquity (Biblical Hebrew). It is therefore most unlikely to revive a clinically-dead language without cross-fertilization from the revivalists' mother tongue(s). Thus, when most native Israeli-speakers speak Israeli, their intonation is much more similar to that of Yiddish, the mother tongue of most revivalists, than to that of Arabic or any other Semitic language. It is high time to acknowledge that Israeli is very different from ancient Hebrew. We should embrace—rather than chastise—the multi-sourcedness of Israeli.

That said, the Hebrew revival cannot be considered a failure because without the zealous, obsessive, enthusiastic efforts of Ben-Yehuda and of teachers, writers, poets, journalists, intellectuals, social activists, political figures, linguists and others, Israelis would have spoken a language (such as English, German, Arabic or Yiddish) that could hardly be considered Hebrew. To call such a hypothetical language 'Hebrew' would have not only been misleading but also wrong. To call today's Israeli 'Hebrew' may be puristic but not wrong: hybridic Israeli is based on Hebrew as much as it is based on Yiddish. So, although the revivalists could not avoid the *subconscious* influence of their mother tongue(s), they did indeed manage at the same time to consciously revive important components of Hebrew.

## HYBRIDITY, CAMOUFLAGE AND THE CONGRUENCE PRINCIPLE

Israeli is a new hybrid language rather than an evolutionary phase of Hebrew. Yiddish is not a 'foreign language' vis-à-vis Israeli, and the word *intuítsya* 'intuition'—to give but one example out of thousands of alleged loan words—is not a loan word (from Yiddish *intuítsye*, Russian *intuítsiya*, Polish *intuicja* etc., all meaning 'intuition') but rather an integral part of Israeli from its very beginning.

According to the Congruence Principle, the more revivalists speak contributing languages with a specific linguistic feature, the more likely this feature is to prevail in the emergent language. Based on feature pool statistics, this principle weakens August Schleicher's famous **Family Tree theory** in historical linguistics, which may give the wrong impression that every language has only one parent. For example, most revivalists spoke languages, mainly Yiddish, that lacked that Semitic pharyngeal gulp *'ayin* (represented, for instance, by the apostrophe in Zuckermann's Christian—actually Jewish—name Ghil'ad). Naturally, their children—the ones who, in fact, shaped the real character of Israeli—could not buy the argument 'do as I say, don't do as I do!' The result is that most Israelis do not have this sound in their speech.

Similarly, *má nishmà*, the common Israeli 'what's up?' greeting, looks like a **calque**—loan translation—of the Yiddish phrase *vos hért zikh*, usually pronounced *vsértsekh* and literally meaning 'what's heard?' but functioning as a common greeting. However, a Romanian-speaking immigrant to Israel might have used *má nishmà* because of Romanian *ce se aude*, a Polish-speaker Jew because of Polish *co słychać*, and a Russian-speaker [что слышно] *chto slyshno*, all meaning the same and functioning in the same way.

The distinction between forms and patterns is crucial here as it demonstrates multiple causation. In the 1920s and 1930s, *gdud meginéy hasafà*, 'the language defendants regiment' (cf. Shur 2000), whose motto was *ivrí, dabér ivrít* 'Hebrew [i.e. Jew], speak Hebrew', used to tear down signs written in 'foreign' languages and disturb Yiddish theatre gatherings. However, the members of this group only looked for Yiddish **forms**, rather than **patterns** in the speech of the Israelis who did choose to speak 'Hebrew'. The language defendants would thus not attack an Israeli speaker saying *má nishmà*. Ironically, even the language defendants regiment's anthem included calques from Yiddish.

Zuckermann (2011, Zuckermann forthcoming) analyzes the hitherto-overlooked camouflaged semantic networking transferred from one language to another. Whereas mechanisms as calques (loan translations such as *superman*, from German *Übermensch*), phono-semantic matches (e.g. *crayfish*, from Old French *crevice*, a cognate of *crab* that has little to do with *fish*) (Zuckermann 2003) and **portmanteau** blends (e.g. *motel*, from *motor+hotel*, or *sprummer*, from *spring+summer*) have been studied, there is a need to uncover concealed semantic links between words in the Target Language which reflect—often subconsciously—semantic networking in the Source Language. Consider the Israeli word *gakhlilít* 'firefly, glow-worm'—coined by poet laureate Hayyim Nahman Bialik (1873–1934). This word is semantically and etymologically linked to the Biblical Hebrew word *gaħelet* 'burning coal, glowing ember'. Morphologically, Israeli *gakhlilít* derives from Hebrew *gaħelet* plus the reduplication of its third radical [1]. However, no Israeli dictionary reveals the crucial semantic networking aspect, namely that the Israeli concoction, *gakhlilít*, in using an element associated with 'glow', in fact replicates a European mindset, apparent for example in the Yiddish word *glivórem*, literally 'glow' (cf. *gaħelet*) + 'worm', or in German *Glühwürmchen*.

## Native Israeli Speech and the Academy of the Hebrew Language

Since its conception, Israeli has been the subject of **purism** (the dislike of foreign words—as in Icelandic: Sapir & Zuckermann 2008) and the enforcement of 'correct' pronunciation. Brought into being by legislation in 1953 as the supreme institute for 'Hebrew', the Academy of the Hebrew Language (known in Israeli as *haakademya lalashón haivrít*) is funded by Israel's Ministry of Education. It superseded the (Hebrew) Language Council [*váad halashón (haivrít)*], which was established in 1889—as a branch of *Safá Brurá* (Clear Language)—by Ben-Yehuda and colleagues. As defined in its constitution, the Academy's functions are: (1) to investigate and compile the Hebrew lexicon according to its historical strata and layers; (2) to study the structure, history, and offshoots of the Hebrew language; and (3) to direct the development of Hebrew in light of its nature, requirements, and potential, its daily and academic needs, by setting its lexicon, grammar, characters, orthography and transliteration [in fact, transcription].

The first goal is most useful, as Israeli is indeed a multilayered language. For example, one could say both (a) *khashkhú enáv*, literally 'His eyes became dark', meaning 'He saw black' ('black' in this context meaning 'bad news'), and (b) *niyá/naasá lo khóshekh baenáim*, meaning the same, albeit structurally different. While *khashkhú enáv* is Hebrew, *niyá lo khóshekh baenáim* is a calque of the Yiddish phrase *siz im gevórn fíntster in di óygn*, which might in turn be an adaptation of the very Hebrew *khashkhú enáv* (transcribed here in its Israeli form, which would have been unintelligible for an ancient Hebrew-speaker).

Israeli has many other minimal pairs, such as *asá din leatsmó* and *lakákh et hakhók layadáim*, both referring to a person violating the law, with the latter being more colloquial; as well as *lelót kayamím*, literally 'nights as days' (also *yamím kelelót*, literally 'days as nights'), and *misavív lashaón*, literally 'round the clock', both often referring to hard work.

Somewhat resembling the 'catastrophic success' of the 1928–1936 Turkish Language Revolution (see Lewis 1999), many referents have several Israeli signifiers, one of which is puristically Hebrew and the other, often more commonly used, 'foreign' (in fact, Israeli *ab initio*). These include many internationalisms such as *opozítsya* 'Opposition' (according to the Academy, the word should be *negdá*—cf. Hebrew *néged* 'against') and *koalítsya* 'Coalition' (according to the Academy: *yakhdá*—cf. Hebrew *yaħad* 'together').

However, goal (3), *to **direct** the development of Hebrew in light of its **nature***, is oxymoronic (cf. Zuckermann 2008b: 139). If the nature of a language is to evolve in a specific direction [cf. Sapir's 'drift' (1921), the pattern of change in which the structure of a language shifts in a determinate direction], why direct its evolution by language policing?

## From the Promised Land to the 'Lucky' Country

The three principles of linguistic revival and survival are:

1. If your language is **endangered** → Do not allow it to die!
2. If your language died → Stop, revive, survive!

3. If you revive your language → Embrace the **hybridity** of the emergent language!

Questions of this kind, albeit in an implicit and sometimes confused fashion, are being raised within the context of Australian Aboriginal languages. Current language revival activities are worthy but often under-theorized. The tendency has been to attempt to revive the language *en masse* despite what has been indicated about the Hebrew rate of success for take up of particular components of language. There is a need to examine a range of existing language revitalization programmes with a view to assessing the rate of success for take up of particular components of language and at the same time adduce the preferences (and sometimes the prejudices) of the group in question (cf. Couzens and Eira forthcoming).

Indigenous Australians have been living in Australia for more than 40,000 years. Today Aboriginal people and Torres Strait Islanders make up 2.6% of Australia's population. Unfortunately, one of the main findings of the most recent National Indigenous Languages Survey Report (2005) was that the situation of Australia's languages is grave (in both senses). Of an original number of over 250 known Australian Indigenous languages, only about 145 Indigenous languages are still spoken and the vast majority of these, about 110, are critically endangered: they are spoken only by small groups of people, mostly over 40 years old. Eighteen languages are strong in the sense of being spoken by all age groups, but three or four of these are showing some disturbing signs of moving into endangerment. So of an original number of over 250 known Australian Indigenous languages, only 6% (i.e. 15) are in a healthy condition.

Aboriginal language revival began recently—from the late 1970s (Amery & Gale 2007)—and has therefore much to learn from other revival efforts, especially that of Hebrew, which began in the late nineteenth century. There has been little coordination among the geographically-scattered language revival efforts in Australia. Most recently, language revitalization practitioners have begun to share experiences at various conferences and workshops (Hobson *et al.* 2010). There is thus an urgent need for an on-the-ground, ongoing input, creating intellectual and practical synergy and complementing the mission of the regional Aboriginal language centres and the recently-established mobile language team based at the University of Adelaide—by adding significant advice based on scholarly and universal perspectives. Practical outcomes will include a useful handbook of the best practices for language revival in Australia (Christina Eira, pers. comm.), and an improved sense of well being in the local Aboriginal community.

There is community support in some parts of the country for revival and heritage learning programmes: either in reclamation proper (e.g. extensive courses similar to Israel's *ulpaním*) or only in symbolic, postvernacular maintenance [teaching Aboriginal people some words and concepts related to the dead language—cf. postvernacular Yiddish among secular Jews in the United States (see Shandler 2005)]. At its broadest level, language revival refers to the range of strategies for increasing knowledge and use of a language which is no longer spoken fully across all generations. In practice, however, this can range from largely symbolic uses of ancestral languages like naming buildings or places through to more constant involvement with the language through school-based language instruction (Walsh 2005).

## Comparative Analysis of Hebrew and Aboriginal Language Revival

Although they too were, at the beginning, very few in number, and encountered great hostility and animosity (e.g. by those who saw the revival as the desecration of a holy tongue), the Hebrew revivalists had several advantages compared with Australian revivalists. Consider the following:

1. *Documentation*: extensive—consider, for example, the Hebrew Bible and the Mishnah.
2. *Accessibility*: Jews have been exposed to literary Hebrew throughout the generations, e.g. when praying in the synagogue or when saying the blessing over the meal. It would be hard to find a Jew who did not have access to Hebrew (unless in totalitarian regimes such as the Soviet Union).
3. *Prestige*: Hebrew was considered a prestigious language (as opposed to Yiddish, for instance, whose Australian sociolinguistic parallel might be Aboriginal English). It is true that some Aboriginal languages are held in high regard by their owners/custodians but unfortunately usually not by the wider Australian society.
4. *Uniqueness*: Jews from all over the globe only had Hebrew in common (Aramaic was not as prominent), whereas there are dozens of 'sleeping' Aboriginal languages and it would be hard to choose only one unifying tongue, unless one resorts to Aboriginal English. The revival of a single language is much more manageable than that of numerous tongues in varying states of disrepair.
5. *National self-determination*: revived Hebrew was aimed to be the language of an envisioned state, where speakers of revived Hebrew would eventually have the political power (cf. Yadin & Zuckermann 2010).
6. *Lack of ownership*: unlike in the case of Aboriginal languages (cf. Walsh 2002), anybody has the right to speak Hebrew, without getting permission from the Jews.
7. *Easy borrowing*: loanwords and foreign words are not considered theft. In fact, Eliezer Ben-Yehuda loved borrowing from Arabic, Aramaic and other Semitic languages.
8. *Lack of place restriction*: Hebrew could be and was revived all over the globe—consider Haim Leib Hazan's coinage *mishkafáim* 'glasses' in 1890 in Grodno (see Zuckermann 2003: 1–4).

9. *Multi-lingualism*: Jews arriving in *Eretz Israel* in the time of the revival were used to multilingualism and did not have a 'monolingual mindset'. For example, back in Europe many of them spoke Yiddish at home and Polish in the market, and prayed in Hebrew (and Aramaic) in the synagogue.
10. *Number*: There are many more Jews than Aboriginal people in Australia.

But, as it happens, Aboriginal revivalists actually have some advantages vis-à-vis Hebrew revivalists. Consider the following:

1. *Deontological reason for the revival*: as we see it, Aboriginal tongues deserve to be revived for historical, humanistic and social justice, *inter alia* addressing inequality (cf. Thieberger 1990). This can provide strength to the revival attempts. We hear again and again 'native title' but where is the 'native tongue title'? Is *land* more important than *langue* and (cultural) *lens*? And if land, langue and heritage are bound together as a trinity, then why ask for **reparation** only for land?
2. *Numerous utilitarian reasons for the revival*: the revival of sleeping Aboriginal languages can result in personal, educational and economic empowerment, sense of pride and higher self-esteem of people who have lost their heritage and purpose in life (see concluding remarks). The Hebrew revival had many less utilitarian purposes, the main one being simply the constitution of a unifying tongue to Jews from all over the world. It would have been unfair, for example, for Ladino-speaking Sephardim if German were selected.
3. *Governmental support*: although it could obviously be greater, the Australian government does support the reclamation and maintenance of Aboriginal languages, or at least there is an obvious address to apply for money from. This has not been the case in fin-de-siècle Palestine.
4. *Similarities between Aboriginal English and Aboriginal languages*: Aboriginal English (e.g. Nunga English in Adelaide), spoken by some revivalists, contains various linguistic features—such as connotations, associations, sounds and morphological characteristics like the dual—of the reclaimed Aboriginal languages at stake. One might perspicaciously argue that Israeli semantics, which is deeply modelled on Yiddish semantics, also maintains the original Hebrew semantics after all because Yiddish, a Germanic language with Romance substratum, was deeply impacted by Hebrew and Aramaic. However, the Yiddish dialects that have been the most influential ones in Israel, e.g. Polish Yiddish, are, in fact, the ones that underwent Slavonization from the thirteenth century onwards, when Jews moved from Germany to Slavonic-speaking areas in Eastern Europe. Aboriginal English is much younger and therefore is much more likely to retain features of Aboriginal languages, than Yiddish is to retain features of Hebrew.

## Universal Constraints of Language Revival

And yet, although obviously language revival attempts should be tailored to the specific contexts, needs and desires of each community, there are some universal constraints that should be recognized. As we have already seen, Hebrew revivalists, who wished to speak pure Hebrew, failed in their *imprisoning purism prism*, the result being a multi-faceted and fascinating fin-de-siècle Israeli language, both multi-layered and multi-sourced. Most relevantly, some Australian interest groups (cf. Tiwi in Dorian 1994: 481–484) get hung up on misled views akin to the slogan 'Give me authenticity or give me death!' (cf. 'Give me Liberty, or give me Death!', the famous quotation attributed to Patrick Henry from a speech he made to the Virginia Convention in America on 23 March 1775), where the death, of course, ends up being the Indigenous language they wish to save from 'contamination'! [On authenticity and language revival, see also Wong (1999) and Hinton and Ahlers (1999).]

Why should we encourage revivalists and Aboriginal leaders to be realistic rather than puristic? Purism creates unrealistic expectations that may discourage learners from acquiring the emerging language. A revived language should not be viewed negatively if it is seen to be influenced by a neighbouring language or by English. The use of words from a neighbouring language should not discredit the revived language. There might be some rare occasions when it is more appropriate for revivalists to favour purism—see Harlow (1993) on Maori. However, in the case of reclamation proper (i.e. the revival of a language that has no native speakers such as Hebrew), one must learn to embrace, celebrate and champion—rather than chastise—the inevitable hybridity of the emerging language.

One might argue that the difference between the conditions that surround Aboriginal languages and Israeli are so large that it is impossible to learn across these contexts, but denying universal traits or constraints in human language in general, and in reversing language shift in particular, is counter-productive. Linguistic reality lies between relativism and universalism. No progress will be made by turning a blind eye to any of these extremes. Based on a critical analysis of Israeli, one can predict accurately the situation in various reclaimed Aboriginal languages such as Kaurna [ga:na], a resurrected language spoken around Adelaide, which is the result of one of the most successful revival attempts in Australia—cf. Gumbaynggirr (Ash *et al.* 2010), Ngarrindjeri, Walmajarri and Kamilaroi/Gamilaraay.

There are scholars, e.g. Dalby (2003: 250), who scoff at some attempts at reviving the use of an endangered language: 'this is no longer a language, any more than musicians are speaking Italian when they say *andante* and *fortissimo*. These are simply loanwords used in a special context'. A more balanced view is manifested in Crystal's (2000: 162) comments on Kaurna:

> The revived language is not the same as the original language, of course; most obviously, it lacks the breadth of functions which it originally had, and large amounts of old vocabulary are missing. But, as it continues in present-day use, it will develop new functions and new vocabulary, just as any other living language would, and as long as people value it as a true marker of their identity, and are prepared to keep using it, there is no reason to think of it as anything other than a valid system of communication.

The impact of English (Aboriginal or Australian English) on reclaimed Kaurna is far-reaching. Consider the following:

1. At the level of phonology, there are often spelling pronunciations, especially for sequences of *er* (as in *yerlo* 'sea' and *yerta* for instance), *ur* (as in *purle* or *purlaitye*). In classical Kaurna, the *r* in these words belonged with the consonant (it was be retroflex) but many times we hear an *er* vowel as in English *slur* or *sir*. The original vowel was /a/ in *yerlo* and *yerta*, and /u/ in *purle* and *purlaitye*. Stress is often placed on the second syllable rather than on the first (Amery 2000: 121–122; Amery & Rigney 2004: 2–3).
2. At the level of vocabulary, there are many calques—see Amery (2000: 124), as well as Chapter 12 *Wodlingga* 'In the Home' (pp. 63–70), Chapter 15 *Tidnaparndo* 'Football' (pp. 81–84) and Chapter 16 *Kuya Pirri-wirkindi* 'Fishing' (pp. 85–88) in Amery (2007), where a range of calques have been developed—especially evident in the names of AFL football teams such as *Kuinyunda Meyunna* (lit. 'sacred men') for the St Kilda Saints. Knowingly—and jocularly—*cricket* (the sport game) was replicated as *yertabiritti* (the term for the insect with the same name in English) (Amery 2003: 86). It should be noted, however, that in reclaimed Kaurna there are relatively few loanwords/foreignisms from English *per se*, far less than we see in any 'strong' language such as Pitjantjatjara or Yolngu Matha.
3. Constituent/word order is free in classical Kaurna as in other Aboriginal languages, though it tended to be SOV (Subject–Object–Verb). Naturally, there are contemporary users of Kaurna who tend to produce more SVO (Subject–Verb–Object) sentences, replicating English (Amery & Rigney 2004: 5).
4. English semantics tends to carry through to Kaurna words (Amery & Rigney 2004: 5–7).
5. The most pervasive influence from English is at the level of discourse. Almost everything said or written is translated from English. Thus, the turn of phrase and the idiom are from English (Amery 2001a: 190–194, 2001b; see also Amery & Rigney 2006).

And still, the impact of English on Kaurna is less than in many other revived languages in Australia—cf. the neighbouring Ngarrindjeri, where published texts are practically English calques: an isomorphic one-to-one translation of English, including the use of interrogative 'where' for 'were' and 'thus' for 'the'. Case suffixes are used as prepositions—see p. iii of *Reviving Languages* (1999), as well as Rhonda Agius in Proctor and Gale (1997: 4–6).

We predict that any attempt to revive an Aboriginal language will result in a hybrid, combining components from Australian English, Aboriginal English, Kriol, other Aboriginal languages and the target Aboriginal tongue, but we are going to assist Aboriginal revivalists to make their efforts more efficient and to embrace hybridity.

## CONCLUDING REMARKS

> If you talk to a man in a language he understands, that goes to his head. If you talk to him in his language, that goes to his heart. (Nelson Mandela)

This article contributes towards the establishment of **Revival Linguistics**, a new linguistic discipline and paradigm. Zuckermann's term Revival Linguistics is modelled upon 'Contact Linguistics' (<language contact). Revival Linguistics *inter alia* explores the universal constraints and mechanisms involved in language reclamation, renewal and revitalization. It draws perspicacious comparative insights from one revival attempt to another, thus acting as an epistemological bridge between parallel discourses in various local attempts to revive sleeping tongues all over the globe.

There is a need to map the revival attempts throughout Aboriginal Australia by: (1) assessing the success of the revival so far; and (2) categorizing the specific need on a continuum of revival efforts, e.g. reclamation (e.g. Kaurna), renewal (e.g. Ngarrindjeri) and revitalization (e.g. Walmajarri)—cf. other RE-terms to be defined such as restoration, resurrection, resuscitation, reinvigoration, reintroduction, regenesis, revernacularization, reawakening, rebirth and renaissance.

Needless to say, even if there is eventually a sound understanding and awareness of the linguistic/sociolinguistic issues involved and even if the endeavour is well-theorized, language revival efforts may well still fail. Internal factional politics are likely to be far more influential in deciding the fate of a language revival movement than any linguistic theory or lack of one. There is no doubt that the first stage of any desire by professional linguists to assist in language revival involves a long initial period of carefully observing, listening, learning and characterizing each indigenous community specifically. Only then can we inspire and assist. That said, this article proposes that there are linguistic constraints applicable to all revival attempts. Mastering them would be most useful to endangered languages in general and to Aboriginal linguistic revival in particular.

While we know that language revitalization can have numerous beneficial effects, we also know that some revival efforts are more successful than others (see Walsh 2010). A better understanding of success in this arena by surveying numerous language reinvigoration efforts in Australia, and by drawing on lessons from the Hebrew revival, will enable less waste of resources and better outcomes. Besides significant scholarly impact and intellectual benefits, the results of such endeavours will also improve substantially the future of Australia's Indigenous communities, promoting and maintaining their physical, spiritual and cultural good health through:

1. transformation of disturbed individuals;
2. capacity building: some Aboriginal people will undertake training only because they are interested in language(s). However, what they will learn in the process are useful generic skills such as literacy, computer literacy, conducting research and giving speeches in public;
3. improved sense of well being in the local Aboriginal community;
4. reconciliation and potential decrease in racism towards Aboriginal people in some country centres; and
5. promoting cultural tourism to Aboriginal areas in order to learn about their cultures and languages.

Regaining language is a life-changing experience for many Aboriginal people. One Aboriginal person has told us that he used to be angry, often drunk and in trouble with the police and his home life was a mess. Two years later, when he had regained his language, his situation had turned around and his family life had greatly improved.

Through this and other experiences we became convinced that a small investment in language revitalization could yield very significant dividends. Language revival can result in the saving of vast amounts of money and resources going into housing, social services and health intervention to little effect. A small investment into language revitalization can make an enormous difference to society. Public health can benefit from language intervention.

To date such money as has been devoted to Aboriginal language revival and maintenance has not been well targeted. This is partly because Australian Indigenous language policies have been piecemeal and un-coordinated at best or otherwise non-existent or implicit (Liddicoat 2008; McKay 2007, 2009; Truscott & Malcolm forthcoming; see also http://www.anu.edu.au/linguistics/nash/aust/policy.html, accessed 6 July 2010). We aim at a better informed Indigenous language policy at the national level, as well as in particular institutional contexts. For instance, in considering Indigenous policies of Australian universities, Gunstone (2008: 107) complains: 'it is apparent that universities are still largely failing to adequately address the educational needs of Indigenous staff, students and communities'.

As cellist Yo Yo Ma said on 28 November 2000 at the White House Conference on Culture and Diplomacy:

> A Senegalese poet said 'In the end we will conserve only what we love. We love only what we understand, and we will understand only what we are taught'. We must learn about other cultures in order to understand, in order to love, and in order to preserve our common world heritage.

## References


Amery, R. 2000. *Warrabarna Kaurna: reclaiming an Australian language* Lisse, The Netherlands: Swets and Zeitlinger.

Amery, R. 2001a. 'Language planning and language revival' *Current Issues in Language Planning* 2: 141–221.

Amery, R. 2001b. 'Regenerating a Kaurna literature' Paper presented at the *AULLA Conference*, University of Adelaide, February.

Amery, R. (ed.). 2003. *Warra Kaurna: a resource for Kaurna language programs* 3rd edition (revised and expanded) University of South Australia: Kaurna Warra Pintyandi, c/-. Reprinted September 2005, Image and Copy Centre, The University of Adelaide. (Includes corrections, addition of introductory notes about the Kaurna language, translations and protocols, timeline of significant events, recent neologisms and sections on modern clothing, modern artefacts and new technologies.)

Amery, R., with Kaurna Warra Pintyandi. 2007. *Kulluru Marni Ngattaitya! Sounds good to me! A Kaurna learner's guide* Draft prototype version (publication forthcoming).

Amery, R. & M.-A. Gale. 2007. 'But our language was just asleep: a history of language revival in Australia' in W. B. McGregor (ed.) *Encountering Aboriginal Languages: studies in the history of Australian linguistics* Canberra: Pacific Linguistics. pp. 339–82.

Amery, R. & A. W. Rigney, with N. Varcoe, C. Schultz & Kaurna Warra Pintyandi. 2006. *Kaurna Palti Wonga—Kaurna Funeral Protocols* (book, CD and sympathy cards) Adelaide: Kaurna Warra Pintyandi (launched 20 May 2006).

Amery, R. & L. I. Rigney. 2004. 'Authenticity in language revival' Paper presented at the *Applied Linguistics Association of Australia (ALAA) Annual Conference* held at the University of South Australia, 17 July.

Ash, A., P. Hooler, G. Williams & K. Walker. 2010. 'Maam Ngawaala: Biindu Ngaawa Nyanggan Bindaayili. Language centres: Keeping language strong' in J. Hobson, K. Lowe, S. Poetsch & M. Walsh (eds) *Re-Awakening Languages: Theory & practice in the revitalisation of*

*Australia's Indigenous languages* Sydney: Sydney University Press. pp. 106–18.

Clark, I. D. & Kostanski. 2005. 'Reintroducing indigenous placenames—lessons from Gariwerd, Victoria, Australia, or, how to address toponymic dispossession in ways that celebrate cultural diversity and inclusiveness' Abstract submitted to *'Names in Time and Space', Twenty Second International Congress of Onomastic Sciences*, 28 August–4 September 2005, Università Di Pisa, Italy.

Couzens, V. & C. Eira. Forthcoming 'Meeting point: parameters for a typology of revival languages' in P. Austin & J. Sallabank (eds) *Endangered Languages: ideologies and beliefs* Oxford: Oxford University Press.

Crystal, D. 2000. *Language Death* Cambridge: Cambridge University Press.

Dalby, A. 2003. *Language in Danger: the loss of linguistic diversity and the threat to our future* New York: Columbia University Press.

Dorian, N. C. 1994. 'Purism vs. compromise in language revitalization and language revival' *Language in Society* 23: 479–94.

Evans, N. 2010. *Dying Words. Endangered languages and what they have to tell us* Malden & Oxford: Wiley-Blackwell.

Fishman, J. A. 1991. *Reversing Language Shift: theoretical and empirical foundations of assistance to threatened languages* Clevedon, UK: Multilingual Matters.

Fishman, J. A. (ed.). 2001. *Can Threatened Languages Be Saved? Reversing language shift, revisited: a 21st century perspective* Clevedon, UK: Multilingual Matters.

Gunstone, A. 2008. 'Australian university approaches to Indigenous policy' *Australian Journal of Indigenous Education* 37: 103–08.

Hagège, C. 2009. *On the Death and Life of Languages* New Haven, CT: Yale University Press.

Haldane, J. B. S. 1963. 'Review of *The Truth About Death*' *Journal of Genetics* 58: 463–64.

Harlow, R. 1993. 'Lexical expansion in Maori' *Journal of the Polynesian Society* 102(1): 99–107.

Hinton, L. & J. Ahlers, 1999. 'The issue of "authenticity" in California language restoration' *Anthropology and Education Quarterly* (Authenticity and Identity: lessons from Indigenous language education, March) 30(1): 56–67.

Hobson, J., K. Lowe, S. Poetsch & M. Walsh. (eds) 2010. *Re-awakening languages: theory & practice in the revitalisation of Australia's Indigenous languages* Sydney: Sydney University Press.

Horvath, J. & P. Wexler. (eds) 1997. *Relexification in Creole and Non-Creole Languages—with special attention to Haitian Creole, modern Hebrew, Romani, and Rumanian* (Mediterranean Language and Culture Monograph Series, vol xiii) Wiesbaden: Otto Harrassowitz.

Lewis, G. L. 1999. *The Turkish Language Reform: a catastrophic success* Oxford: Oxford University Press.

Liddicoat, A. J. 2008. 'Models of national government language-in-education policy for indigenous minority language groups' in T. J. Curnow (ed.) *Selected Papers from the 2007 Conference of the Australian Linguistic Society* Adelaide Available at: http://www.als.asn.au/proceedings/als2007/liddicoat.pdf accessed 6 July 2010.

McKay, G. 2007. 'Language maintenance, shift and planning' in G. Leitner & I. Malcolm (eds) *The Habitat of Australia's Aboriginal Languages: past, present, and future* Berlin: Mouton de Gruyter. pp. 101–30.

McKay, G. 2009. 'English and Indigenous languages in the Australian language policy environment' in H. Chen & K. Cruickshank (eds) *Making a Difference: challenges for applied linguistics* Newcastle upon Tyne: Cambridge Scholars Press. pp. 283–97.

Mühlhäusler, P. & R. Damania. 2004. *Economic Costs and Benefits of Australian Indigenous Languages* Available at: http://www.arts.gov.au/indigenous/MILR/publications accessed 6 July 2010.

Proctor, J., & M.-A. Gale. (eds). 1997. *Tauondi Speaks from the Heart: Aboriginal poems from Tauondi College* Port Adelaide: Tauondi College.

*Reviving Languages: warranna purruttiappendi: tumbelin tungarar: renewal and reclamation programs for indigenous languages in schools.* 1999. Adelaide: Department of Education, Training and Employment (DETE). Notes by Guy Tunstill.

Sapir, E. 1921. *Language. An introduction to the study of speech* New York: Harcourt, Brace.

Sapir, Y., & G. Zuckermann. 2008. 'Icelandic: phonosemantic matching' in J. Rosenhouse & R. Kowner (eds) *Globally Speaking: motives for adopting English vocabulary in other languages* Clevedon, UK: Multilingual Matters. pp. 19–43 (Chapter 2, References: 296–325).

Shandler, J. 2005. *Adventures in Yiddishland: postvernacular language and culture* California: University of California Press.

Shur, S. A. 2000. *Gdud meginéy hasafá beérets israél 1923–1936* [*The Language Defendants Regiment in Eretz Yisrael 1923–36*] Haifa: Herzl Institute for Research and Study of Zionism.

Sutton, P. 2009. *The Politics of Suffering: Indigenous Australia and the end of the liberal consensus* Melbourne: Melbourne University Press.

Thieberger, N. 1990. 'Language maintenance: why bother?' *Multilingua—Journal of Cross-Cultural and Interlanguage Communication* 9(4): 333–58.

Thieberger, N. 2002. 'Extinction in whose terms? Which parts of a language constitute a target for language maintenance programmes?' in D. Bradley & M. Bradley (eds) *Language Endangerment and Language Maintenance* London: Routledge Curzon. pp. 310–28.

Truscott, A. & I. Malcolm. Forthcoming. 'Closing the policy–practice gap: making Indigenous language policy more than empty rhetoric' in J. Hobson, K. Lowe, S. Poetsch

& M. Walsh (eds) *Re-Awakening Languages: theory and practice in the revitalisation of Australia's Indigenous languages* Sydney: Sydney University Press.

Walsh, M. 2002. 'Language ownership: a key issue for Native Title' in J. Henderson & D. Nash (eds) *Language and Native Title* Canberra: Native Title Research Series, Aboriginal Studies Press. pp. 230–44.

Walsh, M. 2005. 'Indigenous languages of Southeast Australia, revitalization and the role of education' *Australian Review of Applied Linguistics* 28(2): 1–14.

Walsh, M. 2008. 'Is saving languages a good investment?' in R. Amery & J. Nash (eds) *Warra Wiltaniappendi Strengthening Languages: Proceedings of the Inaugural Indigenous Languages Conference (ILC), 24–27 September 2007, University of Adelaide* Adelaide: Discipline of Linguistics, University of Adelaide. pp. 41–50.

Walsh, M. 2010. 'Why language revitalization sometimes works' in J. Hobson, K. Lowe, S. Poetsch & M. Walsh (eds) *Re-Awakening Languages: Theory & practice in the revitalisation of Australia's Indigenous languages* Sydney: Sydney University Press. pp. 22–36.

Walsh M. Forthcoming. 'The link between language revitalization and Aboriginal health: mental, physical and social' *Medical Journal of Australia* to be submitted.

Wong, L. 1999. 'Authenticity and the revitalization of Hawaiian' *Anthropology and Education Quarterly* (Authenticity and Identity: lessons from Indigenous language education, March) 30(1): 94–115.

Yadin, A. & G. Zuckermann. 2010. 'Blorít: Pagans' mohawk or Sabras' forelock?: Ideologically manipulative secularization of Hebrew terms in socialist Zionist Israeli' in T. Omoniyi (ed.) *The Sociology of Language and Religion: change, conflict and accommodation* London & New York: Palgrave Macmillan: 84–125 (Chapter 6).

Zuckermann, G. 1999. 'Review article of Nakdimon Shabbethay Doniach and Ahuvia Kahane (eds), *The Oxford English-Hebrew Dictionary*. Oxford & New York: Oxford University Press, 1998' *International Journal of Lexicography* 12: 325–46.

Zuckermann, G. 2003. *Language Contact and Lexical Enrichment in Israeli Hebrew* London & New York: Palgrave Macmillan.

Zuckermann, G. 2005. 'Abba, why was Professor Higgins trying to teach Eliza to speak like our cleaning lady?: Mizrahim, Ashkenazim, prescriptivism and the real sounds of the Israeli language' *Australian Journal of Jewish Studies* 19: 210–31.

Zuckermann, G. 2008a. *Israelít safá yafá [Israeli—A Beautiful Language]* Tel Aviv: Am Oved.

Zuckermann, G. 2008b. '"Realistic prescriptivism": the Academy of the Hebrew Language, its campaign of "good grammar" and lexpionage, and the native Israeli speakers' *Israel Studies in Language and Society* 1(1): 135–54.

Zuckermann, G. 2009. 'Hybridity versus revivability: multiple causation, forms and patterns' *Journal of Language Contact* 2: 40–67.

Zuckermann, G. 2010. 'Do Israelis understand the Hebrew bible?', *The Bible and Critical Theory* 6.1–6.7. DOI:10.2104/bc100006.

Zuckermann, G. 2011. 'Hebrew revivalists' goals vis-à-vis the emerging Israeli language' in J. A. Fishman & O. García (eds) *The Handbook of Language and Ethnic Identity: the success and failure continuum*, Vol II Oxford: Oxford University Press.

Zuckermann, G. Forthcoming. *Language Revival and Multiple Causation* New York: Oxford University Press.

## Critical Thinking and Application

- Do you think that greater understanding of the linguistic features of the Hebrew-Israeli revival would be helpful to those wishing to undertake revitalization efforts in other settings? Why?
- Some language revitalization efforts, such as described by Hinton (1998) for California, involve using words from an indigenous language in limited situations rather than insisting that the language be used completely, for all communication, or not at all. In some cases, the language learned is a simplified, or pidginized, version of the original language. Discuss the benefits and disadvantages of using an endangered language only partially.
- Select one group whose language is currently endangered but is undertaking language revitalization activities. Conduct research into its most recent situation: Have language revitalization efforts borne fruit? What activities have continued? What activities have been dropped or added? Have the prospects for this language improved or declined? What factors have contributed to this fate?

## Vocabulary

aboriginal
calque
diaspora
endangered
Family Tree theory
hybridity
indigenous
language revitalization
lingua franca
loan word
portmanteau
purism
reclamation
reparation
reversing language shift (RLS)
Revival Linguistics
structural linguistics
substratum
superstratum

## Suggested Further Reading

Blau, Joshua. 1981. *The Renaissance of Modern Hebrew and Modern Standard Arabic: Parallels and Differences in the Revival of Two Semitic Languages*. Berkeley: University of California Press.

Bradley, David, and Maya Bradley, eds. 2002. *Language Endangerment and Language Maintenance*. London and New York: RoutledgeCurzon.

Crystal, David. 2000. *Language Death*. Cambridge: Cambridge University Press.

Dalby, A. 2003. *Language in Danger: The Loss of Linguistic Diversity and the Threat to Our Future*. New York: Columbia University Press.

Fellman, Jack. 1973. *The Revival of a Classical Tongue: Eliezer Ben Yehuda and the Modern Hebrew Language*. The Hague: Mouton.

Fishman, Joshua. 1991. *Reversing Language Shift: Theoretical and Empirical Foundations of Assistance to Threatened Languages*. Clevedon: Multilingual Matters.

Hinton, Leanne. 1994. *Flutes of Fire: Essays on California Indian Languages*. Berkeley: Heyday Books.

Hinton, Leanne. 1998. Language Loss and Revitalization in California: Overview. *International Journal of the Sociology of Language* 132: 83–93.

Hinton, Leanne, and Kenneth L. Hale, eds. 2001. *The Green Book of Language Revitalization in Practice*. San Diego: Academic Press.

Nettle, Daniel, and Suzanne Romaine. 2000. *Vanishing Voices: The Extinction of the World's Languages*. Oxford: Oxford University Press.

Segal, Miryam. 2010. *A New Sound in Hebrew Poetry: Poetics, Politics, Accent*. Bloomington: Indiana University Press.

Stavans, Ilan. 2008. *Resurrecting Hebrew*. New York: Schocken (Nextbook).

Walsh, Michael. 2005. Will Indigenous Languages Survive? *Annual Review of Anthropology* 34: 293–315.

Wright, Sue. 1996. *Language and the State: Revitalization and Revival in Israel and Eire*. Clevedon: Multilingual Matters.

# UNIT 7

## Language and Identity

Since we speak every time we interact, and since language varies, the ways we speak are evident and available to everybody. They advertise our origins and our identifications, whether we are proud or ashamed of them. All people reveal many aspects of identity with each word and sentence they utter: which nation they are identifying with (in terms of broader linguistic variety), which region, which social class, which ethnic group, which gender, and each speaker's age.

When sociolinguists first discovered the regularities of linguistic variation and could demonstrate a correlation between linguistic variation and social segment, there was a heady sense of explanatory power. In recent years, a number of critiques of this approach have pointed out that all people have a number of different aspects of their gender; that we are not so easily compartmentalized; and that we do not stay in statistical boxes very readily. A new approach to the study of sociolinguistic variation relies on the notion of "communities of practice," a little like old-fashioned network theory. It suggests that any kind of identity is *accomplished in interaction* rather than existing in some abstract way prior to any action (see, e.g., Fought 2004, Schilling-Estes 2004). Further, people can play with their identities, consciously, in what Ben Rampton has so vividly described as "crossing." Rather than speak of static linguistic *style*, as was the foundational sociolinguistic custom, Rampton has suggested we think of *styling*, an active strategic activity.

### Region

Just as there is no intrinsic linguistic reason for a particular linguistic variety to become a world language, so there is no inherent feature of a language that causes it to become "standard." That is purely a matter of history and the power that certain speakers end up having because of economic and political conditions. The speech of certain areas of the United States, like regions elsewhere, derives from their precise history: who settled there when, where they came from, what other groups moved in and what the relations were among various groups, and any number of other social factors.

But regional language is often given a kind of social meaning and value, so that it is possible for outsiders to develop stereotypes about the speech—and speakers—of a particular region. There is a tendency to applaud one's own language variety and to denigrate that of others. Regional linguistic differences are the subject of humor, of friends' conversation, and of scholarly inquiry.

### Class

Though Americans don't typically name or acknowledge their social classes, there is no doubt that such classes exist. Classes are stratified (layered) by means of income, education, occupation, and general "cultural capital." Language is one of the enduring aspects of a person's class identity, and it is changed only with difficulty. Language correlates with social class everywhere it has been studied in the world, with some linguistic features seen as marking identification with one class or another.

There is no intrinsic superiority of the linguistic features associated with "superior" social classes, only their association with a particular social group. For instance, the presence of postvocalic (r) (as in the word *fourth*) in postwar New York City, as you will see described in Chapter 29, is associated with higher social status, but before World War II it was associated with lower social status. Thus, any study of the relations among status and language must be done with deep knowledge of social setting and context.

### "Race" and Ethnicity

*Ethnicity* is the identity that comes from belonging to a group, often with a sense of shared background or descent, shared cultural practices, and shared social situation. In the United States, we have ethnic groups on the basis of "race" (African Americans), national heritage (Asian Americans, Irish Americans), language ("Hispanics," to use the government category), and religion (Jews). Generally, these ethnic categories are meaningful only in contrast and in relation to other groups.

The term "race" is put in scare quotes because as a biological entity there is no such phenomenon. It does exist, powerfully and consequentially, however, as a social phenomenon.

All countries in the world are multiethnic, even those that have an ideology of homogeneity, such as Japan and Korea. Some celebrate their multiethnicity, like Brazil and, maybe, the United States. Some attempt to eradicate all ethnic differences, as in the "ethnic cleansing" campaigns of Bosnia in the 1990s and former Yugoslavia, and Darfur, Sudan beginning in 2003. (There are usually significant cultural and economic strains leading to this "solution" to social problems.) For many, the ideology of nationalism requires a homogeneous populace, though in reality none has ever existed.

The role of language in the construction of ethnicity can vary quite significantly, from ethnicity based on language (Hispanics in the United States) to language having almost no role (Irish Americans, Jews). The language of others is often stereotyped, in the Ebonics jokes of the 1990s and what Jane Hill calls "Mock Spanish," and pejorative views of speakers with ethnic features are often found throughout the world.

## GENDER

The study of language and gender got its major boost with the publication of Robin Tolmach Lakoff's *Language and Woman's Place* in 1975. Though researchers had written about this topic before, Lakoff's clear style and the feminist movements in the air at the time combined to create a research agenda that has been pursued avidly ever since. Though "gender" meant primarily "women" at the time, it is understood now that the speech of both women and men must be studied; there is no nongendered speech (which is not to say that women's speech is essentially and entirely distinct from men's, and vice versa).

Two principal approaches to the study of language and gender are that (1) women are essentially different from men (though this can be culturally shaped) and (2) women are seen as generally less powerful than men, and thus, they use speech that corresponds to the less powerful party in an interaction.

Some researchers set out to demonstrate absolute differences between women's and men's language, while others showed more of a continuum or more strategic choices dependent on the particular context of use. We could consider the first category *essentialist* and the second *social constructionist*. The latter have built on the idea of "communities of practice," in which speakers' specific choices stem from interactions in particular groups, which may yield language associated stereotypically with their gender—but may not.

Gender interacts with many other aspects of identity, including class, ethnicity, and age. In many ways, the topic of gender has been fully integrated into the study of language in society, as you can see from the many chapters in this book that touch on gender but are placed in different units. The chapters in this unit focus specifically and centrally on language and gender.

## GENERATION

Age is conveyed by many factors, and language also plays a role. Language is never unchanging no matter how static it appears to its speakers. Laments and complaints about the deterioration of language can be found in writings of the ancient Greeks, in Roman times, in the essays of Jonathan Swift, and of course, in the present: the young are destroying Greek/Latin/English/French.... Not only that, but their morals are far inferior to those of their elders!

There is a nugget of truth in these laments, however: language change does seem to originate with youth, whose speech differs ever so slightly, in some cases, or considerably, in others, from that of older speakers. Whether it is in slight differences in pronouncing vowels, in new and shocking vocabulary, or even in grammatical novelty, the changes that begin with teenagers and adolescents sometimes persist. Some of the changes spread upward, as older speakers inadvertently are influenced by the speech of youth, and endure throughout the lifetimes of the teenagers. Over time, such tiny changes can add up, yielding new forms. This is how the Latin of Roman times became the offspring Romance languages. (Such changes also involve physical, political, economic, and social distance.)

Sociolinguists have always studied the combination of age and language change, just as specialists in biological evolution study speciation and diversity/mutations. Language and its specific forms may convey aspects of age and generational identity and are also significant variables in the study of language change. In this section, I provide two studies focused on specific words (*like* and *dude*) that have particular social meaning connected with youth. In the process, you should also be able to learn something about the more general principles of linguistic variation.

Though I have divided this unit into components of region, class, ethnicity, gender, and age, in fact these (and there are more aspects, as well) are all entirely intersecting. At all times we reveal all these facets of our identity— and more.

### Suggested Further Reading

SOCIOLINGUISTIC VARIATION AND THEORY

Eckert, Penelope, and John R. Rickford, eds. 2001. *Style and Sociolinguistic Variation*. Cambridge: Cambridge University Press.

Fought, Carmen, ed. 2004. *Sociolinguistic Variation: Critical Reflections*. Oxford and New York: Oxford University Press.

Hansen, Alan D. 2005. A Practical Task: Ethnicity as a Resource in Social Interaction. *Research on Language and Social Interaction* 38(1): 63–104.

Labov, William. 1972. *Sociolinguistic Patterns*. Philadelphia: University of Pennsylvania Press.

Rampton, Ben. 1995. *Crossing: Language and Ethnicity Among Adolescents*. London and New York: Longman.

Schilling-Estes, Natalie. 2004. Constructing Ethnicity in Interaction. *Journal of Sociolinguistics* 8/2: 163–195.

REGION

Blount, Roy. 2007. *Long Time Leaving: Dispatches from Up South*. New York: Knopf.

Carver, Craig M. 1987. *American Regional Dialects: A Word Geography*. Ann Arbor: University of Michigan Press.

Cassidy, Frederic G. (editor-in-chief). 1985. *Dictionary of American Regional English* (Vol. 1, A–C). Cambridge, MA: Harvard University Press, Belknap.

Cassidy, Frederic G., and Joan Houston Hall, eds. 1991. *Dictionary of American Regional English* (Vol. 2, D–H). Cambridge, MA: Harvard University Press, Belknap.

Cassidy, Frederic G. 1996. *Dictionary of American Regional English* (Vol. 3, I–O). Cambridge, MA: Harvard University Press, Belknap.

Francis, Nelson. 1983. *Dialectology: An Introduction*. New York: Longman.

Francis, Nelson, and Joan Houston Hall (editor-in-chief). 2002. *Dictionary of American Regional English* (Vol. 4, P–Sk). Cambridge, MA: Harvard University Press, Belknap.

Labov, William, Sharon Ash, and Charles Boberg. 2006. *The Atlas of North American English: Phonetics, Phonology, and Sound Change*. Berlin: Mouton de Gruyter.

MacNeil, Robert, and William Cran, eds. 2005. *Do You Speak American?* New York: Doubleday.

Milroy, James. 1992. *Linguistic Variation and Change: On the Historical Sociolinguistics of English*. Oxford: Blackwell.

Trudgill, Peter. 1983. *On Dialect: Social and Geographical Perspectives*. New York: New York University Press.

Trudgill, Peter. 1990. *The Dialects of England*. Cambridge, MA: Blackwell.

Wolfram, Walt. 1991. *Dialects and American English*. Englewood Cliffs, NJ: Prentice Hall.

Wolfram, Walt, and Natalie Schilling-Estes. 2006 [1998]. *American English: Dialects and Variation*. 2nd ed. Malden, MA: Blackwell.

Wolfram, Walt, and Ben Ward, eds. 2006. *American Voices: How Dialects Differ from Coast to Coast*. Malden, MA: Blackwell.

CLASS

Corfield, Penelope J., ed. 1991. *Language, History, and Class*. Oxford: Blackwell.

Edwards, John. 1994. *Multilingualism*. London: Routledge.

Fasold, Ralph. 1984. *The Sociolinguistics of Society*. Oxford: Blackwell.

Fasold, Ralph, 1990. *The Sociolinguistics of Language*. Oxford: Blackwell.

Giglioli, Pier Paolo, ed. 1972. *Language and Social Context*. Harmondsworth: Penguin.

Grillo, Ralph D. 1989. *Dominant Languages: Language and Hierarchy in Britain and France*. Cambridge: Cambridge University Press.

Labov, William. 1972. *Sociolinguistic Patterns*. Philadelphia: University of Pennsylvania Press.

Labov, William. 1996. *The Social Stratification of English in New York City*. Washington, DC: Center for Applied Linguistics.

Macaulay, R. K. S. 1977. *Language, Social Class, and Education: A Glasgow Study*. Edinburgh: University of Edinburgh Press.

Milroy, James. 1991. *Linguistic Variation and Change: On the Historical Sociolinguistics of English*. Oxford: Blackwell.

Milroy, James, and Lesley Milroy. 1985. *Authority in Language: Investigating Language Prescription and Standardization*. London: Routledge & Kegan Paul.

Mugglestone, Lynda. 1995. *"Talking Proper": The Rise of Accent as a Social Symbol*. Oxford: Oxford University Press.

Romaine, Suzanne, ed. 1982. *Sociolinguistic Variation in Speech Communities*. London: Arnold.

Romaine, Suzanne. 2000. *Language in Society: An Introduction to Sociolinguistics*. 2nd ed. Oxford: Oxford University Press.

Trudgill, Peter. 1974. *The Social Differentiation of English in Norwich*. Cambridge: Cambridge University Press.

"RACE" AND ETHNICITY

Abrahams, R. D. 1974. Black Talking on the Street. In *Explorations in the Ethnography of Speaking*, edited by Richard Bauman and Joel Sherzer, pp. 240–262. Cambridge: Cambridge University Press.

American Anthropological Association. Race: Are We So Different? http://www.understandingrace.org/home.html

Baugh, John. 1983. *Black Street Speech: Its History, Structure, and Survival*. Austin: University of Texas Press.

Baugh, John. 1999. *Out of the Mouth of Slaves: African American Language and Educational Malpractice*. Austin: University of Texas Press.

Fought, Carmen. 2003. *Chicano English in Context*. New York and Basingstoke: Palgrave Macmillan.

Gumperz, John J. 1982. *Discourse Strategies*. Cambridge: Cambridge University Press.

Hansen, Alan D. 2005. A Practical Task: Ethnicity as a Resource in Social Interaction. *Research on Language and Social Interaction* 38(1): 63–104.

Herskovitz, Melville J. 1958. *The Myth of the Negro Past*. Boston: Beacon Press.

Hill, Jane H. 1998. Language, Race, and White Public Space. *American Anthropologist* 100: 680–689.

Labov, William. 1972. *Language in the Inner City: Studies in the Black English Vernacular*. Philadelphia: University of Pennsylvania Press.

Leap, William L. 1993. *American Indian English*. Salt Lake City: University of Utah Press.

Morgan, Marcyeliena. 2002. *Language, Discourse, and Power in African American Culture*. Cambridge: Cambridge University Press.

Rampton, Ben. 1995. *Crossing: Language and Ethnicity Among Adolescents*. London and New York: Longman.

Rickford, John R., and Russell J. Rickford. 2000. *Spoken Soul: The Story of Black English*. New York: Wiley.

Schilling-Estes, Natalie. 2004. Constructing Ethnicity in Interaction. *Journal of Sociolinguistics* 8(2): 163–195.

Smitherman, Geneva. 1977. *Talkin and Testifyin: The Language of Black America*. Boston: Houghton Mifflin.

Smitherman, Geneva. 1994. *Black Talk: Words and Phrases from the Hood to the Amen Corner*. Boston: Houghton Mifflin.

Urciuoli, Bonnie. 1996. *Exposing Prejudice: Puerto Rican Experiences of Language, Race, and Class*. Boulder, CO: Westview Press.

Wolfram, Walt, and Erik R. Thomas. 2002. *The Development of African American English*. Malden, MA: Blackwell.

Gender

Bucholtz, Mary, A. C. Liang, and Laurel A. Sutton, eds. 1999. *Reinventing Identities: The Gendered Self in Discourse*. New York: Oxford University Press.

Cameron, Deborah. 1992. *Feminism and Linguistic Theory*. 2nd ed. London: Routledge.

Cameron, Deborah, and Jennifer Coates, eds. 1988. *Women in Their Speech Communities: New Perspectives on Language and Sex*. London: Longman.

Coates, Jennifer, ed. 1998. *Language and Gender: A Reader*. Malden, MA: Blackwell.

Eckert, Penelope, and Sally McConnell-Ginet. 1992. Think Practically and Look Locally: Language and Gender as Community-Based Practice. *Annual Review of Anthropology* 21: 461–490.

Eckert, Penelope, and Sally McConnell-Ginet. 2003. *Language and Gender*. Cambridge: Cambridge University Press.

Goodwin, Marjorie Harness. 1990. *He-Said-She-Said: Talk as Social Organization Among Black Children*. Bloomington: Indiana University Press.

Graddol, David, and Joan Swann. 1989. *Gender Voices*. Oxford: Blackwell.

Hall, Kira, and Mary Bucholtz, eds. 1995. *Gender Articulated: Language and the Socially Constructed Self.* New York and London: Oxford University Press.

Holmes, Janet. 1995. *Women, Men, and Politeness*. London and New York: Longman.

Ide, Sachiko, and Naomi Hanaska McGloin, eds. 1990. *Aspects of Japanese Women's Language*. Tokyo: Kurosio.

Inoue, Miyako. 2006. *Vicarious Language: Gender and Linguistic Modernity in Japan*. Berkeley and Los Angeles: University of California Press.

Irvine, Judith T. 1979. Formality and Informality in Communicative Events. *American Anthropologist* 81(4): 773–790.

Johnson, Sally, and Ulrike Hanna Meinhof, eds. 1997. *Language and Masculinity*. Oxford: Blackwell.

Lakoff, Robin Tolmach. 1975. *Language and Woman's Place*. New York: Harper & Row.

Lakoff, Robin Tolmach. 2004. *Language and Woman's Place: Text and Commentaries*. Revised and expanded edition, edited by Mary Bucholtz. Oxford and New York: Oxford University Press.

Livia, Anna, and Kira Hall, eds. 1997. *Queerly Phrased: Language, Gender, and Sexuality*. Oxford and New York: Oxford University Press.

Mehl, Matthias R., et al. 2007. Are Women Really More Talkative Than Men? *Science* 317 (July 6): 82.

Mori, Kyoko. 1997. *Polite Lies: On Being a Woman Caught Between Cultures*. New York: Holt.

Ochs, Elinor. 1991. Indexing Gender. In *Rethinking Context*, edited by Alessandro Duranti and Charles Goodwin, pp. 335–358. Cambridge: Cambridge University Press.

Philips, Susan U., Susan Steele, and Christine Tanz, eds. 1987. *Language, Gender, and Sex in Comparative Perspective*. Cambridge: Cambridge University Press.

Romaine, Suzanne. 1999. *Communicating Gender*. Mahwah, NJ: Erlbaum.

Smith, Janet Shibamoto. 1985. *Japanese Women's Language*. New York: Academic Press.

Spender, Dale. 1980. *Man Made Language*. London: Routledge & Kegan Paul.

Tannen, Deborah. 1990. *You Just Don't Understand: Women and Men in Conversation*. New York: Ballantine Books.

Thorne, Barrie, and Nancy Henley, eds. 1975. *Language and Sex: Difference and Dominance*. Rowley, MA: Newbury House.

Thorne, Barrie, Cheris Kramarae, and Nancy Henley, eds. 1983. *Language, Gender, and Society*. Rowley, MA: Newbury House.

Generation

Coupland, Nikolas. 2007. *Style: Language Variation and Identity*. Cambridge: Cambridge University Press.

Eckert, Penelope. 1988. *Jocks and Burnouts: Social Categories and Identity in High School*. New York: Teachers College Press.

Eckert, Penelope. 1997. Age as a Sociolinguistic Variable. In *The Handbook of Sociolinguistics*, edited by Florian Coulmas, pp. 151–167. Oxford: Blackwell.

Eckert, Penelope, and John R. Rickford, eds. 2001. *Style and Sociolinguistic Variation*. Cambridge: Cambridge University Press.

Kerswill, Paul. 1996. Children, Adolescents and Language Change. *Language Variation and Change* 8: 177–202.

Labov, William. 1994. *Principles of Linguistic Change. Vol. 1: Internal Factors*. Oxford: Blackwell.

Mendoza-Denton, Norma. 2008. *Homegirls: Language and Cultural Practice Among Latina Youth Gangs*. Malden, MA: Blackwell.

Milroy, James. 1998 [1969]. Children Can't Speak or Write Properly Any More. In *Language Myths*, edited by Laurie Bauer and Peter Trudgill, pp. 58–65. London: Penguin.

Rampton, Ben. 1995. *Crossing: Language and Ethnicity Among Adolescents*. London and New York: Longman.

Romaine, Suzanne. 2000. *Language in Society: An Introduction to Sociolinguistics*. 2nd ed. Oxford: Oxford University Press.

Sankoff, Gillian. 2004. Adolescents, Young Adults, and the Critical Period: Two Case Studies from "Seven Up." In *Sociolinguistic Variation: Critical Reflections*, edited by Carmen Fought, pp. 121–139. Oxford: Oxford University Press.

Trudgill, Peter. 1998 [1990]. The Meanings of Words Should Not Be Allowed to Vary or Change. In *Language Myths*, edited by Laurie Bauer and Peter Trudgill, pp. 1–8. London: Penguin.

# Region and Class

## CHAPTER 29

# The Social Stratification of (r) in New York City Department Stores

*William Labov*

1972 [1966]

*William Labov's classic study—elegant, inexpensive, clear—of New York City department stores showed that people who worked in these stores tended to have the speech corresponding to that of their social class (working class, middle class, upper-middle class) but that this speech lay on a continuum. Further, their speech showed greater similarity to "standard" American English in formal contexts—such as when they had to repeat something—than in casual contexts.*

*Labov's findings are considered "robust." They have been replicated in a wide range of societies and languages, from various areas in England to Belgium, France, and elsewhere. What was especially novel in his account was the observation that the variation in even a given speaker's speech was not random and unpredictable; on the contrary, it could be quantified, predicted, and explained.*

*Labov is well known for both his methodological care and his decades-long attention to dialects, especially in Philadelphia, where it is said he can identify speakers' origins to the block or neighborhood. A recent outgrowth of this work is his editing of the* Atlas of North American English *(with Ash and Boberg). He was one of the first prominent researchers to point out what he called the "logic" of African American English, having developed more appropriate methods of studying the speech of young black men than interviewing them one by one in a formal office. Labov has testified about Black English in several prominent legal cases, helping win recognition that African American Vernacular English, or Black English Vernacular, as it was formerly called, is a genuine, distinct variety of English. He has worked on the question of narrative, which grew out of his attempt to set speakers at ease so he could study their most natural ways of speaking. Finally, he has been working for quite some time on the question of how best to reduce the reading gap for African American children.*

### Reading Questions

- What exactly was Labov trying to find out in the three department stores? Why did he choose the particular phonological variable he did?
- How does (r) differ among the three stores and why?
- What pattern is revealed by the correspondence between participants' age and degree of r-less speech?
- How has (r) changed over time?

---

"As this letter is but a jar of the tongue, . . . it is the most imperfect of all the consonants."

—John Walker, Principles of English Pronunciation. 1791

William Labov, The Social Stratification of (r) in New York City Department Stores. From *Sociolinguistic Patterns*. Philadelphia:University of Pennsylvania Press, 1972, pp. 43–69.

Anyone who begins to study language in its social context immediately encounters the classic methodological problem: the means used to gather the data interfere with the data to be gathered. The primary means of obtaining a large body of reliable data on the speech of one person is the individual tape-recorded interview. Interview speech is formal speech—not by any absolute measure, but by comparison with the vernacular of everyday life. On the whole, the interview is public speech—monitored and controlled in response to the presence of an outside observer. But even within that definition, the investigator may wonder if the responses in a tape-recorded interview are not a special product of the interaction between the interviewer and the subject. One way of controlling for this is to study the subject in his own natural social context—interacting with his family or peer group (Labov, Cohen, Robins, and Lewis 1968). Another way is to observe the public use of language in everyday life apart from any interview situation—to see how people use language in context when there is no explicit observation. This chapter is an account of the systematic use of rapid and anonymous observations in a study of the sociolinguistic structure of the speech community.

This chapter is the first of a series of six which deal primarily with the sociolinguistic study of New York City. The main base for that study (Labov 1966) was a secondary random sample of the Lower East Side.... But before the systematic study was carried out, there was an extensive series of preliminary investigations. These included 70 individual interviews and a great many anonymous observations in public places. These preliminary studies led to the definition of the major **phonological variables** which were to be studied, including (r): the presence or absence of consonantal [r] in **postvocalic** position in *car, card, four, fourth*, etc. This particular variable appeared to be extraordinarily sensitive to any measure of social or stylistic stratification. On the basis of the exploratory interviews, it seemed possible to carry out an empirical test of two general notions: first, that the linguistic variable (r) is a social differentiator in all levels of New York City speech, and second, that rapid and anonymous speech events could be used as the basis for a systematic study of language. The study of (r) in New York City department stores which I will report here was conducted in November 1962 as a test of these ideas.

We can hardly consider the social distribution of language in New York City without encountering the pattern of **social stratification** which pervades the life of the city. This concept is analyzed in some detail in the major study of the Lower East Side; here we may briefly consider the definition given by Bernard Barber: social stratification is the product of social differentiation and social evaluation (1957:1–3). The use of this term does not imply any specific type of class or caste, but simply that the normal workings of society have produced systematic differences between certain institutions or people, and that these differentiated forms have been ranked in status or prestige by general agreement.

We begin with the general hypothesis suggested by exploratory interviews: *if any two subgroups of New York City speakers are ranked in a scale of social stratification, then they will be ranked in the same order by their differential use of (r).*

It would be easy to test this hypothesis by comparing occupational groups, which are among the most important indexes of social stratification. We could, for example, take a group of lawyers, a group of file clerks, and a group of janitors. But this would hardly go beyond the indications of the exploratory interviews, and such an extreme example of differentiation would not provide a very exacting test of the hypothesis. It should be possible to show that the hypothesis is so general, and the differential use of (r) pervades New York City so thoroughly, that fine social differences will be reflected in the index as well as gross ones.

It therefore seemed best to construct a very severe test by finding a subtle case of stratification within a single occupational group: in this case, the sales people of large department stores in Manhattan. If we select three large department stores, from the top, middle, and bottom of the price and fashion scale, we can expect that the customers will be socially stratified. Would we expect the sales people to show a comparable stratification? Such a position would depend upon two correlations: between the status ranking of the stores and the ranking of parallel jobs in the three stores; and between the jobs and the behavior of the persons who hold those jobs. These are not unreasonable assumptions. C. Wright Mills points out that salesgirls in large department stores tend to borrow prestige from their customers, or at least make an effort in that direction.[1] It appears that a person's own occupation is more closely correlated with his linguistic behavior—for those working actively—than any other single social characteristic. The evidence presented here indicates that the stores are objectively differentiated in a fixed order, and that jobs in these stores are evaluated by employees in that order. Since the product of social differentiation and evaluation, no matter how minor, is social stratification of the employees in the three stores, the hypothesis will predict the following result: salespeople in the highest-ranked store will have the highest values of (r); those in the middle-ranked store will have intermediate values of (r); and those in the lowest-ranked store will show the lowest values. If this result holds true, the hypothesis will have received confirmation in proportion to the severity of the test.

The three stores which were selected are Saks Fifth Avenue, Macy's, and S. Klein. The differential ranking of these stores may be illustrated in many ways. Their locations are one important point:

Highest-ranking: Saks Fifth Avenue
at 50th St. and Fifth Ave., near the center of the high-fashion shopping district, along with other high-prestige stores such as Bonwit Teller, Henri Bendel, Lord and Taylor

Middle-ranking: Macy's
Herald Square, 34th St. and Sixth Ave., near the garment district, along with Gimbels and Saks-34th St., other middle-range stores in price and prestige
Lowest-ranking: S. Klein
Union Square, 14th St. and Broadway, not far from the Lower East Side

The advertising and price policies of the stores are very clearly stratified. Perhaps no other element of class behavior is so sharply differentiated in New York City as that of the newspaper which people read; many surveys have shown that the *Daily News* is the paper read first and foremost by working-class people, while the *New York Times* draws its readership from the middle class.[2] These two newspapers were examined for the advertising copy in October 24–27, 1962: Saks and Macy's advertised in the *New York Times*, where Kleins was represented only by a very small item; in the *News*, however, Saks does not appear at all, while both Macy's and Kleins are heavy advertisers.

**No. of pages of advertising October 24–27, 1962**

| | NY Times | Daily News |
|---|---|---|
| Saks | 2 | 0 |
| Macy's | 6 | 15 |
| S. Klein | ¼ | 10 |

We may also consider the prices of the goods advertised during those four days. Since Saks usually does not list prices, we can only compare prices for all three stores on one item: women's coats. Saks: $90.00, Macy's: $79.95, Kleins: $23.00. On four items, we can compare Kleins and Macy's:

| | Macy's | S. Klein |
|---|---|---|
| Dresses | $14.95 | $5.00 |
| Girls' coats | 16.99 | 12.00 |
| Stockings | 0.89 | 0.45 |
| Men's suits | 49.95–64.95 | 26.00–66.00 |

The emphasis on prices is also different. Saks either does not mention prices, or buries the figure in small type at the foot of the page. Macy's features the prices in large type, but often adds the slogan, "You get more than low prices." Kleins, on the other hand, is often content to let the prices speak for themselves. The form of the prices is also different: Saks gives prices in round figures, such as $120; Macy's always shows a few cents off the dollar: $49.95; Kleins usually prices its goods in round numbers, and adds the retail price which is always much higher, and shown in Macy's style: "$23.00, marked down from $49.95."

The physical plant of the stores also serves to differentiate them. Saks is the most spacious, especially on the upper floors, with the least amount of goods displayed. Many of the floors are carpeted, and on some of them, a receptionist is stationed to greet the customers. Kleins, at the other extreme, is a maze of annexes, sloping concrete floors, low ceilings; it has the maximum amount of goods displayed at the least possible expense.

The principal stratifying effect upon the employees is the prestige of the store, and the working conditions. Wages do not stratify the employees in the same order. On the contrary, there is every indication that high-prestige stores such as Saks pay lower wages than Macy's.

Saks is a nonunion store, and the general wage structure is not a matter of public record. However, conversations with a number of men and women who have worked in New York department stores, including Saks and Macy's, show general agreement on the direction of the wage differential.[3] Some of the incidents reflect a willingness of sales people to accept much lower wages from the store with greater prestige. The executives of the prestige stores pay a great deal of attention to employee relations, and take many unusual measures to ensure that the sales people feel that they share in the general prestige of the store.[4] One of the Lower East Side informants who worked at Saks was chiefly impressed with the fact that she could buy Saks clothes at a 25 percent discount. A similar concession from a lower-prestige store would have been of little interest to her.

From the point of view of Macy's employees, a job in Kleins is well below the horizon. Working conditions and wages are generally considered to be worse, and the prestige of Kleins is very low indeed. As we will see, the ethnic composition of the store employees reflects these differences quite accurately.

A socioeconomic index which ranked New Yorkers on occupation would show the employees of the three stores at the same level; an income scale would probably find Macy's employees somewhat higher than the others; education is the only objective scale which might differentiate the groups in the same order as the prestige of the stores, though there is no evidence on this point. However, the working conditions of sales jobs in the three stores stratify them in the order: Saks, Macy's, Kleins; the prestige of the stores leads to a social evaluation of these jobs in the same order. Thus the two aspects of social stratification—differentiation and evaluation—are to be seen in the relations of the three stores and their employees.

The normal approach to a survey of department store employees requires that one enumerate the sales people of each store, draw random samples in each store, make appointments to speak with each employee at home, interview the respondents, then segregate the native New Yorkers, analyze and resample the nonrespondents, and so on. This is an expensive and time-consuming procedure, but for most purposes there is no short cut which will give accurate and reliable results. In this case, a simpler method which relies upon the extreme generality of the linguistic behavior of the subjects was used to gather a very limited type of data. This method is dependent upon the systematic sampling of casual and anonymous speech events. Applied in a poorly defined environment, such a method is open to many biases and it would be difficult to say what population had been studied. In this case, our population is well defined as the sales people (or more generally, any employee whose speech might be heard by a customer) in three specific stores at a specific time. The result will be a view of the role that speech would play in the overall social imprint of the employees upon the customer. It is surprising that this simple and economical approach achieves results with a high degree of consistency and regularity, and allows us to test the original hypothesis in a number of subtle ways.

## The Method

The application of the study of casual and anonymous speech events to the department-store situation was relatively simple. The interviewer approached the informant in the role of a customer asking for directions to a particular department. The department was one which was located on the fourth floor. When the interviewer asked, "Excuse me, where are the women's shoes?" the answer would normally be, "Fourth floor."

The interviewer then leaned forward and said, "Excuse me?" He would usually then obtain another utterance, *"Fourth floor,"* spoken in careful style under emphatic stress.[5]

The interviewer would then move along the aisle of the store to a point immediately beyond the informant's view, and make a written note of the data. The following independent variables were included:

the store
floor within the store[6]
sex
age (estimated in units of five years)
occupation (floorwalker, sales, cashier, stockboy)
race
foreign or regional accent, if any

The dependent variable is the use of (r) in four occurrences:

casual: fou<u>r</u>th floo<u>r</u>
emphatic: *fou<u>r</u>th floo<u>r</u>*

Thus we have **preconsonantal** and final position, in both casual and emphatic styles of speech. In addition, all other uses of (r) by the informant were noted, from remarks overheard or contained in the interview. For each plainly constricted value of the variable, (r-1) was entered; for unconstricted **schwa,** lengthened vowel, or no representation, (r-0) was entered. Doubtful cases or partial constriction were symbolized *d* and were not used in the final tabulation.

Also noted were instances of **affricates** or **stops** used in the word *fourth* for the final consonant, and any other examples of nonstandard (th) variants used by the speaker.

This method of interviewing was applied in each aisle on the floor as many times as possible before the spacing of the informants became so close that it was noticed that the same question had been asked before. Each floor of the store was investigated in the same way. On the fourth floor, the form of the question was necessarily different:

"Excuse me, what floor is this?"

Following this method, 68 interviews were obtained in Saks, 125 in Macy's, and 71 in Kleins. Total interviewing time for the 264 subjects was approximately 6.5 hours.

At this point, we might consider the nature of these 264 interviews in more general terms. They were speech events which had entirely different social significance for the two participants. As far as the informant was concerned, the exchange was a normal salesman-customer interaction, almost below the level of conscious attention, in which relations of the speakers were so casual and anonymous that they may hardly have been said to have met. This tenuous relationship was the minimum intrusion upon the behavior of the subject; language and the use of language never appeared at all.

From the point of view of the interviewer, the exchange was a systematic elicitation of the exact forms required, in the desired context, the desired order, and with the desired contrast of style.

## Overall Stratification of (r)

The results of the study showed clear and consistent stratification of (r) in the three stores. In Figure 29.1, the use of (r) by employees of Saks, Macy's, and Kleins is compared by means of a bar graph. Since the data for most informants consist of only four items, we will not use a continuous numerical index for (r), but rather divide all informants into three categories.

all (r-1): those whose records show only (r-1) and no (r-0)
some (r-1): those whose records show at least one (r-1) and one (r-0)
no (r-1): those whose records show only (r-0)

From Figure 29.1 we see that a total of 62 percent of Saks employees, 51 percent of Macy's, and 20 percent of Kleins used all or some (r-1). The stratification is even sharper for the percentages of all (r-1). As the hypothesis predicted, the groups are ranked by their differential use of (r-1) in the same order as their stratification by extralinguistic factors.

Next, we may wish to examine the distribution of (r) in each of the four standard positions. Figure 29.2 shows this type of display, where once again, the stores are differentiated

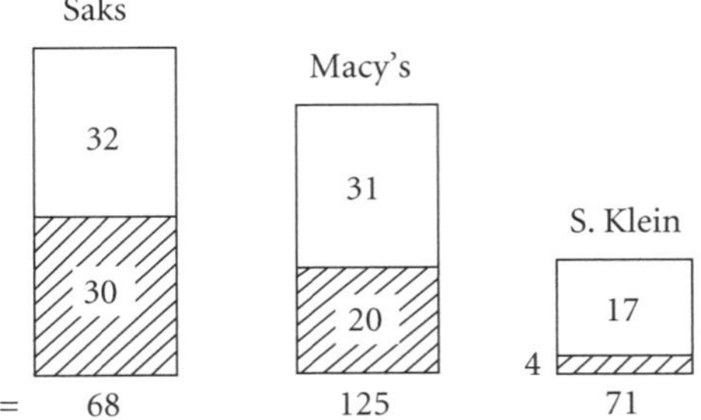


**Figure 29.1** *Overall stratification of (r) by store. Shaded area = % all (r-1); unshaded area = % some (r-1); % no (r-1) not shown; N = total number of cases.*

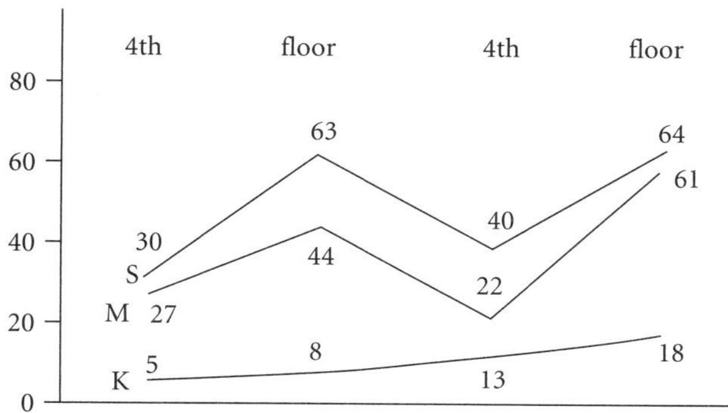


**Figure 29.2** *Percentage of all (r-1) by store for four positions (S = Saks, M = Macy's, K = Kleins).*

in the same order, and for each position. There is a considerable difference between Macy's and Kleins at each position, but the difference between Macy's and Saks varies. In emphatic pronunciation of the final (r), Macy's employees come very close to the mark set by Saks. It would seem that *r*-pronunciation is the norm at which a majority of Macy's employees aim, yet not the one they use most often. In Saks, we see a shift between casual and emphatic pronunciation, but it is much less marked. In other words, Saks employees have more *security* in a linguistic sense.[7]

The fact that the figures for (r-1) at Kleins are low should not obscure the fact that Kleins employees also participate in the same pattern of stylistic variation of (r) as the other stores. The percentage of *r*-pronunciation rises at Kleins from 5 to 18 percent as the context becomes more emphatic: a much greater rise in percentage than in the other stores, and a more regular increase as well. It will be important to bear in mind that this attitude—that (r-1) is the most appropriate pronunciation for emphatic speech—is shared by at least some speakers in all three stores.

Table 29.1 shows the data in detail, with the number of instances obtained for each of the four positions of (r), for each store. It may be noted that the number of occurrences in the second pronunciation of *four* is considerably reduced, primarily as a result of some speakers' tendency to answer a second time, "Fourth."

**Table 29.1** Detailed Distribution of (r) by Store and Word Position

| | Saks | | | | Macy's | | | | S. Klein | | | |
|---|---|---|---|---|---|---|---|---|---|---|---|---|
| (r) | Casual 4th floor | | Emphatic 4th floor | | Casual 4th floor | | Emphatic 4th floor | | Casual 4th floor | | Emphatic 4th floor | |
| (r-1) | 17 | 31 | 16 | 21 | 33 | 48 | 13 | 31 | 3 | 5 | 6 | 7 |
| (r-0) | 39 | 18 | 24 | 12 | 81 | 62 | 48 | 20 | 63 | 59 | 40 | 33 |
| *d* | 4 | 5 | 4 | 4 | 0 | 3 | 1 | 0 | 1 | 1 | 3 | 3 |
| No data* | 8 | 14 | 24 | 31 | 11 | 12 | 63 | 74 | 4 | 6 | 22 | 28 |
| Total no. | 68 | 68 | 68 | 68 | 125 | 125 | 125 | 125 | 71 | 71 | 71 | 71 |

* The "no data" category for Macy's shows relatively high values under the emphatic category. This discrepancy is due to the fact that the procedure for requesting repetition was not standardized in the investigation of the ground floor at Macy's, and values for emphatic response were not regularly obtained. The effects of this loss are checked in Table 29.2, where only complete responses are compared.

**Table 29.2** Distribution of (r) for Complete Responses

| (r) | | % of Total responses in Saks | Macy's | S. Klein |
|---|---|---|---|---|
| All (r-1) | 1 1 1 1 | 24 | 22 | 6 |
| Some (r-1) | 0 1 1 1 | 46 | 37 | 12 |
| | 0 0 1 1 | | | |
| | 0 1 0 1 etc. | | | |
| No (r-1) | 0 0 0 0 | 30 | 41 | 82 |
| | | 100 | 100 | 100 |
| *N* = | | 33 | 48 | 34 |

Since the numbers in the fourth position are somewhat smaller than the second, it might be suspected that those who use [r] in Saks and Macy's tend to give fuller responses, thus giving rise to a spurious impression of increase in (r) values in those positions. We can check this point by comparing only those who gave a complete response. Their responses can be symbolized by a four-digit number, representing the pronunciation in each of the four positions respectively (see Table 29.2).

Thus we see that the pattern of differential ranking in the use of (r) is preserved in this subgroup of complete responses, and omission of the final "floor" by some respondents was not a factor in this pattern.

## The Effect of Other Independent Variables

Other factors, besides the stratification of the stores, may explain the regular pattern of *r*-pronunciation seen above, or this effect may be the contribution of a particular group in the population, rather than the behavior of the sales people as a whole. The other independent variables recorded in the interviews enable us to check such possibilities.

### Race

There are many more black employees in the Kleins sample than in Macy's, and more in Macy's than in Saks. Table 29.3 shows the percentages of black informants and their responses. When we compare these figures with those of Figure 29.1, for the entire population, it is evident that the presence of many black informants will contribute to a lower use of (r-1). The black subjects at Macy's used less (r-1) than the white informants, though only to a slight extent; the black subjects at Kleins were considerably more biased in the *r*-less direction.

The higher percentage of black sales people in the lower-ranking stores is consistent with the general pattern of social stratification, since in general, black workers have been assigned less desirable jobs. Therefore the contribution of black speakers to the overall pattern is consistent with the hypothesis.

**Table 29.3** Distribution of (r) for Black Employees

| (r) | % of Responses in Saks | Macy's | S. Klein |
|---|---|---|---|
| All (r-1) | 50 | 12 | 0 |
| Some (r-1) | 0 | 35 | 6 |
| No (r-1) | 50 | 53 | 94 |
| | 100 | 100 | 100 |
| *N* = | 2 | 17 | 18 |
| % of black informants: | 03 | 14 | 25 |

## Occupation

There are other differences in the populations of the stores. The types of occupations among the employees who are accessible to customers are quite different. In Macy's, the employees who were interviewed could be identified as floorwalkers (by red and white carnations), sales people, cashiers, stockboys, and elevator operators. In Saks, the cashiers are not accessible to the customer, working behind the sales counters, and stockboys are not seen. The working operation of the store goes on behind the scenes, and does not intrude upon the customer's notice. On the other hand, at Kleins, all of the employees seem to be operating on the same level: it is difficult to tell the difference between sales people, managers, and stockboys.

Here again, the extralinguistic stratification of the stores is reinforced by objective observations in the course of the interview. We can question if these differences are not responsible for at least a part of the stratification of (r). For the strongest possible result, it would be desirable to show that the stratification of (r) is a property of the most homogeneous subgroup in the three stores: native New York, white sales women. Setting aside the male employees, all occupations besides selling itself, the black and Puerto Rican employees, and all those with a foreign accent,[8] there are still a total of 141 informants to study.

Figure 29.3 shows the percentages of (r-1) used by the native white sales women of the three stores, with the same type of graph as in Figure 29.1. The stratification is essentially the same in direction and outline, though somewhat smaller in magnitude. The greatly reduced Kleins sample still shows by far the lowest use of (r-1), and Saks is ahead of Macy's in this respect. We can therefore conclude that the stratification of (r) is a process which affects every section of the sample.

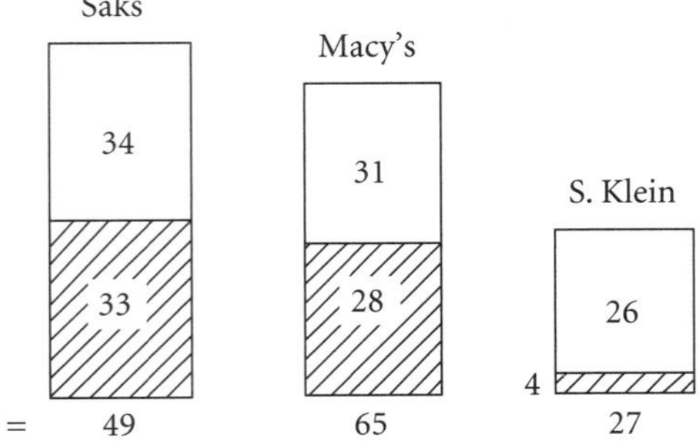


**Figure 29.3** *Stratification of (r) by store for native New York white sales women. Shaded area = % all (r-1); unshaded area = % some (r-1); % no (r-1) not shown; N = total number of cases.*

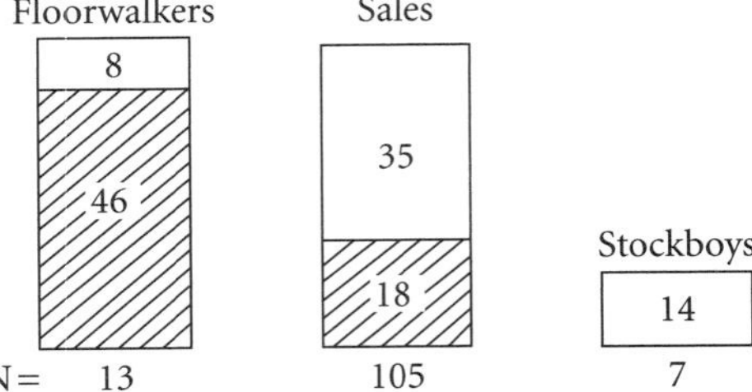


**Figure 29.4** *Stratification of (r) by occupational groups in Macy's. Shaded area = % all (r-1); unshaded area = % some (r-1); % no (r-1) not shown. N = total number of cases.*

We can now turn the heterogeneous nature of the Macy's sample to advantage. Figure 29.4 shows the stratification of (r) according to occupational groups in Macy's: in line with our initial hypothesis, this is much sharper than the stratification of the employees in general. The total percentage of those who use all or some (r-1) is almost the same for the floorwalkers and the sales people but a much higher percentage of floorwalkers consistently use (r-1).

Another interesting comparison may be made at Saks, where there is a great discrepancy between the ground floor and the upper floors. The ground floor of Saks looks very much like Macy's: many crowded counters, salesgirls leaning over the counters, almost elbow to elbow, and a great deal of merchandise displayed. But the upper floors of Saks are far more spacious; there are long vistas of empty carpeting, and on the floors devoted to high fashion, there are models who display the individual garments to the customers. Receptionists are stationed at strategic points to screen out the casual spectators from the serious buyers.

It would seem logical then, to compare the ground floor of Saks with the upper floors. By the hypothesis, we should find a differential use of (r-1). Table 29.4 shows that this is the case.

In the course of the interview, information was also collected on the (th) variable, particularly as it occurred in the word *fourth*. This is one of the major variables used in the study of social stratification in New York (Labov 1966) and elsewhere (Wolfram 1969; Anshen 1969). The most strongly stigmatized variant is the use of the stop [t]

**Table 29.4** Distribution of (r) by Floor in Saks

| (r) | Ground floor | Upper floors |
|---|---|---|
| % all (r-1) | 23 | 34 |
| % some (r-1) | 23 | 40 |
| % no (r-1) | 54 | 26 |
| | 100 | 100 |
| *N* = | 30 | 38 |

in *fourth, through, think*, etc. The percentage of speakers who used stops in this position was fully in accord with the other measures of social stratification which we have seen:

| | |
|---|---|
| Saks | 00% |
| Macy's | 04 |
| S. Klein | 15 |

Thus the hypothesis has received a number of semi-independent confirmations. Considering the economy with which the information was obtained, the survey appears to yield rich results. It is true that we do not know a great deal about the informants that we would like to know: their birthplace, language history, education, participation in New York culture, and so on. Nevertheless, the regularities of the underlying pattern are strong enough to overcome this lack of precision in the selection and identification of informants.

## DIFFERENTIATION BY AGE OF THE INFORMANTS

The age of the informants was estimated within five-year intervals, and these figures cannot be considered reliable for any but the simplest kind of comparison. However, it should be possible to break down the age groups into three units, and detect any overall direction of change.

If, as we have indicated, (r-1) is one of the chief characteristics of a new prestige pattern which is being superimposed upon the native New York City pattern, we would expect to see a rise in *r*-pronunciation among the younger sales people. The overall distribution by age shows no evidence of change, however, in Table 29.5.

**Table 29.5** Distribution of (r) by Estimated Age

| | Age Groups | | |
|---|---|---|---|
| (r) | 15–30 | 35–50 | 55–70 |
| % all (r-1) | 24 | 20 | 20 |
| % some (r-1) | 21 | 28 | 22 |
| % no (r-1) | 55 | 52 | 58 |

This lack of direction is surprising, in the light of other evidence that the use of (r-1) as a prestige variant is increasing among younger people in New York City. There is clearcut evidence for the absence of (r-1) in New York City in the 1930s (Kurath and McDavid 1951) and a subsequent increase in the records of Hubbell (1950) and Bronstein (1962). When we examine the distributions for the individual stores, we find that the even distribution through age levels disappears. Figure 29.5 shows that the expected inverse correlation with age appears in Saks, but not in Macy's or Kleins. Instead, Macy's shows the reverse direction at a lower level, with older subjects using more (r-1), and Kleins no particular correlation with age. This complex pattern is even more puzzling, and one is tempted to dismiss it as the absence of any pattern. But although the numbers of the subgroups may appear to be small, they are larger than many of the subgroups used in the discussions of previous pages, and as we will see, it is not possible to discount the results.

The conundrum represented by Figure 29.5 is one of the most significant results of the procedures that have been followed to this point. Where all other findings con-

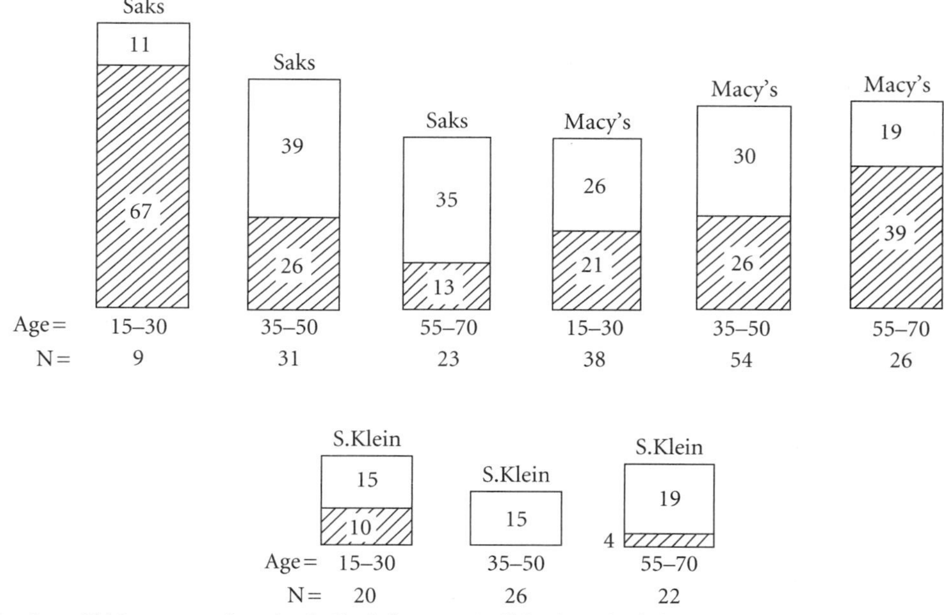


**Figure 29.5** *Stratification of (r) by store and age level. Shaded area = % all (r-1); unshaded area = % some (r-1); % no (r-1) not shown; N = total number of cases.*

firm the original hypothesis, a single result which does not fit the expected pattern may turn our attention in new and profitable directions. From the data in the department store survey alone, it was not possible to account for Figure 29.5 except in speculative terms. In the original report on the department store survey, written shortly after the work was completed, we commented:

> How can we account for the differences between Saks and Macy's? I think we can say this: the shift from the influence of the New England prestige pattern (*r*-less) to the Midwestern prestige pattern (*r*-ful) is felt most completely at Saks. The younger people at Saks are under the influence of the *r*-pronouncing pattern, and the older ones are not. At Macy's, there is less sensitivity to the effect among a large number of younger speakers who are completely immersed in the New York City linguistic tradition. The stockboys, the young salesgirls, are not as yet fully aware of the prestige attached to *r*-pronunciation. On the other hand, the older people at Macy's tend to adopt this pronunciation: very few of them rely upon the older pattern of prestige pronunciation which supports the *r*-less tendency of older Saks sales people. This is a rather complicated argument, which would certainly have to be tested very thoroughly by longer interviews in both stores before it could be accepted.

The complex pattern of Figure 29.5 offered a considerable challenge for interpretation and explanation, but one possibility that always had to be considered was that it was the product of the many sources of error inherent in rapid and anonymous surveys. To confirm and explain the results of the department store survey it will be necessary to [anticipate] the results of [our] systematic interviewing program (Labov 1972b, Chs. 3–7). When the results of [our] major study of the Lower East Side were analyzed, it became clear that Figure 29.5 was not an artifact of the method but reflected real social patterns (Labov 1966: 342 ff). The Lower East Side data most comparable to the department store study are the distribution of (r) by age and class in Style B—the relatively careful speech which is the main bulk of the individual interview.... To Saks, Macy's, and Kleins, we can compare upper middle class, lower middle class, and working class as a whole. The age ranges which are most comparable to the department store ranges are 20–29, 30–39, and 40–. (Since the department store estimates are quite rough, there would be no gain in trying to match the figures exactly.) Figure 29.6 is then the age and class display for the Lower East Side use of (r) most comparable to Figure 29.5. Again, we see that the highest-status group shows the inverse correlation of (r-1) with age: younger speakers use more (r-1); the second-highest-status group shows (r) at a lower level and the reverse correlation with age; and the working-class groups at a still lower level with no particular correlation with age.

This is a very striking confirmation, since the two studies have quite complementary sources of error. The Lower East Side survey was a secondary random sample, based on a Mobilization for Youth survey, with complete demographic information on each informant. The interviews were tape-recorded, and a great deal of data on (r) was obtained from each speaker in a wide variety of styles. On the other hand, the department store study involved a much greater likelihood of error on a number of counts: the small amount of data per informant, the method of notation, the absence of tape recording and reliance on short-term memory, the method of sampling, the estimation of age of the informant, and the lack of background data on the informants. Most of these sources of error are inherent in the method. To compensate for them, we had the uniformity of the interview procedure, the location of the informants in their primary role as employees, the larger number of cases within a single cell, the simplicity of the data, and above all the absence of the biasing effect of the formal linguistic interview. The Lower East Side [LES] survey was weak in just those areas where the department store [DS] study was strong, and strong where it was weak. The methodological differences are summed up in the table below.

| | Lower East Side Survey | Department Store Study |
|---|---|---|
| LES > DS | | |
| Sampling | Random | Informants available at specific locations |
| Recording of data | Tape-recorded | Short-term memory and notes |
| Demographic data | Complete | Minimal: by inspection and inference |
| Amount of data | Large | Small |
| Stylistic range | Wide | Narrow |

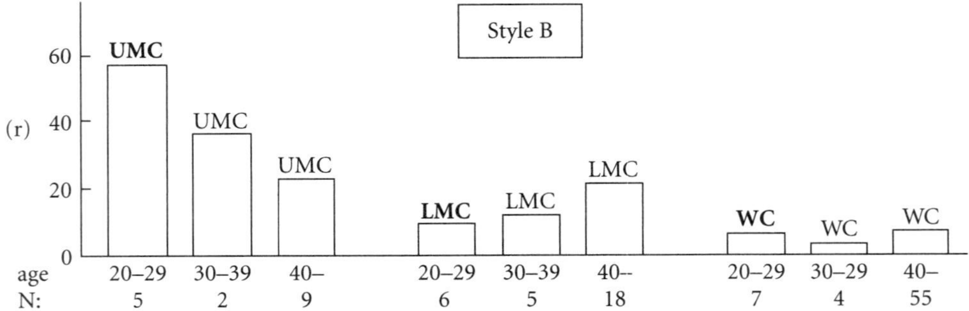


**Figure 29.6** *Classification of (r) by age and class on the Lower East Side: in style B, careful speech.*

| DS > LES | | |
|---|---|---|
| Size of sample | Moderate | Large |
| Location | Home, alone | At work, with others |
| Social context | Interview | Request for information |
| Effect of observation | Maximal | Minimal |
| Total time per subject (location and interview) | 4–8 hours | 5 minutes |

The convergence of the Lower East Side survey and the department store survey therefore represents the ideal solution to the Observer's Paradox [Labov 1972b, Ch. 8]: that our goal is to observe the way people use language when they are not being observed. All of our methods involve an approximation to this goal: when we approach from two different directions, and get the same result, we can feel confident that we have reached past the Observer's Paradox to the structure that exists independently of the analyst.

Given the pattern of Figure 29.5 as a social fact, how can we explain it? The suggestions advanced in our preliminary note seem to be moving in the right direction, but at that time we had not isolated the **hypercorrect** pattern of the lower middle class nor identified the **crossover pattern** characteristic of change in progress. We must draw more material from the later research to solve this problem.

Figures 29.5 and 29.6 are truncated views of the three-dimensional distribution of the new *r*-pronouncing norm by age, style, and social class. Figure 29.7 shows two of the stylistic cross sections from the more detailed study of the Lower East Side population, with four subdivisions by age. The [dashed] line shows us how the highest-status group (Class 9) introduces the new *r*-pronouncing norm in casual speech. In Style A only upper-middle-class speakers under 40 show any sizable amount of (r-1). None of the younger speakers in the other social groups show any response to this norm in Style A, though some effect can be seen in the middle-aged subjects, especially in the second-highest-status group (Class 6–8, lower middle class). In Style B, this imitative effect is exaggerated, with the middle-aged lower-middle-class group coming very close to the upper-middle-class norm. In more formal styles, not shown here, this subgroup shows an even sharper increase in *r*-pronunciation, going beyond the upper-middle-class norm in the "hypercorrect" pattern that has appeared for this group in other studies (see Levine and Crockett 1966; Shuy, Wolfram, and Riley 1967;) [Labov 1972b, Ch. 5]). Figure 29.7 is not a case of the reversal of the age distribution of (r-1); rather it is a one-generation lag in the peak of response to the new norm. The second-highest status group responds to the new norm with a weaker form of imitation in connected speech, with middle-aged speakers adopting the new norm of the younger high-status speakers; Figure 29.8 shows this schematically. Our studies do not give the exact profile of the use of (r) among younger upper-middle-class

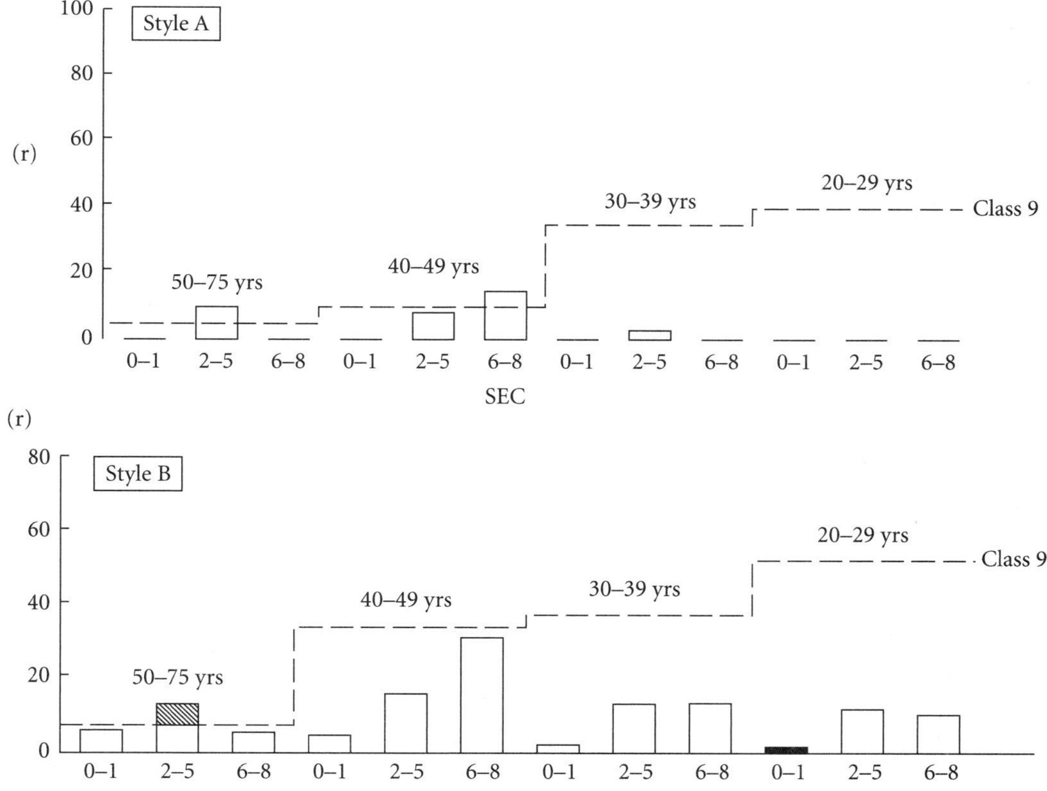


**Figure 29.7** *Development of class stratification of (r) for casual speech (Style A) and careful speech (Style B) in apparent time;* **SEC** = *socioeconomic class scale.*

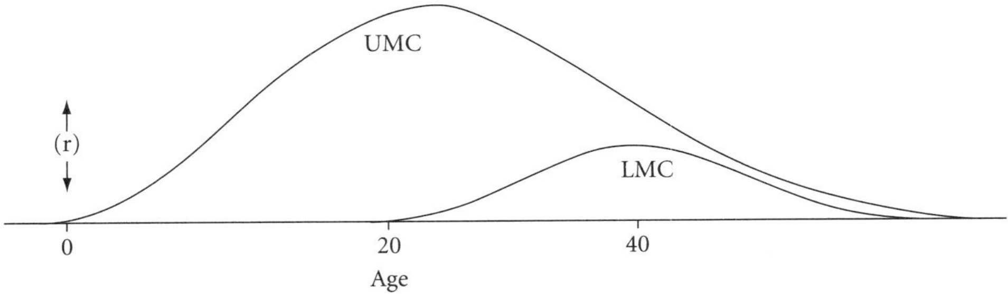


**Figure 29.8** *Hypothetical distribution of (r) as an incoming prestige feature.*

speakers, since we did not focus on that age range. In later observations, I have met some upper-middle-class youth who use 100 percent (r-1), but in most families, (r-1) is still a superposed pronunciation in adolescence and Figure 29.8 reflects this. If we wish to express the (r-1) distribution in a single function, we can say that it is inversely correlated with distance from the highest-status group (taking Class 9 as 1, Classes 6–8 as 2, Classes 2–5 as 3, and Classes 0–1 as 4). It is also directly correlated with the formality of style and the amount of attention paid to speech (taking casual speech, Style A, as 0, careful speech, Style B, as 1, etc.). The slope of style shifting is modified by a function which may be called the "Index of Linguistic Insecurity" (ILI), which is maximized for the second-highest-status group.... The age distribution must be shown as greatest for the upper middle class at age 20 and at age 40 for the lower middle class. We can formalize these observations by writing

(r-1) = –a (Class) + b (Style)(ILI) – c|(Class) · 20 – (Age)| + d

The third term is minimized for the upper middle class at age 20, for the lower middle class at age 40, the working class at age 60, etc. Figure 29.7 supports this semiquantitative expression of a wave effect, which still has a number of unspecified constants.

There is a considerable difference between the behavior of the highest-status group and the others. The upper middle class develops the use of (r-1) early in life—as a variable expression of relative formality to be found at all stylistic levels. For the other groups in New York City, there is no solid basis for (r-1) in the vernacular style of casual speech; for them, (r-1) is a form which requires some attention paid to speech if it is realized at all. As in so many other formal marks of style-shifting, the lower middle class overdoes the process of correction. This is a process learned late in life. When speakers who are now 40–50 were growing up, the prestige norm was not (r-1) but (r-0). Before World War II, the New York City schools were dominated by an Anglophile tradition which taught that (r-1) was a provincial feature, an incorrect inversion of the consonant, and that the correct pronunciation of **orthographic** *r* in *car* was (r-0), [*ka* · ], in accordance with "international English."[9] No adjustment in the pronunciation of this consonant was then necessary for New Yorkers who were trying to use the prestige norm—it was only vowel quality which had to be corrected. This *r*-less norm can be seen in the formal speech of upper-middle-class speakers over 40, and lower-middle-class speakers over 50. It also appears in subjective-reaction tests for older speakers. The lower-middle-class speakers who now shift to (r-1) in formal styles have abandoned their prestige norm and are responding to the form used by the younger high-status speakers that they come into contact with. On the other hand, many upper-middle-class speakers adhere to their original norm, in defiance of the prevailing trend. The pattern which we have observed in the department store survey is therefore a reflection of the **linguistic insecurity** of the lower middle class, which has led the older generation to adopt the most recent norm of (r-1) in preference to the older norm. The process of linguistic socialization is slower for lower-middle-class groups who do not go to college than for upper-middle-class speakers, who begin adjusting to the new norm in the upper class tracks of the academic high schools. For those who do not follow this path, it takes 10 or 20 years to reach maximum sensitivity to the hierarchical organization of formal language in their community.

## Some Methodological Directions

The most important conclusion of the department store study is that rapid and anonymous studies can be a valuable source of information on the sociolinguistic structure of a speech community. There are a number of directions in which we can extend and improve such methods. While some sources of error are inherent in the method, others can be eliminated with sufficient attention.

In the department store survey, the approach to sampling might have been more systematic. It would have been preferable to select every *nth* sales person, or to use some other method that would avoid the bias of selecting the most available subject in a given area. As long as such a method does not interfere with the unobtrusive character of the speech event, it would reduce sampling bias without decreasing efficiency. Another limitation is that the data were not tape-recorded. The transcriber, myself, knew what the object of the test was, and it is always possible that an unconscious bias in transcription would lead to some doubtful cases being recorded as (r-1) in Saks, and as (r-0) in Kleins.[10] A third limitation is in the method used to elicit emphatic speech. Figure 29.2 indicates that the effect of stylistic variation may be slight as compared to the internal phonological constraint of preconsonantal vs. final position. The total percentages for all three stores bear this out.

| % of All (r-1) for Each Position | | | |
|---|---|---|---|
| **Casual** | | **Emphatic** | |
| *fourth* | *floor* | *fourth* | *floor* |
| 23 | 39 | 24 | 48 |

A simple request for repetition has only a limited effect in inducing more formal speech. The use of reading passages, word lists, and minimal pairs in the Lower East Side study gave a wider range of styles. It might be possible to enlarge the stylistic range in rapid and anonymous studies by emphasizing the difficulty in hearing by one technique or another.

The sources of error in the department store study are offset by the comparability of the three subsections, the size of the sample, and the availability of the population for rechecking. Though the individual speakers cannot be relocated, the representative population can easily be reexamined for longitudinal studies of change in progress. There are limitations of such a "pseudopanel" as compared to a true panel study of the same individuals; but the advantages in cost and efficiency are overwhelming.

With such promising results in hand, it should be possible to refine and improve the methods used, and apply them in a wider range of contexts. In large cities it is reasonable to select single large institutions like department stores, but there is no reason to limit rapid and anonymous surveys to sales people or to institutions of this character. We can turn to any large body of individuals located at fixed "social addresses" and accessible to interaction with the public: policemen, postal clerks, secretaries, ushers, guides, bus drivers, taxi drivers, street peddlers and demonstrators, beggars, construction workers, etc. The public groups which are most clearly identified tend to be concentrated towards the lower end of the social scale, with sales people at the upper end. But we can reach a more general public by considering shoppers, spectators at sports events, parades, or construction sites, amateur gardeners, park strollers, and passersby in general; here the general character of the residential area can serve the same differentiating function as the three department stores mentioned above. Many professionals of relatively high social standing are available for public interaction: particularly teachers, doctors, and lawyers. Such public events as courtroom trials and public hearings allow us to monitor the speech of a wide range of socially located and highly differentiated individuals.[11]

There is in all such methods a bias towards those populations that are available to public interaction, and against those which are so located as to insure privacy: business and social leaders, or those engaged in aesthetic, scholarly, scientific, or illegal activities. Any of these groups can be studied with sufficient ingenuity: sociolinguistic research should certainly rise to the challenge to develop rapid and anonymous studies that will escape the limitations of convenience. But it should be emphasized that since those who are most available to public interaction may have the most direct effect upon linguistic change and the sociolinguistic system, the bias through missing the more extreme and obscure ends of the social spectrum is not as great as it may first appear.

Since the department store survey was carried out in Manhattan, several parallel studies have been made. In Suffolk County, Long Island, rapid and anonymous observations of the use of (r) were made by Patricia Allen (1968). In three stratified stores, 156 employees were observed. In the highest-status store (Macy's), only 27 percent of the subjects used no (r-1); in the intermediate store (Grant City), 40 percent; and in the low-status store (Floyd's), 60 percent. We see that the general New York City pattern has moved outward from the city, producing a comparable stratification of (r) in three stores of a somewhat narrower range than those studied in Manhattan. Our own analysis of the New York City situation shows that rapid and anonymous surveys of this kind cannot be interpreted fully without detailed knowledge of the dialect history of the area, and a more systematic study of the distribution of linguistic variables and subjective norms.[12] In this case, rapid and anonymous surveys should be considered a supplement or preliminary to other methods, not substitutions for them. Yet there are cases where rapid methods can give solutions to problems that have never been circumnavigated by conventional techniques. We have used observations of the speech of telephone operators to construct a national map of the merger of the low back vowels in *hock* and *hawk*, and the merger of *i* and *e* before nasals in *pin* and *pen*. In our recent study of the Puerto Rican speech community in New York City, we utilized such natural experimentation to find out what percentage of those heard speaking Spanish on the street were raised in the United States, and what percentage were born in Puerto Rico (Labov and Pedraza 1971).

Future studies of language in its social context should rely more heavily on rapid and anonymous studies, as part of a general program of utilizing unobtrusive measures to control the interactive effect of the observer (Webb et al. 1966). But our rapid and anonymous studies are not passive indices of social use, like observations of wear and tear in public places. They represent a form of nonreactive experimentation in which we avoid the bias of the experimental context and the irregular interference of prestige norms but still control the behavior of subjects. We are just beginning to study speech events like *asking for directions,* isolating the invariant rules which govern them, and on this basis develop the ability to control a large body of socially located public speech in a natural setting. We see rapid and anonymous observations as the most important experimental method in a linguistic program which takes as its primary object the language used by ordinary people in their everyday affairs.

## Notes

This chapter is based upon Chs. 3 and 9 of *The Social Stratification of English in New York City* (1966), revised in the light of further work with rapid and anonymous observations. I am indebted to Frank Anshen and Maverick Marvin Harris for reference to illuminating replications of this study (Allen 1968, Harris 1969).

1. C. Wright Mills, *White Collar* (New York: Oxford University Press, 1956), p. 173. See also p. 243: "The tendency of white-collar people to borrow status from higher elements is so strong that it has carried over to all social contacts and features of the work-place. Salespeople in department stores...frequently attempt, although often unsuccessfully, to borrow prestige from their contact with customers, and to cash it in among work colleagues as well as friends off the job. In the big city the girl who works on 34th Street cannot successfully claim as much prestige as the one who works on Fifth Avenue or 57th Street."

2. This statement is fully confirmed by answers to a question on newspaper readership in the Mobilization for Youth Survey of the Lower East Side. The readership of the *Daily News* and *Daily Mirror* (now defunct) on the one hand, and the *New York Times* and *Herald Tribune* (now defunct) on the other hand, is almost complementary in distribution by social class.

3. Macy's sales employees are represented by a strong labor union, while Saks is not unionized. One former Macy's employee considered it a matter of common knowledge that Saks wages were lower than Macy's, and that the prestige of the store helped to maintain its nonunion position. Bonuses and other increments are said to enter into the picture. It appears that it is more difficult for a young girl to get a job at Saks than at Macy's. Thus Saks has more leeway in hiring policies, and the tendency of the store officials to select girls who speak in a certain way will play a part in the stratification of language, as well as the adjustment made by the employees to their situation. Both influences converge to produce stratification.

4. A former Macy's employee told me of an incident that occurred shortly before Christmas several years ago. As she was shopping in Lord and Taylor's, she saw the president of the company making the rounds of every aisle and shaking hands with every employee. When she told her fellow employees at Macy's about this scene, the most common remark was, "How else do you get someone to work for that kind of money?" One can say that not only do the employees of higher-status stores borrow prestige from their employer—it is also deliberately loaned to them.

5. The interviewer in all cases was myself. I was dressed in middle-class style, with jacket, white shirt, and tie, and used my normal pronunciation as a college-educated native of New Jersey (*r*-pronouncing).

6. Notes were also made on the department in which the employee was located, but the numbers for individual departments are not large enough to allow comparison.

7. The extreme style shifting of the second-highest status group appears throughout the New York City pattern, and is associated with an extreme sensitivity to the norms of an exterior reference group [. When the number of items in which a speaker distinguishes between his own pronunciation of a word and the correct pronunciation was given, the second-highest group had the highest scores on our metric, the Index of Linguistic Insecurity.] We find parallel phenomena in Shuy, Wolfram, and Riley 1967, Wolfram 1969, and Levine and Crockett 1966, who found in their study of Hillsboro, North Carolina, that the second-highest group on the basis of education showed the most extreme stylistic shift of (r).

8. In the sample as a whole, 17 informants with distinct foreign accents were found, and one with regional characteristics which were clearly not of New York City origin. The foreign language speakers in Saks had French, or other western European accents, while those in Kleins had Jewish and other eastern European accents. There were three Puerto Rican employees in the Kleins sample, one in Macy's, none in Saks. There were 70 men and 194 women. Men showed the following small differences from women in percentages of (r-1) usage:

| | **Men** | **Women** |
|---|---|---|
| all (r-1) | 22 | 30 |
| some (r-1) | 22 | 17 |
| no (r-1) | 57 | 54 |

9. See for example *Voice and Speech Problems*, a text written for New York City schools in 1940 by Raubicheck, Davis, and Carll (1940:336):

> There are many people who feel that an effort should be made to make the pronunciation conform to the spelling, and for some strange reason, they are particularly concerned with *r*. We all pronounce *calm, psalm, almond, know, eight, night*, and *there* without worrying...Yet people who would not dream of saying kni: or psai'kplədʒi insist on attempting to sound the *r* in words like p*a*˙k or f*a*ðə just because an *r* marks the spot where our ancestors used a trill....More often than not, people do not really say a third sound in a word like p*a*˙k but merely say the vowel *a*: with the tongue tip curled back toward the throat. This type of vowel production is known as "Inversion."

Letitia Raubicheck was the head of the speech program in the New York City schools for many years and exerted a powerful influence on the teaching of English there. The norm of "international English" was maintained by William Tilly of Columbia and followed by Raubicheck and many others in the 1930s and 1940s. As far as I know, this norm has lost entirely its dominant position in the school system: a detailed study of its disappearance from the radio networks and the school system in the 1940s would tell us a great deal about the mechanism of such shifts in the prestige form.

10. When the phonetic transcriptions were first made, doubtful cases were marked as *d* and were not included in the tabulations made later. There is however room for interviewer bias in the decision between (r-0) and *d* and between *d* and (r-1).

11. Hearings of the New York City Board of Education were recorded during the study of New York City, and preliminary analysis of the data shows that the pattern of social and stylistic stratification of (r) can easily be recovered from the wide variety of speakers who appear in these hearings. Courtroom proceedings at the New York Court of General Sessions are a natural focus for such studies, but speakers often lower their voices to

the point that spectators cannot hear them clearly. Only a small beginning has been made on the systematic study of passersby. Plakins (1969) approached a wide variety of pedestrians in a Connecticut town with requests for directions to an incomprehensible place, phrased at three levels of politeness. She found systematic differences in mode of response according to dress (as an index of socioeconomic position) and mode of inquiry; there were no "rude" responses [huh?] to polite inquiries.

12. Allen's tables resemble the New York City patterns but with one major difference; the number of speakers who use all (r-1) is roughly constant in all three stores: 27 percent in Floyd's, 27 percent in Grant City, 32 percent in Macy's. Examination of the distribution in apparent time showed that this phenomenon was due to the presence of a bimodal split in the lower-store adults (over 30 years old). Eighty percent used no (r-1) and 20 percent used a consistent all (r-1): there were none who varied. On the other hand, 50 percent of the adults were showing variable (r) in the two other stores. This points to the presence of an older *r*-pronouncing vernacular which is now dominated by the *r*-less New York City pattern (Kurath and McDavid 1961), but survives among working-class speakers. The disengagement of such bimodal patterns is a challenging problem (Levine and Crockett 1966), and certainly requires a more systematic survey. Similar complexity is suggested in the results of rapid and anonymous survey of stores in Austin, Texas, by M. M. Harris (1969). In this basically *r*-pronouncing area, the prestige norms among whites appear to be a weak constricted [r], with a strongly retroflex consonant gaining ground among younger speakers. But for the few blacks and Mexican-Americans encountered, this strong [r] seems to be the norm aimed at in careful articulation. Although these results are only suggestive, they are the kind of preliminary work which is required to orient a more systematic investigation towards the crucial variables of the sociolinguistic structure of that community.

## References

Allen, P. 1968. /r/ variable in the speech of New Yorkers in department stores. Unpublished research paper SUNY, Stony Brook.

Anshen, F. 1969. Speech variation among Negroes in a small Southern community. Unpublished dissertation, New York University.

Barber, Bernard. 1957. *Social stratification*. New York: Harcourt, Brace.

Bronstein, A. 1962. Let's take another look at New York City speech. *American Speech* 37: 13–26.

Harris, M. M. 1969. The retroflexion of postvocalic /r/ in Austin. *American Speech* 44: 263–271.

Hubbell, A. F. 1950. *The pronunciation of English in New York City*. New York: Columbia University Press.

Kurath, H., and R. McDavid. 1961. *The pronunciation of English in the Atlantic states*. Ann Arbor: University of Michigan Press.

Labov, W. 1966. *The social stratification of English in New York City*. Washington, DC: Center for Applied Linguistics.

Labov, W. 1972a. *Language in the inner city: studies in the black English vernacular*. Philadelphia: University of Pennsylvania Press.

Labov, W. 1972b. *Sociolinguistic patterns*. Philadelphia: University of Pennsylvania Press.

Labov, W., P. Cohen, C. Robins, and J. Lewis. 1968. A study of the non-standard English of Negro and Puerto Rican speakers in New York City. Final report, Cooperative Research Project 3288. 2 vols. Philadelphia: U.S. Regional Survey, 204 N. 35th St., Philadelphia 19104.

Labov, W. and P. Pedraza. 1971. *A Study of the Puerto Rican speech community in New York City*. Report to the Urban Center of Columbia University.

Levine, L. and H. J. Crockett, Jr. 1966. Speech variation in a piedmont community: postvocalic r. *In* S. Lieberson, *Explorations in Sociolinguistics*. Special issue of *Sociologies Inquiry* 36(2).

Shuy, R., W. Wolfram, and W. K. Riley. 1967. *A study of social dialects in Detroit*. Final report, Project 6–1347. Washington, DC: Office of Education.

Webb, Eugene J., et al. 1966. *Unobtrusive measures: nonreactive research in the social sciences*. Chicago: Rand McNally.

Wolfram, W. 1969. Linguistic correlates of social stratification in the speech of Detroit Negroes. Unpublished thesis, Hartford Seminary Foundation.

---

## Critical Thinking and Application

- Why is it important that Labov chose not to tape-record speech for this article? Are his methods reliable? Why? What does he mean by saying that "our goal is to observe the way people use language when they are not being observed"? What can researchers do?
- If speakers are aware that their speech may be stigmatized, why do they not simply use the standard form?
- Identify a sociolinguistic variable in your area (with an independent and dependent variable). Devise a "rapid, anonymous" study like Labov's. What did you find? How did your method work?

## Vocabulary

affricate
crossover pattern
hypercorrect
linguistic insecurity
LMC
orthographic
phonological variable
postvocalic
preconsonantal
schwa
SEC
social stratification
stop
UMC
WC

## Suggested Further Reading

Corfield, Penelope J., ed. 1991. *Language, History, and Class*. Oxford: Blackwell.

Edwards, John. 1994. *Multilingualism*. London: Routledge.

Fasold, Ralph. 1984. *The Sociolinguistics of Society*. Oxford: Blackwell.

Fasold, Ralph. 1990. *The Sociolinguistics of Language*. Oxford: Blackwell.

Giglioli, Pier Paolo, ed. 1972. *Language and Social Context*. Harmondsworth: Penguin.

Grillo, Ralph D. 1989. *Dominant Languages: Language and Hierarchy in Britain and France*. Cambridge: Cambridge University Press.

Labov, William. 1972. *Sociolinguistic Patterns*. Philadelphia: University of Pennsylvania Press.

Labov, William. 1996. *The Social Stratification of English in New York City*. Washington, DC: Center for Applied Linguistics.

Macaulay, R. K. S. 1977. *Language, Social Class, and Education: A Glasgow Study*. Edinburgh: University of Edinburgh Press.

Milroy, James. 1991. *Linguistic Variation and Change: On the Historical Sociolinguistics of English*. Oxford: Blackwell.

Milroy, James, and Lesley Milroy. 1985. *Authority in Language: Investigating Language Prescription and Standardization*. London: Routledge & Kegan Paul.

Mugglestone, Lynda. 1995. *"Talking Proper": The Rise of Accent as a Social Symbol*. Oxford: Oxford University Press.

Romaine, Suzanne, ed. 1982. *Sociolinguistic Variation in Speech Communities*. London: Arnold.

Romaine, Suzanne. 2000. *Language in Society: An Introduction to Sociolinguistics*. 2nd ed. Oxford: Oxford University Press.

Trudgill, Peter. 1974. *The Social Differentiation of English in Norwich*. Cambridge: Cambridge University Press.

# CHAPTER 30

# New York Jewish Conversational Style

## *Deborah Tannen*

(1981)

*Some stereotypes about regional linguistic varieties have a basis in actual practice. One such stereotype is that of the "pushy New York Jews." Though most people could not provide a detailed technical description of what that consists of, they can talk animatedly about its features: people talk fast, they "crowd" out others, they talk about themselves.... Americans similarly have a sense of "Midwestern reserve" and its concomitant politeness. Regional and ethnic stereotypes often bring with them judgment and evaluation.*

*Deborah Tannen stumbled upon this phenomenon accidentally as she went to analyze a tape-recorded Thanksgiving dinner conversation that included half New York Jews and half Midwesterners (or Californians). Herself a New Yorker, she was startled to find that there was not a single interchange in which New Yorkers did not take part. How to describe and explain this?*

*This chapter uses two important approaches to the study of language: the study of politeness, based largely on the work of Erving Goffman, Robin Lakoff, Penelope Brown, and Stephen Levinson, and the detailed study of conversation, called conversation analysis (a subfield of discourse analysis), inspired by sociologists/ethnomethodologists Harvey Sacks, Emanuel Schegloff, and others. In this kind of analysis, transcripts are made that show not only the words people uttered but their relationship to one another, almost like a musical score, showing when each person entered the talk, when they speak together (overlap), and something about the volume and other* paralinguistic *features of their talk.*

### Reading Questions

- What are the three rules of politeness (or rules of rapport)? Which one do people usually associate with "politeness"?
- What are positive face and negative face?
- How does cross-stylistic interchange, as in the first long example with Peter, David, and Tannen, prove disconcerting? What happens in co-stylistic interchange, as in the second long example with Peter and Tannen?
- What does Tannen mean by saying "People tend to take their conversational habits as self-evident and draw conclusions not about others' linguistic devices but about their intentions or personalities"? Do you think this is true? Have you ever had this experience?

---

A pause in the wrong place, an intonation misunderstood, and a whole conversation went awry. —E. M. FORSTER, A PASSAGE TO INDIA

Conversation, New York's biggest cottage industry, doesn't exist in San Francisco in the sense of sustained discourse and friendly contentiousness.

—EDMUND WHITE, STATES OF DESIRE[1]

Deborah Tannen, New York Jewish Conversational Style. *International Journal of the Sociology of Language* 30 (1981): 133–149.

Take, for example, the following conversation.[2]

F: How often does your acting group work?
M: Do you mean how often we rehearse or how often we perform?
F: Both.
M: [Laughs uneasily.]
F: Why are you laughing?
M: Because of the way you said that. It was like a bullet. Is that why your marriage broke up?
F: What?
M: Because of your aggressiveness.

Of the many observations that could be made based on this interchange, I would like to focus on two: the general tendency to extrapolate personality from **conversational style,** and the specific attribution of aggressiveness to a speaker who uses fast pacing in conversation. In the discussion that follows, I will suggest that the stereotype of the "pushy New York Jew" may result in part from discourse conventions practiced by some native New Yorkers of East European Jewish background. After examining some evidence for the existence of such a stereotype, I will (1) briefly present my notion of conversational style, (2) outline the linguistic and **paralinguistic** features that make up New York Jewish style, and (3) demonstrate their use in cross-stylistic and co-stylistic interaction. In conclusion, I will (4) discuss the personal and social uses of conversational style.

## The Negative Stereotype

Evidence abounds of the negative stereotype of New York speech in general and New York Jewish speech in particular. The most widely recognized component of this speech is, of course, **phonology.** An Associated Press release (Boyer, 1979) reports on California therapists who help cure New York accents. One such therapist is quoted: "It's really a drag listening to people from New York talk. It upsets me when I hear a New York accent.... We're here to offer a service to newcomers to this area, especially to New Yorkers.... When they open their mouths, they alienate everyone. We're here to help them adjust to life in Marin County."

A third-grade teacher in Brooklyn wrote to Ann Landers complaining of native-born children who say, for example, "Vot's the kvestion?," "It's vorm ottside," and "heppy as a boid." Ann Landers advised the teacher, "With consistent effort, bad speech habits can be unlearned. I hope you will have the patience to work with these students. It's a real challenge."

Teachers in New York City have been rising to the challenge for a long time. Not so long ago one of the requirements for a license to teach in the New York City public schools was passing a speech exam, which entailed proving that one did not speak with the indigenous "accent." I myself recall being given a shockingly low midterm grade by a speech teacher in a Manhattan high school who promised that it would not be raised until I stopped "dentalizing." I am not aware of any other group whose members feel that their pronunciation is wrong, even when they are comfortably surrounded by others from the same group and have never lived anywhere else. Labov (1970) has documented the **hypercorrection** that results from the **linguistic insecurity** of middle-class Jewish New York women. I confronted this myself each time I recognized a fellow New Yorker in California by her or his accent. The most common response was, "Oh is it THAT obvious?" or "Gee, I thought I'd gotten rid of that."

Unfortunately, moreover, evaluations of "accent" are not applied merely to the speech itself but form the basis of personality judgments. In an attempt to evaluate the effect of Southern-accented speech on judgments of employability, Van Antwerp and Maxwell (1982) serendipitously tapped the negative valence of New York speech. One of their sample non-Southern speakers happened to be a woman from northern New Jersey whose speech approximated the dialect of New York City. Commentators from the Washington, D.C., area evaluated her employability negatively, attributing to her such characteristics as "inability to articulate," "disorganized and dull," "seemed educated but not very together," "a little too energetic, sort of in a hurry to get it over with," "didn't seem to have things straight in her head before she spoke," "sounded aggressive." These findings demonstrate the possible consequences of negative evaluations based on speech style when cross-stylistic interaction takes place in "gatekeeping" (Erickson, 1975) situations.

## Background of the Study

My own findings on New York Jewish conversational style were in a way serendipitous as well. I had begun with the goal of discovering the features that made up the styles of each participant in two-and-a-half hours of naturally occurring conversation at dinner on Thanksgiving 1978. Analysis revealed, however, that three of the participants, all natives of New York of East European Jewish background, shared many stylistic features which could be seen to have a positive effect when used with each other and a negative effect when used with the three others. Moreover, the evening's interaction was later characterized by three of the participants (independently) as "New York Jewish" or "New York." Finally, whereas the tapes contained many examples of interchanges between two or three of the New Yorkers, it had no examples of talk among non–New Yorkers in which the New Yorkers did not participate. Thus, what began as a general study of conversational style ended by becoming an analysis of New York Jewish conversational style (Tannen, 1979).

The dinner at which this conversation was taped took place in the home of Kurt, a native New Yorker living in Oakland, California. The guests, who were also New Yorkers living in California, were Kurt's brother, Peter, and myself.[3] The three other guests were Kurt's friend David, a native of Los Angeles of Irish, Scotch, and English parents from Iowa and North Dakota; David's friend Chad, a native and resident of Los Angeles whose father was of Scotch/English extraction and whose mother was from New York, of Italian background; and Sally, born and raised in England, of a Jewish father and American mother.[4] Complex as these ethnic backgrounds are, the group split into two when looked at on the basis of conversational style.

## Theoretical Background

My notion of conversational style grows out of R. Lakoff's (1973; 1979) work on communicative style and Gumperz's (1977; 1982) on conversational inference. "Style" is not something extra, added on like frosting on a cake. It is the stuff of which the linguistic cake is made: pitch, amplitude, intonation, voice quality, lexical and syntactic choice, rate of speech and **turntaking,** as well as what is said and how discourse cohesion is achieved. In other words, style refers to all the ways speakers encode meaning in language and convey how they intend their talk to be understood. Insofar as speakers from similar speech communities share such linguistic conventions, style is a social phenomenon. Insofar as speakers use particular features in particular combinations and in various settings, to that extent style is an individual phenomenon. (See Gumperz and Tannen, 1979, for a discussion of individual vs. social differences.)

Lakoff (1973) observes that speakers regularly avoid saying precisely what they mean in the interest of social goals which they pursue by adhering to one of three *rules of* **politeness,** later renamed *rules of rapport* (Lakoff, 1979). Each rule is associated with a communicative style growing out of habitual application of that rule:

1. Don't impose (distance).
2. Give options **(deference).**
3. Be friendly (camaraderie).

To illustrate (with my own examples), if a guest responds to an offer of something to drink by saying, "No thank you; I'm not thirsty," s/he is applying R1. If s/he says, "Oh, I'll have whatever you're having," s/he is applying R2. If s/he marches into the kitchen, throws open the refrigerator, and says, "I'm thirsty. Got any juice?" s/he is applying R3. Individuals differ with regard to which sense of politeness they tend to observe, and cultural differences are reflected by the tendency of members of a group to observe one or the other sense of politeness in conventionalized ways.

These differing senses of politeness are associated as well with two goals of indirectness: *defensiveness* and *rapport*. Defensiveness, associated with R1 "don't impose," is the desire to be able to renege, to say, "I never said that," or "That's not what I meant." Rapport, associated with R3 "be friendly," refers to the fine feeling of being "on the same wavelength," which accrues when one gets what one wants without asking for it or feels understood without having explained.

Another deeply related strand of research in sociology is brilliantly elaborated by Goffman, building on the work of Durkheim. Durkheim (1915) distinguishes between negative and positive religious rites. Negative rites are "a system of abstentions" which prepares one for "access to the positive cult." Goffman (1967: 72–73) builds upon this dichotomy in his notion of *deference*, "the appreciation an individual shows of another to that other, whether through avoidance rituals or presentational rituals." Presentational rituals include "salutations, invitations, compliments, and minor services. Through all of these the recipient is told that he is not an island unto himself and that others are, or seek to be, involved with him..." Avoidance rituals "lead the actor to keep at a distance from the recipient" (Goffman 1967: 62) and include "rules regarding privacy and separateness" (Goffman 1967: 67). Following Lakoff and Goffman, Brown and Levinson (1978) refer to two overriding goals motivating linguistic forms of politeness: **negative face,** "the want of every adult member that his actions be unimpeded by others," and **positive face,** "the want of every adult member that his actions be desirable to at least some others."

All these schemata for understanding human interaction recognize two basic but conflicting needs: to be involved with others and to be left alone. Linguistic systems, like other cultural systems, represent conventionalized ways of honoring these needs. I would like to suggest that the conversational style of the New Yorkers at Thanksgiving dinner can be seen as conventionalized strategies serving the need for involvement, whereas the non–New York participants expected strategies serving the need for independence.

## Features of New York Jewish Conversational Style

Following are the main features found in the talk of three of the six Thanksgiving celebrants. (More detailed discussion of these can be found in Tannen, 1979; 1980a; 1981; 1987.)

1. ***Topic*** (a) prefer personal topics, (b) shift topics abruptly, (c) introduce topics without hesitance, (d) persistence (if a new topic is not immediately picked up, reintroduce it, repeatedly if necessary).
2. ***Genre*** (a) tell more stories, (b) tell stories in rounds, (c) internal evaluation (Labov, 1972) is preferred over external (i.e., the point of a story is dramatized rather than lexicalized), (d) preferred point of a story is teller's emotional experience.
3. *Pacing* (a) faster rate of speech, (b) inter-turn pauses avoided (silence is evidence of lack of rapport), (c) faster turntaking, (d) cooperative **overlap** and participatory listenership.
4. *Expressive paralinguistics* (a) expressive phonology, (b) pitch and amplitude shifts, (c) marked voice quality, (d) strategic within-turn pauses.

All of these features were combined to create linguistic devices which enhanced conversational flow when used among the New Yorkers, but they had an obstructive effect on conversation with those who were not from New York. Comments by all participants upon listening to the tape indicated that they misunderstood the intentions of members of the other group.

Perhaps the most easily perceived and characteristic feature of this style is the fast rate of speech and tendency to overlap (speak simultaneously) and **latch** (Sacks' term for allowing no pause before turntaking). I have demonstrated at length elsewhere (Tannen, 1979; 1980a) that overlap is used cooperatively by the New Yorkers, as a way of showing enthusiasm and interest, but it is interpreted by non–New Yorkers as just the opposite: evidence of lack of attention. The tendency to use fast pace and overlap often combines, moreover, with preference for personal topics, focusing attention on another in a personal way. Both the pacing and the personal focus can be seen repeatedly to cause Sally, Chad, and David to become more hesitant in their speech as they respond in classic complementary schismogenetic fashion (Bateson, 1972). That is, the verbal devices used by one group cause speakers of the other group to react by intensifying the opposing behavior, and vice versa.

## Cross-Stylistic Interchange

The following conversation illustrates how both Peter and I use fast pacing and personal focus to show interest in David's discourse, with the result that he feels "caught off guard" and "on the spot." (This is only one of many such examples.) David, a professional sign interpreter, has been talking about American Sign Language.

(1) D So: and thís is the one that's Bèrkeley. This is the Bérkeley... sign for.. for [Christmas
*p*

(2) T [Do yòu figure oút those..
*f*

those um correspòndences?
Or do? when you learn the signs, /does/ somebody télls you.

(3) D Oh you mean [watching it? like

(4) T [Cause I can imagine knówing that sígn,... and not.. figuring out that it had anything to do with the decorátions.

....

(5) D No. Y you knów that it has to do with the decorátions. ]

(6) T [Cause somebody télls you? Or you figure ]it oút.
D: [No]

(7) D Oh.... You you talking about mé, or a deàf person. ]

(8) T [Yeah.] [You. You.

(9) D Me? uh: Someone télls me, ùsually.... But a lót of em I can tèll. I mean they're óbvious..... The bétter I get the mòre I can tell. The lónger I do it the mòre I can tell what they're talking about.

.....Withoút knowing what the sign is.]

(10) T [Huh.] [That's interesting.]

(11) P [But how do you learn a new sign.

....

(12) D How do I learn a new sign? ]

(13) P [Yeah. I mean supposing... Víctor's talking and all of a sudden he uses a sign for Thanksgíving, and you've never séen it before.

My questions (2) (4) and (6) and Peter's questions (11) and (13) overlap or latch onto David's preceding comments. In contrast, David's comments follow our questions after "normal" or even noticeable (5, 12) pauses.

My question (2) about how David learns about the symbolism behind signs not only is latched onto David's fading comment (1) but is spoken loudly and shifts the focus from a general discourse about signs to focus on David personally. The abrupt question catches him off guard, and he hesitates by rephrasing the question. I then interrupt David's rephrasing to supply more information (4), interpreting his hesitation as indication that I had been unclear. The real trouble, however, was the suddenness of my question and its shift from general to personal. Thus, I hoped to make David comfortable by acknowledging the fault had been mine and rectifying the matter by supplying more information right away, but the second interruption could only make him more uncomfortable; hence, the pause.

David answers my question (4) by commenting (5) "You know that it has to do with the decorations," but he avoids the more personal focus of my question (2) about *how* he knows. I therefore become more specific (6) and again latch my question. David stalls again, this time by asking (7) for clarification. His question comes after a filler, a pause, a slight stutter: "Oh.... You you talking about me.... " He expresses his surprise at the shift in focus. Yet again, I clarify in machine-gun fashion: (8) "Yeah. You. You." David then answers the question and my response (10) overlaps his answer.

Just as this interchange between David and me is settled, Peter uses precisely the strategy that I was using, with the same results. Latching onto David's answer (9), Peter asks another question focusing on David (11); David hesitates by rephrasing the question after a pause (12); Peter barely waits for the rephrasing to finish before he makes his question more specific (13).

The rhythm of this segment is most peculiar. Normally, a question–answer are seen as an **"adjacency pair"** (Sacks, Schegloff, and Jefferson, 1974), and in a smooth conversation they are rhythmically paired as well. The differences in David's pacing on the one hand and Peter's and mine on the other, however, create pauses between our questions and his delayed answers, so that the resultant rhythmic pairs are made up of an answer and the next question. This is typical of how stylistic differences obstruct conversational rhythm. While participants in this conversation were friends and disposed to think well of each other, the operation of such differences in other settings can leave participants with the conviction that the other was uncooperative or odd.

## Co-stylistic Interchange

In the previous example, Peter and I directed similar questions to David, with unexpected results. The following segment shows how the same device serves to enhance conversational flow when used with each other. This segment begins when I turn to Peter suddenly and address a question to him.

(1) T Do you réad?
....
(2) P Do I ˈréad?
...
(3) T Do you reàd things just for fún?
....
(4) P Yeah.....Right now I'm reading Norma Jean the Términte Queen. [Laughs]
(5) T ˈ*f*Whàt's thát?....Norma Jean like uh:....Marilyn Monˈróe?
(6) P It's.. ˈNo:. It's a book about......a housewife /??/ *dec*
(7) T Is it a ˈnóvel or whàt.
(8) P ˈIt's a ˌnóvel.
(9) T ˈYeah?
(10) P Before that...I read the French Lieutenant's Woman?
ˈHave you [ read that?
(11) T [ ˈOh yeah? No. Whó wrote that?
(12) P John Fowles.
(13) T Yeah I've heárd that he's good.
(14) P ˈHé's a ˌgréat writer. ˈÍ think he's one of the ˌbést writers.
T: hm
(15) T /?/
(16) P ˈHé's really ˌgoòd.
(17) T /?/
........
(18) P But Í get very bùsy..... [Yknow?
(19) T [Yeah. I ?.. hardly éver read.
....
(20) P What I've been dòing is cutting down on my sléep.
(21) T Oy! ] [sighs]
(22) P ] And I've been .....and I[s
[K laughs]
(23) T [Í do that tòo but it's páinful.]
(24) P ]Yeah. Fi:ve, six hours a ˈníght, and]
(25) T ]Oh Gód, hòw can you dó it. You survíve?
....
(26) P Yeah làte afternoon méetings are hàrd.....But
T: mmm
outside of thát I can keep gòing [pretty well.
(27) T [Not sleeping enough is térrible.....I'd múch rather not eàt than not sleèp. *p*
[S laughs]
(28) P I próbably should not eàt so much, it would..it would uh...sáve a lot of tìme.
(29) T If I'm /like really/ busy I don't I don't I don't eat. I don't yeah I just don't eat but[I
(30) P [I?I tend to spend a lòt of time eáting and prepáring and [/?/
(31) T [Oh: I néver prepare foòd.......I eat whatéver I can get my hánds on.]
(32) P ] Yeah.

This interchange exhibits many features of New York Jewish conversational style. In addition to the characteristic use of overlap, fast pacing, and personal focus, it exhibits devices I have called (Tannen, 1979) persistence, mutual revelation, and expressive paralinguistics.

Both Peter and I use overlap and latching in this segment: Peter's (22) (24) and (30) and my (19) (23) (25) (27) and (31). The interchange begins with a sudden focus of attention on him by my question (1). Like David, Peter is initially "caught off guard," so he repeats the question after a pause. But then he not only answers the question but supplies specific information (4) about the book he is reading. A common feature of participatory listenership is seen in (5) and (6). While (6) is ostensibly an answer to my question (5), it is clear that Peter would have gone on to give that information in any case. He begins, "It's...," has to stop in order to answer my question with "No," and then repeats the beginning and continues, "It's a book about a housewife."

*Persistence* refers to the pattern by which speakers continue trying to say something despite lack of attention or interruption. In this example it can be seen in (22) and (24), in which Peter makes three attempts to say that he sleeps only five or six hours a night. Persistence is a necessary concomitant to overlap. It reflects a conversational economy in which it is not the business of a listener to make room for another speaker to speak. Rather, it is the business of the listener to show enthusiasm; the speaker, in this system, can be counted on to find room to speak. The conversational burden, in other words, is to serve the need for involvement at the risk of violating independence.

The mutual revelation device can be seen in the series of observations Peter and I make about our own habits. In (19) I state that I hardly ever read as a way of showing understanding of Peter's tight schedule (18). (23) is a similar response to his statement that he cuts down on sleep. (27) is a statement of my preference to balance his statement (26) about sleeping. In (28) Peter makes a statement about his eating habits; in (29) I describe mine; in (30) he reiterates his, and in (31) I reiterate mine. It might seem to some observers that we are not "communicating" at all, since we both talk only about ourselves. But the juxtaposition of comments and the relationship of topics constitutes thematic cohesion and establishes rapport. In this system, the offer of personal information is encouragement to the other to volunteer the same, and volunteered information is highly valued.

Throughout the Thanksgiving conversation, Peter, Kurt, and I use exaggerated phonological and paralinguistic cues. For example, my question (5) "What's that?" is loud and high pitched. When any of the New Yorkers uses such features with Chad or David, the result is that they stop talking in surprise, wondering what caused the outburst. When used in talk among the New Yorkers, introduction of exaggerated paralinguistics spurs the others to follow suit, in a mutually escalating way such as Bateson (1972) has characterized as symmetrical. In the present segment, many of the words and phrases are uttered with extra high or low pitch as well as heavily colored voice quality.

It seems likely that my use of high pitch on "What's that?" as well as on the last syllable of "Monroe" in (5) was triggered by Peter's laughter while uttering the book title. In any case, Peter's response (6) uses sharp contrasts in pitch and pacing to signal the message, "I know this is a silly book." The pitch on "No" is very low, the vowel is drawn out, the sentence is uttered slowly, and it contains a very long pause before the key word "housewife" is uttered. Similar sharp shifts from high to low pitch can be seen repeatedly.

(8) P ˈIt's a ˌnovel.
(14) P ˈHe's a ˌgreat writer. I think he's one of the ˌbest writers.
(16) P ˈHe's really ˌgood.

These pitch shifts, together with voice quality, signal in (8) denigration of the book discussed and in (14) and (16) great earnestness.

Exaggerated paralinguistics can be seen as well in my expressions of concern for Peter's loss of sleep in (23) (25) and (27). These are all uttered with marked stress and breathy voice quality that demonstrate exaggerated and stylized concern.

Yet another stylized response to Peter's assertion that he doesn't sleep enough is a Yiddish nonverbal "response cry" (Goffman 1978), "Oy!" This utterance is rapport-building in a number of ways. Obviously, the choice of a Yiddish expression signals our shared ethnic background. At the same time, the exaggerated nature of my response—the utterance of a great sigh along with "oy"—is a way of mocking my own usage, making the exclamation ironic in much the way Peter was mocking his own reading material while telling about it. (In a similar way, Kurt often mocks his own hosting behavior by offering food in an exaggerated Yiddish accent.) Finally, I utter this cry as if it were an expression of my own feeling, thus taking Peter's point of view as a show of empathy.

The interchange between Peter and me ends with another cooperative use of overlap and repetition. The conversation has turned to dating, and it has continued to be characterized by the features seen in the earlier segment. It ends this way:

(1) P And you just cán't get to know.... <u>ten</u> people <u>really well</u>.
[breathy]
You can't dó it.
*p*
(2) T Yeah right. Y'have to there's no? Yeah there's no tíme.
(3) P There's not tíme.
(4) T Yeah.... 'strue.

Peter's statements (1) and (3) flow in a continuous stream, ending with "You can't do it. There's not time." However the last phrase echoes my words in (2). The end of the talk is signaled by a quieting down of voices as well as the pattern of blended voices and phrases.

## The Opacity of Style

To those unfamiliar with the workings of particular stylistic strategies, their use seems like evidence of lack of communication—which is simply to say they don't see how they work. More often than not the features used have meaning in the speech habits of the different group, so conclusions are drawn based on what the signals would mean if the hearer had used them. To those who do not expect overlap to be used cooperatively, and would not use it in that way themselves, another's overlap will be interpreted as lack of attention. Thus an article in *New West* magazine (Esterly, 1979) tells of the work of a UCLA psychologist, Gerald Goodman, who believes that fast talkers are a conversational menace. Calling them "crowders," he eloquently articulates the effect they have on those unaccustomed to this style:

> There's a dehumanizing aspect to being crowded; there's a lack of respect involved. Interrupting arises from a variety of factors—anxiety, a desire to dominate, boredom, the need to express freshly stimulated thoughts.... People walk away from conversations with crowders feeling upset or dissatisfied or incompetent, though they may not understand why. (p. 68)

Clearly, this is the interpretation of fast pacing made by David, Chad, and Sally during Thanksgiving, at least at times. It is the feeling of being imposed upon, in violation of Brown and Levinson's (1978) negative politeness. However, the "dehumanizing aspect," the vague feeling of dissatisfaction and incompetence, is not a response to others' use of specific linguistic features but rather to their use of such features in an unexpected way. It is the lack of sharedness of style that is disconcerting. Fast talkers walk away from those same conversations feeling similar discomfort, most likely having interpreted the slower pacing as a failure of positive politeness.

Style is often invisible. People tend to take their conversational habits as self-evident and draw conclusions not about others' linguistic devices but about their intentions or personalities. Moreover, few speakers are aware of ways in which others' linguistic behavior may be a reaction to their own.

## The Coherence of Conversational Style

As Reisman (1974: 110) points out, "The conventions which order speech interaction are meaningful not only in that they order and mediate verbal expression, but in that they participate in and express larger meanings in the society which uses them." Becker (1979a: 18) explains, "The figure a sentence makes is a strategy of interpretation" which "helps the people it is used by understand and feel coherent in their worlds." The structure and habits of language which seem self-evidently natural, serve not only as a way to communicate meaning but also to reestablish and ratify one's way of being in the world. In another paper, Becker (1979b: 241) explains:

> The universal source of language pathology is that people appear to say one thing and "mean" another. It drives people mad (the closer it gets to home). An aesthetic response is quite simply the opposite of this pathology.... Schizophrenia, foreign language learning, and artistic expression in language all operate under the same set of linguistic variables—constraints on coherence, invention, intentionality, and reference. The difference is that in madness (and in the temporary madness of learning a new language or a new text) these constraints are misunderstood and often appear contradictory, while in an aesthetic response they are understood as a coherent integrated whole.... The integration of communication (art) is, hence, as essential to a sane community as clean air, good food, and, to cure errors, medicine.

The emotional/aesthetic experience of a perfectly tuned conversation is as ecstatic as an artistic experience. The satisfaction of having communicated successfully goes beyond the pleasure of being understood in the narrow sense. It is a ratification of one's place in the world and one's way of being human. It is, as Becker calls a well-performed shadow play, "a vision of sanity."

To some extent there is for everyone a discontinuity between the private code, i.e., communicative habits learned at home and on the block (or in the fields) around one's home, and the public code, i.e., the form of language used in formal settings. Hence the anxiety most people feel about communicating with strangers. But the degree of discontinuity may be greater or lesser. Those who learned and have reinforced at home norms of interaction which are relatively similar to those which are widely accepted in society at large have a certainty about their linguistic convictions. If they proclaim that it is rude to interrupt or that one ought to state the point of a story outright, it is without ambivalence. But those who have grown up hearing and using norms of interaction which differ significantly from more widely accepted ones may feel ambivalent about their own styles. Thus New Yorkers of Jewish background cannot complain "Why don't you interrupt?" On hearing a tape recording of a conversation they thoroughly enjoyed in the process, they often feel critical of themselves and slightly embarrassed. They, too, believe that it is rude to interrupt, to talk loudly, to talk too much. The "interruption" may actually be the creation of the interlocutor who stopped when s/he was expected to continue talking over the overlap, but the cooperative overlapper is no more likely to realize this than the overlap-resistant speaker.

The greater the discontinuity between ingroup style and public expectations, the more difficult it is for one to feel sane in both worlds. Hence it is not surprising that many speakers reject one or the other style, and New York Jews who have moved away from New York may be heard to proclaim that they hate New York accents, hate to go back to New York, or hate to go home, because "no one listens to anyone else" or "it's so loud" or "people are so rude." There are probably few speakers of this background who have not at times felt uncomfortable upon seeing through public eyes someone from their own background talking in a way that is attracting attention in an alien setting, just as American travelers may feel embarrassed on seeing another American tourist who fits too neatly the stereotype of the ugly American abroad. In contrast, the comfort of interaction in a setting in which one's home style predominates goes far to explain what often appears as clannishness—the preference for the company of those of similar ethnic background. The coherence principles (to borrow a term from Becker) that create conversational style operate on every level of discourse and contribute to, at the same time that they grow out of, people's attempts to achieve coherence in the world.

## Afterword on Accountability

Perhaps a word is in order on the validity of the case-study method. How generalizable are findings based on close observation and interviews with six speakers? The most reassuring confirmation is a phenomenon I have called "the aha factor" (Tannen, 1979). When I explain these style differences in public or private forums, a cry of relief goes up from many of my hearers—especially from intermarried couples, of whom only one partner is Jewish and from New York City. They invariably report that these style differences have been the cause of complaints; the non–New York spouse chronically complains of being interrupted, not listened to, not given a chance to talk, while the New York–bred partner feels unjustly accused and in turn complains that the other partner is unaccountably withholding. If the family does not live in New York City, the misunderstanding often extends as well to children who complain that the New York parent does not listen to them and overreacts to their talk.

In a recent column in *The Washington Post*, Judith Martin, assuming the persona of an etiquette expert named Miss Manners, addressed the question of conversational norms. A disgruntled reader wrote to complain that she is "a good listener," but "there are so many people in this world who will just talk right over me. Sometimes I'm halfway into a sentence or an idea when they burst in with their own."

Miss Manners responded in the spirit of cooperative overlap and participatory listenership:

> If you are, in fact, a practiced "good listener," you have not been traveling through life in silence. You have been asking questions, inserting relevant information and providing commentary on what the chief talkers to whom you have been listening are saying. A good listener is not someone who has to be checked every now and then by the speaker to see if he or she is awake.... Once in the driver's seat, you should try to be a good talker. That is to say, you must allow proper interruptions that are in the tradition of good listening, and even encourage them....

Surprised to find such linguistic values articulated in the popular press, I contacted the writer and was not surprised to learn that Martin is Jewish.

This raises the question of the extent to which the linguistic conventions I have discussed are "New York" and/or "Jewish." My hypothesis is that the style (i.e., the combination of linguistic devices used in the way described) I have discussed represents a prototype of a kind of conversation that is familiar to most New York Jews and unfamiliar to most midwestern and western Americans of non-Jewish background. My impression is that New Yorkers of non-Jewish background and Jews not from New York City use many of the devices I have described and that there are New York Jews who use few of them. I suspect that the existence of this style represents the influence of conversational norms of East European Jewish immigrants and that similar norms are probably general to the Levant.[5] I have not encountered evidence to indicate that Jews of German background necessarily share this style.

The precise distribution of these and related linguistic devices, like the distribution of dialect features, can only be determined by the painstaking research of many workers in many settings, if there turn out to be enough researchers who find this a thing worth doing. In any case, there is no doubt that the acquisition, maintenance, and accommodation of conversational style is a crucial linguistic and social process.

## Notes

1. My thanks to Stephen Murray for this reference.

2. This conversation was reconstructed from memory. Others presented are transcribed from tape recordings. The following transcription conventions are used, as gleaned from Schenkein (1978) and from those developed at the University of California, Berkeley, by Gumperz and Chafe and their respective collaborators.

   ...  half second pause. Each extra dot represents another half-second of pause.
   /  marks primary stress
   \  marks secondary stress
   underline  indicates emphatic stress
   |  marks high pitch on word
   ⌈  marks high pitch on phrase, continuing until punctuation
   |  marks low pitch on word
   .  sentence-final falling intonation
   ,  clause-final intonation (more to come)
   ?  yes/no question rising intonation
   ʔ  glottal stop
   ·  lengthened vowel sound
   *p*  spoken softly (piano)
   *f*  spoken loudly (forte)
   *dec*  spoken slowly
   /?/  inaudible segment
   ⌈ Brackets connecting lines show overlapping speech.
   ⌊ Two people talking at the same time.
   Brackets with reversed flaps ⌉
   ⌊ indicate latching (no intraturn pause)

3. Thus I was both perpetrator and object of my analysis, making me not a participant observer (an observer who becomes a participant) but a participant who is also an observer. At the time of taping, I was in the habit of taping many interactions and had not decided to use this one, let alone what I would look for in analysis. Nonetheless there is a problem of objectivity which I have tried to correct for by pains taking review of the analysis with participants as well as others. I believe that the loss of objectivity is a disadvantage outweighed by the advantage of insight into what was going on which is impossible for a nonparticipant to recover, and that only by taping an event in which one is a natural participant can one gather data not distorted by the presence of an alien observer.

4. With the exception of my own, names have been changed. Now, as always, I want to express my gratitude to these friends who became my data, for their willingness and insight during taping and later during playback. The transcripts will reflect initials of these pseudonyms, except for my own, which is rendered "T" to avoid confusion with "D" (David).

5. The use of cooperative overlap has been reported among American blacks, throughout the West Indies (see in particular Reisman, 1974), and the Middle and Near East.

## References

Bateson, Gregory. 1972. *Steps to an Ecology of Mind.* New York: Ballantine.

Becker, Alton. 1979a. The figure a sentence makes. In *Discourse and Syntax*, T. Givon (ed.). New York: Academic Press.

Becker, Alton. 1979b. Text-building, epistemology, and aesthetics in Javanese Shadow Theatre. In *The Imagination of Reality: Essays in Southeast Asian Coherence Systems*, A. L. Becker and A. A. Yengoyan (eds.). Norwood, NJ: Ablex.

Boyer, Peter J. 1979. Therapists cure New York accents. *The Tribune*, Sunday February 4, 6E.

Brown, Penelope, and Levinson, Stephen. 1978. Universals in language usage: Politeness phenomena. In *Questions and Politeness*, E. Goody (ed.), 56–289. Cambridge: Cambridge University Press.

Durkheim, Émile. 1915. *The Elementary Forms of the Religious Life*. New York: The Free Press.

Erickson, Frederick. 1975. Gatekeeping and the melting pot: Interaction in counseling interviews. *Harvard Education Review* 45(1), 44–70.

Esterly, Glenn. 1979. Slow talking in the big city. *New West*, 4(11) (May 21, 1979), 67–72.

Forster, E. M. 1924. *A Passage to India*. New York: Harcourt Brace Jovanovich.

Goffman, Erving. 1967. *Interaction Ritual: Essays on Face-to-Face Behavior*. Garden City, NY: Doubleday.

Goffman, Erving. 1978. Response cries. *Language* 54(4), 787–815.

Gumperz, John. 1977. Sociocultural knowledge in conversational inference. In *Georgetown University Round Table on Languages and Linguistics 1977*, M. Saville-Troike (ed.), 191–211. Washington, DC: Georgetown University.

Gumperz, John. 1982. *Discourse Strategies*. Cambridge and New York: Cambridge University Press.

Gumperz, John, and Tannen, Deborah. 1979. Individual and social differences in language use. In *Individual Differences in Language Ability and Language Behavior*, C. J. Fillmore, D. Kempler, and W. S.-Y. Wang (eds.). New York: Academic Press.

Labov, William. 1970. The study of language in its social context. *Studium Generale* 23, 30–87.

Labov, William. 1972. *Language in the Inner City*. Philadelphia: University of Pennsylvania Press.

Lakoff, Robin. 1973. The logic of politeness; or, minding your p's and q's. *Papers from the Ninth Regional Meeting of the Chicago Linguistics Society*. Chicago: University of Chicago Department of Linguistics.

Lakoff, Robin. 1979. Stylistic strategies within a grammar of style. In *Language, Sex, and Gender*, J. Orasanu, M. Slater, and L. Adler (eds.), 327. Annals of the New York Academy of Sciences.

Reisman, Karl. 1974. Contrapuntal conversations in an Antiguan village. In *Explorations in the Ethnography of Speaking*, R. Bauman and J. Sherzer (eds.), 110–124. Cambridge: Cambridge University Press.

Sacks, Harvey, Schegloff, Emanuel, and Jefferson, Gail. 1974. A simplest systematics for the organization of turn-taking for conversation. *Language* 50(4), 696–735.

Schenkein, Jim. 1978. *Studies in the Organization of Conversational Interaction*. New York: Academic Press.

Tannen, Deborah. 1979. Processes and consequences of conversational style. Unpublished thesis, University of California, Berkeley.

Tannen, Deborah. 1980a. When is an overlap not an interruption? *First Delaware Symposium on Languages and Linguistics*. Newark: University of Delaware Press.

Tannen, Deborah. 1981. The machine-gun question: An example of conversational style. *Journal of Pragmatics* V(5): 383–397.

Tannen, Deborah. 1987. Conversation style. In *Psycholinguistic Models of Production*, H. Dechert and M. Raupach (eds.). Hillsboro, NJ: Erlbaum.

Van Antwerp, Caroline, and Maxwell, Monica. 1982. Speaker sex, regional dialect, and employability: A study in language attitudes. In *Linguistics and the Professions*, R. DiPietro (ed.). Norwood, NJ: Ablex.

White, Edmund. 1980. *States of Desire: Travels in Gay America*. New York: Dutton.

## Critical Thinking and Application

- Do you consider your own speech preferences to be more like the New Yorkers' or more like the Californians' (to take two iconic cases)? Have you had experience talking with people who tend to use the other style? What happens?
- What is "good listening"? Might rules for this vary across cultures? Ask classmates about the norms in their home settings.
- Why are some people proud of and others embarrassed about their own speech styles? In the latter case, why don't people abandon the "embarrassing" styles?
- Assign parts and read aloud the transcripts as if they are the script of a play. Be sure to overlap and interrupt when appropriate. How does this kind of reading change your understanding of this topic? Is it difficult for some speakers to read some parts? Why?

## Vocabulary

| | | |
|---|---|---|
| adjacency pair | linguistic insecurity | politeness |
| deference | negative face | positive face |
| genre | overlap | style, conversational |
| hypercorrection | paralinguistic | topic |
| latch | phonology | turn taking |

## Suggested Further Reading

Brown, Penelope, and Stephen C. Levinson. 1978. Universals in Language Usage: Politeness Phenomena. In *Questions and Politeness: Strategies in Social Interaction*, edited by Esther N. Goody. Cambridge: Cambridge University Press.

Goffman, Erving. 1959. *The Presentation of Self in Everyday Life*. Garden City, NY: Doubleday.

Goffman, Erving. 1967. *Interaction Ritual: Essays on Face-to-Face Behavior*. Garden City, NY: Doubleday.

Lakoff, Robin Tolmach, and Sachiko Ide, eds. 2005. *Broadening the Horizon of Linguistic Politeness*. Amsterdam and Philadelphia: Benjamins.

Ochs, Elinor, Emanuel A. Schegloff, and Sandra A. Thompson, eds. 1996. *Interaction and Grammar*. Cambridge and New York: Cambridge University Press.

Sacks, Harvey. 1995. *Lectures on Conversation*, edited by Gail Jefferson. Oxford and Cambridge, MA: Blackwell.

Schegloff, Emanuel A. 2007. *Sequence Organization in Interaction: A Primer in Conversational Analysis* (Vol. 1). Cambridge and New York: Cambridge University Press.

# CHAPTER 31

# Regional Dialects

*William A. Kretzschmar Jr.*

(2004)

*William Kretzschmar takes up the fascinating topic of regional dialects—one form of sociolinguistic variation—in U.S. English. As he shows, dialects are constantly remade from habits that have many sources. While even in a single area individuals may not speak in identical ways, "dialects" are tendencies that many individuals may approximate.*

*Dialect geographers, or dialectologists, observe tendencies in word use or pronunciation and map where one or another variant is found. Kretzschmar relies heavily on work done by Kurath in the middle of the twentieth century—using a number of terms that have now vanished (demonstrating the rapidity of language change, though this was not the intention of the research). He also summarizes more recent research on language areas from the* Dictionary of American Regional English *and work by William Labov and his collaborators on sound changes. Overall, we find that language differences are uneven but significant. The principles of language change are evident, however, in the patterns of greater and lesser homogeneity.*

## Reading Questions

- What are the three major speech areas of the eastern United States? What were the dominant influences of each of them?
- Though many specific words have disappeared between the middle and late twentieth-century studies of American dialects, the two major studies cited here suggest that the regional dialect *patterns* themselves persist. What areas do we tend to find?
- What are the three major patterns of sound change that Labov and others have identified in the late twentieth century? Do they ever give rise to misunderstanding?

## Background

While all Americans know there are regional **dialects** of American English…, it is actually quite difficult to prove them right. Detailed investigation of what Americans say – their pronunciation, their grammar, the words they use for everyday things and ideas – shows that each of us is an individual in our language use, not quite the same as any other person studied. All English speakers do of course share a great many words, a core grammar, and much the same sound system but, despite all that we share, American English speakers also vary in their speech. Some, for example, know that a *dragonfly* can be called a *snake feeder* or a *mosquito hawk*, others that it can be called a *darning needle*. Some rhyme the word pairs *cot* and *caught* and *Don* and *dawn*, but others do not rhyme them. To say how they got into the swimming pool last summer, some would say *dived*, others *dove*. There are various possible pronunciations and word choices and grammatical constructions for almost anything that any American would ever want to say – and thus the number of possible combinations of the choices that anyone could make is practically infinite. Surveys carried out in the middle of the twentieth century for the American Linguistic Atlas Project (ALAP) demonstrated that no two speakers in the extensive survey gave exactly the same set of responses to its questionnaire about everyday speech (cf. Houck 1969). It is simply not true that all Americans from a particular region share exactly the same choices of words, pronunciations, and grammar, or that a complete set of choices from one region (say, the North) is different from the set chosen by speakers from another region (say, the South). Moreover, speakers from different social groups within the same locality, and even the same speaker in different situations and at different times, will make different linguistic choices….

Yet we are not wrong to notice that people from different regions of the USA do seem to speak English differently.

William A. Kretzschmar Jr. Regional Dialects. In *Language in the USA: Themes for the Twenty-first Century*, ed. Edward Finegan and John R. Rickford. Cambridge: Cambridge University Press, 2004, pp. 39–57.

In large terms, the speech of people from one region is generally more similar to the speech of people from the same region and less similar to the speech of people from other regions. Americans can often (though not always) recognize the speech of a fellow American as coming from a different part of the country from our own, just as we can recognize an American speaker as talking differently from, say, a speaker of British English or Australian English – though we often cannot recognize a Canadian speaker so readily. What we are recognizing in any of these cases is a tendency for people from a particular place to make some of the same choices of words, pronunciations, and grammar as other people from the same place. Analysis of data from the American Linguistic Atlas Project shows that among a wide range of linguistic features tested, any particular feature tends to be used by people who live relatively close to each other (Kretzschmar 1996a, Lee and Kretzschmar 1993). Words that are not known by very many people in the ALAP survey tend to be known by people who live near each other; and words known by larger numbers of speakers tend to be found in geographical clusters, rather than distributed evenly across the survey area. Other studies also suggest that geography is one of the most important factors for sharing variant linguistic features (e.g., LePage and Tabouret-Keller 1985, Johnson 1996). Such tendencies for any given linguistic feature to be used in specific places can be described statistically for the ALAP survey data. In real life, when we hear relatively unfamiliar words or pronunciations or grammar in someone's speech, we have to guess where those features might be used according to our own sense of probability.

The relative association of particular features of English with Americans from some particular part of the country has its roots in American history. Unlike England, where the English language has a history stretching back to the fifth century CE, North America has a history of settlement by English speakers of only about 400 years. The relatively short period of settlement has not allowed time for dialect differences as sharp as those found in Britain (e.g., between Scottish English and the English of the Thames Valley) to develop in North America – and it is not likely that such sharp regional differences will emerge in the future, given mass public education and other social conditions that do not favor the development of sharp dialect differences. Yet regional differences have in fact emerged in North America and they show no sign of disappearing.

Two factors led to the development of dialects in America. First, and by far the most important, settlements in the American colonies began as separate isolated communities, and each developed somewhat different speech habits during the early colonial period. As settlement proceeded inland from the coastal outposts, the speech habits of the coastal communities were carried to the interior by sons and daughters of the established colonists and by new immigrants who landed at the coast and acquired speech habits as they made their way to the frontier (which for some immigrants took years). Settlement proceeded generally westward in three large geographical bands as far as the Mississippi River, corresponding to what is now the Northern tier of states, a Midland region, and the Southern region. In the North the speech habits that became established in Upstate New York (which differed from the speech of New York City and its environs, originally Dutch in settlement, and from the speech of New England, which was separated from the Inland North by mountains) were carried westward by means of water travel on the Erie Canal and Great Lakes as far as northern Illinois, Wisconsin, and Minnesota. The South had no convenient waterway to facilitate travel, and the varied topography of the land – mountains, the piney woods, wiregrass – was not all well suited to the pattern of plantation agriculture that dominated the colonial economies of Virginia and the Carolinas. Southern settlement thus proceeded more slowly, and in a patchwork of communities across Georgia and Alabama until settlers reached more generally suitable plantation lands in the plains and Mississippi Basin areas of Tennessee, Mississippi, Louisiana, and East Texas. Philadelphia was the focal city for settlement in the Midland region, which proceeded west in two broad streams. The National Road was built through Pennsylvania, eventually as far as central Illinois, close to the present-day route of Interstate 80. Settlement took place along the road, and settlers could also reach the Ohio River valley and then use the waterway to settle farther inland. This more northerly stream of Midland settlement carried Midland speech habits, which mixed to some degree with the speech habits of the Northern region. The more southerly stream of Midland settlement followed the course of the Shenandoah River south through Virginia towards the Cumberland Gap in Tennessee. Mostly these South Midland settlers were subsistence farmers, and they occupied whatever land could support them throughout the Appalachian Mountain region and the uplands as far west as Arkansas, and also in the lowlands of the Southern states where the land was not suitable for plantations. In addition to Midland speech habits, these settlers also acquired speech habits characteristic of the Southern region, especially those Midlanders who found their way to marginally productive land near plantation country. These historical patterns of settlement – North, Midland, and South – created the basic framework of regional American dialects that we still see – and hear – today. (See Figure 31.1 [Kurath 1949: Fig. 3], which we will discuss further below.)

The second historical factor that influenced regional varieties was the people who originally settled the separate colonies. Each colony had its own particular mix of colonists who spoke dialects from different areas of England, or who did not speak English at all. Undoubtedly, some traces of these immigrant speech habits have survived. Lists are available that highlight the contributions to the American English vocabulary of Native Americans, Germans, the Spanish, and other non-English-speaking groups (Marckwardt 1958: 22–58). A list of the contribution of words from African languages to Gullah, a Creole variety still spoken in the Sea Islands off the southern coast is also available (Turner 1949), along with a list of words of African origin still used in the southeast (McDavid and McDavid 1951). As for British dialect influences, special studies of the relationship between Scottish English and Appalachian English have been made (e.g., Montgomery 1989, 1997, Montgomery and Nagle 1993). However, so-called "colonial leveling" resulted from a tendency not to preserve any more than occasional distinctive habits of regional English dialects or isolated words or usages from immigrant languages other than English. Speculative accounts (e.g., Trudgill 1986) of a colonial American **koiné** (a regional dialect used as the common language of a larger area) perhaps overstate the case, since we see that different settlement patterns have created different and long-lasting dialect regions, but there were indeed reasons for settlers not to maintain the sets of speech habits that marked British dialects of English (Kretzschmar 1997). Whole communities of speakers of a dialect or language did not usually settle together, and most communities that began as homogeneous settlements in time blended into the surrounding culture. The strict religious communities of the Pennsylvania Dutch that still preserve their (now archaic) German language are the exception that proves the rule. Thus it is not true that any American regional variety of speech derives particularly from one British dialect source. Appalachian English, for instance, is not particularly descended from Scottish English, although it does show some Scottish influence. Because of population mixture, each colony had a range of speech habits out of which its own regional characteristics could eventually emerge (see, e.g., Miller 1999). ALAP evidence shows that dialect areas in the eastern USA share essentially the same original word stock, but have preserved it differently (Kretzschmar 1996b). While we cannot discount influences from British dialects and the non-English-speaking population, these influences were secondary to the formation of their

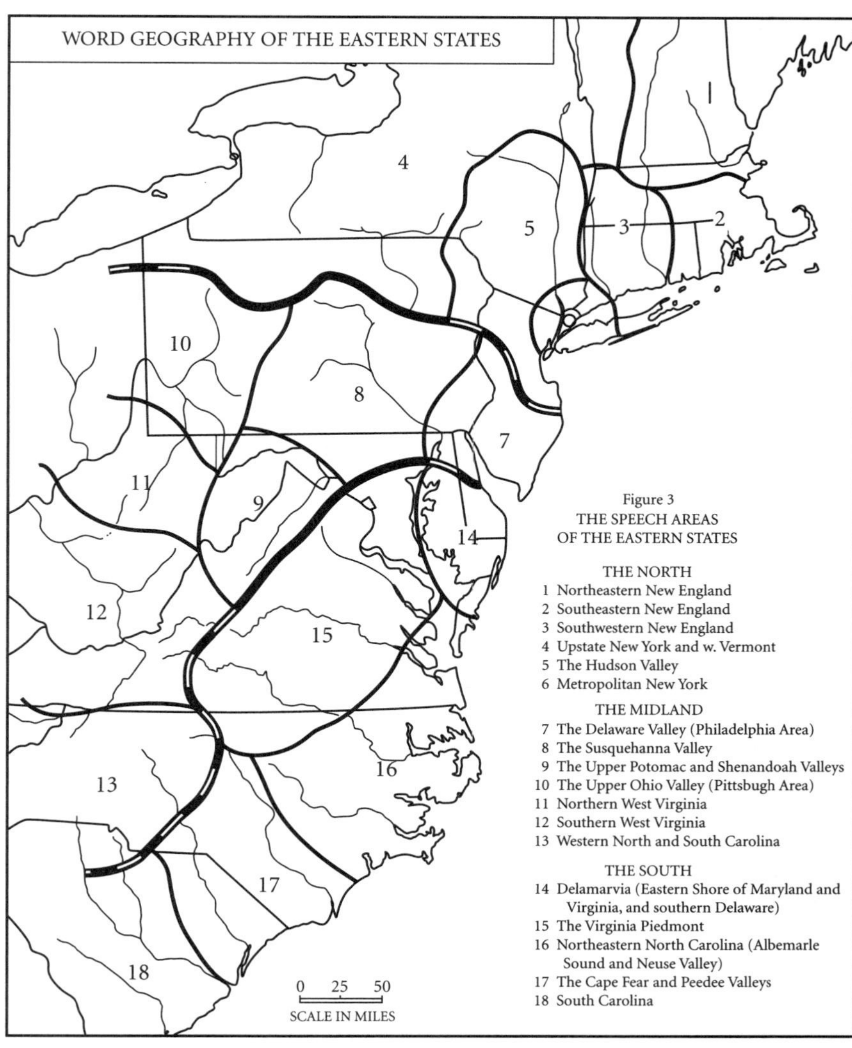


**Figure 31.1** *The Speech Areas of the Eastern States*
Source *From Kurath 1949*

own speech habits by the early populations of the different colonies.

Finally, it is unwise to assume that speech habits that we associate with a particular region have been used there for a long time. Among features most commonly associated with Southern American English, the pronunciation of the vowel in *fire* as a near rhyme with *far*, the pronunciation of *pin* and *pen* as words that rhyme, and the vocabulary item *fixin' to* 'preparing to, about to' were rare or non-existent before the last quarter of the nineteenth century (Bailey 1997). Likewise, other features commonly associated with Southern speech such as lack of pronunciation of *-r* after vowels (as in words like *four* pronounced as *foa* or *foe*) and *a*-prefix on verbs with *-ing* endings (like *a-running*) are also in rapid decline. Similarly, the relatively infrequent variant terms for *chest of drawers* in ALAP data from the eastern USA actually recapitulate terms found in old furniture pattern books (Burkette 2001). The most common American term for this piece of bedroom furniture is now *dresser*, but in the ALAP data of the 1930s and 1940s the most common term was *bureau*, and other terms, now relics, may have been prominent still earlier (Burkette 2001). While individual habits of speech – whether words or pronunciations or grammatical usages – are likely to come and go, the tendency to use different habits in different regions will nonetheless continue. As a consequence, regional variation may well persist in much the same geographical patterns even after such changes in speech habits (cf. Bailey and Tillery 1996). It is thus fair to say that regional dialects of American English are continuously rebuilding themselves, simultaneously dying away with the loss of some speech habits that formerly characterized them and being reborn with new speech habits that speakers might recognize as probably coming from a particular region.

The remainder of this chapter presents evidence for the status of regional dialects in the mid-twentieth century and the beginning of the twenty-first century. First, evidence collected for the ALAP project is used to characterize mid-twentieth century regional varieties; then, more recent evidence is given for regional variation. For both periods it is important to remember that "speaking a regional dialect" is really nothing more than a tendency for a speaker to make some of the same linguistic choices as other people from the same location. A "dialect" is thus a generalization, an abstraction that seizes upon a few selected linguistic features to characterize a variety of the language. A dialect is not a social contract or a comprehensive set of linguistic rules by which all the residents of an area must abide.

## Regional Dialects at Mid-Twentieth Century

Figure 31.1, a 1949 map of dialect areas in the eastern USA based on ALAP evidence, is an example of a dialect generalization. In order to make the map, Hans Kurath, one of the most accomplished **dialect geographers**, began with individual words, like those used to designate the *dragonfly*, and he plotted where ALAP speakers used them, as in Figure 31.2 (Kurath 1949: Map 141). You can see that *darning needle* mostly occurs in the North, *mosquito hawk* and *snake doctor* in the South, and *snake feeder* in Pennsylvania and areas of the Appalachian Mountains as far south as western North Carolina. Such a neat pattern, where each different variant seems to occupy its own part of the map, is extremely unusual in the ALAP evidence; most patterns of distribution for words (or for pronunciations or grammatical features) show a rather spotty areal distribution, with more than one alternative in use in any given area. The *dragonfly* variants, however, show only a relatively small number of words out of their own areas, for example, occurrences of *snake doctor* too far north in Pennsylvania or *darning needle* too far south in West Virginia. From maps like these, the dialect geographer carefully selected features from which to make a different kind of map such as is shown in Figure 31.3 (Kurath 1949: Figure 5a). He drew best-fit lines, called **"isoglosses,"** to indicate the boundary of the majority usage of his carefully chosen words. Here, the dotted line shows the Southern boundary for *darning needle*, which matches where *darning needle* occurred most of the time in Figure 31.2, except for the stray occurrences in West Virginia. To speak in terms of tendencies, if someone heard an American from the time of the ALAP survey say the word *darning needle* in reference to an insect, it would be a very good guess to say that the speaker came from north of the isogloss – but the guess might be wrong because *darning needle* was also used occasionally elsewhere.

Figure 31.3 also shows the next stage of that older process for making a dialect generalization. In this case, the researcher tried to find words whose isoglosses would run in about the same place. Here *darning needle* is combined with isoglosses for *whiffletree* (a variant term for part of the equipment for hitching horses to a wagon – still an everyday rural practice in the 1930s and 1940s) and *pail* (as opposed to *bucket*), all terms used in the North. Such a combination of isoglosses is called a "bundle," and **bundles of isoglosses** are represented by the boundaries of dialect areas shown in Figure 31.1. The heavy black lines in Pennsylvania and Maryland/Virginia represent the thickest bundles of isoglosses. At each end of the heavy black lines, their continuation has been represented with a double line to indicate less agreement in the path of the bundled isoglosses. For instance, in Figure 31.3 the isoglosses diverge in eastern Pennsylvania and New Jersey, just where the double lines appear in Figure 31.1. All of the thinner lines separating the subsidiary dialect areas of the region also represent bundles of isoglosses, but the bundles have fewer constituents than the ones represented by the heavy black or double lines. There was no fixed rule for how many isoglosses had to be present to make a bundle, but the numbers were quite small in relative terms. Out of the thousands available in the ALAP data, only about 400 words were plotted for Kurath's (1949) *Word Geogra-*

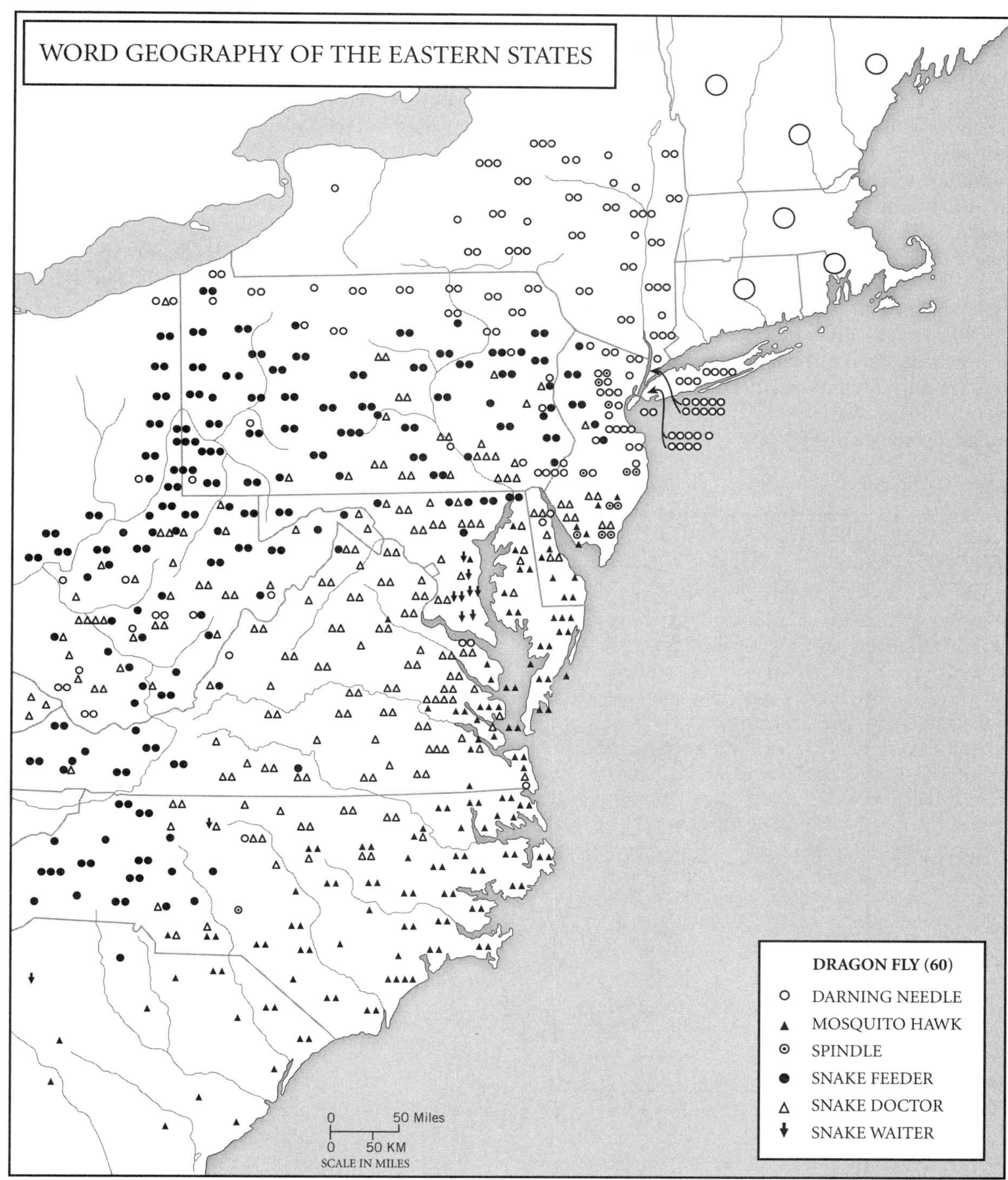


**Figure 31.2** *Dragon fly*
Source *From Kurath 1949*

*phy*, and only a very small number of the mapped words yielded clear isoglosses at all, much less isoglosses that ran together to form bundles that could mark major and subsidiary dialect boundaries. This earlier technique allowed Kurath to confirm judgments he had made about American dialect areas on the basis of his experience and his study of historical settlement patterns: all he needed was a small number of representative isoglosses for that purpose (see Kretzschmar 1992, 1996a). A later study showed that patterns of American pronunciation in the ALAP data largely matched the patterns derived from the vocabulary variants (Kurath and McDavid 1961). The dialect boundaries of Figure 31.1 are thus more suggestive of tendencies rather than being sharp boundaries where, if speakers crossed them while traveling, they could hear sharply different dialects in the speech of the local population on each side. Travelers who go long distances before stopping are apt to hear greater differences in speech habits between stops than they would have heard if they had stopped more frequently along the way.

In addition to these famous maps, Kurath also produced tables indicating whether a word was used regularly (marked by X), fairly commonly (marked by—), rarely (marked by · or a blank space), or not at all in the subsidiary dialect areas of a major dialect region. Figure 31.4 is the table for the Northern region (Kurath 1949: Table I). Only a few terms such as *pail* and *darning needle* are shown as being used throughout the North, and a few more occur in most of the North but are lacking in one of the subsidiary dialect areas. (The numbers in parenthesis after each word – e.g., pail (17) – refer to discussion elsewhere in Kurath's book and are not germane to our discussion here.) The tables also show that some words are used in only two of the major dialect regions, but not in all three. For example, Figure 31.5 shows words that were used in the Midland and the South, but not as much in the North (Kurath 1949: Table V). Figure 31.6 shows words used in the North and the South, but not throughout the Midland (Kurath 1949: Table VI). The table for the Southern region (Figure 31.7; Kurath 1949: Table III), which includes a column for the South Midland, indicates clearly the complexity of speech habits in different areas of this most recognizable of American regional dialects. These tables show us again that Kurath's major American dialect regions are generalizations that, while not wrong, are based on a small number of representative words and that the dialect regions contain large degrees of internal variation within them.

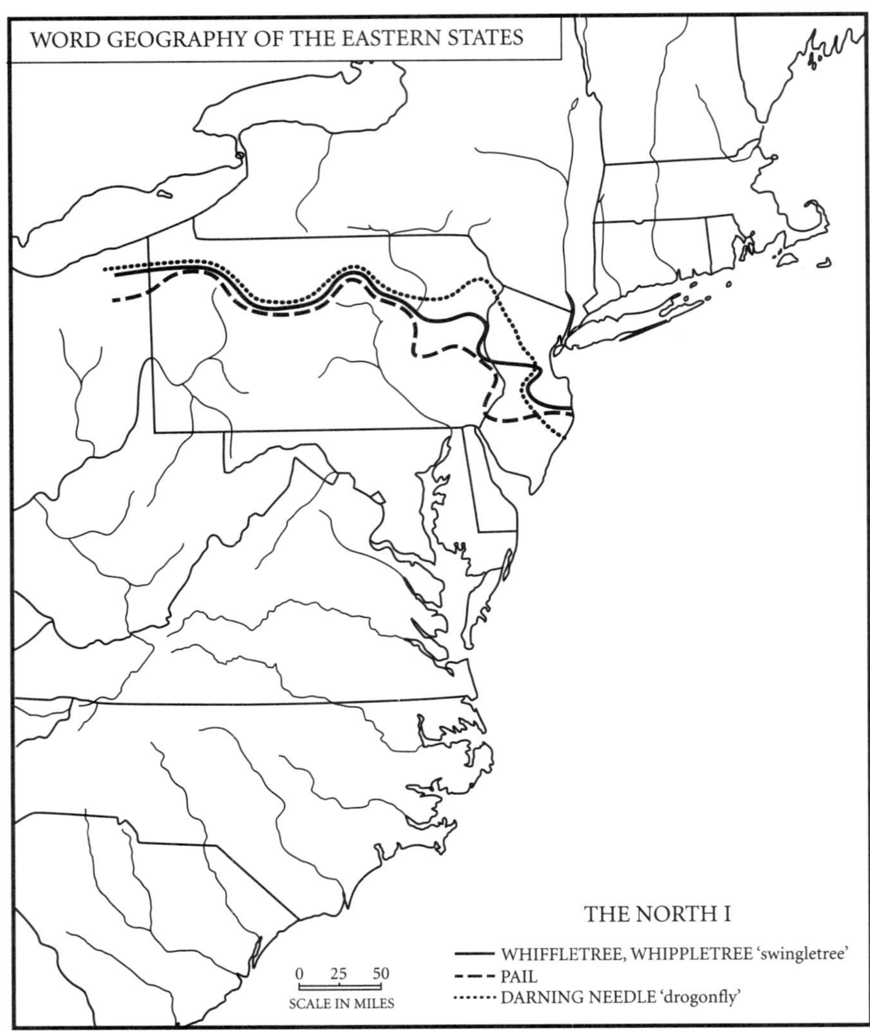


**Figure 31.3** *The North I*
Source *From Kurath 1949*

### THE NORTHERN AREA

| X regular<br>– fairly common<br>rare | Ohio | New York State | | New England | |
|---|---|---|---|---|---|
| | | Upstate | Hudson Valley | Western | Eastern |
| *(1) The North* | | | | | |
| pail (17) | X | X | X | X | X |
| whiffletree (21) | X | X | X | X | X |
| boss! (37) | X | X | X | X | X |
| johnny cake (44) | X | X | X | X | X |
| darning needle (60) | X | X | X | X | X |
| angle worm 60) | | X | – | X | X |
| stone wall (16) | | – | X | X | X |
| nigh-horse (39) | – | – | – | – | X |
| *(2) The North without Eastern New England* | | | | | |
| stoop (10) | X | X | X | X | |
| stone boat (21) | X | X | X | X | |
| fried-cakes (45) | X | X | – | – | |
| lobbered milk, loppered milk (47) | X | X | X | X | |
| sugar bush (61) | X | X | X | – | |
| button ball (61) | | X | X | X | |
| belly-gut(ter) (95) | X | X | – | – | |
| *(3) The North without the Hudson Valley* | | | | | |
| buttry (10) | – | – | | – | – |
| spider (17) | X | X | | X | X |
| fills, thills (20) | X | X | | X | X |
| teeter board (22) | X | X | | X | X |
| coal hod (23) | – | – | | X | X |
| hasty-pudding, Indian pudding (50) | X | X | | X | X |
| Dutch cheese (47) | X | X | | X | – |
| horning (82) | X | X | | – | |

**Figure 31.4** *The Northern Area*
Source *From Kurath 1949*

In addition to the plotting of separate pronunciations as they occurred throughout the ALAP survey area, mid-twentieth-century dialect geographers also wished to construct vowel systems that showed the relationship between vowel sounds within dialect regions. They isolated four types of vowel systems in the eastern USA, as shown in Figure 31.8 (Kurath and McDavid 1961: 6–7).

Differences between the systems are subtle and still noticeable in the speech of Americans from the regions specified. The vowels found in the words *crib, three, ten, eight,* and *bag* are shared by all four regional pronunciation systems, as are those in the words *thirty* and *down* and those in the words *wood* and *tooth*. By contrast, the other vowels vary in the relationships within the four systems of Figure 31.8, and the variation increases in the separate subareas included in the four systems (Kurath and McDavid 1961). In type III for Eastern New England, for instance, the vowel of *car* (and other words like it) is fronted so that it is close in pronunciation to the vowel of *bag* (this is the "Boston" pronunciation often imitated in the phrase "pahk the cah"). Eastern New England also shows a merger of two vowel sounds kept separate in types I and II, the vowels of *crop* and *law*. The vowel system of Western Pennsylvania also has merged these two vowel sounds, but does not have the (fronted) Boston vowel in *car*. The type II system (Metropolitan New York, the Upper South, and the Lower South) does not merge the vowels of *crop* and *law*, but those vowels are more retracted into the low-back vowel range. Metropolitan New York does not share one of the features strongly associated with Southern and South Midland pronunciation, namely, the "slow

## THE MIDLAND AND THE SOUTH

| X regular<br>– fairly common<br>. rare | South | | | | Midland | | | | North |
|---|---|---|---|---|---|---|---|---|---|
| | South Carolina | North Carolina | Virginia Piedmont | Eastern Shore | South Midland | Western Pennsylvania | Eastern Pennsylvania | West Jersey | |
| dog irons, fire dogs (8) | X | X | X | . | X | – | . | . | . |
| paling fence (16) | X | X | X | X | X | X | X | – | |
| bucket (17) | X | X | X | X | X | X | X | X | . |
| spicket (18) | – | X | X | X | X | X | X | X | |
| singletree (21) | X | X | X | X | X | X | X | X | |
| seesaw (22) | X | X | X | X | – | X | X | – | – |
| comfort (29) | X | X | X | X | X | X | X | X | |
| pully-bone (37) | X | X | X | X | X | – | . | X | |
| corn pone (44) | X | X | X | X | X | X | – | | |
| roasting ears (56) | X | X | X | X | X | X | – | | |
| pole cat (59) | X | X | X | X | X | X | X | . | |
| ground squirrel (59) | X | X | X | – | X | X | – | – | |
| granny (woman) (65) | X | X | X | X | X | – | X | . | |
| right smart (74) | X | X | X | X | X | X | X | X | . |
| agin I get there (89) | – | – | – | – | X | – | . | | |
| Christmas gift! (93) | X | X | X | X | X | – | – | | |

**Figure 31.5** *The Midland and the South*
Source *From Kurath 1949*

## THE NORTH AND THE SOUTH

| X regular<br>– fairly common<br>. rare | South | | | | Midland | | North | | | |
|---|---|---|---|---|---|---|---|---|---|---|
| | South Carolina | North Carolina | Virginia Piedmont | Eastern Shore | South Midland | North Midland | Hudson Valley | Upstate New York | Western New England | Eastern New England |
| quarter to (4) | – | – | X | – | | . | – | – | – | – |
| curtains (9) | . | – | – | – | | – | . | – | X | X |
| piazza (10) | X | X | . | | | | – | | X | X |
| gutters (11) | X | X | X | – | | – | X | . | – | X |
| corn house (14) | – | . | X | – | | | . | . | – | – |
| spider (17) | – | – | . | . | | . | – | X | X | X |
| low, loo (36) | X | X | X | X | . | . | | – | – | – |
| harslet (37) | X | X | X | X | – | | – | | – | X |
| nanniel (38) | – | – | – | X | . | | . | – | – | – |

**Figure 31.6** *The North and the South*
Source *From Kurath 1949*

THE SOUTHERN AREA

| **X regular**<br>**– fairly common**<br>**. rare** | **South Midland** | | | **South** | | | | | |
|---|---|---|---|---|---|---|---|---|---|
| | | | | **Virginia Maryland** | | | **The Carolinas** | | |
| | **Western N. C.** | **West Virginia** | **Valley of Virginia** | **Piedmont** | **Tidewater** | **Eastern Shore** | **Albemarle Sound** | **Cape Fear** | **South Carolina** |
| *(1) The South and the South Midland* | | | | | | | | | |
| light-bread (44) | X | X | X | X | X | X | X | X | X |
| clabber (47) | X | X | X | X | X | X | X | X | X |
| snack (48) | X | – | – | X | X | X | X | X | – |
| middlins (46) | X | X | – | X | X | X | – | X | |
| ash cakes (44) | – | . | – | X | X | – | – | – | – |
| (hay) shocks (14) | X | X | X | X | X | . | X | X | |
| (corn) shucks (56) | X | X | X | X | X | – | X | X | X |
| you-all (43) | – | – | X | X | X | – | X | X | X |
| waiter (82) | – | – | – | – | – | – | – | – | – |
| pallet (29) | X | – | X | X | X | . | X | X | X |
| gutters (11) | X | . | X | X | X | . | X | X | X |
| (barn) lot (15) | X | – | . | X | . | | X | X | |
| roll the baby (64) | – | | – | X | – | – | – | – | X |
| salad (55) | – | | . | X | X | . | X | X | |
| rock fence (16) | X | X | X | X | – | . | | | |
| *(2) The South* | | | | | | | | | |
| low (36) | – | . | | X | X | X | X | X | X |
| hasslet (37) | – | | | X | X | X | X | X | X |
| lightwood (8) | | | – | X | X | X | X | X | X |
| turn of wood (19) | | | | X | X | X | X | X | – |
| co-wench! (37) | | | | X | X | X | X | X | X |
| *(3) Virginia and the South Midland* | | | | | | | | | |
| garden house (12) | | | – | – | X | . | X | | |
| wesket (27) | | . | – | – | – | . | – | | |
| lumber room (10) | . | | – | X | – | . | . | | |
| soft peach (54) | . | | . | X | – | | . | | |
| nicker (36) | – | X | – | X | – | – | | | |
| snake doctor (60) | . | – | X | X | . | . | | | |
| come up! (38) | – | – | – | X | . | | | | |
| batter bread (44) | | | . | X | X | | | | |
| *(4) The Carolinas and the South Midland* | | | | | | | | | |
| whicker (36) | – | | | | – | X | X | X | X |
| johnny cake, a griddle cake (44) | – | . | . | | . | X | – | – | – |
| clabber cheese (47) | X | – | | | . | . | X | X | – |
| breakfast strip (46) | – | | | | – | | – | – | – |
| kerosene (24) | X | | | | – | | X | X | X |
| woods colt (65) | X | X | – | | | | – | X | X |
| goop! (38) | – | | | | . | | | X | X |
| *(5) The Southern Coast* | | | | | | | | | |
| curtains (9) | | . | . | . | X | – | X | | . |
| spider (17) | | | | | – | . | X | X | |
| mosquito hawk (60) | | | | | – | X | X | X | X |
| press peach (54) | | | | | – | – | X | X | X |
| piazza (10) | | | | | – | | – | X | X |
| earthworm (60) | | | | | – | | X | X | X |

**Figure 31.7** *The Southern Area*
Source *From Kurath 1949*

Type I: *Upstate New York, Eastern Pennsylvania, and the South Midland*

| | | | | | | |
|---|---|---|---|---|---|---|
| *crib : three* | ɪ | i | | ʊ | u | *wood : tooth* |
| *ten : eight* | ɛ | e | ɜ | ʌ | o | *sun : road* |
| *bag* | æ | | ɑ | | ɔ | *law* |
| *five* | | ai | au | | ɔi | *boil* |
| | | | *thirty* | | | |
| | | | *crop* | | | |
| | | | *down* | | | |

Type II: *Metropolitan New York, the Upper South, and the Lower South*

| | | | | | | |
|---|---|---|---|---|---|---|
| *crib : three* | ɪ | i | | ʊ | u | *wood : tooth* |
| *ten : eight* | ɛ | e | ɜ | ʌ | o | *sun : road* |
| *bag* | æ | | | | ɔ | *law* |
| | | | | ɑ | ɑ˞ | *crop : car* |
| *five* | | ai | au | | ɔi | *boil* |
| | | | *thirty* | | | |
| | | | *down* | | | |

Type III: *Eastern New England*

| | | | | | | |
|---|---|---|---|---|---|---|
| *crib : three* | ɪ | i | | ʊ | u | *wood : tooth* |
| *ten : eight* | ɛ | e | ɜ | θ | o | *road : rode* |
| *bag : car* | æ | a | | ʌ | ɒ | *sun : law, crop* |
| *five* | | ai | au | | ɒi | *boil* |
| | | | *thirty* | | | |
| | | | *down* | | | |

Type IV: *Western Pennsylvania*

| | | | | | | |
|---|---|---|---|---|---|---|
| *crib : three* | ɪ | i | | ʊ | u | *wood : tooth* |
| *ten : eight* | ɛ | e | ɜ | ʌ | o | *sun : road* |
| *bag* | æ | | | | ɒ | *law, crop* |
| *five* | | ai | au | | ɒi | *boil* |
| | | | *thirty* | | | |
| | | | *down* | | | |

**Figure 31.8** *Vowels Systems in the Eastern USA*
Source *From Kurath and McDavid 1961*

diphthong" that makes speakers from other regions hear the word *fire* as *far*. It is one of the "phonic and incidental features" that color the pronunciation of every subarea (Kurath and McDavid 1961).

## American Regional Dialects for the Twenty-First Century

The ALAP researchers described regional American dialects as they existed in the middle of the twentieth century. We now consider what has happened to the regional patterns during the rapid technological and cultural change that has swept America along since World War II, and we consider future prospects for regional dialects.

A more recent treatment by Carver (1987) has mapped American vocabulary with reference to the *Dictionary of American Regional English (DARE)* for which field work was carried out in the 1960s and 1970s (Cassidy et al. 1985–). He found essentially the same dialect areas that Kurath and McDavid had found, although he used a different method to create his maps and preferred different names for some areas. He often noted that some of the words earlier selected for the mid-twentieth century ALAP isoglosses were rare at the time of the *DARE* field work, or no longer found at all. This does not mean that the earlier regional dialect areas had disappeared. Quite the opposite: since the later dialect areas are much the same as the earlier ones, the more recent lists of words from the different areas are successors of the earlier ones. The speakers of the regional dialects changed their habits, but the basic regional patterning of American speech remained in place.

An index of entries in the first two *DARE* volumes provides lists of the words for which all of the different regional labels were used (*An Index* 1993). For instance, there are 1,540 words labeled as "South" and 1,318 as "South Midland," although 851 of these words actually carried both labels (Metcalf 1997: 267). These counts give an indication of the extent to which words can be associated with American dialect regions. The figure for the label "Northern" is smaller (624), but still substantial. Hawaii had the most words (133), followed by Texas (125), California (123), Pennsylvania (113), and Louisiana (110); New York is also prominent if labels for New York City are added to those for the state (87 + 35 = 122) (Metcalf 1997: 273–74). It is not unreasonable to talk about the speech of a state, although state boundaries are political and not usually defined by isoglosses or other linguistic means. As the counts show, however, a smaller number of words associates with any state than with labels for dialect areas. From Kurath's earlier maps, it is evident that a state often has more than one major dialect region within its borders. Only 56 words in the first two volumes of *DARE* were associated with cities, and more than half of those were associated with New York City (Metcalf 1997). *DARE* evidence thus confirms the persistence of large American regional dialect patterns into the second half of the twentieth century, even if some words have become obsolete and others have emerged to take their place. *DARE* suggests that these large regional patterns may be more salient, at least according to word counts, than states or cities as ways to describe and recognize American dialect patterns.

Extensive work in urban areas, particularly in Philadelphia and New York City, has confirmed the vitality of regional dialects. William Labov and his associates found "increasing diversity" in the pronunciation of US English and sought to highlight

> the main finding of our research, one that violates the most commonsense expectation of how language works and is supposed to work. In spite of the intense exposure of the American population to a national media with a convergent network standard of pronunciation, sound change continues actively in all urban dialects that have been studied, so that the local accents of Boston, New York, Philadelphia, Atlanta, Buffalo, Detroit, Chicago, and San Francisco are more different from each other than at any time in the past...Though the first findings dealt with sound change in Eastern cities, it is now clear that it is equally true of Northern, Western and Southern dialects. (Labov and Ash 1997: 508)

Three large patterns of **sound change** have been identified, and they are called the Northern Cities Shift, the Southern Shift, and Low Back Merger (Labov 1991). The term *sound change* refers to the fact that the pronunciation of both vowel and consonant sounds is not eternally fixed but may change over time. For discussion of regional dialects, such changes are important because they are not uniform for all speakers. Different changes occur within different groups of speakers. The term ***shift*** refers to the apparent tendency of English vowels to change not one at a time but according to larger characteristic patterns. The Low Back Merger is best characterized by the fact that the words *cot* and *caught*, and the names *Don* and *Dawn*, are homophones in the area of the merger, while people elsewhere pronounce them differently. One ongoing change of the Southern Shift is the seeming reversal (the facts are actually somewhat more complicated) of the pronunciation of what in the USA are traditionally called the *long e* (IPA [i]) and *short i* (IPA [ɪ]) sounds. Among Southern Shift speakers, the name *Bill* is pronounced much like the name *Beale* would be pronounced in other parts of the country, and vice versa, and *steel mill* is pronounced close to what most people in the rest of the country would recognize as *still meal*. The Northern Cities Shift involves a sequence of changes so that each of the following words might be heard and interpreted as something else by speakers from outside the area: *Ann* as *lan*, *bit* as *bet*, *bet* as *bat* or *but*, *lunch* as *launch*, *talk* as *tuck*, *locks* as *lax* (Labov 1991: 19).

The resulting patterns of sound change have specific geographic extension, as shown in Figure 31.9 from the Atlas of North American English.

As Labov explains the map,

> A remarkable finding of [Figure 31.9] is that the major phonological boundaries of the U. S. as determined by new and vigorous sound changes which arose in the twentieth century coincide with the major lexical boundaries based on vocabulary.

In other words, the Northern Cities Shift occurs in the region occupied by what Kurath had called the Northern dialect area. Like the ALAP data, the Atlas of North American English also describes subsidiary areas. Thus, Eastern New England and the Inland North correspond to areas that Kurath also suggested (Labov's North Central region is farther west than Kurath's surveys). Kurath's Midland dialect region is recapitulated in Labov's Midland and West, which is characterized by the Low Back Merger pattern. As Figure 31.8 shows, Western Pennsylvania shows a merger of *crop* and *law*, and it is this merger that serves as the centerpiece of Labov's description of the western part of Kurath's Midland and Far West. (The Low Back Merger pattern also applies in Canada.) Finally, the region for the Southern Shift corresponds to the Coastal and Upper South areas identified in the mid-twentieth century, and the Southern Shift has urban extensions in Philadelphia and New York City (Labov 1991: 36–37). As Figure 31.8 shows, Kurath and McDavid had previously associated the vowel pattern of New York City with that of the South.

Observation of ongoing sound change confirms the one constant we expect for all languages: they will continue to change as long as people speak them. We are perhaps surprised that changes in American English seem to be occurring *within* the dialect regions described on mid-century evidence, in regions that have their foundations in the history of American primary settlement patterns. American regional dialects show no signs of disappearing; they are simply showing natural internal changes in the habits of their speakers.

What should we think of Labov's surprise, probably shared by many readers of this chapter, that "intense exposure of the American population to a national media with a convergent network standard of pronunciation" has not broken down regional dialects? This paradox – the strong continued existence of regional dialects when most educated Americans think that dialect variation is fading – is the topic for another essay (Kretzschmar 1997), but it is possible to say here that American English has developed a national dialect for the usually well-educated participants in a national marketplace for goods, services, and jobs. The

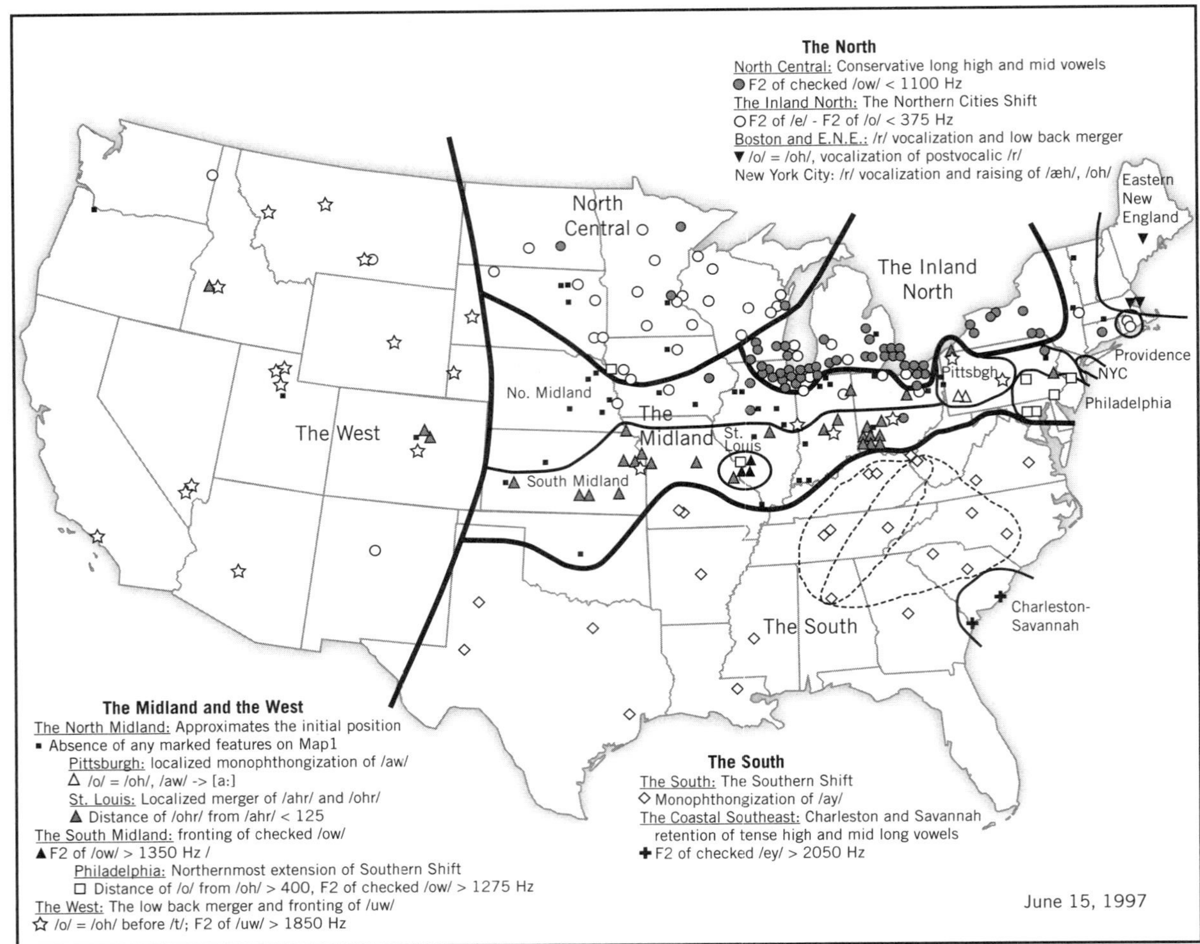


**Figure 31.9** *Urban dialect areas based on the acoustic analysis of the vowel system of 240 Telsar informants.*
Source *http://www.ling.upenn.edu/phono_atlas/NationalMap/NatMap1/.html*

well-educated share a national speech pattern within their own social stratum, unlike earlier periods in the history of American English when they shared regional dialects with working-class and lower-middle-class speakers. The solution to the paradox of the rise of national speech habits and the continuing existence of regional ones as set forth by Labov is that regional dialects are not separate from the social factors that influence the language habits of speakers – which should not surprise us at all once we come to think about it.

## Suggestions for Further Reading and Exploration

For information about the different regional surveys and for examples of complete lists of what people said in response to particular survey questions for the American Linguistic Atlas Project (ALAP), go to *http://www.us.english.uga.edu.* The most recent handbook describing the methods used is Kretzschmar et al. (1993). For early summaries of findings, see Kurath (1949), Atwood (1953), McDavid (1958), and Kurath and McDavid (1961). For dialect developments toward the end of the twentieth century, see Carver (1987). One of the best informed and most entertaining writers on regional American English was Raven McDavid, some of whose essays have been republished in McDavid (1979; see especially "Postvocalic -r in South Carolina," "The Position of the Charleston Dialect," and "Sense and Nonsense About American Dialects") and McDavid (1980; see especially "New Directions in American Dialectology"). Other collections of articles that treat regional American variation include Glowka and Lance (1993), Frazer (1993), and Schneider (1996). Evidence about early regional variation may be found in Mathews (1931). A synthesis of ideas on colonial development of varieties is Kretzschmar (2002). For Southern American English, Pederson's monumental *Linguistic Atlas of the Gulf States* (1986–92) is complemented by Bernstein et al. (1997) and Johnson (1996). The *Oxford Dictionary of Pronunciation for Current English* (2001) offers side-by-side American and British pronunciations, and its discussion of American English points out many differences in regional pronunciations. For lots of linguistic fun, browse in any volume of *DARE* (Cassidy and Hall 1985–2002) or visit the website for the Atlas of North American English at *http://www.ling.upenn.edu/phono_atlas.*

## References

*An Index by Region. Usage, and Etymology to the* Dictionary of American Regional English, Vols. I and II. 1993. *Publication of the American Dialect Society* 77.

Atwood, E. Bagby. 1953. *A Survey of Verb Forms in the Eastern United States.* Ann Arbor: University of Michigan Press.

Bailey, Guy. 1997. "When Did Southern American English Begin?" In *Englishes Around the World: Studies in Honor of Manfred Görlach.* Vol. 1, ed. Edgar Schneider. Amsterdam: John Benjamins, pp. 255–76.

Bailey, Guy and Jan Tillery. 1996. "The Persistence of Southern American English," *Journal of English Linguistics* 24: 308–21.

Bernstein, Cynthia, Thomas Nunnally, and Robin Sabino, eds. 1997. *Language Variety in the South Revisited.* Tuscaloosa: University of Alabama Press.

Burkette, Allison. 2001. "The Story of Chester Drawers," *American Speech* 76: 139–57.

Carver, Craig. 1987. *American Regional English: A Word Geography.* Ann Arbor: University of Michigan Press.

Cassidy, Frederic G. and Joan Houston Hall, eds. 1985–2002. *Dictionary of American Regional English.* Cambridge: Belknap/Harvard University Press.

Frazer, Timothy, ed. 1993. *Heartland English.* Tuscaloosa: University of Alabama Press.

Glowka, Wayne and Donald Lance, eds. 1993. *Language Variation in North American English.* New York: Modern Language Association.

Houck, Charles. 1969. "A Statistical and Computerized Methodology for Analyzing Dialect Materials." Unpublished Ph.D. dissertation, University of Iowa.

Johnson, Ellen. 1996. *Lexical Change and Variation in the Southeastern United States 1930–1990.* Tuscaloosa: University of Alabama Press.

Kretzschmar, William A., Jr. 1992. "Isoglosses and Predictive Modeling," *American Speech* 67: 227–49.

Kretzschmar, William A., Jr. 1996a. "Quantitative Areal Analysis of Dialect Features," *Language Variation and Change* 8: 13–39.

Kretzschmar, William A., Jr. 1996b. "Foundations of American English." In Schneider, pp. 25–50.

Kretzschmar, William A., Jr. 1997. "American English for the Twenty-First Century." In *Englishes Around the World: Studies in Honor of Manfred Görlach*, Vol. 1, ed. Edgar Schneider. Amsterdam: John Benjamins, pp. 307–23.

Kretzschmar, William A., Jr. 2002. "American English: Melting Pot or Mixing Bowl?" In *Of Dyuersitie and Change of Language: Essays Presented to Manfred Görlach on the Occasion of His Sixty-Fifth Birthday*, eds. Katja Lenz and Ruth Möhlig. Heidelberg: C. Winter, pp. 224–39.

Kretzschmar, William A., Jr., Virginia G. McDavid, Theodore K. Lerud, and Ellen Johnson, eds. 1993. *Handbook of the Linguistic Atlas of the Middle and South Atlantic States.* Chicago: University of Chicago Press.

Kurath, Hans. 1949. *A Word Geography of the Eastern United States.* Ann Arbor: University of Michigan Press.

Kurath, Hans and Raven I. McDavid, Jr. 1961. *The Pronunciation of English in the Atlantic States.* Ann Arbor: University of Michigan Press. [rpt. 1982, Tuscaloosa: University of Alabama Press].

Labov, William. 1991. "The Three Dialects of English." In *New Ways of Analyzing Sound Change*, ed. Penelope Eckert. Orlando: Academic Press, pp. 1–44.

Labov, William and Sharon Ash. 1997. "Understanding Birmingham." In Bernstein, Nunnally, and Sabino, eds, pp. 508–73.

Lee, Jay and William A. Kretzschmar, Jr. 1993. "Spatial Analysis of Linguistic Data with GIS Functions," *International Journal of Geographical Information Systems* 7: 541–60.

LePage, Robert and Andrée Tabouret-Keller. 1985. *Acts of Identity.* Cambridge: Cambridge University Press.

Marckwardt, Albert H. 1958. *American English.* New York: Oxford University Press.

Mathews, Mitford. 1931. *The Beginnings of American English.* Chicago: University of Chicago Press.

McDavid, Raven I., Jr. 1958. "The Dialects of American English." In W. Nelson Francis, *The Structure of American English.* New York: Ronald Press, pp. 480–543.

McDavid, Raven I., Jr. 1979. *Dialects in Culture.* Ed. William A. Kretzschmar, Jr., with the assistance of James McMillan, Lee Pederson, Roger Shuy, and Gerald Udell. Tuscaloosa: University of Alabama Press.

McDavid, Raven I., Jr. 1980. *Varieties of American English.* Ed. Anwar Dil. Stanford: Stanford University Press.

McDavid, Raven I., Jr. and Virginia G. McDavid. 1951. "The Relationship of the Speech of American Negroes to the Speech of Whites," *American Speech* 26: 3–17.

Metcalf, Allan. 1997. "The South in *DARE*." In Bernstein, Nunnally, and Sabino, eds, pp. 266–76.

Miller, Michael. 1999. *Dynamics of a Sociolinguistic System: Plural Formation in Augusta, Georgia.* Eds. Ronald Butters and William A. Kretzschmar, Jr., *Journal of English Linguistics* 27, Number 3.

Montgomery, Michael. 1989. "Exploring the Roots of Appalachian English," *English World Wide* 10: 227–78.

Montgomery, Michael. 1997. "Making Transatlantic Connections Between Varieties of English: The Case of Plural Verbal -s," *Journal of English Linguistics* 25: 122–41.

Montgomery, Michael and Stephen Nagle. 1993. "Double Modals in Scotland and the Southern United States: Trans-Atlantic Inheritance or Independent Development?" *Folia Linguistica Historica* 14: 91–107.

*Oxford Dictionary of Pronunciation for Current English.* 2001. Eds. Clive Upton, William A. Kretzschmar, Jr., and Rafal Konopka. Oxford: Oxford University Press.

Pederson, Lee. 1986–92. *Linguistic Atlas of the Gulf States*. 7 vols. Athens: University of Georgia Press.

Schneider, Edgar, ed. 1996. *Focus on the USA*. Philadelphia: John Benjamins.

Trudgill, Peter. 1986. *Dialects in Contact*. Oxford: Blackwell.

Turner, Lorenzo D. 1949. *Africanisms in the Gullah Dialect*. Chicago: University of Chicago Press.

## Critical Thinking and Application

- Why do you think it is important for Kretzschmar to emphasize that dialects are generalizations and abstractions rather than rules or contracts that every individual must follow?
- Kretzschmar quotes Labov and Ash saying that urban dialects are "more different from each other than at any time in the past." Does this seem counterintuitive to you? How is it possible that national media have not eradicated differences in regional ways of speaking? Why would people want to differentiate their speech from that of others?
- How do people *feel* about these linguistic differences? Why do you think this is the case?
- Find a word or pronunciation that you believe will vary. Survey the members of your class, residence hall, or workplace. How do you account for the variation you find? What tools do you need to conduct this research?

## Vocabulary

bundle of isoglosses
dialect
dialect geography
dialectologist
isogloss
koiné
shift
sound change

## Suggested Further Reading

Blount, Roy. 2007. *Long Time Leaving: Dispatches from Up South*. New York: Knopf.

Carver, Craig M. 1987. *American Regional Dialects: A Word Geography*. Ann Arbor: University of Michigan Press.

Cassidy, Frederic G. (editor-in-chief). 1985. *Dictionary of American Regional English* (Vol. 1, A–C). Cambridge, MA: Harvard University Press, Belknap.

Cassidy, Frederic G. 1996. *Dictionary of American Regional English* (Vol. 3, I–O). Cambridge, MA: Harvard University Press, Belknap.

Cassidy, Frederic G., and Joan Houston Hall, eds. 1991. *Dictionary of American Regional English* (Vol. 2, D–H). Cambridge, MA: Harvard University Press, Belknap.

*Dictionary of American Regional English*. Dare.wisc.edu

*Do You Speak American?* www.pbs.org/speak/

Eckert, Penelope, and John R. Rickford, eds. 2001. *Style and Sociolinguistic Variation*. Cambridge: Cambridge University Press.

Fought, Carmen, ed. 2004. *Sociolinguistic Variation: Critical Reflections*. Oxford and New York: Oxford University Press.

Francis, Nelson. 1983. *Dialectology: An Introduction*. New York: Longman.

Hall, Joan Houston (editor-in-chief). 2002. *Dictionary of American Regional English* (Vol. 4, P–Sk). Cambridge, MA: Harvard University Press, Belknap.

Labov, William. 1972. *Sociolinguistic Patterns*. Philadelphia: University of Pennsylvania Press.

Labov, William, Sharon Ash, and Charles Boberg. 2006. *The Atlas of North American English: Phonetics, Phonology, and Sound Change*. Berlin: Mouton de Gruyter.

MacNeil, Robert, and William Cran, eds. 2005. *Do You Speak American?* New York: Doubleday.

Milroy, James. 1992. *Linguistic Variation and Change: On the Historical Sociolinguistics of English*. Oxford: Blackwell.

Preston, Dennis R. 1998. They Speak Really Bad English Down South and in New York City. In *Language Myths*, edited by Laurie Bauer and Peter Trudgill, pp. 139–149. London: Penguin.

Trudgill, Peter. 1983. *On Dialect: Social and Geographical Perspectives*. New York: New York University Press.

Trudgill, Peter. 1990. *The Dialects of England*. Cambridge, MA: Blackwell.

*Urban Dictionary*. Urbandictionary.com

Wolfram, Walt. 1991. *Dialects and American English*. Englewood Cliffs, NJ: Prentice Hall.

Wolfram, Walt, and Natalie Schilling-Estes. 2006 [1998]. *American English: Dialects and Variation*. 2nd ed. Malden, MA: Blackwell.

Wolfram, Walt, and Ben Ward, eds. 2006. *American Voices: How Dialects Differ from Coast to Coast*. Malden, MA: Blackwell.

# "Race" and Ethnicity

## CHAPTER 32

# Suite for Ebony and Phonics

## *John R. Rickford*

(1997)

*In late 1996, the Oakland School Board in California declared that "Ebonics"—a newly coined term combining "ebony" and "phonics"—was the native language of most of its students, almost all African American. As speakers of a distinct language, students attempting to learn Standard English were in effect learning a second language and thus would be entitled to funding to help them with this.*

*Oakland had some of the worst-performing schools in the country. What could be the cause of this? It seemed that language might play a role in students' inability to test well. It was worth a try; most other efforts had failed. The board wanted teachers to teach the systematic differences between the two languages rather than continue to reprimand students for using their home language, because decades of reprimanding had not succeeded in teaching minority students to use Standard English consistently.*

*But the political storm that followed this mild cloud was thunderous: the effort was dismissed as racist, defeatist, wrong-headed, and many other things. When linguists weighed in, however, they tended to side with the school board, though they wished to correct some of the misconceptions that accompanied the initial proclamation, making sure to point out that there was no necessary biological connection between "race" and language spoken.*

*This was not the first time school boards had tried to connect what was then called African American English and achievement in school; among other cases, in 1979 the case of* Martin Luther King Junior Elementary School Children, et al., v. Ann Arbor School District Board *included testimony from linguists such as William Labov about the regular differences between Black English and Standard English. But public understanding of language issues has not substantially improved. (Note the frequently changing terms!)*

*John Rickford has been writing about language, especially African American Vernacular English and creole languages, since the early 1980s. This widely circulated article not only explains the Ebonics issue but also discusses relationships among different types of related languages, often called "dialects" or "slang." At the same time, Rickford shows very clearly some of the distinctiveness of African American Vernacular English (Ebonics), supporting the school board's claims that it is a separate "language" from Standard English.*

### Reading Questions

- What are the three basic principles that linguists agree on in studying the Ebonics controversy?
- What are some of the distinct features of Ebonics in contrast with Standard English?

John R. Rickford, Suite for Ebony and Phonics. http://www.stanford.edu/~rickford/papers/SuiteForEbonyAndPhonics.html. Published in *Discover* magazine, December 1997.

- What are the three common accounts of the origins of African American Vernacular English?
- What practical educational solutions were offered to help improve the educations of speakers of Ebonics (and other minority "dialects")?

---

To James Baldwin, writing in 1979, it was "this passion, this skill, . . . this incredible music." Toni Morrison, two years later, was impressed by its "five present tenses," and felt that "The worst of all possible things that could happen would be to lose that language." What these African American novelists were talking about was Ebonics, the **vernacular** or informal speech of many African Americans, which rocketed to public attention after the Oakland school board approved a resolution in December 1996 recognizing it as the primary language of African American students.

The reaction of most people across the country—in the media, at holiday gatherings, and on electronic bulletin boards—was overwhelmingly negative. In the flash-flood of email on America Online, Ebonics was variously described as "lazy English," "bastardized English," "poor grammar," and "fractured slang." Oakland's decision to recognize Ebonics and use it to facilitate mastery of Standard English [SE] also elicited superlatives of negativity: "ridiculous, ludicrous," "VERY, VERY STUPID," "a terrible mistake." Linguists—the scientists who carefully study the sounds, words, and grammars of languages and **dialects**—were less rhapsodic about Ebonics than the novelists, but much more positive than most of the media and the general public. At their January 1997 annual meeting, members of the Linguistic Society of America [LSA] unanimously approved a resolution describing Ebonics as "systematic and rule-governed like all natural speech varieties," and referring to the Oakland resolution as "linguistically and pedagogically sound." In order to understand how linguists could have had such a different take on the Ebonics issue, we need to understand how linguists study language and what their studies of Ebonics over the past thirty years have led them to agree on (and what [they have] not).

Although linguists approach the study of language from different perspectives—some are keener on language change, for instance, while others are more interested in language as a formal system, in what language tells us about human cognition, or how language reflects social divisions—we agree on a number of general principles. One of these is that linguistics is **descriptive** rather than **prescriptive,** our goal being to describe how language works rather than to prescribe how people should or shouldn't speak. A second principle is that all languages have dialects—regional or social varieties which develop when people are separated by geographical or social barriers and their languages change along different lines, as they develop their own pronunciations, for instance, or their own ways of referring to things. When linguists speak of "dialects" they don't do so in the pejorative way that many non-linguists do. A dialect is just a variety of a language; everyone speaks at least one. A third principle, vital for understanding linguists' reactions to the Ebonics controversy, is that all languages and dialects are systematic and rule-governed. To some extent, this is a theoretical assumption—for if individuals made up their own sounds and words and did NOT follow a common set of rules for putting them together to express meaning, they would be unable to communicate with each other, and children would have a hard time acquiring the "language" of their community. But it is also an empirical finding. Every human language and dialect which we have studied to date—and we have studied thousands—has been found to be fundamentally regular, although its rules may differ from those of other varieties.

Now is Ebonics just **"slang,"** as so many people have characterized it? Well, no, because slang refers just to the vocabulary of a language or dialect, and even so, just to the small set of new and (usually) short-lived words like *chillin* ("relaxing") or *homey* ("close friend") which are used primarily by young people in informal contexts. Ebonics includes non-slang words like *ashy* (referring to the appearance of dry skin, especially in winter) which have been around for a while, and are used by people of all age groups. Ebonics also includes distinctive patterns of pronunciation and grammar, the elements of language on which linguists tend to concentrate because they are more systematic and deep-rooted.

But is Ebonics a different language from English or a different dialect of English? Linguists tend to sidestep questions like these, noting, as the 1997 LSA resolution did, that the answers often depend on sociohistorical and political considerations rather than on linguistic ones. For instance, spoken Cantonese and Mandarin are mutually unintelligible, but they are usually regarded as "dialects" of Chinese because their speakers use the same writing system and see themselves as part of a common Chinese tradition. By contrast, although Norwegian and Swedish share many words and their speakers can generally understand each other, they are usually regarded as different languages because they are the autonomous varieties of different political entities (Norway, Sweden). Despite this, most linguists might agree that Ebonics is more of a dialect of English than a separate language, insofar as it shares most of its vocabulary and many other features with other informal varietes of American English, and insofar as its speakers can understand and be understood by speakers of most other American English dialects.

At the same time, Ebonics is one of the most distinctive varieties of American English, differing from Standard English [SE]—the educated standard—in several ways. Consider, for instance, its verb **tenses** and **aspects**. ("Tense" refers to WHEN an event occurs, e.g., present or past, and "aspect" to HOW it occurs, e.g., habitually or not.) When Toni Morrison referred to the "five present tenses" of Ebonics, she didn't give examples, but it is probably usages like these—each one different from SE—which she had in mind:

1. Present progressive: He Ø runnin (=SE "He is running" or "He's running").
2. Present habitual progressive: He be runnin (=SE "He is usually running").
3. Present intensive habitual progressive: He be steady runnin (=SE "He is usually running in an intensive, sustained manner").
4. Present perfect progressive: He bin runnin (=SE "He has been running").
5. Present perfect progressive with remote inception: He BIN runnin (=SE "He has been running for a long time, and still is").

The distinction between events which are non-habitual or habitual, represented in 1 and 2 respectively by the non-use or use of an invariant *be* form, can only be expressed in SE with adverbs like "usually." Of course, SE can use simple present tense forms (e.g., "He runs") for habitual events, but then the meaning of an ongoing or progressive action signalled by the "-ing" suffix is lost. Note too that *bin* in 4 is unstressed, while *BIN* in 5 is stressed. The former can usually be understood by non-Ebonics speakers as equivalent to "has been" with the "has" deleted, but the stressed BIN form can be badly misunderstood. Years ago, I presented the Ebonics sentence "She BIN married" to twenty-five Whites and twenty-five Blacks from various parts of the US, and asked them, individually, if they understood the speaker to be still married or not. While almost all the Blacks (23, or 92%) said "Yes," only a third of the whites (8, or 32%) gave this correct answer. In real life, a misconstrual of this type could be disastrous!

OK, so it's not just slang, but an English dialect, sharing a lot with other English varieties, but with some pretty distinctive features of its own. What of characterizations of Ebonics as "lazy" English, as though it were the result of snoozing in a hammock on a Sunday afternoon, or the consequences of not knowing or caring about the rules of "proper" English? Well, if you remember the linguistics principle that all languages are rule-governed, you'll probably be ready to reject these characterizations as a matter of general principle, but you can also challenge them on specific grounds.

One problem with statements like these is that they fail to recognize that most of the "rules" we follow in using language are below the level of consciousness, unlike the rules that we're taught in grammar books or at school. Take for instance, English plurals. Although grammar books tell us that you add "s" to a word to form a regular English plural, as in "cats" and "dogs," that's only true for writing. (Let's ignore words that end in s-like sounds, like "boss," which add "-es," and irregular plurals like "children.") In speech, what we actually add in the case of "cat" is an [s] sound, and in the case of "dog" we add [z]. (Linguists use square brackets to represent how words are pronounced rather than how they are spelled.) The difference is that [s] is **voiceless,** with the vocal cords in the larynx or voice box in our throats (the Adams apple) spread apart, and that [z] is **voiced,** with the vocal cords held closely together and noisily vibrating. You can hear the difference quite dramatically if you put your fingers in your ears and produce a "ssss" sequence followed by a "zzzz" sequence followed by a "ssss" sequence: sssszzzzssss. Every time you switch to "zzzz" your voice box switches on (voiced), and every time you switch to "ssss" your voice box switches off (voiceless). Now, how do you know whether to add [s] or [z] to form a plural when you're speaking? Easy. If the word ends in a voiceless consonant, like "t," add voiceless [s]. If the word ends in a voiced consonant, like "g," add voiced [z]. Since all vowels are voiced, if the word ends in a vowel, like "tree," add [z]. Because we spell both plural endings with "s," we're not aware that English speakers make this systematic difference every day, and I'll bet your English teacher never told you about "voiced" [z] and "voiceless" [s]. But you follow the "rules" for using them anyway, and anyone who didn't—for instance, someone who said "book[z]"—would strike an English speaker as sounding funny.

One reason people might regard Ebonics as "lazy English" is its tendency to omit word-final consonants, especially if they come after another consonant, as in "tes(t)" and "han(d)." But if one were just being lazy or cussed or both, why not also leave out the final consonant in a word like "pant"? This is NOT permitted in Ebonics, and the reason (building on your newly acquired knowledge about voicing) is that Ebonics does not allow the deletion of the second consonant in a word-final sequence unless both consonants are either voiceless, as with "st," or voiced, as with "nd." In the case of "pant," the final "t" is voiceless, but the preceding "n" is voiced. Not only is Ebonics systematic in following this rule, but even its exceptions to the rule—negative forms like "ain'" and "don'"—are non-random. In short, Ebonics is no more lazy English than Italian is lazy Latin. To see the (expected) regularity in both we need to see each in its own terms, appreciating the complex rules that native speakers follow effortlessly and unconsciously in their daily lives.

Talking about native speakers naturally brings up the question of who speaks Ebonics. If we made a list of all the ways in which the pronunciation or grammar of Ebonics differs from that of SE, we probably couldn't find anyone who uses all of them 100% of the time. There is certainly no gene that predisposes one to speak Ebonics, so while its features are found most commonly among African American speakers ("Ebonics" is itself derived from "Ebony" and "phonics," meaning "Black sounds"), not all African Americans speak it. Ebonics features, especially distinctive tense-aspect forms like those in examples 1–5 above, are more common among working class than among middle class speakers, among adolescents than among the middle aged, and in informal contexts (a conversation in the street) rather than formal ones (a sermon at church) or writing. These differences are partly the result of differences in environment and social network (recall our point about geographical and social conditions forging dialects), and partly the result of differences in identification. Lawyers and doctors and their families have more contact than blue collar workers and the unemployed do with Standard English speakers, in their schooling, their work environments, and their neighborhoods. Moreover, working class speakers, and adolescents in particular, often embrace Ebonics features as markers of Black identity, while middle class speakers (in public at least), tend to eschew them.

What about Whites and other ethnic groups? Some Ebonics pronunciations and grammatical features are also found among other vernacular varieties of English, especially Southern White dialects, many of which have been significantly influenced by the heavy concentration of African Americans in the South. But other Ebonics features, including **copula** absence, **habitual *be*,** and remote *BIN* are rarer or non-existent in White vernaculars. When it comes to vocabulary, the situation is different. Partly through the influence of rap and hip-hop music, a lot of African American slang has "crossed over" to whites and other ethnic groups, particularly among the young and the "hip" (derived from Wolof *hipi* "be aware"). Expressions like *givin five* ("slapping palms in agreement or congratulation") and *Whassup?* are so widespread in American discourse that many people don't realize they originated in the African American community. This is also true of older, non-slang words like *tote* ("carry," derived from Kongo -*tota*, Swahili -*tuta*).

By this point, some readers... might be fuming. It's one thing to talk about the distinctiveness and regularity of Ebonics and its value as a marker of Black identity and hipness, you might say, but don't linguists realize that nonstandard dialects are stigmatized in the larger society, and that Ebonics speakers who cannot shift to SE are less likely to do well in school and on the job front? Well, yes. As the January 1997 LSA resolution emphasized, "there are benefits in acquiring Standard English." But there is experimental evidence both from the United States and Europe that the goal of mastering the standard language might be better achieved by approaches that take students' vernaculars into account and teach them explicitly to bridge the gap to the standard than by conventional approaches which ignore the vernacular altogether. (Most conventional approaches show a shockingly poor success rate, I should add.) To give only one example: at Aurora University, outside Chicago, African American inner-city students taught by a contrastive analysis approach in which SE and Ebonics features were systematically contrasted through explicit instruction and drills showed a 59% REDUCTION in their use of Ebonics features in their SE writing after eleven weeks, while a control group taught by conventional methods showed an 8.5% INCREASE in such features. Despite ambiguities in their original wording, what the Oakland school board essentially wanted to do is help their students increase their mastery of SE and do better in school through an extension of the Standard English Proficiency program, a contrastive analysis approach widely used in California and already in use in some Oakland schools. It was considerations like these that led the Linguistic Society of America to endorse the Oakland proposal as "linguistically and pedagogically sound."

Let us turn now to the issue of the origins of Ebonics, on which there is much less agreement among linguists. The Oakland resolution referred to the influence of West African languages as the source of Ebonics' distinctive features, and as one reason for its recognition. The African ancestors of today's African Americans came to America mostly as slaves, and mostly between 1619 and 1808, when the [British] slave trade officially ended. Like the forebears of many other Americans, these waves of African "immigrants" spoke languages other than English. Their languages were from the Niger-Congo language family, especially the West Atlantic, Mande and Kwa subgroups spoken from Senegal and Gambia to the Cameroons (e.g., Wolof, Mandingo, Twi, Ewe, Yoruba, Igbo), and the Bantu subgroup spoken further South (e.g., Kimbundu, Umbundu, Kongo). Arriving in an American milieu in which English was dominant, the slaves learned English. But how quickly and completely they did so, and with how much influence from their African languages, are matters of dispute.

One view, the Afrocentric or ethnolinguistic view, is that most of the distinctive pronunciation and grammatical features of Ebonics represent transfers or continuities from Africa, since West Africans acquiring English as slaves restructured it according to the patterns of Niger-Congo languages. On this view, Ebonics simplifies word final consonant clusters ("pas'") and omits linking verbs like *is* and *are* ("He Ø happy") because these features are generally absent from Niger-Congo languages, and Ebonics creates verbal forms like habitual *be* and remote *BIN* because these tense-aspect categories are present in Niger-Congo languages. However, most Afrocentrists don't specify the particular West African languages and examples which support their argument, and given the wide array of languages in the Niger-Congo family, some historically significant Niger-Congo languages don't support them. For instance, while Yoruba does indeed lack a linking verb like *is* for some adjectival constructions, it has another linking verb *rí* for other adjectives, and SIX other linking verbs for non-adjectival constructions where English would use *is* or *are*. Moreover, features like consonant cluster simplification are also found among other English vernaculars (for instance, in England) which had little or no West African influence, and this weakens the Afrocentric argument. Many linguists acknowledge continuing African influences in some Ebonics and American English words (direct loans like *hip* and *tote* were cited earlier, and we can add to these loan-translations of West African concepts into English words, as with *cut-eye* "a glance of derision or disgust"). But when it comes to Ebonics pronunciation and grammar, they want more specific proof.

A second view, the Eurocentric or dialectologist view, is that African slaves learned English from White settlers, and that they did so relatively quickly and successfully, with little continuing influence from their African linguistic heritage. Vernacular or non-SE features of Ebonics, including consonant cluster simplification and habitual *be*, are seen as transfers from vernacular dialects spoken by colonial English, Irish, or Scotch Irish settlers, many of whom were indentured servants, or as features which developed in the 20th century, after African Americans became more isolated in urban ghettoes. (Habitual *be* appears to be commoner in urban than in rural areas.) However, as with Afrocentric arguments, we still don't have enough details of the putative source features in British and settler English varieties, and crucial Ebonics features like the absence of linking *is* appear to be rare or non-existent in them, so they're unlikely to have been the source. Moreover, even with relatively low proportions of Blacks to Whites in the early colonial period, and the fact that they worked alongside each other in households and fields, particularly in the North, the assumption that slaves rapidly and successfully acquired the dialects of the Whites around them requires a rosier view of their social relations and interactions than the historical record and contemporary evidence suggest.

A third view, the creolist view, is that many African slaves, in acquiring English, developed a simplified fusion of English and African languages which linguists call a **pidgin** or **creole,** and that this influenced the subsequent development of Ebonics. A *pidgin* is a contact vernacular, used to facilitate communication between speakers of two or more languages. Native to none of its speakers, a pidgin is a mixed language, incorporating elements of its users' native languages, and it also has a less complex grammar and a smaller vocabulary than its input languages. A *creole*, as traditionally defined, is a pidgin which has become the primary or native language of its users (e.g., the children of pidgin speakers), expanding its vocabulary and grammatical machinery in the process, but still remaining simpler than the original language inputs in some respects. Most creoles, for instance, don't use inflectional suffixes to mark tense ("he walk*ed*"), plurality ("boy*s*"), or possession ("John'*s* house").

Where are creoles common? All over the world, but particularly on the islands of the Caribbean and the Pacific, where large plantations brought together huge groups of slaves or indentured laborers, speaking various ethnic languages, and smaller groups of colonizers and settlers whose European languages (English, French, Dutch) the former had to learn. Under such conditions, with minimal access to European speakers, new restructured varieties like Haitian Creole French and Jamaican Creole English arose. These do show African influence, as the Afrocentric theory would predict, but where the patterns of various African languages were conflicting, the creolist theory would provide for elimination or simplification of more complex alternatives, like the seven linking verbs of Yoruba referred to above. Within the United States, one well-established English creole is Gullah, spoken on the Sea Islands off the coast of South Carolina and Georgia, where Blacks constituted 80% to 90% of the local population in places. When I did research on one of the South Carolina Sea Islands some years ago, I recorded the following creole sentences, much like what one would hear in Caribbean Creole English today:

6. E.M. *run an gone* to *Suzie* house (=SE "E.M. went running to Suzie's house").
7. But I *does* go to see people when they Ø sick (=SE "But I usually go to see people when they are sick").
8. De mill *bin* to Bluffton *dem time* (=SE "The mill was in Bluffton in those days").

Note the characteristically creole absence of past tense and possessive inflections in 6, the absence of linking verb *are* and the presence of unstressed habitual *does* in 7, and the use of unstressed *bin* for past and *dem time* (without *s*, but with pluralizing *dem*) in 8.

What about creole origins for Ebonics? One way in which creole speech might have been introduced to many of the American colonies is through the large numbers of slaves who were imported in the 17th and 18th centuries from Caribbean colonies like Jamaica and Barbados where creoles definitely did develop. Some of those who came directly from Africa may also have brought with them pidgins or creoles which developed around West African trading forts. Moreover, some creole varieties—apart from well-known cases like Gullah—might have developed on American soil. While the percentages of Blacks in the local population might have been too low in 18th-century New England and Middle Colonies for creoles to develop (3% and 7% respectively, compared with 50% to 90% in the early Caribbean), they were higher in the South (40% overall, 61% in South Carolina), where the bulk of the Black population in America was concentrated. There are also observations from travelers and commentators through the centuries to Black speech being different from White speech (contra the Eurocentric scenario), and repeated textual attestations of Black speech with creole-like features. Even today, certain features of Ebonics, like the absence of linking *is* and *are*, are widespread in Gullah and Caribbean English creoles, while rare or non-existent in British dialects.

My own view, perhaps evident from the preceding, is that the creolist hypothesis most neatly incorporates the strengths of the other hypotheses, while avoiding their weaknesses. But there is no current consensus among linguists on the origins issue, and research from these competing perspectives is proceeding at fever pitch. One of the spinoffs of this kind of research is the light it sheds on aspects of American history which we might not otherwise consider. Whatever the final resolution of the origins issue, we should not forget that linguists from virtually all points of view agree on the systematicity of Ebonics, and on the potential value of taking it into account in teaching Ebonics speakers to read and write. That position may strike non-linguists as unorthodox, but that is where our science leads us.

## Critical Thinking and Application

- Why is it important to show that African American Vernacular English has consistent grammatical patterns?
- Why do you think traditional teaching methods have failed to teach Standard English to speakers of minority "dialects"?
- Investigate the contrastive analysis approach (sometimes called the bridge method) of teaching Standard English to speakers of nonstandard varieties of English. How does it work? How effective has it been? How has it fared politically?

## Vocabulary

| | | |
|---|---|---|
| aspect | habitual *be* | vernacular |
| copula | pidgin | voiced |
| creole | prescriptive | voiceless |
| descriptive | slang | |
| dialect | tense | |

## Suggested Further Reading [See also list following Language and Identity; "Race" and Ethnicity unit introduction]

Linguistics Society of America (LSA). 1997. *Linguistics Society of America (LSA) Resolution on the Oakland "Ebonics" Issue.* http://www.stanford.edu/~rickford/ebonics/LSAResolution.html

Rickford, John R., and Russell J. Rickford. 2000. *Spoken Soul: The Story of Black English.* New York: Wiley.

## CHAPTER 33

# Hip Hop Nation Language

*H. Samy Alim*

(2004)

*Hip Hop Communities... Hip Hop Nation... Black America... African America... Linguists and linguistic anthropologists have been analyzing the language found among African Americans in cities since the 1960s. The earliest sociolinguistic work showed that Black English, or Black English Vernacular, was grammatically regular (Labov 1972). Some scholars showed how discourse functioned in interaction. Some recorded vocabulary that was unique to African American English. H. Samy Alim here adds the subject of hip hop to the other forms of ever-innovating language generated in part by oppositional culture from the cities. Sometimes self-consciously coming from "the street," it is increasingly connected to music and other forms of popular culture. Language is manipulated, played with, and analyzed metalinguistically.*

### Reading Questions

- Why is it insufficient to study the linguistic aspects of Hip Hop Nation Language? What else must be included to get a full picture?
- What are some of the features of Hip Hop Nation Language? Alim lists ten tenets.
- Give examples of the extreme linguistic awareness of rappers.
- How do hip hop modes of discourse build on black modes of discourse?

## Hip Hop Culture and Its Investigation in the Street

> The Black Language is constructed of – alright let me take it all the way back to the slave days and use something that's physical. All the slavemasters gave our people straight chittlins and greens, you feel me, stuff that they wasn't eating. But we made it into a delicacy. Same thing with the language. It's the *exact* same formula. How our people can take the *worst*, or take our bad condition, and be able to turn it into something that we can benefit off of. Just like the drums. They didn't want the slaves playing drums because we was talkin through the drums. "What the hell did my slaves do? Oh, no, cut that! Take them drums!" you feel me? So through the music, that's kinda like going on now with the rap thang. It's *ghetto* music. People talkin about they issues and crime and, you feel me? "Don't push me cuz I'm close to the eeedge!" [Rappin Grandmaster Flash and the Furious Five's "The Message"] You feel me? He talkin about, "Man, I'm so fed up with you people in this society, man." So this is the voice of the ghetto. The rap come from the voice of the ghetto... Hip hop and the streets damn near is one, you might as well say that... Straight from the streets. [Interview with rapper JT the Bigga Figga, cited partially in Alim 2000]

**Hip hop** culture is sometimes defined as having four major elements: MCing (rappin), DJing (spinnin), breakdancing (streetdancing), and graffiti art (writing). To these, KRS-One adds knowledge as a fifth element, and Afrika Bambaata, a founder of the Hip Hop Cultural Movement, adds overstanding. Even with six elements, this definition of a culture is quite limited in scope, and it is useful to distinguish between the terms hip hop and **rap. Rappin**, one aspect of hip hop culture, consists of the aesthetic placement of verbal rhymes over musical beats, and it is this element that has predominated in hip hop cultural activity in recent years. Thus, language is perhaps the most useful means with which to read the various cultural activities of the Hip Hop Nation (HHN). This chapter provides a sociolinguistic profile of language use within the HHN in the sociocultural context of the streets. The chapter also examines the varied and rich hip hop cultural modes of **discourse**.

**Sociolinguists** have always been interested in analyzing language and language use within varying contexts. Given a healthy respect for vernacular languages among

H. SamyAlim, Hip Hop Nation Language. In *Language in the USA: Themes for the Twenty-first Century*, ed. Edward Finegan and John R. Rickford. Cambridge: Cambridge University Press, 2004, pp. 387–409.

sociolinguists, and given the richly varied and diverse speech acts and communicative practices of the HHN, it is surprising that until the late 1990s no American sociolinguist had written about hip hop culture in any major academic journal. It was a Belgian student of African history and linguistics at the University of Ghent who first collected data about hip hop culture in the Lower East Side of New York City in 1986–87. In his quest to learn about the social and cultural context of rap performances, Remes (1991) produced one of the earliest sociolinguistic studies of rappin in a hip hop community (the borderless HHN comprises numerous hip hop communities around the world). His pioneering study provided a brief account of the origin of rap, identified several "Black English" linguistic features found in rap, and highlighted the communicative practices of **call-and-response** and **verbal battling**. Only in 1997 did sociolinguist Geneva Smitherman publish her pioneering analysis of the communicative practices of the HHN (Smitherman 1997, presented before an audience in South Africa in 1995).

Since then sociolinguists have presented papers at professional conferences and published in academic journals. In 2001 at the thirtieth anniversary meeting of New Ways of Analyzing Variation (or NWAV) Conference, the major gathering of sociolinguists, several scholars participated in a panel called "The **Sociolinguistics** of Hip Hop: New Ways of Analyzing Hip Hop Nation Language." To paraphrase the poet-dramatist Amiri Baraka, a leading figure of the Black Arts Movement of the 1960s and 1970s, African American linguists are now celebrating hip hop culture and beginning to see that the "Hip Hop Nation is Like Ourselves."

To be fair, at least since 1964, there has been considerable scholarship on language use within what are now called hip hop communities. It started with investigations "deep down in the jungle" in the streets of South Philly ("it's like a jungle sometimes it makes me wonder how I keep from goin under"[1]) that recorded "black talkin in the streets" of America (Abrahams 1964, 1970, 1976) and the analysis of "language behavior" of Blacks in Oakland (Mitchell-Kernan 1971) to the analysis of the narrative syntax and **ritual insults** of Harlem teenagers "in the inner city" (Labov 1972) to the critical examination of "the power of the rap" in the "Black Idiom" of the Black Arts Movement rappers and poets (Smitherman 1973, 1977) and an elucidation of the "language and culture of black teenagers" who skillfully "ran down some lines" in South Central Los Angeles (Folb 1980). In myriad ways, then, scholars had prepared the field for the extraordinary linguistic phenomenon that was about to leave an indelible mark on the language of parts of the English-speaking world. This linguistic phenomenon is, of course, hip hop culture. Most of the works cited above were published before the advent of the first hip hop recording in 1979, the Sugar Hill Gang's "Rapper's Delight." By describing the linguistic patterns and practices of African Americans in the "inner cities," these scholars were studying the linguistic forebears of the HHN. Some of the remaining sections of this chapter will show that language use within the HHN is intricately linked to language use within other African American institutions, such as churches and mosques, as well as to the everyday linguistic practices of Black folk in their communities from the hood to the amen corner.

The work of these pioneering scholars and others demonstrated the creativity, ingenuity, and verbal virtuosity of Africans in America by examining language use at the very loci of linguistic-cultural activity. What is the locus of the linguistic-cultural activity known as hip hop? "The **street** is hardcore and it is the rhythmic locus of the Hip Hop world" (Spady 1991: 406, 407). Foregrounding the streets as the site, sound, and soul of **hiphopological** activity allows one to gain a more thorough understanding of the origins and sociocultural context of hip hop culture, which is critical to understanding language use within this Nation. Rapper Busta Rhymes, often introduced on stage as being "straight from the muthafuckin street," defends the introduction with his characteristic tenacity:

> What do you mean what it mean?! It's straight and plain, plain and simple. Hip hop is street music! It ain't come from nobody's house! You know what I'm saying? It's something that we all gathered in the street to do. As far as the founders of the hip hop thing, you know what I'm saying, the hip hop way of life, it was established in the street. It wasn't established in people's houses, in people's homes, you know what I'm saying? People came from their homes to celebrate the culture of hip hop in the parks, in the streets, on the street corners, you know what I'm saying? (Spady, Lee, and Alim 1999: 183)

"Rap artists affirm that one has to come from the streets, or understand the urban black street tradition, in order to properly interpret and perform rap music," according to one ethnomusicologist (Keyes 1991). In the new millennium, the streets continue to be a driving force in hip hop culture. On "Streets Done Raised Us" (2001), rappers Drag-On and Baby Madison extend the notion that the streets are the center of hip hop cultural activity because for many young Black hip hop artists the streets are the locus of life itself. And as if to make certain of no misunderstanding, the L.O.X. proudly proclaim *We Are the Streets* – equating self and street (2000).

Answering calls for Black linguists to set the standards for linguistic research on the language of Black Americans (Labov 1972, Hymes 1981), Baugh (1983: 36) went straight "to the people" in a variety of social contexts where "black street speech breathes." He writes: "It is one thing to recognize the need to gather data from representative consultants, but it is another matter altogether to get the job done." The "code of the streets" (Anderson 1999) does not look fondly upon someone carrying a tape recorder and asking too many questions, particularly in a cultural environment where people avoid "puttin their business out in the street" at all costs.

The hip hop saturated streets of America today are quite different from the streets of yesteryear. The changing nature of the city streets in the last decade of the twentieth century has been captured by Spady (1991: 407): "Changing. Those streets of yesteryear are no more. Now it is crack-filled and gang-banged. Loose and cracked. Yet most of our people walk straight through these streets night and day. Risking lives. But this is a risqué world... The street is hardcore and it is the locus of the Hip Hop world." What do we mean by hip hop saturated streets? In urban areas across the nation, it is clear that young hip hop heads exist in a state of **hiphopness** – their experience is saturated with the sights, sounds, smells, and stares of what it means to be a hip hop being. It is the "dynamic and constant sense of being alive in a hip hop, rap conscious, reality based world," Spady (1993: 95–96) explains. He writes:

> Hip hop is preeminently a cultural free space. Its transformatory and emancipatory powers are evident each time you see a young blood locked to the music being transmitted through the earphone. They exist in a community of expressive rebellion, in states of **always always,** altering what has traditionally been the culture of the ruling class.

The streets are saturated on multiple levels. An illuminating study of the "New Black Poetry" of the 1960s and 1970s uses the term "saturation" to mean both "the communication of Blackness in a given situation" and "a sense of fidelity to the observed and intuited truth of the Black Experience" (Henderson 1973: 62). In the hip hop saturated streets of America, we are speaking of the communication of the hip hop mode of being (Spady and Alim 1999) and the sense of fidelity to the absolute truth of existing in a state of hiphopness. A close examination of the hip hop saturated streets of America reveals that the street is not just a physical space – it is a site of creativity, culture, cognition, and consciousness. When Jigga (Jay-Z) said "the streets is watchin," and Beans (Beanie Sigel) turned it into "the streets is not only watchin, but they talkin now," they extended the notion of the streets into a living, breathing organism, with ears to hear, eyes to see, and a mouth to speak. Examination of hip hop culture and language must begin in the streets.

## Hip Hop Nation Language [HHNL]

My own research on Hip Hop Nation Language and hip hop culture in general has led to the streets, homes, cars, jeeps, clubs, stadiums, backstage, performances, hotels, religious centers, conferences and ciphers (highly competitive lyrical circles of rhymers) where hip hop lives – up inside the "actual lived experiences in the corrugated spaces that one finds reflected in the lyrical content of rap songs" (Spady, Dupres, and Lee 1995). The centrality of language to the HHN is evident in such song and album titles as the "New Rap Language" (Treacherous Three 1980), "Wordplay" (Bahamadia 1996), "Gangsta Vocabulary" (DJ Pooh 1997), "Project Talk" (Bobby Digital 1998), "Slang Editorial" (Cappadonna 1998), *Real Talk 2000* (Three-X-Krazy 2000), "Ebonics" (Big L 2000), *Country Grammar* (Nelly 2000), and *Project English* (Juvenile 2001). In numerous ethnographic interviews, I have found that language is a favorite topic of discussion in the HHN, and its members are willing to discuss it with great fervor – and to defend its use.

What do we mean by "Nation Language"? In exploring the development of nation language in Anglophone Caribbean poetry, Caribbean historian, poet, and literary and music critic Kamau Brathwaite (1984: 13) writes: "Nation language is the language which is influenced very strongly by the African model, the African aspect of our New World/ Caribbean heritage. English it may be in terms of some of its lexical features. But in its contours, its rhythm and timbre, its sound explosions, it is not English."

Concerned with the literature of the Caribbean and the sociopolitical matrix within which it is created, Brathwaite used the term "nation language" in contrast to "dialect." Familiar with the pejorative meanings of the term "dialect" in the folk linguistics of the people, he writes that while nation language can be considered both English and African at the same time, it is an English which is like a "howl, or a shout, or a machine-gun or the wind or a wave." Then he likened it to the blues. Surely, nation language is like hip hop (as rapper Raekwon spits his "machine-gun-rap" (1999)). HHNL is, like Brathwaite's description, new in one sense and ancient in another. It comprises elements of orality, total expression, and conversational modes (Brathwaite 1984).

Rapper Mystikal, known for having a unique, highly energetic rhyming style highlighted with lyrical sound explosions, provides a perfect example of Nation Language when he raps: "You know what time it is, nigga, and you know who the fuck this is/ DAANNN-JAH!!! [Danger] DAANNN-JAH!!! [Danger]/Get on the FLO' [floor]!/ The nigga right, yeaaahhHHH!"[2] (2000). Mystikal starts out speaking to his listener in a low, threatening growl, asserting his individuality ("you know who the fuck this is"), and then explodes as if sounding an alarm, letting everyone know that they have entered a dangerous verbal zone! "Get on the FLO'!" has a dual function – simultaneously warning listeners to lie down before the upcoming lyrical "DAANNN-JAH!" and directing them to get on the dance floor. When rapper Ludacris (2001) commands his listeners to "ROOOLLLL OUT!" and raps: "Oink, Oink, PIG! PIG! Do away with the POORRK-uh/ Only silverwuurrr [silverware] I need's a steak knife and FOORRK-uh!" he stresses his words emphatically, compelling one to do as he says. In that brief example, he is in conversation with African American Muslim and Christian communities currently dialoguing about the eating of swine flesh (which Muslims consider unholy).

When we speak of "language," we are defining the term in a sense that is congruent with the HHN's "linguistic culture" (Schiffman 1996), and HHNL can be situated in the broader context of African American speech:

> There is no single register of African American speech. And it's not words and intonations, it's a whole attitude about speech that has historical rooting. It's not a phenomenon that you can isolate and reduce to linguistic characteristics. It has to do with the way a culture conceives of the people inside of that culture. It has to do with

> a whole complicated protocol of silences and speech, and how you use speech in ways other than directly to communicate information. And it has to do with, certainly, the experiences that the people in the speech situation bring into the encounter. What's fascinating to me about African American speech is its spontaneity, the requirement that you not only have a repertoire of vocabulary or syntactical devices/constructions, but you come prepared to do something in an attempt to meet the person on a level that both uses the language, mocks the language, and recreates the language. (Wideman 1976: 34)

On her single recording "Spontaneity" (1996), Philadelphia rapper Bahamadia validates Wideman's assertion. She raps about her "verbal expansion" in a stream of consciousness style: "Rip here be dizz like everybody's on it cause eternal verbal expansion keeps enhancin brain child's ability to like surpass a swarm of booty-ass-no-grass-roots-havin-ass MC's." The verbal architect constructs her rhymes by consciously stretching the limitations of the "standard" language. In describing her lyrical influences, she cites rappers Kool Keith of the Ultramagnetic MCs, De La Soul, and Organized Konfusion as "masters at what they do in that they explore the English language and they try to push the boundaries and go against the grains of it, you know what I mean?" (Spady and Alim 1999: xviii).

"It's a very active exchange," says Wideman (1976: 34). "But at the same time as I say that, the silences and the refusal to speak is just as much a part, in another way, of African American speech." Rapper Fearless of the group Nemesis exemplifies the point: envisioning rappers, including himself, among the great orators and leaders in the Black community, he says:

> I always looked up to great orators like Martin Luther King, Malcolm X. Anybody who could ever stand up and persuade a group of young men or a nation... Just the way they were able to articulate. The way they emphasized their words. And the way they would use pauses. They would actually use *silence* powerfully... Just the way they made words cause feelings in you, you know what I'm saying? Just perpetuate thought within people, you know. (Spady and Alim 1999: xviii)

So "language" in HHNL obviously refers not only to the syntactic constructions of the language but also to the many discursive and communicative practices, the attitudes toward language, understanding the role of language in both binding/bonding community and seizing/smothering linguistic opponents, and language as concept (meaning clothes, facial expressions, body movements, and overall communication).

In addition to the above, HHNL can be characterized by ten tenets.

(1) HHNL is rooted in **African American Language (AAL)** and communicative practices (Spady 1991, Smitherman 1997, Yasin 1999). Linguistically, it is "the newest chapter in the African American book of folklore" (Rickford and Rickford 2000). It is a vehicle driven by the culture creators of hip hop, themselves organic members of the broader African American community. Thus HHNL both reflects and expands the African American Oral Tradition.

(2) HHNL is just one of the many language varieties used by African Americans.

(3) HHNL is widely spoken across the country, and used/borrowed and adapted/transformed by various ethnic groups inside and outside of the United States.

(4) HHNL is a language with its own grammar, **lexicon**, and phonology as well as unique communicative style and discursive modes. When an early hip hop group. The Treacherous Three, rhymed about a "New Rap Language" in 1980, they were well aware of the uniqueness of the language they were rappin in.

(5) HHNL is best viewed as the synergistic combination of speech, music, and literature. Yancy (1991) speaks of rap as "*musical literature* (or rhythmic-praxis discourse)." Henderson (1973) asserts that the Black poetry of the 1960s and 1970s is most distinctly Black when it derives its form from Black speech and Black music. HHNL is simultaneously the spoken, poetic, lyrical, and musical expression of the HHN.

(6) HHNL includes attitudes about language and language use (see Pharcyde dialogue below).

(7) HHNL is central to the identity and the act of envisioning an entity known as the HHN.

(8) HHNL exhibits regional variation (Morgan 2001a). For example, most members of the HHN recognize Master P's signature phrase, *Ya heeeaaard may?* ('You heard me?') as characteristic of a southern variety of HHNL. Even within regions, HHNL exhibits individual variation based on life experiences. For example, because California rapper Xzibit grew up in the hip hop saturated streets of Detroit, New Mexico and California, his HHNL is a syncretization of all these Hip Hop Nation Language varieties.

(9) The fundamental aspect of HHNL – and, to some, perhaps the most astonishing aspect – is that it is central to the lifeworlds of the members of the HHN and suitable and functional for all of their communicative needs.

(10) HHNL is inextricably linked with the sociopolitical circumstances that engulf the HHN. How does excessive police presence and brutality shift the discourse of the HHN? How do disproportionate incarceration rates and

> urban gentrification impact this community's language? As Spady (1993) writes: "Hip Hop culture [and language] mediates the corrosive discourse of the dominating society while at the same time it functions as a subterranean subversion... Volume is turned up to tune out the decadence of the dominant culture."

Rappers are insightful examiners of the sociopolitical matrix within which HHNL operates. Discussing the role of HHNL in hip hop lyrics, Houston's Scarface concludes that HHNL functions as a communal "code of communication" for the HHN:

> It's a code of communication, too... Because we can understand each other when we're rapping. You know, if I'm saying, [in a nasal, mocking voice] "Well, my friend, I saw this guy who shot this other guy and..." I break that shit down for you and you say, "Goddamn, man! Them muthafuckas is going crazy out where this dude's from." You know what I'm saying? It's just totally different. It's just a code of communication to me. I'm letting my partner know what's going on. And anything White America can't control they call "gangsters." *Shit!* I get real. Politicians is gangsters, goddamn. The presidents is the gangsters because they have the power to change everything. That's a gangster to me. That's my definition of gangster. (Spady, Lee, and Alim 1999: 301)

Members of Tha Pharcyde actively debated the concept of HHNL:

BOOTY BROWN: There's more than just one definition for words! We talk in slang. We always talk basically in slang. We don't use the English dictionary for every sentence and every phrase that we talk!

PHARCYDE: No, there's a lot of words out of the words that you just said which all...

BOOTY BROWN: Yeah, but the way I'm talking is not the English language... We're not using that definition... We're making our own... Just like they use any other word as a slang, *my brotha*! Anything. I'm not really your brother. Me and your blood aren't the same, but I'm your brother because we're brothas. That's slang... We make up our *own* words. I mean, it depends whose definition you glorify, okay? That's what I'm saying. Whose definition are you glorifying? Because if you go by my definition of "Black," then I can say "a Black person." But if you go by the *Webster Dictionary's*... You have your own definition. It's your definition.

(Spady, Lee, and Alim 1999: xix)

Sociolinguistically, so much is happening in the first exchange above. The HHN continues to "flip the script" (reverse the power of the dominant culture). Scarface is reacting to the media's labeling of reality-based rap lyrics as "gangster." By redefining gangster, he effectively turns the tables on what he believes is an oppressive state. If the presidents have the power to change everything, why ain't a damn thing changed?

In Tha Pharcyde conversation, when the *brotha* says the way he is talking is not the English language, he is talking about much more than slang. He asks pointedly, "Whose definition are you glorifying?" By making up your own words, he attests, you are freeing yourself from linguistic colonization (Wa Thiongo 1992). In an effort to combat the capitalistic comodification of hip hop culture, and to "unite and establish the common identity of the HHN," KRS-One refined the definition of hip hop terms and produced a document known as "The Refinitions" (2000) – putting the power of redefinition to action. KRS defines the language of hip hop culture as "street language" and proposes that "Hiphoppas" speak an Advanced Street Language, which includes "the correct pronunciation of one's native and national language as it pertains to life in the inner-city." KRS is reversing "standard" notions of correctness and appropriateness, realizing that the HHN has distinct values and aesthetics that differ from the majority culture. Clearly, members of the HHN would agree that the use of AAL stems "from a somewhat disseminated rejection of the life-styles, social patterns, and thinking in general of the Euro-American sensibility," as the writer of the first AAL dictionary outside of the Gullah area put it (Major 1970: 10).

## The Relationship Between HHNL and AAL: Lexicon, Syntax, and Phonology

> "Dangerous dialect/Dangerous dialect/I elect... to impress America." That's it, that's what it was about... Dangerous dialect, dangerous wording, you know what I mean? "I elect," that I pick, you know. "To impress America." That's what I pick to impress America, that dangerous dialect, you know. (San Quinn, 2000. Alim and Spady, Unpublished Interview)

The relationship between HHNL and AAL is a familial one. Since hip hop's culture creators are members of the broader African American community, the language that they use most often when communicating with each other is AAL. HHNL can be seen as the *submerged area* (Brathwaite 1984: 13) of AAL that is used within the HHN, particularly during hip hop centered cultural activities, but also during other playful, creative, artistic, and intimate settings. This conception of HHNL is broad enough to include the language of rap lyrics, album interludes, hip hop stage performances, and hip hop conversational discourse. African Americans are on the cutting edge of the sociolinguistic situation in the USA (as evidenced by abundant recent sociolinguistic research on the topic). HHNL, thus, is the cutting edge of the cutting edge.

A revised edition of the lexicon of "Black Talk" (Smitherman 1994, 2000) begins with a chapter entitled, "From Dead Presidents to the Benjamins." The term *dead presidents* (meaning 'money' and referring to American notes with images of dead presidents) has been in use in the African American community since the 1930s. In the late 1990s, hip hop group dead prez both shortened the term and made explicit its multivariate meanings (within the revolutionary context of their rhymes and philosophy, they are surely hinting at assassination – a form of verbal subversion). The *benjamins* is a term from the late 1990s popularized by rapper Sean "Puffy" Combs (P. Diddy).

While several scholars and writers have produced work on the lexicon of AAL (Turner 1949, Major 1970, 1994, Anderson 1994, Smitherman 1994, 2000, Stavsky, Mozeson and Mozeson 1995, Dillard 1977, Holloway and Vass 1997), it is important to note that hip hop artists, as street linguists and **lexicographers,** have published several dictionaries of their own. Old school legend Fab Five Freddy (Braithwaite 1992, 1995) documented the "fresh fly flavor" of the words and phrases of the hip hop generation (in English and German). Atlanta's Goodie Mob and several other artists have published glossaries on the inside flaps of their album covers. Of course, as lexicographers hip hop artists are only continuing the tradition of Black musicians, for many jazz and bebop artists compiled their own glossaries, most notable among them Cab Calloway (1944), Babs Gonzales, and Dan Burley.

Vallejo rapper E-40 discusses the genesis of *E-40's Dictionary Book of Slang, vol. 1* (2003):

> I feel that I *am* the ghetto. The majority of street slang... "It's all good." "Feel me." "Fo' shiiiiiziiie," all that shit come from 40. "What's up, folks?" As a matter of fact, I'm writing my own dictionary book of slang right now... It's a street demand [for it]. Everywhere I go people be like, "Dude, you need to put out a dictionary. Let them know where all that shit come from," you know what I mean? (Spady, Lee, and Alim 1999: 290)

E-40 is credited with developing a highly individualized repertoire of slang words and phrases. If he were to say something like, "What's crackulatin, pimpin? I was choppin it up wit my playa-potna last night on my communicator – then we got to marinatin, you underdig – and I come to find out that the homie had so much fedi that he was tycoonin, I mean, pimpin on some real boss-status, you smell me?" not very many people would understand him. ("crackulatin" = happening, an extended form of "crackin"; "pimpin" is sometimes used as a noun to refer to a person, like, "homie"; "choppin it up" = making conversation; "playa-potna" = partner, friend; "communicator" = cell phone; "marinatin" = a conversation where participants are reasoning on a subject; "underdig" = understand; "fedi" = money; "tycoonin" = being a successful entrepreneur; "pimpin" = being financially wealthy; "boss-status" = managing things like a CEO; "you smell me?" = you feel me? or, you understand me?)

In HHNL, *pimp* refers not only to someone who solicits clients for a prostitute; it has several other meanings. One could be *pimpin a Lex* ('driving a Lexus while looking flashy'), suffering from *record company pimpin* ('the means by which record companies take advantage of young Black artists lacking knowledge of the music industry') or engaging in *parking lot pimpin* ('hanging around the parking lot after large gatherings'). As we also saw above, *pimpin* can also refer generally to an individual, or specifically to one who sports a flashy lifestyle. The word *politickin* can refer to the act of speaking about political subjects relevant to the Black community, simply holding a conversation, or trying to develop a relationship with a female. One might catch *frostbite* or get *goosebumps* from all of the *ice* they got on [*ice* = 'diamonds']. In the HHN, *rocks* can be a girl's best friend ('diamonds') or a community's silent killer ('crack cocaine'), while *to rock* can mean 'to liven up a party,' 'to wear a fashionable article of clothing,' or 'to have sexual intercourse.'

Given the fluidity of HHNL, speakers take a lot of pride in being the originators and innovators of terms that are consumed by large numbers of speakers. Rappers, as members of distinct communities, also take pride in regional lexicon. For instance, the term *jawn* emerged in the Philadelphia hip hop community. *Jawn* is what can be called a context-dependent substitute noun – a noun that substitutes for any other noun, with its definition so fluid that its meaning depends entirely upon context. For instance, you can say, *Oh, that's da jawn!* for *da bomb!* if you think something is superb; "Did you see that *jawn*?" for 'female' when an attractive female walks by; "I like that new Beanie *jawn*" for 'song,' when the song is played on the radio, and so on. Recently, Philadelphia's Roots have handed out T-shirts with "JAWN" written on the front, advocating the use of the distinctive Philly hip hop term. Placed in a broader context, the meaning of the distinct lexicon of HHNL can be nicely summed up: "Slick lexicon is hip-hop's Magna Carta, establishing the rights of its disciples to speak loudly but privately, to tell America about herself in a language that leaves her puzzled" (Rickford and Rickford 2000: 86).

Several scholars have written that the syntax of HHNL is essentially the same as that of AAL (Remes 1991, Smitherman 1997, 2000, Morgan 1999, Spady and Alim 1999, Yasin 1999, Rickford and Rickford 2000, Morgan 2001b). This is true. We must also examine the syntax of HHNL closely enough to elucidate how the language users are behaving both within and beyond the boundaries of AAL syntax. What is happening syntactically when Method Man gets on the air and proclaims, "Broadcasting live from the Apocalypse, it be I, John Blazzzazzziiinnnyyyyy!" (KMEL 2001b)? What is happening when Jubwa of Soul Plantation writes in his autobiography: "Jubwa be the dope mc, freestylin' to the beat deep cover" (cited in Alim 2001). An important question is, How does HHNL confirm our knowledge of AAL syntax – and how does it challenge that knowledge?

Probably the most oft-studied feature of AAL is **habitual** or **invariant be**.... Early studies of AAL syntax (Labov

1968, Wolfram 1969, Fasold 1972) noted the uniqueness of this feature and were in agreement that it was used for recurring actions (*We be clubbin on Saturdays*) and could not be used in finite contexts (*She be the teacher*). Building upon this research, we see that HHNL provides numerous examples of what I call $be_3$ or the **"equative copula"** in AAL (Alim 2001b). Some examples of this construction (Noun Phrase *be* Noun Phrase) follow:

*I be the truth.* – Philadelphia's Beanie Sigel
*Dr. Dre be the name.* – Compton's Dr. Dre
*This beat be the beat for the street.* – New York's Busta Rhymes
*Brooklyn be the place where I served them thangs.* – New York's Jay-Z
*I be that insane nigga from the psycho ward.* – Staten Island's Method Man

These are but a few of countless examples in the corpus of hip hop lyrics, but this equative copula construction can also be found in everyday conversation, as in these examples:

*We be them Bay boys.* – Bay Area's Mac Mall in a conversation with James G. Spady
*It [marijuana] be that good stuff.* – Caller on the local Bay Area radio station
*You know we be some baaad brothas.* – Philadelphia speaker in conversation

It is possible that speakers of AAL have begun using this form only recently and that AAL has thus changed. Alternatively, the form may always have been present in the language but escaped the notice of investigators. Certainly it is present in the writings of Black Arts Movement poets of the 1960s and 1970s, most notably in Sonia Sanchez's *We Be Word Sorcerers*. We also find the form being cited in one linguistic study of Black street speech (*They be the real troublemakers; Leo be the one to tell it like it is*) (Baugh 1983). It is possible that members of the HHN, with their extraordinary linguistic consciousness and their emphasis on stretching the limits of language, have made this form much more acceptable by using it frequently (Alim, in press).

The HHN's linguistic consciousness refers to HHNL speakers' conscious use of language to construct identity. Addressing the divergence of AAL from standard English, Smitherman and Baugh (2002: 20) write:

> Graffiti writers of Hip Hop Culture were probably the coiners of the term "phat" (meaning excellent, great, superb)... although "phat" is spelled in obvious contrast to "fat," the former confirms that those who use it know that "ph" is pronounced like "f." In other words, those who first wrote "phat" diverged from standard English as a direct result of their awareness of standard English: the divergence was not by chance linguistic error. There is no singular explanation to account for linguistic divergence, but Hip Hop Culture suggests that matters of personal identity play a significant role.

This conscious linguistic behavior deals with matters of spelling and phonemic awareness. (See Morgan 2001a and Olivo 2001 on "spelling ideology.") One case – one of the more controversial uses of language in hip hop culture – is the term *nigga*. The HHN realized that this word had various positive in-group meanings and pejorative out-group meanings, and thus felt the need to reflect the culturally specific meanings with a new spelling (*nigger* becomes "nigga"). A *nigga* is your 'main man,' or 'one of your close companions,' your 'homie.' Recently the term has been generalized to refer to any male (one may even hear something like, "No, I was talkin about Johnny, you know, the white nigga with the hair") although it usually refers to a Black male. Demonstrating hip hop's affinity for acronyms, Tupac Shakur transformed the racial slur into the ultimate positive ideal for young Black males – **N**ever **I**gnorant **G**etting **G**oals **A**ccomplished.

As with the highlighting of regional vocabulary, HHNL speakers intentionally highlight regional differences in pronunciation by processes such as vowel lengthening and syllabic stress (Morgan 2001b). When Bay Area rappers JT the Bigga Figga and Mac Mall announced the resurgence of the Bay Area to the national hip hop scene with "Game Recognize Game" (1993), they did so using a distinctive feature of Bay Area pronunciation. The Bay Area anthem's chorus repeated this line three times: "Game recognize game in the Bay, man (mane)." *Man* was pronounced "mane" to accentuate this Bay Area pronunciation feature. Also, as fellow Bay Area rapper B-Legit rhymes about slang, he does so using the same feature to stress his Bay Area linguistic origins: "You can tell from my slang I'm from the Bay, mane" (2000).

When Nelly and the St. Lunatics "busted" onto the hip hop scene, they were among the first rappers to represent St. Louis, Missouri on a national scale. Language was an essential part of establishing their identity in a fiercely competitive world of hip hop culture. For example, in a single by the St. Lunatics featuring Nelly they emphasize every word that rhymes with "urrrr" to highlight a well-known (and sometimes stigmatized) aspect of southern/midwest pronunciation (here → *hurrrr*; care → *currrr;* there → *thurrrr;* air → *hurrrr* and so on). By intentionally highlighting linguistic features associated with their city (and other southern cities), they established their tenacity through language as if to say, "We have arrived."

Nelly and the St. Lunatics are conscious not only of their pronunciation, but also of their syntax. On his platinum single "Country Grammar" (2000), Nelly proclaims, "My gramma bees Ebonics." Clearly, HHNL speakers vary their grammar consciously. An analysis of copula variation in the speech and the lyrics of hip hop artists concluded that higher levels of copula absence in the artists' lyrics represented the construction of a street conscious identity – where the speaker makes a linguistic-cultural connection to the streets, the locus of the hip hop world (Alim 2002). John Rickford has suggested (in a conference comment made in 2001) that the use of creole syntactic and phonological features by many rappers supports the ability of HHNL speakers to manipulate their grammar consciously. Like San Quinn (see opening quote in this section) HHNL speakers elect dialects to demonstrate their high degree of linguistic consciousness and in order to construct a street-conscious identity.

## Hip Hop Cultural Modes of Discourse and Discursive Practices

Keyes (1984: 145) applied Smitherman's (1977) Black modes of discourse to HHNL. Working in hip hop's gestation period, she wrote that "Smitherman schematized four broad categories of black discourse: narrative sequencing, call-response, signification/dozens, and tonal semantics. All of these categories are strategically used in rap music." We know that rappin in and of itself is not entirely new – rather, it is the most modern/postmodern instantiation of the linguistic-cultural practices of Africans in America. Rappers are, after all, "postmodern African griots" (a class of musicians–entertainers who preserved African history through oral narratives) (Smitherman 1997). This section will demonstrate how the strategic use of the Black modes of discourse is manifested in HHNL and how the new ways in which these modes are practiced generate correspondingly new modes of discourse. This section is based on various forms of HHNL data – rap lyrics, hip hop performances and hip hop conversational discourse.

### Call and Response

Here is perhaps the most lucid definition of call and response:

> As a communicative strategy this call and response is the manifestation of the cultural dynamic which finds audience and listener or leader and background to be a unified whole. Shot through with action and interaction, Black communicative performance is concentric in quality – the "audience" becoming both observers and participants in the speech event. As Black American culture stresses commonality and group experientiality, the audience's linguistic and paralinguistic responses are necessary to co-sign the power of the speaker's rap or call. (Daniel and Smitherman 1976, Cited in Spady 2000: 59)

The quintessential example of the HHN's use of call and response grows out of the funk performances and is still heard at nearly every hip hop performance today. "[Rapper] Say 'Hoooo!' [Audience] 'Hoooooooo!' [Rapper] Say 'Ho! Ho!' [Audience] 'Ho! Ho!' [Rapper] 'Somebody screeeaaaaammm!' [Audience] 'AAAHHHHHHHHHHHHH!!!'" Anyone who has ever attended a hip hop performance can bear witness to this foundational call and response mechanism.

A description of a hip hop performance by Philadelphia's Roots paints a picture of a scene where lead MC Black Thought senses that there is a communicative schism developing between him and his Swiss audience (Jackson et al. 2001: 25). The rapper says, "Hold it, hold it, hold it!" and stops the music abruptly. What follows is an "impromptu instruction" in the call and response mode of Black discourse: "Y'all can't get the second part no matter what the fuck I say, right… I wonder if it's what I'm saying… A-yo! We gonna try this shit one more time because I like this part of the show." Providing more explicit instruction, Thought slows it down a bit: "Aight, Aight this is how I'm gonna break it down. I'm gonna be like "ahh," then everybody gonna be like "ahhh." Then – I don't know what I'm gonna say second but y'all gotta listen close cause then y'all gotta repeat that shit – that's the fun of the game!" Thought is not only providing instruction but he is also administering a challenge to his European audience: either *git sicwiddit* [get sick with it] *or git hitwiddit* [get hit with it]*!* (in this context meaning, 'Become active participants in this activity or get caught off guard looking culturally ignorant!')

Call and response mechanisms are so pervasive in HHNL that talented MCs (rappers, Masters of Ceremonies) have taken this mode to new heights. Mos Def describes one of the elements that made Slick Rick a legendary rapper:

> Slick Rick is one of the greatest MC's ever born because he has so many different facilities that he would use. Style. Vocal texture. The way he would even record. Like, he was doing call and response with himself! He would leave four bars open, and then do another character, you understand what I'm saying? (Alim 2000, Unpublished Interview)

The individualized uses of call and response in the hip hop cultural mode of discourse deserve more attention. Also, as is evident from Mos Def's comments, HHNL speakers can be cognizant of the fact that they are operating within and expanding upon the African American Oral Tradition. The linguistic and communicative consciousness of the HHN also needs to be explored.

### Multilayered Totalizing Expression

Beyond the explicit instruction, one can witness the multilayered nature of the call and response mode at hip hop performances where both performer and audience are fully conversant with hip hop cultural modes of discourse. At the first Spit-kicker Tour (2000) in San Francisco's Maritime Hall, I observed this multilayered, multitextual mode. Here's an excerpt from my fieldnotes:

> Maaan, all performers are on stage at once – [DJ] Hi-Tek, Talib [Kweli], Common, Biz [Markie], De La [Soul], Pharoahe [Monch] – and they just kickin it in a fun-loving communal-type hip hop atmosphere! Common and Biz are exchanging lines from his classic hit… The DJ from De La starts cuttin up the music and before you know it, Common is center stage freestylin. The DJ switches the pace of the music, forcing Common to switch up the pace of his freestyle [improvisational rap],

> and the crowd's lovin it! 'Ooooooohhhhh!'... Hi-Tek and Maseo are circling each other on stage giving a series of hi-fives timed to the beat, smilin and laughin all along, as the crowd laughs on with them. Common, seizing the energy of the moment, says, "This is hip hop music, y'all!" Then he shouts, "It ain't nuthin like hip hop music!" and holds the microphone out to the crowd. "It ain't nuthin like hip hop music!" they roar back, and the hall is transformed into a old school house party frenzy... Gotta love this hip hop music.

What is striking about this description is that there are multiple levels of call and multiple levels of response, occurring simultaneously and synergistically, to create something even beyond "total expression" (Brathwaite 1984: 18). This is a *multilayered totalizing expression* that completes the cipher (the process of constantly making things whole). We witness a call and response on the oral/aural, physical (body), and spiritual/metaphysical level. My final note ("Gotta love this hip hop music") captures a moment of realization that meaning resides in what I've just witnessed – in the creation of a continuum beyond audience and performer. We hear varied calls made by the DJ and responded to by a freestylin MC; by the two MC's exchanging lines and by their impromptu leading of the audience in celebration of hip hop; by the physical reaction of performers to each other and the audience (who were also slappin hands with the performers); and by the spirited and spiritual response created during the climax of the performance. Like Common says, "Find heaven in this music and God / Find heaven in this music and God / Find heaven in this music and God" (cited in Jackson et al. 2001).

## Signifyin and Bustin (Bussin)

Scholars have studied **signification** or **signifyin** – or, in more contemporary, semantically similar Black terms, *bustin, crackin*, and *dissin* (Abrahams 1964, Kochman 1969, Mitchell-Kernan 1971, 1972, Smitherman 1973, 1977). Signifyin has been described as a means to encode messages or meanings in natural conversations, usually involving an element of indirection (Mitchell-Kernan 1972). Ironically noting the difficulty in pin-pointing a dictionary definition for the speech act, Rickford and Rickford (2000: 82) cite Mitchell-Kernan's (1972: 82) attempt:

> The black concept of *signifying* incorporates essentially a folk notion that dictionary entries for words are not always sufficient for interpreting meanings or messages, or that meaning goes beyond such interpretations. Complimentary remarks may be delivered in a left-handed fashion. A particular utterance may be an insult in one context and not in another. What pretends to be informative may intend to be persuasive. Superficially, self-abasing remarks are frequently self-praise.

In Scarface's comments and Tha Pharcyde dialogue given earlier, we see evidence of this folk notion that "standard" dictionaries are insufficient to interpret Black language and life. But looking more closely at Tha Pharcyde dialogue, we witness an extremely sly (skillful and indirect) signification in hip hop conversational discourse. In the dialogue, Booty Brown is advocating the Black folk notion described by Kernan above. He implies that his partner is glorifying a Eurocentric meaning-making system over a meaning-making system that is African derived. This does not become clear until Brown chooses his examples – carefully and cleverly. "Just like they use any other word as a slang, *my brotha!*" He emphasizes the "slang phrase" *my brotha*, as it is usually used as a sign of cultural unity and familial bond between African American males (females will use *my sista* in a similar way).

Then he proceeds to ask the direct question, "Whose definition are you glorifying?" which is, in fact, a statement. Finally, as if to *really* lay it on thick (add insult to injury), he chooses to use the word *Black* to show that *Webster's Dictionary* is inadequate. The heat is diffused when "P" says, "I'm sayin, I'm sayin, that's what I'M sayin!" and they – and others around them – break into laughter. This dialogue is an example of how language is used to remind, scold, shame, or otherwise bring the other into a commonly shared ethic through signification.

We see an example of signifyin in Rapper Bushwick Bill's (of Houston's Geto Boys) description of the ever-changing, fluid and flexible nature of "street slang" and the dangers of not "keepin your ear to the street" (being aware of what's happening around you at all times). In this case, Bushwick is referring to the rapidly evolving street terminology for law enforcement officials. Bushwick takes us deep into the locus of hip hop linguistic-cultural activity:

> You lose flavor. You lose the slang. You lose the basic everyday kickin it, you know, knowing what's going on at all times, you know what I'm saying? Knowing the new names for "5–0s". They ain't even 5–0s no more. They call them "po-pos". That means everything changes. And they call them "one-time", you know what I'm saying? But you got to be in there to know that the police might know these words already. So they got to change up their dialect so that way it sounds like Pig Latin to the police. (Spady, Lee, and Alim 1999: 308)

Bushwick's comment refers us directly to tenet (10) above. He is describing the changing nature of the various terms for *police* in the streets – from *5–0s* to *po-pos* to *one time*. At one time, bloods referred to the *one-time* as *black and whites* (Folb 1980). The socio-political contexts of many depressed and oppressed Black neighborhoods necessitate these speedy lexical transformations.

Even though the police are not present in the dialogue above, Bushwick signifies on them with a clever one-liner that also serves to buttress his point. After runnin down all of the various terms (which have gone out of vogue as quickly as the police comprehended them), he concludes, "So they got to change up their dialect so that way it sounds like Pig Latin to the police." *Pig Latin* is chosen here, rather than Greek, Chinese, Swahili, or other unfamiliar languages, to echo the fact that at one time police officers were called *pigs*. Bushwick is not only signifyin on the police, but he is also demonstrating yet another term for 'police' that has gone out of fashion! In addition, he is referencing an old form of Afroamericanized Pig Latin that employs innuendo, wordplay, letter and syllabic shifting, rhyming and coded language designed to communicate with those in the know.

Like call and response, signifyin is ubiquitous in hip hop lyrics. In an example of male-female urban verbal play, in "Minute Man" (2001) with Missy Elliot and Ludacris, Jay-Z signifies on female R & B group Destiny's Child. Some insider knowledge is required to fully understand this speech act. Earlier that year, Destiny's Child had released "Independent Women," in which they asked a series of questions of men who dogged ('treated poorly') females. For example, they introduced each question with the word *question* and then proceeded, "How you like them diamonds that I bought?" (to demonstrate to such men that they had their own income). Given that one of Jay-Z's many personas is the *playa-pimp*-type ('one who uses women for sex and money'), he rhymes to the listeners (including Destiny's Child): "I'm not tryin to give you love and affection / I'm tryin to give you 60 seconds of affection / I'm tryin to give you cash, fare and directions / Get your independent-ass outta here. Question!" The signification doesn't become clear until the last line or, really, the last word, when Jay-Z borrows the word *question* from their song (saying it in such a way as to match their rate of speech, tone and pronunciation). The only thing left to do is say, "Oooohhhhhh!"

We also witnessed signification in the call and response section of the Black Thought performance described above. As Jackson (2001) notes, Thought appears to be signifyin on the audience by highlighting their lack of familiarity with Black cultural modes of discourse: "I wonder if it's what I'm saying... A-yo!" The Roots have been known to signify on audiences that are not as culturally responsive as they would like them to be. During a 1999 concert at Stanford University, they stopped the music and began singing theme songs from 1980s television shows like "Diff'rent Strokes" and "Facts of Life," snapping their fingers and singing in a corny (not cool) way. The largely white, middle-class audience of college students sang along and snapped their fingers – apparently oblivious to the insult. After the show, the band's drummer and official spokesman, Ahmir, said: "Like if the crowd ain't responding, we've done shows where we've stopped the show, turned the equipment around, and played for the wall, you know" (Alim 1999). In this sense, the Roots remove any hint of indirection and blatantly *bust on* the unresponsive audience.

The examples above make clear that HHNL speakers readily incorporate *signifyin* and *bustin* into their repertoire. Whether hip hop heads are performing, writing rhymes, or just "conversatin," these strategies are skillfully employed. Other hip hop cultural modes of discourse and discursive practices, which fall out of the purview of this chapter, are tonal semantics and poetics, narrative sequencing and flow, battling and entering the cipher. Linguistic scholars of the hip hop generations (we are now more than one) are needed to uncover the complexity and creativity of HHNL speakers. In order to *represent* – reflect any semblance of hip hop cultural reality – these scholars will need to be in direct conversation with the culture creators of a very widely misunderstood Nation.

## Acknowledgments

It is my pleasure to acknowledge the assistance and encouragement of John Baugh, Mary Bucholtz, Austin Jackson, Marcyliena Morgan, Geneva Smitherman, James G. Spady, and Arthur Spears in the preparation of this chapter. I would also like to thank Ed Finegan for his scrupulous reading of the manuscript and for his insight and many helpful suggestions, and John Rickford for his support and careful review of an early draft of the manuscript. The chapter has been greatly improved by their efforts as editors. Lastly, much props to my students in Linguistics 74: "The Language of Hip Hop Culture"; they have challenged me to represent to the fullest.

## Suggestions for Further Reading and Exploration

For a thorough understanding of the philosophies and aesthetic values of hip hop's culture creators, the Umum Hip Hop Trilogy is an excellent source. Its three volumes (Spady and Eure 1991, Spady et al. 1995, Spady et al. 1999) offer extensive hip hop conversational discourse with such members of the HHN as Ice Cube, Busta Rhymes, Chuck D, Kurupt, Common, Eve, Bahamadia, Grandmaster Flash, and others. These volumes also provide primary source material for scholars of language use within the HHN. For early works on hip hop culture, see Hager (1984), Toop (1984, 1994, 1999), Nelson and Gonzales (1991), Rose (1994), and Potter (1995).

For updates on what's happening in the HHN, the most informative website is Davey D's Hip Hop Corner (www.daveyd.com). Useful hip hop periodicals include *Murder Dog, The Source, XXL, Vibe* and *Blaze*. One might gain the most insight by "reading" the hip hop saturated streets of America.

### Notes

1. Grandmaster Flash and the Furious Five released "The Message" in 1982 and it became one of the first major hip hop records to document street life and street consciousness. The line, "It's like a jungle sometimes it makes me wonder how I keep from goin under" is perhaps one of the most frequently quoted hip hop choruses to this day. In the epigraph to this chapter, we see JT the Bigga Figga rappin another part of the chorus, "Don't push me cuz I'm close to the eeedge!"

2. The transcription of HHNL into print often leaves a lot to be desired. I have attempted to reconstruct the verbal agility of these hip hop artists on the printed page, but, as Brathwaite (1984) admits, it is best for the reader to listen along to the music whenever possible (see discography).

## References


Abrahams, Roger. 1964. *Deep Down in the Jungle: Negro Narrative Folklore from the Streets of Philadelphia*. Chicago: Aldine Publishing Co.

Abrahams, Roger. 1970. "Rapping and Capping: Black Talk as Art." In *In Black America*, ed. John Szwed. New York: Basic Books.

Abrahams, Roger. 1976. *Talking Black*. Rowley, MA: Newbury House.

Alim, H. Samy. 1999. "The Roots Rock Memorial Auditorium." "Intermission" section of *The Stanford Daily*. Stanford University.

Alim, H. Samy. 2000. "360 Degreez of Black Art Comin at You: Sista Sonia Sanchez and the Dimensions of a Black Arts Continuum." In *360 Degreez of Sonia Sanchez: Hip Hop, Narrativity, Iqhawe and Public Spaces of Being*, ed. James G. Spady. Special issue of *BMa: the Sonia Sanchez Literary Review*, 6.1, Fall.

Alim, H. Samy, ed. 2001a. *Hip Hop Culture: Language, Literature, Literacy and the Lives of Black Youth*. Special issue of *The Black Arts Quarterly*. Committee on Black Performing Arts: Stanford University.

Alim, H. Samy. 2001b. "I Be the Truth: Divergence. Recreolization, and the 'New' Equative Copula in African American Language." Paper presented at NWAV 30, Raleigh, North Carolina, October.

Alim, H. Samy. 2002. "Street Conscious Copula Variation in the Hip Hop Nation," *American Speech* 77: 288–304.

Alim, H. Samy. 2003a. "On some serious next millenium rap ishhh: Pharoahe Monch, Hip Hop poetics, and the internal rhymes of Internal Affairs." *Journal of English Linguistics* 31(1): 60–84.

Alim, H. Samy. 2003b. "'We are the streets': African American Language and the strategic construction of a street conscious identity." In Makoni, S., G. Smitherman, A. Ball, and A. Spears (eds.). *Black Linguistics: Language, Society, and Politics in Africa and the Americas*. New York: Routledge.

Alim, H. Samy. In Press. *'You know my Steez': an Ethnographic and Sociolinguistic Study of Styleshifting in a Black American Speech*.

Anderson, Elijah. 1999. *Code of the Street: Decency, Violence, and the Moral Life of the Inner City*. New York: W. W. Norton.

Anderson, Monica. 1994. *Black English Vernacular (From "Ain't" to "Yo Mama": the Words Politically Correct Americans Should Know)*. Highland City FL: Rainbow Books.

Baugh, John. 1983. *Black Street Speech: Its History, Structure, and Survival*. Austin TX: University of Texas Press.

Baugh, John. 1991. "The Politicization of Changing Terms of Self-Reference Among American Slave Descendants," *American Speech* 66: 133–46.

Braithwaite. Fred. (Fab Five Freddy). 1992. *Fresh Fly Flavor: Words and Phrases of the Hip-Hop Generation*. Stamford CT: Longmeadow Press.

Braithwaite, Fred. 1995. *Hip Hop Slang: English-Deutsch*. Frankfurt am Main: Eichborn.

Brathwaite, Kamau. 1984. *History of the Voice: the Development of Nation Language in Anglophone Caribbean Poetry*. London: New Beacon Books.

Calloway, Cab. 1944. *Hepster's Dictionary: Language of Jive*. Republished as an appendix to Calloway's autobiography. *Of Minnie the Moocher and Me*. 1976. New York: Thomas Y. Crowell.

Daniel, Jack, and Geneva Smitherman. 1976. "How I Got Over: Communication Dynamics in the Black Community," *Quarterly Journal of Speech* 62 (February): 26–39.

Dillard, J. L. 1977. *Lexicon of Black English*. New York: Seabury.

Fasold, Ralph. 1972. *Tense Marking in Black English: a Linguistic and Social Analysis*. Washington DC: Center for Applied Linguistics.

Folb, Edith. 1980. *Runnin' Down Some Lines: the Language and Culture of Black Teenagers*. Cambridge: Harvard University Press.

Hager, Steven. 1984. *Hip Hop: the Illustrated History of Breakdancing, Rap Music, and Graffiti*. New York: St. Martin's Press.

Henderson, Stephen. 1973. *Understanding the New Black Poetry: Black Speech and Black Music as Poetic References*. New York: William Morrow.

Holloway, Joseph E, and Winifred K. Vass. 1997. *The African Heritage of American English*. Bloomington: University of Indiana Press.

Hymes, Dell. 1981. "Foreword." In *Language in the U.S.A.*, eds. Charles A. Ferguson and Shirley B. Heath. New York: Cambridge University Press.

Jackson, Austin. Tony Michel, David Sheridan, and Bryan Stumpf. 2001. "Making Connections in the Contact Zones: Towards a Critical Praxis of Rap Music and Hip Hop Culture." In *Hip Hop Culture: Language, Literature, Literacy and the Lives of Black Youth*, ed. H. Samy Alim. Special issue of *The Black Arts Quarterly*. Committee on Black Performing Arts: Stanford University.

JT the Bigga Figga, Personal interview with H. Samy Alim, November, 2000.

Keyes, Cheryl. 1984. "Verbal Art Performance in Rap Music: the Conversation of the 80s," *Folklore Forum* 17(2): 143–52.

Keyes, Cheryl. 1991. "Rappin' to the Beat: Rap Music as Street Culture Among African Americans." Unpublished Ph.D. diss., Indiana University.

Kochman, Thomas. 1969. "'Rapping' in the Black Ghetto," *Trans-Action* (February): 26–34.

KRS-One. 2000. "The First Overstanding: Refinitions." The Temple of Hip Hop Kulture.

Labov, William. 1972. *Language in the Inner City: Studies in the Black English Vernacular*. Philadelphia: University of Pennsylvania Press.

Labov, William, Paul Cohen, Clarence Robins, and John Lewis. 1968. *A Study of the Nonstandard English of Negro and Puerto Rican Speakers in New York City*. Report on Co-operative Research Project 3288. New York: Columbia University.

Major, Clarence. 1970 [1994]. *Juba to Jive: a Dictionary of African American Slang*. New York and London: Penguin.

Mitchell-Kernan, Claudia. 1971. *Language Behavior in a Black Urban Community*. University of California, Berkeley: Language Behavior Research Laboratory.

Mitchell-Kernan, Claudia. 1972. "Signifying and Marking: Two Afro-American Speech Acts." In *Directions in Sociolinguistics*, eds. John J. Gumperz and Dell Hymes. New York: Holt, Rinehart and Winston, pp. 161–79.

Morgan, Aswan. 1999. "Why They Say What Dey Be Sayin': an Examination of Hip-Hop Content and Language." Paper submitted for LING 073, *Introduction to African American Vernacular English*. Stanford University.

Morgan, Marcyliena. 2001a. "Reading Dialect and Grammatical Shout-Outs in Hip Hop." Paper presented at the Linguistic Society of America Convention. Washington DC. January.

Morgan, Marcyliena. 2001b. "'Nuthin' But a G Thang': Grammar and Language Ideology in Hip Hop Identity." In *Sociocultural and Historical Contexts of African American Vernacular English*, ed. Sonja L. Lanehard. Amsterdam: John Benjamins, pp. 187–210.

Mos Def, Personal interview with H. Samy Alim. October 2000.

Nelson, Havelock, and Michael Gonzales. 1991. *Bring the Noise: a Guide to Rap Music and Hip Hop Culture*. New York: Harmony Books.

Olivo, Warren. 2001. "Phat Lines: Spelling Conventions in Rap Music," *Written Language and Literacy* 4(1): 67–85.

Potter, Russell. 1995. *Spectacular Vernaculars: Hip-Hop and the Politics of Postmodernism*. Albany: State University of New York Press.

Remes, Pieter. 1991. "Rapping: a Sociolinguistic Study of Oral Tradition in Black Urban Communities in the United States," *Journal of the Anthropological Society of Oxford*, 22(2): 129–49.

Rickford, John, and Russell Rickford. 2000. *Spoken Soul: the Story of Black English*. New York: John Wiley.

Rose, Tricia. 1994. *Black Noise: Rap Music and Black Culture in Contemporary America*. Middletown CT: Wesleyan University Press.

San Quinn, Personal interview with H. Samy Alim and James G. Spady, November 2000.

Schiffman, Harold. 1996. *Linguistic Culture and Language Policy*. London and New York: Routledge.

Smitherman, Geneva. 1973. "The Power of the Rap: the Black Idiom and the New Black Poetry," *Twentieth Century Literature: a Scholarly and Critical Journal* 19: 259–74.

Smitherman, Geneva. 1977 (1986). *Talkin and Testifyin: the Language of Black America*, Houghton Mifflin; reissued, with revisions, Detroit: Wayne State University Press.

Smitherman, Geneva. 1991. "'What Is African to Me?': Language, Ideology and *African American*." *American Speech* 66(2): 115–32.

Smitherman, Geneva. 1994 [2000]. *Black Talk: Words and Phrases from the Hood to the Amen Corner*. Boston and New York: Houghton Mifflin.

Smitherman, Geneva. 1997. "'The Chain Remain the Same': Communicative Practices in the Hip-Hop Nation," *Journal of Black Studies*, September.

Smitherman, Geneva. 2000. *Talkin That Talk: Language, Culture and Education in African America*. London and New York: Routledge.

Smitherman, Geneva, and John Baugh. 2002. "The Shot Heard from Ann Arbor: Language Research and Public Policy in African America." *Howard Journal of Communication* 13: 5–24.

Spady, James G. 1993. "'IMA PUT MY THING DOWN': Afro-American Expressive Culture and the Hip Hop Community," *TYANABA: Revue de la Société d'Anthropologie*, December.

Spady, James G. 2000. "The Centrality of Black Language in the Discourse Strategies and Poetic Force of Sonia Sanchez and Rap Artists." In *360 Degreez of Sonia Sanchez: Hip Hop, Narrativity, Iqhawe and Public Spaces of Being*, ed. James Spady. Special issue of *BMa: the Sonia Sanchez Literary Review*, 6.1, Fall.

Spady, James G., and H. Samy Alim. 1999. "Street Conscious Rap: Modes of Being." In *Street Conscious Rap*. Philadelphia: Black History Museum/Umum Loh Publishers.

Spady, James G., and Joseph D. Eure, eds. 1991. *Nation Conscious Rap: the Hip Hop Vision*. New York/Philadelphia: PC International Press/Black History Museum.

Spady, James G., Stefan Dupres, and Charles G. Lee. 1995. *Twisted Tales in the Hip Hop Streets of Philly*. Philadelphia: Black History Museum/Umum Loh Publishers.

Spady, James G., Charles G. Lee, and H. Samy Alim. 1999. *Street Conscious Rap*. Philadelphia: Black History Museum/Umum Loh Publishers.

Stavsky, Lois, Isaac Mozeson, and Dani Reyes Mozeson. 1995. *A 2 Z: the Book of Rap and Hip-Hop Slang*. New York: Boulevard Books.

Toop, David. 1984 (1994, 1999). *Rap Attack: from African Jive to New York Hip Hop*. London: Pluto Press.

Turner, Lorenzo. 1949. *Africanisms in the Gullah Dialect*. Chicago: University of Chicago Press.

Wa Thiongo, Ngugi. 1992. *Moving the Center: the Struggle for Cultural Freedom*. London: Heinemann.

Wideman, John. 1976. "Frame and Dialect: the Evolution of the Black Voice in American Literature," *American Poetry Review* 5(5): 34–37.

Wolfram, Walter. 1969. *A Sociolinguistic Description of Detroit Negro Speech*. Washington, DC: Center for Applied Linguistics.

Yancy, George. 1991. "Rapese." Cited in Spady and Eure, eds.

Yasin, Jon. 1999. "Rap in the African-American Music Tradition: Cultural Assertion and Continuity." In *Race and Ideology: Language, Symbolism, and Popular Culture*, ed. Arthur Spears. Detroit: Wayne State University Press.

## Discography

B-Legit. 2000. *Hempin Ain't Easy*. Koch International.

Bahamadia. 1996. *Kollage*. EMI Records.

Big L. 2000. *The Big Picture*. Priority Records.

Cappadonna. 1998. *The Pillage*. Sony Records.

DJ Pooh. 1997. *Bad Newz Travels Fast*. Da Bomb/Big Beat/Atlantic Records.

Drag-On and Baby Madison. 2001. *Live from Lenox Ave*. Vacant Lot/Priority Records.

Grandmaster Flash and the Furious Five. 1982. *The Message*. Sugarhill Records.

JT the Bigga Figga. 1993. *Playaz N the Game*. Get Low Recordz.

Juvenile. 2001. *Project English*. Universal Records.

L.O.X. 2000. *We Are the Streets*. Ruff Ryders Records.

Ludacris. 2001. *Word of Mouf*. Universal Records.

Missy Elliot f/ Jay-Z and Ludacris. 2001. *Miss E... So Addictive*. Elektra/Asylum.

Mystikal. 2000. *Let's Get Ready*. Jive Records.

Nelly. 2000. *Country Grammar*. Universal Records.

Raekwon. 1999. *Immobilarity*. Sony.

Rza. 1998. *Rza as Bobby Digital in Stereo*. V2/BMG Records.

Three X Krazy. 2000. *Real Talk 2000*. DU BA Records.

Treacherous Three (Kool Moe Dee, LA Sunshine, Special K and DJ Easy Lee). 1980. "New Rap Language." Enjoy Records.

---

### Critical Thinking and Application

- Give examples of how AAL speakers deliberately use language in opposition to Standard English.
- Given that hip hop language is partially intended to include and exclude those who can use it, it must evolve rapidly as outsiders begin to "get hip" to its meanings. Where do you think the new innovations come from?
- Select an example of hip hip lyrics and analyze them using the concepts presented in this chapter. Reflect on the use of scholarly concepts to analyze popular culture. What can you learn this way? What is elusive?

### Vocabulary

| | | |
|---|---|---|
| African American Language (AAL) | hiphopness | ritual insults |
| call-and-response | hiphopological | signification |
| discourse | invariant *be* | signifyin' |
| equative copula | lexicographer | sociolinguistics, sociolinguists |
| habitual *be* | lexicon | "street" |
| hip hop | rap, rappin | verbal battling, verbal duel |

### Suggested Further Reading [See also list following Language and Identity; "Race" and Ethnicity unit introduction]

Chang, Jeff. 2005. *Can't Stop, Won't Stop: A History of the Hip-Hop Generation*. New York: St. Martin's Press.

Condry, Ian. 2006. *Hip Hop Japan: Rap and the Paths of Cultural Globalization*. Durham, NC: Duke University Press.

Morgan, Marcyliena. 2001. "Nothin' but a G Thang": Grammar and Language Ideology in Hip Hop Identity. In *Sociocultural and Historical Contexts of African American English*, edited by Sonja L. Lanehart, pp. 187–209. Amsterdam and Philadelphia: Benjamins.

Smith, Marc Kelly, and Mark Eleveld. 2003. *The Spoken Word Revolution: Slam, Hip-Hop, and the Poetry of a New Generation*. Naperville, IL: Sourcebooks MediaFusion.

Watkins, S. Craig. 2005. *Hip Hop Matters: Politics, Pop Culture, and the Struggle for the Soul of a Movement*. Boston: Beacon Press.

# CHAPTER 34

# Aria

## *Richard Rodriguez*

(1982)

*This chapter is excerpted from Richard Rodriguez's* Hunger of Memory, *in which he ruminates beautifully on his transformation from a Latino boy to a successful English-speaking American man. Quite controversially, Rodriguez rejects the possibility of bilingual education. For him, that would have muddled his identity. He stops short of rejecting bilingual education for everyone, speaking only for himself. Still, his position as a success has made him the target of anger and resentment, as others aim to create circumstances for all children that might lead them to similar success—while maintaining their connections to their home languages.*

*Whatever the reader's view of Rodriguez's solution, the dilemma is nevertheless there to be faced: How can a child of minority identity, constructed as "brown" by others even before he opens his mouth, decide what to do about his or her linguistic and cultural options? What will the ramifications be, whichever way he decides to go? Whom will she alienate and whom enlist? How do social, linguistic, and psychological identities sort themselves out?*

### Reading Questions

- How does Rodriguez describe the sounds of English and of Spanish as they appeared to him prior to his entering school? What were his associations with the two languages? What does he mean when he writes: "I lived in a world magically compounded of sounds"?
- How does Rodriguez regard the choice between public and private? What happened when the nuns visited his house? What made him make the linguistic choice he did? What were the effects of that choice?
- What does Rodriguez mean when he writes, "Intimacy is not created by a particular language; it is created by intimates"? If the language has no effect on intimacy, why doesn't he use more Spanish?

---

### I

I remember to start with that day in Sacramento – a California now nearly thirty years past – when I first entered a classroom, able to understand some fifty stray English words.

The third of four children, I had been preceded to a neighborhood Roman Catholic school by an older brother and sister. But neither of them had revealed very much about their classroom experiences. Each afternoon they returned, as they left in the morning, always together, speaking in Spanish as they climbed the five steps of the porch. And their mysterious books, wrapped in shopping-bag paper, remained on the table next to the door, closed firmly behind them.

An accident of geography sent me to a school where all my classmates were white, many the children of doctors and lawyers and business executives. All my classmates certainly must have been uneasy on that first day of school – as most children are uneasy – to find themselves apart from their families in the first institution of their lives. But I was astonished.

The nun said, in a friendly but oddly impersonal voice, 'Boys and girls, this is Richard Rodriguez.' (I heard her sound out: *Rich-heard Road-ree-guess.*) It was the first time I had heard anyone name me in English. 'Richard,' the nun repeated more slowly, writing my name down in her black leather book. Quickly I turned to see my mother's face dissolve in a watery blur behind the pebbled glass door.

---

Many years later there is something called bilingual education – a scheme proposed in the late 1960s by Hispanic-American social activists, later endorsed by a congressional

Richard Rodriguez, Aria. From *Hunger of Memory*. Boston: David R. Godine, 1982, pp. 12–40.

vote. It is a program that seeks to permit non-English-speaking children, many from lower-class homes, to use their family language as the language of school. (Such is the goal its supporters announce.) I hear them and am forced to say no: It is not possible for a child – any child – ever to use his family's language in school. Not to understand this is to misunderstand the public uses of schooling and to trivialize the nature of intimate life – a family's 'language.'

Memory teaches me what I know of these matters; the boy reminds the adult. I was a bilingual child, a certain kind – socially disadvantaged – the son of working-class parents, both Mexican immigrants.

In the early years of my boyhood, my parents coped very well in America. My father had steady work. My mother managed at home. They were nobody's victims. Optimism and ambition led them to a house (our home) many blocks from the Mexican south side of town. We lived among *gringos* and only a block from the biggest, whitest houses. It never occurred to my parents that they couldn't live wherever they chose. Nor was the Sacramento of the fifties bent on teaching them a contrary lesson. My mother and father were more annoyed than intimidated by those two or three neighbors who tried initially to make us unwelcome. ('Keep your brats away from my sidewalk!') But despite all they achieved, perhaps because they had so much to achieve, any deep feeling of ease, the confidence of 'belonging' in public was withheld from them both. They regarded the people at work, the faces in crowds, as very distant from us. They were the others, *los gringos*. That term was interchangeable in their speech with another, even more telling, *los americanos*.

I grew up in a house where the only regular guests were my relations. For one day, enormous families of relatives would visit and there would be so many people that the noise and the bodies would spill out to the backyard and front porch. Then, for weeks, no one came by. (It was usually a salesman who rang the doorbell.) Our house stood apart. A gaudy yellow in a row of white bungalows. We were the people with the noisy dog. The people who raised pigeons and chickens. We were the foreigners on the block. A few neighbors smiled and waved. We waved back. But no one in the family knew the names of the old couple who lived next door; until I was seven years old, I did not know the names of the kids who lived across the street.

In public, my father and mother spoke a hesitant, accented, not always grammatical English. And they would have to strain – their bodies tense – to catch the sense of what was rapidly said by *los gringos*. At home they spoke Spanish. The language of their Mexican past sounded in counterpoint to the English of public society. The words would come quickly, with ease. Conveyed through those sounds was the pleasing, soothing, consoling reminder of being at home.

During those years when I was first conscious of hearing, my mother and father addressed me only in Spanish; in Spanish I learned to reply. By contrast, English (*inglés*), rarely heard in the house, was the language I came to associate with *gringos*. I learned my first words of English overhearing my parents speak to strangers. At five years of age, I knew just enough English for my mother to trust me on errands to stores one block away. No more.

I was a listening child, careful to hear the very different sounds of Spanish and English. Wide-eyed with hearing, I'd listen to sounds more than words. First, there were English (*gringo*) sounds. So many words were still unknown that when the butcher or the lady at the drugstore said something to me, exotic polysyllabic sounds would bloom in the midst of their sentences. Often, the speech of people in public seemed to me very loud, booming with confidence. The man behind the counter would literally ask, 'What can I do for you?' But by being so firm and so clear, the sound of his voice said that he was a *gringo*; he belonged in public society.

I would also hear then the high nasal notes of middle-class American speech. The air stirred with sound. Sometimes, even now, when I have been traveling abroad for several weeks, I will hear what I heard as a boy. In hotel lobbies or airports, in Turkey or Brazil, some Americans will pass, and suddenly I will hear it again – the high sound of American voices. For a few seconds I will hear it with pleasure, for it is now the sound of *my* society – a reminder of home. But inevitably – already on the flight headed for home – the sound fades with repetition. I will be unable to hear it anymore.

When I was a boy, things were different. The accent of *los gringos* was never pleasing nor was it hard to hear. Crowds at Safeway or at bus stops would be noisy with sound. And I would be forced to edge away from the chirping chatter above me.

I was unable to hear my own sounds, but I knew very well that I spoke English poorly. My words could not stretch far enough to form complete thoughts. And the words I did speak I didn't know well enough to make into distinct sounds. (Listeners would usually lower their heads, better to hear what I was trying to say.) But it was one thing for *me* to speak English with difficulty. It was more troubling for me to hear my parents speak in public: their high-whining vowels and guttural consonants; their sentences that got stuck with 'eh' and 'ah' sounds; the confused syntax; the hesitant rhythm of sounds so different from the way *gringos* spoke. I'd notice, moreover, that my parents' voices were softer than those of *gringos* we'd meet.

I am tempted now to say that none of this mattered. In adulthood I am embarrassed by childhood fears. And, in a way, it didn't matter very much that my parents could not speak English with ease. Their linguistic difficulties had no serious consequences. My mother and father made themselves understood at the county hospital clinic and at government offices. And yet, in another way, it mattered very much – it was unsettling to hear my parents struggle with English. Hearing them, I'd grow nervous, my clutching trust in their protection and power weakened.

There were many times like the night at a brightly lit gasoline station (a blaring white memory) when I stood uneasily, hearing my father. He was talking to a teenaged attendant. I do not recall what they were saying, but I cannot forget the sounds my father made as he spoke. At one point his words slid together to form one word – sounds as confused as the threads of blue and green oil in the puddle next to my shoes. His voice rushed through what he had left to say. And, toward the end, reached falsetto notes, appealing to his listener's understanding. I looked away to the lights of passing automobiles. I tried not to hear anymore. But I heard only too well the calm, easy tones in the attendant's reply. Shortly afterward, walking toward home with my father, I shivered when he put his hand on my shoulder. The very first chance that I got, I evaded his grasp and ran on ahead into the dark, skipping with feigned boyish exuberance.

But then there was Spanish. *Español*: my family's language. *Español*: the language that seemed to me a private language. I'd hear strangers on the radio and in the Mexican Catholic church across town speaking in Spanish, but I couldn't really believe that Spanish was a public language, like English. Spanish speakers, rather, seemed related to me, for I sensed that we shared – through our language – the experience of feeling apart from *los gringos*. It was thus a ghetto Spanish that I heard and I spoke. Like those whose lives are bound by a barrio, I was reminded by Spanish of my separateness from *los otros, los gringos* in power. But more intensely than for most barrio children – because I did not live in a barrio – Spanish seemed to me the language of home. (Most days it was only at home that I'd hear it.) It became the language of joyful return.

A family member would say something to me and I would feel myself specially recognized. My parents would say something to me and I would feel embraced by the sounds of their words. Those sounds said: *I am speaking with ease in Spanish. I am addressing you in words I never use with* los gringos. *I recognize you as someone special, close, like no one outside. You belong with us. In the family.*

*(Ricardo.)*

At the age of five, six, well past the time when most other children no longer easily notice the difference between sounds uttered at home and words spoken in public, I had a different experience. I lived in a world magically compounded of sounds. I remained a child longer than most; I lingered too long, poised at the edge of language – often frightened by the sounds of *los gringos*, delighted by the sounds of Spanish at home. I shared with my family a language that was startlingly different from that used in the great city around us.

For me there were none of the gradations between public and private society so normal to a maturing child. Outside the house was public society; inside the house was private. Just opening or closing the screen door behind me was an important experience. I'd rarely leave home all alone or without reluctance. Walking down the sidewalk, under the canopy of tall trees, I'd warily notice the – suddenly – silent neighborhood kids who stood warily watching me. Nervously, I'd arrive at the grocery store to hear there the sounds of the *gringo* – foreign to me – reminding me that in this world so big, I was a foreigner. But then I'd return. Walking back toward our house, climbing the steps from the sidewalk, when the front door was open in summer, I'd hear voices beyond the screen door talking in Spanish. For a second or two, I'd stay, linger there, listening. Smiling, I'd hear my mother call out, saying in Spanish (words): 'Is that you, Richard?' All the while her sounds would assure me: *You are home now; come closer; inside. With us.*

'*Sí*,' I'd reply.

Once more inside the house I would resume (assume) my place in the family. The sounds would dim, grow harder to hear. Once more at home, I would grow less aware of that fact. It required, however, no more than the blurt of the doorbell to alert me to listen to sounds all over again. The house would turn instantly still while my mother went to the door. I'd hear her hard English sounds. I'd wait to hear her voice return to soft-sounding Spanish, which assured me, as surely as did the clicking tongue of the lock on the door, that the stranger was gone.

Plainly, it is not healthy to hear such sounds so often. It is not healthy to distinguish public words from private sounds so easily. I remained cloistered by sounds, timid and shy in public, too dependent on voices at home. And yet it needs to be emphasized: I was an extremely happy child at home. I remember many nights when my father would come back from work, and I'd hear him call out to my mother in Spanish, sounding relieved. In Spanish, he'd sound light and free notes he never could manage in English. Some nights I'd jump up just at hearing his voice. With *mis hermanos* I would come running into the room where he was with my mother. Our laughing (so deep was the pleasure!) became screaming. Like others who know the pain of public alienation, we transformed the knowledge of our public separateness and made it consoling – the reminder of intimacy. Excited, we joined our voices in a celebration of sounds. *We are speaking now the way we never speak out in public. We are alone – together*, voices sounded, surrounded to tell me. Some nights, no one seemed willing to loosen the hold sounds had on us. At dinner, we invented new words. (Ours sounded Spanish, but made sense only to us.) We pieced together new words by taking, say, an English verb and giving it Spanish endings. My mother's instructions at bedtime would be lacquered with mock-urgent tones. Or a word like *sí* would become, in several notes, able to convey added measures of feeling. Tongues explored the edges of words, especially the fat vowels. And we happily sounded that military drum roll, the twirling roar of the Spanish *r*. Family language: my family's sounds. The voices of my parents and sisters and brother. Their voices insisting: *You belong here. We are family members. Related. Special to one another. Listen!* Voices singing and sighing, rising, straining, then surging, teeming with pleasure that burst syllables into fragments of laughter. At times it seemed there was steady quiet only when, from another room, the rustling whispers of my parents faded and I moved closer to sleep.

## 2

Supporters of bilingual education today imply that students like me miss a great deal by not being taught in their family's language. What they seem not to recognize is that, as a socially disadvantaged child, I considered Spanish to be a private language. What I needed to learn in school was that I had the right – and the obligation – to speak the public language of *los gringos*. The odd truth is that my first-grade classmates could have become bilingual, in the conventional sense of that word, more easily than I. Had they been taught (as upper-middle-class children are often taught early) a second language like Spanish or French, they could have regarded it simply as that: another public language. In my case such bilingualism could not have been so quickly achieved. What I did not believe was that I could speak a single public language.

Without question, it would have pleased me to hear my teachers address me in Spanish when I entered the classroom. I would have felt much less afraid. I would have trusted them and responded with ease. But I would have delayed – for how long postponed? – having to learn the language of public society. I would have evaded – and for how long could I have afforded to delay? – learning the great lesson of school, that I had a public identity.

Fortunately, my teachers were unsentimental about their responsibility. What they understood was that I needed to speak a public language. So their voices would search me out, asking me questions. Each time I'd hear them, I'd look up in surprise to see a nun's face frowning at me. I'd mumble, not really meaning to answer. The nun would persist, 'Richard, stand up. Don't look at the floor. Speak up. Speak to the entire class, not just to me!' But I couldn't believe that the English language was mine to use. (In part, I did not want to believe it.) I continued to mumble. I resisted the teacher's demands. (Did I somehow suspect that once I learned public language my pleasing family life would be changed?) Silent, waiting for the bell to sound, I remained dazed, diffident, afraid.

Because I wrongly imagined that English was intrinsically a public language and Spanish an intrinsically private one, I easily noted the difference between classroom language and the language of home. At school, words were directed to a general audience of listeners. ('Boys and girls.') Words were meaningfully ordered. And the point was not self-expression alone but to make oneself understood by many others. The teacher quizzed: 'Boys and girls, why do we use that word in this sentence? Could we think of a better word to use there? Would the sentence change its meaning if the words were differently arranged? And wasn't there a better way of saying much the same thing?' (I couldn't say. I wouldn't try to say.)

Three months. Five. Half a year passed. Unsmiling, ever watchful, my teachers noted my silence. They began to connect my behavior with the difficult progress my older sister and brother were making. Until one Saturday morning three nuns arrived at the house to talk to our parents. Stiffly, they sat on the blue living room sofa. From the doorway of another room, spying the visitors, I noted the incongruity – the clash of two worlds, the faces and voices of school intruding upon the familiar setting of home. I overheard one voice gently wondering, 'Do your children speak only Spanish at home, Mrs. Rodriguez?' While another voice added, 'That Richard especially seems so timid and shy.'

*That Rich-heard!*

With great tact the visitors continued, 'Is it possible for you and your husband to encourage your children to practice their English when they are home?' Of course, my parents complied. What would they not do for their children's well-being? And how could they have questioned the Church's authority which those women represented? In an instant, they agreed to give up the language (the sounds) that had revealed and accentuated our family's closeness. The moment after the visitors left, the change was observed. '*Ahora*, speak to us *en inglés*,' my father and mother united to tell us.

At first, it seemed a kind of game. After dinner each night, the family gathered to practice 'our' English. (It was still then *inglés*, a language foreign to us, so we felt drawn as strangers to it.) Laughing, we would try to define words we could not pronounce. We played with strange English sounds, often over-anglicizing our pronunciations. And we filled the smiling gaps of our sentences with familiar Spanish sounds. But that was cheating, somebody shouted. Everyone laughed. In school, meanwhile, like my brother and sister, I was required to attend a daily tutoring session. I needed a full year of special attention. I also needed my teachers to keep my attention from straying in class by calling out, *Rich-heard* – their English voices slowly prying loose my ties to my other name, its three notes, *Ri-car-do*. Most of all I needed to hear my mother and father speak to me in a moment of seriousness in broken – suddenly heartbreaking – English. The scene was inevitable: One Saturday morning I entered the kitchen where my parents were talking in Spanish. I did not realize that they were talking in Spanish however until, at the moment they saw me, I heard their voices change to speak English. Those *gringo* sounds they uttered startled me. Pushed me away. In that moment of trivial misunderstanding and profound insight, I felt my throat twisted by unsounded grief. I turned quickly and left the room. But I had no place to escape to with Spanish. (The spell was broken.) My brother and sisters were speaking English in another part of the house.

Again and again in the days following, increasingly angry, I was obliged to hear my mother and father: 'Speak to us *en inglés*.' (*Speak*.) Only then did I determine to learn classroom English. Weeks after, it happened: One day in school I raised my hand to volunteer an answer. I spoke out in a loud voice. And I did not think it remarkable when the entire class understood. That day, I moved very far from the disadvantaged child I had been only days earlier. The belief, the calming assurance that I belonged in public, had at last taken hold.

Shortly after, I stopped hearing the high and loud sounds of *los gringos*. A more and more confident speaker of English, I didn't trouble to listen to *how* strangers sounded, speaking to me. And there simply were too many English-speaking people in my day for me to hear American accents anymore. Conversations quickened. Listening to persons who sounded eccentrically pitched voices, I usually noted their sounds for an initial few seconds before I concentrated on *what* they were saying. Conversations became content-full. Transparent. Hearing someone's *tone* of voice – angry or questioning or sarcastic or happy or sad – I didn't distinguish it from the words it expressed. Sound and word were thus tightly wedded. At the end of a day, I was often bemused, always relieved, to realize how 'silent,' though crowded with words, my day in public had been. (This public silence measured and quickened the change in my life.)

At last, seven years old, I came to believe what had been technically true since my birth: I was an American citizen.

But the special feeling of closeness at home was diminished by then. Gone was the desperate, urgent, intense feeling of being at home; rare was the experience of feeling myself individualized by family intimates. We remained a loving family, but one greatly changed. No longer so close; no longer bound tight by the pleasing and troubling knowledge of our public separateness. Neither my older brother nor sister rushed home after school anymore. Nor did I. When I arrived home there would often be neighborhood kids in the house. Or the house would be empty of sounds.

Following the dramatic Americanization of their children, even my parents grew more publicly confident. Especially my mother. She learned the names of all the people on our block. And she decided we needed to have a telephone installed in the house. My father continued to use the word *gringo*. But it was no longer charged with the old bitterness or distrust. (Stripped of any emotional content, the word simply became a name for those Americans not of Hispanic descent.) Hearing him, sometimes, I wasn't sure if he was pronouncing the Spanish word *gringo* or saying gringo in English.

Matching the silence I started hearing in public was a new quiet at home. The family's quiet was partly due to the fact that, as we children learned more and more English, we shared fewer and fewer words with our parents. Sentences needed to be spoken slowly when a child addressed his mother or father. (Often the parent wouldn't understand.) The child would need to repeat himself. (Still the parent misunderstood.) The young voice, frustrated, would end up saying, 'Never mind' – the subject was closed. Dinners would be noisy with the clinking of knives and forks against dishes. My mother would smile softly between her remarks; my father at the other end of the table would chew and chew at his food, while he stared over the heads of his children.

My *mother!* My *father!* After English became my primary language, I no longer knew what words to use in addressing my parents. The old Spanish words (those tender accents of sound) I had used earlier – *mamá* and *papá* – I couldn't use anymore. They would have been too painful reminders of how much had changed in my life. On the other hand, the words I heard neighborhood kids call *their* parents seemed equally unsatisfactory. *Mother* and *Father; Ma, Papa, Pa, Dad, Pop* (how I hated the all-American sound of that last word especially) – all these terms I felt were unsuitable, not really terms of address for *my* parents. As a result, I never used them at home. Whenever I'd speak to my parents, I would try to get their attention with eye contact alone. In public conversations, I'd refer to 'my parents' or 'my mother and father.'

My mother and father, for their part, responded differently, as their children spoke to them less. *She grew restless, seemed troubled and anxious at the scarcity of words exchanged in the house.* It was she who would question me about my day when I came home from school. She smiled at small talk. She pried at the edges of my sentences to get me to say something more. (What?) She'd join conversations she overheard, but her intrusions often stopped her children's talking. By contrast, my father seemed reconciled to the new quiet. Though his English improved somewhat, he retired into silence. At dinner he spoke very little. One night his children and even his wife helplessly giggled at his garbled English pronunciation of the Catholic Grace before Meals. Thereafter he made his wife recite the prayer at the start of each meal, even on formal occasions, when there were guests in the house. Hers became the public voice of the family. On official business, it was she, not my father, one would usually hear on the phone or in stores, talking to strangers. His children grew so accustomed to his silence that, years later, they would speak routinely of his shyness. (My mother would often try to explain: Both his parents died when he was eight. He was raised by an uncle who treated him like little more than a menial servant. He was never encouraged to speak. He grew up alone. A man of few words.) But my father was not shy, I realized, when I'd watch him speaking Spanish with relatives. Using Spanish, he was quickly effusive. Especially when talking with other men, his voice would spark, flicker, flare alive with sounds. In Spanish, he expressed ideas and feelings he rarely revealed in English. With firm Spanish sounds, he conveyed confidence and authority English would never allow him.

The silence at home, however, was finally more than a literal silence. Fewer words passed between parent and child, but more profound was the silence that resulted from my inattention to sounds. At about the time I no longer bothered to listen with care to the sounds of English in public, I grew careless about listening to the sounds family members made when they spoke. Most of the time I heard someone speaking at home and didn't distinguish his sounds from the words people uttered in public. I didn't even pay much attention to my parents' accented and ungrammatical speech. At least not at home. Only when I was with them in public would I grow alert to their accents. Though, even then, their sounds caused me less and less concern. For I was increasingly confident of my own public identity.

I would have been happier about my public success had I not sometimes recalled what it had been like earlier, when my family had conveyed its intimacy through a set of conveniently private sounds. Sometimes in public, hearing a stranger, I'd hark back to my past. A Mexican farmworker approached me downtown to ask directions to somewhere. '¿*Hijito*...?' he said. And his voice summoned deep longing. Another time, standing beside my mother in the visiting room of a Carmelite convent, before the dense screen which rendered the nuns shadowy figures, I heard several

Spanish-speaking nuns – their busy, singsong overlapping voices – assure us that yes, yes, we were remembered, all our family was remembered in their prayers. (Their voices echoed faraway family sounds.) Another day, a dark-faced old woman – her hand light on my shoulder – steadied herself against me as she boarded a bus. She murmured something I couldn't quite comprehend. Her Spanish voice came near, like the face of a never-before-seen relative in the instant before I was kissed. Her voice, like so many of the Spanish voices I'd hear in public, recalled the golden age of my youth. Hearing Spanish then, I continued to be a careful, if sad, listener to sounds. Hearing a Spanish-speaking family walking behind me, I turned to look. I smiled for an instant, before my glance found the Hispanic-looking faces of strangers in the crowd going by.

---

Today I hear bilingual educators say that children lose a degree of 'individuality' by becoming assimilated into public society. (Bilingual schooling was popularized in the seventies, that decade when middle-class ethnics began to resist the process of assimilation – the American melting pot. But the bilingualists simplistically scorn the value and necessity of assimilation. They do not seem to realize that there are *two* ways a person is individualized. So they do not realize that while one suffers a diminished sense of *private* individuality by becoming assimilated into public society, such assimilation makes possible the achievement of *public* individuality.

The bilingualists insist that a student should be reminded of his difference from others in mass society, his heritage. But they equate mere separateness with individuality. The fact is that only in private – with intimates – is separateness from the crowd a prerequisite for individuality. (An intimate draws me apart, tells me that I am unique, unlike all others.) In public, by contrast, full individuality is achieved, paradoxically, by those who are able to consider themselves members of the crowd. Thus it happened for me: Only when I was able to think of myself as an American, no longer an alien in *gringo* society, could I seek the rights and opportunities necessary for full public individuality. The social and political advantages I enjoy as a man result from the day that I came to believe that my name, indeed, is *Rich-heard Road-ree-guess*. It is true that my public society today is often impersonal. (My public society is usually mass society.) Yet despite the anonymity of the crowd and despite the fact that the individuality I achieve in public is often tenuous – because it depends on my being one in a crowd – I celebrate the day I acquired my new name. Those middle-class ethnics who scorn assimilation seem to me filled with decadent self-pity, obsessed by the burden of public life. Dangerously, they romanticize public separateness and they trivialize the dilemma of the socially disadvantaged.

My awkward childhood does not prove the necessity of bilingual education. My story discloses instead an essential myth of childhood – inevitable pain. If I rehearse here the changes in my private life after my Americanization, it is finally to emphasize the public gain. The loss implies the gain: The house I returned to each afternoon was quiet. Intimate sounds no longer rushed to the door to greet me. There were other noises inside. The telephone rang. Neighborhood kids ran past the door of the bedroom where I was reading my schoolbooks – covered with shopping-bag paper. Once I learned public language, it would never again be easy for me to hear intimate family voices. More and more of my day was spent hearing words. But that may only be a way of saying that the day I raised my hand in class and spoke loudly to an entire roomful of faces, my childhood started to end.

## 3

I grew up victim to a disabling confusion. As I grew fluent in English, I no longer could speak Spanish with confidence. I continued to understand spoken Spanish. And in high school, I learned how to read and write Spanish. But for many years I could not pronounce it. A powerful guilt blocked my spoken words; an essential glue was missing whenever I'd try to connect words to form sentences. I would be unable to break a barrier of sound, to speak freely. I would speak, or try to speak, Spanish, and I would manage to utter halting, hiccuping sounds that betrayed my unease.

When relatives and Spanish-speaking friends of my parents came to the house, my brother and sisters seemed reticent to use Spanish, but at least they managed to say a few necessary words before being excused. I never managed so gracefully. I was cursed with guilt. Each time I'd hear myself addressed in Spanish, I would be unable to respond with any success. I'd know the words I wanted to say, but I couldn't manage to say them. I would try to speak, but everything I said seemed to me horribly anglicized. My mouth would not form the words right. My jaw would tremble. After a phrase or two, I'd cough up a warm, silvery sound. And stop.

It surprised my listeners to hear me. They'd lower their heads, better to grasp what I was trying to say. They would repeat their questions in gentle, affectionate voices. But by then I would answer in English. No, no, they would say, we want you to speak to us in Spanish. ('... *en español*.') But I couldn't do it. *Pocho* then they called me. Sometimes playfully, teasingly, using the tender diminutive – *mi pochito*. Sometimes not so playfully, mockingly, *Pocho*. (A Spanish dictionary defines that word as an adjective meaning 'colorless' or 'bland.' But I heard it as a noun, naming the Mexican-American who, in becoming an American, forgets his native society.) '¡*Pocho*!' the lady in the Mexican food store muttered, shaking her head. I looked up to the counter where red and green peppers were strung like Christmas tree lights and saw the frowning face of the stranger. My mother laughed somewhere behind me. (She said that her children didn't want to practice 'our Spanish' after they started going to school.) My mother's smiling voice made me suspect that the lady who faced me was not really angry at me. But, searching her face, I couldn't find the hint of a smile.

Embarrassed, my parents would regularly need to explain their children's inability to speak flowing Spanish during those years. My mother met the wrath of her brother, her only brother, when he came up from Mexico one summer with his family. He saw his nieces and nephews for the very first time. After listening to me, he looked away and said what a disgrace it was that I couldn't speak Spanish, '*su proprio idioma*.' He made that remark to my mother; I noticed, however, that he stared at my father.

I clearly remember one other visitor from those years. A long-time friend of my father from San Francisco would come to stay with us for several days in late August. He took great interest in me after he realized that I couldn't answer his questions in Spanish. He would grab me as I started to leave the kitchen. He would ask me something. Usually he wouldn't bother to wait for my mumbled response. Knowingly, he'd murmur: '*¿Ay Pocho, Pocho, adónde vas?*' And he would press his thumbs into the upper part of my arms, making me squirm with currents of pain. Dumbly, I'd stand there, waiting for his wife to notice us, for her to call him off with a benign smile. I'd giggle, hoping to deflate the tension between us, pretending that I hadn't seen the glittering scorn in his glance.

I remember that man now, but seek no revenge in this telling. I recount such incidents only because they suggest the fierce power Spanish had for many people I met at home; the way Spanish was associated with closeness. Most of those people who called me a *pocho* could have spoken English to me. But they would not. They seemed to think that Spanish was the only language we could use, that Spanish alone permitted our close association. (Such persons are vulnerable always to the ghetto merchant and the politician who have learned the value of speaking their clients' family language to gain immediate trust.) For my part, I felt that I had somehow committed a sin of betrayal by learning English. But betrayal against whom? Not against visitors to the house exactly. No, I felt that I had betrayed my immediate family. I *knew* that my parents had encouraged me to learn English. I *knew* that I had turned to English only with angry reluctance. But once I spoke English with ease, I came to *feel* guilty. (This guilt defied logic.) I felt that I had shattered the intimate bond that had once held the family close. This original sin against my family told whenever anyone addressed me in Spanish and I responded, confounded.

But even during those years of guilt, I was coming to sense certain consoling truths about language and intimacy. I remember playing with a friend in the backyard one day, when my grandmother appeared at the window. Her face was stern with suspicion when she saw the boy (the *gringo*) I was with. In Spanish she called out to me, sounding the whistle of her ancient breath. My companion looked up and watched her intently as she lowered the window and moved, still visible, behind the light curtain, watching us both. He wanted to know what she had said. I started to tell him, to say – to translate her Spanish words into English. The problem was, however, that though I knew how to translate exactly *what* she had told me, I realized that any translation would distort the deepest meaning of her message: It had been directed only to me. This message of intimacy could never be translated because it was not *in* the words she had used but passed *through* them. So any translation would have seemed wrong; her words would have been stripped of an essential meaning. Finally, I decided not to tell my friend anything. I told him that I didn't hear all she had said.

This insight unfolded in time. Making more and more friends outside my house, I began to distinguish intimate voices speaking through *English*. I'd listen at times to a close friend's confidential tone or secretive whisper. Even more remarkable were those instances when, for no special reason apparently, I'd become conscious of the fact that my companion was speaking only to me. I'd marvel just hearing his voice. It was a stunning event: to be able to break through his words, to be able to hear this voice of the other, to realize that it was directed only to me. After such moments of intimacy outside the house, I began to trust hearing intimacy conveyed through my family's English. Voices at home at last punctured sad confusion. I'd hear myself addressed as an intimate at home once again. Such moments were never as raucous with sound as past times had been when we had had 'private' Spanish to use. (Our English-sounding house was never to be as noisy as our Spanish-speaking house had been.) Intimate moments were usually soft moments of sound. My mother was in the dining room while I did my homework nearby. And she looked over at me. Smiled. Said something – her words said nothing very important. But her voice sounded to tell me (*We are together*) I was her son.

(*Richard*!)

Intimacy thus continued at home; intimacy was not stilled by English. It is true that I would never forget the great change of my life, the diminished occasions of intimacy. But there would also be times when I sensed the deepest truth about language and intimacy: *Intimacy is not created by a particular language; it is created by intimates.* The great change in my life was not linguistic but social. If, after becoming a successful student, I no longer heard intimate voices as often as I had earlier, it was not because I spoke English rather than Spanish. It was because I used public language for most of the day. I moved easily at last, a citizen in a crowded city of words.

## 4

This boy became a man. In private now, alone, I brood over language and intimacy – the great themes of my past. In public I expect most of the faces I meet to be the faces of strangers. (How do you do?) If meetings are quick and impersonal, they have been efficiently managed. I rush past the sounds of voices attending only to the words addressed to me. Voices seem planed to an even surface of sound, soundless. A business associate speaks in a deep baritone, but I pass through the timbre to attend to his words. The crazy man who sells me a newspaper every night mumbles something crazy, but I have time only to pretend that I have heard him say hello. Accented versions of English make little impression on me.

In the rush-hour crowd a Japanese tourist asks me a question, and I inch past his accent to concentrate on what he is saying. The Eastern European immigrant in a neighborhood delicatessen speaks to me through a marinade of sounds, but I respond to his words. I note for only a second the Texas accent of the telephone operator or the Mississippi accent of the man who lives in the apartment below me.

My city seems silent until some ghetto black teenagers board the bus I am on. Because I do not take their presence for granted, I listen to the sounds of their voices. Of all the accented versions of English I hear in a day, I hear theirs most intently. They are *the* sounds of the outsider. They annoy me for being loud – so self-sufficient and unconcerned by my presence. Yet for the same reason they seem to me glamorous. (A romantic gesture against public acceptance.) Listening to their shouted laughter, I realize my own quiet. Their voices enclose my isolation. I feel envious, envious of their brazen intimacy.

I warn myself away from such envy, however. I remember the black political activists who have argued in favor of using black English in schools. (Their argument varies only slightly from that made by foreign-language bilingualists.) I have heard 'radical' linguists make the point that black English is a complex and intricate version of English. And I do not doubt it. But neither do I think that black English should be a language of public instruction. What makes black English inappropriate in classrooms is not something *in* the language. It is rather what lower-class speakers make of it. Just as Spanish would have been a dangerous language for me to have used at the start of my education, so black English would be a dangerous language to use in the schooling of teenagers for whom it reenforces feelings of public separateness.

This seems to me an obvious point. But one that needs to be made. In recent years there have been attempts to make the language of the alien public language. 'Bilingual education, two ways to understand…,' television and radio commercials glibly announce. Proponents of bilingual education are careful to say that they want students to acquire good schooling. Their argument goes something like this: Children permitted to use their family language in school will not be so alienated and will be better able to match the progress of English-speaking children in the crucial first months of instruction. (Increasingly confident of their abilities, such children will be more inclined to apply themselves to their studies in the future.) But then the bilingualists claim another, very different goal. They say that children who use their family language in school will retain a sense of their individuality – their ethnic heritage and cultural ties. Supporters of bilingual education thus want it both ways. They propose bilingual schooling as a way of helping students acquire the skills of the classroom crucial for public success. But they likewise insist that bilingual instruction will give students a sense of their identity apart from the public.

Behind this screen there gleams an astonishing promise: One can become a public person while still remaining a private person. At the very same time one can be both! There need be no tension between the self in the crowd and the self apart from the crowd! Who would not want to believe such an idea? Who can be surprised that the scheme has won the support of many middle-class Americans? If the barrio or ghetto child can retain his separateness even while being publicly educated, then it is almost possible to believe that there is no private cost to be paid for public success. Such is the consolation offered by any of the current bilingual schemes. Consider, for example, the bilingual voters' ballot. In some American cities one can cast a ballot printed in several languages. Such a document implies that a person can exercise that most public of rights – the right to vote – while still keeping apart, unassimilated from public life.

It is not enough to say that these schemes are foolish and certainly doomed. Middle-class supporters of public bilingualism toy with the confusion of those Americans who cannot speak standard English as well as they can. Bilingual enthusiasts, moreover, sin against intimacy. An Hispanic-American writer tells me, 'I will never give up my family language; I would as soon give up my soul.' Thus he holds to his chest a skein of words, as though it were the source of his family ties. He credits to language what he should credit to family members. A convenient mistake. For as long as he holds on to words, he can ignore how much else has changed in his life.

It has happened before. In earlier decades, persons newly successful and ambitious for social mobility similarly seized upon certain 'family words.' Working-class men attempting political power took to calling one another 'brother.' By so doing they escaped oppressive public isolation and were able to unite with many others like themselves. But they paid a price for this union. It was a public union they forged. The word they coined to address one another could never be the sound (*brother*) exchanged by two in intimate greeting. In the union hall the word 'brother' became a vague metaphor; with repetition a weak echo of the intimate sound. Context forced the change. Context could not be overruled. Context will always guard the realm of the intimate from public misuse.

Today nonwhite Americans call 'brother' to strangers. And white feminists refer to their mass union of 'sisters.' And white middle-class teenagers continue to prove the importance of context as they try to ignore it. They seize upon the idioms of the black ghetto. But their attempt to appropriate such expressions invariably changes the words. As it becomes a public expression, the ghetto idiom loses its sound – its message of public separateness and strident intimacy. It becomes with public repetition a series of words, increasingly lifeless.

The mystery remains: intimate utterance. The communication of intimacy passes through the word to enliven its sound. But it cannot be held by the word. Cannot be clutched or ever quoted. It is too fluid. It depends not on word but on person.

My grandmother!

She stood among my other relations mocking me when I no longer spoke Spanish. '*Pocho*,' she said. But then it made no difference. (She'd laugh.) Our relationship continued. Language was never its source. She was a woman in her eighties during the first decade of my life. A mysterious woman to me, my only living grandparent. A woman of Mexico. The woman in long black dresses that reached down to her shoes. My one relative who spoke no word of English. She had no interest in *gringo* society. She remained completely aloof from the public. Protected by her daughters. Protected even by me when we went to Safeway together and I acted as her translator. Eccentric woman. Soft. Hard.

When my family visited my aunt's house in San Francisco, my grandmother searched for me among my many cousins. She'd chase them away. Pinching her granddaughters, she'd warn them all away from me. Then she'd take me to her room, where she had prepared for my coming. There would be a chair next to the bed. A dusty jellied candy nearby. And a copy of *Life en Español* for me to examine. 'There,' she'd say. I'd sit there content. A boy of eight. *Pocho.* Her favorite. I'd sift through the pictures of earthquake-destroyed Latin American cities and blond-wigged Mexican movie stars. And all the while I'd listen to the sound of my grandmother's voice. She'd pace round the room, searching through closets and drawers, telling me stories of her life. Her past. They were stories so familiar to me that I couldn't remember the first time I'd heard them. I'd look up sometimes to listen. Other times she'd look over at me. But she never seemed to expect a response. Sometimes I'd smile or nod. (I understood exactly what she was saying.) But it never seemed to matter to her one way or another. It was enough I was there. The words she spoke were almost irrelevant to that fact – the sounds she made. Content.

The mystery remained: intimate utterance.

---

I learn little about language and intimacy listening to those social activists who propose using one's family language in public life. Listening to songs on the radio, or hearing a great voice at the opera, or overhearing the woman downstairs singing to herself at an open window, I learn much more. Singers celebrate the human voice. Their lyrics are words. But animated by voice those words are subsumed into sounds. I listen with excitement as the words yield their enormous power to sound – though the words are never totally obliterated. In most songs the drama or tension results from the fact that the singer moves between word (sense) and note (song). At one moment the song simply 'says' something. At another moment the voice stretches out the words – the heart cannot contain! – and the voice moves toward pure sound. Words take flight.

Singing out words, the singer suggests an experience of sound most intensely mine at intimate moments. Literally, most songs are about love. (Lost love; celebrations of loving; pleas.) By simply being occasions when sound escapes word, however, songs put me in mind of the most intimate moments of my life.

Finally, among all types of song, it is the song created by lyric poets that I find most compelling. There is no other public occasion of sound so important for me. Written poems exist on a page, at first glance, as a mere collection of words. And yet, despite this, without musical accompaniment, the poet leads me to hear the sounds of the words that I read. As song, the poem passes between sound and sense, never belonging for long to one realm or the other. As public artifact, the poem can never duplicate intimate sound. But by imitating such sound, the poem helps me recall the intimate times of my life. I read in my room – alone – and grow conscious of being alone, sounding my voice, in search of another. The poem serves then as a memory device. It forces remembrance. And refreshes. It reminds me of the possibility of escaping public words, the possibility that awaits me in meeting the intimate.

---

The poems I read are not nonsense poems. But I read them for reasons which, I imagine, are similar to those that make children play with meaningless rhyme. I have watched them before: I have noticed the way children create private languages to keep away the adult; I have heard their chanting riddles that go nowhere in logic but harken back to some kingdom of sound; I have watched them listen to intricate nonsense rhymes, and I have noted their wonder. I was never such a child. Until I was six years old, I remained in a magical realm of sound. I didn't need to remember that realm because it was present to me. But then the screen door shut behind me as I left home for school. At last I began my movement toward words. On the other side of initial sadness would come the realization that intimacy cannot be held. With time would come the knowledge that intimacy must finally pass.

I would dishonor those I have loved and those I love now to claim anything else. I would dishonor our closeness by holding on to a particular language and calling it my family language. Intimacy is not trapped within words. It passes through words. It passes. The truth is that intimates leave the room. Doors close. Faces move away from the window. Time passes. Voices recede into the dark. Death finally quiets the voice. And there is no way to deny it. No way to stand in the crowd, uttering one's family language.

The last time I saw my grandmother I was nine years old. I can tell you some of the things she said to me as I stood by her bed. I cannot, however, quote the message of intimacy she conveyed with her voice. She laughed, holding my hand. Her voice illumined disjointed memories as it passed them again. She remembered her husband, his green eyes, the magic name of Narciso. His early death. She remembered the farm in Mexico. The eucalyptus nearby. (Its scent, she remembered, like incense.) She remembered the family cow, the bell round its neck heard miles away. A dog. She remembered working as a seamstress. How she'd leave her daughters and son for long hours to go into Guadalajara to work. And how my mother would come running toward her in the sun – her bright yellow dress – to see her return. '*Mmmaaammmmááá*,' the old lady mimicked her daughter (my mother) to her son. She laughed. There was the snap of a cough. An aunt came into the room and told me it was time I should leave. 'You can see her tomorrow,' she promised. And so I kissed my grandmother's cracked face. And the last thing I saw was her thin, oddly youthful thigh, as my aunt rearranged the sheet on the bed.

At the funeral parlor a few days after, I knelt with my relatives during the rosary. Among their voices but silent, I traced, then lost, the sounds of individual aunts in the surge of the common prayer. And I heard at that moment what I have since heard often again – the sounds the women in my family make when they are praying in sadness. When I went up to look at my grandmother, I saw her through the haze of a veil draped over the open lid of the casket. Her face appeared calm – but distant and unyielding to love. It was not the face I remembered seeing most often. It was the face she made in public when the clerk at Safeway asked her some question and I would have to respond. It was her public face the mortician had designed with his dubious art.

## Critical Thinking and Application

- Why does Rodriguez emphasize the two different pronunciations of his name (*Rich-heard* and *Ri-car-do*)? Is it possible to unify someone's identity and make it a combination of the two rather than a choice between them?
- Interview someone who learned English after learning another language. Ask about their feelings, sensations, and associations with each of their languages. Do they feel loyalty primarily to one or the other? Which one and why? If not, how do they balance them?
- Bilingual education has both political and psychological aims. Rodriguez dismisses this because he argues for a particular form of individuality. Look carefully at his argument and place it in the context of contemporary discussions of bilingual education.
- Interview someone whose parents were migrants to another country but who themselves were born in the new country. Did they have any experience with their parents' struggles with the new language? How did it make them feel? Did the children have any responsibilities on behalf of the family?

## Suggested Further Reading


Anzaldúa, Gloria. 1987. *Borderlands: The New Mestiza = La Frontera*. San Francisco: Spinsters/Aunt Lute.

Cisneros, Sandra. 1991. *The House on Mango Street*. New York: Vintage.

Flores, Juan, and Renato Rosaldo. 2007. *A Companion to Latina/o Studies*. Malden, MA: Blackwell.

Martínez, Glenn A. 2006. *Mexican Americans and Language: Del Dicho al Hecho!* Tucson: University of Arizona Press.

Omi, Michael, and Howard Winant. 1994. *Racial Formation in the United States: From the 1960s to the 1980s*. New York: Routledge & Kegan Paul.

Rivera, Christopher. 2010. *Admission as Submission: Richard Rodriguez's Autobiographies as an Epistemology of Penetration*. PhD dissertation. New Brunswick, NJ: Rutgers University.

Rodriguez, Richard. 1982. *Hunger of Memory: The Education of Richard Rodriguez*. New York: Dial Press (Random House).

Schechter, Sandra R., and Robert Bayley. 2002. *Language as Cultural Practice: Mexicanos en el Norte*. Mahwah, NJ: Erlbaum.

Stavans, Ilan. 2001. *On Borrowed Words: A Memoir of Language*. New York: Vintage.

Stavans, Ilan. 2004. *Spanglish: The Making of a New American Language*. New York: Rayo.

Zentella, Ana Celia. 1997. *Growing Up Bilingual: Puerto Rican Children in New York*. Malden, MA: Blackwell.

# Gender

## CHAPTER 35

# "Women's Language" or "Powerless Language"?

*William M. O'Barr and Bowman K. Atkins*

(1998 [1980])

*William O'Barr and Bowman Atkins set about to test the hypothesis that there were absolute differences in the ways women and men talk. They looked in particular at the ways witnesses speak and are spoken to during courtroom trials.*

*There has been a lot of research on linguistic interactions in various institutions, such as law, medicine, and schools. In each institution, individuals play particular roles, which always have linguistic dimensions. Sometimes they reflect broader social roles and sometimes they are particular to that setting.*

*O'Barr and Atkins summarize Robin Lakoff's findings about the features of women's language, features that appear obvious through introspection but may not be empirically evident. They find that in some cases their data corresponded quite well to Lakoff's, but in other cases there were significant differences. This led them to suggest an alternative explanation for the features they found.*

### Reading Questions

- What advice do trial practice manuals give about special treatment for women?
- Which features of "women's language" did O'Barr and Atkins find used by women? By men? Under what circumstances? How did O'Barr and Atkins explain their findings?

---

The understanding of language and sex in American culture has progressed far beyond Robin Lakoff's influential and provocative essays on "women's language" written only a few years ago (Lakoff 1975). The rapid development of knowledge in what had been so significantly an ignored and overlooked area owes much to both the development of sociolinguistic interest in general and to the women's movement in particular. But as a recent review of anthropological studies about women pointed out, this interest has grown so quickly and studies proliferated so fast that there is frequently little or no cross-referencing of mutually supportive studies and equally little attempt to reconcile conflicting interpretations of women's roles (Quinn 1977). A similar critique of the literature on language and sex would no doubt reveal many of the same problems. But in one sense, these are not problems—they are marks of a rapidly developing field of inquiry, of vitality, and of saliency of the topic.

Our interest in language and sex was sharpened by Lakoff's essays. Indeed, her work was for us—as it was for many others—a jumping off point. But unlike some other studies, ours was not primarily an attempt to understand language and sex differences. Rather, the major goal of our recent research has been the study of language variation in a specific institutional context—the American trial courtroom—and sex-related differences were one of the kinds of variation which current sociolinguistic issues led us to consider. Our interest was further kindled by the discovery that trial practice manuals (how-to-do-it books by successful trial lawyers and law professors) often had special sections on how female witnesses behave differently from males and thus special kinds of treatment they require.

In this [chapter], we describe our study of how women (and men) talk in court. The research we report here is part of a 30-month study of language variation in trial courtrooms which has included both ethnographic and experimental components. It is the thesis of this study that so-called women's language is in large part a language of powerlessness, a condition that can apply to men as well as women. That a complex of such features should have been called "women's language" in the first place reflects the generally powerless position of many women in American society, a point recognized but not developed extensively by Lakoff (1975: 7–8). Careful examination in one institutional

William M. O'Barr and Bowman K. Atkins. 1998. "Women's Language" or "Powerless Language"? In *Language and Gender: A Reader*, ed. by Jennifer Coates. Oxford: Blackwell, pp. 377–387.

setting of the features which were identified as constituting "women's language" has shown clearly that such features are simply not patterned along sex lines. Moreover, the features do not, in a strict sense, constitute a ***style*** or ***register*** since there is not perfect co-variation.

[This chapter proceeds] as follows: first, it examines the phenomenon of "women's language" in the institutional context of a court of law; second, it shows that the features of "women's language" are not restricted to women and therefore suggests renaming the concept "powerless" language due to its close association with persons having low social power and often relatively little previous experience in the courtroom setting; [...] and finally, it calls for a refinement of our studies to distinguish powerless language features from others which may in fact be found primarily in women's speech.

## How to Handle Women in Court—Some Advice from Lawyers

One of the means which we used in our study of courtroom language to identify specific language variables for detailed study was information provided to us in interviews with practicing lawyers. More useful, however, were *trial practice manuals*—books written by experienced lawyers which attempt to discuss systematically successful methods and tactics for conducting trials. Typically, little effort is devoted to teaching and developing trial practice skills in the course of a legal education. Rather it is expected that they will be acquired through personal experimentation, through watching and modeling one's behavior after successful senior lawyers, and through reading the advice contained in such manuals. Those who write trial practice manuals are experienced members of the legal profession who are reporting on both their own experiences and the generally accepted folklore within the profession. In all these situations, the basis for claims about what works or what does not tends to be the general success of those who give advice or serve as models—judged primarily by whether they win their cases most of the time.

One kind of advice which struck us in reading through several of these manuals was that pertaining to the special treatment which should be accorded women. The manuals which discuss special treatment for women tend to offer similar advice regarding female witnesses. Readers are instructed to behave generally the same toward women as men, but to note that, in certain matters or situations, women require some special considerations. Some of this advice includes the following:

1. *Be especially courteous to women.* ("Even when jurors share the cross-examiner's reaction that the female witness on the stand is dishonest or otherwise undeserving individually, at least some of the jurors are likely to think it improper for the attorney to decline to extend the courtesies customarily extended to women.") (Keeton 1973: 149.)
2. *Avoid making women cry.* ("Jurors, along with others, may be inclined to forgive and forget transgressions under the influence of sympathy provoked by the genuine tears of a female witness." "A crying woman does your case no good.") (Keeton 1973: 149; Bailey and Rothblatt 1971: 190.)
3. *Women behave differently from men and this can sometimes be used to advantage.* ("Women are contrary witnesses. They hate to say yes.... A woman's desire to avoid the obvious answer will lead her right into your real objective—contradicting the testimony of previous prosecution witnesses. Women, like children, are prone to exaggeration; they generally have poor memories as to previous fabrications and exaggerations. They also are stubborn. You will have difficulty trying to induce them to qualify their testimony. Rather, it might be easier to induce them to exaggerate and cause their testimony to appear incredible. An intelligent woman will very often be evasive. She will avoid making a direct answer to a damaging question. Keep after her until you get a direct answer—but always be the gentleman.") (Bailey and Rothblatt 1971: 190–1.)

These comments about women's behavior in court and their likely consequences in the trial process further raised our interest in studying the speech behavior of women in court. Having been told by Lakoff that women do speak differently from men, we interpreted these trial practice authors as saying that at least some of these differences can be consequential in the trial process. Thus, one of the kinds of variation which we sought to examine when we began to observe and tape record courtroom speech was patterns unique to either women or men. We did not know what we would find, so we started out by using Lakoff's discussion of "women's language" as a guide.

Briefly, what Lakoff had proposed was that women's speech varies from men's in several significant ways. Although she provides no firm listing of the major features of what she terms "women's language" (hereafter referred to...as WL), we noted the following features, said to occur in high frequency among women, and used these as a baseline for our investigation of sex-related speech patterns in court.

1. ***Hedges.*** ("It's sort of hot in here."; "I'd kind of like to go."; "I guess..."; "It seems like..."; and so on.)
2. *(Super)polite forms.* ("I'd really appreciate it if..."; "Would you please open the door, if you don't mind?"; and so on.)
3. ***Tag questions.*** ("John is here, isn't he?" instead of "Is John here?"; and so on.)

4. *Speaking in italics.* (Intonational emphasis equivalent to underlining words in written language; emphatic *so* or *very* and so on.)
5. *Empty adjectives.* (*Divine; charming; cute; sweet; adorable; lovely*; and so on.)
6. *Hypercorrect grammar and pronunciation.* (Bookish grammar; more formal enunciation.)
7. *Lack of a sense of humor.* (Women said to be poor joke tellers and to frequently "miss the point" in jokes told by men.)
8. *Direct quotations.* (Use of direct quotations instead of paraphrases.)
9. *Special lexicon.* (In domains like colors where words like *magenta, chartreuse*, and so on are typically used only by women.)
10. *Question intonation in declarative contexts.* (For example, in response to the question, "When will dinner be ready?", an answer like "Around 6 o'clock?", as though seeking approval and asking whether that time will be okay.)

## What We Found

During the summer of 1974, we recorded over 150 hours of trials in a North Carolina superior criminal court. Although almost all of the lawyers we observed were males, the sex distribution of witnesses was more nearly equal. On looking for the speech patterns described by Lakoff, we quickly discovered some women who spoke in the described manner. The only major discrepancies between Lakoff's description and our findings were in features which the specific context of the courtroom rendered inappropriate, for example, *tag questions* (because witnesses typically answer rather than ask questions) and *joking* (because there is little humor in a courtroom, we did not have occasion to observe the specifically female patterns of humor to which she referred).

In addition to our early finding that some women approximate the model described by Lakoff, we also were quick to note that there was considerable variation in the degree to which women exhibited these characteristics. Since our observations were limited to about ten weeks of trials during which we were able to observe a variety of cases in terms of offense (ranging from traffic cases, drug possession, robbery, manslaughter, to rape) and length (from a few hours to almost five days), we believe that our observations cover a reasonably good cross-section of the kinds of trials, and hence witnesses, handled by this type of court. Yet, ten weeks is not enough to produce a very large number of witnesses. Even a single witness may spend several hours testifying. In addition, the court spends much time selecting jurors, hearing summation remarks, giving jury instructions, and handling administrative matters. Thus, when looking at patterns of how different women talk in court, we are in a better position to deal with the range of variation we observed than to attempt any precise frequency counts of persons falling into various categories. Thus, we will concentrate our efforts here on describing the range and complement this with some non-statistical impressions regarding frequency.

Our observations show a continuum of use of the features described by Lakoff.[1] We were initially at a loss to explain why some women should speak more or less as Lakoff had described and why others should use only a few of these features. We will deal with our interpretation of these findings later, but first let us examine some points along the continuum from high to low.

A. Mrs. W,[2] a witness in a case involving the death of her neighbor in an automobile accident, is an extreme example of a person speaking WL in her testimony. She used nearly every feature described by Lakoff and certainly all those which are appropriate in the courtroom context. Her speech contains a high frequency of *intensifiers* ("*very* close friends," "*quite* ill," and so on often with intonation emphasis); *hedges* (frequent use of "you know," "sort of like," "maybe just a little bit," "let's see," and so on); *empty adjectives* ("this *very* kind policeman"); and other similar features. The first example below is typical of her speech and shows the types of intensifiers and hedges she commonly uses.[3] (To understand what her speech *might* be like without these features, example (2) is a rewritten version of her answers with the WL features eliminated.)

(1) L. State whether or not, Mrs. W, you were acquainted with or knew the late Mrs. E. D.
W. Quite well.
L. What was the nature of your acquaintance with her?
W. Well, we were, uh, very close friends. Uh, she was even sort of like a mother to me.

(2) L. State whether or not, Mrs. W, you were acquainted with or knew the late Mrs. E. D.
W. Yes, I did.
L. What was the nature of your acquaintance with her?
W. We were close friends. She was like a mother to me.

Table 35.1 summarizes the frequency of several features attributed to WL by Lakoff. Calculated as a ratio of WL forms for each answer, this witness's speech contains 1.14—among the highest incidences we observed.

B. The speech of Mrs. N, a witness in a case involving her father's arrest, shows fewer WL features. Her ratio of features for each answer drops to .84. Her testimony contains instances of both WL and a more assertive speech style. Frequently, her speech is punctuated with responses like: "He, see, he thought it was more-or-less me rather than the police officer." Yet it also contains many more straightforward and assertive passages than are found in A's speech. In example (3), for instance, Mrs. N is anything but passive. She turns questions back on the lawyer and even interrupts him. Example (4) illustrates the ambivalence of this speaker's style better. Note how she moves quickly to qualify—in WL—an otherwise assertive response.

(3) L. All right. I ask you if your husband hasn't beaten him up in the last week?
W. Yes, and do you know why?
L. Well, I...
W. Another gun episode.
L. Another gun episode?
W. Yessiree.

(4) L. You've had a controversy going with him for a long time, haven't you?
W. Ask why—I mean not because I'm just his daughter.

C. The speech of Dr. H, a pathologist who testifies as an expert witness, exhibits fewer features of WL than either of the other two women. Her speech contains the lowest incidence of WL features among the female witnesses whose speech we analyzed. Dr. H's ratio of WL features is .18 for each answer. Her responses tend to be straightforward, with little hesitancy, few hedges, a noticeable lack of intensifiers, and so on. (See Table 35.1.) Typical of her speech is example (5) in which she explains some of her findings in a pathological examination.

(5) L. And had the heart not been functioning, in other words, had the heart been stopped, there would have been no blood to have come from that region?
W. It may leak down depending on the position of the body after death. But the presence of blood in the alveoli indicates that some active respiratory action had to take place.

What all of this shows is the fact that some women speak in the way Lakoff described, employing many features of WL, while others are far away on the continuum of possible and appropriate styles for the courtroom. Before discussing the reasons which may lie behind this variation in the language used by women in court, we first examine an equally interesting finding which emerged from our investigation of male speech in court.

We also found men who exhibit WL characteristics in their courtroom testimony. To illustrate this, we examine the speech of three male witnesses which varies along a continuum of high to low incidence of WL features.

D. Mr. W exhibits many but not all of Lakoff's WL features.[4] Some of those which he does employ, like intensifiers, for example, occur in especially high frequency—among the highest observed among all speakers, whether male or female. His ratio of WL features for each answer is 1.39, actually higher than individual A. Example (6), while an extreme instance of Mr. W's use of WL features, does illustrate the degree to which features attributed to women are in fact present in high frequency in the speech of some men.

**Table 35.1** Frequency Distribution of Women's Language Features[a] in the Speech of Six Witnesses in a Trial Courtroom

| | Women | | | Men | | |
|---|---|---|---|---|---|---|
| | A | B | C | D | E | F |
| Intensifiers[b] | 16 | 0 | 0 | 21 | 2 | 1 |
| Hedges[c] | 19 | 2 | 3 | 2 | 5 | 0 |
| Hesitation forms[d] | 52 | 20 | 13 | 26 | 27 | 11 |
| W asks L questions[e] | 2 | 0 | 0 | 0 | 0 | 0 |
| Gestures[f] | 2 | 0 | 0 | 0 | 0 | 0 |
| Polite forms[g] | 9 | 0 | 2 | 2 | 0 | 1 |
| Sir[h] | 2 | 0 | 6 | 32 | 13 | 11 |
| Quotes[i] | 1 | 5 | 0 | 0 | 0 | 0 |
| Total (all powerless forms) | 103 | 27 | 24 | 85 | 47 | 24 |
| No. answers in interview | 90 | 32 | 136 | 61 | 73 | 52 |
| Ratio (no. powerless forms for each answer) | 1.14 | 0.84 | 0.18 | 1.39 | 0.64 | 0.46 |

[a] The particular features chosen for inclusion in this table were selected because of their saliency and frequency of occurrence. Not included here are features of WL which either do not occur in court or ones which we had difficulty operationalizing and coding. *Based on direct examinations only.*
[b] Forms which increase or emphasize the force of assertion such as *very, definitely, very definitely, surely, such a*, and so on.
[c] Forms which reduce the force of assertion allowing for exceptions or avoiding rigid commitments such as *sort of, a little, kind of*, and so on.
[d] Pause fillers such as *uh, um, ah*, and "meaningless" particles such as *oh, well, let's see, now, so, you see*, and so on.
[e] Use of question intonation in response to lawyer's questions, including rising intonation in normally declarative contexts (for example, "thirty?, thirty-five?") and questions asked by witness of lawyer like "Which way do you go...?"
[f] Spoken indications of direction such as *over there*, and so on.
[g] Include *please, thank you*, and so on. Use of *sir* counted separately due to its high frequency.
[h] Assumed to be an indication of more polite speech.
[i] Not typically allowed in court under restrictions on hearsay which restrict the situations under which a witness may tell what someone else said.
*Source:* Original data.

(6) L. And you saw, you observed what?
W. Well, after I heard—I can't really, I can't definitely state whether the brakes or the lights came first, but I rotated my head slightly to the right, and looked directly behind Mr. Z, and I saw reflections of lights, and uh, very, very, very instantaneously after that, I heard a very, very loud explosion—from my standpoint of view it would have been an implosion because everything was forced outward, like this, like a grenade thrown into a room. And, uh, it was, it was terrifically loud.

E. Mr. N, more toward the low-frequency end of the continuum of male speakers, shows some WL features. His ratio of features for each answer is .64, comparable to individual B. Example (7) shows an instance of passages from the testimony of this speaker in which there are few WL features. Example (8), by comparison, shows the same hedging in a way characteristic of WL. His speech falls between the highest and lowest incidences of WL features we observed among males.

(7) L. After you looked back and saw the back of the ambulance, what did you do?
W. After I realized that my patient and my attendant were thrown from the vehicle, uh, which I assumed, I radioed in for help to the dispatcher, tell her that we had been in an accident and, uh, my patient and attendant were thrown from the vehicle and I didn't know the extent of their injury at the time, to hurry up and send help.

(8) L. Did you form any conclusion about what her problem was at the time you were there?
W. I felt that she had, uh, might have had a sort of heart attack.

F. Officer G, among the males lowest in WL features, virtually lacks all features tabulated in Table 35.1 except for hesitancy and using *sir*. His ratio of WL forms for each answer is .46. Example (9) shows how this speaker handles the lack of certainty in a more authoritative manner than by beginning his answer with "I guess. . .". His no-nonsense, straightforward manner is illustrated well by example (10), in which a technical answer is given in a style comparable to that of individual C.

(9) L. Approximately how many times have you testified in court?
W. It would only have to be a guess, but it's three or four, five, six hundred times. Probably more.

(10) L. You say that you found blood of group O?
W. The blood in the vial, in the layman's term, is positive, Rh positive. Technically referred to as a capital r, sub o, little r.

Taken together these findings suggest that the so-called women's language is neither characteristic of all women nor limited only to women. A similar continuum of WL features (high to low) is found among speakers of both sexes. These findings suggest that the sex of a speaker is insufficient to explain incidence of WL features, and that we must look elsewhere for an explanation of this variation.

Once we had realized that WL features were distributed in such a manner, we began to examine the data for other factors which might be associated with a high or low incidence of the features in question. First, we noted that we were able to find *more* women toward the high end of the continuum. Next, we noted that all the women who were aberrant (that is, who used relatively few WL features) had something in common—an unusually high social status. Like Dr. H, they were typically well-educated, professional women of middle-class background. A corresponding pattern was noted among the aberrant men (that is, those high in WL features). Like Mr. W, they tended to be men who held either subordinate, lower-status jobs or were unemployed. Housewives were high in WL features while middle-class males were low in these features. In addition to social status in the society at large, another factor associated with low incidence of WL is previous courtroom experience. Both individuals C and F testify frequently in court as expert witnesses, that is, as witnesses who testify on the basis of their professional expertise. However, it should be noted that not all persons who speak with few WL features have had extensive courtroom experience. The point we wish to emphasize is that a powerful position may derive from either social standing in the larger society and/or status accorded by the court. We carefully observed these patterns and found them to hold generally.[5] For some individuals whom we had observed in the courtroom, we analyzed their speech in detail in order to tabulate the frequency of the WL features as shown in Table 35.1. A little more about the background of the persons we have described will illustrate the sort of pattern we observed.

*A* is a married woman, about 55 years old, who is a housewife.

*B* is married, but younger, about 35 years old. From her testimony, there is no information that she works outside her home.

*C* is a pathologist in a local hospital. She is 35–40 years old. There is no indication from content of her responses or from the way she was addressed (always *Dr.*) of her marital status. She has testified in court as a pathologist on many occasions.

*D* is an ambulance attendant, rather inexperienced in his job, at which he has worked for less than 6 months. Age around 30. Marital status unknown.

*E* is D's supervisor. He drives the ambulance, supervises emergency treatment, and gives instructions to D. He has worked at his job longer than D and has had more experience. Age about 30–35; marital status unknown.

*F* is an experienced member of the local police force. He has testified in court frequently. Age 35–40; marital status unknown.

## "Women's Language" or "Powerless Language"?

In the previous section, we presented data which indicate that the variation in WL features may be related more to social powerlessness than to sex. We have presented both observational data and some statistics to show that this style is not simply or even primarily a sex-related pattern. We did, however, find it related to sex in that more women tend to be high in WL features while more men tend to be low in these same features. The speech patterns of three men and three women were examined. For each sex, the individuals varied from social statuses with relatively low power to more power (for women: housewife to doctor; for men: subordinate job to one with a high degree of independence of action). Experience may also be an important factor, for those whom we observed speaking with few WL features seemed more comfortable in the courtroom and with the content of their testimony. Associated with increasing shifts in social power and experience were corresponding decreases in frequency of WL features. These six cases were selected for detailed analysis because they were representative of the sorts of women and men who served as witnesses in the trials we observed in 1974. Based on this evidence, we would suggest that the phenomenon described by Lakoff would be better termed *powerless language*, a term which is more descriptive of the particular features involved, of the social status of those who speak in this manner, and one which does not link it unnecessarily to the sex of a speaker.

Further, we would suggest that the tendency for more women to speak powerless language and for men to speak less of it is due, at least in part, to the greater tendency of women to occupy relatively powerless social positions. What we have observed is a reflection in their speech behavior of their social status. Similarly, for men, a greater tendency to use the more powerful variant (which we will term *powerful language*) may be linked to the fact that men much more often tend to occupy relatively powerful positions in society.

## Conclusion

In this study, we have attempted to argue that our data from studying male–female language patterns in trial courtrooms suggest that Lakoff's concept of "'woman's' language" is in need of modification. Our findings show that, in one particular context at least, not all women exhibit a high frequency of WL features and that some men do. We have argued that instead of being primarily sex-linked, a high incidence of some or all of these features appears to be more closely related to social position in the larger society and/or the specific context of the courtroom. Hence, we have suggested a re-naming of the phenomenon as "powerless language." What has previously been referred to as "women's language" is perhaps better thought of as a composite of features of powerless language (which can but need not be a characteristic of the speech of either women or men) and of some other features which may be more restricted to women's domains.

Thus, Lakoff's discussion of "women's language" confounds at least two different patterns of variation. Although our title suggests a dichotomy between "women's language" and "powerless language," these two patterns undoubtedly interact. It could well be that to speak like the powerless is not only typical of women because of the all-too-frequent powerless social position of many American women, but is also part of the cultural meaning of speaking "like a woman." Gender meanings draw on other social meanings; analyses that focus on sex in isolation from the social positions of women and men can thus tell us little about the meaning of "women's language" in society and culture.

## Notes

The research reported here was supported by a National Science Foundation Law and Social Science Program Grant (No. GS-42742), William M. O'Barr, principal investigator. The authors wish to thank especially these other members of the research team for their advice and assistance: John Conley, Marilyn Endriss, Bonnie Erickson, Bruce Johnson, Debbie Mercer, Michael Porter, Lawrence Rosen, William Schmidheiser, and Laurens Walker. In addition, the cooperation of the Durham County, North Carolina, Superior Court is gratefully acknowledged.

1. Actually each feature should be treated as a separate continuum since there is not perfect co-variation. For convenience, we discuss the variation as a single continuum of possibilities. However, it should be kept in mind that a high frequency of occurrence of one particular feature may not necessarily be associated with a high frequency of another.
2. Names have been changed and indicated by a letter only in order to preserve the anonymity of witnesses. However, the forms of address used in the court are retained.
3. These examples are taken from both the direct and cross examinations of the witnesses, although Table 1 uses data only from direct examinations. Examples were chosen to point out clearly the differences in style. However, it must be noted that the cross examination is potentially a more powerless situation for the witness.
4. This speaker did not use some of the intonational features that we had noted among women having high frequencies of WL features in their speech.
5. We do not wish to make more of this pattern than our data are able to support, but we suggest that our grounds for these claims are at least as good as Lakoff's. Lakoff's basis for her description of features constituting WL are her own speech, speech of her friends and acquaintances, and patterns of use in the mass media.

## References

Bailey, F. Lee and Rothblatt, Henry B. (1971) *Successful Techniques for Criminal Trials.* Rochester, NY: Lawyers Cooperative Publishing Co.

Keeton, Robert E. (1973) *Trial Tactics and Methods.* Boston: Little, Brown.

Lakoff, Robin (1975) *Language and Woman's Place.* New York: Harper & Row.

Quinn, Naomi (1977) "Anthropological studies of women's status." *Annual Review of Anthropology*, 6, 181–225.

## Critical Thinking and Application

- Does the list of features of "women's language" seem plausible to you? Why or why not? Would you change this list? How?
- Where besides a courtroom might you expect to find evidence of "powerless language," and which groups would be likely to use the features of powerless language?
- O'Barr and Atkins wrote this article based on research conducted in the 1970s. Since that time, there has been considerable social change, including some change in gender roles. Gain permission to record at a trial, analyze the data using the features in O'Barr and Atkins's analysis, and compare the similarities and differences between their results and yours. Alternatively, you could analyze trial scenes on television or in movies. This would convey people's stereotypes about courtroom behavior rather than actual behavior.

## Vocabulary

| | |
|---|---|
| hedge | style |
| register | tag question |

## Suggested Further Reading [See list following Language and Identity; Gender unit introduction]

# CHAPTER 36

# Power and the Language of Men

*Scott Fabius Kiesling*

(1997)

*Researchers on language, gender, and society have shown that many features of language can be explained by power asymmetries: who has the right to control the floor, who is considered higher in status, who performs "action that modifies action." Though we can generalize and say that "men have more power than women," it is clearly not true that all men have more power than all women.*

*Rather than make vague statements about power, Kiesling and many other analysts have delved into the details of language-in-use, or* discourse *(adjective,* discursive*), looking at the kinds of words people use, their tone, the flavor of vocabulary, their pacing, and much more. Many of the broader generalizations people make derive from the interactive details, even though we are often unaware of many of them.*

*In his analysis of language in a college fraternity, Kiesling uses notation from* conversation analysis, *which tries to convey in a transcript as many details of an interaction as are relevant. (No transcript can ever convey* all *details.) Punctuation is not according to grammar, but according to what people actually said and how they said it. While it may seem that many of the speakers Kiesling quotes fumble, repeat themselves, and are not consistent in their sentence structures, this is typical of all informal speech. The kind of well-crafted sentences that some fluid speakers can produce are not the norm in ordinary conversation. In fact, in this chapter, the speakers are generally speaking one at a time because they are participating in a meeting with rules for regulating speakers. In ordinary talk, people often overlap with one another, making a much messier (and more complex) transcript and reality. Kiesling includes, at the end of his article, the conventions for the transcription, rather like the legend for a map.*

## Reading Questions

- What are the types of power that Kiesling analyzes? Which are the most powerful and why? How is power connected to roles?
- Why are fraternities (and sororities) ideal places to study language and society? What other similar settings can you think of that would similarly show important social features?
- Which aspects of the fraternity Kiesling studied are hierarchical?
- How is masculinity—or at least men's identities—enacted through the speech event depicted here?

---

Power is usually cited as the most important factor when discussing the ways in which men's identities are constructed.[1] For example, in "Men, inexpressiveness, and power," Jack Sattel argues that: "the starting point for understanding masculinity lies, not in its contrast with femininity, but in the asymmetric dominance and prestige which accrues to males in this society" (1983, p. 119). In this chapter, I aim to show how issues of power and dominance as they relate to male identities are more complex than previously suggested. I will provide examples of some of the **discursive** strategies used by individual men in order to create and demonstrate power, showing how each man adopts a unique

Scott Fabius Kiesling, Power and the Language of Men. In *Language and Masculinity*, ed. Sally Johnson and Ulrike Hanna Meinhof. Oxford, UK: Blackwell, 1997, pp. 65–85.

and personal approach when doing so. In particular, I will demonstrate how sequentiality and activity type must be taken into account when exploring the construction of men's identities through language.

It cannot be denied that men have more power than women in modern Western society. Men still dominate the upper echelons of government and business, and women continue to perform most of the unpaid labour of housework and child care. In addition, women still frequently earn less than men for comparable work, and professions dominated by women are less valued monetarily than those dominated by men (see Hewlett, 1986). Along with the freedom brought by power, however, comes the expectation (or requirement) that a man will somehow embody this power in his identity. This expectation is by no means as restrictive as those which obtain where women's identities are concerned; when a man constructs a powerful identity, it is usually connected in some way to "real" power. Thus, the expectation of a "powerful" identity for men is not symmetrical to the expectation of a "powerless" identity for women, since a man's powerful identity is *rewarded* (with power), whereas a woman's non-powerless identity may be *punished*.

Following Sattel's suggestion, therefore, I take the power of men as a starting point for investigating how men construct their identities through language; I unpack the concept, describe different kinds of power, and show how these work with specific regard to four individual men.

My analysis is based on data gathered during a continuing ethnographic study of a fraternity in the United States. A fraternity is an all-male social club at a university, in which membership is selective. Typically, the fraternity becomes the central organization around which members structure their college lives, especially socially. It is a **"community of practice"** (Eckert and McConnell-Ginet, 1992), defined sharply from the rest of the university through various means—initiation rituals, secret ceremonies, and exclusive social events. Cynthia McLemore (1991) has worked on intonation in the female counterpart to the fraternity—the sorority. She showed that this type of community is ideal for studying language and society, especially the language of society's privileged members, because it is an intensely social, well-defined community, and its activities are based primarily on talk (e.g., meetings and parties). In addition, fraternities exhibit processes typical of other social groups more intensely: entrance into the community is carefully guarded, its members change completely every four years, and yet it manages to retain a unique history and ideology. Finally, fraternities are important to study because they prepare their members for the world of work after college. By analysing the strategies that men learn in fraternities, we can therefore gain insights into how men acquire, construct, and reproduce certain social practices in anticipation of dominance over others in later life.

In this chapter, I will explore how the fraternity's ideology and the immediate speech situation work together to constrain the members' identities. I use the term "constrain," rather than "affect" or "determine," because identity construction is, to some extent, a creative endeavour. In theory, the men are free to create any identity they want, but in practice, they are pushed (and push themselves) towards identities which do not challenge the perceived values of the fraternity or of dominant US society. Each man also has different discursive resources (e.g., storytelling ability, joking ability, a powerful structural role, a loud voice, etc.) in order to draw upon disparate types of power. And crucially, each member has his own personal history within the fraternity, which further constrains the kind of identity he can display at any given time. Each time he speaks, then, the man must produce an utterance (and posture, gaze, etc.) that satisfies these constraints as far as possible. At the same time, he must make the utterance coherent within each current speech situation.

Because I am focusing on power, I will begin by outlining the framework of power used in my analysis. I will then discuss the specific ideology of power at work in the fraternity in question, exploring, for example, the kinds of constraints which the community places on a member's presentation of self. Finally, I will analyse excerpts from my **corpus** in order to illustrate how men draw upon, and construct, different types of power through their use of language.

## A Framework for Power

Before [a concept is applied] to any analysis, it should be well defined. When power is used as an explanation in sociolinguistic analyses, however, it is frequently undefined and unanalysed. Because I am taking power as the starting point for my work, I will briefly sketch the theoretical approach which is to be employed.

Following Foucault (1982), power is action that modifies action. The effect of this action need not be immediate, direct, or even real. So, for example, because power takes place in actions, it is exercised to the extent that people *believe* that they should perform an action because of another action. However, power is not something that individuals may suddenly pull out and use. It must be salient to the situation; the people being acted on must believe in it. Thus, illusions can be powerful motivators. People believe that they should act in certain ways with certain people because they feel that not acting in these ways would have serious consequences. The reasons for performing a given action might therefore seem irrational, such as the avoidance of embarrassment, or the appearance of foolishness or "weakness." But what constitutes a serious consequence is, in turn, dependent on the community in question and its own particular values. This means that any analysis exploring issues of power must be based on a primary analysis of the local community's values and its ideology.

Whilst this view of power is flexible, it lacks analytical force. At a practical level, therefore, I assume that people have power because they occupy roles—some so enduring as to seem eternal and necessary, some fleeting and unnoticed, and some newly created within specific interactions.

People place themselves in roles by using language because different ways of speaking are associated with such roles. A new role may be thrown together out of bits of others, and, in some cases, a single role may dominate a personality. But such roles can only really be discovered by analysing the **discourse** of community members, and by examining the community's formal and informal structures through ethnographic observation and interviewing.

On the basis of my own study, I have identified seven types of power processes from which local roles may be built: physical (coercive and ability), economic, knowledge, structural, nurturant, demeanour, and ideological. I distinguish between two types of physical power: *coercive physical power* is the power of the mugger, while *ability physical power* is an action made possible by physical ability or skill. *Economic power* is the process that rewards one action (e.g., labour) with the possibility of another action (e.g., purchasing goods). *Knowledge power* is the process of gaining knowledge in order to perform an action. *Structural power* is the power of a place within a structure, classically (but not necessarily) a hierarchy. *Nurturant power* is the process of helping another, as in teaching or feeding. *Demeanour power* is the power of solidarity: moral authority, being liked, being "a good guy." The process of demeanour is not normally addressed by views of power, because the actions in this type of power act on emotions. Thus a person exhibits demeanour power when others feel happy, entertained, involved, respectful, etc.

But it is the ideological process which is the most important. This is a "defining process," because individuals evaluate the other types of power processes through the ideological process. This defining process—which I will refer to as *ideological power*—ratifies certain traits as powerful, and determines which of the other processes are available (i.e., identifies the roles in the community). Within each of the other processes, ideological power identifies what is, and what is not, powerful. Thus, ideological power is the process of power whereby ways of thinking about the world are naturalized into a community's behaviour.

Each of the seven types of power outlined is not isolated from the others, but all are closely connected to form what Foucault refers to as: "a net-like organization [...] something which circulates, or rather (as) something which only functions in the form of a chain" (1980, p. 98). In this way, an ideology such as the competitive, hierarchical, group ideology frequently identified as typical of all-male interaction is likely to affect the way in which men structure their groups, change their demeanour, and learn disciplines. Men may be inclined to form hierarchical communities, act in ways that always seem competitive, and see education and work as a competition. The success with which they learn to think and act in these ways will, in turn, affect their ability to use economic, structural, physical, knowledge, and demeanour processes of power.

Power is therefore a way of viewing local practices globally: an **etic** framework filled in by **emic** values. Power in this view (as a role focused on—or created in—a community-defined structure) is similar to concepts of footing and alignment (see Goffman, 1981). However, by using the framework I have outlined, we can identify the types of roles which are available and created vis-à-vis power. As a consequence, we will not be limited to analyses using broad, universal categories. Moreover, we can approach some comparability across communities by looking at the ways in which different communities deal with similar ideologies of power, and similar communities deal with different ideologies of power.

## "Ideology Power" in a Fraternity

In the light of the framework I have outlined, I need to discuss the ideology of the fraternity in question before analysing how power works in the fraternity's discourse. The way a man presents himself within a fraternity is of ultimate importance because he becomes a member of and gains status in the fraternity by projecting the right kind of identity.

Gaining membership to a fraternity is contingent upon successfully negotiating the process of "rush," which is not unlike courtship. In this process, current members meet prospective members (known as "rushes") at organized social functions; they also socialize informally, for example, by talking in dormitory rooms. Prospective members gauge whether they want to be a part of the fraternity, and current members consider whether they want to invite the prospective members to join. The rushes selected by the current members are then offered an invitation for membership, and can accept or reject the "bid," as the offer is known. Once they have accepted a bid, the rushes become probationary members, or "pledges." During the "pledge period," which lasts for six to eight weeks, pledges learn the fraternity's traditions, and pledge education activities take place in unofficial secret ceremonies, which are similar to military "boot camps." Pledges are treated as second-class citizens, subordinating their autonomy and identities to the fraternity as an institution, and to individual older "brothers," as members are called. Pledges "earn respect" and the privilege to become members themselves. They also learn the fraternity's customs, traditions, and oral history. During this time, a strong bond tends to form between so-called pledge brothers, who are members of the same "pledge class," because of their common adversity as second-class citizens.

The pledge period culminates in initiation, a formal clandestine ceremony where the secrets, rights, and responsibilities of membership are imparted. However, the newly initiated brother—known by the acronym "nib"—is still inexperienced in the eyes of the fraternity. He lacks knowledge and past accomplishments in order to prove that he will function well in a fraternity office. In the social sphere, nibs normally follow the older brothers' lead, show respect to them, and defer to their judgement. But nibs still have more latitude here than in the fraternity's "business" sphere, which will be discussed below. As a brother becomes older, he has a chance to prove himself by performing services for the fraternity. Also, simply by becoming older, he gains the respect of younger 'generations' of members.

In the fraternity I studied for over a year, which I will call Gamma Chi Phi (ΓΧΦ), almost all of the men were Caucasian. Out of fifty-seven members, one was Korean-American, and four were Arab-American. Most were of college age (17–22 years old); three alumni members were in their late twenties. By comparison, the university as a whole is 88 percent Caucasian, 10 percent Asian, and 6 percent African-American.

I was able to gain entry into this fraternity because, as an undergraduate, I was a member of the same national fraternity. I first contacted the national fraternity to describe my project, attending several meetings of the steering committee, the National Council. Once I had chosen the local chapter, I contacted the president of that chapter (whom I had met previously at the National Council meeting), and described the project to him in detail in a letter. I told him that I was interested in studying interaction among men, and that I would be observing and audio-tape-recording, as well as conducting interviews with members. He then asked the members for permission to allow me to go ahead with my research at a general meeting of the fraternity, and the members approved. I was permitted to attend any function and visit any individual member. I was also allowed to attend secret ritual ceremonies, but not to tape the ceremonial portion of the ritual activities. The names of the fraternity and all members are aliases.

At ΓΧΦ, there is an overt distinction between the formal, governing sphere of the fraternity, on the one hand, and the social sphere, on the other. However, the border between the two is fuzzy; older, office-holding members tend to associate together, and personality plays a large role in deciding who is elected into fraternity offices. Nonetheless, the ideological organization is the same throughout the fraternity, and can best be described as hierarchic.[2]

The hierarchical nature of the fraternity is already evident in the stages of acquiring membership outlined above. First, because only certain men are accepted into membership, the fraternity experience begins by valuing one identity over another. In ΓΧΦ, demeanour and physical power are highly valued. If someone is rich, caring, or gets good grades, he is not more likely to be offered membership. The current members value skill at playing sports[3]—so a prospective member who played baseball in high school will be highly respected because he can help the fraternity win at intramural softball. Demeanour power is, however, most important in terms of gaining membership.[4] Members told me in interviews that the main reason they joined was because they thought the fraternity was "a good group of guys"; similarly, bids are offered because a prospective member seems like "a good guy."

But what is "a good guy"? Members themselves had difficulty defining this characteristic. For them, a good guy would seem to be someone who others enjoy being with, and someone who would appear to exemplify the members' own ideology. Thus, it may be someone who tells funny stories, or who is the subject of funny stories. Because of the hierarchic, competitive ideology of the organization, a man who acts strong, competitive, and quick is valued. Friendship and community is shown through what seems like competitive talk filled with insults, boasts, orders, and embarrassing jokes and stories. A "good guy" is someone who exemplifies powerful, competitive traits in all spheres: he works hard, gets things accomplished, is seen as a leader, and is verbally skilled in the "competitive cooperative" style through which the men build solidarity. By selecting only men with certain characteristics, the fraternity creates a hierarchy between its members and outsiders (although non-members are also ranked).

Once access to the fraternity has been gained, there is still an implicit hierarchy evident in all stages of membership. The pledges begin their fraternity experience by being treated as unknowledgeable, childlike servants, and even when the pledges become full members, they are still not valued as highly as older members. Usually, only after at least one year of membership does a man have the power to affect, through his own actions, the actions of the fraternity and its members. When attempting to influence the fraternity in this way, ability and demeanour power are highly valued, along with knowledge power. This is especially evident during elections, for example, where members evaluate candidates' work ethic, experience, personality, and skills.

Thus, the main constraint that the men place on each other is to present a competitive, successful, confident identity. The fraternity ideology also values hard work, especially work that promotes the good of the group. In this way, members are taught to protect and care for each other.

## DATA ANALYSIS: POWER AND IDENTITY IN PRACTICE

In this section, I will explore how four men employ different discursive means in order to construct powerful identities. The excerpts I analyse come from an election meeting involving the entire fraternity membership. Ordinary meetings are held every Sunday evening in a campus classroom, but elections are held only once a year, usually in the autumn.

Because they are speaking in a meeting, the four men in question have much at stake. Initially, they must show that they have the authority to speak. But because their identities are on public display in the business sphere, the men are more constrained than usual by the competitive, hierarchic ideology of the fraternity. Through the varying employment of **mitigation,** mood, pronoun use, and personal experience, these members orient themselves towards different processes of power. The processes they draw upon are consistent with the identities that they have constructed previously in the fraternity, but are nevertheless specific to the time of speaking.

The excerpts I analyse are taken from a discussion during elections for the office of chapter correspondent, whose job it is to communicate with the national fraternity through letters published in the fraternity's national magazine. The position traditionally goes to a younger member because it requires little experience or knowledge of how the fraternity works. After the four candidates—Kurt, Ritchie, Mullin, and Ernie—give their speeches, they leave the room so that other members can discuss the candidates' strengths and weaknesses. The four members I shall focus on are Darter, Speed, Ram, and Mack.

## Darter

The first speaker I consider is Darter, a newly initiated brother. He no doubt still feels deferential to those men who, until a few weeks ago, had almost total control over his life. Although he was the president of the pledge class, and is recognized as a possible future leader of the fraternity, he is not in a position to exercise demeanour or structural power because he is a nib, and does not hold a high position. In his comments, the first he has made in the elections, Darter bases his argument on his knowledge of the candidates' abilities. Two of the candidates are his pledge brothers, Ritchie and Ernie. Kim is Korean-American; Speed is an older brother.

EXCERPT 1

48 Darter: Um *Ri:tchie* may come off like he's really like a dumb ass<br>
49 and everything but uh<br>
50 he's like one of the smartest people<br>
51 I know y'know<br>
52 I went to high school with him<br>
53 and he was like ranked *fifth* in our class.<br>
54 and he can he can write like rea:lly well<br>
55 Kim: He's<br>
56 *A:*sian man, what do you expect?<br>
57 Speed: (sarcastic) Is he really?<br>
58 Darter: I mean he he *types* like unbelievably<br>
59 ...quick. um I just think this would be a good position for him<br>
60 to hold because he's a really good writer,<br>
61 I mean I've read a lot of papers o.f his.

Because he is young and a new brother, Darter does not normally speak in meetings. But in this comment Darter draws from his specialized knowledge—his high school friendship with Ritchie—to assert his right to speak. He begins by acknowledging the identity that Ritchie has in the fraternity (line 48).[5] Darter then contrasts this identity with the identity he remembers from high school (lines 50–4). He then states his position: "I just think this would be a good position for him to hold." He mitigates his statement through the use of "I just think," which suggests his opinion is not very valuable. By using "I think" and the conditional "would," he frames his statement as a suggestion, rather than a fact (e.g., "this is a good position for him"). Instead of simply making this more direct statement, he includes a dependent clause that explicitly highlights his reasoning ("because he's a really good writer"), which is implicit from his statements in lines 50–4. (I show below that the older brothers do not need to provide this kind of justification.) Darter then emphasizes once again how he knows that Ritchie is a good writer. He thus explicitly justifies his support for Ritchie through his knowledge of the latter's writing abilities. His power is therefore not based on his demeanour or position in the fraternity, but on knowledge, which he is careful to highlight extensively. He presents himself as holding information important to the debate, but as unsure of its worth.

## Speed

The next speaker I introduce is Speed, a third-year member. Of the four men I am considering, he speaks next in the meeting. His statement is short and to the point.

EXCERPT 2

83 Mick: Speed.<br>
84 Speed: Ri:tchie. I like Ritchie 'cause he's smart<br>
85 and he probably writes really good too:<br>
86 so let him do it dude.

Speed at first does not justify his statement. He merely states Ritchie's name. Then he notes that Ritchie is smart and (extrapolating from line 84) that Ritchie is capable of doing the job. His short statement indicates that for him the choice, based on Ritchie's ability, is simple. It is just a matter of "letting him do it." In addition, by first only uttering Ritchie's name, Speed implies that members should be swayed by the mere fact that he is for Ritchie.

## Ram

Ram presents his powerful identity in a different way. An older brother, he has just finished a year as treasurer. He creates a fatherly, "wise elder" identity through his comment:

EXCERPT 3

119 Ram: um I'd like to endorse David here, surprisingly<br>
120 I mean the kid—<br>
121 I don't want to see him fall into another—<br>
122 and I'm not saying that he would<br>
123 Kevin Fierst type thing,<br>
124 I think we need to make him—<br>
125 we need to strongly involve him *now*<br>
126 I think he's pretty serious about it, y'know<br>
127 and with a little guidance I mean he'll do a fine job.

Ram creates a powerful identity by putting himself in the role of a person with age and experience: he refers to David as "the kid," and he shows off his knowledge of past members of the fraternity (Kevin Fierst was a member who dropped out of school because of substance abuse problems). He further highlights his position through his use of the phrase "with a little guidance," suggesting that he is qualified to give that guidance. He also shows concern for David ("I don't want to see him fall into another...Kevin Fierst type thing"), which suggests a fatherly position. Thus, he draws on the part of the fraternity ideology that stresses "looking out for" another brother. Finally, he also uses the device of speaking on behalf of the fraternity ("we need to strongly involve him now"), although he mitigates his statement more than Mack, in the next section, by embedding it in "I think."

## Mack

Contrast Darter's and Speed's comments with those made by Mack, a fourth-year member, who was Darter's pledge educator (in charge of the programme and activities during the pledge period). Mack affects actions through his demeanour, using little mitigation in his statements, and through the imperative mood. Mick is the president, Pencil is the graduate advisor.

EXCERPT 4

184 Mick: Mack.
185 Mack: *Okay…*
186 This is *it…*
187 Somebody said something about =
188 Pencil: =Again, we need to reorganize (?).
189 Mack: yeah somebody's—
190 we need to look at what we have left here,
191 and there are certain positions
192 that everybody fits into perfectly.
193 Ernie does *not* fit into this: (0.1)
194 I'm not sure where Ernie fits in just yet.
195 ?: historian
196 Mack: *but* I: a:m afraid that we are going to *waste* uh
197 one of the few brains *left*. in someplace that that
198 uh historian has potentially been a
199 non-existent position. uh I think for a couple
200 semesters yahoo took some pictures,
201 Pencil: We're talking about chapter correspondent now
202 Mack: what's that? I know
203 Pencil: and he can hold *both* positions
204 Mack: I understand that. (0.3)
205 But he won't.
206 (0.5)
207 I see—I see *Kurt*—I see Kurt—I see *Kurt*—
208 Pencil: Then talk about chapter correspondent.
209 point of order.
210 ?: we have we have four left.
211 Pencil: point of order.
212 Mack: I see Kurt as chapter correspondent.
213 not Ritchie damn it.

Mack begins by serving notice that his word is gospel: "This is it." It is unmitigated and imperative. Unlike Darter, Mack does not justify his statement at all. This non-mitigation and non-justification presents a role of someone who can make a proclamation—someone with power. In line 190, he emphasizes this view by instructing the members on how to go about making a decision ("We need to look at what we have left"). He does this by using the first person plural subject without any **hedges** (or "I think," as Darter does), and by using "need" instead of "should." Contrast his statement with what might be termed its "opposite": Mack might have said "I think we should look at what's left." By using a bald imperative, then, Mack implicitly puts himself in a role of structural power. However, Mack is not constructing a new place for himself in the fraternity, but continuing in a carefully constructed role: that of the elder, wise, behind-the-scenes manipulator. In an interview, he indicated this manipulator role was the one he seeks for himself. Although he has held few fraternity offices, he goes to other members before elections, and suggests that they run for certain positions, then makes comments in their favour during elections.

Mack was also the pledge educator for the newly initiated brothers, which may affect his comments in two ways. First, he has had a position of supreme authority over the new members until recently—he was their teacher and "drill sergeant"—so that they perceive him as an authority within the fraternity. Second, he can claim to know the new members better than any other member (except perhaps the new members themselves). Thus, he can claim to be qualified to make these pronouncements. He can use his structural and demeanour power to influence the new members, many of whom will vote in the election, and he can employ his knowledge power to influence older brothers.

Mack also demonstrates his role by where he sits in the classroom in which the meeting is held. Older members sit on the right-hand side of the room, and Mack sits as far to the right as possible. Darter, in contrast, sits on the "younger" left-hand side, towards the middle (the extreme left-hand side is empty). Mack's cadence is also significant. Though not evident in the transcript, he speaks with a slow, pause-filled cadence that gives the impression of thoughtfulness and wisdom, while Darter speaks very quickly.

Mack continues to use unmitigated, authority-laden devices throughout his comments. In lines 191–4, he sets up a system in which each member has his place, and Mack knows who belongs where. He presents his statements as axiomatic truths by using "there are" without any indication that he is actually voicing a personal opinion. Had he used modality markers, such as "may," he would be implying that members can decide the issue for themselves. Instead, he leaves no room for doubt. In line 196, he presents himself as advisor to the fraternity ("I am afraid"). In contrast, instead of using these devices to speak for the collective in a leader-like role, he might have said something like "I think Ritchie is overqualified for this position." It is unclear where his argument is going from line 197 forward, because he stops his sentence, and begins to discuss the historian position. It looks as if he planned to highlight his age, by discussing the past worth of the historian position in lines 198–200 ("historian has potentially been a non-existent position"). Pencil then argues with him about discussing one position at a time (lines 201–11), which prompts Mack to finish his statement. Mack ends by simply stating that he "sees" Kurt as correspondent, again without any justification (in fact, with less justification than at the beginning of his comments). This construction, "I see," is used by other brothers to create a similar air of authority, as though the speaker were a visionary, who speaks with the wisdom of the ages.

Thus, there is a large difference between the way in which the older brothers and a younger brother present themselves. The older brother has a position of experience and respect that he can implicitly draw upon, while the younger brother, lacking this structural and demeanour power, is explicit about his reasoning to sway votes in his direction. While both are under similar general pressures to present a "powerful" identity, each has different resources and solves the problem in his own way.

## Speed

Now contrast Mack and Ram's remarks with a later comment by Speed. After Mack speaks, other older members have taken up the discussion of finding offices for the newly initiated brothers. Speed responds to this trend, and returns to his utilitarian theme. Speed's comments are given in a hurried, shouting voice, as if he is angry.

EXCERPT 5

245 Speed: All right look.
246 first of all, you guys need to realize we do *not*
247 *ha:ve* to ne- necessarily make a:ll the new
248 brothers, put them in positions right away.
249 a *lot* of the new brothers already have positions.
250 they can get elected next year *or* next semester.
251 there *are* some positions that are semesterly.
252 we don't have to make sure that every one of them
253 has a position. they need time to *learn* and grow–
254 it's better that//they're– that they're=
255 ?: I need an assistant
256 Speed: =shut the fuck up.
257 it's better that they're–
258 that they're almost like I was with Tex.
259 I was Tex's like little bitch boy...graduate
260 affairs, and I learned a lot more there,
261 than I would if I got stuck in some leadership
262 role, *so fuck 'em,*
263 I don't care if *a*ny of 'em don't get a position.
264 but I'm telling you right now,
265 I think Ritchie should do it because like Kim
266 said, people are gonna read this shit,
267 Kurt might get *ha:mm*ered and write some shitty..
268 fuckin' letter, Ernie *can't* write,
269 fuckin' Mullin already has a position,
270 so put Ritchie in there,
271 and stop fuckin' trying to.. set everybody up in
272 a position. Christ.
273 Mick: Alex.
274 Speed: I:'d like one
275 (laughter)

Speed is an older brother, but he has created an adversarial identity in the fraternity, resisting those in formal offices. He relies on a different presentation of power, one that sets him up in opposition to others. Even though he is a third-year member, he always sits on the "non-powerful" left-hand side, in the back of the room, thus showing his contempt for the fraternity hierarchy. Speed's argumentative identity is evident in this speech, but he uses some of the same linguistic devices as Mack. Like Mack, Speed uses the imperative. He begins by saying "All right look," which is similar in tone to Mack's "This is it." In line 246, Speed states that "you guys need to realize," which is similar to Mack's "we need to look at what we have left." Speed then shows his knowledge of the fraternity, continuing in an imperative mood, saying "we don't have to make sure that every one of them has a position," which contrasts with Mack's "we need to look at what we have left here."

Speed then draws on his personal experience (as Ram did) in the fraternity for an example in lines 259–62 (notably in a low position— "I was Tex's like little bitch boy"). This statement disparages "leadership positions," and implicitly the organizational structure of the fraternity. Next, he uses an aggravated, bold statement to show his indifference to the brothers' aspirations in lines 262–3 ("*so fuck 'em*..."). Speed then again presents a utilitarian argument for voting for Ritchie by pointing out why other candidates are unqualified (lines 264–70). In line 264, he uses a pedagogic tone similar to Mack's ("I'm telling you right now"). Note that this rhetoric is consistent with his argumentative, impatient identity: he sums up each person quickly, with aggravation and profanity. Then, at the very end (line 274), he injects some self-directed humour. Throughout the elections, he has been unable to get elected, and this has become a running joke. When he says "I'd like one," he adds to his demeanour with a joke making fun of himself. Ending with a joke is a common device used by the members in these comments; it builds demeanour power by easing the tedium that accompanies the election meetings.

Thus Speed, while staying within the constraints of the hierarchic fraternity ideology, manages to construct an identity that appears to reject the manipulative structural power used by some of the older brothers. He accomplishes his identity by focusing on the value of competing against a structure of power; rebellion and independence are consistent with the fraternity's competitive ideology. He also focuses on the need to do what is best for the group by highlighting why Ritchie is best qualified for the position. Thus, Speed, Mack, and Ram, while using similar linguistic devices to convince the members and present their identities, nevertheless construct very different identities. Because he is younger, Darter, on the other hand, has different constraints on the identity he presents in the meeting. He does not have a demeanour or structural power process working in his favour, so the problem presented to him—of creating an identity consistent with the fraternity ideology—is much different than the problem presented to Speed, Mack, and Ram. Darter must create a means of influencing voting (an action that will affect other actions) without any prior history of being able to do so. He must also construct a role for himself that fits within the constraints of being a nib, but nevertheless convinces people to vote for his favoured candidate. Darter therefore draws on his specialized knowledge of the candidate.

It is important to notice also that Speed was genuinely impatient with the discussion at the time of his second statement, as seen by a comparison of his two utterances. In the first statement, he simply says why Ritchie is qualified for the position. In the second, however, he is arguing *against* other members—especially Mack—as much as *for* Ritchie, in addition to arguing about the progress of the debate generally. This place in the discussion (he is nearly the last speaker) sets up a context in which he can position himself as the defender of ability power over structural power for its own sake. In other words, he can make clear his dislike of voting members into structural positions without any clear functional reason for doing so. This secondary argument was not possible in Speed's first comments because none of the older members had suggested considering all the new members, and what offices they should occupy. His identity construction in the second statement therefore shows the situated, sequence-dependent nature of identity.

Speed also exhibited this adversarial identity in an interview, however. The semester before the interview, Speed had been the pledge educator, but was ousted because of what he sees as his "independence":

EXCERPT 6

1 SCOTT: Did you keep it ((the pledge period)) the way
2 you had it?
3 SPEED: I tried to, man, but they wouldn't let me so:
4 I had to I had to succumb to their rules
5 th th- th- they got all pissed off at me and tried to take my
6 position away from me and all that shit,
7 man. (1.0) Bunch a dicks.

Speed's independence shows through in this excerpt when he says "I had to succumb to their rules." Speed also sees that he lost his position because he didn't follow the dominant ideology, but evaluates that ideology—or its proponents—negatively ("Bunch a dicks"). Thus, Excerpt 6 provides more evidence for an ideological clash between Speed's alleged independence, and the fraternity's expectation of sacrifice in return for structural power.

All the men discussed create powerful identities, but they each use disparate strategies in order to achieve a different kind of power. Differences can be seen in how the men orient themselves to various features of the fraternity ideology. Most appeal to what will be best for the fraternity. Darter and Speed focus on the ideology of being rewarded for ability. They both argue that Ritchie is simply the most qualified candidate, and voting for him will benefit the fraternity the most. They therefore appeal to the part of the ideology that puts the group before the individual. Ram also appeals to this value, but in another way. He argues that the fraternity will lose Kurt if they don't involve him in it. Mack, however, focuses on the fraternity's hierarchical nature; for him, some jobs are more important than others, and must be "assigned" to more important members. Thus, he wants Ritchie to have a job other than chapter correspondent. Mack also sees his own role as that of manipulator, and uses his structural position of age to put members in the offices that he "sees" for them. Finally, Speed fights against this focus on structural power.

The elections are very important to the members. They care deeply about the fraternity and its future. Who they elect very much affects what happens in the fraternity. In addition, the outcomes affect their own power within the fraternity and, even more important perhaps, their ability to affect the actions of others in the future.[6]

## DISCUSSION

I have thus shown how four men employ both similar and varied discursive devices in order to construct a particular kind of identity, given certain constraints on that identity. All four manage to present some kind of identity valued by the competitive, hierarchic fraternity ideology. Darter had to justify his statements overtly. Ram created a fatherly image. Mack spoke with a voice of the elder. Speed "resisted" the dominance of structural power over ability, and the good of the fraternity and its members over trying to control every detail of the fraternity's future. While being men in a fraternity affected their language in similar ways, their individual solutions in time and space were unique. It is worth pointing out, however, that I have only had sufficient space to consider one speech activity here; in fact, the men's identities vary even more when other speech activities are analysed.

Sociolinguists often group people together based on criteria external to the community, and focus on how people of certain groups use language in a similar way. Generalizations about men and women are among the most common. But within these generalizations we find many variations. Within the fraternity community, for example, we can group older members together, because they tend to use less mitigation and justification and, more importantly, because age is one way the members group themselves. Clearly, then, it is essential, when considering the language of men, to explore how gender is mediated by age, status, and so on, in the same way that this has been necessary when analysing the speech of women. But even grouping Speed, Ram, and Mack together as elder members of the fraternity ignores their very different individual presentations of self.

Meaningful generalizations are, however, still possible and necessary. We can still say that, in some general sense, many men in the United States construct powerful, competitively oriented identities. Moreover, due to the ideology of difference in US society, the motivation for men to construct these identities is of a different nature than for women, and the outcomes for "resistance" are different for each of the two sexes. Men who construct the "preferred" gender identity are rewarded with power, while women are not rewarded in the same sense when they construct the identity that society "prefers" for their gender. In fact, a "powerless" identity that many researchers have shown to be the "preferred" identity for a North American woman could actually be seen as punishing women. Real resistance to the gender order, for instance a "powerful female" identity or a "powerless male" identity, may have similar consequences. But many men arguably have little motivation for such resistance. Speed, for example, appears to be resisting "the establishment," but he is nevertheless using that "resistance" as an alternative way of constructing a powerful, individualistic identity that is ultimately ratified by the fraternity ideology.

The way in which the fraternity men create different yet powerful identities suggests that particular roles, such as workplace and family roles, may be the specifics that make up what people idealize as "masculinity" and "femininity." The men discussed here adopt elements of archetypal male roles: loyal friend, concerned father, wise elder, pragmatic individualist. In addition, two of the men identify *themselves* as having the identities they present in the election.

As Sattel (1983) points out, many men are expected to take on positions of leadership. But the direction of the indexing of men's identities and leadership is not clear; we might also say that society expects leadership positions to be held by men. Work such as Bonnie McElhinny's (1993) study of female police officers in Pittsburgh similarly highlights the importance of work and family roles in society's view of masculinity and femininity. Further research is needed in this area to learn more about such roles and their relationship to the construction of gender. In my research, I plan to return to the fraternity to test whether new members take on the same kinds of roles as older members who have left. Does Darter become a "wise elder," a "concerned father figure," an "impatient individualist"? Or does he create an entirely new role, or a combination of all?

## Conclusion

In this chapter, I have explored the way in which the identities of four fraternity members are constructed through interaction in an election meeting. My findings have, however, a number of implications for work on language and gender in more general terms. For example, I have shown how the four men construct their own identities, drawing upon both the same, and different, types of power processes through the language they use. Thus, although all the men manage to evoke some type of power with their language, it would be extremely difficult to draw specific conclusions on the types of linguistic structures (e.g., tag-questions, hedging, etc.) used by men "as a group" on the basis of my data since their usage is highly contextualized....

TRANSCRIPTION CONVENTIONS

*Turn-taking*

| | |
|---|---|
| // | Bounds simultaneous speech. |
| = | Connects two utterances that were produced with noticeably less transition time between them than usual. |
| (number) | Silences timed in tenths of seconds. |
| (.) | Noticeable silence less than 0.2 second. |
| # | Bounds passage said very quickly. |

*Sound Production*

| | |
|---|---|
| ^ | Falsetto. |
| TEXT | Upper-case letters indicate noticeably loud volume. |
| * | Indicates noticeably low volume, placed around the soft words. |
| *text* | Italics indicate emphatic delivery (volume and/or pitch). |
| – | Indicates that the sound that precedes it is cut off, stopped suddenly and sharply. |
| : | Indicates that the sound that precedes it is prolonged. |
| , | Indicates a slight intonational rise. |
| ? | Indicates a sharp intonational rise. |

*Breathiness, Laughter, Comments*

| | |
|---|---|
| h | An audible outbreath. |
| 'h | An audible inbreath. |
| he, ha | Laughter. |
| (text) | Transcript enclosed in single parentheses indicates uncertain hearing. |
| ((comment)) | Double parentheses enclose transcriber's comments. |

## Notes

1. I have chosen the term "men's identities," rather than "masculinity," for several reasons. First, "masculinity" is not a neutral term; it connotes a single stereotype of male identity, for example, John Wayne and Arnold Schwarzenegger in their movie roles. However, the majority of men in Western culture do not present themselves as copies of these movie heroes (Kessler and McKenna, 1978; Segal, 1990). Some men even contradict this view of men's identities. Thus, masculinity, as I use the term, is but one possible (idealized) type of male identity. Similarly, that there is no "natural," single identity to which men aspire is an important point; hence, I use the plural "identities." Men's (and women's) identities are constructed, negotiated, and changing, but they are also constrained by social structures that value some types of identities over others. Furthermore, I use the term "men" rather than "male" or "masculine" in order to highlight the fact that the identity is a social as opposed to biological construction; it is gender, not sex. "Identity" is an intersection between a social presentation of self, and a psychological understanding of that self.

2. This hierarchic ideology is similar to Connell's characterization of hegemonic masculinity (1987, 1995).

3. Interest in sports, of course, is also connected to competition; in this case, the desire is to be the best fraternity on campus in intramural sports.

4. The fact that demeanour is of primary importance in the fraternity supports its inclusion as a type of power, and not something other than power.
5. Line numbers match those from a complete transcript.
6. Ritchie won the election.

## References


Connell, R. W. 1987. *Gender and Power*. Stanford, CA: Stanford University Press.

Connell, R. W. 1995. *Masculinities*. Oxford: Polity Press.

Eckert, Penelope and McConnell-Ginet, Sally. 1992. Think practically and look locally: language and gender as community-based practice. *Annual Review of Anthropology* 21, 461–90.

Foucault, Michel. 1980. *Power/Knowledge: Selected Interviews and Other Writings*. New York: Pantheon Books.

Foucault, Michel. 1982. The subject and power. *Critical Inquiry* 8, 777–95.

Goffman, Erving. 1981. *Forms of Talk*. Philadelphia: University of Pennsylvania Press.

Hewlett, Sylvia Ann. 1986. *A Lesser Life: The Myth of Women's Liberation in America*. New York: Warner Books.

Kessler, S. and McKenna, W. 1978. *Gender: an Ethnomethodological Approach*. New York: John Wiley & Sons.

McElhinny, Bonnie. 1993. We all wear the blue: language, gender and police work. Unpublished Ph.D. dissertation. Stanford, CA: Stanford University.

McLemore, Cynthia. 1991. The pragmatic interpretation of English intonation: sorority speech. Unpublished Ph.D. dissertation. Austin: University of Texas at Austin.

Sattel, Jack. 1983. Men, inexpressiveness and power. In B. Thorne, C. Kramarae and N. Henley (eds.), *Language, Gender and Society*. Cambridge, MA: Newbury House, 119–24.

Segal, L. 1990. *Slow Motion: Changing Masculinities, Changing Men*. London: Virago.


## Critical Thinking and Application

- What does it mean that identity has to be constructed? How is language involved in the construction of identity?
- Why are men's identities especially connected to competition and power? Might this connection differ among men of different ages?
- Record a gathering of men and analyze their discourse, following the model in Kiesling's chapter. Do your observations support or refute Kiesling's? In what ways?

## Vocabulary

| | | |
|---|---|---|
| community of practice | discursive | hedge |
| corpus | emic | mitigate |
| discourse | etic | |

## Suggested Further Reading [See list following Language and Identity; Gender unit introduction]

# CHAPTER 37

# "Unnatural" Gender in Hindi

*Kira Hall*

(2002)

*Gender by itself means "kind," and it is relevant to language in two different ways: in the language itself (in terms of both "grammatical" and "natural" gender) and in the ways language is used by people of differing genders. The language used by hijras, the "third sex," in Varanasi, India (referred to by its former name, Banaras, in this chapter), exemplifies the convergence of these two aspects of language and gender, as hijras strategically and consciously manipulate a two-gender linguistic system to reflect their own transformation into a third category of gender. Kira Hall has been studying this population for several decades and here lays out their linguistic usage with great clarity. We can see that there is no identity that precedes speech, or as Judith Butler has noted, there is no "prediscursive self."*

## Reading Questions

- Summarize the patterns of grammatical gender in standard Hindi.
- What are hijras? What do they wish to accomplish through their adoption of a particular way of speaking?
- How are insults made through the gender used in speaking to or about other hijras?
- When do hijras use masculine forms to refer to themselves? Why is this the case?

## Introduction

Hindi (*hindī*), adopted by the Indian constitution as a **national-official language,** is an **Indo-Aryan** language that is claimed as a mother tongue by roughly 40% of the Indian population.[1] Boasting over 450 million first- and second-language speakers worldwide, Hindi is one of the three most widely spoken languages in the world today, along with English and Mandarin Chinese. When speakers of **Urdu** are included in this estimate, a language that shares the same basic syntax as Hindi but in certain registers draws much of its vocabulary from **Perso-Arabic** sources as opposed to **Sanskritic,** this number is even greater. Hindi has also been designated the official language of several states, among them Bihar, Haryana, Himachal Pradesh, Madhya Pradesh, Rajasthan, and Delhi; the central government has endorsed its use along with English (identified as the "associate official language") in administrative functions. But these facts obscure the complex internal politics regarding the position of Hindi in the Indian social landscape, where several sectors of the population oppose its ascendancy in politics and government, particularly in southern India where the **Dravidian** languages Tamil and Telugu are dominant. Opposition to Hindi has also steadily increased among Urdu speakers in response to nationalist embracements of a *śuddh* or 'pure' Sanskritic Hindi by various Hindu fundamentalist groups, whose leaders reject Perso-Arabic influences on the language as part of an anti-Muslim political platform. The linguistic correlate, according to some scholars, has been an ever-increasing divergence between Hindi on the one hand and Urdu on the other, with noncomprehensibility sometimes existing between radical versions of each (see Shapiro & Schiffman 1983, King 1999).

Modern grammars of the many dialects now grouped together under the label "Hindi" grew out of 18th and 19th century attempts to link Sanskrit to the known classical and vernacular languages of Europe. Beames' *Comparative grammar of the modern Aryan languages of India* (1872–79) offers the first taxonomy of Indo-Aryan languages and the position of Hindi therein, followed by Kellogg's *A grammar of the Hindi language* (1875) and Grierson's highly influential *Linguistic survey of India* (1903–28). Since the publication of these early surveys, there has been constant debate regarding the appropriate taxonomy of the languages and dialects of Indo-Aryan, a debate that points to the impossibility of

Kira Hall, "Unnatural" Gender in Hindi. In *Gender Across Languages: The Linguistic Representation of Women and Men*, edited by Marlis Hellinger and Hadumod Bussman. Amsterdam: John Benjamins, 2002, pp. 133–162.

defining the difference between "language" and "dialect" in purely linguistic terms (see Shapiro & Schiffman 1983 for an engaging summary of this debate in the Indian context). For the state of Uttar Pradesh, where I conducted my fieldwork, contemporary scholars generally categorize dialects of Hindi as belonging to either Eastern Hindi or Western Hindi. The eastern group includes the dialects of Avadhi, Bagheli, Bhojpuri, and Chattisgarhi, and the western group Braj, Bundeli, Kanauji, and Bangru. Standard Hindi is based on a Western Hindi dialect referred to by academics as *khaṛī bolī*, though only a small percentage of Hindi speakers can be said to have spoken this variety as a mothertongue. In addition to these dialects, there are also several local varieties of Hindi that have developed as **lingua francas** or **pidgins,** most notably *bambaiyā hindī* in Bombay (Chernyshev 1971, Apte 1974) and *bāzārū hindī* in Calcutta (Chatterji 1931). For traditional grammars of regional dialects of Hindi and their classification see Guru (1920), Vajpeyi (1967, 1968) and Sharma (1958); for more contemporary descriptions of Hindi written in English see McGregor (1972), Mohanan (1994), Shapiro (1989), and Srivastava (1969).[2]

Although India has been an important center of sociolinguistic research since the 1950s, fostering insightful debate on the complex relationship between language and social identity, discussions of gender are largely absent in the literature. This has less to do with scholarly neglect than it does with the way in which sociolinguistics has developed on the Indian subcontinent, where **caste** was established early on as the central variable of concern for the study of linguistic variation. Following Bloch's pioneering study "Castes et dialectes en Tamoul" at the beginning of the 20th century (Bloch 1910), much of the early scholarship on social stratification focused on Dravidian languages, particularly Tamil, Tulu, and Kannada. But sociolinguistic research on Hindi also helped to further the preoccupation with caste, when prominent linguistic anthropologists like Gumperz (1958) called our attention to caste influences on Hindi with his important article "Dialect differences and social stratification in a North Indian village". Gumperz's work stands out from many of the studies that preceded it in that he argues for the consideration of other variables in addition to caste, among them place of residence, religion, informal friendship contacts, and occupation. Most critically, he brings the notion of "context" into the sociolinguistic literature when he stresses the importance of studying patterns of individual and group interaction.

But gender takes the backseat in Gumperz's study, as it does in the majority of **variationist** studies that followed, even when sociolinguistic scholarship on South Asian languages broadened its focus to include variables like urbanization, education, economic status, literacy, and age. While we might want to blame this gap on the intellectual climate at the time – after all, the field of language and gender did not really emerge until after the publication of Lakoff's "Language and Woman's Place" in 1973 – it should be noted that Bloch himself considered the role of gender in language use as early as 1910. He notes, for example, that Tamil-speaking women exerted conservative influences on the social dialects of their time, attributing this to their comparative lack of education. In fact, Bloch points to the speech of women and men in early Sanskrit theatre as evidence for a long history of dialect stratification in South Asia, which often represents men of high *varṇas* (e.g. Brāhmaṇa and Kṣhatriya) as speaking Sanskrit and men of low *varṇas*, servants, and women as speaking Prakrit. Nevertheless, few articles to date have explored gender differentiation with respect to language choice, with the notable exception of Simon's recent work (1993, 1996) on gendered attitudes toward the use of Hindi vs. Banarsi Bhojpuri in Banaras.[3]

Certainly the sociolinguistic literature on Hindi has involved much more than variationist studies, especially in the past two decades where we find a boom of research on topics ranging from code-switching and bilingualism to language and nationalism. When we consider these other areas of inquiry, among them the feminist analysis of sexist language (e.g. Valentine 1987) and the **pragmatic** analysis of terms of address, pronoun choice, greetings, and kinship terminology (e.g. Jain 1969, 1973; Khubchandani 1978; Mehrotra 1977, 1985a, 1985b; Vatuk 1969a, 1969b; Misra 1977), we do find a few discussions of gender as a grammatical and as a social category. The study of address terminology is noteworthy in this respect, particularly as its emphasis on language in context has taken Hindi sociolinguistics in more dynamic directions. The fact that Hindi has three **second-person pronouns,** for instance, whose employment is dependent on a complex array of social considerations, disallows descriptions of language that rely on a static conception of social role or identity. The choice of address forms in Hindi, as the authors named above all illustrate, is not simply a function of the social positions of addresser and addressee, predetermined by the gender, marital status, and age of the conversational participants. It is also dependent on how these social positions interact with the context of the speech event, where the topic of discourse, intention of the speaker, degree of intimacy and solidarity between interlocutors, emotional attitudes, and linguistic creativity all play a role.

The study of address terminology, then, moves us squarely into the field of **discourse analysis.** Yet even with this shift in research direction, there has been little subsequent scholarship on how gender materializes in conversational practice. Valentine's work in the mid-1980s (1985, 1986) remains one of the few attempts to apply contemporary interactional sociolinguistics to the Indian context, though the bulk of her data comes from contemporary Hindi novels, plays, and short stories. Paralleling research results for middle-class speakers of English in the United States, Valentine finds, for example, that male speakers of Hindi successfully initiate more conversational topics while female speakers do more of the conversational maintenance work. But her appropriation of a two-cultures model of gender to explain the discursive practices of communication in mixed groups won her sharp criticism from Singh & Lele (1990), who disagree with the way she conceptualizes power in structural-functional rather than hierarchical terms.[4]

I offer this description of the speech patterns of Hindi-speaking **hijras** as an example of how discourse analysis, when applied to a particular **community of practice,** can reveal profound insights about the workings of gender in society. Given that the speech patterns of women and men have been so little studied in Hindi sociolinguistics, some may disagree with my choice to focus on a group of speakers who themselves identify as *na mard na aurat* 'neither man nor woman'. Often discussed as a "third gender" by anthropologists, most hijras were raised as boys before taking up residence in one of India's many hijra communities and adopting the feminine dress, speech, and mannerisms associated with membership. Yet the gendered **liminality** of these speakers is precisely what provoked my initial interest in their language habits, since the hijras alternate between feminine and masculine linguistic reference in ways that reflect both local and dominant ideologies regarding the position of women and men in north Indian society. Since 1993 I have been visiting and researching a variety of hijra communities in northern India. Most of the data are taken from my fieldwork in the city of Banaras, where I conducted extensive interviews with hijras from four different communities and recorded their everyday conversations. Constrained by a linguistic system which allows for only two **morphological genders,** i.e., feminine and masculine, Banaras hijras must gender themselves and fellow community members as either feminine/female or masculine/male. Because nouns, verbs, adjectives, and **postpositions** in Hindi are marked for feminine and masculine gender, with verbs being marked in all three persons, the hijras' attempts at alternating constructions of female and male selves becomes apparent in quite basic choices of feminine and masculine forms.

In this chapter I explore how we might go about analyzing these alternations, particularly given the traditional linguistic distinction between **"grammatical gender"** on the one hand and **"natural gender"** on the other. In the first kind of system, according to conventional linguistic thought, gender is an arbitrary grammatical category that has syntactic consequences throughout the grammar; in the second, gender is a "natural" category that merely reflects the "biological sex" of the referent. Feminist linguists since the 1970s (early articles include Bodine 1975; Martyna 1980a, 1980b) have argued against the first of these classifications, illustrating, sometimes quite convincingly, that grammatical gender is not a purely arbitrary phenomenon. Others have argued against the second of these classifications, suggesting that no classification system is purely "natural".[5] English, for instance, while often discussed as a language exhibiting natural gender, not only allows the usage of male generics for female referents, it also permits the assignment of metaphorical gender to inanimates, as when a ship, boat, or car is referred to as *she*. But I want to move beyond these arguments in order to challenge the very assumption implicit in the term "natural gender", i.e. that gender is a fixed phenomenon, rooted in biology and therefore free of ideological influences. What happens to a language's classification system in instances when the referent's gender can no longer be assumed as either male or female? And what might these instances of "unnatural gender" tell us about the relationship between gender in language and gender in society?

## Gender in the Hindi Language System

### Grammatical Gender: Assignment and Agreement

Any discussion of the workings of gender in the Hindi language system requires a few disclaimers. While a two-way gender system of masculine and feminine is present in all dialects (with the exception of lingua franca or pidginized varieties where grammatical gender is often lost altogether), the specifics of the system materialize differently. Instantiations of grammatical gender for **inanimate** nouns vary from dialect to dialect, with nouns treated as feminine in one sometimes appearing as masculine in another, and vice versa (see Nespital 1990: 8–9 for several examples). The noun *dahī* 'yogurt', for example, is often marked as masculine in eastern dialects and feminine in western ones, a difference most likely caused by a western reinterpretation of the final vowel *-ī* as a feminine morphological marker. And in many of the Hindi dialects emerging in urban areas as a result of contact with other languages, only **animate** nouns referring to female individuals are treated as feminine. Originally feminine nouns such as *hindī* 'Hindi', *nadī* 'river', and *śādī* 'marriage' are classified as masculine, a phenomenon Bhatia (1992: 174) attributes to a "weakening of grammatical gender and the preference for the natural gender". In other words, nouns in these dialects are normally not feminine unless they specifically reference female persons.

Moreover, while speakers of Hindi in the *khaṛī bolī* area[6] most closely produce the kind of gender agreement outlined in instructional grammars, speakers of certain eastern varieties often perceive this same gender agreement as stylistically **marked** when employed across syntactic distance. Because Hindi is a kind of "communication amalgam" (Khubchandani 1991: 273), speakers generally exhibit neutral attitudes toward variations in speech, grammatical gender notwithstanding. But the gender variability described above leads Simon (ms.) to make the interesting claim that the employment or non-employment of standard gender agreement sometimes serves as a **register** marker, **indexing** the speaker's gender, linguistic proficiency, education level, and/or insider/outsider status. Thus in the western Hindi area, according to Simon, elite speakers of standard Hindi will often perceive a speaker who uses non-standard gender agreement as *purbī* (a person from eastern Uttar Pradesh) or *dehātī* (a villager, a rural illiterate). But in Banaras, where the local dialect of Banarsi Bhojpuri is spoken along with standard Hindi, it is the use of standard gender agreement that is sometimes deemed suspect. Simon offers evidence that this is particularly the case among uneducated female speakers of the local dialect, who frequently perceive speakers who maintain the strict gender agreement of standard Hindi as either foreign or over-educated.

Simon's observations regarding Banarsi Bhojpuri cannot easily be applied to the Banaras hijra community, however, since its members rarely come from the city. Hijras are notorious travelers, moving from state to state, city to city, and community to community for years before they settle in any one place. Indeed, their life narratives are constructed around movement: Because so many of them were forced out of their homes at an early age for exhibiting behavior deemed to be "hijra-like" or effeminate, their stories reveal an ongoing state of homelessness and displacement. Those hijras that eventually come to settle in Banaras, then, are rarely native speakers of Banarsi Bhojpuri, and its employment in the community is usually quite marked. What we find instead is a kind of lingua franca loosely based on standard Hindi, which facilitates communication among speakers from a variety of regional and linguistic backgrounds. The hijras' language, which they call *hijṛā bolī* in Banaras,[7] most closely parallels those varieties of Hindi designated by some Hindi speakers as *khicṛī* or *milijhulī* (see, for example, Sachdeva 1982), terms which translate roughly as 'mixed'. Such varieties, among them the Panjabi-ized Hindustani spoken around Delhi, usually develop on the borders of language or dialect areas and reflect features from the divergent bordering varieties. In this context, Hijra Boli might best be thought of as a kind of *sadhukkaṛī*, a term coined by the medieval mystical poet Kabir for the 'mixed' language of travelers (literally, the language of *sādhus* or religious mendicants).[8] This term is especially fitting for the hijras' language, given the hijras' traditional religious role at birth and wedding celebrations, where their blessing is thought to secure a long and fruitful lineage of sons for the recipient.

But where Hijra Boli differs from the lingua francas or pidgins reported for, say, the streets of Bombay and Calcutta is in the use of grammatical gender. In contrast to those varieties, which exhibit a loss of grammatical gender, the variety of Hindi adopted by the hijras tends to overemphasize gender, using masculine and feminine gender in places where it would normally not appear in *khaṛī bolī*, or treating nouns that are masculine in standard Hindi as feminine and vice versa. To give one illuminating example: The word *hijṛā* is grammatically masculine in standard Hindi, but the hijras frequently treat the noun as feminine through verbal agreement when it acts as the subject of a sentence. As I argue here, this usage reflects a kind of gender overcompensation or even **hypercorrection.** Upon entering the community, Banaras hijras work to distance themselves from masculine representations, with many of them even choosing to undergo a ritualized penectomy and castration operation. The fact that the term *hijṛā* is grammatically masculine sometimes gets in the way of this communal distancing, so hijras will mark the noun as feminine as part and parcel of "doing gender". The two-gender system exhibited in standard Hindi, then, is quite relevant to a discussion of the language practices of this community, since grammatical gender is most often overemphasized, not underemphasized, in the hijras' constructions of a more feminine self.

The alternation between feminine and masculine reference in standard Hindi is quite easy to discern linguistically, since many nouns, verbs, postpositions, and adjectival modifiers inflect for gender. Nominals, for instance, exhibit both a two-way gender system of masculine and feminine as well as a two-way number system of singular and plural. While the gender of animate nouns to a certain extent corresponds to the **referent's** gender (i.e. exhibiting "natural gender"), gender designation in inanimate nouns is comparatively arbitrary (though see Valentine 1987 for a discussion of the sexist basis of some of these designations, and Börner-Westphal 1989 for a discussion of lexical gaps in the gender system). Hindi nominal forms are classified as either direct (nominative) or oblique (non-nominative), with the latter normally signaled by the presence of a postposition. For the majority of nouns in the direct case, the *-a* ending signals masculine singular, *-e* masculine plural, *-ī* feminine singular, and *-iyā̃* feminine plural; in the oblique case these endings become *-e, -ō, -ī, and -iyō*, respectively. Not all adjectival modifiers exhibit **inflection,** but those that do agree with their **head noun** in gender, number, and case. Masculine forms of inflecting adjectives end in *-ā* in the singular direct and *-e* in the plural direct, singular oblique, and plural oblique cases; the feminine forms always end in *-ī*, whether singular or plural, direct or oblique. Examples illustrating gender agreement in nominals are given in (1) and (2):

(1) Masculine agreement
a. *acchā* *laṛkā*
good.NOM.MASC.SG boy.NOM.MASC.SG
'good boy'
b. *acche* *laṛke*
good.NOM.MASC.PL boy.NOM.MASC.PL
'good boys'
c. *acche* *laṛke* *ko*
good.OBL.MASC.SG boy.OBL.MASC.SG to
'to the good boy'
d. *acche* *laṛkō* *ko*
good.OBL.MASC.PL boy.OBL.MASC.PL to
'to the good boys'

(2) Feminine agreement
a. *acchī* *laṛkī*
good.NOM.FEM.SG girl.NOM.FEM.SG
'good girl'
b. *acchī* *laṛkiyā̃*
good.NOM.FEM.PL girl.NOM.FEM.PL
'good girls'
c. *acchī* *laṛkī* *ko*
good.OBL.FEM.SG girl.OBL.FEM.SG to
'to the good girl'
d. *acchī* *laṛkiyō* *ko*
good.OBL.FEM.PL girl.OBL.FEM.PL to
'to the good girls'

The **genitive** postposition also agrees with the gender of the head noun, appearing as *kā* when modifying a singular masculine noun, *ke* when modifying a plural masculine noun, and *kī* when modifying a singular or plural feminine noun. For concentrated discussions of grammatical gender in Hindi nominals, see Pathak (1976) and Gosvāmī (1979).

Verbals in standard Hindi also show gender agreement, agreeing with the subject in gender, number, and person if it is in the nominative case. If the subject is in an oblique case – i.e. ergative, dative, instrumental, locative, or genitive – the verb agrees with the object when it is nominative.[9] In general, the appearance of one of the vowels *-ā*, *-e*, *-ī*, or *-ī̃* on the verb signals number and gender, with *-ā* used for masculine singular, *-e* for masculine plural, *-ī* for feminine singular, and *-ī̃* for feminine plural. For example, the intransitive verb *honā* 'to be' is realized as *thā* with masculine singular controllers, *the* with masculine plural controllers, *thī* with feminine singular controllers, and *thī̃* with feminine plural controllers, as illustrated in Table 37.1.

**Table 37.1** Past Tense Forms of *Honā* 'to Be'

| | | Masculine | Feminine | English Translation |
|---|---|---|---|---|
| SG | 1 | *maĩ thā* | *maĩ thī* | I was |
| | 2 | *tū thā* | *tū thī* | you (intimate) were |
| | 3 | *vah thā* | *vah thī* | he was/she was |
| PL | 1 | *ham the* | *ham thī̃* | we were |
| | 2 | *tum the* | *tum thī̃* | you (familiar) were |
| | 3 | *ve/ap the* | *ve/ap thī̃* | they/you (polite) were |

I should add that many speakers of standard Hindi do not employ the feminine plural ending- *ī̃* with any regularity, particularly when the subject of the sentence is in the oblique case and the verb therefore agrees with the object, as in the sentence reproduced in example (3):

(3) a. Standard Hindi
*āp-ne* *kitnī* *kitābẽ*
you.POL-ERG how.many.NOM.FEM book.
NOM.FEM.PL
*paṛh-ī̃?*
read.PF-FEM.PL
'How many books did you read?'

b. Colloquial Hindi
*āp-ne* *kitnī* *kitāb*
you.POL-ERG how.many.NOM.FEM book.
NOM.FEM.SG
*paṛh-ī/paṛh-ī̃?*
read.PF-FEM.SG/PL
'How many books did you read?'

Here, where the second person subject is in the ergative case, even standard Hindi speakers will frequently say 'book' (*kitāb*) instead of 'books' (*kitābẽ*) and employ the singular feminine verbal ending in agreement, as in (3b). Again, examples like this point to the fact that when it comes to conversational practice, there is no singular way to explain "gender in Hindi".

I can only hint at the complexity of the Hindi verbal system, since auxiliaries and modals combine in various ways with either the verb root or its inflected forms to yield numerous distinctions of tense, aspect, mood, and voice. In the imperfective, continuous, and perfective verb forms, aspect is indicated through the addition of explicit markers of various kinds to the stem while tense is indicated through the presence of one of the basic forms of *honā* 'to be' (i.e. present, past, presumptive, subjunctive). Here, too, the appearance of one of the vowels *-ā*, *-e*, *-ī*, or *-ī̃* will signal the gender and number of the NP with which the verb agrees, and each element in the complex that is not in the root form will reflect these agreement features. First-person feminine and masculine agreement for several tenses of the verb *jānā* 'to go' are illustrated in Table 37.2.

The import of this kind of verbal morphology for the hijras, of course, is that even when pronouncing simple first-person statements like 'I am going', hijras must gender themselves as either feminine or masculine.

## Generic Masculines

The hijras' alternating uses of feminine and masculine morphological forms for the same referent appears in very limited contexts in non-hijra Hindi-speaking communities. With perhaps the exception of second language learners unfamiliar with the gender system, Hindi speakers rarely, if ever, betray their "natural" gender when referring to themselves. Likewise, they generally respect the gender of the referent or addressee in question – except, of course, when the generic masculine is used as inclusive of both female and male persons, as in the nouns reproduced in (4):

(4) *dost* 'friend (male or female)'
*sāthī* 'companion (male or female)'
*mitra* 'friend, ally (male or female)'
*yātrī* 'traveler (male or female)'
*ghuṛsavār* 'rider (male or female)'

**Table 37.2** Selected Examples of First Person Verbal Marking with *Jānā* 'to Go'

| Verb Tense | 1st Person Masculine | 1st Person Feminine | English Translation |
|---|---|---|---|
| Future | *maĩ jāū̃gā* | *maĩ jāū̃gī* | I will go |
| Past | *maĩ gayā* | *maĩ gayī* | I went (definite) |
| General Present | *maĩ jātā hū̃* | *maĩ jātī hū̃* | I go |
| Imperfective Past | *maĩ jātā thā* | *maĩ jātī thī* | I went (indefinite) |
| Continuous Present | *maĩ jā rahā hū̃* | *maĩ jā rahī hū̃* | I am going |
| Continuous Past | *maĩ jā rahā thā* | *maĩ jā rahī thī* | I was going |
| Perfective Present | *maĩ gayā hū̃* | *maĩ gayī hū̃* | I have gone |
| Perfective Past | *maĩ gayā thā* | *maĩ gayī thī* | I had gone |

Feminine counterparts to many of the masculine nouns in (4) exist, such as *sahelī* for 'female friend', but these terms are never used generically; rather, their usage expresses specific reference to a female individual. Most females will use *sahelī* for their female friends, for instance, and will rarely call a female friend *dost*. The same is true with respect to verbal agreement with a pronoun like *koī* 'someone'. As the two sentences in (5) illustrate, masculine verbal agreement with *koī* could point to either a male or female subject, but feminine verbal agreement will always denote a female subject.

(5) a. *koī āyā hai*
someone come.PF.MASC.SG be.PRES
'Someone (male or female) has come.'
b. *koī ayī hai*
someone come.PF.FEM.SG be.PRES
'Someone (female) has come.'

And so it is that we find the generic masculine in proverbs such as those reproduced in (6):

(6) a. *sab ādmī barābar haĩ*
all man.MASC.PL equal be.PRES
'All men are equal (i.e. all people are equal).'
b. *har manuṣya kā*
every man.OBL.MASC.SG GEN.MASC.SG
*dharm hai*
duty.NOM.MASC be.PRES
'Every man has his duty (i.e. every person has his/her duty).'
c. *jo boyegā so kaṭegā*
who sow.FUT.MASC.SG he reap.FUT.MASC.SG
'He who sows will reap.'

There is a limited set of feminine epicene terms in standard Hindi, among them the term *savārī* (f) 'passenger' which is used for both male and female referents, but this is comparatively rare, cf. (7);

(7) *savārī āyī*
passenger.FEM.SG come.PF.FEM.SG
'The passenger came.'

As with many of the languages discussed in *Gender across Languages*, such examples point to an asymmetry in the grammatical gender system of Hindi, a point Valentine (1987) made over a decade ago from a feminist perspective. This asymmetry is also reflected in the verbal agreement in sentences with a complex subject that includes both a masculine and a feminine animate noun; in such cases, the masculine form is always used. When the complex subject involves inanimate objects of different genders, however, the verb will normally agree with the noun nearest to it in word order.

## Gender Reversal: Terms of Endearment and Insult

Outside of these uses of the generic masculine, however, speakers generally match morphological gender with referential gender. But there are a few notable exceptions. One of these is the occasional use of the masculine term *beṭā* (m) 'boy' instead of the feminine *beṭī* (f) 'girl' in direct address to a younger woman or daughter. When used in this way, particularly by parents to their children, the term becomes a term of endearment and best translates as 'dear'. One might argue that this gender reversal works as endearment because of the traditional value given to sons, as opposed to daughters, in Indian culture. When masculine terms are used for female persons, then, they tend to elevate the status of the referent.[10] So when women use the term *bhāī* (m) 'brother' for one another, as often happens between intimates, it signals equality and informality (cf. also Tobin, vol. I for gender switch in Hebrew).[11] A parallel might be drawn here with the honorific masculine term *sāhab* (m) 'sir', which is frequently used in reference to women, as in *memsāhab* (m) 'lady', *dākṭar sāhab* (m) 'doctor', and *profesar sāhab* (m) 'professor' (see Valentine 1987 for further discussion). These masculine address terms are highly respectful when used for women, underscoring the recipient's social status. When Indian journalists referred to Mrs. Gandhi as "the only man in the cabinet", they were highlighting her ability to run the affairs of the state (and the inability of male cabinet members to do so).[12]

But male persons are rarely addressed or referenced in the feminine gender. There are a number of insult terms which "imply" effeminacy and act as an insult to the recipient's masculinity, among them the term *hijṛā* when used by non-hijra men. The term, which literally means 'impotent', is frequently employed either in joking or anger to indicate the ineffectiveness of the referent in question. Other masculine terms of insult that connote effeminacy are included in (8). The hijras I knew in Banaras all, with much grief, reported having been called several of these names as young children (see Hall 1997).

(8) Selected masculine insult terms used for males

| | |
|---|---|
| *hijṛā* | 'eunuch, impotent' |
| *nacaniyā̃* | 'little dancer' |
| *bhosṛī vālā* | 'vagina-owner' |
| *chakkā* | 'a set of six, effeminate man' |
| *chah nambar* | 'number six, effeminate man' |
| *gāṇḍū* | 'passive partner in sodomy' |
| *jankhā* | 'effeminate man' |

These terms are all grammatically masculine, and this again points to an asymmetry in the Hindi gender system. While the use of masculine terms for female persons does occur and tends to carry positive implications, the use of feminine terms for male persons is virtually non-existent,[13] and when femininity (or effeminacy) is implied, as in the terms listed in (8) above, the connotations are extremely negative.

It is much less common for a male speaker to make use of the first-person feminine or a female speaker to employ the first-person masculine. There are infrequent accounts of young girls who, as a result of spending their formative years playing in predominantly male environments, speak in the masculine until taught to do otherwise in the Indian school system. But it is much rarer to find a boy speaking as a girl, particularly when there is such stigma attached to doing so. This might explain why the Hindi speakers in Banaras who reviewed my transcripts of hijra conversations were shocked at the hijras' use of feminine forms for themselves and other community members. Although the hijras produce an exaggerated feminine ideal in their mannerisms and dress, most non-hijras nevertheless consider them male and normally refer to them in the masculine gender (see Hall & O'Donovan 1996). The idea that hijras use feminine self-reference comes as a complete surprise to many Hindi speakers, who see the claiming of feminine morphology by speakers they identify as male (albeit "inadequately" male) as highly abnormal.[14] As I argue in the subsequent two sections, the hijras' varied uses of feminine and masculine first, second, and third person verbal forms reflects a unique dual-gender position in a society that views them as neither fully female nor fully male.

## USES OF THE GENDER SYSTEM BY HINDI-SPEAKING HIJRAS

When a hijra joins a Banaras hijra community, she quickly learns a variety of ways to distance herself from the masculine **semiotics** in which she was raised: She begins to wear traditional feminine dress (e.g. saris, jewelry, make-up), adopt hijra gestures (such as their distinctive flat-handed clap), sing and dance like a hijra, and most critically for this article, speak in a more feminine manner. Language is a critical component of this second gender socialization process, so much so that the hijras readily distinguish between what they refer to as *mardānā bolī* 'masculine speech' on the one hand and *zanānā bolī* 'feminine speech' on the other, with the latter variety accepted as the preferred way of speaking. The precise definition of these two terms varies among the hijra communities I worked with in Banaras, but members generally agree that *mardānā bolī* involves direct speech, "stronger" curses, and masculine first person verb forms, while *zanānā bolī* entails indirect speech (and is therefore deemed more polite), "weaker" curses, and feminine first-person verb forms. Whether or not these qualities play out in the ordinary speech of non-hijra men and women has not yet been studied, but the hijras are no doubt identifying stereotypical perceptions of masculine and feminine behaviors in dominant north Indian culture (which, incidentally, are not altogether different from those identified for many middle-class European-American communities). But the hijras accept these distinctions as fact, and use them to instruct each other on how to build a "less masculine" gender presentation.

### Language in Hijra Socialization

The hijras' discussions of their socialization into the community is extensive in my data, but I offer typical excerpts from these discussions here so as to give some indication of the importance of language to this process. The first is taken from Rupa,[15] a Banaras hijra who came to the community at the comparatively late age of 18 and found the change from *mardānā* to *zanānā bolī* particularly difficult. Raised in a prestigious Brahman family, Rupa spent all of her boyhood conforming to masculine roles and representations. But she never felt comfortable with her gender and ultimately decided to join the hijra community, undergo a castration operation, and take on the religious role of *pūjārī* (Hindu priest). As she describes in the following passage (9), the acquisition of "feminine speech" was an especially

(9) "Changing that takes time" Rupa 1993

Rupa: ghar mẽ, to –
mardānā rahate$^{m}$ the$^{m}$,
to mardānā bolī bolte-bolte$^{m}$ haī.
jab hijṛe ko jānā paṛtā hai
to parivartan karnā paṛtā hai....
vahī to bolā, na beṭā? –
jab ghar se cale$^{m}$,–
jab ghar se āye$^{m}$,
to ghar kī bolī mardānā to mẽ,
to mardānā bolī bolā$^{m}$. (3.0)

Kira: laṛkõ kī tarah se āpas mẽ vyavhār karte the?

Rupa: hā̃. bhaīyā$^{m}$ ko "bhaīyā$^{m}$" bol rahe$^{m}$ haī,–
cācā$^{m}$ ko "cācā$^{m}$" bol rahe$^{m}$ haī, –
aise bol rahe$^{m}$ hai. (2.0)
to usko parivartan karne mẽ
to ṭāīm lagta hī hai. (2.0)
to usko parivartan karne mẽ
ṭāīm lagta hai. –
bolte-bolte bolte-bolte,
ādat ho gayī (1.5)
sāt-chah mahīne mẽ.

R: At home –
they were$^{m}$ living$^{m}$ in a *mardānā* way,
so they're always speaking$^{m}$ *mardānā bolī*.
When a hijra has to leave,
then a change has to be made....
That's exactly what I told you, right dear? –
When I left$^{m}$ home, –
When I came$^{m}$ from home,
the speech at home was *mardānā* so I,
so I spoke$^{m}$ *mardānā bolī*.

K: You behaved like boys with each other?

R: Yes, they're calling$^{m}$ brothers$^{m}$
"brothers$^{m}$".
They're calling$^{m}$ their uncle$^{m}$ "uncle$^{m}$".
They're speaking$^{m}$ like that.
So changing that
just takes time.
Changing that
takes time.
But gradually after speaking continously,
it became a habit
in about six or seven months.

long and laborious process. (The transcription symbols used here are identified in the Appendix.)

Here, Rupa is in part illustrating the same-sex nature of socializing in her home village, where men associate with men (e.g. brothers and uncles) and women with women. Her entry into the hijra community involved a shift in play-group, so to speak, as she suddenly found her primary companions identifying as feminine and shunning masculine self-reference altogether. Rupa's transition from masculine to feminine speech, then, was a highly conscious process, one that required several months of practice. In Rupa's own words, it was only after *bolte-bolte bolte-bolte* 'speaking and speaking, speaking and speaking' before it *ādat ho gayī* 'became a habit'.

What is even more interesting in the hijras' discussions of this socialization process, however, is their frequent conflation of *zanānā bolī* with intimacy and solidarity and *mardānā bolī* with social distance. In their discussions with me, the hijras often offered examples of how they talk with one another, listing a host of feminine-marked first and second person verb forms. But in many of these discussions, the hijras also point to the use of the intimate second person pronoun *tū* as an example of *zanānā bolī*, a juxtaposition that suggests an association of feminine speech with intimacy. In excerpt (10), for example, Megha lists both kinds of phrases as examples of what she calls *auratõ kī bolī*, literally the 'speech of women':

(10) "We always speak women's speech" Megha 1993

Megha: hā̃, hameśā auratõ kī bolī boltī$^{f}$ haī<br>
kabhī bhī ādmī ke jaisā nahī̃ boltī$^{f}$ haī, – jaise,<br>
"maī jā rahī$^{f}$ hū̃ jī",<br>
"jā rahī$^{f}$ bahan",<br>
"tū$^{intimate}$ khā le",<br>
"tū$^{intimate}$ pakā le",<br>
"maī abhī ā rahī$^{f}$ hū̃".

M: Yes, we always speak$^{f}$ women's speech.<br>
We never ever speak$^{f}$ like a man.<br>
It's like, "I'm going$^{f}$ sir/mam",<br>
"Sister is going$^{f}$",<br>
"You (intimate) eat!"<br>
"You (intimate) cook!"<br>
"I'm coming$^{f}$ now".

Unlike Rupa, who lives in a house with an Indian family and dresses like a man in her "off-hours", Megha lives with a community of hijras and sees any admission of masculinity as a threat to her already marginalized status as a hijra (hence the strength of her assertion "we always speak women's speech; we never speak like men"). The very fact that Rupa in excerpt (9) refers to both herself and fellow community members in the masculine undermines Megha's claim, and points to divergent embracements of feminine self-reference by community members. Although speaking *zanānā bolī* is clearly the norm for hijras living in the four Banaras communities I researched (even Rupa uses feminine self-reference when discussing her activities with the community), members do not always use feminine forms for themselves and others, as Megha claims here. When a speaker wishes to express social distance between herself and another community member, whether it be out of respect (as for her guru) or disgust (as for an estranged hijra), she will often refer to that member in the masculine. Moreover, the hijras will sometimes use the first-person masculine for reasons of emphasis – for example, when angry or upset, when stressing a particular point, or when referring to their pre-hijra selves.

This again reminds us of the care we must take with folk-linguistic observations, as perceived speech patterns rarely match actual language use. But the hijras' perceptions of their language habits are nevertheless worthy of study, for the ideologies of gender uncovered therein influence their discursive interactions in important ways. In excerpt (11), for instance, we find Sulekha erroneously claiming that she speaks like a woman when speaking with a woman and like a man when speaking with a man:

(11) "I do the same speech of the person I meet" Sulekha 1993

Sulekha: mujh ko koī bāt nahī̃ rahatā hai,<br>
maī aurat jaisī boltī$^{f}$ hū̃, –<br>
ādmī *se* ādmī jaisā bāt kartī$^{f}$ hū̃, –<br>
jo jaisā miltā hai us se bāt kartī$^{f}$ hū̃,...<br>
jaise ab ham- hai na? -<br>
ab- ab- auratõ mē haī, (0.5)<br>
to – aurat ā gayī to aurat vālā hī bolū̃gī$^{f}$,<br>
"dīdī bahan" kahū̃gī$^{f}$. –<br>
ādmī ā jātā hai to<br>
((softly)) "kyā khāte haī$^{polite}$. (1.0)<br>
kyā bāt hai āpko$^{polite}$. (1.0)<br>
kyā kām hai".

S: It's just not a big deal to me.<br>
[Normally] I speak$^{f}$ like a woman,<br>
[but] with a man I speak$^{f}$ like a man.<br>
I do$^{f}$ the same speech of the person I meet....<br>
For example, take my case, okay?<br>
If I'm socializing with women<br>
and a woman comes by I'll just speak$^{f}$ like a woman.<br>
I'll say$^{f}$, "*Dīdī*! *Bahan*!"<br>
If a man comes by [I'll say]<br>
((softly)), "What are you (polite) eating?<br>
What's the matter, sir (polite)?<br>
What brings you here?"

By the end of the passage it becomes clear that what Sulekha means is that she makes her speech correspond to the social distance she perceives as existing between herself and her addressee. Women, for Sulekha, appear to represent intimacy and informality, and so she quotes herself as using familiar terms of address like *dīdī* and *bahan* when speaking with them, both of which translate as 'sister' (the first suggesting respect and intimacy, the second equality and informality). In contrast, men appear to represent distance and formality, hence Sulekha's repeated uses of the polite second person plural *āp* when reproducing her conversations with them. This short passage, even though it reveals little (if anything) about Sulekha's actual language use, does suggest that Sulekha, like Megha, associates feminine speech with intimacy and masculine speech with social distance.

It is this association that governs the choice of feminine or masculine forms among community members. Because hijras are considered "neither men nor women", they have at their disposal an added resource for marking social relations – that of grammatical gender. Indeed, their use of the gender system in many respects parallels the use of second person pronouns in the general population, where the choice of intimate *tū*, familiar *tum*, or polite *āp* indicates the respective social positions of addresser and addressee, as well as a host of other social attitudes and dimensions dependent on the context of the speech event. The pronoun *tū*, for example, is used in cases of heightened intimacy, e.g. to address a god, to address a close friend of equal status, to call a small child, to express anger or disgust. On the opposite end of the relational scale, the pronoun *āp* is used in situations involving any degree of formality, particularly in situations of social inequality when the speaker wishes to signal respect for the addressee – e.g. for a guru, an elder, a parent, an employer. Between these two extremes we find the pronoun *tum*, a form most often used in informal situations by friends and colleagues but also in situations of social inequality; for example, when an individual addresses someone of lesser status. Gender also plays an important role in pronominal choice: A classic example comes from the traditional Hindu family, where the husband will use the intimate *tū* or *tum* when addressing his wife while she will use the formal *āp* when addressing him. As this brief discussion suggests, the social rules governing the varying employments of these three pronouns are terribly complex, and speakers create social relations with pronominal choice as much as they affirm them. The same is true with the hijras' choice of feminine or masculine reference for members of their own community. Equipped with an extra linguistic resource, the hijras have developed their own system for marking social relations, one that has gender at its center.

## The Exploitation of Grammatical Gender in Everyday Hijra Conversation

In the next few pages, I offer selected examples of how the hijras exploit the grammatical gender system in their everyday conversations. Since feminine reference is expected within the community (the hijras even take on female names when initiated), I focus on those conversational excerpts which diverge from this expectation – that is, when the hijras use masculine reference for themselves and for one another. The hijras regularly use feminine reference to express solidarity with the referent in question, in the same manner that the familiar pronoun *tum* is used among good friends. Fellow *celā*'s 'disciples' quickly learn to use feminine reference for one another after joining the community; they will also use feminine reference for a superior or inferior when wishing to show affection. But when status is a point of emphasis, masculine reference is favored. The hijra community relies upon elaborate familial structures which delegate various feminine roles to different members of the group, among them *dādī* 'paternal grandmother', *nānī* 'maternal grandmother', *mausī* 'mother's sister', *cācī* 'uncle's wife', and *bahin* 'sister'. But these designations are also extremely hierarchical, with elders enjoying the respect of newcomers and both young and old members deferring to the community guru. The guru-chela relationship is fundamental to the hijra kinship system, and in any given group one will find a guru surrounded by a hierarchy of chelas, grand-chelas, great grand-chelas, and great great grand-chelas. While chelas will normally use feminine forms when addressing a superior directly, they will often use masculine reference when talking about her in the third person so as to mark their respect for her position. Conversely, hijras will frequently refer to newer chelas in the masculine, first to differentiate them as inferiors and second to indicate that they are still in the learning stages of hijrahood. This use of masculine reference, then, could be said to parallel the use of the intimate second person pronoun *tū* in the larger population, which can be used to address both a god and a servant. What we have here, then, is a neat linguistic pattern whereby feminine forms are used for hijras considered social equals and masculine forms are used for hijras of either higher or lower status.

Because the hijras associate the masculine with both hierarchy and social distance, they also employ it to express their dissatisfaction with other hijras. This kind of masculine reference can readily be seen in their uses of the hijra naming system. When a new member enters the hijra community, she is given a woman's name to replace the name of her former, more male self. The hijras are discouraged from referring to each other with these remnants of their previous lives, yet tellingly, they often employ them in disputes. If a hijra is in a fierce argument with another member of her community, one of the most incisive insults she can give is to question her addressee's femininity by using her male name. Likewise, in example (12), we see Sulekha insulting Muslim hijras by referring to them in the third-person masculine. Although Muslims and Hindu hijras often live together harmoniously in the same communities – an arrangement rarely found in mainstream Banaras where the tension between Muslims and Hindus is quite pervasive – Sulekha, raised Hindu, feels somewhat threatened by Muslim hijras, as they hold powerful positions within the Banaras hijra network, and indeed, throughout all of northern India. The distance Sulekha feels towards Muslim hijras is reflected in her use of third person masculine verb forms when Muslim hijras act as subjects, as in the following exchange between her and my research assistant Vinita:

(12) "I'd be a small mouth with big talk" Sulekha 1993

Sulekha: bazarḍīhā mē jo channū hai,
to vah bhī ādmī$^{m}$ hai.
hijṛā to hai nahī̃....
vo buzurg hai.
vah sab se mălik$^{m}$ vahī hai. (1.0)
sab se mālik$^{m}$ vahī hai.
bazarḍīhā kā$^{m}$. -
ye vo channū iske sab ādmī$^{m}$ haī,
sab āte$^{m}$ haī jāte$^{m}$ haī.
kurtā lungī pahan lete$^{m}$ haī,
nācne samay sāṛī pahan lete$^{m}$ haī, -
sabhī jānte$^{m}$ haī, (2.0)
maī hamko kahne se kyā?
Vinita: lekin vo sab āpreśan karāye hue haī̃?
Sulekha: nahī̃
Vinita: kuch nahī̃ <hai?>
Sulekha: <nahī̃.>
Vinita: tabhī aisī <hai?>
Sulekha: <hā̃.>
Vinita: o:::h. (1.0) acchā?
Sulekha: usko- unko maī kaise kahū̃?
usko kahū̃gī$^{f}$ to merā bāt kāṭ dēge$^{m}$....
maī kah dū̃gī$^{f}$ (0.5) to
((softly)) maī choṭe mūh baṛī bāt,
hamko isī mē rahnā hai. (0.5)
sab māregā$^{m}$ pīṭegā$^{m}$ bāl kāṭ degā$^{m}$.

S: That Channu who lives in Bazarḍīhā
is a man$^{m}$.
He's not a hijra....
He's very old.
He's the chief master$^{m}$ over there,
the chief master$^{m}$ over there.
Of$^{m}$ Bazarḍīhā.
All of the ones under Channu are men$^{m}$,
all of them who come$^{m}$ and go$^{m}$ over there.
They wear$^{m}$ *kurtās* and *lungīs*,
but when they dance they wear$^{m}$ sarees.
Everybody knows$^{m}$ it
so what's the use of my saying so?
V: But haven't they all had operations?
S: No.
V: Nothing at all?
S: No.
V: So they're just that way?
S: Yes.
V: O:::h. Really?
S: How can I say anything about them?
If I'd say$^{f}$ anything, they'd just contradict$^{m}$ me
anyway. If I'd give$^{f}$ anything away then
((softly)) I'[d be] a small mouth with big talk.
I have to live in this [community], after all.
They'd all hit$^{m}$ me, beat$^{m}$ me up, cut$^{m}$ my hair.

(13) "Now he left" Megha 1993

Megha: bacpan se yahī̃ kā$^{m}$ hai, –
ab jākar [place name] mē rah rahā$^{m}$ hai, –
merā jajmānī hai,
to maī un logō ko de detī$^{f}$ hū̃.

M: He belonged$^{m}$ to this household since childhood,
now he left and is living$^{m}$ in [place name].
I had clients there,
but I transferred$^{f}$ those people to him.

Sulekha's use of the third-person masculine to describe the 78-year-old Channu stands in stark contrast to her repeated use of feminine forms for herself and fellow community members in other conversations. But Sulekha appears to view Muslims as below her on the social hierarchy, evidenced in her insistence throughout her interviews with us that Hindu hijras existed long before Muslim hijras, and moreover, that it is only hijras from low caste backgrounds who convert to Islam and eat meat. Displeased with her own "smallness" relative to these Muslim hijras, Sulekha refuses to grant the entire community any acknowledgement of femininity, whether it be linguistic or anatomical.[16]

A comparable instance of such distancing can be found in Megha's references to Sulekha. After a fairly serious argument with Megha, Sulekha left Megha's community in Banaras and went to live with a male partner in a neighboring village outside the city. In a manner consistent with her claims in (10), Megha almost always uses feminine forms when referring to other hijras; yet when she refers to Sulekha, who apparently insulted her authority as *mālkin* (f) 'chief' of her community, Megha uses the masculine. Two examples of this employment are reproduced in excerpt (13).

Through the use of masculine postpositions like *kā* (m) 'of (m)' and masculine verb forms like *rah rahā* (m) *hai* 'he is living (m)', Megha signals that Sulekha is estranged from her.

## The Use of Masculine Self-Reference

Even more interesting than the above uses of the third-person masculine is the hijras' use of the first-person masculine. While this rarely surfaces in conversation, there are at least three situations in which the Banaras hijras do use it. The first of these is perhaps the most predictable: The hijras will regularly use the first-person masculine when referring to themselves as boys or telling of their childhoods. This linguistic shift follows from the fact that many hijras have what might be called a discontinuous gender identity which gradually changes from male to non-male after arrival in the hijra community. It is perhaps for this reason that the hijras sometimes refer to fellow hijras as masculine when referring to them in a pre-hijra state, such as when they tell of each other's childhoods. Here masculine marking will often perform as a tense marker, suggesting a time period prior to the hijra's entry into the community. Nanda (1990: xviii) alludes to similar linguistic shifts in the preface to her ethnography of the hijras when she explains her translation techniques, pointing out that she translates pronouns which refer to the hijras as feminine, unless "referring to the hijra in the past, when he considered himself a male". A hijra's use of the masculine in such instances seems to reflect her own distancing from a previous self, a self that continuously provides an unpleasant reminder that her femininity is appropriated instead of genuine.

A second kind of masculine self-reference occurs when hijras wish to add emphasis to a particular conversational statement. A beautiful example of this is reproduced in excerpt (14), when Sulekha wants to express her disagreement with Megha's portrayal of the hijra community. As I mentioned earlier, Megha is very protective of her community's reputation, and as a result, she painted for us a rather conservative portrait of the hijra lifestyle. Many hijras supplement their income through sex-work, particularly now that their traditional role as the blessers of newborns has become suspect in some segments of the general population. Many educated middle-class Indians, for instance, no longer believe in the hijras' power over procreation, and refuse to pay them money for their song and dance performances at birth celebrations. But Megha nevertheless denied any community involvement with prostitution, and insisted throughout her conversations with us that hijras were nothing but respected religious **ascetics.** In the excerpt below, Sulekha contradicts Megha's claims, punctuating her opposition with the first-person masculine singular:

(14) "No, I don't tell lies!" Sulekha 1993

| | | | |
|---|---|---|---|
| Vinita: | kaise kah rahī thī | V: | Then why was [Megha] saying, |
| | "ham log ko dukh hotā hai, | | "We have a lot of sadness. |
| | ham log kā parivār nahī̃ rahtā, | | We no longer have a family. |
| | ham log kā sambandh nahī̃ rahtā, | | We no longer have relationships. |
| | ham log bhī sote uṭhte baiṭhte". | | All we do is sleep, get up, sit around"? |
| Sulekha: | nahī̃. ye galat bāt hai. – | S: | No, that's wrong. |
| | galat bāt hai. | | That's wrong. |
| | maī isko nahī̃ māntā$^{m}$. – | | I don't believe$^{m}$ that. |
| | galat bāt hai. | | That's wrong. |
| | admī ke sāth kartā hai sab. – | | They all have relationships with men. |
| | jaise aurat *mard sambandh hota hai, – | | *Hijras have relationships with men |
| | usī tarah *hijṛe mard ke sāth sambandh | | just like women have relationships |
| | hotā hai. | | with *men. |
| | kitne *hijṛe- | | So many *hijras- |
| | kitne hijṛe rakh lete haī ādmī ko, – | | So many hijras keep men. |
| | kitnā peśāvar hotā hai, (1.0) | | So many are professionals. |
| | peśā kartī, | | Those who do it as a profession |
| | tab (1.0) *sau, pacās, do sau, cār sau, | | charge *100, 50, 200, 400, |
| | *sabkā peśā kartī haī. – | | *anything they can get. |
| | maī jhūṭh kahtā$^{m}$ hū̃? | | Do I tell$^{m}$ lies? |
| | nahī̃ kahtā$^{m}$ hū̃. | | No, I don't tell$^{m}$ lies. |

Here, Sulekha also repeatedly employs the infamous hijra flat-palmed clap, indicated in my transcription system by an asterisk. Clapping five times in this short passage (and the hijras' clap, incidentally, is extremely sharp and loud), Sulekha denies everything Megha has told us: "Yes, we have relationships with men; yes, we work as prostitutes; yes, we charge anything we can get." Use of the first-person masculine helps to bring her point home, and as this is highly uncharacteristic for Sulekha, she commands our attention: "maī jhūṭh kahtā (m) hū̃? nahī̃ kahtā (m) hū̃!" 'Do I tell (m) lies? No, I don't tell (m) lies!'

A final example of the hijras' use of the first-person masculine comes from a hijra community on the outskirts of the city. The four hijras who make up this comparatively isolated community, all born into Hindu families who ostracized them, have now adopted the religious practices of the Muslim families they live beside – families who in many ways suffer a similar marginalization as residents of a city that is thought of throughout northern India as the "holy Hindu city". The 80 year old Shashi is the guru of the group, and after 69 years of speaking like a woman (she became a hijra when she was eleven years old), we rarely heard her use masculine self-reference. But during one visit we accidentally instigated a family dispute that disrupted this small community. We often gave gifts to the hijras the first few times we met with them, so as to express our gratitude for the time they spent with us and show respect for their profession. On this day, however, we decided to give a gift of 101 rupees to Shashi's chela Mohan, since we had given Shashi a colorful saree on our previous visit. But this is not how the hijra hierarchy works: Only the guru is allowed to accept gifts, and the guru then distributes the group's earnings among her chelas. By giving Mohan a gift, we inadvertently (and regrettably) upset the community balance. After we left that day, Mohan apparently refused to hand over the rupees to her guru, and when confronted with Shashi's rage, she fled back to her home village outside of Delhi.

When we returned a week later, we immediately sensed that something was wrong. The hijras' house was deserted except for Shashi, who we found sitting on a small cot, slumped against a wall. She was devastated by Mohan's departure, and was grieving for the loss of her favorite chela. No apology we gave could remedy the situation or sufficiently express our regret, so we sat with her nervously and listened to what she had to say. Wailing *merā beṭā, merā beṭā* 'my son, my son' and clapping in anger, Shashi screamed about what had happened, venting her anger entirely through use of the masculine first- and third- person. It would seem that for Shashi, anger is an emotion best expressed in the masculine. Perhaps rage is a gut-level reaction that recalls the masculine forms she produced prior to her entry into the community, or perhaps rage requires the kind of emphatic masculinity used by Sulekha in the previous passage. Whatever the case, Shashi's use of masculine self-reference became a dramatic and forceful tool for venting this rage, and it remains with me as a painful reminder of the inherent imbalance between a researcher and her subject.

## Conclusions

But what has this discussion of what we might call "unnatural" gender by Hindi-speaking hijras told us about gender in non-hijra Hindi-speaking communities? Although the morphological shifting exhibited here is perhaps unique to the hijra community, I suggest that the conversations of women and men are also subject to comparable kinds of "gendered negotiations". As language and gender theorists have begun to demonstrate (see the articles in Hall & Bucholtz 1995, for instance), men and women in a variety of communities exploit cultural expectations of femininity and masculinity in order to establish positions of power and solidarity. The hijras have an added resource for accomplishing this, as their between male- and female-position allows them to access and claim both sides of the grammatical gender divide. But non-hijras "do gender" in conversational interaction too, working with and against ideologies of feminine and masculine speech that are themselves rooted in cultural expectations of gender-appropriate behavior. It is here that Judith Butler's (1990, 1993) Derridean reworking of J. L. Austin's concept of **performativity** becomes useful. Her argument that gender works as a performative, constituting the very act that it performs, leads us away from sociolinguistic approaches to identity that view the way we talk as directly indexing a **prediscursive self.** For Butler, there is no prediscursive self, as even our understanding of "biological sex" is discursively produced. This theoretical perspective throws a decisive wrench in the distinction between "natural gender" and "grammatical gender", since there is no "natural" in Butlerian theory. Without the concept of natural gender to fall back on, sociolinguists can no longer make the circular claim that speaker X speaks like X because he is male or that speaker Y speaks like Y because she is female. Rather, we must turn our focus to the speech event itself, uncovering how speakers manipulate ideologies of femininity and masculinity in the ongoing production of gender.

In the case of the hijras, we located some of these ideologies in the association of *mardānā bolī* with directness, hierarchy, and anger, and *zanānā bolī* with indirectness, solidarity, and intimacy. The Banaras hijras at times challenge such associations in their creative employments of masculine and feminine self-reference, but their use of grammatical gender is nevertheless constrained by a rather traditional and dichotomous understanding of gender. While the hijras tend to use the masculine when speaking to a superior or inferior, emphasizing particular points, recalling their past selves as non-hijras, or expressing intense anger, they are more likely to employ the feminine when expressing solidarity and intimacy with fellow community members. Because they occupy an ambiguous gender position in a city that continues to marginalize them, Banaras hijras are perhaps more attentive to the role speech plays in the performance of gender. With a heightened awareness of how language can index gender identity, they enact and contest ideologies of gendered speech in their daily interactions. The research is not yet here to tell us whether "monosexed" Hindi-speaking communities in India share these same expectations of male and female verbal behavior; nor do we yet know how such expectations might influence the actual language practices of men and women in specific communities of practice. I offer this analysis of a rather unusual community to excite more research on gender in Hindi sociolinguistics. The language practices of these Banaras hijras, extraordinary as they are, are not created in a cultural vacuum. Their discursive choices are influenced by dominant ideologies of gender in northern India – ideologies that no doubt affect linguistic behavior in a variety of Hindi-speaking communities.

**Appendix**

The transcription conventions used for the Hindi passages in this article include the following; I have not used all of these conventions in the English translations since extralinguistic features like intonation and emphasis are not parallel.

$x^f$ superscripted *f* indicates feminine morphological marking in the Hindi
$y^m$ superscripted *m* indicates masculine morphological marking in the Hindi
(0.5) indicates length of pause within and between utterances, timed in tenths of a second
a – a a dash with spaces before and after indicates a short pause, less than 0.5 seconds
but- a hyphen immediately following a letter indicates an abrupt cutoff in speaking
(()) double parentheses enclose nonverbal movements \and extralinguistic commentary
[] brackets enclose words added to clarify the meaning of the text
**what** bold print indicates syllabic stress
: a colon indicates a lengthening of a sound (the more colons, the longer the sound)
. a period indicates falling intonation
, a comma indicates continuing intonation
? a question mark indicates rising intonation at the end of a syllable or word
... deletion of some portion of the original text
"a" quotation marks enclose quoted or reported speech
* flat-palmed clap characteristic of the hijras
< > overlapping talk

## Notes

* I began this field research in a joint project with Veronica O'Donovan after concluding an advanced language program during the 1992–1993 academic year in Banaras, India. I am grateful to the American Institute of Indian Studies for sponsoring my participation in the program. Some of the data discussed in this essay also appears in Hall & O'Donovan (1996). My thanks are extended to the many people who helped me with this project in both India and America, to my friend and Hindi teacher Ved Prakash Vatuk, and to the Banaras hijras who participated in these discussions.

1. This percentage is taken from the 1991 Census of India, in which 4022 of every 10,000 people listed Hindi as their primary language and another 518 listed Urdu. These and other language statistics are available at the Census of India website: www.censusindia.net.
2. See Kachru (1980: 3–11) for an interesting discussion of the grammatical tradition of Hindi.
3. There are, however, a number of insightful studies on women's uses of various South Asian oral traditions, such as Raheja & Gold's (1994) ethnography on the poetics of women's resistance in the songs, stories, and personal narratives of women in northern India.
4. For a more extensive discussion of Valentine's work, see Hall (forthcoming).
5. See Romaine (1999: 63–90) for a recent discussion of the "leakage" between grammatical gender and natural gender.
6. The standard Hindi *khaṛī bolī* area is generally said to be located in western Uttar Pradesh between the Ganges and Jumna rivers, stretching from Dehradun in the north to Bulandshahar in the south.
7. In Delhi the hijras have named their language *Farsi*. While their "hijralect" has very little, if anything, to do with what is generally known as Farsi, the term is fitting given that the hijras see themselves as descended from the eunuchs of the medieval Moghul courts, where Farsi was the dominant language.
8. I am grateful to Ved Vatuk for bringing to my attention the parallel between *sadhukkaṛī* and *hijṛā bolī*.
9. I use the term subject in the sense of syntactic subject, not morphological subject. The syntactic subject may be in an oblique case form and does not necessarily determine agreement. The term is usually used for the NP which corresponds to the subject of the English translation.
10. In recent years, however, parents in some Hindi-speaking areas have begun to use the feminine term *beṭī* in direct address to a son, also for reasons of endearment (Ved Vatuk, personal communication).
11. The term *bhāī*, like the masculine term *yār* 'friend', is used in a variety of contexts to index informality. Wives, for instance, will sometimes refer to their husbands as *bhāī*.
12. Ved Vatuk (personal communication).
13. Except, of course, in theatrical situations when men play women's roles, as in folk-dramas known as *nautankī* or *sāng*.
14. A similar reaction would most likely occur towards women using masculine self-reference, except for the fact that there has recently been a number of public female figures who have challenged the assumption of "natural" linguistic gender by assuming a male speaking voice. Most notable in this regard is one of the lead characters in the sitcom *Ham Panch*, whose use of the masculine first-person is intended to reflect her tomboyish personality. Moreover, the popular singer Milan Singh, who is known for singing both male and female parts of traditional Bollywood film songs, regularly speaks in the first person plural when interviewed so as to keep her gender ambiguous before the public.
15. I have chosen pseudonyms for all of the hijras appearing in this article and have avoided giving the names of the four hijra communities mentioned to protect their anonymity. I have also chosen to use *her* and *she* to refer to the hijras since they prefer to be referred to and addressed in the feminine.
16. It could also be quite possible that the group of people Sulekha is referring to here are actually *jankhās* (as called in Banaras) or *kotīs* (as called in Delhi), i.e. men who dress and dance as women but do not publicly identify as hijras or officially belong to the hijra community. As these "non-castrated" men continue to remain in their extended family structures, undergoing arranged marriages and bearing children, they sometimes receive a certain amount of animosity from the hijras. See Hall (forthcoming) for a more lengthy discussion of these different groups.

## References

Apte, Mahadev L. 1974. "Pidginization of a Lingua Franca: A linguistic analysis of Hindi-Urdu spoken in Bombay." *Contact and Convergence in South Asian Languages. International Journal of Dravidian Linguistics* 3: 21–41.

Beames, John. 1872–79. *A comparative grammar of the modern Aryan languages of India*. 3 vols. London.

Bhatia, Tej K. 1992. "Variation in Hindi: Parameters for a pan-dialectal grammar." In *Dimensions of sociolinguistics in South Asia: Papers in memory of Gerald B. Kelley*, eds. Edward C. Dimock & Braj B. Kachru & Bhadriraju Krishnamurti. New Delhi: Oxford & IBH Press, 163–97.

Bloch, Jules. 1910. "Castes et dialectes en Tamoul." *Mémoires de la Société de Linguistique de Paris* 16: 1–30.

Bodine, Ann. 1975. "Androcentrism in prescriptive grammar: Singular 'they', sex-indefinite 'he', and 'he or she'." *Language in Society* 4: 129–46.

Börner-Westphal, Barbara. 1989. "Sexus-Genus-Beziehungen im Hindi." *Zeitschrift für Phonetik, Sprachwissenschaft und Kommunikationsforschung* 42: 762–70.

Butler, Judith. 1990. *Gender trouble: Feminism and the subversion of identity*. New York: Routledge.

Butler, Judith. 1993. *Bodies that matter: On the discursive limits of "sex"*. New York: Routledge.

Chatterji, Suniti Kumarr. 1931. "Calcutta Hindustani: A study of a jargon dialect." *Indian Linguistics* 1: 2–4. Reprinted 1972 in *Select papers*. New Delhi: People's Publishing House, 204–56.

Chernyshev, V. A. 1971. "Nekotorye cherty Bombeiskogo Govora Khindustani, (na materiale sovremennoi prozy khindi)" [Some features of Bombay Hindustani speech (in modern Hindi prose material)]. In *Indiiskaia i Iranskaia Filologiia (Voprosy Dialektologii)*, ed. Nikolai Dvoriankov. Moscow: Izdatel'stvo "Nauka", 121–41.

Gosvāmī, Pūranagira. 1979. *Hindī meṃ linga-bheda kā adhyayana* [A study of gender distinctions in Hindi]. Varanasi: Sañjaya Prakāśana.

Grierson, George Abraham. 1903–1928. *Linguistic survey of India (1903–28)*. 11 vols. Reprint 1967. Delhi: Motilal Banarsidass.

Gumperz, John J. 1958. "Dialect differences and social stratification in a North Indian village." *American Anthropologist* 60: 668–82.

Guru, Karnta Prasad. 1920. "*Hindī Vyākaraṇ*" [Hindi grammar]. Varanasi: Kashi Nagri Pracharini Sabha.

Hall, Kira. 1997. "'Go suck your husband's sugarcane!' Hijras and the use of sexual insult." In *Queerly phrased: Language, gender, and sexuality*, eds. Anna Livia & Kira Hall. New York: Oxford University Press, 430–60.

Hall, Kira (forthcoming). *From tooth to tusk: Language and gender in an Indian hijra community*. Unpublished manuscript.

Hall, Kira & Mary Bucholtz, eds. 1995. *Gender articulated: Language and the socially constructed self*. New York: Routledge.

Hall, Kira & Veronica O'Donovan. 1996. "Shifting gender positions among Hindi-speaking Hijras." In *Rethinking language and gender research: Theory and practice*, eds. Victoria L. Bergvall & Janet M. Bing & Alice F. Freed. London: Longman, 228–66.

Jain, Dhanesh Kumar. 1969. "Verbalization of respect in Hindi." *Anthropological Linguistics* 11: 79–97.

Jain, Dhanesh Kumar. 1973. *Pronominal usage in Hindi: A sociolinguistic study*. Ph.D. dissertation, University of Pennsylvania.

Kachru, Yamuna. 1980. *Aspects of Hindi grammar*. New Delhi: Manohar Publications.

Kellog, Samuel H. 1875. *A grammar of the Hindi language*. London: Routledge.

Khubchandani, Lachman M. 1978. "Towards a selection grammar: Fluidity in modes of address and reference in Hindi-Urdu." *Indian Linguistics* 39: 1–4.

Khubchandani, Lachman M. 1991. "India as a sociolinguistic area." *Language Sciences* 13: 265–88.

King, Christopher R. 1999. *One language two scripts: The Hindi movement in nineteenth century northern India*. New York: Oxford University Press.

Lakoff, Robin. 1973. "Language and woman's place." *Language in Society* 2: 45–80.

Martyna, Wendy. 1980a. "Beyond the he/man approach: The case for nonsexist language." *Signs: Journal of Women in Culture and Society* 5: 482–93.

Martyna, Wendy. 1980b. "The psychology of the generic masculine." In *Women and language in literature and society*, eds. Sally McConnell-Ginet & Ruth Borker & Nancy Furman. New York: Praeger, 69–78.

McGregor, Ronald Stuart. 1972. *Outline of Hindi grammar*. Delhi: Oxford University Press.

Mehrotra, Raja Ram. 1977. "Fluidity in kinship terms of address." *Anthropological Linguistics* 19: 123–32.

Mehrotra, Raja Ram. 1985a. *Sociolinguistics in Hindi context*. New Delhi: Mohan Primlani. ("Hindi address forms", 39–79)

Mehrotra, Raja Ram. 1985b. *Sociolinguistics in Hindi context*. New Delhi: Mohan Primlani. ("Modes of greeting in Hindi: A sociolinguistic statement", 80–122)

Mehrotra, Raja Ram. 1985c. "Sociolinguistic surveys in South Asia: An overview." *International Journal of the Sociology of Language*, 55: 115–24.

Misra, K. S. 1977. *Terms of address and second person pronominal usage in Hindi: A sociolinguistic study*. New Delhi: Bahri Publications.

Mohanan, Tara. 1994. *Argument structure in Hindi*. Stanford: CSLI Publications.

Nanda, Serena. 1990. *Neither man nor woman: The hijras of India*. Belmont, CA: Wadsworth.

Nespital, Helmut. 1990. "On the relation of Hindi to its regional dialects." In *Language versus dialect: Linguistic and literary essays on Hindi, Tamil, and Sarnami*, ed. Mariola Offredi. New Delhi: Manohar Publications, 3–23.

Pathak, Anand Swarup. 1976. *Hindī kā linga vidhāna* [On gender in Hindi: A study]. Mathura: Pramod Prakāśan.

Raheja, Gloria Goodwin & Ann Grodzins Gold. 1994. *Listen to the Heron's words: Reimagining gender and kinship in North India*. Berkeley, CA: University of California Press.

Romaine, Suzanne. 1999. *Communicating gender*. Mahwah, NJ: Erlbaum.

Sachdeva, Rajesh. 1982. *Sociolinguistic profile of Milijhuli around Delhi*. Ph.D. Dissertation, Poona University, India.

Shapiro, Michael C. 1989. *A primer of modern standard Hindi*. Varanasi: Motilal Banarsidass.

Shapiro, Michael C. & Harold F. Schiffman. 1983. *Language and society in South Asia*. Dordrecht: Foris.

Sharma, Aryendra. 1958. *A basic grammar of Hindi*. Delhi: Government of India.

Simon, Beth Lee. 1993. "Language choice, religion, and identity in the Banarsi community." In *Living Banaras: Hindu religion in cultural context*, eds. Bradley R. Hertel & Cynthia Ann Humes. Albany: State University of New York Press, 245–68.

Simon, Beth Lee. 1996. "Gender, language, and literacy in Banaras, India." In *Gender and belief systems: Proceedings of the Fourth Berkeley Women and Language Conference*, eds. Natasha Warner & Jocelyn Ahlers & Leela Bilmes & Monica Oliver & Suzanne Wertheim & Mel Chen. Berkeley: Women and Language Group, 679–87.

Simon, Beth Lee. *Glass River*. Unpublished manuscript.

Singh, Rajendra & Jayant K. Lele. 1990. "Language, power, and cross-sex communication strategies in Hindi and Indian English revisited." *Language in Society* 19: 541–46.

Srivastava, Murlidhar. 1969. *The elements of Hindi grammar*. Varanasi: Motilal Banarsidass.

Vajpeyi, Kishoridass. 1967. *Hindii shabdaanushaasan* [Hindi grammar]. Varanasi: Kashi Nagri Pracharini Sabha.

Vajpeyi, Kishoridass. 1968. *Acchii Hindi* [Good Hindi]. Meerut: Minakshi Prakashan.

Valentine, Tamara M. 1985. "Sex, power, and linguistic strategies in the Hindi language." *Studies in the Linguistic Sciences* 15: 195–211.

Valentine, Tamara M. 1986. "Language and power: Cross-sex communicative strategies in Hindi and Indian English." *Economic Political Weekly* (Special Issue: Review of Women Studies), 75–87.

Valentine, Tamara M. 1987. "Sexist practices in the Hindi language." *Indian Journal of Linguistics* 14: 25–55.

Vatuk, Sylvia. 1969a. "Reference, address, and fictive kinship in urban North India." *Ethnology* 8: 255–72.

Vatuk, Sylvia. 1969b. "A structural analysis of the Hindi kinship terminology." *Contributions to Indian Sociology, New Series* 3: 94–115.

## Critical Thinking and Application

- Why are feminine forms used by hijras for other hijras they consider their social equals, while masculine forms are used for those they consider either socially superior or socially inferior?
- Why do you think the change in language described by Rupa in Excerpt 9 was so conscious and took so much time to complete effectively?
- Are there any similar shifts in gender in the linguistic system that you are most familiar with? Are these shifts easy or difficult to make?
- Research other groups that challenge the notion that there are simply two fixed genders and analyze their language use. Compare what you find to Hall's account of hijra language.

## Vocabulary

animate
ascetic
caste
community of practice
discourse analysis
Dravidian
genitive
grammatical gender
head noun
*hijṛā*
hypercorrection
inanimate
index (verb)
Indo-Aryan
inflection
liminality
lingua franca
marked
morphological gender
national language
natural gender
official language
performativity
Perso-Arabic
pidgin
postposition
pragmatic
prediscursive self
referent
register
Sanskritic
second-person pronoun
semiotics
Urdu
variationist

## Suggested Further Reading [See also list following Language and Identity; Gender unit introduction]

Bucholtz, Mary. 2011. *White Kids: Language, Race, and Styles of Youth Identity*. Cambridge: Cambridge University Press.

Butler, Judith. 1990. *Gender Trouble: Feminism and the Subversion of Identity*. New York: Routledge.

Cameron, Deborah. 2007. *The Myth of Mars and Venus*. Oxford: Oxford University Press.

Eckert, Penelope. 1989. *Jocks and Burnouts: Social Categories and Identity in the High School*. New York: Teachers College Press.

Mendoza-Denton, Norma. 2008. *Homegirls: Language and Cultural Practice Among Latina Youth Gangs*. Malden, MA: Blackwell.

CHAPTER 38

# Language, Socialization, and Silence in Gay Adolescence

*William Leap*

(1999)

*We create or change identities in large part by speaking, and by silence. Identities that are stigmatized, such as gay and lesbian identity, may have certain linguistic features associated with them. This is especially true for the "coming-out" story that is the central ritual in the contemporary United States for these individuals. Speaking the self may be the most powerful action in the creation of an identity, and gay and lesbian identities may illustrate this better than other mainstream identities.*

*William Leap has been writing about gay language since the mid-1990s. We learn, certainly, about the ways gay youth construct an identity and may be able to learn as well about the ways all speakers employ language to create identity. Opposition to the mainstream may require reappropriation of stigmatized terms, such as* queer, *which has become the preferred term in the study of alternative sexualities. Language plays a central role in the work of these, and many other, activists.*

## Reading Questions

- What are the linguistic features that Leap interprets as "expressions of personal agency"? How do such expressions play a role in their speakers' "self-managed socialization"?
- On what sources did Leap's consultants rely in the course of their development of a gay identity?
- How did the accumulation of a repertoire of words, phrases, and sentences prepare youth for their adult lives?

This chapter explores a component of the "coming-out" experience that remains largely overlooked in the literature on gay adolescence: How do gay teenagers go about acquiring the language of gay culture?[1] My discussion of this question builds on three assumptions: (1) that something called "gay culture" (as distinct from gay "lifestyle" or erotic interests) really exists; (2) that "gay culture" includes distinctive "ways of talking" within its inventory of symbolics and **semiotics;** and (3) that these "ways of talking" are sufficiently rich and complex to justify being termed gay *language*, rather than an **argot,** "secret code," or rhetorical style.[2]

William Leap, Language, Socialization, and Silence in Gay Adolescence. In *Reinventing Identities: The Gendered Self in Discourse*, edited by Mary Bucholtz, A. C. Liang, and Laurel A. Sutton. New York: Oxford University Press, 1999, pp. 259–272.

By exploring the convergence of language, identity construction, and gay socialization, this chapter joins other recent studies exploring the close connections between language and culture that underlie, for example, recollections of childhood in a "lesbian living room" (Morgan & Wood 1995), dialogue between entertainer and audience at a black drag club (Barrett 1995; 1999), menu-planning for a lesbian seder (Moonwomon 1996), or the in-flight disclosure of gay identities between an airline passenger and an airline steward (Leap 1993). These studies show how participation in lesbian- and gay-centered text-making in different social settings builds familiarity with the rules of lesbian- and gay-centered grammar and discourse and with other cultural practices relevant to those domains. They also demonstrate how participation in such social moments assumes some degree of familiarity with lesbian- and gay-centered language and cultural practices. In the absence of such information, text-making becomes highly dependent on situated (rather than prediscursive) meanings, on negotiation and inference, on "double (that is, hearer- as well as speaker-based) subjectivity" (Goodwin 1989: 12), and in some instances on conditions of risk (Leap 1996: 72–73).

None of these processes is uniquely lesbian or gay in its basis, but all the same, text-making conducted on such terms has clear implications for lesbian and gay experience. Particularly vulnerable in this regard are young persons who are just beginning to lay claim to lesbian or gay identities and who turn to lesbian- and gay-centered text-making as a format for acting on those claims. Text-making in these cases ranges from the disclosure of same-sex desires to close friends or adult authority figures to the construction of silence as agemates use an individual's ambiguous sexuality as a focus for teasing and taunting. Overlapping with the construction of textual silence, of course, is the almost epidemic-like incidence of attempted suicide reported for American teenagers struggling to come to terms with their homosexuality.[3]

Understandably, when gay men look back on their adolescence, they often speak of this period of their gender career as a time of loneliness and isolation, conditions that one gay man summarized powerfully with the phrase "a vast desert of nothing" (Leap 1996: 127).[4] But some gay men also describe this period as a time when they set out to make sense out of newly discovered feelings, emotions, and interests; when they assembled information that would help them better understand those discoveries; and when they tried to locate other individuals who might share (or understand or at least not dismiss) these concerns. And—of particular importance to this chapter—gay men talk about attempts to find a language through which they can describe, interpret, and account for the new directions now taking shape within their lives.

Some examples of such statements appear below. They were chosen from a larger set of texts I collected during a recent study of gay language socialization (reported, in part, in Leap 1994, 1996: 125–139).[5] Each example describes a young man's attempts to make sense out of a male-centered sexual identity, even though the details of that identity were just beginning to be disclosed. And each example shows how language became a resource during this process.

*Jim* (a 22-year-old gay white man who was born in Buffalo, New York, and lived there until he started college in Washington, D.C.) told me:

> I was never sat down by my mom and dad and told the heterosexual version of the birds and the bees. Um, you know, when you get to the time where you are twelve, thirteen, or fourteen, you begin to be sexually aware, you really look, strive for sources of information.
>
> I started looking for information about homosexuality... and eventually I branched off into the *Encyclopaedia Britannica* we had in the house. I looked up in the index as far as sexual goes: penis, phallus, every single adjective, synonym of that.... I eventually went to the public library, school library and that wasn't easy because it was public and you had to build up your confidence....
>
> I tried to do as much as possible, reading, whatever I thought might have gotten somewhere. For example, if I came across a column like for example Ann Landers might have mentioned it, I'd be her fan for a couple of months so maybe she'd bring it up again.

*Sam* (a 21-year-old gay white man who was born and raised in central Ohio and attended college in Washington, D.C.) told me:

> *Brothers* (a cable television sitcom) had an effeminate stereotyped gay man. That was a good example of how not to talk. I didn't believe gay people talked like that. *Consenting Adult* related a view which I knew was true and was looking for: a normal guy can be gay. *Deathtrap*—my mom was disgusted by the kissing scene. I was distracted.

*Wallace* (a gay white man in his early 30s who grew up in the Washington, D.C. suburbs and is a professional actor with several companies in the Washington area) noted in an interview published in the *Washington Post* (Brown & Swisher 1994):

> I grew up in Maryland, right outside of D.C., and spent my childhood listening to *West Side Story* and *A Chorus Line*. Those cast albums and movie musicals on TV were sort of secret messages from a world we didn't experience in our suburban, private school upbringing. That saved us.

*Robert* (a 27-year-old gay white man who was born in northern Florida, finished graduate school in North Carolina, and is now on the faculty of a junior college in northern Virginia) told me:

> Later in high school, my junior year, I guess, people started calling me faggot. I don't know if it was a joke or what, but they called me that. A lot. Even my teammates, they'd toss me a towel and say, "Hey faggot, catch this," or someone'd say, "Hey faggot, the coach needs to talk to you."
>
> (Q: did you get angry? Did this upset you?)
>
> You know, it's funny. I didn't get mad at all. I was uncomfortable, but I was not mad. See, I knew by then that I was gay so—without even knowing it, they were right! They were telling the truth. I couldn't get mad at them for telling the truth.

*Joe* (a 24-year-old gay white man and a campus and community activist) told me:

> I have been gay since the womb: I started experimenting with sex when I was very young and when I found others doing the same thing I knew there was something to all of this—but I didn't know exactly what it was.
>
> (Q: So when did you come out?)
>
> You mean, telling anybody about all this experimentation? Not 'til I was a teenager. I met an older woman, middle-aged, who had lots of gay friends. She introduced me to some other, older gay men and they took

> me under their wing. That is how I learned the rest of it, the social thing, the networks.

Sam continues:

> (Q: Did you know or know about gay people in [your hometown] when you were in high school?)
>
> No, not at first, but by the time I ended ninth grade, I had learned about five people: one aged thirty-five, three older than that, and one my own age. He became my best friend in high school.
>
> (Q: How did you find these people?)
>
> Pure luck.... I wanted to find someone like me. Found him by pure luck. Met him in the eighth grade. I told him in the ninth grade. He told me he was bisexual in the tenth grade. Both of us were scared. Having been friends, we did not want to jeopardize each other's secret. We talked a lot. No topic was safe. Though really, it was me doing the talking. He was the novice, someone for me to talk to.

Jim continues:

> I, later in my senior year, when I was seventeen or eighteen, I had an English teacher, too. It was real interesting, our relationship, because he was very pull-students-aside-and-get-into-their-lives kind of thing. I do not know for what reason, but he did that with me. He was very helpful in that he knew I was gay and kind of brought me out a bit more. I remember that, for some reason, he approached me, and said: How does your mother feel about this? And I said: Wow! And I told him, and the dam was lifted, and all the information I needed in my life was there, me seeking advice from him, that sort of thing.

## CHARTING A PATH THROUGH THE "DESERT OF NOTHING"

Although life stories are subjective (and in some sense fictional) documents, they do provide a *detail* of gay experience that cannot be retrieved from statistical surveys or other broadly based forms of data-gathering.[6] And in the present case, many details in these narratives speak directly to the importance of language and language learning for gay socialization and for the construction of gay identity during adolescence.

The close connection between language, identity, and **heteronormativity** provides the background for the present discussion, and I begin my analysis with some general comments on this connection.

### Heteronormativity Versus the Gay Imaginary

By *heteronormativity*, I mean the principles of order and control that position heterosexuality as the cornerstone of the American sex/gender system and obligate the personal construction of sexuality and gender in terms of heterosexual norms. Heteronormativity assumes, for example, that there are two sexes and therefore two genders. Heteronormativity then requires that all discussions of gendered identity and opportunity be framed strictly in terms of this dichotomy, forcing gendered actors to be labelled as either 'woman' or 'man', regardless of the identification that the actors might give to themselves.

An abundance of institutions, "a pervasive cluster of forces" (Rich 1980: 640), in Western society conspire to give heteronormativity its natural and normal façade. Importantly, however, while heteronormativity is certainly powerful and pervasive in late modern Western societies, it is not entirely totalizing. Alternative constructions of sexuality and gender are possible within this system, although particular alternatives do not always intersect smoothly with normative claims to authority. Hence the regulation of heteronormativity unfolds through distinctions between acceptable and unacceptable sexual/gendered identities and practices and through an ordering of the social worth of individuals on the basis of their allegiance to such distinctions.

In this way, heteronormativity co-occurs with, and profits from, the social presence of the ***subaltern*** (an "identity-in-differential" which is set apart from both the ideal and the elite [Spivak 1988: 284]), the *queer* ("a unity...of shared dissent from the dominant organization of sex and gender" composed of lesbian, gay, and other lifestyles "whose icons are heavily associated by cultural outsiders with the culture of gay life, politics and practices" [Whittle 1994: 27]); the *stigmatized* (persons who, through various means, must contend with a "spoiled identity" [Goffman 1963]), as well as other stances situated on the margins of late modern society.

Language holds a prominent place in the intersection of the heteronormative and the marginal. In English and other Western languages, conversation, narration, and other forms of text-making provide contexts within which heteronormative messages are produced and reproduced in everyday life. **Morphemic** and **lexical** contrasts, processes of reference and inference, and other structural details provide the framework through which heteronormative messages become inscribed in, remembered within, and retained beyond the textual moment.

Unavoidably, language keeps heteronormative stances in the foreground of daily activity and keeps alternative forms of reference in the background, the margins, and the shadows. Such arrangements ensure that normative assumptions become expectable, reasonable, and acceptable components of the local cultural inventory and that alternative stances remain less familiar, more mysterious, and less desirable.

But even while it imposes such limitations on social reference, language-based normativity does not always disrupt the workings of the personal imaginary. Individuals still construct their own sense of sexual/gendered possibilities and apply their own meanings to those constructions, even if they do not find referential support for these imagined constructions within normatively sanctioned sex/gender discourse. Hence the pervasive presence of silence within heteronormative domains, a silence that reflects an absence of articulation but not necessarily an absence of personal voice. And hence the delight in the discovery of labels, even when the points of reference are not intended to be complimentary or to have any positive implications.

By my reading of his statement cited above, this is the point of Robert's reactions to his peers' taunting and teasing in the high school locker room. Robert's teammates called him *faggot*, but rather than becoming angry at this name-calling, Robert diffuses the statements by acknowledging the truthfulness of their reference: He admits that he *was* gay, after all, and says that he could not be upset at his colleagues for telling the truth. We must not be sidetracked by Robert's seemingly naive rewriting of logical argument. Instead, we must consider how Robert's interpretation of these statements gives him a way of living through moments when he was the target of invective, moments when he had no alternative but either to "confirm" his manhood through a fistfight or some other form of competitive force, thereby directing the team's teasing toward the vanquished party, or simply to maintain his silence. As he told me in our interview, the latter seemed the more reasonable option for a young man growing up in a small Southern town.

Such choices are familiar parts of the gay adolescent social landscape; they are found not only in the narratives collected here but also in more overtly fictional work representing gay adolescent experience. Robert Reinhardt's character Billy in his novel *A History of Shadows* (1986), for example, would understand Robert's decision. Like Robert, in the novel Billy remembers thinking that he "was the only homosexual in the world." He continues:

> Well, that's not quite true.... But I felt I was the only homosexual. It's hard being something for which one doesn't even have a name. And I didn't for a long time. I used to wonder, what am I? I saw the boys in my class and longed for them, but I couldn't figure out what the vague aching was, and I couldn't recognize it in others. I couldn't see that anyone looked at me with the same longing.
>
> I found out about sex in the streets. The first name I had for what I was, was "cocksucker."... (It) was an awful word the way they used it, but it meant that my condition was nameable. I knew I was awful, but I finally had a name for all those odd feelings. I wasn't nothing. I was awful, but I wasn't nothing. (Reinhardt 1986: 25)

*My condition was nameable. I finally had a name for those odd feelings. I wasn't nothing.* Here, the relief in finding a label for "those odd feelings" outweighs the negative content surrounding this usage. And once again, rather than being overwhelmed by negative sentiment, Billy found a way to pull something useful from the statements and to disregard the remainder of the message. Wallace did the same thing, as he reports in the passage cited above, when he began to locate "secret messages from a world we didn't experience" in cast albums and Broadway musicals. Sam did the same thing when he rejected the stereotyped homosexual's use of language on *Brothers* because he "didn't believe gay people talked like that." And Jim did the same thing when he searched through Ann Landers's columns for her occasional comments on homosexuality.

All of these narratives speak to a process that Julia Kristeva (1982) describes in some detail. Even though I may willingly subordinate myself to some object that "precedes and possesses me," an object over which I have no control, "sublimation" allows me to "dissolve [it] in the raptures of a bottomless memory."[7] Then, "as soon as I perceive [the now-sublimated object], as soon as I name it, the sublime triggers—as it has always triggered—a spree of perceptions and words that expands memory boundlessly. I then forget the point of departure and find myself removed to a secondary universe, set off from the other where I 'am'—delight and loss" (1982: 10–11). Kristeva's description speaks to a re-creation of awareness, a construction of a personal imaginary, that does not challenge the dominant and oppressive heteronormativity but does enable individuals to make their own way in spite of heterosexual norms. For Robert and Billy, for Sam and Wallace and Jim, and for the other men contributing life stories to this chapter, the journey of self-discovery moves them through the "desert of nothing." Expressions of personal agency are central to this journey, and—as I will show below—familiarity with a gay-centered language is central to expressions of personal agency. But first, I must say more about personal agency.

## Self-Managed Socialization

A striking feature in the life stories I have collected from gay men has been the consistent presence of the first-person active voice. That is, narrators position themselves as narrative agents, not merely as objects, in their stories. They describe personal struggles to take charge of their gay socialization and present the socialization process itself as a self-initiated, self-managed experience, even while they discuss the frustration and pain it causes.

It is tempting to view such claims as a consequence of the life-story genre: that is, stories that describe events in the speaker's own life are likely to position the speaker as the central character. But genre alone is an inadequate explanation for this component of textual design, because speakers can always adapt narratives to their own needs (see Sawin 1999). If the events in these narratives reflect the tensions between social heteronormativity and the personal gay imaginary as they unfold in adolescent lives, then the pervasiveness of first-person reference must be part of this reflection and its presence must be explained in similar terms.

What then are the narrators telling me when they describe gay adolescence as a time of self-managed socialization? First, these references suggest that gay socialization is quite different from the socialization experiences that unfold elsewhere in the life course. The complex of institutional support that enables the transmission of heteronormative conventions and practices between and within generations (some of which are described in Coates 1999) has very little parallel within gay adolescence, even with the expanding numbers of gay community centers, youth outreach programs, and religious support groups that have emerged in recent years. Understandably, then, statements like *I knew I was different but didn't have a word for it* and *I thought I was the only such person in the world* continue to assume an almost trope-like status in gay men's descriptions of their teenage years. Nothing like these statements appears in the ethnographic descriptions of normative language socialization (e.g., Heath 1983; Ochs 1988; Schieffelin 1990; Ward 1971) or in the comments on socialization experiences that these researchers have collected from members of the speech communities under study. The predominant socialization processes in those settings have to do with incorporating the individual into the social group, not with enabling individuals to claim space on its margin. Claiming space on the margin is, however, the predominant theme in gay men's socialization narratives, as the examples reviewed here have shown. Support for such efforts could come from external sources such as guidance from friends, family members, teachers, or other authority figures, but the narratives always describe such support as accidental and unplanned occurrences, as interventions over which the individual has no control. Sam refers to his relationship with a sympathetic agemate as "pure luck"; Jim "do[es]n't know for what reason" a high school teacher started asking him helpful questions about his sexuality. The point is that although external support is always possible in gay socialization, the availability of such support is in no sense reliable. This leaves only one resource to provide accessible guidance to the individual as he struggles to understand male-centered desire and gay-centered identity: the individual himself.

For this reason, I find it imperative to read the pervasive references to personal agency, to narrator-as-actor, in these life-story segments not as indications of "what I really did to learn about gay life" but as after-the-fact realization that "this (self-managed socialization) was the only way, at this point in my life, that I could have learned about gay experience." Such an analysis places the narrative's emphasis on first-person agency squarely within the narrative strategy that Arthur Kleinman (1988: 50) terms "retrospective narratization." This emphasis reflects the narrator's sense of "significance and validity in the creation of life story," not his "fidelity to historical circumstances" (51): In this case, it is the depiction of loneliness and emptiness combined with the discussions of self-managed socialization that gives these narratives their intended significance and validity.

## Retrieving Gay Messages

Also important is the narrators' descriptions of the sources they consulted while conducting their individualized, personalized search for information about gay experience and about themselves: library books, magazines, newspaper columns, motion pictures, television sitcoms, talk shows, Broadway musicals, gay folklore, jokes, supportive responses from friends and strangers. As already discussed, even derogatory homophobic statements become useful resources in this process.

The particular items that narrators include in this inventory are not as important as the range and variety of materials. Perhaps no single source provided sufficient information to answer the narrators' questions, or the narrators were not satisfied with deriving information from only one source. Either way, the narratives suggest that seeking out information about gay experience is an important part of self-managed socialization.

But seeking out information assumes that the individual knows where to find appropriate sources or is willing to search sufficiently broadly until he stumbles across the right locations. Events in the narratives cited here position both of these practices within the gay socialization process, and they also imply that, once the searching begins, locating gay-relevant materials is not a difficult task. Indeed, as Alexander Doty (1993) argues, any text in today's mass culture contains (at least potentially) a queer message and hence contains information that could be relevant to gay socialization.

At the same time, Doty continues, "unless the text is *about* queers, it seems to me that the queerness of most mass culture texts is less an essential waiting-to-be-discovered property than the result of acts of production and reception" (1993: ix). It would be valuable to know more about the specifics of the reception process described in these narratives. It seems easy enough (as Jim explained) to scan the index of the *Encyclopaedia Britannica* "as far as sexual goes: penis, phallus, every single adjective, synonym of that." But Sam's rereading of the gay character on *Brothers* and Wallace's "queering" of *West Side Story* speak to a more complex interpretation of textual material. What are the clues, the cues, the signals, the signifiers that call forth gay-centered interpretation of such texts?

Answering these questions is similar to answering questions about the mechanics of *gaydar*, the recognition strategy which Michael Musto describes as "the art of spotting sisters [i.e., other gay men], no matter how concealed, invisible or pretending to be straight they are" (1993: 120). Gay men who freely discuss using gaydar are not necessarily explicit regarding the criteria that guide their evaluation of "suspect gay" status; and, when described, such criteria differ greatly from one gay man to the next (see discussion in Leap 1996: 49–66). It is likely that the interpretive processes relevant to queer reading in such encounters are closely linked to the processes that underlie location and retrieval of information about gay-centered culture and language during gay adolescence. If so, then interpretive skills that are central to self-managed socialization during gay adolescence continue to be valuable resources throughout the gender career.

## Homophobia, Rehearsal, and the Language of the Closet

Particularly important in regard to the movement from adolescence to adulthood are the ways in which a retrieval of gay-centered messages from written and other media texts provides *rehearsal* for encounters with gay-centered messages in social settings. Learning how to recognize and make sense out of gay-centered messages in seemingly heteronormative texts is one part of rehearsal. And so is building a personal repertoire of gay commentary by memorizing words, phrases, and sentences from novels, motion pictures, or plays with explicitly gay themes. *Boys in the Band* (Crowley 1968) and *Consenting Adult* (Hobson 1975) remain two popular sources for this purpose. Equally helpful, reported gay men in their 20s, were the dialogues from television soap operas; for gay men in their 40s, additional sources included memorable lines from the films of Bette Davis and the numerous anecdotes attributed to the private life of Tallulah Bankhead.

These sets of information gave gay adolescents opportunities to anticipate the linguistic skills (both of reception and of production—see the previous comment by Doty) that they would need in conversation with another gay, gay-friendly, or potentially gay-friendly individual. On some occasions, as Sam's discovery of "someone like me" suggests, being prepared for those conversations helped both parties secure a long-lasting friendship or led to other successful outcomes. Unfortunately, modeling real-life exchanges around media-derived images of gay communication and its social dynamics can also yield misleading expectations about a conversation and its effects. Often, the resulting (mis)communication leads to unpleasant consequences, as the following story (from Rhoads 1994) suggests.

Andrew (one of Rhoads's key informants) had sex with his best friend in junior high school, and he "found the experience eye-opening":

> "I thought, 'Oh wow, maybe this isn't so wrong.'" ... He learned all his life that having sex with a man was wrong, but his experience seemed to tell him something different. "I thought it seemed like he enjoyed it and I enjoyed it. So it was something we shouldn't do? I was like, 'Oh this is great. There is someone else who feels like I do.'"
>
> The next day, Andrew's friend (the one with whom he had sex) spread it all over school that Andrew had sexually assaulted him. "It was horrendous; I mean it was my first real encounter with homophobia." (1994: 74)

There was little Andrew could do to prevent his "friend" from spreading stories about sexual assault. To deny the charge would be a predictable reaction and would only draw greater attention to the event. Besides, to whom would Andrew voice his denial? Such events require more subtle responses on the part of the gay-accused: silence, secrecy, abjection, erasure, and disguise—each of which gains representation through a language of restraint, a language that parallels the restricted discussions of gay life and gay opportunity in public heteronormative discourse and that transfers those restrictions into the personal linguistic inventory.[8]

Silence, secrecy, disguise, privacy, and restraint are, of course, features that define the experience of "the closet" in Western tradition. Understandably, many gay theorists view "the closet" as a primary obstacle to gay self-determination and consider "coming out of the closet" as the culmination of the move from individuation to disclosure (Davies 1992: 76ff.), "the most momentous act in the life of any lesbian or gay person" (Plummer 1995: 82), and the primary rite of passage in contemporary gay experience (Rhoads 1994: 7–8). The life stories that I have collected contain ample documentation of the damage created when the closet becomes the long-term anchor for a person's gay identity. At the same time, these stories also point out that the closet is not a site of gay denial. Certainly, being "in the closet" discourages explicit expressions of gay identity, but gay socialization is still possible within that enclosure—especially if the socialization process unfolds in personalized, self-managed terms. Closets have keyholes, closet doors have cracks, and closet walls are thin.

So although it is often appropriate to theorize the closet in terms of regulation and repression, it is also possible to theorize this construction as a simpler and less threatening form of gay experience, a subdued alternative to the more explicit demands of a public gay voice. The term *voice* is important here. If the closet is part of gay culture, then the closet, too, has a language—a language that privileges silence over speech, restraint over expression, concealment over cooperation, safety over risk (see also Liang 1999). And for some gay adolescents, learning the language of the closet is as integral to gay self-managed socialization as are the gay messages in TV sitcoms and rock and roll lyrics, the negotiations of gay disclosure between good friends, or the other strategies that guide their journey through the "desert of nothing."

## LANGUAGE AND SURVIVAL

As my analysis of "the closet" suggests, interpreting gay adolescence in terms of self-managed socialization offers a somewhat different perspective on gay adolescence from that usually presented in the scholarly literature. Certainly, as Rhoads argues: "Adolescence is a stressful time for everyone.... For gay and bisexual men, this period of life is even more traumatic because in addition to the typical stressors such as leaving home, dating and thoughts of career, they must also come to terms with their same-sex attractions" (1994: 67). Yet the narratives that Rhoads discusses, like the life stories in Gilbert Herdt and Andrew Boxer's (1993) study of the Horizon Project in Chicago, the life stories in Jim Sears's *Growing Up Gay in the South* (1991), or the life-story segments I have discussed here, are not just narratives of trauma and frustration. They are also survivors' stories. They describe the narrators' efforts—to use Plummer's (1995: 50) formulation—to "move from secrecy, suffering and an often felt sense of victimization toward a major change: therapy, survival, recovery or politics." These efforts may still be continuing at the time of narration, the move may be ongoing, but the narrative stance is consistently the same in these collections: Narrators may find homosexuality to be disruptive, painful, and isolating, yet they search out ways to define gay identity to their own satisfaction and to articulate it successfully with other components of adolescent experience.

Worth interrogating, then, are the reasons why other gay teenagers are not successful in such efforts at self-managed socialization and why still others do not undertake such efforts in the first place. We can move this interrogation forward by recognizing that gay adolescents are not, in any categorical sense, neurotic, maladjusted, and self-destructive, but they are likely to become so when their search for information about gay experience and their other efforts toward self-discovery are devalued, thwarted, and ridiculed at every turn. We can ask, accordingly, whether our own institutions and communities provide teenagers with the opportunities, incentives, and resources on which self-managed socialization depends; we can ask what support each of us is providing to that end.

## Notes

This chapter builds on a discussion of gay English and language socialization that first appeared in Leap (1994) and that I develop further in Leap (1996). I presented versions of this work as an invited lecture at Pennsylvania State University's Lesbian/Gay Studies Series (February 1995) and in a session on lesbian and gay discourse held at the annual meeting of the American Association for Applied Linguistics (Long Beach, CA, March 1995). Mary Bucholtz gave a close reading to the chapter in preliminary draft, and her guidance helped immeasurably in the development of the final argument. My thanks, as well, to Liz Sheehan (American University), Tony D'Augeli (Penn State), Rick Arons (St. John's), and the other editors of this volume for their useful contributions to this project.

1. By the term *gay teenagers* I mean male teenagers who are in the process of discovering male-centered desire and constructing personal identity in response to those discoveries.

2. These assumptions are warranted by a number of works of scholarship: Ken Plummer (1995: 91–95) traces the factors that prompted the emergence of gay culture in recent years; Gilbert Herdt and Andrew Boxer (1992: 3–13, 1993: 1–24) explore the ways in which an authentically gay culture provides a moral critique of contemporary U.S. society; Esther Newton (1993) employs historical perspectives to show how gay culture offers complex if often subtle sites for resistance to heteronormativity; Plummer assigns stories and storytelling a prominent place in gay culture; Birch Moonwomon's (1995) distinction between linguistic and societal discourses in such stories argues powerfully in favor of the existence of lesbian and gay language(s), as well as lesbian and gay texts; Leap (1995: xi–xvii, 1996: 1–11 and introduction) offers additional arguments to that end.

3. Recent estimates suggest that gay teenagers are twice as likely to attempt suicide as are their heterosexual agemates and that as many as three out of every five gay teenagers give serious thought to suicide at least once during their adolescent years (Gibson 1989; Rhoads 1994: 67–68).

4. The remainder of this chapter focuses on gay men's experiences with linguistic and cultural socialization during adolescence. How closely these experiences parallel the socialization experiences of lesbians remains to be determined.

5. The statements below come from a collection of quotations assembled for Leap (1996) and are reproduced here with permission of the University of Minnesota Press. Statements without a bibliographic citation come from interviews I conducted between 1989 and 1992 with self-identified European American and African American gay men aged 18 to 25 and 40 to 55. My lead-in questions for this discussion established my interest in learning about the respondent's experience with gay adolescence. I intentionally kept the focus of discussion open-ended and unstructured, so that I could hear how the respondent himself would talk about his "discovery" of a "gay self."

6. I recognize the limitations of using life-story narratives as a database for studies of gay socialization. Life stories are not factual documents but a form of fiction—that is, they are constructed, crafted texts; they emerge out of the respondent's subjective (re)framing and (re)claiming of a life experience; and, as retrospective narratives (Kleinman 1988: 50–51), their vision of "the past" is likely to be influenced by the politics of the present. But as I see it, the subjective, reflexive nature of these texts makes them especially valuable to the study of gay life as lived experience. In fact, just as telling these stories allows respondents to experiment with presentations of memory, listening to them allows the audience (in this case, the researcher) to coparticipate in those experiments, and by extension to coparticipate in the events that the respondents' narratives now reclaim. Ellen Lewin (1993, especially pages 9–11) reached similar conclusions when she examined the life-story narratives of lesbian mothers. So did Faye Ginsberg (1989, especially pages 141–145) when she studied abortion-rights controversies in Fargo, North Dakota. A particularly vivid example of researcher coparticipation in retold events is found in Kathleen Wood's (1999) discussion of a lesbian coming-out story told in American Sign Language.

7. The wording here retains Kristeva's pronominal usage.

8. I want the term *language* in the phrase *language of restraint* to be read literally. Silence, abjection, and so on are not arbitrary components of conversational or narrative structure; their presence conforms to linguistic rules derived from the *grammar* (that is, the knowledge of language) that the gay adolescent brings into the speech event and from the *discourse practices* that actualize this knowledge within specific text-making settings. By referring here to a language of restraint, I position the textual occurrences of silence, abjection, and so on as products of a particular aggregation of linguistic knowledge and linguistic practices, some of which I have described in Leap (1996: 24–48). Gay teenagers build familiarity with this aggregation of knowledge and practice, this "language," as a part of their experiences with gay socialization and their everyday encounters with heteronormative living; what happened to Andrew in the example cited here is telling in both regards.

## References

Barrett, Rusty. 1995. Supermodels of the world unite: Political economy and the language of performance among African-American drag queens. In William Leap (ed.), *Beyond the lavender lexicon*. Newark: Gordon & Breach, 207–26.

Barrett, Rusty. 1999. Indexing polyphonous identity in the speech of African American drag queens. In Mary Bucholtz, A. C. Liang, and Laurel Sutton (eds.),

*Reinventing identities: The gendered self in discourse.* New York: Oxford University Press, 313–31.

Brown, Joe, & Kara Swisher. 1994. Backstage: The one who fit the bill. *Washington Post* (August 6): C2.

Coates, Jennifer. 1999. Changing Femininities: The talk of teenage girls. In Mary Bucholtz, A. C. Liang, and Laurel Sutton (eds.), *Reinventing identities: The gendered self in discourse.* New York: Oxford University Press, 123–44.

Crowley, Matt. 1968. *Boys in the band.* New York: Samuel French.

Davies, Peter. 1992. The role of disclosure in coming out among gay men. In Ken Plummer (ed.), *Modern homosexualities.* New York: Routledge, 75–85.

Doty, Alexander. 1993. *Making things perfectly queer: Interpreting mass culture.* Minneapolis: University of Minnesota Press.

Gibson, Paul. 1989. Gay male and lesbian youth suicide. In M. R. Feinlieb (ed.), *Report of the Secretary's Task Force on Youth Suicide.* Washington, DC: U.S. Department of Health and Human Services, 110–42.

Ginsberg, Faye. 1989. *Contested lives: The abortion debate in an American community.* Berkeley: University of California Press.

Goffman, Erving. 1963. *Stigma: Notes on the management of spoiled identity.* Englewood Cliffs, NJ: Prentice Hall.

Goodwin, Joseph P. 1989. *More man than you'll ever be: Gay folklore and acculturation in Middle America.* Bloomington: Indiana University Press.

Heath, Shirley Brice. 1983. *Ways with words: Language, life, and work in communities and classrooms.* Cambridge: Cambridge University Press.

Herdt, Gilbert, & Andrew Boxer. 1992. Introduction: Culture, history and life course of gay men. In Gilbert Herdt (ed.), *Gay culture in America: Essays from the field.* Boston: Beacon Press, 1–27.

Herdt, Gilbert, & Andrew Boxer. 1993. *Children of horizons: How gay and lesbian teens are leading a new way out of the closet.* Boston: Beacon Press.

Hobson, Laura Z. 1975. *Consenting adult.* Garden City, NY: Doubleday.

Kleinman, Arthur. 1988. *The illness narratives: Suffering, healing and the human condition.* New York: Basic Books.

Kristeva, Julia. 1982. Approaching abjection. In Kristeva, *Powers of horror.* New York: Columbia University Press, 1–31.

Leap, William L. 1993. Gay men's English: Cooperative discourse in a language of risk. *New York Folklore* 19(1–2): 45–70.

Leap, William L. 1994. Learning gay culture in a "desert of nothing": Language as a resource in gender socialization [Special issue]. *High School Journal* 77(1–2): 122–31. "The Gay Teenager."

Leap, William L. 1995. Introduction. In William Leap (ed.), *Beyond the lavender lexicon.* Newark: Gordon & Breach, vii–xxix.

Leap, William L. 1996. *Word's out: Gay English in America.* Minneapolis: University of Minnesota Press.

Lewin, Ellen. 1993. *Lesbian mothers: Accounts of gender in American culture.* Ithaca: Cornell University Press.

Liang, A. C. 1999. Conversationally implicating lesbian and gay identity. In Mary Bucholtz, A. C. Liang, and Laurel Sutton (eds.), *Reinventing identities: The gendered self in discourse.* New York: Oxford University Press, 293–310.

Moonwomon, Birch. 1995. Lesbian discourse, lesbian knowledge. In William Leap (ed.), *Beyond the lavender lexicon.* Newark: Gordon & Breach, 45–64.

Moonwomon, Birch. 1996. Lesbian conversation as a site for ideological identity construction. Paper presented at the annual meeting of the American Association for Applied Linguistics, Chicago.

Morgan, Ruth, & Kathleen Wood. 1995. Lesbians in the living room: Collusion, co-construction and co-narration in conversation. In William Leap (ed.), *Beyond the lavender lexicon.* Newark: Gordon & Breach, 235–48.

Musto, Michael. 1993. Gaydar: Using that intuitive sixth sense. *Out* 12: 120–24.

Newton, Esther. 1993. *Cherry Grove, Fire Island.* Boston: Beacon Press.

Ochs, Elinor. 1988. *Culture and language development: Language acquisition and language socialization in a Samoan village.* Cambridge: Cambridge University Press.

Plummer, Ken. 1995. *Telling sexual stories: Power, change and social worlds.* London: Routledge.

Reinhardt, Robert C. 1986. *A history of shadows.* Boston: Alyson Press.

Rhoads, Richard. 1994. *Coming out in college: The struggle for a queer identity.* Westport, CT: Bergin & Garvey.

Rich, Adrienne. 1980. Compulsory heterosexuality and lesbian existence. *Signs* 5: 631–60.

Sawin, Patricia E. 1999. Gender, context, and the narrative construction of identity: Rethinking models of "women's narrative". In Mary Bucholtz, A. C. Liang, and Laurel Sutton (eds.), *Reinventing identities: The gendered self in discourse.* New York: Oxford University Press, 241–58.

Schieffelin, Bambi. 1990. *The give and take of everyday life: Language socialization of Kaluli children.* Cambridge: Cambridge University Press.

Sears, Jim. 1991. *Growing up gay in the South: Race, gender and journeys of the spirit.* Binghamton, NY: Harrington Park Press.

Spivak, Gayatri Chakravorty. 1988. Can the subaltern speak? In Cary Nelson & Lawrence Grossberg (eds.), *Marxism and the interpretation of culture.* Basingstoke, England: Macmillan, 271–313.

Ward, Martha. 1971. *Them children: A study in language learning.* New York: Holt, Rinehart & Winston.

Whittle, Stephen. 1994. Consuming differences: The collaboration of the gay body with the cultural state. In Stephen Whittle (ed.), *The margins of the city: Gay men's urban lives.* Brookfield, VT: Ashgate, 27–41.

Wood, Kathleen M. 1999. Coherent identities amid heterosexist ideologies: Deaf and hearing lesbian coming-out stories In Mary Bucholtz, A. C. Liang, and Laurel Sutton (eds.), *Reinventing identities: The gendered self in discourse.* New York: Oxford University Press, 46–63.

## Critical Thinking and Application

- Why is the socialization of gay and lesbian youth different from other forms of socialization, with and without language?
- What is "the closet" and how does this play a central role in the socialization of gay youth?
- Gay teenagers are clearly at odds with the heteronormative society in which they find themselves. What other groups may also be oppositional to the larger society? What linguistic actions might they undertake to create a positive identity for themselves? Is this process similar to or different from what Leap describes in this chapter?

## Vocabulary

| | |
|---|---|
| argot | morphemic |
| heteronormativity | semiotics |
| lexical | subaltern |

## Suggested Further Reading

Bucholtz, Mary, A. C. Liang, and Laurel A. Sutton, eds. 1999. *Reinventing Identities: The Gendered Self in Discourse*. New York: Oxford University Press.

Cameron, Deborah. 2006. *The Language and Sexuality Reader*. London and New York: Routledge.

Leap, William. 1995. *Beyond the Lavender Lexicon: Authenticity, Imagination, and Appropriation in Gay and Lesbian Language*. Amsterdam: Gordon & Breach.

Leap, William. 1996. *Word's Out: Gay Men's English*. Minneapolis: University of Minnesota Press.

Leap, William. 1999. *Public Sex/Gay Space*. New York: Columbia University Press.

Leap, William, and Tom Boellstorff, eds. 2004. *Speaking in Queer Tongues: Globalization and Gay Language*. Urbana: University of Illinois Press.

Lewin, Ellen, and William Leap. 1996. *Out in the Field: Reflections of Lesbian and Gay Anthropologists*. Urbana: University of Illinois Press.

Lewin, Ellen, and William Leap, eds. 2009. *Out in Public: Reinventing Lesbian/Gay Anthropology in a Globalizing World*. Chichester and Malden, MA: Wiley-Blackwell.

Livia, Anna, and Kira Hall, eds. 1997. *Queerly Phrased: Language, Gender, and Sexuality*. New York: Oxford University Press.

Morrish, Liz, and Helen Sauntson. 2007. *Language and Sexual Identity*. Basingstoke: Palgrave Macmillan.

## Generation

# CHAPTER 39

# *Like* and Language Ideology: Disentangling Fact from Fiction

*Alexandra D'Arcy*

(2007)

*What are the most annoying linguistic habits of young people? Ask their elders; they'll surely have an answer. And since the 1990s, one answer American English speakers would probably give is that kids use "like" every time they open their mouths. Not only that, but they have all kinds of random thoughts that they can't express articulately.*

*The use of* like *has now been studied by linguists from a number of angles. Most point out that it is regular, like most other linguistic practices, but it has several different uses and meanings, so it appears with great regularity.*

*Using data from a range of sources, D'Arcy examines the ages and locations where English speakers use various forms of* like *in order to ask how long it has existed, where it is derived from, and how it has spread through different age groups. One technique used, "apparent-time study," takes a snapshot of a specific linguistic form at a single moment in time and looks at how it is used by people of different ages. It assumes that a form used predominantly by younger people and decreasing over the age of the speakers is a "change in progress," something that is in the process of increasing in use. Given that language is changing at all times, it is powerful to be able to capture a change as it is occurring.*

### Reading Questions

- Why does D'Arcy say that criticism of new forms of language, for example, as "sloppy, lazy, ignorant, or vulgar," is social rather than linguistic?
- What are the "facts" and what are the "fictions" with regard to *like*?
- What are the four vernacular uses of *like* in casual conversation, aside from its more traditional meanings?
- How does D'Arcy explain that *like* is used as a discourse particle by speakers in their eighties and nineties in the United Kingdom and by speakers in their seventies (one version) or fifties (other version) in North America? What does this say about the *countercultural* nature or American genesis of the nonquotative forms of *like*?
- Who are Valley Girls? How has this group become associated with the frequent use of *be + like*? What is the relationship between Valley Girls, *like*, and the impression that women use *like* more than men do?

---

Throughout the inhabited world, in all times and under every circumstance, the myths of man have flourished.

[Campbell 1949, 13]

Campbell was referring to traditional mythology, yet there is a link here to **language ideology**, since it is likely that myths about language have flourished for as long as language has functioned in social contexts, that is, from the beginning. Modern examples include the belief that right-handed people are more proficient linguistically than left-handed people, that double negatives are illogical, that women talk too much, that King Arthur spoke English, and most notably, that the media/America/teenagers are ruining the language. This final grouping belongs to the overarching and timeless gestalt that the language is degenerating.[1] Ideologies such

Alexandra D'Arcy, *Like* and Language Ideology: Disentangling Fact from Fiction. *American Speech* 82 (4), 2007: 386–419.

as these are widespread, virtually intractable, and so deeply ingrained as part of one's cultural heritage that they often cease to be recognized for the myths they are (see also Bauer and Trudgill 1998, xvi). As a result, they tend to be accepted, generally unquestioningly, as fact.

From a linguistic perspective, the veracity of individual language myths is often dubious if not fictional. But like traditional myths, language myths reflect the society that produces them, and for this reason they offer important insights into cultural attitudes and mores. For example, ongoing language change is often met with derision. This may reflect a general unease with change in any form, but when considering language, it typically results in the characterization of new forms as sloppy, lazy, ignorant, or vulgar. These are, of course, social rather than linguistic notions, but the recurrence of such comments underlies the poignancy of the sentiment. A particularly interesting aspect of the social context of language change is that from a **diachronic** perspective, the cumulative effects of change are unexceptional, yet in **synchronic** time individual changes are synonymous with degradation. As Ogden Nash writes in "Laments for a Dying Language" (cited in Aitchison 1981, 17): "Farewell, farewell to my beloved language / Once English, now a vile orangutanguage."

Inevitably, language change is always most advanced among younger speakers. A peak in the progress of change among adolescent cohorts is a recurrent finding of **apparent-time studies** (Labov 2001, 454; Chambers 2003, 223; Tagliamonte and D'Arcy 2007b) and has come to be seen as a criterial feature of ongoing change (Labov 2001, 455). Because this peak typically occurs among speakers between the ages of 13 and 17, it is not a coincidence that children and adolescents are singled out as the primary offenders in the linguistic arena. The proposed solution to the "language misuse" of younger generations is often more rigid teaching standards, a suggestion that undoubtedly draws on another folk belief: that children learn the fundamentals of the spoken language at school. As James Milroy (1998, 63) points out, since children have already acquired the basic spoken grammar by the time they arrive at school, complaints about the way young people speak are not about language ABILITY; they are about language VARIETY. And as just discussed, it is adolescent varieties that are at the forefront of ongoing linguistic changes.

One feature of contemporary vernaculars currently subject to widespread condemnation is *like* when used in the ways highlighted in (1).

1. a. He WAS LIKE, "Yeah so I'm going out with Clara now." And then she sounded really disappointed; she WAS LIKE, "Yeah she's really smart." So then he WAS LIKE, "I kind of feel bad, but then again, I don't." [N/f/18][2]
   b. He looks like he's LIKE twelve or LIKE eight. [2/f/16]
   c. LIKE if you're doing your undergrad, no big deal. LIKE it's not that bad, but LIKE I'm in a professional school. I want to be a professional. [N/f/26]
   d. Like the first hour I was LIKE totally fine, like I wasn't LIKE drunk. [3/m/18]

As with all forms involved in change, *like* is associated in popular culture with adolescents and young adults, and perceptual investigations by Dailey-O'Cain (2000) and Buchstaller (2006b) have documented the strength of this belief. Older speakers seldom claim to use *like* themselves, characterizing its occurrence in their vernaculars as rare or nonexistent, while younger age groups stipulate to its regularity in their own speech (Dailey-O'Cain 2000, 69).

There is an intricate and multifaceted lore surrounding *like*. The belief that younger speakers alone are responsible for the propagation of *like* constitutes just one part of the complex. This conglomerate of beliefs is the focus of the current analysis. As with other language ideologies, those surrounding *like* have been cultivated by popular consensus, but such consensus is not necessarily informed by **empirical** truth(s). Thus, in examining beliefs about *like*, my intention is to disentangle fact from fiction. Many of the commonly held beliefs about *like* will be shown to be false, while others are simply too broad to reflect any coherent reality. In such cases, certain aspects of the myth may bear merit, though as encapsulated the belief itself remains unmotivated. However, in examining individual beliefs about *like*, it becomes clear that each contributes to the perpetuation of others in important and nontrivial ways to create a unified whole.

## The *Like* Language Myth

Entwined with the multitude of beliefs about *like* are a number of subjective reactions to the use of this form. These include the feeling that it is an exasperating tic and that it makes those who use it seem less educated, intelligent, or interesting (Dailey-O'Cain 2000, 73; Buchstaller 2006b, 371). Indeed, general attitudes toward *like* are overtly negative (De Quincey 1840–41, 224; Jespersen 1942, 417; Schourup 1983, 29; Dailey-O'Cain 2000, 69–70). It is not the aim of this article to address or to change such attitudes, though such consequences may inadvertently result from the discussion. Rather, the focus is centered on those aspects of the myth that can be dispelled objectively, drawing on empirical data. Thus, the beliefs to be examined are those listed here, for which there is evidence of the ways in which the folklore either reflects or obscures actual usage:

*Like* is just *like*, that is, there is one *like* that is recycled repeatedly.
*Like* is meaningless; it simply signals a lack of articulacy.
Women say *like* more than men do.
*Like* began with the Valley Girls.
Only young people, and adolescents in particular, use *like*.
*Like* can be used anywhere in a sentence.

## METHOD

The primary body of evidence brought to bear here on the issues encompassed by the *like* myth consists of **corpus data** from a large archive of spoken contemporary English. The materials were collected in Toronto, Canada, in the period between 2002 and 2004, using a combination of quota-based random sampling and social networking.[3] The full Toronto English Archive comprises over 350 hours of casual conversational data with speakers between the ages of 9 and 92, all of whom were born and raised in the city; the sample used for the current analysis is outlined in Table 39.1.

With the largest metropolitan population in Canada, Toronto presents an ideal context in which to examine urban vernacular usage. Toronto is also the fourth largest city in English-speaking North America; only New York, Los Angeles, and Chicago have larger populations (WorldAtlas.com 2006). Although General Canadian English differs from General American English in a number of respects, the uses of *like* exemplified in (1) are shared by both varieties. Consequently, Toronto English is taken here to represent North American English more generally, an assumption that is further supported by two factors. First, models of spatial diffusion (Trudgill 1974; Bailey et al. 1994; Labov 2003) highlight the crucial role of cities in the spread of linguistic features. Typically, new forms spread hierarchically from an originating center. Although some changes are seemingly arrested by national boundaries (e.g., the Northern Cities Shift), others are not (e.g., uvular (r) in Europe; Trudgill 1974). Second, the vast body of research investigating **quotative** *be like* (as in 1a) has revealed regular trends across American and Canadian Englishes, showing that this form is consistently constrained in the U.S. and Canada (e.g., Blyth, Recktenwald, and Wang 1990; Singler 2001; Cukor-Avila 2002; Tagliamonte and D'Arcy 2004, 2007a). Similarly, there is striking consistency in observations about non-quotative uses of *like* (as in 1b–1d) regardless of locale (e.g., Schourup 1983; Underhill 1988; Meehan 1991; Romaine and Lange 1991; Dailey-O'Cain 2000; D'Arcy 2005, 2006). From this we can extrapolate that regardless of issues of origin, *like* is a feature of North American English more generally....

**Table 39.1** The Sample

| Age | Male | Female | Total |
|---|---|---|---|
| 10–12 | 5 | 5 | 10 |
| 15–16 | 4 | 4 | 8 |
| 17–19 | 5 | 5 | 10 |
| 20–24 | 5 | 5 | 10 |
| 25–29 | 5 | 5 | 10 |
| 30–39 | 5 | 5 | 10 |
| 40–49 | 4 | 4 | 8 |
| 50–59 | 4 | 4 | 8 |
| 60–69 | 4 | 4 | 8 |
| 70–79 | 3 | 4 | 7 |
| 80+ | 4 | 4 | 8 |
| Total | 48 | 49 | 97 |

## DISENTANGLING FACT FROM FICTION

In discussing the beliefs surrounding *like*, it is important to bear in mind that certain aspects of the myth are more general than others, which may be somewhat restricted regionally. For example, while the association of *like* with younger speakers seems to hold across the English-speaking world, there is evidence that its associations with both women and the United States are variably salient. In North America, the frequency of *like* in the speech of women and the focus on California are overtly acknowledged as key elements in the received wisdom surrounding vernacular uses (e.g., Dailey-O'Cain 2000). In the New Zealand context, the pivotal role of women remains fundamental, but the Valley Girl link is more tenuous, especially among older speakers who may not be familiar with this particular social grouping. This is not to say that the perception of *like* as either an American or more specifically a Californian feature does not persevere. Indeed, anecdotal evidence clearly associates *like* with the United States. In the United Kingdom, Buchstaller (2006b, 369–70) investigated attitudes toward quotative *be like* and found that although a substantial proportion of speakers associate the form with women (34%; $N = 101$), the majority (59%) are in fact noncommittal to any gender pattern. Moreover, only 12% of responses associated *be like* with America, compared to the 74% response rate for "no idea" for its regional affiliation ($N = 90$; Buchstaller 2006b, 374). Thus, the details of the *like* language myth clearly differ somewhat across varieties of English. That such is the case serves as an important reminder of the culturally dependent nature of myths in general. In what follows, however, I attempt to address each part of the myth apart from cultural context, focusing on the content of the belief itself rather than the social milieu that may have led to its formation in the communal consciousness.

***Like* Is Just *Like* (and It Is Meaningless)** In the media there is a tendency to talk of *like* as a single, monolithic entity, and metalinguistic commentary typically involves performative speech in which most, if not all, the uses demonstrated in (1) are modeled. There are, however, four uses that draw attention in vernacular speech. Each is functionally distinct and can be distinguished from the "grammatical" and largely unremarkable uses in (3).[4]

3. a. VERB: I don't really LIKE her that much. [2/f/12]
   b. NOUN: He grew up with the LIKES...of all great fighters. [N/m/60]
   c. ADVERB: It looks LIKE a snail; it just is a snail. [I/f/19]
   d. CONJUNCTION: It felt LIKE everything had dropped away. [I/m/40]
   e. SUFFIX: I went, "[mumbling]" or something like stroke-LIKE. [N/f/31]

To distinguish between the forms in (3), which have long been features of both written and spoken English (Romaine and Lange 1991, 244), and the forms in (1), which are largely restricted to informal discourse, I will refer to the latter as VERNACULAR USES/FUNCTIONS OF *LIKE*. This signals quite clearly the existence of more than one *like* in discourse. The functions included in the vernacular category are quotative complementizer (as in 4), approximative adverb (as in 5), **discourse marker** (as in 6), and **discourse particle** (as in 7).[5]

4. QUOTATIVE COMPLEMENTIZER
   a. And we WERE LIKE, "Yeah but you get to sleep like three-quarters of your life." He WAS LIKE, "That's an upside." [2/f/12]
   b. I WAS LIKE, "Where do you find these people?" [1/f/19]
5. APPROXIMATIVE ADVERB
   a. It could have taken you all day to go LIKE thirty miles. [N/f/76]
   b. You-know, it was LIKE a hundred and four [degrees], but it lasted for about two weeks. [N/m/84]
6. DISCOURSE MARKER
   a. Nobody said a word. LIKE my first experience with death was this Italian family. [N/f/82]
   b. I love Carrie. LIKE Carrie's like a little like out-of-it but LIKE she's the funniest. LIKE she's a space-cadet. [3/f/18]
7. DISCOURSE PARTICLE
   a. Well you just cut out LIKE a girl figure and a boy figure and then you'd cut out LIKE a dress or a skirt or a coat, and like you'd color it. [N/f/75]
   b. And they had LIKE scraped her. [I/m/35]
   c. She's LIKE dumb or something. Like I love her but she's LIKE dumb. [3/f/18]

As a quotative, *like* occurs with the dummy form *be* to support inflection and to satisfy the requirement that the clause have a lexical verb (see Romaine and Lange 1991, 261–62). This **collocation** performs the specialized role of introducing **reported speech**, thought, and nonlexicalized sounds, among a range of other content (i.e., CONSTRUCTED DIALOGUE; Tannen 1986, 315). Since Butters's (1982) editor's note in *American Speech*, quotative *be like* has received vast attention in the sociolinguistic literature (e.g., Schourup 1983; Blyth, Recktenwald, and Wang 1990; Meehan 1991; Romaine and Lange 1991; Ferrara and Bell 1995; Tagliamonte and Hudson 1999; Singler 2001; Cukor-Avila 2002; Buchstaller 2004, 2006a; D'Arcy 2004; Tagliamonte and D'Arcy 2004, 2007a); there is little more to add here. I will simply reiterate what has been said elsewhere: *be like* is an innovation, representing ongoing change.[6]

Use of the quotative is constrained by both language-internal (e.g., person, tense, and temporal reference, content of the quote) and language-external (e.g., gender, age) factors. The relevance of the linguistic factors is twofold: one, the operation of grammatical constraints reveals systematicity; and two, such constraints highlight the unique function of *be like*, not only within the quotative paradigm but vis-à-vis other vernacular uses of *like* which do not share these same conditions on use. The relevance of the social factors will be broached later in the discussion. Finally, the quotative is referentially contentful, functioning as a synonym for a range of verbs within the quotative repertoire, such as *say, think, ask*, and the like. This last point is demonstrated in (8), which restates the examples from (4) using more traditional verbs of quotation in place of *be like*.

8. a. And we SAID, "Yeah but you get to sleep like three-quarters of your life." He SAID, "That's an upside."
   b. I THOUGHT, "Where do you find these people?"

The second vernacular use of *like* denotes concise propositional content as well. It is used to signal approximation, and it is an adverb (D'Arcy 2006). Thus (5b), repeated here as (9a), in which *like* and *about* alternate, can be paraphrased straightforwardly with *about* alone as in (9b), or simply with *like*, as in (9c), without affecting the meaning.

9. a. You-know, it was LIKE a hundred and four [degrees] but it lasted for ABOUT two weeks. [N/m/84]
   b. You-know, it was ABOUT a hundred and four [degrees] but it lasted for ABOUT two weeks.
   c. You-know, it was LIKE a hundred and four [degrees] but it lasted for LIKE two weeks.

The synonymy illustrated in (9) has been noted since the earliest work on vernacular uses of *like*. Schourup (1983, 30) notes that before numerical expressions, "*approximately* or *about* or *around* can be substituted for *like*...without noticeably altering their meaning or acceptability," and Underhill (1988, 234) excludes *like* a priori as an approximative when it precedes quantified phrases. That *like* should convey such meanings falls out from processes of semantic change, since it has long conveyed approximative content in English (Meehan 1991; Romaine and Lange 1991), yet it is rarely seen as grounds for distinguishing a distinct function in the folk linguistic lore surrounding *like*. It is interesting to note, for example, that Newman (1974, 15) illustrates "meaningless speech" with the phrase *like six feet tall* (cited in Schourup 1983, 29).

The third vernacular function of *like* is the discourse marker. [Discourse markers have a] **pragmatic** role, which is to signal the sequential relationship between units of discourse, whether it be one of exemplification, illustration, explanation, or the like (Fraser 1988, 1990; Brinton 1996). As such, they operate in the textual component, marking discourse and information structure. Consequently, markers are sometimes referred to as "discourse deictics" (Schiffrin 1987) or "discourse connectives" (Blakemore 1987).

The examples in (6) illustrate the use of *like* as a discourse marker, where it brackets elements of talk (e.g., Schiffrin 1987, 31). Although the bracketing is local in that *like* links contiguous utterances, discourse markers may also link noncontiguous stretches of discourse (see Schiffrin 1992). Other markers in English include *so, then,* and *well,* as well as parentheticals such as *I/you know, I guess,* and *I think* (Brinton 1996; Traugott and Dasher 2002). Indeed, these last can often be felicitously substituted for *like* without affecting the **epistemic stance** of the utterance. This is exemplified in (10). A characteristic trait of pragmatic features in general is their lack of lexical meaning (Östman 1982). Nonetheless, markers are not a trivial resource in discourse despite the difficulties inherent in trying to define them in referential terms. Rather, they are "essential to the rhetorical shape of any argument or narrative" (Traugott and Dasher 2002, 154).

10.a. LIKE one of my cats meows so much, 'cause LIKE he's really picky and everything. [3/m/11]

b. I MEAN one of my cats meows so much, 'cause YOU KNOW he's really picky and everything.

The final vernacular function of *like* to be discussed here is the discourse particle, which—in contrast to the marker—occurs within the clause as demonstrated in (7). A number of pragmatic functions have been proposed for this use of *like*, including pausal interjection (Schourup 1983), focus (Underhill 1988), and nonequivalence between form and intention (Schourup 1983; Andersen 1997, 1998, 2001). Unlike quotative *be like*, approximative adverb *like*, and discourse marker *like*, particle *like* cannot be **glossed**. This does not mean, however, that it serves no purpose. Whereas markers function at the textual level, particles operate in the interpersonal realm, aiding cooperative aspects of communication such as checking or expressing understanding. They may also generate a sense of sharing or intimacy between interlocutors (Östman 1982; Schourup 1983, 1999; Schiffrin 1987). Indeed, the discourse saliency of particles is quite high, since interactions in which particles do not occur can be perceived as unnatural, awkward, dogmatic, or even unfriendly (Brinton 1996, 35). Such is also the case with *like*. In a **matched-guise** experiment, Dailey-O'Cain (2000, 73) found that although *like* guises were rated as less intelligent than non-*like* guises, speakers were rated significantly more attractive, cheerful, and friendly when they used *like* as opposed to when they did not. Thus, regardless of subjective attitudes toward *like* more generally (i.e., whether speakers like *like* or not), it serves important and palpable social functions in face-to-face interactions.

In sum, there is clearly more than one *like* in discourse. Even though what is heard consistently is /laɪk/, this unit of sounds is not simply recycled in various frames as an undifferentiated entity. Rather, it is a versatile form, performing multiple—and distinct—vernacular functions. In attending to the belief that *like* is just *like*, we simultaneously address another part of the myth, which is that *like* is a meaningless interjection. Each vernacular form of *like* has a unique function. It therefore follows that each has a unique meaning, whether such meaning is primarily referential or pragmatic. To suggest that *like* is no more than a linguistic crutch, signaling hesitancy and a lack of fluency or articulation (e.g., Siegel 2002, 47; see also citations in Diamond 2000, 2 and Levey 2003, 24), trivializes the complex juxtaposition of functions performed by this **lexeme** in the spoken language (see Levey 2003). In recognizing that numerous functions of *like* are operative in vernacular usage, the myth of meaninglessness is simultaneously demystified.

**Women Say *Like* All the Time** Another widely held belief concerning the vernacular forms of *like* is that men use them less often than women do, an ideology substantiated by Dailey-O'Cain (2000, 68–69). She gave her participants a written questionnaire that included two sample sentences, one demonstrating the particle and one demonstrating the quotative. Asked whether they associate *like* with men or women, the overwhelming majority of the participants, nearly 83% ($N = 40$), responded in favor of women. Given the multiple vernacular functions of *like*, however, this question is not as straightforward as it may seem. There is also the issue of quantification. What counts as "more"?...

I considered the approximative adverb, the marker, and the particle separately, carefully constraining the variable contexts according to syntactic structure (for the detailed methodology, see D'Arcy 2005).... The findings of this proportional comparison are reported in Figure 39.1, where the overall distributions are given for each use of *like* according to gender.[7]

As Figure 39.1 demonstrates, the gender puzzle is finely articulated: the question of men versus women depends on which vernacular form of *like* is at issue. In the case of the quotative, women use *be like* significantly more than their male peers do overall ($N = 6{,}364$; Tagliamonte and D'Arcy 2007a). Concerning the discourse marker, women use this form more frequently than men do as well, and despite the narrow margin in the overall results, this too is significant ($N = 3{,}363$; D'Arcy 2005, 97). The results for the approximative adverb reveal a slight female edge (19% vs. 18%), but these proportional results fail to be selected as significant in a multivariate analysis, where the probabilities for both men and women hover near .50 ($N = 3{,}068$; D'Arcy 2006, 349). Thus, whereas the quotative and the marker are significantly favored by women, gender is not a conditioning factor on the adverb. Both distributionally and in terms of probabilities, men and women are equally likely to use this form.

What of *like* as a particle? The results for this function are divided into three syntactic environments in Figure 39.1: (1) DP, the functional projection that dominates noun phrases ($N = 2{,}213$); (2) vP, the functional projection that is located hierarchically between the tense phrase (which hosts auxiliaries and other functional categories in the verb phrase) and the lexical verb projection ($N = 4{,}389$); and (3) AP, which represents predicate adjective constructions ($N = 3{,}455$).[8] In each of these three contexts, *like* is more frequent among men than it is among women. Strikingly, the proportional differences between the two genders—though narrow—are statistically significant across the board (D'Arcy

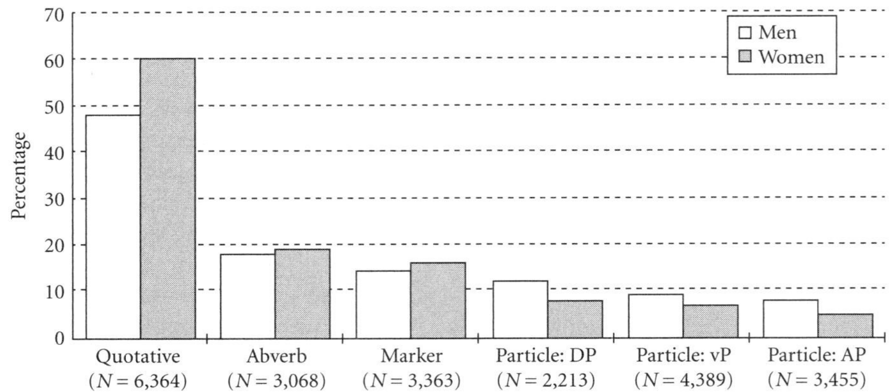


**Figure 39.1** *Overall Distribution of Vernacular Functions of* like *Across Gender Groups*

2005, 155, 160, 196). This is likely due to the consistency of the gender pattern across the age groups that use the particle in each of the relevant contexts....

In short, there are distinct gender patterns associated with the vernacular functions of *like*. The quotative and the marker are correlated with women, the adverb exhibits no gender conditioning at all, and the particle is more frequent in the speech of men. Thus, even though popular belief makes women the "great offenders" in the *like* arena, the winner in this battle of the sexes depends on function. Such a result underscores the discussion in the previous section. If *like* truly were just *like*, we might expect all manifestations to be similarly constrained by gender. Such is not the case.

**Blame It on the Valley Girls and Adolescents** The differences in function and in social conditioning displayed by the various forms of *like* raise the question of where the vernacular uses came from. As discussed above, popular ideology situates the epicenter of *like* usage in California, and the Valley Girls in particular are attributed with launching *like* into the general social consciousness (Blyth, Recktenwald, and Wang 1990, 224; Dailey-O'Cain 2000, 70). It is difficult, however, to divorce the issue of genesis from that of practice, because the truth of one impinges directly on that of the other. It is a common assumption that vernacular uses of *like* are age-graded, frequently marking the speech of adolescents and younger adults only to be outgrown in adulthood. In other words, *like* use is presumed ephemeral and temporally banded, appropriate for a certain stage of life and then shrugged off when its suitability wanes. In addressing the history of the various discourse functions, issues are raised concerning its social embedding, of which age is an important concomitant.

It is generally assumed that the vernacular uses of *like* discussed here have their origins in American English (e.g., Andersen 2001, 216). In popular lore, no distinctions are made beyond "America" and/or "California." Among linguists, however, it is possible to find some degree of differentiation. For example, it has been suggested that the marker and the particle (and most likely the approximative adverb as well) developed among the counterculture groups (i.e., jazz, cool, and Beat) of New York City during the 1950s and 1960s (Andersen 2001, 216, and references therein), while the quotative complementizer emerged some time later in California (see Blyth, Recktenwald, and Wang 1990). This last hypothesis is the most easily defensible on the basis of empirical findings; I will concentrate on the rise of the remaining vernacular uses before subsequently returning to the issue of the quotative.

It is entirely plausible that counterculture groups drew on *like* as a resource in constructing their sociolinguistic identities, and attestations demonstrate that they did use *like* as both a discourse marker and a discourse particle. Chapman (1986, 259) describes these uses as characteristic of "1960s counterculture and bop talk," which he exemplifies with the sentence "Like I was like groovin' like, you know?" and as shown in (11), a quote from Jack Kerouac's monument to the Beat generation, *On the Road*, and in (12), from *Neurotica*, a Beat journal published from 1948 to 1951, both uses were already features of English in the mid- and early 1950s.

11. "Man, wow, there's so many things to do, so many things to write! How to even begin to get it all down and without modified restraints and all hung-up on LIKE literary inhibitions and grammatical fears...." [ellipsis in original; Jack Kerouac, *On the Road* (New York: Viking, 1957), 7]
12. "...LIKE how much can you lay on [i.e., give] me?..." [Lawrence Rivers, *Neurotica*, Autumn 1950, 45 (*OED2*)]

The attribution of the discourse marker and the discourse particle to particular groups in a specific place at a specific time suggests that use of either form among speakers over a certain age in North America (or elsewhere) would be unexpected. For example, if we assume that the apparent time hypothesis (Labov 1966) provides a valid premise on which to model ongoing language change (for discussion, see Bailey 2002 and Sankoff 2004), then in North America, use of both the marker and the particle should be roughly circumscribed to speakers aged 65 years and under. This figure is based on the following calculation: speakers who were 17 years old in 1955 (roughly the purported dawn of the *like* age in the United States) would today be in their mid-sixties. To allow for the transatlantic diffusion of these forms to the United Kingdom, the cutoff should be somewhat younger in British varieties.

As the examples in (14) demonstrate, *like* is used as a discourse marker by speakers well beyond 65 years of age. Moreover, not only is this form used by elderly speakers in the North American context (as in 14a–14d), but it also occurs in the speech of septa-and octogenarians living in isolated, rural villages across the United Kingdom (as in 14e–14h).

14. a. LIKE our daughter was turning sixteen, and the little girl down the street is sixteen, was given a car for her birthday. [N/m/83]
 b. LIKE we were above the tracks but um it was a pretty good company. [N/f/87]
 c. LIKE we always said "karkey" but now I hear them saying "khaki." [N/f/80]
 d. LIKE we were quite close and when I went away, he just closed the doors and went to work for someone else. [N/m/84]
 e. LIKE my neighbors and we got on fine. [AYR/f/78]
 f. LIKE you forget that's on at the finish, don't you? [MPT/m/78]
 g. LIKE it was my thinking bit of road. [MPT/f/81]
 h. LIKE it was a kind-of wee bit of tongue-twister. [CLB/f/89]

An important question to consider is whether the occurrences in (14) represent isolated or rare tokens in the speech of individuals that could result from the late adoption of lexical forms or whether they represent a more regular pattern of use in discourse. While no distributional analysis has been performed on the British dialect data, figures are available concerning the overall rate of use in the Toronto materials. Among the oldest speakers in the sample, those in their eighties, *like* marks 8% of matrix-level clauses, while all other discourse markers combined (*well, I mean, so, you see, actually*, etc.) account for 11% of contexts overall ($N$ = 299). In other words, *like* accounts for almost half of the total discourse markers used by speakers in their eighties; we can surmise that it is a relatively high-frequency item in the speech of this generation, who were already in their thirties and early forties in 1955.

Evidence from the particle presents a further twist. In (15) *like* is shown in two distinct syntactic positions: on the left edge of a noun phrase (as in 15a–15c), and on the left edge of the lexical verb (as in 15d–15f). These data illustrate the use of the particle by elderly speakers of regional British varieties. In (16), the same contexts are illustrated from the Toronto materials.

15. a. It was only LIKE a step up to this wee loft. [CLB/m/91]
 b. Oh, it was LIKE boots we wore. [CLB/f/89]
 c. That was LIKE the visitors and we says we would nae mind ken. [AYR/f/78]
 d. We were LIKE walking along that Agohill road. [CLB/f/86]
 e. They were just LIKE sitting waiting to dies. [AYR/m/75]
 f. We were like ready to LIKE mutiny. [YRK/f/74]
16. a. We stayed at LIKE a motel. [N/f/76]
 b. Now Tim would be going more for LIKE Fred Flintstone. [N/f/72]
 c. They didn't have windows. They had LIKE a box. [N/m/62]
 d. So we bought it and LIKE moved five houses over. [N/f/55]
 e. They were LIKE living like dogs. [N/m/52]
 f. I'm not sure if my eight-year-old LIKE understands that. [N/m/46]

In the North American data, the oldest speakers to use the particle in the context of noun phrases are in their seventies (in 16a and 16b), much younger than is the case, for example, in Culleybackey, Northern Ireland (in 15a and 15b). In the case of lexical verbs, the oldest speakers to use *like* in Toronto are in their fifties (in 16d and 16e), again well behind communities in Northern Ireland, Scotland, and England (in 15d–15f). These two contexts form the basis of comparison here because they illustrate an important point: there is no context where *like* occurs among, for example, the 80-year-olds from Toronto where it does not also occur among the 80-year-olds from the rural U.K. locales. The reverse does not obtain.

In isolation, the Toronto data are somewhat problematic for the counterculture genesis hypothesis. Not only is the marker used by speakers older than 65 years of age, but the examples do not represent random occurrences. As noted, the marker is highly productive among Torontonians in their eighties, occurring nearly as often as all other discourse markers combined in the speech of this cohort. This suggests that the marker was already a feature of the vernacular before it was associated with the Beat and jazz groups of the 1950s and 1960s. In fact, working from the apparent-time hypothesis, in the 1930s, when these 80-year-olds were teenagers, *like* must have been relatively frequent in the ambient language as a discourse marker, a usage inherited by these speakers from the previous generations. The added perspective afforded by the British data further jeopardizes the plausibility of the counterculture genesis hypothesis. As both a marker and a particle, *like* is attested among the oldest speakers in the English, Scottish, and Northern Irish communities considered here, raising troubling questions about the American roots of these forms more generally. If we interpret the differences between the North American and the British dialect data as temporal analogues, then *like* was used as a particle in certain contexts approximately 10–20 years earlier in the British varieties than it was in comparable syntactic frames in North American English.

There is a further complication. A form that is highly reminiscent of the use of *like* as a discourse marker is attested in literary sources from the nineteenth century, as in (17a) from the *OED2*, as is its use as a discourse particle, as illustrated in (17b).

17. a. "Why LIKE, it's gaily nigh like to four mile like." [De Quincey 1840–41, 224][9]
    b. He would not go LIKE through that.... They are LIKE against one another as it is. [C. Clough Robinson, *A Glossary of Words Pertaining to the Dialect of Mid-Yorkshire*, English Dialect Society no. 14 (London: Trübner, 1876), 76 (Wright 1902)]

Shown in (18), the marker is also attested in recordings of elderly speakers made by the New Zealand National Broadcasting Service in 1946–48. These data document the speech of native New Zealanders born in the period from 1851 to 1919. The vast majority of these speakers' parents had emigrated to New Zealand from England, Ireland, and Scotland; none had come from the United States.

18. a. LIKE until his death he used to write to me quite frequently. [Thomas Steel, b. 1874, Waikato]
    b. LIKE you'd need to see the road to believe it. [John McLew, b. 1875, Otago]
    c. You know, LIKE you would be going to the hotel to stay for a day or two. [Catherine Dudley, b. 1886, Central Otago]
    d. LIKE once we got the milk from the cows he'd take it into town. [Eric Robinson, b. 1919, Canterbury]

Examples such as these support Romaine and Lange's (1991, 270) assertion that nonquotative uses of *like* have probably been functioning in the vernacular for more than a century. In fact, in the case of the marker, they suggest a much longer history. Moreover, the early sources in (17) are British, not American, and an American link would be difficult to construct for the New Zealand examples in (18). Thus, both the historical record and synchronic facts contradict the notion that American English is the origin of the vernacular uses of *like* as both a marker and a particle.

New linguistic forms may occur at extremely low rates for extended periods before reaching a point of widespread diffusion, assuming they survive at all. Language change is not deterministic. In order to advance, innovative forms must develop an association with some desirable social construct (Labov 2001, 462). Although it seems clear that the jazz, cool, and Beat groups of the 1950s and 1960s were not the SOURCE of *like* as a marker and a particle, it also seems incontestable that these uses were associated with the counterculture groups. In other words, they exploited a resource already available in the ambient language. A reasonable deduction, therefore, is that these groups provided the means for *like* to accelerate in the vernacular. In short, I suggest that circa the middle of the twentieth century, *like* was an incipient form in the vernacular and its connection with certain groups cultivated the appropriate social context for the marker and the particle to advance. These forms represent **change in progress**.

That *like* has functioned as a marker and a particle for some time in the English language itself indicates that such uses are not restricted to adolescents and young adults. The data in (14)–(16) further substantiate this observation: speakers in their seventies, eighties, and nineties use *like* in the same ways speakers more than sixty years their juniors do. Why, then, does the *like* language myth consistently point to younger speakers? The answer is as obvious as it is timeless. As with any form involved in change, adolescents are in the vanguard. They are not the only members of the community using these forms, but they use them at higher frequencies than older age cohorts within the population.[10]

To this end, consider Figure 39.2, which tracks the frequencies of the marker and the particle across apparent time in Toronto. For the particle, the same contexts from Figure 39.1 are included. There are two critical observations to draw from these results. First, in each vernacular function, the frequency of *like* increases steadily across apparent time. This monotonic association of frequency with age is characteristic of change in progress (Labov 2001, 460). Second, a peak occurs in each trajectory, either among the 17–19-year-olds or the 15–16-year-olds. According to Labov (2001), these peaks are not, for example, indicators of age grading whereby we can expect a retrenchment toward adult norms following adolescence. Rather, the peaks are a general requirement of ongoing change, falling out from the logistic progression of innovative forms. In short, *like* the marker and *like* the particle are not simply passing fads of the adolescent years. It is incontrovertible that younger speakers use them more frequently than older speakers do. This has been established in other research as well (e.g., Dailey-O'Cain 2000, 66). It is also incontrovertible, however, that despite popular belief, adolescents are not alone. Other age groups also use *like* for these functions; they simply do not do so as often, exactly as predicted by all models of language change.

Similarly, the use of *like* as an approximative adverb has increased dramatically over the past 65 years within this same population. Interestingly, the adverbial function provides an example of lexical replacement. As shown in Figure 39.3, it has been ousting *about* in the spoken vernacular for most of the period we can track with this corpus, providing a trajectory of weak complementarity (Sankoff and Thibault 1981, 207). Although a minority form among the oldest speakers in the community, *like* has gained significant currency across apparent time as an approximative strategy. While speakers over the age of 30 tend to prefer the traditional form, *about*, speakers under that age favor *like* (D'Arcy 2006). In other words, the form has changed: where one increases, the other decreases. This is the defining characterization of weak complementarity (Sankoff and Thibault 1981, 207).

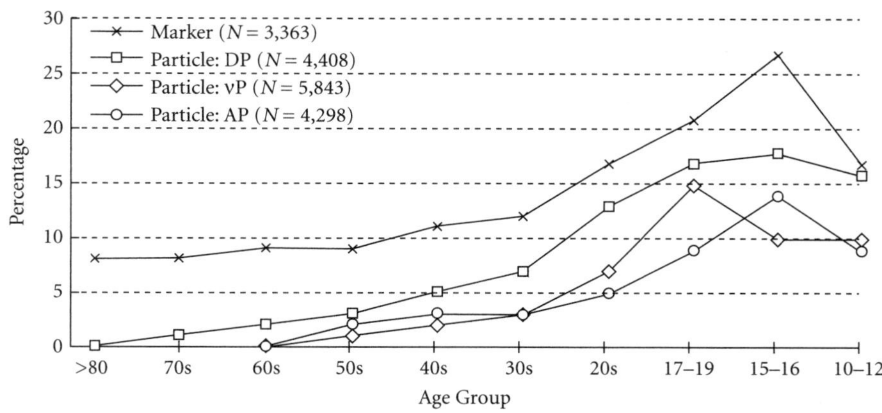


**Figure 39.2** *Frequencies of* like *as a Discourse Marker and a Discourse Particle Across Apparent Time in Toronto*

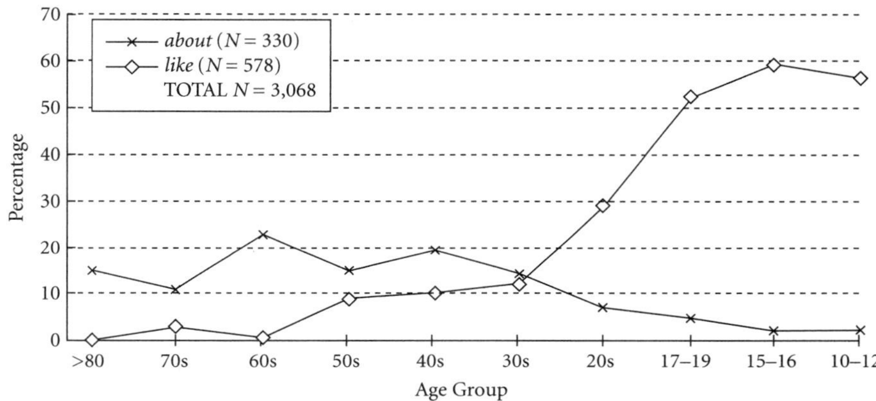


**Figure 39.3** *Overall Distributions of* like *and* about *as Lexical Approximations Across Apparent Time*

None of this, however, relates to the Valley Girls. Songs like Frank Zappa's "Valley Girl" (1982) and Atlantic Pictures's 1983 movie by the same name provide snapshots of life as a teenage girl in the San Fernando Valley, iconic images that continue to be perpetuated in pop culture (e.g., Paramount's 1995 *Clueless*). The vernacular forms of *like* are salient features of the Valley Girl persona, but as with the counterculture groups, the Valley Girls were not the only speakers to use these forms, nor were they the innovators. This much is obvious. Furthermore, while it is likely—as one reviewer rightly points out—that the linguistic and cultural style associated with the category "Valley Girl" was established prior to its being popularized by media representations in the early 1980s, it remains nonetheless that the category only became available to the broader social context at this time. Stated differently, outside its local milieu, "Valley Girl" was not an active model for association, linguistic or otherwise, until after 1980. The apparent-time trajectories in Figures 39.3 and 39.4, however, suggest that as a marker, particle, and approximative adverb, *like* was already increasing in frequency before this time. For each use that is tracked in these figures, the upward slope begins 20, and in some cases 30, years earlier than can be reasonably postulated for the Valley Girl branch of the myth to be upheld. Nonetheless, this belief seems too robust in the North American psyche to be utterly without substance. It is possible, for example, that vernacular uses of *like* were recycled as a Valley Girl phenomenon once their initial association with the counterculture groups waned among subsequent generations of speakers. As Milroy (2004, 169) states, "different groups may be foregrounded at different times." In other words, the saliency of social categories can be variable across time, and linguistic forms associated with one may later come to be associated with another as each rises to prominence in the cultural landscape of the time. There is some support for this in the apparent-time trajectories. In Figures 39.2 and 39.3, some of the slopes steepen visibly within the cohort of speakers in their thirties. These speakers would have been in their pre- and young teens when the Valley Girl persona rose to popularity....

Thus, the sum of the apparent-time evidence indicates that *like* was functioning in the vernacular as a discourse marker, a discourse particle, and an adverb of approximation well before the Valley Girl category was popularized in the early 1980s. These functions were also increasing in frequency before this time. However, the rate of change seems to increase among speakers between the ages of 30 to 39, and this momentum is then maintained across apparent time. In fact, it is among the subsequent age groups that the vernacular uses of *like* attain significance, favored among speakers aged 29 and under. All together, the results suggest that while the Valley Girls were not solely responsible for launching these forms in discourse, they did seem to get a boost during the height of the Valley Girl period, which may in turn have helped to propel them into the vernacular faster than they would have otherwise.

The one form that probably can be identified as "Valley Girl" is quotative *be like*, since in this instance the chronology seems to corroborate popular belief. The first mention of *be like* in the sociolinguistic literature is dated 1982 (Ronald Butters's editor's note in *American Speech*), at which time it appeared to be an incipient form (see also Tannen 1986). There are attestations of this use available from the pop culture of the time (e.g., "She's like 'Oh my God'" in Zappa's "Valley Girl"), yet none predating the Valley Girls of which I am aware. The inception of quotative *be like* for introducing constructed dialogue thus seems to be fairly well circumscribed to the early 1980s. Apparent-time data provide further support for this accounting. Figure 39.4 displays the frequency of the quotative across the Toronto population.

The results demonstrate that although *be like* appears in the speech of Torontonians in their forties and fifties, such uses are extremely rare. In contrast, *be like* is used productively by speakers in their thirties, accounting for 26% of quotative verbs overall within this cohort ($N = 453$). This is the generation—born in the late 1960s and early 1970s—that comprised the teenagers of the 1980s. The divide between the results for this group and those for the 40-year-olds in Figure 39.4 is critical to disentangling the developmental history of *be like*. Similar data from 1995 demonstrated that the overall distribution of *be like* among speakers aged 18 to 27 was then 13% (Tagliamonte and Hudson 1999). The real-time trend comparison from Tagliamonte and D'Arcy (2007a) reveals that use has since increased substantially: *be like* now accounts for 58% of quotatives among 25–29-year-olds, and 31% of quotatives among speakers aged 30–34. In other words, the frequency of *be like* has more than doubled across two similar populations in the seven intervening years. Results such as these provide compelling evidence for communal change, with speakers increasing their use of innovative features throughout their lifetimes (Labov 1994, 84). Relative to the genesis of *be like*, this suggests that the odd tokens which occur in the speech of 40- and 50-year-olds do not mark the inception of this form, but rather reflect the late adoption of a new feature during adulthood (see Tagliamonte and D'Arcy 2007a; also Buchstaller 2006a).

In short, of the vernacular forms of *like* that occur in discourse, only quotative *be like* may have Valley Girl origins. The discourse marker and particle have long histories in the language, predating the Valley Girls by at least a century (cf. 17 and 18; also Romaine and Lange 1991), and the conversational use of *like* to mean *about* has likewise been a feature of English throughout most of the twentieth century (cf. 5; also Figure 39.3). Moreover, the apparent-time data indicate that the use of nonquotative forms of *like* was increasing prior to 1980. Nonetheless, a distinct change in the rate of this increase coincides with the rise of the Valley Girl persona. It is unlikely that these are disparate phenomena. Given the general perception that *like* is just *like*, it is possible that the association of quotative *be like* with the Valley Girl image led to concomitant increases in the use of other functions performed by *like* in the vernacular. It may also have contributed to the belief that the Valley Girls are responsible for all of the vernacular forms.

However, to acknowledge that the Valley Girls may have contributed to the advancement of these forms in North America must not be confused with saying that they are responsible for their spread more generally. As I have

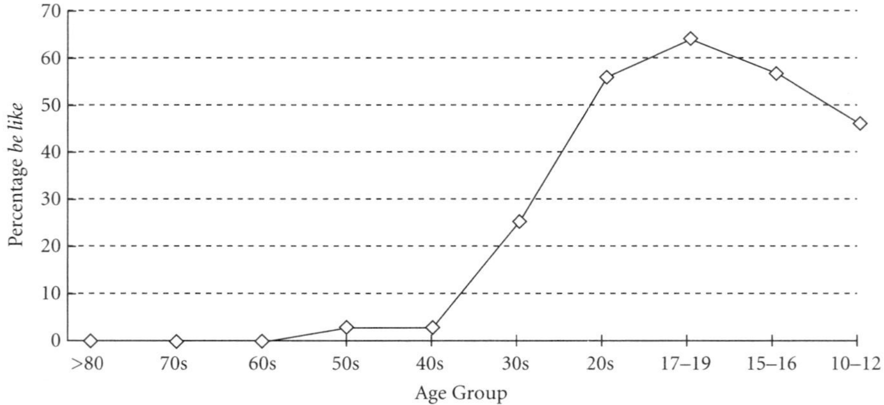


**Figure 39.4** *Overall Distribution of Quotative* be like *Across Apparent Time in Toronto (after Tagliamonte and D'Arcy 2007, 205, fig. 2; N = 6,364)*

argued above, outside quotative *be like*, the other forms of *like* have been increasing in the vernacular for as long as we are able to ascertain with synchronic data. Moreover, these functions are not unique to North America. They are found in the discourse of elderly speakers of isolated, rural varieties across both the United Kingdom and New Zealand. To these observations can be added the evidence from perceptual investigations. The social baggage of one region does not straightforwardly—or even necessarily—carry to another region. For example, quotative *be like*, the only vernacular form for which a North American genesis can be supported, appears to carry no coherent regional affiliation for speakers in the United Kingdom (Buchstaller 2006b). Thus, notions like 'Valley Girl', 'California', or even 'American' may not be as salient outside the North American context as they are within it. We must, therefore, be very cautious about claims that the American media are responsible for exporting the vernacular functions of *like* to other varieties. While it is possible that use by iconic media figures reinforced these functions, it is more than likely that they were already in existence in the vernacular. In other words, it is important to distinguish between the development and subsequent embedding (social and linguistic) of linguistic forms, their transmission across nonproximate contexts, and the possible influence of other varieties as "targets" for adoption and/or appropriation to the local context (for discussion of "Americanization" in language variation and change more generally, see Meyerhoff and Niedzielski 2003).

**Anything Goes** The apparent-time perspective also provides insights on how the current state of adolescent vernaculars has come into being. The trajectories in Figures 39.2 and 39.3 reveal quite clearly that nonquotative uses of *like* have not appeared ex nihilo. Each function and each syntactic frame has developed gradually across the generations. The net result is that frequency of use is the primary criterion distinguishing adolescent cohorts from adult ones.[11]

However, it is also the general impression that vernacular forms of *like* can be used anywhere, inserted into an utterance at whichever point in the syntax a speaker wishes. As with other aspects of the *like* language myth, this belief is propagated by the media (e.g., Diamond 2000) and by language commentators (e.g., Wilson 1987, 92). It can also be found in various guises in the linguistic literature. Siegel (2002, 64) maintains that *like* can "occur grammatically anywhere in a sentence," and Romaine and Lange (1991, 261) state that *like* is characterized by "syntactic detachability and positional mobility." While it is true that the combined functions of marker and particle account for a wide range of contexts across clause structure, it is also the case that these positions are not random. To see this, it is necessary to observe not only where these forms of *like* do occur, but also where they do not. I will concentrate here on the position of the particle vis-à-vis verbs. However, similar types of argumentation can be applied to the other clause-internal contexts where *like* functions as a particle, as well as to the use of *like* as a discourse marker (see D'Arcy 2005).

In the current data set, the **syntagmatic** order of *like* and verbs is highly fixed: the particle categorically occurs to the immediate left of the lexical verb. Thus, when functional morphemes such as modal verbs, auxiliary verbs, and infinitival *to* are present, *like* appears between these and the main verb, as exemplified in (19) (see also 15d–15f and 16d–16f above). This observation was made by Underhill (1988, 243) for American English and by Andersen (2001, 280) for London English, and it also holds in the Toronto materials (D'Arcy 2005; $N = 4389$).[12]

19. a. I'd LIKE wake up and feel good. [2/m/15]
    b. I've LIKE grown into that. [3/m/12]
    c. They like to LIKE intervene a lot. [3/m/18]
    d. Everyone is LIKE calling stuff out. [1/m/22]
    e. They kept LIKE jumping around. [N/m/26]

The consistency and regularity of the pattern in (19) refutes the notion of arbitrariness in the use of the particle. It also suggests that *like* targets a specific adjunction site in the syntax, since its position is systematic.... As the examples in (20) demonstrate, all three patterns are attested in the Toronto data.

20. a. They LIKE want to Ø get together. [3/f/16]
    b. I didn't Ø want to LIKE walk up to them [2/f/15]
    c. You're Ø trying to LIKE pull it out of the water. [3/f/17]
    d. As long as they LIKE try to LIKE merge with Canadian culture.... [1/m/22]

...Jackendoff (1972, 1997, 2002) has proposed that adverbs can be grouped into three basic classes: speaker = oriented, subject = oriented, and degree/manner. Examination of the Toronto data reveals two distinct patterns: (1) adverb + *like* and (2) *like* + adverb. This first pattern is demonstrated in (21) and (22); the second pattern is shown in (23) and (24). Crucially, these patterns are not accidental; they correlate with adverb type. In (21) and (22), where the particle co-occurs with speaker-and subject-oriented adverbs, *like* follows the modifier. In (23) and (24), where the particle appears with degree and manner adverbs, it precedes the modifier.

21. SPEAKER-ORIENTED
    a. I don't REALLY [epistemic 'truly'] LIKE judge people on what music they listen to. [2/m/15]
    b. We LITERALLY LIKE cooked all the food. [N/m/26]
    c. He ACTUALLY LIKE stood up. [I/m/21a]
    d. They HONESTLY LIKE threatened me. [I/m/21b]
22. SUBJECT-ORIENTED
    a. Andrea STILL LIKE comes to lunch with us. [2/f/16]
    b. Me and my friends, we ALWAYS LIKE took rulers. [3/m/11]

c. They like it but they NEVER LIKE played. [3/f/17]

23. DEGREE
    a. A trade that I LIKE REALLY [intensification] like was the one they had got from Jersey. [3/H/m/12]
    b. Some people LIKE TOTALLY fell into the mold. [2/i/f/19]
    c. The glue LIKE SLIGHTLY falls off your hair. [2/r/f/11]
24. MANNER
    a. But people will LIKE SLOWLY get into it. [2/f/19]
    b. And then he LIKE SLOWLY added more and more things. [S/m/15]
    c. And then they LIKE GRADUALLY changed like how they looked. [2/m/15]

Thus, in examining just one syntactic context in which the discourse particle occurs, it becomes fairly evident that *like* is not a random element of the vernacular. Nonetheless, the PERCEPTION that it is ad hoc is likely to endure in popular belief. There are at least three reasons for this. First, as a lexeme, *like* is remarkably versatile. It functions as a lexical verb, a noun, a preposition, a conjunction, a suffix, a quotative complementizer, an approximative adverb, a discourse marker, and a discourse particle. As noted by Wilson (1987, 92), "the only part of speech *like* isn't is a pronoun." In terms of raw occurrence, this translates directly into increased token frequency. Second, the marker and the particle together account for at least eight adjunction sites in the syntax, and probably more: CP, TP, DP, NP, DegP, AP, vP, AdvP (D'Arcy 2005; see also note 11). Thus, not only is *like* multifunctional, but certain of these functions cover a wide array of contexts. The third compounding factor is that, as discussed above, the vernacular forms of *like* have recently undergone a period of vigorous development. All together, these facts have contributed to its saliency, and because each form sounds like every other, it creates the illusion that *like* can go anywhere grammatically. In other words, we have returned to the first ingredient of the *like* language myth, that *like* is just *like*, which it is not.

## Conclusion

To summarize, I have argued the following. First, there are minimally four vernacular functions of *like* occurring in discourse: quotative complementizer, approximative adverb, discourse marker, and discourse particle. Because they all sound the same, they resound in the communal ear simply as 'like'. Second, each function connotes a distinct referential and/or pragmatic meaning. Third, gender does not condition use of the vernacular forms uniformly. Women are favored for the quotative and discourse marking functions, but men are favored across the range of contexts examined here in which the particle occurs. The adverb exhibits no gender pattern, being equally probable as an approximation strategy in the speech of either gender. Fourth, the vernacular forms are not twentieth-century innovations that originate from the Valley Girls. Only the quotative may be sourced to this group; the rest have extended histories in the English language. Fifth, adolescents use the vernacular forms more frequently than adult cohorts do, but adults of all ages use them to some extent or another. Sixth and finally, vernacular uses of *like* are systematic, not arbitrary.

Returning to the various components of the *like* myth, a little bit of truth has been disentangled from the fiction. These truths in turn suggest some of the factors that may have been instrumental in the rise of the myth more generally. The combination of empirical data from regional dialects of British English and the apparent-time results from Toronto suggest that the nonquotative vernacular functions of *like* have been increasing in frequency over the last 65 years or so, and the marker for seemingly longer still. In other words, they represent change in progress and cannot be isolated to the North American context. In the interim, quotative *be like* was likely introduced by the Valley Girls in the early 1980s, and the other forms were concomitantly associated with this group as well. Since this time, all vernacular forms of *like* have subsequently increased in frequency to the point where they are now significantly favored among speakers under the age of 30 and disfavored (though not absent) among older age groups. As a consequence of the typical trajectory of change, these uses are most frequent in the speech of adolescents, and the stigma associated with the vernacular forms draws overt attention and commentary.

From here it is possible to hypothesize a scenario that could have led to the cultivation of a number of beliefs about *like*. In North America at least, Valley Girls remain a well-defined category. This not only perpetuates the Valley Girl image, but it also perpetuates stereotypes of Valley Girl behavior. *Like* is one aspect of this image. Crucially though, Valley Girls are young and female. While this might seem obvious, it helps to explain why the myth perseveres, focusing on the use of teenagers and women in particular, even though it is clear that vernacular uses are not, nor have they been historically, confined to these segments of the population. The adolescent peak that is a general requirement of language change then feeds the adolescent connection, as does the strong female preference for quotative *be like*. If *like* is just *like*, then it follows that what holds for one holds for all.

This, however, raises an interesting issue for theories of language change more generally. The gender conditioning displayed by the vernacular functions of *like* does not correlate with the social affiliation that has emerged within its attendant ideology. The iconic figures of the counterculture movements were predominantly male (e.g., William S. Burroughs, Neal Cassady, Lawrence Ferlinghetti, Allen Ginsberg, Jack Kerouac, Peter Orlovsky, etc.), yet the discourse marker, which was a part of the Beat vernacular (as in 12 and 13), has been more frequent in the speech of women than in that of men across apparent time. Only the particle displays a regular association with men. Valley Girls are young women, and while the quotative—for which they are credited—has more or less consistently been favored among women throughout its development (Tagliamonte and D'Arcy 2007a), the particle remains more frequent in the speech of men. At the same time, the use of *like* as an approximative adverb is independent of gender. This suggests that social patterns of use are not tied to the groups with which a form comes to be associated for a time. In other words, social perception and language use can operate independently of one another. Thus, even though *like* might simply be regarded as a single form in the received cultural wisdom, in the grammar these various functions remain distinct.

To conclude, teasing apart the individual beliefs that contribute to popular *like* ideology has revealed what the vernacular uses of *like* are as well as what they are not. On one hand, they are complex and historically long-standing features of English dialects. Only quotative *be like* can be defined as a late-twentieth-century innovation. On the other hand, these uses are not simply "a girl thing," "a teenager thing," or some combination of the two (e.g., "a Valley Girl thing"), nor can it be said that they are a strictly "American thing." Instead, to a certain extent, these forms are everybody's thing.

## Notes

I gratefully acknowledge Sali Tagliamonte for granting me access to the Toronto English and Roots of English archives, without which this research would not have been possible. I also thank Isabelle Buchstaller, Suzanne Romaine, Johanna Wood, and three anonymous reviewers for their careful and insightful comments on earlier versions of this manuscript. Finally, I acknowledge the Social Sciences and Humanities Research Council of Canada (SSHRC), who supported this work with Doctoral Fellowship no. 752-2002-2177.

1. On language myths in general, see Bauer and Trudgill (1998) and articles therein; for attitudes toward language change, see Aitchison (1981) and L. Milroy (2004); and on the state of the language, see Cameron (1995).

2. Parenthetical information following examples marks the subcorpus from which the datum was extracted, followed by the speaker's sex and age. The following corpora, housed in the Sociolinguistics Laboratory at the University of Toronto, document Toronto English: 2 = data collected by students in the 2002 Research Opportunities Program (ROP) in Linguistics; 3 = data from the 2003 ROP course; I = data collected in 2003 as part of the "In-TO-vation" (TO) research project; and N = data collected in 2004 for the TO project. For British dialect data, the relevant codes are: AYR = Ayrshire; PVG = Portavogie; MPT = Maryport; and YRK = York (see Tagliamonte and Smith 2002; Tagliamonte forthcoming).

3. For discussion of the design and construction of the individual corpora within the Toronto Archive, see Tagliamonte and D'Arcy (2004, 497) and Tagliamonte (2006).

4. Despite being a feature of colloquial English since the fourteenth century (Romaine and Lange 1991, 244, n. 7), the use of *like* as a conjunction created an uproar during the 1950s in North America when R. J. Reynolds Tobacco Company released the advertising slogan "Winston tastes good like a cigarette should." Interestingly, this usage recently drew a reaction from a New Zealand audience of older, educated speakers during a presentation about the vernacular uses of *like* (Sept. 5, 2006). It seems the conjunction was perceived along the lines of *like* in (1d), suggesting that despite the longevity of constructions such as (3d), there are sectors of the population who continue to advocate the use of 'as (though)' in speech.

5. This [chapter], which draws largely on data from North American English, presents evidence for four vernacular functions, though it is clear that some varieties of English may distinguish between five or more. For example, English English and Scottish English include a sentence-final adverbial, discussed by Andersen (2001) and Miller and Weinert (1995) and exemplified profusely in the *OED2* (see also 17a), which takes backward scope and can be glossed as 'as it were' or 'so to speak.' In North American English, this function is marginal, restricted in the Toronto materials to speakers over the age of 60 (e.g., "We need to smarten it up a bit LIKE" [N/f/76]), though even within this cohort its use is extremely rare. It has also been suggested that *like* functions as a pause-filler, equivalent to *um* and *er* (e.g., Siegel 2002, 38; Fought 2006). While it is possible that as a particle *like* may function this way in some of its uses, it should be noted that most instances of *like* are prosodically integrated; co-occurrence with self-repair and hesitation phenomena constitute the exception, not the norm, in vernacular use (Andersen 2000, 19; Levey 2003, 28). Consequently, this function is not considered here.

6. See Tagliamonte and D'Arcy (2007a) for discussion of the actuation problem with reference to *be like*.

7. The results for quotative *be like* in Figure 39.1 are drawn from Tagliamonte and D'Arcy (2007a), while the results for the approximative adverb, the discourse marker, and the particle are drawn from D'Arcy (2005, 2006). It should be noted that this figure reports overall distributions across the age groups who use each form of *like*. This age range differs from function to function (see Figures 39.2–39.4).

8. This list is intended to be representative, not exhaustive.

9. Notably, in his discussion of "vulgarities," De Quincey (1840–41, 224) provides the sentence in (17a) as an example of the speech typical of uneducated, older, rural males of Westmoreland. That he associates *like* with this particular social group suggests that it was already at that time well-entrenched as a feature of the vernacular. De Quincey goes on to state that *like* is used so frequently that "if the word were proscribed by Parliament, he ["an ancient father of his valley"] would have no resource but everlasting silence."

10. Buchstaller and Traugott (2006) discuss adverbial *all* (e.g., John is *all* wet), tracing its history from Old English through to the present day. Though not new, this adverbial function is often considered such (e.g., Waksler 2001), linked with the genuinely innovative form quotative *be all*. Buchstaller and Traugott (2006, 364) suggest that the perception of newness for adverbial uses results from a "social selective attention effect," what Zwicky (2005) has called the "adolescent illusion." A similar effect may be at work with vernacular *like*. Specifically, the emergence of quotative *be like*, a form whose diffusion has progressed with extreme rapidity, may have

increased the saliency of the other vernacular functions, triggering a "perceptual generalization" (Buchstaller and Traugott 2006, 365) whereby adolescents, associated with quotative *be like* as a recent change in progress (as opposed to slower, long-standing ones), become associated with all functions.

11. In fact, when language-internal constraints are factored into the analysis, they are revealed to operate uniformly across the sample, regardless of speaker age. In short, the entire speech community shares a single variable grammar for each of the vernacular functions of *like* (D'Arcy 2005, 139, 213–14).

12. This does not rule out the possibility that *like* may subsequently generalize beyond this position and begin to occur in an increasing array of syntactic contexts. In D'Arcy (2005, 219), I hypothesize that grammaticalization of the particle is incomplete, which, if correct, would allow for its spread to projections not yet in evidence in either the Toronto materials or the earlier corpora used by Underhill (1988) and Andersen (1997). Indeed, I thank Isa Buchstaller for sending the below examples from the Web, found using Google (pers. comm., Feb. 10, 2007), which demonstrate just that. In other words, the suggestion being made is that the restriction of *like* to the immediate left of the lexical verb represents an earlier stage of development in this ongoing change.

    a. Like, something like when you get LIKE to see if you have like strep throat or something. [interview with "low-risk teen" about AIDS, Center for Risk Perception and Communication, Carnegie Mellon University, http://www.hss.cmu.edu/departments/sds/risk/HIV%20interview%2004.pdf (accessed Feb. 10, 2007)]

    b. ... but when you get LIKE to go and see them and help out, same people that you've robbed. [David Smith, Harry Blagg, and Nick Derricourt, "Mediation in South Yorkshire," *British Journal of Criminology* 28 (1988): 378 (http://bjc.oxfordjournals.org/cgi/content/abstract/28/3/378)]

    c. ... and she LIKE is walkin to the banster and when she gets there she like hippbummps the air! [ps_iluvyou_xo, post on High School Musical Club discussion board, Picture Trail, http://www.picturetrail.com/club/forums/viewTopic.php?topicID=5419. July 10, 2006]

## References


Aitchison, Jean. 1981. *Language Change: Progress or Decay?* London: Fontana.

Andersen, Gisle. 1997. "*They gave us these yeah, and they like wanna see like how we talk and all that:* The Use of *like* and Other Discourse Markers in London Teenage Speech." In *Ungdomsspråk i Norden*, ed. Ulla-Britt Kostinas, Anna-Brita Stenström, and Anna-Malin Karlsson, 82–95. Stockholm: Institutionen för Nordiska Språk, Stockholms Univ.

Andersen, Gisle. 1998. "The Pragmatic Marker *like* from a Relevance-Theoretic Perspective." In *Discourse Markers: Descriptions and Theory*, ed. Andreas H. Jucker and Yael Ziv, 147–70. Amsterdam: Benjamins.

Andersen, Gisle. 2000. "The Role of Pragmatic Marker *like* in Utterance Interpretation." In *Pragmatic Markers and Propositional Attitude*, ed. Gisle Andersen and Thorstein Fretheim, 17–38. Amsterdam: Benjamins.

Andersen, Gisle. 2001. *Pragmatic Markers and Sociolinguistic Variation: A Relevance-Theoretic Approach to the Language of Adolescents.* Amsterdam: Benjamins.

Bailey, Guy. 2001. "Real and Apparent Time." In *The Handbook of Language Variation and Change*, ed. J. K. Chambers, Peter Trudgill, and Natalie Schilling-Estes, 312–32. Malden, Mass.: Blackwell.

Bailey, Guy, Tom Wilke, Jan Tillery, and Lori Sand. 1994. "Some Patterns of Linguistic Diffusion." *Language Variation and Change* 5: 359–90.

Bauer, Laurie, and Peter Trudgill, eds. 1998. *Language Myths.* London: Penguin.

Blakemore, Diane. 1987. *Semantic Constraints on Relevance.* Oxford: Blackwell.

Blyth, Carl, Jr., Sigrid Recktenwald, and Jenny Wang. 1990. "I'm like, 'say what?!': A New Quotative in American Oral Narrative." *American Speech* 65: 215–27.

Brinton, Laurel J. 1996. *Pragmatic Markers in English: Grammaticalization and Discourse Functions.* Berlin: Mouton de Gruyter.

Buchstaller, Isabelle. 2004. "The Sociolinguistic Constraints on the Quotative System: British English and US English Compared." Ph.D. diss., Univ. of Edinburgh.

Buchstaller, Isabelle. 2006a. "Diagnostics of Age-Graded Linguistic Behaviour: The Case of the Quotative System." *Journal of Sociolinguistics* 10: 3–30.

Buchstaller, Isabelle. 2006b. "Social Stereotypes, Personality Traits and Regional Perception Displaced: Attitudes Towards the 'New' Quotatives in the U.K." *Journal of Sociolinguistics* 10: 362–81.

Buchstaller, Isabelle, and Elizabeth Closs Traugott. 2006. "*The lady was al demonyak*: Historical Aspects of Adverb *all*." *English Language and Linguistics* 10: 345–70.

Butters, Ronald. 1982. Editor's note [on 'be + like']. *American Speech* 57: 149.

Cameron, Deborah. 1995. *Verbal Hygiene.* London: Routledge.

Campbell, Joseph. 1949. *The Hero with a Thousand Faces.* New York: Pantheon. Repr. Abacus ed. London: Sphere Books, 1975.

Chambers, J. K. 2003. *Sociolinguistic Theory: Linguistic Variation and Its Social Significance.* 2nd ed. Oxford: Blackwell.

Chapman, Robert L., ed. 1986. *New Dictionary of American Slang.* New York: Harper and Row.

Cukor-Avila, Patricia. 2002. "*She say, She go, She be like*: Verbs of Quotation over Time in African American Vernacular English." *American Speech* 77: 3–31.

Dailey-O'Cain. Jennifer. 2000. "The Sociolinguistic Distribution of and Attitudes Toward Focuser *like* and Quotative *like*." *Journal of Sociolinguistics* 4: 60–80.

D'Arcy, Alexandra. 2004. "Contextualizing St. John's Youth English within the Canadian Quotative System." *Journal of English Linguistics* 32: 323–45.

D'Arcy, Alexandra. 2005. "Like: Syntax and Development." Ph.D. diss., Univ. of Toronto.

D'Arcy, Alexandra. 2006. "Lexical Replacement and the Like(s)." *American Speech* 81: 339–57.

De Quincey, Thomas. 1840–41. "Style." *Blackwood's Magazine*. Repr. in *De Quincey's Works*, vol. 10, *Style and Rhetoric and Other Essays*, 158–292. Edinburgh: Black.

Diamond, S. J. 2000. "Like It or Not, 'Like' is Probably Here to Stay." *Los Angeles Times*, August 21, 2.

Ferrara, Kathleen, and Barbara Bell. 1995. "Sociolinguistic Variation and Discourse Function of Constructed Dialogue Introducers: The Case of *be + like*." *American Speech* 70: 265–90.

Fought, Carmen. 2006. Interviewed on the *Today Show*, May 9. Cited in "Like It or Not, a Discourse Marker Making Its Mark on a Wider Stage," Voice of America News, May 6, 2006. Transcript and audio files available at http://www.voanews.com/specialenglish/archive/2006-05/2006-05-09-voa5.cfm.

Fraser, Bruce. 1988. "Types of English Discourse Markers." *Acta Linguistica Hungaria* 38: 19–33.

Jackendoff, Ray S. 1972. *Semantic Interpretation in Generative Grammar*. Cambridge, Mass.: MIT Press.

Jackendoff, Ray S. 1997. *The Architecture of the Language Foculty*, Cambridge, Mass.: MIT Press.

Jackendoff, Ray S. 2002. *Foundations of Language: Brain, Meaning, Grammar, Evolution*, Oxford: Oxford Univ. Press.

Jespersen, Otto. 1942. *A Modern English Grammar on Historical Principles*. Part 6, *Morphology*. Copenhagen: Munksgaard.

Labov, William. 1966. *The Social Stratification of English in New York City*. Washington, D.C.: Center for Applied Linguistics.

Labov, William. 1994. *Principles of Linguistic Change*. Vol. 1, *Internal Factors*. Oxford: Blackwell.

Labov, William. 2001. *Principles of Linguistic Change*. Vol. 2, *Social Factors*. Oxford: Blackwell.

Labov, William. 2003. "Pursuing the Cascade Model." In *Social Dialectology: In Honour of Peter Trudgill*, ed. David Britain and Jenny Cheshire, 9–22. Amsterdam: Benjamins.

Levey, Stephen. 2003. "He's like 'Do it now!' and I'm like 'No!': Some Innovative Quotative Usage Among Young People in London." *English Today* 19: 24–32.

Meehan, Teresa. 1991. "It's Like, 'What's Happening in the Evolution of *like*?': A Theory of Grammaticalization." *Kansas Working Papers in Linguistics* 16: 37–51.

Miller, Jim, and Regina Weinert. 1995. "The Function of *like* in Dialogue." *Journal of Pragmatics* 23: 365–93.

Milroy, James. 1998. "Children Can't Speak or Write Properly Anymore." In Bauer and Trudgill, 58–65.

Milroy, Lesley. 2004. "Language Ideologies and Linguistic Change." In *Sociolinguistic Variation: Critical Reflections*, ed. Carmen Fought, 161–77. New York: Oxford Univ. Press.

Newman, Edwin. 1974. *Strictly Speaking: Will America Be the Death of English?* Indianapolis, Ind.: Bobbs-Merrill.

*OED2. The Oxford English Dictionary*. 1989. 2nd ed. 20 vols. Oxford: Clarendon.

Östman, Jan-Ola. 1982. "The Symbiotic Relationship Between Pragmatic Particles and Impromptu Speech." In *Impromptu Speech: A Symposium*, ed. Nils Erik Enkvist, 147–77. Turku, Finland: Åbo Akademi.

Romaine, Suzanne, and Deborah Lange. 1991. "The Use of *like* as a Marker of Reported Speech and Thought: A Case of Grammaticalization in Progress." *American Speech* 66: 227–79.

Sankoff, David, and Pierrette Thibault. 1981. "Weak Complementarity: Tense and Aspect in Montreal French." In *Syntactic Change*, ed. Brenda B. Johns and David R. Strang, 205–15. Ann Arbor: Dept. of Linguistics, Univ. of Michigan.

Sankoff, Gillian. 2004. "Adolescents, Young Adults, and the Critical Period: Two Case Studies from *Seven Up*." In *Sociolinguistic Variation: Critical Reflections*, ed. Carmen Fought, 121–39. New York: Oxford Univ. Press.

Schiffrin, Deborah. 1987. *Discourse Markers*. Cambridge: Cambridge Univ. Press.

Schiffrin, Deborah. 1992. "Anaphoric *then*: Aspectual, Textual, and Epistemic Meaning." *Linguistics* 30: 753–92.

Schourup, Lawrence. 1983. *Common Discourse Particles in English Conversation*. Ohio State Working Papers in Linguistics 28. Columbus: Dept. of Linguistics, Ohio State Univ.

Schourup, Lawrence. 1999. "Discourse Markers." *Lingua* 107: 227–65.

Siegel, Muffy. 2002. "*Like*: The Discourse Particle and Semantics." *Journal of Semantics* 19: 35–71.

Singler, John Victor. 2001. "Why You Can't Do a VARBRUL Study of Quotatives and What Such a Study Can Show Us." *University of Pennsylvania Working Papers in Linguistics* 7.3: 257–78.

Tagliamonte, Sali A. 2006. "*So cool, right*: Canadian English Entering the 21st Century." In *Canadian English in the Global Context*, ed. Peter Avery, Alexandra D'Arcy, Elaine Gold, and Keren Rice, 309–31. Special issue of *Canadian Journal of Linguistics* 51.2/3.

Tagliamonte, Sali A. Forthcoming. *Roots of English: Exploring the History of Dialects*. Cambridge: Cambridge Univ. Press.

Tagliamonte, Sali, and Alex D'Arcy. 2004. "*He's like, she's like*: The Quotative System in Canadian Youth." *Journal of Sociolinguistics* 8: 493–514.

Tagliamonte, Sali A., and Alexandra D'Arcy. 2007a. "Frequency and Variation in the Community Grammar: Tracking a New Change Through the Generations." *Language Variation and Change* 19: 199–217.

Tagliamonte, Sali A., and Alexandra D'Arcy. 2007b. "To Peak or Not to Peak: Exploring the Incrementation of Linguistic Change." Paper presented at the xxth annual conference on New Ways of Analyzing Variation (NWAV xx), Philadelphia, Oct. 11–14.

Tagliamonte, Sali, and Rachel Hudson. 1999. "*Be like* et al. Beyond America: The Quotative System in British

and Canadian Youth." *Journal of Sociolinguistics* 3: 147–72.
Tagliamonte, Sali A., and Jennifer Smith. 2002. "'Either It Isn't or It's Not': Neg/Aux Contraction in British Dialects." *English World-Wide* 23: 251–81.
Tannen, Deborah. 1986. "Introducing Constructed Dialogue in Greek and American Conversational and Literary Dialogue." In *Direct and Indirect Speech*, ed. Florian Coulmas, 311–32. Berlin: Mouton de Gruyter.
Traugott, Elizabeth Closs, and Richard B. Dasher. 2002. *Regularity in Semantic Change*. Cambridge: Cambridge Univ. Press.
Trudgill, Peter. 1974. "Linguistic Change and Diffusion: Description and Explanation in Sociolinguistic Dialect Geography." *Language in Society* 3: 215–46.
Underhill, Robert. 1988. "*Like* Is, Like, Focus." *American Speech* 63: 234–46.
Waksler, Rachel. 2001. "A New *all* in Conversation." *American Speech* 76: 128–38.
Wilson, Kenneth G. 1987. *Van Winkle's Return: Change in American English, 1966–1986*. Hanover, N.H.: Univ. Press of New England.
WorldAtlas.Com. 2006. "Largest Cities of the World: by Population." http://worldatlas.com/citypops/htm (accessed Sept. 27, 2006).
Wright, Joseph, ed. 1902. *The English Dialect Dictionary*. London: Frowde.
Zwicky, Arnold. 2005. "More Illusions." Post on Language Log. Aug. 17. http://itre.cis.upenn.edu/~myl/languagelog/archives/002407.html.

## Critical Thinking and Application

- Consider D'Arcy's account of linguistic change. Are you aware of any other linguistic forms that are associated in the popular imagination with younger people? Could you conduct a similar study of this variable?
- Why do you think there is a tendency to criticize the speech of young people rather than to accept that change is a constant aspect of human life (including speech)?
- Record fifteen minutes of casual conversation (take a slice from the middle). Transcribe a section. Do you see examples of *like* similar to those D'Arcy analyzes? Do they follow the patterns she suggests?

## Vocabulary

| | | |
|---|---|---|
| apparent-time study | discourse particle | matched-guise test |
| change in progress | empirical | pragmatic |
| collocation | epistemic stance | quotative |
| corpus data | gloss | reported speech |
| diachronic | language ideology | synchronic |
| discourse marker | lexeme | syntagmatic |

## Suggested Further Reading

Aitchison, Jean. 1981. *Language Change: Progress or Decay?* London: Fontana.
Chudacoff, Howard P. 1989. *How Old Are You? Age Consciousness in American Culture*. Princeton, NJ: Princeton University Press.
Eckert, Penelope. 1989. *Jocks and Burnouts: Social Categories and Identity in the High School*. New York: Teachers College Press.
Jones, Mari C., and Edith Esch. 2002. *Language Change: The Interplay of Internal, External, and Extra-Linguistic Factors*. Berlin: Mouton de Gruyter.
Jones, Mari C., and Ishtla Singh. 2005. *Exploring Language Change*. London and New York: Routledge.
Labov, William. 1994. *Principles of Linguistic Change. Vol. 1: Internal Factors*. Oxford: Blackwell.
Labov, William. 2001. *Principles of Linguistic Change. Vol. 2: Social Factors*. Oxford: Blackwell.
McMahon, April M. S. 1994. *Understanding Language Change*. Cambridge: Cambridge University Press.
Romaine, Suzanne, and Deborah Lange. 1991. The Use of *Like* as a Marker of Reported Speech and Thought: A Case of Grammaticalization in Progress. *American Speech* 66: 227–279.

# CHAPTER 40

# Dude

## Scott F. Kiesling

(2004)

*Sometimes a single word can index an entire stance. Such is the case for* dude *in contemporary American English. This word has meanings and functions for its users as well as its hearers, and it is possible to examine the word in use by collecting information about who uses it and in what circumstances. In this case, the word, as Scott Kiesling says, indexes a stance of cool solidarity, something particularly desirable among certain groups of young men. Such terms, which arise at identifiable moments, are often connected with popular culture and with disadvantaged social groups, yet they wind their way into the mainstream.*

*Although the particularities of this term will certainly change over time—indeed,* dude *has now spread widely among women as well as men—the issues raised by studying something in such fine-grained detail are more general: How are age, gender, social group, ethnicity, sexuality, relationship, and stance signaled, or indexed, through the specific choice of a word and its pronunciation or any other linguistic behavior? How does linguistic behavior create in- and out-groups? How are attitudes toward speech related to attitudes toward people?*

*These are questions that each of us may ask every time we observe people speaking.*

### Reading Questions

- What does Kiesling mean by *dude* "indexing" a "stance" of "cool solidarity"?
- What are the five interactional functions for *dude*?
- How did Kiesling conduct his research? Is it persuasive?
- What are the relationships that his consultants aim to convey through their use of *dude*?

---

Older adults, baffled by the new forms of language that regularly appear in youth cultures, frequently characterize young people's language as "inarticulate," and then provide examples that illustrate the specific forms of linguistic mayhem performed by "young people nowadays." For American teenagers, these examples usually include the **discourse marker** *like*, rising final intonation on **declaratives,** and the address term *dude*, which is cited as an example of the inarticulateness of young men in particular. As shown in the comic strip in Figure 40.1, this stereotype views the use of *dude* as unconstrained—a sign of inexpressiveness in which one word is used for any and all utterances. These kinds of stereotypes, however, are based on a fundamental misunderstanding of the functions and meanings of these linguistic forms. As analyses of *like* and rising intonation have shown (e.g., Guy et al. 1986; McLemore 1991; Andersen 2001; Siegel 2002), these forms are constrained in use and precisely expressive in meaning. *Dude* is no exception. This article outlines the patterns of use for *dude* and its functions and meanings in interaction and provides some explanations for its rise in use, particularly among young men, in the early 1980s, and for its continued popularity since then.

Indeed, the data presented here confirm that *dude* is an address term that is used mostly by young men to address other young men; however, its use has expanded so that it is now used as a general address term for a group (same or mixed gender) and by and to women. *Dude* is developing into a discourse marker that need not identify an **addressee**, and more generally encodes the speaker's **stance** to his or her current addressee(s). The term is used mainly in situations in which a speaker takes a stance of **solidarity** or **camaraderie**, but crucially in a nonchalant, not-too-enthusiastic manner. *Dude* indexes a stance of effortlessness (or laziness, depending on the perspective of the hearer), largely because of its origins in the "surfer" and "druggie"

Scott F. Kiesling, Dude. *American Speech* 79 (3), 2004: 281–305.

**Figure 40.1** *Use of* dude *in the "Zits" Comic Strip*

subcultures in which such stances are valued. This **indexicality** also explains where *dude* appears in **discourse** structure and why it tends to be used in a restricted set of speech events. The reason young men use this term is precisely that *dude* **indexes** this stance of cool solidarity. Such a stance is especially valuable for young men as they navigate cultural **Discourses** of young masculinity,[1] which simultaneously demand masculine solidarity, strict heterosexuality, and nonconformity.

The discussion that follows illuminates not only the meanings and use of this address term but also the broader linguistic issue of how language-in-interaction creates and displays social relationships and identities, that is, how language is socially meaningful. An understanding of the ways in which *dude* works thus leads to a better understanding of how everyday language-in-interaction is related to widespread, enduring cultural Discourses (i.e., the relationship between **first**- and **second-order indexical** meanings, in Silverstein's 1996 terms). In this article I focus on gender meanings and on how cultural Discourses of gender are recreated in interaction with the help of *dude*.

The crucial connection between these cultural Discourses and the everyday use of *dude* is the stance of cool solidarity which *dude* indexes. This stance allows men to balance two dominant, but potentially contradictory, cultural Discourses of modern American masculinity: masculine solidarity and **heterosexism.** Connell (1995) argues that different types of masculinities are hierarchically ordered in Western cultures and that the most desired and honored in a particular culture is its **hegemonic** masculinity. Along with Carrigan et al. (1985), he shows that heterosexuality is one component of hegemonic masculinities in Western cultures, especially in the United States. Kimmel (2001, 282) argues more forcefully that "homophobia, men's fear of other men, is the animating condition of the dominant definition of masculinity in America, [and] that the reigning definition of masculinity is a defensive effort to prevent being emasculated," where "emasculated" is equivalent to being perceived as gay by other men. At the same time, there is a cultural Discourse of masculine solidarity—close social bonds between men. In this cultural Discourse, a bond with, and loyalty to, other men is a central measure of masculinity. This Discourse is epitomized in the ideal of loyalty within a military unit, as outlined for American war films by Donald (2001) and illustrated vividly in Swofford's (2003) *Jarhead*, a first-person account of the author's experiences as a U.S. Marine in the 1991 Persian Gulf War. Although this ideal of masculine solidarity could be understood to be consonant with the Discourse of heterosexism (i.e., by having a set of loyal close friends, a man need not be afraid that they will think he is gay), on another level masculine solidarity, in emphasizing closeness between men, is opposed to heterosexism, which emphasizes distance between men. Masculine solidarity and heterosexism thus delimit a narrow range of ratified, dominant, and hegemonic relationships between American men, since masculine solidarity implies closeness with other men, while heterosexism entails nonintimacy with other men. *Dude* allows men to create a stance within this narrow range, one of closeness with other men (satisfying masculine solidarity) that also maintains a casual stance that keeps some distance (thus satisfying heterosexism).

What follows provides evidence for these claims about *dude* in the details of its use. Data are drawn from a number of complementary sources. Survey data come from three surveys of two types performed by classes at the University of Pittsburgh. Ethnographic and interaction data are drawn from my observations in 1993 of an American college fraternity.[2] I also draw from various media sources and from my own experience as a bona fide "*dude*-user" in the 1980s. These multiple sources of data come together to present a consistent picture of the uses, meanings, and recent history of the address term.

I first investigate the wider use of the term and then excerpt several uses in the fraternity to illustrate its discourse functions and how it is used in interaction. I also discuss the personalities of the men who use *dude* the most in the fraternity, then describe the most salient phonological characteristics of the term—a **fronted** /u/—and possible connections between this feature of *dude* and the ongoing fronting of this vowel across North America. Finally, I explain the rise and use of *dude* by exploring cultural Discourses of masculinity and American identity more generally in the 1980s.

## HISTORY AND ORIGINS

The recent history of *dude* provides insight into its indexicalities as well as its rise in use in the United States. The discussion that follows is based on Hill's (1994) history of the term until approximately the 1980s. *Dudes* originally referred to 'old rags', and a *dudesman*, 'scarecrow'. In the latter half of the nineteenth century, "*dude* became synonymous with *dandy*, a term used to designate a sharp dresser in the western territories [of the United States]" (321). There was for a time a female version of the word, but it fell out of use. According to Hill, the use of *dude* as an address term developed in the 1930s and 1940s from groups of men, "Urban Mexican-American *pachuchos*[3] and African-American *zoot-suiters*" (323), known for their clothes consciousness. These groups began to use *dude* as an in-group term, and it soon was used as a general form of address among men. Then *dude* followed a well-worn linguistic path from stigmatized groups such as urban African Americans and Mexicans to whites through African American music culture (much as *cool* and *groovy* did). In the 1980s, "young people began to use *dude* as an exclamation of delight and/or affection" (325). Hill predicts that *dude* may follow *fuck* and its derivatives as being able to function in any grammatical slot or as a single-word utterance that can mean anything in the right context. The history of the term, however, shows that from the time it began to be used as an address term, it was an in-group term that indicated solidarity.

It is this cool solidarity and in-group meaning that has remained with *dude* until the present, and it is the kind of stance indexed when the men in the fraternity use it. However, I show below that, while it is true that *dude* is used as more than simply an address term, it is restricted in where and how it is used grammatically in discourse structure and with what intonation.

## THE *DUDE* CORPUS

As an assignment for two introductory undergraduate sociolinguistics classes at the University of Pittsburgh (in 2001 and 2002), students were required to listen for and record the first 20 **tokens** of *dude* that they heard throughout a three-day period. They recorded the entire utterance as best as they could remember it, the gender and ethnicity of the speaker and addressee(s), the relationship between speaker and hearer, and the situation. I have compiled the results from both classes into a 519-token Dude **Corpus** (DC).[4] The impression that *dude* is used by young men (under 30) is confirmed by the survey, but young women also used the term a significant amount, particularly when speaking to other women, as shown in Figure 40.2.[5]

In addition to the overwhelming predominance of male-male uses of *dude* in these data,[6] it is important to note that the second most common speaker-addressee gender type is female-female, while in mixed-gender interactions there were relatively fewer uses of *dude*. This correlational result suggests that *dude* indexes a solidary stance separate

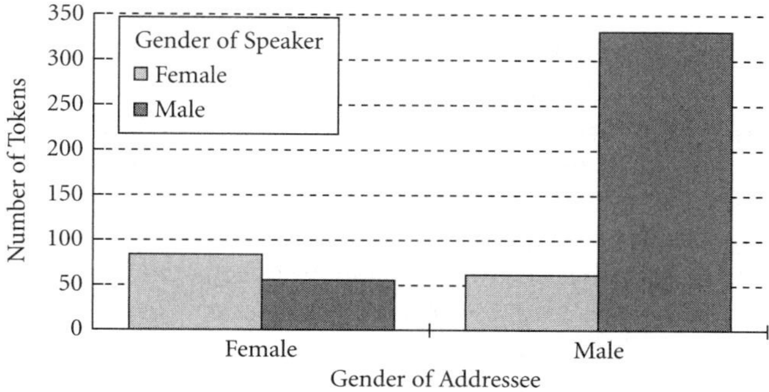


**Figure 40.2** *Use of* dude *by Gender of Speaker and Addressee for People Under 30 Years of Age*

from its probable indexing of masculinity, unless for some reason women are apt to be more masculine (and men, less masculine) when speaking to women.[7]

More clues to the solidarity component of *dude*'s indexicality can be found in the actual tokens used by women speakers to women addressees, however. The all-women tokens were not used in simple greetings, but mostly in situations where camaraderie was salient: only 1 of the 82 woman-woman tokens (1.2%) was a simple greeting (*Hey dude* or *What's up, dude*), as opposed to 7.6% (25/329) of the men's tokens. The women tended to use *dude* (1) when they were commiserating about something bad or being in an unfortunate position, (2) when they were in confrontational situations, or (3) when they were issuing a directive to their addressee. In these last two uses by women, *dude* seems to function to ameliorate the confrontational and/or hierarchical stance of the rest of the utterance.

For example, one token of commiserating was said in a whisper during a class: "Dude, this class is soooo boring." An even clearer example of commiseration (and clearly not masculinity) was recorded after the addressee had been describing a situation in which a man had been trying to "hit on" her. Following the story, the woman who heard the story replied simply, "Dude," with "a tone of disbelief and disgust." An instance of a confrontational situation in which *dude* is used was recorded after the addressee had been teasing the speaker, who then said, "Dude, that's just not cool." Finally, a token used with a direct order while in a car: "Dude, turn signal!" There were also several instances of **constructed dialogue**[8] with men as addressees in the woman-woman tokens, which inflates the woman-woman tokens. However, these tokens also reveal information about the indexicality of *dude*, because all of these constructed dialogue tokens are used to express a stance of distance—or at least nonintimacy—from a man. For example, one token was recorded in the midst of telling a story about talking to a man. In the course of the narrative, the narrator says to the man "I'm like, dude, don't touch me!" Such tokens are clearly being used to create stances of distance between the speaker and the addressee ("don't touch me"), and these tokens thus reveal the nonintimate indexicality of the term.

*Dude* thus carries indexicalities of both solidarity (camaraderie) and distance (nonintimacy) and can be deployed to create both of these kinds of stance, separately or together. This combined stance is what I call COOL SOLIDARITY. The expansion of the use of *dude* to women is thus based on its usefulness in indexing this stance, separate from its associations with masculinity. *Dude* is clearly used most by young, European American men and thus also likely indexes membership in this identity category. But by closely investigating women's use of the term, the separation between the first-order stance index (cool solidarity) and the second-order group-identity index (men) becomes evident. These data also suggest, as would be intuitively predicted by anyone living in North American Anglo culture, an indexical connection between the stance of cool solidarity and young Anglo masculinity, thus showing an indirect indexical connection, of the kind outlined by Ochs (1992), between *dude* and masculinity.

## SELF-REPORT STUDY

The connection between the category 'men' and *dude* was further investigated by a project of a language and gender class at the University of Pittsburgh in fall 2002. This class administered a self-report survey to their friends on the terms *dude, babe,* and *yinz* (the latter being a Pittsburgh dialect term for second person plural). Respondents were asked how often they used the term and then whether they would use the term with particular addressees (boyfriend/girlfriend, close friend, acquaintance, stranger, sibling, parent, boss, and professor) using a **Likert scale** of 1 to 5. They were also asked why they used the term and what kind of people they typically think use the term. The survey is reproduced in the appendix.

These self-report data corroborate the findings of the survey above: that *dude* is used primarily by men speaking to other men, but not exclusively so. The highest average frequency rating was for man-man interactions (3.34), but men reported using *dude* with women as well (the average man-woman frequency rating was 3.24). As shown in Figure 40.3, the gender of the survey respondent was more important than the gender of the addressee, since the difference between male and female speakers is greater than the difference between male and female addressees (i.e., the difference between the endpoints of the lines is greater than the difference between the two lines). However, there are again clues that *dude* is restricted to nonintimate solidarity stances. Consider Figure 40.4.[9] The first noticeable pattern in this figure is that the gender of the addressee makes more of a difference to the men than the women: for women respondents (represented by the squares and diamonds), there is almost no difference between male and female addressees in any category, while for men respondents (the triangles), the gender of the addressee makes a striking difference, especially in the close friend category. In fact, in Figure 40.4 the female lines are almost always within the male lines. These data thus show that *dude* is associated with a male friendship for the men and a nonhierarchic relationship for all respondents, indicated by the low values for parent, boss, and professor.

In addition, intimacy is NOT indexed by *dude*, especially for the men, as shown by the low ratings in the "heterosexual intimate relationship" (Hetero.) category. More importantly, the difference between the "different-gender, close-friend" and "heterosexual relationship" category is greater for men than for women (a difference of 0.63 for men and 0.55 for women). The disparity is even greater between "same-gender, close-friend" and "heterosexual relationship" (the difference for men is 1.85, while for women it is 0.33). Thus, intimate relationships with women are among the least likely addressee situations in which men will use *dude*, while a close female friend is the most likely woman to be addressed with *dude* by a man. In simple terms, men report that they use *dude* with women with whom they are close friends, but not with women with whom they are intimate.

This survey, combined with the DC, thus supports the claim that *dude* indexes a complex and somewhat indeterminate combination of distance, casualness, camaraderie, and equality. The survey also suggests that speakers are aware of the association between *dude* use and masculinity: in the open-ended question asking who uses *dude*, all responses suggested men, specifically young, drug-using men, often with descriptions such as *slacker, skater* (one who skateboards), or *druggie*. This second-order indexicality, or **metapragmatic awareness** (Silverstein 1996; Morford 1997), is one which connects the term to counter-culture, nonserious masculinity.

These indexicalities are clearly represented in films such as *Fast Times at Ridgemont High* (1982), *Bill and Ted's Excellent Adventure* (1989), *Clerks* (1994), and *Dude, Where's My Car?* (2000), and in other popular representations of the term. In these films, some or all of the young male characters frequently use the term *dude*. The character Jeff Spicoli in *Fast Times at Ridgemont High*, played by Sean Penn, is one of the earliest, perhaps the best known and most prototypical, of these characters. This film is a comedy about a year in a southern Californian high school, with Spicoli as the do-nothing, class-cutting, stoned surfer. While he is

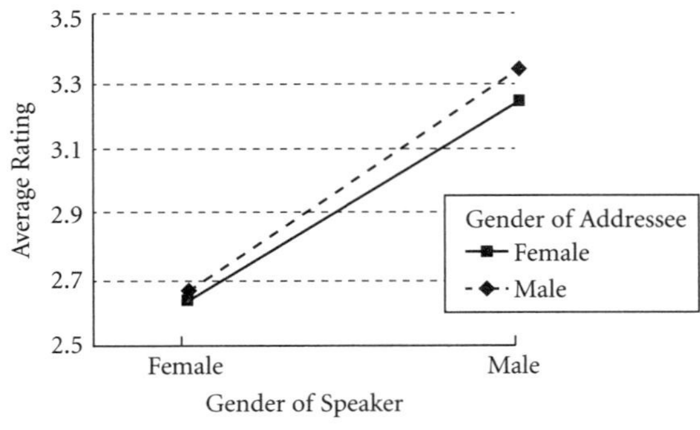


**Figure 40.3** *Reported Frequency of Use of* dude *by Gender of Speaker and Addressee*

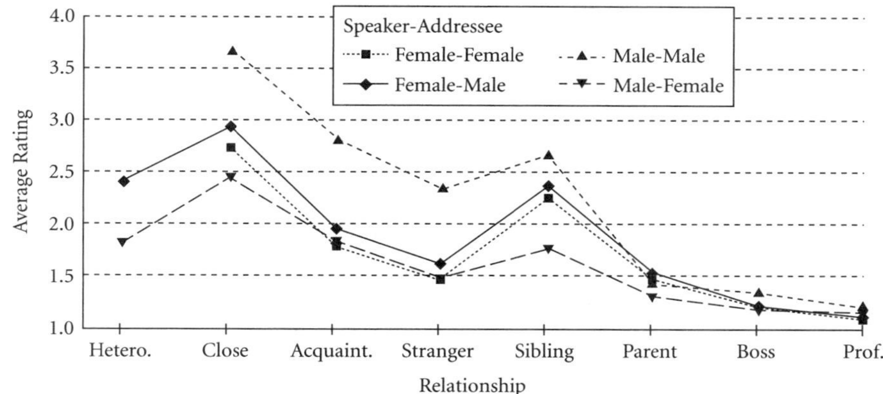


**Figure 40.4** Dude *Reported Use by Gender of Speaker, Addressee, and Relationship (see note 9 for descriptions of the relationship labels)*

"clueless" and often falls on hard times, Spicoli is consistently laid back, even in exasperation, and especially in encounters with authority. The male characters who use *dude* in the other films mentioned here have similar personalities. Although they manifest it in slightly different ways, all take a laid-back stance to the world, even if the world proves to be quite remarkable, as in *Bill and Ted's Excellent Adventure* (in which the protagonists travel through time). I was a teenager at the time *Fast Times* was released. The characters in this film resonated with me and my peers because they represented (and satirized) a distillation of the dominant identity types found in my high school of mostly middle-class European Americans. As such, these characters, especially Spicoli, became media "linguistic icons" in Eckert's (2000) terminology. Many young men glorified Spicoli, especially his nonchalant blindness to authority and hierarchical division; in the early 1980s we often spoke with Spicoli's voice. At first these quotes were only in stylized situations where we quoted from the movie, but eventually many of the features of Spicoli's speech, especially *dude*, became commonplace as we endeavored to emulate the stance Spicoli takes toward the world. I will return to this film when discussing the rise of *dude*, but here it is evidence of the stances associated with *dude* as represented in popular media.

*Dude* has also been featured in comic strips, as shown in Figure 40.1, from the comic strip "Zits," which has as its main characters American teenagers. *Dude* is implicated in stereotypes of male communication as inexpressive and monosyllabic (see also Sattel 1983), but in this episode of "Zits" the speakers are actually performing an act of solidarity (offering and accepting chewing gum), but with limited enthusiasm. *Dude* is perfect for such an interaction, and again bolsters the understanding of *dude* as indexing cool solidarity, especially among men. Figure 40.5 is a "Doonesbury" comic strip of a dialogue between two male college roommates. One of the roommates, distressed that the other has stopped calling him *dude*, interprets this as a symptom of becoming a more serious student overall. Here *dude* is clearly indexed with not being serious, since not using *dude* is seen as evidence of becoming serious. All of these representations suggest that *dude*'s first-order indexicality is one of cool solidarity, with a related second-order indexicality of men who shun authority and the establishment. Cartoonist Gary Trudeau uses this indexicality to humorous effect in a later strip when one of the characters in Figure 40.5 joins the CIA; the humor is created by the clash inherent in the "slacker" working for the agency that arguably represents the height of establishment power. The indexicalities of *dude* thus encompass not just stances but also specific kinds of masculinity, and the two are intimately bound with one another in an indexical web.

## *Dude* in Interaction

To understand how these indexicalities are put to use, this section investigates how *dude* is used in contextualized interactions among college-aged men in 1993 and views some examples of its use in interaction. I first outline where *dude* appears, and then the various functions it fulfills in interaction.

In reviewing the tokens of *dude* in the tapes from my year's ethnographic work in an American all-male fraternity (see Kiesling 1997, 1998, 2001a, 2001b) and in the DC, I have found that *dude* appears overwhelmingly in utterance-initial or utterance-final position. The frequencies with which *dude* appears in these positions are presented in Table 40.1. It is also used regularly in **sequential** locations in interaction, such as in greetings, leave-takings, the prefacing of important information, and exclamations.

I also identify five specific interactional functions for *dude*: (1) marking discourse structure, (2) exclamation, (3) confrontational stance **mitigation**, (4) marking **affiliation** and connection, and (5) signaling agreement. Almost all of these functions overlap and derive from its indexicalities of cool solidarity and laid-back masculinity, although these indexicalities are employed in different ways depending on the function. These functions also show how *dude* encapsulates the men's **homosociality**, that is, the small zone of "safe" solidarity between camaraderie and intimacy.

**Figure 40.5** Dude *in "Doonesbury" Comic Strip*

**Discourse Structure Marking** An individual use of *dude* may indicate a discourse structure, as described below, although the cool solidarity stance is simultaneously indexed when *dude* is used in this way. When this function marks off a new segment of discourse from a previous segment (as in the example below), it usually has a sharply falling intonation.

**Exclamation** *Dude* may be used on its own as an exclamation, to express both positive and negative reactions (commonly with another exclamative, especially *whoa*). The **prosody** used for *dude* in this function varies depending on the exclamation; in most instances it can be extremely elongated and falling in pitch, but not as sharply as in the discourse-structure-marking function.

**Table 40.1** Frequency of Positions of *dude*

| Position | | |
|---|---|---|
| Initial | 309 | (59.5%) |
| Final | 140 | (27.0%) |
| Medial | 19 | (3.7%) |
| Greeting | 36 | (6.9%) |
| *Dude* as entire utterance | 7 | (1.3%) |
| Exclamation with *whoa* | 8 | (1.5%) |
| Total | 519 | |

Note: Dude *is final in all greetings and exclamations.*

**Confrontational Stance Attenuator** *Dude* is often used when the speaker is taking a confrontational or "one-up" stance to the addressee. Through its indexing of solidarity, *dude* can **attenuate** or ameliorate the confrontation, signaling that the competitive or hierarchical component of the utterance is not serious. The DC has many instances of this kind of use, especially in woman-woman situations. In the terms of Brown and Levinson's (1987) politeness theory, this use is as a **positive politeness** strategy in situations of **negative face threat.** These instances are typically found at the end of the phrase and exhibit a low pitch that rises slightly on a slightly elongated syllable (not as elongated as in exclamations, however).

**Affiliation and Connection** When *dude* is used as a true address term (i.e., it identifies the addressee), it is used to indicate a stance of affiliation or connection, but with cool solidarity as well. The pitch in this function is usually higher than in others, often slightly rising.

**Agreement** *Dude* is commonly used when a stance of agreement is taken, either sympathizing with something the addressee said, or agreeing with the content of the utterance. As with the affiliation and connection function, when sympathy or agreement is expressed and *dude* is used, this sympathetic stance retains a measure of cool. The prosody for this function is very similar to the confrontational *dude*, the only difference being that in the agreement function the pitch tends to be higher.

---

These functions are not all mutually exclusive; *dude* can perform more than one function in a single utterance, or it can be left ambiguous. Some examples of each of the functions in use show how speakers use this term in particular situations and how its indexicalities work in these situations.

The first example, in which *dude* is used in its discourse-structure-marking function, is from a narrative told by Pete at the end of a meeting of fraternity members (see Kiesling 2001a). In this excerpt, Pete is telling about a road trip that he and Hotdog had taken during the previous weekend, in which they got lost. (This excerpt is not the entire narrative, which is very long and has numerous points which might be counted as **evaluation** and/or **climax**.)

EXCERPT 1[10]

1 PETE: I was like fuck it just take this road we'll be there.
2 end up,
3 at one o'clock in the morning,
4 in south Philly.
5 I don't know if any y'all been at south Philly,
6 but it ain't where you wanna be at one o'clock in the morning
7 HOTDOG: it's it's the northeast of Washington D.C.
8 PETE: it is it's the southeast of Philadelphia
9 that's what it is.
10 I mean it's southeast
11 DUDE.
12 we're driving a 94 Geo Prism (.) with no tags, (1.1)
13 two White boys,
14 and we're like stuck behind this bu-
15 at one point,
16 we were stuck in an alley,
17 in an alley like cars parked on both sides, (.)
18 behind a bus,
19 and there's like two bars
20 like on both sides.
21 like (1.0) all these black people everywhere.
22 WASTED.
23 fucked up.
24 lookin at us.
25 *just like* (1.8)
26 I was scared shitless,
27 I 'as like Hotdog GO GO.
28 he was like there's a bus.
29 I don't care GO GO (0.7)
30 most nerve-racking time of my life-

Pete's use of *dude* in line 11 marks off an important segment of the narrative, a part in which he tells about the "danger" he and Hotdog were in. In lines 1–4 he is setting up their arrival in South Philadelphia. In lines 5–10, he describes in general that South Philly is dangerous, with help from Hotdog in line 7, who explains the status of South Philadelphia by relating it to a similar neighborhood in Washington, D.C., with which his audience is familiar. He has some **disfluency** getting exactly the form he is looking for, and then in line 11 utters *dude*, with a complete intonation contour that has a sharply falling intonation and is low in his pitch range. *Dude* thus serves to break off the string of disfluencies from the following utterances, which Pete "resets" by giving it more volume and beginning with a higher pitch. The utterances following *dude* then resume his evocation of danger more specifically, and the climax of this part of the story comes in lines 21–29, in which he describes the "dangerous" people around them, and then an evaluation in line 26 ("I was scared shitless").

In this example, *dude* is not picking out a single addressee: Pete is addressing the entire meeting. Rather, *dude* has two functions related to the narrative structure and purpose. First, it delays the climax and resets the narrative, calling attention to the climax and evaluation to come. In this sense it is a discourse marker rather than an address term. So why does Pete use *dude* here and not something more "discourse-focused" like *so* or *anyway*, which are sometimes used to return to the main thread of a conversation or narrative once it has been left? The answer is the second function—that *dude* also retains its indexicality of cool solidarity and allows Pete to bring the audience into his story as if he were telling it to one person rather than many. Moreover, it invites the hearers to take Pete's perspective, thus further creating a separation between himself and the dangerous denizens of South Philly. Pete uses *dude* to build involvement, to use Tannen's (1989) term.

Later in the story, before Hotdog begins to conarrate, Pete again uses *dude*:

EXCERPT 2

40 PETE: DUDE it was like boys in the hood man ai:n't no: lie:
41 HOTDOG: And they're all they're fucked up on crack, wasted
42 they're all lookin' at us they start comin' to the car,
43 so Pete's like FLOOR IT.
44 so I take off (.) and (.)

In this instance, Pete uses *dude* with an exclamatory function, with a slightly elongated vowel and a level intonation; *dude* is the most prominent syllable in the phrase, which lowers in pitch and amplitude throughout. But notice that the statement that follows is also a summary and evaluation of the situation he and Hotdog found themselves in, and continues the same involved, affiliative stance he used in the previous excerpt. We can infer this from his concurrent use of Southern vernacular English forms in *ain't no lie* and the address term *man*, which is similar to *dude* but less pervasive in this group.

An instance in which Pete uses *dude* to both attenuate a competitive stance and create connection is shown in the following excerpt from the Monopoly game:

EXCERPT 3

44 PETE: Fuckin' ay man.
45 Gimme the red Dave. DUDE. (1.0)

46 DAVE: No.
47 PETE: Dave DUDE, DUDE Dave hm hm hm hm
48 DAVE: I'll give you the purple one
49 PETE: Oh THAT's a good trade

Pete is of course playing with the alliteration between Dave's name and *dude* in line 47 (Dave's real name also has an initial /d/). But Pete's use of *dude* in line 45 is coupled with a bald imperative ("gimme the red"), and *dude* is in fact added almost as an afterthought, with a falling intonation on Dave, before *dude* (although there is no pause between the two words). Dave responds with his own bald refusal ("no"), which continues the confrontational stance initiated by Pete. The next line serves a purely interactional purpose, as it contains only Dave's name and *dude* repeated once in **chiasmus**. This "contentless" use of *dude* then can be performing only an interactional function (it is not performing a necessary address term function, since Pete also uses Dave's first name). Pete's chuckles after his use of the term indicate that he is not taking a truly confrontational stance, so he is probably changing his strategy to get the red property by emphasizing his and Dave's friendship. Dave follows suit in this "toning down" of the competition; he makes a conciliatory move after Pete's initial plea by offering Pete another property. In this excerpt, then, we see *dude* used in a purely **affiliative** way and in its mitigating function, especially useful because Pete is in an inherently competitive but friendly activity (the Monopoly game). These uses show how *dude* can be strategically placed so that the confrontation and the competition stay on a playful level. In this sense, it is a **framing** device as well as a stance indicator, indexing a "play" frame for the men (see Bateson 1972; Tannen 1979).

In the next example, Pete uses *dude* to create a stance of affiliation, but also to project coolness. Pete is in a bar with Dan, an out-of-town friend visiting another fraternity member. In this conversation, Pete agrees with many of the comments Dan enthusiastically makes but plays down his enthusiasm (see Kiesling 2001b). Particularly important here is that Pete is not just agreeing but doing so while keeping a cool, nonchalant stance that contrasts with Dan's enthusiasm about playing caps (a drinking game).

EXCERPT 4

DAN: I love playin' caps.
That's what did me in last [last week.
PETE: [that's]
Everybody plays that damn game, DUDE.

Pete's use of *dude* in this excerpt matches the nonchalant stance of Pete's statement, thus helping to create that stance.

The next excerpt indexes a similar cool stance, but this time in a meeting. This example is Speed's first comment about which candidate should be elected chapter correspondent in an election meeting (see Kiesling 1997).

EXCERPT 5

SPEED: Ri:tchie. I like Ritchie 'cause he's smart and he probably (writes really good) too:.
so let him do it DUDE.

*Dude* helps Speed create a "stand-offish" stance in this excerpt, as it is used with the phrase "let him do it." Speed could have used something more active, such as "elect Ritchie," or "we need to put Ritchie in this position," but he frames his comments as a matter of simply stepping aside and letting Ritchie do the job. His relatively short comments are also consistent with this stance. Note also that Speed is speaking not to a single person, but to a roomful of members who are collectively his addressee, as Pete did in (1). *Dude* in this instance, then, is used purely to help create this stance of nonintervention, letting things take their course.

In the next excerpt, taken from a rush event (a social function held to attract potential members to the fraternity), Saul agrees with a potential member's (or rushee's) assessment of the University of Virginia men's basketball team.

EXCERPT 6

RUSHEE: Junior Burroughs is tough he's gonna be (tough to beat)
SAUL: Oh HELL yeah DUDE

This use of *dude* is especially interesting because it appears with an **intensifier.** The main part of Saul's utterance is his agreement with the rushee, as expressed simply by "yeah." But he intensifies this agreement with the use of "oh hell" before it with the primary sentence stress on *hell.* This indexes a stance not just of agreement but of enthusiastic agreement, in contrast to Pete's nonchalant agreement with Dan in (4). This difference is characteristic of Saul and Pete's personal styles: the former more often takes an enthusiastic interpersonal stance while the latter more often takes a cool stance. So it is not surprising that Saul should employ *dude* in a less cool, affiliative stance than Pete. Nevertheless, *dude* still serves to index both affiliation and distance, "toning down" the enthusiasm.

Finally, let us consider an instance of *dude* used in an interview. Mack uses it in (7) in an answer to a question I had asked about who gets elected to offices and whether the person who works hard or has the most ability actually gets elected to the office. In his answer, Mack takes me into his confidence about "the way things really work."

EXCERPT 7

60 MACK: You've been getting DUDE, what-
61 and this is, again what I'm coming down to
62 SK: ??
63 MACK: It really- the guys have been telling you what is supposed to happen
64 they don't know.

Mack here takes a stance of the knowledgeable insider, one he takes habitually (see Kiesling 1997, 1998). In lines 63 and 64, he creates a dichotomy between what is supposed to happen and what really happens, which only he and a few others know about. In line 60, he begins this course of argument ("you've been getting" refers to the answers I had received from other members about how people are elected to office), and he uses *dude* to signal that he is taking me into his confidence, into the inner circle of members. So here *dude* has solidarity function.

Although *dude* is used by almost all the men at some times, some use the term much more frequently than others. Pete uses *dude* at least sometimes in many different kinds of speech activities, as does Speed. Hotdog, Mack, and another member, Ram, by contrast, do not use *dude* in meetings but do use it in in-group narratives. Mack, as in (7), uses *dude* in the interview, but Hotdog and Ram do not. This pattern is strikingly similar to the patterns for the men's *-ing/-in'* use I have found (Kiesling 1998), suggesting that there is a similarity in the stances indexed and identities performed by the vernacular variant ([In]) and *dude*. However, both of these linguistic forms (*dude* and [In]) can index many kinds of stance while retaining core abstract indexicality of casual, effortless, or nonconformist (in the case of [In]), and affiliation and "cool" (in the case of *dude*). They overlap in their indexing of effortlessness and coolness and are thus likely to be used by the same men.

In sum, these examples show how the general stances indexed by *dude* can be used as a resource in interaction. By using *dude*, the men are not rigidly encoding a relationship with an addressee or addressees. Rather, they are using the indexicalities of the term to help create an interpersonal stance, along with many other resources that interact with various parts of context (the nature of the speech event, participants' previous interactions and identities within the institution, etc.). I will acknowledge the vagueness with which I have been describing the stance indexed by *dude* and at the same time argue that this indeterminacy is characteristic of the overwhelming majority of social indexes (see also Silverstein 1996, 269). Without context there is no SINGLE meaning that *dude* encodes, and it can be used, it seems, in almost any kind of situation (as shown by the "Zits" comic). But we should not confuse flexibility with meaninglessness; rather, the complex of stances indexed by the term—distance, camaraderie, cool, casualness, solidarity—can be made salient through different contexts. *Dude*, then, shows us two important ways indexicality, and meaning more generally, work in language. First, the meaning that speakers make when using language in interaction is about stance-taking at least as much as it is about **denotation**. Nor is this social meaning-making most often focused on signaling group affiliation or "acts of identity" (Le Page and Tabouret-Keller 1985). Rather, it is about specific relationships speakers create with each other in interaction. Second, meaning is made in contextualized interactions; words and sounds are indeterminate resources that speakers combine to perform and negotiate stances, and it is these stances which are the primary focus of interaction.

## How to Say *Dude*

If context is important to interpretation, then the linguistic and sociohistorical moment in which an utterance takes place is significant. Using *dude* in 2003 is different from using it in 1983, and certainly different from in 1963. This historical view also relates to the manner in which *dude* is pronounced. The importance of, and differences in, prosody has been discussed above; here I refer to the vowel quality of /u/ in *dude*. As shown by Labov (2001, 475–97), /u/ is being fronted across North America, especially after **coronal onsets.** *Dude* is thus a strongly favored environment for this fronting to take place. In fact, *dude* is almost always spoken with a fronted /u/ by the young speakers who use it, especially when it is used in a stylized manner (that is, when someone is performing while using the term, in the sense that they are marking it as not an authentic use of their own). I suggest that when older speakers pronounce *dude* with a backed /u/, younger speakers identify the token as unauthentic, uncool, or simply "old." There is thus a close connection between the fronted /u/ and *dude*. **Phonology** and **lexis** work together in this case to further make *dude*, in its most general sense, indexical of American youth. I would not go so far as to suggest that *dude* is driving this **sound change**, although Labov does argue that **outliers** (which are likely to be found in *dude* given its stylized uses) are important in the continuation of a sound change. While *dude* is not causing nor necessarily driving the sound change, it is certainly emblematic of it and is one of the ways that the sound change has been imbued with social meanings.

## Discussion

The casual and cool stance that is the main indexicality of *dude* is an important feature of men's homosociality in North America. While masculine solidarity is a central cultural Discourse of masculinity in North America, this solidarity is nevertheless ideally performed without much effort or dependence. *Dude* helps men maintain this balance between homosociality and hierarchy. It is not surprising, then, that *dude* has spread so widely among American men because it encodes a central stance of masculinity. If *dude* use by men is related to the dominant cultural Discourses of masculinity, then why did this term expand significantly in middle-class, European American youth in the early 1980s? What are the cultural currents that made the particular kind of masculinity and stance indexed by *dude* desirable for young men (i.e., for the post-baby-boom generation)?

Youth in general often engage in practices that are meant to express rebellion or at least differentiate them in some way from older generations (Brake 1985). In language, this nonconformity can be seen in the **"adolescent peak"**—the rise in nonstandard language use by teenagers (see Labov 2001, 101–20), a peak which flattens out as teenagers become older. The rise of *dude* likely took place because cool solidarity became a valuable nonconformist stance for youth in the 1980s. While I can find no studies analyzing dominant cultural Discourses of masculinity in the 1980s, I would characterize this time—the Reagan years particularly—as one in which "yuppie consumerism" and wealth accumulation were hegemonic. Edley and Wetherell (1995, 141), moreover, comment that

> it could be argued that the 1980s were characterized by the reinstatement of a new form of puritanist philosophy, once again emphasizing hard work and traditional family values (Levitas 1986). Typified in the character played by Michael Douglas in the film *Wall Street*, the stereotypical or ideal 1980's man was portrayed as a hard, aggressive person single-mindedly driven by the desire for power and status.

In perhaps the most well-known scenes in *Fast Times at Ridgemont High* (1982), a conflict is set up between Spicoli and his history teacher, Mr. Hand. In the first scene Spicoli is late on the first day of class, and in the second he has a pizza delivered to class. Mr. Hand is represented as a demanding, uptight teacher who takes stances that could hardly be further from those Spicoli adopts. Mr. Hand, of course, becomes outraged that Spicoli does not even seem to realize his behavior is unacceptable. From the eyes of a 1980s teenager, the conflict between Spicoli and Mr. Hand is an allegory for competing norms of masculinity and shows how the stances associated with *dude* are set up in conflict with stances of hard work and other "adult" values.[11] The "slackers" in the film *Clerks* (1994) are also the opposite of Edley and Wetherell's "hard, aggressive person single-mindedly driven by the desire for power and status," but in *Clerks*, the fun-loving of Spicoli has been replaced by nihilism: more "why bother?" than "who cares?" All of these portrayals, which can be connected to the use of *dude*, are part of a general American cultural Discourse which represents the post-baby-boom generation as having little or no career ambition—a whole generation of slackers. There is also a component of the surfer subculture associated with *dude* that valorizes not just skill and success, but the appearance of effortless, yet authentic, achievement. This kind of success is also quite different from the 1980s image of success based on hard work. So in many ways the stances indexed by *dude* were (and still are) nonconformist and attractive to adolescents.

This view of the motivations for the rise of *dude* in American English shows that sociolinguistic norms are much more complex than, for example, associating a sound with prestige. The kinds of meanings indexed by language can be numerous, even if connected by a common thread, and change with each use. More importantly, *dude* shows that it is not just the indexicalities of a form that might change, but that the values and aspirations of the speakers might change as well. What was cool in 1982 is not necessarily cool in 2002 but may become cool again in 2005. In other words, the very definition of prestige changes over time. The casual stance indexed by *dude* is becoming more "prestigious" throughout the United States, so perhaps it will eventually be used by all ages and in most situations in America. For the time being, it is clear that *dude* is a term that indexes a stance of cool solidarity for everyone and that it also has second orders of indexicality relating it to young people, young men, and young counterculture men. It became popular because young men found in *dude* a way to express dissatisfaction with the careerism of the 1980s, and it has later been a way of expressing the nihilism of the 1990s. Perhaps we are becoming a nation of skaters and surfers, at least in certain cultural trappings, who only wish for, in Spicoli's words, "tasty waves and cool buds," and *dude* is the harbinger of things to come.

## APPENDIX

### *Dude* Survey

(This form modified from the original: *yinz* has been removed.)

**Language Survey**

Please help me with a survey for a linguistics class. The answers should take you only a few minutes. If you are interested in the topic, I can explain what we are studying after you have taken the survey.

Your answers are anonymous and confidential. No one will know who gave your answers, and the paper will be destroyed at the end of the course.

This survey asks you to answer questions about [two] words in English. These words are all terms of address. That is, they are used to greet someone or get their attention to talk to them in a sentence like this: "Hey, sir, you dropped something!"

The terms are *Dude* and *Babe*.

DUDE

1. How often do you use this term as an address term (circle one)?
   Many times each day
   About once a day
   About once a week
   Hardly ever
   Never

2. What kind of person are you likely to use it to address?
   1 = Not likely at all, will never use it with someone like this
   5 = Very likely, use it all the time with people like this

| *The person is your* | *The person is also a man* | *The person is also a woman* |
|---|---|---|
| Girl/boyfriend | 1 2 3 4 5 N/A | 1 2 3 4 5 N/A |
| Close friend | 1 2 3 4 5 N/A | 1 2 3 4 5 N/A |
| Acquaintance | 1 2 3 4 5 N/A | 1 2 3 4 5 N/A |
| Stranger | 1 2 3 4 5 N/A | 1 2 3 4 5 N/A |
| Sibling | 1 2 3 4 5 N/A | 1 2 3 4 5 N/A |
| Parent | 1 2 3 4 5 N/A | 1 2 3 4 5 N/A |
| Boss | 1 2 3 4 5 N/A | 1 2 3 4 5 N/A |
| Professor | 1 2 3 4 5 N/A | 1 2 3 4 5 N/A |

3. Why do you use the term? That is, what do you think it says about you to the person you are talking to?
4. What kind of person do you think uses it frequently?

BABE

1. How often do you use this term as an address term (circle one)?
   Many times each day
   About once a day
   About once a week
   Hardly ever
   Never
2. What kind of person are you likely to use it to address?
   1 = Not likely at all, will never use it with someone like this
   5 = Very likely, use it all the time with people like this

| *The person is your* | *The person is also a man* | *The person is also a woman* |
|---|---|---|
| Girl/boyfriend | 1 2 3 4 5 N/A | 1 2 3 4 5 N/A |
| Close friend | 1 2 3 4 5 N/A | 1 2 3 4 5 N/A |
| Acquaintance | 1 2 3 4 5 N/A | 1 2 3 4 5 N/A |
| Stranger | 1 2 3 4 5 N/A | 1 2 3 4 5 N/A |
| Sibling | 1 2 3 4 5 N/A | 1 2 3 4 5 N/A |
| Parent | 1 2 3 4 5 N/A | 1 2 3 4 5 N/A |
| Boss | 1 2 3 4 5 N/A | 1 2 3 4 5 N/A |
| Professor | 1 2 3 4 5 N/A | 1 2 3 4 5 N/A |

3. Why do you use the term? That is, what do you think it says about you to the person you are talking to?
4. What kind of person do you think uses it frequently?

NOW PLEASE ANSWER A FEW QUESTIONS ABOUT YOURSELF:

1. What is your age?
2. What is your ethnicity?
3. What is your gender?
4. In what city did (do) you go to high school?
5. What is your occupation?
6. If you are a college student, what is your major (or school, if undecided):

## Notes

1. I use the term *cultural Discourse* in the sense of poststructuralists, following Foucault (1980). Cultural Discourses are similar to ideologies, yet leave open the possibility of contradiction, challenge, and change, and describe more than idea systems, including social practices and structures. For a review of the term and its relevance to masculinities, see Whitehead (2002). I will always use a capital *D* with *cultural Discourses* to distinguish them from the linguistic notion of discourse, which is talk-in-interaction.
2. Fraternities are social clubs, with membership typically limited to men, on college campuses across North America.
3. *Pachuchos*, also spelled *pachucos*, refers to members of groups, or gangs, of young Mexicans and Mexican Americans known for their flamboyant dress, especially the zoot suit. The origin of the term is not completely clear, but it is likely derived from a native American word (Kiowa or Kiliwa). See Cummings (2003) and Sharp (2004).
4. The corpus results, class assignment, and an electronic version of the survey instrument are available at http://www.pitt.edu/~kiesling/dude/dude.html. I encourage instructors of linguistics courses to use the survey in their own courses, but please inform me that you have used it and, if possible, the results.
5. Of the 519 tokens collected, 471 (91%) were in situations with speakers and addressees under 30 years of age. This result may reflect the age population of the class, of course, but it is a relatively valid representation of *dude* use for that age group. In terms of class, most students were middle class or upper working class. Statistics were gathered for ethnicity, with European Americans providing the vast proportion of tokens, but again these results are probably skewed by the predominance of European Americans in the class.
6. These tokens could, of course, be influenced by who collected them. Both classes had more women than men, however, so if the results are skewed because of the sex of the observer, it is women's use of the term that has been artificially expanded.
7. It has been pointed out to me that there was also a time when *dudette* was used, but that this term was unsuccessful. I do not remember hearing many instances of *dudette* used as an address term except with *dude* ("Hi, dudes and dudettes!"). I do remember it being used to refer to "female dudes." In any case, it was not a successful term, perhaps because of its inequality with the male form as a diminutive derivative.
8. CONSTRUCTED DIALOGUE is more commonly called **reported speech**, which is essentially quoted speech; that is, it would be written in quotation marks in a novel. For example, "I'm like, dude, don't touch me," *dude, don't touch me* is reported speech. Tannen (1989) shows that such representations of other people's speech are often not what was actually said. Rather, the speech is CONSTRUCTED by the person doing the "quoting" to promote involvement in talk. The speaker in this example likely did not say exactly what she "quoted." Her use of a direct quote, however, makes her story much more vivid for the audience.
9. Some of the relationship labels need explanation. The first is "Hetero." This category is "heterosexual intimate relationships," labeled on the survey as girlfriend/boyfriend. There were responses for male-male and female-female categories, but it is clear from the students who gathered the data that not all respondents understood the intimate nature of this category for same-sex situations. That is, not all male respondents who gave a rating for "boyfriend" are homosexual. This confusion makes the response problematic, and so I have removed the same-sex boyfriend/girlfriend data from this table, thus making it represent heterosexual relationships only. "Close" refers to a close friend, and "Aquaint." is an acquaintance. The rest of the labels should be self-explanatory.

10. Transcription conventions are as follows: Each line is roughly a breath group, and unless otherwise noted there is a short pause for breath at the end of each line in the transcripts.

| | |
|---|---|
| (text) | indicates the accuracy of transcription inside parentheses is uncertain |
| (?) | indicates an utterance that could be heard but was not intelligible |
| a: | indicates the segment is lengthened |
| (#.#) | indicates a pause of #.# seconds |
| (.) | indicates a pause of less than 0.5 seconds |
| = | indicates that the utterance continues on the next line without a pause |
| A⌊B⌊<br>⌈C⌈D | indicates overlapping speech: B and C are uttered simultaneously, not A nor D. |
| TEXT | indicates emphasis through amplitude, length, and/or intonation |
| *text* | indicates noticeably lower amplitude |
| bu- | indicates an abrupt cutoff of speech |
| ((text)) | indicates comments added by the author |

11. See http://www.netwalk.com/~truegger/ftrh/ for plot summaries and audio clips of the film, including a "film strip" of the famous scenes (http://www.netwalk.com/~truegger/ftrh/pizza.html).

## References


Andersen, Gisle. 2001. *Pragmatic Markers and Sociolinguistic Variation: A Relevance-Theoretic Approach to the Language of Adolescents.* Amsterdam: Benjamins.

Bateson, Gregory. 1972. *Steps to an Ecology of Mind.* New York: Ballantine.

*Bill and Ted's Excellent Adventure.* 1989. Written by Chris Matheson and Ed Solomon. Directed by Stephen Herek. U.S.: De Laurentiis Entertainment Group, Interscope Communication, and Nelson Entertainment.

Brake, Mike. 1985. *Comparative Youth Culture: The Sociology of Youth Cultures and Youth Subcultures in America, Britain, and Canada.* London: Routledge.

Brown, Penelope, and Stephen Levinson. 1987. *Politeness: Some Universals in Language Use.* Cambridge: Cambridge Univ. Press.

Carrigan, Tim, Bob Connell, and John Lee. 1985. "Toward a New Sociology of Masculinity." *Theory and Society* 14: 551–604.

*Clerks.* 1994. Written and directed by Kevin Smith. U.S.: Miramax Films and View Askew Productions.

Connell, R. W. 1995. *Masculinities.* Cambridge: Polity.

Cummings, Laura L. 2003. "Cloth-Wrapped People, Trouble, and Power: Pachuco Culture in the Greater Southwest." *Journal of the Southwest* 45: 329–48.

Donald, Ralph R. 2001. "Masculinity and Machismo in Hollywood's War Films." In *The Masculinities Reader*, ed. Stephen M. Whitehead and Frank J. Barrett, 170–83. Cambridge: Polity.

*Dude, Where's My Car?* 2000. Written by Philip Stark. Directed by Danny Leiner. U.S.: Alcon Entertainment.

Eckert, Penelope. 2000. *Linguistic Variation as Social Practice: The Linguistic Construction of Identity in Belten High.* Malden, Mass.: Blackwell.

Edley, Nigel, and Margaret Wetherell. 1995. *Men in Perspective: Practice, Power, and Identity.* London: Prentice Hall/Harvester Wheatsheaf.

*Fast Times at Ridgemont High.* 1982. Written by Cameron Crowe. Directed by Amy Heckerlin. U.S.: Refugee Films and Universal Pictures.

Foucault, Michel. 1980. *Power/Knowledge: Selected Interviews and Other Writings 1972–1977.* Ed. Colin Gordon. 1st American ed. New York: Pantheon.

Guy, Gregory, Barbara Horvath, Julia Vonwiller, Elaine Daisley, and Inge Rogers. 1986. "An Intonational Change in Progress in Australian English." *Language in Society* 15: 23–52.

Hill, Richard. 1994. "You've Come a Long Way, Dude—A History." *American Speech* 69: 321–27.

Kiesling, Scott Fabius. 1997. "Power and the Language of Men." In *Language and Masculinity*, ed. Sally Johnson and Ulrike Hanna Meinhof, 65–85. Oxford: Blackwell.

Kiesling, Scott Fabius. 1998. "Men's Identities and Sociolinguistic Variation: The Case of Fraternity Men." *Journal of Sociolinguistics* 2: 69–99.

Kiesling, Scott Fabius. 2001a. "Stances of Whiteness and Hegemony in Fraternity Men's Discourse." *Journal of Linguistic Anthropology* 11: 101–15.

Kiesling, Scott Fabius. 2001b. "'Now I Gotta Watch What I Say': Shifting Constructions of Masculinity in Discourse." *Journal of Linguistic Anthropology* 11: 250–73.

Kimmel, Michael. 2001. "Masculinity as Homophobia: Fear, Shame, and Silence in the Construction of Gender Identity." In *The Masculinities Reader*, ed. Stephen M. Whitehead and Frank J. Barrett, 266–87. Cambridge: Polity.

Labov, William. 2001. *Principles of Linguistic Change.* Vol. 2, *Social Factors.* Oxford: Blackwell.

Le Page, R. B., and Andrée Tabouret-Keller. 1985. *Acts of Identity: Creole-based Approaches to Language and Ethnicity.* Cambridge: Cambridge Univ. Press.

Levitas, Ruth, ed. 1986. *The Ideology of the New Right.* Cambridge: Polity.

McLemore, Cynthia Ann. 1991. "The Pragmatic Interpretation of English Intonation: Sorority Speech." Ph.D. diss., Univ. of Texas at Austin.

Morford, Janet. 1997. "Social Indexicality in French Pronominal Address." *Journal of Linguistic Anthropology* 7: 3–37.

Ochs, Elinor. 1992. "Indexing Gender." In *Rethinking Context: Language as an Interactive Phenomenon*, ed. Alessandro Duranti and Charles Goodwin, 335–58. Cambridge: Cambridge Univ. Press.

Sattel, Jack. 1983. "Men, Inexpressiveness, and Power." In *Language, Gender and Society*, ed. Barrie Thorne, Cheris Kramarae, and Nancy Henley, 119–24. Rowley, Mass.: Newbury.

Sharp, Charles. 2004. "Pachucos." Zoot Suit Riot Web page. http://www.ethnomusic.ucla.edu/estudent/csharp/pachucos.html (accessed July).

Siegel, Muffy E. A. 2002. "*Like*: The Discourse Particle and Semantics." *Journal of Semantics* 19: 35–71.

Silverstein, Michael. 1996. "Indexical Order and the Dialectics of Sociolinguistic Life." In *Salsa III: Proceedings of the Third Annual Symposium about Language and Society—Austin*, ed. Risako Ide, Rebecca Parker, and Yukako Sunaoshi, 266–95. Austin: Dept. of Linguistics, Univ. of Texas.

Swofford, Anthony. 2003. *Jarhead: A Marine's Chronicle of the Gulf War and Other Battles*. New York: Scribner.

Tannen, Deborah. 1979. "What's in a Frame? Surface Evidence for Underlying Expectations." In *New Directions in Discourse Processing*, ed. Roy Freedle, 137–81. Norwood, N.J.: Ablex.

Tannen, Deborah. 1989. *Talking Voices: Repetition, Dialogue, and Imagery in Conversational Discourse*. Cambridge: Cambridge Univ. Press.

Whitehead, Stephen M. 2002. *Men and Masculinities: Key Themes and New Directions*. Cambridge: Polity.

## Critical Thinking and Application

- Kiesling uses *dude* as an index but ultimately argues that the stance indexed by *dude* is vague: "Without context there is no SINGLE meaning that *dude* encodes." How does this differ from a view of language as essentially a set of words with meanings? What implications does this have for how language should be studied and analyzed?
- Kiesling has a brief discussion in "How to Say *Dude*" about the pronunciation of the vowel /u/ in *dude*, pointing out that it is usually fronted. There is some disagreement among scholars about how sounds change in a language, with some arguing that they change as a whole, systematically, and others that individual words can sometimes drive later, more systematic changes. Learn more about theories of sound change and the role played by youth in initiating that change.
- Kiesling posts his survey instrument at http://www.pitt.edu/~kiesling/dude/dude.html. Using this instrument, conduct your own survey (and inform Kiesling of your results). Are your results similar to his? If not, how would you explain any discrepancies?
- Identify another linguistic variable that indexes generation or age. Record its actual use. What are the linguistic functions and what are the corresponding interactional or social functions?

## Vocabulary

addressee
adolescent peak
affiliation, affiliative
attennate, attenuator
camaraderie
chiasmus
climax
constructed dialogue
coronal onset
corpus
declarative
denotation
discourse
Discourse
discourse marker
disfluency
evaluation
first-order index
framing
fronted
hegemony, hegemonic
heterosexism
homosociality
index, indexicality
intensifier
lexis
Likert scale
metapragmatic awareness
mitigation
negative face, negative face threat
outlier
phonology, phonological
positive politeness
prosody
reported speech
second-order index
sequential
solidarity
sound change
stance
token

## Suggested Further Reading

Coupland, Nikolas. 2007. *Style: Language Variation and Identity*. Cambridge: Cambridge University Press.

Eckert, Penelope. 2001. Style and Social Meaning. In *Style and Sociolinguistic Variation*, edited by Penelope Eckert and John R. Rickford, pp. 119–126. Cambridge: Cambridge University Press.

Eckert, Penelope, and John R. Rickford, eds. 2001. *Style and Sociolinguistic Variation*. Cambridge: Cambridge University Press.

Fought, Carmen, ed. 2004. *Sociolinguistic Variation: Critical Reflections*. Oxford: Oxford University Press.

Jaffe, Alexandra M., ed. 2009. *Stance: Sociolinguistic Perspectives*. Oxford: Oxford University Press.

Johnson, Sally, and Ulrike Hanna Meinhof, eds. 1997. *Language and Masculinity*. Oxford: Blackwell.

Kiesling, Scott F. 2009. Style as Stance: Stance as the Explanation for Patterns of Sociolinguistic Variation. In *Stance: Sociolinguistic Perspectives*, edited by Alexandra M. Jaffe, pp. 171–194. Oxford: Oxford University Press.

Rampton, Ben. 1995. *Crossing: Language and Ethnicity Among Adolescents*. London and New York: Longman.

Wong, William S-Y. 1979. Language Change—A Lexical Perspective. *Annual Review of Anthropology* 8: 353–371.

# PART III

# Language as Social Action

Language has structure; language creates the human race; language operates to create, enforce, and perform our various identities. But language does many more things than that. Since J. L. Austin published his striking *How to Do Things with Words*, philosophers of language, linguists, and anthropologists have busily established some of the many ways humans make use of language in carrying out the specific activities of their lives. This focus on action has developed in a number of different directions, some of which are introduced in this part of the book.

In contrast to a *referential* view of language, in which language conveys information ("says something"), or an *indexical* view of language, in which language conveys social identities, a focus on how language *does* things is called a *pragmatic* view of language. That is, it focuses on consequences and effects of language in context.

Austin's and the later Wittgenstein's new way of regarding language drew attention to many of the performative aspects of language or "language games." (The early Wittgenstein focused more on language as a self-contained system.) In works from this perspective, terms used include *performance*, *emergence*, and *action*. The study of discourse and performance emerged in the 1980s as folklorists, linguists, and anthropologists began to study complex forms of language use in their contexts. One prominent pursuit in this was the study of what had previously been called "folklore" but began to be called "verbal art"; the new field of "ethnopoetics" was formed.

Units of analysis were necessarily much larger than sentences, and a variety of creative approaches were invented to understand "discourse." In discourse analysis, there is always a focus on details of conversation (conversation analysis is the most prominent subset of discourse analysis) with a concomitant consideration of the broader context with, which it took place.

Beyond art, however, this study also showed how thoroughly political every aspect of performance was. Power was the newest ingredient in the study of language.

Some of the many topics investigated from this perspective include language socialization (how children are socialized into and through language), religious ritual (in which language is often seen as having efficacy), emotion (in which language is seen to create emotion), politics and power (in which language creates and reinforces power differences), and healing (in which language is often seen as bringing about improvements in health). In all such studies, language has to be looked at in its full social and cultural context. It cannot be dissociated from the conditions in which it is used because the *meaning* lies in its use, not simply in a combination of words and grammar. Here we find a breathtaking range of human uses of language throughout the world.

The final topic here is that of language ideology. This involves what the uses of language are for its speakers: how they see language functioning, what kinds of language they see as more desirable or even more beautiful, and where language should and should not be used. These aspects of language have been studied increasingly in the decades since the term *language ideology* was first widely used in the 1990s.

## Suggested Further Reading


Abu-Lughod, Lila. 1986. *Veiled Sentiments: Honor and Poetry in a Bedouin Society*. Berkeley: University of California Press.

Abu-Lughod, Lila, and Catherine Lutz, eds. 1990. *Language and the Politics of Emotion*. Cambridge: Cambridge University Press.

Briggs, Charles. 1986. *Learning How to Ask: A Sociolinguistic Appraisal of the Role of the Interview in Social Science Research*. Cambridge: Cambridge University Press.

Brown, Penelope, and Stephen C. Levinson. 1987. *Politeness: Some Universals in Language Usage*. Cambridge: Cambridge University Press.

Feld, Steven. 1982. *Sound and Sentiment: Birds, Weeping, Poetics, and Song in Kaluli Expression*. Philadelphia: University of Pennsylvania Press.

Grice, Paul. 1989. *Studies in the Way of Words*. Cambridge, MA: Harvard University Press.

Keenan, Elinor Ochs. 1976. The Universality of Conversational Postulates. *Language in Society* 5(1): 67–80.

Lutz, Catherine A. 1988. *Unnatural Emotions: Everyday Sentiments on a Micronesian Atoll and Their Challenge to Western Theory*. Chicago: University of Chicago Press.

Malinowski, Bronislaw. 1923. The Problem of Meaning in Primitive Languages. In *The Meaning of Meaning*, edited by C. K. Ogden and I. A. Richards. New York: Harcourt, Brace.

Malinowski, Bronislaw. 1935. *Coral Gardens and Their Magic: A Study of the Methods of Tilling the Soil and of Agricultural Rites in the Trobriand Islands*. New York: American Book.

Malinowski, Bronislaw. 1948. *Magic, Science, and Religion, and Other Essays*. Boston: Beacon Press.

Rosaldo, Michelle Z. 1982. The Things We Do with Words: Ilongot Speech Acts and Speech Act Theory in Philosophy. *Language in Society* 11: 203–235.

Searle, John R. 1969. *Speech Acts: An Essay in the Philosophy of Language*. Cambridge: Cambridge University Press.

# UNIT 8

# Discourse, Performance, and Ritual

Language, treated as social action, focuses on the ways people accomplish things by means of language; in Austin's terms, we perform actions rather than simply reporting on them. The context of use is always relevant because the words used have an effect on the world in which they are spoken.

This tradition extends back also to the pioneering anthropologist Bronislaw Malinowski, who noted that in the Trobriand Islands of Papua New Guinea, people often used language for reasons quite different from that of conveying information, which is known as the *referential* function of language.

Other fascinating things people do with language include all the ways language is used in religion—for supplication, for exorcism, to testify to things seen—in emotion, in politics, and in every facet of life. In such studies, the veracity of language is often secondary to the effectiveness of language-in-use.

Discourse analysis takes language in context and examines its consequences and mechanisms. How does power emanate from the exchange of words? Whose voices are involved? Such questions drive a lively field that analyzes everything from intimate conversation to international politics.

## Suggested Further Reading


Abrahams, Roger D. 1983. *The Man-of-Words in the West Indies: Performance and the Emergence of Creole Culture.* Baltimore: Johns Hopkins University Press.

Bakhtin, Mikhail M. 1981. *The Dialogic Imagination*, edited by Michael Holquist, translated by Caryl Emerson and Michael Holquist. Austin: University of Texas Press.

Bauman, Richard, and Charles L. Briggs. 1990. Poetics and Performance as Critical Perspectives on Language and Social Life. *Annual Review of Anthropology* 19: 59–88.

Bloch, Maurice, ed. 1975. *Political Language and Oratory in Traditional Society.* London: Academic Press.

Brown, Gillian, and George Yule. 1983. *Discourse Analysis.* Cambridge: Cambridge University Press.

Duranti, Alessandro. 1994. *From Grammar to Politics: Linguistic Anthropology in a Western Samoan Village.* Berkeley: University of California Press.

Fairclough, Norman. 1989. *Language and Power.* London and New York: Longman.

Hymes, Dell. 1975. Breakthrough into Performance. In *Folklore: Performance and Communication*, edited by D. Ben-Amos and K. S. Goldstein, pp. 11–74. The Hague: Mouton.

Hymes, Dell. 1981. *"In Vain I Tried to Tell You": Essays in Native American Ethnopoetics.* Philadelphia: University of Pennsylvania Press.

Keating, Elizabeth. 1998. *Power Sharing: Language, Rank, Gender, and Social Space in Pohnpei, Micronesia.* New York: Oxford University Press.

Sherzer, Joel. 2002. *Speech Play and Verbal Art.* Austin: University of Texas Press.

Tambiah, S. J. 1979. *A Performative Approach to Ritual.* Proceedings of the British Academy 65. London: Oxford University Press.

Tedlock, Dennis. 1983. *The Spoken Word and the Work of Interpretation.* Philadelphia: University of Pennsylvania Press.

## CHAPTER 41

# How to Do Things with Words


*J. L. Austin*


(1962)

*Philosophers of language such as Bertrand Russell worked hard to explain how language derived its meaning, aiming to describe it like mathematics or formal logic. They looked principally at the grammar and the logical operators that linked words such as nouns and verbs. What was critical was to determine its "truth value," since its primary function seemed to be to convey factual information.*

*J. L. Austin followed a different path. Known as an* ordinary language philosopher, *he looked at the actual* acts *people performed in ordinary life by means of language. Thus, what was most important was what happened through use of language, or what language* does, *rather than what language* means. *He is considered the founder of Speech Act Theory and also influential in the development of the* pragmatics *branch of linguistics, both very rich sources of inspiration for the study of language.*

*This chapter is the first of the twelve chapters in his book* How to Do Things with Words, *originally a series of lectures given at Harvard University in 1955. Although Austin is not the first to note that looking at sentences for their "truth value" is not adequate to account for every use of language, he put it extremely clearly, using ordinary, everyday examples.*

*In later chapters in the book, Austin distinguishes the* locutionary act *(what people say) from the* illocutionary act *(what people intend) and the* perlocutionary force *(what results from the utterance). Though he initially applied this analysis principally to what he names in this chapter the* performative utterance*—that special kind of sentence that accomplishes something in the world, like christening a ship by using the present-tense form of a verb and potentially using the word* hereby*—he later made clear that in some sense all language is performative. This was a revolution in the study of language, and we are all its beneficiaries.*

### Reading Questions

- What kinds of sentences do philosophers usually analyze?
- What examples does Austin give of "constatives" and of "performatives"? What is each type of utterance for?
- Why can't performatives be true or false?
- Are there some utterances that *must* be made for an action to take place? What examples can you think of?

---

What I shall have to say here is neither difficult nor contentious; the only merit I should like to claim for it is that of being true, at least in parts. The phenomenon to be discussed is very widespread and obvious, and it cannot fail to have been already noticed, at least here and there, by others. Yet I have not found attention paid to it specifically.

It was for too long the assumption of philosophers that the business of a **'statement'** can only be to 'describe' some state of affairs, or to 'state some fact', which it must do either truly or falsely. Grammarians, indeed, have regularly pointed out that not all 'sentences' are (used in making) statements:[1] there are, traditionally, besides (grammarians') statements, also questions and exclamations, and sentences expressing commands or wishes or concessions. And doubtless philosophers have not intended to deny this, despite some loose use of 'sentence' for 'statement'. Doubtless, too, both grammarians and philosophers have been aware that it is by no means


J. L. Austin, How to Do Things with Words. Lecture I. From *How to Do Things With Words*, 2nd ed. Cambridge, Mass.: Harvard University Press, 1975 [1962], pp. 1–11.

easy to distinguish even questions, commands, and so on from statements by means of the few and jejune grammatical marks available, such as word order, mood, and the like: though perhaps it has not been usual to dwell on the difficulties which this fact obviously raises. For how do we decide which is which? What are the limits and definitions of each?

But now in recent years, many things which would once have been accepted without question as 'statements' by both philosophers and grammarians have been scrutinized with new care. This scrutiny arose somewhat indirectly—at least in philosophy. First came the view, not always formulated without unfortunate dogmatism, that a statement (of fact) ought to be 'verifiable', and this led to the view that many 'statements' are only what may be called pseudo-statements. First and most obviously, many 'statements' were shown to be, as KANT perhaps first argued systematically, strictly nonsense, despite an unexceptionable grammatical form: and the continual discovery of fresh types of nonsense, unsystematic though their classification and mysterious though their explanation is too often allowed to remain, has done on the whole nothing but good. Yet we, that is, even philosophers, set some limits to the amount of nonsense that we are prepared to admit we talk: so that it was natural to go on to ask, as a second stage, whether many apparent pseudo-statements really set out to be 'statements' at all. It has come to be commonly held that many **utterances** which look like statements are either not intended at all, or only intended in part, to record or impart straightforward information about the facts: for example, 'ethical propositions' are perhaps intended, solely or partly, to evince emotion or to prescribe conduct or to influence it in special ways. Here too KANT was among the pioneers. We very often also use utterances in ways beyond the scope at least of traditional grammar. It has come to be seen that many specially perplexing words embedded in apparently descriptive statements do not serve to indicate some specially odd additional feature in the reality reported, but to indicate (not to report) the circumstances in which the statement is made or reservations to which it is subject or the way in which it is to be taken and the like. To overlook these possibilities in the way once common is called the 'descriptive' fallacy; but perhaps this is not a good name, as 'descriptive' itself is special. Not all true or false statements are descriptions, and for this reason I prefer to use the word **'constative'**. Along these lines it has by now been shown piecemeal, or at least made to look likely, that many traditional philosophical perplexities have arisen through a mistake—the mistake of taking as straightforward statements of fact utterances which are *either* (in interesting non-grammatical ways) nonsensical *or else* intended as something quite different.

Whatever we may think of any particular one of these views and suggestions, and however much we may deplore the initial confusion into which philosophical doctrine and method have been plunged, it cannot be doubted that they are producing a revolution in philosophy. If anyone wishes to call it the greatest and most salutary in its history, this is not, if you come to think of it, a large claim. It is not surprising that beginnings have been piecemeal, with *parti pris*, and for extraneous aims; this is common with revolutions.

## PRELIMINARY ISOLATION OF THE PERFORMATIVE[2]

The type of utterance we are to consider here is not, of course, in general a type of nonsense; though misuse of it can, as we shall see, engender rather special varieties of 'nonsense'. Rather, it is one of our second class—the masqueraders. But it does not by any means necessarily masquerade as a statement of fact, descriptive or constative. Yet it does quite commonly do so, and that, oddly enough, when it assumes its most explicit form. Grammarians have not, I believe, seen through this 'disguise', and philosophers only at best incidentally.[3] It will be convenient, therefore, to study it first in this misleading form, in order to bring out its characteristics by contrasting them with those of the statement of fact which it apes.

We shall take, then, for our first examples some utterances which can fall into no hitherto recognized *grammatical* category save that of 'statement', which are not nonsense, and which contain none of those verbal danger-signals which philosophers have by now detected or think they have detected (curious words like 'good' or 'all', suspect auxiliaries like 'ought' or 'can', and dubious constructions like the hypothetical): all will have, as it happens, humdrum verbs in the first person singular present indicative active.[4] Utterances can be found, satisfying these conditions, yet such that

A. they do not 'describe' or 'report' or constate anything at all, are not 'true or false'; and
B. the uttering of the sentence is, or is a part of, the doing of an action, which again would not *normally* be described as, or as 'just', saying something.

This is far from being as paradoxical as it may sound or as I have meanly been trying to make it sound: indeed, the examples now to be given will be disappointing.
Examples:

(E. *a*) 'I do (sc. take this woman to be my lawful wedded wife)'—as uttered in the course of the marriage ceremony.[5]
(E. *b*) 'I name this ship the *Queen Elizabeth*'—as uttered when smashing the bottle against the stem.
(E. *c*) 'I give and bequeath my watch to my brother'—as occurring in a will.
(E. *d*) 'I bet you sixpence it will rain tomorrow.'

In these examples it seems clear that to utter the sentence (in, of course, the appropriate circumstances) is not to *describe* my doing of what I should be said in so uttering to be doing[6] or to state that I am doing it: it is to do it. None of the utterances cited is either true or false: I assert this as obvious and do not argue it. It needs argument no more than that 'damn' is not true or false: it may be that the utterance 'serves to inform you'—but that is quite different. To name the ship *is* to say (in the appropriate circumstances) the words 'I name, &c.'. When I say, before the registrar or altar, &c., 'I do', I am not reporting on a marriage: I am indulging in it.

What are we to call a sentence or an utterance of this type?[7] I propose to call it a *performative sentence* or a performative utterance, or, for short, 'a **performative**'. The term 'performative' will be used in a variety of cognate ways and constructions, much as the term 'imperative' is.[8] The name is derived, of course, from 'perform', the usual verb with the noun 'action': it indicates that the issuing of the utterance is the performing of an action—it is not normally thought of as just saying something.

A number of other terms may suggest themselves, each of which would suitably cover this or that wider or narrower class of performatives: for example, many performatives are *contractual* ('I bet') or *declaratory* ('I declare war') utterances. But no term in current use that I know of is nearly wide enough to cover them all. One technical term that comes nearest to what we need is perhaps 'operative', as it is used strictly by lawyers in referring to that part, i.e., those clauses, of an instrument which serves to effect the transaction (conveyance or what not) which is its main object, whereas the rest of the document merely 'recites' the circumstances in which the transaction is to be effected.[9] But 'operative' has other meanings, and indeed is often used nowadays to mean little more than 'important'. I have preferred a new word, to which, though its etymology is not irrelevant, we shall perhaps not be so ready to attach some preconceived meaning.

## Can Saying Make It So?

Are we then to say things like this:

> 'To marry is to say a few words', or
> 'Betting is simply saying something'?

Such a doctrine sounds odd or even flippant at first, but with sufficient safeguards it may become not odd at all.

A sound initial objection to them may be this; and it is not without some importance. In very many cases it is possible to perform an act of exactly the same kind *not* by uttering words, whether written or spoken, but in some other way. For example, I may in some places effect marriage by cohabiting, or I may bet with a totalisator machine by putting a coin in a slot. We should then, perhaps, convert the propositions above, and put it that 'to say a few certain words is to marry' or 'to marry is, in some cases, simply to say a few words' or 'simply to say a certain something is to bet'.

But probably the real reason why such remarks sound dangerous lies in another obvious fact,...which is this. The uttering of the words is, indeed, usually a, or even *the*, leading incident in the performance of the act (of betting or what not), the performance of which is also the object of the utterance, but it is far from being usually, even if it is ever, the *sole* thing necessary if the act is to be deemed to have been performed. Speaking generally, it is always necessary that the *circumstances* in which the words are uttered should be in some way, or ways, *appropriate*, and it is very commonly necessary that either the speaker himself or other persons should *also* perform certain *other* actions, whether 'physical' or 'mental' actions or even acts of uttering further words. Thus, for naming the ship, it is essential that I should be the person appointed to name her, for (Christian) marrying, it is essential that I should not be already married with a wife living, sane and undivorced, and so on: for a bet to have been made, it is generally necessary for the offer of the bet to have been accepted by a taker (who must have done something, such as to say 'Done'), and it is hardly a gift if I *say* 'I give it you' but never hand it over.

So far, well and good. The action may be performed in ways other than by a performative utterance, and in any case the circumstances, including other actions, must be appropriate. But we may, in objecting, have something totally different, and this time quite mistaken, in mind, especially when we think of some of the more awe-inspiring performatives such as 'I promise to...'. Surely the words must be spoken 'seriously' and so as to be taken 'seriously'? This is, though vague, true enough in general—it is an important commonplace in discussing the purport of any utterance whatsoever. I must not be joking, for example, nor writing a poem. But we are apt to have a feeling that their being serious consists in their being uttered as (merely) the outward and visible sign, for convenience or other record or for information, of an inward and spiritual act: from which it is but a short step to go on to believe or to assume without realizing that for many purposes the outward utterance is a description, *true or false*, of the occurrence of the inward performance. The classic expression of this idea is to be found in the *Hippolytus* (1. 612), where Hippolytus says

> ἡ γλῶσσ' ὀμώμοχ', ἡ δὲ φρὴν ἄνω μοτός,

i.e., 'my tongue swore to, but my heart (or mind or other backstage artiste) did not'.[10] Thus 'I promise to...' obliges me—puts on record my spiritual assumption of a spiritual shackle.

It is gratifying to observe in this very example how excess of profundity, or rather solemnity, at once paves the way for immodality. For one who says 'Promising is not merely a matter of uttering words! It is an inward and spiritual act!' is apt to appear as a solid moralist standing out against a generation of superficial theorizers: we see him as he sees himself, surveying the invisible depths of ethical space, with all the distinction of a specialist in the *sui generis*. Yet he provides Hippolytus with a let-out, the bigamist with an excuse for his 'I do' and the welsher with a defence for his 'I bet'. Accuracy and morality alike are on the side of the plain saying that *our word is our bond*.

If we exclude such fictitious inward acts as this, can we suppose that any of the other things which certainly are normally required to accompany an utterance such as 'I promise that...' or 'I do (take this woman...)' are in fact described by it, and consequently do by their presence make it true or by their absence make it false? Well, taking the latter first, we shall next consider what we actually do say about the utterance concerned when one or another of its normal concomitants is *absent*. In no case do we say that the utterance was false but rather that the utterance—or rather the *act*,[11] e.g., the promise—was void, or given in bad faith, or not implemented, or the like. In the particular case of promising, as with many other performatives, it is appropriate that the person uttering the promise should have a certain intention, viz., here to keep his word: and perhaps of all concomitants this looks the most suitable to be that which 'I promise' does describe or record. Do we not actually, when such intention is absent, speak of a 'false' promise? Yet so to speak is *not* to say that the utterance 'I promise that...' is false, in the sense that though he states that he does, he doesn't, or that though he describes he misdescribes—misreports. For he *does* promise: the promise here is not even *void*, though it is given *in bad faith*. His utterance is perhaps misleading, probably deceitful, and doubtless wrong, but it is not a lie or a misstatement. At most we might make out a case for saying that it implies or insinuates a falsehood or a misstatement (to the effect that he does intend to do something): but that is a very different matter. Moreover, we do not speak of a false bet or a false christening; and that we *do* speak of a false promise need commit us no more than the fact that we speak of a false move. 'False' is not necessarily used of statements only.

## Notes

1. It is, of course, not really correct that a sentence ever *is* a statement: rather, it is *used* in *making a statement*, and the statement itself is a 'logical construction' out of the makings of statements.
2. Everything said in these sections is provisional, and subject to revision in the light of later sections.
3. Of all people, jurists should be best aware of the true state of affairs. Perhaps some now are. Yet they will succumb to their own timorous fiction, that a statement of 'the law' is a statement of fact.
4. Not without design: they are all 'explicit' performatives, and of that prepotent class later called 'exercitives'.
5. [Austin realized that the expression 'I do' is not used in the marriage ceremony too late to correct his mistake. We have let it remain in the text as it is philosophically unimportant that it is a mistake. *J.O. Urmson*, ed.]
6. Still less anything that I have already done or have yet to do.
7. 'Sentences' form a class of 'utterances', which class is to be defined, so far as I am concerned, grammatically, though I doubt if the definition has yet been given satisfactorily. With performative utterances are contrasted, for example and essentially, 'constative' utterances: to issue a constative utterance (i.e., to utter it with a historical reference) is to make a statement. To issue a performative utterance is, for example, to make a bet. See further below on 'illocutions'.
8. Formerly I used 'performatory': but 'performative' is to be preferred as shorter, less ugly, more tractable, and more traditional in formation.
9. I owe this observation to Professor H. L. A. Hart.
10. But I do not mean to rule out all the offstage performers—the lights men, the stage manager, even the prompter; I am objecting only to certain officious understudies, who would duplicate the play.
11. We deliberately avoid distinguishing these, precisely because the distinction is not in point.

## Critical Thinking and Application

- What is the difference between looking at language as *utterances* and looking at language as *sentences*? What difference would it make to study language by following these two different approaches?
- If the important thing about performatives is that they accomplish something in the world, is it the case that speaking always makes things happen? Why or why not? Can you declare yourself ruler of a kingdom? Can you christen a ship by smashing a bottle of champagne over the prow and declaring the vessel christened?
- Do utterances have a single function? How can you determine it?
- Keep track of all the ways people are using language (their goals, the effects) for an hour. How often are people attempting to make referential statements, and how often are they doing something different? Could you create a list of those functions? Do you think this would be a finite list? Why or why not?

## Vocabulary

constative statement
performative utterance

## Suggested Further Reading

Austin, John L. 1975 [1962]. *How to Do Things with Words*, 2nd ed. Cambridge, MA: Harvard University Press.

Rosaldo, Michelle Z. 1982. The Things We Do with Words: Ilongot Speech Acts and Speech Act Theory in Philosophy. *Language in Society* 11: 203–235.

Searle, John R. 1969. *Speech Acts: An Essay in the Philosophy of Language*. Cambridge: Cambridge University Press.

CHAPTER 42

# Discourse in the Novel

## *Mikhail Bakhtin*

(1934–1935)

*In the 1980s, Mikhail Bakhtin's work from the Stanlinist days of 1930s Russia was translated into English and transformed the way literary scholars thought about literature. No longer was it sufficient to think about the author's voice in a text, but it was necessary to consider multiple voices, all the different possible ways of writing and speaking that were available to any given author. In* Discourse in the Novel, *the focus was clearly on the genre of the novel, but linguists and anthropologists extracted the ideas of multivocality, of heteroglossia (other + voice), of dialogism, of intertextuality, and of performance and found them to possess a huge range of applicability. Suddenly, the idea of "voices" was everywhere, and Bakhtin's heteroglossia was all the rage.*

*In the decades since then, Bakhtin's ideas have saturated the study of discourse. It is impossible to count all the scholars influenced by his work or to trace the multifaceted inspiration that he provided. Just as Bakhtin's work has been taken as a critique of the stifled political system within which he was writing of literature, so have contemporary scholars located liberation, protest, and escape through speakers' many voices.*

*This short excerpt comes from* Discourse in the Novel, *which is in turn published with three other essays in the seminal* The Dialogic Imagination. *It should not be regarded as definitive of Bakhtin's work but simply as providing a slice of the thinking of one of the most influential writers of the twentieth century. You should feel free to look for more!*

### Reading Questions

- What are some of the ways that languages, which nonetheless cohabit, differ from each other?
- One of the most famous phrases of Bakhtin's is that "The word in language is half someone else's." What does this mean? Why do you think it has come to define Bakhtin's thought?
- How does the prose writer cope with, or even revel in, heteroglot languages?

Language—like the living concrete environment in which the consciousness of the verbal artist lives—is never unitary. It is unitary only as an abstract grammatical system of normative forms, taken in isolation from the concrete, ideological conceptualizations that fill it, and in isolation from the uninterrupted process of historical becoming that is a characteristic of all living language. Actual social life and historical becoming create within an abstractly unitary national language a multitude of concrete worlds, a multitude of bounded verbal-ideological and social belief systems; within these various systems (identical in the abstract) are elements of language filled with various semantic and axiological content and each with its own different sound.

Literary language—both spoken and written—although it is unitary not only in its shared, abstract, linguistic markers but also in its forms for conceptualizing these abstract markers, is itself **stratified** and **heteroglot** in its aspect as an expressive system, that is, in the forms that carry its meanings.

This stratification is accomplished first of all by the specific organisms called ***genres***. Certain features of language (lexicological, semantic, syntactic) will knit together with the intentional aim, and with the overall accentual system inherent in one or another genre: oratorical, publicistic, newspaper and journalistic genres, the genres of low literature (penny dreadfuls, for instance) or, finally, the various genres of high literature. Certain features of language take on the specific

Mikhail Bakhtin, Discourse in the Novel. In *The Diaelogic Imagination*, edited by Michael Holquist; translated by Caryl Emerson and Michael Holquist. Austin: University of Texas Press, 1981 [1934–35], pp. 288–300.

flavor of a given genre: they knit together with specific points of view, specific approaches, forms of thinking, nuances and accents characteristic of the given genre.

In addition, there is interwoven with this **generic** stratification of language a *professional* stratification of language, in the broad sense of the term "professional": the language of the lawyer, the doctor, the businessman, the politician, the public education teacher and so forth, and these sometimes coincide with, and sometimes depart from, the stratification into genres. It goes without saying that these languages differ from each other not only in their vocabularies; they involve specific forms for manifesting intentions, forms for making conceptualization and evaluation concrete. And even the very language of the writer (the poet or novelist) can be taken as a professional jargon on a par with professional jargons.

What is important to us here is the intentional dimensions, that is, the denotative and expressive dimension of the "shared" language's stratification. It is in fact not the neutral linguistic components of language being stratified and differentiated, but rather a situation in which the intentional possibilities of language are being expropriated: these possibilities are realized in specific directions, filled with specific content, they are made concrete, particular, and are permeated with concrete value judgments; they knit together with specific objects and with the belief systems of certain genres of expression and points of view peculiar to particular professions. Within these points of view, that is, for the speakers of the language themselves, these generic languages and professional jargons are directly intentional—they denote and express directly and fully, and are capable of expressing themselves without mediation; but outside, that is, for those not participating in the given purview, these languages may be treated as objects, as typifactions, as local color. For such outsiders, the intentions permeating these languages become *things*, limited in their meaning and expression; they attract to, or excise from, such language a particular word—making it difficult for the word to be utilized in a directly intentional way, without any qualifications.

But the situation is far from exhausted by the generic and professional stratification of the common literary language. Although at its very core literary language is frequently socially homogeneous, as the oral and written language of a dominant social group, there is nevertheless always present, even here, a certain degree of social differentiation, a social stratification, that in other eras can become extremely acute. Social stratification may here and there coincide with generic and professional stratification, but in essence it is, of course, a thing completely autonomous and peculiar to itself.

Social stratification is also and primarily determined by differences between the forms used to convey meaning and between the expressive planes of various belief systems—that is, stratification expresses itself in typical differences in ways used to conceptualize and accentuate elements of language, and stratification may not violate the abstractly linguistic dialectological unity of the shared literary language.

What is more, all socially significant world views have the capacity to exploit the intentional possibilities of language through the medium of their specific concrete instancing. Various tendencies (artistic and otherwise), circles, journals, particular newspapers, even particular significant artistic works and individual persons are all capable of stratifying language, in proportion to their social significance; they are capable of attracting its words and forms into their orbit by means of their own characteristic intentions and accents, and in so doing to a certain extent alienating these words and forms from other tendencies, parties, artistic works and persons.

Every socially significant verbal performance has the ability—sometimes for a long period of time, and for a wide circle of persons—to infect with its own intention certain aspects of language that had been affected by its semantic and expressive impulse, imposing on them specific semantic nuances and specific axiological overtones; thus, it can create slogan-words, curse-words, praise-words and so forth.

In any given historical moment of verbal-ideological life, each generation at each social level has its own language; moreover, every age group has as a matter of fact its own language, its own vocabulary, its own particular accentual system that, in their turn, vary depending on social level, academic institution (the language of the cadet, the high school student, the trade school student are all different languages) and other stratifying factors. All this is brought about by socially typifying languages, no matter how narrow the social circle in which they are spoken. It is even possible to have a family jargon define the societal limits of a language, as, for instance, the jargon of the Irtenevs in Tolstoy, with its special vocabulary and unique accentual system.

And finally, at any given moment, languages of various epochs and periods of socio-ideological life cohabit with one another. Even languages of the day exist: one could say that today's and yesterday's socio-ideological and political "day" do not, in a certain sense, share the same language; every day represents another socio-ideological semantic "state of affairs," another vocabulary, another accentual system, with its own slogans, its own ways of assigning blame and praise. Poetry depersonalizes "days" in language, while prose, as we shall see, often deliberately intensifies difference between them, gives them embodied representation and dialogically opposes them to one another in unresolvable dialogues.

Thus at any given moment of its historical existence, language is heteroglot from top to bottom: it represents the co-existence of socio-ideological contradictions between the present and the past, between differing epochs of the past, between different socio-ideological groups in the present, between tendencies, schools, circles and so forth, all given a bodily form. These "languages" of **heteroglossia** intersect each other in a variety of ways, forming new socially typifying "languages."

Each of these "languages" of heteroglossia requires a methodology very different from the others; each is grounded in a completely different principle for marking differences and for establishing units (for some this principle is functional, in others it is the principle of theme and content, in yet others it is, properly speaking, a socio-dialectological principle). Therefore languages do not *exclude* each other, but rather intersect with each other in many different ways (the Ukrainian language, the language of the epic poem, of early Symbolism, of the student, of a particular generation of children, of the run-of-the-mill intellectual, of the Nietzschean and so on). It might even seem that the very word "language" loses all meaning in this process—for apparently there is no single plane on which all these "languages" might be juxtaposed to one another.

In actual fact, however, there does exist a common plane that methodologically justifies our juxtaposing them: all languages of heteroglossia, whatever the principle underlying them and making each unique, are specific points of view on the world, forms for conceptualizing the world in words, specific world views, each characterized by its own objects, meanings and values. As such they all may be juxtaposed to one another, mutually supplement one another, contradict one another and be interrelated dialogically. As such they encounter one another and co-exist in the consciousness of real people—first and foremost, in the creative consciousness of people who write novels. As such, these languages live a real life, they struggle and evolve in an environment of social heteroglossia. Therefore they are all able to enter into the unitary plane of the novel, which can unite in itself parodic stylizations of generic languages, various forms of stylizations and illustrations of professional and period-bound languages, the languages of particular generations, of social dialects and others (as occurs, for example, in the English comic novel). They may all be drawn in by the novelist for the orchestration of his themes and for the refracted (indirect) expression of his intentions and values.

This is why we constantly put forward the referential and expressive—that is, intentional—factors as the force that stratifies and differentiates the common literary language, and not the linguistic markers (lexical coloration, semantic overtones, etc.) of generic languages, professional jargons and so forth—markers that are, so to speak, the sclerotic deposits of an intentional process, signs left behind on the path of the real living project of an intention, of the particular way it imparts meaning to general linguistic norms. These external markers, linguistically observable and fixable, cannot in themselves be understood or studied without understanding the specific conceptualization they have been given by an intention.

Discourse lives, as it were, beyond itself, in a living impulse [*napravlennost'*] toward the object; if we detach ourselves completely from this impulse all we have left is the naked corpse of the word, from which we can learn nothing at all about the social situation or the fate of a given word in life. *To study the word as such, ignoring the impulse that reaches out beyond it, is just as senseless as to study psychological experience outside the context of that real life toward which it was directed and by which it is determined.*

By stressing the intentional dimension of stratification in literary language, we are able, as has been said, to locate in a single series such methodologically heterogeneous phenomena as professional and social dialects, world views and individual artistic works, for in their intentional dimension one finds that common plane on which they can all be juxtaposed, and juxtaposed dialogically. The whole matter consists in the fact that there may be, between "languages," highly specific dialogic relations; no matter how these languages are conceived, they may all be taken as particular points of view on the world. However varied the social forces doing the work of stratification—a profession, a genre, a particular tendency, an individual personality—the work itself everywhere comes down to the (relatively) protracted and socially meaningful (collective) saturation of language with specific (and consequently limiting) intentions and accents. The longer this stratifying saturation goes on, the broader the social circle encompassed by it and consequently the more substantial the social force bringing about such a stratification of language, then the more sharply focused and stable will be those traces, the linguistic changes in the language markers (linguistic symbols), that are left behind in language as a result of this social force's activity—from stable (and consequently social) semantic nuances to authentic dialectological markers (phonetic, morphological and others), which permit us to speak of particular social dialects.

As a result of the work done by all these stratifying forces in language, there are no "neutral" words and forms—words and forms that can belong to "no one"; language has been completely taken over, shot through with intentions and accents. For any individual consciousness living in it, language is not an abstract system of normative forms but rather a concrete heteroglot conception of the world. All words have the "taste" of a profession, a genre, a tendency, a party, a particular work, a particular person, a generation, an age group, the day and hour. Each word tastes of the context and contexts in which it has lived its socially charged life; all words and forms are populated by intentions. Contextual overtones (generic, tendentious, individualistic) are inevitable in the word.

As a living, socio-ideological concrete thing, as heteroglot opinion, language, for the individual consciousness, lies on the borderline between oneself and the other. The word in language is half someone else's. It becomes "one's own" only when the speaker populates it with his own intention, his own accent, when he appropriates the word, adapting it to his own semantic and expressive intention. Prior to this moment of appropriation, the word does not exist in a neutral and impersonal language (it is not, after all, out of a dictionary that the speaker gets his words!), but rather it exists in other people's mouths, in other people's contexts, serving other people's intentions: it is from there that one must take the word, and make it one's own. And not all words for just anyone submit equally easily to this appropriation, to this seizure and transformation into private property: many words stubbornly resist, others remain alien, sound foreign in the mouth of the one who appropriated them and who now speaks them; they cannot be assimilated into his context and fall out of it; it is as if they put themselves in quotation marks against the will of the speaker. Language is not a neutral medium that passes freely and easily into the private property of the speaker's intentions; it is populated—overpopulated—with the intentions of others. Expropriating it, forcing it to submit to one's own intentions and accents, is a difficult and complicated process.

We have so far proceeded on the assumption of the abstract-linguistic (dialectological) unity of literary language. But even a literary language is anything but a closed dialect. Within the scope of literary language itself there is already a more or less sharply defined boundary between everyday-conversational language and written language. Distinctions between genres frequently coincide with dialectological distinctions (for example, the high—Church Slavonic—and the low—conversational—genres of the eighteenth century); finally, certain dialects may be legitimized in literature and thus to a certain extent be appropriated by literary language.

As they enter literature and are appropriated to literary language, dialects in this new context lose, of course, the quality of closed socio-linguistic systems; they are deformed and in fact cease to be that which they had been simply as dialects. On the other hand, these dialects, on entering the literary language and preserving within it their own dialectological elasticity, their other-languagedness, have the effect of deforming the literary language; it, too, ceases to be that which it had been, a closed socio-linguistic system. Literary language is a highly distinctive phenomenon, as is the linguistic consciousness of the educated person who is its agent; within it, intentional diversity of speech [*raznorečivost'*] (which is present in every living dialect as a closed system) is transformed into diversity of language [*raznojazyčie*]; what results is not a single language but a dialogue of languages.

The national literary language of a people with a highly developed art of prose, especially if it is novelistic prose with a rich and tension-filled verbal-ideological history, is in fact an organized microcosm that reflects the macrocosm not only of national heteroglossia, but of European heteroglossia as well. The unity of a literary language is not a unity of a single, closed language system, but is rather a highly specific unity of several "languages" that have established contact and mutual recognition with each other (merely one of which is poetic language in the narrow sense). Precisely this constitutes the peculiar nature of the methodological problem in literary language.

Concrete socio-ideological language consciousness, as it becomes creative—that is, as it becomes active as literature—discovers itself already surrounded by heteroglossia and not at all a single, unitary language, inviolable and indisputable. The actively literary linguistic consciousness at all times and everywhere (that is, in all epochs of literature historically available to us) comes upon "languages," and not language. Consciousness finds itself inevitably facing the necessity of *having to choose a language*. With each literary-verbal performance, consciousness must actively orient itself amidst heteroglossia, it must move in and occupy a position for itself within it, it chooses, in other words, a "language." Only by remaining in a closed environment, one without writing or thought, completely off the maps of socio-ideological becoming, could a man fail to sense this activity of selecting a language and rest assured in the inviolability of his own language, the conviction that his language is predetermined.

Even such a man, however, deals not in fact with a single language, but with languages—except that the place occupied by each of these languages is fixed and indisputable, the movement from one to the other is predetermined and not a thought process; it is as if these languages were in different chambers. They do not collide with each other in his consciousness, there is no attempt to coordinate them, to look at one of these languages through the eyes of another language.

Thus an illiterate peasant, miles away from any urban center, naively immersed in an unmoving and for him unshakable everyday world, nevertheless lived in several language systems: he prayed to God in one language (Church Slavonic), sang songs in another, spoke to his family in a third and, when he began to dictate petitions to the local authorities through a scribe, he tried speaking yet a fourth language (the official-literate language, "paper" language). All these are *different languages*, even from the point of view of abstract socio-dialectological markers. But these languages were not dialogically coordinated in the linguistic consciousness of the peasant; he passed from one to the other without thinking, automatically: each was indisputably in its own place, and the place of each was indisputable. He was not yet able to regard one language (and the verbal world corresponding to it) through the eyes of another language (that is, the language of everyday life and the everyday world with the language of prayer or song, or vice versa).[1]

As soon as a critical interanimation of languages began to occur in the consciousness of our peasant, as soon as it became clear that these were not only various different languages but even internally variegated languages, that the ideological systems and approaches to the world that were indissolubly connected with these languages contradicted each other and in no way could live in peace and quiet with one another—then the inviolability and predetermined quality of these languages came to an end, and the necessity of actively choosing one's orientation among them began.

The language and world of prayer, the language and world of song, the language and world of labor and everyday life, the specific language and world of local authorities, the new language and world of the workers freshly immigrated to the city—all these languages and worlds sooner or later emerged from a state of peaceful and moribund equilibrium and revealed the speech diversity in each.

Of course the actively literary linguistic consciousness comes upon an even more varied and profound heteroglossia within literary language itself, as well as outside it. Any fundamental study of the stylistic life of the word must begin with this basic fact. The nature of the heteroglossia encountered and the means by which one orients oneself in it determine the concrete stylistic life that the word will lead.

The poet is a poet insofar as he accepts the idea of a unitary and singular language and a unitary, monologically sealed-off utterance. These ideas are immanent in the poetic genres with which he works. In a condition of actual contradiction, these are what determine the means of orientation open to the poet. The poet must assume a complete single-personed hegemony over his own language, he must assume equal responsibility for each one of its aspects and subordinate them to his own, and only his own, intentions. Each word must express the poet's *meaning* directly and without mediation; there must be no distance between the poet and his word. The meaning must emerge from language as a single intentional whole: none of its stratification, its speech diversity, to say nothing of its language diversity, may be reflected in any fundamental way in his poetic work.

To achieve this, the poet strips the word of others' intentions, he uses only such words and forms (and only in such a way) that they lose their link with concrete intentional levels of language and their connection with specific contexts. Behind the words of a poetic work one should not sense any typical or reified images of genres (except for the given poetic genre), nor professions, tendencies, directions (except the direction chosen by the poet himself), nor world views (except for the unitary and singular world view of the poet himself), nor typical and individual images of speaking persons, their speech mannerisms or typical intonations. *Everything that enters the work must immerse itself in Lethe, and forget its previous life in any other contexts: language may remember only its life in poetic contexts (in such contexts, however, even concrete reminiscences are possible).*

Of course there always exists a limited sphere of more or less concrete contexts, and a connection with them must be deliberately evidenced in poetic discourse. But these contexts are purely semantic and, so to speak, accented in the abstract; in their linguistic dimension they are impersonal or at least no particularly concrete linguistic specificity is sensed behind them, no particular manner of speech and so forth, no socially typical linguistic face (the possible personality of the narrator) need peek out from behind them. Everywhere there is only one face—the linguistic face of the author, answering for every word as if it were his own. No matter how multiple and varied these semantic and accentual threads, associations, pointers, hints, correlations that emerge from every poetic word, one language, one conceptual horizon, is sufficient to them all; there is no need of heteroglot social contexts. What is more, the very movement of the poetic symbol (for example, the unfolding of a metaphor) presumes precisely this unity of language, an unmediated correspondence with its object. Social diversity of speech, were it to arise in the work and stratify its language, would make impossible both the normal development and the activity of symbols within it.

The very rhythm of poetic genres does not promote any appreciable degree of stratification. *Rhythm, by creating an unmediated involvement between every aspect of the accentual system of the whole* (via the most immediate rhythmic unities), destroys in embryo those social worlds of speech and of persons that are potentially embedded in the word: in any case, rhythm puts definite limits on them, does not let them unfold or materialize. Rhythm serves to strengthen and concentrate even further the unity and hermetic quality of the surface of poetic style, and of the unitary language that this style posits.

As a result of this work—stripping all aspects of language of the intentions and accents of other people, destroying all traces of social heteroglossia and diversity of language—a tension-filled unity of language is achieved in the poetic work. This unity may be naive, and present only in those extremely rare epochs of poetry, when poetry had not yet exceeded the limits of a closed, unitary, undifferentiated social circle whose language and ideology were not yet stratified. More often than not, we experience a profound and conscious tension through which the unitary poetic language of a work rises from the heteroglot and language-diverse chaos of the literary language contemporary to it.

This is how the poet proceeds. The novelist working in prose (and almost any prose writer) takes a completely different path. He welcomes the heteroglossia and language diversity of the literary and extraliterary language into his own work not only not weakening them but even intensifying them (for he interacts with their particular self-consciousness). It is in fact out of this stratification of language, its speech diversity and even language diversity, that he constructs his style, while at the same time he maintains the unity of his own creative personality and the unity (although it is, to be sure, unity of another order) of his own style.

The prose writer does not purge words of intentions and tones that are alien to him, he does not destroy the seeds of social heteroglossia embedded in words, he does not eliminate those language characterizations and speech mannerisms (potential narrator-personalities) glimmering behind the words and forms, each at a different distance from the ultimate semantic nucleus of his work, that is, the center of his own personal intentions.

The language of the prose writer deploys itself according to degrees of greater or lesser proximity to the author and to his ultimate semantic instantiation: certain aspects of language directly and unmediatedly express (as in poetry) the semantic and expressive intentions of the author, others refract these intentions; the writer of prose does not meld completely with any of these words, but rather accents each of them in a particular way—humorously, ironically, parodically and so forth;[2] yet another group may stand even further from the author's ultimate semantic instantiation, still more thoroughly refracting his intentions; and there are, finally, those words that are completely denied any authorial intentions: the author does not express *himself* in them (as the author of the word)—rather, he *exhibits* them as a unique speech-thing, they function for him as something completely reified. Therefore the stratification of language—generic, professional, social in the narrow sense, that of particular world views, particular tendencies, particular individuals, the social speech diversity and language-diversity (dialects) of language—upon entering the novel establishs its own special order within it, and becomes a unique artistic system, which orchestrates the intentional theme of the author.

Thus a prose writer can distance himself from the language of his own work, while at the same time distancing himself, in varying degrees, from the different layers and aspects of the work. He can make use of language without wholly giving himself up to it, he may treat it as semi-alien or completely alien to himself, while compelling language ultimately to serve all his own intentions. The author does not speak in a given language (from which he distances himself to a greater or lesser degree), but he speaks, as it were, *through* language, a language that has somehow more or less materialized, become objectivized, that he merely ventriloquates.

The prose writer as a novelist does not strip away the intentions of others from the heteroglot language of his works, he does not violate those socio-ideological cultural horizons (big and little worlds) that open up behind heteroglot languages—rather, he welcomes them into his work. The prose writer makes use of words that are already populated with the social intentions of others and compels them to serve his own new intentions, to serve a second master. Therefore the intentions of the prose writer are refracted, and refracted *at different angles*, depending on the degree to which the refracted, heteroglot languages he deals with are socio-ideologically alien, already embodied and already objectivized.

The orientation of the word amid the utterances and languages of others, and all the specific phenomena connected with this orientation, takes on *artistic* significance in novel style. Diversity of voices and heteroglossia enter the novel and organize themselves within it into a structured artistic system. This constitutes the distinguishing feature of the novel as a genre.

Any stylistics capable of dealing with the distinctiveness of the novel as a genre must be a *sociological stylistics*. The internal social dialogism of novelistic discourse requires the concrete social context of discourse to be exposed, to be revealed as the force that determines its entire stylistic structure, its "form" and its "content," determining it not from without, but from within; for indeed, social dialogue reverberates in all aspects of discourse, in those relating to "content" as well as the "formal" aspects themselves.

The development of the novel is a function of the deepening of dialogic essence, its increased scope and greater precision. Fewer and fewer neutral, hard elements ("rock bottom truths") remain that are not drawn into dialogue. Dialogue moves into the deepest molecular and, ultimately, subatomic levels.

Of course, even the poetic word is social, but poetic forms reflect lengthier social processes, i.e., those tendencies in social life requiring centuries to unfold. The novelistic word, however, registers with extreme subtlety the tiniest shifts and oscillations of the social atmosphere; it does so, moreover, while registering it as a whole, in all of its aspects.

When heteroglossia enters the novel it becomes subject to an artistic reworking. The social and historical voices populating language, all its words and all its forms, which provide language with its particular concrete conceptualizations, are organized in the novel into a structured stylistic system that expresses the differentiated socio-ideological position of the author amid the heteroglossia of his epoch.

## Notes

1. We are of course deliberately simplifying: the real-life peasant could and did do this to a certain extent.

2. That is to say, the words are not his if we understand them as direct words, but they are his as things that are being transmitted ironically, exhibited and so forth, that is, as words that are understood from the distances appropriate to humor, irony, parody, etc.

## Critical Thinking and Application

- Though Bakhtin is writing principally of literary language, and even more specifically of the novel, what are the applications of this chapter to language in general? Are there ways in which these ideas would not apply to nonliterary language?
- Bakhtin argues strongly that it is useless "to study the word as such" and that "there are no...words and forms that can belong to 'no one.'" What does this mean, why is it useless "to study the word as such," and what should be done instead?
- Bakhtin gives the example of an illiterate Russian peasant and all his languages. Record someone speaking—any person, in any context, in any language. Analyze the multiple forms of language contained in your recording along the lines given by Bakhtin.

## Vocabulary

generic
genre
heteroglossia
heteroglot
stratified

## Suggested Further Reading

Bakhtin, Mikhail M. 1981 [1975]. *The Dialogic Imagination*, edited by Michael Holquist, translated by Caryl Emerson and Michael Holquist. Austin: University of Texas Press.

Bakhtin, Mikhail M. 1984 [1965]. *Rabelais and His World*, translated by Hélène Iswolsky. Bloomington: Indiana University Press.

Bakhtin, Mikhail M. 1986 [1979]. *Speech Genres and Other Late Essays*, edited by Caryl Emerson and Michael Holquist, translated by Vern McGee. Austin: University of Texas Press.

Bauman, Richard. 2004. *A World of Others' Words: Cross-Cultural Perspectives on Intertextuality*. Malden, MA: Blackwell.

Bauman, Richard, and Charles L. Briggs. 1990. Poetics and Performance as Critical Perspectives on Language and Social Life. *Annual Review of Anthropology* 19: 59–88.

Briggs, Charles L., and Richard Bauman. 1992. Genre, Intertextuality, and Social Power. *Journal of Linguistic Anthropology* 2: 131–172.

Hanks, William. 1987. Discourse Genres in a Theory of Practice. *American Ethnologist* 14(4): 666–692.

Hanks, William. 1996. *Language and Communicative Practice*. Boulder, CO: Westview Press.

Hill, Jane. 1995. The Voices of Don Gabriel: Responsibility and Self in a Modern Mexicano Narrative. In *The Dialogic Emergence of Culture*, edited by Dennis Tedlock and Bruce Mannheim, pp. 97–147. Urbana: University of Illinois Press.

Silverstein, Michael, and Greg Urban, eds. 1996. *Natural Histories of Discourse*. Chicago: University of Chicago Press.

## CHAPTER 43

# Naming Practices and the Power of Words in China

*Susan D. Blum*

(1997)

*Kinship, or family relations, have been at the center of anthropological research for more than a century. How people are related, and then how they act once they are related, as well as variations in human views of relationships, are an unendingly fascinating topic. For his research on property among the Iroquois, the influential nineteenth-century anthropologist Lewis Henry Morgan depended largely on his understanding of the responsibilities that accompanied kin relations. This led, ultimately, to his seeking information about kinship terms worldwide and to both his* Systems of Consanguinity and Affinity of the Human Family *and to his systematizing work,* Ancient Society, *which undergirded almost a century of anthropological studies.*

*Key to our understanding of human relations are the terms we use for and with those relations, whether we use what we would consider names or the commonly used kinship terms.*

*In terms of naming, we might wish to distinguish* reference *(how we refer to someone) and* address *(how we address someone). The terms used are rather different. Further, in many cases, we have a variety of relationships with people and can choose how to make use of one or another in a given situation.*

*This article argues that rather than naming being a single once-and-for-all affair of choosing a name for a baby, naming as* practice *occurs daily in all social interactions in China. It points out that relationships are constructed, in part, through the choice of title or form of address used at a particular moment in a particular interaction. Moreover, these utterances are too important to be left to the whims of young children, so children are shown, exactly, how to address the important people in their lives. Despite an egalitarian ideology that governed China during its most radical and revolutionary years, there was never a challenge to the idea that relationships are frequently unequal. The term* comrade (tongzhi) *which was proposed to replace virtually all social titles has waned; it is now used for gay partners.*

### Reading Questions

- What is meant by "naming practices"? How are such practices observed? What considerations are made when people engage in naming practices?
- Who has the responsibility in a relationship for uttering the proper naming term? How do people know what name to use with someone else?
- Why is inequality not considered anathema to participants in the Chinese naming system?
- Why are kin terms often preferred to personal names?

---

Susan D. Blum, Naming Practices and the Power of Words in China. *Language in Society* 26 (3) (1997): 357–379.

> Nets are for catching fish; after one gets the fish, one forgets the net. Traps are for catching rabbits; after one gets the rabbit, one forgets the trap. Words are for getting meaning; after one gets the meaning, one forgets the words. Where can I find people who have forgotten words, and have a word with them?
>
> —ZHUĀNGZI, CHAP. 26

Names are often regarded as one-time labels fixed to solid objects, useful for identifying them but without any real substance or inherent interest. Philosophers of language, anthropologists, linguists, and ordinary people have often been drawn to the topic, each with their own idea of the origins of names: Adam created them in the Judeo-Christian tradition; the mythical sage-emperor Fúxī discovered the Eight Trigrams (*bā guà*) that developed into characters in one version of the Chinese myth; "society" creates them in a sociological interpretation; a child's parents select names in a commonsense explanation. Contemporary structural linguists, from Saussure on, write of the arbitrariness of the sign (but see Benveniste 1966b, Friedrich 1979). Most assume the primacy of the thing/object/signified, and the subsequence of the label/name/signifier. The underlying ontology of a split between substance and surface appears in much analysis of language (see Derrida 1982 for a critique of this position), and in mainstream anthropological considerations of language use. When the distance between word and object appears collapsed, practices revolving around language are often termed "magical"—notwithstanding almost a century of critique of the category of magic as opposed, say, to science (Malinowski 1935, 1948, O'Keefe 1982).

[Here] I analyze a wide range of practices revolving around naming in a very well-known society: China. I use the term "naming" as the superordinate category, within which I include the categories of **"proper names,"** "kinship terms," and pronouns.[1] The ambiguity of the term "naming" between a nominal and a verbal reading emphasizes that this is an active set of practices rather than a static system.

In the process I hope to demonstrate an alternative approach to conceptualizing naming practices and indeed language use in general, while explaining some specific features of Chinese language use. Chinese naming practices reveal a view of the Chinese person as thoroughly embedded in a world of speakers and hearers whose relationships to each other and the world are constituted through speaking certain terms, and where sound, object, and name are in some important senses combined. I will show further that what accounts for the success of a language act is not that it springs spontaneously from an emotion-filled, intention-driven, sincere individual, as might be presumed in the West, but that it demonstrates respect through willingness to be educated by others—often by rehearsal through verbatim routines, which function also as a sort of three-way negotiation of place in the hierarchy. Language acts in China are seen as continuous with other sorts of action rather than as belonging to a separate domain. As such, they are managed as other behavior is, and socialized as other forms of social practice are—through imitation and direct repetition. Finally, I will show that solidarity is built through affectionate affirmation of hierarchy, and that hierarchy is often seen as involving no contradiction to affection.

The Chinese term *míng* 'name' refers to both proper and **common names,** including people's names; in political philosophy, it often refers to public or social roles. The most famous discussion of the importance of appropriate naming is in the *Analects* of Confucius (3rd century B.C.E.) with its discussion of *zhèng míng*, usually translated 'rectification of names' (Waley 1938: 171, D. C. Lau 1979: 118, Huáng 1990). Throughout the Warring States period (5th through 3rd centuries B.C.E.) political philosophers contemplated the proper way to conduct moral and effective government. Correct naming was the proper method for *rú*-ists ("Confucians") and Legalists. Other philosophical schools, including those of the Logicians and Daoists, were more playful. Thus Zhuāngzi argued (Guō 1983: 944) that one could forget a name once one attained the thing to which it referred; and that before language there was a real world, so the linguistic distinctions over which people fought so hard were really beside the point (see Guō 1983, Hansen 1992: 291, and cf. Granet 1934, Munro 1969, Hansen 1983, Graham 1989, Makeham 1994).

The importance of personal naming also is visible throughout imperial China. Reign periods were segments of emperors' rules that had propitious names; a single ruler could have several different reign periods, changing the names of the periods to change the fortunes of the empire. Emperors' personal names were powerful, tabooed both during life and after death. If their names contained ordinary syllables, like *guāng* 'glorious', that word had to be replaced in all written texts.

Public figures had names that were public currency. By the Sòng dynasty (960–1279), writers commonly selected *zì* 'style names' or *hào* 'courtesy names' that indicated something about their character that they wished to have known, or about their biography. Sū Shì, for instance, selected his style name as Dōngpō 'Eastern Slope'; a famous dish is known as "Dongpo's soup" after a recipe he described in an essay. The Míng philosopher Wáng Shǒurén's selection of his style name, Yángmíng 'bright yang-ness', indicates the centrality of illumination to his thought. Ever since, the name Yángmíng is widely known to refer to that thinker. The mountain just north of Taibei, Yángmíng Shān, is named for him.

Philosophical ruminations about the nature of naming pervade China's intellectual history. In recent years, Mao insisted that what counted was practice, rather than idealism and intellectual work. Nevertheless, the 20th century focus has been on selecting appropriate names for individuals.

Are they "enemies of the people"? What kind of "contradiction" (i.e., conflict) exists in a particular case? Assigning roles has been a central activity of contemporary China; those who stray have to be 'rectified' (*zhèng*), using the term of the Warring States thinkers, though in this case it is the PERSON who most critically must be rectified, not the name. Crimes are assigned to appropriate categories such as disagreement, or counter-revolution. Clearly, the place of naming has had significant ramifications for much of public life throughout China's long history. However, the remainder of this [discussion] does not refer to philosophical writings on names, but rather attempts to account for patterns in observable naming behavior.

The analysis here focuses on the contemporary mainland of China, and on the political economic circumstances that surround the use of language. I add material reported for other Chinese societies, especially Taiwan, when this helps explain naming practices I have observed. This account is based in part on fieldwork conducted in Kunming, capital of Yunnan province in southwest China, as well as other stays in the People's Republic of China (PRC) and Taiwan over the course of the last 14 years, and on other written analyses of naming practices in China. I also sent a general inquiry out on the Internet in 1996 over the H-ASIA network, soliciting comments on contemporary PRC naming practices and speculating about a possible return of more "traditional" practices.

I begin with a routine which I have observed hundreds of times,[2] and which goes something like this. In the presence of C (father's father), A (parent) prompts B (child) to speak:

| | | |
|---|---|---|
| A (parent): | *Jiào "yéye."* | Say "Grandfather." |
| B (child): | *Yéye.* | Grandfather. |
| | or | |
| A (parent): | *Jiào "yéye zàijiàn."* | Say "Goodbye grandfather." |
| B (child): | *Yéye zàijiàn.* | Goodbye grandfather. |

*Jiào* 'call', meaning both 'address someone as' and 'utter', opens the routine, signaling that what follows is to be repeated verbatim. The intonation of the repeated phrase is often fairly flat, not enthusiastic—because, I believe, what matters is not the heartfelt depth of the utterance, but the mere fact of its being stated. It is also meaningful not merely because it gauges the child's knowledge, but because it evokes compliance and produces the desired object: the spoken kinship term. Such routines, for greetings and partings in particular, are common in Chinese communities and persist into the child's adulthood, when it is no longer caregivers but the all-important *zhōngjiānrén* 'middle-person, intermediary' who gives these instructions. The importance of knowing and UTTERING the proper kinship term is illustrated by the ubiquity of these routines. I will place this example in the context of other possible forms of address and reference, accounting for the importance of the utterance of kinship terms by juniors through their ability to invoke prototypes of relationships.

## KINSHIP TERMS

Kinship terms are the ultimate expression of solidarity. Many anthropologists who have written about **"classificatory" kinship** (Morgan 1871, Schneider 1984, Trautmann 1987) have shown that, in some societies, all persons are assigned the nearest kinship term in order to create a meaningfully populated world (cf. Witherspoon 1977: 88, Kondo 1990: 11–26, Chagnon 1992).[3] Even strange outsiders like anthropologists are often assigned to one group or another (Bell 1993: 18–21), permitting persons in small communities to have an identity. This has been referred to rather problematically as **"fictive" kinship.** In the case of anthropologists who look vastly different from those among whom they work, it is easy enough to recognize the fictitious nature of the relationship; but calling native terms "fictive" suggests that only the anthropologist's system reflects "reality"—a reality where "blood" relations are paramount—while those participating are somehow simple-minded and ignorant of the real state of affairs (see Bowen 1964: 64, 74, 75).

Chinese kinship was a general problem in anthropology for a time; even Kroeber wrote an analysis of it (1933). The Chinese kinship terms are often considered classificatory, of the "bifurcate-collateral" type (Kroeber 1952: 192). Friends and patrilateral cousins call one another by sibling terms, e.g., *mèimei* 'Younger sister'; friends of the family are called "Aunt" and "Uncle," while older women on the street are called *pópo* 'Grandmother'.

Yet considering kinship relations to be emergent in interaction, rather than reflected or expressed by use of kinship terms, clarifies our opening puzzle: only by speaking the terms does the relationship emerge (Mannheim & Tedlock 1995: 8). Prototypes of the expression-construction are viewed daily; rare is the family drama on television that does not end with some scene like that of a tearful child murmuring "Mama, Ma" as her mother dies, moves away on the train, or walks off. Movies and TV dramas are filled with dialog that may consist of little more than the exchange of kinship terms—and these evoke sobs from audiences. The use of such terms in address is mandatory for the closest relationships; it is preferable for medium-distance ones; and it is usable even with strangers, such as old women from whom one wishes to ask directions. The use of pronouns, which is quite common in many languages for addressing people of all different classes, has rather limited scope in China, in contrast to kinship terms. In fact, it is often considered insulting and impudent to use a pronoun. But kinship terms may be too intimate in some cases, and a junior may use a proper title instead.

In most cases lexical reciprocity exists, an automatic pair of relationships signaled by kinship terms and by some titles: *Māma* 'mother' implies *háizi* 'child', *gēge* 'older brother' implies *dìdi* 'younger brother' or *mèimei* 'younger sister', *lǎo X* 'elder/superior surname-X' implies *xiǎo Y* 'younger/inferior surname-Y', *pópo* 'grandmother' implies *sūnzi/sūnnǚ* 'grandson/granddaughter', *lǎoshi* 'teacher' implies *xuésheng* 'student'. But reciprocity does not mean actual symmetry;

a senior can use the junior's name, but the junior can only use the proper (kinship) term. The kinship terms referring to the junior are rarely used in address, except sometimes in melodrama (Chao 1956: 237). Thus it falls to the junior to name the relationship and assent to the hierarchy. The junior must desire seniors with whom to maintain solid, affectionate relationships; and these are by nature, in the Chinese case, hierarchical. Reminiscent of the Japanese notion of ***amae,*** affectionate dependence of a junior on a senior (Doi 1971), children's earliest experiences include the willing act of naming their seniors.

In contrast to the way face is usually regarded, the junior in a close relationship confers face on the senior, especially before a third party. Indeed, the prototypical case described above of addressing others—visible throughout the life cycle in China—involves at least three participants.[4]

For children, a parent—often a mother, but also possibly another caregiver—initiates the exchange. The child does her part, and the elder kinsperson receives the utterance as a kind of gift. Teachers similarly remind their young students to address visitors: *Āyí shūshu zàijiàn!* 'Goodbye, aunt(s) (*āyí*) and uncle(s) (*shūshu*)!' In the traditional literature on speech act theory and linguistic analysis, the prototypical exchange is of two equal partners (but see Goffman [1979] 1981a: 129–30); in China, however, it seems to be a hierarchy of three graded participants, seeking to determine places for themselves vis-à-vis one another. Animators of authors' words speaking to a third person are seen as in no way less "authentic" or "genuine" than someone speaking alone and from the heart. Here the contrast with a generalized Western linguistic ideology is sharp: the intention or originality of an utterance is much less central than mastery of a form through practice.

Failures occur not when the junior somehow doesn't mean what is said, but rather when the term is not uttered. When a child refuses to perform—a rare occurrence in my experience—there is often much consternation on the part of the parent. The person who should have been named may say *Méi guānxi, tā hái xiǎo* 'It doesn't matter, s/he's young.' But learning to be a full person presupposes mastery of this kinship-naming routine. This hierarchical, familial relationship is the ultimate endpoint of solidarity, in which a kinship term must be uttered to acknowledge, illustrate, and create the desired relationship.

The same principle is visible when a young woman marries into a family. The essential transformative moment occurs—not, as in the US, in an overt performative statement *I do* [agree to be and am hereby married]—but when she speaks the kinship terms appropriate for a husband and wife to use. She becomes a wife by uttering the terms for his relatives. The film *Small Happiness* (Hinton 1984) has a memorable scene where a young bride in North China is forced to *kètóu* (kneel and bow her head, preferably by knocking it on the ground) as her husband's relative reads the kinship terms of the husband's relatives; she protests and resists. This is often seen as an educational ritual in which the bride learns the terms; but it may also be regarded as performative. While the resistance seems somewhat stylized, that does not necessarily make it less genuine.[5] The likely explanation is that the sudden incorporation into a husband's family through the use of these kinship terms is painful and undesired. She has no genuine bond with these new **affines;** but by acquiescing to the terms, she is agreeing that such bonds will inevitably develop and the behavior associated with the terms will be produced—and she is assenting to enter a world in which she has little power. Concomitantly, the bonds with her natal family will weaken.[6]

Changing a title can change the relationship. Topley (1974: 246–47) describes a certain diagnosis of incompatible horoscopes, accompanying physical symptoms of a culture-bound ailment in the Canton delta, similar to what Western pediatricians call "failure to thrive." This ailment is explained as stemming from a problematic relationship, a lack of bonding, between a mother and child. One cure is to change the term that the child uses for her mother:

> There is no real solution if such a child remains with its mother, but one could try to redefine the problem, adjusting the role to the behavior rather than behavior to the role. By changing the term of address, one suggests that the mother is not really the mother. The child is taught to call her either *a- tse*, "elder sister," *a-so*, "brother's wife," or *a-naai*, "wet-nurse"... I was told that when the term of address was modified, the child should not really treat its mother as elder sister or brother's wife, but the mother need not feel so bad if the child who did not call her mother was difficult to control.

The terms chosen as replacement indicate close relationships which are not as difficult as that between mother and child. This is said to modify the bad feelings the mother has if her child treats her poorly, not as a mother should properly be treated; it is more acceptable for a greater degree of indifference in a relationship between older sibling and younger sibling than between mother and child. The names—here, kinship terms—are not merely descriptive, but potent. They are inevitably hierarchical; selection is made among alternative forms of hierarchy that are nonetheless intimate and affectionate.

Socialization of children in China, as in many societies, includes much attention to the proper use of naming practices, as the above example suggests. But by contrast with many societies, the routine in which a third party clarifies the forms of address that should be used by the other two participants is not limited to childhood. It is not something that is supposed to be internalized and mastered, and thereafter volunteered by the two participants. The presence of a third party is presumed as the default case. After describing other forms of naming, I will return to this point.

## Nicknames

Within a family and outside most official contexts, and before entering school, children are known by and addressed almost exclusively with nicknames. So-called *xiǎomíng* 'small names' or *nǎimíng* 'milk names' are often (in Mandarin) reduplicated syllables from a child's formal personal name; thus Chén Qīngzhū 'dark pearl' might be called Zhūzhu. (In Taiwanese—also called Fujianese, Hokkien, Southern Min, or Minnanhua—they are often prefaced by *a*-, and then one syllable of a child's personal name is used: Qīngzhū would be addressed as Āzhū.) These are the names by which a child is called at home by elders, and sometimes by all the family members. R. Watson 1986 and Farris 1988 have shown that adult women may have only such small names, which blur the boundary between proper and common nouns, e.g., *xiǎomèi* 'little sister' or *sānmèi* 'third daughter'. Farris shows how **marked** many of the terms referring to women are, even when words referring to women have related terms referring to men. But these are only loosely related pairs. Those referring to women often suggest sexuality and depravity, e.g., *biǎozi* 'prostitute, bitch'; in contrast, the insulting term for males is *biǎozi yǎngde* 'raised by a bitch' or *biǎozi érzi* 'son of a bitch' (Farris, 293–95). Alice Murong Pu Lin (1988) has a story titled "Grandmother Had No Name," which dealt with exactly this matter: her grandmother was known only as "wife of Li," and even Lin's mother did not know her own mother's name (she knew her only by the local term meaning Mom, *Muma*, p. 14). Kingston (1975: 3–16) writes of an unmarried aunt who violated the family honor by having a child out of wedlock, and who was thereafter never referred to; her existence was presumed erased, her name never uttered.

Those at the lower end of the economic ladder, like women, may have no real formal name, or names that verge into mere designation (Alleton 1993: 173, 205–8). Nicknames are sometimes recorded by officials sent to record the names of the illiterate villagers under their jurisdiction, but at their limit they may simply be kinship terms.

In contrast, upper-class men have often had a multitude of names—courtesy names, pen names, studio names, style names. They have also been certain of their "real" names. In Chinese traditional times (which were far from unitary), men of the elite classes often selected names for themselves to correspond to given attributes of their (desired) character, and these were included in their biographies as pen names.[7] Though this practice is in some ways obsolete, people in public life often change their names to reflect attitudes toward the world. The well-known political figure Dèng Xiǎopíng is unofficially reported to have had the original name Kàn Zégāo; his five children all use his adopted surname Dèng (Hsu 1982: 351).[8] The 20th century writers Lǔ Xùn (born Zhōu Shùrén [J. Lau & H. Goldblatt 1995:xxxii]), Bā Jīn (Lǐ Fèigān [Lau & Goldblatt 1995:xxv]), Lǎo Shě (born Shū Qìngchūn [Lau & Goldblatt 1995:xxx]), and Máo Dùn (born Shěn Yànbīng [Lau & Goldblatt 1995:xxxiii]) all selected these as their public names—sometimes called Party names. The tightness of fit that many Westerners often claim to exist (or wish to exist) between their unitary individual essence and name appears more malleable for people in China. The more manipulation on the part of the name-holder, the higher the status.

Ordinary people's names, in contrast, appear to vary, and it is impossible to draw boundaries between types of naming practices. If some kinship terms become nicknames which are then recorded as formal names—or if people adopt politically fashionable names that give an impression of revolutionary ardor, and then pass them on to their children—then it is necessary to include within a single analysis all these naming practices. In a sense there is a single "system" or universe that includes social and occupational titles, pronouns, introductions, status, nicknames, and multiple names. Indeed, only now we arrive at "proper" names.

## "Proper" Names

Names are fascinating to people in China. They are discussed avidly and frequently, and have been written about voluminously. Hansen argues (1992, 4n.) that names (*míng*) rather than sentences are central to all Chinese philosophy—and that this fact distinguishes the Chinese approach to reality, which is more important than a theory of truth. Proper names in China have been dealt with in great detail by Alleton 1993, following earlier treatments by Chao 1956, Sung 1979, 1981, Liu 1981, R. Watson 1986, Wáng 1988, Zhào 1988, Chén 1990, and Erbaugh 1993. I will not repeat this information here, except to state that parents and grandparents (usually) select infants' names according to a given set of criteria:[9] they should be auspicious; they are viewed as governing the child's fate in some ways; they should harmonize with the time, and often the place, of the child's birth; they may be changed if, through illness or misfortune, a diagnosis of mismatch with the name is made; they may indicate membership in a generation in a family of intellectuals; they may be female names which typically come from a much reduced and stereotypical stock, compared to that for male names; they may reflect changes in naming styles resulting from various political and intellectual trends.

However, what most analysts skim over is the very role of naming: after the first bestowing of a personal name, many other things are still done with names. People are accustomed to being addressed and referred to by an assortment of names, and they do not necessarily retain any of them as their "real" name or as the one that they feel reflects their identity. A friend in Kunming told me that though "her name" in Mandarin was Zhào Hóngdá, everyone called her Xiǎohóng ([Xiaohom] in Kunming dialect); to her, both dialect versions were acceptable. Another friend, a member of a minority group, had one "proper" name in her native Yi language, another in Kunming dialect, still another in Standard Mandarin; engaged to a foreign man who did not speak much Chinese, she had an English name ("Priscilla") by which he called her; most other foreigners called her with *xiǎo* (little) and her surname. Which one is her name? All of them, in a way. And there are other variants as well: her family called her by a familiar name at home, and school friends by yet another.

Personal names play very little role in the actual exchanges of everyday life, though they are often included in introductions (they do sit, baldly, on identification cards in the PRC, Taiwan, Hong Kong, and Singapore.)[10] When two people of approximately equal status and some education meet, in the absence of a mutual acquaintance who can perform the introduction, one person may say something like "I am Yang Jihua." The **interlocutor** will respond with a query about the characters constituting the name, since there are so many homophones in Chinese and the names may be made of virtually any words that are not inauspicious (Alleton 1993: 21–32). But this will occur only with virtual equals: students in the same class, friends of friends, etc. In most other circumstances, a *zhōngjiānrén* 'middle-person, intermediary' will perform the introductions, which are followed by attempts to work out the relationships and settle on the proper title. This replicates the prototypical routine described at the beginning of this [chapter], where there are necessarily three participants and where the junior must utter the proper terms for the ensuing relationship:

| | | |
|---|---|---|
| A: | *Zhèiwèi shi Jì Chăngzhăng.* | This distinguished person (C) is Factory-head Ji. |
| B: | *Jì Chăngzhăng.* | (Repeating the surname and title) |
| C: | *Nĭ hăo.* | Hello. |

Repetition of the surname *Jì* with the title *Chăngzhăng* constitutes acknowledgment of the introduction and acceptance of this title; C's moving on to a greeting demonstrates that the relationships have been properly cared for. A person who will be called by a name that indicates speaker's superiority to that person, such as an employee, will be introduced by full name, and called either by full name or by a diminutive and the surname: *Xiăo Wáng*, comparable to English use of surname alone (especially British: *Jones*).

| | | |
|---|---|---|
| A: | *Zhè shì Wáng Shĕn.* | This is Wáng Shĕn. |
| B: | *Xiăo Wáng.* | [I am acknowledging you as] Wang (i.e., Hello). |
| C: | *Jì Chăngzhăng hăo.* | Hello Factory-head (Mr.) Ji. |

Assenting to the forms of address, each person utters them for the first time. The junior has the obligation to utter the form of naming, but is expected to say nothing else. In negotiating a new relationship, the participants will sometimes dispute the terms gently—the senior or superior perhaps reluctant to accept the honor and responsibility that follow greater distance. A young woman might say *Gūmā* 'Older aunt', and the older woman say *Jiào wŏ āyí* 'Call me *āyí* (younger aunt)'. Such struggles seem at first glance to be attempts to diminish any sense of hierarchy, but I suggest that we view it rather as an attempt to diminish the distance while retaining the hierarchy. The recipient of the correction tries to maintain the original greater distance, but only with difficulty. The names are murmured, rather than spoken in the same volume as other exchanges—thus marking this part of the exchange, the **FRAME** (Goffman 1981b: 174–78), conducted in **metalinguistic** terms about what will be said in the future, as a separate piece of discourse. It will be altered only with great difficulty in the future.[11] In our putative prototypical case, the goal was to agree about participants' relative position and statement of these terms; but especially with "fictive" kinship, the positions are often unclear and require negotiation.

Instruction and guidance about these matters is often desired, but not forced. Children, but not only children, rely on others to help them figure out which term and which relationship is appropriate. In a novel about a Cantonese family in San Francisco's Chinatown, Fae Myenne Ng's protagonist (the native-born daughter of immigrants) describes her discomfort at being alone with her mother's new husband—not because of any sense of danger, but because she doesn't know how to address him: "This is what I'd worried about all through the bus ride up here: What to call him after they married. I expected Mah to give me instructions, but she didn't, and now Leon and I were alone" (Ng 1993: 186). Though it is possible for a junior to ask directly *Wŏ zĕnme jiào nĭ?* or *Wŏ zĕnme chēnghu nĭ?* 'How do I address you?'—a metalinguistic act that occurs with great regularity—it is greatly preferable for a third person to give the instructions.

In China as elsewhere, one can disparage people by calling them by a lesser term than expected; or one can try to oblige others by calling them by an "undeserved" higher term. One can also flatter through choice of naming practice, and these strategies are often considered very carefully by adults. Jianying Zha, a writer born in China who came to the US as a young woman, returned to China as an adult to try to grasp and describe the contemporary climate. She reports deliberately choosing a title desired by her interlocutor in order to gain entry into a particular informant's good graces:

> I call her "Teacher Bei," instead of "Aunt Bei" as Chinese normally call somebody her age, because of a warning from the friend who introduced us: It is very important, he said, to make her feel that she belongs to the educated class and is someone with culture. Teacher Bei was so pleased by our visit and got to talking so much that she skipped her nap and made a big pot of tea. (Zha 1995: 25)

Here the speaker is quite conscious of the flattery, but its effectiveness is nonetheless clear. Note too the inclusion in this brief discussion of "the friend who introduced us"; he had conferred with Zha about the proper way to address "Teacher Bei."

In a story by the contemporary author Zhāng Jié, a very calculating, middle-aged Communist party member named Yue meets a former classmate and current colleague while out jogging. He chooses his naming practices deliberately as well, but to bolster his own position, not to flatter his acquaintance:

> He caught up with Little Duan. They had called him "little" in college because he was the youngest in the class. Though he was growing bald now, Yue still addressed him this way. Since becoming section chief he had taken to prefacing the names of many of his subordinates with

"little." Apart from sounding fatherly, it also conveyed his own seniority. (Zhang 1986: 65)

These two had been classmates (*tóngxué*) and hence had a relationship institutionalized as egalitarian. (This is something like age-mates in some African societies, though without the ritual rites of passage that are so anthropologically famous.) Classmates spend their entire time at the school together, moving from subject to subject while remaining in their classroom—a room for which they are responsible. Even in higher education, entering students take the same subjects, study together, graduate together, and often marry one another. (Indeed, the closeness of classmates is known as an unparalleled opportunity for young people of the opposite sex to meet. The many people in the countryside who leave school well before marriageable age, often after fifth grade—at age 12 or so—are aware of the fact that they have few opportunities to meet appropriate partners, and they rely on introductions from mutual acquaintances to succeed in setting up a marriage.)

Students at the same school but in different years are also *tóngxué*, but are clearly distinguished as in the class above (*xuéxiōng* 'older-brother student' and *xuéjiě* 'older-sister student') or the class below (*xuédì* 'younger-brother student' and *xuémèi* 'younger-sister student'), in contrast to *tóngbān tóngxué* 'classmates of the same class'.

Classmates keep in touch throughout their lives, having reunions whenever possible and helping one another through difficulties. During my last visit to China (1994), one of my husband's former students learned that we were there after a three-year absence, and on almost no notice—in a day—assembled a group of eight or so classmates who were now scattered throughout the city of Kunming. They had all graduated, a few were engaged (one is now married), and several had gone home to rural locations, but most kept track of one another. This is the most egalitarian relationship that a Chinese person encounters, and it also takes place in the setting most likely to include frequent hearing of people's full personal names. Hence classmates are likely to know one another's full names, and sometimes even to use them. As Chao points out (1956: 239, 1968: 514) spouses may even use these names to address one another, especially in certain circumstances: when a wife addresses her husband, before they have children and begin to use **teknonyms,** if the personal name is monosyllabic and thus bound, and if they met as classmates and grew accustomed to hearing and using the combination of surname with personal name. Clearly, these conditions are rarely all met, and other forms of naming are much more common. As in the vignette quoted above, we see that other forms of address may even be employed among classmates: some are selected as superior, others as junior.

This nuanced way of addressing even the most equal of people in China helps explain what might be seen as puzzling to Western linguists in China: avoidance of pronouns. While it might seem desirable to use pronouns for their social neutrality, I argue that this neutrality is precisely what is UNDESIRABLE, indeed insupportable, to those who insist on maintaining strict hierarchy. This is most true when referring to exalted others, particularly in their presence.

## PRONOUNS

Pronouns are names in the sense that they "stand in for names." We all know of the familiarity and slight insult used when a husband says, without antecedent, *She won't let me go to the game*. It is somewhat different when a student says of a professor, *She gave me a C on my paper*, without ever mentioning a "real name." (I think it reflects a desire to challenge the power of the professor, a challenge that would not be voiced in her presence.) Chinese pronouns are fascinating, especially when we bring in the written evidence of the last 2,000 years. They have varied from period to period, and in the present vary greatly among dialects (Chao 1956: 240, Norman 1988: 182, 190, 196, 203, 205, 208, 220, 223, 227, 234). Plural markers are fairly recent, and number does not have the importance that it has in English and other Indo-European languages. Only animate, human nouns may even be distinguished with a plural marker; but they may also be left **unmarked.** Pronouns are the only obligatory location for plural/singular distinctions, and this distinction is felt rather more loosely than in English; even pronouns can be considered neutral between singular and plural in some cases (e.g., *nín*; see below). Elsewhere I have treated Chinese pronouns in reference to ethnic groups (Blum 1994a, 1994b: 296–310, 1998), showing that those groups that are seen as equivalent agents to Han speakers are more likely to be referred to in the 3rd person plural (*tāmen*), while those that are non-individuated and known as a type are more likely to be referred to in the singular (*tā*).

Still, pronouns are used more commonly in Chinese than, say, in Japanese (Hendry 1993, Bachnik & Quinn 1994) or in Javanese (Errington 1985, 1988) (see also P. Brown & S. Levinson 1987). In some areas in North China, 1st person plural pronouns can be distinguished by inclusive and exclusive varieties (*zámen* 'we the people involved in this conversation' vs. *wǒmen* 'I and some people not now present'). A 2nd person polite pronoun (*nín*) is said to be unmarked for number—quite unlike the Indo-European pronouns for politeness, which seem to have come from the plural (R. Brown & A. Gilman 1960). Use of *nín* has increased steadily over the past decade, as the norms governing deference have increased and egalitarian ideals have been less enforced. (On pronouns see also Benveniste 1966a, Friedrich 1972, P. Brown & S. Levinson 1987, Urban 1996: 28–65.)

But use of pronouns is commonly seen as neutral with respect to hierarchy and relationship; and within the entire naming system, it is believed to confer little meaning. So it ends up conveying the meaning of LACK of respect; ultimately one flatters by using a title in place of a pronoun: *Lǎoshi shénme shíhou dào wǒmen zhèr lái?* 'When will the teacher come to our house?', which can only be translated as "When will [you] come to our home?"—though there is no literal "you" (*nǐ/nín*). Again, *Xiānsheng de shūfa wànshì wúxiǔ* 'Master's/Teacher's calligraphy will not fade for ten thousand generations'—i.e., "Your calligraphy, Teacher/ Master, will endure through the generations." One uses names and forms of address in a manner identical to reference, as if honoring the addressee by speaking to a third person—which recalls the suggestion made earlier that prototypical interactions in China involve three parties.

Young (1994: 149–52) demonstrates how employees can threaten the face of employers by publicly performing functions that are supposed to be to the credit of the superior. What is crucial here is the observation of a third person. Similarly, Kipnis (1995: 126–27), following the suggestion of one of his consultants, shows how face requires the participation of three people. Without too great a divergence into the topic of "face," I invoke these two authors' works to demonstrate how interwoven the notion of threesomes is with naming.[12]

So how can we understand the significance of Chinese naming practices in the context of Chinese culture and in the context of the anthropological concern with naming in general? Individual psychological identity appears not to be critical; but factors such as face, where other participants must be considered, are essential. In this sense language can be seen as continuous with other forms of social action. To understand this fully, we must consider how words in general function in Chinese culture.

## The Power of Words

The act of naming events (with "common," not "proper" names) is regarded as powerful in China, as in many other cultures. Taboos against "bad luck" words are well known (Sung 1979), especially on otherwise happy (but liminal and dangerous) occasions—e.g., New Year (see Lu Hsun [1924] 1972: 130) or weddings. One avoids saying words that sound like *sǐ* 'die', in order to avoid a bad beginning of the year (Sung 1979: 24); and on all occasions one tries to avoid giving gifts that could be counted as *sì* 'four' (stems of flowers, apples, etc.) because of the similarity of sound (disregarding tone) with *sǐ*. Words and the objects of the events to which they refer are intimately connected; this extends to homophones of such words, and to the objects to which the homophones refer.

Many "traditional" ritual practices involve the use of objects of which the "name" (common noun) is auspicious:[13] *zǎozi* 'dates' are eaten at weddings to encourage the early coming of sons (*zǎo* 'early', *zǐ* 'son'); *chángmiàn* 'long noodles' are homophonous with 'long life'; *yú* 'fish' is homophonous with 'surplus', so banquets end with fish so that one can say *Niánnián chī yú* 'Eat fish/have surplus every year'. This is rather different from the sort of magical power usually attributed to words (Frazer [1890] 1981: 9–12, Malinowski [1935] 1978: 52–62, Tambiah 1968, O'Keefe 1982: 39–56), in which either a **metaphoric** or **metonymic** relationship is seen as accounting for the efficacy of words in ritual. Here it is a demonstration of the continuum of language and object: when one utters a word, it (and its homophones) are psychologically and actually present; when one focuses on an object, its names and homophones are also present.[14]

These matters may not be left to whim; children are not allowed to make grave mistakes in these practices. (Others have pointed out that the general style of socializing children in China is intolerant of experimentation, and hence of error. Children are shown the proper procedure and are rehearsed in it, but only when they have become competent to learn. Children walk, for instance, at an average age older than in the US.) Recall that even adult children are told *Jiào Wáng Shūshu* 'Call him (younger) uncle Wang' when meeting a new adult. Emotions are not what is primarily being indexed; rather, respect for proper authority and form, demonstrated through mastery of the proper words, demonstrates the speaker's sincere desire to be guided by teachers (Blum 1996) and an eagerness to define hierarchy properly. The critical factor is not emotional (Potter 1988, Abu-Lughod & Lutz 1990); the power of words is that they invoke prototypes which then guide people's actions. This is the key to understanding Chinese naming practices.

## Chinese Naming Practices

Treatments of naming in China usually focus on proper names (Chao 1956, Sung 1979, 1981, R. Watson 1986, Alleton 1993), though all mention the rarity of their use (Alleton 201–4). What has not been discussed in much detail is the strategic way in which speakers select from among their options for various purposes in particular contexts. Liu 1981 and Chao 1956 describe certain linguistic aspects of forms of address, especially kinship terms. Chao gives a chart with choices that should cover every social or linguistic situation, but his discussion is limited to the semantic and social meanings of terms—and it describes usage from his youth in China in the early 20th century. I suggest that cultural meanings can be grasped only if we situate naming in a broader context that includes the **ontology of language**—a consideration of the nature of language in the Chinese world, and what language is seen as being able to do.

Given structures of meaning and status, individuals employ means at their disposal to create/enforce relationships at every turn. In Japan (Bachnik & Quinn 1994) and Java (Errington 1985, 1988, Siegel 1986: 15–33), a speaker cannot evade commitment to one social level or another; in China, the choice about which name to use (or not) commits one to a particular position. There is no neutrality; relationship and status are evident at all times. This is common throughout virtually all non-egalitarian societies; what varies is the particular means through which the principle is effected, and the homologies with other aspects of the culture.

In traditional Chinese domestic religious practice, now being revived to some degree in the mainland of China (see Siu 1989, Feuchtwang 1992, Dean 1993), the ontological categories of living and dead, human and godlike intersect with the otherwise vital ones of female and male, adult and child, married and unmarried, educated and illiterate, senior and junior, kin and stranger. Ghosts discovered to be powerful sometimes get renamed and are worshipped as gods (Harrell 1974), while gods retain their names until they fade completely from memory. Ancestors too may be forgotten; but unlike strangers, they have once been named. Ghosts are the spiritual counterpart to strangers, the undesirable element in the well-researched triad of god, ghost, and ancestor—corresponding to officials, strangers, and kin (see Jordan 1972, Ahern 1973, 1981, A. Wolf 1974a, Feuchtwang 1992). Ghosts are blamed for all manner of ailment, and are feared. Ancestors for whom proper rituals are not maintained can be ghosts, as when a woman commits suicide in a family well (Kingston 1975: 1–16, M. Wolf 1975, Spence 1978, Tan 1989). Kinship relations are disturbed by the death's occurrence in an unnatural and undesirable way; and the person is then often left unnamed, as if no longer in the family. Such improper death results in taboo of the name: powerful but silenced.

Like ghosts, strangers can easily pass in the street, and can negotiate use of space without verbal interaction. The difference between words used and words not used, between silence and speaking (Becker 1984: 136, Tannen & Saville-Troike 1985), is a basic aspect of discourse that must be described for each society. There may be words to name those encountered, even if these words are unuttered. Strangers may be referred to or addressed or both or neither. Chinese public life, especially urban life, involves daily contact with countless strangers. Most are ignored and unaddressed.

## Conclusion

Words that name people also name and thus create relationships among speakers, hearer(s), and persons named. The relative statuses of all three, if all are present, is an important factor in determining which term will be used. Considerations of closeness sometimes override those of distance: closeness can be part of distance if it is generational or conventional. Unlike Americans, who usually seek the most egalitarian forms of address (*Professor Jones? Is it okay if I call you Linda?*), Chinese usually seek to be told about their status relative to one another through the help of a mutual acquaintance, and they do so throughout their lives.

A common cultural prototype in China is of the benevolent (paternalistic?) older kin who takes care of the younger ones, who reciprocate with affection, later in life with care, and finally (traditionally) with the performance of ritual remembrances ("ancestor worship"). Invocation of the kinship term calls up images of the prototype for speaker and hearer, reminding all of the full potential for practice implied by the term. But speakers do not always have the right to use close kinship terms, and relationships do not always fall into kinship patterns. However, prototypical relationships may still be hierarchical, such as that of employer and employee. Clearly, hierarchy does not impede formation of close attachments; the literature on politeness, however, tends to portray a world of instrumental manipulators of limited goods.[15] I have suggested [here] that in China, even when speaking with and of one's closest intimates, choices may be made about the term that embodies the proper relationship, which may be one of hierarchy, but not distance. The maintenance of face can be signaled and granted by selecting intimate terms, and in fact requires this labeling for the relationship to be forged. Silently knowing how one feels is not expected to be adequate; nor does one speak volumes about relationships (*I love you so much*...). Affection is conveyed through the naming patterns over which one has control; and the socialization of children into this mastery is a powerful way in which they learn to be persons among others.

I have examined the role of language, and especially naming, in the face-to-face interactions of everyday Chinese life; names are one element to be deployed in strategies of giving, withholding, and exchanging face. I have shown that face is bestowed through naming practices, and that this can operate in terms of solidarity (which is not the same as equality) as well as authority. This occurs in some cases through the utterance of certain terms which have the power to affect the world. I have also explained some of the principles underlying the choice of particular terms, from the available font of naming possibilities, in particular situations—showing that reliance on prototypical relationships allows speakers to employ selected terms, in anticipation that the relationship will embody features common to that prototype. But intention and emotion are not especially important here. I have shown further that naming practices reveal distinctions among what may be said, what may not be said, and what must be said, in monitoring the delicate balance of self and world.

What we often refer to as "language," easily and casually, designates diverse entities. Words are imbued with different sorts of qualities in different cultures. Language may be seen as separate from other social practices, or as isomorphic with them, or as contradictory. It may be seen as ideally expressing the speaker's innermost thoughts, or it may be seen as exemplifying the speaker's knowledge of what is expected on certain occasions and in certain contexts. It can be performative (Austin 1962) or descriptive of the state of affairs of the world (but see Kripke 1980, Rosaldo 1982). It can be, and usually is, a source of social information about identities of many sorts: gender, age, status, occupation, and ethnic identity (Li 1994). In some areas, language is seen as efficacious (Tambiah 1968); in others, it is superfluous (Bauman 1983); in many societies, it is dangerous (Favret-Saada 1977, Wagner 1978). Writing of this plethora of ways in which language is viewed, Woolard & Schieffelin (1994: 55) have defined "language ideology" as the often explicit "notions of how communication works as a social process." I have discussed [here] one aspect of Chinese language-in-use—naming—as a preliminary contribution to a broader explicit understanding of the diverse ways in which language functions in social life.

## Notes

This research relies in part on observations made while I conducted fieldwork for my dissertation during the 1990–91 academic year under the auspices of the Committee on Scholarly Communication with the People's Republic of China (National Academy of Sciences), now the Committee on Scholarly Communication with China. I thank Norma Diamond, Sergei Kan, Donald Munro, Bruce Mannheim, Haun Saussy, Sara Davis, and Lionel Jensen for reading drafts of this article in its various incarnations. William Bright and two reviewers for *Language in Society* made invaluable suggestions; it is not their fault if I did not follow all of them. Sara Davis also helped with enthusiastic bibliographic and other assistance, thanks to support from Greg Posseh1 and the Department of Anthropology at the University of Pennsylvania; H-ASIA subscribers responded to my request for current information about naming practices. I am grateful to the Department of Asian Studies at the University of Texas (Austin) and the Center for East Asian Studies at the University of Pennsylvania for opportunities to present material related to this article.

1. Social and occupational titles and on-the-spot terms should also be included, but in the interest of brevity I have omitted them here.

2. Yunnan province borders Burma, Laos, and Vietnam, as well as Guizhou and Sichuan provinces and the autonomous areas of Tibet and Guangxi. It is ethnically quite diverse: Yunnan counts 24 officially recognized ethnic minority groups among its inhabitants. Its capital city, Kunming, has also been home to many migrations of the majority Han Chinese from elsewhere in China; hence its linguistic stock is quite diverse. *Kūnmínghuà* 'Kunming dialect' is a variant of southwest Mandarin, somewhat similar to Sichuan dialects. Other Chinese dialects in the province, all termed *Hànhuà* 'language of the Han,' are similar enough to be intelligible to natives of Kunming, but distinctive enough to be (it is claimed) identifiable. Most ethnic minorities have languages associated with them, though not all members of those groups speak "their" language. *Pǔtōnghuà*, Standard Mandarin, is found in official and formal contexts, though when spoken by natives of the area it usually carries a "southern accent." Migrants from northern areas sometimes retain their more standard pronunciation, which may be perceived as odd by Yunnan natives (see Blum 1994b: 150–78).

   My general argument about strategies reflects my observations in Yunnan; but I believe that many of the principles can be observed elsewhere, at least among Han Chinese in the People's Republic. Regional variation among Han Chinese causes less variation in underlying principles than do factors such as social status and gender, among others, in particular situations.

   The question of the speech community intersects with that of the national community. Claims about essential cultural homogeneity in China (Cohen 1994, Tu Wei-ming 1994a, etc.) and in other Chinese societies (Erbaugh 1995) sit alongside predictions that China will soon unravel (Friedman 1994). Practices like those described here must be considered when any such conclusions are drawn. How prevalent are these practices—at least the underlying principles? It is possible that, in addition to the unification provided by the use of a single script and the ideology of unity accompanying it, China is unified by certain pragmatic principles. I welcome comments from researchers in other areas of China who can support or refute notions of the uniformity of pragmatics in the nation-state. Comments from scholars in China would be especially welcome.

3. See Urban (1996: 99–133) for a fresh account of the history of the term "classificatory," and of the offhand way in which Morgan announced that he had "discovered" classificatory kinship—as if it were a solid object available to be picked up and put in a backpack.

4. The model of a prototype that is psychologically present is a useful one; but like all models, it is a construct of analysts (see Lakoff 1987, Quinn & Holland 1987, MacLaury 1991).

5. See Urban 1988 on ritual laments and Johnson 1988 on funeral laments. Emotion in these cases is inseparable from its expression.

6. There is little anthropological treatment of wedding ceremonies with the degree of detail necessary to draw conclusions about this moment; one wishes for a conference and volume akin to that for death ritual (see J. Watson & E. Rawski 1988). See M. Wolf 1978 for discussion of the good wife's infrequent contact with her natal family, and Judd 1989 for a correction of the view that women severed ties with their natal families upon marriage.

7. Many famous people are remembered principally in terms of their studio names (Sū Dōngpō rather than Sū Shì, Pú Sōnglíng). Wáng Shǒurén, the Ming philosopher, took "Yángmíng" as his style name, and it now refers to him even without his surname. Zhōngshān, Sun Yat-sen's style name pronounced in Mandarin, is another case.

8. Huà Guófēng, Mao's immediate successor, is unofficially reported to have been born Su Zhu, and his children are reported to retain his natal name of Su (cf. Hsu 1982: 351–52). Mao's wife Jiāng Qīng was reported to have been born Li Zhongjin (Snow 1968: 459), Li Jin (Witke 1977: 45), Luan Shumeng (Chung & Miller 1968: 12), Lǐ Yúnhè (Bartke 1981: 576), or Lǐ Nà (Wang Jie, p.c.) She took the name Lán Píng as a film actress, and later took Jiāng Qīng as her Party name. Most Chinese sources fail to give the original names for many people, such as Huà or Jiāng Qīng, while English-language sources fail to provide tonal marks for the romanized names. It is more common for English-language sources to inquire into the original names, while Chinese-language sources tend to retain the name that was used after a person became well known.

9. See He Liyi (1993: 121–27) and Miller (1993: 7) for descriptions of naming among the Bai minority. The Bai, one of Yunnan's dominant ethnic minorities, rely on chance to select the bestower of a child's name on his or her full-month birthday. Miller reports being asked to select a child's name, and feeling a tremendous degree of undesired responsibility for this stranger's child.

10. Thanks to a reviewer for *Language in Society* for pointing out this obvious but unremarked point.

11. Chao (1956: 224, 225, 237) describes meeting an illustrious person of superior age, but equal status: the speaker chooses to use the courtesy name with title, knowing that in the future the title may be dropped. It would be more difficult to move from a formal name and title to the bald courtesy name. These elaborate social considerations are no longer part of Chinese etiquette, to my knowledge—and certainly were never part of common folks' practices. However, in responses to an inquiry I made over the Internet, several people reported a significant

increase in the use of the personal name during the last two or three years, often with a title but without the surname.

12. Face in China and face in general have been treated extensively. It is often, as Kipnis 1995 points out, a virtual "fetish" of Chineseness, with even theoretical treatments returning to classic sources on China (Hu 1944, Martin Yang 1945, Goffman 1967: 5–6). Face has been central in the extensive literature on politeness (P. Brown & S. Levinson 1987) and is one aspect of the person discussed in the literature on personhood (Goffman 1967, Geertz 1973, Mauss 1985). It is somewhat surprising, however, to notice how seldom issues of face have surfaced in recent accounts of the anthropology of the self and the person. This may be because of the American folk ideology of the self which privileges interior experience over practice and surface; however, see Potter 1988, Abu-Lughod & Lutz 1990, Wikan 1995.

    Negative and positive face—the desire to be left alone, the desire to be acknowledged for achievement—and their involvement in politeness are often treated as clustering around poles of power and solidarity, but these factors are not always easy to sort out. Kinship relations are solidary and yet hierarchical, as many feminist analysts have pointed out (Collier & Yanagisako 1987); but intimacy, affection, and respect are intermingled most evidently within family relations. A degree of pleasure may be derived from uttering a kinship term, or being called by a kinship term, because one gains "face" from it. However, another source of pleasure comes from performing scripts—acting in accord with a prototype of kinship relations—in which the relationship is enforced and in some sense created by the utterance or invocation of the proper term.

    Children can give face to their parents through achievements, just as they can lose face for them through misdeeds. There is a sense in which the face of a family is shared by all its members. Thus Daniel (1984, chaps. 2 and 3), writing about India, describes the substance of a *jati* being shared by its members in Tamil Nadu, and indeed by the very soil of its homeland. *Jati* is usually translated as 'caste' but is more accurately described as an endogamous, ranked, localized, corporate group.

    Face is prototypically involved in two types of cases: first, instrumental public relations, where factors of power and status must be considered (see Hu 1944, Martin Yang 1945, Mayfair Yang 1994, Kipnis 1995), and second, intimate relations within the family, where affective factors must also be considered (see Potter 1988, Jankowiak 1993)—but not necessarily egalitarian relations. In fact, relations in the family are, according to predominant Chinese ideology, all hierarchical.

13. See Siu 1989 on the transformation of the meaning of traditional practices despite continuity of form; and see Dean 1993. The question of cultural continuity alongside "modernity," socialism, or nationalism is in many ways a central one in anthropology now. Siu argues in a Saussurean way (like Sahlins 1981) that a "traditional" practice in a changed context has an entirely different meaning (value) than it had in the past. Pemberton 1994 makes basically the same point about the use of "tradition" in New Order Indonesia.

14. Ahern 1979 writes that her informants in Taiwan explained similar actions as expressing wishes, rather than as actually capable of bringing about changes in the world. She terms these "weak illocutionary acts," in contrast to the more literal reading of them as illocutionary acts.

15. A reviewer of this article pointed out that "hierarchy is often equated with hegemonic discourse, and hegemonic discourse is universally disvalued" in our "social scientific climate." I think this is true, and it is an important example of how the cultural values of social scientists affect our analysis of other cultures.

## References

Abu-Lughod, Lila, & Lutz, Catherine A. 1990. Introduction: Emotion, discourse, and the politics of everyday life. In Catherine A. Lutz & Lila Abu-Lughod (eds.), *Language and the politics of emotion*, 1–23. Cambridge & New York: Cambridge University Press.

Ahern, Emily Martin. 1973. *The cult of the dead in a Chinese village*. Stanford, CA: Stanford University Press.

Ahern, Emily Martin. 1979. The problem of efficacy: Strong and weak illocutionary acts. *Man* 14: 1–17.

Ahern, Emily Martin. 1981. *Chinese ritual and politics*. Cambridge & New York: Cambridge University Press.

Alford, Richard D. 1988. *Naming and identity: A cross-cultural study of personal naming practices*. New Haven: HRAF Press.

Alleton, Viviane. 1993. *Les Chinois et la passion des noms*. Paris: Aubier.

Austin, John L. 1962. *How to do things with words*. Cambridge, MA: Harvard University Press.

Bachnik, Jane M., & Quinn, Charles J., Jr. 1994. *Situated meaning: Inside and outside in Japanese self, society, and language*. Princeton, NJ: Princeton University Press.

Bartke, Wolfgang. 1981. *Who's who in the PRC*. Hamburg: Institute of Asian Affairs.

Bauman, Richard. 1983. *Let your words be few: Symbolism of speaking and silence among seventeenth-century Quakers*. Cambridge & New York: Cambridge University Press.

Becker, Alton L. 1984. Biography of a sentence: A Burmese proverb. In Edward Bruner & A. L. Becker (eds.), *Text, play, and story*, 135–55. Washington, DC: American Ethonological Society.

Bell, Diane. 1993. *Daughters of the dreaming*. 2d ed. Minneapolis: University of Minnesota Press.

Benveniste, Emile. 1966a. La nature des pronoms. In his *Problèmes de linguistique générale* 1: 251–57. Paris: Gallimard. [Translated by Mary Elizabeth Meek as The nature of pronouns, in *Problems in general linguistics*, 217–22. Coral Gables, FL: University of Miami Press, 1971.]

Benveniste, Emile. 1966b. Nature du signe linguistique. In his *Problémes de linguistique générale* 1: 49–55. Paris: Gallimard. [Translated by Mary Elizabeth Meek as The nature of the linguistic sign, in *Problems in general linguistics*, 43–48. Coral Gables, FL: University of Miami Press, 1971.]

Blum, Susan D. 1994a. Constructing a "Chinese" identity in the modern nation-state. Paper presented at the annual meeting of the Association for Asian Studies, Boston.

Blum, Susan D. 1994b. *Han and the Chinese other: The language of identity and difference in Southwest China*. Dissertation, University of Michigan, Ann Arbor.

Blum, Susan D. 1996. The power of words in China. Paper presented at the Center for East Asian Studies, University of Pennsylvania, Philadelphia, February 2.

Blum, Susan D. 1998. Pearls on the string of the Chinese nation: Pronouns, plurals, and prototypes in talk about identities. *Michigan Discussions in Anthropology*, 13: 207–237.

Bowen, Elenore Smith [Laura Bohannan]. 1964. *Return to laughter: An anthropological novel*. New York: Doubleday.

Brown, Penelope, & Levinson, Stephen C. 1987. *Politeness*. Cambridge & New York: Cambridge University Press. [Originally published in 1978.]

Brown, Roger, & Gilman, Albert. 1960. The pronouns of power and solidarity. In Thomas A. Sebeok (ed.), *Style in language*, 253–76. Cambridge, MA: MIT Press.

Chagnon, Napoleon. 1992. *Yanomamo*. 4th ed. Fort Worth, TX: Harcourt Brace Jovanovich.

Chao, Yuan-ren. 1956. Chinese terms of address. *Language* 32: 212–41.

Chao, Yuan-ren. 1968. *A grammar of spoken Chinese*. Berkeley: University of California Press.

Chén Ruìjùn. 1990. Xìngmíngxué qǐguān [A glance at naming]. *Dōngxiàng* 6: 551.

Chung Hua-min, & Miller, Arthur C. 1968. *Madame Mao: A profile of Chiang Ch'ing*. Hong Kong: Union Research Institute.

Cohen, Myron L. 1994. Being Chinese: The peripheralization of traditional identity. In Tu Weiming (ed.), 88–108.

Collier, Jane Fishburne, & Yanagisako, Sylvia Junko. 1987, eds. *Gender and kinship: Essays toward a unified analysis*. Stanford, CA: Stanford University Press.

Daniel, E. Valentine. 1984. *Fluid signs: Being a person the Tamil way*. Berkeley: University of California Press.

Dean, Kenneth. 1993. *Taoist ritual and popular cults of Southeast China*. Princeton, NJ: Princeton University Press.

Derrida, Jacques. 1982. White mythology: Metaphor in the text of philosophy. In his *Margins of philosophy*, 207–71. Chicago: University of Chicago Press.

Doi, Takeo. 1971. *Amae no koozoo*. Tokyo: Koobundoo Ltd. [Translated by John Bester as *The anatomy of dependence*. Tokyo: Kodansha, 1973.]

Erbaugh, Mary S. 1993. The making of modern Chinese: Language and power in modern China. MS.

Erbaugh, Mary S. 1995. Southern Chinese dialects as a medium for reconciliation within Greater China. *Language in Society* 24: 79–94.

Errington, J. Joseph. 1985. *Language and social change in Java: Linguistic reflexes of modernization in a traditional royal polity*. Athens: Ohio University Center for International Studies.

Errington, J. Joseph. 1988. *Structure and style in Javanese: A semiotic view of linguistic etiquette*. Philadelphia: University of Pennsylvania Press.

Farris, Catherine S. 1988. Gender and grammar in Chinese, with implications for language universals. *Modern China* 14: 277–308.

Favret-Saada, Jeanne. 1977. *Les mots, la mort, les sorts*. Paris: Gallimard. [Translated by Catherine Cullen as *Deadly words: Witchcraft in the bocage*. Cambridge & New York: Cambridge University Press, 1980.]

Feuchtwang, Stephan. 1992. *The Imperial metaphor: Popular religion in China*. London: Routledge.

Frazer, James G. 1890. *The golden bough: A study in magic and religion*. Abridged ed. New York: Macmillan. [Reprinted 1981.]

Friedman, Edward. 1994. Reconstructing China's national identity: A southern alternative to Mao-era anti-imperialist nationalism. *Journal of Asian Studies* 53: 67–91.

Friedrich, Paul. 1972. Social context and semantic feature: The Russian pronominal usage. In John J. Gumperz & Dell Hymes (eds.), *Directions in sociolinguistics: The ethnography of communication*, 270–300. New York: Holt, Rinehart & Winston.

Friedrich, Paul. 1979. The symbol and its relative nonarbitrariness. In his *Language, context, and the imagination*, 1–61. Stanford, CA: Stanford University Press.

Geertz, Clifford. 1973. Person, time, and conduct in Bali. In his *Interpretation of cultures*, 360–411. New York: Basic Books.

Goffman, Erving. 1967. On face-work: An analysis of ritual elements in social interaction. In his *Interaction ritual: Essays on face-to-face behavior*, 5–45. New York: Pantheon.

Goffman, Erving. 1979. Footing. *Semiotica* 25: 1–29. [Reprinted in Goffman 1981a: 124–57.]

Goffman, Erving. 1981a. *Forms of talk*. Philadelphia: University of Pennsylvania Press.

Goffman, Erving. 1981b. The lecture. In Goffman 1981a: 160–96.

Graham, Angus. 1989. *Disputers of the Tao: Philosophical argument in Ancient China*. La Salle, IL: Open Court.

Granet, Marcel. 1934. *La pensée chinoise*. Paris: Albin Michel.

Guō Qìngfān. 1983. ed. *Zhuāngzi Jíshì* [Annotated Zhuāngzi]. (Sìbù Kānyào.) Táiběi: Hànjīng wénhuà shìyè.

Hansen, Chad. 1983. *Language and logic in ancient China*. Ann Arbor: University of Michigan Press.

Hansen, Chad. 1992. *A Daoist theory of Chinese thought: A philosophical interpretation*. Oxford & New York: Oxford University Press.

Harrell, Stevan A. 1974. When a ghost becomes a god. In Arthur P. Wolf (ed.), 193–206.

He Liyi. 1993. *Mr. China's son: A villager's life*. Boulder, CO: Westview Press.

Hendry, Joy. 1993. *Wrapping culture: Politeness, presentation, and power in Japan and other societies*. Oxford: Clarendon Press.

Hinton, Carma. 1984. director. *Small happiness: Women of a Chinese village* (film). Long Bow Productions. Produced by Richard Gordon, Kathy Kline, and Daniel Sipe. Distributed by New Day Films, Wayne, NJ.

Hsu, R. S-W. 1982. Personal and family names. In Brian Hook (ed.), *The Cambridge Encyclopedia of China,* 351–52. Cambridge & New York: Cambridge University Press.

Hu, Hsien Chin. 1944. Chinese concepts of face. *American Anthropologist* 46: 45–64.

Huáng Kǎn. 1990. ed. Lùnyǔ Zhùsù [Critical commentaries on the Analects]. (Shísānjīng zhùsù.) Shanghai: Gǔjí chūbǎnshè.

Jankowiak, William R. 1993. *Sex, death, and hierarchy in a Chinese city: An anthropological account.* New York: Columbia University Press.

Johnson, Elizabeth L. 1988. Grieving for the dead, grieving for the living: Funeral laments of Hakka women. In Watson & Rawski (eds.), 135–63.

Jordan, David K. 1972. *Gods, ghosts, and ancestors: Folk religion in a Taiwanese village.* Berkeley: University of California Press.

Judd, Ellen R. 1989. *Niangjia:* Chinese women and their natal families. *Journal of Asian Studies* 48: 525–44.

Kingston, Maxine Hong. 1975. *The woman warrior: Memoirs of a girlhood among ghosts.* New York: Vintage.

Kipnis, Andrew. 1995. "Face": An adaptable discourse of social surfaces. *Positions: East Asia Cultures Critique* 3: 119–48.

Kondo, Dorinne K. 1990. *Crafting selves: Power, gender, and discourses of identity in a Japanese workplace.* Chicago: University of Chicago Press.

Kripke, Saul A. 1980. *Naming and necessity.* Cambridge, MA: Harvard University Press.

Kroeber, Alfred L. 1933. Process in the Chinese kinship system. *American Anthropologist* 35: 151–57. [Condensed and reprinted in his *The nature of culture,* 190–95. Chicago: University of Chicago Press, 1952.]

Lakoff, George. 1987. *Women, fire, and dangerous things: What categories reveal about the mind.* Chicago: University of Chicago Press.

Lau, Dim Cheuk. 1979. trans. *The Analects.* Harmondsworth: Penguin Books.

Lau, Joseph S. M., & Goldblatt, Howard. 1995. eds. *The Columbia anthology of modern Chinese literature.* New York: Columbia University Press.

Li Wei. 1994. *Three generations, two languages, one family.* Clevedon, UK: Multilingual Matters.

Lin, Alice Murong Pu. 1988. *Grandmother had no name.* San Francisco: China Books.

Liu, Charles A. 1981. Chinese kinship terms as forms of address. *Journal of the Chinese Language Teachers Association* 16: 35–45.

Lu Hsun. 1924. The New Year's sacrifice. Translated in *Selected stories of Lu Hsun,* trans. by Yang Hsien-yi & Gladys Yang, 125–43. Beijing: Foreign Languages Press, 1972.

MacLaury, Robert E. 1991. Prototypes revisited. *Annual Review of Anthropology* 20: 55–74.

Makeham, John. 1994. *Name and actuality in early Chinese thought.* Albany: State University of New York Press.

Malinowski, Bronislaw. 1935. *Coral gardens and their magic.* New York: American Book Co. [Reprinted, New York: Dover, 1978.]

Malinowski, Bronislaw. 1948. *Magic, science and religion, and other essays.* Boston: Beacon. [Reprinted, Garden City, NY: Doubleday, 1954.]

Malkolkin, Anna. 1992. *Name, hero, icon: Semiotics of nationalism through heroic biography.* Berlin: Mouton de Gruyter.

Mannheim, Bruce, & Tedlock, Dennis. 1995. Introduction. In D. Tedlock & B. Mannheim (eds.), *The dialogic emergence of culture,* 1–32. Urbana: University of Illinois Press.

Mauss, Marcel. 1985. A category of the human mind: The notion of person; the notion of self. In Michael Carrithers et al. (eds.), *The category of the person: Anthropology, philosophy, history,* 1–25. Cambridge & New York: Cambridge University Press. [Originally published in 1938.]

Miller, Lucien. 1993. The ethnic chameleon: Bakhtin and the Bai. Paper presented at the International Society for the Comparative Study of Civilizations, Scranton, PA.

Morgan, Lewis Henry. 1871. *Systems of consanguinity and affinity of the human family.* Washington, DC: Smithsonian Institution.

Munro, Donald J. 1969. *The concept of man in early China.* Stanford, CA: Stanford University Press.

Ng, Fae Myenne. 1993. *Bone.* New York: Hyperion.

Norman, Jerry. 1988. *Chinese.* Cambridge & New York: Cambridge University Press.

O'Keefe, Daniel Lawrence. 1982. *Stolen lightning: The social theory of magic.* New York: Continuum.

Pemberton, John. 1994. *On the subject of "Java."* Ithaca, NY: Cornell University Press.

Potter, Sulamith Heins. 1988. The cultural construction of emotion in rural Chinese social life. *Ethos* 16: 181–208.

Quinn, Naomi, & Holland, Dorothy. 1987. Culture and cognition. In D. Holland & N. Quinn (eds.), *Cultural models in language and thought,* 3–40. Cambridge & New York: Cambridge University Press.

Rosaldo, Michelle. 1982. The things we do with words: Ilongot speech acts and speech act theory in philosophy. *Language in Society* 11: 203–37.

Sahlins, Marshall. 1981. *Historical metaphors and mythical realities: Structure in the early history of the Sandwich Islands Kingdom.* Ann Arbor: University of Michigan Press.

Schneider, David M. 1984. *A critique of the study of kinship.* Ann Arbor: University of Michigan Press.

Siegel, James T. 1986. *Solo in the new order: Language and hierarchy in an Indonesian city.* Princeton, NJ: Princeton University Press.

Siu, Helen F. 1989. *Agents and victims in South China: Accomplices in rural revolution.* New Haven, CT: Yale University Press.

Snow, Edgar. 1968. *Red star over China.* New York: Grove Press.

Spence, Jonathan D. 1978. *The death of Woman Wang*. New York: Viking Press.

Sung, Margaret M. Y. 1979. Chinese language and culture: A study of homonyms, lucky words, and taboos. *Journal of Chinese Linguistics* 7: 15–30.

Sung, Margaret M. Y. 1981. Chinese personal naming. *Journal of the Chinese Language Teachers Association* 16: 67–90.

Tambiah, Stanley J. 1968. The magical power of words. *Man* 3: 175–208.

Tan, Amy. 1989. *The Joy Luck Club*. New York: Ballantine Books.

Tannen, Deborah, & Saville-Troike, Muriel. 1985. eds. *Perspectives on silence*. Norwood, NJ: Ablex.

Topley, Marjorie. 1974. Cosmic antagonisms: A mother–child syndrome. In A.P. Wolf (ed.), 233–49.

Trautmann, Thomas R. 1987. *Lewis Henry Morgan and the invention of kinship*. Berkeley: University of California Press.

Tu Wei-ming. 1994a. Cultural China: The periphery as the center. In Tu Wei-ming (ed.), 1–34.

Tu Wei-ming. 1994b. ed. *The living tree: The changing meaning of being Chinese today*. Stanford, CA: Stanford University Press.

Urban, Greg. 1988. Ritual wailing in Amerindian Brazil. *American Anthropologist* 90: 385–400.

Urban, Greg. 1996. *Metaphysical community: The interplay of the senses and the intellect*. Austin: University of Texas Press.

Wagner, Roy. 1978. *Lethal speech: Daribi myth as symbolic obviation*. Ithaca, NY: Cornell University Press.

Waley, Arthur. 1938 trans. *The Analects of Confucius*. London: Allen & Unwin. [Reprinted, New York: Vintage, 1967.]

Wáng Quàngēn. 1988. *Huáxià Xìngmíng Miànmiàn Guān* [A comprehensive look at Chinese names]. Nánníng: Guǎngxī rénmín chūbǎnshè.

Watson, James L., & Rawski, Evelyn S. 1988. eds. *Death ritual in late imperial and modern China*. Berkeley: University of California Press.

Watson, Rubie S. 1986. The named and the nameless: Gender and person in Chinese society. *American Ethnologist* 13: 619–31.

Wikan, Unni. 1995. The self in a world of urgency and necessity. *Ethos* 23: 259–85.

Witherspoon, Gary. 1977. *Language and art in the Navajo universe*. Ann Arbor: University of Michigan Press.

Witke, Roxane. 1977. *Comrade Chiang Ch'ing* [Jiang Qing]. Boston: Little Brown.

Wolf, Arthur P. 1974a. Gods, ghosts, and ancestors. In A. P. Wolf (ed.), 131–82.

Wolf, Arthur P. 1974b. ed. *Religion and ritual in Chinese society*. Stanford, CA: Stanford University Press.

Wolf, Margery. 1975. Women and suicide in China. In M. Wolf & R. Witke (eds.), 111–41.

Wolf, Margery. 1978. Child training and the Chinese family. In A. P. Wolf (ed.), 221–46.

Wolf, Margery, & Witke, Roxane. 1975. eds. *Women in Chinese society*. Stanford, CA: Stanford University Press.

Woolard, Kathryn A., & Schieffelin, Bambi B. 1994. Language ideology. *Annual Review of Anthropology* 23: 55–82.

Yang, Martin C. 1945. *A Chinese village*. New York: Columbia University Press.

Yang, Mayfair Mei-hui. 1994. *Gifts, favors, and banquets: The art of social relationships in China*. Ithaca, NY: Cornell University Press.

Young, Linda W. L. 1994. *Crosstalk and culture in Sino-American communication*. Cambridge & New York: Cambridge University Press.

Zha, Jianying. 1995. *China pop: How soap operas, tabloids, and bestsellers are transforming a culture*. New York: New Press.

Zhang Jie. 1986. The time is not yet ripe. Trans. by Gladys Yang. In *Love must not be forgotten*, 63–77. San Francisco: China Books.

Zhào Ruìmín. 1988. *Xìngmíng yú Zhōngguó Wénhuà* [Names and Chinese culture]. Chóngqìng: Hǎinán rénmín chūbǎnshè.

## Critical Thinking and Application

- This [chapter] emphasizes that performance is more important than how the speaker feels about the utterance. How do you regard what you say? Is it your own choice? Are you coerced by others' expectations to say what you do?
- Discuss the suggestion made here that a prototypical exchange in China involves three parties rather than two.
- Keep track for an hour or two of all the ways you and people around you interact, jotting down the ways people address one another (by nickname, title, first name, etc.). What kinds of equalities and inequalities can you observe through these interactions? Would changing the form of address change the relationship?

## Vocabulary

affine
*amae* (Japanese)
classificatory kinship
common name
face
fictive kinship
frame
interlocutor
marked
metalinguistic
metaphoric
metonymic
ontology of language
proper name
teknonym
unmarked

## Suggested Further Reading

Abu-Lughod, Lila. 1986. *Veiled Sentiments: Honor and Poetry in a Bedouin Society*. Berkeley: University of California Press.

Abu-Lughod, Lila, and Catherine Lutz, eds. 1990. *Language and the Politics of Emotion*. Cambridge: Cambridge University Press.

Austin, J. L. 1975 [1962]. *How to Do Things with Words*, 2nd ed. Cambridge, MA: Harvard University Press.

Blum, Susan D. 2007. *Lies That Bind: Chinese Truth, Other Truths*. Lanham, MD: Rowman & Littlefield.

Briggs, Charles. 1986. *Learning How to Ask: A Sociolinguistic Appraisal of the Role of the Interview in Social Science Research*. Cambridge: Cambridge University Press.

Brown, Penelope, and Stephen C. Levinson. 1987. *Politeness: Some Universals in Language Usage*. Cambridge: Cambridge University Press.

Grice, Paul. 1989. *Studies in the Way of Words*. Cambridge, MA: Harvard University Press.

Keenan, Elinor Ochs. 1976. The Universality of Conversational Postulates. *Language in Society* 5(1): 67–80.

Lutz, Catherine A. 1988. *Unnatural Emotions: Everyday Sentiments on a Micronesian Atoll and Their Challenge to Western Theory*. Chicago: University of Chicago Press.

Malinowski, Bronislaw. 1923. The Problem of Meaning in Primitive Languages. In *The Meaning of Meaning*, edited by C. K. Ogden and I. A. Richards. New York: Harcourt, Brace.

Rosaldo, Michelle Z. 1982. The Things We Do with Words: Ilongot Speech Acts and Speech Act Theory in Philosophy. *Language in Society* 11: 203–235.

Searle, John R. 1969. *Speech Acts: An Essay in the Philosophy of Language*. Cambridge: Cambridge University Press.

CHAPTER 44

# Rewritten Rites: Language and Social Relations in Traditional and Contemporary Funerals

*Guy Cook and Tony Walter*

(2005)

*Ritual requires both action and speech. Action may include symbols, objects, people, situations, and movement, often analyzed by the use of common-sense categories. Speech can be analyzed using the tools of discourse analysis to reveal profound cultural elements. Death rituals—usually funerals in the West—are part of every society but differ in what they are attempting to accomplish and in what ways. Over the last century or so, in the United Kingdom and elsewhere, assumptions of unchanging, shared religious tradition have yielded to comprehension that individuals may choose to participate in religious ritual—or not—and that participants may not share beliefs or practices. This is just one aspect of the changing background of funeral rituals. In this chapter, Guy Cook and Tony Walter call attention to details of language that uncover significant new meanings of funeral rituals. They show that discourse analysis provides an essential and powerful set of techniques and principles by means of which we can know something not evident to common sense.*

## Reading Questions

- What is a "transition ritual"? Give some examples.
- What are the ritual characteristics of traditional Christian funerals? contemporary Christian funerals? contemporary secular funerals?
- What are "ritualists" and "anti-ritualists"? What does this have to do with "elaborated" and "restricted" codes?
- What is the funeral expected to accomplish? How has this shifted in the last several centuries?
- Why do Cook and Walter argue that the differences between traditional and contemporary Christian funerals are more profound than those between contemporary Christian and secular funerals?
- What is the difference between funerals enacted and prayers spoken because of religion and those carried out because of choice, individuation, and personalization?
- What is *language play*? What role does this have in ritual? What does the lack of language play mean in contemporary rituals?

## Introduction

People need language for **ritual,** just as much as for communication, and rituals can be found in all human societies. Yet the ritual functions of language have, with some notable exceptions, received less attention in **discourse analysis** than either its ideational or interpersonal functions (Halliday, 1973). While rituals do in some measure fulfil these more fully researched functions, they have something else besides: a negotiation with the unknown (Handelman, 1996), and an expression of identity that is as much intrapersonal as interpersonal (du Bois, 1986). At a time of rapid ideological and religious change, in an era of intense multilingual and multicultural contact, the choices that need to be made by individuals and societies about rituals are quite as important as those in more practical matters, and can—as we hope to demonstrate—be elucidated by discourse analysis. Although our article focuses upon one particular type of

Guy Cook and Tony Walter, Rewritten Rites: Language and Social Relations in Traditional and Contemporary Funerals. *Discourse & Society* 16 (3) (2005): 365–391.

ritual in one particular society, the issues that it raises are, we believe, of far wider significance.

Although there is considerable cultural and historical variation in their forms, and in the events that inspire them, those rituals which mark transitions in the human life course—birth, marriage, and death—are, in all societies, of particular potency and significance, bearing out Firth's definition of ritual as 'a formal procedure of a communicative but arbitrary kind, having the effect of regularizing a social situation' (cited in Kuiper and Flindall, 2000: 184). The traditional religious ritualization of these transitions continues in contemporary western societies to varying degrees. In England (the country on which we focus in this article), almost everyone still has a funeral,[1] even though this is not required by law as long as the body is decently disposed of.

The forms and functions of **transition rituals** have been profoundly affected by religious and other changes. For some people, there is the absence or loss of any religious faith. For others, loss of belief in the religion of their own tradition is mitigated, if not by actual conversion to another, by some notion of 'personal spirituality' (Heelas and Woodhead, 2004), sometimes tinged with sympathy for elements of Paganism and Buddhism (Hardman and Harvey, 1995). In addition, in multicultural societies, there is often a practical need to incorporate into a transition ritual the presence of people holding different beliefs to those expressed in the ceremony itself. Even in contexts where the religious faith of those attending is both strong and homogenous, there are likely to be significant differences from the past. Contemporary Christians, for example, compared with their forebears, typically have radically revised ideas about the absolute need for ritual observance, the nature of a resurrection and afterlife, and the authority of the Church.

In addition to the ancient transitions common to all societies, the secular life of modern urban democracies gives rise to 'new' events, felt to be significant enough to benefit from ritual recognition, but unknown in earlier ages and other societies. The past decade has witnessed a proliferation in secular **rites of passage.** One book that is influential and widely used in Australia (Messenger, 1979) includes, in addition to alternative versions for baby-namings, marriages and funerals, ceremonies for divorce, gay commitment, the acceptance of new 'step relationships', house moving, and career changing. In England from 2004, citizenship ceremonies are available for new in-migrants. Unlike the revision of church rites, over which liturgical commissions ponder long and hard, these new ceremonies are written by a haphazard range of authors, including—in England—individual celebrants, registrars, voluntary organizations,[2] at least two commercial companies,[3] as well as the parents, couples, and mourners themselves.

All this leads to a very interesting situation for discourse analysis—from both a linguistic and a sociological standpoint. Rituals are still used to mark life transitions, but the typical reliance on those religious rituals which have evolved over hundreds of years is no longer able to fulfil everyone's demands. In this situation, those who still feel the need for rituals often write their own or radically revise existing ones—sometimes beyond recognition. With each individual having more choices over their life course (Giddens, 1991), transitions become more individualized, reflected in rites that are tailor-made, at least in part, by the individual or individuals concerned. This raises a question as to whether these later ceremonies can be described as rituals at all.

Transition rituals are then an ideal area of study for revealing how changes in language use relate to changes and variations in values, beliefs and social relations. It is not possible in the space of one article to examine such rituals in their entirety, or even changes in one kind of transition ritual across a variety of cultures and languages. In this article we therefore examine changes in the openings of one kind of transition ritual only, the funeral, in one particular social context, mainstream English culture,[4] contrasting the language used in the opening of a traditional Christian funeral (The Order for the Burial of the Dead in *The Book of Common Prayer* of 1662) both with the new authorized rite of 2000 and with one contemporary secular alternative.[5] Despite this apparently narrow scope, however, our claim is that this apparently limited study reveals facts about the general relation of ritual, language and society which are transferable not only to other rituals in English life, but more generally to changes in language use which are happening on a global level. Our study also, we believe, draws attention to the relative neglect of ritual language, not only in discourse analysis, but also in sociolinguistics and in the sociology of language.

## Some Earlier Work on Ritual Language

In her book *Natural Symbols*, first published in 1970, the anthropologist Mary Douglas discusses intensively the nature of ritual as communication, and advances an explanation for the alternating ascendancy of those whom she terms 'ritualists', who believe in the necessity and value of rituals, and 'anti-ritualists', who use the term 'ritual' pejoratively, regarding rituals as empty and insincere (Douglas, 1970/2003). Two examples of anti-ritualist movements in Europe are the Reformation, which overturned the rituals of medieval Catholicism, and the protest movements of the 1960s, which sought to replace 'empty' adherence to social rituals with more individual, spontaneous and unpredictable expression. The distinction is not, however, confined to Europe or the west. Examples of this dichotomy are legion in diverse societies and religions, and one of Douglas's aims and achievements is to dispel the myth that ritualism is most intense in tribal societies, being gradually replaced in subsequent forms of social organization. She does this by illustrating the alternation between ritualism and anti-ritualism in a variety of societies.

In explanation of this contrast, Douglas makes extended use of Bernstein's sociolinguistic theory of **restricted** and

**elaborated codes** (Bernstein, 1964, 1972),[6] and advances a cogent argument for ritual as a form of communication employing a restricted code, and anti-ritualism as one employing an elaborated code. Traditional rituals, in this view, will have all of the conditions for the development of a restricted code: namely differentiated power, a close-knit group who know each other well and share values and beliefs, and a particular physical context. Some quotations from Douglas will make this point more eloquently than we can:

> It is illuminating to consider ritual as a restricted code. (...) Bernstein argued that the restricted code has many forms; any structured group that is a group to the extent that its members know each other very well, for example in cricket, science or local government, will develop its special form of restricted code which shortens the process of communication by condensing units into pre-arranged coded forms. —1970/2003: 57

> Clearly the words (...) carry a small part only of the significance of the occasion. The comparable situations in family life would be the spatial layout of the chairs in the living room which convey the hierarchy of rank and sex, the celebration of Sunday dinner, and for some families, presumably those in which a restricted code is used, every meal and every rising, bathing and bed-time is structured to express and support the social order. —1970/2003: 36

At one point in her analysis, Douglas seems on the verge of going into linguistic detail:

> At first sight, all ritual would seem to be a form of restricted code. It is a form of verbal utterance whose meanings are largely implicit; many of them are carried along standardized non-verbal channels. (...) Its units are organized to standard types in advance of use. Lexically its meanings are local and particular. Syntactically it is available to all members of the community. The syntax is rigid, it offers a small range of alternative forms. —1970/2003: 35

Yet, unsurprisingly for an anthropologist, she goes no further, and despite the richness of her social commentary, she has little to say about the wording of any ritual. Subsequent studies of religious ritual from a sociological/anthropological perspective do the same (Douglas, 1970/2003; Flanagan, 1991; Turner, 1977), even those such as Fenn (1982) that discuss ritual language at length. Although funeral rites produce what Davies (1997) calls 'words against death', anthropologists who have studied these ritual words focus on their symbolic meaning (Danforth, 1982; Nenola-Kallio, 1982) rather than on the language itself—even though the Orthodox texts and laments amply cited by Danforth and Nenola-Kallio manifestly have power through rhythm alone, apart from any meaning.[7] Conversely, when linguists write about religious ritual (Crystal, 1965) they focus almost exclusively on language. There has been, as far as we are aware, little analysis of religious ritual which combines sociology and linguistics[8]—despite the fact that, as rituals are largely constructed from language and perform major social functions, the combination of the two would seem to be essential to understanding.

One relevant attempt at such a combination, however, can be found in du Bois (1986), who identifies a number of typical features of ritual speech. These are usefully summarized by Rampton (1999) as follows (our lineation and order):

(a) a mode of delivery that entails 'a high degree of fluency, without hesitations, in a stylized intonation contour', accompanied by 'prescribed postures, proxemics, behaviours, attitudes, and trappings';
(b) the mediation of speech through additional people, so that there is more than a simple relation of speaker and hearer;
(c) local *belief* in the archaism and ancestral origins of ritual speech;
(d) a tendency for speakers to disclaim any credit or influence on what is said, paying tribute instead to a traditional source;
(e) obscurity in propositional meaning;
(f) the use of 'archaic, borrowed, tabooed or formulaic' elements that mark the ritual 'register' off from colloquial speech;
(g) **parallelism** (e.g. with couplets formed according to simple but strict syntactic rules of repetition with substitution).

This list of features forms a useful guide to which we shall refer. Yet even here there is less attention than it might seem to the actual language used. Of these eight characteristics, (a) and (b) are aspects of performance, (c) and (d) a question of belief about the origin of the words, while (e) concerns propositional meaning rather than linguistic form. This leaves only (f) and (g) about the nature of the language used, and it is upon these two that we shall mostly concentrate. Our intention is to provide a commentary on linguistic detail in relation to social change, of the kind that distinguishes discourse analysis from sociological analysis.

## The Wider Social Context

In line with this intention, and in order to provide the necessary context for linguistic analysis, we start by considering some of the broader issues concerning contemporary funerals in England.

The 1990s in England have witnessed more innovative rites of passage than any decade in the previous 150 years, and this spate of innovation seems set to continue. Civil weddings no longer need be held in the often-dour surroundings of the register office, but may now be conducted in stately homes, castles, hotels, and other stylish locations. Secular baby-namings are now offered by registrars, while The Baby Naming Society enables couples to produce their own ceremony.

It has also been a revolutionary period in funeral rites. Woodland burial sites expanded from zero to over a hundred; the number of humanist funerals has risen rapidly;[9] while stories of innovatory funeral practices (such as burial in hand-painted cardboard boxes) could be found in the broadsheet newspapers, radio and television almost every week throughout the 1990s (Weinrich and Speyer, 2003). Although such secular, humanist, woodland or do-it-yourself ceremonies remain a tiny fraction of all funerals, the majority of which are still led by clergy of the Church of England, nevertheless funerals in general—especially in the South of England—became much more personal through the decade (Walter, 1994). The widely broadcast funeral (technically, memorial) service in Westminster Abbey for Diana Princess of Wales in 1997 (Walter, 1999) both reflected, and possibly encouraged, the personalizing of religious funerals. Although North American funerals comprise very different specific elements, a similar trend towards personalization and individualization has been observed there (Garces-Foley and Holcomb, 2005).

More generally, and even within a religious context, innovation has been made possible by a long-term shift in the meaning of rites of passage. In much of traditional Christian religion—Catholicism and the Orthodox churches, for example—a rite of passage has power. The prayers of the priest and of the faithful actually help the deceased into the next world; the magic words[10] of the baptism actually induct the infant into membership of the Church, on earth and in heaven; the couple are not married in the eyes of God until the priest has uttered the words, 'I pronounce that they be Man and Wife'.[11] It is this perceived function of ritual language which contributes to the aura of 'negotiation with the unknown' to which we referred earlier. A key question for any discourse analysis of such rituals is whether and how specific linguistic forms may add to, or even create, this aura.

This aspect of the funeral services was removed by Protestant reformers, who stripped them of magical power half a millennium ago, as they believed the living had no power to affect the destiny of the departed (Duffy, 1992; Gittings, 1984; Rowell, 1977). In a secular world, this reform is taken further. Rites no longer change the participants' status with each other or with God; rather they are primarily ceremonies that mark a change that has already happened (Pickering, 1974). The baby-naming ceremony welcomes the child into family and society, but does not actually create membership; the wedding acknowledges a union that may have begun years ago when the couple first starting living together; the funeral celebrates a life lived. There is, therefore, no absolute need for the person conducting the ritual to have magical status; anyone can lead the recognition and celebration of what has already occurred.[12] This is not to say, however, that the ceremony only affirms what has already happened, or is little more than a party. There are still very serious matters to be undertaken. Weddings, renewal of vows, and baby-namings all entail the making of promises. Funerals include, or are a prelude to, the necessary disposal of a corpse.

In England, it was not until 2002 that a small number of registrars began to lead civil funeral ceremonies[13]—though not in their statutory capacity as registrars but rather as employees of a private company, Civil Ceremonies Ltd.[14] In these civil funerals there is no legal exclusion of any reference to religion, as there is in civil naming ceremonies and weddings. Clearly, however, a registrar is not going to recite the entire Anglican funeral service: a client who wants that should hire a minister of religion. But religious elements are allowable. The first registrar-led civil funeral, in Liverpool in March 2002, for example, included the Lord's Prayer. The wording with which it was introduced, however, is highly significant, namely that the deceased's daughter 'has requested that we should all say the Lord's Prayer together'. The authority for saying the prayer, in other words, lay not in the celebrant being a minister of religion (she wasn't), or in the ceremony being conducted in a church (it wasn't), but in the prayer being the choice of a member of the deceased's family. And if we accept du Bois' characterization of ritual speakers as having 'a tendency...to disclaim any credit or influence on what is said, paying tribute instead to a traditional source' we might see this attribution as evidence of, in Douglas' terms, anti-ritualism. The bottom line of this kind of funeral in other words is neither religion, nor atheism, but personal choice, reflecting a wider trend towards individualization in death, dying and bereavement (Walter, 1994), and indeed in late modern culture in general (Beck and Beck-Gernsheim, 2002). Thus what at first sight appears to be a process of secularization is, at least in the case of funerals, arguably more a process of individuation and personalization, not least because, as we hope to show later, the same process of personalization is evident within religious funerals too. This is clearly demonstrated when we consider changing funeral liturgy in detail.

## The Three Openings

Let us turn now to the opening words of the services we intend to contrast.

Like its predecessors of 1549 and 1552, the 1662 *Book of Common Prayer* was ratified by Act of Parliament in an attempt to impose by law uniform liturgical practice upon a whole country, and is permanently authorized, even today. Its funeral service (which we shall refer to as the 'traditional funeral') is entitled 'The Order for the Burial of the Dead', and begins with two instructions:

> Here it is to be noted that the Office ensuing is not to be used for any that die unbaptized, or excommunicate, or have laid violent hands upon themselves.
>
> The Priest and Clerks meeting the Corpse at the entrance of the Church-yard, and going before it, either into the Church, or towards the Grave, shall say, or sing.

It then proceeds to the opening words, a trio of quotations from the Bible:

> I am the resurrection and the life, saith the Lord: he that believeth in me, though he were dead, yet shall he live: and whosoever liveth and believeth in me shall never die. —ST. JOHN XI 25, 26
>
> I know that my Redeemer liveth, and that he shall stand at the latter day upon the earth. And though after my skin worms destroy this body, yet in my flesh shall I see God: whom I shall see for myself, and mine eyes shall behold, and not another. —JOB XIX 25–27
>
> We brought nothing into this world, and it is certain that we can carry nothing out. The Lord gave, and the Lord hath taken away: blessed be the Name of the Lord. —1 TIMOTHY VI 7: JOB I 21

From the outset the instructions in the traditional funeral are authoritative and uncompromising, with no apology or provision made for the absolute exclusion of the unbaptized, excommunicate and suicides. There is explicit direction too for the procession: where it shall begin, and who shall lead it. Very few options are given. The service may be held in the church or at the graveside, spoken or sung—but that is all.[15] And there are no alternative words given. All three extracts from the Bible are to be used, and in the order given. This 'Order for the Burial of the Dead' lives up to its name. It is very much an 'order' in both (related) senses of the word. It tells us both what must be done and said, and the sequence.

The opening of the traditional funeral is very much in tune with the notion of a restricted code: authoritative, following a beaten track, and quoting an authoritative source rather than using the participants' own words. Indeed, not only this opening, but also the greater part of this traditional funeral is a pastiche of biblical quotation—reminding us of du Bois' description of ritual language as frequently 'borrowed'. In adaptations and departures from this traditional form, though they remain Christian, we can see a movement away from these characteristics towards what is, in Douglas' terms, a gradual de-ritualization of the event.

Thus in the most recent authorized prayer book *Common Worship* (Church of England, 2000), although the first of these opening quotations is retained, it is optional, and is followed by a list of six alternatives, with the much looser instruction 'One or more sentences of Scripture may be used.' In addition, 20 supplementary texts are provided for use at any stage of the funeral, and 5 further suggestions are made for introductory Biblical quotations for a child's funeral. The second quotation ('I know that my Redeemer liveth...') has been relegated to one of the supplementary texts and its reference to the **taboo** topic of physical decomposition—'And though after my skin worms destroy this body, yet in my flesh shall I see God'—has been dropped. Taboo, we may remember, is one of du Bois' characteristics of ritual language so its omission can be regarded as further evidence of de-ritualization.

In addition to these changes, *Common Worship* also prefaces the recitation of Biblical quotation with the following—significantly optional—passage

> **This may be read by those present before the service begins**
>
> God's love and power extend over all creation. Every life, including our own, is precious to God. Christians have always believed that there is hope in death as in life, and that there is new life in Christ over death.
>
> Even those who share such faith find that there is a real sense of loss at the death of a loved one. We will each have had our own experiences of their life and death, with different memories and different feelings of love, grief and respect. To acknowledge this at the beginning of the service should help us to use this occasion to express our faith and our feelings as we say farewell, to acknowledge our loss and our sorrow, and to reflect on our own mortality. Those who mourn need support and consolation. Our presence here today is part of that continuing support.

These words, by talking of what 'Christians have always believed...' seem implicitly to acknowledge and accommodate the presence of non-Christians, as well as perhaps, by the words 'even those who share such faith...' some variation in reaction to death among the faithful. This is followed by a very explicit reference to differences among the mourners.

In contrast to these changing Christian funeral services, the 2002 Civil Funerals Training Manual, produced by Civil Ceremonies Ltd. for the training of its celebrants, provides the following suggested options for an opening (three others are included but not quoted here).

FUNERAL CEREMONY

> **(F)** = immediate family mourner/s.
> **(D)** = deceased person's name.
>
> Good morning/afternoon everyone. On behalf of **(F),** I thank you for being here today for this ceremony. I am..., a Funeral Celebrant and I will be leading today's ceremony.
> Please sit.

SECTION 1—OPENING

> **Option 1A**
> You may well ask why, exactly, we are here, what is a funeral really for. A funeral has to do three things. First, and simplest, it must enable each of us to say farewell, in a way that allows for the natural variations of feeling among you. Second, it should try to give a reasonably accurate account of the quality and character we have lost. And third, it should articulate the love, affection and regard in which the deceased was held. These things we shall try to do.
>
> **Option 1B**
> It has been traditional in our culture to regard a funeral as a grimly sad occasion. We all know that **(D)** was a man/woman of immense wit and great realism, and he/she left very clear instructions that we were neither to wear black nor indulge in overt grief. (If appropriate

insert he/she used to say...). We shall try to carry out **(D)**'s wish, and the way to do that is to honour his/her achievements and celebrate his/her life.

The leeway for variation, however, is much more than is apparent here, for the manual (given to trained celebrants on CD-Rom) merely provides templates, which the celebrant is expected to personalize for the funeral in hand. One actual and by no means untypical ceremony (with names changed) began as follows:

> The family has asked me to conduct the ceremony here today on their behalf, so I need to introduce myself. I am Andrew Brown and some of you know me in my previous roles in education for the borough for very many years or in my current work in the registration of births, deaths and marriages in Brent. I have to point out that my role as funeral celebrant is separate from my other duties and I am privately employed by Civil Ceremonies Limited for this purpose.
>
> As you know we are assembled here today to honour the memory of Thomas Arthur Smith, to salute his life and make our last sad farewells. I will, if I may from now on simply call him Tom as that was the name by which he was known by everyone. So on behalf of Tom's family may I welcome all of you who have come here today. He would I am sure have very much appreciated the efforts you have made to be here but as you know he would not have expected it because he was so modest a man.
>
> As you will see, we will concentrate on celebrating Tom's life rather than mourning his death because this is the family's last wish...

This secular service has moved, it seems, so much further down the path of deritualization than the revised Christian version in *Common Worship*, that it creates a problem for our analysis. For it is so dissimilar from the traditional service that we are to an extent no longer contrasting like with like. The words are no longer a pastiche of quotations from a traditional source (the Bible), as the Christian services are, but recently written for the purpose. And although there is an option to introduce other texts, which may indeed be more traditional (a popular choice being poems),[16] their identity is not stipulated, and thus varies from service to service. Lastly, there are no instructions, no orders: the 'order of service' becomes 'suggestions for a ceremony'. In the opening, and throughout, decisions about what to do and say, and when, seem to be open.

This lessening of authority does not, however, seem to be simply a feature of the transition from religious to secular services. It is also evident in the 2000 religious funeral, suggesting that the loss of faith is only part of the changes taking place, and that the later Christian version forms an intermediate stage in a process of change. Compare, for example, the instructions given in the 1662 prayer book with those in the 2000 version, and the very striking replacement of the **modal** verb 'shall' with the far less stringent modality of 'may'.

> After they are come into the church, *shall* be read one or both of the following
>
> When they come to the Grave while the Corpse is made ready to be laid into the earth, the Priest *shall* say, or the Priest and Clerks *shall* sing
>
> Then while the earth *shall* be cast upon the Body by some standing by, the Priest *shall* say
>
> Then *shall* be said or sung
>
> —1662 (ITALICS ADDED)

> The coffin *may* be received by the minister
>
> One or more sentences of Scripture *may* be used
>
> The minister *may* say one of these prayers
>
> A hymn *may* be sung
>
> A brief tribute *may* be made
>
> The service *may* end with a blessing.
>
> —2000 (ITALICS ADDED)

There are also in the 2000 version, in addition to these auxiliary modal verbs, numerous phrases which function in effect as **epistemic modals** by diminishing the certainty of what will be done:

> in these *or other* suitable words
>
> These *or similar* words
>
> This *or another* psalm *or* hymn is used

Indeed, *Common Worship* is explicit that its publication on the worldwide web enables clergy to customize the texts for their own local use.

In some areas, though, *Common Worship* attempts to reinstate authority. Whereas an interim 1986 version suggested only that 'A SERMON *may* be preached', *Common Worship* requires that 'A sermon is preached' and gives firm guidance as to its purpose (Churches' Group, 1986; Sheppy, 2004: ch. 3). Both linguistically and theologically, *Common Worship* is somewhat more traditional than some of the liturgies developed in the previous three decades which it replaces. These emerged from a period in which both Protestant and Catholic Christianity was very much on the defence against modernism; attempts to make the liturgy comprehensible to 'modern man' arguably ended up not with making it intelligible, but with making it secular (Flanagan, 1991; Nichols, 1996). In the more postmodern 1990s, in which tradition and non-scientific language were re-instated, not as absolutes but as possible options for individuals to choose, it became possible for liturgists to reassemble theologically and linguistically more traditional elements. The result, in *Common Worship*, is a prayer book far longer than any of its predecessors: the postmodern salad bar takes up more space than the simple meals both of tradition and of modernism. *Common Worship* expects clergy to provide both a sermon, *and* a personal tribute.

The much greater authority of the older service is warranted of course, as already observed, by the fact that the Priest speaks for God, the Church, and the State. He is not, as in the secular services, there on the invitation of the family, or as an employee of a commercial organization. And he makes no acknowledgement of the individual identities of himself, the mourners, or (at this point in the service) 'the Corpse'; participants have **roles** rather than individual identities: priest, congregation, corpse—although ironically, in the contexts in which the traditional service was used, it was much more likely that the priest would actually have known the deceased. The apparent individualization of contemporary services, moreover, is often only superficial. Many are personalized scripts composed using a computerized option[17] by celebrants who never met the deceased while they were alive. Even Humanist officiants, though not reliant on a computerized template, may have their own preferred format which shapes most, if not all, of the funerals they conduct.[18] The production of the contemporary funeral resembles the production of the contemporary automobile—in each case a production line/computer program is used to mass produce not a standard product but one individually tailored to the customer: mass-produced individualization. One person's car may look different from another's and seem to express their personality in its walnut veneer, wire wheels and other accessories, but in essence the two are the same.

Greater religious certainty allows the traditional service to look towards the future: both the immediate grim physical decomposition, and the later glorious physical resurrection, references to which have significantly declined in contemporary versions, despite an attempt to reaffirm the physical resurrection in *Common Worship* compared with versions of the previous three decades (Sheppy, 2004). In contrast to the traditional religious emphasis on a future afterlife, civil funerals look backwards to the past, seeking to give only a 'reasonably accurate account of the quality and character we *have lost*' (our italics), dwelling upon 'the love, affection and regard in which the deceased *was* held' (our italics).

Even in talking of the past, there is no certainty—only a 'reasonably accurate' account. This tension between the traditional Christian future and the modern backward glance is evident in *Common Worship*'s advice to relegate the personal tribute to the deceased to the early stages of the service, so as 'not to interrupt the flow of the readings and sermon'. But even this ordering is 'preferable' rather than mandated. *Common Worship* makes clear that 'the sermon is not a celebration of the life of the deceased; it is a celebration of Christ, risen from the dead' (Sheppy, 2004: ch. 3), and is not to be interrupted by human vanity. This tension between backward-looking celebration of the deceased and forward-looking Christian hope is even clearer in *Common Worship's* discussion of memorial services, where mourners gather in church some weeks or months after the death for a celebratory memorial service; these are becoming increasingly popular.

The different time foci are further emphasized by the stark contrast between the terms 'Corpse' in the traditional service and 'Deceased' in the modern ones. 'Corpse' speaks of what the person is now, 'deceased' of what has happened to them. The traditional service moreover speaks of what will happen to this corpse ('body worms destroy') and reflects a much harsher image of death, though this is mitigated by faith in physical resurrection ('in my flesh') and belief in the one true God ('and not another')[19]. It would be hard to imagine any reference to 'body worms' or 'flesh' in contemporary funerals, secular or Anglican. *Common Worship*'s references to the physical reality of death are rather more gentle:

> Like a flower we blossom and then wither;
> like a shadow we flee and never stay.

The traditional service presents a view of death as universal within a Christian cosmology which makes no allowance for alternatives. What happens is determined by God rather than Man, and no distinction is made between different types of deceased, as it is in the contemporary secular services, where variants (not quoted here) cater for differences of age, personality, relationship, etc. Ironically, for our age which considers itself much more egalitarian than its predecessors, it is the traditional service, originating in a more rigidly stratified society, which presents Death as the great leveller.

## Ritual Movement

A further striking difference—not unconnected perhaps to the deflection of attention from the corpse as a physical object—is the absence in the modern versions, whether religious or secular, of any reference to procession or movement or action by the participants. (And in practice, more recent services are notably short of the 'prescribed postures, proxemics, behaviours, attitudes, and trappings' attributed to ritual by du Bois.) This is a notable change, as a rite of passage is a distinctly embodied rite: there is a bride and groom to be married, a baby to be named, a coffin to be buried. The rite entails movement of these key actors in space and time; indeed their journeys (of the bride up the aisle accompanied by her father, of the coffin from sight) symbolize the social journeys (from single to married, from wife to widow, from child to orphan) that the rite marks and enables. This sense of physical movement is facilitated by buildings such as gothic and neo-gothic churches with long central aisles along which brides and coffins may process, not to mention lych-gates at which they may rest en route. Significantly, possibilities for ritual movement are more limited in modern locations such as English crematoria, register offices, and other secular settings which were never designed for it. In these, the celebrant typically stands motionless, addressing a motionless audience that listens rather than a congregation that moves and participates (Walter, 1990). In the wording of traditional liturgies, by contrast, the physical reality of the corpse is acknowledged, and the sense of physical movement is reflected in the rhythm of the language: the mode of delivery described by du Bois that entails 'a high degree of fluency, without hesitations, in a stylised intonation contour'. In the opening words of the funeral, the old words are ones the funeral party may process to, the new words are not. There is thus an intimate inseparable connection between the actions of the ritual and its words—to which we now turn.

## Linguistic Form and Function in the Traditional Funeral

Two striking linguistic features in the traditional service are its parallel structures and—from a contemporary viewpoint—the archaism of its language. In this section we examine both.

Even allowing for very considerable variation in the ways in which they might be delivered, the three texts that open the traditional service are markedly rhythmic. Stress location might vary to emphasize different interpretations.[20] Nevertheless, the following stress patterns will characterize all readings, whatever variations might be added by an individual celebrant. (Here x and upper case letters indicate a stressed syllable, and - and lower case letters an unstressed syllable.)

I am the re su RREC tion and the LIFE, saith the LORD:
- - - - - x - - - x -[21] - - x
he that be LIEV eth in me, though he were DEAD, yet shall
- - - x - - x - - - x - -
he LIVE:
- x
and who so e ver LIV eth and be LIEVE eth in ME shall
- - - - - x - - - x - - x -
never DIE.
- - x

Represented diagrammatically in three lines as follows this attribution reveals some striking regularities,

- - - - - x - - - x / - - - x
- - - x - - x - - - x / - - - x
- - - - - x - - - x - - x / - - - x

most noticeably the repeated pattern —x, coinciding with **syntactic boundaries** and **semantic** parallels. There is, moreover, a **caesura** effect (/) in each line, which lends itself to a very marked enunciation of the last words

saith the Lord

yet shall he live

shall never die

There are in addition in this opening text, numerous **assonantal** and consonantal parallels

he/ believeth/ me; Life/ Lord; believeth/ liveth

and **lexical** repetitions

life/ live/ liveth/ liveth/ die/ dead/

In short, the overall character of this text is highly poetic (in the sense established by Jakobson, 1960), with a **set** towards the form of the message as much as its meaning. It lends itself to dramatic incantation.

The language is also, or at least has become, archaic, and therefore both a distinct **register**, and obscure in propositional meaning: all features designated by du Bois (1986) as typical of ritual language. The two aspects—parallelism and archaism—are inseparably entwined. Thus in their anti-ritualist efforts to update these passages through the removal of archaic words and forms without regard to the effect on rhythm and other sound effects, later versions have sacrificed some, though not all, of this poetic linguistic patterning. An interim, 1986, version, for example, has the following (Churches' Group, 1986):

> Jesus said, I am the resurrection, and I am the life; he who believes in me, though he die, yet shall he live, and whoever lives and believes in me shall never die.

*Common Worship* (2000), however, has attempted to restore some of the lost rhythm:

> 'I am the resurrection and the life,' says the Lord. 'Those who believe in me, even though they die, will live, and everyone who lives and believes in me will never die.'

The second and third texts which open the traditional service are also poetic in this sense, though less so than the first. The second has no regular rhythm, but might nevertheless be lineated as **blank verse** as follows:

I know that my Redeemer liveth,
and that he shall stand at the latter day upon the earth.
And though after my skin worms destroy this body,
yet in my flesh shall I see God:
whom I shall see for myself,
and mine eyes shall behold,
and not another.

The third text, curiously constructed by putting together two separate half verses from different parts of the Bible (the first from the Book of Job and the second from St Paul's First Epistle to Timothy), has markedly parallel and symmetrical grammatical and lexical echoes.[22]

We brought    nothing into    this world,    and it is certain
    that
we can carry    nothing out.    (Ø of this world)
                The Lord        gave,        and
                the Lord    hath    taken away;
blessed be the Name of    the Lord.

As with any parallel structures there is a degree of rhythm, though it is not as marked as in the first quotation.

*Common Worship*, in the optional Pastoral Introduction quoted earlier, does seem to make some attempt to create **alliterative** sound sequences (faith... feelings... farewell) and parallel grammatical structures, as in the repeated infinitive + direct object structures of the sentence:

To acknowledge this at the beginning of the service
    should help us to use this occasion
to express    our faith and our feelings as we
    say farewell,
to acknowledge    our loss and our sorrow,
and to reflect on    our own mortality.

The secular service by contrast has very little in the way of rhythm or other poetic features—a loss which many seek to compensate by incorporating poems. The presence of one mild attempt at parallelism, lost in the otherwise colourless prose, only emphasizes this absence.

> First, and simplest, it must enable each of us...
>
> Second, it should try to give a reasonably accurate account...
>
> And third, it should articulate the love, affection and regard...

What is the nature of the relation between parallelism, obscure archaisms, and ritual? Is it only the superficial one that parallel phonological and linguistic structures lend themselves to memorization, incantation, and verbatim repetition, while archaic language marks off a particular register? Or is there some deeper relation, which explains the ritualist's passionate attachment, and the anti-ritualist's vehement aversion, to such language?

One explanation has been offered by Cook (2000) in a book on **language play**, defined as discourse which combines linguistic patterning and repetition, semantic obscurity and reference to alternative realities, and the **pragmatic** functions of inclusion or exclusion from a group. These linguistic, semantic and pragmatic features occur together across a range of apparently diverse genres including inter alia, children's rhymes and lore, intimate banter, jokes, verbal duels, advertisements, tabloid news, song, poetry, oratory, liturgy, prayer and ritual. Despite their diversity, they have a tendency to be widely distributed, frequently repeated, remembered, enjoyed and valued. Cook investigates the relation between parallelism, the high value attached to these genres, and the kinds of meaning and effect that they create. One aspect of the argument is that by allowing formal coincidences such as rhyme and grammatical parallelism to determine, to a greater degree than usual, the meaning of what is said, such genres aid innovative and creative thought by generating meanings, which might not otherwise have emerged. Another aspect is that this process of partial surrender to form, being unpredictable, also introduces a sense of the unknown and of forces beyond human control. It is this perhaps which explains its appeal and use in many religious traditions. Punning, for example, in which meaning is determined by formal coincidence, is regarded in Zen Buddhism as a 'navigator of thought' (Redfern, 1984: 146). Riddles perform sacred functions both in classical religion and in non-western religions (Hasan-Rokem and Shulman, 1996). In the Judaeo-Christian tradition, Kabbalistic interpretations treat the scriptures as, in effect, a word game to be solved (Dan, 1993; Eco, 1997; Steiner, 1975). In this context it is perhaps significant that in societies that reject ritual, genres such as puns and riddles become disparaged as trivial, ephemeral and childish. The language of the funeral openings we have examined could be said to illustrate this theory. The marked surrender to incantatory and patterned language in the traditional service goes together with a submissive faith and belief in mystery, whereas the later versions, both Christian and secular, abandon both this encounter with the unknown and the language which suggests it.

## PARTICIPANT RELATIONS

Changes in the three funerals are not only linguistic, however, but also pragmatic. New forms of words, and the new meanings they express, have been accompanied by changes to the relationships between participants. These are most evident in the contrast between the traditional Christian service and modern secular service, harder to pin down in the *Common Worship*.

Participants in the traditional service can be represented as shown in Figure 44.1. (The inclusion of the corpse as a 'participant' may seem macabre, but he or she is undoubtedly a real presence.) For believers (and that means, at the time that it was written, almost everybody) the funeral, composed almost entirely of quotations from the scriptures, is in a very real sense the word of God on the subject of death. The direction of communication is *from* God *through* prayer book and priest *to* the laity. The writers of the prayer book are mere orchestrators and choreographers of those words; the priest is a mere channel through which the words are conveyed. He is not the sender of the message, i.e. its **originator,** but rather the **addresser**, the person who passes it on (Jakobson, 1960), not the **author** but the **animator** (Goffman, 1981), with no more freedom to change the words and actions than a faithful messenger. The mourners are receivers of what is said, even perhaps only **'bystanders'** (Goffman, 1981; Levinson, 1983). Although they actively participate, their words are only 'responses', stipulated for them in advance, displaying that peculiarly circular attribute of established prayer and worship in which the faithful address God in his own words.

The 1662 funeral rite is written for a society in which (notwithstanding the substantial doctrinal differences of the time between Christian denominations) there was no significant doubt in the biblical promise of an afterlife. Interpretation of this faith is imposed upon the ceremony by church and state. All this is reflected in the relation between participants. The priest speaks on behalf of higher powers. Few options are allowed, or concessions made to the wishes of the congregation or the deceased, which are in any case assumed to coincide with those expressed in the text. The presence of atheists, agnostics or believers in other religions is not an issue. In the later funerals, however, we begin to see the demise of this uniformity, confidence and authority. The crucial changes, significantly occurring in later Christian versions as much as in their secular successors, concern the introduction of alternatives, and with them a shift of authority for what is being said and done from the priest (speaking for God, church and state) to the mourners. Their decisions are based, not upon what God wants, but upon what the deceased is deemed to have wanted. Indeed, in contemporary English society, the very choice of having a Christian funeral, reflects the decision of mourners or deceased, and not, as in 1662, a religious and legal obligation.[23]

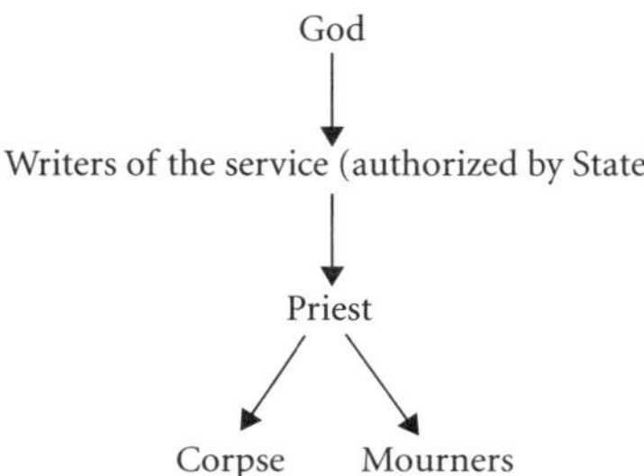


**Figure 44.1** *Participant Relations in the Traditional Funeral*

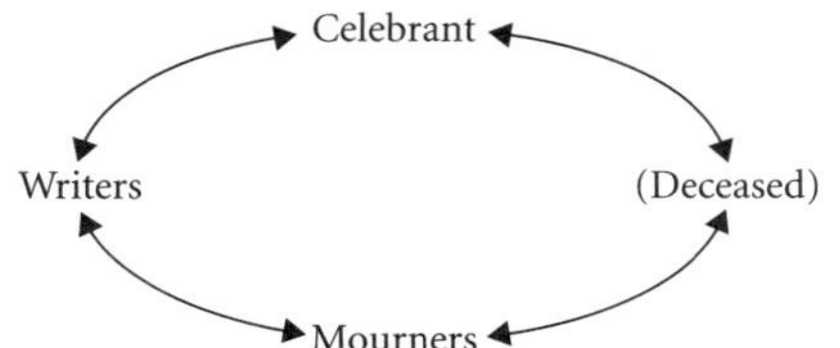


**Figure 44.2** *Participant Relations in a Secular Funeral*

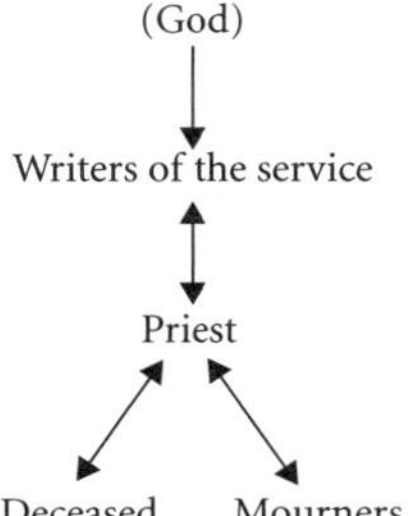


**Figure 44.3** *Participant Relations in the Revised Christian Funerals*

Once loss of faith removes the presence of God from this interaction, its nature changes radically. Although the form of what is happening remains to some extent the same—there is a person leading the ceremony, a book from which it is taken and an order of events—the source of what is said is no longer so clear. In the secular services, this source is often claimed to be (as already noted earlier) the wishes of the deceased or the mourners themselves, and the celebrant and writers appear to have made every effort to construct a service which gives as much opportunity as possible for these to be included. In effect, writers and celebrant seek to preserve the role of mouthpiece (addresser) traditionally assigned to priests—only this time it is not the word of God that they claim to voice to the congregation, but the words of the congregation itself! If we try to locate the source of what is said diagrammatically we end up with something circular (Figure 44.2).

The cynical might say that in both cases—the traditional religious and the secular—the writers disguise their own influence by attributing what they say elsewhere!

This contrast between traditional Christian and modern secular services is relatively straightforward. The more complicated case is that of the revised Christian service, in which belief in God, and consequently in the authority of prayer book and priest, although still overtly present, seems to be somewhat hedged. *Common Worship* bristles with alternatives and choices to be decided by celebrant and mourners, with opportunities to insert individualized references that reflect the wishes of the family and the deceased (expressed as we have seen with 'may' being used much more often than 'shall'). In many ways, with its 180 pages of options and alternatives, it resembles more the Civil Funerals Manual than the 1662 *Book of Common Prayer*'s eight required pages for The Order for the Burial of Dead. All this perhaps reflects diminished religious certainty among the faithful and a less specific belief in an afterlife. It may also tacitly recognize that the Christian faith of the congregation or even the deceased cannot be taken for granted. We could say that in today's Church of England funeral, although the participants apparently remain as they were in the traditional service, God needs to be bracketed—to indicate that for believers he is a major presence, for the non-believer not present at all, whereas for others he flashes—as it were—on and off (Figure 44.3).

## Discussion

Our aim in this conclusion is twofold: first, to consider what our analysis reveals about the connection between social and linguistic changes within the limited data that we have examined (the openings of funerals in English), and second, to speculate on whether the changes we have described here have a more general relevance, to other rituals, languages, and societies.

The changes we have described are of three kinds, moving in parallel. First, there are changes at the macro-level, in the society in which the funeral takes place. Second, there are changes at the micro-level, in the relations between participants. Third, there are changes in the nature of the language (and **paralanguage)** that is used. The relationship between macro- and micro-social relations is straightforward enough, and for brevity, in what follows, we shall refer to these together as 'social changes'. The relation between these social changes, however, and the linguistic ones which have accompanied them, is more problematic, and less well understood. In this analysis—writing together as a sociologist and an applied linguist—we have striven to bridge this gap. We hope to have shown how, in our limited data, social and linguistic changes are moving in tandem. The social changes include a weakening of religious belief, an unwillingness to confront the physical nature of death, a diminution of authority, increases in individualization and choice, and more scope for reciprocal interaction between celebrant and mourners. The linguistic changes include a lowering of register from the highflown to the everyday, an absence of reference to the physical facts of death (the corpse and its decomposition) and a reduction in the use of rhythm and other sound effects, of grammatical and lexical parallelism. The overall result is a lessening of incantatory power, and a greater convergence between the language of the funeral and that of other more everyday genres such as conversation. There seems in short to be a process of de-ritualization. This is already evident in the later Christian service, and even more apparent in the civil funerals. The large question which this raises, and we have tried in part to answer, is whether there is any motivated connection between these social and linguistic changes.

Poetic language is of its nature, as has often been observed, unparaphrasable. The effects that it creates are the consequence of precise linguistic choices and as such admit no options. The text must remain exact, if the specific poetic effects are to be preserved. There is an analogy here perhaps with the attitude of the faithful to the 'word of God'. The 1662 funeral service can admit, in its own words, 'not another'. Poetry, like Scripture, despite literary theoretical arguments for 'the death of the author' (Barthes, 1977), remains the expression, through performers, of one single authoritative voice, rather than being arrived at through a democratic consensus. It cannot be tampered with and remain itself.[24] In a similar way, Christian theology must yield to the authority of its founder—and such debates as there are among the faithful, are attempts not to replace but to interpret that teaching. The priest's role is analogous to that of the director or performer of a literary work; the congregation's to that of an audience.

Perhaps also, poetic language introduces a sense of a power beyond that of literal meaning. By allowing the formal demands of rhythm and rhyme to determine the wording, and thus the meaning, of what is said (Cook, 2000) poetic language mimics a surrender of autonomy, and an acknowledgement of greater authority, which fits well with traditional religious beliefs. Yet the need for such language, especially at times of transition, is by no means a monopoly of the religious. It is apparently felt equally by the agnostic and the atheist. As already noted, the banal literalism and poetic poverty of secular ceremonies may be compensated, ironically often at the mourners' behest, by the inclusion of poems and poetic literary prose, reintroducing into the ceremony precisely the kind of language use which has been lost in the erosion of belief in traditional religion. There is some connection here too perhaps with unease at the passing of decision-making about the ceremony from a higher authority to celebrant and mourners. Rhythmic and incantatory language belong to traditional societies; it is to be repeated verbatim[25] not freely re-worked. If poetry, especially in its more incantatory incarnations, belongs more to tribal, non-democratic, non-individualist societies (Jakobson, 1959) then it is not surprising that many people revert to it from choice at moments of life-phase transition. Such points make us more aware of our common humanity than our individual identity, of our powerlessness rather than our power.

At this point, we may note that Douglas (1970/2003), following Durkheim (1965), tends to see ritual as reflecting normal social relationships. There is, however, a contrary scholarly tradition which argues that rituals typically reverse normal social relationships (Jacobson-Widding, 1988; Turner, 1977), transgress everyday social rules (Bakhtin, 1981), or entail a psychological reversal in which adult participants temporarily regress to infantile dependency (Reed, 1978). This tradition may, perhaps, prove fruitful in understanding the re-insertion into contemporary rites of elements that reflect the language of traditional societies.

## Conclusion

Our account has described changes in funeral rites in a traditionally Christian English-speaking society. Although we have dealt only with the opening words of Church of England and secular funerals, our research suggests that we could have demonstrated, had space and readers' patience allowed, similar social and linguistic changes in the later parts of these ceremonies, in those of other Christian denominations[26] and in other secular funerals, as well as in other rites marking life stages such as births and marriages.[27] Whether, in Christian, and post-Christian societies more generally, similar changes can be found in rites of languages other than English is a matter for further research. Our view is that they most probably can. A broader question concerns whether similar changes have occurred in non-Christian societies, indicating perhaps a globalized tendency to de-ritualization. Are they to be found, for example, in the spectrum of beliefs and practices that differentiate orthodox, liberal and secular Judaism (Glinert, 1993), or in differences between Sufi, Sunni or Shiite Islam (Ruthven, 1997)? And are there, in non-Abramic religions, for example in Buddhism or Hinduism, similar linguistic changes accompanying weakening of faith and authority? Again, from what we know of these issues, and from other investigations we have made, our impression is that similar contrasts might be found.

Another question is whether personalized secular funerals are, in any recognizable sense, rituals? In three key ways we have considered, they are not: the leader speaks only by authority of the family, there is no longer any supernatural dimension, and linguistic parallelism and obscurity (together with prescribed actions) have declined.

Sociologically, however, we can see three ways in which personalized funerals represent not so much ritual's destruction as its continuing evolution.

First, in both their preparation and execution, personal funerals still bring mourners together and bind them together (Garces-Foley and Holcomb, 2005). For Durkheim (1965), this is the essence of religious ritual. In the personalized funeral, the binding together is of mourners, 'some of whom may be strangers, into a temporary community in a world where it is difficult to form communal bonds' (Garces-Foley and Holcomb, 2005). Walter (1996) has observed that contemporary mourners are typically separated geographically; not only funerals, but also a whole a range of contemporary rituals comprise a temporary congregation of nomads who normally do not meet, or even know, one another. These need not be 'second-rate' rituals, however, for the small bands of hunter-gatherer aboriginals on whom Durkheim based his theory were also nomads, meeting one another occasionally through funerary and other rituals (Couldry, 1999; Walter, 2001). For Wouters (2002), following Elias (1991) and Maffesoli's (1996) theories of individualization, the temporary gathering together to celebrate a unique life reflects a broader cultural trend in which, while protesting their individuality, people want to belong, if only symbolically, to a wider group; for Wouters, these celebrations are therefore not non-rituals but new rituals.

Second, following Beck and Beck-Gernsheim (2002), we suggest that the focus on the individual entails a new form of social solidarity, which they term 'co-operative individualism'. All relationships, not just politics, are now being freed from paternalistic authority: partners, for example, are provided no fixed template for marriage and are expected constantly to negotiate and renegotiate their relationship. Funerals are no longer given; they too must be negotiated. We might term them democratic, rather than authoritative, rites. If social relationships are becoming less fixed, more fluid, it is not surprising if rites that mark life transitions are also becoming more fluid in a process which is mirrored in the use of far more fluid and less predictable linguistic structures. That said, it seems very likely, third, that Garces-Foley and Holcomb's (2005) judgement on the personalized American funeral may also, with time, prove true in England: 'Personalized funerals have by now been around long enough that they have begun to develop their own "tradition" in the sense of frequently used elements.' Tradition has a habit of returning through the back door of even the most dramatic revolutions.

There is clearly a great deal of research to be done. The lack of such research results, as we remarked in our opening, from discourse analysts' marginalization of language's ritual functions in favour of language's **transactional** functions—which, we argue, do not easily account for ritual uses of language. Yet, ritual clearly remains one of the most important and powerful uses of language in society. This is especially true when the religious faith expressed in more traditional rituals has either changed or disappeared, but people still feel a need to create new 'ceremonies and celebrations'. The various attempts to compensate for the ritual power which has been lost along with religious certainty is surely a classic case of an area of language use of vital importance to society, and one in which discourse analysis could offer both insight and advice.

**Acknowledgements**

The authors thank Paul Sheppy and Anne Barber for their comments on the manuscript and Civil Ceremonies Ltd for permission to use material.

## Notes

1. Church weddings, by contrast, although still popular, have fallen in number and infant baptisms have declined dramatically (Pickering, 1974).
2. Such as the British Humanist Association.
3. Civil Ceremonies Limited and the Baby Naming Society.
4. As a multicultural society, the population of England includes believers in a variety of religions. Alternative and secular funerals seem to appeal more to those from the more individualistic Christian Protestant tradition than to people from outside the majority English culture who have lost faith in their own religious tradition. Adherence to a non-Christian religious tradition is often sustained by ethnic minority families as an important badge of cultural identity, making it difficult for individual family members to depart from it, especially during family-controlled rites of passage.
5. The full texts of the two Christian funerals are available at [http://www.eskimo.com/~lhowell/bcp1662/occasion/burial.html] and [http://www.cofe.anglican.org/commonworship/funeral/funeralfront.html]. The template for the secular funeral service cannot be reproduced in full for copyright reasons.
6. Douglas gives only the 1964 reference, as her work precedes Bernstein (1972).
7. Another kind of analysis is that of liturgists such as Sheppy (2004) who are primarily concerned with theological meaning, although Nichols (1996), writing in this tradition, also addresses aesthetic and sociological critiques of modern Catholic liturgies.
8. There are, however, numerous sociolinguistic analyses of other kinds of ritual. See, for example, Abrahams (1962), Dundes et al. (1970), Gossen (1976) on verbal duelling; Shippey (1993) on ritual boasting; Kaivola-Bregenhøj (1996) on ritual functions of riddle; Rampton (1999) on the ritual nature of foreign language use between school children. There is also work, such as Carter (2004), Cook (2000), and Crystal (1998), which comments on the relation between ritual, language play and creativity.
9. From a handful for members only to around 6000 per year for any who ask. This is still only about 1 percent of all funerals.
10. The boundary between magic and religion is hotly debated. Here we use the term (contra Glucklich, 1997; Malinowski, 1948; Mauss, 1972) to mean the power to effect change through words and actions.
11. The words of the 1662 *Book of Common Prayer*. Such utterances provide classic examples of what Austin (1962) termed declarations: in which the performative speech act must depend upon a particular form of words. There are also secular declarations, notably in law, such as 'I sentence you to . . .'.
12. Although in England, for a couple to be legally married, the ceremony at present must be led by a registrar or authorized minister, and a certain form of words must be followed.
13. Secular civil weddings conducted by a registrar, by contrast, date back to 1837, and secular baby-naming ceremonies conducted by a registrar to 2001.

14. Only a few registrars in a few local authorities have done this. They may in future be employed in this capacity by the local authority.

15. This option of going straight to the grave, however, may have had a very practical cause—to dispose of decomposing corpses as quickly as possible (Rowell, 1977).

16. Popular funeral poems in England include Kipling's 'If' and, inspired by its use in the film *Four Weddings and a Funeral*, the first of W. H. Auden's 'Two Songs for Hedli Anderson' (also known as 'Funeral Blues') beginning 'Stop all the clocks, cut off the telephone...'.

17. Civil Funerals Software. CD-Rom, Civil Ceremonies Ltd. (2002; revised 2003).

18. For examples, of formats, and variations within them, see Wynne Willson (1989).

19. A phrase which presumably excludes all other faiths in as uncompromising a manner as the exclusions at the opening.

20. ˈ*I am the resurrection*, for example, might highlight the uniqueness and humanity of Jesus; *I* ˈ*<u>am</u> the resur*ˈ*rection* belief in his continuing living presence; *I am the resur*ˈ*<u>rec</u>tion* the prospects for the future.

21. 'Saith' is pronounced by some English speakers as /seIJeθ/ and by others as /seθ/. This unstressed syllable is only present in the former.

22. While the first two texts were also used in earlier medieval burials, the third was an innovation of the 1552 prayer book (Rowell, 1977).

23. Rowell (1977) notes that from 1662 until 1880 burial in an Anglican churchyard following the Anglican service was obligatory, but notes how non-conformists would remain silent. Jews and other non-Christians would at that time have followed their own practices in secret.

24. This is even more marked in the case of the Koran, which, unlike the Christian Bible, loses its holiness in translation.

25. Notwithstanding the widely accepted claim (Lord, 1960) that verbatim repetition does not characterize oral traditions as popularly believed, nevertheless rhyme, rhythm and other devices serve to reinforce the likelihood of some repeated wording (Buchan, 1972).

26. For the Catholic requiem the linguistic change is of a different nature as it involves the switch from Latin to English. Nichols (1996) has argued that, in recent developments within vernacular liturgies, the everyday language and focus on the congregation are at the expense of a focus on God, a parallel argument to our own.

27. In Britain and the USA, one may get married in a number of geographical locations; in many continental European countries, the wedding must take place in the town hall of the home town of one of the partners, suggesting, perhaps, that the rite marks not so much a contract between individuals as a rearrangement of relationships within the community. As far as we are aware, scholars have yet to comment on individualization in the Anglo-American wedding, though Beck and Beck-Gernsheim (1995, 2002) have analysed in some detail individualization in marriage.

## References


Abrahams, R. D. 1962. 'Playing the Dozens', *Journal of American Folklore* 75: 209–20.

Austin, J. L. 1962. *How to Do Things with Words*. Oxford: Clarendon Press.

Bakhtin, M. M. 1981. 'From the Prehistory of Novelistic Discourse', in M. Holquist (ed.) *The Dialogic Imagination*. Austin: University of Texas Press.

Barthes, R. 1977. 'The Death of the Author', in R. Barthes *Image, Music, Text* (S. Heath, ed. and trans.), pp. 142–9. London: Fontana.

Beck, U. and Beck-Gernsheim, E. 1995. *The Normal Chaos of Love*. Oxford: Polity Press.

Beck, U. and Beck-Gernsheim, E. 2002. *Individualization: Institutionalised Individualism and its Social and Political Consequences*. London: Sage.

Bernstein, B. 1964. 'Social Class and Psycho-therapy'. *British Journal of Sociology* 15: 54–64.

Bernstein, B. 1972. 'Social Class, Language and Socialisation', in P. Giglio (ed.) *Language and Social Context*. Harmondsworth: Penguin.

Buchan, D. 1972. *The Ballad and the Folk*. London: Routledge & Kegan Paul.

Carter, R. A. 2004. *Language and Creativity*. London: Routledge.

Church of England. 2000. *Common Worship: Pastoral Services*. London: Church House.

Churches' Group on Funeral Services at Cemeteries and Crematoria. 1986. *Funeral Services*. Norwich: Canterbury Press.

Civil Ceremonies Ltd. 2002. *Civil Funerals Training Manual*. Huntingdon: Civil Ceremonies.

Cook, G. 2000. *Language Play, Language Learning*. Oxford: Oxford University Press.

Couldry, N. 1999. 'The Geography of Celebrity and the Politics of Lack'. *New Formations* 36: 77–91.

Crystal, D. 1965. *Linguistics, Language and Religion*. London: Burns and Oates.

Crystal, D. 1998. *Language Play*. Harmondsworth: Penguin.

Dan, J. 1993. 'Language for Mysticism', in L. Glinert (ed.) *Hebrew in Ashkenaz: A Language in Exile*. New York: Oxford University Press.

Danforth, L. 1982. *The Death Rituals of Rural Greece*. Princeton, NJ: Princeton University Press.

Davies, D. 1997. *Death, Ritual and Belief*. London: Cassell.

Douglas, M. 1970/2003. *Natural Symbols*. London: Routledge. (Originally published 1970.)

du Bois, J. 1986. 'Self Evidence and Ritual Speech', in W. Chafe and J. Nichols (eds.) *Evidentiality*. Norwood, NJ: Ablex.

Duffy, E. 1992. *The Stripping of the Altars: Traditional Religion in England 1400–1580*. New Haven, CT: Yale University Press.

Dundes, A. L., Leach, J. W. and Ozkök, B. 1970. 'Strategy of Turkish Boys' Verbal Duelling Rhymes', *Journal of American Folklore* 83: 325–49.

Durkheim, E. 1965. *The Elementary Forms of the Religious Life*. New York: Free Press. (Originally published 1912.)

Eco, U. 1997. *The Search for the Perfect Language*. London: HarperCollins, Fontana.

Elias, N. 1991. *The Society of Individuals*. Oxford: Blackwell.

Fenn, R. K. 1982. *Liturgies and Trials: The Secularization of Religious Language*. New York: Pilgrim.

Flanagan, K. 1991. *Sociology and Liturgy*. Basingstoke: Macmillan.

Garces-Foley, K. and Holcomb, J. S. 2005. 'Contemporary American Funerals: Personalizing Tradition', in K. Garces-Foley (ed.) *Death and Religion in a Changing World*. Armonk, NY: Sharpe.

Giddens, A. 1991. *Modernity and Self-Identity*. Oxford: Polity Press.

Gittings, C. 1984. *Death, Burial and the Individual in Early Modern England*. London: Croom Helm.

Glinert, L. 1993. 'Language as Quasilect: Hebrew in Contemporary Anglo-Jewry', in L. Glinert (ed.) *Hebrew in Ashkenaz: A Language in Exile*. New York: Oxford University Press.

Glucklich, A. 1997. *The End of Magic*. New York: Oxford University Press.

Goffman, E. 1981. *Frame Analysis: An Essay on the Organisation of Experience*. Boston: Northeastern University Press.

Gossen, G. H. 1976. 'Verbal Duelling in Chamula' in B. Kirschenblatt-Gimblett (ed.) *Speech Play*. Philadelphia: University of Pennsylvania Press.

Halliday, M. A. K. 1973. *Explorations in the Function of Language*. London: Arnold.

Handelman, D. 1996. 'Traps of Transformation: Theoretical Convergences', in G. Hasan-Rokem and D. Shulman (eds.) *Untying the Knot: On Riddles and Other Enigmatic Modes*. New York: Oxford University Press.

Hardman, C. and Harvey, G. (eds.). 1995. *Pagan Pathways*. London: Thorsons.

Hasan-Rokem, G. and Shulman, D. (eds.). 1996. *Untying the Knot: On Riddles and Other Enigmatic Modes*. New York: Oxford University Press.

Heelas, P. and Woodhead, L. 2004. *The Spiritual Revolution: Why Religion is Giving Way to Spirituality*. Oxford: Blackwell.

Jacobson-Widding, A. 1988. 'Death Rituals as Inversions of Life Structures: A Comparison of Swedish and African Funerals', in S. Cederroth, C. Corlin and J. Lindström (eds.) *On the Meaning of Death: Essays in Mortuary Rituals and Eschatological Beliefs*, pp. 137–53. Stockholm: Almqvist & Wiksell.

Jakobson, R. 1959. 'Linguistic Aspects of Translation', in R. A. Brower (ed.) *On Translation*. Cambridge, MA: Harvard University Press.

Jakobson, R. 1960. 'Closing Statement: Linguistics and Poetics', in T. A. Sebeok (ed.) *Style in Language*. Cambridge, MA: MIT Press.

Kaivola-Bregenhøj, A. 1996. 'Riddles and Their Uses', in G. Hasan-Rokem and D. Shulman (eds.) *Untying the Knot: On Riddles and Other Enigmatic Modes*. New York: Oxford University Press.

Kuiper, K. and Flindall, M. 2000. 'Social Rituals, Formulaic Speech and Small Talk at the Supermarket Checkout', in J. Coupland (ed.) *Small Talk*, pp. 183–207. Harlow: Longman.

Levinson, S. 1983. *Pragmatics*. Cambridge: Cambridge University Press.

Lord, A. 1960. *The Singer of Tales*. Cambridge, MA: Harvard University Press.

Maffesoli, M. 1996. *The Time of the Tribes: The Decline of Individualism in Mass Society*. London: Sage.

Malinowski, B. 1948. *Magic, Science and Religion, and Other Essays*. Boston: Beacon Press.

Martin, D. 1980. *The Breaking of the Image*. Oxford: Blackwell.

Mauss, M. 1972. *A General Theory of Magic*. London: Routledge. (Originally published 1902.)

Messenger, D. 1979. *Ceremonies for Today*. Armadale, Vic: Zouch.

Nenola-Kallio, A. 1982. 'Studies in Ingrian Laments', PhD thesis, University of Turku, Finland.

Nichols, A. 1996. *Looking at the Liturgy: A Critical View of Its Contemporary Form*. San Francisco: Ignatius Press.

Pickering, W. 1974. 'The Persistence of Rites of Passage: Towards an Explanation', *British Journal of Sociology* 25: 63–78.

Rampton, B. 1999. 'Dichotomies, Difference and Ritual in Second Language Learning and Teaching', *Applied Linguistics* 20: 316–41.

Redfern, W. 1984. *Puns*. Oxford: Blackwell.

Reed, B. 1978. *The Dynamics of Religion*. London: Darton, Longman, Todd.

Rowell, G. 1977. *The Liturgy of Christian Burial: An Introductory Survey of the Historical Development of Christian Burial Rites*. London: SPCK/Alcuin Club.

Ruthven, M. 1997. *Islam*. Oxford: Oxford University Press.

Sheppy, P. 2004. *Death Liturgy and Ritual. Vol. 2: A Commentary on Liturgical Texts*. Abingdon: Ashgate.

Shippey, T. A. 1993. 'Principles of Conversation in Beowulfian Speech', in J. M. Sinclair, M. Hoey and G. Fox (eds.) *Techniques of Description: Spoken and Written Discourse*. London: Routledge.

Steiner, G. 1975. *After Babel*. Oxford: Oxford University Press.

Turner, V. 1977. *The Ritual Process*. Ithaca, NY: Cornell University Press.

Walter, T. 1990. *Funerals—And How to Improve Them*. London: Hodder.
Walter, T. 1994. *The Revival of Death*. London: Routledge.
Walter, T. 1996. 'A New Model of Grief: Bereavement and Biography', *Mortality* 1: 7–25.
Walter, T. 1999. *The Mourning for Diana*. Oxford: Berg.
Walter, T. 2001. 'From Cathedral to Supermarket: Mourning, Silence and Solidarity', *Sociological Review* 49: 494–511.
Weinrich, S. and Speyer, J. (eds.). 2003. *The Natural Death Handbook*. London: Rider.
Wouters, C. 2002. 'The Quest for New Rituals in Dying and Mourning: Changes in the We–I Balance', *Body & Society* 8: 1–27.
Wynne Willson, J. 1989. *Funerals Without God: A Practical Guide to Non-Religious Funerals*. London: British Humanist Association.

## Critical Thinking and Application

- Compare this reading's three illustrations in terms of the various participants in the rituals. Analyze another type of ritual. What are the participant relations in that ritual?
- How does poetic language differ from other language? Why does it have a central role in traditional rituals? Are de-ritualized rituals as effective as traditional rituals? Why?
- What do Cook and Walter claim about the need for discourse analysis in genuine comprehension of rituals? Why is symbolic, sociological, or anthropological analysis insufficient? Do you agree?
- Observe a funeral or other transition ritual (perhaps using film or television). Analyze its language using some of the features included in this chapter. Where does it lie on the traditional-contemporary-secular continuum? What is your evidence for this claim?

## Vocabulary

addresser
alliterative
animator
assonantal
author
blank verse
bystander
caesura
discourse analysis
elaborated code
epistemic modal
language play
lexical
modal verb
originator
paralanguage
parallelism
pragmatic
register
restricted code
rite of passage
ritual
role
semantic
set
syntactic boundary
taboo
transaction, transactional
transition rituals

## Suggested Further Reading

Bernstein, Basil. 1964. Elaborated and Restricted Codes: Their Social Origins and Some Consequences. *American Anthropologist* 66(6 [2]): 55–69. DOI: 10.1525/aa.1964.66.suppl_3.02a00030.
Blommaert, Jan. 2005. *Discourse: A Critical Introduction*. Cambridge: Cambridge University Press.
Brown, Gillian, and George Yule. 1983. *Discourse Analysis*. Cambridge: Cambridge University Press.
Fairclough, Norman. 1995. *Critical Discourse Analysis: The Critical Study of Language*. London: Longman.
Jakobson, Roman. 1960. Closing Statement: Linguistics and Poetics. In *Style in Language*, edited by Thomas A. Sebeok, pp. 350–377. Cambridge, MA: MIT Press.
Jaworski, Adam, and Nikolas Coupland, eds. 2006. *The Discourse Reader*. 2nd ed. London and New York: Routledge.
Johnstone, Barbara. 2002. *Discourse Analysis*. Oxford: Blackwell.

Schiffrin, Deborah, Deborah Tannen, and Heidi Ehernberger Hamilton, eds. 2001. *The Handbook of Discourse Analysis*. Oxford: Blackwell.

Sherzer, Joel. 2002. *Speech Play and Verbal Art*. Austin: University of Texas Press.

van Dijk, Teun A., ed. 1985. *Handbook of Discourse Analysis* (4 vols.). New York: Academic Press.

van Gennep, Arnold. 1960 [1909]. *The Rites of Passage*, translated by Monika B. Vizedom and Gabrielle L. Caffee. Chicago: University of Chicago Press.

## CHAPTER 45

# Narrative Embodiments: Enclaves of the Self in the Realm of Medicine

*Katharine Young*

(1989)

*Humans are storytelling mammals. We narrate ourselves, our histories, our meanings. Even in the physical realm of something as material as medicine, we must tell our tale. Indeed, much of narrative analysis has been conducted in the realm of medical encounters, though many other types of institutions also operate predominantly through narrative interactions. Patients tend to be in quite vulnerable positions—stripped of power, clothing, and self. Some acquiesce and others resist this powerlessness. Much of the jockeying for dignity and power occurs through language.*

*Narrative analysis, or narratology, has been developed in linguistics and linguistic anthropology, in part out of William Labov's efforts in the 1960s to make speakers comfortable so he could analyze their specific pronunciation and dialect. He discovered certain features of their stories, or narratives. In the intervening decades, the study of narrative has become sophisticated, nuanced, and powerful, with the suggestion that narrative is central to our nature as social and symbol-constituted beings. It has now become a central part of literary theory, rhetoric, and psychoanalysis in addition to remaining significant in linguistics and anthropology.*

### Reading Questions

- When does the patient in this reading offer each of the three stories? Are they welcome as appropriate? How does the doctor respond? Would you regard the stories as effective? In what sense?
- How does the narrator make himself a character in his stories?
- What does Young mean by "centration" and how does this challenge the more typical view of social scientists that an orderly temporal sequence is appropriate for narration?

---

To write the body. Neither the skin, nor the muscles, nor the bones, nor the nerves, but the rest: an awkward, fibrous, shaggy, raveled thing, a clown's coat —ROLAND BARTHES

Persons are tender of their bodies as if their selves inhered in its organs, vessels, tissues, bones and blood, as if they were embodied. For us, the body is the locus of the self, indistinguishable from it and expressive of it. As the **phenomenologist**, Maurice Natanson, writes.

> The immediacy of my experience of corporeality should be understood as an indication of the interior perspective I occupy with respect of 'my body'. I am neither 'in' my body nor 'attached to' it, it does not belong to me or go along with me. *I am my body*. (Natanson, 1970, p. 12).

I experience myself as embodied, incorporated, incarnated in my body. To appear in my own person is to evidence this implication of my self in my body.

Medical examinations threaten this embodied self with untoward intimacies. The accoutrements of propriety are stripped away: I appear in nothing but my body. What follows has the structure of a transgression, an infringement, but one in which I am complicit. I disclose my body to the other, the stranger, the physician (see Berger and Mohr, 1976, p. 68). To deflect this threat to the embodied self,

Katharine Young, Narrative Embodiments: Enclaves of the Self in the Realm of Medicine. In *Texts of Identity*, edited by John Schotter and Kenneth J. Gergen. London: Sage, 1989, pp. 152–165.

medicine constitutes a separate realm in which the body as lodgement of the self is transformed into the body as object of scrutiny: persons become patients. This transformation is intended to protect the sensibilities of the social self from the trespasses of the examination. Whatever the medical business of the examination, its phenomenological business is to displace the self from the body (see Young, in press). However, persons can perceive rendering the body an object as depersonalizing, dehumanizing or otherwise slighting to the self.[1] The disparity between the physician's intention and the patient's perception establishes the context for 'gaps', 'distortions' and 'misunderstandings' between patients and physicians (Mishler, 1984, p. 171).

Because of their sense of the loss of self – a well-founded sense if also a well-intentioned loss – patients can have some impulse to reconstitute a self during medical examinations. This reconstitution can be undertaken by the patient in one of two moves:[2] either by breaking the framework of the realm of medicine by disattending, misunderstanding or flouting its conventions[3] or by maintaining the framework but inserting into the realm of medicine an enclave of another **ontological** status, specifically, a **narrative** enclave.

Rules for producing narratives on ordinary occasions require that they be set off by their **frames** from the discourses in which they are embedded (see Young, 1982, pp. 277–315). Narrative frames – **prefaces, openings, beginnings, endings, closings, codas** – create an enclosure for stories within medical discourse. The **discourse** within the frames is understood to be of a different ontological status from the discourse without. In particular, the Storyrealm, the realm of narrative discourse, conjures up another realm of events, or Taleworld, in which the events the story recounts are understood to transpire (see Young, 1987, pp. 15–18). It is in this alternate reality that the patient reappears as a person. This move depends on the existence of what Alfred Schutz calls 'multiple realities' (1967, pp. 245–62), the different realms of being, each with its own 'metaphysical constants' (Natanson, 1970, p. 198), which individuals conjure up and enter into by turning their attention to them.

Embodying the self in a narrative enclave respects the conventions of the realm of medicine and at the same time manages the presentation of a self, but of one who is sealed inside a story. An inverse relationship develops between the uniquely constituted narrative enclosure in which a patient presents a self and the jointly constituted enclosing realm in which the patient undergoes a loss of self. Stories become enclaves of self over the course of an occasion on which medicine inhabits the realm of the body.

Erving Goffman argues that persons are in the way of presenting themselves, guiding controlled impressions, not necessarily to deceive, but to sustain a reality, an event, a self. Structurally, the self is divided into two aspects: (1) the performer who fabricates these impressions, and (2) the character who is the impression fabricated by an ongoing performance which entails them both (Goffman, 1959, p. 252). On ordinary occasions, then, persons do not provide information to recipients but present dramas to an audience (Goffman, 1974, p. 508). It is here that the **theatrical metaphor** for which Goffman is famous takes hold: talk about the self is not so far removed from enactment. We do not have behaviours and descriptions of them but a modulation from embodied to disembodied performances. Storytelling is a special instance of the social construction of the self in which 'what the individual presents is not himself but a story containing a protagonist who may happen also to be himself' (Goffman, 1974, p. 541). On the occasion investigated here, embodying the self in stories occurs in circumstances in which the self is being disembodied, a complication of the matter Goffman has called 'multiple selfing', that is, the evolving or exuding of a second self or several selves over the course of an occasion on which the self is being presented (Goffman, 1974, p. 521 fn.).

The natural occurrence of these 'texts of identity' in the course of a medical examination suggests implications about the uses of **narrativity** in social scientific discourse. Kenneth and Mary Gergen write that 'rules for narrative construction guide our attempt to account for human actions across time', both in making ourselves intelligible informally and in social scientific discourse (Gergen and Gergen, 1986, p. 6). Individuals use narratives, they argue, to reflexively reconstruct a sense of self. 'The fact that people believe they possess identities fundamentally depends on their capacity to relate fragmentary occurrences across temporal boundaries' (Gergen and Gergen, 1983, p. 255). What the Gergens call 'self-narratives' then 'refer to the individual's account of the relationship among self-relevant events across time' (p. 255). Kenneth Gergen's speculation that 'lives are constructed around pervading literary figures or **tropes**' (Gergen, 1986, p. 3) is an instance of his more general claim 'that scientific theory is governed in substantial degree by what are essentially aesthetic forms' (Gergen and Gergen, 1986, p. 20).

Note that two claims are being made here: that individuals use stories to make sense of events, and that so, in the same vein, do social scientists. The narrativity of social scientific discourse, then, takes its legitimation from storytelling in everyday life. This in turn warrants the application of narrative theory to social scientific discourse. However, discovering the structures of narrative in discourses about the self must be distinguished from imputing narrative structures to discourses about the self. The first is an ethnographic enterprise; the second an analytic one. To regard social scientific discourse as narrative is to treat it under a metaphor, in the same way that it is to regard cultures as texts or minds as **cybernetic systems** or reality as mechanistic. Analysts' uses of the devices of narrative to structure their approaches to discourses about the self render problematic the conventions that narrativity imports into the social sciences. My concern as a **narratologist** is to distinguish these approaches from persons' presentations of self in narrative modes. It is crucial to return to the social disposition of stories, to their linguistic coding, their contexts of use, to see how they illuminate the way individuals construe their lives. Doing so lays the groundwork for pursuing enquiries into narrativity as an interpretive structure for social scientific discourses about the self.

This is an analysis of a medical examination in the course of which the patient tells three stories in which he appears as a character. The links and splits between the realm of medicine and the realm of narrative illuminate the nature of narrative, the nature of medicine, and the nature of the self.

Medical examinations are divided into two parts: the history-taking, and the physical examination. These internal constituents of the realm of medicine are bounded by greetings and farewells which mark the transition between the realm of the ordinary and the realm of medicine. The shift from greetings, in which the physician emerges from his professional role to speak to his patient as a social person, to history-taking, in which the physician elicits information from the patient about his body, is the first move towards dislodging the self from the body. The patient's social person is set aside to attend to his physical body.

The patient on this occasion is Dr Michael Malinowski, a seventy-eight-year-old professor of Jewish history and literature. He has come to University Hospital to consult an internist, Dr Mathew Silverberg.[4] Dr Silverberg shakes hands with the professor and his son in the waiting room, escorts them to his office, and there begins to take the patient's history. The shift from the waiting room to the office reifies the transition between realms. The history-taking reorients the person's attitude towards his body in two respects: it invites him to regard his body from outside instead of from inside, and it invites him to see it in parts instead of as a whole. Dr Silverberg's enquiries direct the patient to attend to his body as an object with its own vicissitudes which he recounts with the detachment of an outsider. In so doing, Dr Malinowski suffers a slight estrangement from his own body. In making these enquiries, Dr Silverberg asks about the parts of the body separately, disarticulating it into segments. So Dr Malinowski's body undergoes a fragmentation. Since the self is felt to inhere in the body as a whole from the inside, these shifts of perspective tend to separate the self from the body. It is against the thrust of this ongoing estrangement and fragmentation that the professor sets his first story, the story of the liberation. Dr Silverberg has shifted from general enquiries about the whole body – height, weight, age, health – to specific enquiries about the eyes, the throat and the blood. He continues:

### STORY I

#### THE LIBERATION[5]

Dr S: Have you ever had any problems with your heart.
Dr M: No.
Dr S: No heart attacks?
Dr M: Pardon me?
Dr S: Heart attacks?
Dr M: No.
Dr S: No pain in the chest?
Dr M: No pain in the chest.
Dr S: I
noticed that =
Dr M: I am a graduate from Auschwitz.
Dr S: I know— I heard already =
Dr M: Yeah.
I went there when— I tell Dr Young about this
and
after Auschwitz
I went through a lot of— I lost this
Dr S: Umhm.
Dr M: top finger there
and
I was in a—
after the liberation we were under supervision of American doctors.
Dr S: Yeah?
Dr M: American doctors.
Dr S: Right.
Dr M: And it uh
I was sick of course after two years in Auschwitz I was quite uh uh exhausted.
And later I went through
medical examination
in the American Consul
in Munich
Dr S: Yeah?
Dr M: and I came to the United States.
Dr S: Right?
Dr M: In nineteen hundred forty-seven.
Nineteen forty-six—
about nineteen forty-seven.
One day—
I lived on Fairfield Avenue
I started to spit
blood.
Dr S: Right?
Dr M: Yeah?
And I called the doctor
and he found that something here ((*gestures to his chest*))
Dr S: Tuberculosis?
Dr M: Somethin— yeah.
And I was in the Deborah
Sanitorium for a year.
Dr S: In nineteen forty-seven.
Dr M: I would say forty-seven and about
month of forty-eight.
...
Dr S: Back
to your heart.

The story conjures up a Taleworld, the realm of Auschwitz, which is juxtaposed to the ongoing history-taking. The preface, 'I am a graduate from Auschwitz', opens onto the other realm. Prefaces are a conventional way of eliciting permission to take an extended turn at talk in order to tell a story

(Sacks, 1970, II, p. 10). In response to what he perceives as a divagation from the realm of medicine, Dr Silverberg says, 'I know – I heard already.' Having heard a story is grounds for refusing permission to tell it again (Goffman, 1974, p. 508). Dr Malinowski persists in spite of this refusal, thus overriding one of the devices available to physicians for controlling the course of an examination, namely, a relevancy rule: that the discourse stay within the realm of medicine. To insert the realm of narrative into the realm of medicine, the professor initially breaks its frame. But in so doing, he substitutes another relevancy rule: topical continuity. Like the history-taking, the Taleworld focuses on a part of the body, the chest. It is this part of the body that the professor uses to produce topical continuity between the history-taking and the story. However, it is not the chest but the heart on which the physician is focusing. When he returns talk to the realm of medicine with the remark, 'Back to your heart', he is at the same time protesting the irrelevance of the excursion.[6] As is apparent from this, the rule for topical continuity, the selection of a next discourse event which shares at least one element with a previous discourse event, permits trivial connections between discourses and, by extension, between realms. But there is a deeper continuity here. Both the realm of Auschwitz and the realm of medicine address the body.

In the realm of medicine, the dismantling of the body continues with Dr Silverberg's enquiries about the heart, breath, ankles and back; he recurs to whole body concerns with enquiries about allergies, habits and relatives; then he goes on to segment the body into the skin, head, eyes again, nose, throat again, excretory organs, stomach again, muscles, bones and joints. Into this discourse, the professor inserts his second story, the story of the torture. This story is also about a part of the body, the finger, and so again maintains a parallel with the realm in which it is embedded, although not the strict tie of topical continuity. Having created an enclosure in medical discourse for the Auschwitz stories earlier on, Dr Malinowski now feels entitled to extend or elaborate that Taleworld (see Young, 1987, pp. 80–99). This story is tied not to the discourse that preceded it but to the previous story in which he mentions his finger. As if in acknowledgement of the establishment of this enclosure, Dr Malinowski's preface, 'I was not sick except this finger', elicits an invitation from Dr Silverberg to tell the story: 'What happened to that finger.' The Taleworld is becoming a realm of its own.

### STORY 2

### THE TORTURE

Dr M: No.
I don't know.
I tell you— I told you Dr. ((*to me*)) I don't—during the twenty-three months in Auschwitz
Dr S: Yeah?
Dr M: I was not sick except this finger.
Dr S: What happened to that finger.
Dr M: I wa—
I tell Dr. Young
I was sitting
((*coughs*)) you have something to drink
Dr S: Yeah.
I have for you.
Dr M: Yeah.
I was sitting at the press—
the machine
I don't know how to say in English
[— a machine or]
Dr S: [I understand.]
Dr M: Anyway I had to put in this was
iron
and I had to put in— in here with the right hand to put this which made a hole or whatever it did.
Dr S: Made a hole in your finger.
Dr M: No.
Made a hole here. ((*in the piece of iron*))
My finger got it.
And behind me was an SS man.
The SS was walking.
And he stood behind me
and at one moment he pushed me.
Just— this was a— a— a—
daily sport.
And instead to put the iron in I put my finger in.
/
But otherwise I wasn't sick.

The shift from taking the history to giving the physical examination involves moving to another space, the examining room, which is an even more narrowly medical realm. Dr Silverberg closes the history-taking by saying:

Dr S: I would like to examine you.
Dr M: For this I came.
Dr S: I will lead you into the examining room?
Dr M: All right.
Dr S: I would like you to
take everything off
Down to your undershorts.
And have a seat on the table.

Dr Silverberg then takes his patient to the examining room down the hall and leaves him to take off his clothes. Clothes are the insignia of the social self. Their removal separates the body from its social accoutrements. This reduction of the social self along with the enhancement of the medical realm completes the dislodgement of the self. What remains is the dispirited, unpersoned, or dehumanized body.

During the physical examination, the body is handled as an object. When Dr Silverberg returns he finds the professor lying on the examining table in old-fashioned long white shorts that button at the top, with his arms folded across his chest. They speak to each other and then Dr Silverberg comes up to the examining table, picks the patient's right hand up off his chest, holds it in his right hand, and feels the pulse with his left fingertips. Here is the inversion of the initial handshake which enacted a symmetry between social selves; the physician touches the patient's hand as if it were inanimate. The examination is the rendering in a physical medium of the estrangement of the self and the fragmentation of the body. The external perspective is substituted for the internal perspective and the whole is disarticulated into parts. Of course, there is still talk – questions, comments, instructions; but now such remarks are inserted into interstices between the acts, the investigations, the physical manipulations the structure the examination. Henceforth, for the course of the physical examination, the patient's body is touched, lifted, probed, turned, bent, tapped, disarranged and recomposed by the physician. It is here that the absence of the self from the body can be intended as a protection: the social self is thereby preserved from the trespasses of the examination. These are committed only on an object.

The physical examination proceeds from the hands up the arms; then Dr Silverberg sits the patient up, looks at his head, ears, eyes, nose, mouth, throat, back, chest and heart; then he lays the patient back down on the table, tucks down the top of his shorts, examines his genitals, and folds the shorts back together at the top. He continues down the legs to the feet, then sits him up again and returns to the arms and hands. At this point, Dr Silverberg asks the patient to touch his nose with the tips of his fingers and as he does so the patient alludes to a bump on his skull: 'I have to tell you how I got that.' And the physician responds, 'How.' Despite this invitation, Dr Malinowski appears uncertain about the propriety of inserting a story into this realm.

### STORY 3

### THE CAPTURE

Dr M: I have to tell you how I got that. ((*the bump*))
Dr S: How.
Dr M: Should I talk here?
Dr S: You
Dr M: Can I talk here?
Dr S: Sure.
/
Dr M: You already know. ((*to me*))
When I (s— try) to go the border
between Poland and Germany
Dr S: Yeah?
Dr M: I wanted to escape
to the border over Switzerland=
Dr S: Umhm.
Dr M: as a Gentile.
Dr S: Yeah?
Dr M: When they caught me
they wanted investigation.
/
Dr S: That it?
Dr M: (At)
the table was (sitting) near me
and (his arm) was extending behind me
with— how the police ha— how do you call it.
A police club?
Dr S: Nightstick.
Dr M: Nightstick.
Dr S: Umhm.
Dr M: And they—
I had to count
and they hit me twenty
times over the head.
And er— he told me zählen
zähle means you count.
And after the war—
after the liberation shortly about two three days
American Jewish doctors came
they (examined us)
and he told me
that I have
a nerve splint here?
Dr S: Yeah.
Dr M: And this made me be deaf.

The physician then examines the patient's ears, and finally his prostate and rectum. So here, suspended between the genital and rectal examinations, the two procedures towards which the displacement of the self from the body are primarily oriented, is the professor's third and last story. Once again, the story is about a part of the body, the ears, which maintains a continuity with the realm of medicine. But it is also about another part of the body, the genitals. As he mentions, Dr Malinowski has already told me this story when I talked to him in the waiting room to get his permission to observe and tape-record his examination. He told me that he and a friend had decided, boldly, to cross the border out of Poland into Germany and work their way across Germany to the Swiss border. They carried forged papers. He himself got through the border and was already on the other side when something about his friend aroused the border guard's suspicion and they called him back. To check their suspicions, the guards pulled down his pants and exposed his genitals. Jews were circumcised. This story is concealed as a subtext directed to me within a text directed to the physician. On this understanding, the positioning of the story between the genital and rectal examinations has a tighter topical continuity than is apparent on the surface.

Stories are sealed off from the occasions on which they occur – here, the realm of medicine – as events of a different ontological status. For that reason they can be used to reinsert into that realm an alternate reality in which the patient can reappear in his own person without disrupting the ontological conditions of the realm of medicine. Stories about the realm in which he appears, the world of Auschwitz, might be supposed to be inherently theatrical, on the order of high tragedy. But the boundary between realms insulates medicine in some measure from the tragic passion. The apertures along the boundary through which the realms are connected are here restricted to parts of the body. In telling these stories, Michael Malinowski is not intending to play on his hearers' emotions. He is rather reconstituting for them the ontological conditions of his world and, having done so, inserting himself into that realm as a character. Besides creating a separate reality, telling stories during a medical examination creates a continuity between the two realms which converts the ontological conditions of the realm of medicine precisely along the dimension of the body.

The stories are tokens of the man, talismans of the salient and defining history which has shaped him. They are not, on that account, unique to this occasion, but are invoked as touchstones of his presence (as they were, for instance, for me when we talked before the examination). They present a person whose life is wrought around an event of existential proportions. Auschwitz was a life-pivoting, world-splitting event: time is reckoned before-Auschwitz and after-Auschwitz; space is divided by it. Not only has he lost a country, a language and a childhood, but he has also lost a life-form. Before Auschwitz, he had a wife and child in Poland; the son who has brought him today is the only child of a second marriage made in the USA after the war. Dr Malinowski mentions once that he had two sisters: one perished, the other died a few years ago of cancer.

The sequential order of events in a story replicates the temporal unfolding of events in the realm it represents (Labov, 1972, pp. 359–60). This replication is supposed by social scientists to extend to the sets of stories which are strung together to make a life history. In this instance, the sequential order in which these stories are told does not replicate the temporal order in which the events they recount occurred. He tells about the liberation first, then the torture, and finally the capture. There are of course clear contextual reasons for this which have been detailed here in terms of topical continuity. But I would like to suggest a deeper reason for their array. These stories cluster around Michael Malinowski's sense of self. Auschwitz provides what I would like to call **centration:** life is anchored here, everything else unfolds around this. The set of stories that make up the Auschwitz experience could be told in any order. There is an implication here for the use of narrativity in the social sciences. In insisting either on the notion that temporally ordered events are presented sequentially in stories or on re-ordering stories to present them so, social scientists have misunderstood the shape of experience: a life is not always grasped as a linear pattern. Serious attention to narrativity in stories of the self will not force the sense of self into the pattern of narrative, but will deploy narrative to discover the sense of self.

In so presenting the man and reconstituting the ontological conditions of his world, these stories attain the status of moral fables and lend the medical examination a delineation which renders the etiquette of touch an ethical condition. Not that the stories are warnings to the physician against similar transgressions. Rather, in the existential context of these stories, what might otherwise be seen as indignities to the body are transmuted into honours: the physician is a man whose touch preserves just those proprieties of the body that are infringed at Auschwitz.

The body in the Taleworld is the analogue of the body in the realm of the examination, connected to it part for part, but inverted. The stories spin out existential situations in which the self is constrained to the body. In the first story, 'The Liberation', the part of the body is the chest and the mode of insertion of the self in the body is sickness. The self cannot transcend its absorption in its bodily discomforts: its sensibilities are sealed in its skin. In the second story, 'The Torture', the part of the body is the finger and the mode of insertion of the self in the body is pain. The self is jolted into the body, its sensibilities concentrated in its minutest part, the tip of a finger. In the third story, 'The Capture', the parts of the body are the head and the genitals, and the mode of insertion is humiliation. Here the body is emblematic of the man, literally inscribed with his identity. Its degradations are his.

The phenomenological cast of the Taleworld is set against the phenomenological cast of the realm of the examination in which the self is extricated from the body. The medical history of the tuberculosis, the severed fingertip, the deafness, which could be detached, is instead enfolded in the personal history of the concentration camp and recounted as a story. So Auschwitz is invoked not as the cause of these dissolutions of the flesh, but as the frame in terms of which we are to understand what has befallen the body and, it transpires, the frame in terms of which we are to understand what has become of the man. To see the fact that both the realm of medicine and the realm of narrative are about the body as topical continuity is a trivial rendering. The stories are transforms of the ontological problem that is central to the examination: the fragile, stubborn, precarious, insistent insertion of a self in the body.

APPENDIX: TRANSCRIPTION CONVENTIONS

| Line-ends | Pauses |
|---|---|
| From Tedlock, 1978: | |
| = | Absence of obligatory end-pause |
| / | One turn pause |
| Capital letters | Start of utterance |
| . | Down intonation at end of utterance |
| ? | Up intonation at end of utterance |
| — | Correction phenomena |
| () | Doubtful hearings |
| (()) | Editorial comments |
| [[ | Simultaneous speech |
| [] | Extent of simultaneity |

Adapted by Malcah Yeager from Schenkein, 1972:

... Elisions

Initials before turns are abbreviations of speakers

English spelling indicates English speaking

## Notes

This paper was first given in 1985 at the American Folklore Society Meetings in Cincinnati, Ohio. The present version was clarified by a critical reading by Kenneth Gergen.

1. This sense of dehumanization is well attested to in both popular and social scientific literature. Elliot Mishler locates

dehumanization in the discourse of medicine, where he describes it as the conflict between the voice of medicine, which is understood to dominate during medical examinations, and the voice of the life-world, which is suppressed in a way, he argues, that leads to an 'objectification of the patient, to a stripping away of the life-world contexts of patient problems' (Mishler, 1984, p. 128).

2. Mishler points out that the conventions could be shifted by the physician (1984, p. 162).

3. Mishler would say, by interrupting the voice of medicine with the voice of the life-world (1984, p. 63).

4. To protect confidentiality, the names of the patient, the physician and the hospital are fictitious.

5. The text is transcribed from tapes of medical examinations collected during my research on the phenomenology of the body in medicine in 1984. Transcription devices are appended.

6. Mishler notes that the struggle between voices for control is associated with disruption of the flow of discourse (1984, p. 91). As he says, to see departures from the medical paradigm as interruptions is to privilege the physician's perspective (p. 97). 'I am proposing an interpretation of the medical interview as a situation of conflict between two ways of constructing meaning. Moreover, I am also proposing that the physician's effort to impose a technocratic consciousness, to dominate the voice of the life-world by the voice of medicine, seriously impairs and distorts essential requirements for mutual dialogue and human interaction. To the extent that clinical practice is realized through this type of discourse, the possibility of more humane treatment in medicine is severely limited.' I should like to reiterate my point that the objectification of the body can be intended to protect the sensibilities of the person. To see the dominance of the medical paradigm as an imposition is to privilege the patient's perspective. The rhythm of interplay between perspectives, discourses or realms is my concern here.

## References


Barthes, R. 1977. *Roland Barthes*. New York: Hill & Wang.

Berger, J. and J. Mohr. 1976. *A Fortunate Man: The Story of a Country Doctor*. New York: Pantheon.

Gergen, K. 1986. *If Persons Are Texts*. New Brunswick, NJ: Rutgers University Press.

Gergen, K. and M. Gergen. 1983. 'Narratives of the Self', in T. R. Sarbin and K. E. Scheibe (eds.), *Studies in Social Identity*. New York: Praeger.

Gergen, K. and M. Gergen. 1986. 'Narrative Form and the Construction of Psychological Theory'. Unpublished paper, Swarthmore College/Pennsylvania State University.

Goffman, E. 1959. *The Presentation of Self in Everyday Life*. New York: Doubleday.

Goffman, E. 1974. *Frame Analysis*. New York: Harper & Row.

Labov, W. 1972. 'The Transformation of Experience in Narrative Syntax,' in *Language in the Inner City*. Philadelphia: University of Pennsylvania Press.

Mishler, E. G. 1984. *The Discourse of Medicine: Dialectics of Medical Interviews*. Norwood, NJ: Ablex.

Natanson, M. 1970. *The Journeying Self: A Study in Philosophy and Social Role*. Reading, MA: Addison-Wesley.

Sacks, H. 1968. Unpublished lecture notes, University of California, Irvine, 17 April 1968.

Sacks, H. 1970. Unpublished lecture notes, University of California, Irvine, 17 April 1970.

Schenkein, J. 1972. *Foundations in Sociolinguistics*. Philadelphia: University of Pennsylvania Press.

Schutz, A. 1967. *On Phenomenology and Social Relations*. Chicago and London: University of Chicago Press.

Tedlock, D. 1978. *Finding the Center: Narrative Poetry of the Zuni Indians*. Lincoln and London: University of Nebraska Press.

Young, K. 1982. 'Edgework: Frame and Boundary in the Phenomenology of Narrative Communication', *Semiotica*, 41(1/4): 277–315.

Young, K. 1987. *Taleworlds and Storyrealms: The Phenomenology of Narrative*. Dordrecht: Martinus Nijhoff.

Young, K. In press. 'Disembodiment: The Phenomenology of the Body in Medicine', *Semiotica*.


## Critical Thinking and Application

- What does Young suggest is the relationship among self, body, and story? Do you think this applies only in this situation or more generally? Why?
- How does telling the three stories during the medical examination permit the patient to maintain control over himself and his identity? Discuss Young's statement: "[I]n the existential context of these stories, what might otherwise be seen as indignities to the body are transmuted into honours: the physician is a man whose touch preserves just those proprieties of the body that are infringed at Auschwitz."
- Record someone telling her or his life story. Analyze the components of the narrative, looking especially at prefaces, openings, beginnings, endings, closings, and codas.

## Vocabulary

| | | |
|---|---|---|
| beginning | coda | ending |
| centration | cybernetic | frame |
| closing | discourse | narrative |

narrativity
narratologist
ontology, ontological
opening
phenomenology, phenomenologist
preface
theatrical metaphor
trope

## Suggested Further Reading


Bal, Mieke. 1997. *Narratology: Introduction to the Theory of Narrative*. 2nd ed. Toronto: University of Toronto Press.

Bamberg, Michael G. W. 1997. *Oral Versions of Personal Experience: Three Decades of Narrative Analysis*. Mahwah, NJ: Erlbaum.

Bamberg, Michael G. W., Anna De Fina, and Deborah Schiffrin. 2007. *Selves and Identities in Narrative and Discourse*. Amsterdam: Benjamins.

Cortazzi, Martin. 1993. *Narrative Analysis*. London: Falmer Press.

Goffman, Erving. 1959. *The Presentation of Self in Everyday Life*. New York: Doubleday.

Herman, David, Manfred Jahn, and Marie-Laure Ryan, eds. 2005. *Routledge Encyclopedia of Narrative Theory*. London and New York: Routledge.

Labov, William, and David Fanshel. 1977. *Therapeutic Discourse: Psychotherapy as Conversation*. New York: Academic Press.

Labov, William, and Joshua Waletzky. 1967. Narrative Analysis. In *Essays on the Verbal and Visual Arts*, edited by J. Helm, pp. 12–44. Seattle: University of Washington Press.

Norrick, Neal R. 2000. *Conversational Narrative Storytelling in Everyday Talk*. Amsterdam: Benjamins.

Prince, Gerald. 1982. *Narratology: The Form and Functioning of Narrative*. Berlin: Mouton.

Shotter, John, and Kenneth J. Gergen. 1989. *Texts of Identity*. London: Sage.

Toolan, Michael J. 1988. *Narrative: A Critical Linguistic Introduction*. London and New York: Routledge.

Young, Katharine Galloway. 1987. *Taleworlds and Storyrealms: The Phenomenology of Narrative*. Dordrecht: Nijhoff.

# UNIT 9

# Language Ideology

As occasionally happens in intellectual matters, the concept *language ideology* named something that anthropologists, linguists, and other analysts of language had been aware of for some time: different values are placed on various aspects of language at different times and in different places. We see it as early as in Malinowski's "The Problem of Meaning in Primitive Languages," in much work on the ethnography of speaking [including in Joel Sherzer and Regna Darnell's "Outline Guide for the Ethnographic Study of Speech Use" (especially the section on "Attitudes Toward the Use of Speech")], and in a good portion of the work of Michael Silverstein. When Kathryn Woolard and Bambi Schieffelin gave a name to this approach to the understanding of language in 1994, they unleashed a new creative energy in this study (see also Schieffelin, Woolard, and Kroskrity 1998, Kroskrity 2000). The term *ideology* (in contrast to *idea*) links notions of power and politics to questions of how people regard the very nature of language.

Writing on language ideology is very broad and very rich. Elsewhere in this book we have also seen it applied to norms of socialization (Chapter 9), to attitudes toward literacy (Chapter 17), and to the meanings of the English word *like* (Chapter 39). The term is now used in studies of gender, multilingualism, language policy, language standardization, prejudice, language shift, language socialization, and many more topics.

## Suggested Further Reading


Bauman, Richard, and Joel Sherzer, eds. 1989 [1974]. *Explorations in the Ethnography of Speaking*. 2nd ed. Cambridge: Cambridge University Press.

Blommaert, Jan, ed. 1999. *Language Ideological Debates*. Berlin: Mouton de Gruyter.

Gumperz, John J., and Dell Hymes, eds. 1986 [1972]. *Directions in Sociolinguistics: The Ethnography of Communication*. Oxford: Blackwell.

Johnson, Sally, and Tommaso M. Milani, eds. 2010. *Language Ideologies and Media Discourse: Texts, Practices Politics*. London: Continuum.

Kroskrity, Paul V., ed. 2000. *Regimes of Language: Ideologies, Polities, and Identities*. Santa Fe, NM: School of American Research Press.

Malinowski, Bronislaw. 1923. The Problem of Meaning in Primitive Languages. In *The Meaning of Meaning*, edited by C. K. Ogden and I. A. Richards. New York: Harcourt, Brace.

Ryan, Ellen Bouchard, and Howard Giles, eds. 1982. *Attitudes Towards Language Variation: Social and Applied Contexts*. London: Arnold.

Schieffelin, Bambi B., Kathryn A. Woolard, and Paul V. Kroskrity, eds. 1998. *Language Ideologies: Practice and Theory*. New York and Oxford: Oxford University Press.

Sherzer, Joel, and Regna Darnell. 1986 [1972]. Outline Guide for the Ethnographic Study of Speech Use. In *Directions in Sociolinguistics: The Ethnography of Communication*, edited by John J. Gumperz and Dell Hymes, pp. 548–554. Oxford: Blackwell.

Silverstein, Michael. 1979. Language Structure and Linguistic Ideology. In *The Elements: A Parasession on Linguistic Units and Levels*, edited by Paul R. Clyne, William F. Hanks, and Carol L. Hofbauer, pp. 193–247. Chicago: Chicago Linguistic Society.

Silverstein, Michael. 1998. The Uses and Utility of Ideology: A Commentary. In *Language Ideologies: Practice and Theory*, edited by Bambi B. Schieffelin, Kathryn A. Woolard, and Paul V. Kroskrity, pp. 123–145. New York: Oxford University Press.

Silverstein, Michael, and Greg Urban, eds. 1996. *Natural Histories of Discourse*. Chicago and London: University of Chicago Press.

van Dijk, Teun A. 1998. *Ideology: A Multidisciplinary Approach*. London: Sage.

Woolard, Kathryn A., and Bambi B. Schieffelin. 1994. Language Ideology. *Annual Review of Anthropology* 23: 55–82.

# CHAPTER 46

# Communication of Respect in Interethnic Service Encounters

## *Benjamin Bailey*

(1997)

*Linguistic differences can lead to social differences, which in turn can produce anything from indifference to violence. People often believe that others are disrespectful of them, when in fact there are different ideologies about the norms of interaction. Riots broke out in Los Angeles in the 1990s, as depicted fictionally in Spike Lee's film* Do the Right Thing, *in which Korean shopkeepers were often regarded as privileged outsiders by African Americans resentful of inequalities. In this article, Benjamin Bailey looks carefully at interactions between shopkeepers and their customers, revealing that something as subtle as whether a laugh is reciprocated can lead to conclusions about respect. The ideologies people hold, and enact, regarding the proper use of language is part and parcel of their view of proper human behavior. We tend to regard our ideologies as universal morality, but when one group's norms are contrasted with those of another, we can see how variable these guidelines are.*

### Reading Questions

- How did African Americans in Bailey's study regard Korean shopkeepers? How did Korean shopkeepers regard African American customers?
- How did African Americans and Koreans demonstrate respect? How did each group interpret the other group's interactional behavior?
- What are *involvement politeness* and *restraint politeness*? How do these relate to *socially minimal* and *socially expanded service encounters*?
- How do African Americans and Koreans interact among themselves? How does each group tend to regard exchanges at the stores?
- What are norms of affective personal involvement for African Americans, as displayed in Encounter 1? How would call-and-response work? What happens when people have different expectations about their interlocutors' responses? (Compare Tannen, Chapter 30.)
- What communicative activities with strangers are typical for African Americans? for Koreans? How does this norm play out in Encounter 2? Why do you think the storekeeper becomes more reticent while the customer becomes more animated at the end of the encounter?

---

Conflict in face-to-face interaction between immigrant Korean retail merchants and their African American customers has been widely documented since the early 1980s. Newspapers in New York, Washington, DC, Chicago, and Los Angeles have carried stories on this friction; and the 1989 movie *Do the Right Thing* depicted angry confrontations of this type. By the time that the events of April 1992 – referred to variously as the Los Angeles "riots," "uprising," "civil disturbance" or, by many immigrant Koreans, *sa-i-gu* 'April 29' – cast a media spotlight on such relations, there had already been numerous African American boycotts of immigrant Korean businesses in New York and Los Angeles; politicians had publicly addressed the issue; and academics (e.g. Ella Stewart 1989 and Chang 1990) had begun to write about this type of friction.

There are multiple, intertwined reasons for these interethnic tensions in small businesses. An underlying source

Benjamin Bailey, Communication of Respect in Interethnic Service Encounters. *Language in Society* 26 (3) (1997): 327–356.

is the history of social, racial, and economic inequality in American society. In this broader context, visits to any store can become a charged event for African Americans. Thus, according to Austin (1995: 32),

> Any kind of ordinary face-to-face retail transaction can turn into a hassle for a black person. For example, there can hardly be a black in urban America who has not been either denied entry to a store, closely watched, snubbed, questioned about her or his ability to pay for an item, or stopped and detained for shoplifting.

Specific features of small convenience/liquor stores, such as the ones studied here, exacerbate the potential for conflict. Prices in such stores are high, many customers have low incomes, and the storekeepers are seen by many as the latest in a long line of economic exploiters from outside the African American community (Drake & Cayton 1945, Sturdevant 1969, Chang 1990, 1993). Shoplifting is not uncommon, and the late hours and cash basis of the stores make them appealing targets for robbery. Nearly all the retailers interviewed had been robbed at gunpoint; this had led some to do business from behind bulletproof glass, making verbal interaction with customers difficult.

In this socially, racially, and economically charged context, subtle differences in the ways that respect is communicated in face-to-face interaction are of considerable significance, affecting relationships between groups. This [chapter] documents how differences in the ways that immigrant Korean storekeepers and African American customers communicate respect in service encounters have contributed to mutual, distinctively intense feelings of disrespect between the two groups, and serve as an ongoing source of tension. These contrasting practices for the display of politeness and respect are empirically evident in the talk and behavior that occur in stores, and the negative perceptions that result are salient in interviews of retailers and customers alike.

## Respect

The issue of "respect" in face-to-face encounters has been stressed both in the media and in academic accounts of relations between African Americans and immigrant Korean retailers. Ella Stewart (1991: 20) concludes that "respect" is important for both groups in service encounters:

> Both groups declared rudeness as a salient inappropriate behavior. The underlined themes for both groups appear to be respect and courtesy shown toward each other. Each group felt that more respect should be accorded when communicating with each other, and that courtesy should be shown through verbal and nonverbal interaction by being more congenial, polite, considerate, and tactful toward each other.

Such analysis suggests that good intentions are all that is required to ameliorate relationships: each group simply has to show more "respect and courtesy" to the other. However, the data presented in this [chapter] suggest that, even when such good intentions seem to be present, respect is not effectively communicated and understood. The problem is that, in a given situation, there are fundamentally different ways of showing respect in different cultures. Because of different conventions for the display of respect, groups may feel respect for each other, and may continuously work at displaying their esteem – yet each group can feel that they are being disrespected. This type of situation, in which participants communicate at cross-purposes, has been analyzed most notably by Gumperz 1982a,b, 1992 regarding intercultural communication, though not regarding respect specifically.

The communication of respect is a fundamental dimension of everyday, face-to-face interaction. As Goffman says (1967: 46), "the person in our urban secular world is allotted a kind of sacredness that is displayed and confirmed by symbolic acts." These symbolic acts are achieved, often unconsciously, through the manipulation of a variety of communicative channels including **prosody**, choice of words and topic, **proxemic distance,** and timing of utterances. Gumperz 1982a, 1992 has shown how cultural differences in the use of such **contextualization cues** – at levels ranging from the perception and categorization of sounds to the global framing of activities – can lead to misunderstandings in intercultural communication. The focus of this article is the ways in which constellations of interactional features can communicate (dis)respect in service encounters.

The intercultural (mis)communication of respect between African American customers and immigrant Korean retailers is particularly significant for interethnic relations because behavior that is perceived to be lacking in respect is typically interpreted as actively threatening. Thus, according to Brown & Levinson (1987: 33), "non-communication of the polite attitude will be read not merely as the absence of that attitude, but as the inverse, the holding of an aggressive attitude." When conventions for paying respect in service encounters differ between cultures, as they do between immigrant Koreans and African Americans, individuals may read each other's behavior as not simply strange or lacking in social grace, but as aggressively antagonistic.

Brown & Levinson posit a classification system for politeness practices that is useful for conceptualizing the contrasting interactional practices of immigrant Korean retailers and African American customers. Following Durkheim 1915 and Goffman 1971, they suggest two basic dimensions of individuals' desire for respect: **NEGATIVE FACE** wants and **POSITIVE FACE** wants. Negative face want is "the want of every 'competent adult member' that his actions be unimpeded by others," while positive face want is "the want of every member that his wants be desirable to at least some others" (Brown & Levinson, 62). Stated more simply, people do not want to be imposed on (negative face want); but they do want expressions of approval, understanding, and solidarity (positive face want). Because the labels "positive" and "negative" have misleading connotations, I use the word ***involvement*** to refer to positive politeness phenomena, and **RESTRAINT** to refer to negative politeness phenomena. These terms denote the phenomena to which they refer more mnemonically than the terms POSITIVE and NEGATIVE.

Strategies for paying respect include acts of "involvement politeness" and acts of "restraint politeness." Involvement politeness includes those behaviors which express approval of the self or "personality" of the other. It includes acts which express solidarity between interactors – e.g. compliments, friendly jokes, agreement, demonstrations of personal interest, offers, and the use of in-group identity markers. Data from store interactions show that these acts are relatively more frequent in the service encounter talk of African Americans than of immigrant Koreans.

Restraint politeness includes actions which mark the interactor's unwillingness to impose on others, or which lessen potential imposition. These strategies can include **hedging** statements, making requests indirect, being apologetic, or simply NOT demanding the other's attention to begin with. Restraint face wants are basically concerned with the desire to be free of imposition from others, where even the distraction of one's attention can be seen as imposition. Behaviors that minimize the communicative demands on another – e.g. NOT asking questions, NOT telling jokes that would call for a response, and NOT introducing personal topics of conversation – can be expressions of restraint politeness or respect. Such acts of restraint are typical of the participation of immigrant Korean store-owners in service encounters.

## METHODS

Fieldwork for this study took place in Los Angeles between July 1994 and April 1995. Data collection methods included ethnographic observation and interviewing in immigrant Korean stores, interviews with African Americans outside of store contexts, and videotaping of service encounters in stores.

I made repeated visits to six stores in the Culver City area, five in South Central, and two in Koreatown. Visits to stores typically lasted from one-half hour to two hours; with repeated visits, I spent over 10 hours at each of three stores in Culver City and one in South Central, and over five hours in one Koreatown store.

Service encounters in two immigrant Korean stores, one in Culver City and one in Koreatown, were videotaped for a total of four hours in each store. Video cameras were set up in plain view, but drew virtually no attention, perhaps because there were already multiple surveillance cameras in each store. The tapes from the Koreatown store are used for the current study because the Culver City store had no Korean customers and a lower proportion of African American customers. During the four hours of taping in this Koreatown store, there were 12 African American customers and 13 immigrant Korean customers.

The encounters with African American customers were transcribed using the conventions of conversation analysis (Atkinson & Heritage 1984),[1] resulting in over 30 pages of transcripts. The encounters in Korean were transcribed by a Korean American bilingual assistant according to McCune–Reischauer conventions, and then translated into English. Transcription and translation of Korean encounters were accompanied by interpretation and explanation – some of which was audio-recorded – by the bilingual assistant while watching the videotapes. In addition, the storekeeper who appears throughout the four hours of videotape watched segments of the tapes and gave background information on some of the customers appearing in the tapes, e.g. how regularly they came to the store. Transcripts of encounters in Korean comprise over 25 pages.

## SERVICE ENCOUNTER INTERACTION

In the following sections, I first consider the general structure of service encounters as an activity, delineating two types: **SOCIALLY MINIMAL** vs. **SOCIALLY EXPANDED** service encounters. Second, I consider the characteristics of convenience store service encounters between immigrant Koreans, presenting examples from transcripts that show socially minimal service encounters to be the common form. Third, I consider the characteristics of service encounters between immigrant Korean storekeepers and African American customers, using transcripts of two such encounters to demonstrate the contrasting forms of participation in them.

Merritt (1976: 321) defines a service encounter as:

> an instance of face-to-face interaction between a server who is "officially posted" in some service area and a customer who is present in that service area, that interaction being oriented to the satisfaction of the customer's presumed desire for some service and the server's obligation to provide that service. A typical service encounter is one in which a customer buys something at a store…

Service encounters in stores fall under the broader category of **institutional talk**, the defining characteristic of which is its goal-orientation (Drew & Heritage 1992a). Levinson (1992: 71) sees the organization, or structure, of such activities as flowing directly from their goals: "wherever possible I would like to view these structural elements as rationally and functionally adapted to the point or goal of the activity in question, that is the function or functions that members of the society see the activity as having."

The structural differences between Korean-Korean service encounters and those with African American customers that will be described below suggest that the two groups have different perceptions of the functions of such encounters. Even when goals are seen to overlap, participants in intercultural encounters frequently utilize contrasting means of achieving those goals (Gumperz 1992: 246). Although African American customers and immigrant Korean shopkeepers might agree that they are involved in a service encounter, they have different notions of the types of activities that constitute a service encounter and the appropriate means for achieving those activities.

The service encounters involving immigrant Koreans and African Americans that are transcribed in this article took place in a Koreatown liquor store between 3 P.M. and 7 P.M. on a Thursday in April 1995. The store does not use bulletproof glass, and from the cash register one has an unobstructed line of sight throughout the store. The cashier is a 31-year-old male employee with an undergraduate degree from Korea; he attended graduate school briefly, in both Korea and the US, in microbiology. He has been in the US for four years and worked in this store for about three and a half years.

Service encounters in this corpus vary widely both in length and in the types of talk they contain. They range from encounters that involve only a few words, and last just seconds, to interactions that last as long as seven minutes and cover such wide-ranging topics as customers' visits to Chicago, knee operations, and race relations. More common than these two extremes, however, are encounters like the following, in which an immigrant Korean woman of about 40 buys cigarettes:

Cash: *Annyŏng haseyo.*
'Hello/How are you?' ((Customer has just entered store.))
Cust: *Annyŏng haseyo.*
'Hello/How are you?'
Cust: *Tambae!*
'Cigarettes!'
Cash: *Tambae tŭryŏyo?*
'You would like cigarettes?' ((Cashier reaches for cigarettes under counter.))
Cash: *Yŏgi issŭmnida.*
'Here you are.' ((Cashier takes customer's money and hands her cigarettes; customer turns to leave.))
Cash: *Annyŏnghi kaseyo.*
'Good-bye.'
Cust: *Nye.*
'Okay.'

The basic communicative activities of this encounter are: (a) greetings or openings, (b) negotiation of the business exchange, and (c) closing of the encounter.

**Greetings,** as **"access rituals"** (Goffman 1971: 79), mark a transition to a period of heightened interpersonal access. In these stores, greetings typically occur as the customer passes through the doorway, unless the storekeeper is already busy serving another customer. Greetings in these circumstances include *Hi, Hello, How's it going, How are you?* – or, in Korean, *Annyŏng haseyo* 'Hello/How are you?'

The second basic activity is the negotiation of the business transaction, which includes such elements as naming the price of the merchandise brought to the counter by the customer, or counting out change as it is handed back to the customer. While explicit verbal greetings and closings do not occur in every recorded encounter, each contains a verbal negotiation of the transaction. The negotiation of the business exchange can be long and full of **adjacency pairs** (Schegloff & Sacks 1973) – involving, e.g., requests for a product from behind the counter, questions about a price, repairs (Schegloff et al. 1977), and requests or offers of a bag. Merritt calls these adjacency pairs **"couplets,"** and she gives a detailed structural flow chart (1976: 345) that shows the length and potential complexity of this phase of a service encounter.

The third and final activity of these encounters, the **closing,** often includes formulaic exchanges: *See you later, Take care, Have a good day*, or *Annyŏnghi kaseyo* 'Goodbye'. Frequently, however, the words used to close the negotiation of the business exchange also serve to close the entire encounter:

Cash: One two three four five ten twenty ((Counting back change.))
Cash: (Thank you/okay)
Cust: Alright

This type of encounter – limited to no more than greetings/openings, negotiation of the exchange, and closings – I call a SOCIALLY MINIMAL service encounter. The talk in it refers almost entirely to aspects of the business transaction, the exchange of goods for money; it does not include discussion of more sociable, interpersonal topics, e.g. experiences outside the store or the customer's unique personal relationship with the storekeeper.

However, many service encounters do NOT match this socially minimal pattern. SOCIALLY EXPANDED service encounters typically include the basic elements described above, but also include activities that highlight the interpersonal relationship between customers and storekeepers. These socially expanded encounters are characterized by practices that increase interpersonal involvement, i.e. involvement politeness strategies such as making jokes or small-talk, discussing personal experiences from outside the store, and explicitly referring to the personal relationship between customer and storekeeper.

The initiation of a social expansion of a service encounter is evident in the following excerpt. The African American customer has exchanged greetings with the Korean owner and cashier of the store; the cashier has retrieved the customer's habitual purchase, and begins to ring it up. The customer, however, then reframes the activity in which they are engaged, initiating (marked in boldface) a new activity – a personable discussion of his recent sojourn in Chicago – which lasts for several minutes.

Cash: That's it?
Cust: Tha:t's it ((Cashier rings up purchases.)) ((1.5))
Cust: **I haven't seen you for a while**
Cash: hehe Where <u>you</u> been
Cust: Chicago. ((Cashier bags purchase.))
Cash: Oh really?

The customer's comment *I haven't seen you for a while* instantiates and initiates a new type of activity and talk. The discussion of the customer's time in Chicago is a fundamentally different type of talk from that of socially minimal service encounters. Specifically, it is characterized by talk that is not directly tied to the execution of the business transaction at hand, but rather focuses on the ongoing relationship between the customer and storekeeper. Discussing the customer's trip to Chicago both indexes this personal relationship and, at the same time, contributes to its maintenance.

Such sharing of information helps constitute social categories and co-membership. To quote Sacks (1975: 72),

> Information varies as to whom it may be given to. Some matters may be told to a neighbor, others not; some to a best friend, others, while they may be told to a best friend, may only be told to a best friend after another has been told, e.g., a spouse.

In introducing talk of his trip to Chicago, the customer asserts **solidarity** with the cashier: they are co-members of a group who can not only exchange greetings and make business exchanges, but who can also talk about personal experiences far removed from the store.

This type of talk, which **indexes** and reinforces interpersonal relationships, distinguishes socially expanded service encounters from minimal ones. My data contain a wide range of such talk which enhances personal involvement. Specific practices include, among many others, talk about the weather and current events (*Some big hotel down in Hollywood, all the windows blew out*), jokes (*I need whiskey, no soda, I only buy whiskey*), references to commonly known third parties (*Mr. Choi going to have some ice?*), comments on interlocutors' demeanor (*What's the matter with you today?*), and direct assertions of desired intimacy (*I want you to know me.*).[2] Through their talk, customers and retailers create, maintain, or avoid intimacy and involvement with each other. These individual service encounters – an everyday form of contact between many African Americans and immigrant Koreans – are fundamental, discrete social activities that shape the nature and tenor of interethnic relations on a broader scale.

## Service Encounters Between Immigrant Koreans

Before examining immigrant Korean interaction with African Americans, I consider service encounters in which the customers as well as the storekeepers are immigrant Koreans. These Korean–Korean interactions provide a basis for comparison with African American encounters with Koreans. If, for example, the taciturnity and restraint of retailers in their interaction with African Americans were due solely to racism, one would expect to find retailers chatting and joking with their Korean customers and engaging in relatively long, intimate conversations.

In fact, the retailers in Korean–Korean encounters display the same taciturn, impersonal patterns of talk and behavior that they display with African American customers, even in the absence of linguistic and cultural barriers. The Korean–Korean interactions are even shorter and show less intimacy than the corresponding interactions with African American customers. Ten of the 13 service encounters with immigrant Korean customers were socially minimal, while only 3 of the 12 encounters with African Americans were socially minimal. Unlike their African American counterparts, immigrant Korean customers generally do not engage in practices through which they could display and develop a more personal relationship during the service encounter, e.g. making small talk or introducing personal topics. The example of a Korean woman buying cigarettes, transcribed above, is typical of encounters between Korean merchants and customers. Racism or disrespect are not necessarily reasons for what African Americans perceive as distant, laconic behavior in service encounters.[3]

I have no recorded data of service encounters involving African American store-owners with which to compare these encounters with immigrant Korean ones. I did, however, observe many interactions between African American customers and African American cashiers who were employed in stores owned by immigrant Koreans. Interactions between customers and such African American cashiers were consistently longer, and included more social expansions and affective involvement, than the corresponding encounters with immigrant Korean cashiers in the same stores.

Of the three socially expanded service encounters among immigrant Koreans, two involve personal friends of the cashier from contexts outside the store, and the third is with a child of about 10 years who is a regular customer at the store. According to Scollon & Scollon (1994: 137), the communicative behavior that East Asians display toward those whom they know and with whom they have an ongoing personal relationship ("insiders") differs drastically from the behavior displayed toward those in relatively anonymous service encounters ("outsiders"):

> One sees quite a different pattern [from "inside" encounters] in Asia when one observes "outside" or service relationships. These are the situations in which the participants are and remain strangers to each other, such as in taxis, train ticket sales, and banks. In "outside" (or nonrelational encounters) one sees a pattern which if anything is more directly informational than what one sees in the West. In fact, Westerners often are struck with the contrast they see between the highly polite and deferential Asians they meet in their business, educational, and governmental contacts and the rude, pushy, and aggressive Asians [by Western standards for subway-riding behavior] they meet on the subways of Asia's major cities.

In my data, service encounter communicative behavior among Korean adults could be predicted by the presence or absence of personal friendship from contexts outside the store. Socially expanded encounters with immigrant Korean adults occurred only when those adults were personal friends of the cashier, with whom he had contact outside the store. The cashier did not have a relationship with the child customer outside the store; but criteria for expanding encounters with children, and the nature of the expansions, may be different than for adults. In this case, the social expansion included a lecture to the child on the necessity of working long hours, and the child formally asked to be released from the interaction before turning to go.

Even in socially expanded service encounters among adult Korean friends, **interlocutors** may at times display a relatively high degree of restraint. For example, in the following segment, the cashier encounters a former roommate whom he has not seen in several years, who has by chance entered the store as a customer. The cashier and this customer had shared an apartment for two months in Los Angeles, more than three years prior to this encounter, and the customer had later moved away from Los Angeles.

When the customer enters the store, he displays no visible surprise or emotion at this chance encounter with his former roommate. He initially gives no reply to the cashier's repeated queries, "Where do you live?", and gazes away from the cashier as if nothing had been said. After being asked five times where he lives, he gives a relatively uninformative answer, "Where else but home?"

Cash: *Ŏ:!*
'He:y!' ((Recognizing customer who has entered store. Cashier reaches out and takes customer's hand. Customer pulls away and opens cooler door.)) ((3.0))
Cash: *Ŏdi sarŏ.*
'Where are you living?'
Cash: *Ŏ?*
'Huh?' ((7.0))
Cash: *Ŏdi sarŏ.*
'Where are you living?' ((.5))
Cash: *Ŏdi sarŏ.*
'Where are you living?' ((Cashier and customer stand at the counter across from each other.)) ((2.5))
Cash: *Ŏ?*
'Huh?' ((Customer gazes at display away from cashier. Cashier gazes at customer.))
Cash: *Ŏdi sarŏ::*
' C'mon, where are you living?' ((1.0))
Cust: ( )
Cash: *Ŏ?*
'Huh?' ((Cashier maintains gaze toward customer; customer continues to gaze at display.)) ((7.0))
Cash: *Ŏdi sanyanikka?*
'So, where are you living?' ((3.0))
Cust: *Ŏdi salgin, chibe salji.*
'Where else, but home?' ((1.0))
Cash: *Ŏ?*
'huh?'
Cash: *Chibi ŏdi nyago?*
'So where is your house?'

In this opening segment of transcript, the cashier has asked the customer six times where he lives – 10 times if the follow-up *Huh?'s* are included. The customer does not reveal to his former roommate where he lives, even as he stands three feet away from him, directly across the counter.

The customer's initial unresponsiveness in this encounter is striking by Western standards of conversational cooperation (Grice 1975). The cashier, however, does not seem to treat the customer's behavior as excessively uncooperative, e.g. by becoming angry or demanding an explanation for his interlocutor's lack of engagement. A Korean American consultant suggested that the customer's restraint was a sign not of disrespect, but of embarrassment (perhaps regarding his lack of career progress), which could explain the cashier's relative patience with uninformative responses.

This apparent resistance to engagement, however, is precisely the type of behavior cited by African Americans as insulting, and as evidence of racism on the part of immigrant Korean storekeepers:

> When I went in they wouldn't acknowledge me. Like if I'm at your counter and I'm looking at your merchandise, where someone would say "Hi, how are you today, is there anything I–" they completely ignored me. It was like they didn't care one way or the other.
>
> They wouldn't look at you at all. They wouldn't acknowledge you in any way. Nothing. You were nobody... They'd look over you or around you. (46-year-old African American woman)
>
> ...to me, many, not all, many of them perceive Blacks as a non-entity. We are treated as if we do not exist. (50-year-old African American male gift shop owner)

The customer's reluctance to acknowledge the cashier verbally or to respond to his questions – and the cashier's lack of anger at this – indicate that, at least in some situations, relatively dispassionate and impassive behavior is not interpreted by Koreans as insulting or disrespectful.

The taciturnity of the customer in this interaction, and of immigrant Korean storekeepers and customers more generally, is consistent with descriptions of the importance of *nunch'i* among Koreans – roughly 'perceptiveness', 'studying one's face', or 'sensitivity with eyes' (M. Park 1979, Yum 1987). It is a Korean interactional ideal to be able to understand an interlocutor with minimal talk, to be able to read the other's face and the situation without verbal reference. Speaking, and forcing the interlocutor to react, can be seen as an imposition: "to provide someone with something before being asked is regarded as true service since once having asked, the requester has put the other person in a predicament of answering 'yes' or 'no'" (Yum 1987: 80).

This ideal, of communicating and understanding without talk, is present in the two most important religio-philosophical traditions of Korea – Confucianism and Buddhism. Confucian education stresses reading and writing, rather than speaking. Talk cannot be entirely trusted and is held in relatively low regard:

> To read was the profession of scholars, to speak that of menials. People were warned that "A crooked gem can be straightened even by rubbing; but a single mistake in your speech cannot be corrected. There is no one who

> can chain your tongue. As one is liable to make a mistake in speech, fasten your tongue at all times. This is truly a profound and urgent lesson..." (Yum 1987: 79)

In Buddhism, communication through words is generally devalued: "there is a general distrust of communication, written or spoken, since it is incomplete, limited, and ill-equipped to bring out true meaning" (Yum 1987: 83). Enlightenment and understanding in Korean Buddhism is achieved internally, unmediated by explicit utterances: "The quest for wordless truth – this has been the spirit of Korean Buddhism, and it still remains its raison d'être" (Keel 1993: 19).

The data from service encounters presented here suggest that this cultural ideal, of understanding without recourse to words, exists not only in religio-philosophical traditions, but may extend in certain situations to ideals of behavior in everyday face-to-face interaction.

## SERVICE ENCOUNTERS BETWEEN IMMIGRANT KOREANS AND AFRICAN AMERICANS

As noted above, the service encounters with African American customers are characterized by more personal, sociable involvement and talk than the Korean–Korean encounters. While **social expansions** with Korean adult customers occurred only with personal friends of the cashier from contexts outside the store, only one of the nine African American customers in socially expanded encounters was friends with the cashier outside the store context.

Although the encounters with African Americans are longer and in many ways more intimate than the corresponding ones with Korean customers, close examination reveals consistently contrasting forms of participation in the service encounters. Overwhelmingly, it is the African American customers who make the conversational moves that make the encounters more than terse encounters focusing solely on the business transaction. Repeatedly, African American customers, unlike the immigrant Korean storekeepers and customers, treat the interaction not just as a business exchange, but as a sociable, interpersonal activity – by introducing topics for small-talk, making jokes, displaying affect in making assessments, and explicitly referring to the interpersonal relationship between cashier and customer.

Immigrant Korean retailers in these encounters are interactionally reactive, rather than proactive, in **co-constructing** conversation. Videotaped records reveal, for example, repeated instances where African American customers finish turns when discussing issues not related to the business transaction, and then re-initiate talk when no reply is forthcoming from the storekeepers. African American customers carry the burden of creating and maintaining the interpersonal involvement.

When immigrant Korean storekeepers do respond to talk, many responses display an understanding of **referential** content of utterances – but no alignment with the emotional stance, of the customer's talk, e.g. humor or indignation. Consider the reaction to ASSESSMENTS, i.e. evaluative statements that show one's personal alignment toward a phenomenon (Goodwin & Goodwin 1992). These are not met by storekeepers with second-assessments of agreement. When they do respond to assessments with affect, e.g. smiling at a customer's joke and subsequent laughter, their displayed levels of affect and interpersonal involvement are typically not commensurate with those of the customers.

The relative restraint of storekeepers in interaction with African American customers is not only a function of cultural preference for socially minimal service encounters and situated, interactional restraint; it also reflects limited English proficiency. It is more difficult to make small-talk, to joke, or to get to know the details of a customer's life if communication is difficult. Restraint politeness can be expressed by NOT using the **verbal channel**, i.e. silence; but involvement politeness requires more complex verbal activities – e.g. using in-group identity markers, showing interest in the other's interests, and joking.

The **phonological, morphological**, and **syntactic** differences between Korean, an **Altaic** language, and English, an **Indo-European** one, make it difficult to achieve fluency, and store-owners have limited opportunities for study. Even among those who have been in America for 20 years, many cannot understand English spoken at native speed, and many express embarrassment about speaking it because of limited proficiency.[4]

Videotaped records of interaction do NOT reveal constant hostility and confrontations between immigrant Korean retailers and African American customers; this finding is consistent with many hours of observation in stores. Some relationships, particularly those between retailers and regular customers, are overtly friendly: customers and storekeepers greet each other, engage in some small talk, and part amicably. Observation and videotape do not reveal the stereotype of the inscrutably silent, non-greeting, gaze-avoiding, and non-smiling Korean storekeepers which were cited by African Americans in media accounts and in interviews with me. However, videotaped records do reveal subtle but consistent differences between African Americans and immigrant Koreans in the forms of talk and behavior in service encounters. These differences, when interpreted through culture-specific frameworks, can contribute to and reinforce pejorative stereotypes of store-owners as unfriendly and racist, and of customers as selfish and poorly bred.

In the following section I detail these differences in interactional patterns in transcripts of two socially expanded service encounters. The first interaction is with a middle-aged African American man who is a regular at the store. The cashier was able to identify him immediately on videotape in a follow-up interview; he said that the customer had been coming to the store two or three times a week for at least three and a half years. This encounter shows notably good and comfortable relations, typical of encounters with regular customers, but at the same time it displays the asymmetrical pattern of involvement described above. The second interaction is a much longer one that occurs with a 54-year-old customer who is new to the area and the store, and who may be under the influence of alcohol at the time. Contrasting forms of participation are particularly evident in this second interaction.

### Encounter 1

In this interaction, a neatly dressed African American man in his 40s, carrying a cellular phone, comes into the store to buy a soda and some liquor. He is a regular at the store, but at the time of videotaping he had been away in Chicago for a month. The cashier is behind the counter, and the store-owner is standing amid displays in the middle of the store. The store-owner, about 40, has been in America for 20 years. He received his undergraduate degree from the University of California, Los Angeles; he studied math and computer science, he told me, because his English was not good enough for other subjects. He is more outgoing and talkative with customers than most of the storekeepers of his age, or older, who were observed.

Following greetings, the customer begins to treat the activity not just as a business transaction, but as an opportunity to be sociable, e.g. by introducing personal narratives about his long absence from Los Angeles and his experiences in Chicago:

((Customer enters store and goes to soda cooler.))
Cust: [Hi ]
Own: [How ar]e you?
((Customer takes soda toward cash register and motions toward displays.)) ((7.5))
Cust: Wow you guys moved a lot of things around
Cash: Hello:, ((Cashier stands up from where he was hidden behind the counter.))
Cash: Heh heh
Cash: How are you? ((Cashier retrieves customer's liquor and moves toward register))
Cust: What's going on man? ((Cashier gets cup for customer's liquor.)) ((.8))
Cust: How've you been?
Cash: Sleeping
Cust: eh heh heh ((1.8))
Cash: That's it?
Cust: Tha:t's it ((Cashier rings up purchases.)) ((1.5))
Cust: I haven't seen you for a while
Cash: hehe Where you been
Cust: Chicago. ((Cashier bags purchase.))
Cash: Oh really?
Cust: [yeah]
Cash: [How] long?
Cust: For about a month ((1.2))
Cash: How's there.
Cust: Co:l'!
Cash: [Co:ld?]
Cust: [heh ] heh heh heh
Own: Is Chicago cold?
Cust: u::h! ((lateral headshakes)) ((1.4)) man I got off the plane and walked out the airport I said "Oh shit."
Cust: heh heh heh
Own: I thought it's gonna be nice spring season over there
Cust: Well not now this is about a month– I been there– I was there for about a month but you know (.) damn ((lateral headshakes))
((Customer moves away from cash register toward owner.)) ((1.4))
Cust: Too co:l'
Cust: I mean this was really cold
Own: (They have snowy) season there
Cust: I've known it to snow on Easter Sunday ((.))
Cust: Alright this Sunday it'll be Easter ((.))
Cust: I've seen it snow Easter Sunday
((15-second discussion, not clearly audible, in which the owner asks if there are mountains in Chicago, and the customer explains that there are not.))
Cust: See th– this– California weather almost never changes.
Cust: ((Spoken slowly and clearly as for non-native speaker.)) back there it's a seasonal change, you got fall, winter, spring
Own: mm hm
Cust: You know
Cust: But back there the weather sshhh ((lateral headshake))
Cust: It's cold up until June
Cust: I mean these guys like they– they wearing lon:g john:s from September until June
Own: (It's hot season, June)
Cust: He– here it's hot, but there it's ((lateral headshake))
Cust: (Really ) ((Customer moves toward exit.))
Own: Kay [see you later]
Cust: [see you later]
Cust: Nice talking to you

Although this customer has come into the store to buy a soda and liquor, he also displays interest in chatting, particularly about his sojourn in Chicago and the climate there. After the initial greetings, he comments on how much the store displays have changed: *Wow you guys moved a lot of things around*. This comment is consistent with the fact that he's been away; it provides an opening for a reply such as *We moved those a long time ago*, or another such comment that would display acknowledgment that the customer hasn't been in the store for some time. But neither cashier nor owner responds to his comment. The customer's use of the present perfect tense (*How've you been?*) – as opposed to present tense (*How are you?* or *How ya doing?*) – draws attention to the fact that he hasn't had contact with these storekeepers for a period of time beginning in the past and ending as he speaks; again this invites discussion of the fact that he hasn't been to the store for an unusually long time. The cashier answers the question *How've you been?* with *Sleeping*, treating it as referring to the present. The English present perfect tense is expressed with a past tense form in Korean, and may have led the cashier to interpret the question as a form of present tense.

The cashier places the customer's habitually preferred liquor on the counter without the customer's requesting the item. In doing so, the cashier, without talk, shows that he knows the customer, at least his business exchange habits. As the cashier rings up the purchase, the customer again uses the present perfect tense, indexing his relatively long absence from the store, commenting: *I haven't seen you for a while.* This comment not only indexes his long absence from the store, but draws the cashier into conversation. The comment is typically made by a person who has remained in one place while another has left and come back. In this case there is no indication that the cashier has been away. In fact, as an immigrant Korean working in a liquor store, he probably spends 80 or more hours a week in the store, up to 52 weeks each year.

The customer's seeming reversal of roles – speaking as if the cashier, rather than he, had been away – has the function, however, of drawing the cashier into conversation. The customer does not simply introduce the topic he wants to discuss; he compels the cashier to ask him about the topic. If the customer had simply stated, *I've been in Chicago for a month and it was cold*, his audience could simply have nodded and acknowledged it. Instead the speaker chooses an interactional strategy that compels a question from his interlocutors, increasing interpersonal involvement.

The customer's delivery displays a relatively high level of affective personal involvement: he uses profanity (*Oh shit*), falsetto voice, hyperbole (*they wearing long johns from September until June*), elements of African American English syntax (*they wearing*) and phonology (*col'*), and relatively high-volume laughter. The cashier and owner, however, do not display such a high level of affective personal involvement in the interaction, even through channels which are not dependent on linguistic proficiency. They do not laugh during the encounter, for example, and the owner is looking down unsmiling when the customer recounts his reaction (*Oh shit*) when getting off the plane in Chicago.

This disparity in levels of personal involvement is particularly apparent as the customer makes repeated assessments that display his alignment toward the weather in Chicago. According to Goodwin & Goodwin (1992: 166),

> this alignment can be of some moment in revealing such significant attributes of the actor as his or her taste and the way in which he or she evaluates the phenomena he or she perceives. It is therefore not surprising that displaying congruent understanding can be an issue of some importance to the participants.

Assessments provide a locus for interlocutors to show a common understanding and orientation through verbal and/or non-verbal markers of agreement with the assessment. Even when an individual has little knowledge of the referent of an assessment, positive response to the assessment will show emotional understanding and alignment with the assessor.

Explicit practices for displaying this alignment are highly developed among African Americans in the interactional pattern of "call-and-response," in which one actor's words or actions receive an immediate, often overlapping, response and confirmation from others (Smitherman 1977). Call-and-response marks involvement and congruent understanding with explicit vocal and non-verbal acts. Responses that **overlap** the caller's action are not seen as disrespectful interruptions, but rather as a means of displaying approval and of bringing caller and responder closer together.

While most often studied in formal performances – e.g. concerts, speeches, or sermons – relatively animated **back-channel responses** also characterize everyday talk of (and particularly among) many African Americans. Smitherman (1977: 118) points out that differing expectations and practices of back-channel responses can lead to the breakdown of interethnic communication:

> "call-response" can be disconcerting to both parties in black–white communication... When the black person is speaking, the white person... does not obviously engage in the response process, remaining relatively passive, perhaps voicing an occasional subdued "Mmmmmmhhm." Judging from the white individual's seeming lack of involvement, the black communicator gets the feeling that the white isn't listening... the white person gets the feeling that the black person isn't listening, because he "keeps interrupting and turning his back on me."

In the encounter under consideration, the storekeepers display little reaction to the customer's assessments – much less animated, overlapping responses. The customer makes repeated assessments of the extreme cold of Chicago, e.g. *Co:l'!; Oh shit; damn; Too col'; this was really cold; back there the weather sshhh; it's cold up until June; they wearing lon:g john:s from September until June*; and *there it's* [lateral headshake]. The cashier smiles at the customer's *Oh shit* and immediately succeeding laughter, but other assessments get no such show of appreciation. The owner's responses to these dramatic assessments tend toward checks of facts: *Is Chicago cold?; I thought it's gonna be nice spring season over there*; and *It's hot season, June.* The Korean storekeepers show little appreciation for the cold of Chicago, thereby failing to align themselves and display solidarity with the customer making these assessments.

Following two of these assessments (*co:l'* and *I got off the plane and walked out the airport I said "Oh shit"*), the customer laughs. According to Jefferson (1979: 93),

> Laughter can be managed as a sequence in which speaker of an utterance invites recipient to laugh and recipient accepts that invitation. One technique for inviting laughter is the placement, by speaker, of a laugh just at completion of an utterance, and one technique for accepting

> that invitation is the placement, by recipient, of a laugh just after onset of speaker's laughter.

The customer's laughter following his utterances matches this pattern precisely, but cashier and owner do not accept the invitation to laugh. Not only do they fail to accept the invitation to laugh, but the owner actively declines the invitation to laugh. He does this not through silence, which would allow the speaker to pursue recipient laughter further, but by responding to the customer's laughter with serious talk of facts, i.e. the temperature in Chicago: *Is Chicago cold?* and *I thought it's gonna be nice spring season over there.* As Jefferson says,

> In order to terminate the relevance of laughter, recipient must actively decline to laugh. One technique for declining a postcompletion invitation to laugh is the placement of speech, by recipient, just after onset of speaker's laughter, that speech providing serious pursuit of topic as a counter to the pursuit of laughter.

The owner's response to the customer's invitation to laugh serves as an effective counter to the invitation.

Finally, the customer's comment upon leaving (*Nice talking to you*) suggests his attitude toward this service encounter: it wasn't just an encounter about doing a business transaction, it was a time to enjoy talking personally and make connections to people. Such an attitude is consistent with observations and videotaped records, which show African American customers consistently engaging in a relatively high degree of sociable, interpersonal interaction in service encounters.

The customer's parting comment, *Nice talking to you*, has no equivalent in Korean. The closest expression might be *sugo haseo*, which has a literal meaning close to 'Keep up the good work,' but is used to mean 'Thank you and goodbye'. Reference to work may serve as a more appropriate social currency ('Keep up the good work') than reference to talk ('Nice talking to you'), consistent with cultural ideals of relative taciturnity in service encounters.

This asymmetrical pattern of interaction occurs despite apparent attempts by both parties to accommodate to the perceived style or linguistic proficiency of the other. Both cashier and owner, for example, make repeated inquiries about the customer's trip to Chicago (*How long?; How's there.*) and the weather there (*Is Chicago cold?; They have snowy season there*). Showing interest in one's interlocutor's interests is a basic form of involvement politeness (Brown & Levinson 1987: 103), and one that is absent in the encounters between immigrant Koreans that do not involve intimate friends or children. The cashier and owner are adopting a relatively involved style. The customer also appears to adapt his speech behavior to his interlocutors, in this case for non-native speakers. He explains and repeats his assessments after they draw no second-assessment of agreement (*I've known it to snow on Easter Sunday... Alright this Sunday it'll be Easter... I've seen it snow Easter Sunday*); and he shifts to a slow and enunciated register to explain the seasonal weather of Chicago (*back there it's a seasonal change, you got fall, winter, spring*). Thus both parties **accommodate** to the other, narrowing differences in communication patterns; but the accommodation is not necessarily of the type or degree that can be appreciated by the other, to result in a more synchronous, symmetrical interaction.

## Encounter 2

This second encounter of a Korean immigrant shop-owner and cashier with an African American customer is much longer, lasting about 7 minutes, with distinct episodes – including two instances when the customer moves to the exit as if to leave, and then returns to re-initiate conversation. Five excerpts from the encounter are presented and discussed.

The customer's talk and communicative behavior are in sharp contrast to that of immigrant Korean customers. He not only engages in interactional practices that increase interpersonal involvement, e.g. talk of personal topics; he also explicitly states that he wants the storekeepers to know him, and he pledges extreme solidarity with them – e.g. he tells them to call him to their aid if their store is threatened in future "riots." His interaction with the storekeepers suggests that he has different ideas about the relationship between customers and storekeepers than do immigrant Koreans, and different ideas about the corresponding service encounter style.

This customer's explicit expressions of solidarity and intimacy with the storekeepers are matched with an interactional style that includes many of the characteristics – e.g. relatively high volume, volubility, and use of profanity – that immigrant Korean retailers have characterized as disrespectful (Ella Stewart 1989, 1991, Bailey 1996). While this customer's interactional style is "emotionally intense, dynamic, and demonstrative" (Kochman 1981: 106), relative to most of the African American customers at this Koreatown store, it shares many features with the style regularly observed in stores in low-income South Central Los Angeles.

The customer, a male in his 50s, has visited the store just once before, the previous night. He is accompanied by his nephew, who does not speak during the encounter. The customer is wearing a warm-up suit and has sunglasses resting on top of his head. His extreme expressions of co-membership with the storekeepers as he talks to them, along with the jerkiness of some of his arm motions, suggest that he may have been drinking. It is not uncommon for customers at mom-and-pop liquor stores to display signs of alcohol use when they are at the store. This customer's speech is not slurred, however, and he does not appear to be unsteady on his feet.

This new customer arrives at the store speaking to his nephew at relatively high volume. The encounter proceeds as a socially minimal service encounter until the African American customer, following the pattern described above, reframes the activity by introducing a personal topic from outside the store context (his recent move to the area) and referring to his personal relationship with the cashier:

((Customer arrives talking to his companion, who is later identified as his nephew.))

Cust: ( ) thirty-seven years old (in this) ass

Cust: Motherfucker ((1.0))

Cash: Hi ((Customer approaches counter.)) ((.2))

Cust: How's it going partner? euh ((Cashier nods.)) ((1.0))

Cust: You got them little bottles?

Cash: (eh) ((Customer's gaze falls on the little bottles.)) ((3.5))

Cust: One seventy-fi:ve! ((Customer gazes at display of bottles.)) ((2.0))

Cust: You ain't got no bourbon? ((1.2))

Cash: No: we don't have bourbon ((1.0))

Cust: I'll get a beer then.

Cust: ((turns to nephew)) What would you like to drink? what do you want? ((Customer selects beverages and brings them to the cash register.)) ((7.5))

Cash: Two fifty ((Cashier rings up purchase and bags beer.)) ((4.5))

Cust: I just moved in the area. I talked to you the other day. You [remember me]?

Cash: [Oh yesterday ] last night

Cust: Yeah

Cash: [(O:h yeah ) ] ((Cashier smiles and nods.))

Cust: [Goddamn, shit] [then you don't- ]

Own: [new neighbor, huh?] ((Customer turns halfway to the side toward the owner.))

Cust: Then you don't know me

Cash: [(I know you ) ] ((Cashier gets change at register.))

Cust: [I want you to know] me so when I walk in here you'll know me. I smoke Winstons. Your son knows me

Cash: [Ye::ah]

Cust: [The yo]ung guy

Cash: There you go ((Cashier proffers change.))

Cust: [Okay then]

Cash: [Three four] five ten ((Cashier steps back from counter.))

The interaction with the storekeepers proceeds as a socially minimal service encounter until the customer volunteers personal information about himself (*I just moved in the area*) and raises the history of his relationship with the cashier (*I talked to you the other day. You remember me?*). Although the cashier shows that he remembers the customer (*Oh yesterday, last night*), the customer continues as if the cashier didn't know or remember him. The customer's *goddamn, shit.... then you don't know me* is spoken at high volume, but with a smile, suggesting humor rather than anger.

Though the cashier acknowledges having seen the customer before, his turns are oriented toward completing the transaction. Except for the words *last night*, his acknowledgments of this customer's history with the store (*Oh yeah, I know you, Yeah*) are spoken in overlap with the customer's words, and only in response to the customer's assertions.

The customer does not acknowledge it when the cashier shows that he remembers him. Perhaps the recognition does not count when it requires prompting (*Then you don't know* me), but rather must be done immediately and spontaneously. The customer then explicitly states that he wants the cashier and the owner to know him (he moves his gaze back and forth between them): *I want you to know me so when I walk in here you'll know me. I smoke Winstons. Your son knows me*. This customer is concerned with the storekeepers "knowing" him: he wants them to know him now and on future store visits, and he finds it worth noting that one of the other employees (*your son*) already knows him.

Knowing a customer's habitual purchases and brand preferences (e.g. Winstons) is one way of "knowing" the customer, and storekeepers frequently ready a customer's cigarettes or liquor without being asked; minimally, this customer wants to be known in this way. Subsequent talk, however, suggests that "knowing" him will involve a more personal, intimate relationship, and one that involves specific types of talk and behavior.

The data presented here suggest that immigrant Korean retailers and African American customers have differing notions of what it means to "know" someone in a convenience store context, and differing ideas about the kinds of speech activities entailed by "knowing" someone in this context. Different ideas about what it means to know someone may apply not just to service encounters, as described above, but to any encounter between relative strangers. Thus M. Park (1979: 82) suggests that, by Western standards, Koreans are restrained and impersonal with those who are not intimate friends or part of a known group:

> The age-old cliché, "Koreans are the most courteous people in the East" is rather rightly applied only to inter-personal interaction among ingroups or hierarchical groups. Koreans tend to be [by Western standards] impolite or even rude when they interact with outgroups like outsiders or strangers. Everyone outside the ingroup is likely to be treated with curiosity or caution or even a bit of suspicion...

It may be difficult for these storekeepers to extend what for them is an intimate communicative style to a relative stranger.

In America, many communicative activities – e.g. greetings, smiles, and small-talk – occur in interactions both with friends and with relative strangers. The communicative style extended to both strangers and friends relatively emphasizes the expression of casual solidarity and explicit recognition of personal details.

> Personal treatment in American life includes use of the first name, recognition of biographical details and acknowledgements of specific acts, appearances,

> preferences and choices of the individual. Cultural models are given by salesmen and airline hostesses. Their pleasant smiles, feigned and innocuous invasions of privacy, "kidding" and swapping of personal experiences constitute stereotypes of personal behavior... Signs of friendship, the glad handshake, the ready smile, the slap on the back... have become part of the normal way of behavior. (Edward Stewart 1972: 55, 58)

Everyday speech behavior among strangers in America includes practices that would be reserved for talk among relative intimates in Korea.

Such differing assumptions about appropriate communicative style in service encounters, and about the relationship between customer and server, may underlie the contrasting forms of participation in the encounter under consideration. When the customer states that he wants the storekeepers to know him, the cashier's *Yeah* and subsequent *There you go*, as he hands back change, fail to engage the topic of knowing the customer. The cashier is reframing the activity as a business transaction, specifically the closing of the business negotiation component, and perhaps the entire encounter. The return and counting of change (*There you go; Three four five ten*) is used in many service encounters as a way of closing not only the business negotiation, but also the entire interaction.

The customer however, does not treat this as the end of the encounter. Instead, he treats this as a time to discuss details of his life outside the store:

Cust: And then I– I've got three months to be out here.
Cash: How's [here ] ((Cashier steps back from counter and gazes down.))
Cust: [I'm going] to school
Cash: How's here
Cust: I'm going to– (.2) locksmith school
Cash: Oh really
Cust: Yeah. so after that– because I had a (.) knee operation ((Customer rolls up pant leg to show scars.)) ((4.2))
Cust: I had a total knee so my company is retiring my– old black ass at fifty-four ((Customer smiles and gazes at owner.)) ((.6))
Own: (mmh) ((Owner shakes his head laterally and gazes away from the customer.))
Cust: And they give me some money
Cash: Huh ((Cashier bares his teeth briefly in a smile.))
Cust: So I'm spending my money at your store on liquor heh heh heh heh hah hah hah hah hah ((Customer laughs animatedly, turning toward the owner who does not smile, but who continues lateral headshakes as he takes a few steps to the side.))
Own: You still can work?

The business exchange has been completed, and the customer initiates discussion of a series of personal topics. He volunteers how long he will be in Los Angeles, what he is doing there, details of his medical history, and his current employment status. He goes so far as to roll up his pant-leg to show the scars from his knee replacement operation. He has said that he wants these storekeepers to "know" him, and he's giving them some of the information they need to know him. In doing so he is treating them as co-members of an intimate group, i.e. the circle of people who can see his knee scars, even though by some standards they are virtual strangers. The customer is treating the social distance between himself and the storekeepers as small; his interactional style increases involvement between him and the storekeepers.

The cashier's talk displays some interest in the interaction, e.g. his initial query *How's here* displays understanding of the customer's statement (*I've got three months to be out here*) and invites further comment. The customer, however, does not answer the question. The non-standard form *How's here* (for 'How do you like it here?') may not have been understood by the customer, and comprehension may have been further hindered by the cashier's non-verbal actions. During the first *How's here*, the cashier's arm is in front of his face, and his gaze is not on the customer; during the second, he's shifting his weight to lean on a counter to the side. The even intonation contour of *How's here* may also prevent the customer from realizing that a question is being asked. Even when a storekeeper expresses involvement in an interaction, his or her limited English proficiency may prevent the customer from understanding the expression of interest.

The customer concludes this introduction with a joke that stresses the humorous nature of his relationship with the liquor store owners: he is sharing the proceeds from his disability payments with them. His smile and laughter at this situation are an invitation to his audience to share in his laughter (Jefferson 1979). The store-owner and cashier fail to join in this laughter; the cashier displays a fleeting, stiff smile, and the owner none at all. Not only do cashier and owner fail to accept the invitation to laughter, but as in the previous encounter, the owner, through his subsequent question, ACTIVELY DECLINES the invitation to laughter. His question *You still can work?* is a serious pursuit of a topic that effectively counters the customer's pursuit of laughter. The question proves his comprehension of the customer's prior talk, but displays no **affective alignment** or solidarity with the customer's humor. Even though the store-owner can understand the referential content of the words, he does not participate in the interactional activity of laughing – the preferred response to the customer's laughter.

It is also, of course, possible that the owner is displaying a dispreferred response because he does NOT want to display alignment: perhaps he thinks that people take advantage of social programs when they could support themselves through their own work – a sentiment voiced in interviews with immigrant Korean retailers in a variety of forms. This active declination to laugh, however, also occurs in my data during talk about morally less sensitive topics, e.g. the weather, with both African American and Korean customers; this suggests a pattern of declining invitations to laughter that is unrelated to personal opinions about the topic at hand.

In the next two minutes of talk and interaction (not transcribed here), the customer gets change for a five-dollar bill, and then explains to the owner that his former employer doesn't want him to work for fear that they would have to redo his knee operation if he resumed work. The customer takes his bag of purchases from the counter, and moves to the door as if to leave (the owner says *See ya*); but he stops in the doorway, then re-enters the store to resume talking. He discusses the exact amount of money he receives per month for his disability, compares it to the amount of money he made previously, and reiterates that if he goes to work now, his disability benefits will be cut off.

In the next segment, transcribed below, the customer explains that he is being re-trained for a new job. He begins to depart, and then once again returns from the threshold of the exit door to re-initiate talk:

Cust: So I gotta get another trade. Just like if you get hurt in the liquor store business, you gotta go get another trade. So I gotta go get another trade. For them to pay me the money. So I'm gonna get another trade. But then like– after I get another trade they pay me (a sum) a lump sum of money? And I'm gonna do what I wanna do. ((.8))
Cust: They only gonna give me about sixty or seventy thousand. ((1.4))
Cust: Plus– my schooling– ((1.0))
Cust: So:– I got to take it easy for a little bit. ((Customer moves toward exit.))
Cust: That's why I'm gonna buy enough of your liquor (so I can take it)
Own: Alright, take care
Cust: Okay ((Customer pauses in doorway.))

This segment is characterized by dramatically asymmetrical contributions to the interaction. Not only does the customer do most of the talking, but there is a noticeable absence of response to his statements. He gives up his turn at talk five times in this short segment, but receives a verbal response only once. The customer only gets verbal collaboration, in this segment, in leaving the store – which suggests that these storekeepers may be more proficient at closing interactions with customers than they are at sociable, personal discussion with them.

The lack of verbal response to the customer's talk is particularly noteworthy because he is making statements that invite easy responses. The fact that he's going to get a lump sum of money and *do what I wanna do* makes relevant such questions as: *How much are you going to get?* or *What are you going to do when you get the money?* The amount of money he's going to get (*sixty or seventy thousand*) similarly invites comment, e.g. *That's great*, or *That's a lot of money*, or again, *What are you going to do with it?* The customer's *Plus my schooling* invites questions about the details of the schooling, beyond the fact (stated earlier) that it's locksmith school. The customer's reference to buying *enough of your liquor* also provides an opening for storekeeper recognition of his patronage, e.g. *We appreciate your business.* The silence of the storekeepers displays restraint, but not interest or involvement.

The immigrant Korean storekeepers' lack of overt response to the customer's talk forms a stark contrast with the African American pattern of call-and-response described above. Smitherman (1977: 108) emphasizes the importance of responding to a speaker, regardless of the form of the response: "all responses are 'correct'; the only 'incorrect' thing you can do is not respond at all." By this standard, the storekeepers' lack of response is inappropriate.

In the next segment, although the customer has once again moved to the door, and the owner has said goodbye, the customer re-enters the store and more talk follows. After learning the storekeepers' names, the customer invokes the events of April 1992. He tells the store-owners that he will come to their aid if they have problems in the future, and goes on to discuss his philosophy of race relations:

Cust: What's your name? ((Customer re-enters store and approaches the owner.))
Own: Han Choi ((.6))
Cust: Han? ((Customer shakes hands with the owner.)) ((1.2))
Cust: What's your name? ((Customer shakes cashier's hand.))
Cash: Shin
Cust: Chin?
Cash: No. [Shin ]
Cust: [Okay] (.) Shin?
Cash: Yeah
Own: What's yours (then)?
Cust: Larry
Own: Larry
Cust: I'm a gangsta from Chicago, Larry Smith. Anybody fuck with you, this black– I seen them riots and things. and they was fucking up with the Korean stores and the– and the what's his name stores? And I was in Vietnam and everything like that
Own: [(Our) neighbors friendly (here)]
Cust: [Well– (.) well let me ] tell you something– nobody fuck with your store, if I catch 'em making fuck with your store (.) you just ca:ll me: dow:n
Own: Alright
Cust: I:'ll fuck 'em up ((Customer reaches out and shakes the owner's hand; the owner's arm is limp and he is pulled off balance by the handshake.)) ((.8))
Cust: Because I believe in people not Koreans, not Blacks, not Whites, not this, I believe in people. ((.4))
Cust: Right there. ((Customer taps the owner on the chest twice, in rhythm with the two words *right there*))

The customer, who has created and emphasized solidarity with the storekeepers throughout their interaction, continues to reinforce his solidarity and co-membership with them. After learning their names and shaking their hands – an act of physical intimacy – he makes two explicit assertions of solidarity.

His initial assertion of solidarity is dramatic: he promises with high volume and affect that he will respond to their call for help, and "fuck up" anyone who is harming them or their store. He has seen the havoc of Los Angeles in April 1992 on TV; but he is a Vietnam veteran, so he has the capacity to deal with such events. The storekeepers' enemies are his enemies; he and the storekeepers are co-members of an intimate group, a group whose members will risk harm to protect each other.

He reiterates this sentiment of solidarity by explaining his readiness to act on their behalf based on his personal philosophy: *Because I believe in people not Koreans, not Blacks, not Whites.* Social distance between him and these storekeepers is low; race is not a barrier. He emphasizes his intimacy with the store-owner by tapping him on the chest, once more making physical contact, and citing this specific store-owner as an example of the people in whom he has faith.

Following the segment transcribed above, there are two minutes of talk (not transcribed here) during which the customer discusses his beliefs about the basic sameness of people, regardless of race, and his criticisms of those who make society racist. The customer utters more than 10 words for each of the store-owner's words during this period. The service encounter comes to an end with the following turns:

((The customer speaks with high volume and animation, and sounds almost angry during these penultimate two turns. He is gesticulating so strongly that his sunglasses become dislodged from atop his head and he has to reposition them as he talks.))

Cust: Okay what I'm saying is (.) if you throw five kids (in the middle of the floor) and don't tell them what they are nothing like that they just grow up to be people ((.))

Cust: They don't even know (.) that they Black. they don't even know they Korean they don't know that they White they don't know this and that. It have to be an old person like you or me, George Washington and all these motherfuckers. Martin Luther King and all these motherfuckers.

((The customer has begun moving toward the exit. His vocal register shifts suddenly to one of low volume and affect for his final turn. He gazes first at the owner and then the cashier as he waves goodbye.))

Cust: Anyway– have a good day.

Own: Later ((Customer turns and exits.))

As this interaction progresses, the storekeepers become more and more reticent while the customer becomes more and more outspoken. Although the customer has dominated the talk throughout the interaction, his volume and affect level get higher as it progresses, and he holds the floor an ever higher proportion of the time. In the final two minutes of talk, the customer is literally following the owner from place to place in the store, leaning over the shorter man, and repeatedly touching him on the chest as he makes his points.

This asymmetry in participation occurs despite apparent efforts at accommodation by both customer and storekeepers. Thus the storekeepers ask more questions that display interest in the customer – *How's here; You still can work?* – than they ask of non-intimate adult Korean customers. The customer adapts his speech for non-natives, e.g. by using an example to explain his job retraining (*Just like if you get hurt in the liquor store business, you gotta go get another trade*); and he introduces a topic that might be of particular interest to them, e.g. Los Angeles civil unrest that could threaten their store. As in the first encounter, however, the mutual accommodation may not be of the degree or type that can be fully appreciated by the other party, or can result in more symmetrical participation in the encounter.

Mismatch in politeness orientations can have a self-reinforcing, spiraling effect that exaggerates differences in politeness style as interaction continues; this can exacerbate misunderstandings and mutual negative evaluations. The more this African American customer cheerfully talks and stresses his camaraderie with the store-owner, the more the retailer withdraws and declines involvement. This may be a more general phenomenon in interethnic communication. Borrowing a term from Bateson, 1972 Tannen (1981: 138) concludes that speakers from backgrounds with contrasting linguistic practices frequently respond to each other in "complementary schismogenetic fashion"; i.e., "the verbal devices used by one group cause speakers of the other group to react by intensifying the opposing behavior, and vice versa."

Since, for many African Americans the nature of good and respectful service encounter relations involves relatively great personal involvement, this customer may be redoubling his efforts to create solidarity as he encounters the retailers' increasing reticence. For the store-owner, the appropriate response to a customer's increasing intimacy may be the silence or avoidance that demonstrates restraint. In this instance, the pattern does not escalate out of control. The owner maintains a degree of engagement, although he appears uncomfortable at times; and the customer does not react as if he is being ignored, although his increasing affect as the interaction proceeds may well be related to the low level of response he gets from the storekeepers.

However, this self-escalating cycle may contribute to confrontations that have occurred elsewhere. Media and informant accounts of confrontations between retailers and African Americans often stress the seeming suddenness with which storekeepers, perceived to be inscrutably impassive, suddenly explode in anger at customers. As customers persist in behaviors that the retailer perceives as invasive, the storekeeper will remain silent; the customer will not know that he or she is doing something that the storekeeper finds inappropriate, and will increase the intensity of the involvement behaviors in reaction to the restraint of storekeepers. When the weight of the trespass against sensibilities becomes too grave, the store-owner will feel justified in lashing out (Kochman 1981: 118, 1984: 206). Conversely, the increasingly restrained behavior of store-owners, as customers express ever-greater friendliness, can lead to customer outbursts and accusations of storekeeper racism. Storekeepers report repeated instances in which customers have suddenly (and to the storekeepers, inexplicably) accused them of being racists.

## Conclusion

Divergent practices for displaying respect in service encounter interaction are an ongoing cause of tension between immigrant Korean retailers and their African American customers. The two groups have different concepts of the relationship between customer and storekeeper, and different ideas about the speech activities that are appropriate in service encounters. The talk of immigrant Koreans focuses almost exclusively on the business transaction at hand, while the talk of African American customers includes efforts toward more personal, sociable interaction.

The interactional patterns that are apparent in videotaped records are consistent with data that come from dozens of hours of observation in various stores, and from interviews with storeowners, customers, and consultants. The seeming avoidance of involvement on the part of immigrant Koreans is frequently seen by African Americans as the disdain and arrogance of racism. The relative stress on interpersonal involvement among African Americans in service encounters is typically perceived by immigrant Korean retailers as a sign of selfishness, interpersonal imposition, or poor breeding (Bailey 1996).

The focus of this article on miscommunication should not be taken to mean that immigrant Korean merchants and African American customers can never communicate effectively, or never have friendly relationships. The overwhelming majority of African American customers and immigrant Korean retailers that I observed get along, and relationships between retailers and regular customers (40–80% of the clientele at stores I visited) are often very positive. Retailers often know regular customers' family members and other details of their lives; and many retailers engage in friendly small-talk with such customers, even when limited English proficiency makes it difficult. This type of relationship, which often results only after longer contact, can change mutual perceptions, as described by an African American woman in her 50s:

> I find that they shy away from you until you get to know them. Like this lady, the Korean store, I've been in the neighborhood for years and years, and she's friendly with everybody cause she knows everybody but when they don't know you, they're shy, and you think they're prejudice. They might be, but you just have to get to know them. They're nice people once you get to know them.

This article has focused on one source of interethnic tensions: miscommunication due to cultural and linguistic differences. Socio-historical conditions – e.g. social, economic, and racial inequality – are also clearly sources of tensions between African Americans and immigrant Korean storekeepers. Within a social and historical context, however, there are specific linguistic and cultural practices that can ameliorate or exacerbate tensions between groups. The goal of this essay has been to shed light on communicative processes that can lead to tensions between groups in face-to-face interaction, in the hope that understanding linguistic and cultural bases of differences in communication patterns can make these differences less inflammatory.

### Notes

Initial fieldwork for this research was funded by a Research Institute for Man/Landes Training Grant. Many thanks to Alessandro Duranti for extensive comments on repeated drafts of the UCLA M.A. thesis on which this article is based. Thanks also to Jae Kim, who transcribed and translated the Korean service encounters, and who shared much with me about the language, lives, and perceptions of Korean immigrants in Los Angeles.

1. Transcription conventions are as follows: Speakers are identified with an abbreviation in the far left column, e.g. "Cust" for "Customer," "Cash" for "Cashier," and "Own" for "Owner." A question mark in this column indicates that the speaker's identity is not clear to the transcriber. Descriptions of non-verbal activities are in double parentheses, e.g. ((Customer enters store.)) Note also the following:

| | |
|---|---|
| ((4.3)) | Numbers in parentheses indicate the length of time in seconds during which there is no talk. Single parentheses are used for intra-turn silences, double parentheses for silences between turns. |
| (.) | A period in parentheses or double parentheses indicates a stretch of time, lasting no more than two-tenths of a second, during which there is no talk. |
| : | A colon indicates that the preceding sound was elongated in a marked pronunciation. |
| ? | A question mark indicates a marked rising pitch. |
| . | A period indicates a marked falling pitch. |
| ( ) | Parentheses that are empty indicate that something was said at that point, but it is not clear enough to transcribe. Parentheses around words indicate doubt about the accuracy of the transcribed material. A slash between words in parentheses indicates alternate possibilities. |
| hhh | *h*'s connected to a word indicate breathiness, usually associated with laughter. |
| [ ] | Brackets enclose those portions of utterances that are spoken in overlap with other talk. The overlapping portions of talk are placed immediately above or below each other on the page. |
| ! | An exclamation point indicates an exclamatory tone. |
| , | A comma indicates a marked continuing intonation in the sound(s) preceding the comma. |
| _ | Text that is underlined was pronounced with emphasis, i.e. some combination of higher volume, pitch, and greater vowel length. |
| ' | A single apostrophe replaces a letter that was not pronounced, e.g. *col'* for *cold*, when the *d* is not pronounced. |
| - | A hyphen or dash indicates that speech was suddenly cut-off during or after the preceding word. |

Transcriptions of Korean data follow Martin et al. (1967: xv).

2. This category includes practices that might seem to vary significantly in degree of intimacy; however, immigrant Koreans do not treat such distinctions as relevant in most encounters with immigrant Korean customers. As described in the section on encounters between immigrant Koreans, small-talk about the

weather (for example) does not occur independently of, or more frequently than, talk of more personal matters.

3. This is not meant to deny the role of racism in tensions between African Americans and immigrant Korean retailers. Racism permeates American society; and it provides a cogent explanation for a wide variety of historical, social, and economic phenomena, including behavior in face-to-face interaction. Quotes from store-owners interviewed in other studies (e.g. Ella Stewart 1989, K. Park 1995), attest the blatant racism of some storekeepers. The point here is not that immigrant Korean merchants are or are not racist, but rather that many immigrant Korean interactional practices upon which African American customers base assumptions of racism are not valid indices of racism, because retailers use identical practices with immigrant Korean customers.

4. The difficulty of mastering English for adult speakers of Korean is suggested by the grammatical interference evident in the following utterance by a storekeeper who had been in Los Angeles over 20 years. When asked where her husband was, she replied: *Husband some merchandise buy* (i.e., 'My husband is buying some merchandise.') The subject-object-verb word order of Korean is used, rather than the subject–verb–object word order of English. The present tense form of *buy* is used, rather than present progressive; this parallels Korean usage, in which the present tense form of action verbs can indicate present progressive meaning. The possessive pronoun *my* is elided, since it would be understood from context in Korean (Lee 1989: 90).

## References


Atkinson, J. Maxwell, & Heritage, John. 1984. Eds. *Structures of social action: Studies in conversation analysis.* Cambridge & New York: Cambridge University Press.

Austin, Regina. 1995. Moving beyond deviance: Expanding Black people's rights and reasons to shop and to sell. *Penn Law Journal* 30: 30–34.

Bailey, Benjamin. 1996. *Communication of respect in service encounters between immigrant Korean retailers and African-American customers.* M.A. thesis, University of California, Los Angeles.

Bateson, Gregory. 1972. *Steps to an ecology of mind.* New York: Ballantine.

Brown, Penelope, & Levinson, Stephen. 1987. *Politeness: Some universals in language usage.* Cambridge & New York: Cambridge University Press.

Chang, Edward. 1990. *New urban crisis: Korean–Black conflicts in Los Angeles.* Dissertation, University of California, Berkeley.

Chang, Edward. 1993. Jewish and Korean merchants in African American neighborhoods: A comparative perspective. *Amerasia Journal* 19: 5–21.

Drake, St. Clair, & Cayton, Horace. 1945. *Black metropolis: A study of Negro life in a northern city.* New York: Harper & Row.

Drew, Paul, & Heritage, John. 1992a. Analyzing talk at work: An introduction. In Drew & Heritage (eds.), 3–65.

Drew, Paul, & Heritage, John. 1992b. Eds. *Talk at work: Interaction in institutional settings.* Cambridge & New York: Cambridge University Presss.

Duranti, Alessandro, & Goodwin, Charles. 1992. Eds. *Rethinking context: Language as an interactive phenomenon.* Cambridge & New York: Cambridge University Press.

Durkheim, Emile. 1915. *The elementary forms of the religious life.* London: Allen & Unwin.

Goffman, Erving. 1967. The nature of deference and demeanor. In his *Interaction ritual: Essays on face-to-face behavior*, 47–95. New York: Pantheon.

Goffman, Erving. 1971. *Relations in public: Microstudies of the public order.* New York: Basic Books.

Goodwin, Charles, & Goodwin, Marjorie. H. 1992. Assessments and the construction of context. In Duranti & Goodwin (eds.), 147–90.

Grice, Paul. 1975. Logic and conversation. In Peter Cole & Jerry Morgan (eds.), *Syntax and semantics*, 3: 41–58. New York: Academic Press.

Gumperz, John. 1982a. *Discourse strategies.* Cambridge & New York: Cambridge University Press.

Gumperz, John. 1982b. Ed. *Language and social identity.* Cambridge & New York: Cambridge University Press.

Gumperz, John. 1992. Contextualization and understanding. In Duranti & Goodwin (eds.), 229–52.

Jefferson, Gail. 1979. A technique for inviting laughter and its subsequent acceptance declination. In George Psathas (ed.), *Everyday language: Studies in ethnomethodology*, 79–96. New York: Irvington.

Keel, Hee-Sung. 1993. Word and wordlessness: The spirit of Korean Buddhism. *Korea Journal* 33: 11–19.

Kochman, Thomas. 1981. *Black and White styles in conflict.* Chicago: University of Chicago Press.

Kochman, Thomas. 1984. The politics of politeness: Social warrants in mainstream American public etiquette. *Georgetown University Roundtable on Languages and Linguistics* 1984: 200–209.

Lee, Hansol H. B. 1989. *Korean grammar.* Oxford & New York: Oxford University Press.

Levinson, Stephen. 1992. Activity types in language. In Drew & Heritage (eds.), 66–100.

Martin, Samuel, et al. 1967. *A Korean-English dictionary.* New Haven, CT: Yale University Press.

Merritt, Marilyn. 1976. On questions following questions (in service encounters). *Language in Society* 5: 315–57.

Park, Kyeyoung. 1995. The re-invention of affirmative action: Korean immigrants' changing conceptions of African Americans and Latin Americans. *Urban Anthropology* 24: 59–92.

Park, Myung-Seok. 1979. *Communication styles in two different cultures: Korean and American.* Seoul: Han Shin.

Sacks, Harvey. 1975. Everyone has to lie. In Mary Sanches & Ben Blount (eds.), *Sociocultural dimensions of language use*, 57–79. New York: Academic Press.

Schegloff, Emanuel, Jefferson, Gail, & Sacks, Harvey. 1977. The preference for self-correction in the organization of repair in conversation. *Language* 53: 361–82.

Schegloff, Emanuel, & Sacks, Harvey. 1973. Opening up closings. *Semiotica* 7: 289–327.

Scollon, Ron, & Scollon, Suzanne Wong. 1994. Face parameters in East–West discourse. In Stella Ting-Toomey (ed.), *The challenge of facework*, 133–58. Albany: State University of New York Press.

Smitherman, Geneva. 1977. *Talkin' and testifyin': The language of Black America*. Boston: Houghton Mifflin.

Stewart, Edward. 1972. *American cultural patterns*. Chicago: Intercultural Press.

Stewart, Ella. 1989. *Ethnic cultural diversity: An interpretive study of cultural differences and communication styles between Korean merchants/employees and Black patrons in South Los Angeles*. M.A. thesis, California State University, Los Angeles.

Stewart, Ella. 1991. Ethnic cultural diversity: Perceptions of intercultural communication rules for interaction between Korean merchants/employees and Black patrons in South Los Angeles. Paper presented to the 19th Annual Conference of the National Association for Ethnic Studies at California State Polytechnic University, Pomona, CA.

Sturdevant, Frederick. 1969. Ed. *The ghetto marketplace*. New York: Free Press.

Tannen, Deborah. 1981. New York Jewish conversational style. *International Journal of the Sociology of Language* 30: 133–49.

Yum, June-Ock. 1987. Korean philosophy and communication. In D. Lawrence Kincaid (ed.), *Communication theory: Eastern and Western perspectives*, 71–86. San Diego: Academic Press.

## Critical Thinking and Application

- Bailey presents laughter as a sequence of invitation and response. Record conversations and analyze the role of laughter. Who "invites" it and who accepts—or declines—the invitation? What is the effect on the interaction?
- This article focuses on Korean–African American interactions in Los Angeles shops. Using the same concepts of interactional norms, observe interactions among individuals from other ethnic groups in other settings. What norms of interaction can you identify? Are the forms of politeness and respect in harmony with both groups? What results from the interactions?
- The concept of *accommodation* or *convergence* supposes that when people interact, their styles become more alike. This has been demonstrated in pacing, intonation, vocabulary, pronunciation, and gesture. At the same time, people may regard their own norms as correct and good and may *diverge* from their interlocutor to emphasize differences. Discuss the opposing tendencies toward divergence and convergence of interactional style. What factors may foster one or the other?

## Vocabulary

| | | |
|---|---|---|
| accommodate, accommodation | index | prosody |
| adjacency pair | Indo-European | proxemic distance |
| affective alignment | institutional talk | referential |
| Altaic | interlocutor | restraint politeness |
| back-channel response | involvement | socially expanded, social expansion |
| closing | morphological | socially minimal |
| co-construct | negative face | solidarity |
| contextualization cues | overlap | syntactic |
| couplet | phonological | verbal channel |
| hedging | positive face | |

## Suggested Further Reading

Brown, Penelope, and Stephen C. Levinson. 1978. *Politeness: Some Universals in Language Usage*. Cambridge: Cambridge University Press.

Gumperz, John J. 1982. Interethnic Communication. From *Discourse Strategies*, pp. 172–186. Cambridge: Cambridge University Press.

Sacks, Harvey, Emanuel A. Schegloff, and Gail Jefferson. 1974. A Simplest Systematics for the Organization of Turn-Taking for Conversation. *Language* 50(4) (part 1): 696–735.

Smitherman, Geneva. 1977. *Talkin' and Testifyin': The Language of Black America*. Boston: Houghton Mifflin.

Tannen, Deborah. 2005 [1984]. *Conversational Style: Analyzing Talk Among Friends*. Rev. ed. New York: Oxford University Press.

CHAPTER 47

# On Mother and Other Tongues: Sociolinguistics, Schools, and Language Ideology in Northern India

*Chaise LaDousa*

(2010)

*Multilingualism is never neutral. One language tends to be elevated over others, at least for certain purposes and for use in certain domains.*

*India, the largest nation in the South Asian subcontinent, is characterized by a swirl of languages and cultures. Its precolonial linguistic situation was full of multilingualism; it was normal for individuals to know many languages and to know how to switch from one to the other for a variety of functions and in a variety of situations. The official language of India is Hindi, but as a legacy of colonialism English is also widely used as a language of education, technology, business, and government. Twenty-two other languages are recognized as national languages in the constitution of India. Some states, further, recognize other languages as official languages.*

*Hindi is a descendant language of Sanskrit, the sacred language of India and the language in which Indian religious texts are written. It is an Indo-European language. (Not all languages in India are Indo-European.) Despite its status as the official language, not everybody can speak it. There is a standard variety of Hindi, but many speakers speak variants of it, such as Bhojpuri. Still, it holds a certain ideological importance.*

*Beyond officially recognized languages, however, there are many varieties that are used regularly even if they have no official status. (Charles Ferguson, in his seminal article "Diglossia," found that the Arabic vernaculars were so unofficial that people denied using them, even when he had taped them doing so!) Many have not been studied, and most are probably named, simply, the language of such-and-such a place.*

*In this selection, Chaise LaDousa provides a complicated view of the complexity of the linguistic situation in the famous holy city of Banaras (also spelled Benares and Benaras, and now more frequently called Varanasi) located on the banks of the Ganges (Ganga) River. It is here, among the colorful temples, that many people come to send off the dead, and Banaras is the frequent destination of pilgrims and tourists. In Banaras, among other languages, we find English, Hindi, and Bhojpuri, a largely unwritten vernacular that may not even be acknowledged.*

*Education is a focus of many people's attention, with choices existing between "English-medium" and "Hindi-medium" schools, which are stratified with English regarded as superior. Students are supposed to make a choice, partially dependent on their "mother tongue," something also measured in inconsistent ways on India's census, which has existed for more than a century. The census relies on people's responses to questions, which are interpreted in wildly varying ways. Experts change their categories (sometimes treating separately and sometimes together "dialects" of major languages), and respondents have varying interpretations of what* mother tongue *means.*

*LaDousa connects this somewhat technical question to language ideology, in which ideas of value, power, beauty, and utility are connected with ideas of linguistic variety. Individuals may also develop a "complex" if they regard their own language and schooling as superior or inferior to those of others.*

Chaise LaDousa, On Mother and Other Tongues: Sociolinguistics, Schools, and Language Ideology in Northern India. *Language Sciences* 32 (2010): 602–614.

## Reading Questions

- What is the difficulty in assessing someone's mother tongue?
- What is the "three-language formula" that guides education in India? How is this evident in the schools LaDousa hears about?
- What is Bhojpuri? How does it differ from Hindi?
- What is the connection between the medium of education and the development of a "complex"?
- Why does LaDousa claim that these practices have to do with language ideology?

---

## INTRODUCTION

Scholars have shown that the notion that a person or a group can possess a "mother tongue" is an ideology reflecting "the situated, partial, and interested character of conceptions and uses of language" rather than an objective, **unmediated** feature of the world (Errington, 1999, p. 115). As such, scholars and lay people alike have used various grounds on which to define or argue for a "mother tongue's" existence. These include the notion that a language was learned first, that a language is known best, and/or that a language is used most (Skutnabb-Kangas and Phillipson, 1989, p. 453). In turn, such arguments have been shaped by historically and politically particular notions like the "insistence on the authenticity and moral significance of 'mother tongue' as the one first and therefore *real* language of a speaker, transparent to the true self" that can be traced to the **Herderian** equation of a people and a language (Woolard, 1998, p.18). The uses of such arguments are legion and include the call for the recognition of, the call for the inclusion of, or the valorization of some practice or group associated with the "mother tongue." Mitchell (2009, p. 23) explains that "the defense of one's 'mother tongue,' whether in public or in private, is a learned behavior rather than a natural impulse. Yet, this does not mean that such a learned behavior is insignificant or should be dismissed." Thus, Pattanayak's claim that "'mother tongue' is both a sociolinguistic reality and a product of the mythic consciousness of a people" is correct insofar as the notion is understood to have rather powerful ideological effects (1981, p. 54).[1]

This article aims to trace some of the institutional lives of the notion of "mother tongue" in northern India, the site of my own ethnographic research. Doing so necessitates the exploration of both scholarly and ethnographic domains. The exploration of the ways in which the notion of "mother tongue" is used in scholarly publications in sociolinguistics helps to explain why the ethnographic domain of the school is not only underrepresented therein, but also treated as un-Indian. In another institutional domain, the **census** of India, scholars of sociolinguistics have been adept at tracing multiple **denotational** values for the term "mother tongue," and have shown how such values presuppose and produce ideological effects from census to census. They have been less willing to trace such effects in the institutional domain of the school, however. This article explores select key publications in sociolinguistic work on India, noting that schools' use of **standardized** language proved to be anathema to scholars' arguments about India's lasting **plurilingualism**. Indeed, according to such work, schools provide no place for the "mother tongue."

What, then, can be learned in an exploration of schooling and its relationship to language in northern India? This article illustrates some of the ways in which talk about schools is productive of **language ideology**, and that such ideology involves the notion of "mother tongue." The article traces the ways in which schools do indeed exclude languages, but at the same time provide a way for people to assert the existence and institutional location of the "mother tongue." Such assertions are hardly uncomplicated, however, and people who reflect on languages and schools often become entangled in contradictions. In one extended narrative presented herein, for example, a university professor establishes schools as types via language, and makes claims about students' dispositions within them based on notions of "mother tongue." She then subverts her assertions by claiming herself to be an exception. In the second extended narrative presented herein, a secretary and mother invokes a language variety excluded by schooling to lampoon a girl who claims not to know the language that makes one subordinate in distinctions between schools as types.

This [chapter] presents the two interview excerpts because they show the dual necessity of considering languages as ideological constructs and considering languages' social locations and values. Indeed, they illustrate people grappling with the lack of fit between language ideology, the institutional location of languages, and the ways in which the two fail to account [for] the complexities characteristic of the lives from which the narratives emerge. It is the exploration of such complexity that has largely been missing in sociolinguistic scholarship on India. In sum, this [chapter] argues that rather than arguing for India's uniqueness or difference from some Western sociolinguistic paradigm that leads to the neglect of the school because it emerges as an exemplar of standardization, scholars should explore the complex ways in which schools serve as a vehicle for ideologies focused on the notion of the "mother tongue" as well as a site of particularly dense ideological contradiction. The next section offers an explanation of why the school has been neglected in sociolinguistic work on India.

## "MOTHER TONGUE," THE CENSUS, AND EDUCATION IN THE SOCIOLINGUISTICS OF INDIA

Scholars of language variation in India have been especially adept in describing the bewildering number of meanings and uses of the notion of "mother tongue." I mean for my review of scholars' valuable assertions about the multiple and sometimes incommensurable and distorting meanings and uses of "mother tongue" to serve two purposes. On the one hand, I want to note that such scholars were aware of multiple meanings of the idea of "mother tongue." They were adept at tracing the ways in which certain denotational values of the term were linked to different usages. And, most importantly for my argument, they were willing to explore the ways in which the census of India was an institution in whose hands the meanings of "mother tongue" might change, and in whose reports the enumeration of sociolinguistic realities might be shown to be inherently inaccurate. On the other hand, I want to show that such scholars were relatively unwilling to explore another institutional domain, the school, with the same intellectual distance. In discussions of schooling, scholars working in the sociolinguistics of India have tended to treat the "mother tongue" as a residual realm of knowledge to be valorized. Indeed, the "mother tongue" emerges as something to be upheld and praised as Indian in opposition to the language of the school which emerges as something to be dismissed.

In a classic critique, Pattanayak (1981) presents a great number of possibilities for what "mother tongue" can mean. He decries the commonplace understanding of "mother tongue" as "one's own language" as too vague for sociolinguistic use because two or more languages might fit appropriate criteria (p. 47). The gloss "language of nature," applied to the deaf and their "language of signs," he explains, presupposes no language community at all (p. 47). He invokes Rabindranath Tagore's assertion that "Sanskrit is the mother of Indic languages in the same sense as the earth is the mother of the worm" to critique the notion that the "mother tongue" is "the original language from which others spring" (p. 47). Pattanayak explains that "learning a language without formal training" can be understood to make a language a "mother tongue" (p. 50). He questions the idea that "language which allows one to have the cognizance of the world is the mother tongue" by noting the vagueness of "cognizance" (p. 51). He proceeds to explain that "mother tongue" has rested on the emotional attachment one feels to a language that is often underpinned by the notion of "mother land," one's nation or would-be nation (p. 51). Yet another meaning of "mother tongue" can be comprised by the capacity for "cognitive development" and "creativity." Pattanayak cites a commonly held belief that "precision of thought and clarity of ideas are considerably hampered without the ability to speak effectively and to read and write correctly and lucidly in one's mother tongue" (p. 52). Finally, Pattanayak notes that "mother tongue" can mean something like "home language," and argues that such can be subverted by the existence of more than one language spoken at home (p. 53).[2]

Pattanayak illustrates the institutional vicissitudes of the meanings of "mother tongue" by examining the questions meant to solicit respondents' ideas about language in the Indian censuses. Pattanayak (1981, pp. 47–48) writes:

> In the census of 1881, 1931, 1941, and 1951 a question on mother tongue was asked. In the 1881 census mother tongue was defined as "the language spoken by the individual from the cradle." In the 1891 census the term was changed into "Parent tongue" which was defined to mean the language spoken by the parents of the individual. In the 1901 census it was further modified into "Language ordinarily spoken in the household." In the case of bilingual respondents, the language used with the enumerator was noted. In 1921 the question was simply "language ordinarily used."

The very notion of "mother tongue" shifted from census to census.

The instructions given to census enumerators, Pattanayak proceeds to demonstrate, treated the idea of "mother tongue" in such a way as to skew sociolinguistic realities sought in the questions. Pattanayak (1981, p. 48) notes:

> According to the instruction given to the enumerators in the 1961 Indian census, "Mother tongue is language spoken in the childhood by persons' mother. If the mother died in infancy write the language mostly spoken in the person's home in childhood."

Pattanayak (p. 48) notes the potential for two possible answers:

> in the case of a Bihari mother tongue speaker (as declared in the census) marrying a Hindi speaker. Assuming that the mother was a speaker of a language/dialect which she could have declared as Bihari in the census, then if she were living that would probably be recorded as the mother tongue of the child even if she was married to a man who would have recorded his mother tongue as Hindi. However, if at the time of recording the mother tongue the mother was dead then the language mostly spoken in the person's home being Hindi would be recorded as the "Child's mother tongue."[3]

Two aspects of Pattanayak's disposition toward the idea of the "mother tongue" are important to the argument to come. There is, on the one hand, a profound ambivalence on the part of Pattanayak about the use of the term as a sociolinguistic descriptor. On the other hand, there exists the possibility of the emergence of both standardized (Hindi) and non-standardized (Bihari or Hindi) language varieties as candidates.

Key to understanding the relationship between the notion of the "mother tongue" and the institution of the school in the sociolinguistics of India is the pervasive idea that there exists in societies such as India the possibility of a lasting and contextually appropriate multilingualism.[4] Ostensibly, some societies are unlike India because they do not provide such a possibility. For example, in their review of sociolinguistic work on India, Agnihotri and Khanna (1997, pp. 33–34) claim that:

> In heterogenous societies such as that of India, languages are learnt in non-authoritarian contexts leading to continuous sociocultural and cognitive enrichment. Variations in linguistic behaviour act as facilitators rather

> than as barriers in communication. Languages are kept distinct as they perform different functions in different domains. On the other hand, there are several domains in which different languages converge towards a common lingua franca... Although there is an underlying sociolinguistic unity that characterizes Indian multilingualism, it is this unity that nurtures rather than forbids flexibility and variability.

Although Agnihotri and Khanna's focus is on languages rather than institutions, the scholars' depiction of India as a place of lasting multilingualism – where languages are learned outside of authoritarian contexts such as the school – involves institutional contexts. Against the backdrop that Agnihotri and Khanna create, the school emerges as unnatural and dangerous for its use and dissemination of language varieties incompatible with flexibility, variability, or accommodation.[5]

Schooling emerges in Agnihotri and Khanna's overview as an alien institution. They turn to policy measures undertaken by the Government of India during the 1960s in order to critique the artificial, arbitrary impositions of schooling on students, as well as the official acknowledgement of the value of languages that have been deemed fit for use in schools:

> Two assumptions that have often guided the deliberations of these [government] committees are firstly, that every child in the country should learn the same number of languages and secondly, that learning Hindi and English are of paramount importance for everyone. Both of these assumptions militate against the fluid plurilingual texture of Indian society (Agnihotri and Khanna, 1997, p. 35).

Here, Agnihotri and Khanna are critiquing the three-language formula constructed by the Kothari Commission of the Central Government of India from 1964 to 1966 (Chaturvedi and Mohale, 1976; Jayaram, 1993; Sridhar, 1991; Srivastava, 1990). The commission decided that students should study in three languages to foster national linguistic integration.

One should be the official language of the state in which the school is located. The second language should be another language such as English, or in the case of students from minority language-speaking communities, there being at least 40 in a school or ten of them in a grade level, the second language should be that language (Government of India, 1971, p. 8). Sridhar (1996, pp. 331–332) notes that there are five ways of understanding a sociolinguistic situation to constitute a minority status in India: a language not recognized in Schedule VIII of the constitution; a major recognized language outside of its area of dominance; a language of a **scheduled caste** or tribe; a language of a religious minority; a major recognized language whose speakers lack numerical strength (such as Kashmiri); and a language of an ethnic minority (such as Anglo-Indians). It is speakers of tribal languages, Sridhar explains, who suffer the worst disadvantages because their languages are the most quickly dispensed with as a medium of instruction in school. What the third language should be depends on the axis of northern (Indo-Aryan) and southern (Dravidian) language difference. For students from the states of Andhra Pradesh, Karnataka, Kerala, or Tamil Nadu, speakers of Telugu, Kannada, Malayalam, or Tamil, respectively, Hindi or some other official state language of the north should be required. For students from one of the northern states, outside of the Dravidian language area, one of the four aforementioned languages should be required. The three-language formula is underpinned by a desire to facilitate communicative competence in an Indian language with people residing elsewhere in the country. Agnihotri and Khanna (1997) find such legislation and its vehicle, the school, to be incompatible with the linguistic ethos and the sociolinguistic realities of Indian society. Schools and their language varieties are rendered un-Indian.[6]

In another classic critique, Dasgupta (1993) uses the distinction between high (H) and low (L) varieties of language in Fishman's (1967) sense of extended **diglossia** to characterize an essential division in education in India.[7] For Dasgupta, the distinction can be used to depict the relationship between language and education, H and L emerging as something like styles of cognition. One is reminded of Bernstein's (1971) distinction between "elaborated" and "restricted" codes, respectively.

> Education is thus a relation between two discourses. The H discourse level of systematic knowledge codifies and organizes the textual and practical complexes in terms of the simple primes into which serious and systematic thought analyzes the complexes. The L discourse level of the learner – and, in his or her ordinary life, the teacher – conceptualizes items as being difficult, or remote from experience, versus easy, or accessible to common perception. Education is a mapping between the simple primes of the H world and the easy percepts of the L world (Dasgupta, 1993, p. 104).

Dasgupta's usage differs from Bernstein's in that in India, the classroom and ultimately the textbook become the locus of H, whereas the "ordinary life" of teacher and student becomes the locus of L. It is in L that education, or the translation between H and L can take place.

Much later in the book, we find that another distinction serves to anchor H and L. Drawing on the first line of the constitution, Dasgupta argues that the referent of "India" is H and the referent of **"Bharat"** is L. Rather than bemoaning the advance of standardizing tendencies in government policy and the decline of India's natural plurilingual ethos as Agnihotri and Khanna (1997) do, Dasgupta (1993, pp. 182–183) celebrates the resurgence of that same ethos in the return of "Bharat."

> As a consequence of this shift from the teaching mode, where the Indian elite took the social and cognitive initiative, to the learning mode, in which Bharat's many collectivities unevenly and regionally initiate processes

> of learning whose very brokenness reflects the (plural) pleasure of the people and marks the limits beyond which the modernization project cannot proceed, the nation-image of Bharat begins to emerge as a new reality, capable of constructing a credible past and future for itself, and of contesting the India image's presence as well as its projections into the past and the future.

Thus, Dasgupta equates H with the "teaching mode," "India's elite," and a single "modernization project" and L with the "learning mode" and "Bharat's many collectivities" which are "regionally" situated. Only outside of the institution of the school do teacher and student have the ability to render H as difficult, arcane, and disembodied.

This quotation from Dasgupta is prescient to my argument because it intimates what happens to the notion of "mother tongue" once schooling is invoked. The "mother tongue" ceases to have the range of possibilities emergent, for example, in Pattanayak's critique of the census, where standardized and non-standardized languages both emerge as possibilities, and begins to mean that knowledge that exists in the shadow of the school or language legislation. The "mother tongue" emerges in contrast to the "other tongue" (Pattanayak, 1981) or to the "auntie tongue" (Dasgupta, 1993) that derives its lifeblood from the lifeless school. Pattanayak (1981, p. 63) sums up the set of oppositions supporting the identity of the "mother tongue" as that language variety quashed by the school: "Schooling is a major break in the natural acquisition of language where ignorant pedants teach the non-existent logic, identify varieties as incorrect, create a low self-image by branding the home language as non-standard and try to establish their right to teach the correct as the standard."

On the one hand, it is not my intention to contest these scholars' assertions that processes of standardization present hurdles to policy makers, those who are charged with instituting policy decisions, or those who lack access to or control of standardized varieties. As will become apparent in the discussion below of varieties of language in Banaras and northern India and the varieties that are deemed acceptable for use in schools, many of the assertions made by the scholars cited herein ring true. Schools do indeed exclude certain languages, especially those that officials feel have not been standardized. On the other hand, I mean to call attention to the absence in sociolinguistic work in India of the kind of discursive activity to be presented in two narratives below, that which focuses on schools as sites constituted, in part, by distinctions between language varieties. The absence seems likely given the ways in which sociolinguistic work in India has pined for a plurilingualism that the standardizing tendencies of the school as a site of language use, primarily in the form of the textbook, embodies. Almost all sociolinguistic work conducted in India acknowledges the existence of schools, but assumes that they are places where standardized language varieties can be found. One learns little about schools as places in which people might have an interest and use schooling as a way to engage in discursive practice that exhibits language ideology.[8] Indeed, one learns little apart from what particular standardized languages are taught there or, more minimally, what languages a particular state's policies allow for use in schools. This article finds this state of affairs particularly in need of attention because notions of what constitutes the "mother tongue" play an especially prominent and important role in the language ideology that emerges.

## SCHOOLS AND LANGUAGE (ERASURE) IN BANARAS

Talk about schools in Banaras, the site of my field research for a year from the end of the monsoon (late September) in 1996 to the same time of year in 1997, for several weeks in 2005–2006, and for two months in 2007, often invoked language distinctions whether or not language difference was an explicit topic of talk. Indeed, a common way in which one can refer to a school is to call it either "Hindi medium" or "English medium," **"medium"** referring to the primary language of classroom discourse and language materials in a school. As per the three-language formula described above, Hindi and one other language are taught in English-medium schools as subjects, and English and one other language are thus taught in Hindi-medium schools. The nomenclature of schooling in Banaras and in urban areas across northern India is quite complicated. In addition to the distinction in medium, there is a distinction in ownership (government vs. private, often called "public" schools); board certification (Uttar Pradesh Board in Allahabad, Uttar Pradesh or UP being the state in which Banaras is located vs. Central Board of Secondary Education, among many other private boards); religious affiliation ("convent" schools run by Christian denominations vs. madrassas run by Islamic foundations vs. schools run by the Rashtriya Swayamsevak Sangh, the National Self-service Society, a militant Hindu organization, among many more), NGO (non-governmental organization) affiliation; and gender (all-girls, all-boys, co-educational); all in addition to the clustering of grade levels (nursery (lower kindergarten and upper kindergarten), primary (classes 1–5), secondary (classes 6–10), and inter-college (classes 11–12)).

In a number of articles, I have described the ways in which language medium distinctions based on the difference between Hindi and English align with other institutional distinctions such as low versus high cost, government support versus private ownership, and an orientation toward Banaras and its environs versus an orientation outward, primarily toward Delhi, respectively, to recreate and contribute to a particularly robust and salient dichotomy (LaDousa, 2002, 2004, 2005, 2006, 2007). By invoking the division between Hindi- and English-medium schools, people in Banaras often "erase," in the rubric of Gal and Irvine (1995), a number of languages and institutions that fail to be salient to the division.[9]

Bhojpuri is one of these languages. Bhojpuri is a language variety that exhibits regional variation different than Hindi.

Yet, like that of Hindi, the sociolinguistic history of Bhojpuri is extremely complex. Both Hindi and Bhojpuri can be found in locations throughout the world as a result of migration underpinned by indentured servitude in the 19th century (Barz and Siegel, 1988; Eisenlohr, 2006; Gambhir, 1981; Mesthrie, 1991; Mohan, 1978) and later migrations partly dependent on policy shifts in various countries. The allure of employment opportunities has drawn speakers of Bhojpuri to various urban areas of northern India, especially Delhi, and away from the area still associated with Bhojpuri speakers, the western part of the state of Bihar, the eastern part of the state of Uttar Pradesh, and the northern part of the state of Jharkhand. In that region, from the colonial period to the present, officials and linguists have identified regional variation in Bhojpuri (Grierson, 1967; Masica, 1991). The intersection of regional variation and names that people use to identify variants is messy such that some laypeople, on the one hand, and officials and scholars, on the other hand, use "Bihari" to refer to Bhojpuri found in parts of the state of Bihar and Jharkhand or in the speech of migrants from such areas residing in eastern Uttar Pradesh and beyond, while other scholars dispute the term's reflection of sociolinguistic variation (Masica, 1991). My purpose is not to weigh in on such discussions, but rather to acknowledge that Bhojpuri is a language with complex and variation that has been the target of some controversy in the scholarly literature. Less controversial is that people in Banaras are said to speak a variety called "Banarsi Boli" or "Banaras Talk."

Hindi differs from Bhojpuri in two respects, among others. First, Hindi covers a much wider territory, stretching across entire states in northern and central India. People across this massive ***Sprachbund*** typically speak a language such as Bhojpuri, Avadhi, or Marwari in addition to some level of competence in Hindi (Gumperz, 1958, 1964). Shapiro and Schiffman (1981, p. 65) rightly explain:

> In large portions of South Asia it is difficult to construct a model of standardized languages directly subsuming discrete classes of regional dialects. Most of the spoken vernaculars of North India, for instance, comprise a virtual continuum of speech forms extending across the subcontinent from Bombay to Ahmadabad in the west to Calcutta in the East.

Nevertheless, Hindi can be said to contrast with the more regionally delimited languages such as Bhojpuri because Hindi is realizable as a variety that has undergone standardization for use in domains such as the newspaper, government publications, and school texts (Dua, 1994; Gumperz, 1961; Orsini, 2002). Many people throughout the Hindi-speaking region call this variety of Hindi *śuddh* Hindi (pure Hindi). Some people will laud and some people will complain about its use of Sanskrit-derived elements (Rai, 2000). The use of Persian- and Arabic-derived linguistic elements will often cue the language label Urdu. What distinguishes Urdu and Hindi has become an increasingly complicated issue over the late-19th and 20th centuries (King, 1994; Lelyveld, 1993; Rai, 1984). Some stress similarity and mutual comprehension and enrichment in spoken forms especially, while others stress difference and even moral incompatibility. Certainly, script has come to demarcate one from the other (King, 2001). The use of the Nastaliq script has come to be associated with Urdu and the use of the Devanagari script with Hindi.

The mere existence of a school with its textbooks and exams rendered in standardized language, Hindi, Urdu, or English, banishes Bhojpuri.[10] I asked about the possibility of using Bhojpuri in schools often. My queries were met with an absolute stance, always negative and sometimes peppered with amusement. Sometimes, outside of a discussion of schools, people told me that Banarasi Boli, Bihari, or Bhojpuri provided the basis of *śuddh* Hindi. A few particularly well-educated people pointed to the efforts of Bharatendu Harischandra in the late-19th century to vouch for the use of a Sanskritized, *śuddh* Hindi. Harischandra's home was Banaras. The city was also home to journals and other publications inspired by him (Dalmia, 1997). But people found the idea of using Bhojpuri in school texts and exams, much less in interaction, ridiculous. They had at their disposal a whole set of descriptors to explain why Bhojpuri is not meant for school. People I knew consistently contrasted Bhojpuri as *gāv kī bhāsā* (language of the village) and *ghar kī bhāsā* (language of the house) to Hindi as *rāstrabhāsā* (national language) or *deś kī bhāsā* (language of the land/nation). As such, Hindi could stand proudly next to English, often described as *antarrāstrabhāsā* (international language).

Simon (1986, 2003) rightly argues that Bhojpuri and Hindi do not have fixed ideological underpinnings, but rather embody a salient distinction that speakers can partially manipulate in a given context. For example, she notes that Bhojpuri can connote something that is Banarsi or Banaras-like, especially when the particular variety, Banarsi Boli, or Banaras Talk, is used or mentioned. It can become local with respect to a more universal Hindi. But, in certain situations, Hindi can connote something particular to Banaras vis-à-vis Bhojpuri, associated with neighboring Bihar. These pragmatic possibilities are erased in the school as well because Bhojpuri is banished in favor of Hindi. Only one, the next section of the article demonstrates, emerges as the "mother tongue." This is true in both the senses of a language variety used in school and a type of school.

## NOTES ON A "COMPLEX"

While it is true that schools do banish Bhojpuri, and this reflects what sociolinguists claim about schools in northern India, they also provide a means for talking about Hindi as "mother tongue." Schools are so important to consider in the study of language ideology in northern India because schooling presupposes a divide between Hindi- and English-medium institutions, but also the dispositions of students who attend them. Students attending Hindi-medium institutions are said to be studying in their "mother tongue" while students attending English-medium schools are not. The notion that a student can develop a "complex" rests on the distinction between Hindi- and English-medium schools, and thus is a particularly rich notion for the investigation of language ideology.[11]

The use of the term "complex" presupposes the institutional labels of Hindi and English medium, but focuses on the student. Specifically, a "complex" can "develop" in the person who moves from a Hindi-medium school to an English-medium school, or a "complex" can develop in the person who has been educated in an English-medium school and comes into contact with a person who, until joining the English-medium school, has been educated in a Hindi-medium school. The student in the former situation is said to feel "inferior" and the student in the latter situation is said to feel "superior." The use of the term "complex" presupposes much else besides. A "complex" is likely to develop at specific times during a student's progression through school. Students can "develop a complex" at any age, and some teachers at English-medium schools did use the term to describe youngsters who had transferred from Hindi-medium schools anywhere from the first level to the ninth level. And though most teachers chalked up a reticence to talk on the part of children in the first, second, third, or fourth level to bashfulness and insecurity of the very young, a few claimed the culprit to be a lack of practice in talking in English that attendance at Hindi-medium schools is said to entail. The most common moment of the onset of a "complex," however, coincided with the point at which students educated in Hindi-medium schools most commonly find themselves amid students educated in English-medium schools for the first time, the university classroom. Even those people who talked about a "complex" being relevant at the high school level, such as the woman in the second example to be presented below, noted that the shift from a Hindi-medium to an English-medium high school was undertaken in anticipation of minimizing the possibility of a "complex" in forthcoming university courses.

Ramanathan (2005, p. 6) offers a description of institutional forces that contribute to the dilemma facing Hindi-medium students desiring higher education:

> ...if the English proficiency of students educated in the Vernacular [Gujarati in the case Ramanathan describes; Hindi in the case described herein] is deemed insufficient at the end of the 12th grade, which by and large is the case, they are denied access to these 'prestigious disciplines.' Furthermore, in instances when VM [Vernacular-medium] students are admitted to EM [English-medium] colleges, they face the uphill task of not only taking classes with their EM counterparts but of having to make the same set of state-mandated examinations in English. In many cases, this proves to be insurmountable for many low-income VM students and many of them drop out of the education system during and after college.

Ramanathan's invocation of "prestigious disciplines" demonstrates yet another way in which the notion of "complex" is grounded in a highly complex intersection of language difference and institutional structure. At Banaras Hindu University and at many other central universities around the country, courses in science, technology, medicine, and management are offered in English whereas many courses in the social sciences and arts are offered in either English or Hindi. During fieldwork in 1997, students in primary and secondary schools claimed higher education in the sciences to be their own or some "bright" sibling's ambition. By 2005, the answers "commerce" or "computers" had taken the place of "science" entirely. The language deemed necessary for higher education in such prestigious fields has remained the same, English, and the notion still holds that students coming from Hindi-medium schools who want to study "commerce" or "computers" will likely develop a "complex."

The first example presented below, the case of a university professor in Banaras, shows the ways in which the notion of a "complex" rests on ideas about the "mother tongue" of students. The professor's narrative quickly makes apparent the assumption that Hindi is the "mother tongue" of students. The professor uses this idea to argue that students at the university level coming from Hindi-medium schools are severely but unfairly disadvantaged. The professor later explains that she studied in Hindi-medium schools. In order to account for the incongruity between her past and present, the professor invokes a status common to all schools, regardless of language medium, that trumps the "complex." Her narrative shows that the institution of the school must be taken into account in sociolinguistic work on India not only because it provides an institutional focus for language ideology based on the notion of the "mother tongue," but also because people like the professor reproduce that ideology just as they embody an exception to it. The second example presented below, the case of a government secretary, argues for the consideration of language ideology emergent from talk about schooling for a different purpose. The secretary presupposes ideas about the "complex" just as the professor does. In her narrative, however, Bhojpuri, the language banished from school, provides an ironic twist. Though the notion of "complex" presupposes the fact that Hindi is the student's "mother tongue," in the secretary's narrative, one is left wondering whether it is really Hindi or Bhojpuri. None of these ideological constructs or the contradictions that arise in narrative reflection are able to emerge in sociolinguistic work on India that imagines the school solely as a place of standardized language varieties. (See Fig. 47. 1)

## The "Complex" and the "Topper"

The first example comes from an interview I conducted in December 2005 with a professor, Shona Shastri, in the social sciences at Banaras Hindu University, a major university known throughout India. This [chapter] presents a lengthy section of the interview because the professor recreates the notion

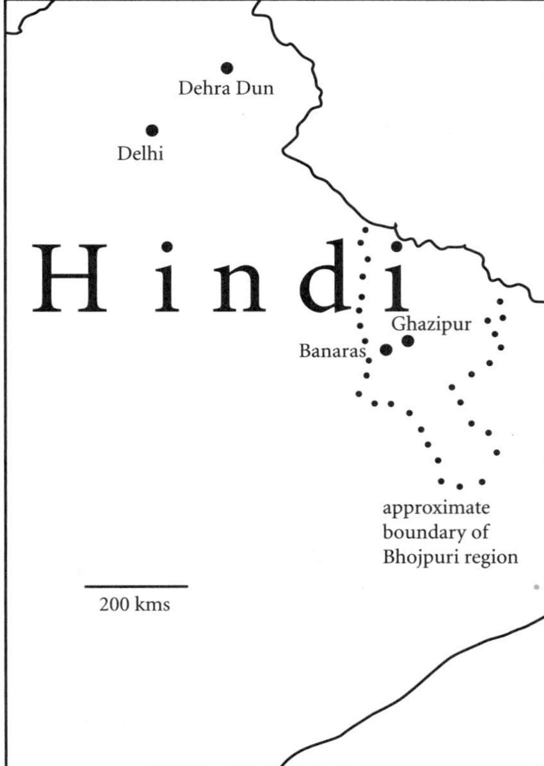


**Figure 47. 1** *Language and Places Mentioned in the [Chapter].*

of a "complex" arising from language medium difference, only to claim herself as an exception by virtue of a disposition in school that has nothing to do with language, per se. Initially the professor talks of the "complex" as relevant to those students in the university who have studied in English medium at the undergraduate level who meet and feel superior to students at the graduate level who have taken their bachelor's degrees in Hindi-medium courses. She thus shows that the most salient structural insecurity in schooling underpinned by the language-medium divide – the Hindi-medium intercollege student desiring admission to an undergraduate course of study – can be extended further upward to characterize the Hindi-medium undergraduate desiring admission to select disciplines grouped by the language in which they are offered.

Shona Shastri (SS hereafter):

> English still dominates. But, ultimately, the drawback, what is there, that here those students who come from lower-middle class or from the rural background, actually they do not, they do not know English. And because they are poorly nourished, their brains are also not that very sharp sometimes, you know, so they find it really very difficult to learn a new language. Yeah. And for them it is very easy to learn their own mother tongue, learn the subjects in their own mother tongue. Sometimes they are very bright, but they have not been exposed to English-medium education because in the villages where there is less facility of schooling it is so difficult to get the English-medium education, you know. These children, they pass out in under... in BA, in undergraduate level, with good marks. But when they come to this university, ah, they find it very difficult. They generally... unfortunately, English-medium boys, they suffer from some kind of superiority.

The professor lumps together a lack of nutrition, a rural background, lower-middle class economic status, and access to education via the "mother tongue," all in juxtaposition to an English-medium student. Her usage of "mother tongue" nicely represents the shifting referential capacities of the term. Generally in Banaras, the term "mother tongue" can refer to any linguistic variety that is not English. Reflecting the discussion of "erasure" above, when "mother tongue" is used to talk about languages used in schools, the term's referential possibilities narrow and Bhojpuri, for one, is excluded. The professor relies on and reproduces the erasure of Bhojpuri when she states that subjects are easier to study in one's "mother tongue." Indeed, in primary, grammar, and high school levels, teachers told me that Hindi is often the most difficult subject for students, more difficult than English, because students have a very difficult time producing the correct *mātrā* forms, or combinations of consonants and vowels. Some teachers exclaimed with humor that students "do not know" or "cannot write" their own "language" or "mother tongue." In this explanation, "language" and "mother tongue" meant Hindi specifically to the exclusion of Bhojpuri. The amused exasperation about a situation in which students make mistakes in their own "language" or "mother tongue" makes sense of the fact that Hindi and not English would seem to be the more difficult subject. In any case, the professor's explanation takes for granted that Hindi is one's "mother tongue," in juxtaposition to English.

In her next few comments, the professor explains that she protests to her own students that the complex is unjustified because one's language medium background is an inaccurate measure of one's intelligence. She explains that she chastises students coming from an English-medium background for "not knowing your mother tongue" at the same time that she "encourages" students coming from a Hindi-medium background, "try to learn that language" [English].

SS: what happens generally you will find that the English-medium students, uh, somehow or the other, they dominate other students.
Chaise LaDousa (hereafter CL): I see.
SS: Because uh, uh, snobbish, snobbish is a word, *na*? Snobbish, *hã̃* [yes].
CL: Yes.
SS: Yeah. Snobbish. A snobbish value comes to them that they, they are perfect in English, they know English.
CL: I see.
SS: *hã̃, hã̃, hã̃, hã̃.*
CL: What kinds of things do they say?
SS: Do they say because they will only mix up with those children who know English. They will not mix up with those children who know Hindi. And they form a different group, an elitist group.
CL: I see.
SS: You know? So that is exhibited through their behavior and other things, you know? So, those, those who are good in Hindi, uh, they feel bad about it. They complain. They come to us and then they say *ki* [that] they feel so sorry that they do not know English, you know? But what we try to do in the class, we give equal importance to both of them. And we always tell our English-medium students it is not a great thing that you know English, because you have been educated in English medium, that's why you know, but not knowing your mother tongue is not a thing to be complimented. If a Hindi-medium student asks a good question, I will always encourage him or her. So it very much depends on the attitude of the teacher also. How do you take them, you know? So they are... and I always tell Hindi-medium students never feel inferior that you do not know that language. Try to learn that language. If I can learn French at this age you can learn English at that age, you know? And you should learn English because there is so much of literature. There is, you can get, most of the good books are in English. They have not been translated in Hindi. So for your survival and progress you should learn English. So try to learn English. Even at this stage you can learn it.

In this excerpt, the professor wrestles with the medium divide and, in so doing, becomes entangled in some of the contradictions common to discourse about language, schooling, and notions of "mother tongue" in northern India. For example, the professor begins by arguing that the "complex" felt by students who have been schooled in English-medium schools can be chalked up to snobbishness. She then states that those students of hers who are good at Hindi feel bad about their proficiency. We gradually learn that proficiency in Hindi implies a lack of knowledge of English. She then asserts that those students who have been schooled in the English medium might claim not to know their mother tongue, but that this is not a stance of which one should be proud. In keeping with the ideological nature of the nexus of schooling and language medium, one has the impression that were students disabused of the "complex," the superiority and inferiority associated with English and Hindi medium backgrounds, then one's ability in one or the other language would disappear as a concern. The excerpt of the interview with the professor, however, hints at why this might not occur. The benefit of the "mother tongue" to students who have attended English-medium schools is never addressed, for example.

In the final excerpt, the professor introduces a surprise: she was educated in Hindi-medium schools. Given that she is now a professor at a major university, this embodies a contradiction to most all of what she has claimed thus far about the "complex" emergent from the language-medium divide.

SS: You will be very surprised to know, because you take up my case, throughout I studied in Hindi medium. Throughout. Because, not because I belonged to a lower-middle class, because the place where I was living, all the nearby schools were in Hindi medium.
CL: I see,
SS: English-medium schools were very, very very far, you know? So, I studied there, but English I always learned as a subject. And because I learned...
CL: And which area are you from?
SS: Banaras only. Banaras. The ghats. I was living near ghats.[12]
CL: In the old city.
SS: The old city, yes, very near ghats. And, but English I learned as a subject. And as a subject I felt that my writing in English was much much better than those, you know. When I joined here MA, then I joined English medium because I thought I should also be good in the spoken English, so I should also learn, you know? Because unless until you communicate, and if you are sharp you can pick up the things very fast, you know? So at the age of MA when I was studying then I joined English medium. And then I picked it up and then I started teaching in English and other things, you know? So I know through what stage the students go, you know, and feel, and all that, you know?
CL: Did you ever face this complex yourself?

SS: I, my case actually, you know, I was a topper throughout. *Hã̃*, so actually to whatever language you may be, but if you are a topper, generally you are taken in a high esteem, you know?

Although the professor uses the school medium as the basis for describing an essential difference between her students, and describes herself in terms of the language divide, such distinctions disappear when she describes herself with a term common to both Hindi- and English-medium schools, the "topper." In every school, those students who have "topped" their board exams, especially at the 10th and 12th levels, have their names and photos displayed temporarily, sometimes permanently, in prominent places including the school's entrance, hallways, or principal's office. In the professor's rendition of the relationship of languages to schooling through medium designations, becoming a "topper" seems to offer esteem that can overcome the "complex." The professor thus demonstrates the ways in which schooling presupposes the idea that Hindi is one's "mother tongue" and that this understanding rests on an institutional juxtaposition with English. She also demonstrates that success in the institution can nullify the very challenges posed by the institutional distinction of Hindi and English. The professor emerges as an exception to the state of affairs she has just narrated.

## "Like All Her Life She was Speaking Bhojpuri with Her Parents, and Naturally She Would Not Have Known Any Hindi"

The second example comes from an interview conducted in the summer of 1997 with another woman, Arti Aggarwal, who was working as a secretary for a relatively low-ranking government official. Arti worked near the place where I took lunch after morning visits to schools and before afternoon visits to teachers or the families of schoolchildren after the school day. While the example of the professor illustrates the importance of studying the school because success in it provides an exception to the contradictions of language ideology, this second example does so because Arti launches a rather complicated critique of the "complex" that invokes Bhojpuri, a language erased from the language-medium division in schooling. Arti exhibits a possibility missing in the professor's ruminations: the possibility of irony and subversion.

Arti had a three-year-old daughter at the time of our interview. Arti focuses the first part of the excerpt with a consideration of the decisions she has made regarding her daughter's education, and turns to her own youth to consider the medium divide.

Arti Aggarwal (hereafter AA):

And one thing is there that the public, though I want to send my kid to a public school, an English-medium school, that has several reasons that I told you, that, like for higher studies she will be needing this and, I mean, she should not be developing this complex that "my mother didn't send me to an English-medium school and now I don't know how to cope up with my further studies."

CL: Right.

AA: But, it's a, like, superiority complex.

CL: The public school. Superiority complex.

AA: *Hã̃*, they think, they think they are superior to the other Hindi-medium school-going children.

CL: How so? I mean, like, can you give an example?

AA: Yes. Um, uh, for class.... I went to, uh, Central Hindu Girls School for Class IX and, uh, as I, as you know, I was studying in Kendriya Vidyalaya.[13]

CL: Right

AA: And, the girls coming from, uh, Saint John's School, when they, when they got to know that I, OK, I, I am, the medium of instruction I'm opting is English, they were just like, "you wanna come in English-medium class?" I mean, they, they thought, "OK, she's coming from the Kendriya Vidyalaya, so no way she can do it in English medium."

CL: Right

AA: So it was like, "are you coming? In this class?" I said, "why not?"

CL: In English, you mean, you said this.

AA: Yeah, yeah. [clears throat]

Arti reiterates the professor's assertion that English is the medium of choice for higher, post-secondary education, and introduces another term, "public," that is used only for fees-taking schools in which the medium of instruction is English. Of course, not all fees-taking schools in Banaras are English-medium, but Arti illustrates that high cost, entailed in her use of "public school," serves as a vehicle for a language-based institutional choice, ignoring the complex ways that fees and language co-vary in the city. Furthermore, Arti demonstrates the reproductive power of the language-medium divide by talking about it as a choice, one about which she has personal knowledge, and, therefore, one for which she can envision consequences for her three-year-old daughter.

Arti has, prior to the excerpt presented here, expressed her desire that the possibility of her daughter's future in science be left open by attendance at an English-medium school. But what happens in Arti's excerpt here speaks to the social circulation of the notion that a complex can develop in a student and the risk the development embodies for a parent. Arti shifts to the first person – from her daughter's perspective, that is – in order to explain, "my mother didn't send me to an English-medium school and now I don't know how to cope up with my further studies." In parallel fashion, Arti uses first person quotations to animate her own pain involved in switching from Hindi-medium to English-medium education. Thereby, the "complex" is dramatized. She herself has been met with the question "are you coming? In this class?" It is a question posed by students coming from the English-medium St. John's School to her because she has come from the Hindi-medium Kendriya Vidyalaya. The Central Hindu Girls School, where the question was posed, is exceptional in Banaras because it is a government school in which English-medium education in considered to be quite good. It is a question that she does not want for her child to be asked. Indeed, Arti finishes her narration of the experience of changing schools and joining the students coming from the English-medium school by clearing her throat and pausing for nearly ten seconds before beginning again.

As Arti continues in the next segment in the excerpt, however, she complicates depictions of the language-medium divide offered by the professor and herself by focusing on the hypocrisy on which the superiority felt by English-medium students might be based. In order to do this, she introduces Bhojpuri, a language that plays no part in the institutional dichotomy of English- and Hindi-medium schools. Particularly interesting is that she draws on distinctions such as those between the rural and the urban mentioned by the professor, but does so in order to complicate and destabilize the disposition claimed by the girl she mocks toward the social value of language medium.

AA: And there were some uh, some students from Valiant School, Dehra Dun, it's called Valiant Girls' School Dehra Dun, and her background was like she belonged to Ghazipur, it's a totally rural area.
CL: Near Banaras, right.
AA: Yeah, near Banaras, and she would tell other students of my class that she doesn't know a word of Hindi. She doesn't know a word of Hindi as she was in an English-medium school. And this, Chaise, she was very proud of this. OK, "I don't know any Hindi." And as I belong to Dehra Dun, my hometown is Dehra Dun, the other students will come and ask me, "Arti, is this school like this that they don't teach at all in, any Hindi at all? Or the students do not know any Hindi?" I said, "it's not that." And then, they say, "but the girl who has come from Valiant School in Dehra Dun, she doesn't know a word of Hindi." I said, "of course, how do you expect her to know Hindi because she must be knowing Bhojpuri because she's coming from Ghazipur!" And, the other day, her parents came, her father was wearing *dhotī, kurtā*.[14]
CL: Right.
AA: Very traditional dress. And then, they were, my friends were, they came running to me, "see, her father has come, her father has come." I said, "so? What do you realize now?" They said like, "I think you're right."
CL: Yeah.
AA: Like all her life she was speaking Bhojpuri with her parents, and naturally she wouldn't have known any Hindi.
CL: So it's a joke [laughingly]
AA: Yeah [laughingly] So this is the kind of mentality these English-medium, uh, students have.
CL: Wow.
AA: I guess they think, as they can converse in English, they are very superior.

Arti begins by introducing the case of a student who has come to Central Hindu Girls School in Banaras from the Valiant School, a private, fees-taking, English-medium school in Dehra Dun. Arti's relatives live in Dehra Dun while the girl's relatives live in Ghazipur, a town close to Banaras. In the narrative, Arti uses her transcendence of her classmates' knowledge of other locations in order to lampoon a girl's claim that she cannot speak Hindi. The girl has claimed maximal distance from Hindi, presumably to attain maximal identification with English. Arti, however, turns the girl's claim of superiority on its head. Bhojpuri functions – ironically in a narrative about schools wherein the language is considered unfit for use – as the element that lends the story a ridiculous twist. The girl does not (even) know Hindi because she comes from Ghazipur, a place that is not (even) Banaras. Certainly, Bhojpuri occupies the lowest position among languages because it is the secret that unmasks a claim. But its use in the narrative is unanticipated by the dichotomy of Hindi-medium and English-medium schools. In this case, Arti uses an association with Bhojpuri to show-up the claim not to know Hindi as utterly ridiculous. In the meantime she critiques what the language-medium divide presupposes, the rather confident feeling that those educated in English-medium schools are superior to those educated in Hindi-medium schools. And just like in the previous example, this critique rests on the idea that Hindi-medium schools teach in the students' "mother tongue." Indeed, when I asked if anyone might not know Hindi at a place like Central Hindu Girls School, she answered that the very idea is ridiculous given that Hindi is the students' "mother tongue."

## Conclusion

This article has explored several domains, scholarly and social, in which the notion of "mother tongue" can be found in northern India. In showing that the notion of the "mother tongue" changes in its denotational value as its uses in various censuses are traced, scholars of sociolinguistics in India have made a valuable contribution to the understanding of language itself as always situated and anything but natural and unmediated. In their zeal to argue for a lasting plurilingualism in India, however, those same scholars came to disregard the school as a site of exploration for its standardizing tendencies. This has been a mistake, this article contends, because just as the census teaches us valuable insights about the ideological disposition of the notion of "mother tongue," so does the school. People in northern India believe one type of educational institution to embody the "mother tongue." The "mother tongue" gains its institutional recognition through its juxtaposition with English. So salient is the institutional divide that students believed to have studied in the medium of their "mother tongue" suffer anxiety when confronted with someone who has studied in an English-medium school. The two people whose narratives are presented in the examples argue against various aspects of the institutional divide, but do not imagine an institutional arrangement apart from it.

The narrative activity and the language ideology that emerges from it is important to consider seriously because it demonstrates the contradictions that the institutionalized linguistic divide entails, on the one hand, and the unexpected possibilities for critique that involve languages outside the institutional divide, on the other hand. The narrator of the first example presented above, for example, was trained exclusively in Hindi-medium schools until master's coursework, yet she now is a professor in an English-medium university. The category that allows her to emerge as exceptional to the state of affairs she has just narrated – in which such shifts seem so unlikely – is the "topper." Thus, success in school in either medium serves to prove exceptional to the language-medium divide between one's "mother tongue" and English. It is thus important to realize that the institution of the school is crucial to the study of language ideology lest language ideology come to mask the possibility of contradiction. The second example shows that the language ideology presupposed by the language-medium divide does not exhaust the languages relevant to critique. Indeed, the narrator employs Bhojpuri, a language excluded from the language medium of schooling, to question the "superiority" of English-medium-trained students. These reflections show that languages and schools are not entities to be coordinated and counted, although this is a pervasive idea presupposed by the notion of "medium," but also components of the world with which people struggle to conceptualize such unstable notions as "mother tongue."

**Acknowledgments**

The field research on which this [chapter] is based was made possible by a grant from the National Science Foundation, a Faculty Development Grant from Southern Connecticut State University, and Hamilton College's Dean of Faculty. Discussions with Lavanya Murali Proctor, Bonnie Urciuoli, and Susan Wadley helped to clarify the arguments. For guidance and friendship in India, thanks are due to Neelam Bohra, Ravinder Gargesh, Krishna Kumar, Nita Kumar, Chandrakala Padia, and Rakesh Ranjan. Special thanks are due to Nigel Love and Umberto Ansaldo for being such excellent organizers, hosts, and critics.

## Notes

1. For other explanations of the concept of language ideology, see Blommaert (2006), Kroskrity (2000) and Silverstein (1979).

2. Many critiques of the census and the changing denotational values of its linguistic descriptors exist. A particularly rich example is Khubchandani (1983).

3. Downright arbitrary is the procedure described by Pattanayak (1981, p. 49) whereby "respondents [in the 1961 census] who spoke and understood more than one language in addition to their mother tongue, two languages were recorded by the census enumerator, the tabulation was based only on the language recorded first by him."

4. There have been a few exceptions, but no study of an institutional domain of language ideology as offered here. Vaughier-Chatterjee (2007, p. 360) quotes Khubchandani (1991) in order to explain:

   > The five decades since independence [of India] have seen the birth of a new linguistic order and, to quote an Indian scholar, India is "turning away from an organically accommodating plurilingual nation into an institutionally assertive multilingual nation."

   See Aggarwal (1997) for a critique of the sociolinguistic notion of India's plurilingualism that ignores institutional domains such as the school.

5. Lachman Khubchandani (1981, p. 2) claims similarly (but with less emphasis on national identity): Under the present educational system, the easy-going *grassroot* multilingualism of the illiterate masses is being replaced by an *elegant* bilingualism (or trilingualism) with standardisation pulls from different directions, e.g., neo-Sanskritic Hindi, Perso-Arabicised Urdu, BBC [British Broadcasting Corporation] or AIR [All India Radio] English, medieval literary Telugu and classicised modern Tamil. The emphasis on distinct normative systems (i.e. standard languages), nurtured in historically and geographically unrelated "traditions," is at variance with the requirement of active bilingualism in a society. We do not learn more about schools' relationships to languages beyond this, however.

6. This assertion, I would point out, begs the question of whether resistance to these tendencies of policy – especially in the South as noted by Brass (1990), Das Gupta (1970) and Ramaswamy (1997) – were indeed fueled by the "fluid plurilingual texture of Indian society."

7. In Charles Ferguson's (1959) original formulation, H and L are varieties of the same language, whereas in Fishman's (1967) reformulation, H and L are differentiated by the dichotomies of the original formulation – textual versus oral, formal versus vernacular, institutionally acquired versus mother tongue – but not necessarily related linguistically.

8. Though he does not approach the relationship between languages and schools in a closely considered case, as this article does, Khubchandani (2003, p. 251) outlines some of the dimensions of the relationship:

   > One needs to adopt a pragmatic approach to linguistic usage in education (such as when phasing the shift and/or combining the mediums of instruction) and take into account the mechanisms of language standardization in plural societies when tackling the literary problems through varying demands in the spoken and written genre of the same language.

9. Note the difference, for example, between the ethnographic account of the notion of language medium and the account of Khubchandani (1984, p. 55): Owing to the rigorous academic base and to selective education, English, in spite of such intense use by non-native speakers, has not been so greatly pidginized in the Indian context, but it definitely has acquired a certain regional flavor which distinguishes South Asian English from native standard varieties (British English, American English, etc.). The most prominent characteristic of South Asian English is the cheerful acceptance of regional deviations in pronunciation.

   To people in Varanasi with whom I worked, much more important than schools' effect on the nativeness of English was its juxtaposition with Hindi as a medium of instruction. I present Khubchandani as an exemplar because his is one of the most ethnographically sophisticated approaches.

10. See Benei (2008) for the case of the state of Maharashtra where Marathi achieves the status of "mother tongue" in a way very different from the case of Hindi and the languages in its geographic domain.

11. "Complex," like "medium" and "topper," is a "bivalent" term in Woolard's (1999) sense. One might even render them as *kāmpleks, mīdiam*, and *tāpār* because they can be used in utterances in Hindi without any recognition that any other language is being used. Indeed, I often heard utterances like "he got a complex" (*usko kāmpleks gayī hai*), "she studies in Hindi medium" (*vaha hindī mīdiam mẽ parhtī hai*), and "she was a topper" (*vaha tāpart thī*). See LaDousa (2007) for an explanation that the bivalent use of English words in matters of education, but not Hindi words, might be understood to **index** the school system's colonial origins.

12. The ghats are the steps leading up to the city from the Ganges River.

13. A school run by its own board meant to serve the children of central government employees who may be posted far away from their last assignment.

14. A *dhotī* is a piece of cloth that is worn by men around the waist and legs. A *kurtā* is the stitched shirt worn on the upper body. The *dhotī* can be considered traditional and/or formal depending on the context.

## References


Aggarwal, K. 1997. What's Indian about Indian plurilingualism. Language Problems and Language Planning 21(1): 35–50.

Agnihotri, R. K., Khanna, A. L. 1997. Problematizing English in India. Sage Publications, New Delhi.

Barz, R. K., Siegel, J. (Eds.). 1988. Language Transplanted: The Development of Overseas Hindi. Otto Harrassowitz, Wiesbaden.

Benei, V. 2008. Schooling Passions: Nation, History, and Language in Contemporary Western India. Stanford University Press, Palo Alto.

Bernstein, B. 1971. Class, Codes, and Control. Theoretical Studies Towards a Sociology of Language, vol. 1. Routledge and Kegan Paul, London.

Blommaert, J. 2006. Language ideology. In: Brown, K. (Ed.), Encyclopedia of Language and Linguistics, vol. 6. Elsevier, Oxford, pp. 510–22.

Brass, P. 1990. The New Cambridge History of India. Part 1: The Politics of India Since Independence, vol. 4, Cambridge University Press, Cambridge.

Chaturvedi, M. G., Mohale, B. V. 1976. Position of Languages in School Curriculum in India. National Council of Educational Research and Training, Delhi.

Dalmia, V. 1997. The Nationalization of Hindu Traditions: Bharatendu Harischandra and 19th-Century Banaras. Oxford University Press, Delhi.

Das Gupta, J. 1970. Language Conflict and National Development: Group Politics and National Language Policy in India. University of California Press, Berkeley.

Dasgupta, P. 1993. The Otherness of English: India's Auntie Tongue Syndrome. Sage Publications, New Delhi.

Dua, H. 1994. Hindi language spread policy and its implementation: achievements and prospects. International Journal of the Sociology of Language 107: 115–43.

Eisenlohr, P. 2006. Little India: Diaspora, Time, and Ethnolinguistic Belonging in Mauritius. University of California Press, Berkeley.

Errington, J. J. 1999. Ideology. Journal of Linguistic Anthropology 9(1–2): 115–17.

Ferguson, C. 1959. Diglossia. Word 15: 325–40.

Fishman, J. 1967. Bilingualism with and without diglossia; diglossia with and without bilingualism. Journal of Social Issues 23: 29–38.

Gal, S., Irvine, J. 1995. The boundaries of language and disciplines: how ideologies construct differences. Social Research 62(4): 967–1001.

Gambhir, S. 1981. The East Indian Speech Community in Guyana: A Sociolinguistic Study with Special Reference to Koiné Formation. Ph.D. Thesis, University of Pennsylvania.

Government of India. 1971. The 12th Report of the Commissioner of Linguistic Minorities in India. Ministry of Home Affairs, New Delhi.

Grierson, G. A., [1903–1928]. 1967. Linguistic Survey of India: Vol. V Part 2 Bihari and Oriya Languages and Vol. VI Eastern Hindi. Motilal Banarsidass, Delhi.

Gumperz, J. 1958. Dialect differences and social stratification in a North Indian Village. American Anthropologist 60(4): 668–81.

Gumperz, J. 1961. Speech variation and the study of Indian civilization. American Anthropologist 63(5, part 1): 976–87.

Gumperz, J. 1964. Linguistic and social interaction in two communities. American Anthropologist 66(6, part 2): 137–51.

Jayaram, N. 1993. The language question in higher education: trends and issues. Higher Education 26(July): 93–114.

Khubchandani, L. 1981. Language Identity: Miscellaneous Papers. Studies in Linguistics, Number 16. Centre for Communication Studies, Pune.

Khubchandani, L. 1983. Plural Languages, Plural Cultures: Communication, Identity, and Sociopolitical Change in Contemporary India. University of Hawai'i Press, Honolulu.

Khubchandani, L. 1984. Sociolinguistics in India: the decade past, the decade to come. International Journal of the Sociology of Language 45: 47–64.

Khubchandani, L. 1991. Language, Culture, and Nation-building: Challenges of Modernisation. Manohar, Delhi.

Khubchandani, L. 2003. Defining mother tongue education in plurilingual contexts. Language Policy 2: 239–54.

King, C. 1994. One Language, Two Scripts: The Hindi Movement in Nineteenth Century North India. Oxford University Press, Delhi.

King, C. 2001. The poisonous potency of script: Hindi and Urdu. International Journal of the Sociology of Language 150: 43–59.
Kroskrity, P. 2000. Regimenting languages: language ideological perspectives. In: Kroskrity, P. (Ed.), Regimes of Language: Ideologies, Polities, and Identities. School of American Research Press, Santa Fe, NM, pp. 1–34.
LaDousa, C. 2002. Advertising in the periphery: languages and schools in a North Indian City. Language in Society 31(2): 213–42.
LaDousa, C. 2004. In the mouth but not on the map: visions of language and their enactment in the Hindi belt. Journal of Pragmatics 36(4): 633–61.
LaDousa, C. 2005. Disparate markets: language, nation, and education in North India. American Ethnologist 32(3): 460–78.
LaDousa, C. 2006. The discursive malleability of an identity: a dialogic approach to language "Medium" schooling in North India. Journal of Linguistic Anthropology 16(1): 36–57.
LaDousa, C. 2007. Of nation and state: language, school, and the reproduction of disparity in a North Indian City. Anthropological Quarterly 80(4): 925–59.
Lelyveld, D. 1993. The fate of Hindustani. In: Breckenridge, C., van der Veer, P. (Eds.), Orientalism and the Postcolonial Predicament: Perspectives on South Asia. University of Pennsylvania Press, Philadelphia, pp. 189–214.
Masica, C. 1991. The Indo-Aryan Languages. Cambridge University Press, Cambridge.
Mesthrie, R. 1991. Language in Indenture: A Sociolinguistic History of Bhojpuri-Hindi in South Africa. Witwatersrand University Press, Johannesburg.
Mitchell, L. 2009. Language, Emotion, and Politics in South India: The Making of a Mother Tongue. Indiana University Press, Bloomington.
Mohan, P. 1978. Trinidad Bhojpuri: A Morphological Study. Ph.D. Thesis, University of Michigan.
Orsini, F. 2002. The Hindi Public Sphere 1920–1940: Language and Literature in the Age of Nationalism. Oxford University Press, Delhi.
Pattanayak, D. P. 1981. Multilingualism and Mother Tongue Education. Oxford University Press, Delhi.
Rai, A. I. 2000. Hindi Nationalism. Orient Longman, Hyderabad.
Rai, A. M. 1984. A House Divided: The Origin and Development of Hindi/Hindavi. Oxford University Press, Delhi.
Ramanathan, V. 2005. The English-Vernacular Divide: Postcolonial Language Politics and Practice. Multilingual Matters, Clevedon.
Ramaswamy, S. 1997. Passions of the Tongue: Language Devotion in Tamil India, 1891–1970. University of California Press, Berkeley.
Shapiro, M. C., Schiffman, H. F. 1981. Language and Society in South Asia. Motilal Banarsidass, Delhi.
Silverstein, M. 1979. Language structure and linguistic ideology. In: Clyne, P., Hanks, W., Hofbauer, C. (Eds.), The Elements: A Parasession on Linguistic Units and Levels. Chicago Linguistic Society, Chicago, pp. 193–247.
Simon, B. 1986. Bilingualism and Language Maintenance in Banaras. Ph.D. Thesis, University of Wisconsin, Madison.
Simon, B. 2003. Here we do not speak Bhojpuri: a semantics of opposition. In: Toffolo, C. E. (Ed.), Emancipating Cultural Pluralism. State University of New York Press, Albany, pp. 147–62.
Skutnabb-Kangas, T., Phillipson, R. 1989. "Mother Tongue": the theoretical and sociopolitical construction of a concept. In: Ammon, U. (Ed.), Status and Function of Languages and Language Varieties. Walter de Gruyter, Berlin, pp. 450–77.
Sridhar, K. K. 1991. Bilingual education in India. In: García, O. (Ed.), Bilingual Education: Focusschrift in Honor of Joshua A. Fishman on the Occasion of His 65th Birthday, vol. I. John Benjamins, Amsterdam, pp. 89–101.
Sridhar, K. K. 1996. Language in education: minorities and multilingualism in India. International Review of Education 42(4): 327–47.
Srivastava, A. K. 1990. Multilingualism and school education in India: special features, problems, and prospects. In: Pattanayak, D. (Ed.), Multilingualism in India. Multilingual Matters, Clevedon, UK, pp. 37–53.
Vaughier-Chatterjee, A. 2007. Politics of language in education: policies and reforms in India. In: Kumar, K., Oesterheld, J. (Eds.), Education and Social Change in South Asia. Orient Longman Private Limited, New Delhi, pp. 359–89.
Woolard, K. 1998. Introduction: language ideology as a field of inquiry. In: Schieffelin, B., Woolard, K., Kroskrity, P. (Eds.), Language Ideologies: Practice and Theory. Oxford University Press, New York, pp. 3–50.
Woolard, K. 1999. Simultaneity and bivalency as strategies in bilingualism. Journal of Linguistic Anthropology 8: 3–29.

## Critical Thinking and Application

- How is prestige connected with the medium of education?
- LaDousa shows how difficult it is to ask about language on the census that India administers every decade. Discuss the various terms and their meanings. Develop a preferable term and explain how it solves some of the problems in the other terms.
- The United States has many language ideological associations with English and Spanish. Learn about policies with regard to Spanish-medium education in the United States. How is it similar to and different from the situation in northern India?

## Vocabulary

Bharat
census
denotational
diglossia
Herderian
index
language ideology
-medium
plurilingualism
scheduled caste
*Sprachbund*
standardized
unmediated

## Suggested Further Reading


Bénéï, Véronique. 2008. *Schooling Passions: Nation, History, and Language in Contemporary Western India*. Stanford, CA: Stanford University Press.

Edwards, John R. 1994. *Multilingualism*. London and New York: Routledge.

Ferguson, Charles. 1972 [1959]. Diglossia. In *Language and Social Context*, edited by Pier Paolo Giglioli, pp. 232–251. Middlesex: Penguin.

Goel, B. S., and S. K. Saini. 1972. *Mother Tongue and Equality of Opportunity in Education*. New Delhi: National Council of Educational Research and Training.

Gopal, Ram. 1966. *Linguistic Affairs of India*. Bombay: Asia Publishing House.

Gumperz, John J. 1958. Dialect Differences and Social Stratification in a North Indian Village. *American Anthropologist*, new series, 60(4): 668–682.

Gumperz, John J. 1982. *Discourse Strategies*. Cambridge: Cambridge University Press.

Heller, Monica, ed. 1988. *Codeswitching: Anthropological and Sociolinguistic Perspectives*. Berlin and New York: Mouton de Gruyter.

Mitchell, Lisa. 2009. *Language, Emotion, and Politics in South India: The Making of a Mother Tongue*. Bloomington: Indiana University Press.

Myers-Scotton, Carol. 1988. Codeswitching as Indexical of Social Negotiations. In *Codeswitching: Anthropological and Sociolinguistic Perspectives*, edited by Monica Heller, pp. 151–186. Berlin and New York: Mouton de Gruyter.

Pattanayak, D. P. 1981 *Multilingualism and Mother-Tongue Education*. Delhi: Oxford University Press.

Ramaswamy, Sumathi. 1997. *Passions of the Tongue: Language Devotion in Tamil India, 1891–1970*. Berkeley: University of California Press.

Romaine, Suzanne. 1989. *Bilingualism*. Oxford: Basil Blackwell.

Simon, Beth. 1993. Language Choice, Religion, and Identity in the Banarsi Community. In *Living Banaras: Hindu Religion in Cultural Context*, edited by Bradley R. Hertel and Cynthia Ann Humes, pp. 245–268. Buffalo: State University of New York Press.

CHAPTER 48

# "To Give Up on Words"
## Silence in Western Apache Culture

*Keith H. Basso*

(1970)

*Stereotypes of others are part and parcel of human experience. Not all stereotypes are entirely erroneous; there is often a kernel of truth behind them, though stereotypes often make it seem unnecessary to understand the context or nuances surrounding a mysterious way of doing things.*

*Keith Basso has been interpreting Apache culture since the 1960s, shattering stereotypes or explaining reasons that might lie behind them. In this case, he examines some of the circumstances under which Western Apache may remain silent. Using the* ethnography of speaking *approach pioneered by Dell Hymes, Basso focuses on the function of silence, in appropriate settings, rather than on the form. (And, as he says so succinctly, "the form of silence is always the same.")*

*Basso gives six types of situation in which he has observed restraint from speech. He discusses the reasons for silence with local people, usually at a later time, coming up with a fairly powerful reason in each of these cases. He ends with a more synthetic generalization that accounts for all six cases, suggesting that this might or might not explain silence in other cultures.*

### Reading Questions

- What are the circumstances in which Apaches refrain from speech? Would you do the same in some of these situations? For the same or different reasons?
- What is the unifying reason for the Apache to remain silent?
- Why is the stereotype of the silent American Indian misleading?

---

It is not the case that a man who is silent says nothing.
—Anonymous

## I

Anyone who has read about American Indians has probably encountered statements which impute to them a strong predilection for keeping silent or, as one writer has put it, "a fierce reluctance to speak except when absolutely necessary." In the popular literature, where this characterization is particularly widespread, it is commonly portrayed as the outgrowth of such dubious causes as "instinctive dignity," "an impoverished language," or, perhaps worst of all, the Indians' "lack of personal warmth." Although statements of this sort are plainly erroneous and dangerously misleading, it is noteworthy that professional anthropologists have made few attempts to correct them. Traditionally, ethnographers and linguists have paid little attention to cultural interpretations given to silence or, equally important, to the types of social contexts in which it regularly occurs.

This study investigates certain aspects of silence in the culture of the Western Apache of east-central Arizona. After considering some of the theoretical issues involved, I will briefly describe a number of situations—recurrent in Western Apache society—in which one or more of the participants typically refrain from speech for lengthy periods of time.[1] This is accompanied by a discussion of how such acts

Keith Basso, "To Give Up on Words": Silence in Western Apache Culture. *Southwestern Journal of Anthropology* (1970) 26 (3): 213–30.

of silence are interpreted and why they are encouraged and deemed appropriate. I conclude by advancing an hypothesis that accounts for the reasons that the Western Apache refrain from speaking when they do, and I suggest that, with proper testing, this hypothesis may be shown to have relevance to silence behavior in other cultures.

## II

A basic finding of sociolinguistics is that, although both language and language usage are structured, it is the latter which responds most sensitively to **extra-linguistic** influences (Hymes 1962, 1964; Ervin-Tripp 1964, 1967; Gumperz 1964; Slobin 1967). Accordingly, a number of recent studies have addressed themselves to the problem of how factors in the social environment of speech events delimit the range and condition the selection of message forms (cf. Brown and Gilman 1960; Conklin 1959; Ervin-Tripp 1964, 1967; Frake 1964; Friedrich 1966; Gumperz 1961, 1964; Martin 1964). These studies may be viewed as taking the now familiar position that verbal communication is fundamentally a decision-making process in which, initially, a speaker, having elected to speak, selects from among a repertoire of available codes that which is most appropriately suited to the situation at hand. Once a code has been selected, the speaker picks a suitable channel of transmission and then, finally, makes a choice from a set of referentially equivalent expressions within the code. The intelligibility of the expression he chooses will, of course, be subject to grammatical constraints. But its acceptability will not. Rules for the selection of linguistic alternates operate on features of the social environment and are commensurate with rules governing the conduct of face-to-face interaction. As such, they are properly conceptualized as lying outside the structure of language itself.

It follows from this that for a stranger to communicate appropriately with the members of an unfamiliar society it is not enough that he learn to formulate messages intelligibly. Something else is needed: a knowledge of what kinds of codes, channels, and expressions to use in what kinds of situations and to what kinds of people—as Hymes (1964) has termed it, an **"ethnography of communication."**

There is considerable evidence to suggest that extra-linguistic factors influence not only the use of speech but its actual occurrence as well. In our own culture, for example, remarks such as "Don't you know when to keep quiet?," "Don't talk until you're introduced," and "Remember now, no talking in church" all point to the fact that an individual's decision to speak may be directly contingent upon the character of his surroundings. Few of us would maintain that "silence is golden" for all people at all times. But we feel that silence is a virtue for some people some of the time, and we encourage children on the road to cultural competence to act accordingly.

Although the form of silence is always the same, the function of a specific act of silence—that is, its interpretation by and effect upon other people—will vary according to the social context in which it occurs. For example, if I choose to keep silent in the chambers of a Justice of the Supreme Court, my action is likely to be interpreted as a sign of politeness or respect. On the other hand, if I refrain from speaking to an established friend or colleague, I am apt to be accused of rudeness or harboring a grudge. In one instance, my behavior is judged by others to be "correct" or "fitting"; in the other, it is criticized as being "out of line."

The point, I think, is fairly obvious. For a stranger entering an alien society, a knowledge of when *not* to speak may be as basic to the production of culturally acceptable behavior as a knowledge of what to say. It stands to reason, then, that an adequate ethnography of communication should not confine itself exclusively to the analysis of choice within verbal repertoires. It should also, as Hymes (1962, 1964) has suggested, specify those conditions under which the members of the society regularly decide to refrain from verbal behavior altogether.

## III

The research on which this [work] is based was conducted over a period of sixteen months (1964–1969) in the Western Apache settlement of Cibecue, which is located near the center of the Fort Apache Indian Reservation in east-central Arizona. Cibecue's 800 residents participate in an unstable economy that combines subsistence agriculture, cattle-raising, sporadic wage-earning, and Government subsidies in the form of welfare checks and social security benefits. Unemployment is a serious problem, and substandard living conditions are widespread.

Although Reservation life has precipitated far-reaching changes in the composition and geographical distribution of Western Apache social groups, **consanguineal kinship**—real and imputed—remains the single most powerful force in the establishment and regulation of interpersonal relationships (Kaut 1957; Basso 1970). The focus of domestic activity is the individual "camp," or *gową́ą́*. This term labels both the occupants and the location of a single dwelling or, as is more apt to be the case, several dwellings built within a few feet of each other. The majority of *gową́ą́* in Cibecue are occupied by nuclear families. The next largest residential unit is the *gotáá* (camp cluster), which is a group of spatially localized *gową́ą́*, each having at least one adult member who is related by ties of **matrilineal kinship** to persons living in all the others. An intricate system of **exogamous clans** serves to extend kinship relationships beyond the *gową́ą́* and *gotáá* and facilitates concerted action in projects, most notably the presentation of ceremonials, requiring large amounts of manpower. Despite the presence in Cibecue of a variety of Anglo missionaries and a dwindling number of medicine men, diagnostic and curing rituals, as well as the girls' puberty ceremonial, continue to be performed with regularity (Basso 1966, 1970). Witchcraft persists in undiluted form (Basso 1969).

## IV

Of the many broad categories of events, or scenes, that comprise the daily round of Western Apache life, I shall deal here only with those that are coterminous with what Goffman (1961, 1964) has termed "focused gatherings" or "encounters." The concept *situation,* in keeping with established usage, will refer inclusively to the location of such a gathering, its physical setting, its point in time, the standing behavior patterns that accompany it, and the social attributes of the persons involved (Hymes 1962, 1964; Ervin-Tripp 1964, 1967).

In what follows, however, I will be mainly concerned with the roles and statuses of participants. The reason for this is that the critical factor in the Apache's decision to speak or keep silent seems always to be the nature of his relationships to other people. To be sure, other features of the situation are significant, but apparently only to the extent that they influence the perception of status and role.[2] What this implies, of course, is that roles and statuses are not fixed attributes. Although they may be depicted as such in a static model (and often with good reason), they are appraised and acted upon in particular social contexts and, as a result, subject to redefinition and variation.[3] With this in mind, let us now turn our attention to the Western Apache and the types of situations in which, as one of my informants put it, "it is right to give up on words."

## V

**1. "Meeting strangers"** *(nda dòhwáá'iłtsééda)* The term, *nda,* labels categories at two levels of contrast. At the most general level, it designates any person—Apache or non-Apache—who, prior to an initial meeting, has never been seen and therefore cannot be identified. In addition, the term is used to refer to Apaches who, though previously seen and known by some external criteria such as clan affiliation or personal name, have never been engaged in face-to-face interaction. The latter category, which is more restricted than the first, typically includes individuals who live on the adjacent San Carlos Reservation, in Fort Apache settlements geographically removed from Cibecue, and those who fall into the category *kii dòhandáágo* (non-kinsmen). In all cases, "strangers" are separated by social distance. And in all cases it is considered appropriate, when encountering them for the first time, to refrain from speaking.

The type of situation described as "meeting strangers" (*nda dòhwáá'iłtsééda*) can take place in any number of different physical settings. However, it occurs most frequently in the context of events such as fairs and rodeos, which, owing to the large number of people in attendance, offer unusual opportunities for chance encounters. In large gatherings, the lack of verbal communication between strangers is apt to go unnoticed, but in smaller groups it becomes quite conspicuous. The following incident, involving two strangers who found themselves part of a four-man round-up crew, serves as a good example. My **informant**, who was also a member of the crew, recalled the following episode:

> One time, I was with A, B, and X down at Gleason Flat, working cattle. That man, X, was from East Fork [a community nearly 40 miles from Cibecue] where B's wife was from. But he didn't know A, never knew him before, I guess. First day, I worked with X. At night, when we camped, we talked with B, but X and A didn't say anything to each other. Same way, second day. Same way, third. Then, at night on fourth day, we were sitting by the fire. Still, X and A didn't talk. Then A said, "Well, I know there is a stranger to me here, but I've been watching him and I know he is all right." After that, X and A talked a lot.... Those two men didn't know each other, so they took it easy at first.

As this incident suggests, the Western Apache do not feel compelled to "introduce" persons who are unknown to each other. Eventually, it is assumed, strangers will begin to speak. However, this is a decision that is properly left to the individuals involved, and no attempt is made to hasten it. Outside help in the form of introductions or other verbal routines is viewed as presumptuous and unnecessary.

Strangers who are quick to launch into conversation are frequently eyed with undisguised suspicion. A typical reaction to such individuals is that they "want something," that is, their willingness to violate convention is attributed to some urgent need which is likely to result in requests for money, labor, or transportation. Another common reaction to talkative strangers is that they are drunk.

If the stranger is an Anglo, it is usually assumed that he "wants to teach us something" (i.e., give orders or instructions) or that he "wants to make friends in a hurry." The latter response is especially revealing, since Western Apaches are extremely reluctant to be hurried into friendships—with Anglos or each other. Their verbal reticence with strangers is directly related to the conviction that the establishment of social relationships is a serious matter that calls for caution, careful judgment, and plenty of time.

**2. "Courting"** *(líígoláá)* During the initial stages of courtship, young men and women go without speaking for conspicuous lengths of time. Courting may occur in a wide variety of settings—practically anywhere, in fact—and at virtually any time of the day or night, but it is most readily observable at large public gatherings such as ceremonials, wakes, and rodeos. At these events, "sweethearts" (*zéédé*) may stand or sit (sometimes holding hands) for as long as an hour without exchanging a word. I am told by adult informants that the young people's reluctance to speak may become even more pronounced in situations where they find themselves alone.

Apaches who have just begun to court attribute their silence to "intense shyness" (*'isté'*) and a feeling of acute "self-consciousness" (*dàyéézi'*) which, they claim, stems from their lack of familiarity with one another. More specifically, they complain of "not knowing what to do" in each other's presence and of the fear that whatever they say, no matter how well thought out in advance, will sound "dumb" or "stupid."[4]

One informant, a youth 17 years old, commented as follows:

> It's hard to talk with your sweetheart at first. She doesn't know you and won't know what to say. It's the same way towards her. You don't know how to talk yet...so you get very bashful. That makes it sometimes so you don't say anything. So you just go around together and don't talk. At first, it's better that way. Then, after a while, when you know each other, you aren't shy anymore and can talk good.

The Western Apache draw an equation between the ease and frequency with which a young couple talks and how well they know each other. Thus, it is expected that after several months of steady companionship sweethearts will start to have lengthy conversations. Earlier in their relationship, however, protracted discussions may be openly discouraged. This is especially true for girls, who are informed by their mothers and older sisters that silence in courtship is a sign of modesty and that an eagerness to speak betrays previous experience with men. In extreme cases, they add, it may be interpreted as a willingness to engage in sexual relations. Said one woman, aged 32:

> This way I have talked to my daughter. "Take it easy when boys come around this camp and want you to go somewhere with them. When they talk to you, just listen at first. Maybe you won't know what to say. So don't talk about just anything. If you talk with those boys right away, then they will know you know all about them. They will think you've been with many boys before, and they will start talking about that."

**3. "Children, coming home"** ***(čəgəše nakáii)*** The Western Apache **lexeme** *iltá'inatsáá* (reunion) is used to describe encounters between an individual who has returned home after a long absence and his relatives and friends. The most common type of reunion, *čəgəše nakáii* (children, coming home), involves boarding school students and their parents. It occurs in late May or early in June, and its setting is usually a trading post or school, where parents congregate to await the arrival of buses bringing the children home. As the latter disembark and locate their parents in the crowd, one anticipates a flurry of verbal greetings. Typically, however, there are few or none at all. Indeed, it is not unusual for parents and child to go without speaking for as long as 15 minutes.

When the silence is broken, it is almost always the child who breaks it. His parents listen attentively to everything he says but speak hardly at all themselves. This pattern persists even after the family has reached the privacy of its camp, and two or three days may pass before the child's parents seek to engage him in sustained conversation.

According to my informants, the silence of Western Apache parents at (and after) reunions with their children is ultimately predicated on the possibility that the latter have been adversely affected by their experiences away from home. Uppermost is the fear that, as a result of protracted exposure to Anglo attitudes and values, the children have come to view their parents as ignorant, old-fashioned, and no longer deserving of respect. One of my most thoughtful and articulate informants commented on the problem as follows:

> You just can't tell about those children after they've been with White men for a long time. They get their minds turned around sometimes...they forget where they come from and get ashamed when they come home because their parents and relatives are poor. They forget how to act with these Apaches and get mad easy. They walk around all night and get into fights. They don't stay at home.
>
> At school, some of them learn to want to be White men, so they come back and try to act that way. But we are still Apaches! So we don't know them anymore, and it is like we never knew them. It is hard to talk to them when they are like that.

Apache parents openly admit that, initially, children who have been away to school seem distant and unfamiliar. They have grown older, of course, and their physical appearance may have changed. But more fundamental is the concern that they have acquired new ideas and expectations which will alter their behavior in unpredictable ways. No matter how pressing this concern may be, however, it is considered inappropriate to directly interrogate a child after his arrival home. Instead, parents anticipate that within a short time he will begin to divulge information about himself that will enable them to determine in what ways, if any, his views and attitudes have changed. This, the Apache say, is why children do practically all the talking in the hours following a reunion, and their parents remain unusually silent.

Said one man, the father of two children who had recently returned from boarding school in Utah:

> Yes, it's right that we didn't talk much to them when they came back, my wife and me. They were away for a long time, and we didn't know how they would like it, being home. So we waited. Right away, they started to tell stories about what they did. Pretty soon we could tell they liked it, being back. That made us feel good. So it was easy to talk to them again. It was like they were before they went away.

**4. "Getting cussed out"** ***(šiłditéé)*** This lexeme is used to describe any situation in which one individual, angered and enraged, shouts insults and criticisms at another. Although the object of such invective is in most cases the person or persons who provoked it, this is not always the case, because an Apache who is truly beside himself with rage is likely to vent his feelings on anyone whom he sees or who happens to be within range of his voice. Consequently, "getting cussed out" may involve large numbers of people who are totally innocent of the charges being hurled against them. But whether they are innocent or not, their response to the situation is the same. They refrain from speech.

Like the types of situations we have discussed thus far, "getting cussed out" can occur in a wide variety of physical settings: at ceremonial dance grounds and trading posts, inside and outside wickiups and houses, on food-gathering expeditions and shopping trips—in short, wherever and whenever individuals lose control of their tempers and lash out verbally at persons nearby.

Although "getting cussed out" is basically free of setting-imposed restrictions, the Western Apache fear it most at gatherings where alcohol is being consumed. My informants observed that especially at "drinking parties" (*dá'idlą́ą́*), where there is much rough joking and ostensibly mock criticism, it is easy for well-intentioned remarks to be misconstrued as insults. Provoked in this way, persons who are intoxicated may become hostile and launch into explosive tirades, often with no warning at all.

The silence of Apaches who are "getting cussed out" is consistently explained in reference to the belief that individuals who are "enraged" (*hasˇkéé*) are also irrational or "crazy" (*bìné'idį́į́*). In this condition, it is said, they "forget who they are" and become oblivious to what they say or do. Concomitantly, they lose all concern for the consequences of their actions on other people. In a word, they are dangerous. Said one informant:

> When people get mad they get crazy. Then they start yelling and saying bad things. Some say they are going to kill somebody for what he has done. Some keep it up that way for a long time, maybe walk from camp to camp, real angry, yelling, crazy like that. They keep it up for a long time, some do.
>
> People like that don't know what they are saying, so you can't tell about them. When you see someone like that, just walk away. If he yells at you, let him say whatever he wants to. Let him say anything. Maybe he doesn't mean it. But he doesn't know that. He will be crazy, and he could try to kill you.

Another Apache said:

> When someone gets mad at you and starts yelling, then just don't do anything to make him get worse. Don't try to quiet him down because he won't know why you're doing it. If you try to do that, he may just get worse and try to hurt you.

As the last of these statements implies, the Western Apache operate on the assumption that enraged persons—because they are temporarily "crazy"—are difficult to reason with. Indeed, there is a widely held belief that attempts at mollification will serve to intensify anger, thus increasing the chances of physical violence. The appropriate strategy when "getting cussed out" is to do nothing, to avoid any action that will attract attention to oneself. Since speaking accomplishes just the opposite, the use of silence is strongly advised.

**5. "Being with people who are sad"** ***(nde dòbíłgòzóóda bigą́ą́ )*** Although the Western Apache phrase that labels this situation has no precise equivalent in English, it refers quite specifically to gatherings in which an individual finds himself in the company of someone whose spouse or kinsman has recently died. Distinct from wakes and burials, which follow immediately after a death, "being with people who are sad" is most likely to occur several weeks later. At this time, close relatives of the deceased emerge from a period of intense mourning (during which they rarely venture beyond the limits of their camps) and start to resume their normal activities within the community. To persons anxious to convey their sympathies, this is interpreted as a sign that visitors will be welcomed and, if possible, provided with food and drink. To those less solicitous, it means that unplanned encounters with the bereaved must be anticipated and prepared for.

"Being with people who are sad" can occur on a footpath, in a camp, at church, or in a trading post; but whatever the setting—and regardless of whether it is the result of a planned visit or an accidental meeting—the situation is marked by a minimum of speech. Queried about this, my informants volunteered three types of explanations. The first is that persons "who are sad" are so burdened with "intense grief" (*dółgozóóda*) that speaking requires of them an unusual amount of physical effort. It is courteous and considerate, therefore, not to attempt to engage them in conversation.

A second native explanation is that in situations of this sort verbal communication is basically unnecessary. Everyone is familiar with what has happened, and talking about it, even for the purpose of conveying solace and sympathy, would only reinforce and augment the sadness felt by those who were close to the deceased. Again, for reasons of courtesy, this is something to be avoided.

The third explanation is rooted in the belief that "intense grief," like intense rage, produces changes in the personality of the individual who experiences it. As evidence for this, the Western Apache cite numerous instances in which the emotional strain of dealing with death, coupled with an overwhelming sense of irrevocable personal loss, has caused persons who were formerly mild and even-tempered to become abusive, hostile, and physically violent.

> That old woman, X, who lives across Cibecue Creek, one time her first husband died. After that she cried all the time, for a long time. Then, I guess she got mean because everyone said she drank a lot and got into fights. Even with her close relatives, she did like that for a long time. She was too sad for her husband. That's what made her like that; it made her lose her mind.
>
> My father was like that when his wife died. He just stayed home all the time and wouldn't go anywhere. He didn't talk to any of his relatives or children. He just said, "I'm hungry. Cook for me." That's all. He stayed that way for a long time. His mind was not with us. He was still with his wife.
>
> My uncle died in 1941. His wife sure went crazy right away after that. Two days after they buried the

> body, we went over there and stayed with those people who had been left alone. My aunt got mad at us. She said, "Why do you come over here? You can't bring my husband back. I can take care of myself and those others in my camp, so why don't you go home." She sure was mad that time, too sad for someone who died. She didn't know what she was saying because in about one week she came to our camp and said, "My relatives, I'm all right now. When you came to help me, I had too much sadness and my mind was no good. I said bad words to you. But now I am all right and I know what I am doing."

As these statements indicate, the Western Apache assume that a person suffering from "intense grief" is likely to be disturbed and unstable. Even though he may appear outwardly composed, they say, there is always the possibility that he is emotionally upset and therefore unusually prone to volatile outbursts. Apaches acknowledge that such an individual might welcome conversation in the context of "being with people who are sad," but, on the other hand, they fear it might prove incendiary. Under these conditions, which resemble those in Situation No. 4, it is considered both expedient and appropriate to keep silent.

**6. "Being with someone for whom they sing"** *(nde bìdádìstááha bigą´ą´)* The last type of situation to be described is restricted to a small number of physical locations and is more directly influenced by temporal factors than any of the situations we have discussed so far. "Being with someone for whom they sing" takes place only in the context of "curing ceremonials" (*gòjˇitáł; èdotáł*). These events begin early at night and come to a close shortly before dawn the following day. In the late fall and throughout the winter, curing ceremonials are held inside the patient's wickiup or house. In the spring and summer, they are located outside, at some open place near the patient's camp or at specially designated dance grounds where group rituals of all kinds are regularly performed.

Prior to the start of a curing ceremonial, all persons in attendance may feel free to talk with the patient; indeed, because he is so much a focus of concern, it is expected that friends and relatives will seek him out to offer encouragement and support. Conversation breaks off, however, when the patient is informed that the ceremonial is about to begin, and it ceases entirely when the presiding medicine man commences to chant. From this point on, until the completion of the final chant [the] next morning, it is inappropriate for anyone except the medicine man (and, if he has them, his aides) to speak to the patient.[5]

In order to appreciate the explanation Apaches give for this prescription, we must briefly discuss the concept of "supernatural power" (*diyí'*) and describe some of the effects it is believed to have on persons at whom it is directed. Elsewhere (Basso 1969:30) I have defined "power" as follows:

> The term *diyí'* refers to one or all of a set of abstract and invisible forces which are said to derive from certain classes of animals, plants, minerals, meteorological phenomena, and mythological figures within the Western Apache universe. Any of the various powers may be acquired by man and, if properly handled, used for a variety of purposes.

A power that has been antagonized by disrespectful behavior towards its source may retaliate by causing the offender to become sick. "Power-caused illnesses" (*kásit ídiyí' bił*) are properly treated with curing ceremonials in which one or more medicine men, using chants and various items of ritual paraphernalia, attempt to neutralize the sickness-causing power with powers of their own.

Roughly two-thirds of my informants assert that a medicine man's power actually enters the body of the patient; others maintain that it simply closes in and envelops him. In any case, all agree that the patient is brought into intimate contact with a potent supernatural force which elevates him to a condition labeled *gòdiyó'* (sacred, holy).

The term *gòdiyó'* may also be translated as "potentially harmful" and, in this sense, is regularly used to describe classes of objects (including all sources of power) that are surrounded with **taboos.** In keeping with the semantics of *gòdiyó'*, the Western Apache explain that, besides making patients holy, power makes them potentially harmful. And it is this transformation, they explain, that is basically responsible for the cessation of verbal communication during curing ceremonials.

Said one informant:

> When they start singing for someone like that, he sort of goes away with what the medicine man is working with (i.e., power). Sometimes people they sing for don't know you, even after it (the curing ceremonial) is over. They get holy, and you shouldn't try to talk to them when they are like that... it's best to leave them alone.

Another informant made similar comments:

> When they sing for someone, what happens is like this: that man they sing for doesn't know why he is sick or which way to go. So the medicine man has to show him and work on him. That is when he gets holy, and that makes him go off somewhere in his mind, so you should stay away from him.

Because Apaches undergoing ceremonial treatment are perceived as having been changed by power into something different from their normal selves, they are regarded with caution and apprehension. Their newly acquired status places them in close proximity to the supernatural and, as such, carries with it a very real element of danger and uncertainty. These conditions combine to make "being with someone for whom they sing" a situation in which speech is considered disrespectful and, if not exactly harmful, at least potentially hazardous.

## VI

Although the types of situations described above differ from one another in obvious ways, I will argue in what follows that the underlying determinants of silence are in each case basically the same. Specifically, I will attempt to defend the hypothesis that keeping silent in Western Apache culture is associated with social situations in which participants perceive their relationships vis-à-vis one another to be ambiguous and/or unpredictable.

Let us begin with the observation that, in all the situations we have described, *silence is defined as appropriate with respect to a specific individual or individuals.* In other words, the use of speech is not directly curtailed by the setting of a situation nor by the physical activities that accompany it but, rather, by the perceived social and psychological attributes of at least one focal participant.

It may also be observed that, in each type of situation, *the status of the focal participant is marked by ambiguity*—either because he is unfamiliar to other participants in the situation or because, owing to some recent event, a status he formerly held has been changed or is in a process of transition.

Thus, in Situation No. 1, persons who earlier considered themselves "strangers" move towards some other relationship, perhaps "friend" (*šìdikéé*), perhaps "enemy" (*šikédndíí*). In Situation No. 2, young people who have had relatively limited exposure to one another attempt to adjust to the new and intimate status of "sweetheart." These two situations are similar in that the focal participants have little or no prior knowledge of each other. Their social identities are not as yet clearly defined, and their expectations, lacking the foundation of previous experience, are poorly developed.

Situation No. 3 is somewhat different. Although the participants—parents and their children—are well known to each other, their relationship has been seriously interrupted by the latter's prolonged absence from home. This, combined with the possibility that recent experiences at school have altered the children's attitudes, introduces a definite element of unfamiliarity and doubt. Situation No. 3 is not characterized by the absence of role expectations but by the participants' perception that those already in existence may be outmoded and in need of revision.

Status ambiguity is present in Situation No. 4 because a focal participant is enraged and, as a result, considered "crazy." Until he returns to a more rational condition, others in the situation have no way of predicting how he will behave. Situation No. 5 is similar in that the personality of a focal participant is seen to have undergone a marked shift which makes his actions more difficult to anticipate. In both situations, the status of focal participants is uncertain because of real or imagined changes in their psychological makeup.

In Situation No. 6, a focal participant is ritually transformed from an essentially neutral state to one which is contextually defined as "potentially harmful." Ambiguity and apprehension accompany this transition, and, as in Situations No. 4 and 5, established patterns of interaction must be waived until the focal participant reverts to a less threatening condition.

This discussion points up a third feature characteristic of all situations: *the ambiguous status of focal participants is accompanied either by the absence or suspension of established role expectations.* In every instance, non-focal participants (i.e., those who refrain from speech) are either uncertain of how the focal participant will behave towards them or, conversely, how they should behave towards him. Stated in the simplest way possible, their roles become blurred with the result that established expectations—if they exist—lose their relevance as guidelines for social action and must be temporarily discarded or abruptly modified.

We are now in a position to expand upon our initial hypothesis and make it more explicit.

1. In Western Apache culture, the absence of verbal communication is associated with social situations in which the status of focal participants is ambiguous.
2. Under these conditions, fixed role expectations lose their applicability and the illusion of predictability in social interaction is lost.
3. To sum up and reiterate: keeping silent among the Western Apache is a response to uncertainty and unpredictability in social relations.

## VII

The question remains to what extent the foregoing hypothesis helps to account for silence behavior in other cultures. Unfortunately, it is impossible at the present time to provide anything approaching a conclusive answer. Standard ethnographies contain very little information about the circumstances under which verbal communication is discouraged, and it is only within the past few years that problems of this sort have engaged the attention of sociolinguists. The result is that adequate cross-cultural data are almost completely lacking.

As a first step towards the elimination of this deficiency, an attempt is now being made to investigate the occurrence and interpretation of silence in other Indian societies of the American Southwest. Our findings at this early stage, though neither fully representative nor sufficiently comprehensive, are extremely suggestive. By way of illustration, I quote below from portions of a preliminary report prepared by Priscilla Mowrer (1970), herself a Navajo, who inquired into the situational features of Navajo silence behavior in the vicinity of Tuba City on the Navajo Reservation in east-central Arizona.

> I. *Silence and Courting:* Navajo youngsters of opposite sexes just getting to know one another say nothing, except to sit close together and maybe hold hands.... In public, they may try not to let on that they are interested in each other, but in private it is another matter. If the girl is at a gathering where the boy is also present, she may go off by herself. Falling in step, the boy will generally follow. They may just walk around or find some place to sit down. But, at first, they will not say anything to each other.

II. *Silence and Long Absent Relatives:* When a male or female relative returns home after being gone for six months or more, he (or she) is first greeted with a handshake. If the returnee is male, the female greeter may embrace him and cry—the male, meanwhile, will remain dry-eyed and silent.

III. *Silence and Anger:* The Navajo tend to remain silent when being shouted at by a drunk or angered individual because that particular individual is considered temporarily insane. To speak to such an individual, the Navajo believe, just tends to make the situation worse.... People remain silent because they believe that the individual is not himself, that he may have been witched, and is not responsible for the change in his behavior.

IV. *Silent Mourning:* Navajos speak very little when mourning the death of a relative.... The Navajo mourn and cry together in pairs. Men will embrace one another and cry together. Women, however, will hold one another's hands and cry together.

V. *Silence and the Ceremonial Patient:* The Navajo consider it wrong to talk to a person being sung over. The only people who talk to the patient are the medicine man and a female relative (or male relative if the patient is male) who is in charge of food preparation. The only time the patient speaks openly is when the medicine man asks her (or him) to pray along with him.

These observations suggest that striking similarities may exist between the types of social contexts in which Navajos and Western Apaches refrain from speech. If this impression is confirmed by further research, it will lend obvious cross-cultural support to the hypothesis advanced above. But regardless of the final outcome, the situational determinants of silence seem eminently deserving of further study. For as we become better informed about the types of contextual variables that mitigate against the use of verbal codes, we should also learn more about those variables that encourage and promote them.

## Notes

At different times during the period extending from 1964–1969 the research on which this paper is based was supported by U. S. P. H. S. Grant MH-12691-01, a grant from the American Philosophical Society, and funds from the Doris Duke Oral History Project at the Arizona State Museum. I am pleased to acknowledge this support. I would also like to express my gratitude to the following scholars for commenting upon an earlier draft: Y. R. Chao, Harold C. Conklin, Roy G. D'Andrade, Charles O. Frake, Paul Friedrich, John Gumperz, Kenneth Hale, Harry Hoijer, Dell Hymes, Stanley Newman, David M. Schneider, Joel Sherzer, and Paul Turner. Although the final version gained much from their criticisms and suggestions, responsibility for its present form and content rests solely with the author. A preliminary version of this paper was presented to the Annual Meeting of the American Anthropological Association in New Orleans, Lousiana, November 1969.

1. The situations described [here] are not the only ones in which the Western Apache refrain from speech. There is a second set—not considered here because my data are incomplete—in which silence appears to occur as a gesture of respect, usually to persons in positions of authority. A third set, very poorly understood, involves ritual specialists who claim they must keep silent at certain points during the preparation of ceremonial paraphernalia.
2. Recent work in the sociology of interaction, most notably by Goffman (1963) and Garfinkel (1967), has led to the suggestion that social relationships are everywhere the major determinants of verbal behavior. In this case, as Gumperz (1967) makes clear, it becomes methodologically unsound to treat the various components of communicative events as independent variables. Gumperz (1967) has presented a hierarchical model, sensitive to dependency, in which components are seen as stages in the communication process. Each stage serves as the input for the next. The basic stage, i.e., the initial input, is "social identities or statuses." For further details see Slobin 1967: 131–134.
3. I would like to stress that the emphasis placed on social relations is fully in keeping with the Western Apache interpretation of their own behavior. When my informants were asked to explain why they or someone else was silent on a particular occasion, they invariably did so in terms of *who* was present at the time.
4. Among the Western Apache, rules of exogamy discourage courtship between members of the same clans (*kii àłhánigo*) and so-called "related" clans (*kii*), with the result that sweethearts are almost always "non-matrilineal kinsmen" (*dòhwàkíída*). Compared to "matrilineal kinsmen" (*kii*), such individuals have fewer opportunities during childhood to establish close personal relationships and thus, when courtship begins, have relatively little knowledge of each other. It is not surprising, therefore, that their behavior is similar to that accorded strangers.
5. I have witnessed over 75 curing ceremonials since 1961 and have seen this rule violated only 6 times. On 4 occasions, drunks were at fault. In the other 2 cases, the patient fell asleep and had to be awakened.

## References

Basso, Keith H. 1966. *The Gift of Changing Woman.* Bureau of American Ethnology, bulletin 196.

Basso, Keith H. 1969. *Western Apache Witchcraft.* Anthropological Papers of the University of Arizona, no. 15.

Basso, Keith H. 1970. *The Cibecue Apache.* New York: Holt, Rinehart & Winston.

Brown, R. W., and Albert Gilman. 1960. "The Pronouns of Power and Solidarity," in *Style in Language* (ed. by T. Sebeok), pp. 253–276. Cambridge: The Technology Press of Massachusetts Institute of Technology.

Conklin, Harold C. 1959. Linguistic Play in Its Cultural Context. *Language* 35:631–636.

Ervin-Tripp, Susan. 1964. "An Analysis of the Interaction of Language, Topic, and Listener," in *The Ethnography of Communication* (ed. by J. J. Gumperz and D. Hymes), pp. 86–102. *American Anthropologist*, Special Publication, vol. 66, no. 6, part 2.

Ervin-Tripp, Susan. 1967. *Sociolinguistics.* Language-Behavior Research Laboratory, Working Paper no. 3. Berkeley: University of California.

Frake, Charles O. 1964. "How to Ask for a Drink in Subanun," in *The Ethnography of Communication* (ed. by J. J. Gumperz and D. Hymes), pp. 127–132. *American Anthropologist*, Special Publication, vol. 66, no. 6, part 2.

Friedrich, P. 1966. "Structural Implications of Russian Pronominal Usage," in *Sociolinguistics* (ed. by W. Bright), pp. 214–253. The Hague: Mouton.

Garfinkel, H. 1967. *Studies in Ethnomethodology.* Englewood Cliffs, NJ: Prentice-Hall.

Goffman, E. 1961. *Encounters: Two Studies in the Sociology of Interaction.* Indianapolis: Bobbs-Merrill Co.

Goffman, E. 1963. *Behavior in Public Places.* Glencoe, IL: Free Press.

Goffman, E. 1964. "The Neglected Situation," in *The Ethnography of Communication* (ed. by J. J. Gumperz and D. Hymes), pp. 133–136. *American Anthropologist*, Special Publication, vol. 66, no. 6, part 2.

Gumperz, John J. 1961. Speech Variation and the Study of Indian Civilization. *American Anthropologist* 63: 976–988.

Gumperz, John J. 1964. "Linguistic and Social Interaction in Two Communities," in *The Ethnography of Communication* (ed. by J. J. Gumperz and D. Hymes), pp. 137–153. *American Anthropologist*, Special Publication, vol. 66, no. 6, part 2.

Gumperz, John J. 1967. "The Social Setting of Linguistic Behavior," in *A Field Manual for Cross-Cultural Study of the Acquisition of Communicative Competence (Second Draft)* (ed. by D. I. Slobin), pp. 129–134. Berkeley: University of California.

Hymes, Dell. 1962. "The Ethnography of Speaking," in *Anthropology and Human Behavior* (ed. by T. Gladwin and W. C. Sturtevant), pp. 13–53. Washington, DC: The Anthropological Society of Washington.

Hymes, Dell. 1964. "Introduction: Toward Ethnographies of Communication," in *The Ethnography of Communication* (ed. by J. J. Gumperz and D. Hymes), pp. 1–34. *American Anthropologist*, Special Publication, vol. 66, no. 6, part 2.

Kaut, Charles R. 1957. *The Western Apache Clan System: Its Origins and Development.* University of New Mexico Publications in Anthropology, no. 9.

Martin, Samuel. 1964. "Speech Levels in Japan and Korea," in *Language in Culture and Society* (ed. by D. Hymes), pp. 407–415. New York: Harper & Row.

Mowrer, Priscilla. 1970. Notes on Navajo Silence Behavior. MS, University of Arizona.

Slobin, Dan I. (ed.). 1967. *A Field Manual for Cross-Cultural Study of the Acquisition of Communicative Competence (Second Draft).* Berkeley: University of California.

## Critical Thinking and Application

- What are some of the assumptions you tend to make when someone doesn't speak?
- When are you comfortable and when uncomfortable with silence? On what does this difference depend?
- Are you familiar with cultural prescriptions about the proper time to speak and the proper time to remain silent? Collect slogans and clichés about this. Then observe actual behavior and see what caveats must be made about silence.

## Vocabulary

consanguineal kinship
ethnography of communication
exogamous clans
extralinguistic
informant
lexeme
matrilineal kinship
taboo

## Suggested Further Reading

Basso, Keith H. 1986 [1970]. *The Cibecue Apache.* Prospect Heights, IL: Waveland Press.

Basso, Keith H. 1979. *Portraits of the "Whiteman": Linguistic Play and Cultural Symbols Among the Western Apache.* Cambridge and New York: Cambridge University Press.

Gumperz, John J., and Dell Hymes, eds. 1986. *Directions in Sociolinguistics: The Ethnography of Communication.* Oxford: Blackwell.

Tannen, Deborah, and Muriel Saville-Troike, eds. 1985. *Perspectives on Silence.* Norwood, NJ: Ablex.

# GLOSSARY

*Note: Many of these terms have multiple meanings, and quite a few have been the subject of lengthy discussion or controversy. Some have been invented by or associated with particular individuals, whose names are provided. These definitions are intended to aid you in understanding the chapters in which the terms appear in this book.*

**AAVE:** African American Vernacular English
**aboriginal:** from Latin, *ab origine*, there from the beginning; "native" or indigenous
**aborigine, aboriginal:** native or indigenous group; for example, Native American tribes in the United States
**absolute coordinate system:** a frame of reference for describing the locations of objects in a geocentric way (e.g., *The house is south of the mountain.*)
**accent (nontechnical term):** a set of features of pronunciation associated with a particular geographic location or a social group
**accommodate, accommodation:** when speakers adjust their speech (accent, dialect, language of choice) to match that of their interlocutors
**acquisition planning:** official determination of teaching of specific languages in multilingual settings
**acrolect:** a linguistic variety accorded greater status
**addressee:** the person who receives the communication
**addresser:** the person who sends the communication
**adjacency pair:** two utterances that belong together (e.g., *Thank you. You're welcome.*)
**adolescent peak:** rise in nonstandard language use by teenagers
**affective alignment:** when speakers match their language to that of their interlocutor to have similar emotional experiences
**affective commentaries:** a school routine in which students are asked about their emotional responses to texts
**affective stance:** the emotions and attitudes attributed to a language
**affiliation, affiliative:** having a relationship with a person or group
**affine:** a person related by marriage
**affix:** something added to a word, such as a prefix or suffix
**affricate:** a class of sound that stops the flow of air and then continues with friction in the same position, such as the initial sound in *chop*
**African American Language (AAL):** African American variety of standard English
**A-Level:** standardized tests taken in order to qualify for admission to universities in Great Britain
**algorithm:** a step-by-step procedure to carry out in solving a problem
**alliterative:** relating to the repetition of two or more initial sounds, usually consonants, in adjacent words
**alphabet:** a writing system in which each symbol is used to represent a sound in the language
**Altaic:** language family consisting of the Turkic, Mongolic, and Tungusic languages; Japanese and Korean may also be a part of this family
**alternate sign languages:** sign languages used in addition to another, usually spoken, language
***amae* (Japanese):** a sense of dependence and love felt by the junior in a relationship
**analog:** a system in which elements may grade infinitely
**analogical questions:** questions that compare people, things, and events with others
**analogous:** in evolution, having similar function despite different origins
**anglophone:** describing areas or persons that use English; English-speaking
***angular gyrus*:** association area of the brain especially activated in reading (from Norman Geschwind)
**animate:** (adj.) a class of words and structures that refer to living things
**animate:** (verb) to "give life" to words, to utter them (even if they originate elsewhere) (from Erving Goffman)
**animator:** the one who is uttering the words in a communication event
**apparent-time study:** a study in which different age groups are observed, to detect language change in progress
**apprehension:** in reading, seizing the material and preparing to comprehend it
**arbitrariness;** see *arbitrary*
**arbitrary:** related by convention and rules, not by natural necessity, bond, or connection; unmotivated
**argot:** a secret language or vocabulary
**argument:** in syntax, a category of words that can fill a particular slot
**ascetic:** denying pleasure
**aslexia:** loss of ability to read

**aspect:** a characteristic of verbs that conveys whether the action is complete or incomplete, ongoing or punctual
**aspirate:** producing air on pronunciation
**aspiration:** hearable puff of air that is part of some speech sounds, as in the sound at the beginning of English *puff*
**assimilationist:** a person who advocates for cultural, racial, or linguistic integration
**assonantal:** relating to repetition of vowel sounds with different consonants in adjacent words
**asymmetrical bilingualism:** situation in which one group has command of two languages while the other group only has command of only one; for example, in a colony
**attachment:** in syntax, combination of one linguistic structure to another
**attenuate, attenuator:** something that makes an utterance less direct or strong
**author:** the originator of the words in a communication event (from Erving Goffman)
**autonomous model:** of literacy, suggesting that literacy was universal and identical, when it existed (from Brian Street)
**baby-talk register:** way of talking to or like a baby; for example, using words like *horsie* or *baba*
**back-channel response:** response from a listener which indicates that she is paying attention to the speaker (e.g., *yeah, right*)
**basilect:** a linguistic variety accorded lesser status
**beginning:** in narrative analysis, the initial part of a story
**behaviorism:** a psychological theory that sees all human behavior (including thought) as learned; associated with the idea of the mind as "blank slate"
**beneficiary:** the intended recipient of an utterance
**Bharat:** the name for India in Sanskrit
**bilingual education:** education in two languages simultaneously
**binocular:** using two eyes for depth perception
**bipedalism:** walking upright, on two legs
**blank verse:** unrhymed verse
**blending:** a form of linguistic productivity that combines elements of more than one call or utterance
**borrowing:** use of terms from one language in another
**Broca's area:** named for Paul Broca, area in the left cerebral hemisphere connected to speech production
**bundle of isoglosses:** grouping of several features that mark the boundary between dialects
**bystander:** someone who is perceived as a witness to an event or conversation
**caesura:** a pause in a line of verse
**call system:** nonlinguistic communicative repertoire of animals (including humans)
**call-and-response:** a system of communication in which one person's utterances expect a voiced response
**calque:** a way of translating from one language to another, using "loan translation"
**camaraderie:** goodwill and friendship among people
**cardinal numbers:** numbers that count things
**caregiver:** someone who regularly cares for a child
**caste:** (in India) an inherited, named, and ranked social group
**census:** an official survey of a population
**centration:** placing an event at the center; placing stories around it (from Katharine Young)
**change in progress:** a linguistic change occurring at the moment of observation
**chiasmus:** a literary device in which the order of words or sounds is reversed (to create a parallel construction) (e.g., *I don't eat to live, I live to eat.*)
**chunking:** in learning to read, a step in which students are able to recognize familiar combinations within larger units
**classificatory kinship:** a kinship system that combines individuals from what are considered "different categories" into a single category
**click:** a rare type of speech sound made by two points of contact at the same time, producing a vacuum between them and a loud sound when released; found in some South African and East African languages
**climax:** in narrative analysis, the tensest, most central, and important part of a narrative
**closed call-system:** a communicative system in which there are a fixed number of calls
**closing:** in narrative analysis, the final section of a narrative
**co-construct:** when two people work together to understand and create meaning
**coda:** in morphology and phonology, the final element of a linguistic unit; in narrative analysis, the evaluative element of a narrative, often providing the moral, significance, or relevance of the story
**code switching, code-switching:** use of more than one identifiable linguistic code in a single stretch of discourse
**cognitive sciences:** fields of study devoted to the study of cognition; sometimes used in the singular as an interdisciplinary field
**cognitive:** relating to conscious mental processes, such as thinking and problem solving
**collocation:** two or more words that are commonly used together (e.g., *dead serious, black and white*)
**colloquial:** informal language
**colonialism:** a form of governance in which an outside power controls or strongly influences a less-powerful territory or group of people
**colony:** a country or territory under the political control of another country
**common name:** a noun referring to a thing
**community of practice:** a group of people who interact for a shared purpose, often producing shared modes of communication (from Jean Lave and Etienne Wenger)
**comparative method (of historical linguistics):** a method of reconstructing a parent language by comparing lexical items and phonological systems of descendant languages
**computational linguistics:** study of the formal, grammatical rules of language (related to generative grammar as traced ultimately to Noam Chomsky)

**consanguineal kinship:** relationships by "blood" or descent

**conspecific:** of the same species

**constative:** a statement that conveys information; an utterance that can be judged true or false

**constituent structure:** the property of language that combines medium-sized groups of words into units

**constructed dialogue:** allegedly reporting and quoting what someone else said, though it is often not the actual speech; also called *reported speech*

**contact variety:** a form of language influenced by the language of another group with which there is frequent contact

**contextualization cues:** signals or clues that lead to a particular meaning or interpretation of an utterance

**continuity paradox:** the apparent similarity among species

**convention:** agreement; often used to emphasize the social but arbitrary nature of meaning; in the context of international policy, agreements and contracts

**copula:** a verb that links a subject and predicate; in English it is the verb *to be*

**coronal onset:** pronunciation of the beginning of consonants made with the front part of the tongue (e.g., /t/, /d/)

**corpus:** a collection of data

**corpus data:** written documents or audio recordings of speech

**corpus planning:** official determination of writing and grammar of national languages in multilingual settings

**couplet:** adjacency pair

**creole:** a language evolved from the pidgin formed through the interaction of speakers of unrelated languages; a creole takes on some characteristics of each of its donor languages and has regular syntax and vocabulary

**crossing:** people of a particular social group using linguistic forms often associated with a different social group (from Ben Rampton 1995)

**crossover pattern:** in sociolinguistics, a type of linguistic behavior in which members of the middle class employ standard linguistic forms more than those of the upper-middle class at greater levels of formality

**cultural capital:** educational or intellectual resources or assets that promote social mobility (from Pierre Bourdieu 1991)

**culturally constructed:** a concept or practice that is created by a social group

**cuneiform:** wedgelike writing developed by Sumerians, made by reed stylus on soft clay, for recording accounts and administrative affairs

**cybernetic:** related to the study of information systems

**cyborg:** a being made of both biological and mechanical or technological components

**declarative:** a speech act in which speakers assert their beliefs, opinions, or feelings

**decoding:** deciphering or working out the meaning

**deference:** respect conveyed through interaction (this usage often attributed to Erving Goffman)

**deixis:** the property of languages to "point to" proximity or distance, or to derive meaning from context

**denotation:** the literal meaning of a sign; its dictionary definition

**denotational:** the meaning of a sign that is broadly agreed upon by members of a social group

**description, descriptive grammar or linguistics:** analysis that describes the actual usage of language users

**design features:** the analytic components of a communicative system (from Charles Hockett)

**desinential inflections:** modifications at the ends of words in Arabic to indicate case and mood

**diachronic:** across time

**diacritical:** a mark added to other written symbols to add nuance for pronunciation

**dialect:** a variety of a language; "nonstandard" linguistic variety

**dialect geography:** study of dialects, their distribution, and the ways physical features like mountains may have affected their distribution

**dialectal:** related to dialects

**dialectologist:** someone who studies dialects or variants of a language

**dialogic:** the idea that language exists in response to things that have already been said (from Mikhail Bakhtin)

**dialogism:** an instance of discourse which explicitly addresses its relationship to other instances (from Mikhail Bakhtin); dialogue, interaction

**diaspora:** the dispersal of a population from its original home territory; a population that no longer lives in its original home territory

**diasporic:** related to diaspora

**digital:** a system in which elements are discrete, with absolute distinctions

**diglossia:** a situation in which an H ("high") and an L ("low") language coexist in a speech community and are used for complementary functions (from Charles Ferguson)

**discourse:** a unit of language above the level of the sentence

**discourse, Discourse:** Scott Kiesling distinguishes *discourse* and *Discourse*, where the former is used in its linguistic and linguistic anthropological meaning of connected speech in context, and the latter is used more in its Foucaultian sense of, essentially, *culture*.

**discourse analysis, discourse analysts:** a field of study that looks at language in its social context; analysis of language above the level of the sentence. One kind of discourse analysis is conversation analysis.

**discourse function:** the role and effect of a particular linguistic element in its larger contexts

**discourse markers:** units in a stretch of discourse that have communicative functions

**discourse particles:** small, frequently used words with pragmatic rather than semantic function, used in conversation to indicate relationships and stances (e.g. English *well, but, so*)

**discrete, discreteness:** divided, distinct, noncontinuous (said, for example, of speech sounds)

**discursive:** related to discourse

**discursive style:** the style of a stretch of speech or language

**disfluency:** breaks or irregularities in speech such as repetitions or sounds and syllables

**displacement:** the ability to refer to things outside the immediate situation, often removed in time and space from the moment of utterance

**domain:** in syntax, the unit within which a certain operation applies

**double articulation:** another term for *duality of patterning*

**double-voiced:** an utterance that has more than one origin, source, or author; it often appears to accept inequality while simultaneously challenging it (from Mikhail Bakhtin); see also *dialogism*

**dragon bones:** oracle bones from China that are a significant collection of early Chinese writing, usually on turtle shells or ox scapulae

**Dravidian:** a language family of eighty-five languages, mostly in southern India, not related to Indo-Aryan languages; one well-known member is Tamil

**dual immersion:** a form of bilingual education in which two languages are used for academic purposes; also called *two-way immersion*

**duality of patterning:** the property of smaller meaningless elements combining at a higher level to create meaning

**dyad, dyadic:** group of two people interacting

**elaborated code:** a more universal style of speaking which uses explicit or easily recognizable meanings of words (from Basil Bernstein)

**ELT:** English language teaching

**emergent:** arising or coming into being

**emic:** from the participant's point of view; derived from *phonemic* (from Kenneth Pike)

**empirical:** concerned with verifiable observations and experience

**endangered:** at risk of going extinct

**endangered language:** a language in danger of becoming extinct

**ending:** in narrative analysis, the concluding, synthesizing portion of a story

**English immersion:** an approach to teaching English as a new language that puts learners immediately into a setting in which only English is used

**enregisterment:** the process through which forms of speech become socially recognized and come to be associated with speaker attributes (from Asif Agha)

**entextualization:** the process of making oral language into written texts

**epiphenomena (plural), epiphenomenon (singular):** something that arises as a secondary effect of something else

**epistemic modal:** the speaker's evaluation or confidence in what he or she is saying; the way a speaker expresses his or her doubts, certainties, or guesses

**epistemic stance:** how certain a speaker is about what he or she is saying

**epistemology:** how we understand the world

**equative copula:** a construction where two things are equated or linked

**equipotential:** having equal potential

**eros:** the drive for love (from Sigmund Freud); named for the Greek god of love

**essentialism; linguistic essentialism:** the idea that language and culture are identical

**essentialize:** reduce to an essence without regard for differences

**ether:** an allusion to a substance believed until the twentieth century to fill apparently empty space and sky; used to speak about the medium for transmission of invisible electromagnetic waves

**ethnographic, ethnography:** a study of a particular setting, using participant observation; or an account of such a study

**ethnography of communication:** an approach to the study of language in society that looks at who says what to whom in what way, incorporating social, cultural, and linguistic dimensions of particular speech events; also called *ethnography of speaking* (from Dell Hymes, John Gumperz)

**ethnography of speaking:** an approach to the study of language in society that looks at who says what to whom in what way, incorporating social, cultural, and linguistic dimensions of particular speech events; also called *ethnography of communication* (from Dell Hymes, John Gumperz)

**etic:** from an outsider's point of view; derived from *phonetic* (from Kenneth Pike)

**evaluation:** in narrative analysis, the summarizing and concluding portion of a story, often providing an emotional or moral meaning

**evidential marker:** a component of an utterance that indicates the source or validity of the information conveyed

**exclusivist:** those who accept as writing *only* systems of graphic symbols that can express all thought

**exogamous clans:** clans that do not marry each other's members

**expansion:** spelling out more explicitly or at greater length what another—often a novice—said in abbreviated form

**extraction:** in syntax, removing one element from within another

**extragenetic:** outside genetic transmission (usually through cultural transmission)

**extralinguistic:** outside language

**face:** reputation, honor, dignity, prestige, value in the eyes of others

**false etymology:** a mistaken history of a word, usually based on resemblance to another term

**Family Tree theory:** a system of language classification which groups related languages into treelike structures (from August Schleicher)

**fetish:** an object believed to have magical powers or to be inhabited by a spirit

**fictive kinship:** a relationship expressed through the idiom of kinship, though without actual kin relations

**field dependent:** in cognitive styles of learning, requiring interaction with and knowledge of the context of learning
**field independent:** in cognitive styles of learning, not requiring interaction with and knowledge of the context of learning
**First Nation:** Canadian aboriginals
**first-order index:** the pragmatic meaning inferred from an utterance
**first-person pronoun:** a pronoun referring to the speaker (in English, *I* or *we*)
**floor:** the right to speak and be listened to
**focal:** the individuals whose actions are central in a particular study
**footing:** the attitude, identity, or stance taken by speakers in particular interactions (from Erving Goffman)
**frame:** of writing, a basic unit of writing and the space around it
**frame:** the expected structure of an interaction
**framing:** taking context into account by recognizing the different expectations that speakers have regarding interactions
**francité:** Frenchness; characteristics specific to the French
**francophone:** describing areas or people that use French; French-speaking
**frontal lobes:** located at the front of each cerebral hemisphere of the brain, involved with higher mental functions
**fronted:** a vowel made with the tongue forward in the mouth
**full writing:** a system of graphic symbols that can convey any and all thought
**GCSE:** General Certificate of Secondary Education, in the United Kingdom, a certification of knowledge of particular subjects
**gender:** a class of words; this can be masculine, feminine, neuter, animate, etc.
**generative grammar:** a theory of language that looks at the ways novel sentences are generated through rules for movement and combination (from Noam Chomsky)
**generic:** having to do with genre
**genitive:** having to do with possession (a grammatical term)
**genre:** a style of a particular communicative variety with recognizable form and function
**gesticulation:** waving arms and hands accompanying speech
**gesture-call:** a system of communication that has a number of gestures combined with vocalizations
**gloss:** as noun, explanation of a word; as verb, to define, to put into words; to reword
**glossolalia:** meaningless speech often associated with religious worship; speaking in tongues
**grammatical gender:** usually considered an arbitrary division of linguistic forms into categories
**grammatical gender marking:** a class of words; this can be masculine, feminine, neuter, animate, etc.
**grapheme:** basic unit of writing
**habitual *be*:** the verb *be* used to indicate an ongoing, rather than momentary, state of affairs, often associated with African American English (e.g., *He be practicing for the marathon every day at 5 A.M.*)
**HE:** Hispanized English
**head noun:** the main noun in a phrase that includes modifiers
**hedge, hedging:** a verbal form that makes a stance less clear or firm, or indicates a speaker's hesitancy
**hedonism:** the pursuit of pleasure (*hedonize*)
**hegemony, hegemonic:** domination (often more ideological than physical or political)
**Herderian:** the idea that each language and culture reflects the unique experience of a people (national or ethnic group) (from Johann Gottfried von Herder)
**heritable, heritability:** the quality of traits' variation stemming from genes
**heritage language:** a language learned in homes where the dominant language of the area is not spoken or is not the sole language; for example, Polish in the United States
**hermeneutics:** the study of interpretation, from the Greek god Hermes
**heteroglossia:** the diversity of voices within a single text, especially in the novel (from Mikhail Bakhtin)
**heteroglot:** characterized by heteroglossia
**heteronormativity:** the assumption that heterosexuality is normal, with two genders and two sexes
**heterosexism:** discrimination and bias against homosexuals based on the belief that opposite-sex relationships are natural
**hieroglyphic writing:** pictorial writing system
**hijra:** in South Asia, biological males who have a feminine gender identity and therefore dress, act, and speak like women; the "third sex"
**hip hop:** a type of music developed by African Americans and Latinos
**hiphopness:** the characteristics of hip hop
**hiphopological:** related to hip hop
**holistic:** taking a unified view; indivisible
**holophrase:** a one-word utterance
**holophrastic:** utterances that consist of a single word
**home language:** a language spoken at home but not at work or school
**hominid, hominin:** erect, bipedal members of the Hominidae primate family. The human lineage emerges from the hominin (or hominids).
**hominoid:** apes and humans
**homologous:** corresponding in structure and origin (evolution)
**homosociality:** same-sex relationship that is not romantic or sexual
**hybridity:** mixing
**hypercorrect, hypercorrection:** beyond correct; using a formal form in a situation where a more casual one may be expected (from William Labov)
**iconic, iconic signs:** signs that resemble their referent

**iconicity:** the trait of signs resembling the concept to which they refer

**ideological model:** of literacy, suggesting that literacy has varying meanings connected with particular forms of power, culture, and practices (from Brian Street)

**illocutionary force:** the intended effect of an utterance (from J. L. Austin)

**immediacy:** the quality of acting in the present and responding to stimuli actually there

**inanimate:** a category of words and structures referring to beings that are not alive

**inclusivist:** those who accept as writing *any* systems of graphic symbols that convey some thought

**index:** (as verb) point to or indicate a relationship, state of affairs, or social context; (as noun) a sign whose meaning is understood from the context in which it is used

**indexical, indexicality:** term whose reference or meaning shifts with context (e.g., *I, today*) or with association (e.g., *y'all* is indexical of southern U.S. identity)

**indigeneity:** the condition of being indigenous

**indigenous:** native or aboriginal

**Indo-Aryan:** a language family, part of Indo-European, dominant in South Asia, including most notably Hindi

**Indo-European:** language family that includes Romance, Slavic, Germanic, Indo-Iranian, Greek, and others

**inference-making skills:** skills related to eliciting consequences and suppositions from reading

**inflected:** a category of languages that indicate grammatical relations through inflections

**inflected:** a category of languages that indicate grammatical relations through inflections

**inflection:** elements added to base words to provide information about relationships, time, and other grammatical or semantic features, such as the past-tense marker of *walk**ed***

**informant:** a participant in a culture consulted by an ethnographer

**initialism:** an abbreviation made from the first letter of each word, such as *LOL* for *laugh out loud*

**initiation-reply-evaluation sequence:** a routine in which children or students are tested on their answers to questions initiated by adults or teachers

**innate:** inborn

**innatist:** a theory of language acquisition which holds that humans' ability to learn language is inborn

**institutional talk:** type of speech that is relatively restricted and used in settings like hospitals and courts

**intensifier:** a word which emphasizes or intensifies another word or phrase

**interactional frame:** a structure for interacting that provides guidance and expectations for interpretation

**interlocutor:** a partner in a conversation

**intersubjective:** sharing a subjective or personal state with two or more people

**intonation:** rhythm, stress, and pitch changes accompanying ordinary speech

**intrasentential (intra-sentential) code-switching:** code-switching within a sentence boundary

**intrinsic coordinate system:** a frame of reference for describing the locations of objects in an object-centered way (e.g., *The house is in front of the school.*)

**invariant be:** the verb *be* used to indicate repeated or ongoing states, usually associated with African American English (e.g., *He be workin' at the restaurant every day till midnight.*)

**involvement:** the willingness and ability of participants in a conversation to start and continue a conversation

**isogloss:** boundary between dominant uses of a particular language form

**isolating:** describing a category of languages that indicate grammatical relations by the use and position of particular words

***kana*:** Japanese syllabic writing system; there are two types of kana: *katakana* and *hiragana*

***kanji*:** Chinese characters used in written Japanese

**koiné:** a regional dialect used as the common language of a larger area

**la francophonie:** the countries in which French is spoken

**labeling game:** a routine of pointing out the names of objects to young children

**laminated:** a layering of different kinds of speakers in a single stretch of talk

**language academy:** institution that determines how a language should change (e.g., the *Académie française*)

**language death:** the disappearance of a language when it is no longer spoken, usually as a result of a shift in language used

**language ecology:** the study of languages and their relationships (originally from Einar Haugen 1972)

**language endangerment:** a situation in which a language is at risk of dying

**language ideology:** ideas about language held by people in a particular society; a set of beliefs about language or particular languages

**language loss:** the discontinued use of a particular language variety

**language maintenance:** ongoing use of an earlier-learned language after a new one has been learned

**language planning:** study and implementation of policies with regard to language, often institutionally

**language play:** the manipulation of the forms and functions of language

**language policy:** legislation and regulation regarding language

**language preservation:** efforts to ensure continued existence of a potentially endangered language

**language revitalization:** effort to increase language use of an endangered language, especially in younger speakers

**language revival:** bringing back to full use a language that has been moribund

**language rights:** the political right to learn and speak one's native language

**language shift:** change in dominant language
**language socialization:** the inculcation of linguistic and communicative abilities in culture; socialization into and through language
**language transfer:** when speakers' native language interferes with their use of a second language
**latch:** no pause before turn taking
**lexeme:** word
**lexical:** having to do with words
**lexicographer:** someone who investigates a language's vocabulary, or the author of a dictionary
**lexicon:** a mental dictionary; the collection of words in a language
**lexis:** lexicon
**Likert scale:** used in questionaires and surveys, the scale is designed to indicate how strongly a person agrees or disagrees with a statement
**liminal:** an intermediary or transitional phase or stage
**liminality:** the quality of being marginal or in a transitional phase
**linear:** moving from one stage to another sequentially
**lingua franca:** a language spoken across a region, often learned by people whose mother tongues differ, to foster communication across language boundaries
**linguistic determinism:** the notion that language determines people's thought
**linguistic ecology:** a way of studying language that draws on the image of an ecosystem to explain the relationship between languages and the people who speak them (originally from Einar Haugen 1972)
**linguistic equilibrium:** a hypothesized situation prior to the development of agriculture and settled human communities in which human languages were born, changed, and died in equal numbers
**linguistic insecurity:** speakers' worries about whether their speech is "correct", often visible as hypercorrection
**linguistic market:** the entire range of linguistic resources
**literacy event:** an event in which the focus is on a written text
**literacy practices:** different ways of approaching reading depending on cultural context
**LMC:** lower-middle class
**loan word:** use of a word from one language in another
**logographic writing:** a system of writing in which each symbol represents a word
**logosyllabary:** a writing system that combines concepts and sounds
**ludic:** having to do with play
**manual:** using the hands
**manual language:** a language involving use of the hands rather than speech
**manualism:** the use of signed languages for communication
**marked, markedness:** atypical, not the default case; having to be indicated by some particular mark; for example, in English, the singular is unmarked, and the plural tends to be marked, as in *car - cars*
**matched-guise test:** a test of attitudes toward languages in which bilingual speakers are recorded and listeners are asked to evaluate them; the listeners do not realize that the speakers have two "guises" or identities
**matrilineal kinship:** relationships through the female line
**MC:** middle class
**meaning making:** a way that people understand events by imposing meaning on the world around them or deriving meaning from written texts
**media (plural), medium (singular):** a way of conveying something; a channel for communication
**-medium:** in the specific language, as *Hindi-medium*
**-medium school:** the dominant language within which education takes place, as in *English-medium schools*
**mesolect:** a linguistic variety between acrolect and basilect; of moderate prestige
**metacognition:** thought about thought
**metacommentary:** a way of commenting on someone's claims
**metalinguistic:** relating to language about language
**metalinguistic awareness:** awareness of language
**metaphor, metaphoric:** a figure of speech which uses one term nonliterally to represent another
**metaphorical code-switching:** code-switching done because of an association between a code and a topic, a stance, a feeling, or something related to a particular code within a single conversation (from John Gumperz 1982)
**metaphorical concept:** linguistic expressions that structure thought by conceiving of one thing in terms of another
**metapragmatic awarness:** consciousness of what speech does (in a particular context)
**metapragmatic function:** the use of language to comment on its own uses and effects
**metonym, metonymic:** a figure of speech in which a part stands for a whole or a feature stands for something associated with it, as in *the crown* for *the ruler*
**mitigate, mitigating:** softening, reducing the impact
**mitigation:** the act of softening or reducing the impact of something
**mixed codes:** speech with elements from two languages mixed together
**modal verb:** a verb which combines with another verb to indicate likelihood, ability, permission, or obligation (e.g., *can, shall, should*)
**modality, communicative modality:** a type of communication, such as spoken or signed languages
**monolingualism (as language ideology):** the idea that it is natural to be monolingual
**moral panic:** a public panic over something that is thought to be a threat to "proper" society
**morpheme:** the smallest meaningful element in language
**morphemic:** relating to morphemes
**morphological gender:** gender marked by a specific linguistic form
**morphology, morphological:** study of morphemes; study of the structure and form of words

**morphonological:** related to the interaction between morphology and phonology
**morphophonemic:** of writing, indicating some aspects of both sound and meaning
**mother tongue:** the language spoken earliest and at home
**multimodal:** having more than one mode, such as combining song and speech
**mutually intelligible:** able to be understood by speakers of both varieties; said of related languages
**narrative:** a story or portion of discourse that reports events sequentially, with a beginning, middle, and end
**narrativity:** the presentation and interpretation of a narrative
**narratologist:** someone who studies narratives
**national language:** a language which has been legally recognized and adopted for widespread use, often with symbolic and representational power
**nativism:** a view of human features as innate
**nativist:** someone who holds that human characteristics, such as linguistic abilities, are innate or inborn
**natural gender:** usually regarded as linguistic categories corresponding to social and cultural categories of beings in the world
**Neanderthal, Neandertal:** *Homo sapiens neanderthalensis* (according to some scholars; others call it its own species): a hominid living about 200,000 to 30,000 years ago in Europe, western Asia, and northern Africa
**negative face:** honoring people by giving them options (from Erving Goffman)
**negative face threat:** when a person impedes an interlocutor's freedom of action (from Erving Goffman)
**network:** an interconnected system of nodes, lines, or persons
**nomic:** customary, ordinary
**nonce:** momentary, temporary; just on this occasion
**NSPRS:** Nonstandard Puerto Rican Spanish
**nucleus:** the most sonorous (rich, full) part of a syllable
**number:** the grammatical feature in some languages that distinguishes singular and plural, and sometimes other categories such as dual
**numeracy:** the ability to work with and understand numbers
**occipital area:** the visual center of the brain
**official language:** a language used for administrative and national communication, often without symbolic power
**onset:** the beginning of something, often a sound
**ontogeny:** the development of an organism from conception to adulthood
**ontology, ontological:** a theory about the nature of being
**ontology of language:** a view of the nature of language; see also *language ideology*
**opening:** in narrative analysis, the beginning part of a story
**oralism:** advocacy of teaching the deaf to speak
**ordinals:** numbers that order things (e.g., English *first, second*, etc.)
**originator:** the person who came up with or created the message, even if it is voiced by someone else
**orthographic:** having to do with the writing or spelling system
**orthography:** writing or spelling system
**outlier:** a data point that is significantly distant from other points
**overlap:** to speak simultaneously; also a noun referring to this phenomenon
**paralanguage:** nonverbal communication; for example, tone of voice
**paralinguistic:** related to elements in addition to words said (including intonation, volume, etc.)
**parallelism:** similarity in structure of two or mores words, phrases, or clauses
**parietal lobe:** portion of the brain that integrates sensory information
**partial writing:** a system of graphic symbols that can convey only some thought
**participant frame:** a frame which is relevant to the participants, giving them a way of making sense of the interaction and their roles
**party line:** early telephone systems in which households shared a telephone line and number
**performance:** idea that one is playing a role when interacting with others (from Erving Goffman)
**performative:** a type of utterance that performs an action (from J. L. Austin)
**performativity:** a theory of human culture in which meanings and identities emerge from performance or action (from Judith Butler)
**Perso-Arabic:** said of Hindi and Urdu: source languages that influenced contemporary vocabulary in contrast to those deriving more directly from Sanskrit
**phenomenology, phenomenologist:** the study of consciousness and events based on direct experience
**philology, philological:** the study of the origins of languages, sometimes as they appear in literature
**phoneme:** the smallest unit of sound that makes a difference in meaning (e.g., the initial sounds of *bat* and *pat*)
**phonological:** relating to the sound pattern in a language
**phonological variables:** aspects of the sound pattern that vary systematically
**phonologists:** people who study sound patterns in language
**phonology:** the study of the systematic sound pattern of a particular language
**phrase structure:** the structure of the syntactic constituents of sentences
**phrase-structure rules:** the principles by which categories of elements in language are related and structured (from generative grammar)
**phylogenetic(ally):** based on evolutionary development
**phylogeny:** history and evolution of a species or other grouping of organisms
**pidgin:** a rudimentary, possibly unstable, form of language produced out of necessity for communication by people whose native languages differ

**pidginized:** the process of a language developing features of a pidgin (simplification, etc.)
***pinyin*:** official transcription system for Mandarin Chinese
**plasticity:** the capacity of the brain to change
**plurality:** the grammatical quality of number beyond one
**plurilingualism:** a situation in which a speaker is competent in more than one language and can switch between them easily, or an ideology that accepts such a situation
**politeness:** principles of human linguistic interaction that give face to others
**polyglot:** someone who speaks several or many languages
**pongid:** the family of apes that includes gorillas, chimpanzees, and orangutans
**portmanteau:** a word whose meaning is derived from the combination of two or more words (e.g., *blog* from ***web*** and ***log***)
**positive face:** honoring people by showing enthusiasm or sharing
**positive politeness:** seeks to indicate enthusiasm and similar interest; support for the hearer's positive face (from Erving Goffman and Penelope Brown and Stephen Levinson)
**postposition:** a grammatical marker that follow the words it modifies (the mirror image of a preposition)
**postvocalic:** following a vowel
**pragmatic:** relating to context and use
**pragmatics:** study of language in use and how context contributes to meaning
**PRE:** Puerto Rican English
**preconsonantal:** before a consonant
**prediscursive self:** a self that exists prior to speech
**preface:** in narrative analysis, matters preliminary to the story itself
**prefix:** a bound morpheme that precedes the root or stem that it modifies
**prescription, prescriptive, prescriptive grammar, prescriptivism:** describing analysis or attitudes that tell people how their language should be
**primary sign languages:** sign languages used as the main form of communication
**primate:** an order of mammals with binocular vision, the ability to grasp, and a large brain; this includes humans, apes, and monkeys
**principal:** the primary person associated with an utterance (from Erving Goffman)
**productivity:** the capacity to say things that have never been said before
**proper name:** a unique or limited term by which to identify individuals
**prosodic, prosodically:** relating to the length, stress, and tone of speech
**prosody:** the length, stress, and tone of speech
**proto:** the original, hypothesized earlier form of a language
**proto-Indo-European:** the hypothetical original language of which the descendants are other living (and extinct) languages in Europe and South Asia
**protolanguage:** in historical linguistics, a language that is the ancestor of one or more modern languages, as Proto-Indo-European is ancestral to contemporary European languages; in language evolution, the precursor phase to full-fledged human language (from Derek Bickerton)
**proxemic distance:** the measurable distance between people as they interact
**pull theory of media evolution:** aspects of the new media that attract users (from Marshall Poe)
**purism:** the idea that a language needs to be kept free from foreign or outside influences that might cause it to decline
**push theory of media evolution:** aspects of the situation that impel users to seek new technologies (from Marshall Poe)
**quotable gestures:** conventional hand and other gestures that must be learned; also called *emblems*
**quotable vocalizations:** conventional expressions that are not words, such as *m-hm* or *uh-oh*
**quotative:** a word or words that introduce quoted speech
**rank:** place within a hierarchy or grading system
**rap, rappin:** aesthetic placement of verbal rhymes over musical beats
**ratified participant:** a person acknowledged to have a right to take part in a conversation or interaction (from Erving Goffman)
**reappropriation:** using proudly and deliberately a term that is otherwise stigmatized
**reason-explanations:** a routine of asking children or students to explain observed events
**rebus:** representation of words through images or symbols which, when pronounced, sound like those words, such as *ICU* for *I see you*, or a combination of phonetic and logographic elements, such as *gr8* for *great*
**reclamation:** taking a word that used to mean something negative and making it acceptable to use
**recursive:** able to be repeatedly applied, as in recursive grammatical rules
**referent:** what is being referred to
**referential:** pointing to a linguistic sign; having to do with literal or informational meaning
**reflexive, reflexivity:** the idea that we can use language to talk about language
**register:** a more-or-less consistent version of a language that is used in a professional, social, or other setting or context
**reify:** make something real
**relative coordinate system:** a frame of reference for describing the locations of objects in a viewpoint-dependent way (e.g., *The map is to the right of the car keys.*)
**reparation:** the process of making up for past wrongs
**reported speech:** when a speaker's words are repeated by someone else
**reproduction:** the tendency of social structures to replicate themselves; Bourdieu emphasizes the social agents' role in reproducing these structures (from Pierre Bourdieu and Jean-Claude Passeron)

**resistance:** refusal to accept subordinate treatment
**restitution:** making amends for past ill treatment
**restraint politeness:** giving people options or distance; another term for *negative politeness*
**restricted code:** style of speaking in which the meanings of words are drawn from context (from Basil Bernstein)
**Reversing language shift (RLS):** establishes how much shift to another language has occurred and then attempts to revive the original language through establishing new speaker populations
**Revival Linguistics:** an attempt to reverse the decline and extinction of languages (from Ghil'ad Zuckermann)
**rhythm and speed:** a repeated pattern of sound and how quickly the action goes; prosodic features
**rite of passage:** a ritual which marks a person's move from one stage of life to the next
**ritual:** a ceremonial act; for example, marriages, church services, funerals
**ritual insults:** insults which occur as part of accepted social interactional frames
**role:** the connected behaviors, rights, and obligations a person has in a given social situation
**routine:** a scripted, regularly occurring interactional event
**RP:** in United Kingdom, Received Pronunciation, or prestige variety of Standard English; also called *Queen's* or *King's English*
**sacralize:** to make something scared
**SAE:** usually Standard American English; for Whorf, Standard Average European
**Sanskritic:** said of Hindi: direct vocabulary source from earlier phases of Hindi
**scaffolding:** adults preparing an interaction to elicit a child's correct but simple action to complete it
**scheduled caste:** in India, groups of historically disadvantaged people who are given special recognition in the Indian constitution
**schwa:** an unstressed vowel, such as the two last vowels pronounced in the word *vegetable*, written /ə/
**SEC:** socioeconomic class
**second-order index:** the relationship between linguistic variables and people's ideas about what those variables mean
**second-person pronoun:** a pronoun referring to the person addressed (in English, *you*)
**semantic:** relating to meaning
**semanticity:** the quality of conveying meaning through utterances
**semi-official language:** a language with some official status but that cannot be used in all official settings; for example, Catalan or Welsh in the European Union
**semiology:** the science of the study of signs; more commonly called *semiotics*
**semiotic:** related to signs and meaning
**semiotics:** the science of the study of signs
**sequential:** in order
**set:** an orientation or emphasis on a particular aspect of a communicative event; for example, in much poetry, the dominant *set* is toward the *poetic* function (from Roman Jakobson)
**shift:** the process in which a language community changes from speaking one language to another or in which sound patterns change
**sign:** something that points to something else
**sign language:** a language using hand shapes, arms, and face
**signification:** see *signifyin'*
**signified:** the "meaning" of a sign
**signifier:** the form taken by a sign; the outside appearance of a sign
**signifyin':** in African American English, a genre of playful teasing or boasting with clever putdowns, sometimes competitive
**"Simple Nativism":** the view that all major properties of language are dictated by inbuilt mental apparatus (see Chapter 8 by Levinson)
**slang:** a set of terms associated with a particular social group and context
**SMS:** in text-messaging, short message service
**social capital:** a person's accomplishments, social sophistication, and connections (from Pierre Bourdieu 1991)
**social engineering:** managing people and modifying their behavior according to social principles
**social stratification:** levels of social differentiation with evaluative differentiation
**socially expanded, social expansion:** voluble and involved interaction
**socially minimal:** uninvolved and businesslike interaction
**sociolinguistics:** a branch of linguistics that investigates the relationships between linguistic and social factors
**sociolinguists:** linguistic scholars who investigate the relationship between linguistic and social factors
**socio-semiotic:** a branch of semiotics which examines the social dimensions of meaning
**solidarity:** mutual support within a group
**sound change:** a process which changes the pronunciation and sound system of a language
**speech community:** a group of people who regularly interact and communicate.
***Sprachbund*:** linguistic area in which several nonrelated languages share linguistic features
**SPRS:** Standard Puerto Rican Spanish
**stance:** a speaker's position toward the implications of his or her speech
**standard (as language ideology):** the idea that a particular language is and should be an unchanging, idealized object
**standard, standard language:** a language variety defined as the correct version against which other varieties are measured
**standardize, standardization:** the process by which a particular linguistic variety becomes established as the standard
**standardized:** of a linguistic variety, codified and accepted by a group of people as proper or correct

**statement:** an utterance that provides information or facts
**status:** the honor or prestige attached to one's social position
**status planning:** official determination of functions and domains of specific languages in multilingual settings
**stem:** the basic part of a word, which may be combined with other elements
**stigmatized:** regarded as flawed or inferior
**stop:** a class of sounds that stops the flow of air, such as the two consonants in *tad*
**stratified, stratification:** hierarchically, to have graded levels of social status
**"street":** popular opinion, often used for urban youth
**structural linguistics:** approach to linguistics that holds that the components of a system have no meaning by themselves but rather gain meanings through their relationship to other components in the system
**structure:** relations and rules or principles
**style, conversational:** the paralinguistic and discursive aspects of speech: pitch, amplitude, intonation, voice quality, lexical and syntactic choice, rate of speech and turn taking; what is said; how discourse cohesion is achieved
**subaltern:** people socially, politically, and geographically outside the power structure
**substratum:** used of *creoles*, the source language; the language that is being replaced in a contact situation but often provides the basic grammatical structure and categories
**suffix:** a bound morpheme that follows the stem or root that it modifies
**superlaryngeal vocal tract:** the part of the vocal tract above the larynx
**superstratum:** used of *creoles*, the target language; the language that is replacing the original language in a contact situation, often providing the lexicon and often a colonial language
**syllabary:** a collection of written syllables, each symbol referring to a syllable
**symbol:** something that designates a linguistic sign; more generally, something that represents an idea (from Ferdinand de Saussure)
**symbolic:** relating to symbols
**symbolic units:** elements that have meaning, often with arbitrary connections
**symbolism:** the meaning of a sign
**synchronic:** at a given moment in time
**syntactic:** relating to the rules of syntax (sentence construction)
**syntactic boundary:** a place in an utterance between syntactic, grammatical units
**syntagmatic:** relating to linguistic units in sequence
**syntax:** the arrangement of items in an utterance
**synthetic:** describing a category of languages that indicate grammatical relations by internal transformations within words
**taboo:** something powerful, often with strict prohibitions in some circumstances or for some individuals or classes
**tag question:** a question appended to an utterance, as in *She's a top-notch researcher, isn't she?*
**teknonym:** a term of address indicating parenthood or grandparenthood, named for the child, as in *Rachel's mother*
**temporal lobe:** located in the cerebral cortex of the brain, involved with auditory reception
**tense:** a characteristic of verbs indicating temporal relationships
**tertiary education:** higher education; postsecondary education
**textism:** the language used in text messages
**theatrical metaphor:** the idea that people are actors who must present their intentions and characteristics to others through performances (from Erving Goffman); also *dramaturgical*
**theme:** in syntax, a linguistic category
**third-person pronoun:** a pronoun referring to neither the addressee nor the speaker (e.g., in English, *she, he, it, they*)
**token:** an instance of a linguistic type or term
**topic:** the subject of an utterance or conversation
**traditional transmission:** the passing on of knowledge through contact with people in society
**transaction, transactional:** an agreement to exchange something
**transition ritual:** a ritual that marks a person's move from one stage of life to another
**transitional bilingual education:** bilingual education intended to be temporary, while students are in the process of learning a new language
**triadic:** a group of three parts or an interaction involving three people
**trope:** figurative language in which words are used with a sense that differs from their literal meaning
**tuition:** (British) teaching, instruction
**turn:** an instance of having the floor in a conversation
**turn taking:** alternation of turns
**typology:** a branch of linguistics dealing with classification and study of languages based on structural features; or a classification based on types
**UMC:** upper middle class
**Universal Grammar (UG):** theory which suggests that there is some deep grammatical structure that all languages share
**unmarked:** the default or typical case (as singular versus plural)
**unmediated:** direct; without anyone or anything intervening
**Urdu:** a language spoken primarily in Pakistan and closely related to Hindi
**utterance:** something said, of any length or quality
**validity-forms:** classes of verbs indicating the source of information or evidence
**variationist:** an approach to the study of linguistic variation that correlates it with social identity; usually a part of sociolinguistics

**variety:** any distinctive spoken, written, printed, electronic, or other aspect of a language

**verbal battling, verbal duel:** the rapid exchange of nonserious insults between two or more people

**verbal channel:** spoken means of communication

**vernacular:** sometimes refers to a nonstandard variety of a language that also has a standard; local language, in contrast to a "high," sacred, or official language

**visual-manual:** the mode or channel of signed languages

**vocal-auditory:** the mode or channel of spoken languages

**voice:** the characteristic of a sound in terms of vibration or lack of vibration of the vocal cords

**voiced:** involving vibration of the vocal cords, as in the initial consonant of *zoo*

**voiceless:** without the vibration of the vocal cords, as in the initial consonant of *soon*

**WC:** working class

**"ways of taking":** approaches to eliciting meaning from written material

**what-explanations:** a routine of asking factual questions of children or students to which adults or teachers have the answer

**what-question:** a question that seeks to elicit basic factual information

**Whorfianism:** shorthand expression for the approach to the relationship between language and thought associated with Benjamin Lee Whorf; also called *linguistic relativity*

**working language:** a language given legal status as the primary means of communication at an international organization, company, or society; for example the United Nations has six working languages

# INDEX